Chronicle
of
World History

Chronicle
of
World History

KONECKY&KONECKY

Konecky & Konecky
72 Ayers Point Rd.
Old Saybrook, CT 06475

Originally published in German by Chronik Verlag
Copyright © 2007 & 2008 by Chronik Verlag im Wissen Media Verlag GmbH
Translation copyright © 2008 by Konecky & Konecky LLC.
Chronolgy sections originally appeared in *Chronicle of the World* copyright © 1996 by Dorling Kindersley
and used by permission of Dorling Kindersley, Ltd.

10 digit ISBN: 1-56852-680-6
13 digit ISBN: 978-1-56852-680-5

Project director: Sean Konecky
Managing editor: Chuck Gidley
Translations provided by: Sibylle Dausien-Konecky, Ilka Schlueter,
Rosetta Translations and Transperfect Translations
Text adaptations: Anne Depue, David Reinhardt, Andrew Stevens,
Janet Foster and Fola Sumpter
Line editors: Avra Romanowitz and Cher Paul
Special thanks to Michael Cook

Typography by E-Book Services.

Printed and bound by Replika Press, India

Text design by Chris Ciccone

To understand history we need to look through a wide-angle lens. To then relate its disparate events and processes requires a great deal of work and study. But the rewards are great since the knowledge of history is an irreplaceable component to an awareness of the political, social and cultural circumstances in which we find ourselves. The German philosopher Gottfried von Herder wrote: "All human doubts and complaints regarding the confusion and apparent lack of progress of the Good arise from the troubled wanderer's too narrow outlook on his way."

The ambitious task of *The Chronicle of World History* is to offer the reader a wider and more comprehensive perspective on the human story: from the earliest hominids to leave impressions on the fossil and archaeological record, through Classical antiquity in Europe, Asia, and the Americas, to geographical and scientific discovery, religious conflict and revolution, industrialization and the internet. The book is divided into three parts. First, over 1500 articles address specific topics, tracing the rise and fall of great empires, crucial political, religious and intellectual innovations, key moments of conflict and encounter, and the personalities that have left their imprint upon their times and succeeding generations. Second, detailed chronologies with nearly 5000 annalistic entries provide a comprehensive overview of unfolding events. Third, in-depth essays examine major areas of interest such as the emergence of Christianity, the achievements of pre-Columbian civilizations, and the growth of nation states.

Just as history is a dynamic process, so the writing of history cannot remain static. Changing times generate changing approaches, and received wisdom has to be continually updated in the light of new discoveries. So, for example, the dating of some epochs in ancient Egyptian history still remains a source of scholarly disagreement. The crowded tapestry of recent events and the powerful trend of globalization of recent decades necessarily entail extreme selectivity. There is not enough space within the compass of one book to give every new idea and every important event its just due.

The Chronicle of World History presents a concentrated picture of humanity: its breakthroughs in awareness and improbable accomplishments, its tragic failures and terrible cruelties. Even the most cursory consideration results in the inescapable conclusion that we possess both the impulse to good and the impulse to evil. As we look to the uncertain prospects of the new millennium, a backward glance at what we have achieved for good and for ill may help light our way forward.

The Publisher

CONTENTS

THE ROAD TO HOMO SAPIENS

In reading the earth's geologic strata, we can trace the history of changes in climate and life forms. One such strata represents the Miocene epoch, about 25 to 14 million years ago. We know that during this epoch the earth was in a warm phase. Europe, northern Asia and parts of North America were covered by marshy forests. Further south, in central Africa and southern Asia, the land was covered by extensive areas of savannah. During the Miocene and over a period of millions of years, the climate became cooler. Fauna adapted to these new conditions, particularly in Africa, where the savannah continued to spread over increasingly large areas. This change caused a surge in the number of large herds of grazing animals, and then the development of many new genera.

During this period there evolved several genera of large apes. One of the earliest was northern India and China, whose large numbers enabled it to populate a wide geographic range for some twelve million years, twenty to eight million years ago. *Dryopithecus* is today the earliest known precursor of the line of development from which humans evolved.

DRYOPITHECUS AND *RAMAPITHECUS*

However, during these millions of years, *Dryopithecus* did not evolve in a straight line with clearly recognizable intermediate stages leading to *Homo sapiens*. It survived for a long time more or less unchanged until about 14 million years ago when a new genus branched off and developed separately as *Ramapithecus*, a creature barely over 3 feet tall and the first true ancestor of *Homo sapiens*. Even so, *Ramapithecus* was still much closer to the genus represented by apes than that of humans.

The only fossil remains of *Ramapithe-cus* are jaw bones and teeth. But these are cus ate nuts, seeds, roots, and other solid food. Accordingly, its incisors were shorter than those of other apes and its jaw was less prominent—dental and facial structures that were a step towards the development of human features. As was already the case with those of *Dryopithecus*, *Ramapithecus*' molars had the same grooved pattern as human back teeth. And, like its ancestor *Dryopithecus*, *Ramapithecus* lived in east Africa, southern Asia, and, possibly, Europe as well.

WORLDWIDE CLIMATE CHANGE

The Pliocene epoch (about 12 to 2.8 million years ago), the last phase in the Tertiary period, marks the beginning of the Ice Age. While an abundance of biological genera and forms had developed in the course of the previous millions of years, the sudden change of climate resulted in a reduction in the number of living creatures. Mammals in central Europe, North America and central Asia were adversely affected by these climate changes in which the North and South Poles began to ice over. Flora became scarce. *Ramapithe-cus* made its first appearance in the initial phase of the Pliocene. How it developed in the course of the next phase, from 8 to 4 million years ago, is not certain. But it is known that during those four million years considerable changes took place, because at the end

Important prehistoric sites have been discovered in the Olduvai Gorge in what is now Tanzania. Remains of Homo habilis have been dug up there.

Pliopithecus, a long-armed primate that today is believed to be an ancestor of the gibbon. Another was *Proconsul*, an ancestor of the chimpanzee and the gorilla. *Oreopithecus* and *Dryopithecus* also made their appearance during the Miocene epoch. *Oreopithecus* was an anthropoid which stood 4 feet tall, weighed about 90 pounds, and inhabited the regions of present day southern Europe and Africa. *Dryopithecus*, also an early form of anthropoid, was a great ape native to east Africa, enough to provide the paleontologists with significant information. Like many chimpanzee species that developed from *Proconsul*, *Ramapithecus* was a tree-dweller. However, its teeth show that it survived on a diet different than of the *Proconsul* line. While many of these early primates ate mainly soft fruits, *Ramapithecus* fed on harder food. Thick tooth enamel, traces of wear and tear and large back teeth suggest that *Ramapithe-* of this period there were two *Ramapithecus* descendants who clearly had human-like features. These were members of the genus *Australopithecus*, which the famed paleontologists, the Leakeys, had decided to include in the genus *Homo*.

AUSTRALOPITHECINES—ONLY A SIDE BRANCH?

The genus *Australopithecus* ("southern ape") had long been considered to be a link between *Ramapithecus* and the genus *Homo*, but today many scientists doubt this analysis. They believe that *Australopithecus* was a side branch that was developing in the direction of humans, but that this group became extinct about 1.5 million years ago. This means that the *Pithecanthropus* genus, described by the paleontologist Louis Leakey as *Homo habilis*, was not only a contemporary of *Australopithecus*, but that it already had much more pronounced human features. From 4 to 1.5 million years ago the African continent was inhabited by three different species of *Australopithecus*: *Australopithecus africanus*, approximately 4 feet tall, who inhabited southern and eastern Africa; *Australopithecus robustus* (also *Paranthropus robustus*), 4 to 5 feet tall, who lived in eastern and southern Africa; and the east African *Australopithecus boisei* (also *Paranthropus boisei*).

As their pelvic structure reveals, all three were bipeds. *Australopithecus africanus* lived in open grassland, while the powerful *Australopithecus robustus* and closely related *Australopithecus boisei* preferred the dense bush. They all fed on plants, but *Australopithecus africanus* in particular was quite partial to small prey that it ate using simple found objects, such as sharp animal bones, in addition to his sharp teeth. The forehead of *Australopithecus* was barely larger than that of the anthropoid ape.

HOMO HABILIS— ALREADY HUMAN?

In contrast to *Australopithecus*, which inhabited present-day Kenya and northern Tanzania, *Homo habilis* (its classification in the *Homo* genus is disputed) may have created simple stone tools. The species name, *habilis*, refers to this use of tools: *Homo habilis* means "skillful man." The skull of *Homo habilis* is surprisingly similar to the head of a modern human but the volume of its brain, ranging between 40 and 49 cubic inches, is still considerably smaller than that of *Homo sapiens*, which is, on average, 85 cubic inches. With a height of only about 4 feet, *Homo habilis* was considerably smaller than modern man. For a creature of that height, the brain of *Homo habilis* was undoubtedly well developed.

Because of *Homo habilis'* larger brain, his forehead was higher and more domed than that of *Australopithecus*, which, unlike *Homo habilis*, had a large bony bulge longitudinally across the skull. The massive, bony bulges above the eye sockets were hardly visible in *Homo habilis*. His feet were also much more like those of the modern human. His arched metatarsal bones made it possible

for the erect *Homo habilis* to absorb shocks when running. His strongly developed large toes enabled him to propel himself. In contrast to *Australopithecus*, *Homo habilis* could stretch his knee out completely. His hands were more dexterous, a fact, reflected in the deliberate manufacturing of stone tools, that was an essential part of human evolution.

THE UPRIGHT WALKING MAN

Australopithecus and *Homo habilis* were followed by *Homo erectus*, the "upright man". Walking upright resulted not only in changes in the head area—the brain volume increased and the teeth became smaller— but the hands and feet also adapted to their new functions. This process took millions of years.

How *Homo erectus* developed from these various predecessors is not certain. Although some paleontologists see it as descendant of *Australopithecus*, it is much more probable that it is a descendant of *Homo habilis*. But even this is not certain.

What is certain is that 2 to 1.5 million years ago, representatives of *Homo erectus* were geographically widespread. Some 2 million years ago, Java was inhabited by *Homo erectus modjokertensis*, a hominid about 5-1/2 feet tall, which foraged through the tropical forests in small hordes, collecting fruit, digging up worms, and killing wild animals with primitive stone tools. Some 600,000 years ago *Homo erectus modjokertensis* was succeeded by *Homo erectus erectus* (also known as *Pithecantropus erectus*) or Trinil Man. Trinil Man did not live in dwellings but roamed free in the jungle. Then, approximately half-a-million years ago, *Homo erectus erectus* became extinct on Java.

At about the same time that *Homo erectus* existed in Java, it also appeared in Europe, at first as *Homo erectus heidelbergensis*, in what is now Germany, and later as *Homo erectus paleohungaricus* in what is now Hungary. Like their relatives on Java, they roamed through the forests in hordes without any fixed dwelling. They lived amidst herds of elephants, rhinoceroses, elks, and beavers.

In Africa the first hominids of the *Homo erectus* type made their appearance about 1.6 to 1.3 million years ago as *Homo erectus leakeyi*. More recent discoveries in Kenya and Ethiopia suggests that they may be much older. The hominids lived here like their human-like ancestors, in the savannah, in the bush and in sparse primeval forests, congregating near large freshwater lakes such as present-day Lake Turkana. Some 1 million years ago representatives of this type of

hominid spread throughout the African continent: *Homo erectus mauritanicus* in the far north of Africa and Homo erectus capensis in the Cape region of South Africa.

PEKING MAN

The youngest member of the Homo

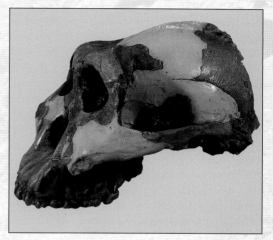

A side branch of the hominids: skull fragment of an Australopithecus (site of discovery: Olduvai Gorge).

erectus type appeared in present-day China some 500,000 to 400,000 ago as *Homo erectus pekinensis* (also known earlier as *Sinanthropus pekinensis*), or Peking Man. Peking Man was possibly the descendant of a sub-species 500,000 years older, *Homo habilis officinalis*, and was the most developed representative of his kind. His brain volume was on average about 64 cubic inches and his average height slightly over 5 feet tall. Besides plants, Peking Man lived off what he hunted, mainly deer and wild boar. Moving in bands, he would catch prey by forcing it over the edges of cliffs.

This subspecies of *Homo erectus* made simple tools from quartz, sandstone, flint, and limestone. It has been established that he overcame his fear of fire and learned to make use of it for warmth and for cooking. The layers of ash in his hearths, often several meters high, suggest that Peking Man had not learned how to set fires but did know how to keep them burning. It was only later that humans learned how to start fires, at first using the bow and drill method, then later by the "striking technique" whereby sparks were created with flint and sulfur.

It is possible that Peking Man had developed a kind of sign language. Hunting had not only resulted in a division of labor between the sexes but had also led to communal eating. This in turn occasioned the development of linguistic skills enabling humans to communicate.

RATIONAL MAN

The earliest representatives of *Homo sapiens*, or "knowing man," were directly descended from *Homo erectus*. They existed in different varieties, inhabiting various parts of the world. *Homo sapiens steinheimensis*, or Steinheim Man, (so named after the site where he was first discovered, Steinheim near Stuttgart), lived during the Mindel-Riss interglacial period about 350,000 and 400,000 years ago. He had a narrow skull and a higher domed forehead compared to that of his ancestors, but he still had the prominent bulges above the eye sockets similar to Peking Man. His brain volume was about 70 cubic inches. *Homo sapiens steinheimensis* was a hunter-gatherer, using stone tools, some of which bore artistic designs.

The first *Homo sapiens* already recognized and appreciated simple geometric shapes. Hand axes have been discovered that are made in a standardized manner, with clearly symmetrical, aesthetically harmonious shapes. *Homo sapiens* also used stone knives and scrapers, as well as fire-treated wooden clubs and lances.

While Steinheim Man lived in Europe and the Mediterranean region in the relatively mild climate of the interglacial period, experiencing the same weather conditions as twenty-first century humans, its phylogenetic descendant, Neanderthal Man, flourished in similarly favorable weather conditions when he first emerged around 150,000 years ago. By 80,000 years ago, Neanderthal Man tried, and ultimately failed, to adapt to a climate that was becoming increasingly harsher.

NEANDERTHAL MAN DEFYING UNFAVORABLE CONDITIONS

Homo sapiens neandertalensis , or Neanderthal Man, (so named after the site where the first skeleton remains were discovered, the Neanderthal region near present-day Dusseldorf), lived on the southern edge of the vast ice mass of the Wurm glacial age. His habitat was similar to that of today's Eskimos. This was a barren, icy tundra of windswept grass steppes and sparse taiga woodland. Survival in such a harsh environment required great strength and mental acumen. Contrary to the present-day stereotype, Neanderthal Man, whose geographic distribution stretched from southern France to Siberia and from Africa to the Near and Far East, was remarkably adaptive and a cunning hunter able to capture big game such as cave bear and Siberian ibex. These animals not only produced meat rich in energy, but they

also provided fur. Simple fur garments and a warm fire protected Neanderthal Man from the cold and frost.

Homo sapiens neandertalensis was about 5 1/2 feet tall, heavy-boned and muscular. In spite of a strong constitution he rarely lived beyond the age of fifty in such harsh

Skull of a Neanderthal man of the Middle Pleistocene (site: Gibraltar).

conditions. The difficult struggle that Neanderthal Man faced everyday required an intelligence that, fortunately, his large brain afforded: Neanderthal's brain volume was about 82 to 105 cubic inches, more or less the same as humans today.

Apparently, this large brain was capable of reflecting on the meaning of life and death. Neanderthal buried his dead and put weapons, tools, and food in the grave for the deceased to take with them, indicating belief in life after death. A recent examination of skeletal remains in Asia Minor suggests that the deceased had been buried on a ceremonial bed of flowers. Such a metaphorical representation in relation to an afterlife suggests that Neanderthal had the ability to think in the abstract and as such, had probably developed some form of language. He even created the first works of art in the shape of small, simple statuettes.

Neanderthal Man had a contemporary who lived on Java: Java Man. He resembled Neanderthal Man in many respects but still had definite features of *Homo erectus*: a primitive skull shape, a broader physique and thicker bulges above the eye sockets than Neanderthal Man. Another early *Homo sapiens* subspecies, *Homo sapiens rhodesiensis* ,or Rhodesian Man, lived in South Africa

at the same time and became extinct only about 30,000 years ago.

A later member of the Neanderthal family lived in the Near East: *Homo sapiens presapiens* or *palaestinensis*. Although definitely Neanderthal, this subspecies was taller and more graceful. Its thigh bones were straighter and longer, its forehead was more strongly domed, the back of its head was higher and much rounder, and the chin was more prominently shaped, as with the Central European Neanderthal. It is even possible that *Homo sapiens presapien* is the ancestor of the present-day Central European, because the European Neanderthal became extinct 40,000 to 35,000 years ago, while at the same time a hunting people immigrated into Europe from the East displaying all the features of *Homo sapiens sapiens*.

CRO-MAGNON MAN AND THE BIRTH OF ART

The people who arrived in Europe from theThe people who arrived in Europe from the East 40,000 to 35,000 years ago were athletically built with high, angular, rather narrow skulls. The pronounced chin was slightly pointed so that the bottom half of the face was almost triangular. The nose was long and narrow, while the forehead was high and domed.

These Cro-Magnon people, so named after the site where they were first discovered, in the former quarry of Cro-Magnon at Les Eyzies-de-Tayac in the Dordogne region of France, were excellent hunters. Moving in bands, they hunted mammoths, cave bears and other big game of the late Ice Age. They had developed coherent speech and could therefore plan and carry out hunting expe-

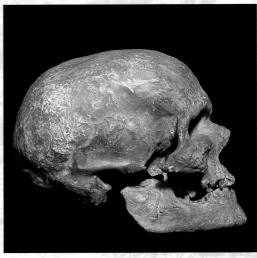

Remains of an ancestor of Homo sapiens, named Cro-Magnon after the site where it was discovered.

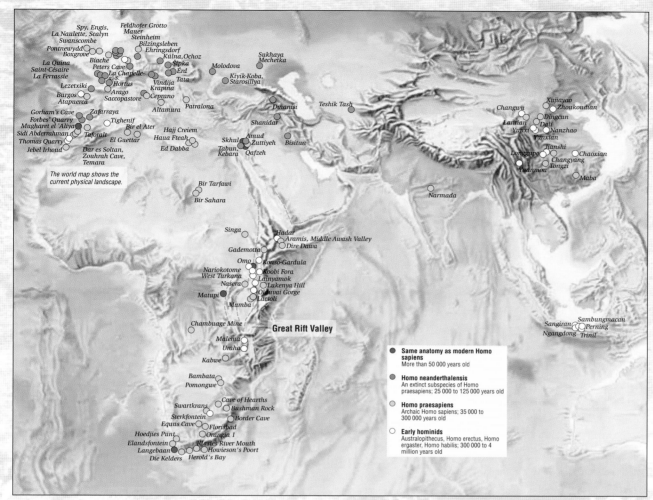

A dense network of sites with hominid fossils stretches along the East African Rift and in the loess landscapes in China.

figurines from clay and crushed animal bones, which were hardened by firing in a primitive kiln. At the site of the mammoth hunters of Dolní Vestonice in Moravia, paleontologists discovered the oldest ceramic kiln in the world, built by Cro-Magnon.

The mother played a major role in Cro-Magnon society, which based its taboos and rituals on matriarchal traditions. The maternal line determined the membership of the tribe, and tribal societies traced their origin back to a first mother, who was viewed as a goddess.

BURIAL RITES AND HOUSING

Cro-Magnon developed an elaborate cult of the dead. Because they were artists, they gave their dead not only items of practical use, such as fur garments, weapons, and food, but also beautifully made jewelry as talismans for their last journey. In many cases make-up was applied to the faces of the dead. Necklaces of mussels and teeth were typical burial objects. Flat stones were placed on the faces of the dead to protect them. The dead were placed in extreme squatting positions, often with the knees touching the chin.

The Cro-Magnon hunters lived in groups of fifteen to thirty and were the first people in history known to have built settlements. Their dwellings were situated under overhanging rock faces and at the entrance of caves. Their settlements were almost always located on southern slopes, protected from the wind. In caves, they covered the floor with a paving made of blocks of stone to provide protection from the damp. Cro-Magnon Man had already developed the art of building fixed tents, made of fur and skins. In eastern Europe, pit dwellings, dug deep into the soil, have been discovered.

Man had already developed the art of building fixed tents, made of fur and skins. In eastern Europe, pit dwellings, dug deep into the soil, have been discovered. ❑

ditions. They hunted with spears, lances, and powerful clubs, and they developed trap hunting, using carefully concealed pits. They had a wide range of tools designed for specific purposes that were made with the utmost precision.

The numerous remains of Cro-Magnon Man throughout Europe reveal their magical approach to hunting. They made clay animals that represented the real prey, pierced with arrows and, so, ritually killed. Hundreds of cave paintings and pictures were scratched, drawn, or painted in deep cave passages. These also had a charmant purpose, and their very creation may have been a ritual act: most of these wall representations are situated far from daylight in underground passages that are often hundreds of yards long.

Thus some of the earliest known "paintings" were born. It is true that on very rare occasions Neanderthal Man had also created small primitive stone figures, but Cro-Magnon Man developed a series of elaborate, polished techniques. About 40,000 years ago he carved the first outlines of the human hand into a rock face in the Bara-Bahau cave in the Vézère valley in the Dordogne. In a nearby cave in Les Combarelles, he carved hundreds of animal figures and a few human representations in the rock. In the cave of Rouffignac in Font-de-Gaume, and in other caves, he drew animals with crayons of manganese oxide. In Niaux, in the famous Altamira cave in northern Spain and in the celebrated cave of Lascaux he created polychrome works of art of great expressive power. He used earth pigments and metal oxide to create color that was applied by hand or with brushes made of small, hollow bones into which tufts of animal hair were inserted. He even developed the technique of spray painting, blowing powdered paint through small hollow bones onto the damp rock face.

Cro-Magnon Man not only carved, drew and painted but also worked in three dimensions. In many caves bas-reliefs of animal heads or almost free-standing sculptures of animals have been found. The two 39 inch tall bison discovered in the cave of Tuc d'Audoubertare are famous examples. Cro-Magnon Man also made small

FROM THE INVENTION OF WRITING TO THE FALL OF ROME

3500 BC – AD 499

REGIONAL KEY
■ Africa
■ Asia
■ Australia
■ Europe
■ North America
  South America

3500 BC – 2001 BC

Mesopotamia, c.3500 BC. At Uruk in southern Mesopotamia, graphic signs appear on stone or slate tablets. They are pictograms representing objects in the concrete world. Pictographic writing soon developed into the more sophisticated cuneiform writing.

Europe, c.3400 BC. Along the Atlantic coast of western Europe, complex architectural structures are being built in which to bury the dead. Most consist of a rectangular or round funeral chamber reached by means of a corridor. Each body is surrounded by polished hatchets, objects made of precious stones, necklaces, and pieces of pottery.

South America, 13 August 3114 BC Mythical founding of the Maya dynastic calendar.

Egypt, c.3100 BC. King Menes unites Upper and Lower Egypt.

Sahara, c.3000 BC. The progressive desiccation of the Sahara region leads to an extension of the desert and the migration of cattle-breeding populations to more fertile areas such as Egypt.

India, c.3000 BC. Farming villages appear all over the Indus Valley. Exploiting the fertile soil and annual river floods, the population is steadily growing, so that there are now many larger settlements, often surrounded by brick walls. With increasing trade and contact between the villages, a common style of life has been established.

Egypt, c.2800 BC. New forms of art and architecture are starting to develop, among them relief carving, metal craftsmanship, sculpture in the round, and furniture making. Tombs known as *mastabas* are being specially made for members of the royal family and other important people.

Mesopotamia, c.2800 BC. A great flood is rumored to have occurred in Mesopotamia, causing extensive destruction and wiping out most of the population. It is believed to have been sent by the gods in order to destroy the sinful human race.

China, c.2700 BC. The inhabitants of China have mastered the art of silk weaving. They are also making bronze artifacts for the first time.

Mesopotamia, c.2675 BC. Gilgamesh fights to keep Uruk independent. He is credited with the building of the city's walls

Egypt, c.2615 BC. Djoser a king of the 3rd Dynasty has his chief architect build the step pyramid of Saqqara.

India, c.2550 BC. The substantial towns at Mohenjo-Daro and Harappa are surrounded by defensive walls of baked brick.

Mesopotamia, c.2500 BC. The world's first libraries are being set up at Shuruppak and Eresh.

Near East, c.2500 BC. Bronze is becoming a popular material for the manufacture of arms and tools.

Mexico, c.2500 BC. Pottery and weaving are developing in central Mexico.

Egypt, c.2350 BC. The Egyptians have adopted the practice of making hieroglyphic inscriptions on the walls of the pharaohs' tombs, in order to protect their occupants after death.

Mesopotamia, c.2330 BC. The advance of Lugalzaggesi, the prince from Umma in Sumer, tries to unify the whole of Mesopotamia under his rule but is stopped by Sargon of Agade.

Europe, c.2300 BC. The development of long-distance trade routes has helped spread the knowledge of advanced metallurgy through Europe, and bronze is now being used more and more widely for making weapons and tools. Sophisticated craftsmanship in metal and stone is particularly prevalent in the region of the Aegean Sea.

Central America, c.2300 BC. Ceramics are being produced here for the first time.

Egypt, c.2290 BC. Marked by great building works, particularly at Abydos, Dendera, and Bubastis, the reign of Pepi has ended. Pepi sent military expeditions to Nubia, the country to the south of Egypt beyond the Nile cataract, and to Palestine. He established a thriving trade between Egypt and Byblos in the Levant.

Egypt, c.2155 BC. Pepi II is dead after a reign of 94 years. He came to the throne at the age of six and ruled during a glorious period, during which Egypt experienced intense commercial activity. The close of his rule was very troubled and the death of Pepi II marks the end of the last illustrious reign of the Egyptian Old Kingdom.

Mesopotamia, c.2150 BC. The Akkadian Empire, founded approximately 200 years ago by Sargon, has been overthrown by an invasion of Guti highlanders from the Zagros Mountains, who have pillaged and sacked the land.

Egypt, c.2040 BC. Mentuhotep I of Thebes unites Upper and Lower Egypt and founds the Middle Kingdom.

Mesopotamia, c.2047 BC. The Sumerian king, Urnammu founds the Third Dynasty of Ur and takes the title King of Sumer and Akkad.

2000 BC – 1501 BC

South America, c.2000 BC. Large-scale maize cultivation is under way in the Peruvian Andes and permanent villages are emerging. Pottery is being made in the Andes for the first time, though elsewhere on the continent the art has been known for at least 1,000 years.

Britain, c.2000 BC. At Stonehenge in Wessex, an impressive circle of standing stones is constructed. Stonehenge has replaced Avebury as the preeminent ritual center of southern Britain.

East Africa, c.2000 BC. A distinctive culture has developed around the practice of carving bowls from stone, probably as cooking pots for stew.

Egypt, c.1925 BC. Sesostris I, whose reign has just ended, led successful expeditions against both Libya and Nubia, and brought Egypt to a new peak of prosperity.

Egypt, c.1840 BC. During his reign of nearly 40 years, Sesostris III, descended from Amenemhat I, has annexed Lower Nubia to Egypt and built fortifications on the Nile to secure his country's southern border. He undertook a military expedition into Palestine. At home he suppressed moves toward provincial independence.

Egypt, c.1800 BC. Egyptian prosperity reaches new heights during the reign of Amenemhat III, which has just ended. Amenemhat III promoted international trade, bringing an influx of foreign peoples into the country.

Babylon, c.1728 BC. The history of Babylon begins with Hammurabi.

Near East, c.1700 BC. A tribal chieftain and religious leader called Abraham is reputed to have led his tribe out of the city of Ur in Sumer and settled at Hebron in Canaan.

Greece, c.1650 BC. Greek mainland culture is breaking free of Cretan influence and developing new forms. One example is the domed beehive tomb known as the *tholos*. This type of monument began at Pylos. Here and at Mycenae, craftsmen also make vases with figurative decorations.

Anatolia, c.1620 BC. The Indo-European intruders known as the Hittites have become a force to be reckoned with. They laid the foundations for a kingdom under Labarnas I, who died c.1650 BC after notable conquests in central Anatolia.

Near East, c.1595 BC. Mursilis, the Hittite king, has taken the town of Babylon, bringing the dynasty of Hammurabi to an end. Earlier, Mursilis brought down the kingdom of Aleppo in northern Syria.

1500 BC – 1001 BC

India, c.1500 BC. The cities of the Indus Valley have been abandoned. Whether the cause was some natural catastrophe, an internal breakdown of order, or attacks by marauders from the hills to the west is unknown.

Crete, c.1450 BC. The palatial complexes are destroyed, apart from Knossos, which is taken over by Mycenaeans from the mainland. The Mycenaeans adopt bureaucratic techniques, such as writing, from the older Cretan culture, and the Greek language is now being written down for the first time.

Egypt, c.1430 BC. Amenhotep II, son of the great soldier Thutmose III, keeps a tight grip on southern Palestine, harshly repressing any rebellion.

Egypt, c.1410 BC. The recent marriage of Thutmose IV—who now rules over the flourishing empire founded by his grandfather, Thutmose III—and the daughter of the Mitanni king promises to promote good international relations.

Anatolia, c.1400 BC. The Hittites have learned how to smelt and forge iron for practical purposes. The first use of the metal in the Near East dates back to c.2500 BC, when a king of Agade made an iron statue of a god. The key discovery of the Hittites is a technique to increase the carbon content of iron, making it much harder.

Greece, c.1400 BC. The Mycenaean civilization on the Greek mainland is opening up to the outside world and establishing trading contacts over large parts of the Mediterranean, especially in the Aegean, Cyprus, and Near East. The Mycenaeans exchange fabric, perfumed oils, cereals, and wine for the basic materials they lack, such as copper, tin, gold, ivory, amber, and jewels.

Crete, c.1375 BC. The palace of Knossos—the only Minoan palace to survive the 1450 BC devastation—is destroyed. The introduction of the *tholos* (stone-built beehive tomb), the wide use of metal in warriors' tombs, and the economic, military, and political organization on the island bear witness to the recent domination of Crete by the Mycenaeans.

Anatolia, c.1350 BC. The bold soldier and diplomat Shuppiluliumash, who became king c.1380 BC, founds a new Hittite kingdom.

Syria, c.1350 BC. The scribes in the Syrian port of Ugarit (Ras Shamra) are developing multilingual skills. Besides their own tongue, written in a cuneiform alphabet, they are using the foreign languages of the Babylonians and the Hittites.

Assyria, c.1350 BC. During the reign of Assur-Uballit, who founded a new kingdom c.1365 BC, Assyria has freed itself from the domination of Mitanni, of which it had been a vassal state for 200 years. The king is the driving force behind the resurgence and expansion of Assyria, which is gradually asserting itself as a great power. He has built a wall around his capital, Assur, and entered into diplomatic relations with Egypt.

Mesopotamia, c.1345 BC. Provoked by the murder of his grandson, Assur-Uballit, king of Assyria, marches on Babylon and sparks off a brief war—the first open conflict between the two kingdoms. The dead child was the son of Assur-Uballit's daughter, whom he gave in marriage to the king of Babylon, Burnaburiash.

Egypt, c.1335 BC. The reign of the controversial pharaoh Amenhotep IV, who succeeded his father Amenhotep III, ends when the Egyptian sphere of influence is crumbling.

Syria, c.1335 BC. Upon the death of Shuppuliuliumash, king of the Hittites, the whole of Syria up to the region of Damascus is under Hittite control.

Egypt, c.1265 BC. The young and ambitious Ramesses II, who succeeded his father Seti to the throne of Egypt, marries a Hittite princess, the daughter of Hattusilis III of Hatti. This consolidates the good relations between Egypt and the Hittites, recently sealed in a peace treaty settling differences that reached their climax in 1285 BC at the Battle of Kadesh.

Assyria, c.1250 BC. The Assyrians have continued their energetic campaign of conquest under the great warrior King Shalmaneser. After subduing the northern mountainous region of Urartu (in Armenia), Assyria has turned on its former allies, the Hurrians, and their Hittite mercenaries, by annexing their lands.

Babylon, c.1235 BC. Tukulti-Ninurta, who became king of Assyria in 1244 BC, marches on Babylon, seizes its king, Kashtiliash IV, whom he deports to Kalah (Nimrud), and takes control of the kingdom. He is the first Assyrian to be named king of Babylon.

Babylon, c.1225 BC. The Babylonians revolt against the Assyrian sponsored rulers.

Near East, c.1200 BC. The Israelite tribes, who were driven out of Egypt c.1230 BC by Ramesses II, are reputed to have arrived in Canaan. They fight to take control of the country under the leadership of Joshua, who is believed to have performed various miracles, such as causing the walls of Jericho to fall at the sound of trumpets.

Greece, c.1200 BC. The four palaces of Mycenae, Tiryns, Pylos, and Thebes have been destroyed and the Mycenaean civilization has collapsed.

Anatolia, 1184 BC. Legendary destruction of Troy.

Babylon/Iran, c.1157 BC. The Elamites defeat and capture the ruler in Babylon after a fierce struggle, and carry off the statue of the god Marduk. The Elamite occupation of Babylon brings the mighty Kassite dynasty to an end, which was founded c.1595 BC.

Aegean, c.1150 BC Following the collapse of the Mycenaean civilization, massive population movements are under way in Greece and the Aegean world. Among the migrants are the first Greeks to settle in Anatolia.

Babylon/Iran, c. 1120 BC. Nebuchadnezzar, king of Babylon, attacks Elam and wins a notable victory, recapturing the statue of Marduk.

Assyria, c.1100 BC. Scribes have begun to compose records to perpetuate the memory of royal conquests and victories. Among them is an epic in honor of the exploits of King Tukulti-Ninurta, who died in 1208BC after attacking and occupying Babylon

Assyria, 1077 BC. The murder of Tiglath-Pileser, king of Assyria, brings to an end a glorious period in the history of the region. Tiglath-Pileser imposed Assyrian authority from the Phoenician coast of the Mediterranean to Babylon, which was conquered only after heavy resistance. He reinforced the city walls of Assur and Nineveh, created a library, and promoted law and social justice in his kingdom.

Egypt, c.1070 BC. Decline sets in after the demise of the New Kingdom, set up 500 years ago. During this period Egypt reached a peak of influence and wealth. There was a great flowering of art and architecture, and the pharaohs achieved numerous conquests.

China, c.1025 BC. The Shang Dynasty is overthrown by the Zhou people, originally vassals of the Shang, from the western border region. They establish a new capital at Hao, near Xi'an.

Israel, c.1020 BC. On the foundation of the Kingdom of Israel, Saul is chosen as first king.

1000 BC – 501 BC

Peru, c.1000 BC. The influence of the civilization centered on Chavin de Huantar now reaches as far as the Moche Valley in the north and the Nazca Valley in the south. Chavin people are skilled at work in stone, pottery, gold, and textiles. Social, military, and religious practices are based on a feline deity cult.

Israel, c.1000 BC. David, Saul's successor as king of Israel, chooses the recently conquered city of Jerusalem as the capital of his kingdom.

Israel, c.925 BC. Jeroboam becomes the first king of a divided kingdom of Israel. After the death of Solomon, Jeroboam led a successful revolt of the northern tribes against Rehoboam, and now heads the Kingdom of Judah.

North Africa, c. 900 BC. The northeast African kingdom of Nubia (Kush), under Egyptian domination for 1,000 years, gains its independence. Its capital is Napata.

Armenia, c.830 BC. Sardur founds a neo-Hurrian kingdom at Urartu in Armenia, on the northern fringes of the Assyrian empire. He chooses as his capital Tushpa, on the banks of Lake Van.

North Africa, c.814 BC. The Phoenicians found Carthage.

Mesopotamia, c.811 BC. The death of Shamshi-Adad V, who succeeded his father Shalmaneser III as Assyrian king, sees Babylon crushed and power restored to Assyria. Shamshi-Adad had to subdue an internal uprising led by his own brother. Taking advantage of the civil war, Babylon imposed a humiliating treaty on Assyria. Before he died Shamshi-Adad wreaked his vengeance by pulverizing the Babylonian forces.

Syria, c.806 BC. Adad-Nirari III, who has just assumed full power as king of Assyria, invades Syria and enters Damascus, where he succeeds in imposing taxes and tributes. When his father died in 811BC, Adad-Nirari was too young to rule, so for five years Assyria was governed by his mother, Sammuramat (also known as Semiramis).

Iran, c.800 BC. The Medes and the Persians, Indo-European peoples who began to enter Iran from the north 300 years ago, are now firmly settled on the Iranian plateau.

India, c.800 BC. The Indo-Aryans who first appeared in India and Pakistan several hundred years ago have spread through northern India. They are integrating with the local agricultural population and establishing permanent farming settlements. Many have reached the Ganges valley where, after clearing the dense forests, they are laying the basis of an urban civilization.

Mexico, c.800 BC. The La Venta culture begins to spread from its homeland on Mexico's gulf coast.

Sardinia, c.800 BC For 200 years a civilization distinctive for its original architecture and sculpture has been evolving in Sardinia. The Sardinians build dry-stone towers in the shape of truncated cones and surrounded by stone walls. Sculptors create bronze statues of men, animals and divinities, including a "great goddess" portrayed as a woman cradling a child in her arms.

Italy, c.790 BC. Small villages of primitive thatched huts are appearing on the Palatine and neighboring hills overlooking the Roman countryside. As well as fishing, hunting and gathering, the inhabitants grow wheat and barley and raise goats and pigs.

Greece, 776 BC. Athletes compete in the first Olympic Games.

China, c.770 BC. After the fall of the Western Zhou capital at Hao, a new Zhou capital is set up at Luoyang. The state of Qin (Ch'in) is established in the area of the former capital in the Wei valley.

Italy, 753 BC. Legendary founding of Rome.

Greece, c.750 BC. The epic poems, *The Iliad and The Odyssey* traditionally attributed to the blind poet Homer, are believed to have been composed around this time.

Italy, c.750 BC. The Etruscan civilization is taking root as immigrants who arrived by sea from the Near East establish settlements in Tuscany. The newcomers are integrating with the Villanovan people and spreading their knowledge of goldworking and other skills.

Israel, c.750 BC. Amos, a peasant prophet from Judah, warns of a coming Day of Judgment. On that day, according to Amos, the justice of the Lord will be seen to be done, and the children of Israel will suffer for their unrighteous ways

Armenia, c.743 BC. Urartu, in Armenia, has reached new heights under Sardur III, a descendant of Sardur I, who founded the kingdom about 100 years ago. Sardur III has now formed a vast coalition with Syria against their common enemy, Assyria.

Syria, c.743 BC. Tiglath-Pileser III, king of Assyria, defeats Arpad after a three-year siege. Arpad was the center of an anti-Assyrian coalition headed by Sardur of Urartu.

Mesopotamia, c.740 BC. The Medes and the Persians, the Indo-European peoples who have been settling Iran for the past few hundred years, have now reached the frontiers of Assyria.

Syria, c.732 BC With the fall of Damascus to the Assyrians, Syria is finally subjected. Samaria, Tyre and Byblos recognized Assyrian authority when Tiglath-Pileser broke up a second Syrian coalition

Babylon, 729 BC. After stamping out a Babylonian revolution, Tiglath-Pileser III, king of Assyria, names himself king of Babylon.

Assyria, 727 BC. At his death, Tiglath-Pileser III leaves behind him a vast and prosperous empire.

Italy, 716 BC. Romulus, the legendary founder and first king of Rome, is reputed to have been carried up to heaven in a chariot of fire. Romulus and his twin brother Remus were said to have been suckled by a she-wolf.

Asia Minor, c.710 BC. The Kingdom of Phrygia reaches its zenith under the rule of King Midas whose great wealth spawns legends.

Assyria, c.710 BC. Sargon II, the brilliant soldier who ascended the Assyrian throne c.721 BC, moves his capital from Nimrud to Khorsabad, 15 miles northeast of Nineveh. Khorsabad, built on a previously virgin site, includes a vast palace and a ziggurat.

Assyria, c.700 BC. Sennacherib has swiftly put an end to the sporadic revolts that broke out after he ascended the Assyrian throne c.704 BC, following the death of his father, Sargon II. Sennacherib is well-informed about the situation prevailing in the provinces because for a long time as crown prince, he was in charge of the reconnaissance service of the Assyrian army.

Asia, c.700 BC. Fierce warrior horsemen known as the Scythians, whose way of life has so far been mostly nomadic, are forming large permanent communities in the western steppes. In addition to rearing cattle, sheep, and horses, they do some farming and hunting. Their settlements are rich and hierarchical.

Greece, c.700 BC. The poetry of Hesiod, a former shepherd born near Mount Helicon in Boeotia, central Greece, is gaining in influence. The first Western writer to embody didacticism in his work, Hesiod has an essentially serious outlook on life and exalts honest labor. His epic poem *Works and Days* creates a vivid impression of everyday life in a contemporary Greek village.

Mesopotamia, c.689 BC. Following Assyria's near defeat in a great battle with the Babylonians and the Elamites (Iranians) on the Tigris, Sennacherib, king of Assyria, takes his revenge by destroying the city of Babylon.

Anatolia, c.687 BC. Gyges, bodyguard of the Lydian king, Candaules, kills his master and takes his place. Rumor has it this was the outcome of a plot devised by Candaules' wife at the time of the plot, whom Gyges has now married.

Mesopotamia, c.680 BC. Under Esarhaddon, youngest son of Sennacherib, the Assyrian Empire reaches its greatest height. In 671 Esarhaddon conquers Egypt, which remains an Assyrian province until 656 BC.

Japan, c.660 BC. The legendary prince Jimmu Tenno, who is descended from the solar goddess Amaterasu, ascends the throne of Japan after vanquishing the Yamato Kingdom. He is reputed to have been born in Kyushu, which he left c.667 BC to conquer eastern Japan.

Anatolia, c.660 BC. The king of Assyria, Ashurbanipal, has refused to answer an appeal for help from Gyges, king of Lydia. Lydia is under severe pressure from the Cimmerians, who have already invaded the young kingdom several times. The Assyrian armies, however,

are fully occupied in putting down the revolt in Egypt.

Egypt, c.656 BC. Psammetichus has driven the Assyrians out of Egypt and restored his country's independence. After an oracle advised him to ally himself with men of bronze who came from the sea, he enlisted the help of Ionian and Carian mercenaries. He has now pursued the Assyrians as far as Ashdod in Palestine.

Babylon, 648 BC. The king of Assyria, Ashurbanipal, is officially recognized as king of Babylon, after the suicide of his brother, Shamash-shuma-ukin—the former Babylonian ruler—in a palace fire.

Iran, 639 BC. The entire land of Elam is devastated by the Assyrians, who have emerged the victors in a long and bloody war with the Elamites. Ashurbanipal, king of Assyria, orders the plundered Elamite capital, Susa, to be razed to the ground.

Egypt, c.630 BC. The king of Egypt, Psammetichus, wards off a threatened Scythian invasion by means of bribes. After his successful attempt, with the help of the Lydians, to expel the Assyrians from Egypt in 655 BC, Psammetichus founded a capital at Sais, in the Nile Delta region, and reunited his country. He has also encouraged an influx of Greeks into Egypt.

Babylon, 626 BC. A Babylonian governor called Nabopolassar, the leader of an insurrection against Assyrian domination, enters Babylon, where he is crowned king. With this event, which follows a year of guerrilla war, the old dream of the Semitic people known as the Chaldeans to ascend the throne of Babylon is at last realized.

Assyria, 612 BC. Nineveh, capital of Assyria, falls to the Medes and Babylonians. The Medes under Cyaxares, and the Babylonians led by Nabopolassar, had mounted a long siege on the city. The sack of Nineveh marks the end of the mighty Assyrian Empire.

Palestine, 609 BC. Necho II, who succeeded Psammetichus as king of Egypt c.610 BC, has won a brilliant victory at the Battle of Megiddo. This battle, the climax of Necho's campaign to restore the Egyptian Empire in Asia, saw the death of Josiah, king of Judah.

Babylon, c.605 BC. Nebuchadnezzar II, the son of Nabopolassar, who has recently been crowned king of Babylon, has surrounded himself with a private cabinet of counselors under the authority of a secretary. Babylonia itself is divided into provinces watched over by governors or their agents.

Greece, c.600 BC. A huge burst of artistic activity is under way. Architectural advances include the development of Doric temples and the sanctuaries at Delphi and Olympia. Sculptors have adopted a new subject: kouroi (youths) and korai (maidens). At first stiff, bulky, and stylized, these statues are growing animated and lifelike. The Corinthians used to dominate the ceramics market with floral and animal decorations of oriental inspiration. Attic potters are now gaining recognition for their vases decorated with scenes from everyday life and mythology.

Persia, c.600 BC. The teachings of the prophet Zoroaster are gaining in influence. Zoroaster argues that the struggle between the benevolent creator and the evil principle is the core of history. He prophecies that good will eventually triumph and evil be destroyed.

Anatolia, c.590 BC. After several failed attempts to conquer the Lydians, Cyaxares, king of the Medes, agrees to fix a frontier with the Kingdom of Lydia; it follows the course of the river Halys.

Near East, 587 BC. Nebuchadnezzar II, king of Babylon, destroys Jerusalem after a Jewish revolt and carries the tribes of Judah off into captivity. Under the leadership of Nebuchadnezzar, Babylon has secured an empire running from Suez, the Red Sea, and Syria across the border of Mesopotamia and the old Kingdom of Elam.

Anatolia, 560 BC. Croesus becomes king of Lydia and extends the borders of his kingdom.

India, c.560 BC. Birth of Siddhartha Gautama Buddha.

Persia, 539 BC. Cyrus, king of Persia, conquers Babylon after defeating King Nabonidus near Sippar. Cyrus secured control of the whole of Persia after vanquishing his grandfather, Astyages, at the Battle of Hamadan (Ecbatana) in 548 BC. He is now master of all Asia from the Hindu Kush to the Mediterranean.

Persia, 538 BC. Cyrus issues an edict putting an end to the Jews' captivity in Babylon and grants them permission to return to their own country.

Egypt, 526 BC. Six months after the coronation of Psammetichus III, the Persians, led by Cambyses II, son of Cyrus, invade and conquer Egypt. Cambyses is declared king of Egypt.

Iran, 515 BC. King Darius lays the foundation stones, of gold and silver, of a new capital at Persepolis. Darius came to the throne in 522 BC, after a bout of palace intrigues following the death of Cambyses II, to whom he is distantly related.

Asia/Europe, c.513 BC. At the head of a large army, Darius, king of Persia, crosses the Bosporus and heads for the Danube, aiming to wage war on the Scythians, who inhabit central Asia and northern Europe. However, the elusive Scythians get the better of him and the Persians are only saved from disaster by the treacherous Greek tyrants who rule the cities of Ionia in the Persian interest.

India, c.510 BC. With the annexation of the Indus Valley by Darius of Persia, the Achaemenid Empire embraces all the lands from the Indus to Thrace in Europe, and Egypt and the Libyan coast in Africa.

Rome, 510 BC. Tarquinius Superbus, seventh king of Rome, and all of his family are banished from the kingdom. Tarquinius was the third member of an Etruscan dynasty to rule in Rome. His tyrannical behavior provoked an uprising led by his nephew, Brutus.

500 BC – 251 BC

, c.500 BC. Temple complexes are being built at Monte Alban in the valley of Oaxaca, in southern Mexico. The mountaintop has been flattened and leveled and the temples have been designed around a large plaza. The settlers have evolved distinctive styles of pottery, sculpture, and architecture; they are also formalizing astronomical observations and a calendar system.

Greece, 492 BC. The Persian general Mardonius at the head of a large army and fleet, subdues Thrace and Macedonia in the aftermath of the Ionian revolt. He retreats after the Persian fleet is dashed to pieces on the rocky promontory of Mount Athos in a storm.

Persia, 486 BC. Xerxes becomes king on the death of his father, Darius, the architect of Persian hegemony.

Anatolia, c.480 BC. Heraclitus, a philosopher from Ephesus, argues that the universe is governed by the conflict of opposites and that everything is achieved by discord. He believes that the elements are caught up in an endless cycle of transformation, which starts from fire, the primordial element.

Sicily, c.480 BC. Gelon, tyrant of Syracuse, in alliance with Theron, tyrant of Acragas, inflicts a crushing defeat on the Carthaginians under Hamilcar at the Battle of Himera. Gelon is the successor to Hippocrates, the tyrant of Gela, who, profiting from a serious social crisis earlier in the century, seized power at Syracuse also. The Punic threat has been growing ever since.

Greece, c.480 BC. A cult is developing centered on the worship of Demeter, goddess of the earth's fertility, and her daughter Persephone, who was carried off by Hades, god of the underworld. The new spirituality finds its most complete expression in the rituals known as the Eleusinian Mysteries.

Greece, 479 BC. After their defeat at the Battle of Salamis, the Persians try unsuccessfully to negotiate a treaty of alliance with the Athenians against the rest of the Greek world.

India, c.478 BC. Siddhartha Gautama Buddha, the founder of Buddhism and one of the great spiritual masters of Asia, dies in Oudh. At the age of 30, he abandoned all earthly ambitions for the life of an ascetic. In his contemplative life, he found the perfect way, and spent over 40 years teaching and gaining many disciples.

Mediterranean, 474 BC. Hieron, who became tyrant of Syracuse on the death of Gelon in 478 BC, wins a great naval victory over the Etruscans, destroying Etruscan sea power. Despite his violent nature, Hieron is a lover of poetry and patronizes Pindar, Aeschylus, Simonides, and Bacchylides. Pindar and Bacchylides have written odes in praise of Hieron's success in the horse races at Olympia.

Greece, 468 BC. The great Athenian politician Aristeides dies in poverty. Known as Aristeides "the Just," he was a general at the Battle of Marathon before being elected *archon* (chief magistrate) in Athens, but his rivalry with Themistocles and the democrats led to his exile. Recalled to command the Athenian forces at the Battle of Plataea in 479 BC, he helped to make Athens the ruling state of the Delian League.

Greece, 467 BC. Cimon, son of Miltiades, the conqueror at Marathon, destroys or captures most of the Persian ships at the mouth of the River Eurymedon, off the coast of Pamphylia, securing Athenian dominance in the Aegean. Having taken advantage of Themistocles' political decline, Cimon is currently the most powerful man in Athens.

Athens, 467 BC. Aeschylus wins the dramatic competition of the Great Dionysia with his trilogy on the Theban legend. The last of the three plays, *Seven Against Thebes*, deals with the final confrontation between the two accursed sons of Oedipus. Eteocles, king of Thebes, and his brother Polynices kill each other in battle and the terrible curse on the house of Laius dies with them.

Persia, 465 BC. Xerxes, king of Persia, is assassinated. Xerxes never fully recovered his power after the Persian defeats by the Greeks, and palace intrigues and revolts followed one another thick and fast. His son, Artaxerxes, succeeds.

Greece, 465 BC. The states of the Delian League make their payments to the shrine of Apollo on Delos. These payments can be in money or in kind, for example by supplying ships to the common fleet. Although the original aim of the League was to protect Greek cities against Persian invasion, it is rapidly becoming an instrument to bolster the power of Athens.

Greece, 454 BC. The Delian League's treasury is moved from Delos to the Acropolis of Athens. The official reason is the threat to its security. More likely, Athens intends to use the funds to further its imperialist policy.

Athens, 451 BC. Pericles, leader of the democrats, is shoring up his position in Athens and restoring order in the Aegean after signing a five-year truce with Sparta. He is faced with an aristocratic opposition led by Cimon who, back in Athens after ten years of ostracism, acted as principal negotiator in the Spartan truce talks.

Greece, 446 BC. Athens and Sparta sign a 30-year peace treaty that obliges Athens to withdraw its troops from territories belonging to the Peloponnesian League.

Rome, 443 BC. The office of *censor* is created. The elected official is responsible for taking a census of the nation, for maintaining a list of senators and for purifying the Roman people. He can exclude from the senate any citizen thought likely to blemish the common good and transfer such a person to a different tribe or social class.

Athens, 443 BC. With his rival Thucydides banished, Pericles is the undisputed authority in Athens.

Athens, 442 BC. Sophocles' new play *Antigone* poses important moral and political questions. It examines in particular the conflict between divine and human justice.

Greece, 431 BC. Sparta's invasion of Attica begins the Second Peloponnesian War between Athens and Sparta for Greek supremacy. Allies of Athens include Thessaly and some of the city-states of western Greece. Allied with Sparta is the Peloponnesian League.

Greece, c.430 BC. Herodotus completes his history of the wars between Greece and the barbarians. From a literary family in Anatolia, Herodotus traveled widely in the Greek world, collecting mythological, historical, and geographical material. Starting with the conquest of the Greek colonies in Anatolia by the Lydian king, Croesus, he gives a history of Lydia and then moves on to deal with Persia, Babylon, and Egypt. The two Persian wars occupy a large part of his work.

Greece, 425 BC. Athens inflicts several defeats on the Peloponnesian League. Aware of an Athenian plot to spark a *helot* revolt in Laconia and Messenia, the Spartans hastily evacuated Attica, but were too late to stop the occupation of Messenian Pylos. Subsequent Peloponnesian attacks were driven back by the Athenians under Demosthenes. Survivors have been taken to Athens as hostages against reinvasion.

Greece, 421 BC. Athens and Sparta sign the Peace of Nicias, marking at least a truce in the Peloponnesian war. The two camps agree to return to their original positions and to exchange prisoners of war.

Greece, 413 BC. While the Athenians are busy fighting in Sicily, the Spartans invade Attica, acting on the unseemly advice of the defector Alcibiades. They establish themselves at Decelea and set about devastating the region.

Asia Minor, 410 BC. Alcibiades, appointed general by the Athenian fleet at Samos, annihilates the Peloponnesian fleet at Cyzicus in Asia Minor (Anatolia).

Athens, 407 BC. Alcibiades, now an Athenian general, returns to the city he betrayed a few years ago. His welcome amounts to a pardon and reflects the euphoria in Athens after recent victories over the Peloponnesians in Asia Minor (Anatolia) and the restoration of democracy.

Greece, 403 BC. The success of the Athenian democrats, led by Thrasybulus, over the Spartans at the Battle of Munychia presages a political change. An amnesty is declared. The restoration of democratic institutions marks the end of a very bloody era.

India, c.400 BC. The scholar Panini analyzes and organizes the grammar of the Sanskrit language, formulating 4,000 grammatical rules.

Athens c.399 BC. The philosopher and teacher Socrates is condemned to death on charges of corrupting the youth of Athens.

Athens, 384 BC. Plato writes a philosophical dialogue and comedy of manners called *The Symposium*. Its characters include Socrates, Aristophanes, and Alcibiades in the role of a slightly inebriated reveler. At the symposium, drinking is interspersed with philosophical conversation: each participant must give a eulogy to love.

Sicily, 367 BC. The reign of Dionysius, tyrant of Syracuse, is at an end. After his election in 405 BC, Dionysius attacked the propertied rich and freed their slaves. He concluded a peace treaty with Carthage, opening the way for Syracuse to become one of the dominant cities of southern Italy.

Macedonia, 359 BC. Philip becomes regent of the small Kingdom of Macedonia on the death of his brother, King Perdiccas, whose son is a mere child. Philip, aged 22, already displays unusual diplomatic and military acumen.

Greece, 357 BC. Supported by Byzantium and Mausolos of Caria, Chios, Rhodes, and Cos leave the Athenian alliance. Meanwhile, Philip of Macedon captures Amphipolis and allies himself with the Chalcidians and the Thessalians.

Macedonia, 356 BC. Amyntas, son of the late King Perdiccas, is deposed and Philip is confirmed as absolute king. He signs a pact with the Chalcidian League, which names Athens as the common enemy, and goes on to take the city of Potidaea. During the year Philip has more good news: His horse wins at Olympia and his wife, Olympias, gives birth to a son, Alexander.

Greece, 355 BC. The historian Xenophon dies at Corinth. Famed for his account in the *Anabasis* of the Greek retreat from Persia after the Battle of Cunaxa, Xenophon also wrote philosophical works, some of which are dedicated to his master, Socrates. Banished from Athens for associating with Sparta, Xenophon spent much of his life in the Peloponnese.

Athens, 351 BC. The orator Demosthenes denounces the expansionist policies of Philip of Macedon and castigates his fellow citizens for their lack of awareness.

Greece, 348 BC. Philip of Macedon takes Olynthus by siege and utterly destroys it, securing control of the Chalcidice peninsula. When the Chalcidian League learned of Philip's intentions, they broke with their former ally and appealed to Athens. Convinced by Demosthenes, Athens at last sent an expeditionary force—but it was too late.

Greece, 347 BC. Plato, the philosophical genius, dies at a wedding feast. Founder of the Academy at Athens, Plato embodied his influential theories on universality in a series of dialogues, including the celebrated *Republic.* Before withdrawing to the world of pure ideas, he tried in vain to convert the tyrant Dionysius of Syracuse.

Greece, 346 BC. After the disaster at Olynthus, Athens is forced to make peace with Philip and end its involvement in the Sacred War.

Sicily, 339 BC. Carthage agrees to withdraw its support for the Greek tyrants in Sicily. This follows the Carthaginian defeat two years prior in the Cape Lilybaeum region by the Syracusans and a Corinthian contingent led by Timoleon. Since its signature of a treaty with Rome in 348 BC, Carthage has been busy attacking the Greek cities of Sicily that threaten its commercial policy.

Greece, 339 BC. Hostilities are renewed between Athens and Macedonia, marking the start of the Fourth Sacred War. Philip II occupies Elateia, two days' march from Attica. Demosthenes saves the day for the panic-stricken Athenians by engineering an alliance between Athens and Thebes.

Greece, 338 BC. Philip II of Macedon defeats the combined forces of Athens and Thebes at the Battle of Chaeronea. With the surrender of Thebes, the Boeotian League is dissolved. Philip imposes peace terms on Athens that include allying with Macedonia and dissolving the Athenian League. Struck by the generosity of their conqueror, the Athenians offer citizenship to Philip and his son, Alexander.

Italy, 338 BC. Rome, which has become the main power in Italy, succeeds in dissolving the Latin League and uniting Latium.

Rome, 336 BC. Plebeians are allowed to become *praetors* (magistrates closely connected with military affairs). This is the latest step in a gradual recognition

of plebeians' rights. The office of dictatorship was opened to them in 356 BC, and the censorship in 351 BC.

Macedonia, 335 BC. After succeeding his father as king of Macedonia, Alexander sets out on his first military campaign, aiming to punish the Triballi for their rebellion of 339 BC and to reestablish order in the Balkans. His victory reinforces Macedonian power in the region of the lower Danube.

Asia Minor, 333 BC. Already in control of a large part of Asia Minor (Anatolia), Alexander defeats Darius III of Persia at Issus. This follows his great victory over the Persians the previous year at the river Granicus. Darius is put to flight and Alexander captures his camp and family, sleeping in the Persian king's tent on the night of his victory.

Persia, 331 BC. After his unopposed expedition to Egypt, Alexander moves into Persia and defeats the Persian army at Gaugamela. Babylonia and Susa surrender to him.

Persia, 330 BC. Alexander marches on Persepolis and allows his army to pillage the royal city. He wants to take Darius alive, but the Persian king is assassinated by rebels. His death marks the collapse of the Achaemenid Dynasty.

China, 325 BC. The prince of Qin takes the title *wang* (king), thereby making a claim to be the legitimate ruler of the whole of China.

Babylon, 323 BC. Alexander dies at the age of 33. His conquests are divided among his generals: Perdiccas is regent in Asia; Antipater remains regent in Europe. Ptolemy becomes ruler of Egypt, Lysimachus of Thrace, Antigonus the One-Eyed of Asia Minor (Anatolia).

Athens, 322 BC. Zeno of Cyprus founds the Stoic school, named after Athens' painted portico, *stoa poikile*, under which he usually teaches. Stoicism centers on the doctrine that virtue, which is based on knowledge, is the only good.

India, 317 BC. Chandragupta, who founded the Mauryan Dynasty in 321 BC with a capital at Pataliputra (Patna) in the east of the country, drives the Greek garrisons out of India.

Macedonia, 316 BC. Olympias, Alexander's mother, is stoned to death on Cassander's orders. This act of revenge stems from the succession crisis created by the death, in 319 BC, of Antipater, made regent of Macedonia and Greece on Alexander's departure for Asia.

Athens, 305 BC. Epicurus, the philosopher who believes that pleasure is the chief good, founds a school in Athens.

India, 302 BC. Chandragupta, founder of the Mauryan Dynasty, signs a peace treaty with Seleucus, the former Macedonian general who now rules Babylon.

Asia Minor, 301 BC. Antigonus the One-Eyed dies at Ipsus, in Phrygia, in a battle with the other successors of Alexander, who agree on a new division of the world. Cassander keeps Macedonia; Lysimachus has Thrace and Asia Minor (Anatolia) as far as the Taurus Mountains; Seleucus gets only northern Syria, the southern part being held by Ptolemy. Demetrius keeps areas of Asia Minor, Greece, the Cyclades, and Phoenicia.

Italy, 295 BC. In the Third Samnite War—which began three years prior, prompted by the expansionist policies of Rome—the Romans defeat a large army of Gauls and Samnites at the Battle of Sentinum. They then force the Etruscans to accept peace.

Alexandria, c.290 BC. The mathematician Euclid sets out the principles of geometry in his *Elements*.

Alexandria, 290 BC. Ptolemy founds the Museum of Alexandria and dedicates it to the Muses. The museum welcomes scholars who wish to devote themselves to study.

Rome, 287 BC. The law of Hortensius, according to which the decisions of the plebeians have legal standing, is vigorously promulgated.

China, 287 BC. To protect themselves against barbarian invasion, the northern states of China begin to build sections of a "Great Wall."

Egypt, 285 BC. Ptolemy, who became ruler of Egypt—one of the richest Greek kingdoms—after the death of Alexander, abdicates in favor of his son. During his reign, Ptolemy devoted himself to annexing neighboring territories and fostering Greek immigration. His capital, Alexandria, is the center of commerce and Greek culture.

Alexandria, 285 BC. Sostratus of Cnidus builds a lighthouse, linked by a dike to dry land, on the island of Pharos. The three-story building is over 300 feet high. At the top, an arrangement of convex mirrors reflects the light from a wood fire.

Egypt, 283 BC. A translation of the Hebrew scriptures into Greek is started. It is known as the Septuagint after the number of translators: seventy.

Macedonia, 281 BC. Seleucus Nicator dies after falling into a trap set by Ptolemy II of Egypt. Seleucus—the last surviving general of those appointed by Alexander—became king of Syria after defeating Lysimachus at Corupedium in Asia Minor (Anatolia) earlier in the year.

Italy, 280 BC. Pyrrhus, king of Epirus, has sent troops to aid Tarentum and the other Greek cities of southern Italy against Rome. At the Battle of Heraclea, Pyrrhus' elephants terrorize the Roman soldiers.

Epirus, 272 BC. King Pyrrhus of Epirus is dead. A brilliant strategist and administrator, he made a great power of his mountainous kingdom, one by one annexing the provinces under Macedonian control.

India, 268 BC. The Indian emperor, Asoka, unites the sub-continent for the first time.

Rome, 264 BC. The Romans have discovered a new kind of spectacle: gladiatorial combat. A violent and cruel sport, often seen at funerals, it is becoming enormously popular.

Asia Minor, 262 BC. Following a victory over the Seleucid army, Eumenes, nephew of Philetaeros—who saved Pergamon from the Gauls in 276 BC—declares Pergamon independent and founds a fourth Hellenistic kingdom in Asia Minor (Anatolia).

Sicily, 260 BC. Rome wins its first great naval victory, over the Carthaginians at Mylae. "Ravens"—grappling hooks designed to hold Roman and enemy ships together—allowed the Romans to fight hand-to-hand on board ship.

Syria, 254 BC. A six-year war between the Seleucids and the Ptolemies for possession of Syria is concluded by a marriage alliance between Antiochus II and Berenice, a daughter of Ptolemy II.

250 BC – 101 BC

China, 247 BC. Prince Zheng ascends to the throne of Qin.

Carthage, 237 BC. After putting an end to the mercenaries' revolt with the aid of Hanno the Great, Hamilcar, the Carthaginian general defeated by Rome in Sicily, embarks for Spain.

Rome/Carthage 226 BC. A treaty makes the Ebro River (in present-day Spain) the boundary between the two warring nations.

Rhodes, 223 BC. The Colossus of Rhodes a 100-foot high statue of the sun god Helios that stood in the island's harbor is destroyed by an earthquake.

Spain, 219 BC. In an effective declaration of war on Rome, the Carthaginian general Hannibal besieges the pro-Roman town of Saguntum. Since Spain became a province of their empire in 236 BC, the Carthaginians have been exploiting the economic resources of the peninsula and swelling the ranks of their army with local recruits.

Palestine, 217 BC. Egyptian *hoplites*, led by the young Ptolemy IV Philopater, crush the Seleucid army under Antiochus III at Raphia. Two years prior, in pursuit of his dream of restoring the grandeur of the Seleucid Empire, Antiochus initiated the Fourth Syrian War and took possession of the coveted province of Coele Syria at the expense of Ptolemaic Egypt.

Italy, 217 BC. Hannibal takes the Roman general Flaminius and his legions by surprise near Lake Trasimene in Umbria. The ensuing battle, in which 15,000 Romans are killed and 15,000 taken prisoner, marks the loss to Rome of the whole of Etruria. In Rome itself, in anticipation of imminent assault, the bridges over the Tiber River are cut and the city walls repaired.

China, c.215 BC. Shi Huang Di, the architect of Chinese political and administrative unity, joins the separate parts of the Great Wall.

China, 213 BC. On the orders of Shi Huang Di, all books, other than those on useful subjects, such as medicine, agriculture, and divination, are burned.

Sicily, 212 BC. The Roman general Marcellus captures the city of Syracuse after a siege. Archimedes, a mathematician who used his expertise to construct formidable war machines to resist the Roman onslaught, dies in the battle. Syracuse, ally of Carthage, had hoped to negotiate with the Romans, but this was vetoed by pro-Carthaginian factions.

Italy, 212 BC. War breaks out between Rome and Macedonia. Philip V of Macedon—an ally of Hannibal since 215 BC—intends to gain control of Illyria and the Greek cities along the Adriatic coast, an area of Roman influence.

Italy, 211 BC. Capua, in Campania, adopted by Hannibal as a key position, surrenders to the Romans after a siege. This

is despite an attempt by Hannibal to protect his ally by marching on Rome.

Italy, 209 BC. Capitalizing on their successes at Syracuse and in Campania, the Romans take Tarentum.

Spain, 209 BC. Led by Scipio Africanus, the Romans defeat the Carthaginians at the town of New Carthage.

Italy, 207 BC. A Carthaginian plan to attack the Romans from both sides ends in failure. Hasdrubal had crossed the Alps and threatened northern Italy. Hannibal, still in the south of the peninsula, advanced northward, but was halted by the Roman consul Gaius Nero. Nero then rejoined his colleague Livius on the Metaurus, where the Romans achieved a decisive victory over Hasdrubal's forces.

Macedonia, 205 BC. In order to concentrate all its efforts against Hannibal, Rome puts an end to a war against Macedonia by signing the Treaty of Phoinike, by which Rome and Macedonia share the protectorate of Illyria.

Rome, 204 BC. Plautus stages a new comedy, *Miles Gloriosus*, diverting the Romans with a spectacle of a swaggering hero boasting of his war exploits.

China, 202 BC. Liu Bang, a former peasant, becomes emperor of China and founds the Han Dynasty.

Carthage 201 BC. Carthage surrenders to Rome, ending the Second Punic War.

Syria, 200 BC. Antiochus III conquers Coele-Syria by winning a victory over the Egyptians at Panion.

Mexico, c.200 BC. The merging of a number of villages in the Teotihuacan Valley, with a total population of about 50,000, has given rise to a large-scale building program. The people follow the cult of the rain-god Tlaloc.

Mexico, c.200 BC. Urban centers are emerging in the Maya area. At the city

of El Mirador, the Tigre and the Danta Pyramids (respectively 178 and 136 feet high) are under construction.

Greece, 197 BC. Defeated by the Romans at the Battle of Cynoscephalae, Philip V is forced to accept all the conditions insisted upon by the consul Flamininus in exchange for peace. Macedonia is stripped of its possessions in European Greece and Asia Minor (Anatolia). This puts an end to three years of fighting between Rome and Macedonia in Illyria.

Greece, 191 BC. Antiochus III, the territorially ambitious Seleucid king, is forced to abandon Greece after a defeat by the Romans in the pass of Thermopylae. Antiochus sent 10,000 men to Greece the prior year after forging an anti-Roman coalition with the Aetolians, Spartans, and Macedonians. The Aetolians in particular felt frustrated at the political reorganization of Greece by Rome, which has declared all Greek cities free.

Asia Minor, 190 BC. After a defeat by the Romans at Magnesia, Antiochus III gives up his claim to Thrace and evacuates Asia Minor as far as the Taurus Mountains. The credit for this development goes to Publius Cornelius Scipio and Publius Scipio Africanus, who were sent by Rome to Greece and then to Asia Minor in order to finally settle the Seleucid problem. The Romans were supported in this task by the kingdom of Pergamon.

Rome, 189 BC. Eumenes II, king of Pergamon, is received by the Senate. They reach an agreement whereby control of Asia Minor will be shared between Pergamon and Rhodes.

Asia Minor, 188 BC. After his defeats at Thermopylae and Magnesia, Antiochus III concludes a peace treaty with the Romans at Apamea in Phrygia. The treaty effectively puts an end to Seleucid influence in the Mediterranean. The Thracian peninsula and most of Seleucid Asia Minor are now controlled by Pergamon.

Rome, 184 BC. Marcius Porcius Cato (the Elder), the censor, endeavors to restore moral virtue in Rome by taxing luxury. He also builds the first basilica in the Forum: the Basilica Porcia. The basilica, which becomes a popular meeting place, reflects the growing Greek influence on the architecture of Rome.

China, 180 BC. Following the death of Empress Dowager Lu, who has dominated court politics since the death of Liu Bang, founder of the Han Dynasty, Emperor Wendi succeeds to the throne.

Judea, 167 BC. Antiochus IV, the Seleucid king of Syria, dedicates the Temple of Jerusalem to the Olympian Zeus.

Rome, 167 BC. Direct taxation of Roman citizens is abolished.

Greece, 167 BC. The third Macedonian War ends in a total Roman victory. The Romans restore order to Greece. The pro-Macedonians are hunted down remorselessly. Exiles, summary executions, forced residence in Italy: Every course is pursued to eliminate the slightest opposition.

Judea, 165 BC. Judas Maccabaeus enters Jerusalem, purifies the temple and reestablishes Judaism. This is the outcome of his rebellion against the Hellenization of the country and the prohibition of Judaism promulgated by Antiochus IV.

North Africa, 151 BC. Masinissa, king of neighboring Numidia, invades the city of Carthage and achieves a military victory. The Numidian invasion has its roots in the king's desire to annex Carthage, which, despite the harsh peace conditions imposed by Rome after the Second Punic War, is on the road to recovery.

North Africa, 149 BC. Rome decides to intervene in the dispute between Numidia and Carthage, triggering the Third Punic War.

Rome, 149 BC. Marcus Porcius Cato, who performed his duties so rigorously that he acquired the permanent surname of "Censor," is dead. After visiting Carthage in 153 BC, he made the statement: "*Delenda est Carthago* (Carthage must be destroyed)."

North Africa, 146 BC. Under the leadership of Scipio Aemilianus, the Romans capture and destroy Carthage after a hard-fought battle with Hasdrubal, bringing the Third Punic War to a conclusion. They then establish the province they call Africa (northern Tunisia).

Mesopotamia, 146 BC. Mithridates the Philhellene has laid the basis for a Parthian empire. After defeating the Seleucids to gain control of Media and Babylonia, he went on to add Elam, Persia, and parts of Bactria (northern Afghanistan) to his kingdom. The Parthian capital is the city of Ctesiphon-Seleucia on the banks of the Tigris.

Corinth, 146 BC. After anti-Roman demonstrations Roman troops raze the city and sell its inhabitants into slavery.

Judea, 142 BC. The Jews liberate Jerusalem and make it their capital.

China, 136 BC. Confucianism becomes the state religion. Emperor Wudi changes the system of officially appointed academicians, of whom there were traditionally 72, establishing chairs for only the five main classical traditions.

Asia Minor, 133 BC. At his death, Attalus III Philometor, last sovereign of the Attalid Dynasty in Pergamon, bequeaths the city to Rome.

Spain, 133 BC. The Romans capture Numantia, in central northern Spain, after a long siege. This marks a decisive turning point in the guerrilla war they have been fighting in the mountains since the creation of two Roman provinces in Spain in 197 BC. It also puts an end, for the time being, to revolts such as those led by Viriathus, provoked by hardening repression.

Rome, 133 BC. After his election as tribune, Tiberius Sempronius Gracchus attempts to introduce reforms to alleviate the plight of the thousands of Roman citizens living in hopeless poverty.

Gaul, 123 BC. The Romans put an end to a series of attacks by the Celto-Ligurian tribe known as the Salluvii on the people of Massilia (Marseilles). This expedition brings Rome's military campaigns in Gaul to a successful conclusion.

Rome, 121 BC. The tribune Caius Sempronius Gracchus, brother of Tiberius, is killed by a slave after a riot in the Forum in which 3,000 of his supporters died. They were protesting the Senate's decision to repeal laws enacted by Gracchus, in the tradition of his brother, to lighten the burden of the poor.

North Africa, 118 BC. On the death of the king of Numidia, his adoptive father, Jugurtha acts against his two brothers, who are joint heirs with him to the Numidian throne. He has one murdered and attacks the other, Adherbal, forcing him to flee to Rome.

Gaul, 118 BC. A new Roman province, Gallia Narbonensis (Provence), is created between the Maritime Alps and the Pyrenees. The Romans begin building roads here to link Italy with Spain. Massilia (Marseilles) is made responsible for maintaining a coast road that runs from the Alps to the Rhone.

Asia, 115 BC. The Parthians have established themselves as rulers of Bactria (northern Afghanistan), Persia, and Mesopotamia.

Gaul, 113 BC. The Cimbri, the Teutons, and the Ambrones, Celtic and Germanic tribes that have migrated to the eastern Alps, are growing restless and posing an increasing threat to Rome.

North Africa, 112 BC. Jugurtha, who has been given control of western Numidia by Rome, again attacks Adherbal, his brother and rival for the Numidian throne. Despite Roman opposition, Jugurtha besieges Adherbal in Cirta, captures the city, and kills his brother.

China, 108 BC. The Chinese are pursuing a ruthless policy of expansion. They have now taken Zhaoxian, a border kingdom in the Korean peninsula.

North Africa, 105 BC. The Roman general Gaius Marius defeats the Numidian king Jugurtha ending the Jugurthine War.

Gaul, 102 BC. The Roman general Marius inflicts a decisive defeat on the Teutons and Cimbri at Aquae Sextiae (Aix-en-Provence).

Asia Minor, 101 BC. Mithridates, king of Pontus (on the Black Sea coast), is pursuing an expansionist policy in the region. To protect both the province of Asia and seaborne trade in the Aegean, the Romans create a new province, Cilicia, in southern Asia Minor.

100 BC – 1 BC

Rome, 90 BC. The consul Lucius Julius Caesar passes the *Lex Julia*, offering basic citizenship to the Italian allies.

Rome, 89 BC. The tribune Marcus Plautius implements the *Lex Plautia Papiria*. The new law supplements the *Lex Julia* of the previous year and gives satisfaction to many of the Italians seeking Roman citizenship. It grants the freedom of the city of Rome to everyone whose name is entered in the praetor's register.

Rome, 88 BC. As the Social War approaches its end, Lucius Cornelius Sulla is elected consul. He is given the responsibility of promoting internal recovery and, above all, of standing up to the threat from Mithridates. Sulla reacts to attempts by the general Marius to block his command against Mithridates by marching on Rome with an army and taking the city by force. Marius is forced to flee.

Asia Minor, 88 BC. Mithridates, the ambitious king of Pontus (on the Black Sea), routs Nicomedes of Bithynia in northwest Asia Minor. He then invades the Roman province of Asia and massacres 80,000 Romans and Italians.

Greece, 87 BC. Prepared to take on Mithridates, who is now in control of much of Greece, Sulla disembarks at Epirus with a large army. He swiftly gains control of the European part of Greece, with the exception of Athens and the port of Piraeus, to which he lays siege.

Rome, 87 BC. Lucius Cornelius Cinna, who distinguished himself in the field during the Social War, is elected consul after swearing to Sulla not to disturb the constitution. Soon after taking office, however, he impeaches Sulla and agitates for the recall of Marius.

Rome, 86 BC. Marius and Cinna march against Rome and declare themselves consuls after a brutal massacre of aristocrats. A fortnight later Marius dies of natural causes.

Asia Minor, 85 BC. Mithridates makes peace with the Romans, on Sulla's terms, at Dardanus, giving up all the territories he has conquered.

Rome, 84 BC. The tyrannical consul Cinna, former ally of Marius, is killed in a mutiny.

Rome, 82 BC. At the Battle of the Colline Gate, Sulla repulses a large force of Samnites from Rome. This is the culmination of a brilliant campaign to subdue his opponents, whom he severely punishes before having himself appointed dictator.

Asia Minor, 81 BC. Rome signs a peace treaty with Mithridates ending the Second Mithridatic War.

Rome, 81 BC. Julius Caesar, the son of a Roman praetor, angers the dictator Sulla by marrying Cornelia, daughter of Sulla's enemy Cinna. Caesar retreats to Asia.

Asia Minor, 74 BC. Mithridates invades the Roman province of Bithynia. The general Lucullus is faced with the task of ejecting him.

Asia Minor, 73 BC. After being driven back by the Romans, who are occupying his kingdom of Pontus, Mithridates flees to the court of Tigranes in Armenia.

Italy, 73 BC. A gladiator from Thrace by the name of Spartacus seizes Mount Vesuvius and sets off a revolt supported by many fugitive slaves. The rebels defeat two Roman armies and devastate southern Italy.

Rome, 71 BC. Pompey returns from Spain and cooperates with Crassus in finishing off the revolt of slaves led by Spartacus. Pompey, after crucifying many surviving fugitives, claims credit for the victory, thereby making an enemy of Crassus.

Parthia, 70 BC. The Kingdom of Parthia has suffered a collapse and been greatly reduced in territory by Tigranes, king of Armenia.

Mediterranean, 67 BC. The Roman general Pompey clears the sea of pirates. Centered on Crete and Cilicia, their activity has been interfering with Rome's grain supply.

Rome, 67 BC. After spending a year as *quaestor* in Spain, Julius Caesar returns to Rome and marries Pompeia, a relative of Pompey and Sulla.

Asia Minor, 66 BC. Pompey vanquishes Mithridates, king of Pontus, and drives him out of Bithynia. He then goes on to capture Tigranes, king of Armenia, who has been attempting to annex Cappadocia and Syria. Tigranes is deprived of all territories except Armenia.

Rome, 66 BC. Lucius Sergius Catilina (Catiline), appointed governor of Africa the previous year, is disqualified for the consulship by charges of maladministration and extortion.

Judea, 63 BC. After nearly a century of freedom, the Jews have once again been conquered by a foreign power. To pacify the country, Pompey has captured Jerusalem and annexed Judea to the Roman Empire, leaving the Maccabaean high priest Hyrcanus in charge.

Rome, 63 BC. Fearful of extremists, the Romans elect the famous statesman and orator Cicero to the consulship. The former "knight," who has held all the main magistracies, puts into effect a moderate policy and unites the Romans against Catiline.

Rome, 61 BC. After his brilliant victories in the east over Mithridates, Tigranes of Armenia, and Antiochus of Syria, and his capture of Jerusalem, Pompey returns in triumph to Rome. The senators, however, are in no hurry to organize a celebration to mark his achievements. At the instigation of the tribune Cato, moreover, measures are taken to undermine Pompey's patrician supporters.

Rome, 60 BC. Julius Caesar forms a triumvirate with Pompey and Marcus Licinius Crassus. Caesar is elected consul for next year, with the support of Crassus.

Rome, 59 BC. Caesar gives his daughter Julia in marriage to Pompey, and has himself married Calpurnia, daughter of Lucius Calpurnius Piso.

Gaul, 58 BC. Having won control of the provinces of Cisalpine Gaul, Transalpine Gaul and Illyricum, Caesar opens a military campaign in Gaul, conquering the Celtic tribe known as the Helvetii at Bibracte (Mont Beuvray) and the German leader Ariovistus near Vesontio (Besancon).

Italy, April 56 BC. The triumvirs meet at Lucca, in Etruria, to renew the clauses of their agreements. They decide that Crassus and Pompey will jointly hold the consulship for the year 55 BC. Caesar's command in Gaul is prolonged five years.

Britain, 55 BC. Caesar crosses the Channel and invades Britain, but withdraws after failing to secure a firm foothold. The southeast of the country is dominated by Belgic people.

Rome, 55 BC. Pompey and Crassus become consuls. Crassus is given control of Syria for five years and Pompey re-ceives both of the Roman provinces in Spain for the same period.

Mesopotamia, 53 BC. Despite being deserted by the Armenians, his former allies, Crassus leads his troops into the Mesopotamian desert in the hope of reaching and conquering Seleucia. The Romans are utterly defeated at Carrhae by the Parthians, and Crassus dies in the battle.

China, 52 BC. In the previous year, the *shanyu* (ruler) Huhanye of the Xiongnu confederacy of nomads sent his son to the Han court. He now pays personal homage to the Han emperor, who treats him more as a rival head of state than as a vassal and rewards him generously for his participation in the Han tributary system. The nomad threat to China is thereby diminished.

Gaul, 52 BC. A serious revolt breaks out in Gaul under the leadership of Vercingetorix, who is declared supreme commander of the Gauls at Bibracte (Mount Beuvray). Vercingetorix is the son of Celtillus, a former king of the Gallic tribe known as the Arverni.

Rome, 52 BC. Pompey is illegally appointed sole consul by the Senate.

Egypt, 51 BC. On his death, Ptolemy XI Auletes leaves his throne jointly to his children, Cleopatra VII and Ptolemy XII.

Rome, 51 BC. In his *De Republica*, just completed, Cicero reflects on contemporary political problems. He advocates a constitution that combines monarchy, oligarchy, and democracy, and he asserts the importance of human rights and the brotherhood of man.

Rome, 50 BC. Alarmed by Caesar's desire to remain in Gaul in command of his army and the province, his opponents in the Senate strive to get him recalled to face charges of wrongdoings during his consulship. Caesar's interests are defended in the Senate by the tribune Mark Antony.

Italy, 10 January 49 BC. Caesar crosses the Rubicon.

Rome, 49 BC. With the support of the *praetor* Marcus Aemilius Lepidus and sympathetic senators remaining in Rome, Caesar is appointed dictator. This follows his investiture with magistracies making him a lawful representative of republican powers.

Greece, 9 August 48 BC. Having landed in northern Epirus in June, Caesar defeats Pompey's troops and those of his father-in-law, Metellus Scipio, at Pharsalus. Pompey flees to Egypt.

Egypt, 28 September 48 BC. Upon landing in Egypt, Pompey is murdered on the orders of Ptolemy XII.

Egypt, 47 BC. Caesar, who has pursued Pompey to Egypt, insists that Cleopatra VII be returned to the throne of Egypt to rule jointly with her brother, Ptolemy XII, by whom she had been expelled.

Egypt, 47 BC. Cleopatra charms Caesar into spending three months with her as her lover in Egypt.

Syria, 2 August 47 BC. At Zela, Caesar defeats Pharnaces, son of Mithridates the Great, who has earlier invaded Pontus. Caesar's comment on the victory is: "*Veni, vidi, vici* (I came, I saw, I conquered)."

Rome, 46 BC. Caesar returns to Rome to quell a mutiny. Among the reforms he undertakes is abandonment of the old calendar of the pontiffs in favor of a calendar in which there are 365 days in a year with an extra day every four years.

Rome, 45 BC. Caesar, who has recently been made consul for ten years, adopts his great-nephew, Octavius. Apart from other royal tributes, Caesar's head appears on Roman coins.

Rome, 44 BC. Mark Antony becomes Caesar's colleague in the consulship.

Rome, 15 March 44 BC. Caesar is murdered by conspirators.

Rome, 44 BC. A succession crisis breaks out after Caesar's death. Mark Antony stakes his claim against that of Octavian, Caesar's great-nephew and adopted son, who has arrived in Rome to receive his inheritance.

Italy, November 43 BC. Octavian meets Mark Antony and Marcus Lepidus, governor of Transalpine Gaul, at Bononia (Bologna), and forges with his former foes an alliance of interest known as the Second Triumvirate.

Rome, 7 December 43 BC. Cicero is assassinated on the orders of Mark Antony.

Rome, 42 BC. Caesar is officially recognized as a god and, at the instigation of the triumvirate, it is decided to erect a temple in his honor in the forum.

Greece, 42 BC. Octavian and Mark Antony defeat Cassius and Brutus, two of Caesar's murderers, at the Battle of Philippi. Brutus commits suicide.

Asia Minor, 41 BC. In the course of reorganizing the eastern part of the empire, Mark Antony meets Cleopatra VII, the Egyptian queen, at Tarsus in Cilicia.

Italy, October 40 BC. A peace treaty is concluded at Brundisium (Brindisi) by which Octavian and Mark Antony share the Roman world between them. The west will be controlled by Octavian and the east by Mark Antony. Lepidus takes control of the African possessions.

Italy, 40 BC. Following the recent death of his wife Fulvia, Mark Antony marries Octavian's sister Octavia.

Judea, 37 BC. The Romans drive the Parthians, who invaded Judea in 40 BC, out of Jerusalem. Herod, who escaped to Rome after the invasion, becomes king.

Egypt, 36 BC. After suffering a defeat by the Parthians, Mark Antony goes to live in Egypt with Cleopatra, whom he weds despite still being married to Octavia. Cleopatra seeks to establish a Hellenistic monarchy with Antony.

Rome, 33 BC. Charges by Octavian that Mark Antony is under the control of the

Egyptian queen, Cleopatra, spark off a campaign of abuse between the two leaders.

Rome, 32 BC. Mark Antony divorces his wife, Octavia, the sister of Octavian.

Greece, 31 BC. Octavian declares war on Mark Antony and Cleopatra, who are now in Greece, and moves into Greece with his general Agrippa; they choose Actium as a base. Antony and Cleopatra are defeated in the ensuing sea battle and flee to Egypt.

Egypt, 31 BC. Mark Antony, after his defeat at the Battle of Actium, and in the belief that Cleopatra has taken her own life, commits suicide.

Egypt, 30 BC. Having failed to seduce the young Octavian, Cleopatra commits suicide. Her death brings to an end the last of the Hellenistic monarchies. The suicides leave Octavian as sole master of the Roman world.

Egypt, 30 BC. Egypt becomes a Roman province. Henceforth it will be directly under the authority of Octavian and its administration will be entrusted to a prefect.

Rome, 29 BC. By closing the temple of Janus for the first time since 235 BC, Octavian signals the achievement of peace throughout the empire.

Rome, 16 January 27 BC. The senate bestows on Octavian the title of *Augustus*, in recognition of his superior position in the state. He will henceforth be known by the new name.

Rome, 23 BC. Augustus gives up the consulship. However, for all intents and purposes, his powers remain unchanged. At the same time he receives the *imperium maius*, which gives him authority over provincial governors, and the "power of a tribune," which allows him to summon the senate.

Balkans, 15 BC. The Roman generals Drusus and Tiberius, the stepsons of Augustus, complete the conquest of

Noricum and Raetia to the south of Germany, in Danubian Europe.

Gaul, 12 BC. Drusus dedicates the altar of Lugdunum (Lyons) in honor of Augustus. This event reflects the extent to which the worship of Augustus has spread through the Roman Empire, and symbolizes the unification of Gaul. While forbidding the deification of his own person, Augustus has willingly received all the marks of piety bestowed upon him.

Germany, 9 BC. Tiberius succeeds Drusus, stepson of Augustus, who died after reaching the Elbe, as commander of the Roman army stationed in Germany. Tiberius is now making great inroads into the territory beyond the Rhine.

Armenia, 6 BC. Tiberius, engaged for the past two years in continuing the conquest of Germany, has now been sent to Armenia.

Asia Minor, c.5 BC. Strabo, a Greek born in Amaseia, northern Asia Minor, has written a vast *Geography*. A general survey of Hellenistic geography and cartography, his work examines the controversies between Eratosthenes, the first systematic geographer, who was writing 200 years prior, and his successors. Regional descriptions cover physical geography, ethnographic features, and myth. Its wide range makes the *Geography* an effective census of the world.

Judea, 4 BC. The brutal reign of Herod the Great, king of Judea, is at an end. On his death, his kingdom is divided between his three sons.

Judea, 4 BC. A Jewish couple, Joseph the carpenter and his wife Mary, have a baby in a stable in Bethlehem and name him Jesus.

AD 1 – 99

Rome, 4. On the death of his only surviving son, Gaius, Augustus adopts Tiberius and makes him his successor.

Germany, 9. Roman troops in Germany under the General Publius Verrus are wiped out by a confederation of German tribes led by Arminius. The eagles, the legion's standards, are captured.

Italy, August 19, 14. Caesar Augustus dies in Nola near Naples. Tiberius becomes emperor.

Rome, 15. Tiberius brings back into force the law of *maiestas*, which punishes acts that undermine the sovereign power and dignity of the Roman people.

Germany, 16. While on the Rhine with his parents, Germanicus (adopted son of Tiberius) and Agrippina, the four-year-old Gaius is nicknamed "Caligula" ("Little Boots") by the soldiers because of the military boots he wears.

Rome, 26 May 17. Germanicus, the son of Drusus who was adopted by Tiberius, celebrates a great victory over the Germans under Arminius—the latest in a two-year campaign to avenge the Romans for the crushing defeat they suffered at the hands of the Germans in the Teutoberger forest eight years ago.

Asia Minor, 17. On the deaths of the kings Archelaus of Cappadocia and Antiochus of Commagene, their kingdoms are annexed to the Roman Empire. Cappadocia is established as a province and Commagene becomes part of Syria.

Asia Minor, 17. The prolific poet Ovid dies in exile at Tomis on the Black Sea. Before writing his controversial love poems, Ovid was a distinguished lawyer and scored his first literary success with the tragedy *Medea*. His epic poem *Metamorphoses*, written in hexameters, is a collection of stories from classical and Near Eastern legend. Since his banishment by Augustus, Ovid has written, among other things, a five-volume work of elegies called the *Tristia*.

Syria, 10 October 19. The Roman general Germanicus dies near Antioch. He was convinced that the mysterious illness that ended in his death was a result of poisoning by the Syrian governor, Gnaeus Calpurnius Piso, who he had ordered to leave the province.

China, 22. The usurper Wang Mang is beaten and killed during a revolt by partisans of the legitimate Han regime. The revolt was provoked by merchants and capitalists employed as administrators, whose underhanded practices Wang Mang was trying to curb. His death sparks off a quarrel between the Han princes over who should rule.

Rome, 23. Sejanus, the sole commander of the Praetorian Guard, concentrates the Guard—until now dispersed throughout Italy—in a permanent camp in Rome. Following the recent death of Tiberius' son Drusus (in which Sejanus may have been implicated), Sejanus occupies a position of enormous influence in the senate.

India, 25. In Gandhara, the Buddha is represented for the first time in human form.

Judea, 26. Pontius Pilate, who recently became the fifth Roman procurator of Judea and Samaria, has offended the Jews by bringing images of the emperor into Jerusalem. He has shown his lack of sympathy with the Jewish religion in other ways.

Italy, 27. On the prompting of Sejanus, the prefect of the Praetorian Guard who has become his chief adviser, Tiberius decides to leave Rome for the island of Capri.

Judea, c.27. Herod Antipas, who became tetrarch of Galilee on the death of his father, Herod the Great, in 4 BC, divorces his wife and marries his niece, Herodias, the daughter of his brother Philip's wife. He is denounced by John the Baptist. John, a cousin of Mary, mother of Jesus, has gained a reputation for his baptisms and his preaching about repentance and forgiveness of sins.

Judea, 30. The procurator Pontius Pilate makes a vain attempt to transfer to Herod Antipas, tetrarch of Galilee—who is in Jerusalem for the Passover—the responsibility for trying the Galilean, Jesus.

Judea, 30 April 30. After being condemned to death by the Jewish court known as the Sanhedrin, Jesus of Nazareth is crucified at Golgotha.

Rome, 31. Tiberius orders the arrest of Sejanus. He is immediately put to death by order of the Senate.

Rome, 33. Interest rates rocket as a the result of a currency shortage. Property prices fall as owners sell their land to pay off debts. Tiberius provides the bankers with 100 million sesterces to finance interest-free loans.

Parthia, 35. Overthrown by his cousin Tiridates III, who enjoys the support of Rome, Artabanus III, king of Parthia, escapes and is given refuge by the nomadic people of Hyrcania.

Judea, 35. Stephen, one of the seven diakone of the early Christian community in Jerusalem is found guilty of blasphemy by the Sanhedrin and stoned to death, becoming the first Christian martyr.

Syria, c.35. On the road to Damascus, the Jew, Saul of Tarsus, is converted to Christianity by a vision of Jesus Christ crucified. Formerly a strenuous Pharisee, Saul had assisted in the persecution of the Christians.

Parthia, 36. Artabanus III regains his throne and comes to an agreement with Rome: he is recognized as king of the Parthians but accepts the Roman protectorate of Armenia.

Italy, March 37. On a trip to the Italian mainland from his home on Capri, the emperor Tiberius dies at Misenum (on the bay of Naples). The Senate proclaims Caligula emperor. Caligula then adopts his cousin Tiberius Gemellus.

Rome, 38. In the year since he became emperor, Caligula has squandered the vast fortune left by Tiberius. He has also banished or murdered many of his relatives, except Drusilla and Claudius.

Judea, 39. At the instigation of his wife, Herodias, the tetrarch Herod Antipas asks Caligula for the title of king. However, he is deposed on a charge of treason trumped up by his nephew, Agrippa, who proceeds to inherit his tetrarchy.

Rome, January 41. Shortly after declaring himself a god, Caligula is assassinated by two Praetorian tribunes. After fruitless discussion about the reestablishment of a republic, the Senate recognizes Caligula's uncle, Claudius, as emperor. The appointment is proclaimed by the Praetorians. Claudius was saved from Caligula's cruelty by his supposed mental deficiency. After his nephew's murder, soldiers found him hiding in the palace.

Judea, 41. Agrippa, nephew of Herod Antipas and grandson of Herod the Great, is made king of all Judea by the Emperor Claudius.

Britain, c.42. Cunobelinus, king of the Catuvellauni from Verulamium (St Albans), is dead. After moving against the Essex tribe called the Trinovantes, Cunobelinus established a capital at Camulodunum (Colchester) and went on to conquer Kent.

Britain, 43. On the orders of Claudius, the Romans, led by Aulus Plautius, invade Britain.

Egypt, 45. The philosopher and commentator Philo dies in his native Alexandria. Philo headed a Jewish embassy to Caligula in 39 to ask for exemption from the duty of worshipping the emperor—an expedition he described in his *De Legatione*. He attempted to reconcile Jewish and Greek thought.

Asia Minor, 45. The Apostle Paul begins a three-year journey through Asia Minor preaching. This will be followed by travels in 49-52 to Galatia and Greece and 54-58 through Galatia, Phrygia, Ephesus, and to Corinth and Illyria.

Rome, 48. The sexual profligacy of Claudius' wife Messalina reaches a climax when, in Claudius' absence, she goes through the formalities of a marriage ceremony with one of her lovers, the consul designate Gaius Silius. Claudius has Messalina and her lover Gaius Silius put to death.

Rome, 48. Claudius marries his niece Agrippina II, the daughter of Germanicus.

Rome, 50. Claudius adopts his stepson Nero, the son of his wife Agrippina.

Jerusalem, c.50. An apostolic council that brings together Paul and Barnabas with the original disciples decides that converts to the new religion need not observe Mosaic law, making it easier for Paul to spread his message to the gentiles.

Parthia, 52. Vologeses, a Mede, comes to the throne of Parthia and restores order to his country after a period of dynastic disturbance.

Britain, 51. The British king Caractacus, son of Cunobelinus, who has been fighting the Roman invaders since 43, is taken prisoner at Ludlow. He sought refuge with Cartimandua, queen of the Yorkshire Brigantes, who handed him over to the enemy. Most of Caractacus' family is already in captivity.

Armenia, 53. In a challenge to Rome, Vologeses, king of Parthia, puts his brother Tiridates on the Armenian throne, laying the ground for an Arsacid dynasty in the country.

Rome, 53. Nero marries his stepsister Octavia, the daughter of Claudius and Messalina.

Rome, 13 October 54. Claudius is murdered by Agrippina and is succeeded by his adopted son, Nero, rather than by Britannicus, his son by Messalina.

Rome, 55. Britannicus, son of Claudius, is poisoned to death by Nero.

Armenia, 58. Corbulo, leader of the Roman armies in Syria, completes a successful invasion of Armenia and makes the country into a Roman protectorate.

Palestine, 58. The Apostle Paul is arrested and held in prison in Caesarea until 60, when he is sent to Rome.

Rome, 59. Nero murders his mother, Agrippina, who herself poisoned her husband, Claudius, in 53.

Armenia, 60. The Roman general Corbulo drives Tiridates, brother of the Parthian king Vologeses, out of Armenia, replacing him by Tigranes V, whose grandfather ruled the country in the Augustan era.

Rome, 62. On the death of Burrus—the prefect of the guard who has effectively been governing Rome with Seneca—Nero divorces Octavia and places her under military surveillance in Campania. He then marries his mistress Poppaea, former wife of his friend Otho, and banishes Octavia to Pandateria, where, on 9 June, she is murdered.

Armenia, 63. With the consent of Rome, the Armenian throne is returned to Tiridates. The six-year conflict following his ejection from Armenia by Corbulo has ended with the peace of Rhandeia.

Rome, 64. Accused by Nero of having started the fire that devastated Rome, Christians are persecuted. Peter, a Jewish fisherman to whom Jesus assigned the task of universal shepherd, is crucified.

Rome, c.64. Paul of Tarsus, who has spent two years as a prisoner in Rome, after suffering much harassment by the Jews, is executed.

Rome, 65. Nero uncovers a conspiracy to assassinate and replace him with Gaius Calpurnius Piso. The writers Seneca, Lucan, Petronius, and the Stoic Thrasea are accused of complicity and forced to commit suicide.

Judea, 67. The Jews rise up against the Romans. Vespasian, a former consul who distinguished himself in the invasion of Britain, is given the task of crushing them.

Greece, 67. Nero has Corbulo executed along with two ex-legates of Germany.

Gaul/Spain, 68. Vindex, the governor of Gallia Lugdunensis (the Lyons region of Gaul), and Galba, a brilliant soldier and the governor of the eastern seaboard of Spain, rise up against Nero. Vindex is beaten, but Galba wins the support of Otho, the governor of Lusitania in western Spain.

Rome, 9 June 68. Deserted by the Praetorians and having lost favor with the Senate, Nero commits suicide.

Rome, October 68. Servius Sulpicius Galba, known as the "legate of the Senate and the Roman people," accepts the invitation of Vindex, the governor of Gallia Lugdunensis who rebelled against Nero, to succeed as emperor. He enters Rome with the support of Otho, governor of Lusitania in western Spain.

Germany, 3 January 69. The Roman legions on the Rhine refuse to declare their allegiance to Galba, instead proclaiming their legate, Aulus Vitellius, as emperor.

Rome, 15 January 69. Weakened by the revolt of the legions in Germany, Galba is overthrown and killed by the Praetorians, who offer the empire to Otho.

Judea, 69. After his previous year's capture of Qumran, stronghold of the Essenes, and Jericho, Vespasian, the commander appointed to suppress the Jewish rebellion, lays siege to Jerusalem.

Italy, 16 April 69. Defeated by Vitellius' troops at Bedriacum, Otho commits suicide.

Egypt, 1 July 69. In Alexandria, Vespasian, the leader of the eastern army and son of a humble tax collector from the Italian municipality of Reate, is hailed as Roman emperor by the Egyptian legions under Tiberius Alexander.

Italy, September 69. Antonius Primus, commander of a legion in Pannonia, declares his support for Vespasian and, having gained the backing of the other Danubian armies, leads an invasion of Italy.

Italy, October 69. The forces of Antonius Primus inflict a crushing defeat on Vitellius at Cremona.

Rome, 20 December 69. Vespasian's supporters enter Rome and discover Vitellius in hiding. He is dragged through the streets before he is brutally murdered.

Rome, 21 December 69. Vespasian enters Rome and is adopted as emperor by the Senate.

Judea, 7 September 70. Under siege by Titus, since his father Vespasian's proclamation as emperor last year, Jerusalem finally falls to the Romans.

Germany, 70. Gaius Julius Civilis, a Batavian who led a great revolt of the Germanic peoples against the Romans, suffers a decisive defeat. The "war of liberation" began in 69 under pretext of providing support for Vespasian, and was joined by Gallic tribes such as the Treveri and Lingones.

Palestine, c.70. Appearance of The Gospel according to Mark.

China, 73. General Ban Chao is sent to the western regions, where he establishes Chinese control over the oasis states. This marks a new peak in later Han military success.

Judea, April 15, 73. After a siege that lasted two years, the Roman general Lucius Flavius Silva captures the Jewish fortress of Masada. All of the defenders and their families commit suicide rather than face imprisonment.

Rome, 75. Flavius Josephus, a Jewish historian and former fighter in the 66 uprising, now with the Romans, recounts the events in his *Bellum Judaicum* (*History of the Jewish Wars*). He has also written a history of his own people from their origins until the present, the *Antiquitates Judaicae* (*Early History of the Jews*).

Syria, 76. With the consent of Vespasian, Johanan ben Zakkai, former spokesman of the Pharisaic pacifist sect, sets up an academy at Jabneh and reestablishes the Sanhedrin. Johanan ben Zakkai took refuge at Jabneh before the Romans captured Jerusalem.

Italy, 23 June 79. On his death at Cutilia, Vespasian is deified. He is succeeded by his elder son Titus, who was responsible for the capture of Jerusalem in 70. Titus appoints his younger brother Flavius Domitianus (Domitian) as heir.

Pompeii, August 24, 79. The city is completely destroyed following the eruption of Mt. Vesuvius.

India, 80. Vima Kadphises, whose father Kujula founded the Kushan Empire, has extended his kingdom's possessions in India as far as Mathura.

Rome, 80. Some 50,000 visitors are in attendance as the Coliseum is dedicated.

Italy, 19 September 81. Titus dies of the plague at Cutilia. He is succeeded by his brother Domitian.

Rome, 81. Domitian consecrates the triumphal arch begun by Titus to celebrate his victory over the Jews.

Balkans, 83. After unifying the Dacian people, who inhabit territory in the southeast corner of the Adriatic, Decebalus becomes king of Dacia.

Britain, 83. Continuing the conquest of Britain started by his predecessors, Julius Agricola defeats the Caledonians at Mount Graupius.

Germany, 83. Domitian crosses the Rhine at Mainz on his campaign against the Chatti, a highly organized Germanic people who live in the region of the upper Weser and the Diemel.

Balkans, 87. The Romans suffer a serious setback in the Dacian war, which broke out in 85. The Praetorian prefect, Cornelius Fuscus, who was entrusted with the Roman command, is defeated and killed.

Balkans, 89. The Romans fail to wipe out the Dacians. Their kingdom has been saved from total destruction by the Marcomanni and the Quadi, who now occupy Bohemia, a western neighbor of Dacia. After defeating the emperor in battle, these peoples forced Domitian to sign a humiliating peace treaty with the Dacian king, Decebalus.

Rome, 90. Domitian has embarked on a campaign of persecution and execution of his opponents.

Central Asia, 91. Continuing his conquest of the Tarim Basin, the Chinese general Ban Chao defeats the Indian Kushans under the leadership of Kaniska.

Rome, 92. The lawyer Quintilian, who was born in Spain c.30, has written the *Institutio Oratorio*, a program of education for future orators. Quintilian, who believes that the supreme orator represents all that is best in morals, education, and stylistic judgment, holds the chair of Latin eloquence created by Vespasian in 72. Among his pupils were Pliny the Younger and the two great-nephews and heirs of Domitian.

Rome, 95. Domitian accuses the consul Flavius Clemens and his wife, Flavia Domitilla, of "atheism" (perhaps Christian or Jewish practices). Clemens—whose two sons Domitian had intended to be his heirs—is executed. Domitilla, meanwhile, is banished to an island.

Rome, 18 September 96. Domitian, who has been conducting a reign of terror for the past three years, is assassinated as the result of a plot by his wife Domitia and two Praetorian prefects.

Nerva, suspected of complicity in the death of Domitian, is declared emperor by the Senate. The Senate then annuls laws passed by Domitian and orders his statues to be destroyed.

Rome, 27 October 97. To placate the Praetorians and legions in Germany, Nerva adopts Trajan, the Spanish-born governor of lower Germany.

Rome, 98. Cornelius Tacitus publishes an account of the life of his father-in-law, Julius Agricola, whose daughter he married in 77. Tacitus has also written a descriptive history of the various tribes north of the Rhine and the Danube, and recently started work on a monumental history of Rome.

Germany, 28 January 98. On the death of Nerva, Trajan is declared Roman emperor in Cologne, the seat of his government in lower Germany.

Rome, 99. Having inspected and organized the frontiers of the Rhine and Danube, and subdued or executed mutinous Praetorians, Trajan leaves Germany and makes his entry into Rome.

Rome, 99. Julius Frontinus, a former governor of Britain who was made superintendent of Rome's water supply by the Emperor Nerva, has completed a detailed account of the city's water system, describing the aqueducts and their history. He has also written studies of land surveying and of Greek and Roman military science.

100 – 199

Mexico, c.100. The Pyramids of the Sun and Moon are under construction at Teotihuacan.

Rome, 100. Among the many social reforms introduced by Trajan is a system of *alimenta*, which is designed to give allowances to children of the poor. Interest paid by landowners on mortgage loans made by the state is distributed among the children—primarily to increase the birth rate in order to swell the ranks of the Roman legions.

Spain, 105. The bridge of Alcantara, which has a straight floor, is constructed over the Tagus River

Balkans, 105. Decebalus, king of the Dacians, attacks the nomadic people known as the Iazyges, who come from the lower Danube region, and besieges the Roman garrisons remaining in Dacia.

China, 105. A form of prototype paper is evolved and made known to the Han government by the eunuch Cai Lun.

Balkans, 106. Having relieved the Roman garrisons in Dacia, Trajan recaptures the Dacian capital and drives Decebalus to suicide. Dacia becomes a Roman province.

Arabia, 106. The Kingdom of Nabataea, which has its capital at Petra, is invaded by Cornelius Palma, governor of Syria, and annexed by Rome. It becomes the Roman province of Arabia.

India, c.110. At the instigation of the Kushan king, Kaniska, a grand Buddhist council is held in Kashmir. It proceeds under the direction of the Buddhist theologian Asvaghosha, a poet, dramatist, musician, and friend of the king. The most important outcome of the council is the division of Buddhism into two branches of belief, those of the Greater and Lesser Vehicle, Mahayana and Hinayana.

Asia Minor, 110. Pliny the Younger is appointed governor of Bithynia.

Rome, 114. The Senate votes to build a triumphal arch at Beneventum, at the end of the new Via Traiana, the construction of which has improved communications with Brundisium (Brindisi) and the east. Dedicated to "Trajan Optimus," it will depict imperial achievements in a series of allegories.

Armenia, 114. Osroes, king of the Parthians, dethrones the Armenian king, a vassal of the Romans, and replaces him with his nephew Parthamasiris. Trajan then declares war on the Parthians, and occipies Armenia aided by the people of Colchis in the Caucasus.

Mesopotamia, 115. With the collaboration of Abgar, king of Osroene, a kingdom in the northwest of the region with a capital at Edessa, Trajan occupies most of Mesopotamia.

Syria, August 117. Hadrian, named by the dying Trajan as his successor, is declared emperor at Antioch. To establish peace on the frontiers of the empire, he abandons Mesopotamia and Assyria.

Rome, 121. Hadrian sets off on a tour of inspection of the Empire that will last until 125.

Britain, 122. On the orders of Hadrian, who is visiting Britain, construction begins on a frontier wall between the Roman province and the unconquered Caledonians. It will stretch from the Solway Firth to the Tyne River.

Armenia, 123. Under a peace treaty signed by Hadrian and the Parthian king, Osroes, Armenia again has an Arsacid ruler under the protection of Rome.

Athens, 124. During a journey to Greece, Hadrian is initiated into the ancient rites known as the Eleusinian Mysteries.

Athens, 128. Hadrian dedicates the Olympieum, the enormous temple of the Olympian Zeus. Work on construction of the temple started under the tyranny of Peisistratus over 700 years prior. The emperor also accepts the title of *Olympius*.

Italy, c.130. On his property at Tibur (Tivoli), Hadrian has had a palatial villa erected to house reproductions of the monuments he has admired during his journeys. At Rome, he has completely rebuilt the Pantheon, the temple in the Campus Martius built in 25 BC by Marcus Vipsanius Agrippa.

Egypt, 130. While on a journey with the emperor up the Nile, Hadrian's lover Antinous is drowned. Rumor has it that he may have given his life for his master. Hadrian founds the city of Antinopolis in his memory.

Judea, 132. Incensed by the creation of a pagan Roman colony and the building of a shrine to Jupiter Capitolinus on the site of the temple at Jerusalem, the Jews rebel. Under the joint leadership of Simon Bar-Kochba ("Son of the Star") and the rabbi Eleazar, they take possession of Judea.

Judea, 135. After two and a half years of fighting, the Jewish revolt is quelled and Hadrian recaptures Jerusalem. The last of the rebels take refuge in the fortress of Bethar to the southwest of the Holy City, but surrender during the summer after a siege of several months. Jerusalem is renamed Aelia Capitolina, and is forbidden to Jews. Judea is renamed Syria Palestine.

Rome, February 138. Hadrian adopts Titus Aurelius Antoninus, a former proconsul of Asia, who is given full imperial powers. Antoninus in turn adopts Commodus' young son and his own nephew, Marcus Annius Verus.

Italy, 10 July 138. Hadrian dies at his residence on the Bay of Naples.

Britain, 143. Quintus Lollius Urbicus, the governor of Britain, has suppressed the revolt of the Brigantes that began last year. Lollius is also responsible for the construction of the turf wall built across the country north of Hadrian's Wall.

Rome, 145. Marcus Aurelius marries his cousin Faustina the Younger, daughter of Antoninus.

Rome, 146. On the birth of his daughter, Marcus Aurelius receives the powers of a tribune and a proconsul, making him the most likely successor to Antoninus.

Rome, 21 April 147. Antoninus celebrates the 900th anniversary of Rome's foundation.

Germany, 160. The *limes* (fortified boundary) of the Rhine is extended beyond the valley of the Neckar.

Italy, March 161. On the death of Antoninus at Lorium, Marcus Aurelius becomes emperor. Marcus Aurelius invests his adoptive brother Lucius Verus with the powers of a tribune and makes him co-emperor. For the first time, the imperial powers are fully shared.

Britain, 165. Following new incursions by the Brigantes, the Romans abandon the Antonine Wall, built in 143, and retreat to Hadrian's Wall.

China, 166. An embassy of Syrian merchants who claim to have been sent by Marcus Aurelius in 162 arrives in China.

Mesopotamia, 166. After Avidius Cassius' victories, including the partial destruction of Ctesiphon, the Emperor Verus enters the Parthian capital and makes peace with Vologaeses III.

Italy, 166. German tribes pour across the upper and lower Danube and invade northern Italy.

Rome, 167. Brought back from the east by Verus' army, the plague ravages Rome. Marcus Aurelius resorts to the most ancient rites to ward it off: *vota publico*, public vows to the gods, and *lectisternia*, by which gods are symbolically entertained as guests at a meal, couches being specially prepared for them.

Rome, 169. Lucius Verus dies of apoplexy on his return to Rome.

Rome, 170. Marcus Aurelius has an equestrian statue of himself erected on the Capitol.

Balkans, 172. Marcus Aurelius imposes peace on the Quadi and the Marcomanni. A strip almost five miles wide to the north of the Danube is forbidden to them.

Egypt, 173. Invested with the control of the whole of the eastern empire since 166, Avidius Cassius, the governor of Syria, crushes the insurrections of the shepherd brigands known as the *boukoloi*.

Syria, 175. At the false rumor of Marcus Aurelius' death, Avidius Cassius, the governor of Syria, has himself proclaimed emperor. However, three months after his accession, abandoned by his supporters, he is killed by a soldier.

Rome, 176. Marcus Aurelius puts his son Commodus on the throne, giving him the title of Augustus.

Balkans, 177. The Quadi and the Marcomanni have again declared war on the Roman Empire.

Balkans, 17 March 180. At the death of his father, Marcus Aurelius, from the plague, Commodus is fighting the Marcomanni on the upper Danube. Commodus, who is now sole emperor, abandons plans for conquest, makes peace with the Marcomanni and hastens to Rome.

Black Sea, c.180. A Germanic people known as the Goths, who originated in southern Scandinavia, have migrated from the Baltic and are settling on the shores of the Black Sea. They are divided into Goths from the west (Visigoths) and Goths from the east (Ostrogoths), on either side of the Dniester.

Germany, 180. Work begins on the Porta Nigra in the Roman capital of Augusta Trevorum (Trier).

Egypt, 190. The country is suffering worsening poverty as a result of the doubling of prices in the past decade. The proportion of silver in the denarius is lowered from 90 to 70 percent.

Southern Africa, c.190. The culture associated with the early users of iron in the continent has spread as far south as the Limpopo Valley to Mabveni (in southern Zimbabwe) and Makodu (in eastern Botswana). The pottery produced here, which is distinct from the east coast tradition, derives from the region of the East African great lakes (Zambia, western Tanzania, and Uganda).

Rome, 191. Considering himself the new founder of Rome, Commodus rebaptizes the city in his own name, calling it *Colonia Lucia Annia Nova Com-*

modiana. He does likewise with the fleet, the wheat, the legions, and all the months of the year.

China, 192. After allowing his soldiers to burn down the capital, Loyang, General Dong Zhuo is assassinated, and China descends into anarchy.

Rome, 31 December 192. His mind unhinged by power, Commodus, who sees himself as the incarnation of Hercules, has expressed a desire to sacrifice the new consuls on 1 January 193. Frightened by this mania for blood, his concubine Marcia and the Praetorian prefect Aemilius Laetus arrange for an athlete called Narcissus to strangle him in his bath. His death brings to an end the Antonine Dynasty. Publius Helvius Pertinax is proclaimed emperor by the Praetorian Guard under its prefect Laetus.

Roman Empire, 193. The year of five emperors. In March, the Praetorian Guard regrets the removal of Commodus and assassinates Pertinax after only three months in office. This is followed by the proclamation of Marcus Didius Julianus—a man unpopular with both the Roman masses and the provincial armies—as emperor. In April, the distinguished soldier Septimus Severus is proclaimed emperor by the army in Illyricum. Later in the month, Pescennius Niger, who became governor of Syria two years ago, is proclaimed emperor by the army in the east. The Emperor Marcus Didius Julianus is murdered in his palace on the first of June, and after his uncontested entry into Rome, Septimius Severus dismisses the Praetorian Guard and replaces it with a new guard. In September, Clodius Albinus, the governor of Britain, is given the title Caesar.

Syria, 194. After several defeats by the army of Septimius Severus, Pescennius Niger, declared emperor by his troops last year, is overtaken and executed while fleeing toward the Euphrates. Syria is then divided into two provinces.

Gaul, 196-197. In an attempt to secure the support of the German legions for

a march on Rome, Clodius Albinus, the governor of Britain, who has been declared Augustus by his army, crosses to Gaul. Septimus Severus defeats Clodius Albinus and reunites he Empire under his command.

Mesopotamia, 197. As retribution for their support of Pescennius Niger, Septimius Severus battles and then vanquishes the Parthians at Seleucia and Ctesiphon and wrests control of Mesopotamia from them.

Mesopotamia, 199. Mesopotamia becomes a Roman province.

200 – 299

West Africa, c.200. The state known as Ghana in the savannah region (where Mauritania and Mali overlap) is gaining in wealth and power. Local Mandingo people have been influenced by incoming Berber traders from the north since c.600 BC.

Rome, 202. An edict is issued against Christianity in the Roman Empire. All Christian or Jewish proselytizing is forbidden, opening the way for local persecutions in Africa, Gaul, and Egypt.

Gaul, c.202. The Christian father Irenaeus is dead—perhaps martyred in the persecution. After becoming bishop of Lugdunum in 178, Irenaeus devoted himself to the conversion of the Rhone Valley. He will be remembered particularly for his controversy with the Gnostics, set out in his great treatise *Against Heretics*.

Rome, 203. An arch dedicated to Septimius Severus is erected in the Forum.

Rome, 203. The jurist Papinian becomes Praetorian prefect, in succession to Plautianus, who was executed in a plot. Papinian's recently published doctrinal analyses *Quaestiones* and *Responsa* link law and humanism.

Egypt, 203. Origen replaces Clement as head of the Christian school of Alexandria.

Britain, 4 February 211. Septimius Severus dies of natural causes at Eburacum (York) during his British campaign. He is succeeded by his sons Marcus Aurelius Antoninus—nicknamed Caracalla on account of his long-hooded Gaulish tunic—and Septimius Antoninus Geta.

Rome, February 212. Geta is murdered on the orders of his brother Caracalla, who proceeds to unleash bloody repression in Rome. Among the 20,000 victims is the famous jurist Papinian.

Rome, 212. Caracalla grants Roman citizenship to virtually all free inhabitants of the empire.

Mesopotamia, 217. After the assassination of Caracalla, the Praetorian prefect Marcus Opellius Macrinus, who is implicated in the killing, becomes the first emperor from the Equestrian Order.

Syria, 218. Defeated in a battle near Antioch, Macrinus is captured and put to death by supporters of Elagabalus, who claims to be the son of Caracalla and has recently been hailed as emperor.

Palestine, 219. A Hebrew edition of the *Mishna*, a collection of sayings and teachings drawn from the Torah, is published. It was produced under the direction of Rabbi Yehuda ha-Kadosh.

China, 220. With the end of the Han Dynasty the country is divided into three kingdoms: Wei, Shu, and Wu.

Rome, 221. On the death of Elagabalus, Alexander Severus becomes emperor.

Rome, 222. Pope Callistus is killed during an anti-Christian popular uprising. This is at a time when the church is undergoing a great expansion and Christians are mostly tolerated by the authorities. They even have contacts with the powerful Empress Julia Mamaea, mother of the Emperor Alexander Severus.

Mesopotamia, 226. Ardashir overthrows Artabanus, the last of the Parthian kings, and founds a new Persian dynasty of the Sassanids.

China, 227. Cao Pi, founder of the Wei Dynasty, is dead. He was the son of Cao Cao, the poet and general who conquered northern China.

Near East, 232. The Romans expel the Sassanid king Ardashir from the provinces of Mesopotamia and Cappadocia, which he invaded in 230.

Germany, 235. Alexander Severus is murdered by his own troops. They proclaim their general, Maximinus, a former Thracian peasant, emperor.

Balkans, 238. Despite the payment of tributes, the Romans have failed to persuade the Goths and Carpi to withdraw from the province of Moesia.

Italy, 238. Maximinus—made emperor in 235—is killed by his troops while besieging Aquileia in northern Italy. The 13-year-old Gordian III becomes emperor.

China, 239. Queen Himiko of Yamatai, in Japan, sends an envoy to China. The envoy is given a gold seal by the Chinese emperor confirming the queen as an ally of China.

Black Sea, 242. Gordian III evacuates the cities of the Cimmerian Bosporus (southern Russia). Cut off from the Roman world, the region falls under the domination of the Ostrogoths who are settling in the Ukraine.

Mesopotamia, March 244. Gordian is murdered by his own soldiers during a war against the Persians that began in 242. The Praetorian prefect, an Arab named Philip, is made emperor and makes peace with the Persians.

Rome, 244: The Greek Neoplatonist philosopher Plotinus travels from Alexandria to Rome. He composes a work in 54 parts setting down his teachings.

Japan, 247. Civil war breaks out in Japan after the death of Queen Himiko when her brother usurps the throne, overthrowing the female right of inheritance. Peace is only restored when Himiko's daughter Iyo regains power as priestess-queen.

Rome, 27 April 247. Philip the Arab marks the millennium of Rome with a celebration of the *ludi saeculares*.

Italy, 249. Philip the Arab is killed in a clash with Decius, his commander in Dacia, at Verona. Decius becomes emperor.

Ethiopia, c.250. Axum is growing into a powerful kingdom under the rule of King Aphilas. Frankincense and myrrh are exported through the Red Sea to the Mediterranean, and Aphilas issues his own coinage. Magnificent obelisks and a royal palace are in the process of construction.

Rome 250. Decius launches a wave of anti-Christian persecution. Among those executed are Fabianus, the Bishop of Rome.

Balkans, 251. As a consequence of the disloyalty of Gallus, the governor of Moesia, Decius and his son are defeated and killed at the Battle of Abrittus by the Goths under Kniva. Gallus becomes emperor.

Persia, 252. The Sassanid emperor, Shapur I, makes Armenia part of his domain, forcing the Armenian king, Tiridates II, to flee.

Balkans, 253. During an attack on Aemilius Aemilianus, his successor as governor of Moesia, Gallus is killed by his own troops.

Rome, September 253. Aemilianus, emperor for just a few months, is killed in a mutiny. The Senate recognizes Valerian as emperor. He chooses his son Gallienus as his colleague.

Palestine, 253. The theologian and philosopher Origen, who headed a Christian school in his native Alexandria for 28 years, dies as a result of torture suffered during the Decian persecution of 250.

Rome, 258. A second edict is issued following one published the previous year, forbidding Christian worship. Pope Sixtus II is martyred.

North Africa, 258. Cyprian, the bishop of Carthage, is martyred.

Roman Empire, 260. The *limes* are trespassed by west Germanic tribes. They attack Gaul and reach Spain.

Rome, 260. Gallienus issues an edict enshrining tolerance of the Christians. It is known as the "little peace of the Church."

Syria, 260. The Persians are repelled in Cappadocia by the Praetorian prefect Macrinus, who has his sons proclaimed emperors at Emesa (Homs). Odenathus, the prince of Palmyra, attacks them while they are retreating and takes control of the Roman Empire.

China, 265. The short-lived Wei Dynasty is ousted by a Wei general, Sima Yan, who founds a new regime, the Jin or Western Jin.

Balkans, 267. The Goths pillage Thrace, Macedonia, and Greece.

Balkans, 269. After crushing the Goths in two great battles at Doberus and Naissus (Nissa), Claudius II—one of Gallienus' chief officers, who succeeded his master the previous year—wins the congratulatory nickname of "Gothicus." Soon after becoming emperor, Claudius defeats the invading Alamanni.

Egypt, 269. Zenobia, the widow of Odenathus of Palmyra, a city centered on an oasis between Syria and Babylonia, conquers Egypt. She has already secured control of Syria and laid waste to the northern Arabia region of Bostra.

Balkans, 270. Claudius II dies of the plague and Lucius Domitius Aurelianus (Aurelian), who distinguished himself in the fight against the Goths after Claudius put him in charge of the cavalry, becomes emperor.

Asia Minor, 270. Zenobia gains control of most of Asia Minor, apart from Bithynia.

Balkans, 271. In their first important withdrawal since the beginning of the empire, the Romans evacuate Dacia.

Rome, 271. An attack by the Juthungi on northern Italy prompts Aurelian to order the building of a sturdy wall around the city of Rome.

Syria, 271. Zenobia declares herself empress and breaks with the Roman Empire. She gives her son Vaballathus the title of Augustus.

Egypt, 271. Aurelian, who has decided to put a stop to Zenobia's activities, sends his troops into Egypt, but loses his general, Probus, in a battle for control of the country.

Syria, 272. Having reoccupied Anatolia and defeated Zenobia's troops in two battles, Aurelian captures Palmyra and takes the queen herself prisoner.

Syria, 273. Aurelian puts down a new revolt in Palmyra and deposes the new king. The city is reduced to a village.

Gaul, 275. The country is pillaged by the Franks and the Alamanni.

Asia Minor, 275. On his way to confront the Persians, Aurelian is murdered near Byzantium as the result of a military plot.

Asia Minor, 276. Tacitus, who was chosen by the Senate late in the previous year to succeed Aurelian, is killed by his own troops after winning a victory over the Goths.

Persia, 26 February 277. Mani, the founder of Manichaeism, is put to death by the Sassanian Persians.

Gaul, 277. Marcus Aurelius Probus, who became sole emperor in 276 after outmaneuvering his rival, Florian, liberates Gaul from the Franks and the Alamanni.

Palestine, 279. Johanan bar Nappacha, the Jewish rabbi who masterminded and edited the Palestinian or Jerusalem Talmud, dies.

Asia Minor, 20 November 284. On the death at Nicomedia of Numerian, younger son and successor of Cams, Diocletian, the commander of the emperor's bodyguard, is proclaimed emperor by his soldiers.

Gaul, 1 April 286. Maximian is made emperor by Diocletian and placed on an equal footing with him, acquiring the title Augustus.

Asia Minor, 1 March 293. Diocletian arranges for two Caesars, Galerius and Constantius Chlorus, to join the two Augusti in the rule of the Roman Empire.

Central America, c.295. The civilizations of Teotihuacan and Monte Alban in Mexico and Central America are reaching new heights of prosperity. In the lands controlled by the Maya numerous city-states are developing, ruled by rival dynastic families.

Britain, 296. The Emperor Constantius Chlorus, Caesar of the west, recovers the province of Britain from the usurper Allectus, an officer in Carasius' army who had murdered the rebel leader and taken control himself.

300 – 399

Armenia, 300. Tiridates, king of Armenia, is converted to Christianity by Gregory the Illuminator, making his the first state to accept Christianity as its official religion.

Rome, 20 November 303. The Augusti and the Caesars, together for the first time, hold a festival in honor of the twentieth anniversary of Diocletian's accession.

Asia Minor, 304. Since his purge of the army and the court in 302, Diocletian has issued four edicts aimed at destroying Christianity in the Roman Empire.

Churches are dismantled, clergy arrested, and Christians forced to sacrifice to the pagan gods on pain of death.

Rome, 1 May 305. Diocletian becomes the first emperor to abdicate; he retires to a palace on the Adriatic. Maximian is forced to abdicate with him. The former Caesars Galerius and Constantius both receive the title of Augustus. The new Caesars are Severus, who is made prefect of Italy, and Galerius' nephew Maximin Daia, who gains control of Syria and Egypt.

Britain, 23 July 306. On the death of his father, the Augustus Constantius Chlorus, Constantine is proclaimed Caesar of the west by the army at York. Severus, the former Caesar, is recognized by Galerius as Augustus of the west.

Rome, 306. Maxentius, son of Maximian, is elevated to the throne by the Praetorian Guard and the people of Rome. He takes control of Italy, Spain, and Africa.

Italy, 306. Severus surrenders to Maxentius at Ravenna after attempting to march on Rome. He is put to death.

Eastern Empire, 307. Galerius is forced to abandon an invasion of Italy because of disloyalty in his army.

Rome, 308. Maxentius takes the title Augustus. His father, the former emperor Maximian, meanwhile, after failing to depose his son, has fled to Constantine.

Balkans, 308. Galerius confers with Diocletian and Maximian at Carnuntum on the Danube. Maxentius is declared a public enemy, and Licinius is proclaimed rightful Augustus of the west.

Persia, 310. After a crisis over the succession, the 17-year-old Shapur II, grandson of Narses, becomes king.

Balkans, April 311. The Emperor Galerius issues the Edict of Sardica, grant-ing toleration to the Christians; he dies shortly afterward. Maximin and Licinius hurry to divide up the eastern empire between them. Maximin resumes persecution of the Christians.

Italy, 28 October 312. After invading Italy, Constantine defeats Maxentius at the Battle of the Milvian Bridge, making him master of the whole Roman west.

Milan, February 313. Licinius marries Constantine's sister, Constantia. The two emperors agree on a policy of religious toleration for Christians, known as the Edict of Milan.

Adrianople, 30 April 313. Licinius eliminates the Caesar Maximin Daia and unifies the whole of the eastern empire under his rule.

Balkans, 313. The ex-emperor Diocletian dies in Dalmatia.

Rome, 315. The Arch of Constantine is built near the Coliseum. Constantine also completes the great basilica begun by Maxentius and places in it a huge statue of himself. These monuments commemorate his victory of 312.

China, 316. The Western Jin collapses following the capture of Changan by the Xiongnu.

China, 317. The survivors of the Western Jin reestablish themselves farther south on the Yangzi River, and the prime minister, Sima Rui, succeeds to the throne of the Eastern Jin in Jiankang (Nanking).

Egypt, 318. Arius, the priest of Alexandria, puts forward his doctrine denying the consubstantiality of the Son with the Father and, therefore, Christ's fully divine nature.

India, 320. Chandragupta, king of Magadha, founds the Gupta Dynasty.

Rome, 3 July 321. Sunday is made a day of rest throughout the empire and Christians are given the right to inherit property.

Asia Minor, 324. After inflicting a series of military defeats on Licinius by land and sea, Constantine captures and soon executes his co-emperor. His hold on the east secured, Constantine is now sole ruler of the empire.

Asia Minor, May 325. Constantine summons and presides over a world council of bishops at Nicaea. An orthodox creed is established.

Palestine, 325. Eusebius, the bishop of Caesarea and a supporter of Arius, publishes his *Ecclesiastical History* and a historical *Chronicle*.

Jerusalem, 326. Helena, mother of Constantine, discovers the Holy Cross and Jesus' tomb, the Holy Sepulcher.

Constantinople, 11 May 330. Constantine makes the town of Byzantium, on the southern end of the Bosporus, the new capital of his empire. It is now dedicated and called Constantinople after the emperor.

Jerusalem, 335. The church of the Holy Sepulcher is consecrated.

India, c.335. Chandragupta, king of Magadha, who founded the Gupta Dynasty in 320, is dead. He is succeeded by Samudragupta, who takes on creating an empire in the Ganges plain.

Constantinople, 336. Having been condemned by the Council of Tyre for his uncompromising attitude toward Arians and Melitans, Athanasius, patriarch of Alexandria since 328, appeals to Constantine. But the Arian bishop Eusebius persuades the emperor to exile Athanasius to Trier in Gaul.

Asia Minor, 22 May 337. After a deathbed baptism, Constantine dies in his villa near Ancyra in Nicomedia. He is buried in the church of the Holy Apostles in Constantinople.

Constantinople, 9 September 337. Constantine's three sons, already Caesars, each take the title of Augustus. Constantine II and Constans share out the west. Constantius II takes control of the east.

Italy, March 340. After defeating and killing his brother Constantine II at Aquileia in northern Italy, Constans unites the whole of the west under his rule.

Rome, 340. Pope Julius holds a synod attended by Athanasius and other exiled eastern bishops. In a letter to the eastern churches, he supports their position and asserts the primacy of his see.

Balkans, 343. The emperors try to heal the split between the eastern and western churches by calling a joint council at Sardia (Sofia) in Thrace. Western bishops support the primacy of Rome, but eastern bishops reject his claims.

Egypt, 21 October 346. Under heavy imperial pressure, the eastern and western churches reach a nervous compromise at Alexandria. Athanasius is restored to his see.

Mesopotamia, 348. The bloody Battle of Singara between Shapur II, king of the Persians, and Constantius II, ends indecisively.

Gaul, 350. Constans is murdered in a coup d'etat by the military commander Magnentius, who defeats his rivals and usurps the Western Empire.

Gaul, August 353. Constantius II follows up his victory over Magnentius at Mursa in 351 by pursuing the usurper into Gaul. Defeated for the second time, Magnentius commits suicide. Constantius II becomes sole emperor.

Gaul, 355. The Alamanni, a Germanic barbarian tribe, crosses the Rhine and wreaks havoc in eastern Gaul.

Constantinople, 19 February 356. Constantius II issues a decree giving orders for all the pagan temples in the Roman Empire to be closed.

Egypt, 356. Athanasius, the former patriarch of Alexandria, takes refuge in a remote desert in upper Egypt after being expelled again from Alexandria by the pro-Arian Emperor Constantius II.

Rome, 28 April 357. Constantius II visits Rome for the first time, to celebrate his victory over Magnentius and to address the Senate and the Roman people.

Gaul, 25 August 357. Julian, who was made Caesar on 6 November 355 by his cousin Constantius II, defeats the Alamanni at Strasbourg and drives them back behind the Rhine.

Syria, 359. Shapur II, the Sassanian king of Persia, invades Syria and captures the Roman town of Amida after a long struggle.

Italy/Mesopotamia, 359. Two separate councils of the western and eastern churches are held, at Rimini and Seleucia. Each is persuaded to accept a pro-Arian creed put forward by the advisers of the Emperor Constantius II.

Constantinople, 360. A council ratifies pro-Arian alterations to the Nicene creed.

Mesopotamia, 360. The Persians, under the leadership of Shapur II, capture Singara and Bezabde in battles with the Romans.

Gaul, February 360. In Paris, Julian who, as Caesar in charge of Gaul and Britain, has subdued the Franks and the Alamanni and restored the Rhine frontier is declared Augustus by his army. This follows a request by the Emperor Constantius II for Julian to send some of his men to the east, at which Julian's troops mutinied.

Asia Minor, November 361. Constantius II dies of fever on his way to fight Julian, who is marching east to attack him. Julian becomes sole emperor.

Syria, 17 June 362. The Emperor Julian passes an edict banning Christians from teaching grammar and rhetoric. He has already revealed himself to be a pagan and has proclaimed toleration for all religions.

Persia, 26 June 363. Julian invades Persia. Having defeated the Persians outside the walls of their capital, Ctesiphon, he is fatally wounded while retreating up the Tigris. His death brings an end to the pagan revival.

Persia, 363. Jovian, who served in the Persian campaign under Julian and was hastily chosen as emperor upon his death, concludes a dishonorable peace treaty with Shapur II. He surrenders all of the territory Diocletian had won in the east to the Persians, as well as the imperial cities of Nisibis and Singara.

Asia Minor, 26 February 364. On the death of Jovian, a conference at Nicaea chooses Valentinian, an army officer who was born in the central European region of Pannonia in 321, to succeed him.

Constantinople, 28 March 364. Valentinian appoints his brother Valens to govern the east. For the first time, the division of rule over the empire is accompanied by a true division of resources and armies between the west and the east.

Roman Empire, 368. A *defensor civitatis* (defender of the city) is appointed in each city to protect humble people against the powerful and to provide them with an inexpensive and accessible court of justice.

Gaul, 372. Martin, a disciple of Hilary of Poitiers, is made bishop of Tours. Born c.316 in Pannonia, Martin served in the Roman army before joining the clergy. He establishes one of the first hermit communities in the west.

Egypt, 2 May 373. Athanasius, the patriarch who fiercely defended Nicene orthodoxy against the Arian heresy, dies at Alexandria. He played an important role in the spread of monasticism.

India, 375. Samudragupta, who came to the throne in 335 and created a vast empire in the Ganges plain, is dead.

Guatemala, 375. In the first recorded royal accession in a Maya city, "Curl Snout" becomes king of Tikal in the Peten jungle.

Ukraine, 375. The nomadic people known as the Huns, moving steadily eastward from the steppes of central Asia, defeat and conquer the Ostrogoths. In consequence, the Ostrogothic king Ermanaric commits suicide.

Central Europe, 17 November 375. Enraged by the insolence of barbarian envoys, Valentinian dies of apoplexy in Pannonia. His elder son Gratian, aged 16, is proclaimed emperor of the west.

Balkans, 376. The Visigoths, who have been inhabiting part of Dacia for the past 150 years, are driven by the Huns to seek Roman permission to cross the lower Danube. Permission is granted.

Asia Minor, August 378. Valens, the emperor of the east, is defeated and fatally wounded in a battle against the Visigoths at Adrianopole.

Balkans, January 379. To help him control the crisis within the empire, Gratian appoints the Spaniard Theodosius as the new Augustus of the east. Theodosius takes charge of the war against the Goths.

Constantinople, 381. The new pro-Nicene Emperor Theodosius summons an ecumenical council to Constantinople, at which Arianism is finally condemned once and for all. Gratian follows suit in the west.

Italy, 382. Gratian formally moves the imperial court from Rome to Milan—probably to be closer to the frontier armies and ready to deal with any crises. Emperors now rarely visit Rome.

Balkans, 15 August 383. Theodosius signs a peace treaty with the Visigoths giving them land and political autonomy within the empire in return for military service.

Gaul, 15 August 383. After Maximus, proclaimed emperor by the troops in Britain, invades Gaul, Gratian is murdered by his troops at Lyons. Maximus is proclaimed emperor by the army.

Southern Africa, 385. Copper mining and smelting has begun at Kansanshi in the Katanga (Shaba) Copperbelt (on the Zaire-Zambia border).

Italy, 387. Maximus invades Italy and drives out Valentinian II, Gratian's younger brother, who appeals to Theodosius.

China, 387. The Northern Wei Dynasty is founded, with its capital at Pingcheng (Datong). Until now China has been a battleground for various short-lived dynasties of non-Chinese origin. The Toba people of Mongolian origin who found this dynasty prove to have a far greater capacity for bringing stability to northern China.

Italy, 388. After two defeats by Theodosius, Maximus surrenders and is executed at Aquileia.

Milan, 25 December 390. Ambrose, the bishop of Milan, forces the Emperor Theodosius to perform public penance for his massacre of thousands of the rebellious citizens of Thessalonica.

Rome, 24, February 391. Theodosius makes Christianity the official state religion of the empire.

Japan, 391. Invaders from Yamato overrun Silla and Paekche and start an expedition into Kokuri.

Italy, 392. Valentinian II, Augustus of Italy and Illyricum, is murdered on 15 May by his Frankish military commander Arbogast, who proclaims Eugenius, a Roman professor of rhetoric, emperor. Eugenius makes vain attempts to restore paganism.

Italy, 6 September 394. Theodosius defeats and kills the usurper Eugenius and his general Arbogast at the Battle of the River Frigidus. Theodosius is now sole emperor.

Milan, 17 January 395. Theodosius dies and is succeeded by his two sons. The empire is once again divided. Arcadius, age 18, controls the east; Honorius, age

10, takes the west. The border dividing the empire crosses the Balkans and the Libyan desert.

400 – 499

Mexico, c.400. Building activity is reaching new heights at the Mexican city of Teotihuacan—with a population of 250,000, the sixth largest city in the world. Teotihuacan is also exerting a strong cultural influence on Maya city-states such as Tikal and the Zapotec capital Monte Alban.

Italy, 401. The Visigoths under Alaric invade northern Italy from the Balkans.

Italy, 402. To escape the Visigothic threat, the court of the Western Empire is moved again, from Milan to Ravenna, a naturally well-defended site.

Verona, 402. The Visigoths are defeated in battle by the Roman army of the west, led by the Vandal Stilicho, supreme military commander and effective ruler of the Western Empire. He forces them out of Italy.

Italy, 23 August 406. On a march to Rome, pillaging barbarians from various tribes under the leadership of King Radagaisus are crushed by Stilicho with the aid of mercenary barbarian troops at Fiesole, near Florence.

Gaul, 31 December 406. Hordes of Vandals, Alans, and Sueves take advantage of the exceptional cold to cross the frozen Rhine. The frontier is lost. Gaul is open for pillaging.

Gaul, 407. The usurper Constantine III leaves Britain, where he has been declared emperor by the army, and sets out to save Gaul from invading tribes.

Constantinople, 1 May 408. On the death of Arcadius, the eastern emperor, his eight-year-old son Theodosius II, succeeds to the throne under the protection of the Praetorian prefect Anthemius, who has been in real control in the east since 405.

Ravenna, 23 August 408. With the Emperor Honorius, the aristocracy, and the Roman troops against him, Stilicho is arrested and executed. The Roman forces massacre the families of the barbarian mercenaries who go off and join Alaric's army.

Spain, 409. The Vandals, Alans, and Sueves move from Gaul into Spain.

Rome, 24 August 410. The Visigoths under Alaric sack Rome.

Gaul, 411. The usurper Constantine III is besieged at Aries and finally captured by forces loyal to the Emperor Honorius.

Constantinople, 413. The Praetorian prefect Anthemius builds the great walls of Constantinople, known as the Theodosian Walls.

Gaul, 1 January 414. At Narbonne, Athaulf, Alaric's successor as king of the Visigoths, marries Galla Placidia, the sister of the Emperor Honorius, who was taken hostage during the sack of Rome in 410. Athaulf led the Visigoths into Gaul in 412 and has seized the southwest of the country.

Constantinople, 414. At the age of only 15, Pulcheria, the sister of Theodosius II, becomes ruler of the Eastern Empire as regent for her weak-minded brother.

Alexandria, 415. The Greek mathematician and philosopher Hypatia, the leading intellectual of Alexandria, is tortured to death by a mob of Christian zealots incited by the patriarch Cyril. The fatal attack was provoked by Hypatia's scientific rationalism and authority as a woman, both of which ran counter to the dogma of emerging Christianity.

China, 420. Eastern Qin (Ch'in) is overthrown by its general, Liu Yu, who becomes the first Liu Song emperor. Liu Yu, born into great poverty, owes his rise to power to an exceptional military career. Fourteen years prior he temporarily recaptured the former cap-ital of Loyang in northern China from its non-Chinese occupiers.

Rome, September 421. Constantius III dies just a few months after being made co-emperor of the West by Honorius. Appointed supreme commander of the Western army in 411, Constantius married Galla Placidia, sister of Honorius, in 417.

Constantinople, 422. The Emperor Theodosius agrees to pay an annual tribute to the Huns in order to buy peace.

Constantinople, 428. Nestorius, the Patriarch of Constantinople, preaches a new doctrine of Christ that emphasizes the distinction between his divine and human natures. Nestorianism is immediately condemned by Pope Celestine and Cyril, the patriarch of Alexandria, as heresy.

North Africa, May 429. The Vandals, led by King Gaiseric, cross the Strait of Gibraltar from Spain into Africa. They are said to number 80,000.

Italy, 429. Aetius, who has defeated the Visigoths and the Franks and reestablished the frontier of the Rhine with the help of Hun mercenaries, is appointed commander of the armies of the Western Empire.

North Africa, 28 August 430. Augustine, the bishop of Hippo, dies while his town is under siege by the Vandals.

Asia Minor, June 431. The Third Ecumenical Council, meeting at Ephesus, condemns the Nestorian doctrine as heresy.

Balkans, 434. The armies of Theodosius II are defeated by the Huns in Thrace. Attila and his brother Bleda set the peace terms. The Romans' annual tribute to the Huns is doubled and a series of other concessions are made.

Constantinople, 29 October 437. Valentinian III, the ruler of the Western Empire, marries Licinia Eudoxia, the daughter of Theodosius II, the ruler of the Eastern Empire.

North Africa, 19 October 439. The Vandals, led by King Gaiseric, take Carthage.

China, 439. With the fall of the Northern Liang to the Northern Wei rulers, the Toba, the northern and southern courts stand in direct conflict. The Northern Wei complete their unification of north China under a single regime.

India, 440. A great center of Buddhist studies is founded on the plain of the Ganges at Nalanda. It consists of some ten monasteries and a group of shrines, all enclosed within a surrounding wall.

Rome 440. Leo I (Leo the Great) becomes pope. He asserts the primacy of the Bishop of Rome over the Patriarchs of Constantinople, Alexandria, Antioch, and Jerusalem.

Balkans, 447. The Huns, under Attila, cross the Danube frontier, invade Thrace, and force the Romans to pay them a heavier tribute and withdraw from a wide strip of land beside the Danube. The annual tribute paid to the Huns by the Eastern Empire had already been tripled from 443 onward.

Asia Minor, 449. At a council held at Ephesus, under the leadership of Dioscurus, Patriarch of Alexandria, the Monophysites push through the acceptance of their doctrine. This takes place in the absence of Pope Leo, a fierce opponent of Monophysitism.

Constantinople, 28 July 450. Theodosius II falls off his horse and dies, after ruling as emperor of the East for 42 years. He leaves no direct heir. Theodosius was prone throughout his reign to follow the advice of others, notably his sister and his wife, but also a series of imperial officials.

Constantinople, August 450. Marcian, a retired army officer, becomes emperor of the East thanks to the all-important backing of Aspar, the barbarian commander of the Eastern armies, and of the Empress Pulcheria, Theodosius II's sister, who duly marries him.

Ireland, c.450. Patrick founds the episcopal see of Armagh.

Gaul, 20 June 451. Having mounted an invasion of Gaul, Attila's army of Huns is defeated in the Battle of the Catalaunian Fields by a combined force of Romans, Visigoths, and several other barbarian peoples, all under the command of Aetius.

Asia Minor, October 451. At Chalcedon, the Fourth Ecumenical Council, summoned by Pope Leo, condemns Monophysitism and completely reverses the decrees of the Council of Ephesus of 449.

Italy, 452. The Huns invade Italy and sack a series of northern Italian cities, including Padua and Verona, before Pope Leo persuades Attila to desist from his planned attack on Rome and withdraw.

Pannonia, 453. On the death of Attila, leader of the Huns since 434, the vast Hun Empire is divided up between his sons.

Italy, 21 September 454. Aetius, the supreme army commander, is murdered at Ravenna by Valentinian III, the emperor of the West.

Pannonia, 454. The Germanic vassals of the Huns, inspired by Ardaric, the king of the Gepids, rebel against Attila's sons and defeat them in Pannonia. The Hun Empire begins to fall apart.

Ethiopia, 454. Following the split in the Roman church, which became more pronounced three years prior after the Council of Chalcedon, the Kingdom of Axum decides to give its support to the Coptic patriarch of Alexandria, who follows the Monophysite doctrine.

Rome, March 455. Valentinian III is assassinated by two barbarian retainers of Ae-

tius. His death brings an end to the Theodosian Dynasty. A very wealthy senator, Petronius Maximus, bribes the troops and is proclaimed emperor by them.

Rome, June 455. The Vandals, led by King Gaiseric, sack Rome. On the death of Valentinian III, they had immediately seized those parts of Africa still in Roman hands, together with the islands of Sardinia and Corsica. In the panic before their arrival in Rome, the new Emperor Maximus tried to flee and was killed by the mob, after a reign of 11 weeks.

Gaul, 9 July 455. Following a two-month period without an emperor, the Gallic senators proclaim Avitus, military commander in Gaul, as emperor of the West. Avitus has the support of Theodoric II, the king of the Visigoths.

Italy, 456. Avitus is defeated in battle at Placentia, in northern Italy, and forced to abdicate by the rebel general Ricimer, an Arian barbarian from the Suevian tribe. Ricimer aims to rule through a puppet emperor, Majorian.

Constantinople, 7 February 457. A Thracian officer by the name of Leo is proclaimed as emperor of the East by the army general, Aspar, on the death of the Emperor Marcian.

Italy, 2 August 461. Majorian is deposed and killed by his military commander, Ricimer, the man responsible for elevating him to the throne. In the event, Majorian had proved too independent for Ricimer's liking.

Italy, 15 August 465. Libius Severus, the puppet emperor elevated by Ricimer to succeed Majorian, dies after a reign of four years.

Rome, August 467. In return for military aid, Ricimer accepts Leo's nominee, the general Anthemius, as Western emperor. Anthemius marches west and is proclaimed Augustus.

Sicily, 468. The Vandals defeat the Western forces decisively and conquer the island of Sicily.

Constantinople, 471. On the orders of the Emperor Leo, the army commander Aspar is assassinated.

Rome, 11 July 472. The barbarian general Ricimer kills the Emperor Anthemius in civil war. He replaces him with Olybrius.

Rome, 19 August 472. The kingmaker Ricimer, who has been responsible for raising a series of emperors to the Western throne, dies. Another barbarian, the Burgundian Gundobad, takes over supreme command of the Western army.

Rome, 2 November 472. Olybrius dies. No emperor is immediately appointed to succeed him.

Rome, 24 June 473. Julius Nepos, backed by Leo, emperor of the East, marches on Rome and ousts Gundobad's nominee Glycerius, becoming emperor of the West himself.

Constantinople, 474. Leo II, who became sole emperor of the East following the death of Leo I earlier in the year, dies after reigning for only a few months and is succeeded by his father, Zeno.

Gaul/Spain, 475. Euric, king of the Visigoths since 466, is granted legal tenure of his conquests by Julius Nepos, emperor of the West. The Visigoths now control southwestern Gaul and most of Spain, except for the Suevian kingdom in the northwest.

Rome, 475. The Roman army commander Orestes drives Julius Nepos out of Italy and puts his own son, Romulus Augustus, on the throne.

Gaul, 476. The Visigothic king, Euric, conquers the remainder of southern Gaul, up to the Italian frontier.

Italy, 476. The imperial army at Ravenna mutinies and proclaims Odoacer, a barbarian officer from Germany, king. Odoacer sets aside the last Western Roman Emperor, choosing to do without a puppet emperor and formally recognizes Zeno as sole emperor, while holding real power himself.

North Africa, 477. The Vandal king, Gaiseric, dies in the province of Africa. His son Huneric, who is an Arian Christian, succeeds him and embarks upon a policy of violent persecution of the Catholics.

China, 477. The Liu Song Dynasty collapses when General Xiao Daocheng has the emperor killed and sets himself up as regent.

China, 477. Buddhism becomes the state religion.

China, 479. Xiao Daocheng has the boy emperor and all the members of the imperial family murdered and creates the Southern Qi Dynasty. Fighting between the Toba and the south begins again.

Britain, c.480. Saxons under the leadership of Aelle land on the south coast and drive the Britons westward. The kingdom of the South Saxons (Sussex) is established.

Dalmatia, 480. Odoacer occupies the Dalmatia region on the death of the exiled former emperor Julius Nepos, who had controlled it.

Gaul, 480. Gundobad, the former Western commander, succeeds his brother Chilperic as king of the Burgundians. The Burgundian kingdom now extends over much of eastern Gaul, with two capitals, at Lyons and Geneva.

Gaul, 481. Childeric, king of the Franks, dies at his capital, Tournai, and is succeeded by his son Clovis.

Constantinople, 482. In order to settle the violent conflict between the Chalcedonian Monophysites and Catholic believers, the Emperor Zeno promulgates a compromise edict.

Constantinople/Rome, 484. A schism splits the Churches of Constantinople and Rome. The pope refuses to accept Zeno's compromise, which he regards as heretical.

Gaul, 486. The Frankish king, Clovis, defeats Syagrius, leader of the Gallo-Romans, at Soissons and conquers much of northern Gaul, except for Armorica (Brittany).

Constantinople, 488. Having survived a series of attacks by rebels and barbarians, Zeno finally ends the troubles besetting his reign by paying the Ostrogothic king Theodoric to go and expel Odoacer from Italy.

Constantinople, 491. Anastaius I becomes emperor.

Ravenna, 493. After a two-year siege of the city the Ostrogoth chief, Theoderic, reaches an agreement with Odoacer, who opens the gates of the city to him. Soon after Theoderic has Odoacer assassinated.

Babylon, 499. The Babylonian Talmud, a compendium of Jewish law and commentary is completed. ❑

THE NEOLITHIC REVOLUTION

During the period between 8000 and 3000 BC, the period that has come to be known as the Neolithic or New Stone Age, the development of agriculture resulted in a quantum leap in the complexity of human society. Archaeological finds confirm that there were two different Stone Ages. The first was characterized by the use of knapped stones or flint, and it is known as the Paleolithic or Old Stone Age. It was followed by the second phase, distinguished by the use of sharpened stones and the first metal tools, that is known as the Neolithic or New Stone Age. Agriculture led

The Neolithic revolution was the springboard for the advanced civilizations of the future: a black, diagrammatic cave painting of the Neolithic period (cave of Pileta, Spain).

to such enormous changes in this period that it is sometimes described as the "Neolithic Revolution."

With agriculture, humans were able for the first time to adapt their natural environment to their own needs and change it for their own purposes. While the hunter-gatherer of the Old Stone Age depended completely on the natural conditions around him, Neolithic man was able to produce food himself. The surplus of food, the development of new technologies, and the development of fixed settlements gave him a relative independence from the uncertainties and threats posed by his natural environment.

Because of the glaciations of the Ice Age, agriculture developed at different times in different regions. Agriculture developed first in about 8000 BC in the region of the fertile crescent of Mesopotamia between the Tigris and the Euphrates Rivers. This was where wild wheat grew naturally, and from it the most important cultivated plant in the Western world developed. It grew so fast that more was harvested by one family within the three-week period of maturity than its members could consume in one year.

THE PROCESS OF DOMESTICATION

The natural characteristic of wild wheat is that the ripe ears split open and the grains fall out. While this process makes sense in nature, it was a disadvantage for the early gatherers of wild wheat because the seeds or grains that were blown away reduced the harvest. So the choice was either to harvest the unripe grains or to lose many grains during the ripening process.

It was this combination of events that led to the cultivation of wheat. Many wheat plants were unable to scatter their ears through genetic defects, and naturally these grains could be harvested in larger quantities when ripe. It has been theorized that many of the harvested grains were lost as they were being carried back to the village, and sometimes they fell on fertile soil. Most of the plants sprouting up the following year would then have been of the non-scattering variety as well as being closer to the village, and as result they were harvested in preference to the others. The constant repetition of this unintentional selection process led to ever larger, higher-yielding wheat fields near the village.

A similar change resulting not from delib-

erate intervention but from a process of adaptation and unintentional selection occurred with all the plants gathered by man. The decisive factor leading to the development of agriculture was the regular storage and systematic sowing of these precious grains.

The first plant to be domesticated in China was millet in about 4000 BC. Rice was domesticated in about 3000 BC, but agriculture goes back even further in southeast Asia: in Thailand the horse bean and a pea variety were already cultivated as far back as 7000 BC. Rice was probably cultivated here thousands of years before it was cultivated in China.

Agriculture also goes back a long time in Mexico and Peru. The great variety in the type of soils led to the development of a wide range of edible plants. The oldest sites where maize has been discovered date from between 5200 and 3400 BC. Pumpkins and beans were domesticated even earlier.

Because of the plentiful food available, fewer hunting accidents, and the reduction in infanticide that had been necessary for nomadic hunting societies to survive, the population began to grow. The number of people in a settlement soon exceeded the amount of food available in a region so that individual groups started to move away. Agriculture thus became the foundation of civilization.

CATTLE BREEDING

The domestication of animals occurred in much the same way as it had with plants, although here deliberate management by man played a greater part. Old Stone Age people must have had some basic knowledge of cattle breeding because they did not kill the best animals but kept them alive for the preservation of the species.

Improved hunting techniques, such as driving entire herds into pens where they were easier to kill, gradually led to the keeping of domestic animals. The first domestic animals were goats and sheep in Persia and Anatolia in about 6500 BC. As these were herd animals, their natural tendency to follow a leader made their domestication easier. Gradually selection by humans led to the natural selective breeding of more productive, more docile animals.

Goats and sheep were kept not only as animals for slaughter but also for their wool and milk. Pigs were domesticated in about 6000 BC, but they played only a minor role because of their fastidious feeding requirements, and the fact that they were carriers of disease. The aurochs that lived in regions of the Near East were attributed magical qualities. The dog became a domestic animal at least 15,000 years ago, but it was used for hunting purposes, not as a source of food.

HOUSE — VILLAGE — TOWN

In various parts of the world, the old hunting groups and encampments of the Paleolithic or Old Stone Age developed into farming villages, new settlements that were independent of each other. These early villages, which developed in about 7000 BC, first appeared in the Near East. In the more developed Neolithic cultures, villages and towns could reach a considerable size, numbering from several hundred to a thousand inhabitants.

The first houses of the now sedentary Neolithic man were circular buildings. A circular frame of poles was mounted on a circular foundation, then covered with skins or straw. Later the houses were built of clay and were soon placed on a solid stone plinth. Besides round houses, there were also rectangular dwellings. At the beginning settlements were surrounded by fortifications, usually in the form of a wide moat with a kind of embankment or earth bank. Later, houses were made of stone, wood, and air-dried bricks, and they acquired second stories and had several rooms.

In southern Europe, houses were mainly rectangular and detached, and often of considerable size. The wooden long houses inhabited by farmers in northern and central Europe could reach a length of 100 to 150 ft. (30 to 45 m) and a width of 20 to 23 ft. (6 to 7 m). Inside was a raised platform that served as granary.

SOCIAL RELATIONSHIPS — PROPERTY AND WAR

Gradually the Neolithic hunting groups that rarely consisted of more than a few dozen members were replaced by farming villages with a completely different social system. The surplus provided by agriculture made it possible for new tasks to be carried out that would have been impossible for a single hunting group, such as the more intensive agriculture achieved through irrigation. The first attempts at specialization were made when craftsmen took over particular tasks such as stonework, pottery, and metalwork, while others looked after producing the food. Early burial objects show a general equality within the settlement and between the sexes.

The greatest change in social behavior was that fighting became a decisive factor in the life of the settlements. The concept of property ownership, involving its acquisition, expansion, and protection, led to the development of warlike attitudes. For the first time craftsmen made weapons to fight people.

In about 3000 BC, the role of ruler developed in Mesopotamia and Egypt. The former social structure of co-existence with equal rights developed into a state with a king and civil servants, while the people lived in a situation of graduated dependence on the king. The functional groups of various "specialists" developed into priests, craftsmen, tradesmen, laborers, and farmers.

RELIGION AND ART

The changes in the Neolithic period also

A burial site of the Neolithic and Bronze Age: dolmen in Poulnabrone, Ireland

had an impact on religion and its expression in art. The male god of the Old Stone Age continued to live among the cattle-breeding nomads. The only fixed place of the herdsmen was the burial place, identifiable from afar. Enormous blocks of stone marked the places where the cult of ancestor worship was followed.

Among the sedentary farmers, the house, herd, seeds, and fertile land were all associated with a female goddess. The four cardinal points, the cycle of the moon and water were all symbols of the woman as the bearer of life. Instead of a male god, worshippers venerated representations of a mother goddess.

While cattle breeders continued to make artistic representations of animals, in farming cultures there was no concrete representation of nature. Shapes were transformed into geometric abstractions and the figures of the goddess did not represent a real woman as much as the general concept of fertility.

TECHNOLOGICAL DEVELOPMENTS

The technological innovations introduced in the Neolithic period included a new kind of stone construction, building with clay and stone, as well as the development of carpentry, pottery, and metalworking.

Knowledge of various kinds of stone led to new techniques of dressing and perforating stone. Important progress was made in pottery with craftsmen changing not only the shape of the raw material but also the state of the material itself: soft clay was fired and thus transformed into a hard material.

One of the most important inventions was the processing of metal. This dates as far back as 8000 BC in Iran, although it only started spreading much later. Not until 4000 BC did metalworkers begin to manufacture metal tools. While in the Stone Age the man's ability to produce new tools and implements was strictly limited by the materials used, the invention of smelting and casting made it possible to create all kinds of shapes. By about 3000 BC metalworking was flourishing in the cities of Mesopotamia. Tin was added to copper to create an alloy, bronze, that was not only easier to cast but could be worked to make harder implements.

The continuous search for new materials led to an increase in trade in the Mediterranean and extended the market for the products manufactured in the highly developed Mesopotamian city-states. The material and intellectual developments at the end of the Neolithic provided the foundations for the development of a written language. ❑

THE DEVELOPMENT OF HIEROGLYPHICS

Egypt, c.3000 BC

At the beginning of the third millennium BC, Egyptian scribes began using drawn symbols to write and record everyday life on a form of paper made from reeds. This "paper" was made by soaking and pressing papyrus reeds from the Nile before drying them. A system of *hieroglyphs*, a form of writing inextricably linked to art, developed in the form of engravings on temple walls and in a parallel form known as *hieratic* on papyri.

The classical language (Middle Egyptian) used some 700 hieroglyphic signs, although over time that number had to increase considerably so the technique could be flexible enough to meet the demands placed upon it. The hieroglyphs showed, for example, human figures, parts of the human body, animals, birds, trees and plants, as well as vari-

Egyptian hieroglyphics

ous tools, vessels, and items of furniture.

These symbolic images were used in horizontal or vertical lines that could be read either from right to left or from left to right. A human or animal head indicated the direction by pointing to the beginning of the line. Words and sentences were not separated.

Scribes used hieroglyphs as an art form as well as a means of communication. They endeavored to group the signs into an imaginary square, often with the sign for the king or a god preceding other words. A sign could have several meanings: It could express an idea or a sound and could be used to explain other signs.

The "grammar" of hieroglyphs was complex. A sign used to convey the name of an object

WRITTEN LANGUAGE INVENTED IN SUMER

Mesopotamia, c.3200 BC

The Sumerian invention of writing in the city of Uruk was a decisive step in the story of mankind and inaugurated the historical era. Students of linguistics have suggested that for many generations, whenever people dwelling in the city paid tribute to the priests to intercede for them with the gods who kept the soil fertile, they would make mental notes. But even the best of memories could sometimes fail or mislead, especially if a bad harvest raised doubts about whether the priests were doing their job.

To answer this challenge the city dwellers in Uruk devised a system of signs for putting

Lexical cuneiform signs

important transactions on record. The priests would use a sharp reed pen to make *pictographs*—marks on clay tablets. These marks, which represented numbers, objects and even ideas, were used to keep grain accounts and other business matters, including land sales. It has been theorized that they stumbled on the idea after a period of keeping records by using clay tokens, which they impressed into wet clay.

The invention was an instant success; soon no business deal was accepted as genuine unless it had been written down. Though Sumerians are believed to be the first people to have devised

a system of writing, the discovery was immediately copied by others. Archaeological finds show that at almost the same time as the Sumerians hit upon their new system for keeping records, a very similar one appeared in the city of Susa in neighboring Elam.

Among the finds from Susa are pictographs on clay tablets much like those adopted in Sumer. Since Sumer was no more than a few days' travel from Susa, and the two places had many cultural affinities, it seems likely that travelers spread the word among the people of Susa.

Sumerian writing was essentially a series of drawings: crude outlines of familiar objects,

Weight with cuneiform signs

such as plants, human heads, and animals. These were used as *ideograms*, pictures expressing ideas. Childbirth was suggested by an egg next to a bird, and darkness by fine parallel lines beneath the arc of a circle—perhaps an image of sunset. However, in a relatively short period, the Sumerian script became increasingly sophisticated. The images used became more schematic, and a script made up with wedge-shaped marks developed.

Cuneiform signs were capable of representing distinct sounds, rather than standing for single words and ideas. This enabled the priests to handle a greater vocabulary with fewer signs. ❑

THE STORY OF GILGAMESH

Sumer, c.2750 BC

or action (an ideogram) could not be easily used, for instance, to convey abstract notions such as thoughts, feelings, professional or family relations, and proper names. A sign representing a sound (a phonogram) expressed only consonants, not vowels. Some signs determined the sense of the sounds that preceded them and were not pronounced.

Sentences were constructed in a very strict order: verb, subject, direct object, and complements. To make writing more efficient, hieroglyphs became stylized. As they began to stand for sounds, the total number of customary signs could be reduced from about 2,000 early on, to somewhere between 350 and 400 in its late stage of development. Only priests and scholars used hieroglyphs in a population that was 99 percent illiterate. ❏

Gilgamesh, king of the Sumerian city of Uruk in southern Mesopotamia, became the subject of a great epic. In actuality, Gilgamesh fought against the Kingdom of Kish and was deified after his death for his heroic exploits. In the epic, Gilgamesh sets out to defy the gods in his quest for immortality.

With his friend Enkidu he kills Huwawa, guardian of the cedar forest, and when the goddess Inanna sends the Bull of Heaven to kill the two heroes, it, too, is slain. But when Enkidu dies, a distraught Gilgamesh seeks out Utnapishtim—an old man who, according to Sumerian legend, survived a great flood by building an ark for his families and animals and was therefore granted eternal life by the gods.

Utnapishtim gives Gilgamesh a magic plant that restores youth, but a serpent steals the plant, and

Relief from the time of Gilgamesh

Gilgamesh again becomes distraught. He returns to Utnapishtim for the secret of immortality, for which he must stay awake for

six days and seven nights. Gilgamesh is only human and falls asleep. But when he awakes he is reconciled to his mortality. ❏

SUMERIAN MYTHOLOGY

Point of Interest

Sumerians were guided in their daily lives by a host of gods worshipped in a hierarchy according to the importance of the field of human life each looked after. In earlier times, each of the Sumerian cities originally had its own particular deity, but political changes in the relations between the cities may have led to the hierarchy of several gods. Sumerian gods had human forms and expressed people's relationships with each other and with Nature. Chief among them were Anu, Enlil, and Enki. Anu, the god of the sky, was also father of the gods. Enlil was the god of air, who made everything possible. It was he who created the order of things. Enki, god of wisdom and cunning, administered this and the underground waters essential to Sumer's well-being. Another important deity was Inanna, goddess of love and war.

Sumerians worshiped their gods in complex ceremonies. In return for these rituals and a life of propriety, they believed the gods would give them longevity and prosperity. The rebirth of creation was celebrated in an annual spring festival, which reassured Sumerians that their existence, vulnerable at all times to natural disasters such as flooding, would continue for another year. ❏

MENES UNITES EGYPTIAN KINGDOMS

Memphis, c.2950 BC

The rise of Menes (Horus Narmer), the first king of Egypt, marked a new phase of development in Egypt. Menes founded the Thinite Dynasty—perhaps named after the district in Upper Egypt, from where the kings of this dynasty came. He established his capital in Memphis, the Inebhedj or White Wall, at the apex of the Nile delta.

His great achievement was to unite the whole of his country under one rule. The new state combined Upper and Lower Egypt, the Nile Valley and delta. This union was indicated by the white and red crowns of Upper and Lower Egypt worn by the king.

This king used several names. The name Narmer was inscribed on ceremonial palettes and mace heads at Hierakonpolis in Southern Egypt in honor of his jubilee, a festival intended to rejuvenate and reinvigorate him for the next part of his reign.

As surviving exam-

ples clearly show, the palettes and mace heads were exquisitely carved with scenes in raised relief, representing the most accomplished examples of this dynasty's art. By assuming the name Horus, Menes equated himself with the god Horus, with whom all Egyptian kings would identify and to whom the temple at Hierakonpolis was dedicated. ❏

STATUARY FOR THE DEAD

Egypt, c. 2550 BC

After the death of the general, Prince Rahotep, statues portraying him accompanied by his wife Nofret were added to his grave. The costume of funerary figures is typical for the Old Kingdom. Men wore short loincloths, and women wore dresses with loose-fitting mantles. As customary with the kings and nobles of this period, Rahotep was laid to rest in a large square-shaped *masta-ba* (freestanding tomb) covered with limestone. Within the tomb were ceremonial and storage chambers.

According to Egyptian belief, the dead journeyed to the next world where their bodies lived on. The soul, which left the body at death, would then return to it in the next life. In early times, only the Pharaoh and his immediate family were thought to be immortal. But by the end of the Old Kingdom, the circle of those who could look forward to a future existence had widened to include various high officials.

Great attention was paid to preparations for the life to come. The walls of the mastabas were painted with scenes depicting the pleasures enjoyed in one's earthly life, such as hunting, sailing, and feasting, as well as pictures of menservants and maids performing such tasks as sewing, cook-

ing, and hunting. These elaborate paintings would ensure that the dead would be accompanied on their coming journey. The graves were also stocked with objects the dead were believed to need, including food, furniture, weapons, and jewelry. Caring for the dead with food and drink was the responsibility of priests or relatives.

In prehistoric times, the dead in Egypt were buried in the sand. Due to the extreme dryness of the climate, many bodies, though subject to decay, did not entirely

disappear. Some evidence of the remains, such as skin and hair, would survive. This may have been where the idea of embalming and mummification came from.

Although attempts to preserve the dead began early on, they were not immediately crowned with success. For this reason, tombs—such as that of General Rahotep—contained statues that resembled the dead and could represent them. The statues could then be offered food and drink to their taste through specially constructed holes in the walls of the tombs. Reflections of these practices are seen in humbler graves as well, where knives, necklaces, and jugs to hold food or drink have been found. ❑

Statues of Prince Rahotep and his wife Nofret (Cairo Museum)

THE PYRAMID OF KING DJOSER

Memphis, c.2620 BC

The high priest, Imhotep, was architect of the great step pyramid of Saqqara. The dimensions of this extant tomb for the late King Djoser of the Third Dynasty are enormous. The site of the pyramid and its funerary temple covers more than 180,000 square yards of desert. A special closed room (*serdab*) was built to contain a magnificent seated statue of the king. A second tomb was built to the south, and chapels dedicated to different gods were built to the east of the pyramid.

The design of the Saqqara pyramid was based on the designs of tombs built in previous dynasties. These consisted of burial mounds of sand consolidated by brickwork and were finally replaced by rectangular mounds with walls sloping toward the center. The *mastaba* (a freestanding tomb with

sloping sides) symbolized the mound emerging from the liquid chaos created by the god Atum during the very first days of the earth.

Imhotep used similar principles in his design, but the Saqqara pyramid was constructed of stone to ensure that this spectacular royal tomb would last

Statue of Imhotep (c. seventh century BC)

THE GREAT PYRAMIDS

Egypt, c.2580 BC

The Great Pyramids are enduring monuments to Egyptian civilization and its religious ideals. According to these principles, eternity was assured for the kings of Egypt who, embalmed and mummified using simple techniques, were laid to rest in colossal stone-built tombs in the desert near the river that made this country fertile. These pyramids—the tallest of which was built by Khufu (Cheops) and is over 480 feet in height—were constructed of limestone quarried in the vicinity of the building site. Stone of better quality was transported from quarries on the opposite bank of the Nile. The remaining blocks of stone, each weighing

over two tons, were transported using logs.

The workers employed in this great task were not slaves. This was sacred work. The men who toiled to raise these vast stones to such heights—using a combination of girders and ropes—were free to work the soil during the rest of the year. They labored for their king, whose influence assured peace, civil order, and har-

Pyramids of Giza

THE NILE AS THE SOURCE OF LIFE

Point of Interest

forever. In the later stages of the design, the architect emphasized the symbolism of the *mastaba* by adding several layers to evoke a "stairway to heaven," which the soul of the pharaoh would climb to rise up to his father, Re. It is possible that the design of the pyramid was also meant to represent beams of light shooting out from the sun.

King Djoser did not live to see the completion of his spectacular tomb. Imhotep's plans called for the pyramid to be covered in limestone and evidences his concern that it be secured against future robbers and vandals. At the bottom of a huge 90-foot shaft, an intricate network of galleries leads to the burial chamber that held the mummified body of the king.

The glazed tiles, the reliefs on the walls, the false doors, and the niches are vivid witnesses to the care taken in the construction of this monument. ❏

Since the time King Menes introduced water engineering to Egypt, the Nile, bringing alluvial silt and fish to the delta, provided life and prosperity to the people of Egypt. Theirs was a peasant economy, and the *fellahin*, mostly small farmers and fishermen, made maximum use of the river's annual floods for their food.

The land was well-irrigated by a system of canals and reservoirs that captured the water and silt. Wheat, barley, emmer (a wheat species), and flax were the main harvests. Orchards and vegetable gardens flourished by the riverside, with broad beans, lentils, chickpeas, lettuces, and cucumbers growing in great quantities. Vineyards were a common sight—wine had been produced since the beginning of third millennium BC.

Most peasants lived in mud-brick houses, keeping their own goats, sheep, and even pigs. Oxen, working in pairs, were the main power source for the wooden plows. Fish products, dried or preserved, and eaten with bread and beer, were an important part of the country's diet.

The Egyptian economy depended greatly on the pharaoh, national stability, and good administration by officials. The people relied on them to supervise the maintenance of canals and reservoirs. In times of crisis agriculture suffered and famine threatened. ❏

Pyramid of Djoser at Saqqara

AVEBURY: A TEMPLE AMID THE HILLS OF SOUTHERN ENGLAND

Britain, c.2600 BC

mony for the country within the universe.

The Egyptians believed in life after death, and that after his death the pharaoh would accompany the sun god during the day. Thus, it was essential that his body be preserved and that he have everything necessary for life within his tomb, like food and drink left within his reach.

At death, the royal body was mummified—to achieve this, it was treated with drugs, filled with aromatic substances, and bandaged. The Egyptians also believed that the pharaoh was reborn at the time of his death, allowing him once again to occupy his royal throne. The social order he maintained in life had to continue; thus the king's wife and his most important officials were also buried close to him. ❏

The magnificent henge (ceremonial structure) at Avebury is thought to have been built at this time. The first phase of the building of this monument was the erection of two stone circles. An outer stone circle was then added, with a massive earth bank and ditch enclosing the ceremonial area approached by two avenues of stones.

The whole structure covers 28 acres and is a marvel of artistry and engineering. The pairs of stones that make up the grand avenue alternate between tall, thin stones and broad, lozenge-shaped ones, representing men and women. The henge at Avebury is the most impressive but by no means the only one of its kind. Many tombs and stone circles in the area date from this period. ❏

THOUGHTS OF AN EGYPTIAN OFFICIAL

Egypt, c.2350 BC

A glimpse into Egyptian life during this period was provided by the discovery of writings by the vizier Ptahhotpe. Ostensibly advice for his son they may have been composed with an eye on future generations. His maxims, recorded in hieratic script on papyrus, make a moving document.

Ptahhotpe bewails the limitations of old age. "You doze during the day, the eyes are dim, the ears are deaf... the mouth is silent and cannot speak, the mind is empty and no longer remembers the past..." He goes on to caution against intellectual arrogance and recommends taking pleasure in life:

"Do not be proud on account of your knowledge; consult the ignorant and the wise...Entertain your friends with that which you possess because you only have these possessions as one whom God favors...bow before your superior...wretched is he who challenges a superior..." ❏

THE FIRST ADVANCED CIVILIZATION IN MESOPOTAMIA

Between 3500 and 3000 BC, the first advanced civilization in the history of the human race began to develop in a bare, alluvial plain in southern Mesopotamia, between the Tigris and Euphrates in the center of present-day Iraq. But archaeologists have traced its roots, especially in northern Mesopotamia, even further into prehistory, to about 7000 BC.

Small agricultural settlements first appeared in the alluvial plain of southern Mesopotamia around 5,000 years ago and developed into the first towns in the history of mankind. The riches of this region attracted new nomadic tribes that soon became sedentary. The various waves of migration and successive rulers determined the civilization and history of the plains of the Euphrates and Tigris in Eastern antiquity.

The greatest achievement of Sumerian civilization was the invention of writing: stones with cuneiform script.

SUMER AND AKKAD

The first of these migratory waves to be historically recorded was that of the Sumerian people, who gave southern Mesopotamia the name Sumer. Exactly when this people arrived from Central Asia is not certain. But it is known that they merged with the region's original inhabitants to form a single entity, creating the first recognized advanced civilization in the world at the turn of the fourth and third millenniums. They founded the first towns, invented writing, developed religious rituals, and organized a communication network. The early dynastic period in Sumer, which began in about 2750 BC and lasted until about 2350 BC, is poorly confirmed by historical sources and its chronological sequence has not been clearly established. However, archaeological finds confirm the existence of small city-states with monumental religious architecture.

The incomplete list of Sumerian kings includes the important leaders Mesilim of Kish (about 2700 BC), Gilgamesh of Uruk (about 2675 BC), Eannatum of Lagash (about 2500 BC), Urukagina of Lagash (until about 2340 BC), and Lugalzaggesi of Umma (about 2340 BC). The kings acted as priest-king over the city, the center of which consisted of monumental temple buildings with a ziggurat.

In about 2340 BC, the Semite king Sargon I (about 2340–2284 BC) came from the north to put an end to Sumerian supremacy. He built a residence named Akkad in central Mesopotamia, which then gave its name to the whole of the northern part of Mesopotamia. Supported by a well-equipped army, Sargon I launched military expeditions as far as the Mediterranean coast and even reached Cyprus. His claim to world supremacy was unambiguous when he took the title, King of the Four Corners of Earth. But barely 200 years later, in about 2200 BC, the Akkadian Empire was invaded by the Gutians, a barbarian people from Iran. It was only after 2070 BC that Utuhegal, King of Uruk, succeeded in driving out the invaders.

This marked the beginning of Sumer's last flowering. Its most famous ruler was Gudea of Lagash (about 2080–2060 BC). Other great rulers, such as Urnammu and Shulgi of the third dynasty of Ur, extended Sumer's supremacy over almost the whole of the large Akkadian Empire. In about 2000 BC, Sumer was attacked from the east by the Elamites who destroyed Ur. Shortly afterwards, the nomadic Amorites invaded from Syria, drove out the Elamites, and made Babylon, a town on the Euphrates, their new capital. This ended the Sumerian age after some 1,500 years, but its cultural heritage lived on and continued to influence history.

BABYLONIA AND ASSYRIA

Two new empires developed from the Mesopotamian city-states: Babylonia in the south and Assyria in the north. Over the course of the next 1,500 years, their influence would extend far beyond the land of Mesopotamia.

In about 1700 BC, Hammurabi of Babylon (1728–1686 BC) established a vast, unified kingdom that stretched from the Persian Gulf to present-day Turkey, from the Zagros mountains in the east to Chabur in Syria. He created a system of administration, commerce, and justice throughout the whole of Babylonia and is famed for the law code he created. In 1531 BC, the Babylonian Empire collapsed after being attacked and invaded by the Hittites, a warlike people of Asia Minor. After the Hittites' withdrawal, the Iranian mountain tribe of the Kassites seized power and ruled Babylonia until 1160 BC when the Elamites invaded again and destroyed the Kassite Empire.

Meanwhile, the Assyrians continued to expand their sphere of influence moving into the vacuum left after the destruction of the mighty Mitanni Empire by the Hittites in 1356 BC. This led to the creation of the Middle Assyrian Empire (1318–1050 BC), the first military power in Asia Minor. The empire continued to extend its boundaries with military expeditions as far as Lake Van in Armenia and the Mediterranean. It was a steady territorial expansion that only ended with the death of Tiglath Pileser I (1115–1077 BC) and was made easier by an alliance with Egypt and the downfall of the rival Hittite Empire, which since 1600 BC had pushed its boundaries ever further out from Central Anatolia. It collapsed in about 1200 BC, when it was invaded by various seafaring peoples, and for centuries Asia Minor sank into the mist of oblivion.

THE ZENITH AND FALL OF THE EMPIRE

In the first half of the millennium before Christ, a new power emerged in Asia Minor with the rise of the Neo-Assyrian Empire (883–612 BC). After heavy fighting, the supremacy of Old Assyria was reestablished and numerous states, including Israel, Judea, and Babylonia were reduced to vassals. Assyrian rule was marked by cruelty and the deportation of whole populations. In the course of just a few decades, the Assyrian Empire had expanded dramatically: In 722 BC the Assyrians conquered Samaria, in 714 BC they defeated the kingdom of Urartu in Armenia, in 689 BC they destroyed Babylon, in 671 BC they conquered Egypt, and in 646 BC they annexed Elam. The wealth of the Assyrians was not only based on goods manufactured in the region, but also on the profits from foreign trade and the spoils of war. In the provinces, which were ruled by governors of the king, officials collected natural produce and precious metals as taxes.

Eventually, wars and internal conflicts contributed to Assyria's inability at the end of the seventh century BC to defend its distant boundaries or to suppress the numerous uprisings that were occurring in the provinces. In 612 BC, the Medes and Babylonians conquered the Assyrian capital of Nineveh. The last ruler, Assuruballit II, probably died in 609 BC. With his death the great Assyrian Empire came to an end.

But the late Babylonian Empire that succeeded the Assyrian kingdom could only survive for 100 years. The most prominent Babylonian ruler was Nebuchadnezzar II (605–562 BC), who became famous for his monumental architecture. During his reign, Babylon became one of the most magnificent cities in the world. In 539 BC, the Neo-Babylonian Empire fell when Babylon was captured by the armies of the Persian king Cyrus II, the Great, (559–530 BC), who had shaken off the Median supremacy of King Astyages (585–550 BC). He did not allow Babylon to be destroyed but made it one of the capitals of his own empire.

STATE ORGANIZATION

The government of ancient eastern city-states, and of the empires that followed, was based on monarchy and religion. But as a result of expansion, governments developed into a centralized vassal or bureaucratic states. In early Sumerian times (from about 2750 BC), the city ruler was at the same time the high priest, and he was advised by a council of elders. From the time of Sargon I of Akkad, the empire had a standardized central administration that was run by a clerical and state civil service. High functionaries such as the treasurer, vizier, and governors of the provinces were usually members of the aristocracy. They often gave their instructions in written form, testimony of which are the 500,000 or so clay tablets that have survived.

The ruler was the lawmaker and supreme judge, as is shown by the codes of laws drawn up by famous kings such as Urnammu of Ur and Hammurabi of Babylon. An appointed judge, helped by an advisory committee, carried out the administration of justice. Ownership of land had originally been the privilege of temples, but in Akkadian times, from about 2350 BC, private land ownership was allowed and registered. In about 1500 BC, the system of feudal tenure with its rigid hierarchical structure of society was established.

THE ORGANIZATION OF SOCIETY

As is illustrated in a mosaic of Ur created in 2650 BC, Mesopotamian society was divided into three classes: the aristocracy, free citizens, and slaves. Aristocratic families, whose power and wealth was based on the possession of land, provided the high secular and clerical administrators and officers. A remarkable fact is that servants followed their master into the grave by committing suicide.

City dwellers and farmers, who were deemed inferior, formed the non-enslaved part of the population. It was the responsibility of the farmers, cattle breeders, gardeners, hunters, and fishermen to supply food to the towns and cities, which in turn boasted highly skilled craftsmen such as bricklayers, cabinetmakers, potters, stonemasons, millers, bakers, butchers, weavers, brewers, curriers, and brickmakers. The Sumerians were also the first to develop wheeled vehicles—chariots with two or four wheels, as well as carts for use in agriculture.

ARCHITECTURE AND ART

In the course of about 3,500 years, Mesopotamia developed its own independent art and civilization. Mesopotamian architecture was remarkable for its monumental buildings—palaces, large temple complexes, ziggurats, and enormous town walls. Houses, on the other hand, were very simple. From about 3000 BC, sculptures were produced in the form of votive statuettes, while in the ninth century BC, statues of rulers started to become significant. Reliefs were also very widespread. During the Neo-Assyrian period, which is from about 1000 BC, the bottom part of palace walls was frequently lined with limestone panels 6 feet 6 inches (2 meters) high, known as orthostates, on which the deeds of the ruler were illustrated. ❏

The army was the main support of monarchic power: chariots on the standard of Ur (Mesopotamian mosaic, dating from about 2650 BC).

THE FIRST GREAT CIVILIZATIONS

Third Millennium BC

The establishment of the first civilizations in Mesopotamia and Egypt ushered in the historical era. All of these early civilizations grew up beside rivers.

The Mesopotamian Kingdoms on the Tigris and the Euphrates
The Egyptian Kingdom on the Nile
The Harappan Culture of the Indus River Valley
The First Dynasty in China on the Yellow River

All of these areas were settled early on. The increased fertility of the soil helped farmers to make the transition from hunting and gathering, and to abandon a nomadic way of life. With an economy based on agriculture, they were able to establish a settled existence and take the first steps toward developing more complex social structures. All of these cultures can be identified by certain common features,

- Technical mastery of the natural world was relatively well-developed.
- Cities began to emerge and were the focal points of government and commerce.
- Societies organized themselves politically into states characterized by a hierarchical structure consisting of different social classes and were subject to governing institutions.
- New, more diverse economies benefited from the division of labor.
- Writing became the dominant mode of communication for government and business.
- Surplus wealth encouraged the flowering of artistic endeavor. Architecture made significant advances, and decorative and literary production flourished.

The Nile River: Lifeline of ancient Egyptian civilization

- Cultural identity was forged through language, art, and religion.

To what extent these early cultures developed independently of each other is still a matter of scholarly debate. There were contacts between Mesopotamia and the Nile Valley relatively early on; the people of the Indus Valley had commercial exchanges with Mesopotamia as well. Some historians have suggested that writing was not an indigenous invention of China but derived from the earlier writing systems of the Near East. ❏

GREAT RIVERS—CRADLES OF CIVILIZATION

Point of Interest

It was not by chance that the great civilizations of antiquity arose on the banks of major rivers. The annual cycle of rivers overflowing their banks brought rich alluvial mud onto their shores and provided excellent farmland when the waters retreated.

Desert land surrounded the rivers where the first great societies in Egypt and Mesopotamia appeared. This caused the life-giving waters to be even more highly treasured. To construct irrigation ditches and dams required a significant degree of social organization and encouraged the emergence of a class of state officials to take responsibility for their maintenance. In addition, water rights had to be shared, giving rise to mechanisms to apportion land holdings and settle disputes.

When the annual floods failed to appear or were insufficient, famine threatened. Thus, a system for storing and distributing goods was required. Ancient economies grew in response to this fact. Evidence of storage facilities has been found in sites in the Indus Valley as well as in Egypt. The Joseph story in the Bible tells of his rise to power in Egypt for accurately foretelling a forthcoming time of famine and instituting measures for storing up grain in its anticipation.

In order to be prepared for the annual flooding, early on in Egypt a reliable calendar was developed. The Egyptian calendar posited a solar year of 365 days. It took account of the necessary intercalation to adjust for leap years. This was arrived by observations of the periodic rising of Sirius: the difference of its cycle and that of the sun was one day in four years. Research into the calendar was the great endeavor of the early Egyptian scientists and can rightly be seen as the beginnings of the study of astronomy. ❏

THE REIGN OF KING SARGON

Mesopotamia, 2279 BC

Sargon I, rose from being a humble cupbearer to founding a great Mesopotamian empire. For 50 years, he ruled his empire from the city of Agade, or Akkad, which he also founded. Even before his death, Sargon, whose name means "righteous" or "true king," had become a legendary figure whose origins were shrouded in myth.

He is said to have been an illegitimate child who was abandoned in a rush basket, rescued by a well drawer, and brought up by the goddess Ishtar (Inanna). He was the cupbearer of Ur-Zababa, the king of Kish, whom he overthrew before marching on Uruk with an army of followers and defeating King Lugalzaggesi, then overlord of Sumer.

Conquering in rapid succession Ur, Lagash, and Umma, Sargon went on to found a new city at Agade, on the Euphrates, where he built a palace and temples to Ishtar and Zababa, the warrior-god of Kish. Agade

became the first true capital of Mesopotamia and for the first time gave the Semites ascendancy over the Sumerians.

Sargon was more than a great warrior. He respected the religious institutions of Sumer, making his daughter the priestess of Nanna, moon-god of Ur. He was also aware of the importance of good, and loyal, administration. After he consolidated his authority over Sumer, and enlarged his army, he advanced across the Tigris toward Iran, and along the Euphrates toward Syria, appointing Akkadians (inhabitants of Agade) as governors of conquered territories.

Sargon's campaigns were directed against regions rich in metals, stone, and timber, some of which could be floated down the Euphrates to Agade. Royal wealth was the foundation of an imperial economy, with governors growing increasingly rich, yet knowing they owed it all to their king.

From the Mediterranean to the highlands of Persia, from the foothills of the Caucasus to the Persian Gulf, Sargon became unchallengeable. He was even able to leave his palace at Agade to retreat to the provinces, where he encouraged art to flourish. Sargon was, in short, the first absolute monarch. He reigned for 55 years, defeating revolts even in his old age.

The empire he bequeathed to his son and successor, Rimush, was not without internal difficulties. The funneling of wealth from the conquered lands to the capital had stirred discontent. Nonetheless, Sargon's rule set the stage for the wider conquests of his successors.

Following Sargon's establishment of an Akkadian dynasty, wars were waged over a much larger area. The kings had two purposes in going to war. First, they needed to harass and destabilize their neighbors to ensure the security of their commercial centers. Second, they sought to enrich thmselves. Thus, their whole economy was based on war.

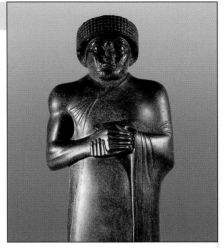
Praying figure from the Gudean period (3rd millennium BC)

After Sargon's death, Akkadian armies marched to the Mediterranean coast and eastward well into Persia. Not even Sargon's great conquests could match the reputation of his grandson Naram-Sin, around whose long reign of at least 36 years seems to have been almost entirely filled with military operations. In the west, he conquered Arman and Ebla in Syria, In the north, he campaigned against Hurrian Namar and built a royal residence in the Khabur basin, But his most important victory was over the powerful Lullubi in the east, commemorated in rock sculpture. ❑

CIVILIZATION RISES ON THE BANKS OF THE INDUS

India, c.2250 BC

A remarkable farming civilization flourished in the fertile plains of the Indus River Valley. Spread over half a million square miles, it was sustained by its agriculture and centered on the two important cities of Harappa and Mohenjo-Daro, which had populations of as many as 30,000 people each. The similar street plans of

both cities bear witness to the highly developed administration and organization of the inhabitants; both were arranged on a grid pattern with wide streets and had dwellings built of kiln-fired bricks. The bricks were also used in complex dyke systems to ward off the dangers of flooding from the Indus. It is hard to say whether this civilization deserves to be called an empire, but it featured a similarity of building methods and the use of standardized weights and measures over a vast area. The Indus culture was probably the first to make cotton cloth, and its craftsmen produced beautiful decorated earthenware vessels and elegant bronze statuettes. ❑

Ruins of Mohenjo-Daro

THE DEMISE OF THE OLD KINGDOM

Egypt c.2160 BC

After an extraordinarily long reign—Egyptian records say that it lasted 94 years—Pepi II finally died. He ascended the throne when he was only six years old. He ruled over one of the most prosperousa periods in Egypt's history, noteworthy for its great commercial activity, particularly with Byblos and Punt in East Africa. The last years of his rule were, however, troubled by decentralization and the decline of Pharaonic power, and his death marked the end of the last illustrious reign of the Egyptian Old Kingdom. ❑

Alabaster vessel of the Pharaoh Pepi II (c.2200 BC)

STONEHENGE: ENIGMATIC CIRCLES OF STONES

England, Second and Third Millennium BC

Stonehenge, built between 2460 and 1500 BC in the county of Wiltshire near Salisbury, is an enduring witness to megalithic culture. It is the largest prehistoric stone monument in Europe.

The arrangement of stones originally consisted of several concentric circles. Although its function remains a matter of dispute, it has been plausibly argued that it served as a cult center for sun worshipers, on the basis that the placement of individual stones corresponds to the rising sun. The axis of the stones' layout seems to have been oriented to the position of sunrise on the day of the summer solstice. Main stones were placed in the circle to mark other positions of the sun over the course of the year.

In the first century AD, the site was used by the Celts for ritual or religious purposes. The numerous mounds in the vicinity suggest some connection with a cult of the dead.

The construction of Stonehenge took place in three stages. The monument was built around 2460 BC, in the midst of the Stone Age, upon a simple circular plan with a trench and an inner wall. Its diameter measured about 350 feet (106 meters). It consisted of a circular bank and ditch. Around the monument 56 holes were dug and possibly used in connection with sacrificial rites. Human remains from this time period have been found there. The entrance to the monument was to the northeast.

A second phase of construction was completed around 2200 BC, and the entire plan was altered. The entrance was modified; sandstone monoliths were used to mark it out. One of these, the still extant "Heelstone" stands about 18 feet high (5.5 meters). During this period, 80 giant bluestones were hauled and arranged in a double circle in the middle of the monument.

The third phase of construction took place between 2000 and 1500 BC. It was at this point that Stonehenge assumed its present form. The existing arrangement of bluestones was replaced by enormous sarsen stones with stone lintels connecting them. Within this circle were five trilithons laid out in a horseshoe shape, possibly a symbol of death. The horseshoe opened to the northeast. Additional stones were placed as to suggest an altar. From there, a 60-foot wide ceremonial avenue that had already been completed during the second phase of construction ran northward. After about 400 yards, the road forked leading to a settlement.

The sarsen blocks came from an area 20 miles to the north of the site; while the bluestones, which in some cases weighed over 100 tons, were transported from quarries in Wales 120 miles away. Moving, preparing, and positioning such huge stones called for remarkable feats of engineering. The laborious process of transporting them required sleds with wheels and the concerted effort of many people. They were dragged up an embankment, erected in specially dug holes, and wedged into place with rocks and boulders. The stones were shaped into the desired convex form with heavy stone hammers so that when standing they did not appear as if they were tapered toward the top. A kind of tongue and groove construction locked in the lintel stones that joined them together and they were raised up with the use of levers. Some of the stones were decorated with engraved representations. ❑

View of Stonehenge outside of Salisbury, England

STANDING STONES

Point of Interest

Stonehenge is the most impressive stone monument in Europe dating from at least as early as the second millennium. But it is in no way unique. The megalithic culture that produced standing stones was widespread throughout continental Europe. It seems to have flourished along the Atlantic coast of France, in Scandinavia, and on the Baltic Sea. Sites have also been found in southern Italy, on Mediterranean islands, in southern Bulgaria, and as far away as in the Caucasus along the Black Sea coast.

The monoliths can be found standing alone or arranged in circles or rows. There are, in addition, many stone graves in different shapes and sizes. The oldest Megalithic tombs are found in Brittany dating from about 3500 BC. For walls, most of the graves used upright stones that were then roofed over with smooth flat stones. The burial chambers had walls constructed without the use of mortar and were supported by more stones. The construction was then covered by earthen mounds or piles of stones. In addition to these dolmens, tombs that included burial chambers and other graves were laid in rows or galleries with side chambers that served as burial places for entire families.

In many places throughout Europe, temples or other cult sites were located near the standing stones and graves. In Malta, in about 2500 BC, the walls of the temples were of hewn stone cunningly joined together. They were originally covered with a clay wash then painted over. Enigmatic flat female figures were left there as offerings to the dead.

As a general rule, the walls of graves and ceremonial sites were covered with ornamental designs and symbolic representations. ❑

THE LIBRARY AT EBLA

Syria, c.2000 BC

Although the oldest cities in the world were in Sumer in southern Mesopotamia, flourishing and influential towns sprang up in other parts of the great Fertile Crescent between the Mediterranean and the mouths of the Tigris and Euphrates.

One of these was Ebla, a town of over 120 acres in northwestern Syria, dominated by a citadel with a royal palace, massive oval ramparts, and four fortified gates on the site of what is known today as Tell Mardikh.

What made Ebla remarkable was its great state archive of clay tablets. These were kept on wooden shelves in the royal palace. They are written in the cuneiform script devised for official records by Sumerian scribes in the preceding centuries. The rise of Ebla testifies to the emergence of many small states around Mesopotamia, especially along the trade routes carrying valuable raw materials. Many of the documents were therefore concerned with trade and diplomacy. The inscribed tablets from Ebla also detail activities of Sumerian professions.

The library itself was an official archive of Ebla's history and considerable influence on—and perhaps also aggression toward—other powers in the region.

In one letter to the king of Ebla, a neighbor, the king of Mari, appears to warn his counterpart against any act of aggression by reminding him of the exploits of his royal predecessors. ❏

SEPARATION OF CHURCH AND STATE

Sumer, early third millennium BC

Under the reforms initiated by Urukagina of Lagash, kings of Mesopotamia ceased to be substitute gods and cast off their priestly functions. This separation of palace and temple outlived his fall.

Under previous kings, Lagash had had a separate high priest called Dudu. After King Enmetena's death, the priests of Ningirsu seized the throne of Lagash, and for the next two decades they enlarged their own influence and property at the expense of the people. Officials interfered in every facet of life: Heavy taxes were levied on burials and weddings, and corruption was rife.

When Urukagina came to the throne he launched an ambitious reform program, removing superfluous officials, cutting taxes, and restoring land and property that had been dedicated to the gods. An inscription of the time reads: "He freed the citizens of Lagash from usury, monopoly, hunger, theft and assault; he established their freedom."

Urukagina's reign lasted eight years then he was driven out of Lagash by the invading army of Lugalzaggesi of Umma. Lugalzaggesi went on to conquer Uruk but was eventually defeated in battle by Sargon. ❏

THE SUMERIAN KINGDOM UNITED

Sumeria c.2047 BC

The Sumerian Urnammu was originally merely a military governor under King Utuhegal. He overthrew his master and founded the last major dynasty in Sumer—and after the collapse of the Akkadian Kingdom incorporated it into his empire.

Assuming the title King of Sumer and Akkad, he controlled a trading network that extended from the Persian Gulf to Syria, developed maritime trade, and secured the kingdom, allowing it to enjoy a period of great prosperity derived from its grain supplies and textile production.

Urnammu improved the country's system of canals and instituted a register recording landholdings. He is also responsible—in part following along the lines of the early Sumerian king of the Akkad Dynasty, Naramsi— for mankind's earliest known law book. The fragments of 10,000 legal and governmental texts that have been found dating to his era testify to the energy and organization of his administration of the kingdom. Countless archaeological finds bear mention of his name, whether written on clay shards, stone, or bronze. The program of new construction he launched was continued by his successor, Shulgi. Shulgi was able to expand Sumerian power to include the neighboring kingdoms of Elam and Anshan.

Within two generations, Sumer was on the defensive against incursions from Amorites and attacks from the resurgent Elamites. Finally, dynastic rule was confined to the city of Ur, as governors of other cities broke away from the central monarchy. One Ishbi-Erra set himself up as king in the rival city of Isin, founding a dynasty that laid claim to the rule of all Sumer and Akkad. But by this time the Sumerian Empire was more a rhetorical than actual political entity. The kingdom continued to exist at least in name until the rise of Hammurabi, but then he incorporated it into the Babylonian Empire. ❏

Babylonian art: Lyre from Ur (reconstruction)

Ani is portrayed worshipping the god Ra (top left in a boat) and the god Osiris (detail of a painting on papyrus, Egyptian art of the Ninth Dynasty).

There is no other country in the world whose development has been so influenced by geographic conditions as Egypt. The country's division into three regions, with the narrow Nile Valley in Upper Egypt, the wide delta, and the western and eastern desert regions, formed a natural disparity between desert and fertile land. It caused the isolation of the people living along the Nile from other equally developed civilizations, and it also resulted in the development of a special form of agriculture. In particular, the annual flooding of the Nile forced people to gather together in groups to regulate the water in order to manage it.

The history of Egypt began with its first king, Menes, who united the two kingdoms of Upper Egypt and Lower Egypt to form a single state around 3100 BC. At the center of this new order was the concept of the kingdom, which was reflected in the dual role of the ruler of Upper and Lower Egypt. The administrative center was the royal residence in Memphis and the entire country was divided into 42 administrative districts. The Egyptian pharaoh was considered the incarnation of the god Horus. During this period the Egyptians invented hieroglyphs, a combination of symbols and a phonetic alphabet.

THE PYRAMID BUILDERS OF THE OLD KINGDOM

The highpoint of the Old Kingdom began in about 2635 BC with the Third Dynasty, the most famous ruling figure of which was King Djoser (about 2624–2605 BC). The step pyramid at Saqqara, 197 feet (60 meters) high, is proof of his power. It marks the beginning of the monumental Egyptian architecture that reached its peak with the pyramids and temples of Giza, built by the pharaohs Khufu, Khafre, and Menkaure of the Fourth Dynasty. These monumental buildings bear witness to the internal structure and economic success of Egypt, while at the same time express the complete integration of political and religious life.

The period of the Fourth Dynasty ended in about 2465 BC with conflicts surrounding succession to the throne. These disputes heralded the beginning of the reduction of power of the central royal government. Under the first kings of the Fifth Dynasty, important political and religious changes took place. The influence of the temple of Ra and the worship of the sun god centered on Heliopolis played decisive roles. Besides the old, official state dogma that the pharaoh was the human transformation of the god Horus, a new concept developed whereby he was considered the human son of the god.

There was another important cultic change at the end of the dynasty in about 2325 BC. Under the influence of the growing worship of Osiris, the dead pharaoh gradually became identified with Osiris, the god of fertility and the underworld. The pyramid texts dating from that period, which are the oldest religious texts in the history of mankind, reveal the Egyptians' attempt to balance the worship of the sun god and the cult of the dead.

Over time the religiously justified, universal claim of the monarchy diminished, as did its political power. The provincial governors became powerful princes in their own right and the priests became ever more independent and increasingly privileged. Under the influence of a barter economy and increasing decentralization, the strictly organized administrative state gradually developed into a kind of feudalism. Still, Egypt continued to increase its power and riches through a combination of trade, which flourished, and successful military expeditions.

During the Sixth Dynasty (2325–2160 BC), Egypt remained on sound footing. But decline set in toward the end. Political and social unrest, together with conflicts on the borders of the kingdom, favored the rise of local rulers—the provincial governors. Attempts by the pharaohs to retain absolute power failed. Finally, the family of the provincial princes of Herakleopolis in the province of Memphis seized power and claimed the throne of the pharaohs. The kingdom broke up. In the south, the provincial governors of Upper Egypt became independent under the rule of Thebes in 2134 BC (Seventh through Tenth Dynasties).

CULTURAL DEVELOPMENT OF THE MIDDLE KINGDOM

The second great renaissance period in the history of Egypt started with the founder of the Twelfth Dynasty, Amenemhat I, who came to power in 1991 BC. It was under the rule of his successors that the copper-rich Sinai Peninsula and southern Palestine came under Egyptian control. Trade links were established with Minoan Crete (which at the time was experiencing a cultural renaissance) and with Mesopotamia.

In Egypt itself, Sesostris III (1878–1841 BC) succeeded in eliminating the dynasties of provincial governor-princes and so restored a central government. Middle Egyptian, the language spoken during the period of the Middle Kingdom, developed into the classical written language. This hieroglyphic script was used on monuments until the Greco-Roman period.

FOREIGN DOMINATION BY THE HYKSOS

After the extinction of the Twelfth Dynasty in 1785 BC, rulers succeeded one other in quick succession. This instability led to a cultural decline and the loss of the outer provinces of Sinai, Nubia, and Palestine as well as the infiltration of the eastern delta by nomadic Semitic tribes. In about 1650 BC, the whole of Egypt fell under the rule of the Hyksos. An indigenous royal house from Thebes started a national struggle to liberate Egypt from the invaders. The Theban king Ahmose I succeeded in driving them out by adopting the fighting technique introduced by the Hyksos, which included the two-wheeled chariot.

THE IMPERIALISM OF THE NEW KINGDOM

The era of Egyptian imperialism began with Thutmose I (1506–1494). As a result of his policies of expansion, Egypt developed into a great power with considerable influence in the Mediterranean. It was at that time that the Valley of the Kings was created, facing the new royal capital of Thebes on the west bank of the Nile.

Hatshepsut (1490–1468 BC), the most powerful Egyptian queen in history, was succeeded by Thutmose III who forced the Hittites, Babylonians, and Assyrians to recognize Egyptian dominance over much of the Near East. Egypt had thus reached the greatest territorial expansion in its history. The arrival of Amenophis III, who ascended the throne in 1402 BC, put an end to the active military campaigns and expansionist policies. This pharaoh presided over a period of stability and economic prosperity until his death in 1364 BC.

The Egyptian kingdom survived a domestic upheaval during the reign of Amenohotep IV (1364–1347 BC), who at the beginning of his reign founded a new religious movement in which the sun god Ra, symbolized by the solar disc "Aten," was considered the source of all life. The king, who was also the high priest of the monotheistic religion he had established, moved his capital from Thebes to the newly founded city of Amarna. He changed his name to Akhenaten, "He who is acceptable to Aten."

However, the resistance against the monotheism imposed by the pharaoh grew in all classes of society at the same time as Egypt's external political power diminished with the loss of Syria to the Hittites. Akhenaten's successor, Tutankhamun, who became famous in the twentieth century when his treasure-filled tomb was discovered, returned to the old religion and moved his capital back to Thebes.

THE RAMESSES RULERS

Under Ramesses II (1290–1224 BC), the most famous ruler of the Nineteenth Dynasty, Egypt regained a position of power. He began a vast building program. As to foreign policy, he managed to make peace with the Hittites, who agreed to share their supremacy over Asia Minor with Egypt. But now the danger was coming from the Libyans in the west and maritime invaders from the north; they had already established bases in Crete and the Aegean as early as the thirteenth century.

It is true that the last great pharaoh of the New Kingdom, Ramesses III, succeeded in repelling a major attack by the Libyans and their seagoing allies. But it was during his reign that the stonemasons working on the royal tombs went on strike for the first time, and the pharaoh's power continued to decline steadily under the rule of his successors. In contrast, the Amun priests in Thebes became so powerful that under the Twenty-first Dynasty (1070–945 BC), Egypt became a de facto Theban-South Egyptian temple-state, while the actual sphere of influence of the royal capital in the northeast delta collapsed. In the tenth century BC, the Kush kingdom was founded in the province of Nubia by a native Egyptianized dynasty that then conquered Memphis in the eighth century BC and gradually subjugated the whole Nile Valley. In 671 BC, the Assyrian king Esarhaddon conquered Memphis and in 663 BC, the Assyrians destroyed Thebes.

RESTORATION AND THE LATE PERIOD

Taking advantage of the major conflicts plaguing the Assyrian Empire, the lords of Sais, Necho I, and Psamtik I, founders of the Twenty-sixth Dynasty (664 BC 525 BC), shook off Assyrian sovereignty and united the Nile Valley under their rule once more. Egypt experienced another artistic and political renaissance. Then Egypt tried again to annex Syria into the empire, but in 605 BC, the Pharaoh Necho II suffered a crushing defeat at the hands of the Babylonians and was forced to give up his plans for expansion in Asia Minor. Under King Amasis, Egypt annexed Cyprus—a military success that confirmed that the pharaoh's Egypt was still a naval power to be reckoned with.

The rise of the Persian Empire under Cyrus II in 559 BC forced Amasis to join the defensive alliance of Babylon, Lydia, and Sparta against the new power. The conquest of Egypt was only a question of time. In 525 BC, the last king, Psamtik III was defeated by the Persians, and Egypt became a Persian satrapy. Although the Persians were very tolerant toward the people they conquered, the Egyptians were extremely hostile to the Persian domination. In 332 BC Alexander the Great was greeted jubilantly as a liberator when he arrived in Egypt. ❑

Pharaoh Ramesses II built the massive pylon (entrance tower) of the Luxor temple.

THE GOD AMUN AND EGYPT'S NEW CAPITAL

Thebes, c.2000 BC

The start of the second millennium BC witnessed the growth and consolidation of Egyptian power. Thebes became the capital of Egypt and massive building work was undertaken to create the temple of Karnak to celebrate Amun's elevation to the country's principal god. He was originally a minor deity, worshipped in Thebes when it was no more than a provincial town. As the town grew to become the capital of Egypt, Amun's prestige grew with it, until he was viewed as the king of the gods—at the top of the Theban trinity with his wife, the goddess Mut, and his son Chons.

Amun was regarded as the physical father of every pharaoh and thus received many gifts from his grateful sons in their temples, which accounts for the enormous privileges granted to his priests. The temples dedicated to him were huge, and the priests became a political power to be reckoned with. The name Amun was an important element of royal names.

Theban legend spoke of Amun's taking part in a public procession in his ship of state each year; in fact, he was brought in statue form on the occasion of the procession of the feast of Opet, the greatest of Thebes' festivals.

Amun was most frequently portrayed wearing a cap decked with two tall feathers with his body sometimes shown as ithyphallic in token of fertility. The ram and the white goose were the two animals associated with him.

His power was considered great indeed. A prayer confirms the popular faith in Amun's justness. "Amun-Re judges the earth with his finger, and speaks to the heart. He assigns the wicked to punishment, but the righteous to the West."

The pharaohs enlarged Karnak into a major complex of temples and built themselves funerary temples—large rock-cut tombs with magnificent facades at el Tarif. It was Mentuhotep I (c.2061–2010 BC) who established Thebes as the capital

One of Mentuhotep's successors, Amenemhat I (1991–1962 BC), abandoned the city and set up his capital at el Lisht in the area near Memphis. The reasons for this move were mainly administrative, due to its strategic location between the Nile delta and Nile Valley. Amenemhat's son Senusret I secured the Nubian frontier, building a series of fortresses. He also established relationships with some cities in Canaan and Syria.

During this time, a major reorganization of the kingdom took place, with the pharaohs aiming to consolidate a single political unit around themselves. Significantly, the god Osiris—at one time the "exclusive property of the kings"—was now associated with every dead person in the kingdom. The problems of royal succession, which contributed to anarchy in the past because of the pharaohs' longevity and proclivity to fatherhood, were resolved by a system of coregency between a king and his son.

Senusret III (r. 1879-1839 BC), the most significant ruler of the Middle Kingdom, presided over a period of significant political expansion, extending Egyptian domination southward into Sudan as far as the second cataract of the Nile. ❑

Pharaoh Sesostris III

BOOK OF THE DEAD

Egypt, c.1700 BC

Egypt's dead were offered more than food, drink, and ceremonial boats for their passage to the world to come. They were provided with spiritual guidance in the form of religious texts.

At first these were inscribed on coffins ("coffin texts"), but later were written on papyrus and placed directly into the sarcophagi or coffins. They came to be known as *The Book of the Dead*.

The texts ranged over a wide variety of subjects. Some themes recurred frequently, in particular, precepts that served to protect the deceased in the hereafter.

Many of books were beautifully illustrated with the names of their dead owners inserted at appropriate places. Magic spells ensured the dead a safe escape from the darkness of the tomb and a return to their homes and gardens where they could enjoy "the sweet breezes of the north wind." ❑

FOREIGN RULE OF EGYPT

Egypt, c.1550 BC

In Northern Egypt, the Hyksos people seized power and established a dynasty. *Hyksos* was the Egyptian word meaning "Lords of a foreign country." However,

The Egyptian God, Osiris

after a lengthy siege, the Hyksos defenders of the fortress capital of Avaris in the northeastern delta capitulated, bringing foreign domination of Egypt to an end. Following its victory, the Egyptian army crossed the Sinai and invaded Palestine and Syria in pursuit of the Hyksos and their allies into western Asia. These tribes from Asia had taken advantage of weak Egyptian leadership to infiltrate the Nile delta and to finally conquer the whole of Egypt, using war chariots and other forms of weaponry unknown to Egypt. Contemporary accounts speak of the "infliction of every kind of barbarity upon the inhabitants, slaying some, and reducing the wives and children of others to a state of slavery." Others speak of the destruction of the great temples built by previous Egyptian rulers, although many of these claims were exaggerated. The groundwork for the Hyksos Dynasty was laid by King Salitis around 1680 BC. It ruled Egypt with garrisons built along the entire length of the Nile. The Hyksos, mostly an illiterate race, adopted Egyptian customs, took Egyptian names, and learned to use the hieroglyphic script. . Organized resistance began in Thebes. The Egyptians had learned the value of the horse-drawn war chariot, of bows and arrows and slings, from their Hyksos masters. Now they turned these same weapons on their invaders. Most of the delta was liberated by the Egyptian king, Ahmose, before he laid siege to the Hyksos stronghold at Avaris. ❑

HAMMURABI THE LAWGIVER

Babylon, c.1760 BC

After winning a series of victories over his neighbors, Hammurabi became the sixth king of Babylon and the first king of the Babylonian Empire. He is best known for a set of laws that he had engraved on stone slabs. Hammurabi promoted Marduk, god of Babylon, to the head of the pantheon of gods, thereby providing a divine sanction to his dynasty. Then, like other Mesopotamian kings, he "ordained justice" by remitting various debts and fixing prices of commodities in the markets.

His laws were essentially a collection of ad hoc edicts, often based on existing laws and customs in order to ensure continuity. They related to the three social classes of citizens: free men, serfs, and slaves. Fees and punishments varied according to class.

Compensation in kind, or money, which was the basis of the Sumerian system, was partially replaced by the Law of Retaliation. Thus, a surgeon or architect whose work resulted in injury to his client, or death, was liable to have his hand cut off or, in extreme cases, to be executed.

Adulterous wives could be saved from sentence of death by their husbands, but their lovers could be spared only by the king's edict. A prisoner's wife could sleep with another man "if there is nothing to eat in her house." Men wishing to divorce their wives had to compensate them financially. Widows had the use of their husbands' property for life.

People in certain positions were granted *il-kum*—corn, land, sheep, and cattle—from the king in return for their loyalty. ❑

Stele engraved with the Code of Hammurabi (Louvre, Paris)

EXCERPTS FROM THE CODE OF HAMMURABI

If a judge try a case, reach a decision, and present his judgment in writing; if later error shall appear in his decision, and it be through his own fault, then he shall pay twelve times the fine set by him in the case, and he shall be publicly removed from the judge's bench, and never again shall he sit there to render judgment. If any one commits a robbery and is caught, he shall be put to death. If the robber is not caught, then shall he who was robbed claim under oath the amount of his loss; then shall the community, and...on whose ground and territory and in whose domain it was compensate him for the goods stolen. If a tavern-keeper (feminine) does not accept corn according to gross weight in payment of drink, but takes money, and the price of the drink is less than that of the corn, she shall be convicted and thrown into the water. If a man takes a woman to wife, but has no intercourse with her, this woman is no wife to him.If a woman quarrels with her husband, saying "You are not congenial to me," her reasons for her prejudice must be presented. If she is guiltless, and there is no fault on her part, but he leaves and neglects her, then no guilt attaches to this woman, she shall take her dowry and go back to her father's house. ❑

HIGH WATER MARK OF THE SHANG DYNASTY

China, c.1600 BC

By the middle of the second millennium BC, the Shang Dynasty had firmly established itself in the Henan Honan province, some 75 miles north of the Yellow River. They were powerful but cruel rulers. The social order they established centered on their king, who was considered a semidivine ruler and regarded as the channel of communication with the ancestors of the royal clan.

In order to keep on good terms with these powerful gods, the Shang offered them human sacrifices, usually prisoners taken from the neighboring peoples with whom they waged constant war.

The Shang conversed with their gods by writing questions on bones and tortoise shells, applying a hot iron, and then analyzing the resultant cracks. The answer given by the cracks was written on the bone or shell, which was then carefully filed away. This divinatory practice gave rise to one of the most famous of all Chinese literary works, the *I Ching*.

The responses, and therefore the gods, controlled every aspect of Shang life. The "oracle bones" were consulted before armies set out on campaigns, at the start of an elephant hunt, and to ask the gods for rain.

Bronze mask from the time of the Shang Dynasty (2nd millennium BC)

Craftsmanship was highly regarded, with bronze and jade being worked into utensils and jewelry. Mulberry trees were cultivated and silk was used for clothing, while many of the surrounding peoples still wore only coarse hemp clothes.

There was also no such thing as equality in this society. The lower classes lived in pit-dwellings with few possessions. They spent their days laboring in the fields, while the ruling aristocrats lived in luxury and devoted themselves to warfare and ritual. ❑

ARTISTIC FLOWERING IN EGYPT

Point of Interest

Pictorial art in Egypt reached new heights during the reign of Amenhotep III. Compositions were larger than ever before; the gestures of the subjects more supple; and the range of colors subtler.

Artists in the service of Amenhotep III preferred white backgrounds rather than the gray-blue of the early days of Egyptian art.

Naturalistic art made great strides, as shown in the fowling scene of Nebamun hunting birds with a throw stick. There a cat snares birds, and butterflies take flight; everything is recorded in the minutest detail.

Another main motif reflected the Egyptian obsession with death; mourners follow a funeral procession, and pictures in the tomb of the vizier Ramose show unrestrained grief, with tears flowing down the cheeks of the wailing women. The artistry is powerful and typical of this pharaoh's reign. ❏

Mask of the face of a prince made from an alloy of gold and silver (Mycenaean))

THE PALACES AT KNOSSOS

Crete, late 15th century BC

A high civilization existed on the island of Crete from late in the third millennium BC. After a massive earthquake brought ruin and desolation to the island, its palaces were rebuilt on an even grander scale than before. The palace at Knossos has associations in legend with King Minos, who was said to have engaged the architect Daedalus to construct the vast complex of buildings surrounding a central court running north and south.

Besides the throne room and the royal apartments there were shrines, administrative offices, an arsenal, granaries, warehouses, and workshops. Near the central court was the Snake Goddess, a statuette of a narrow-waisted woman with a flounced skirt and a tight-fitting blouse, cut away to expose her breasts. In her hands she held out wriggling snakes. The walls were adorned with frescoes, the most famous of which, the *Toreador Fresco*, shows a young man apparently leaping over a bull's back.

In addition to palaces, there were also country houses: centers of estates that produced olive oil and wine. Writing, in a local script based on Egyptian models, was introduced to keep track of these ever more complex commercial arrangements.

The new palaces at Knossos and elsewhere on the island were built on the sites of the original ones. Therefore, much of the evidence of the past construction has been effaced. It is known, though, that the old palaces, like the new ones, consisted of buildings arranged round a large rectangular courtyard.

Around the year 1500 BC, Crete was invaded and conquered by the expanding Mycenaean Empire. ❏

THE MINOTAUR AND THE LABYRINTH

Point of Interest

According to legend, Minos, the son of Zeus and Europa, was the first king of Crete. It was he who had the labyrinth built by the inventor and architect Daedalus. Minos asked Poseidon, the sea-god, for an animal to sacrifice as proof of the divine origin of his rule. But instead of offering Poseidon the bull he was given, he offered a substitute from his own herd.

As a punishment, his wife, Pasiphaë, was made to fall passionately in love with the bull, who gave her a monster for a son: the Minotaur, a man with a bull's head. Minos imprisoned the Minotaur in the labyrinth built by Daedalus.

Athens was required to render a yearly tribute to Minos of fourteen virgins, seven boys and seven girls, who were then offered to the Minotaur. The hero Theseus took upon himself the labor of freeing Athens from this grisly sacrifice. He traveled to Crete and set out to fight the Minotaur. Before entering the labyrinth, the king's daughter Ariadne, who had fallen in love with the Athenian warrior, provided him with a spool of thread. He unwound this as he journeyed to the center of the labyrinth, where he battled and slew the monster. Then by following Ariadne's thread, he was able to find his way out again. ❏

Alabaster sarcophagus of a Holy Triad (14th century BC). Upper right. Statue of Minoan snake goddess from Knossos (17th century BC). Lower right. Vase with flower motif in dark colors on a light background, typical of Minoan pottery.

Statue of the Minotaur, half man, half bull

MYCENAEAN DOMINATION OF THE MEDITERRANEAN

Mycenae, Greece, c.1450 BC

Established in their strategically sited citadel on a plain just to the north of Argos, the lords of Mycenae achieved fame and prosperity without equal on mainland Greece. Not only did they hold sway over the fertile plain, with its cornfields and horse ranches, but they also dominated the trade routes from the southeastern ports through the mountain passes northward to the Isthmus of Corinth. In Homer's *Iliad* the commander of the Greek army is Agamemnon, King of Mycenae, a recognition of its early glory.

The Mycenaeans fostered a vigorous enterprise culture, forging links deep into Europe for trade in gold, bronze. and amber, some of which they reexported, along with their pottery, to the islands of the Aegean and the eastern Mediterranean.

The opulence of the Mycenaean lords' burial customs was famed throughout the ancient world. In the so-called shaft graves, which were enclosed in stone circles, men and women were buried with gold and silver vases, gold rings and necklaces, crowns and tiaras, and bronze daggers with gold inlays. One Mycenaean dignitary was buried with his face covered by a heavy mask fashioned from solid gold.

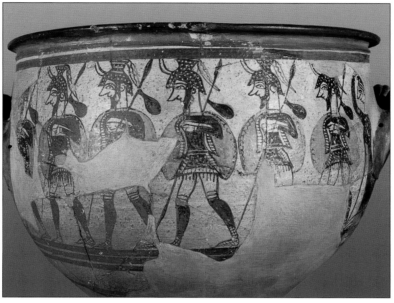

Mycenaean vase decorated with warlike figures (12th century BC)

The Mycenaeans also built massive beehive shaped vaulted tombs, up to 49 (16m.) feet in diameter, outside the citadel itself. Again, the dead were buried with a rich assortment of weapons, tools, jewelry, and vases containing food and drink. Some historians believe that the people buried in the beehive tombs were later moved to the shaft graves where new burials took place.

The Mycenaean ruling classes generally enjoyed a full life of sport and games, spiced by wars with the hill tribes to the north. Boar hunting expeditions and armed combat, with lance and body shield of bull's hide, can be seen portrayed on palace frescoes, tombstones, and vases that also show the womenfolk as large-eyed, with flowing hair, flounced skirts, and low-cut bodices. The women are shown dancing and feasting with the men.

The age of Mycenaean hegemony came to an end in the thirteenth century BC. There have been a number of theories regarding the cause of the decline. Some have suggested the civilization was destroyed by invaders from the north, others that the collapse came from within. Whatever the cause, its empire had disappeared by 1200 BC . ❏

A WOMAN RULES EGYPT

Egypt, c. 1490 BC

In every respect the beautiful Hatshepsut was a pharaoh in her own right. Statues and paintings show her as a bearded Osiris in the traditional manner. She was not buried with royal women in the Valley of the Queens but lies in her spectacular tomb among male pharaohs in the Valley of the Kings.

Historians wonder how a woman could have achieved such power and influence in such a male-dominated society? The answer is found in the complicated marital situation prevailing at the time. Hatshepsut married her half-brother, Thutmose II, who died prematurely leaving a son, Thutmose III, the child of another wife. Thutmose III was a child, incapable of ruling, and thus the forceful, charismatic Hatshepsut stepped in and officially took power until her death.

Hatshepsut's reign saw the expansion of trade and the erection of one of the finest temples in Egypt—its great doors fashioned from black bronze, its inlaid figures in electrum—built for her by Senenmut, her daughter's tutor. A trading expedition to the land of Punt (perhaps in the region of Somalia) that brought back gold, ivory, incense, apes, birds, and trees is recorded in some detail among the inscriptions. They show the very fat queen of Punt, together with the Egyptian envoy, displaying beads and other articles used in the trade.

Hatshepsut's reign was also marked by her support of art and architecture. At Karnak, for instance, she was responsible for the erection of two monumental obelisks. At her death, a vast mortuary temple was built for her by her stepson, Thutmose III. It dominates the cliffs overlooking Karnak, its height and splendor indicating the prestige in which the queen was held. The building is partly cut into rock and fits perfectly with its surroundings. ❏

The great funeral temple built for Queen Hatshepsut by her son Thutmose III

EXPANSION OF HITTITE POWER

Egypt, c.1375 BC

Originally the Hittites occupied a small Anatolian kingdom centered in the city of Hattusa. The capital was fortified with inner and outer walls and solid watchtowers. Hittite society was organized around the person of the king. He was its religious as well as its political leader. Most of the citizenry was engaged in the martial enterpris-

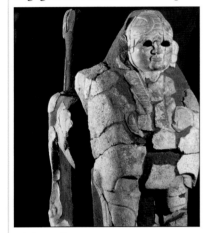

Hittite sculpture

es. Below him in the military hierarchy was a class of knights and below them charioteers and infantry. The king also had his personal bodyguard. At the bottom rung was the slave population. The king presided over all religious functions, and many stone reliefs depict him in this role.

Flexing its muscles, the Hit-

tite Kingdom began to challenge Egypt, the dominant force in the region, with Palestine and Syria the eagerly sought prizes. Egypt had exercised its might in a series of campaigns by Egypt's Thutmose III, and the stage was set for a confrontation between Egypt and the Hittite kingdoms.

The death of Thutmose, the military genius, sparked off fresh uprisings and internecine warfare between the Syrian princes. Though these were quelled by an operation led by Thutmose's son, Amenhotep II, tension remained high throughout the Middle East as the Hittites sought to expand their sphere of influence.

The interests of both countries were focused on the Mitanni Kingdom, which lorded over much of Syria and Mesopotamia. Thutmose never succeeded in conquering the Mitanni; his successor, Amenhotep II, anxious to befriend the nation, arranged to take a Mitanni princess into his harem. Meanwhile, after founding a new Hittite kingdom after 20 years of civil war, King Suppiluliuma cast covetous eyes on Mitanni. He lent his support to a pretender to the Mitanni throne and used this alliance to manufacture a *casus belli*.

Although Suppiluliuma's first

The Lion's Gate. One of the five entrances to the Hittite capital of Hattusa. The city was first excavated at the end of the 19th century.

attack was a failure, his second was a spectacular success. The city capitulated, and Suppiluliuma gained control of most of the Mitanni Kingdom.

Following this victory an uneasy state of truce prevailed btween the Hittite and Egyptian armies, and the Hittites decided to go on to the offensive. In a daring move, Suppiluliuma started a drive south to extend the territory of his empire. He was drawn to the rich cities and manufacturing centers of north Syria: natural targets for the steady expansion of Hittite power.

Despite fierce opposition from the Egyptians, who were also keen to expand their influence in the Levant, Suppiluliuma succeeded in establishing vassal

states in Syria, driving a wedge between the still-dangerous remnants of the Mitanni Kingdom and the Mediterranean Sea. In so doing he assumed control of the major urban centers of Alalah and Carchemish.

Suppiluliuma was succeeded by his son Mursili II, who took power around 1330 BC. He turned his attention westward conquering cities on the Anatolian coast. It was his son, Muwatalli II, who led his troops into battle against the Egyptians. The two armies met at Kadesh, a settlement on the border between Canaan and Syria. They fought to a standoff, but the battle left the Hittites weakened and vulnerable to an increasingly powerful enemy from the east, Assyria. ❑

EGYPTIAN RULE OF THUTMOSE III

Egypt, c.1450 BC

Thutmose III proved himself an outstanding military leader. Over seventeen campaigns, he succeeded in extending the Egyptian Empire to the banks of the Euphrates. The campaigning began when Egypt was threatened by an alliance of the princes of Megiddo and Kadesh. Thutmose took preemptive action and attacked Megiddo, leading his army in single file along a narrow defile—"horse behind horse, man behind man, his Majesty showing the way by his

own footsteps"—and captured the city after a short siege.

Thutmose pursued a strategy of creating "buffer states" around Egypt primarily to defend his country against any repetition of the invasion that produced the Hyksos Dynasty. He also created a novel system under which Syria and Palestine were forced to keep the peace and smaller states were kept under order. The pharaoh established an inspection system for collecting tributes from defeated

nations.

After many years of subordination to his stepmother, Queen Hatshepsut, Thutmose's emergence as the fighting head of such a great empire came as something of a surprise to observers. The pharaoh was not merely a great general: He was a statesman who treated his defeated enemies with considerable humanity. Even those leaders who fought against him were not executed. They were deposed, and their sons and broth-

ers brought to Egypt and held hostage. Under Thutmose, the smaller states enjoyed a kind of prosperity previously unknown.

Thutmose III finally died in 1425 BC, after reigning for 54 years. He had undertaken the construction of over 50 temples, including a major expansion of the great temple at Karnak. ❑

THE BIRTH OF A NEW RELIGION

Egypt, 1353 BC

For centuries Egyptians worshipped the great god Amun Re. But under the rulership of Amenhotep IV they adopted a new religion. In a sign of shifting sentiment, the pharaoh changed his name ("Amun is Satisfied") to Akhenaten ("He who is acceptable to Aten.") He then moved his capital from Thebes to a newly founded desert town, el Amarna, which he renamed after himself. The Aten, the actual disc of the sun, providing heat and prosperity, became the new deity; Amun was regarded as a deity too intimately connected with the old religion to be capable of change. Solar worship had gained greater influence already under Amenhotep III, and proved to be more universal in its appeal.

The name of Amun was erased from monuments, and almost overnight he became a non-

god. The new temples dedicated to the Aten were open and filled with light. Nefertiti, Akhenat-

Akhenaten and his family praying to Aten, the solar disk. Right. Statue of Akhenaten from el Amarna.

en's queen, visited them to offer gifts of flowers and fruits to the god. The worship of the sun disc

was a religion of life, freedom, and love of nature; elements of it appear to have been developed by the priests of Heliopolis who worshipped the sun god Re-Har-akhti.

Akhenaten's refusal to leave his impressive capital ended up causing serious political problems, however. The wealth of the occupied territories in the Levant and other lands in the eastern Mediterranean had been used to enrich Thebes and the priests of the Amun cult. With Hittite incursions, the flow of tribute and taxes diminished. Akhenaten's pacifism—and isolation—also hobbled Egyptian power. As he maintained poetic correspondence with the vassal princes of Asia, the great Egyptian Empire shrank, threatened by the Hittites. ❑

THE BEAUTIFUL ONE APPROACHES

Egypt, mid-fourteenth century BC

The 19-inch (48 cm) bust of Nefertiti was discovered in 1912 and brought to Berlin. It is to this day one of the greatest treasures of the Altes Museum.

During the excavations in el Amarna of the residence built by Akhenaten, the German Oriental Society discovered the bust of Nefertiti, the consort of the pharaoh.

The archaeologists found the statue of the ancient Egyptian queen, whose name translated means "the beautiful one approaches," together with other statuettes in a closed storage room used by sculptors. The work has been attributed to the sculptor Thutmose (the court sculptor, not the pharaoh of the same name).

The beautifully molded and painted bust shows a young woman of extraordinary beauty, adorned with a characteristic headdress, in the shape of a trun-

Bust of Nefertiti. Egyptian ideal of beauty

cated cone. It is a great pity that one ear and eye of the statuette were missing and despite extensive efforts could not be found.

There is no doubt that the statue of Nefertiti represents to many people the Egyptian ideal of beauty, but it is by no means a unique achievement. Rather it is an example—granted the finest—of an artistic transition that characterized the whole of Akhenaten's fifteen-year reign. Art in this period became more naturalistic and expressive. A softer style with greater

attention to detail and figures portrayed with relaxed features was beginning to develop during the time of Akhenaten's predecessor, Amenhotep III. It may have been influenced by the contact with foreign cultures dating back to the time of the Hyksos invasion.

The Pharaoh Akhenaten had himself portrayed in a 12-foot (3.6 m) high statue. It shows him with pronounced lips and a forceful, sensuous mouth. His face is long, his belly protruding, and legs thin. It does not portray his sexual organ. This combined with his slender body has led some scholars to propose that the portrayal deliberately suggests a degree of androgyny. Perhaps Akhenaten's new god, Aten, is expressed by the lack of marked sexual characteristics implying that the god represented the union of opposites, embodying both male and female qualities. ❑

TUTANKHAMUN THE BOY PHARAOH

Egypt c.1338 BC

After a brief and undistinguished reign, Tutankhamun died at the age of 18. His tomb with its fabled riches was discovered unspoiled by the British archaeologist, Howard Carter in November 1922. The following words were found inscribed

Death mask of Tutankhamun made from hammered gold

on the mask of solid gold under which his body is enshrined: "Your right eye is the boat of night (of the sun god), your left eye is the boat of day, your eyebrows are those of the Ennead of Gods, your forehead is that of Anubis, the nape of your neck is that of Horus, your locks of hair are those of Ptah-Sokar. You are in front of the Osiris (Tutankhamun); he sees thanks to you, you guide him to the good paths, you smite for him the confederates of Seth so that he may overthrow your enemies before the Ennead of the Gods in the great mansion of the Prince which is in Heliopolis ..."

These words served to protect the mask and its owner by identifying its various parts with the corresponding parts of the bodies of the gods them-

selves. Such was the total belief in Egypt that any pharaoh, even a minor ruler like this boy-king, would be transported to the hereafter and become a god.

The personal and ritual objects in Tutankhamun's tomb were richly ornamented, many of them covered in gold leaf. The items deposited in the burial chamber were decorated with scenes showing the pharaoh with his queen, Ankhesenamun, daughter of Akhenaten, seated at his feet drinking a beverage he is pouring for her. In another decoration, the young king is seen depicted in the process of killing a lion he is holding by the tail—a favorite theme of the kings of Egypt at this time. ❏

The God Anubis as a jackal.

EGYPTIAN INROADS IN THE NEAR EAST

Egypt, 1303 BC

During the reign of Seti I, Egypt once again asserted its power in the Near East. Seti ascended the throne in 1303 BC during the time of the Nineteenth Dynasty. The territories in Syria and Palestine that Thutmose III had incorporated into the Egyptian Empire had slipped away under the rule of his successors. Bedouin tribes now possessed what was once the pride of Egypt.

Soon after becoming pharaoh, Seti set out on a mission of conquest. He led his army across Gaza into Lebanon. The Hittites who

controlled the north promised the pharaoh that they would not interfere with his plans. At the same time Seti entered into an alliance with the Amorite king, Bentesina, who had once been captured and held prisoner by the Hittites.

Egypt also faced a threat from the west. Defensive action had to be taken against tribes of Libyan nomads that impinged upon its western border.

Seti also supervised construction of temple buildings at Karnak. His tomb at Biban al Muluk surpassed those of his predecessors in

size. His son and successor would carry monumental architecture to even greater heights. ❏

Seti I and Ramesses II (bas-relief)

RAMESSES II

Egypt, c.1250 BC

In the year 1280 BC, the young and ambitious Ramesses II succeeded his father Seti to the Egyptian throne. These two kings were members of the Nineteenth Dynasty founded c.1370 by Ramesses I.

Ramesses was almost immediately occupied in facing the Hittite Kingdom, his main rival for the rich lands of the Near East. In 1275 BC, at Kadesh in Syria, a cunning piece of disinformation brought near disaster to Ramesses II's armies as they prepared to assault this Hittite stronghold on the Orontes River. As the advance guard of the Egyptian army approached the city, two Hittite spies told Ramesses that the entire Hittite army had fled, leaving the city at his mercy.

It was not until Ramesses was preparing to march into Kadesh that the Hittites struck. Their leader, Muwatallis, sprang his trap, ordering a powerful force of war chariots from its hiding place to cut Ramesses' armies into two. The elite Egyptian Re division was wiped out crossing a ford.

As his armies regrouped—the Amun division was completely in disarray after the surprise attack—Ramesses, now left in command of a small force, was encircled by the entire Hittite regiment of more than 2,500 chariots.

In the fierce hand-to-hand fighting that followed, Ramesses, leading his men from his war chariot, made two desperate charges and eventually managed to drive the Hittites back across the river. Even so, the Egyptian king's army remained in grave danger.

As they prepared what must have been the final attack, the Hittites paused to sack the Egyptian tented camp. Only then did Ramesses hear the sound of bugles and drums of an Egyptian division marching from the coast. Despite further fighting, Kadesh

GREAT BUILDER AND WARRIOR

remained in Hittite hands.

It was not until almost 30 years later that the struggle between the two dominant powers abated. In 1256 BC, Ramesses married a Hittite princess, the daughter of Hattusilis III of Hatti. This consolidated the good relations between the Egyptians and Hittites, in effect placing a seal on a peace treaty that was concluded between them shortly before. The princess was not the Pharaoh's only wife. In fact he is said to have fathered more than 100 children.

Nonetheless, the threat of invasion from other regional powers remained ever-present. As a defensive move, Ramesses II moved the country's capital to Pi-Ramesse in the northeastern delta, ushering in the most extensive period of building and rebuilding ever witnessed in Egypt.

The great temple of Abu Simbel in Nubia typifies the scale of Ramesses' approach to architecture. The entire edifice, with its colossal statues both inside and outside the temple, was carved into the rocks overlooking the Nile, facing the sunrise with the falcon-headed Re-Harakhti stepping forward to face the morning sun. The shrine was superbly designed to ensure that the first rays of light fell on the four gods inside: Amun-Re of Thebes, Ptah of Memphis, Re-Harakhti of Heliopolis, and Ramesses himself who was expected to join the others in eternity as a god in his own right.

The statues of the pharaoh, Ramesses II, at the entrance to the Temple of Abu Simbel stand over 66 feet high. The temple was moved between 1964 and 1968 as construction proceeded on the Aswan Dam.

Statue of Ramesses II with sacrificial offerings

The entire temple was dominated by four massive statues of this pharaoh on his throne—carved from different strata of rock to allow them to stand out in every condition of light. A small temple was dedicated to Queen Nofretari on the same site. Ramesses built his mortuary temple, the Ramesseum, west of Thebes. Here, once again, monumental figures of the king dominated the entire scene—one of them (of him seated) is bigger than any other statue carved in ancient Egypt. The temple's surrounding wall also enclosed a great many houses and workshops.

Ramesses is believed to have ruled in Egypt until 1213 BC, a reign of 67 years. He is the pharaoh associated with the Biblical account of the exodus from Egypt.

His rule was a high-water mark of Egyptian power. He was succeeded by his son Merenptah, who was soon faced with incursions from Libyans and Mediterranean pirates. He defeated them in a great navel battle at Pi-yer, killing 6,000 and capturing 9,000. The account of the battle can be found commemorated on a wall in the Temple of Karnak. For Merenptah, it was a magnificent victory, but the victory and the campaign that produced it exhausted Egypt's resources.

The causes of Egypt's conflict with its North African neighbors can be traced back a thousand years, when the fertile plains of the Sahara dried up. The result was a movement of people eastward, the pressure increasing over the centuries. Brilliant horsemen and charioteers, they regularly ravaged the country before being turned back by Merenptah's depleted forces.

In the time leading up to battle at Pi-yer, the Libyans had allied themselves with sea raiders from Corsica, Sardinia, and Sicily—veterans of the sackings of the Levantine cities. They offered to provide the navy that would carry the Libyans around Egypt's flank.

Merenptah also had to contend with Asian migrants from Persia threatening Egypt from the east. Merenptah's land victory against the Asians in southern Palestine, and his sea victory against the Libyans and their maritime allies at Pi-yer, served to temporarily secure Egypt's frontiers. But its empire was entering into period of decline. ❑

THE DEATH OF MOSES

From Deuteronomy

34:1 And Moses went up from the plains of Moab unto the mountain of Nebo, to the top of Pisgah, that is over against Jericho. And the LORD shewed him all the land of Gilead, unto Dan, 34:2 And all Naphtali, and the land of Ephraim, and Manasseh, and all the land of Judah, unto the utmost sea, 34:3 And the south, and the plain of the valley of Jericho, the city of palm trees, unto Zoar.

34:4 And the LORD said unto him, This is the land which I sware unto Abraham, unto Isaac, and unto Jacob, saying, I will give it unto thy seed: I have caused thee to see it with thine eyes, but thou shalt not go over thither.

34:5 So Moses the servant of the LORD died there in the land of Moab, according to the word of the LORD.

34:6 And he buried him in a valley in the land of Moab, over against Bethpeor: but no man knoweth of his sepulchre unto this day.

34:7 And Moses was an hundred and twenty years old when he died: his eye was not dim, nor his natural force abated.

34:8 And the children of Israel wept for Moses in the plains of Moab thirty days: so the days of weeping and mourning for Moses were ended.

34:9 And Joshua the son of Nun was full of the spirit of wisdom; for Moses had laid his hands upon him: and the children of Israel hearkened unto him, and did as the LORD commanded Moses.

34:10 And there arose not a prophet since in Israel like unto Moses, whom the LORD knew face to face, 34:11 In all the signs and the wonders, which the LORD sent him to do in the land of Egypt to Pharaoh, and to all his servants, and to all his land, 34:12 And in all that mighty hand, and in all the great terror which Moses shewed in the sight of all Israel. ❏

Stone relief of an episode from Exodus

THE FALL OF TROY

Asia Minor, C.1240 BC

In the *Iliad*, the Greek poet Homer tells the story of the ten-year war between Greece and the fortified city of Troy.

In the year 1240 BC, the city of Troy lying on the northwest tip of Asia Minor at the entrance to the Dardanelles was completely destroyed by an earthquake.

The ruins of the settlement were the site of continuing excavations from 1870 to 1894 by German archaeologist Heinrich Schliemann—aided by Wilhelm Dörpfeld.

The city whose ruins the archaeologists investigated was an ancient one. There was a settlement there as early as the middle of the third millennium BC. Later it was capital of a kingdom. By the end of the third millennium BC, it had grown in size and was surrounded with walls. According to Schliemann, it was from this epoch that the treasures he described as Priam's gold came—a hoard containing exquisite gold jewelry and other fine objects made from gold, silver, and copper.

Around 1900 BC, after of a period of relative obscurity, the city reemerged as an important urban center engaging in a flourishing trade with the Mycenaean Empire. At that point the city encompassed almost 15 square miles of land. This was the city that the earthquake destroyed. Whether it was this period of the city's history that Homer described is still a matter of dispute. Priam's gold, which Schliemann uncovered, certainly stems from the Mycenaean period. The hostilities that Homer speaks of might well have a basis in fact, since around 1300 BC Mycenae was colonizing Asia Minor, and Mycenae might well have felt its commercial interests threatened by the growing power of Troy.

In his dramatic epic poem, the *Iliad*, Homer narrates the ten-year war between the Greek captains and the city of Troy, which ended in the capture of the city. According to the story, the war started with the abduction of Helen, wife of the Greek King Menelaus, by Paris, son of Priam the king of Troy.

The conflict not only drew in mortals but the gods as well, some supporting Greece and others Troy. Homer describes the battle as being fought on Olympus as well as before the gates of the city. For many years, fortune favored the Trojans, but the dark prophesies of the city's eventual destruction came to pass in the end. The mightiest of Greek warriors, Achilles, had for the greater part of the war with-

THE ISRAELITE EXODUS FROM EGYPT

Egypt, C.1200 BC

In the story that ends the Book of Genesis in the Bible, Joseph, son of Jacob, is sold by his brothers into slavery into Egypt, where with divine help he rises to become the right hand of Pharaoh and brings his father and brothers down to live there with him.

As the next book, Exodus, begins, 400 years have passed, and "there arose a new king over Egypt who did not know Joseph." This pharaoh, traditionally associated with Ramesses II, enslaved the Is-raelites. According to the biblical account, Yahweh heard the cries of his people and appeared to Moses to command him to lead them out of Egypt back to the land of Canaan. Through the hands of Moses and Aaron his brother, Yahweh subjected Pharaoh to ten mighty plagues, the last being the death of every first-born animal and child in Egypt. This final plague broke the will of Pharaoh, and he agreed to let the people go.

The rest of the Torah (the five books of Moses) contains laws and ritual instruction. Gathered at Mount Sinai, God appears to the whole people and delivers through Moses the Ten Commandments, precepts that are considered by many to be the founding moral principles of Western civilization. But it also tells of Israel's uneasy relationship with their God. The fourth book, Numbers, relates the story of their forty years of wandering in the desert before they finally reach Canaan. In a moving passage at the end of Deuteronomy, the last of the five books, God, who does not allow Moses to enter into Canaan, takes him to the top of Mount Nebo and grants him the vision of the Promised Land.

The Bible then goes on to record the Israelite invasion of Canaan and their conquest of the land, under the leadership of Joshua. They wrest it from the tribes inhabiting it and in time found a kingdom under Saul, David, and Solomon. ❏

drawn from battle after a dispute with Agamemnon, captain of the Greek army and brother to Menelaus. When, however, his friend Patroclus was killed, he reentered the fray and slew Hector, son and heir to Priam, and the greatest warrior in Troy. The city was eventually taken not by force, but by stratagem. Odysseus, the most cunning of the Greek captains, ordered a great wooden horse to be built and in its hollow belly concealed thirty soldiers. He then had the Greek

With the gift of a wooden horse the Greeks brought down the great city of Troy.

Ruins of the city of Troy

fleet pretend to sail away. The Trojans brought the horse into the city and that night the Greek soldiers snuck out and opened the gates of the city. The Greek army poured in, killed the king and his retainers, and set Troy aflame. Between the events described in the *Iliad* and the composition of the poem four centuries later, Greek culture went through a period of decline. It was overrun by a series of invasions that spread throughout the Aegean world and lasted until the beginning of the Iron Age. ❑

RAMESSES III, LAST GREAT PHARAOH

Egypt, c.1187 BC

Ramesses III was the second pharaoh of the Twentieth Dynasty. He is considered to be the last great ruler of the New Kingdom. His 30-year rule was characterized by the reaffirmation of Egypt's power in the region. His first test came soon after he ascended the throne. In a bitterly fought, bloody encounter at the mouth of the Nile, Egyptian combined forces smashed an invasion attempt by the Sea Peoples. At the head of his army, Ramesses began a drive far into Palestine and Syria on a punitive expedition against these foreign invaders.

These Sea Peoples were an alliance of tribes living along the

Eastern Mediterranean coast. For years they had been terrorizing neighboring countries in an orgy of pillage and looting. In the eighth year of Ramesses' reign, they joined together for a mass incursion into Egypt. It was a two-pronged attack, with the main body of the invaders marching along the coast, accompanied by ships offshore.

They had clearly assumed that the Egyptians were unprepared, and that landing on the Nile delta would be an easy affair. They had not reckoned with Ramesses' excellent intelligence. The Egyptians were ready and allowed their boats to be lured into the Nile be-

Ramesses was able to fight off attacks but had to give up Syria.

fore the fleet struck.

The Sea Peoples were completely outnumbered, and those who managed to struggle ashore were quickly mopped up by war chariots and foot soldiers. The defenders showed no mercy. The invaders' bodies were stripped, their hands and other parts cut off. This was not the first attempt at an invasion by these Levantine tribesmen, but it was the most dangerous. The invaders were accompanied by their families, and so almost certainly intended to

settle in what they expected to be the newly conquered lands. The coalition included the peoples of Tjekker, Sherden, Shekelesh, Weshesh, Denen, and others.

With this naval victory Ramesses was able to assert firm control in Egypt and ensure the whole of the troubled Near East a period of stability. But his death in 1153 BC signaled the beginning of the end of pharaonic power in Egypt and rise of the political might of the priestly class. ❑

CHINA'S CENTRAL MONARCHY

In 221 BC, China was united for the first time in its history. Prince Zheng, who ruled the small state of Qin, had conquered all the rival states and had proclaimed himself *Qin Shi Huangdi*, the "sublime and divine emperor of the beginning." Before the country's unification, there had been a long period of constant wars between the tyrants of the various ruling houses. Nevertheless, during this period of inner turmoil, intellectual life in China experienced a renaissance during which the foundations were laid for China's cultural development by the "Hundred Schools," in particular by the philosophers Lo Zi (Lao Tzu, sixth century BC), or according to other sources, fourth-third century BC), and Kong Fuzi (Confucius, 551–479 BC).

Sima Qian (145–c.90 BC), who wrote the first general history of China, mentions the first mortal ruler Huangdi, the Yellow Emperor, as well as his successor, to whom all aspects of civilization can be ascribed: administration, finance, housekeeping, cattle breeding, the invention of the compass, the written language, and much more. The equally legendary Yu, the founder (although archaeologically not proven) of the Xia dynasty (2205–1766 BC), is believed to have developed the vitally important river controls. A rebellion against Jie, the last and cruelest Xia ruler, marked the end of that ruling house. The leaders of the rebellion were the Shang, who as the new rulers founded a feudal system of mostly independent territorial lords.

FEUDALISM: THE SHANG AND ZHOU DYNASTY

The Shang rulers created a functional government and promoted agriculture, the surplus of which was used to maintain a permanent army. Nevertheless, the Shang dynasty was unable to develop a tangible superiority over neighboring states. The emergence of the use of bronze in about 1500 BC led to important progress in the fields of art and technology. At the same time, a script was developed from the magical signs used in oracles.

The majority of the Stone Age farming population worshipped divinities close to nature. For the aristocracy, their king was the religious head. Sovereignty was not based on their descent but was seen as a divine mission. This view enabled the Zhou clan to overthrow the last Shang ruler, Zhou-Xian. In 1122 BC, the Zhou conquered the capital Ying. After a lengthy period of fighting, the new dynasty succeeded in establishing itself. It also established its own god, Tian, instead of the

The figurines of the Terracotta Army were to accompany the emperor Qin Shi Huangdi to the "eternal kingdom."

previous supreme god Shangdi, because the dynasty's sovereignty had to be legitimized as a divine mission.

The Zhou dynasty is divided into three periods and was for a time marked by a highly developed feudalism that gradually weakened the central royal power. During the first period (1050–771 BC), the rulers divided the land into fiefs that were handed to noble vassals. In addition, the Zhou rulers provided their vassals with warriors. As a result, the regions along the borders soon became more powerful than the central royal house through the conquest of neighboring territories. In 841 BC, the powerful vassal princes forced Li Wang (878-841 BC) to flee. In 770 BC, the feudal system collapsed and the power of the Zhou dynasty finally fell into the hands of the vassal princes. The Zhou dynasty continued to rule the region round the capital until 249 BC, albeit in name only.

SPRING AND AUTUMN

The period that started after the actual removal of the Zhou rulers in 771 BC and that ran to 481 BC is called *Chunqiu* ("autumn and spring") after the book written by Confucius. Eleven principalities evolved from the numerous city-states. In the sixth century, new state legal principles were established to replace of old common laws. The statute book drawn up by the Zhou rulers laid down the foundations of Chinese society. At the top was the emperor, the emissary sent by Heaven. The affairs of state were run by the nobility on the basis their birth and education. They looked after the large numbers of farmers who lived in patriarchal families and had no voice in public affairs. A Cabinet with several areas of responsibilities managed social and military affairs, enforced justice, and organized the emperor's life. In contrast to this ideal structure, the territorial princes ruled high-handedly and with almost absolute freedom over their territories. Only to defend themselves against external dangers did they join forces under joint leadership. The growth of trade led to the emergence of a new middle class. Merchants played an increasingly important part in society because they collected the taxes that were paid in kind, without which the cities were not viable.

THE ERA OF THE WARRING KINGDOMS

During the periods of the Warring Kingdoms (481-249 BC), seven states emerged after a series military conflicts. These states remained at war with each other since none of them was strong enough to gain supremacy in the "Middle Kingdom," as China had been known since the early Zhou dynasty. In 403 BC, the country separated into three parts and the western state of Qin achieved a dominant position through its efficient organization. Military conquests and, more importantly, clever irrigation and the building of canals, gave the previously underdeveloped Qin the necessary food surplus and resources to create a powerful army. The use of weapons made of iron instead of bronze, the creation of a people's army, and the transition from the limitations of feudal warfare to waging all out war enabled the Qin rulers to control all the other states. After the battle at Zhangping (259 BC), Prince Zheng of Qin planned the conquest of the whole of China. In 230 BC he took over the state of Han, in 228 BC Zhao, in 225 BC Wei, in 223 BC Zhu, and in 222 BC Yan. After the annexation of the most important rival state, Ji, China was once again under the authority of a single ruler.

THE QIN DYNASTY

Zheng, who now called himself Qin Shi Huangdi, replaced the existing feudal system with a centralized monarchy. The power of government was entirely concentrated in the emperor. To protect the constantly threatened northern border against the Hsiung-nu (the Huns), the emperor extended the border fortifications by building the Great Wall. He broke the power of the aristocracy by transforming their estates into districts that were run by a civilian and military administration that was regularly replaced.

Because he wanted to be considered the founder of China, Qin Shi Huangdi ordered all the history books to be burnt. But a few books escaped destruction or were passed on orally. After mass uprisings, the Qin dynasty ended four years after Shi Huangdi's death (210 BC). The power of the first ruler of unified China is reflected in his grave, in which an army of about 7,000 terracotta figurines—life-size soldiers, horses, and chariots—guards the emperor's eternal rest.

The main facade of the Temple of Confucius in Qufu is richly decorated with reliefs and decorative columns.

TECHNOLOGY, SCRIPT AND PHILOSOPHY

These centuries of war were at the same time a period of technical progress. After 1500 BC, the influence of technology in art and tool manufacturing reached a high degree of sophistication resulting from the development and use of bronze: a level that was unequalled in the civilizations of Egypt and the Near East. At the center of technical progress were irrigation and architecture. The script of the Shang dynasty was based on signs used by the oracle priests of the aristocracy. The pictorial signs represented ideas and concepts, not sounds.

Chinese philosophy began with the unique metaphysical book, the *I Ching* (*Book of Changes*) that expounds the ancient philosophy of yin and yang. Chinese medical techniques—for instance, acupuncture—also developed at this time. Little is known about the life Lao Tzu, the "Old Master." The author Sima Qian wrote that Lao Tzu had composed a book in two parts, the *Tao Te Ching*, (*Book of the Way and its Power*) at the request of a tax collector. Because man is considered a part of nature but has distanced himself from the whole and original as a result of the feudal system, the complete man must withdraw from society so as to find harmony and tranquility through simple living. A little later, Confucius developed these thoughts, not as logical arguments, but rather in conversations in which he questioned his pupils. His opinions were based on the attempt to apply wisdom to everyday life and in particular to government. The conservatism advocated by Confucius marked the whole future history of China. ❏

THE ISRAELITE MONARCHY AND SOLOMON'S TEMPLE

Israel, c.925 BC

The Kingdom of Israel was once no more than a home for 12 tribes of nomadic Hebrews who escaped from bondage in Egypt only to wander for 40 years in the desert. But by the middle of the tenth century BC, it had established itself as one of the great nations of the eastern Mediterranean. The former nomads settled down and established a stable state, which was administered by an increasingly complex bureaucracy and defended by a substantial standing army.

This transformation was largely achieved through the efforts of two kings: David, who died in 965 BC after a 40-year reign, and his son Solomon, his successor, whose rule lasted 40 years as well.

King David's major achievement was the unification of twelve disparate tribes, especially those in the northern part of the kingdom, who resented the increasing power of his capital, Jerusalem.

His son Solomon, who was forced to overcome his own half-brother in the struggle for the throne, built on David's success to preside over a golden age for Israel and to establish himself as a monarch whose influence extended far beyond his own nation.

Under Solomon the state enjoyed unprecedented stability, with a strictly hierarchical bureaucracy, arranged in nine departments and based on an Egyptian model, creating a fully unified kingdom. This unity was backed by a professional army that boasted an elite chariot corps of 4,000 horses and 1,400 vehicles.

Against this background Israel underwent an economic boom. Using slave labor, drawn from prisoners of war, the country developed copper mines at the Wadi Araba. Israelite craftsmen garnered an international reputation. Trading was extensive, and the monarchy cultivated close-knit relations with neighboring Phoenician states.

The most notable example of such trade links was the visit of the legendary Queen of Sheba, who traveled 1,500 miles to meet Solomon and to experience for herself his fabled wisdom and wealth.

Solomon's greatest memorial was his extensive program of building. The Temple of Jerusalem, built on Mount Moriah to house the Ark of the Covenant, was his enduring achievement. Over seven years in the making, the Temple combined a vestibule, a *cella* (or internal area) and the Holy of Holies. Here, too, Solomon benefited from his trading partners: King Hiram of Tyre provided craftsmen, raw materials, and the boats to transport them. The Temple lasted until 586 BC when it was destroyed by the Babylonians. Rebuilt upon the Israelites' return from exile, it remained the spiritual heart of Israel until it was finally razed by the Romans in 70 BC. ❑

Painting of the Temple of Solomon

THE ZIGGURAT OF ELAM

Elam c.1180 BC

Elamite civilization first came to prominence at the beginning of the second millennium BC when the Elamites destroyed the Third Dynasty of Ur, but around the beginning of the twelfth century BC its influence increased dramatically. At that time, its ruler, Shutruk-Nakhunte, captured Babylon making the Elamites masters of Mesopotamia.

Untash-napirisha, who became king in about 1240 BC, founded the holy city of Dur-Untash, home to the ziggurat of the temple of the god Inshushi-nak.

This was perhaps the greatest Elamite monument to be seen anywhere in the Middle East. The city, surrounded by a high defensive wall, had at its center the main sanctuary, sheltered by a farther wall.

In the middle of the sanctuary stood the ziggurat. Its first floor comprised a number of vaulted rooms reached by stairways embedded in the main construction—an architectural innovation.

Shutruk-Nakhunte devoted his whole reign to the successful pursuit of the Babylonian war. He was a fierce warrior, and no town in Babylonia was able to resist the forces of Elam. Shutruk-Nakhunte completed his conquest of Mesopotamia taking the principal records of Mesopotamian history, from those of Naram-Sin of Agade to those of Hammurabi of Babylon, back to his capital at Susa.

Elamite glory was short-lived as Nebuchadnezzar I of Babylon overran it around 1125 BC, bringing its empire to an end. ❑

The Construction of the Temple

From The First Book of Kings

2:1 And Solomon determined to build an house for the name of the LORD, and an house for his kingdom.

2:2 And Solomon told out threescore and ten thousand men to bear burdens, and fourscore thousand to hew in the mountain, and three thousand and six hundred to oversee them.

2:3 And Solomon sent to Hiram the king of Tyre, saying, As thou didst deal with David my father, and didst send him cedars to build him an house to dwell therein, even so deal with me.

2:4 Behold, I build an house to the name of the LORD my God, to dedicate it to him, and to burn before him sweet incense, and for the continual shewbread, and for the burnt offerings morning and evening, on the sabbaths, and on the new moons, and on the solemn feasts of the LORD our God. This is an ordinance for ever to Israel….

3:1 Then Solomon began to build the house of the LORD at Jerusalem in mount Moriah, where the Lord appeared unto David his father, in the place that David had prepared in the threshing floor of Ornan the Jebusite.

3:2 And he began to build in the second day of the second month, in the fourth year of his reign…

5:1 [Then] all the work that Solomon made for the house of the LORD was finished: and Solomon brought in all the things that David his father had dedicated; and the silver, and the gold, and all the instruments, put he among the treasures of the house of God. ❑

Chinese Renaissance with the Zhou Dynasty

China, c.1100 BC

Around 1100 BC, the last king of the Shang Dynasty was overthrown in a rebellion. The Zhou became China's next ruling dynasty.

Shang rule ended when the dissolute Emperor Zhou-Xian, upon finding himself deserted by his warriors. set fire to his palace and perished in the flames.

Following their accession to power, the Zhou ruled wisely, delegating authority over much of China to junior members of the royal family and to nobles who had been given fiefs to rule.

Human sacrifice became much less common than it was in the days of the Shangs, whose regime was marked by cruelty.

One of the reasons for this appears to be that the Zhou rulers deserted the old Shang religion of ancestor worship and developed a theology in which they worshiped Tian or "Heaven," a semipersonal divinity.

The founders of the Dynasty, King Wen and his son, attained almost mythic stature and were attributed with the authorship of a substantial part of the great Chinese classic, the *I Ching*.

The Zhou took pride in recording their history, inscribing their achievements on ornate bronze vases and for the first time providing accurate dates. There was much to be recorded, for the ambitious nobles of the Zhou Empire continually expanded its boundaries. The highpoint of the Zhou period seems to have been between 770 and 480 BC and was marked by the use of iron implements that boosted agricultural productivity and an elegantly cultivated court life. ❑

Incense burner from the time of the Zhou Dynasty

Dark Ages in Greece

Greece, c.900 BC

After a period of steep decline, the Greek lands began to regain a little of the prosperity of the Mycenaean age. For 400 years, the inhabitants of Greece were illiterate, living largely in villages and knowing nothing of Greece's illustrious past. Palaces disappeared and the towns were depopulated as Greece slid into a Dark Age.

Much of southern Greece was dominated by the Dorians, invaders from the north. Just how this relatively primitive people came to dominate the Peloponnese is not known, but it seems likely that the Mycenaeans were overwhelmed by internal crises and domestic revolts, creating a power vacuum for the Dorians to fill.

Like other Dark-Age Greeks, the Dorians came to rely on iron to make their tools and weapons. They lived in small communities with land divided into plots owned by the community. But as individuals began to grab larger chunks of land, a more hierarchical society started to develop.

Phoenician traders would visit Greece regularly, bringing jewelry, pottery, and other objects, but the reemergence of Greek art from its hibernation was a slow process. There was nothing in this period comparable to the Mycenaean era in terms of architecture, wall paintings, or decorative metalwork, although there was some painted pottery bearing rather stilted decorations of funeral processions and land and sea battles.

However, the Greeks of this time did perpetuate the Mycenaean religion and emulate their predecessors through a cult of heroes—their tombs marked by great burial mounds like that covering the grave of a chief and his wife at Lefkandi in Euboea. Another sign of greater things to come was the establishment of the Olympic Games at the beginning of the eighth century. ❑

THE FIRST OLYMPIC GAMES

Greece, 776 BC

Greece was the birthplace of the Olympic Games, which were from the beginning designed as a quadrennial event. The first attested Games were held in honor of Zeus, the mightiest of all the gods. They consisted of the integration of religious ceremonies and athletic contests. Each participant—entry being limited to freeborn Greek males—had to boast of a sterling reputation. There was a mandatory training period of nine months at home and then an additional thirty days in Olympia. The four-year cycle served as the basis for the Greek calendar.

The site of the Games consisted of a sacred area, the *Altis*, marked by a boundary wall, and

a secular (nonreligious) area. The sacred area contained the temples, including the one to Zeus, the altars on which sacrifices were made, and the Treasuries, small buildings erected by the city-states in which precious offerings were kept (e.g., vases and statues). The secular area was outside the boundary wall. It contained the sporting structures of the *gymnasium*, *palaestra*, stadium, and hippodrome, plus all the buildings used for the administration of the Games and to welcome important guests.

Only the priests and the staff responsible for looking after the sanctuary lived at Olympia. At the time of the competitions, the atmosphere was very different. In addition to the athletes and spectators, merchants of all kinds flocked to the site: The number of spectators is estimated to have been over 40,000. From 724 BC onward, the victor of the Games was crowned at Delphi with a laurel wreath in the name of the god Apollo. ❑

Discus thrower (Roman copy of Greek statue)

MYSTERIOUS OLMEC CULTURE

Gulf of Mexico, c.800 BC

Great basalt heads, 12 feet (3.6 m) in height, placed next to pyramids amid temples have been found near the religious centers at La Venta, San Lorenzo, and Tres Zapotes in the Central American region of Mexico. The devotion inspired by the religious cults of Central America is spectacularly demonstrated by these huge sculptures carved in the Gulf of Mexico, some of which weigh several tons.

The interiors of the temple buildings are decorated with finely carved pillars, altars, and coffins. Jade, terracotta, and bone sculptures portray fat eunuchs with innocent expressions as well as jaguars and serpents.

The Olmecs designed an accurate calendar from their study of the stars and studied the arts of counting, calculating, and writing.

Many of the ideas and beliefs of these highly developed people spread to neighboring eastern and central Mexico and farther afield to Central America, as far as Guatemala and El Salvador. ❑

One of the monumental basalt heads from La Venta

REVIVAL OF THE

Assyria, c.879 BC

At the height of its power the Assyrian Empire laid claim to an area that stretched from the Red Sea to the Mediterranean coast and included the entire fertile river valley between the Tigris and Euphrates Rivers. To the east it reached as far as the Zagros Mountains of Armenia.

Upon ascending the throne in 883 BC, Ashurnasirpal consolidated past gains and extended Assyrian authority over almost the entire Near East. He moved his capital from Assur to the newly built city of Nimrud. There he constructed a great palace for himself that reflected the strength of the Assyrian revival and the huge resources the empire controlled.

Ashurnasirpal's palace dominated the city's five-mile perimeter. The palace gates were guarded by colossal alabaster lions and bulls. In the throne room and reception rooms, the walls were decorated with life-size bas-reliefs depicting religious scenes, battles, and royal hunts.

One of the more spine-chill-

CARTHAGE FOUNDED

North Africa, 814 BC

Phoenician mariners founded the city of Carthage, about ten miles from the present-day city of Tunis, as a way station on their route to the silver mines of Spain.

The Phoenicians were the most enterprising merchants in the Near East. Starting in 1100 BC, they had set up a network of trading posts across the Mediterranean Sea, Endowed with a rich surrounding area, Carthage experienced rapid growth and soon had a population of 300,000 residents. ❑

THEFT OF STATUE HOLY TO THE BABYLONIANS

Sippar, Babylon, c.879 BC

In an undeniable sign of waning Babylonian might, the statue of the god Marduk was removed from the city by plundering Assyrians. This was a deeply felt blow to a population demoralized by continuing warfare and economic crises.

Without his statue to worship, Babylonians felt that Marduk had gone, and they no longer had his divine protection. For the local economy this sense of desolation proved dire. Without a god to serve and feed, farmers lacked the motivation to bring in harvests. The crisis was further compounded by the arrival of marauding Aramaean and Sutaean nomads plundering granaries and burning buildings on the outskirts of towns.

The Babylonian religion observed a carefully calibrated relationship between men and the gods. They worried that by not being able to worship Marduk the balance of the cosmos would be called into question. Speculation was rife as to how an angry and hungry Marduk would react to being deserted by his faithful followers and shipped off to a place as a prisoner. ❑

ASSYRIAN EMPIRE

ing inscriptions to stop a visitor entering Ashurnasirpal's new palace reads: "I flayed all the chief men who revolted, and I covered the pillar with their skins, some I walled up within the pillar, some I impaled upon the pillar on stakes, and others I bound to stakes round about the pillar; many within the border of my own land I flayed, and I spread their skins upon the walls; and I cut off the limbs of the officers who had rebelled..."

The effect of the message was deliberate. During this era the Assyrian Empire operated a conscious policy of terror. Its army, which had the reputation of being the most effective in the Near East, was equally well-known for its cruelty and ruthlessness.

The army depended on horses. Its two-wheeled chariots and, to a lesser extent, cavalry proved unbeatable at breaking through enemy lines in high-speed phalanxes. Whole communities were uprooted as part of Assyria's security strategy of bringing conquered peoples completely under its control. Non-Assyrians were considered barbarians and subjected to ruthless treatment; official reports detail massacres and mutilation.

To the Assyrians, who saw themselves as being engaged in a cosmic fight against evil on behalf of the supreme god, Ashur, their wars were divinely inspired and commemorated in religious ceremonies. Soldiers would bring back soil from pillaged towns and spread it outside the capital's gates so the Assyrian people could tread it underfoot daily.

To celebrate the glory of his new capital and officially recognize the realization of Assyria's 200-year-old dream of once again controlling an empire that reached to the Mediterranean, the king hosted ten days of feasting. More than 60,000 guests descended on the capital for its

Fresco of lion hunt from the Palace of Til Barsip during the reign of Tiglath Pileser III (745-727 BC)

inaugural feast to pay homage to the king.

It was to Nimrud that conquered peoples would bring their annual tributes of gold, silver, and other precious metals, along with raw materials, goods, herds, flocks, and produce. In addition to the king's palace, the fortified acropolis contained several temples, including one to Ninurta, god of war, who could be said to have taken up the Assyrian cause It had been two centuries since the Assyrians—under Tiglath-

Pileser I—last had access to the Mediterranean. Infighting among his successors weakened the kingdom and led to loss of control of surrounding lands.

After a period of decline a revival began in 911 BC, under Adad-Nirari II, whose six campaigns established strategic strongholds in northern Syria. His grandson Ashurnasirpal II consolidated these before fortifying the eastern border to leave him free to reopen the route to the sea. ❑

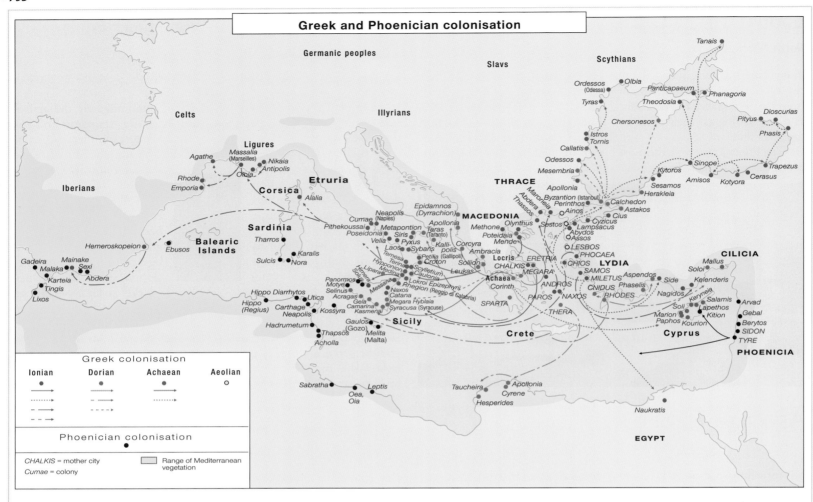

Greek and Phoenician colonisation

Germanic peoples

Celts

Illyrians

Slavs

Scythians

Ligures

Iberians

Corsica

Etruria

Sardinia

Balearic Islands

THRACE

MACEDONIA

LYDIA

CILICIA

Cyprus

PHOENICIA

Sicily

Crete

EGYPT

Greek colonisation

Ionian · Dorian · Achaean · Aeolian

Phoenician colonisation

CHALKIS = mother city
Cumae = colony

Range of Mediterranean vegetation

GREEK COLONIZATION OF THE MEDITERRANEAN

Greece, 733 BC

By the mid-seventh century BC, the slow pace of revival in Greece began to accelerate. Greek expeditions traveled the Mediterranean to set up colonies, some cities founding as many as four or five colonies in one generation. The settlers, young men of fighting age, set out in bands of up to 200 under the command of an *oikistes*, or founder, to a place chosen by the elders of their city. Corinth, for example, established Syracuse in Sicily; other colonies were founded in southern Italy, North Africa, and on the shores of the Black Sea. These colonies were essentially agrarian with land being equally among the settlers.

Sometimes they were welcomed by the original inhabitants, who would give them grants of land, but in other cases they had to fight their way ashore. If they were victorious they would use the conquered natives as slave laborers in the fields. Once established, the new colonies became completely independent from their metropolis, or mother city. Still, the settlers retained close links with their old homes, taking with them their traditional institutions and even carrying their gods with them in the form of wooden statuettes.

There was, however, another form of Greek colonization—trade, which marched hand in hand with the agricultural settlements. These commercial settlements, or *emporia*, usually owed their existence not to a mother city, but to groups of businessmen seeing an opportunity for profitable trade.

One such *emporion* was set up at Naukratis in Egypt. It was strictly a commercial enterprise and, although the pharaoh allowed the Greeks to worship their own gods, he forbade mixed marriages and maintained strict control over the aliens' activities.

Greek art showed Asian influence. The geometric patterns of earlier pottery, for instance, gave way in Corinth and other cities to motifs and patterns borrowed from the ceramic art of the East, bringing a new vitality to decorated vases. ❑

Greek theater in Syracuse, Sicily

THE FOUNDING OF ROME

Rome, 753 BC

According to Roman lore, the city was founded by Romulus, the first of eight legendary kings. In the first century BC, the Roman scholar and historian, Marcus Terentius Varro determined the city's founding date to be April 21, 753 BC.

Romans traced the beginning of their civilization back to the Trojan hero Aeneas, son of Anchises and the goddess Aphrodite, who fled from the ruins of his ravaged city after the Greeks put it to the flame. After a testing seven-year journey, he landed on the coast of Latium. Twin brothers, Romulus and Remus, were considered to be his descendants. They were exposed at birth by the king of Alba and raised by a she-wolf.

In time, Romulus established and fortified a settlement on the Palantine, one of the Seven Hills of Rome. After slaying his brother, he assumed the title of King of Rome. According to the annals of the city, it was he who gave Rome its name, but there is no historical or archaeological evidence to suggest that either he or the seven kings that followed him are anything other than legend.

Archaeological investigation has established the existence of a tenth-century Latin settlement on the Palantine and a Sabine settlement on the Quirinal (another of Rome's seven hills) dating from the seventh century. Excavations from a burial site dated to this period show that Sabines and Latins were buried next to one other, suggesting an alliance against the more powerful Etruscans. The name "Rome" probably stems from the Etruscan "ruma."

The Etruscans first appeared in Italy at this time. Their presence is evidenced by remains of urban settlements and artifacts indicating a fairly high level of cultural development. Traces of Etruscan

According to legend the founders of Rome, Romulus and Remus, were suckled by a she-wolf.

influence have also been found in Rome. The Etruscan king was apparently the dominant figure of this epoch. He assumed the Indo-European title of "Rex." The *fasces* and the *lictores*, the Roman insignia of sovereignty and the courtiers who carried them, seem to have been of Etruscan origin.

The Etruscans also bequeathed arts of telling the future from examining the entrails of animals, the flight of birds, and the movement of celestial bodies. ❏

HOMER'S ODYSSEY

Greece, late eighth century BC

The *Odyssey* recounts the epic tale of the travels and exploits of Odysseus (Latin form: Ulysses). He was the son of King Laertes of Ithaca, and appeared in the *Iliad* as a warrior valued for his bravery and wise counsel. It was Odysseus who conceived of the plan of offering the enemy a great wooden horse, a ruse that brought about the downfall of Troy.

The *Odyssey* begins after the sack of the city. Odysseus sets off to return home to his wife Penelope and son Telemachus. He fights the Cicones soon after leaving Troy, but is beaten off and carried by a storm to the land of the Lotus Eaters from where he wanders to the land of a race of cyclops.

The cyclops Polyphemus captures Odysseus and his men and begins to eat them. But using his characteristic cunning, Odysseus manages to escape with most of his crew and blind Polyphemus. Eventually he reaches the isle of the sorceress Circe. She turns Odysseus' men into swine until he forces her to change them back, after which he lives with her for a year.

He sets out again, careful not to succumb to the Sirens, whose singing attracts sailors to land, where they die. Later, his hungry crew eats cattle belonging to Helios, the Sun.

In revenge, Helios shipwrecks Odysseus, killing his companions; he drifts to the island of the nymph Calypso where she keeps him for seven years. He finally sails away and is once again wrecked; but he swims ashore and is tended by the King of Phaeacia, who sends him home clad as a beggar. In a violent denouement, Odysseus and his son, Telemachus, kill the suitors of his wife Penelope. Finally, ten years after leaving Troy, he is reunited with his family.

The *Odyssey* represents a remarkable advance in literature, not only because of the remarkable artistry with which the complex strands of the tale are woven together, but also in its focus on the individual consciousness. ❏

The blinding of Polyphemus (Greek vase, 6th century BC)

THE BEGINNING OF THE IRON AGE

Europe, c.700 BC

The Bronze Age can be said to have begun in middle and western Europe as early as the seventeenth century BC. Bronze was only slowly replaced by iron. As iron's melting point is higher than that of bronze, it was harder to make tools from it. But once the technical means had been mastered, its introduction had profound effects on culture, society, and warfare.

The widespread bronze-age Urnfield culture was dominant in Europe until around 700 BC. It gave way before the new iron-bearing Hallstatt culture, named after a large burial site found near Salzkammergut in Austria. Its territory stretched from what is now France across the Alps into the Balkans. A prerequisite for the establishment of the Iron Age was the birth of cottage industries that developed manufacturing techniques.

Among the consequences of the introduction of the new

metal were a strengthening of a hierarchical social structure and an increase in trade and specialization of labor.

Artifacts from the end of the Bronze Age: Above. A cult wagon. Left: Above. Knives. Below. Bronze statue of a bull.

CONQUESTS OF ASSYRIAN KING SARGON II

Nimrud, Assyria, c.700 BC

Sargon with noble attendant (bas-relief from Dur-Sharrukin)

With the overthrow of Shalmaneser V by Sargon II, Assyria began to reverse years of declining power. Shalmaneser had proven himself unable to govern and had alienated important sectors of Assyrian society. Although Sargon's background was mysterious, his choice of titles offered a clue to his ambitions. The name Sargon, which has the meaning "the legitimate king," deliberately evoked the glory days of Sargon of Agade, founder of the Akkad Dynasty. The new Sargon moved fast to end the domestic disorder that helped him ride to power and oust Shalmaneser V.

His first act was to overturn the unpopular decision to curtail the privileges of Assyria's holy cities, which had led to civil unrest. Sargon assured the citizens of the temples and city-states that he would not restrict their traditional immunity from taxation and conscription. Once domestic issues were addressed, Sargon was in a position to turn his attention to the two major threats that confronted his empire.

To the west, the Egyptians, still smarting from the loss of Phoenicia to the Assyrians, were lending covert support to the princes of Palestine in the hope of starting a rebellion that could embarrass Sargon II and leave his forces stretched.

On his eastern front, Sargon II faced similar interference in the affairs of Babylon from the Elamites, who reckoned that an independent Babylon would help restore their trade routes, which were cut when Assyria conquered the city.

Sargon's first moves were against the northern Kingdom of Israel. Its existence effectively came to an end following the surrender of the city of Samaria after a siege lasting two years.

PERU'S DISTINCTIVE PARACAS CULTURE

Peru, c.710 BC

Iron manufacture, once a Hittite military secret, was then mastered by Celtic-speaking peoples who carried it across Europe. Their knife blades and long slashing swords were ground sharper—and therefore deadlier—giving them a distinct military advantage.

After the collapse of the Hittite Empire in the east, it took 350 years for their strong and cheap iron-making methods to be used more widely. While the new iron technology was confined to Anatolia, the brilliant kingdoms of Mycenae had time to grow. Trade flourished. They bought amber from the Baltic, tin from Czechoslovakia, and gold from Hungary.

Once these fabulous kingdoms disappeared, there was a gradual recession in the Mediterranean, which coincided with the arrival of iron from the east. The Hallstatt culture was succeeded by the La Tène culture in the sixth century BC. ❑

The Paracas tribe inhabited what is now the southern coastal section of Peru. The complexity of their culture is eloquently shown in their elaborate burial customs.

Dead men's bodies were mutilated and preserved in unusual burial rituals. Indians on the Paracas Peninsula dug subterranean vaults through desert rock to fill with precious "mummy bundles" of their dead.

The hot dry desert climate helped in the mummification process, which involved the removal of the internal organs, after which the body was tied up in a fetal position. Circular holes were gouged out of the top of the skull of the corpse with bone tools.

Bundles of these bodies were brought from north and south of the peninsula to be buried in the tomb at Paracas Cavernas.

At Paracas, necropolis vaults

Above. Colorful textile from the Paracas Culture (3rd to 1st century BC). Right. The Paracas culture preceded the Nazca culture, which is known for its uncanny land art.

were filled with a rich assortment of burial offerings: gold ornaments, weapons, pottery, and textiles. Long mantles were packed with beautifully embroidered cotton and brightly patterned textiles woven in elaborate designs. The Paracas seemed to have been the forerun-

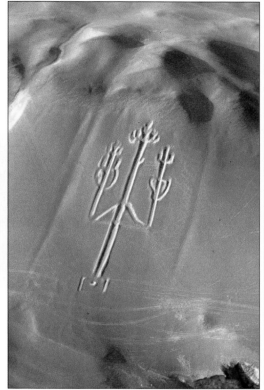

ners of the Nazcas tribes whose enigmatic land art is a riddle that still remains to be solved. ❑

The surrender of Samaria was Sargon II's first victory. The collapse of the siege was the last act in the Israelite uprising that began six years before when King Hoshea ben Elah, a vassal king installed by Tiglath Pileser III, refused to perform an act of allegiance to his son Shalmaneser V on his accession. Although Hoshea was captured in 725 BC, the city of Samaria held out.

Assyrian forces, acting on the orders of their new king, began mass deportations of captured Israelites, removing every trace of their tribes from Samaria. Most of them ended up as slaves in forced labor camps.

Instead of two Israelite kingdoms there was now only one—Judah, to the south, which had opted for Assyrian protection fif-

teen years before.

Sargon next turned his attention to the Kingdom of Urartu in Armenia. In 714 BC, victorious Assyrian forces won complete control over it, ending over a century of conflict. The fall of Urartu on the shores of Lake Van marked the collapse of Assyria's main enemy to the north and a personal triumph for Sargon.

Shrewd use of military intelligence played a key role in the successful timing of the Assyrian assault. Reports that Cimmerian nomads had inflicted a heavy defeat on Urartian forces, including one from Crown Prince Sennacherib listing the names of Urartian commanders killed in battle, convinced Sargon that the time was ripe to move against his weakened enemy.

The conquest of Urartu gave Assyria control of a flourishing economy. Urartu's farming infrastructure was well-organized, with secure granaries and artificial lakes and reservoirs that lessened the threat of drought. Its metal workers were world-famous. Strategically placed on the major trade routes, its annexation further enriched Assyria and secured its northern border. ❑

Head of a gatekeeper (from Nineveh)

HESIOD AND THE GOLDEN AGE

Greece, c.700 BC

The poet Hesiod, who may have been a contemporary of Homer, was the first to compile the rich oral tradition of Greek mythology. In his work *Theogony*, the poet sought to explain what the gods represent. In his book *Works and Days* he set out to explain the state of human existence. He ascribed man's present woeful, weary lot to two causes. The first was the jar of evils opened on the world by the woman Pandora. Secondly, Hesiod said, men have generally deteriorated since the "first age" of mankind.

The people of this wonderful Age of Gold were made by the gods, and lived "with carefree heart, remote from toil and misery." They never grew old, but died "as if overcome by sleep." Backbreaking work on the land was unknown since the soil gave them all the food they needed of its own accord. When these people passed from the earth Zeus made their spirits divine.

The Age of Gold was followed by the inferior Silver Age. The men of silver lived through a childhood of 100 years, and then died shortly afterward, because in their witlessness they failed to properly honor the gods. Zeus put them away beneath the earth as the "mortal blessed," and then made a third—bronze—race of men. These were "terrible and fierce" warriors, who slew each other until none was left.

Zeus improved on the men of bronze with a fourth race, the "godly race of heroes," who were the predecessors of modern men. But these "righteous and noble" men were destroyed by "ugly war and fearful fighting" before the seven gates of Thebes and at Troy "on account of lovely-haired Helen." Those who did not perish were granted a blessed life in the islands at the ends of the earth.

In Hesiod's time men suffered in the Age of Iron, and despite some good things were fated to "never cease from toil and misery." But Hesiod warned that men would soon succumb to envy, dishonor, hatred, and lawlessness. When this happened Zeus would destroy them as surely as he had destroyed their predecessors. ❑

Early Greek sphinx. The smile is characteristic of this period.

PHRYGIA SUCCUMBS TO INVADERS

Gordium, Phrygia, c.695 BC

Cimmerian hordes from the north ransacked the Kingdom of Phrygia, bringing its power to an end. The lifespan of the kingdom was brief; it lasted only one hundred years. Under the legendary King Midas, it reached the highpoint of its influence at the end of the eighth century BC. Defenseless against invaders, the Phrygian monarch, whose fabulous wealth inspired legends that whatever he touched would turn to gold, committed suicide in his capital of Gordium.

Midas' suicide marked the end of Phrygian independence. The country was forced to sign a peace treaty with its southern neighbor, Sargon II of Assyria, which guaranteed protection in return for Phrygia's paying him tribute.

Midas had enhanced the reputation of this kingdom high on the Anatolian plateau by his wealth, his marriage to a Greek princess, and by being the first non-Greek to make offerings at Delphi. Various arts flourished under his rule. Fine geometric patterned mosaics adorned homes and painted reliefs ornamented the facades of temples. The Phrygian architectural legacy included great city walls, monumental altars, and skillful stonework. In addition, the Phrygian mode or scale had a lasting effect on musical composition. Their headwear was adopted by the Jacobins during the French revolution; they saw the Phrygian cap as a symbol of freedom. ❑

Fortress dating from Phrygian era

NEW TEMPLE CONSTRUCTION

Greece, c.690 BC

Early in the seventh century, the Greeks embarked on an active program of temple building. The sites chosen for these sanctuaries had generally been used as places of worship by previous inhabitants. They were usually in the open air, in places with outstanding natural features related to the particular deity with whom the place was connected. The rustling of the leaves on the sacred oak trees at the oracle of Dodona was ascribed to Zeus, to whom the site was dedicated. Delphi, the greatest of the oracles, was rededicated to Apollo, although in former times it had been the shrine of an earth spirit.

Most Greek temples were based on the plan of a rectangular room with an entrance at one end, and a porch created by extending the two side walls, between which there were often columns. The

SPARTA: MILITARY POWER IN ANCIENT GREECE

Sparta, c.660 BC

Sparta, a city-state on the Peloponnesian Peninsula in the far south of Greece, was known for its military prowess. It had a written constitution, attributed to the great lawgiver Lycurgus, aimed at what was called *eunomia*, "good order." The constitution had two main principles: equality and strict discipline. The machinery of the constitution was a mixture of monarchy, oligarchy, and democracy.

However, most of Sparta's inhabitants were not citizens and were excluded from government; they were the freemen and serfs who grew the food for everyone else. Women, as in other Greek states, were excluded from all political power, although their lives were less constrained than in many other places. The city was run along austere, lines. Commerce and the possession of gold and silver was forbidden. Male citizens were brought up as soldiers from the age of seven, lived in dormitories, and ate together in communal messes, even after marriage.

Sparta differed from other Greek states, not only in its social order but also in its form of government. Unique to it was the innovation of having two kings rule together. Their power was, however, limited by the five *ephors* (magistrates) who were elected annually and a council of elders whose members were elected for life but had to be at least 60 years old. This institution dates back to as least as far as 754 BC.

The *ephors* exercised the bulk of power in government. They oversaw the police and the courts. The other main organ of government was a legislative assembly to which only full citizens were admitted. The assembly chose the 28 men who made up the Council of Elders. The final say in legislation was possessed by an assembly of 9,000 citizens.

In questions of foreign policy the *ephors* and the kings often came into conflict. The *ephors* were inclined toward a policy of isolation, while the kings were more likely to want to intervene to support governments ruled by the aristocracy. Occasionally, Sparta would aid those oppressed by tyrants, but they were also willing to fight against democratic cities, such as Athens. Overall, their foreign policy was marked by cautious reserve. However, in the victory over the Persian invaders, Sparta, which possessed the strongest army in Greece, played a decisive role. The sharing of responsibilities and credit in the Persian War, became a contentious issue for Athens and Sparta, and the victory was followed by continuing conflict between rival city-states. ❑

HESIOD'S *WORKS AND DAYS*

Greece, c.700 BC

"Work and let work follow work." This was the key to a decent life of reasonable prosperity, according to Hesiod, the shepherd poet from the agricultural area of central Greece. The advice comes in his poem *Works and Days*, in which he gives a detailed account of the yearly calendar of hard work to serve as an example to moderately well-off farmers.

His primary emphasis was on "the clearing of debts and avoidance of famine," because "a procrastinator does not fill his granary." If you did not do this, Hesiod said, you would have to go begging to your neighbors, who would eventually turn you away.

Hesiod idealized working the land. In his eyes, the prosperous peasant was one who owned a few slaves, or hired laborers, and produced all the food he and his family needed, such as wheat, barley, vegetables, fruit, and grapes. He kept sheep for wool, goats for milk and cheese, oxen or mules for pulling and carrying.

Each part of the year was endowed with its allotted task: plowing, sowing, harvesting, threshing, and storing grain and straw. The women of the household prepared food, spun flax and wool, and wove cloth to make garments.

There were, however, numerous festival days, when the peasant families enjoyed the fruits of their toil. ❑

temple was built as the house of the god rather than as a place in which people congregated to worship. Acts of worship took place at a separate altar that stood opposite the front of the building; only members of the priesthood and lay officials were allowed into the temple itself. At more famous shrines, some cities built "treasuries" next to temples; these were miniature temples to display the cities' piety and wealth. ❑

Spartan bronze sculpture of a soldier (end of 6th century)

THE RISE AND FALL OF THE ASSYRIAN EMPIRE

Nineveh, Assyria, 640 BC

After a bloody civil war, King Ashurbanipal became the undisputed sovereign of the Assyrian Empire by defeating his brother Shamash-shuma-ukin, the viceroy of Babylon. The brothers were sons of King Esarhaddon, who died in 668 BC.

Shamash-shuma-ukin committed suicide in his palace after ordering his men to set fire to it as Assyrian forces made their final assault.

Shamash-shuma-ukin's death ended four years of warfare and left the conspirators who had hoped to overthrow Ashurbanipal without a leader.

The Assyrians were known and widely hated for their aggressive expansionism and the cruelty they displayed toward conquered peoples. The kingdom had been in existence since 1115 BC, and from its home territory of Assur, Nineveh and Nimrud had expanded to become the greatest empire of its time. In 670 BC, it reached its height with its victory over Egypt. At that point the boundaries of the empire stretched from the Mediterranean to East Turkey and the Persian Gulf.

Assyrian success was based upon its military technology, which far surpassed that of its neighbors. From the ninth century BC onward, the Assyrian army employed mounted warriors and then heavy chariots with blades attached to their wheels. Chariots would break through the ranks of their enemies, allowing the infantry to exploit the gaps. The Assyrians also developed sophisticated siege weaponry. The Bible recounts many gruesome details of Assyrian warfare. Massacres and the brutal punishments of leaders of rebellions were the order of the day.

After his victory over his brother and the destruction of Babylon, Ashurbanipal set his sights on the Elamite Kingdom and the city of Susa. His first sally occurred in 645 BC. At the battle of Tulliz on the Kerkha River, the Elamite king, Tempt-humbaninshushinak, was killed, bringing to an end one of the few periods in Elamite history when its uneasy coalition of small principalities had been ruled by one man. Assyria's strategy had long been based on the notion of a divided Elam, too absorbed in its own dynastic squabbles to coordinate attacks against Assyria. To that end it engineered many of Elam's palace plots, with rival factions tearing each other to pieces as they fought for the throne. After his victorious engagement, the emperor ordered the head of Tempt-humbaninshushinak to be hung in the royal garden as a warning to the princes of Elam.

The royal city of Susa finally fell to the Assyrians in 639 BC. The streets of Nineveh were treated to a symbolic and ruthless display of imperial power as three captured Elamite princes and a former king of Arabia were shackled like cart horses to King Ashurbanipal's chariot and made to pull him around the capital.

Assyrian forces under King Ashurbanipal then embarked on a scorched earth policy against the Elamites that culminated in the destruction of the 2000-year-old kingdom.

Those Elamites who survived the massacres were deported to Assyria, as the Assyrian army carried out a defoliation program in Elam, scattering salt to turn its fertile lands into desert.

Nineveh had become the richest city in the world by far, overflowing with treasure, including booty taken from Memphis, Thebes, and Susa during the Egyptian and Elamite wars, tributes from the vassal princes of Judah, Phoenicia, and Lydia, and gifts from the princes of Media and Persia who pledged their allegiance.

Assyrian achievements were not only in the realm of military technology. It also engaged in massive civil engineering programs. A 30-mile long aqueduct was built to ensure the water supply for Nineveh in 691 BC. It comprised a system of bridges, tunnels, and canals. The wealth of conquered nations was also used to fund the building of magnificent palaces for the Assyrian overlords, richly ornamented and adorned with wonderful relief work.

King Ashurbanipal's military victories, coupled with the solution of the long-term Babylonian problem, meant that Assyria's 1,200-mile northern and eastern frontiers were more secure than ever. At the midpoint of his career Ashurbanipal and his empire seemed impregnable. However, the empire's successful military campaigns had left its army overstretched and exhausted, and Assyria's use of force rather than assent did little more than keep the

Excavations in Susa (southwestern Iran). This ancient city was in existence in the fourth millennium BC. It was conquered by the Persians in 550 BC, who built this palace, which is decorated with splendid animal reliefs.

Left: King Ashurbanipal hunting lions. Lion hunts despite the danger they entailed were a custom among Assyrian kings.

LYDIA RULES ASIA MINOR

Asia Minor, c.607 BC

lid on a cauldron of dissent that would grow into open rebellion.

The decline in Assyrian fortunes was already apparent by the end of Ashurbanipal's reign. Following his death, his two sons who succeeded him proved ineffective, while in neighboring Babylon the arrival of a strong ruler, Nabopolassar, altered the balance of power in the region. Babylon's move against the city of Nineveh in 616 BC failed, but its alliance with the Medes, led by Cyaxares, ultimately sealed the fate of Assyria.

Four years later, the Medes and their Babylonian allies succeeded in taking the city. The high point for the Medes was the storming of Nineveh's temple of Ashur, where Median soldiers smashed into tiny pieces the tablet containing the oath of allegiance, which the Medes had been forced to swear to the Assyrians for 70 years. Without Nineveh, Assyria's last king, Ashur-uballit, had little chance of restoring his throne. Although he experienced a number of minor victories after he rallied his forces at Harran, his desperate last-ditch attempt to regain his capital failed. The Assyrian king is believed to have died on the battlefield; his once-mighty empire utterly destroyed. ❑

Lydian coin

Under the monarchy of King Alyattes II, Lydia enjoyed its greatest influence. After the collapse of the Phrygian Kingdom in 695 BC, Lydia was able to fill the vacuum of power. Because of its gold supplies it was already a formidable trading power and under the Mermnad Dynasty it was able to translate this into political power. King Gyges and his son Ardys conquered western Asia Minor. They also took control of several of the Greek trading cities on the Anatolian coast.

Alyattes extended the kingdom's boundaries to the Halys River and acquired more Greek cities. Smyrna, which resisted the Lydian attack, was overrun and destroyed in 575 BC. After that Alyattes failed in his attempt to take Miletus.

Eastward expansion led to a battle with the neighboring Medes for lordship of the Anatolian peninsula. A solar eclipse on May 28, 585 BC, which had been predicted by the Greek philosopher and mathematician Thales of Miletus, brought six years of war to an end. The parties both accepted the Halys as the boundary line between their two nations. Alyattes' son Croesus presided over even greater growth in Lydian might but oversaw its decline as well. The Lydians are credited with the invention of money. Although bronze coins have been found in China that date from as early as the twelfth century BC, these do not seem to have been used outside of a very narrow circle at court. Around 685 BC under the reign of the Lydian king Ardys, coins were first brought into widespread circulation. The coins were made of electrum, an alloy of silver and gold. On one side they bore triangular stamp and on the other the Assyrian lion. The introduction of currency greatly facilitated business and trade. The coins were made to standards and guaranteed by the issuing monarch. ❑

The Kizilirmak, the central Anatolian river, was the boundary between Lydia and Media. In that time it was called the Halys and was hotly contested.

THE DESTRUCTION OF JERUSALEM

Judea, 586 BC

The Kingdom of Judah, which had been threatened for many years by the growing might of Babylon finally fell, and Jerusalem, its holiest city, was taken by the invading armies of King Nebuchadnezzar. The city was utterly destroyed and its entire population deported.

Nebuchadnezzar, who ruled over mighty Babylon with its Hanging Gardens and many other glories, always wished to include Jerusalem in his empire. In 597 BC, he raided the city, replacing the young King Jehoiachin with his uncle Zedekiah, who was to rule as a Babylonian puppet. In the event Zedekiah, backed by his court, preferred rebellion to Babylonian rule, although the prophet Jeremiah constantly preached that submission to Babylon was the only way Judah could atone for years of what he condemned as moral laxity.

Nebuchadnezzar's armies began the invasion of Judah in 587 BC, taking outlying cities before starting an 18-month siege of Jerusalem. Finally, resistance collapsed and the city was forced to submit. The invaders left it in smoldering ruins. The greatest loss was the destruction of the first temple, which had been built by Solomon. This black period in Jewish history is called the Babylonian captivity. It would last for almost 50 years until Babylon itself fell and its van-

King Josiah discovering the Book of Deuteronomy, as recounted in 2 Kings: 23.

quisher Cyrus the Great granted the Jews the freedom to return to Jerusalem. ❑

TYRANTS: A NEW POLITICAL PHENOMENON

Point of Interest

As Greek city-states began to grow in population and power, a new type of ruler appeared, called the tyrant. He was drawn from the aristocracy and would seize power in a periods of crisis. The first tyrant on mainland Greece, was Cypselus of Corinth. Then Theagenes became the ruler of Megara in 640 BC, and ten years later supported an unsuccessful coup by his son-in-law Cylon at Athens.

A distinct pattern in the tyrants' rise to power can be discerned. Anarchy was their breeding ground; they were nurtured on discontent. As a general rule, the tyrant would win the support of a faction of the quarrelling aristocracy or the poor and dispossessed. Sometimes he might engage the assistance of a band of foreign mercenaries.

His immediate task was to solve the particular crisis that brought him to power, and he usually would have the people's support while he did so. He was, in fact, often a popular figure.

To order and institute radical measures, involving the redistribution of land, he would set economic and social measures in motion with building projects and often look to increase his city's international prestige.

Tyrants also often promoted the arts and popular religious cults. Some managed to pass on their rule to their sons but that rarely extended beyond one generation before the Greeks' natural love of freedom reasserted itself. ❑

GLORY DAYS FOR BABYLON

Babylon, c.585 BC

Nebuchadnezzar first appeared in the pages of history with a decisive victory over Egypt, Babylon's chief rival. As crown prince, heir to his father, Nabopolassar, who had reestablished Babylonian independence 20 years before, he led Babylonian troops across the Euphrates and captured the strategically important town of Carchemish from the Egyptians, putting the two-year-old Syrian war on a new footing. During the battle for Carchemish the Egyptian garrison, reinforced by Greek mercenaries, put up a strong fight, but was overrun. Defenders who escaped were massacred in the desert.

The victory at Carchemish by Nebuchadnezzar, who had recently begun to share the reins of

The Hanging Gardens of Babylon

PHOENICIAN SAILORS' EXPLORATION OF UNKNOWN SEAS

Nile Delta, early sixth century BC

An Egyptian-backed Phoenician fleet embarked on the first voyage of circumnavigation—from the Red Sea, back to the Nile delta—returning to Egypt with dramatic reports of Africa. The arduous voyage lasted three years, taking the fleet from the Red Sea down the length of the Indian Ocean and back northward around the Cape of Good Hope to the Pillars of Hercules (the Strait of Gibraltar) and along the length of the Mediterranean to Egypt. This epic voyage was commissioned by Necho II, who had long been anxious to extend Egypt's authority and trading links to the southern seas. It was Necho who ordered the building of a canal between the Nile and the Red Sea, following a dried-up bed of an old arm of the Nile. This undertaking was abandoned after 120,000 men had died and the pharaoh had been told by an oracle that he was "doing the work for a barbarian." This was interpreted as meaning that he was leaving his country exposed to enemy invasion.

The Phoenicians proved themselves the most adventurous mariners in the ancient world. In contrast to the Greeks, who confined themselves to sailing within the Mediterranean, the Phoenicians traveled as far as England and the Canary Islands. In 470 bc they founded a trading post on the west coast of Africa. ❑

ANIMAL SACRIFICE IN ANCIENT GREECE

Greece, early sixth century BC

To the Greeks, animal sacrifice was an important part of daily life, both as a tribute to the gods and as a source of food. No important political decision or military initiative would be taken without first conducting a sacrifice.

The ritual slaughter of domestic animals—goats, sheep, or oxen—was also the principal way of preparing meat for eating.

The precise form of the sacrifice depended on the animal, the god or gods addressed, and the occasion. A common feature, however, was that the animal victim would be festively prepared, groomed, perhaps even have its horns gilded, and be led with apparent willingness to the altar.

The place of slaughter was marked out by carrying around a sacred basket and sprinkling water over both victim and participants. Barley grain was thrown at the animal to secure its acquiescence. Then the head was pulled back to point toward the sky, and the throat was cut.

The animal would be immediately skinned and butchered. The prime lean cuts were roasted, distributed, and eaten. Finally, the remains were boiled and made into sausages or puddings for the less favored. ❑

power with his aging warrior father, was a breakthrough for the Babylonians, who had tried several times without success to create a bridgehead across the Euphrates into Syria and Palestine and reopen their traditional trade routes to the Mediterranean.

Despite taking control of the old Assyrian Empire, the Babylonians showed little interest in occupying or redeveloping the vast tracts of Assyria. They contained the Medes, their allies in the overthrow of Assyria, by giving them the land east of the Zagros Mountains. Babylon's ambitions were focused to their west, toward the Mediterranean.

Upon ascending the throne as Nebuchadnezzar II, the young king turned his attention to making the city into the most imaginative masterpiece in the world.

Much of the work surpassed the glory of the old city, destroyed by Assyrian troops 80 years before. Its centerpiece was the Hanging Gardens, only accessible via the royal apartments and regarded as one of the Wonders of the World. Filled with luxuriant vegetation, including many exotic plants, these artificially irrigated terraced roof gardens offered a stark contrast to the desolation of the surrounding countryside.

The new Babylon contained more than 50 temples dedicated to the gods. The most striking was the Tower of Babel dedicated to the god Marduk. It had seven stories and was built in the form of a step pyramid that tapered toward the top and contained the Marriage House of the God, with a separate temple to Marduk at the base.

In the temple of Ishtar, the goddess of fertility and voluptuousness, local tradition demanded that a Babylonian woman offer herself once in her lifetime to a stranger within the temple, the man having to pay for this fleeting union.

A gate dedicated to Ishtar, who was also a goddess of war, was one of the sights that greeted the visitor to Babylon. The shimmering blue enameled brick decoration of Ishtar's gate depicts symbolic animals of myth and legend, such as griffins and bulls. All the gates were enlarged and embellished, standing farther out as Nebuchadnezzar II increased the city's perimeter and raised the external fortifications to bring the rural population under his protection.

Babylon's glory was short-lived. Following Nebuchadnezzar's death there was a period of struggle between his sons and the priests of Marduk. Then in 539 BC, Cyrus the Great defeated Babylon and reduced it to a province of the Persian Empire. ❑

The Tower of Babel by Peter Brueghel (Kunsthistorisches Museum, Vienna)

SAPPHO POET OF LESBIAN LOVE

Greece, c.580 BC

Already in her lifetime, Sappho's poetry was widely known, her fame reaching far beyond the confines of the island of Lesbos where she lived and worked. Her passionate poetry was written in a pure, unadorned style in the Aeolian dialect.

Sappho was the founder of a unique school for women on Lesbos. Although she was a wife and mother, her enduring poetry celebrated the love between women.

Born into one of the best families in Lesbos, Sappho is said to have been the wife of a rich man from Andros, by whom she had a daughter. She founded a boarding school for well-born young women of the island, and taught them poetry, music, and social graces under

The poet Sappho

the watchful eyes of the Muses, the Graces, and Aphrodite.

Pupils were groomed for marriage, which Sappho exalted in her poems. But Sappho also encouraged the girls to show affection for one another. This may have involved sexual contact and, if so, it would have been no more unusual than male homosexuality, which was more or less institutionalized in Greece at this time. Sappho's poems were not explicitly physical, but full of passion and sensuality. They described the torments of love, with tremulous outpourings of emotion and were often dedicated to her pupils. ❑

XENOPHANES: POET AND SKEPTIC

Brief lives

Xenophanes was a poet who traveled around Greece reciting his verses. These upset many traditionalists by ridiculing their religious beliefs and the conventional explanations offered by Greek mythology. He observed that men give their gods bodies, voices, and clothes like their own; Thracians think of their gods as having red hair and blue eyes; while Ethiopians have gods with snub noses and black faces. Homer and Hesiod even had the gods behaving badly, like humans, committing adultery, stealing, and deceiving one another.

Xenophanes derided these notions by suggesting that if cows, lions, and horses had hands and could paint, they would paint the gods as cows, lions, and horses. He believed that there is one god, more powerful than all other gods and men, who is different from mortals in mind and body. ❑

SOLON AND THE GOVERNMENT OF ATHENS

Athens, early sixth century BC

The first tentative steps toward democracy in Athens can be traced to the time of Dracon. Serving as *archon* (first magistrate) in 621 BC, he devised the first written code of laws for the people. After an attempted coup by the ambitious young aristocrat Cylon and the subsequent upheavals, there was a need for firm rules, widely understood and generally accepted.

Dracon, a deeply religious man, set out a new legal concept that made a clear distinction between manslaughter and premeditated murder. For murder, there was a scale of penalties that even took into account the weapons used. Other crimes, from assault and battery, robbery and theft, on to personal insults and sacrilege, were all identified and allocated appropriate penalties, which included fines that varied according to the importance of the victim, as well as imprisonment, enslavement, and execution.

Some of his fellow citizens criticized his laws as too severe (whence the term Draconian), but they gave Athenians a set of rules applicable to all and sharply curtailed the settling of differences by blood feuds and acts of personal revenge.

A little less than thirty years later Solon, the poet-statesman, was elected *archon*. He introduced a completely new set of laws. These laws guaranteed the freedom of every citizen of Athens. In a poem commemorating this radical move he said, "I wrote down laws alike for base and noble, fitting straight judgment to each."

His dislike of the greed and pride of the Athenian aristocracy recurred throughout his poetry; but that led to disappointment among some of the lower classes who had expected him to be even more radical with his new laws.

The reality of office forced him to compromise. Nevertheless, his social reforms became known as the *seisachtheia*, "the shaking off of burdens." Possibly the most welcome was the abolition of the system whereby a man and his family could fall into slavery through the nonpayment of debts or mortgages.

Solon also reorganized the distribution of political power, taking it from the old aristocracy and dividing it between four new property-owning classes according to the yields from their lands.

In practice, actual power re-sided in the first three of these classes, who filled the public posts either by election or by casting lots, "the choice of the gods." But even the lowest class, the *thetes*, were admitted to the judicial tribunals and Assembly.

Citizens had a voice in the appointment of magistrates and members of the Council. Foreigners were also granted civil rights. These laws could be read by everybody. They were written on wooden tablets set in rotating four-sided frames.

Though a case can be made that Solon brought democracy to Athens, there remained two classes who were denied any part in the political process and had no control over their lives: the slaves and the women of Athens. ❑

Solon the great Athenian law giver

ZOROASTER AND MONOTHEISM IN PERSIA

Persia, c.560 BC

After receiving a divine vision, the 30-year old Zoroaster, also called Zarathustra, founded a new monotheistic religion. Little is known about his life. He is thought to have been born in Bactria (present-day Afghanistan) and died at the age of 77 in Khorosan, where he had spent most of his career. He had been exiled there in 590 BC and two years later converted the lord of the city. Some historians, however, have placed the date of his birth much earlier, in the tenth or eleventh century BC.

Zoroaster based his doctrine on free will, as opposed to the existing religious practice in which many gods were worshiped and ritual, animal sacrifice and drugs were prevalent. Zoroaster conceived of the world as a stage for the conflict between good and evil. Good was represented by the Creator-God, Ahura Mazda, evil by his counterpart, Ahiram. Man must come to an ethical decision regarding his role in this cosmic struggle. He can overcome evil by engaging in right thinking, right speech, and right action.

The *Avesta*, the sacred writings of Zoroastrianism, is a compilation of works of different genres and periods. Most revered are the 17 Gathas, said to stem from the founder himself. Characteristic features of the religion are purification rites involving fire. The religion reached its highpoint in Persia under the Sassanid Dynasty (224 BC–642 AD). Today's Parsis, most of whom live in India, continue to practice the religion. ❑

Parsi temple in Shiraz (Iran)

THE WISE MEN OF ANTIQUITY

The proverbial seven wise men lived in Greece in the sixth and seventh centuries BC. A number of them bequeathed among other things pithily phrased comments on the right way of living.

Cleobulus of Lindos (c.600 BC): The tyrant of Lindos on the Isle of Rhodes is reported to have said: "Moderation is the best."

Solon of Athens (c.640–559 BC): Athens great lawgiver and social reformer embraced as his motto: "Nothing in excess." In his poetry Solon addressed questions of human conduct and ethical relationships.

Chilon of Sparta (early sixth century BC): Venerated as a statesman in his home city, Chilon had as his watchwords: "Know yourself."

Bias of Priene (c.625–540 BC): His experience as a judge made him somewhat pessimistic. He declared: "The majority of men are evil."

Thales of Miletus (c.625–547 BC): Not only as a mathematical genius (who was the first to construct a right triangle with the aid of a compass) but as a philosopher and politician, Thales was widely known. He is considered to be the founder of the Western philosophical tradition, the first to systematically seek rational explanations for natural phenomena.

Pittacus of Mytilene (c.650–580 BC): Pittacus was ranked among the seven wise men because of his political genius. He freed his home city from tyranny and gave it new laws.

Periandros of Corinth (c.626–586 BC): The tyrant of Corinth attacked the institution of slavery and defended the lower middle classes, thus setting the city-state on the road to an era of great achievement. ❏

Pittacus of Mytilene

NEW POWER IN THE NEAR EAST

Persia, 559 BC

The vassal king Cyrus rebelled against his overlord, Astyages, the king of Media, and took over his kingdom, setting Persia on the road to becoming the great world power of its age.

Both the Medes and the Persians were part of a great migration that had come from the north into the Iranian plateau in the middle of the second millennium BC. Each people founded its own kingdom, but beginning around 700 BC, the Persians were forced to acknowledge Median lordship. Media, setting out on a program of conquest, had to contend with the Assyrians During the reign of King Cyaxeres (625–585), it achieved its greatest influence, when along with the Babylonians it destroyed the Assyrian Empire.

With the capture of the Median capital Ecbatana (present-day Hamadan), Cyrus brought to an end a three-year struggle with Astyages, his father-in-law. In place of the existing Median rule, he consolidated the position of the Achmenid Dynasty, which had been founded around 700 BC. Near the site of his victory, Cyrus erected a new capital, Pasargadae.

As with other great leaders—Moses, Sargon of Agade—legends grew up around him. Some said that Cyrus was found abandoned as a small child on a river. Whether adopted or not, he was brought up as the son of King Cambyses, the first Achmenid king to rule all the Persian tribes. When Cyrus succeeded his father, the Persians were still subject to the rule of the Medes. But when in 550 BC the Median army mutinied and the Median king, Astyages, proved unable to control his empire, Cyrus led a Persian revolt, crushing the Medes, capturing Astyages, and establishing Persian dominance. ❏

The wounded Persian king, Cyrus the Great, being cared for in Jerusalem

THE RETURN OF THE JEWS FROM BABYLON

Jerusalem, 538 BC

Forty-seven years after their forefathers were deported from a devastated Jerusalem and carried off into exile in Babylon, the Jews returned to their holy city. Persia's King Cyrus conquered Babylon in 539 BC. One of his first acts thereafter was to repatriate the Jews, as well as others formerly held captive.

More than ever determined to adhere to the worship of their one god, Yahweh, the Jews attributed their return to their Lord.

The Jews homecoming to Israel is well documented in the Books of Ezra and Nehemiah.

The Book of Daniel provides further details of the story of their deliverance. During a banquet given by King Nabonidus' son Belshazzar a mysterious hand wrote on a wall the words *"mene mene tekel upharsin."* The prophet Daniel explained that God had "weighed the king in the balance and found him wanting." Accordingly, his kingdom was handed over to Cyrus. ❏

PHILOSOPHERS AND SCIENTISTS CHALLENGE GREEK GODS

Greek world, c.560 BC

The foundations of the scientific tradition were laid down in Greece during this period. A group of Greek intellectuals in the Ionian cities of Asia Minor (Anatolia) radically changed the way men thought about the world around them and the universe beyond. With their searching questions, Thales, Anaximander, and Heraclitus challenged traditional myths and legends familiar to readers of the poet Hesiod, who cataloged some 300 gods, with Zeus as their king. Besides Atlas, who holds up the sky, and Astraeus, who takes care of the stars, Hesiod had gods for the physical world: earth, sea, mountains, and so on.

The Ionian intellectuals had little patience for these traditional ideas. They rejected the notion of the gods meddling with the natural world. To them thunder was not a loud noise made by an angry Zeus; it was to be explained in natural terms. Likewise, Iris may be goddess of the rainbow, but a rainbow was simply a mul-

ticolored cloud of moisture. The Ionians had a word for their new way of looking at things. *Kosmos* means "the universe," but it also means something more; it comes from the Greek word meaning "to order" or "to arrange" things. So the universe, including our own world, is seen as arranged in an orderly fashion; it can be studied and explained by reasoning. The philosophers did not simply make assertions; they supported their opinions with reasoned argument.

In the seaport town of Miletus, the philosopher Anaximander broadened his countrymen's perspective by designing a controversial map of the world engraved on a tablet of stone. He envisaged the world as rounded, like a pillar, with the inhabited part on one side. But the unusual feature of his map was that it was represented as being viewed from on high, as though by a bird or a god. Nobody had thought of doing that before. The idea probably came to Anaximander because, as

a pupil of Thales, who devised a system of geometry, he was familiar with geometric shapes, such as the circle. He theorized that the earthly cylinder lies at the center of a celestial sphere in a position of perfect equilibrium. Another of Anaximander's theories was that humans were developed from animals, because animals can look after themselves very soon, while humans need to be nursed for a long period of time.

At the same time, the mathematician Pythagoras was gaining renown in the Greek settlements of southern Italy, chiefly because of the missionary zeal of his followers, who had become a political force in several cities. Not only did they expound the Pythagorean theorem (that the square of the hypotenuse of a right angled triangle is equal to the sum of the squares of the other two sides), but they also

told of his discovery that musical harmonies can be expressed mathematically. The Pythagoreans were vegetarians and were opposed to the killing of any living creature. They also carried out physical exercises similar to yoga practices that suggest some contact with the Far East. But numbers were at the center of their beliefs: According to them, numbers can explain the working of the universe. ❑

Greek coin with portrait of Pythagoras

GREEK GLORY SYMBOLIZED BY TEMPLES

Greek world, c.560 BC

With the flourishing of Greek civilization in the Mediterranean, there were no more potent and beautiful displays of Greek genius and prestige than the many temples being built. At the height of the Mycenaean Empire, around 1200 BC, people, including kings, worshiped at shrines in their own homes, or at sacred sites like caves or mountaintops

in the open air. But when Greek culture reemerged from obscurity after the empire's fall, a new architectural form, the temple, emerged with it. This was probably one of the first symbols of the collective government of the *polis*, or city-state, which replaced the monarchy of earlier times. Instead of palaces and tombs of kings, monuments were now to be built for the gods who protected the polis. Indeed, some of the first temples were built on the foundations of old Mycenaean palaces.

Except in Crete, however, temples did not bring religion indoors. They were simply the houses of the gods, where

their images were kept, and only priests were normally allowed in. Religious ceremonies were performed at separate altars outside the temples, a survival of earlier open-air worship.

The earliest temples were made of mud brick, often painted, on stone foundations, with wooden pillars supporting steeply pitched thatched roofs. Decorated clay was often used for the *metopes*, the designs on the frieze between the pillars and the roof. The basic ground plan was of a rectangular main room, or *naos*, with a projecting porch way on pillars. Later, an added colonnade, or peristyle, around the naos allowed a lower-pitched roof and offered better protection for the mud walls. Later still, the use

of heavy clay tiles for the roof led to the replacement of the wooden pillars by stone columns. With few exceptions, soon Greek temples were made entirely of stone. Two distinct styles or "orders" of temple architecture developed in the sixth and seventh centuries BC. On mainland Greece and in the western colonies, the Doric order was popular; its columns, stubby and fluted with plain, cushion-like capitals (column tops), were reminiscent of Mycenae or Egypt. In Anatolia and the Greek islands, the Ionic order prevailed; its columns were slimmer, with bases and curled capitals. It was more oriental in style and more ornamented (for example, with floral designs) than the Doric order. ❑

Cyrus Dies, but Persian Empire Lives

Persia, c.530 BC

Cyrus the Great, founder of the Persian Empire, reigned for 29 years. The king's conquests stretched from Greece to India. His reputation for mercy and justice was exemplified by his decision to help the Jewish exiles in Babylon return to their homeland.

In 547 BC, Cyrus enlarged his territory. Allying himself with Babylon he won a decisive battle against King Croesus of Lydia, his neighbor to the west, making the country a province of Persia. The kingdom, fell in fourteen days, although Cyrus spared the life of its king and employed him as an advisor. He also took territories on the Mediterranean coast formerly belonging to the Greeks including Phoenicia and Palestine. In 539 BC, he brought down the Babylonian Kingdom of Nabonidus and his son Bels-

hazzar. He then restored the Kingdom of Judah to the Jews after their nearly 50 years of captivity in Babylon. He also provided money and support for the rebuilding of temple in Jerusalem.

Just as with the Jews, Cyrus proved himself to be a benefactor to other nations, displaying an extraordinary degree of tolerance for different customs and peoples. The conquered nations were permitted to practice their own religion, customs, and language, often even their own forms of government. In this way he succeeded in building and holding together a mighty empire.

Cyrus had greater difficulties in extending his power eastward. He had temporary success in military campaigns between 545 and 540 BC against the Parthians and Bactrians, but he fell in battle

Legend attributed untold wealth to King Croesus of Lydia.

in 529 BC at the Aral Sea against the Massagetae, a nomadic people of northeastern Iran. His son Cambyses II succeeded him and was able to maintain the empire his father had carved out. ❏

The Delphic Oracle Draws Petitioners

Greece, sixth century BC

During the sixth century BC, the oracle in the temple of Apollo at Delphi became revered throughout Greece for foretelling the future. There, every month, ordinary people and delegates from the cities would come to ask the advice of the god as he spoke by way of the Pythia, a peasant woman chosen for her purity. The petitioner, always male, had to follow a precise ritual. First, he would make an offering, in money or in kind. City spokesmen would pay more than private individuals, but they were given priority. Then, he would make a sacrifice, usually a goat, which was examined by the priests. If the portents were good, he would be allowed to enter the temple.

There the Pythia, carefully purified, sat on a bronze tripod awaiting his question. It has been suggested that she would achieve a trance state by chewing bay leaves; others insist that her tri-

pod was placed over a fissure in the rock, which gave off trance-inducing fumes. She would listen to the question and then make a series of strange utterances that were interpreted and transcribed

in verse by her attendant priests.

However, even after the priests made their interpretation, the Pythia's utterances could be read in many different ways, and often the wrong conclusion was

drawn, with disastrous results. The questions that were asked covered many subjects. Cities asked if they should go to war or make peace. Individuals wanted to know if they should make voyages or should marry.

One of the oracle's most important tasks was to advise cities where to set up colonies. There was a practical aspect to these consultations as well as the religious function, for the priests kept copies of all the Pythia's utterances, and much general information was filed in the temple's library, enabling them to make rational judgments. ❏

The beehive tomb at Delphi dedicated to the Goddess Athena

ROME'S SUPPLANTING OF ETRUSCAN POWER

Rome, c.500 BC

The city of Rome's early flourishing owed much to the Etruscans, its neighbors to the north. Under their influence, Rome developed from a collection of mud hut villages into a major city. Along with the completion of the Forum, the city boasted of a unique drainage system that began as a single ditch before its expansion into a more sophisticated form, which drained the whole city. Pavements were built for its populace; and the city-state founded its own army.

Etruscan origins and culture are somewhat enigmatic. Their descent remains a subject of scholarly dispute, although their forebears were certainly eastern Mediterranean in origin, and Greek influence was paramount in their culture. Rome was up until this time, basically a collection of villages, built on seven hills. It

Etruscan musician (c. 490 BC)

was attractive to the Etruscans because the Tiber River could be easily forded, allowing them access to the rich lands of Latium (an area south of Rome), which could produce as many as three crops per year, and there were valuable salt deposits close by.

The Etruscans passed on their alphabet—derived from Greek—to the Romans, as well as an administrative framework, the work of Servius Tullius, a representative in Rome of the Tarquin Dynasty that ruled Etruria. Even the name *Rome*—despite the legend of Romulus (man of Rome), the city's supposed founder—was Etruscan in origin.

Starting around 600 BC, the Etruscans extended their dominance over Umbria and northern Italy. In 540 BC, they founded the city of Felsina (present-day Bologna). Next, they expanded to the south

and for a time the Tarquins, who were of Etruscan descent, ruled over Rome.

Their power faded away and by the end of the fifth century BC, they were being challenged by their increasingly powerful neighbor. Finally, in 290 BC, they lost their independence to Rome. ❑

Etruscan sarcophagus figure (3rd century BC)

THE ROMAN REPUBLIC

Rome, from 509 BC

After driving the last Etruscan king out of the city, Rome established itself as a republic, in which political power rested primarily in the hands of the patrician class.

At the head of the state stood two officials with equal powers (first named *Praetors* and later called *Consuls*). They served for a one-year term. In times of crisis a dictator was empowered. He was given unrestricted power, but for no longer than a period of six months. During this period he was above the law. Under the consular level were the praetors, who were responsible for the administration of justice. Beneath them were the *curule aediles* who oversaw certain police functions as well as the public games and from 447 BC on, the *quaestors*, who were in charge of the city's finances.

To rise to the highest political power in Rome, one had to

first serve in the lower offices. This was called the *cursus honorum*. Each level had its own age requirements.

For membership in the 300-member senate, the *patres* (the fathers) were chosen from the city's aristocracy and former magistrates. They represented the interests of their class. The senate advised the magistrates—at a later stage their decisions were binding.

The third leg of the city's government had already been established in the days of the monarchy. This was the popular assemblies. Most important of these were the centurion committees. The assembled citizens were ranked according to wealth, not birth, in five classes and 193 centuries. The centuries were responsible for decisions of war and peace and the elections of high officials. ❑

The Roman forum

Temple dedicated to Aphrodite

GOLD AND BRONZE PAY TRIBUTE TO CELTIC ROYALTY IN LAVISH BURIALS

Europe, c.520 BC

Archaeological finds from this period testify to a new prosperity among the Celtic communities in Europe. Tribal chieftains built hilltop palaces where they stored their newfound riches in the form of gold and bronze objects and other precious possessions. Their wealth was also buried with them.

A superb example of the fine art of this age is the Krater (vase) of Vix. It was buried together with an unknown princess. The lavish burial is indisputable evidence of the high regard in which women were held in Celtic culture. The crater itself is about five feet high; its neck is decorated in relief with warriors and with chariots on its lid. It has as its handle a statuette of a young woman, with a gold

diadem on her head. The woman interred was laid out on a wagon with highly decorated elements. Scholars speculate that it may have been a druid priestess.

Clay Athenian cups were among the treasures buried in the graves of Celtic rulers from Bohemia to Burgundy.

These chieftains formed part of a military aristocracy that controlled the trading routes between Europe and the Mediterranean, building fortifications at strategic points, usually on hilltops.
In exchange for raw materials like tin and amber, Greek and Etruscan traders exported to the north luxury items, works of art, and wine—adding to their considerable wealth and enhancing their lifestyles. ❑

INCIPIENT DEMOCRACY IN ATHENS

Athens, 508 BC

In 508 BC, the aristocrat, Cleisthenes, was able to wrest power from his rival, Isagoras by enlisting the help of the *demos*, the people. He then embarked on a program of far-reaching reforms that gave more power to the people but at the same time helped to consolidate his rule over them.

His first major change was to break up the city-state into administrative units called the *deme*, which consisted of a village or a section of Athens. These units were then combined into 30 groups called *trittyes*, which themselves formed ten new *phylai*, or tribes, replacing the old division of four tribes.

Each tribe now had the responsibility of choosing fifty men by lot to send to the *boule* (assembly), which guaranteed that all the citizens of Athens, from the richest to the poorest, were represented. All were now equal in the eyes of the law.

However, while some scholars have argued that that this proves that Cleisthenes had been genuinely converted to the cause of the demos, there are others who believe that the reforms were merely a device to curb the power of his rivals among the the privileged classes.

Theoretcially these reforms could be seen as leading to the dimishment of the distance between the governors and the governed. It worked against the empowerment of a competent, quasi-professional political class that might develop a corporate mentality and lose touch with the people

Cleisthenes has also been credited with the introduction of the system of ostracism, under which, once a year, a man considered to be dangerous to Athens could be sent into exile for ten years. This was done by citizens scratching the name of the man they want exiled on a potsherd. The man who received the most votes was be exiled.

In keeping with these new populist sentiments, the fame of the mighty Theseus, slayer of the Minotaur and hero of many myths, became increasingly pronounced in Athens. His deeds can be seen represented on Attic pottery, festivals were held in his memory, and sacrifices were devoted to him.

Skillfully promoted, this cult had to do not so much with his heroism as with his rule as king of Athens. For it was Theseus who unified the city-state and established Athens as the center of political life.
This fit in very well with the radical reforms instituted by Cleisthenes, and Theseus was conveniently annexed as the hero-father of the new democracy. ❑

Clay shard used as ballot for the ostracism of Themistocles

THE PERSIAN EMPIRE

Between 1500 and 1000 BC Indo-European tribes describing themselves as Aryans pushed forward from the northeast across the Caucasus to the Iranian plateau. There they established their supremacy on the land they called Iran, "Land of the Aryan." The last migrant tribes to arrive were the Medes and Persians, mentioned for the first time in Assyrian annals in the ninth century BC. In the eighth and ninth centuries BC, the Persian tribes moved toward the southeast, occupying Elamite territories and other areas farther to the east, which they called Parsa, "Land of Persia."

Teispes (675–645 BC), son of Achemenes, founder of the dynasty of the "Achmenids" (705–675 BC), was already calling himself king, when in fact he and his successors—for a time there were two Persian kingdoms co-existing next to each other (640–600 BC)—were vassals of the Median rulers. It was only when Cyrus the Great (559–529 BC) came to the throne that the Persians were able to defeat their Median overlords, the Astyages, in about 550 BC, and found the Achemenid Empire.

In about 546 BC, Cyrus conquered Lydia. The Greek cities along the west coast of Asia Minor were also captured, as were the Carians and Lycians. After taking Babylon, the road to Mesopotamia, Syria, Palestine, and Phoenicia was wide open to Cyrus. All the countries he subdued fell under Persian administration, but religion, national customs and traditions, language, and the forms of government were preserved. The official languages of the administration were Persian, Elamite, and Aramaic.

ACHEMENID CONQUESTS

Cambyses II (530–522 BC), who succeeded his father Cyrus, pursued a policy of conquest, occupying Egypt (525 BC), and pushing into Nubia and Libya. During his absence in 522 BC, the magus Gaumata, a follower of the teachings of Zoroaster, seized the throne. Cambyses died in Syria on his way to Persia. His successor, Darius I (522–486 BC), succeeded in killing Gaumata, assisted by a conspiracy of six Persian aristocratic families who also removed Gaumata's followers and restored unity.

Darius divided the empire into twenty satrapies (provinces administered by a governor), introduced a single gold currency and uniform taxes, organized finances, and built roads. In 518 BC, he founded the new capital, Persepolis. Persia achieved its greatest expansion under his rule and that of his successor Xerxes I (486–465 BC). In 513 BC, Darius pushed as far east as the Indus region; his campaign against the Scythians was unsuccessful, but he seized Thrace and Macedonia. His ultimate objective was to control the Black Sea and the Aegean by conquering their shores on either side.

The Persian Wars started in 500 BC with the uprising of the Ionian Greeks in Asia Minor, and these military conflicts between Greeks and Persians continued for some 50 years. During the Persian Wars there were

Emissaries of people obliged to pay tribute to Persia: Sargatians and Parthians (top), Sogdians, Gandarans, and Scythians (middle), Indians, Bactrians, and Lydians (relief from the ruins of Persepolis)

uprisings in other parts of the kingdom, especially in Egypt and Babylonia, that continued under the later Achemenids. At the same time, the ruling house lost its original dynamism. Xerxes I turned into an eastern despot mainly interested in court ceremonies. Succession conflicts among his successors weakened the country's internal stability. Artaxerxes III Ochos, (359 to 338 BC) managed to extend the country to its former size. But he and his son Arses died as the victims of court intrigues in 338 and 336 BC respectively. The defeat of Darius III (336–330 BC) near Gaugamela in 331 BC by Alexander the Great marked the end of the Achemenid rule.

SELEUCIDS AND PARTHIANS

When Alexander the Great (ruled 336–323 BC) incorporated Persia into his realm, he also adopted the Persian system of administration and government. At the same time, the Iranian regions became Hellenized. Alexander's general Seleucus became Satrap of Babylon in 321 BC, and in 312 BC, he founded his own dynasty, proclaiming himself king under the name Seleucus I Nicator. His territories included Mesopotamia, Iran, and Syria. The capital of this kingdom was Babylon, later Seleucia, and finally Antioch. In the third century BC, the satraps in the northeastern provinces used the conflicts opposing the Seleucids and Egyptian Ptolemaic rulers to further their own attempts at independence. Admittedly Antiochus III (223–187 BC) was able to return the kingdom to its former size, but his unsuccessful war against Rome marked the end of the Seleucids once and for all.

In about 250 BC, nomadic tribes invaded the northwestern regions of the Iranian plateau. One of their leaders, Arsakes, proclaimed himself king in 247 BC and founded the dynasty of the Arsacids. During the next 150 years, the Arsacids pushed the Seleucids westward where the Roman commander Pompey defeated them, thus heralding the end of their rule. Meanwhile, their last ruler abdicated, and Syria became a Roman province.

The Parthian Empire reached its zenith under Mithridates I (about 171–138 BC). Rome became involved for the first time in internal Parthian politics in the western territories in 64/63 BC. The Roman emperor Augustus reached an accommodation with Parthia and recognized the Euphrates as the border of the empire. The defensive actions against the people in the east and the wars against the Roman Empire weakened the Parthian kingdom. Internal disputes and a strong national Iranian movement also played an important

role. During the reign of Ardashir I from the House of the Sassanids, this situation resulted in open revolt, and ultimately the end of the Arsacid supremacy in 224 AD.

THE SASSANIDS

When Ardashir I (224–241) ascended the throne, he saw himself as the legitimate heir and reviver of the Acheme-

Persian art: capital with bulls (sculpture in Susa, 5th–4th century BC)

nid kingdom. By the time he died, he had restored the kingdom to its old borders, with the exception of Syria, Egypt, and Asia Minor. His son Shahpur I (241–272) continued the wars against Rome, and his claim to power is clearly expressed in his title "King of Iran and Not-Iran."

Constant wars against Rome, internal conflicts, battles against the Scythians, and disputes with Arab border tribes marked the next hundred years. Actual power was often in the hands of a very powerful feudal aristocracy and the supreme Magus, the Guardian of Zoroastrianism, which had been elevated to become the official state religion.

The last great king was Khosrow I (531–579). He drove back the Byzantines (561/62), defeated the Hephtalites, and pushed the borders as far back as Yemen. But conflicts broke out among his successors, the aristocracy rebelled, and the rulers changed quickly. The Byzantine emperor Heraclius (610–641) took advantage of these weaknesses and defeated the Persian army several times in 627/28. In 637, the Arabs occupied Seleucia. Fifteen years later the vast Sassanid kingdom fell into the hands of the Muslim conquerors.

RELIGION AND CULT

In the pre-Achemenid period, the Iranian religion was polytheistic, and the cult was in the hands of the Median magi. The beginning of the Achemenid rule witnessed the proliferation of the teachings of Zoroaster (630–553 BC). The central idea of his teaching was the worship of one god, the creator of the world, Ahura Mazda, and the cosmic struggle between "justice" and "falsehood." Because

humans could freely choose between these moral principles, they could have a determining influence on their own destiny. The magi adopted these teachings, albeit with major changes. Mithras, the god of light, gained importance.

During the reign of Shahpur Mani (215–275), a new Iranian religion developed. According to Manichaeism, the "evil one" was the creator and ruler of the visible world, and the soul that was part of the "good god" was incarcerated inside the body. The liberation of the soul from the powers of darkness was possible, and this knowledge led to self-knowledge, which would lead to redemption.

STATE AND SOCIETY

The power of the "King of Kings," who was absolute ruler in war and peace, was bestowed unto him by Ahura Mazda. Noble advisers assisted him in legal matters and administration. Military leadership was entrusted to a commander who was only responsible to the "King of Kings." Together with the army, the so-called "10,000 immortals," a literate civil service, formed the main support of the ruler. Socially on the same level as the royal family were the six noble families who had helped Darius I in his struggle against Gaumata. Just below them came the owners of large estates who occupied important positions such as priests, government functionaries, and army officers. All important nobles were given land by the king, and in return they provided troops and served in the army. Free craftsmen, free tradesmen, free day laborers and workers, serfs, and slaves formed the lowest class. ❑

PERSIAN ADVANCE HALTED

Marathon, Greece, September 13, 490 BC.

The crucial Battle of Marathon was fought on this day. The hero of the engagement was Miltiades, who persuaded nine other generals to start fighting without waiting for help from the Spartans. To enlist Sparta's help, Athens had sent Philippides, who, in a remarkable feat of endurance, covered 150 miles in two days to beg for assistance. Nonetheless, the Spartans refused to march during the full moon and would not set forth until their religious festivities were over.

The army of the Persian King Darius had sacked the town of Eretria on the island of Euboea and landed on the eastern coast of Attica. The Persians then massed on the marshy plain of Marathon with the Athenian force of some 10,000 in the hills above.

Miltiades had heard that the Persians had withdrawn some of their cavalry to the ships to prepare for an attack on Athens from the sea. He chose this time to attack, relying on surprise, speed, and a three-pronged assault across a wide front. His forces ran toward the Persian archers, getting underneath their arrows.

At first, the Persians broke through in the center and pursued the Athenians inland. The two armies on the flanks, however, encircled the Persian flanks and made a concerted attack on the main force from the rear. They then captured seven Persian ships. Some 6,400 Persians were killed, against the

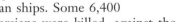

Athenian army's losses, which numbered fewer than 200.

The Athenians, triumphant in their victory over Persia, showed their gratitude to the god Apollo by building a treasury in his honor at Delphi. Inside the miniature temple, they left offerings of silver, plundered from the abandoned Persian camp.

This treasury still stands at Delphi. The sculptures that decorate the metopes were made from Parian marble. They are as fine as any that Greece produced at that time. They depict scenes from the exploits of the Greek heroes, Theseus and Heracles. ❑

Stele depicting hoplite (c. 500 BC)

THE GREEK HOPLITES

Point of Interest

Over the course of a century, Greek city-states developed a new kind of soldier. Each city had a citizens' army, and every Greek was required to take part in the defense of his city. Usually, all men who owned a moderate amount of land had to equip themselves as heavily armed foot soldiers called *hoplites*.

The hoplites wore bronze helmets, breastplates, and greaves, and were armed with long lances, for stabbing rather than throwing, and short swords. They carried stout circular shields of wood on their left arms. The key to the hoplites' success was their formation into compact, highly disciplined formations called *phalanxes*. A typical phalanx was deeper than it was wide; the soldiers would stick very close together, each protecting himself and the man on his left with his shield. The fighting became a matter of shoving and pushing with one's shield, accompanied by stabbing with spear or sword. If the front rank fell it would be trampled underfoot as the next rank replaced it, and so on until one side would give way. Death in battle was often particularly nasty. Because of the hoplites' shields, most wounds were either in the neck or genitals. ❑

Running hoplite with shield, helmet and spear (painted vase c. 500 BC)

ATHENS CREATES A FORMIDABLE FLEET OF WARSHIPS

Athens, 483 BC.

The Greek statesman Themistocles realized that Athens best hope for defending itself against Persia lay in increased naval power. Under his leadership, Athens set out to construct the largest fleet in Greece, seven times bigger than that of its rival, Aegina. He instituted a crash building program of 200 *triremes* to be completed in only three years. The triremes were long, fast ships, each requiring some 200 oarsmen. They were built for fighting, and their square sails were often left on the beach when they went into battle.

Themistocles, who was one of the city's *archons* (chief magistrates), persuaded his fellow citizens to fund the work of construction with the recent big find of silver at the Laurion mines. He also raised money by the *trierarchy*, a tax levied on those who owned very large amounts of property. Effectively, it was a tax on the hundred or so wealthiest citizens.

To house the new fleet the port of Athens, Piraeus, was extensively modernized. The Bay of Munychia was dredged and enormous repair yards were built there.

Themistocles launched his plan ostensibly to help in the war against Aegina. But his real purpose was to build up Athenian defenses against the much stronger potential enemy—Persia. His new navy required 40,000 rowers, more than Athens herself could provide even if all able-bodied men were drafted. If Athens were ever to be defeated by the Persians, or any other power, the triremes could be used for mass emigration of the Athenians to the west of Greece. One result of Athens' recent victories and sizeable investment in its military was to assert its claims to be the preeminent power on the Greek peninsula. ❑

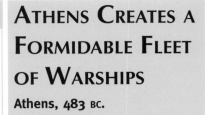

VICTORY AT MARATHON

History of Herodotus, **translated by George Macaulay**

Thus speaking Miltiades gained Callimachos to his side; and the opinion of the polemarch being added, it was thus determined to fight a battle...then the Athenians were drawn up for battle in the order which here follows: On the right wing the polemarch Callimachos was leader...and he leading, next after him came the tribes in order as they were numbered one after another, and last were drawn up the Plataians occupying the left wing: On this occasion however, when the Athenians were being drawn up at Marathon something of this kind was done: their army being made equal in length of front to that of the Medes, came to be drawn up in the middle with a depth of but few ranks, and here their army was weakest, while each wing was strengthened with numbers. And when they had been arranged in their places and the sacrifices proved favourable, then the Athenians were let go, and they set forth at a run to attack the Barbarians...the Persians seeing them advancing to the attack at a run, made preparations to receive them; and in their minds they charged the Athenians with madness which must be fatal, seeing that they were few and yet were pressing forwards at a run, having neither cavalry nor archers. Such was the thought of the Barbarians; but the Athenians when all in a body they had joined in combat with the Barbarians, fought in a memorable fashion...Now while they fought in Marathon, much time passed by; and in the centre of the army...the Barbarians had broken the ranks of their opponents and were pursuing them inland, but on both wings the Athenians and the Plataians severally were winning the victory; and being victorious they left that part of the Barbarians which had been routed to fly without molestation, and bringing together the two wings they fought with those who had broken their centre, and the Athenians were victorious. ❏

HIGH POINT OF THE PERSIAN EMPIRE

Persia, early fifth century BC

Following the death of Cyrus the Great, his son Cambyses II succeeded him to power. Then during a period of political turmoil, Darius, a former spearbearer to King Cambyses seized power in the second revolution in the country in only three months. At the time Cambyses was in Egypt, he was declared king of Upper and Lower Egypt after his defeat of the Egyptian king, Amasis, at the battle of Pelusium.

Cambyses was not popular in Egypt, where his troops often plundered villages. He was accused of killing the divine bull, Apis, as well as his own, pregnant sister. Learning of turmoil at home, he hurried back to Iran but is thought to have died on the way.

Darius' rule coincided with a flowering of Persian culture and political power. In 515 BC, he laid the foundation stones of gold and silver, for his new capitol at Perse-polis. He died in 486 BC, the architect of an expanded Persian Empire, and was succeeded by his son Xerxes. Persia was now the dominant people in an empire that stretched from Greece to India; all Persians were given special privileges. The aristocracy was advisers and officials, who made up the cavalry in time of war. Commoners were exempt from taxes and served as the army's heavy infantry.

Where Cyrus had been content to conquer lands, Darius systematically exploited their resources. The empire itself was divided, as it had been under Cyrus, into 20 *satrapies*, each under its own *satrap*, or governor. Each satrapy had to provide money (collected as taxes), horses, produce, ships, and soldiers. Individual satraps ruled virtually as local kings, administering law and order, commanding troops, and conducting local diplomacy.

An extensive system of new roads crossed the empire, establishing unprecedented standards of communication, and a stable coinage underpinned the flourishing economy.

Although their invasions of Greece were frustrated, the Persians showed their might in other parts of their empire. In 482 BC, Xerxes brutally extinguished a revolt in Babylon—launched to recover the freedom lost to Persia in 539 BC. Many rebels were tortured and slain; Xerxes ordered the city walls destroyed and its temples razed to the ground. As spoils of his victory, he carried off the vast gold statue of the god Marduk and the temple to Marduk, the largest and most prestigious sacred building of its time. Before long the Babylonian rebellion and the manner of its suppression combined to destabilize the empire and undermine Darius' great achievements. Xerxes was assassinated in 465 BC. ❏

Relief depicting Darius I

The city of Persepolis was laid out on a grand open plan. It was destroyed by Alexander the Great in 330 BC.

THE BUDDHA AND THE EIGHTFOLD PATH TO ENLIGHTENMENT

Central India, fifth century BC

There is scholarly dispute about the exact date of the Buddha's death. Traditionally he was considered to have been born around 563 BC, but more recent scholarship suggests a somewhat later date. In any event, the narrative of his life and work are widely accepted. Siddhartha Gautama was born in Kapilavastu, at the foot of the mountains of Nepal. His father was a wise and illustrious ruler; his mother, Maya Devi, died a week after his birth, according to legend "that she might not have her heart broken by seeing her son leave home and take to the life of a beggar."

Quiet and reflective, he was brought up for a life of pomp and politics for which he was temperamentally unsuited. His father, fearing his son would renounce the throne for a contem-plative life, attempted to isolate him from all human suffering. He failed. One day, driving in his chariot through the eastern gate of Kapilavastu, Siddhartha was confronted by the sufferings of an old man. Another day, driving through the southern gate, he was confronted by the sufferings of a diseased man. A third time, driving through the western gate, he was confronted by a dead man. Finally, at the northern gate, he passed a monk with a begging bowl. The four sights concentrated his mind; he renounced his princely inheritance and became a monk.

At this time, religion in India was the monopoly of the Brahmin caste, which taught that birth and rebirth were eternal cycles from which there was no escape. Siddhartha rejected their teach-ings and withdrew to the village of Urevela, on the banks of the Nairanjana, where he stayed for six years. There, under a fig tree, he achieved enlightenment, be-

Bust of Gautama Buddha, the Enlightened One

coming the "Buddha," the "Enlightened One," entering into the state of *Nirvana*.

According to the Buddha's teaching, there are four essential noble truths: Everything is suffering; The cause of suffering is desire; The suppression of desire brings about the suppression of suffering; and To suppress suffering you must follow the noble eightfold path: right opinion, intention, speech, action, livelihood, mindfulness, effort, and concentration. The Buddha preached that enlightenment and salvation are not exclusive to the Brahmins, as the latter maintained, but open to all. ❑

CONFUCIAN PRINCIPLES OF SOCIAL ORDER

China, 479 BC

During a period of nationwide discontent and political instability, Confucius, a Chinese civil servant, set out a body of teachings that has been of paramount importance for the development and flourishing of Chinese culture up to the present day. He propounded a doctrine that would guide people on the best way to govern their lives and live together in harmony. His teachings and recommendations for order focused on the individual and his relations to a model of fair and stable government.

Confucius, the Western pronunciation of Kong Fuzi, was born into the lesser nobility. He worked for a time as a civil servant in charge of supervising granaries. It is said that he turned to private teaching after failing to find a single Chinese ruler who would follow his advice on how to institute sound government; he then went on to refine his doctrines even further until his death.

Confucius believed that long ago people lived in a serene age when everyone knew his place in society and carried out the duties that went with it. His doctrines envisaged a return to that time, the principles of which he claimed had been forgotten or obscured over the centuries. At the heart of Confucian teaching is order—the position of everything in its rightful and natural place in the universe. To ensure order it was absolutely vital that those in government stick to their moral obligations toward one other and toward society as a whole. In practical terms, this ideal favors those institutions that are most inclined to lead to the persistence of order, such as the family group and social hierarchy. It requires honesty, integrity, and respect for elders and betters, as well as an unpatronizing fairness toward people in lower social positions.

For those in government Confucius is said to have asked for four qualities in both rulers and administrators: care and respect for records, decency of conduct, loyalty, and faithfulness toward superiors and colleagues. Confucius took a very dim view of naked ambition, because a good administrator who carries out his duties scrupulously can expect to be rewarded without pursuing success. ❑

Confucius

THE DEATH OF HERACLITUS

Asia Minor c.480 BC

Heraclitus, one the most radical pre-Socratic philosophers, died at about 70 years old at Ephesus in Asia Minor. His discourses baffled many of his contemporaries, who nicknamed him "the Obscure." He argued that the universe is governed by the conflict of opposites and that everything is achieved by discord. In his view, the elements are caught up in an endless cycle of transformation. For him, fire, which is constantly changing, is the primordial element.

His conviction that everything is in flux influenced Socrates and Plato. His work survives only in fragments quoted by later writers. ❑

FLOWERING OF GREEK ART

Greece, fifth century BC

Greek artistic values, which decisively influenced much of the development of Western aesthetics, reached new heights at this time. The innovative nature of Greek artistic production is rooted in the outburst of creative energy dating from almost 100 years prior. At that time, advances in architecture changed the face of Greek communities, as seen in Doric temples and the sanctuaries at Delphi and Olympia. Sculptors adapted new subject matter: creating *kouroi* (youths) and *korai* (maidens). At first bulky and

stylized, these figures grew more animated and lifelike. Corinthian ceramics were characterized by floral and animal decorations of oriental inspiration, while Attic potters drew from the rich mythological tradition and also depicted scenes from everyday life.

But with the emerging self-confidence of Greek culture, artists began to display a new realism, particularly in painting. The concern to portray individual faces rather than types signaled a growing self-awareness. ❑

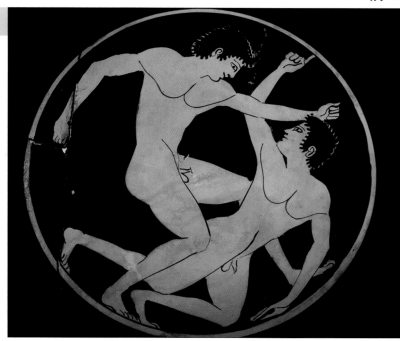

The transition from archaic to classic can be readily seen in vase painting. Left. Painted against a black background red figures are purely ornamental. Above. In the newly emerging classic style the figures have more of an individual character.

GREEKS REPEL PERSIAN INVASION

Greece, 480/479 BC

Thermopylae: After the Persian defeat at Marathon in 490 BC and the death of king Darius, the Persian King Xerxes once again attempted to take possession of the Greek peninsula. The first major engagement took place at the pass of Thermopylae.

King Leonidas, King of Sparta and commander of the Greek forces holding the pass, withstood the attack of the Persian hordes for two days. The contours of the narrow pass and the fighting skill of his men enabled him to repel the enemy with great loss.

On the second day, however, a Greek traitor, Ephialtes, revealed the existence of a mountain path enabling the Persians to take the

Greek general Themistocles

Greeks from behind. When scouts came running with news of Ephialtes' treachery, Leonidas knew that he was doomed. His force was only 4,000 strong, an advance guard designed to hold the Persians until the main force, which was busy with religious celebrations, arrived.

He sent the men from other cities away, keeping with him only the Thebans, whom he mistrusted, and the valiant Thespians, who refused to go. The end was inevitable. The Thebans went over to the Persians, but the Thespians and the Spartans fought to the death.

Salamis: Their heroic resistance, however, gave the Greeks time to regroup and prepare for a decisive naval battle in the Straits of Salamis. Initially, the Greek cities were divided over tactics and strategy, but in the end the Athenian commander, Themistocles, prevailed, and the Greeks sailed out from their anchorages off Salamis to give battle in the main channel. There were 380 Greek ships opposed to some 800 Persian men of war. But the Persians split their forces and, in the confused melee

that ensued, the Athenian triremes with their great prows rammed the Persian ships, sending 200 to the bottom.

The Greeks won the battle as much by cunning as by bravery and seamanship. They tricked the Persians into believing that they had the Greek fleet bottled up in the straits, but when the battle started, it was the Persians who were trapped.

Plataea: Following these reversals, Xerxes withdrew his main force to Asia Minor to protect his line of supply, but left behind a force of 50,000 troops under Mardonius to continue the war. Mardonius ravaged the countryside, setting fire to Athens, and then retreated to Boeotia to force the Greeks to fight in a country in which he could exploit his numerical superiority—the Greeks could field only 39,000 men. Under the command of Spartan, Pausanias, the Greeks met the Persian army outside Plataea and, despite some initial setbacks against the Persian cavalry, inflicted a terrible defeat on the Persians, killing Mardonius. The

Persians, demoralized by the death of their general were overmatched by the phalanxes of heavily armed Greek infantry. Only 3,000 of the Persians survived

The Greeks also won another victory, catching the Persians off guard at Samos where they burnt the Persian fleet and massacred the garrison, thus securing control of the Aegean. ❑

Persian defeat at Salamis

MIGRATIONS CAUSE SOCIAL TENSIONS TO INTENSIFY IN WESTERN EUROPE

Europe, c.450 bc

Rebellions against many Celtic rulers served to usher in a new cultural phase in northern Eu-

La Tène era forge with oven and bellows

rope, typified in the architecture and artifacts of La Tène, beside Lake Neuchâtel, in Switzerland.

Starting with the beginning of the century, the older centers of Celtic power in Burgundy and southern Germany began to lose their importance. Social inequalities and tensions, which self-serving chiefs did little to mitigate, coincided with large growths and movements in population. There were sporadic uprisings. Fortresses like the Heuneburg in Bavaria were overrun, looted, and razed to the ground. Tribes spread into Western France, the British Isles, and Spain. This was

the beginning of a new and more aggressive phase of Celtic culture, based on developing warrior societies whose members launched raids to capture slaves, and who even ventured into Italy and parts of Asia Minor, clashing with Romans and Greeks. Some then ended up as mercenaries in Greek armies.

There were significant regional differences among the Celts, but one unifying factor was religion. They believed in rebirth after death, and worshiped similar gods. The priesthood of the Druids had great power, as educators of the young and with the power to order human sacrifices. Symbols of this emergent civili-

Bronze statuette of a boar

zation can be found at La Tène: long double-edged iron swords and artistic decorations derived from Etruscan, and native sources; fantastic stylized animals are also common, as well as necklaces of solid gold or bronze. ❑

PERICLES RISES TO POWER

Athens, 443 bc

Pericles, the great orator and statesman, lived from about 490 to 429 BC. According to Plutarch, Pericles was the dominant figure in Athenian politics for forty years, which would place his rise to power around 470 BC. He sought to provide an example of citizenship, cultivating an air of frugality and avoiding banquets. In 461 BC, he confirmed his position as the most powerful man in Athens by engineering the ostracism, or exile, of his rival Cimon. He was then able to press for the democratic political reforms initiated by his friend, the murdered Ephialtes.

His ideas extended far beyond domestic reform. It was his intention to make the Athenians fully aware of their power and to use the principle of democracy to bring unity and glory to the city-state.

He had already demonstrated his ability to think beyond the confines of Athens. In 449 BC, he organized a congress of all Greek states to plan the rebuilding of the temples destroyed by the Persians, the establishment of the freedom of the seas, and peace among the states.

Although nothing came of this, Pericles gained much honor and

was subsequently appointed commissioner for the building of the Parthenon. He was an incorruptible official, but his democratic principles won him many enemies among aristocrats. In 444 BC, he was accused of wasting government money in his public works programs. The charge was leveled by Thucydides (not the historian of the same name), the ambitious leader of the conservatives. Pericles passionately defended himself and swayed public opinion. As a result, Thucydides was ostracized, and Pericles continued to rule Athens until his death. ❑

Athenian statesman Pericles

GREEK CITY-STATES IN ALLIANCE TO REBUFF PERSIAN THREAT

Greece, 478 bc

Despite Xerxes' defeats at Plataea and the great sea battle of Salamis, the Persian king still remained a threat to Greece. To defend against the very real possibility of renewed hostilities, Athens took the lead in forming an alliance of Greek cities against their powerful enemy.

Aristides the Just convinced Athens' Ionian allies of the need for these actions. Delos, the small

island home of a religious community, was chosen as the administrative headquarters of the alliance. It was agreed that the congress of this "Delian League" would meet once a year on the island. The alliance was sealed by sinking pieces of iron in the sea to symbolize the fate of those who break oaths.

The first problem to be faced by Aristides was building a joint

navy. It was essential for the league to have a fleet capable of protecting its cities against the Persians. Some of its members, however, were too small to be able to provide the necessary ships and men. In response, Aristides proposed that each member should pay an annual *phoros*, or tribute, to finance a fleet of triremes, with the contribution of each city fixed

according to its means.

The Spartans, believing that the war against Xerxes was over, played no part in the League's affairs. As events unfolded, their typically independent attitude turned out to be a cause of regret, for the Athenians' leadership of the league was a significant factor in their dominant position among Greek city-states. ❑

WAR BETWEEN ATHENS AND SPARTA

Greece, fifth century bc

After successful battles against its Persian invaders, Athens focused on consolidating its power. It became the dominant *polis* (city-state) in the Aegean in a loosely structured empire called the Delian League. Its power was based on the biggest navy in the area, including the 200 triremes built between 483 and 480 BC. This fleet enabled Athens to recover from invasion and win great naval battles against the Persians at Salamis and Mycale.

Although the Delian League was originally a defensive alliance of Greek cities that paid a tribute to Athens mainly to support the navy, over the years the Athenians used it to exert economic and political power over the other city-states, some of which, like Athens, were democracies and others oligarchies. In most of the other cities there were resident Athenians who wielded influence in the local assemblies.

Athens became the judicial capital of the region and its focal point. The Athenian currency was used in all trade in the empire. Thanks to its rich silver mines and the business and craft skills of its citizens, Athens was able to guarantee the grain supply.

Power still resided with old families, and the two main leaders of the period—Pericles and Cimon—stemmed from these established houses. But they depended on the power of their oratorical skills, which won them support in the Assembly, rather than upon any hereditary right to govern.

The rise of Athenian power played out against a backdrop of continued enmity of Sparta. Though treaties resulted in periods of truce, a kind of cold war existed between the two rivals. This broke out into open hostilities in 431 BC when Peloponnesian troops invaded Attica.

The population of Athens swelled with the number of people seeking refuge in the city. But to the general misfortune the invasion under the Spartan king, Archidamus, coincided with the arrival of a devastating plague from Ethiopia, via Egypt and Libya and lands held by the king of Persia. At the start of the war Pericles had gathered the people of Attica behind the defensive walls he had built, allowing the superior Spartan army to ravage the countryside while the Athenian fleet harried the enemy coastline. But Athens now faced an enemy inside the walls.

The disease appeared first in the port of Piraeus. When it reached Athens, the influx of people from the surrounding countryside provided ideal conditions for the spread of the epidemic: people crammed together in badly ventilated huts during the heat of summer.

The historian Thucydides, who caught the disease but survived, described its symptoms: "People in perfect health suddenly began to have burning feelings in the head; their eyes became red and inflamed, there was bleeding from the throat and tongue, their breath became unnatural and fetid. As the disease progressed from chest to stomach, it would cause vomiting and spasms. The skin would break out into pustules and ulcers."

Driven by thirst and heat people plunged into cisterns, which only served to spread the disease. While Spartan troops ravaged Attica, more than a quarter of the population succumbed within the city's boundaries. As despair grew along with the piles of bodies in the streets, citizens resorted to looting, robbery, and sexual abandon. Among the grievous casualties was Pericles, the leader who had urged the city on to war.

The brutal war between Athens and Sparta and their allies devastated Greece. In 429 BC, the city-state of Potidaea was forced to surrender to the besieging Athenians after being reduced to such a state of hunger that its people ended up eating the bod-

The Spartan general Lysander demolishing the walls of Athens.

ies of their dead. The Athenian generals allowed the inhabitants to leave the town without massacring them, but imposed such harsh terms—the men were allowed to take only one garment—that many died in the harsh winter that followed. Even so, the victorious generals were criticized in Athens for not insisting on the unconditional surrender of the city. In truth, the Athenian soldiers were suffering almost as much as the Potidaeans, such was the condition into which the Peloponnesian War had plunged the Greeks. The lion's share of the blame for the war rested on the imperial ambitions of Athens, which led it into conflict with the other Greek city-states.

A truce between the warring parties in 421 BC allowed a return to some semblance of normality and enabled the completion of the temple of Athena Nike, the jewel of the Acropolis, work on which began almost 30 years earlier. But in 414 BC, urged on by Alcibiades, who had always opposed the peace treaty, the Athenians sent an invading fleet against Sparta's ally Syracuse in Sicily. There the Athenian fleet was routed. Finally after years of conflict and political turmoil, in 404 BC the war was brought to an end with the ratification of a general amnesty. But the decades-long hostilities only served to weaken all of the participants and signal the decline of the Greek *polis*. ❑

TEMPLE BUILDINGS ON THE ACROPOLIS

Athens, c.430 BC

Top. Detail of Parthenon. Center. Parthenon Temple complex with the Erechtheum at the right. Bottom. Southern portico of the Erechtheum showing the Porch of the Caryatids.

With the completion of the Erechtheum, the last building in the magnificent complex of temples on the Acropolis towering over their city, Athenians could look up with pride to this symbol of their greatness. The three temples, and the superb entrance structure with its huge Doric columns, required 40 years of labor. It is beyond all question one of the architectural feats of the age.

The whole structure was built as a monument to the recovery of Athens from the devastation of the Persian invasion of 480 BC. Building began in 447 BC on the initiative of Pericles, the aristocratic leader. He diverted some of the funds raised for defense by other Greek cities in the Delian League to finance the undertaking.

He saw it as a massive public works project, providing employment not only for architects, sculptors, and painters, but also for craftsmen and laborers. His critics alleged that it was a vanity and a misuse of the allies' money. He maintained that Athens eaned their support by building up the finest navy in the region.

The Acropolis, which has steep cliffs on three sides, had been a fortress for many years. In the Bronze Age it was topped by a Mycenaean palace. Pericles determined to make it a shrine to the city's patron goddess, Athena, and a showplace for the art of its citizens.

In its final form the complex consisted of four buildings: the Parthenon, the Propylaea, the Erechtheum, and the Temple to Nike. The biggest structure is the Parthenon, flanked on all sides by towering columns of white pentelic marble. It was begun in 447 BC, and the construction took fifteen years to finish. The architects, Ictinus and Callicrates, worked under the supervision of Phidias. The gold and ivory statue of Athena, standing helmeted and armed, was sculpted by Phidias himself. The architrave was dominated by a frieze showing the struggle between the Athenians and the barbarians and symbolizing the triumph of reason over brute force. Other scenes show the capture of Troy and the birth of Athena among the Olympians.

The columns are arranged with a grace and symmetry that can claim to be the finest achievement of the classical period. The statues are a celebration of the human body, male and female, showing a keen attention to anatomy and movement.

The Propylaea, the entrance hall to the Acropolis, was built over a period of six years beginning in 438 BC under the direction of the architect Mnesicles. Its asymmetrical layout is adorned with Ionic and Doric columns.

The Erechtheum, named after the mythical king Erechtheus, was devoted to the veneration of a number of deities including Poseidon, who with his trident, was a guardian of the city. The southern portico is known as the Porch of the Caryatids, with six female forms who function as columns supporting the roof. Work on the Erechtheum began around 421 BC, and it is possible that Mnesicles was responsible for its design as well.

The Temple to Nike, the goddess of victory, was built following the design of Callicrates. Construction started in 430 BC and was completed nine years later. ❑

GREEK COMEDY AND TRAGEDY

Greece, c.425 BC

With the production of *Lysistrata*, in the middle of the Peloponnesian Wars, Greek theater reached new dramatic heights—or, as some contemporaries had it, depths. The play by the comic playwright Aristophanes, describes an imaginary peace movement in which the women of Greece force peace on their warring men by denying them sex. The result is inevitable.

Lysistrata, which concludes with peace breaking out everywhere, was so successful that Cleophon, the leader of the Athenian pro-war party, denounced it as morally offensive and called for Aristophanes' deportation as an alien.

Since the Persian Wars, Athens had become the cultural center of Greece, and it was there that theater reached its full flowering. Theatrical performance was first seen in Greece in the sixth century BC. It stemmed from rituals associated with the cult of Dionysus. Originally it consisted of a chorus and a soloist who would step out and perform songs and dance in the honor of the god. Aeschylus added a second character, and Sophocles a third, which resulted in dialogue and a heightened sense of drama. The chorus acted as commentator on the action of the play and its import. Actors wore masks, each actor playing several parts. Props and scenery were minimal, symbolic rather than used to convey a sense of place or dramatic context; subtle facial expressions and nuances were impossible. Everything depended upon the lines. Drama was serious and tragic, the protagonists pawns of the gods, struggling against the exigencies of fate and necessity.

Tragedy, although gradually divorced from a strictly religous context, still had an elevating purpose. It aimed to provide the audience with the experience of catharsis, which Aristotle defined as the combination of pity and fear.

Euripides, who died in 406 BC and whose life spanned most of the fifth century BC, added a new tone to tragedy, focusing on the passions of men rather than celebrating the greatness of myths. *Iphigenia in Aulis*, in which Agamemnon must choose between the defeat of his army or the death of his daughter, epitomized the new style. In some ways his work humanized Greek drama, though at the cost of sacrificing some of the majestic rigor of his great predecessors.

It was only in the last few decades of the fifth century BC that theater established its reputation for comedy and satire, and this was largely due to Aristophanes. Before Aristophanes, satire, particularly in the hands of his older rival, Cratinus, was a crude matter. Aristophanes, in such plays as *Frogs*, *Birds*, and *Peace*, raised bawdiness to a higher level, giving it a political edge. This made his work very popular with the Athenian public, while earning him the animus of its leaders. ❑

The amphitheater at Epidaurus is the best-preserved theater from ancient Greece.

GREEK PLAYWRIGHTS OF THE GOLDEN AGE

Aeschylus (525/24–456/55 BC).

Extant plays: *The Suppliants, The Persians, The Seven against Thebes, Prometheus Bound, Oresteia*, a trilogy consisting of three works: *Agamemnon, The Choëphoroe* (The Libation Bearers), and *The Eumenides*

Euripides (c.485–406 BC)

Extant plays: *Alcestis* (438 BC); the *Heraclidae, Medea, Hippolytus, Andromache, Hecuba, The Suppliants, Hercules Furens, Electra*, the *Trojan Women, Helena, Ion, Iphigenia in Tauris, The Phoenician Women, Orestes, Iphigenia in Aulis*, and *The Bacchae*

Sophocles (c.496–406 BC)

Extant plays: *Ajax, Antigone, Oedipus Rex, Electra, The Trachiniae, Philoctetes*, and *Oedipus at Colonus*

Aristophanes

Extant plays: *The Acharnians, The Knights, The Clouds, The Wasps, The Peace, The Birds, Lysistrata, The Thesmophoriazusae* or *The Women at Demeter's Festival, The Ecclesiazusae* or *The Women in Politics*, and *Plutus*. ❑

THUCYDIDES AND THE HISTORY OF THE PELOPONNESIAN WAR

Greece, 430 BC

Thucydides was born around 460 BC. He was a devoted follower of the Athenian commander Pericles. As a Greek soldier he revolutionized the annals of warfare by bringing reports from the battlefields of the war between Athens and Sparta, which he labeled "the greatest disturbance in the history of the Greeks."

Thucydides had no doubts about the importance of his work. He said: "It is better evidence than that of the poets, who exaggerate the importance of their themes, or of the prose chroniclers, who are less interested in telling the truth than in catching the attention of their public." His *History of the Peloponnesian War* remains a landmark of military history and unparalleled source for an understanding of the period. ❑

HIPPOCRATES: FOUNDER OF THE SCIENCE OF MEDICINE

Greece, C.420 BC

The teachings of Hippocrates and that of other physicians who adopted his methods transformed the approach to sickness in the city-states of Greece. Hippocrates insisted that disease has natural causes and is not to be explained by divine intervention. His book *On the Sacred Disease* caused a sensation by rejecting the common belief that epilepsy was caused by the gods. Calling the disease sacred, he said, was simply a justification of ignorance. The code of ethics, referred to as the Hippocratic Oath, guides medical practice to this day. It says: "I will use my power to help the sick, according to my ability and judgment, and not for their injury or any evil purpose...Whatever I see or hear in my attendance on the sick, which ought not to be divulged publicly, I will keep secret and tell nobody..." Busts of the great physician show him bearded, with a grave and thoughtful expression. ❑

THE HIPPOCRATIC OATH

"I swear by Apollo Physician and Asclepius and Hygeia and Panacea and all the gods and goddesses, making them my witnesses, that I will fulfill according to my ability and judgment this oath and this covenant. To hold him who has taught me this art as equal to my parents and to live my life in partnership, and if he is in need of money to give him a share of mine, and to regard his offspring as equal to my brother in male lineage and to teach them this art if they desire to learn it without fee and covenant; to give

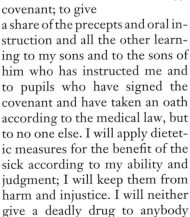

Hippocrates

a share of the precepts and oral instruction and all the other learning to my sons and to the sons of him who has instructed me and to pupils who have signed the covenant and have taken an oath according to the medical law, but to no one else. I will apply dietetic measures for the benefit of the sick according to my ability and judgment; I will keep them from harm and injustice. I will neither give a deadly drug to anybody if asked for it; nor will I make a suggestion to this effect. Similarly I will not give to a woman an abortive remedy. In purity and holiness I will guard my life and my art. I will not use the knife, not even on sufferers from stone, but will withdraw in favor of such men as are engaged in this work. Whatever houses I may visit, I will come for the benefit of the sick, remaining free of all internal injustice, of all mischief and in particular of sexual relation with both female and male persons, be they free or slaves. What I may see or hear in the course of the treatment or even outside the treatment in regard to the life of men, which on no account one must spread abroad, I will keep to myself holding such things shameful to be spoken about. If I fulfill this oath and do not violate it, may it be granted to me to enjoy life and art, being honored with fame among all men for all time to come; if I transgress it and swear falsely, may the opposite of all this be my lot." ❑

GREEK PHILOSOPHY AND PLATO'S ACADEMY

Athens, 385 BC

Greek thought had been undergoing a significant transformation over the two preceding centuries from a worldview based upon mythology to one grounded in the observance of natural phenomenon and rational interpretation.

Plato

rational inquiry and emphasized grammar and rhetoric.

Socrates and his student Plato (427–347 BC) saw human thoughts and actions in relation to a world of eternal ideas. The awareness and contemplation of this world was in their eyes the highest good.

Athens was the center of this new approach. As a dominating sea power in the Mediterranean it became a center for trade and a meeting place for diverse cultures and ideas. The ancient societies of Egypt and Mesopotamia contributed the rich fruits of their mathematical and astronomical observations, which Athenians ordered into a scientific system.

The primary concern of the Greek philosophers was the nature of the universe and man's place within the cosmos. The pre-Socratic thinkers sought to identify the primary element or elements underlying phenomena and arrived at different conclusions. Pythagoras saw numbers, while Heraclitus considered the Logos to be the essence of all things. Empedocles (c.483–424 BC) asserted that existence stems from the interaction of four primal elements: earth, water, fire, and air. Zenon (c.490–430 BC), whom Aristotle claimed was the father of the dialectic method, reduced all phenomena to a tiny indissoluble unitary particle, and Democritus (460–371 BC) developed these ideas into Atomism. This mechanistic and materialistic perspective would underlie much of modern approach to science.

The debate between Socrates and the Sophists centered on human nature. The Sophists held in a famous formulation that "man is the measure of all things." They downplayed the value of

After years of foreign travel, Plato returned to his native Athens to open his own school just outside the city in a garden dedicated to the mythical hero Academus. Plato expressed his philosophical views in lectures that took the form of conversations, or dialogues held between his teacher Socrates and other thinkers and statesmen of his day.

The dialogues discuss such questions as the theory of knowledge, the acquisition of wisdom, the difference between right and wrong, and whether democracy or autocracy is better. Plato argued that ideas have an independent existence and are the archetypes of all concrete things and examined the relationship between the human soul, the state and the universe.

After leaving Athens at the time of Socrates' death, Plato spent some time at the court of Dionysius, the tyrant of Syracuse in Sicily. That experience led him to argue that a just state will only come into existence when philosophers—who comprehend the harmony of the universe—become the rulers and abolish private property and the family, and introduce eugenic mating and an educational system to train each citizen for his place in society. The Academy served as a place where like-minded scholars could develop these ideas. It remained in existence for almost 1,000 years, finally dissolved in AD 529. ❑

THE SOCRATIC METHOD

Athens, 399 BC

Plato's Academy (mosaic, National Archaeological Museum of Naples)

After a controversial trial, the Athenian philosopher Socrates was sentenced to death. The principle charges against him were his refusal to recognize the Gods and claims that he was corrupting Athenian youth. He declined the offer to flee and voluntarily drank the cup of hemlock that was the statutory method of execution.

Socrates' teachings were entirely oral. He left no written works behind. Thus all knowledge of his philosophy and career derive from secondary sources, the most important being the writings of his pupil Plato.

Socrates was born in Athens in 470 BC. His background and

Death of Socrates (Painting by C.A. Dufresnoy)

way of life were modest. Unlike his rivals the sophists, he did not ask to be paid for teaching. The idea that a virtuous life is the product of wisdom, may be seen as the central thesis of his philosophy. He called upon the leading politicians of his time who had the reputation for being wise and questioned them. The effect of his questioning was to bring out the fact that though they thought they were wise they were in fact ignorant, and Socrates, who acknowledged his ignorance, had the advantage.

In time, the Socratic method of getting at the truth by repeated questioning gained him a high reputation among young Athenians, who flocked to his side to study with him. They would then go off and make people contradict themselves as they struggled to answer question after question. Socrates might have been let off with a fine or exile, but he sealed his fate when suggested his sentence should be a pension for life as a reward for helping Athenians to find virtue and wisdom. ❑

GAULS SACK ROME

Rome, 387 BC

The attack on Rome by the Gauls was reckoned by later Roman historians as the blackest day in the city's history. Nonetheless, Rome was able to rebound from its defeat by forging new alliances and instituting a program of military reforms.

The Gauls handed Rome a crushing defeat at the Battle of the Allia and then stormed the largely undefended city destroying most of it. The Gauls had migrated from their original settlements north of the Alps and settled in the northern Po Valley. From there they assembled an army of about 30,000 men and moved south down the Adriatic coast. Their first confrontation with Rome came in 391 BC when they attacked the city of Clusium (Chiusi), an ally of Rome.

Approximately four years later the two armies met by the Allia River in a decisive engagement. Apparently, the Roman army was ill-prepared for the onslaught of their enemy's troops. After this, the road to Rome was open to the invaders. The Gauls met with little resistance. A small band of die-hard troops was able to hold on in a fortified area of the Capitoline, withstanding a long siege. But the rest of the city was razed. In the process the historic records of the city were destroyed, and as a result most of the accounts of events in Rome before the invasion are more legend than history.

The Gauls made the Romans pay dearly for lifting their siege. According to legend the Gauls used falsified weights to measure the booty. When this ploy was discovered their commander retorted, "Vae victis," ("Woe to the losers"). A further legend tells how the squawking of the geese sacred to Juno, which were kept on the Capitoline, alerted the defenders to the danger of a surprise attack.

Aware of Rome's weakened state its allies seized the opportunity to dissolve the bonds that had joined them together. The Latin alliance, which had been gradually built up, broke apart and disappeared.

But as a consequence of its humiliating defeat, Rome took stock of itself and set about making fundamental changes in its defense. The Servian Wall was erected in 380 BC, greatly enhancing the security of the city. In addition a thoroughgoing reform of military tactics was undertaken. Up until this point the Roman army was organized much as the Greek hoplite troops, with the heavily armed infantry in the middle and the poorer and more poorly armed citizens at the flanks. The reorganization called for three categories of infantry. This gave the army much greater flexibility to change formations based upon battle conditions.

To meet the ongoing danger

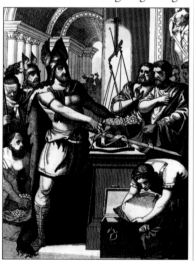

Gauls receiving ransom from Rome

posed by the Gauls, who continued to plunder cities in the middle and south of Italy, Rome renewed its alliances with the Latins in a treaty signed in 358 BC. Ten years later, Rome came to an accord with Carthage that furthered improved its security. Over the next one hundred years, Rome was able to expand its sphere of influence—in part through military means, in part through strategic alliances—to encompass all of central and southern Italy. ❑

GREECE: CRADLE OF THE WESTERN WORLD

The ratification of a general amnesty with Sparta and its allies in 404 BC after thirty years of war, led Athenians to believe that peace would at last prevail. Never had it been more urgently needed. Internal conflicts were tearing at the fabric of the Hellenic world and leaving it vulnerable to foreign domination. Yet, at the same time, its culture gradually conquered the entire Mediterranean.

of many small city-states (*poleis*, singular *polis*) with an urban center, or, as was the case with most of them, a citadel (acropolis) with a sanctuary.

THE EMERGENCE OF THE GREEK CITY-STATES

In Greece the political community was at the same time the ritual community. Besides the awareness of linguistic affinity, all Greeks were united by a common cult that involved

Overpopulation made it necessary to search for suitable places for establishing new settlements outside the territory of the state. Between the eighth and sixth centuries BC, the Greeks founded many cities along the shores of the Mediterranean, in Libya, southern Italy, and Sicily, as well as along the French Mediterranean coast.

Old, aristocratic families were involved in this movement, but the increasing importance

The Parthenon is one of the outstanding marble buildings on the Acropolis in Athens erected during the time of Pericles (5th century BC).

The complexion of the Greek city-states had been formed by various migrations, the geographical composition of the inhabited regions, and the distinctive individualistic character of this highly talented people. The migration that had caused the southward move of the Dorians began after 1000 BC. The fractured landscape of Greece and Asia Minor, with its many valleys open to the sea, together with the numerous islands in the Mediterranean, contributed to the creation

a pantheon of gods ruled by a supreme god, Zeus or his son Apollo.

The relative barrenness of the land meant that most city-states turned to trade, particularly of native products such as wine, olive oil—as well as amphoras for their transport—and later, craft objects. Consequently, they looked toward the sea for outlets. They established close trade relations with the Phoenicians, whose script formed the basis of the Greek alphabet as we know it.

of trade and business led to the emergence of a new class with wealth and influence. There were important changes in military tactics as well. Greek success was a product of heavily armed foot soldiers who provided their own equipment and formed the main part of a closed combat formation, the hoplite phalanx. This formation was much superior to the previous strategy of single combat, because of the power of the joint attack.

Meanwhile, social differences resulted in

the emergence of poor farming and urban classes who were burdened by debts. This in turn led to tensions. These problems could only be resolved by internal reforms, written laws, and the cancellation of debts, ordered from above. The state was not able to achieve all of this everywhere by itself. Where internal conflicts could not be settled, the commonest result was a short-term dictatorship of usually progressive thinking aristocrats, who as "tyrants" removed or ignored these laws.

SPARTA AND ATHENS

Two city-states in particular stood out at this time: Athens and Sparta. It was in the city-state of Athens, which included the whole of Attica covering nearly 1,000 square miles (2,500 km²), that the joint rule of the citizens emerged, settling their interests themselves through the people's assembly and selected officials: a democracy. Sparta, on the other hand, after conquering the fertile region of Messenia and subsequently establishing its supremacy over the Peloponnese in the seventh century BC, had maintained its double kingdom, probably stemming from the period of migrations. However, these two kings were, in fact, important only in wartime, and they were controlled by the people's assembly, the Council of Elders, and the five *ephors* (annually elected magistrates). There were two classes of free citizens without political rights, *perioikoi* and *helots*, who were ruled by a few thousand citizens with full citizenship, *Spartiates*. These citizens with political rights could devote themselves entirely to the craft of war, so Sparta soon possessed the most powerful military force in the Greek world. The battle between the two rivals for hegemony persisted throughout the fifth century.

THE GOLDEN AGE OF ATHENS

The Golden Age of Athens was the result of the important role it played in driving back the Persian advance toward Greece (the Battle of Marathon in 490 BC, and the Battle of Salamis 480 BC), as well as in protecting the freedom of the Greek cities in Asia Minor. During the Persian wars, at the instigation of its leader Themistocles, Athens built a war fleet that remained unbeatable for a long time. In 478/77 BC, Themistocles united most of the Aegean islands under his rule in the Delian League, the members of which supported his naval policy with their contributions.

The fifty years before the outbreak of the Peloponnesian War were a period of cultural renaissance in Athens, particularly after 443 BC under the undisputed political leadership of Pericles. The transfer of the state treasury from Delos to Athens led to a major public works program, including the buildings of the Acropolis, which resulted in a flourishing expansion of the economy. It also led to an intellectual renaissance: Aeschylus, Sophocles, and Euripides took classical tragedy to the heights of perfection, and

The gods Poseidon and Apollo and the goddess Artemis (relief from the frieze on the east side of the Parthenon)

at the same time the ancient literary art of comedy developed with Aristophanes, Eupolis, and Cratinus. Herodotus and Thucydides developed the writing of history, while Hippocrates founded the science of medicine.

THE EMPIRE OF ALEXANDER THE GREAT

Rivalries between the two Greek powers Sparta and Athens led to the Peloponnesian Wars (431–421 BC and 415–404 BC), which ended with the defeat of Athens and the dissolution of the Delian League. In 359 BC, the Macedonian king Philip II came to power. He transformed his kingdom, previously divided into autonomous states, into a strictly ruled, centralized state. While expanding his control over northern Greece and the Aegean, he eventually came into conflict with the Greek states, which he defeated at Chaironeia in 338 BC. He then decided to consolidate his position by organizing a campaign involving all the Greek states under his rule against the increasingly weak Persian Empire. But he was murdered in 336 BC in a palace revolution.

Upon his death, his son and successor Alexander set off for Asia Minor in 334 BC to execute Phillip's plan. Within four years he had conquered the crumbling Persian Empire and by 326 BC, he had extended his power as far as the Indus River, where his troops mutinied when he ordered them to continue farther. He did not have time to realize his plan of merging the Greco-Macedonian elite with the Persian one. When he died in 323 BC, there was no successor able to keep this vast, recently acquired empire together. The generals (the *diadoches*) divided the empire between them. Besides the motherland of Macedonia, the most important parts were the Ptolemaic Empire, which included central Egypt, and that of the Seleucids, which included Syria, Mesopotamia, and Persia itself. In Asia Minor, several smaller states developed, the largest being the kingdom of Pergamon. The Greek city-states constantly formed different alliances but they were never able to shake off Macedonian rule, and they never played an important part in the balance of power again.

HELLENISM AND ROMAN EXPANSION

At the same time, Greek civilization spread inexorably throughout the Mediterranean. Greek became the language of the educated elite. Greek science became established and accepted everywhere. The general "Hellenization" of the Mediterranean also included that of Rome, the new great power in the region that had been expanding since the third century BC. Cultured Romans were educated by Greeks and were fluent in that language as well as their own. Latin became refined, as a language following the Greek example. At the same time, the Hellenization of Rome meant that Roman art came under the influence of Greek art. Combined with local Italic art, this resulted in important creations in the field of painting and the art of mosaic. ❑

THE SEVEN WONDERS OF THE WORLD

Point of Interest

What were the Seven Wonders of the Ancient World? Ancient and medieval writers provided many different answers to the question. A few examples will suffice to indicate the range of possible candidates. Antipater of Sidon compiled a list in the second century before Christ that included the walls of Babylon, which were so wide that a chariot could drive over them. Pliny the Elder considered the hundred-gated city of Thebes as one of the great wonders as well as the entire city of Rome. Five hundred years later, Cassiodorus went further while acknowledging the presence of many of the marvels of antiquity, he wrote that Rome surpassed them all.

Christian authors had different ideas. Gregory the Bishop of Tours (538–594 AD) thought that Noah's Ark and the Temple of Solomon deserved mention in the list. But most of the choices reflect a Hellenistic world view, all being encompassed by the bounds of Alexander's empire.

In the seventeenth century, with the renewed interest in antiquity the topic generated much discussion. Finally in 1721, an Austrian architect, Johann Fischer von Erlach, published what would become the accepted list along with illustrations of what they might have looked like.

Pyramids of Giza. Of all the Seven Wonders of the World the only one still standing is the oldest, the Pyramid of Giza. Lying in the desert near Cairo, it was built between 2650 and 2500 BC as a tomb for the Fourth Dy-

J.B. Fischer von Erlach, *Lighthouse of Pharos* (drawing c. 1700)

nasty Egyptian Pharaoh Khufu. The building blocks were hauled from as far as 500 miles away The placement of stone slabs weighing as much as thirty tons apiece presented awesome engineering challenges. In addition, the proportions of the Pyramid and its orientation demonstrate the penetrating mathematical and astronomical understanding of the builders. By any standard it re-

mains an architectural marvel.

The Hanging Gardens of Babylon. The Babylonian King Nebuchadnezzar II (606–562 BC) set out a lavish garden for his Median wife to evoke the fertile countryside of her homeland. Classical authors report that the gardens occupied approximately two square miles and were adorned with terraces and archways covered with an abundance of vegetation. The gardens were supported by an ingenious irrigation system. In later times, the gardens creation was attributed to the legendary Babylonian queen, Semiramis.

The Mausoleum of Mausolos. Mausolos, the satrap of the Persian province of Caria, ordered the construction of a lasting monument to his memory. The two-story mausoleum rose to a height of 150 feet (45 meters). Built in marble on a stone platform, the construction featured stone warriors mounted on horseback and 36 columns. After the satrap's death, his wife and sister Artemisia completed

the monument. It was leveled to the ground in the sixteenth century.

The Temple of Artemis at Ephesus. Philo of Byzantium called the temple "an immortal heavenly jewel." It was built in 550 BC in honor of the virgin-huntress, Artemis (Diana). Work on it was initiated by Croesus, King of Lydia. It is referred to in the New Testament, where during Paul's visit to Ephesus, the people rioted upon hearing that the temple was to be destroyed. The temple was officially declared closed by the Emperor Theodosius in 391 AD and torn down by a mob led by St. John Chrysostom ten years later.

The Statue of Zeus. The Athenian sculptor Phidias (c.500–423 BC) built a 35-foot high (11 meter) statue of Zeus for the newly built temple to the god in Olympia. Phidias used gold and ivory for the body and constructed his throne from wood. In his right hand Zeus held a figure of Nike, the goddess of victory, in his left a scepter with an eagle, signifying his sovereignty. His head was crowned with a laurel wreath. The fate of the statue is unknown. It may have been sent to Constantinople to be melted down in a bonfire.

The Colossus of Rhodes. For

The Mausoleum of Halicarnassus after a reconstruction and the Colossus of Rhodes (drawing from 1643)

THE PHILOSOPHY OF ARISTOTLE

Athens, 367 BC

Cheops pyramid in Giza (photo. 1880)

only 66 years this gigantic statue of the sun-god Helios overshadowed the harbor of the Island of Rhodes. Rhodes was besieged by Demetrius and an army of 40,000 during the Diadochen wars following the death of Alexander. It was built as a thanksgiving offering to the god after the island's successful defense against the invaders. At a height of 100 feet (32

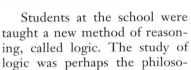

Ruins of the Temple of Artemis.

meters), it was the largest statue built in antiquity. The maquette was constructed from iron and stone, which was then covered in bronze. The building took twelve years. But then it was destroyed in an earthquake in 226 BC.

The Lighthouse of Pharos. The lighthouse rose 350 feet (106 meters) over the harbor of Alexandria. Its light intensified by mirrors was visible as far as twenty miles away. Work on the lighthouse was initiated by Ptolemy I, and it was dedicated by his successor Ptolemy II in 283 BC. ❑

Aristotle was born in 384 BC; his father was physician to King Philip of Macedon. When he was 17, Aristotle came to Athens to study under Plato and remained until Plato's death 20 years later. Many expected him to succeed Plato as head of the Academy. When that did not happen, Aristotle left and became tutor to Alexander, the heir to the Macedonian throne. Upon the death of Philip and Alexander's ascension to power, Aristotle returned to Athens, where he founded the Lyceum, named after the Lyceum park in which it was located.

Students at the school were taught a new method of reasoning, called logic. The study of logic was perhaps the philoso-

Aristotle

pher's greatest contribution to the whole question of human knowledge.

Aristotle introduced his students to the syllogism: All men are mortal (major premise); Socrates is a man (minor premise); therefore Socrates is mortal (conclusion). The syllogism presents in a logical fashion what is necessary in order to prove something.

In every branch of learning on the Lyceum curriculum, Aristotle's teaching rested on close observation of facts. This was especially noticeable in his book *Historia Animalium*, a detailed record of the behavior and habits of animals, earning Aristotle the title of the world's first biologist. "Even in the study of animals unattractive to the senses," he wrote, "the na-

ture that fashioned them offers immeasurable pleasure to those who can learn the causes..."

Aristotle changed the way people think. He divided knowledge into two categories: theoretical and practical. Theoretical knowledge seeks knowledge for its own sake; it includes philosophy, the theory of mathematics, and theoretical chemistry. Practical knowledge deals with such matters as building, politics, and economics.

In addition to his new approach to science, which he believed is properly an investigation of the forms that nature takes, he wrote on metaphysics, ontology, the soul, rhetoric and ethics, which he considered to be, to some extent, part of politics.

For the study of politics Aristotle collected no fewer than 150 different constitutions of Greek city-states in order to discover the best system of government. ❑

THE ELEUSINIAN MYSTERIES

Point of Interest

The Eleusinian Mysteries were the most famous initiatory cult in the Greek world. The cult of the *Mystae* was celebrated in Athens and Eleusis. An elaborate religious festival, the "Greater Eleusinian Mysteries," continued over a period of nine days every September in honor of Demeter, goddess of fertility and resurrection, and her daughter Persephone.

Only the initiated were allowed to attend, but the cult was open to all Greek-speakers, even slaves, regardless of age and gender. The candidates received preliminary instruction during smaller festivals at Agrae at the end of the winter. After their initiation they were sworn to silence.

The principal festival began in Athens and on a beach at

Phaleron, where the *Mystae* sacrificed a pig and bathed in the sea to purify themselves. Then, on the fifth day, they marched in procession to the sanctuary of Demeter and Persephone at Eleusis. It was there, in the Hall of Initiation, that the Eleusinian Mysteries reached their climax.

Details of the rites were shrouded in great secrecy. The priests would mime the legend of Persephone and unveil sacred symbols of fertility.

Demeter had been given refuge in Eleusis after her daughter, Persephone, was abducted by Hades and made queen of the underworld. In return for their hospitality Demeter had given her favorite, Triptolemus, an ear of corn, the symbol of renewed life. Afterward, Zeus intervened with Hades, persuading him to

allow Persephone to visit her mother every summer in Eleusis. The celebrations that marked her return each year were held to symbolize the annual rebirth of the crop. ❑

Aristotle's *Ethics* (illuminated manuscript, 15th century)

THE LIFE OF ALEXANDER THE GREAT

Macedonia, 336 BC

Alexander took over the throne of Macedonia at the age of 20. In spite of his youth, he was already a veteran of warfare and of government. Four years before, while his father, Philip, was on an expedition to Byzantium, Alexander acted as regent of Macedonia and fought his own local war against the Thracian Maedi. His role in the battle of Chaeronea spread his reputation throughout Greece.

Alexander had a rich and complex education. At the age of 13, his father took him to become a pupil of Aristotle. A liberal education with others in residence at Mieza included medicine, geometry, rhetoric, and literature.

In his first few months, the young monarch moved swiftly to put his personal stamp on the Greek Empire. He purged politically unreliable individuals and launched swift punitive expeditions against any regions even hinting at disloyalty. In his absence, however, there was disaffection in Sparta and Athens.

In Thebes, a rebellion broke out, ignited by rumor that Alexander had been killed in action. Thebes promptly split from the Greek federation. After a forced march of 310 miles in 13 days, Alexander stormed the city and systematically destroyed everything except temples and the home of Pindar the poet, who had written poems in praise of one of his ancestors. The city's 8,000 people were sold as slaves and their homeland split into lots that were also sold. Other states tempted to dissent hastily sought the king's pardon.

Alexander then visited Egypt where he established the foundations of a city to be named after him, Alexandria. A great harbor, created by constructing a mole linking the mainland with the island of Pharos, was planned as a naval base for Alexander's war against the Persian Empire. He then launched his campaign into Persia. The Persians had the bigger army, but Alexander had the

better one. The first battle took place at the Granicus River, near the Sea of Marmora. Alexander plunged into the swiftly running waters and with a feigned attack on the Persian left caused the enemy to weaken its center, where the main Greek blow came. It was the first battle of the war in which the phalanx was used. This close formation of long spears behind a wall of overlapping shields devastated the Persian lines.

From Granicus, Alexander went south, liberating the Greek cities of Asia Minor and planning for the following year's campaign, which would begin at Gordium. There he was told of Gordius, the mythical king of Phrygia, whose wagon was fastened to the yoke by a knot that defied all efforts to untie it. An oracle said that whoever untied the knot would rule Asia. Alexander simply cut the Gordian knot with his sword.

Alexander and his army, crossed into western Persia, coming upon the remnants of the once-mighty forces of Darius III. Faced with Alexander's army most of them fled, and when Alexander caught up with the Persian wagons he found Darius in one of them, dead from stab wounds inflicted on the orders of his cousin Bessus. The campaign that had begun three years before, when Alexander crossed into Asia Minor with 30,000 men, was over. He was now master of the Persia and made Susa the capital of his empire. In 325 BC, he returned there after a victorious Indian campaign—his army almost halved in numbers by the toll taken on them by heat, hunger, and thirst on the long march from the Punjab.

Alexander had fought his way across Afghanistan and penetrated the Khyber Pass to descend on to the Punjab plain where he vanquished Porus, the last rajah to have been brought under Persian influence. It was a heroic saga, with Alexander winning battle after battle. He struck through the Hindu Kush into Turkestan, crossed the

Alexander the Great (mosaic first century AD)

Oxus River to reach Samarkand and captured the Scythian chief Oxartes, and married his daughter Roxana.

In his desire to unite his newly conquered empire, he adopted some Persian customs, and as king of the rugged Macedonian tribes he strove to gain acceptance from the cultivated Greeks.

When Alexander came down to Babylon, embassies from all parts of the known world were waiting to pay homage to the conqueror of the east. He was already planning his next great enterprise, the exploration of the seas around his empire.

He devoted himself to overhauling the imperial administration, dismissing officials judged

to be incompetent, and dealing with complaints of corruption. He sought to bind the conquered Persians to his cause by offering satrapies to Persian grandees and recruiting 30,000 Persian youths for his armies. He took the daughter of Darius, as a wife before leaving Susa for Babylon. In Babylon he ordered the construction of an immense fleet, and under his supervision a great basin was excavated in the Euphrates capable of taking 1,000 ships. He wanted to open a maritime route from Babylon to Egypt, around Arabia and later, in the far north of his empire, seek a passage from the Caspian Sea to the Northern Ocean. ❑

Alexander the Great arrives in Babylon (17th century)

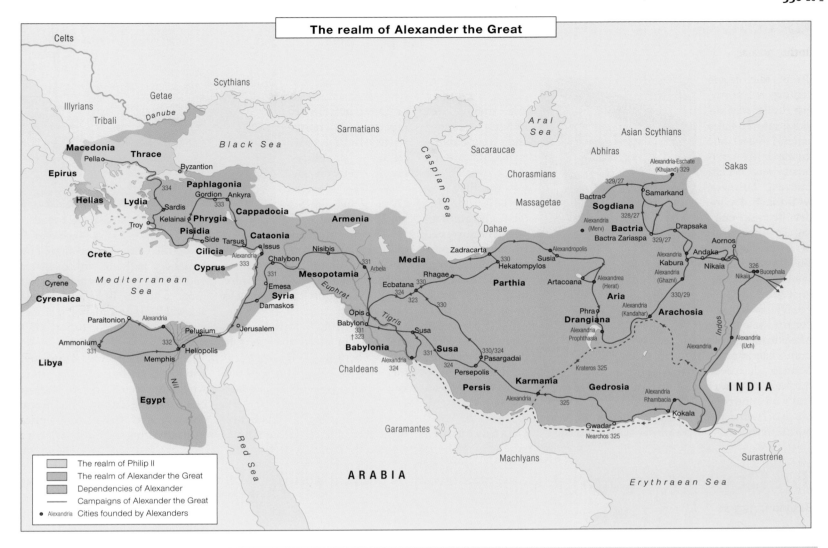

The realm of Alexander the Great

The realm of Philip II
The realm of Alexander the Great
Dependencies of Alexander
Campaigns of Alexander the Great
• Alexandria   Cities founded by Alexanders

PHILIP OF MACEDONIA CREATES A NEW EMPIRE

Greece, 351 BC

During a period of internecine warfare among the Greek city-states, a new power arose in the north. After twenty years at war, Macedonians under Philip II supplanted the Thracian Empire, taking control over lands that stretched from the Danube to the Bosphorus.

Philip then turned his attention to Greece. His first major campaign was the Sacred War, waged for ten years for possession of Greece's oracle at Delphi. It started when the Thebans, who controlled the *Amphictiony*, the multi-state council that administered the shrine, threatened war against the Phocians unless they paid a fine for cultivating sacred ground. The Phocians, who had once had control of Delphi, refused. Then followed a period of cruel, confused

warfare that drew in the ambitious Philip, who saw his opportunity to seize Greek territory.

Athens had already been battling with Philip. The city was able to hold his advance after a long battle in 352 BC to control the strategic Thermopylae Pass. Philip used a temporary peace with Athens to join Thebes in the "Sacred War" against Phocis. Thebes was a hollow victor; the real winner was Philip.

Philip's advance and involvement in Greek affairs drew bitter attacks from the Athenian orator and statesman, Demosthenes, who issued the first of his "Philippics" in 351 BC. Although his arguments often failed—anti-war in 354 BC, and pro-war in 351 BC—he gradually won a reputation for speeches

of powerful logic, withering sarcasm, and use of dialogue that kept his audience enthralled.

From 351 BC onward, his was the one insistent voice warning Athenians, to support cities threatened by Philip, and that war was inevitable. Athens belatedly sent an army to help the Phocians, but to no avail. Philip captured the city and razed it to the ground. Philip had gained a foothold in Greece.

In 341 BC Philip attacked Athens' allies in Thrace. Renewed warfare culminated in his decisive victory over Athens at Chaeronea. The turning point was a cavalry charge, led by Philip's son Alexander.

After this, Athenian leaders accepted peace on terms that effectively ended the traditional in-

dependence of Greek city-states. The war had lasted for 20 years, and the Macedonian "barbarian" proved himself a master of political strategy as well as a military genius. He had used the wiles of diplomacy, marriage, banking, corruption, and sabotage.

In the immediate aftermath of the war, Thebes was occupied by Macedonians. Nominal self-government continued elsewhere, but without autonomy overseas. Most states were required to join Philip's new League of Corinth.

In 336 BC, King Philip II of Macedon died at the hands of an assassin. He was stabbed by a royal bodyguard with a grudge. Philip was succeeded by his son Alexander. ❑

CHANDRAGUPTA AND THE MAURYAN DYNASTY

India, 302 BC

From the fourth century BC, northern India was divided into 16 large states, under one monarch. Government was decentralized, however, with much day-to-day decision-making in the hands of local deputies. Buddhism and Jainism were taking root. The Ganges Valley fell under the sway of the Magadha Kingdom until Chandragupta Maurya destroyed the Nanda Dynasty and won control of much of central and northern India.

East gate of stupa in Sanchi (present-day Madhya Pradesh)

King Chandragupta's reign was notable for military success, and for stability achieved through peace treaties. He was the first man to unite the Indian subcontinent, which he governed from his capital city of Pataliputra with the assistance of a highly developed civil service. This period also witnessed the flowering in India of the great religions of Buddhism and Jainism.

In 305 BC, Chandragupta fought Seleucus Nicator, a former general of Alexander who had remained in northwestern India. A peace treaty established friendly relations between the Mauryan Dynasty and the Seleucid Kingdom.

The magnificence of Pataliputra, capital of the Mauryan Empire, was described by Megasthenes, the ambassador of the *diadochen* king, Seleucus Nicator.

Megasthenes' mission was the result of the peace treaty in 305 BC between Seleucus Nicator, and Chandragupta. The two kings exchanged gifts and ambassadors.

According to Megasthenes, the city extended for ten miles

Indian grave monument (stupa) in Sanchi (c. 150 BC)

along the Ganges, surrounded by a massive palisade with 64 gates and 570 large towers and a broad moat. The magnificent royal palace was built of timber and stone, with richly gilded ornamentation.

Megasthenes was impressed with the organization of the army, which included a large number of elephants. His observations are corroborated by contemporary Indian writings.

THE DEATH OF ALEXANDER AND THE END OF HIS EMPIRE

Babylon, 323 BC

On June 10, 323 BC, Alexander died in the Palace of Nebuchadnezzar of Babylon. The cause of his death is still a matter of dispute. Some have argued that he was poisoned, possibly by the son of his viceroy in Macedonia, Antipater. Others say that he succumbed to malaria, which he contracted some years before. He had spent the previous two nights carousing with friends. Afterward he awoke with a fever, which at first he dismissed as trivial. But soon he became delirious. The palace swarmed with generals, soothsayers, and priests making sacrifices and uttering incantations. Once, during a lucid moment, he was asked who should inherit his empire. His reply: "The strongest man."

One by one the men of his Macedonian army passed through the sick chamber, bidding him farewell. It is said that he recognized each man by name. He died

as the sun was setting on the plain of Babylon. He was 32 years old.

Alexander was a military genius and a man with a vision. He left such an impression on the conquered Persians that they adopted his name, calling members of the royal family Iskander. He was the subject of numerous legendary accounts. He is mentioned in the first Book of the Maccabees, and is identified in the Quran with the figure Dhul-Qamayn. From the middle ages stems a whole cycle of romance poems celebrating his deeds.

The empire that Alexander built did not long survive him. Within twelve years it broke up between his successors, called the *Diadochi*. Soon Alexander's empire was to disintegrate in a welter of bloodshed. In western Asia, the most powerful of the *Diadochi*, Antigonus, assumed for himself the title of king, a move that encouraged others to assert

their own power by doing the same.

In Egypt, Ptolemy declared himself king, as did Seleucus in Babylon and Lysimachus in Asia Minor. In 319 BC, Antipater died and was succeeded by his son Cassander. He attacked and killed Alexander's mother Olympias, who had earlier murdered Alexander's epileptic half-brother Philip Arrhidaeus and his wife Eurydice. He was also responsible for the death of Alexander's widow, Roxana, and his son, who was briefly known as Alexander IV. Intermittent war continued between Antigonus and his rivals. Demetrius, the son of Antigonus, joined his father. He successfully invaded Cyprus but was unable to gain a foothold in Egypt. When Antigonus died in 301 BC at the battle of Ipsus, any realistic hope of reuniting Alexander's empire perished as well. ❑

EUCLID: THE FOUNDER OF GEOMETRY

300 BC

Euclid was a teacher of mathematics in the city of Alexandria. He compiled all of the mathematical rules known at the time and invented important new formulae.

Born in 365 BC, Euclid had his first encounter with philosophy in Athens; he studied at the *Mouseion* in Alexandria, which was founded as a scientific institute in 307 BC. There he was exposed to the great Greek thinkers Pythagoras and Plato. He immersed himself in geometry, optics, astronomy, and music theory. His greatest passion was for mathematics.

His masterwork *Elements*, in thirteen volumes, systematized all of the mathematical knowledge of his time. Volumes 1–4 on plane geometry and volumes 7–10 on number theory were based on the work of the Pythagorean school. Volume 5, which addresses the theory of ratio and proportion, as well as Volume 12 owe much

Even more extraordinary are Megasthenes' observations on life at the court of Seleucus Nicator. He told how the king liked being rubbed with sticks of wood by attendants while hearing cases. His recreations were equally eccentric. He enjoyed hunting from his chariot, surrounded by two or three armed women, in an enclosure with the quarry surrounded by spear carriers—or, in the wild, from the back of an elephant.

Kautilya, Chandragupta's prime minister, wrote a treatise, the *Arthashastra*, describing the Mauryan ideal of government. In 297 BC, Chandragupta abdicated in favor of his son Bindusara. Shortly before his abdication, he converted to Jainism. He withdrew from the world and spent the rest of his life pursuing an ascetic existence. ❏

Euclid: relief from the Cathedral of Florence

to the work of Eudoxus (408–355 BC), a student of Plato. The author of Volumes 10 and 13 on irrational numbers and regular polyhedrons was Theaitetos. *Elements* is the first work that proceeds by deduction from a set of basic axioms and operates according to strict rules of proof. By establishing simple rules, Euclid was able to develop formulae to account for mathematical complexity in a comprehensive fashion. Euclid's two most significant discoveries were his algorithm for finding the greatest common divisor for two rational numbers and his axiom that parallel lines never meet. This is the keystone of his geometric system. His system was the basis of all geometric studies until well into the nineteenth century. ❏

THE PORT OF ADULIS AT THE CENTER OF WORLD TRADE

Ethiopia, 264 BC

The port of Adulis on Ethiopia's Red Sea coast, originally merely a collection of huts, emerged around this time as a center of world trade. Anchored in the harbor were dhows and galleys bringing frankincense and cinnamon from Arabia, silks and spices from India, and manufactured goods from Europe. Rarely a day would go by without a caravan arriving from Kush, carrying wrought iron and gold, or from Ethiopia, carrying timber and ivory.

The opening up of the Red Sea started at the beginning of the third century BC when Ptolemy I of Egypt, interested in securing elephants for his army, established a series of elephant-hunting base camps along the African coast. Equally significant, he built a permanent fleet on Egypt's south coast to protect traders from pirates, and recut the canal linking the Gulf of Suez with the Nile, thus allowing ships to sail directly from the Red Sea to Alexandria and the Mediterranean.

His son, Ptolemy II Philadelphus, continued his father's policies, and under his admiral, Eumenes, his father's elephant-hunting bases were turned into trading and staging posts.

Adulis was the most southerly of these posts. Beyond the Bab el Mandeb, the Red Sea bottleneck where Africa and Arabia almost touch, the Arabian dhows maintained their monopoly of trade with India, Persia, and the rest of Arabia.

It was thus that Adulis, an obscure and godforsaken outpost, became the entrepôt of East and West. ❏

PYRRHIC VICTORIES WON AGAINST ROME

Beneventum, 275 BC

After five years of war, Rome's legions finally held off the superbly trained Greek army of Pyrrhus of Epirus. Following successful—though costly—campaigns on the mainland of Italy and then in Sicily, Pyrrhus returned to help fellow Greeks in their fight against a Rome-Carthage alliance on the Italian mainland. Neither side was a clear victor.

Roman soldiers first faced the tactics of Alexander the Great, including war elephants, when they battled with Pyrrhus' phalanx at the battle of Heraclea, facing elephant charges that scattered their cavalry. The short Roman swords could not cope with the long spears of the Greeks. A total of 7,000 Romans died in that battle. Despite the heavy Roman losses, Pyrrhus' army suffered casualties of more than 4,000 men whom he could ill afford to lose, as he had started his crusade against Rome with an army of 25,000.

Pyrrhus, a relative of Alexander the Great, was invited to lead his army into Italy by the leaders of Tarentum, the Greek city in the south of the country that had won a major sea battle against the Romans and expected massive retaliation. At the same time, Rome was beginning to extend its interests southward with the clear aim of uniting the whole of Italy. The clash became inevitable.

Pyrrhus followed up his victory at Heraclea with a dash to Rome, hoping—in vain—to gain support on the way from other states. It is true his forces were victorious in several engagements with the Romans, particularly at Asculum where rough ground made the going difficult for his phalanx until Pyrrhus could move the fight to level ground. But he could not translate this string of victories into an enduring conquest. Two years later, he led his army into Macedonia and then to the Peloponnesian peninsula, where he died in a street battle, according to legend, from a falling roof tile. ❏

THE FLOURISHING HOPEWELL CULTURE

North America, c.300 BC

Around this time, a tribal migration from the wooded areas in eastern North America gave rise to a highly developed society in the Ohio Valley, that of the Hopewell Culture. The Hopewell people made their living from trade, which was conducted over great distances. They were gifted craftsmen and led lives of luxury as evidenced by their rich burial sites. They were responsible for technical innovations in ceramics and jewelry. They produced tobacco pipes of stone and made use of silver, mica, and obsidian to create a wide variety of other goods. Their religion was also highly developed. Their most impressive legacy was the cult burial mounds of which traces still remain. This first high culture in North America lasted more than 600 years. ❏

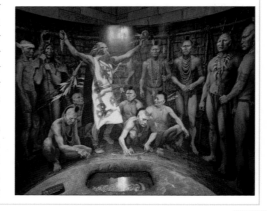

THE BRIEF LIFE OF THE SELEUCID DYNASTY

Asia Minor, 261 BC

Antiochus I, the son of the *Diadochen*, Seleucus Nicator, inherited the Persian part of Alexander's empire.

As Alexander's chief general, Nicator had assumed mastery over Persia in 323 BC when the young conqueror died. During the *Diadochen* wars he emerged victorious at the battle of Corupedium and was able to extend his authority over the greater part of Asia Minor. His attempt to become master of the entire Hellenistic world came to a sudden end with his murder at the hands of a son of his chief rival Ptolemy I.

By the end of his life, Nicator had elevated his son Antiochus to the position of co-ruler for the eastern provinces of his kingdom. As Antiochus assumed sole control he found himself faced with a number of external threats. In Syria, he had to put down a rebellion fomented by Ptolemy II Philadelphus, who had been seeking to expand his reach to the

Black Sea.

The Macedonian King, Antigonus II, was making inroads into Asia and Antiochus was forced to conclude a treaty with him. The combined force of the two kingdoms was needed to stem Celtic invaders that threatened from the north.

Even in Asia Minor itself, Antiochus faced opposition. The city of Pergamon had been handed over to Philetaerus by Nicator. At Nicator's death, Philetaerus took the opportunity to declare Pergamon's independence. This assertion of autonomy within his sphere of influence was unacceptable to Antiochus. In 263 BC, he fought with Pergamon's new king, Eumenes, at the battle of Sardis. Antiochus was defeated. Two years later, he was beaten in renewed fighting with the Celts.

The successors to Antiochus had little more success in bringing peace to the Seleucid Kingdom. Continued conflict with

Ptolemaic Egypt wore down the Seleucids. To unite the vast extent of the lands over which they ruled and their widely different cultures and peoples proved to be an impossible task. Only for a brief period under Antiochus III (Antiochus the Great), who came to power in 223 BC, were the kingdom's boundaries secured and even extended. But in 190 BC,

he was defeated by the Romans. As he sought to plunder a temple in Susa, he was killed by a native Persian. ❑

Head of a statue of Antiochus I (from Nemrut Dag, Turkey)

THE QIN TERRACOTTA ARMY

China, 221 BC

A vast army of terracotta soldiers was arrayed in front of the tomb of the Chinese Emperor Qin Shi

Soldier from Qin terracotta army

Huangdi. They and their animals stood in formation between walls of unexcavated figures, awaiting the command from their dead master.

Qin Shi Huangdi was the first emperor of China. He was known as the First August Lord of Qin. He died, aged 49, in the eleventh year of his reign over the unified empire. He was given a funeral fitting for his accomplishments in a vast tomb beneath a manmade mountain near his capital, Xianyang.

The Emperor conquered the six warring Chinese kingdoms and established a strong central government. He set up 36 new regional territories each ruled by a civilian and a military governor. In order to promote national unity, writing, measures, and even

the wheel width of wagons were regularized.

His state reforms met with resistance from members of the intellectual old guard who recognized that its special position was being threatened. They claimed the support of ancient writings, particularly those of Confucius, for their position. To put an end to their protests, the emperor banned the private possession of books and ordered many books burned. Saved from the fires were works on medicine, fortune telling, and architecture. The leaders of the resistance were either executed or, in a fate to be little more preferred, sent to work on the construction of the Great Wall.

In his tomb, the constellations of the heavens were pic-

tured on the interior of the dome that formed the roof, while the mountains and rivers of China were modeled below. Rich grave goods surrounded the body of the emperor, ready for him to use in the afterlife along with an army of bodyguards.

Recent excavations conducted by the Chinese government have brought to light the incredible artistry that went into the fashioning of this army. It consisted of as many as 7,000 life-sized terracotta soldiers and horses. Each soldier was modeled with care and has distinctive features. The Emperor's guardians were buried in the ground around the tomb; they still seem ready to spring to their master's aid. ❑

ALEXANDRIA: CENTER OF HELLENISTIC CULTURE

Alexandria, 212 BC

The city founded by and named after Alexander the Great was the scientific capital of the Hellenistic world, largely owing to the support and encouragement of Egypt's rulers, the Ptolemy Dynasty, started by one of Alexander's generals, Ptolemy I. His son, Ptolemy II Philadelphus, founded the library as part of the Museum (the *Museion*) of Alexandria.

The Ptolemys made the museum into the leading Greek university, with schools of medicine, mathematics, astronomy, and geography. Scholars from all over the Greek world were attracted to the university and paid by the king. Alexandria's library had no rival in the ancient world. It was reputed to hold 200,000 (some even say 490,000) volumes, although given that each "volume" was, in fact, a papyrus scroll, several of which could have been needed for a

single work, and that there were many duplicates, the true number may be closer to 120,000 titles.

Working under a chief librarian, the library staff carried out an enormous task. New acquisitions arrived continually. All were catalogued as to their origins, former owner and, edition, as well as by author and subject matter. Often they had to be recopied by hand and deviant editions corrected.

The man in charge of the famous library, Eratosthenes of Cyrene, devised a method for measuring the circumference of the earth. He recorded the angle of a shadow cast by a stick at Alexandria on the day of the summer solstice, when there was no shadow at Aswan, about 500 miles (800 km) to the south. Then he divided the figure—7.5 degrees—into 360.

The date and manner of the destruction of the library at Alexandria remains one of the most vexing, unresolved puzzles of antiquity; classicists and historians universally bemoan its loss. ❏

Ptolemy (medallion)

The burning of the Library of Alexandria in 47 BC destroyed an unimaginable store of knowledge.

ASOKA'S RULE OF PEACE AND JUSTICE IN INDIA

India, c.262 BC

Asoka, the grandson of Chandragupta, ascended to the throne of India in 268 BC, becoming the third king of the Mauryan Dynasty. He can lay claim to being the first ruler to extend his government across the entire subcontinent and to providing it with a sense of identity. He was responsible for large-scale building projects in his capital at Pataliputra. His empire, encompassing all of India, was so vast that it was divided into four

provinces, each administered by a prince of the royal blood. Its population, in turn, was divided into seven castes, of which two, the Brahmins and the Kshatriyas, monopolized spiritual and temporal power respectively. Rule was paternalistic, carried out by a centralized bureaucracy.

Shocked by the horrors of the Kalinga war, in which 100,000 were

slain, Asoka converted to Buddhism. He merged spiritual and temporal power, with the goal of establishing a state based on "universal order."

All over India, rocks and stone pillars engraved with Prakrit inscriptions announced his conversion, pledging that he would rule his empire through the principles of "kindness, liberality, truthfulness, and purity

of deed and thought." The philosopher-king practiced what he preached: He founded monasteries, financed irrigation schemes, established a health service, and created a welfare state. In addition, he extended the principle of universal toleration—"the very essence of religion"—to all religions in his kingdom. After his death in 232 BC, the country was thrown into a period of decline, and the Mauryan Dynasty came to an end in 180 BC. ❏

HANNIBAL, SCIPIO, AND THE PUNIC WARS

Carthage, 201 BC

The struggle between Rome and Carthage for dominance of the Mediterranean was fought for much of the second half of the third century BC. Called the First and Second Punic Wars from the Roman name for Phoenicians—the Semite people who had founded the city of Carthage—the first war lasted from 264–241 BC. The arena of battle was Sicily. At that time, part of the island was under Carthaginian control. With the help of the city of Syracuse, Carthage besieged Messana (present-day Messina). Rome was called upon to help and sent troops.

Sea battles ensued. Carthage laid waste to the coast of Italy and in response Rome built up its own fleet, but many of its ships were lost at sea during a storm. Rome rebuilt its navy and then lost two important engagements in 249 BC. Finally in 241 BC, Rome was able defeat its rival in Sicily, and Carthage withdrew. When the two warring nations ceased hostilities, Rome had the upper hand in Sicily, but Carthage under its ruler Hamilcar had seized Spain and declared it a Carthaginian Province.

Following Hamilcar's death, his sons Hasdrubal and Hannibal continued his work of conquest. Hannibal occupied the Spanish city of Sagunto, an ally of Rome, in 218 BC, thus beginning the Second Punic War.

In a brilliant and wholly unanticipated maneuver, Hannibal led an army of 25,000 men with war elephants and horses across the snow-covered Alps and invaded Italy from the north. His army linked up with Gallic allies in the Po Valley and prepared to strike at Rome. Despite Rome's superior army—mobilized and numbering a potential 60,000 men, including allies—Hannibal's surprise move made the second Punic War a much more evenly matched encounter. Historians suggest that Hannibal's ultimate aim was not to take the city of Rome but to negotiate a settlement with Rome on favorable terms.

Rome had relied on its superior sea power to fight off any invasion from Carthage. At the outset of the campaign, Rome prepared squadrons to invade both Carthage and Spain. One of the objectives of the latter attack was the arrest of Hannibal. The Romans, however, had not reckoned with the speed at which the fiery young general could move. Although there was a Roman army stationed in the south of Gaul, he was able to make his way with a veteran army of African horsemen and infantry from Spain across the Rhone to the Alps.

Hannibal's losses were considerable. Thousands were killed by hostile Gauls, more still on the ice-covered passes. However, with his forces replenished with Gauls, the threat Hannibal posed was so serious that Rome abandoned its projected invasion of Carthage and diverted its army northward. In 218/217 BC Hannibal's army beat the Romans at the Ticinus and Trebia Rivers and at Lake Trasimene.

In 216 BC, two years after his brilliant Alpine crossing into Italy, Hannibal's armies inflicted a crushing defeat on the Roman legions. Forty-five thousand Romans lay dead on the fields of the battle of Cannae. Another 20,000 legionaries were captured, and the future of Rome itself seemed in grave doubt as its former allies began to turn on it. Cannae was without a doubt the worst military disaster suffered by Rome until this point.

Blinded by the dust of battle, the Romans were outmaneuvered and outgeneraled, with Hannibal's infantry deliberately retreating in the center to allow the cavalry on the flanks to encircle the Romans.

Rome was so shaken by its defeat that human sacrifices were offered for the first time in living memory. The road to the city lay open to Hannibal's troops, with only two legions blocking the way. But unlooked-for victories in Spain strengthened Roman resolve.

The Roman army under its new commander, Fabius, engaged in a change in tactics, carefully avoiding direct confrontation with the invaders, preferring to harass the enemy until they could be attacked in their winter quarters. With the Romans closing in, Hannibal succeeded in fooling them at nighttime when he tied torches to the horns of a herd of cattle to simulate an army on the move—meanwhile escaping in another direction.

The continuing conflict began to erode the strength of the Carthaginian forces. Though the Carthaginians were victors in a number of small battles they lacked the strength to capture Rome and had little success in peeling away Rome's Italian allies. Finally in 203 BC, Hannibal was recalled by the senate of Carthage, which was facing the

In the Battle of Zama (202 BC) Scipio celebrates his victory over Hannibal (painting, Roman school, 1521)

threat of Roman troops that had landed in Africa. The tide had begun to turn in Rome's favor.

As Hannibal's invasion of Italy was running its course, his brother, Hasdrubal, had been holding off Roman incursions into Spain. The two sides fought to a kind of stalemate, but that changed when Rome gave command of its troops in Spain to Scipio Africanus. The brilliant, young Roman general changed the entire course of the war. At the age of 25, he led a legion behind the lines in Spain and gained the upper hand over what the enemy had called "New Carthage." Hasdrubal was called to reinforce the Carthaginian position in Italy, where he was killed during a terrible defeat in the Battle of the Metaurus, and Scipio proved himself master in Spain, forcing the Carthaginian army to retreat to Africa.

It was Scipio who took the Roman army back to Africa, arriving there in 204 BC. The Romans had learned a great deal from Hannibal—particularly in the use of cavalry—and when the two generals met at Zama, the two armies were equally matched.

For once, Hannibal's elephants—he used 80 in the front line—were of no avail to him. They panicked, scattering their own infantry. Scipio used Hannibal's own cavalry tactics on the flanks, and it was the Carthaginian army that collapsed.

Finally in 201 BC, the once-proud city of Carthage bowed to its Roman victors and accepted terms of surrender. Despite the reverses suffered during Hannibal's early campaign in northern Italy, Rome had triumphed. The great Carthaginian Empire was destined to fade into the dust of the North African desert.

Carthage was forced to surrender almost of all of its fleet and the elephants that made its army such a formidable fighting force. It was required to pay massive

Hannibal

reparations to Rome and could no longer declare war without its prior approval. The terms of the surrender allowed Carthage to retain control of its cities in Africa, together with slaves, herds, flocks, and other property; no Roman garrison would be based in the city.

When these terms were put to the Carthaginians, one senator was about to speak against them when he was pulled from the rostrum by Hannibal.

The responsibility for defeat, he said, was his. The Roman terms were generous. He is reported to have said. "It seems to me amazing that anyone who is a citizen of Carthage should not thank his stars that now we are at their mercy we should receive such leniency." ❑

Scipio Africanus

THE DEATH OF ARCHIMEDES

Sicily, 212 BC

When the Romans took the city of Syracuse from the Carthaginians in the second Punic War, soldiers acting against the express orders of its general Marcus Claudius Marcellus seized and killed the Greek thinker Archimedes. Archimedes was a physicist and engineer and had built, among other things, military apparatus to help defend his home city. To stand up to the might of Rome, Syracuse had allied itself with Hannibal.

The Romans besieged the city for three years, but their efforts were frustrated by the port's bulwarks. Having had the experience of many wars, the lord of the city Hieron II (306–215 BC) and his son Gelon II, who assumed power at his father's death, had built up the city's fortifications. Archimedes' genius contributed to its defense, as he placed his knowledge of physics at its service. He designed catapults and pulley and lever systems that had military applications. By using a surface that reflected the sun's light he was able to set Roman ships on fire. This has been called Archimedes' "death ray."

After their victory over the strategically important city, Rome's way was clear to subdue the rest of the island and make Sicily its province.

Archimedes was responsible for many pioneering inventions and discoveries. He was the son of the astronomer Phidias and was born in Syracuse on the island of Sicily in 287 BC. He then studied mathematics in Alexandria and finally moved back to his home city, where he devoted his energies to the understanding of physical laws and mathematical principles.

His technical innovations

seemed nothing short of miraculous to his contemporaries. His famous remark at the moment of discovery of what became known as Archimedes' Principle of hydrostatics—"Eureka, I have found it!"—has been echoed by scientists and thinkers down through the ages.

Mathematics: One major theoretical breakthrough was his method of arriving at a proof by hypothesizing that a proposition was true and then showing that this would lead to a contradiction. He studied circles, parabolas, and other geometric shapes and devised a method for manipulating very large numbers.

Archimedes' screw: As part of a commission for building a huge boat for the king of Syracuse, the inventor came up with a bailing device that was made from a revolving blade inside a cylinder. Turned by a crank, it transferred water from a lower area to a higher level.

Measurement of weight: Called upon to determine whether the king's crown was made of pure gold or with a mixture of lesser metals without doing damage to the crown, Archimedes discovered the principle of specific weight.

Engineering: Archimedes worked in a number of areas of military engineering. The Claw of Archimedes was a device to be used in naval warfare, consisting of a large crane and hook that could grab a ship, lift it out of the water, and theoretically sink it.

The lever: Though he did not invent the lever, he wrote the first systematic treatise about it. He is quoted as saying: "Give me a place to stand on and I can move the earth." ❑

THE FIRST HAN EMPEROR

China, 200 BC

A man of humble origins, Liu Bang (256–195 BC., consolidated his claim to the imperial throne in China. He named his dynasty the Han after the river that gave its name to the first state he ruled during his rise to power.

That rise was completely unexpected, for when the first emperor, the great First August Lord of Qin died in 210 BC., power passed to his son. But he was weak and fell under the influence of the court eunuch, Zhao Gao, who had designs on the throne.

The tight hold maintained by the first emperor fell away. Differ-ent factions struggled for power. First his son and then the eunuch were assassinated. The shockwaves then spread to the far corners of the empire and the conquered states began to rebel against the oppressive rule of Qin.

From all this turmoil there emerged two main contenders for supreme power. One was an aristocratic general, Xiang Yu, and the other was Liu Bang, a man of humble peasant origins who, nevertheless, was a forceful leader. He found his base of support in rural China, which had been subjected to a crushing burden of taxation.

Liu's cautious approach and careful choice of subordinates brought him victory over Xiang Yu, and he was proclaimed emperor in 202 BC.. At the time, there were those who thought that his humble origins would lead to a relaxation of the harsh laws of Qin, and, indeed, Liu promised that he would repeal those laws.

Upon assuming control, Liu Bang did lighten the tax burden on the peasantry. He set about to restore an economy devastated by years of civil war. In order to do so, he increased taxes on the merchant class and took actions designed to curb what he considered decadent mores. Confucian scholars were welcome at his court, and their moral and social thinking became increasingly influential.

Liu founded a new capital on the Yellow River at Chang'an and continued construction of the Great Wall. Known in China as Gaozu, the emperor's adroit political skills ushered in a golden age for China and the Han Dynasty that he founded lasted almost four hundred years, until AD 220 ❏

ROME FREES GREECE FROM MACEDONIAN RULE

Corinth, 196 BC

Celebrations took place at the Isthmian Games as a decree was issued declaring freedom and autonomy for the Greeks after the defeat of the Macedonians by Rome.

The Roman proconsul, Titus Quinctius Flamininus, was hailed as the country's liberator. He had taken command of the Roman army after his election the previous year, and had led it to a crushing victory over the Macedonians at Cynoscephalae.

This effectively brought an end to the Second Macedonian War, forcing Philip V of Macedon to make peace and promise to stay out of Greece.

The Romans came to the aid of the Greeks after a joint appeal in 201 BC by the city-state of Rhodes and King Attalus of Pergamon. They had themselves declared war on Philip in an effort to halt his conquest of the minor independent states of the Aegean, but with little success.

The Roman army was, at first, poorly disciplined and poorly led. Not all Greeks supported their campaign, and the Macedonians had held their own until the arrival of Flamininus. The victory paved the way for Rome's incorporation of Greece into its growing empire. It became a Roman colony in 148 BC. ❏

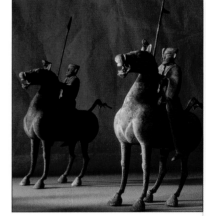

Two riders with spears (Han dynasty)

DEFEAT OF THE SELEUCIDS

Magnesia, 190 BC

In a pitched battle close to Magnesia in Asia Minor, the Roman army defeated the army of the Seleucid King Antiochus III (Antiochus the Great). Six years before, the Roman general Flamininus had proclaimed freedom for Greece after defeating Philip of Macedonia's forces. Rome employed its commitment to the defense of the freedom of Greek cities as justification of its expansionist policies.

Antiochus crossed the Hellespont en route to Europe as Rome sought ways to limit Seleucid ambitions. Up until this point, Antio-chus had experienced nothing but success on the battlefield, winning territories that made the Seleucids the dominant power in the Near East. Following the lead of Alexander the Great, he set his sights on India. In 195 BC, Hannibal fled from Carthage to find a safe haven at his court. In 192 BC, Antiochus entered into an alliance with Aetolia, which had been sparring with Rome. This produced an alliance between nations worried about his increasing might. The unlikely partners were Philip V of Macedonia, Ptolemy V, King Eumenes of Pergamon, and Rome. In the following year, the Roman army drove Antiochus from the Greek mainland at the Battle of Thermopylae and then achieved a decisive victory at Magnesia. Antiochus had to submit to the new order. He yielded control of territories captured in Pergamon; some cities were returned to Rhodes and others freed and entered into the *formula amicorum* (list of friends of Rome). Hannibal, who had taken refuge with Antiochus, was forced to flee, this time to Bithynia where he would meet his death. Roman power and influence was on the rise. ❏

Antiochus III (Seleucid monarch)

BACCHANALIA AND SATURNALIA

Rome, 186 BC

By decree of the senate, secret mystery cults were banned from Rome in the hope of strengthening the official state religion. But despite the senate's action, they continued to attract adherents.

Outrage over Bacchanalian orgies spurred the senate to take energetic action. A purge of the priests and instigators of the cults was decided upon. The decree ordered that cult sites be destroyed. Up to 7,000 people were imprisoned and many sentenced to death. The only exceptions were those cults that had formerly been licensed by Roman officials.

Dionysus (also known as Bacchus) had long been honored in Rome. Numerous pictures and statues of the god testify to his enduring popularity. As early as the fifth century BC, the ancient Italian god wine god Liber had been worshiped. He became identified with the Greek god Dionysus, a son of Zeus. The god overpowered all enemies and promised success to his adherents through the cultivation of vineyards. He was also venerated as a god of fertility. His entourage was composed of nature spirits, such as nymphs and satyrs, and his followers experienced ecstatic states. Through sexual orgies, music, and drunkenness, they sought the condition of *enthusiasmos* (being god-filled). They would meet to enact rituals in the god's honor (the Bacchanalia).

With its popularity on the rise, the cult of Bacchus became a serious rival to the state religion. In the eyes of the authorities, it posed a grave threat to the social order. They condemned the drunkenness, crime, and immorality associated with the celebration of the Bacchanalia.

The origins of these practices remain in question. Whatever their origin, religious festivals were turned into occasions of wine and feasting, with promiscuity between men and women, youths and their elders, accompanied by loud music. Further debaucheries were also alleged, including fraudulent plots, forgeries, and murders of kin.

A different type of festival was the Saturnalia, an officially sponsored celebration in honor of the god Saturn. The Saturnalia began on December 17 and also served to commemorate the founding of the temple of Saturn, the first and oldest temple in the Roman forum. In its joyous mood and relaxation of public strictures, it had much in common with present-day carnival celebrations. All of Rome, even slaves, took part. For as long as the festival lasted, social distinctions were abolished. Slaves were given their freedom; they could eat and drink with their masters and were

Michelangelo, *Bacchus*

even served by them.

Nonetheless, this publicly sanctioned holiday had little power to hinder the spread of mystical cults promising ecstasy and personal spiritual experience. In the years that followed, more mystery religions infiltrated Rome from the Near East. One, Christianity, would in time supplant the veneration of the gods and become the official state religion. ❑

NEW COMEDY IN ROME

Point of Interest

"New Comedy"—a form of entertainment in which live actors performed as gods and mortals in absurd situations—achieved considerable popularity in Rome as practiced by several outstanding writers. The most prolific writer of such comedies was Titus Maccius Plautus. The playwright was notorious for his audacious treatment of once-sacred Greek myths. The pioneer of the genre was Menander (c.342–292 BC), who inspired the writer Terence as well as Plautus. Much of the humor of their works derived from their use of such stock figures as the crafty slave, errant son, cuckolded husband, and motherly whore. Their genius lay in their elaborations of such conventional material.

A fine example of the genre is *Amphitryon* by Plautus'. In the play, a Theban general of that name has gone campaigning with his servant Sosias, leaving their womenfolk, including the general's wife Alcmene, unattended. The gods Jupiter and Mercury (father and son)  adopt the likeness of the absentees. Alcmene shares her bed with her "husband," but the real Amphitryon and Sosias return next day. For Sosias, arriving ahead of his master, the first shock is to be greeted at the door by his double. The plot, laced with song and reed music, involves increasing complications and nonstop action. Unlike his Greek predecessors, Plautus did not like intervals. ❑

THE MACCABEAN REVOLT

Judea, 165 BC

Led by Judas Maccabeus, a priest of the house of Hashmon, the Jews in Judea rebelled against their Seleucid rulers thwarting attempts to turn their holy city, Jerusalem, into a Greek colony. Jewish partisans defeated a large Syrian army under generals Gorgias and Nicanor and rejected all efforts to dedicate their Temple to the Olympian Zeus and suppress the worship of Yahweh.

Maccabeus, whose name in Hebrew means "the Hammerer," was one of the five sons of the priest Mattathias, who had been a major opponent of the Syrian occupiers since 169 BC, when the Seleucid King Antiochus sacked the Temple and began his attempt, spearheaded by the high priest Jason, to impose Hellenism on the Jews. Antiochus displayed utter contempt for Jewish tradition. After plundering the Temple of its treasures and, in 167 BC, installing a garrison in Jerusalem, he systematically desecrated the holy places. Prostitutes set up shop within the Temple precincts, a pig was sacrificed on the altar, and Jews throughout the country suffered wholesale persecution.

Urged on by his father to resist the king, Maccabeus and a few companions gradually built up an army of some 6,000 partisans. A two-year campaign forced Antiochus to give ground, and ended in a victory for the Maccabean party. The Syrians remained in power, but Maccabeus entered Jerusalem in triumph and promised to restore the Temple.

The story of Jewish resistance is told in First and Second Book of Maccabees. Though not part of the Protestant or Hebrew scriptures, they are considered canonical and included in the Catholic Bible. The celebration of Chanukah commemorates an event that occurred after the Seleucid army was driven out of Jerusalem. The Jews found that there was enough oil to keep the light on the altar lit for only one day. According to Jewish law, that light was never to be extinguished. In its account, the Talmud relates that God provided for the oil to last eight days, until new oil could be pressed. For that reason, Jews light one candle of the *menorah* (an eight-branched candelabra) each day for eight days during the celebration of Chanukah. ❑

GREECE LOSES ITS INDEPENDENCE TO ROME

Corinth, 146 BC

Rome's patience with her Greek subordinates came to a savage end with the sacking and destruction of Corinth. The city's male inhabitants were slaughtered; its women, children, and slaves sold; and its masterpieces removed and taken to Rome.

Only fifty years before, Rome had declared itself the champion of the freedom of Greek states. But it soon became clear that freedom meant subordination to Rome's growing power.

The drastic action against Corinth followed years of war between Greek city-states and political unrest. Greece had been allowed to manage its own internal affairs until a pretender tried to seize the Macedonian throne. Rome crushed this uprising, reducing Greece to provincial status. Even so, the Achaean League continued to agitate against the detention of 1,000 deported prisoners and fanned the flames of revolt in Greece. Believing that Rome was fully occupied in Africa and Spain, the Achaeans opposed Roman orders to free Sparta, Corinth, and Argos.

It was when anti-Roman dem-

The destruction of Corinth by Mummius (woodcut, 19th century)

onstrations began in Corinth that Rome acted. The revolt spread quickly to neighboring states. Critolaos, the commanding general of the Achaean League placed himself at the head of the resistance. He is quoted as saying: "The Achaean League hoped to find in Rome a friend, not a master." His battle against the Roman troops resulted in his utter defeat. His successor, Dialos had no better success in stopping the Roman advance. Although a Roman army led by Metellus was held back by Corinthian forces, four legions led by Mummius routed the defenders at the Isthmus and began the systematic destruction of the city.

With the sack of Corinth, Greek pretensions to independence effectively came to an end. But while Rome conquered militarily, Greece achieved its own lasting victory. Rome found itself seduced by the culture of its defeated foe. In 146 BC, Cato the Censor died. He was in many ways the embodiment of Roman virtue. He had campaigned against Greek influence in Roman life, imposed heavy taxes on luxuries, and demanded the destruction of the old enemy Carthage. Of provincial peasant stock, he came to Rome as a young man, fought in the Second Punic War, and held a number of public offices before becoming censor and fiercely defending traditional values in Senate speeches delivered in broad rustic tones. With Cato's death, the most outspoken voice for the preservation of Roman austerity and discipline was silenced.

Meanwhile, Greek culture and customs were making themselves felt in almost all aspects of Roman life. For most Romans, the patrician Scipio family was best known for its military prowess. But Scipio Aemilianus, the heir to the Scipio name, grandson by adoption of the great Scipio Africanus, was an admirer of Greek culture and became the patron of the writer Terence, who won great popularity by presenting

THE ALTAR OF PERGAMON

Pergamon, 160 BC

Pergamon (present-day Bergama in Turkey) under the Hellenistic King Eumenes II, reached levels of artistic magnificence that, in some cases, not even Athens could match. With the decline of Ptolemaic Egypt, it became a cultural capital to rival Alexandria. Among the theaters, palaces, temples, and libraries of the acropolis was its greatest glory, the great altar of Zeus. Construction of the altar began in 180 BC, and lasted for twenty years. This enormous, almost square building was decorated with more than 425 feet (130 meters) of bas-relief frieze, the work of many artists, under the direction of Menecrates of

Rhodes. In honor of Zeus and Athena, patron deities of Pergamon, it commemorated victory over the Gauls by depicting the Olympian gods triumphing over giants representing the forces of barbarism. The altar is now in the Pergamon Museum in Berlin.

The altar is unequivocal testimony of the rise of the city from a provincial backwater to a cultural metropolis. Despite the aggressive moves of its neighbors, the Seleucids and the Ptolemys, Pergamon managed to maintain its independence. When its last king, Attalos III, died in 133 BC, he left his king-

Reconstruction of the great altar of Pergamon (in the Pergamon Museum in Berlin)

dom as a testamentary bequest to the city of Rome. ❑

Greek plays to Latin-speaking audiences in Italy.

Terence was born in North Africa and received a Greek education. Brought to Rome as a slave, he was freed when his talents were discovered. His story was by no means unusual. As Roman power had spread abroad, the greater sophistication of the lands it had conquered began to supplant the city's Republican ethos.

Greek influence went back many years and was reflected in the many Greek words that passed into Latin. Greek deities had also been adopted by the Romans, who would send an embassy to consult the Oracle of Apollo at Delphi in times of danger. But in the aftermath of Rome's conquest, Greek artisans as well as writers settled in Rome, and Greek architecture was widely copied.

Perhaps the most telling observation on Rome's transformation came from the poet Horace, the master of the epigrammatic style: "*Graecia capta ferum victorem cepit.*" "Captive Greece took captive her conqueror." ❑

THE DESTRUCTION OF CARTHAGE

North Africa, 146 BC

In 153 BC, Marcus Porcius Cato, who performed his duties so rigorously that he acquired the permanent surname of "Censor," visited Carthage. Alarmed by the pace of recovery there he made a statement that would foreshadow later events. "*Delenda est Carthago.*" (Carthage must be destroyed.)

Two years later Masinissa, king of Numidia and an ally of Rome, invaded the city of Carthage and achieved a military victory. The invasion had its roots in the king's desire to annex Carthage, before it could regain territory lost in the Second Punic War. Despite Masinissa's victory, the specter of a newly militant Carthage led Rome to intervene, coming down firmly on Numidia's side, triggering the Third Punic War.

Roman troops under the direction of Scipio Aemilianus, whose grandfather had led Rome to victory fifty years be-

Cato the Elder

fore, besieged the city. Despite Scipio's outstanding generalship, the campaign began badly for the Romans. The army was dispirited, lacking experience, and suffered several defeats before Scipio instituted strict discipline and retraining. The move paid off. Scipio's legions captured a strategic fort and began the lengthy blockade of Carthage. A vast mole was built across the harbor to stop supplies arriving by sea. The Carthaginians responded by building a fleet of 50 ships, only to see them smashed by the Roman navy in a bitter battle. The city was doomed, but a defiant Hasdrubal, the Carthaginian leader, refused to surrender his garrison to Scipio's legions. This led to the Roman Senate's order for the sacking and razing of Carthage. A bloody and bitter battle followed. For six days and six

Roman troops take Carthage

nights, the Romans fought from house to house, until the citadel itself capitulated.

Finally the defendrs set fire to the temple of Asclepius they had been occupying, burning themselves to death.

Carthage was utterly destroyed. Every building in this city was flattened, and the ashes of the great citadel were ploughed into the ground. The 50,000 inhabitants—men, women, and children—were sold into slavery. Carthage, once the brightest jewel in North Africa, suffered the full brunt of Roman fury, leaving Rome the undisputed ruler of the Mediterranean. ❑

THE CULT OF VENUS

Rome, C.130 BC

On the Cycladean island of Milo, a sculptor built a statue of Aphrodite out of marble. Aphrodite was venerated in Rome as Venus, the goddess of love. The famous Venus de Milo was not discovered until 1820. It is regarded as one of greatest treasures that has come down to us from antiquity, astonishing viewers with its remarkable beauty. The cult of Aphrodite came from Asia and traveled across different islands until it reached Greece. Places of her worship are found on Cyprus and Cytherea. Aphrodite can be seen as an incarnation of such fertility goddesses, as Inanna, Astarte, and Ishtar. According to Greek mythology, she was the daughter of Zeus. Her name can be interpreted as "risen from the sea foam." She betrayed her husband Hephaestos with Ares the God of War. Out of their union came Eros (Roman Cupid) and his sister Eris (the Goddess of Discord).

Venus was thought to have been the mother of Aeneas, the legendary founder of Rome, having seduced his father, the Trojan lord, Anchises. Aeneas survived the fall of Troy and migrated to Italy with a band of followers. This may explain the high esteem in which the goddess was held in Rome. An official cult was established for her in 295 BC. She was considered to be Rome's *Numina*, the presiding spirit and embodiment of Roman virtues, and took her place among *Spes* (Hope), (Harmony), and *Virtus* (Manliness). After a successful engagement against Hannibal in 217 BC, Fabius Maximus dedicated a temple to her in Rome. It was consecrated two years later. And in the same year, a sacred site was erected in her honor on Mount Eryx in Sicily. The Dictator Sulla (138–78 BC) adopted Venus as his personal guardian. The Delphic Oracle had told him that she would accompany him in battle against Macedonia.

Venus de Milo

Not only Sulla, but also Pompey (106–48 BC) and Julius Caesar (100–44 BC) each presented himself as the direct descendant of the union between Jupiter and Venus. In 48 BC, Caesar dedicated a temple to her, adorned with a magnificent statue by the sculptor Archesilaos. As a sign of his veneration for her, he also had her picture engraved on his personal seal. At his funeral, Caesar's corpse was born aloft in a gilded reproduction of the Venus Temple. Countless statues evidence the high measure of devotion that the goddess inspired throughout the Hellenic-Roman world. ❑

MASSACRE IN ASIA MINOR

Ephesus, 88 BC

In the Kingdom of Pontus in Asia Minor, Mithridates VI strove against Rome's imperial ambitions. He made use of the domestic weakness in Rome to launch a bloody campaign of murderous reprisals. Historians have put the number of Romans murdered at 80,000, which included men, women, children, and even slaves. With this action, Mithridates hoped to send a strong signal discouraging further Roman expansion.

Mithridates emerged during a violent struggle for succession to the crown. It took him twelve years to secure his position. Then he moved against the nearby small principalities, eventually building a kingdom that encompassed the Black Sea. Rome's foothold in Asia Minor was the most serious impediment to his dream of establishing a new Hellenistic empire.

In 89 BC, Mithridates invaded the Roman province of Asia. The Greek residents welcomed him as a liberator. He then proceeded to annihilate its Roman population and seize its property. The bloodbath eliminated Rome's presence in Asia Minor. One half the confiscated goods he divided among his army, the other half went to enrich the royal treasury. Athens took sides with Mithridates. In the war that ensued, Rome, under the Sulla's generalship, defeated Mithridates and drove him from Greece. But it was not until 65 BC, that he was unseated from power by Pompey at the climax of the Third Mithridatic War. ❑

MASSACRE AT EPHESUS

Theodor Mommsen, *The History of Rome*,

From Ephesus king Mithridates issued orders to all the governors and cities dependent on him to put to death on one and the same day all Italians residing within their bounds, whether free or slaves, without distinction of sex or age, and on no account, under severe penalties, to aid any of the proscribed to escape; to cast forth the corpses of the slain as a prey to the birds; to confiscate their property and to hand over one half of it to the murderers, and the other half to the king. The horrible orders were—excepting in a few districts, such as the island of Cos—punctually executed, and eighty, or according to other accounts one hundred and fifty, thousand—if not innocent, at least defenseless—men, women, and children were slaughtered in cold blood in one day in Asia Minor; a fearful execution, in which the good opportunity of getting rid of debts and the Asiatic servile willingness to perform any executioner's office at the bidding of the sultan had at least as much part as the comparatively noble feeling of revenge.

In a political point of view this measure was not only without any rational object—for its financial purpose might have been attained without this bloody edict, and the natives of Asia Minor were not to be driven into warlike zeal even by the consciousness of the most blood-stained guilt—but even opposed to the king's designs, for on the one hand it compelled the Roman senate, so far as it was still capable of energy at all, to an energetic prosecution of the war, and on the other hand it struck at not the Romans merely, but the king's natural allies as well, the non-Roman Italians. This Ephesian massacre was altogether a mere meaningless act of brutally blind revenge, which obtains a false semblance of grandeur simply through the colossal proportions in which the character of sultanic rule was here displayed. ❑

THE NEW ROMAN ARMY

Rome, 107 BC

During the year 113 BC in Gaul, Celtic and Germanic tribes, the Cimbri, the Teutons, and the Ambrones, began migrating to the eastern Alps where they applied increasing pressure on Rome. Recognizing the need to field a greatly expanded army to combat these nomadic warriors, General Gaius Marius, in 107 BC, created a new standing army, which for the first time offered military training to working-class Romans. Traditionally, only landowners were accepted for war service, and then, only while hostilities continued. However, with the threat from the northern provinces and General Marius' recent hard-won victory over the rebellious King Jugurtha in Numidia, North Africa, this military reform, which had been debated in the Roman Senate for over a century, became crucially important to Rome's future defenses.

Critics of this reform had argued that class loyalty and duty to country, the traditional sources of the army's *esprit de corps*, would be corroded and that the loyalty inherent in its aristocratic composition would be replaced by a more mercenary and questionable fealty, one that would result in loyalty to the increasingly empowered generals as opposed to the Roman state itself. However, these fears were palliated

Victorious Germans (woodcut, 1860)

when, despite a resounding defeat in 105 BC by the combined forces of the Cimbri, Teutons, and Ambrones at Arausio (Orange), Marius, and his newly formed army gained a decisive victory over the Teutons and Cimbri at Aquae Sextiae (Aix-en-Provence). ❑

THE GRACCHI AND LAND REFORM

Rome, 133 BC

Armed with the legs of their chairs, Roman senators beat to death the people's tribune Tiberius Sempronius Gracchus (162–133 BC) in the midst of the public assembly. His body, along with those of his murdered followers, was thrown into the Tiber. The unprecedented attack arose out of a dispute over land reform. The conflict was provoked after Gracchus brought forward a proposal that had as its aim a more equitable distribution of farmland in Italy. Gracchus, though serving as tribune, came from one of Rome's noblest families. He was the grandson of Scipio Africanus, who had brought Carthage to its knees in the Second Punic War. He had studied stoic philosophy and had absorbed its concern for justice. As he made his way to Spain, where he was to serve as quaestor, Gracchus saw firsthand the poverty of Italy's farmers. Barbarian slaves were working the fields that free Italians once cultivated.

As a result of its imperial successes, Rome had undergone profound economic changes. Vast amounts of wealth flowed into the city. Roman senators were pro-hibited by law from engaging in business or banking, and such activities were considered somehow beneath the dignity of the patrician class. So a large proportion of this newfound wealth was invested in land. Great estates benefiting from the influx of abundant cheap slave labor swallowed up smaller landholdings. The idealized farmer, exemplified by Cincinnatus, who defended Rome in its hour of need and then returned to his plow, could no longer support himself. In his place sprang up vast estates devoted to producing olive oil and wine for export.

This agrarian upheaval had a deleterious effect on Rome's military. It may well have been this aspect of things that most concerned Gracchus. Roman law stipulated that legionnaires could only be drawn from what were termed *assidui* (those who owned a certain amount of land). The small farmers were the army's backbone, and yet serving soldiers were often the first ones to suffer the loss of their lands. While they were away fighting, their holdings became easy pickings.

Another facet of the problem was the use of public lands. These once played a crucial role in the small farmer's ability to make ends meet. Now they too were falling victim to expanding demands of the major landholders. Gracchus' reforms called for the provision of plots of 18.5 acres to be distributed among the dispossessed farmers and capped at 308 acres, the amount of public land that could be controlled by a single individual.

Not unexpectedly, the tribune's proposal was acclaimed by the bulk of the agrarian population and castigated by the senate and the patrician class. Fearing vengeance if he were to return to private life and abandon the protection afforded by public office, Tiberius Gracchus announced that he would seek a second term as tribune. It was shortly after this announcement that he and 300 of his followers were murdered. The Roman historian Velleius writing two centuries later saw the tribune's bloody end as a turning point in Roman history. "This is the first time that a Roman citizen's blood has been shed in the city of Rome…without fear of punishment. After that law was overwhelmed by force with greater respect given to greater power."

Ten years later, the brother of Tiberius, Gaius Gracchus, took up his brother's struggle. Gaius served as tribune for three successive terms and tried to institute wide-ranging reforms that not only sought to redistribute land, but also extend Roman citizenship to all Italians and ensure that courts allowed to pass capital sentences could only be established by the people. Once again the conservatives gained the upper hand. Frustrated in his designs to bring about change, Gaius took to open rebellion, which was ruthlessly suppressed. His ill-fated attempt ended with his death and that of many of his followers. ❑

Julius Caesar and the Triumvirate

Rome, 60 BC

After Julius Caesar returned from a successful year as governor of Spain, he continued his drive to consolidate power over the Senate oligarchy by securing an alliance with two of Rome's most influential men: Pompey, whose victories in the East over Mithridates of Pontus, Tigranes of Armenia, and Antiochus of Syria, and his capture of Jerusalem, made him the most distinguished and successful Roman military leader; and Crassus, the wealthiest man in Rome. The coalition of these three powerful and ambitious men was to become known as the First Triumvirate and quickly became the dominant power in Roman political, military, and cultural life. Its rise to power represented a symbiotic sharing of power, but one whose undisputed leader was Caesar.

His winning of consular rank and his creation of the powerful triumvirate had been the fruition of years of shrewd political strategy. While Pompey had been campaigning in the East, Caesar had become a champion for the *populares* (the common man), with a series of measures aimed at corrupt members of the Senate. He augmented this populist strategy, while simultaneously winning Pompey's gratitude, by proposing to the Senate a law by which land would be given to the veterans of Pompey's wars. This support was in conjunction with his hectoring the procrastinating Senate with its duty to recognize Pompey's victories by bestowing on him Triumphal honors. He further secured his relation with Pompey by giving him the hand of his daughter, Julia, in marriage. In pursuit of his goals, Caesar had borrowed a considerable amount of money from Crassus, and though in deep debt, was able to finesse an alternative to its payment by including Crassus in this rise to power.

The creation of the triumvirate was a brilliant synthesis of the three men's interconnected ambitions. Caesar wanted to use his position as consul as a stepping stone to extend his influence over Roman political and cultural life, then to assume command of a major province such as Gaul to enhance his military status, and ultimately to assume the role of *pontifex maximus*—the official head of religion. Pompey wanted the Senate to ratify the settlement he made in the East after defeating Mithridates, and to effect the land gifts to his veterans. Crassus, as Caesar's lifelong patron, wanted to use his financial position to gain political and military power equal to his sometime rival, Pompey.

Caesar went on to become consul, and, in 58 BC, achieved his military ambition by winning control of the provinces of Cisalpine and Transalpine Gaul and then commanding the victorious campaign against the Celtic tribe in Gaul known as the Helvetii, as well as defeating the German leader Ariovistus. In 56 BC, the final consolidation of the Triumvirate's power was sealed when the triumvirs met at Lucca, in Etruria, to renew the clauses of their original agreement. They decided that Crassus and Pompey would jointly hold the consulship for the year 55 BC, and that Caesar would maintain his command over Gaul for five more years. Crassus was given control of Syria for five years, and Pompey was made overseer of both of the Roman provinces in Spain. Caesar had created the conditions that would eventually enable him to seize complete control over Rome. ❑

Pompey was murdered in Egypt in 48 BC.

Cicero Exposes the Catiline Conspiracy

Rome, 63 BC

In October of 63 BC, the consul and famed orator, Marcus Tullius Cicero, revealed to the Senate the details of a conspiracy, allegedly devised by Lucius Sergius Catilina (Catiline) to overthrow the Roman Republic. Catiline, scion to one of Rome's most patrician families and former propraetorian governor for Africa, had failed in his bid for a consulship and attributed his loss to what he saw as the aristocratic Senate's political corruption. Cicero, who denied these accusations on behalf of the Senate, relentlessly pursued Catiline and his co-conspirators as unrepentantly traitorous enemies of the Republic. Based partly on information he had received from Catiline's mistress, and from a turncoat deputation of Gallic tribe members, the Allobroges, whom the conspirators had enlisted to support their rebellion, Cicero delivered a vitriolic invective, which would become known as *The First Oration Against Catiline*. Outraged by Cicero's accusations, Catiline announced that he would submit to voluntary exile, leaving Rome to go, purportedly, to Massilia (Marseilles). In fact, he fled to Etruria, where he was to raise a band of mercenaries. Cicero, who in total delivered four such *Catiline Orations*, continued his attack on Catiline in a second speech, this time to the people of Rome. In it, he said of the rebels: "They devote their whole lives and all their waking hours to the vast labor of banqueting. In this herd is found the gambler, the adulterer, and all the filth of Rome."

In December, despite a moving plea for moderation from Julius Caesar, five of the co-conspirators were executed. Catiline himself was at large until January of 62 BC, when he was slain in a

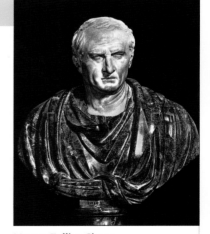

Marcus Tullius Cicero

battle with soldiers of the republican army at Pistoria. His mercenary troops were routed and the conspiracy effectively ended. ❑

THE RISE OF POMPEY AND THE FALL OF SPARTACUS

Rome, 70 BC

In an unmistakable sign of Roman intolerance for any rebellion in the ranks of its burgeoning slave population, 6,000 men, the equivalent of an entire legion, were crucified along the Appian Way after making a break for freedom and war against Rome. It was a grim warning to any slave of a mind to cast off his shackles. This rebellion was different from other such wars in being started and led by one of the servile elite, a Thracian member of the gladiator school at Capua. His name was Spartacus.

A former auxiliary (non-legion) soldier, he took flight two years earlier with ten others and hid in the inactive volcano of Mount Vesuvius. He soon collected an irregular army that scored local victories over official forces. He dominated Campania and Lucania and frightened Rome. In fact, Spartacus wanted to vanish across the Alps, but was overruled by Germans and Gauls in his force who preferred plunder in Italy to farming at home.

With 70,000 men Spartacus defeated Roman armies and bought time to escape to a better life. But he could not elude the brigands in his own ranks and was still in southern Italy when two Roman armies (one landing by sea from Thrace) trapped him. His army, facing two fronts, fragmented. His main force lost three successive battles to the six legions led by Crassus, a soldier politician. During the battle the rebel chief was killed and his "legion" hung like carrion along the Appian Way.

The last chapter of the ill-fated revolt was written by Pompey. On his way back from Spain, where he had served as proconsul, he met with the remaining rebel forces—numbering about 5000—and annihilated them.

Pompey returned to Rome in triumph and immediately thereafter was elected consul for the first time. His rise to power was so swift that, at 36, he was not yet of legal age for the post, neither had he held one of the senatorial positions normally required of a man wishing to become consul.

He owed his success not only to his family connections—his father was consul ten years before—but also to his prowess on the battlefield where he first appeared at the head of three legions raised and equipped from his father's dependents.

He had fought for the dictator Sulla so successfully in Sicily and Africa that Sulla granted him the right to enter Rome in triumph in 81 BC, and gave him the title of Magnus—the Great.

Four years later he helped to drive Sulla's enemy, Lepidus, from Italy and destroyed the army of Sertorius, another of the dictator's rivals, in Spain. He sealed his reputation by mopping up the slaves' revolt.

At this point in his career, Pompey was still an unknown quantity. As consul, he won the support of the lower classes with his populist legislation. After his term of office, he went on to free the Mediterranean from the depredations of pirates. This success followed by military triumphs in the East made him the most highly praised figure in Rome and earned him a place in the triumvirate along with Crassus and Julius Caesar. ❑

Mosaic showing a gladiator scene. In the amphitheaters most of the combatants were slaves.

SULLA: ROMAN DICTATOR

Rome, 88 BC

Lucius Cornelius Sulla's transformation from conservative consul to vengeful dictator began in 88 BC when, at the end of the Social Wars, he was elected consul. His main goals were to promote internal recovery of the republic and defend it against threats from Mithridates of Pontus. He maintained the upper hand over his rival Gaius Marius, who also desired command of the army against Mithridates, by marching on Rome with loyal soldiers and forcing Marius to flee. He consolidated his hold on the republic further by enlisting the support of consul Gnaeus Octavius against the rebellion of Marius' ally, Lucius Cornelius Cinna, whose troops he drove out of Rome. Even after the combined assault on the city of Marius and Cinna and their massacre of a number of aristocrats supporting Sulla, Sulla was able to ultimately claim victory at the Colline Gate, where he defeated all remaining opponents, including Marius' supporters.

His authority now unchallenged, he assumed the role of dictator and launched a reign of terror, wreaking vengeance on remaining enemies and imposing a comprehensively strict discipline on Roman society. He rewarded his soldiers and supporters with land and goods confiscated from his opponents, and proceeded to redefine the constitution to conform to his conservatively aristocratic principles. He increased the power of the Senate, and at the same time took away the tribune's veto power. He also dismantled Marius' inclusively populist military structure, reintroducing a rigidly hierarchical command, predicated on the old class system.

His conservative reign was short lived. In 80 BC, he stunned his supporters and the republic by suddenly resigning his dictatorship, disbanding his army loyalists and reestablishing a consular government. He then ran for and was elected as an ordinary consul. In 78 BC, he retired to his estate at Puteoli. Engaging in a dissipated lifestyle, he died shortly thereafter of liver failure. ❑

CAESAR'S WAR IN GAUL

Gaul, 58 BC

After serving as consul for a year, Julius Caesar was named proconsul and placed in charge of the provinces of South (Cisalpine) Gaul and Narbonensis (present-day Provence). At that point he began his war against the Gallic, Germanic and Celtic tribes. In his multi-volume work, *De bello Gallico* (*The Gallic Wars*), he documents his military campaigns.

Southern Gaul was already under the control of Rome. In 59 BC, the Germanic king Ariovisto led his soldiers across the Rhine to attack Middle Gaul. At this time, Ariovisto still

Battle between Romans and Goths (detail from sarcophagus)

bore the title "Friend of the People of Rome." But at the behest of the tribal leaders of the region, Caesar and his legions came to their aide against the invaders. They met up with Ariovisto's forces in Alsace. Emphasizing Gallic rights and entitlements, Caesar was able to paint himself as the defender of Gaul. In the resulting bloody battle Ariovisto was defeated. With this victory Caesar ensured Rome's lordship over Middle Gaul.

Following the battle, additional tribes entered into the Roman fold, partly out of gratitude and partly out of a desire for the protection Rome provided. Nonetheless, Caesar saw that there was still cause to worry about security. For that reason he renewed the triumvirate with Pompey and Crassus that had been established four years before. In Gaul, he still had to contend with the coastal raids of Venetian pirates and uprisings by the Usipetes and Tencteri. His strategy was a mixture of force and negotiation, which was not applauded by the Senate. However, his successes and the steady stream of booty that he channeled into Rome's coffers silenced his critics.

Caesar could now report that the Rhine was the boundary of the Roman Empire. In a period of ten days in 55 BC, he had a bridge built across it. Gaul still demanded his constant attention. There were more outbreaks from resident tribes in 54/53 BC, in which they joined together to harass Roman garrisons. With 50,000 troops Caesar ruthlessly put down the insurrection. But the resistance was still not broken. One tribe called upon the son of a leader of the Arverni, Vercingetorix. He cleverly was able to unite the resistance under a single banner. Tribes that had been up until that time loyal to Rome broke ranks and went over to his side. But Caesar reinforced his legions, went on the attack and won a decisive victory at the Battle of Alesia. With this capitulation the rebellion in Gaul was effectively brought to an end. Vercingetorix was captured and brought back to Rome where he was displayed as part of the triumph held in Caesar's honor. With his conquest of Gaul complete Caesar was now free to turn his energies to the unfolding political situation in Rome. ❑

ANTONY'S FUNERAL ORATION

From William Shakespeare, *Julius Caesar*

Friends, Romans, countrymen, lend me your ears; I come to bury Caesar, not to praise him. The evil that men do lives after them; The good is oft interred with their bones: So let it be with Caesar. The noble Brutus hath told you Caesar was ambitious: If it were so, it was a grievous fault; And grievously hath Caesar answer'd it. Here, under leave of Brutus and the rest,—For Brutus is an honourable man; So are they all, all honorable men,—Come I to speak in Caesar's funeral. He was my friend, faithful and just to me: But Brutus says he was ambitious; And Brutus is an honourable man. He hath brought many captives home to Rome, Whose ransoms did the general coffers fill: Did this in Caesar seem ambitious? When that the poor have cried, Caesar hath wept: Ambition should be made of sterner stuff: Yet Brutus says he was ambitious; And Brutus is an honourable man. You all did see that on the Lupercal I thrice presented him a kingly crown, Which he did thrice refuse: was this ambition? Yet Brutus says he was ambitious; And, sure, he is an honourable man. I speak not to disprove what Brutus spoke, But here I am to speak what I do know. You all did love him once,— not without cause: What cause withholds you, then, to mourn for him? —O judgment, thou art fled to brutish beasts, And men have lost their reason! — Bear with me; My heart is in the coffin there with Caesar, And I must pause till it come back to me. ❑

CAESAR CROSSES THE RUBICON

Rome, January 11, 49 BC

In what would later be seen as one of history's defining moments, Julius Caesar led his troops across the Rubicon, the stream that divided Italy and Gaul. By so doing he set the stage for a direct confrontation with his erstwhile ally Pompey. In the civil war that followed Caesar would gain mastery over the Roman Empire. With his victory he reaped the benefits of his long hard military campaigns and his clever manipulation of popular sentiment.

Caesar was no stranger to political infighting. In his youth he was targeted by Sulla, because he was the nephew of Marius and son-in-law of Cinna, who had led the resistance to Sulla's dictatorial policies. Although born into a patrician family, he was a populist and stood on the side of the plebes against the *optimates* (the senate's pro-aristocratic faction). On his return from his service as governor in Spain, he formed the first triumvirate with Pompey and Crassus, an informal alliance but one that put most public power in their hands. He was also elected consul for the year 59 BC. At the end of his consular year, he became proconsul for Gaul. The remarkable success of military campaigns extended Roman influence into Britain, pacified the warring Gallic tribes, and secured Rome's boundaries all of which enhanced Caesar's stature,

The death of Caesar

CLEOPATRA

Alexandria, August 12, 30 BC

Cleopatra's dramatic life came to a dramatic end. She and her husband Mark Antony were defeated by Octavian in their struggle for control of the empire. Antony committed suicide, and she killed herself with a snake bite.

Julius Caesar first met Cleopatra in Alexandria in 48 BC, where he had pursued his fleeing rival Pompey.

At this point in time there was a struggle for succession in Egypt following the death of Cleopatra's father Ptolemy XII. Cleopatra gained Caesar's support and with his help deposed her brother the young Ptolemy XIII. Caesar invested her and another of her brothers, Ptolemy XIV with Egypt's crown, thereby guaranteeing the country's loyalty to Rome.

But Caesar had other than political reasons for supporting Cleopatra. He was swept up by her charms. The historian Plutarch tells us that "the sound of her voice made him happy." Cleopatra was a gifted woman. She was well-educated in history, philosophy, and literature, spoke a number of languages and was well-equipped to assume the reins of power in her homeland.

Caesar's reluctance to leave Egypt seems to have provided an occasion for uprisings in the East. In Asia Minor, King Pharnaces of Pontus, tried to take advantage of the situation, invading Colchis and Lesser Armenia.

Caesar left Egypt with his army and easily eliminated the threat. It was on this occasion that he wrote back to Rome: "Veni, vidi, vici." ("I came, I saw, I conquered.") After resolving the situation in Asia, he returned to Rome, where Cleopatra visited him in 46 BC, remaining there until his death. Caesar had a statue of her erected in the Temple of Venus. Whether or not they had a child together is a matter of some dispute. In any event, Cleopatra's son Caesarion was born in Egypt in 47 BC. Upon her return to Egypt she poisoned her brother and set up her son under the name of Ptolemy XV as her co-ruler.

In 41 BC, she entered into an alliance with Mark Antony, who had shared power with Octavian since Caesar's death, and became his lover. In 37 BC, Antony took up residence in Alexandria, and they were married and had four more children. Relations between Octavian and Antony soured, and they met at the Battle of Actium, where

The Egyptian queen Cleopatra VII.

Antony's army was utterly defeated. The couple fled to Egypt only to be followed by Octavian. Hearing the false news that Cleopatra had committed suicide, Antony killed himself. Cleopatra then chose suicide as well, preferring to die by her own hand than be taken captive. ❑

---

but also made him a threat to the political establishment.

Crassus, the third member of triumvirate, had died in a campaign against the Parthians in 53 BC. The senate, led by Pompey, who was now closely allied with the *optimates*, recalled Caesar to Rome as his term of proconsul had ended. It also stipulated that he could not stand for election as consul unless he relinquished control of his army. Caesar rightly saw this as a threat, because as a private citizen he would lose the immunity from prosecution that his office provided him and be liable to various charges that his political enemies were making. Thus for Caesar the civil war was one for political survival.

Upon crossing the Rubicon he was purported to have said: "*Alea jacta est.*" ("The die has been cast.") He set forth to Rome. Within two months his army had overpowered all of Italy and soon after Spain fell under his control as well. In 48 BC, he attacked Epirus where Pompey's general had retreated with his army and won a major victory. Meanwhile, Pompey had taken refuge in Egypt. There he was assassinated by the young king Ptolemy XIII, who thought to curry favor by doing so. Events proved him wrong. Caesar turned away in disgust upon being presented with Pompey's head and he had Ptolemy deposed. It was during this visit to Egypt that Caesar first met Cleopatra, Ptolemy's sister. He installed her as queen of Egypt directly subordinate to Rome. Following this, he marched east where his victory over King Pharnaces of Pontus secured the empire's eastern border.

After his defeat of the remnants of Pompey's army in North Africa and Spain, Caesar returned to Rome where he was made dictator for life. He embarked upon a multifaceted program of reform. He oversaw changes to the calendar that would remain in effect until the adoption of the Gregorian calendar in the sixteenth century. He enacted measures to alleviate the burdens of private debt, made provisions for veterans, and regulated the grain supply. Caesar wrote his will making his great-nephew Octavian his successor.

Even though Caesar had refused the title of king on numerous occasions, resistance grew in the senate at the concentration of power in his hands. Led by his old friend Marcus Junius Brutus, a plot was laid to assassinate Caesar. On the Ides of March (March 15) of 44 BC, Caesar was stabbed to death on the floor of the senate. ❑

After a victorious campaign in Gaul Caesar returned to Rome in triumph.

VIRGIL'S AENEID

Rome, 19 BC

With the completion of his epic poem in twelve books, the *Aeneid*, Virgil created a magnificent myth that was a perfect mirror of Roman pride and ambition in the Augustan age. It also showed how the poet could give patriotic service to his country equally as important as that of soldier or statesman.

The poem, which took him nearly a decade to write, was a radical change from the exaltation of rural virtues of his earlier pastoral poetry and his *Georgics*. Virgil was inspired by the great epic poems of the Greek poet, Homer. His hero, the Trojan Aeneas, was a relative of Hector, an important character in Homer's *Iliad*. Aeneas leaves Troy for long wanderings over the sea, just as Odysseus did in the Odyssey, though for different reasons. In Virgil's poem, Aeneas is near Italy when a storm started by the goddess, Juno, casts him onto the shore of Africa. Venus then puts a spell on him that makes him fall in love with Dido, the queen of Carthage. He tells her the story of the fall of Troy and his wanderings. But Jupiter tells him to get on with his mission of founding a new kingdom. The grief-stricken Dido kills herself when he leaves. After many battles Aeneas arrives in Latium and founds Rome with the help of the Arcadians and Etruscans. ❑

The poet Virgil surrounded by Muses (mosaic from Tunis)

THE CITY OF PETRA

Petra, c.25 BC

From their extraordinary rock-hewn desert city of Petra, located in southwest Jordan, the Nabataeans spread their commercial empire far and wide and maintained their independence against all comers. They grew rich from the caravan trade with southern Arabia.

Petra lies hidden in great folds of mountains. With their wealth, the Nabataeans hollowed caves out of the sides of the ravines and created a whole city in the rock with villas, temples, markets, and tombs. In later times, monks occupied the ruins of the city. The city was discovered at the beginning of the nineteenth century by a Swiss explorer who was ravished by its beauty. It is one of the great marvels of the ancient world. Petra means simply "rock," an apt name for a city hewn from stone. ❑

AUGUSTUS CAESAR AND

Rome, 27 BC

In his last will and testament, Julius Caesar had named Octavian as his beneficiary and with that his successor. Octavian was Caesar's great-nephew and like his adopted father, he was part of the Julian clan that traced its ancestry back to the Goddess Venus and Aeneas, the mythical founder of Rome. He was eighteen years old when Caesar died, but in spite of his young age he had already gained some combat experience. Upon hearing of Caesar's murder he hurried back to Rome.

In Rome, Caesar's friend and supporter Mark Antony saw that his hour had come. Through his exceptional rhetorical skills he succeeded in channeling popular sentiment against those who had carried out the assassination: Marcus Brutus, Gaius Cassius Longinus, and their fellow conspirators. His task was made easier in that Caesar had left a testamentary behest to all of the people of Rome.

Caesar's death brought an abrupt end to his dictatorship but not to the public's desire for a strong leader or to the cult that had been growing up around him. Octavian took advantage of that, appearing before the Roman army as "Gaius Julius Caesar, son of Caesar." With that the name, Octavian became identified with legitimate authority, and the standing of his rival Mark Antony was somewhat diminished. Through clever political maneuvering, Octavian won the support of Cicero and the senate and gained the upper hand. In a confused period of shifting political alliances, he even went so far as to engage him militarily. But their rivalry was set aside to join in the perceived common threat presented by an army raised by Brutus and Cassius. Along with another staunch supporter of the murdered dictator, Marcus Aemilius Lepidus, Octavian and Antony formed the second triumvirate in Rome's his-

ARCHITECTURAL PROGRAMS

27 BC–AD 14

The spreading prosperity and civilizing impulses of the Augustan Age led to the establishment of vibrant urban centers. At the same time, architecture was making great strides. As with other art forms it was brought into the service of Roman politics and ideolo-

Imperial baths in Trier, Germany

gy. Just as Virgil wrote in praise of the founders and by extension the power elite of Rome, so architects reflected the cult of the emperor and Rome's military and political successes. The emperor's cult required temples and associated buildings. Old temples were renovated, new ones built. To bring together large numbers of people, Roman engineers and builders constructed vast halls and theaters, working primarily from Hellenistic models. Stylistic elements from the eastern portion of the empire

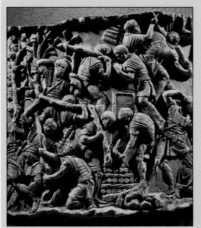

Building a fort (detail from Trajan's column)

THE PAX ROMANA

tory. But this time it was not an unofficial pact; it was recognized and legitimized by the senate, which conferred upon the three leaders a dictatorship of five years' duration.

Together the triumvirs defeated the troops of the conspirators at two battles at Philippi in Macedonia. Their victory was sealed by an agreement of power sharing made at Brundisium. Antony would rule in the eastern part of the Empire, Octavian was given control over the West, and Lepidus, who found himself outmaneuvered, was left with Africa. In 36 BC, Octavian saw to it that Lepidus be removed from power and took over Africa for himself.

In the meantime, Antony had consolidated his power base in the East through his marriage with Cleopatra, Queen of Egypt. In Rome, Octavian was looking for the opportunity to eliminate him as well. Clever use of propaganda and Antony's own excesses rallied senatorial opinion to Octavian. War was declared on Cleopatra's Egypt in 32 bc, and the following year at the Battle of Actium, Octavian handed Antony a crushing defeat. In the aftermath, both Antony and Cleopatra committed suicide. Octavian was now solely in charge of Rome and its empire.

In 27 BC, in a masterfully orchestrated political display, Octavian renounced his position as the remaining triumvir and declared himself ready at the pleasure of the senate to relinquish the provinces of Gaul, Egypt, Syria, and Spain. But he assumed responsibility for the security of their borders. As a gesture of their gratitude, the senate conferred upon him the title of Augustus. In addition as a memorial to his adopted father who had been deified in 42 BC, he assumed the name *Divi Filius* (Son of the God). With his official duty as protector of Rome's borders, Augustus assumed personal control over its legions. He served as consul only until 24 BC. After that he kept for himself only those official powers held by his predecessor combined with the office of Tribune. In this way Augustus maintained the forms and the procedures of the Republic, while consolidating total power within his own hands.

Augustus guided the empire and the people of Rome to new heights of prestige and prosperity. He strengthened the city's power in Gaul and Spain, reorganized provincial governments, and stretched Rome's authority over wide expanses of territory. His goal was to extend the empire's borders to natural easily defended boundaries. He labored to create the remarkable system of roads to bind the empire together and could take credit for establishing the *Pax Romana*, an era of peace in what had been until then a world beset by continuous warfare.

Augustus died in 14 AD—after a period of economic and cultural achievements known as the Augustan Age. His genius for government laid the foundations for the continuation and growth of the Roman Empire. ❑

Augustus Caesar

UNDER AUGUSTUS

can be recognized as well.

As a general rule the Roman home stood on its own. The typical Italian house with a small open court in the middle was extended with a second court used as a garden. In large cities, such as Rome and Ostia, middle-class people and especially the poor had to content themselves with more modest rented lodgings with limited amenities.

These rental properties were as tall as 60 feet high (20 meters) on fairly small pieces of land. One common problem was that the ceilings between the floors were too thin. The houses were crowded together and especially vulnerable to fire.

In the first century BC, arches and domes were added to standard brick and stucco houses that made them more stable and secure. This enabled further developments in large-scale construction. Good examples are the theater in Orange (France), and the theater in Sabratha and the nymphaeum in Leptis Magna (both in present-day Libya). The perfection of the arch is most apparent in the construction of bridges and aqueducts, fine examples of which are still standing. Most impressive are the aqueducts at Pont du Gard near Nimes and in Segovia (Spain) and the bridge over the Tagus River in Spain close to

Pont du Gard, Nîmes, France

the Portuguese border. The best-known example of the Roman use of arches as constituent elements in building is the Colosseum in Rome, which possessed 80 arches when it was built.

During the Augustan Age, major urban centers were founded or expanded throughout the Roman provinces. In Gaul, the capital was Lugundum (Lyons), the residence of the emperors when they were in the province. The city of Augusta Trevorum (Trier) on the banks of the Moselle was founded in 16 BC and would later become the most important city in the Western empire outside of Italy. In Germany, cities sprang up on the sites of legionnaires' camps such as Oppidum Ubiorum (Cologne). In Spain, ancient cities such as Gades (Cadiz) adopted Roman law during this period. ❑

Amphitheater in Pula, Croatia

Shortly before his death in AD 14, Augustus drew up a report that was made public throughout the empire with inscriptions in both Greek and Latin. In it the emperor wrote: "After I put an end to the civil wars, I, who have reached the highest power with the consent of the general public, transferred the state out of my control back to the free rule of the Senate and the Roman people. For this service I have been named Augustus by decision of the Senate... Since then I tower above everyone as regards influence and reputation, but henceforth I do not have any more power than those of my colleagues in my post."

Rome extended its sphere of influence: Roman galleys crossing the Danube (detail from Trajan's column)

These words probably describe the rarest form of dictatorship in history. Although the attempt to institute his autocratic rule had cost the life of Julius Caesar, Augustus's adoptive father, it was nevertheless welcomed by all sides. The golden "Augustan Age" put an end to the state of continual crises that had plagued the Roman Republic for a century. The Roman Empire finally had achieved stability, enabling it to survive for another four centuries.

From City-State to Republic

The city of Rome was an Etruscan settlement that in the mid-sixth century BC consisted of several settlements built on the hills 12 miles (20 km) to the northeast of the Tiber estuary. As part of the Etruscan sphere of influence, the city experienced a remarkable rise that enabled it to develop into a hegemonic power under the Etruscan tribes of the Latins. The city-state ruled over an area of 300 square miles (800 sq km) and was originally governed by kings who toward the end of sixth century BC were driven out by Rome's leading families, the patricians. After many battles and vicissitudes Rome succeeded in establishing its rule over its Latin neighbors and gained control over all of central Italy. With the decisive Roman victory in 290 BC over the Samnites, who had settled near Benevento, it became the leading power in Italy.

The decisive factors in Rome's success were an excellent constitution and the brilliant organization of the army, which was ruled by two consuls who were replaced every year. In times of emergency, one of them could be appointed dictator for a limited period. They were advised and assisted by the heads of the patrician families. By the beginning of the third century BC, conflicts with the general population, the plebeians, led to the more prosperous families of this class acquiring some political privileges. The people's assembly was given the right to participate in political decisions, and tribunes of the people were created to intervene against the decisions of the leading officials if they appeared to be acting unlawfully. The consequent inner stability contributed in turn to Rome's further expansion.

But this territorial expansion led to a confrontation with the second political power in the western Mediterranean basin, the North African merchant city-state of Carthage. The conflict between the two powers flared up suddenly in 264 BC as they both attempted to establish their supremacy over Sicily. The pressure of the First Punic War (264-241 BC) led the Romans to build a fleet that transformed Rome into a leading naval power. The advance of the Carthaginian General Hannibal into Italy unleashed the Second Punic War (218-201 BC), which brought Rome to the verge of complete defeat. But because Carthage lacked the resources to fully project its power onto the Italian peninsula, Hannibal was forced to retreat, and Rome escaped unscathed.

After the final destruction of Carthage in 146 BC, the Romans became drawn into the numerous conflicts among the successor states that had made up the empire of Alexander the Great, and those of the kingdom of Pontus. The Romans became equally involved in the problems of Parthian expansionism. Because the situation became increasingly difficult to control, Greece, Asia Minor, and the coastal regions of the Mediterranean finally became integrated into the Roman Empire or, in effect, subjugated.

Crises in the Republic

But this expansion was not without serious consequences for Rome. Being a city-state, the Republic was not prepared for the administration of such a vast empire. The collection of taxes in the subjugated territories was entrusted to financially powerful citizens who took advantage of the provinces allocated to them. Because of the long war that started in 264 BC, the farmer-soldiers had to leave their land, which became fallow or was seized by rich noble landowners. The reforms of the Gracchi (133-121 BC), whose aim was the distribution of land to the poor, failed. The militia army was turned into a mercenary army by Gaius Marius. But the problem of land distribution remained. Because of these social tensions the equilibrium of the state completely collapsed. Admittedly, Lucius Cornelius Sulla (82-79 BC) succeeded in restoring power to the "nobility," but this failed to provide the fundamental changes needed for the survival of the Republic. Thereafter, policies were determined by people who had close links with the ruling circles, ties with the army, and followers among the people.

Gnaeus Pompeius (Pompey) was the most prominent of these politicians. His successes against the rebellions in Spain, the cleansing of the Mediterranean from piracy, and the reorganization of the Roman rule in the east (64-62 BC) made him one of the most powerful politicians in Rome; he might have ruled Rome without having to occupy the highest office and without infringing the existing constitution. But the Senate's nobility refused to accept this, which led Pompey to form an alliance with the other two important politicians of the time, the financially powerful Marcus Crassus and Gaius Julius Caesar (First Triumvirate, 60 BC). From this position of power, Caesar was eventually able to establish his dictatorship.

FROM CAESAR TO AUGUSTUS

Appointed dictator for life, Julius Caesar was apparently aiming toward royal status. This provoked such fierce opposition in the circles of the Senate that it finally led to his murder. The consequences were further turmoil and civil wars, during which Caesar's adoptive son Octavian and his former commanders Marc Anthony and Lepidus formed the Second Triumvirate in 43 BC. Of the three, Octavian was the most politically astute. After eliminating Lepidus and dividing the empire with Anthony, Octavian then defeated Anthony in the Battle of Actium in 31 BC, thus establishing his dictatorship once and for all.

A PERIOD OF PEACE

Octavian exercised his authority in a circumspect fashion. Because of his reputation he could afford to renounce his special powers in 27 BC and formally restore the old republican constitution. As a result the Senate gave him the honorary title Augustus. In addition he held the military high command (*imperium*) while only acting sporadically as consul. Thus he based his dictatorship as "first citizen" (*princeps*) mainly on his own high standing and that associated with his official authority (*auctoritas*). To establish the Roman peace throughout the empire (*Pax Romana*), Augustus gave the provinces a relative independence that could not be repealed by the Roman provincial governors (legates, proconsuls or procurators). The Julio-Claudian dynasty of which Augustus was a part, ended in 68 BC with the murder of Nero, but a series of capable rulers ensured Rome's peace and prosperity until the middle of the second century AD and the death of Marcus Aurelius. At this point Roman decline set in.

By the third century the circumstances had deteriorated. The state of public finances was desperate. The considerable expenses incurred by the army in defending the empire against the Germanic tribes and the Persians and the lavish lifestyle of the emperors and their courts demanded expanded sources of revenue. In 212, the Emperor Caracalla extended the privileges of Roman citizenship to all residents of the Empire. This meant they could be taxed.

For decades the leadership of the Empire had fallen into the hands of the strongest army commanders (soldier-emperors), who had very little time to consolidate their position. The Emperor Diocletian (284-305) tried to remedy the consequences of this situation. He carried thorough administrative reforms and created the system of tetrarchy, whereby the eastern and western halves of the Empire were each ruled by an Augustus and a subordinate Caesar. This did not prove successful. Constantine the Great (324-337) was able to gather all the reins of power in his hands, but his successors continued to fight among themselves. Constantine did legalize Christianity. In 380, it became the official state religion.

THE SUCCESS OF THE CHURCH

The advance of Christianity in its first centuries was truly breathtaking. During this time the Church was able to cope with heterodoxy and formulate a dogma that is still valid today. Theologians developed an intellectual approach that yielded a bold combination of philosophy and faith.

The most influential early Christian was the Pharisaic Jew Paul. His mission to the gentiles spread Christianity throughout the pagan Mediterranean world and right into Rome. By separating the new religion from Judaism, Paul can lay claim to being the true founder of Christianity.

With remarkable adaptability, the Church adjusted to its environment. But in doing so it had to walk a fine line between preserving its own beliefs while absorbing popular-religious elements from other cults. The religion developed into an orthodox faith through a passionate process that did not remove uncomfortable texts from the Bible or add the theologians' own revelations to the written records. Believers were made to suffer greatly for their faith. Convinced of their redemption, Christians readily accepted the martyrdom to which they were condemned. Later they went as far as to explain that persecution contributed to the spread of the Christian faith.

The distant, self-conscious relationship with the Roman government in the end led—paradoxically—to the alliance between the emperor and Christianity that is most visibly expressed in the state or established Church.

All this could not prevent the decline of the Empire, the capital of which the Emperor Constantine moved to Byzantium (Constantinople). The hostility of the Persians and the surging Germanic tribes made the lasting division between the Western and Eastern Roman Empire necessary in 395. Increasing numbers of Germanic people invaded the empire and, while the Eastern Roman Empire was able to survive because of the more favorable location of its capital, Rome was conquered and plundered in 410 and 455. The Western Roman emperors were forced to watch helplessly. When in 476 the Germanic army commander Odoacer dethroned the last of them, Romulus Augustulus, the ancient Roman Empire with Rome as its center came to an end. ❑

Flute-player (Etruscan fresco, 5th century B.C.)

123

THE LIFE OF JESUS AND THE FOUNDING OF CHRISTIANITY

Palestine, April 7, AD 30

On Golgotha, a hill in front of the city gates of Jerusalem, Jesus of Nazareth was crucified. Found guilty of inciting insurrection, a plaque on the cross read: "INRI" (Jesus of Nazareth, King of the Jews).

Historic sources, above all the New Testament, provide a great deal of information about his religious teachings and mission, but less so regarding the rest of his life. To summarize: Jesus ("God helps") came from a rural region of Palestine. He was born a Jew in the otherwise undistinguished town of Nazareth, probably in the year 4 BC. He grew up within a Jewish community and spoke the language of his country, Aramaic. He took up the trade of his father and learned to become a carpenter. The Gospel of Mark tells us that Jesus had sisters and four brothers: James, Joseph, Judas, and Simon. His mother Mary survived him.

Sometime in year AD 27 , Jesus met John the Baptist, an ascetic preacher who announced that the last days were approaching and called for repentance. Jesus joined with John and was baptized by him in the Jordan River. Upon John's violent death at the hands of the Roman procurator, Herod Antipas, Jesus traveled throughout Galilee. His charismatic preaching drew men and women to him. Following in their master's footsteps, his disciples abandoned their professions and their families to join him in spreading his message through the little towns of Galilee. The town of Capernaum on the west coast of the Sea of Galilee was in all likelihood the center of the Jesus movement at that time.

Jesus preached that the end of time was approaching and enumerated the many signs that foretold the last days, proof of which was his own appearance. In this fashion he partook of the messianic current of thought among the Jewish community of his time

and called upon the Jews to turn back to God, as was written in their scriptures. However, Jesus came into conflict with the Jewish elites over the interpretation of the law, even though like them he taught that the dead would rise again. He criticized the contemporary Jewish scribes and Pharisees (teachers of law) in stark terms charging them with obedience to the law at the expense of the concern they owed to their fellow men. In his eyes this went against God's will. At the same time he spoke of God's universal mercy and compassion. When human relationships were imbued with God's love then the Kingdom of God would be made manifest.

Jesus began to attract attention with these teachings. His entry into Jerusalem caused a great sensation. This was especially true when he chased the money changers off the steps of the Temple where they had been accustomed to do business. Betrayed by Judas, one of his disciples, he was arrested by soldiers of the Temple's high priest and brought before the Sanhedrin—the Jewish court that considered religious questions. The court delivered him over to the Roman authorities. Before a tribunal Jesus was found guilty and sentenced to death. On a Friday, the fifteenth day of the Jewish month of Nisan, he was crucified, following the customary Roman procedure for the punishment of capital crimes.

Upon his death Jesus' disciples first returned to Galilee. His disciple Simon Peter saw Jesus in a vision and reassembled all of the disciples in Jerusalem. Here they founded the first Christian community. Many of his followers testified that Jesus had appeared to them alive and in the flesh. It was their common belief that the appearances were confirmation of his resurrection and triumph over death. They decided to await the *Parousia* (Second Coming) of their Lord

near the Temple. Soon after these appearances the disciples had a common ecstatic experience that is spoken of in the Acts of the Apostles as the descent of the Holy Spirit.

Jesus' disciples, just as their Master, were all Jews and remained closely attached to Jewish practice and customs. But in addition to their desire for reform, the orien-

Matthias Grünewald, *Christ on the Cross*

tation of their beliefs changed. For Jesus the central message was that the Kingdom of God was at hand; his disciples made Jesus as Messiah the cornerstone of their belief. In the eyes of their contemporaries these early Christians were simply another Jewish sect, of which there were several. Under the leadership of three of the disciples, Simon Peter, James, and John, the community grew rapidly. Decisions were at arrived at by consensus; helping the poor, widowed, and orphaned was a primary concern. The rite of baptism assumed particular importance as a ceremony of induction. Prayers were held in common and included wine and food in commemoration of Jesus' last supper with his disciples. The practice of common ownership of goods leveled social distinctions. These practices and the disciples' preaching were direct criticisms of Jewish orthodoxy and led to the first persecution of the new community. Charged with blasphemy by the Jewish assembly, the apostle Stephen was sentenced to death by stoning.

As a result some of the disciples fled to surrounding Hellenistic regions: Phoenicia, Cyprus, and Antioch. Bitter divisions grew

up between them and the original Jerusalem community regarding whether the message should be spread to the gentiles (non-Jewish populations). At an apostolic council held in AD 44 the mission toward non-Jews was more clearly defined. The decision was taken to spread the message of Jesus to "all the nations," laying the groundwork for the worldwide expansion of Christian belief. The principal architect of this missionary work was Saul of Tarsus. Saul was formerly an observant Pharisee who had participated in the persecution of the nascent Christian sect. On his way to Damascus he had a vision of Christ, who spoke to him saying: "Saul, Saul why are you persecuting me?" After this he converted and took the name of Paul. He traveled extensively through Asia Minor and Eastern Europe founding many communities: Corinth, Ephesus, and Galatia among the more important ones. In Athens he defended Christian belief against the questions of the philosophers. His letters to the communities he had established were the first systematic articulation of the theological meaning of the life and death of Jesus. ❑

Roman Defeat in the Teutoburger Forest

Germany, AD 9

German tribes under their general Arminius, leader of the Cheruscis, handed Rome a crushing defeat in wild, trackless land. The bitter engagement fought in swamps and pathless woods lasted for three days and ended in almost total annihilation of three Roman legions. The Roman commander Quinctilius Varus faced with as the magnitude of his defeat committed suicide .

Tiberius, adopted son of Augustus and his chief general, had conquered a wide area of territory in what is now Germany and Austria and established the legionary camp at Augsburg as capital of the new Roman provinces of Raetia and Norica. In AD 7, he handed over control to Varus who was charged with securing the new provinces.

Varus enforced Roman law and raised taxes on the Germanic inhabitants. Resentment toward his program of forced Romanization led to resistance, which coalesced under the banner of Arminius. Arminius had served in the Roman army as commander of an auxiliary troop. Returning to his homeland, he put together an army drawn from a number of Germanic tribes. When negotiations between Varus and Arminius broke down, Varus took three legions and marched from the Weser River in the direction of the Rhine. He sorely underestimated the danger posed by the German enemy, relaxing discipline and security precautions while his troops were on the march. Meanwhile, Arminius had been secretly arming his forces and preparing them for the attack. It was the first time that German tribes had come together in a united effort against the Roman imperium.

They ambushed and trapped the Roman legions, catching them by surprise. After a grim struggle, the Roman army of 25,000 men was almost entirely wiped out. With this defeat Roman aspirations to the territory north of the Danube and east of the Rhine were shattered. For Rome, the most bitter fruit of the calamity was the loss to Arminius of the Eagles, the legion's standards, which were looked upon as sacred. ❑

Monument to Arminius, Germany

The Four Evangelists and the New Testament

Point of Interest

The life and teachings of Jesus of Nazareth have come down to us through the writings of the four Evangelists. Their detailed and often overlapping accounts provide a description unparalleled in antiquity in the multiple perspectives they offer about a single individual. One does need to bear in mind that the four gospel writers, Matthew, Mark, Luke, and John, do not always have the goal of providing a historically accurate portrayal of Jesus' life on earth. Each sees the figure of Jesus through the lens of a cultural and religious environment steeped in the Hebrew scriptures. None of the Evangelists knew Jesus personally. Their writings were based upon oral traditions and earlier written reports that had sprung up around him.

The consensus of scholars is that the Gospel of Mark is the oldest of the four Gospels. It was written around 70 in unadorned but eloquently rendered prose. Mark, who was possibly a Christianized pagan from Syria, concentrates on the events of Jesus' public ministry. It seems clear that in addition to oral traditions, he drew upon more than one written source, which he skillfully redacted. The foundations he laid were built upon by both Matthew and Luke, who combined his account with another source unknown to or not used by Mark. This source is commonly referred to as "Q" (from the German *quelle*, meaning source), a collection of the sayings of Jesus that apparently was already in existence when Mark wrote his account. Among other passages, the Sermon on the Mount (Matthew 5–7; Luke 6) is said to derive from this source.

Matthew puts particular emphasis on Jesus' roots in the Jewish tradition. He uses the text of the Jewish scriptures to show that he was indeed the Son of God, the looked-for Messiah of whom the Jewish prophets had foretold. Because the Jews rejected Jesus' claims, his teachings were to be given to the rest of the world.

Luke described himself as a doctor and an impartial observer. He provided the longest, most detailed and fully thought-out account. We are indebted to Luke for the details of Jesus' birth. He also wrote the Acts of the Apostles, which describes the events that took place after the death of Jesus and the travels of Paul, whom Luke accompanied through Asia Minor, Greece, and finally to Rome. Luke also describes the celebration of Pentecost and the descent of the Holy Spirit, which, after the Ascension of Jesus to heaven, was sent to comfort Christians in the coming time of persecution.

The fourth Gospel, that of John, was written in Asia Minor sometime around the year 100. John is less interested in providing a biographical account. He is more concerned with the meaning of the person of Christ. He begins his Gospel: "In the beginning was the Word, and the Word was with God, and the Word was God."

The Gospels and Acts of the Apostles constitute the historical part of the New Testament. Older than these are Paul's letters as well as other letters by unknown writers. These provide invaluable information on the life and practices of the early Christian communities. Because of strong similarities in their theological viewpoint, the Gospel of John and the Epistles of John are considered the Johannine writings. The last book of the New Testament, the Book of Revelation, is a visionary prophecy of Jesus' Second Coming and the Last Judgment. ❑

Opening page of the Gospel of St. Matthew (Lorscher Gospels, Carolingian school, ninth century)

ROME SUFFERS UNDER DESPOTISM

Rome, 41

In the midst of the Palatine Games a tribune of the Praetorian Guard assassinated the Emperor Caligula (12–41), ending four years of unmitigated horror.

Caligula, whose full name was Gaius Julius Caesar, had come to the throne in 37. His predecessor Tiberius was accused by Roman historians of causing the death of Caligula's father and brothers in order to eliminate them as rivals. Whatever the truth of the charge, Caligula's father Germanicus was the nephew of Tiberius, the son of his deceased brother Drusus, and his adopted son and heir. Germanicus was the Roman general whose main responsibilities lay on the Roman German border. Caligula grew up in army camps and was a favorite among the soldiers, who gave him the nickname Caligula, which means "little boots."

Upon the death of Tiberius, Caligula was elevated to the emperor's throne through the support of the Praetorian Guard. At the beginning of his reign he enjoyed wide popularity, in part due to a general amnesty offered to those imprisoned by Tiberius for political reasons. However, in a very short time he turned into a willful tyrant whose cruelty was unrestrained. It is possible that he suffered from some kind of psychological derangement. In any event, from that time forth his rule was one of unbridled indulgence and megalomania. He quickly exhausted the accumulated wealth of his predecessor on extravagant displays and self-aggrandizing projects. To rid himself of those around him he perceived as unreliable he reinstituted trials for treason. These had a financial benefit as well, since he could then claim the estates of those condemned as property of the emperor. Extortion and executions were the order of the day. He considered himself a godlike being, similar to the ancient Egyptian pharaohs. His wild excesses bankrupted the Roman treasury and did great harm to Rome's foreign and domestic standing. The climate of terror he created with his unpredictable, wanton cruelty finally provoked Cassius Chaerea, captain of the Praetorians—the group that had brought him to power—to assassinate the young emperor.

Caligula was succeeded by his uncle Claudius (12–54). Claudius was denigrated by the Roman historians, such as Tacitus and Suetonius. They describe him as a complete novice in political affairs and a man of weak character, who suffered from some sort of speech impediment. Certainly for a member of the imperial family—Augustus was his great-uncle—he was pointedly passed over for positions of authority. However, he was a devoted scholar, historian, and an able administrator with a great command of detail. He increased the number of officials surrounding the emperor and enlarged their powers, transforming the imperial office from one based upon a cult of personality into a political office. With the help of a talented and well-organized bureaucratic staff, he was able to achieve a great deal during his tenure. He expanded the boundaries of the empire to include Britain, Mauretania, and Thrace, and his general Corbulo led a successful campaign against the Frisians. Claudius was particularly known for his devotion to traditional forms of piety and to Greek language and literature.

Claudius was, however, not as adroit in his choice of women. The promiscuous behavior of his third wife Messalina damaged the reputation of the imperial house. Her numerous affairs, lascivious displays, and general extravagance almost precipitated a crisis of state. The final straw was the marriage ceremony she conducted with her lover Gaius Silius while her husband was away from Rome. Having been informed of this reckless provocation, Claudius had the pair of lovers condemned and put to death. In 49, he married his niece, Agrippina the Younger, despite the warnings of her guardian. Agrippina had one son by an earlier marriage, Lucius Domitius Ahenobarbus (known as Nero), and successfully contrived that he become Claudius' successor in the place of Claudius' own son Britannicus, who was still a child. Roman historians are almost unanimous in charging Agrippina with the murder of her husband.

Nero (37–68) was fated to be the last relation of Augustus to rule as emperor. He was brought up under the tutelage of the philosopher Seneca. With his help he was able to distance himself from

The Apotheosis of Claudius

his mother, who had hoped to be the power behind the throne. Eventually he exiled her and finally had her murdered. Seneca served to some extent as a moderating influence on the emperor, but he was accused of treason and committed suicide, leaving his place to Tigellinus, prefect of the Praetorian Guard. It was at about this time that Nero's despotic tendencies came into full bloom. Nero presented himself to the people as a great artist and patron of the arts. He shocked traditional Roman morals by having the presumption to perform as a singer and musician in public. In 64, Rome was devastated by a terrible fire, and the suspicion for starting it fell on the emperor himself.

Nero persecuted the fledgling Christian sect and subjected its adherents to cruel tortures and punishments. He was devoted to public games and to secure the money needed for his lavish expenditures, condemned senators and confiscated their estates. When a conspiracy led by Piso was discovered; all of the participants paid with their lives. Opposition to the emperor only grew stronger. Nero's response was travel to Greece where he gave further command performances. On his return to Rome, realizing that power was slipping from his hands and that even the Praetorian Guard had turned against him, he retired to his villa, where he committed suicide. ❑

Sir Lawrence Alma-Tadema, *Assassination of Caligula*, 1871

ROME IN FLAMES

Rome, 64

On the night of July 18–19 in the year 64, a fire broke out in the Circus Maximus and quickly spread through the rest of the city. For three days the city burned; in its narrow streets the fire quickly leaped from one wooden rooftop to the next. Citizens fled the city in panic. Of Rome's fourteen districts only four were spared from the fire's destructive path. Hundreds of houses, including the emperor's palace, were burned to the ground. Many thousands of people became homeless. The Emperor Nero hurried back from Antium, where he was staying, to oversee the recovery efforts. He took measures to stop general plundering and prevent famine and the spread of disease. After the conflagration was extinguished Nero planned for the rebuilding of the city. He designed wider streets and new construction was made from stone instead of wood. For himself he designed a new magnificent dwelling called the *Domus Aurea* (Golden House).

It was rumored that Nero had set the fire himself so that he could rebuild Rome on a grander scale. Others said that while the city was in flames he played his lyre and sang of the fall of Troy.

Johann Styka, *Nero Looks on as Rome Burns,* c. 1890

To allay those suspicions and calm the public, Nero accused the fledgling Christian sect of arson. This was the beginning of the persecutions of Christians in Rome. ❏

PETER AND PAUL DIE AS MARTYRS

Rome, 64 (or 67)

After two years of imprisonment, Paul was executed in Rome; shortly after, Peter met the same fate. Their deaths marked the end of the first generation of Jesus' followers. Nonetheless, the missionary groundwork they laid prepared the way for the rapid spread of the new Christian religion.

Peter, the disciple of Jesus, was murdered in the aftermath of the

Crucifixion of St. Peter (15th century fresco)

persecution in Rome instigated by Nero. His last days—just as those of his fellow Christian, Paul—are undocumented outside of the New Testament.

The Evangelist Luke reports in the Acts of the Apostles that Paul continued to do missionary work during his imprisonment in Rome. His arrival in Rome was highly anticipated by Christian "brothers" who met him on the Appian Way. He was allowed to live in private quarters under the supervision of a Roman guard. Members of the Jewish community were permitted to visit him, and he converted some of them to the new religion. The historical evidence goes only so far as to confirm that he died in Rome after having lived there under house arrest for the duration of his trial. Other less reliable sources assert that Paul traveled to Spain.

The circumstances surrounding Peter's death are also unclear. Christian writers have painted a picture of these circumstances that corresponds to his high position within the ranks of the disciples. Peter, whose original name was Simon, was born in Bethsaida, was married, and was a fisherman on the Sea of Galilee. According to the account in the Gospels, Jesus called him along with his brother Andrew and gave him the name Peter ("Rock"). They report that Peter was the first of the disciples to recognize Jesus as the Messiah. In response to this Jesus said: "On this rock will I build my church." These words form the basis for the primacy of the Bishop of Rome and the legitimization of papal authority. Despite this Peter is described as being poor in faith. Matthew reports Peter was able to follow Jesus in walking on water, but then became afraid and would have drowned if Jesus had not saved him. Afterward, Jesus reproved him for his lack of faith. Then during the trial of Jesus, Peter denied his association with Jesus, as his Master had predicted, three times before the cock's crow.

In the First Epistle to the Corinthians, Paul says that upon his resurrection Jesus appeared first to Peter. With the disciples James and John, Peter founded the Jerusalem Church, the first Christian community. He lent his support to Paul's efforts to spread the message of Christianity to the gentiles and was the first to baptize a non-Jew. Later, however, Paul criticized him for wavering in his faith.

Peter was thrown into prison during the first persecution of the followers of Jesus by Herod Agrippa. Somehow he was able to make his way to Rome. The early church historian Eusebius of Caesarea (263–339) states that he was martyred according to his own wish on a cross turned upside down.

The fate of the remains of both Peter and Paul is unclear. Archaeologists dispute the location of Peter's grave. Although the Vatican maintains that St. Peter's Basilica was built over his gravesite, conclusive proof for this claim is lacking. But their heads are held to rest in St. John's Lateran Basilica, the oldest church in Rome. There are suggestions that Christians stole the bones of the saints and deposited them in catacombs and that they were taken from there on the occasion of the erection of a basilica during the reign of the Emperor Constantine. ❏

THE DESTRUCTION OF POMPEII

Pompeii, 79

The eruption of Mount Vesuvius is customarily thought to have occurred on August 24, 79. Its violent activity lasted more than 19 hours, and its volcanic tephra dispersed over a cubic mile. The town of Pompeii was buried under ten feet of ash and rock. The eruption utterly destroyed Pompeii as well as other surrounding communities; the most significant of these was the town of Herculaneum. The population of Pompeii has been estimated to have been between ten to twenty-five thousand, and that of Herculaneum, five thousand. All inhabitants of these towns are believed to

events from a ship in the harbor. In a letter written to the historian Tacitus, he describes the horror of the scene: "...on Mount Vesuvius broad sheets of fire and leaping flames blazed at several points, their

The bodies recovered from the eruption of Mt. Vesuvius in Pompeii were hollow and needed to be filled with plaster to be reconstructed.

Ruins from Pompeii

have perished. Among them was the famed naturalist writer and Prefect (commander) in the Roman Navy, Pliny the Elder. He was found beneath the rubble at Stabiae, nine miles away from Vesuvius; the manner of his death was chronicled by his adopted nephew Pliny the Younger, who witnessed the

bright glare emphasized by the darkness of night...the buildings were shaking with violent shocks and seemed to be swaying to and fro as if being torn from their roots."

History dates the founding of Pompeii to some time in the seventh or sixth century BC by a central Italian people known as the Osci. Pompeii was perched on a hill overlooking the sea, and at the time of its destruction was one of the most popu-

lar Roman holiday resorts. A town bustling with tourists, traders, and craftsmen, its pottery was acclaimed throughout Italy; its houses noted for their frescoes and cloistered gardens; its stone amphitheater reputed to be the oldest in the Roman world. It was also rife with prostitution, for which graffiti advertisements spread the word.

The devastation was so complete that the Roman government decided to leave it buried under the lava and ash.

And so it remained until 1748, when workmen who had been erecting a palace for the King of Naples, Charles of Bourbon, at what had been Herculaneum, rediscovered it.

It is fair to say that Pompeii is the most eloquent testament to life in antiquity that one can imagine. The eruption of the volcano was so sudden that many of the towns' citizens were caught going about their daily business and remain mute witnesses of what life was like 2,000 years ago. ❑

THE FALL OF JERUSALEM

September AD 70

The first Jewish-Roman War, also known as The Great Revolt, ended in September of AD 70 with the sacking of Jerusalem by Roman forces under the command of Titus Flavius. Jerusalem was destroyed and with it, the most sacred of all Jewish places, the Second Temple.

Roman occupation of Palestine began in 63 BC when Pompey's troops overran the country. In 40 BC, the Roman senate placed the province in the hands of a Jewish king, Herod the Great. He kept strict control over the population, even going so far as to execute some Jewish nationalists. But his large public works programs secured the loyalty of the populace. His most significant project was the rebuild-

ing of the Temple, which had fallen into disrepair over the years.

The Jewish revolt against Rome began in AD 6 when detested census and taxation policies were imposed throughout Judea and Syria by the Roman governor Quirinius. A Judean resistance force known as the Zealots engaged in pitched battles with Roman forces for decades, eventually losing in northern Judea and ending with a tenacious defense of Jerusalem, beginning in 66 . The Zealots—led by historically feuding leaders, John of Giscala and Simon Bar Giora, and an extremist sect of Zealots known as the Sicarii—took control of the city, repelling the Roman assaults and, controversially, murdering fellow Jews who called for moderation or accommodation. Their resistance ended in failure. The siege of Jerusalem, mounted first by Titus' father Vespasian, went on for four years until the city finally fell and the Temple was razed. Historians have considered this calamity to be the precipitating event of the Jewish Diaspora.

Titus' victory left the fortress of Masada as the last bastion of Jewish resistance. It was finally captured after a siege lasting two years. The attackers found only seven survivors, two women and five children. The remaining 960 defenders had killed themselves. ❑

The fortress of Masada on the Dead Sea

ROME REBUILT UNDER VESPASIAN

Rome, AD 70

The Arch of Titus, Vespasian's son, built to celebrate his triumph over the Jews.

Vespasian returned from the wars in Judea and was named the new emperor by the Senate on December 21, AD 69. He moved swiftly to repair the damage done by his predecessors in what has become known as the Year of the Four Emperors. Following the disastrous reign of Nero in AD 68, the Roman Empire sank into a period of civil war and a succession of three inept emperors, Galba, Otho, and Vitellius, only exacerbated the chaos that Nero had created.

As the "fourth emperor," Vespasian reversed this decline. With a benignly authoritarian leader-

ship, he expedited the architectural rehabilitation of Rome by allowing anyone with the means to build on empty parcels of land that had not been reclaimed by the original owners. To finance these projects, he raised money by instituting a wide range of new taxes. He tightened his control of the Senate by removing ineffective members, promoting others including non-Romans and provincials whom he knew to be competent and loyal. He widened the role of public education and extended this progressive agenda to the justice system by decreasing the use of executions. ❑

THE ROMAN COLOSSEUM

Rome, 80

The building of the Colosseum (photo to right) was one of the high points of Roman-Hellenic monumental architecture. After eight years of work, the Flavius Amphitheater, which would later be known as the Colosseum, was completed. During the 100-day dedication festival decreed by the Emperor Titus, gladiators slew more than 5,000 wild animals in the arena.

The building was almost 150

feet high and could boast the largest enclosed area of any structure in antiquity. The stadium could hold 50,000 spectators. Above them presided the emperor in the imperial box. The first floor was reserved for members of the court and high government officials. Prominent families were seated on the second floor, while the third and fourth floors were for the common people. Underground there were chambers for gladiators and

animals as well as the amphitheater's personnel and various machinery used in the games. The ruins of the building with its multiple arches is recognized throughout the world as a symbol of the once-great power of the Roman Empire. The last gladiatorial

event was held in the arena in the year 405. ❑

HADRIAN'S WALL

Britain, 128

The Emperor Hadrian (r.117–138) based his foreign policy upon the establishment of the *Pax Romana* rather than military conquest.

After six years of construction, Hadrian's Wall was finally completed. It stretched over 73 miles securing Britain's northern border from the Pictish tribes of Scotland. It was built at Britain's narrowest point between the North and Irish Seas. Its eastern section was made from stone and was approximately 15 feet high; in the west, the wall was built from turf. A system of ditches further

Remnants of Hadrian's Wall

fortified its defenses. In addition to the wall itself, 320 towers, 17 forts, and 80 gates were constructed. The construction work was interrupted many times by the repeated attacks of the Picts.

The boundary line in Britain was part of an overall program launched by Hadrian, who since his accession devoted himself to improving the empire's infrastructure. He built roads and cities and aqueducts. He pursued a policy of reconciliation with his neighbors, concluding a peace treaty with the Parthians whom Rome had attacked under the leadership of his predecessor Trajan.

Some of the most impressive building of antiquity was completed under Hadrian's aegis: the Pantheon and Mausoleum in Rome, Hadrian's Villa in Tivoli, and the Library in Athens. ❑

GERMANIC TRIBES

Point of Interest

The name "German" is a generic term used to designate any of the many tribes that occupied the Northern part of Europe around the time of the birth of Christ. They lived in tribal communities and extended families. An assembly of the tribe had the final say in decisions affecting the tribe's welfare. Judges were also chosen, but they dealt only with crimes of a serious nature. More often crimes were handled privately, which could lead to cycles of vengeance and prolonged feuds. The institution of the *wergild* (monetary compensation for crimes against persons) was devised to alleviate these conflicts. Kings, whose functions were primarily religious and symbolic, served as the embodiment of tribal identity, and relied more on the personal loyalty of attendants than legal authority. The tribes lived in fixed settlements and their economies were based on agriculture and herding. ❑

ROMAN WALLS AT THE EMPIRE'S LIMITS

Rome, 83

The *limites* (meaning "limits," singular *limes*) were gigantic fortification works that marked the boundaries of the Roman Empire and guarded it from invasion. They were built at the edges of the empire and included Hadrian's Wall, the Antonine Wall, the *Limes Germanicus*, *Arabicus*, and *Tripolitanus*. In places they consisted of fenced palisades overlooked by wooden watchtowers and in other places stone walls protected by barriers and ditches. The Rhaetius Germanicus *Limes* is one of the best-known. Over 340 miles long, construction began in 83 under the Emperor Domitian. Work continued under Trajan, Antoninus Pius, and Hadrian. It served an important function in protecting the Roman provinces from the continuing incursions of Germanic tribes looking for new lands in which to settle. For many years, the limes proved to be an insurmountable obstacle with more than 1,000 watchtowers and 100 stone forts. It continued to serve its purpose until the middle of the third century. In 259, the Alamanni broke through, destroying much of the limes. Their way to the richly cultivated provinces was now open. In 406, the Rhine border fell; four years later, Alaric the Visigoth king sacked the city of Rome. ❑

ROME'S EASTERN EMPIRE

Petra, 105–106

Rome annexed the Nabataean Kingdom under the Emperor Trajan. With the establishment of a new province Rome extended its boundaries eastward.

The Roman general Cornelius Palma conquered the Nabataeans and took possession of the rich trading center of Petra. He immediately fortified its borders and established the new Roman province of Arabia.

Petra had been an important trading partner of Rome for over a century. The city was built in a rocky pass on the route between India and the Mediterranean and enjoyed great success as a trading center. Trajan had succeeded to the imperial throne in 98. By seizing control over Petra he gained an important strategic advantage in his planned war against Parthia.

As a result of his successful prosecution of the Dacian Wars, Trajan enriched the Roman treasury with the booty he had garnered and was able to institute popular reforms and lower taxes. He also initiated major public works programs that included building new roads, bridges, and canals. In 113, he led his army in a campaign against the Parthians, capturing their capital, Ctesiphon, in 116 and then proceeding to the Persian Gulf, where he declared the formation of the new Roman province of Mesopotamia.

Under Trajan's rule, the Roman Empire reached the widest extent in its history, stretching from Britain to east of the Tigris River. The senate conferred upon him its highest honor, the title of "Optimus Princeps." ❑

Ruins of Petra

THE INVENTION OF PAPER

China, 105

The invention of paper is attributed to Cai Lun, a high-ranking Chinese civil servant. He combined mulberry wood, bark, cloth, and hemp then mixed the material it yielded into a thin fiber. Using a wooden frame and a sieve made from bamboo stalks, he shaped this into the desired form. Then he dried it in the sun, smoothed it with stones, and arrived at durable sheets of paper.

Before the invention of paper people used different materials to write on, but all had their disadvantages. While clay tablets kept documents relatively secure, were long lasting, difficult to falsify, and fireproof, they required a lot of effort to write on and were difficult to handle and store. Manufactured from papyrus reeds, papyrus had been in use in Egypt since 3000 BC and was similar to paper. Made from the pith of the plant it was then cut into strips laid crosswise over one another, pressed, hammered, and smoothed. Sheets of papyrus were easy to write on and to correct. Inks were made from solutions of soot, ocher, and cinnabar. Pens were made from reeds. For longer texts, sheets of papyrus could be stitched together to the desired length. Long documents were stored in rolls. If needed, one could write on both sides of a sheet of papyrus and after washing, it could be used over again. Papyrus was generally kept in chests or clay boxes. However,

this material also had disadvantages. It was susceptible to fire and dampness and therefore not suitable for the preservation of important political documents. For this reason, official proclamations were often engraved in stone.

Parchment had been used since the second millennium BC in Egypt and Mesopotamia. It was in common use throughout antiquity in many different regions. Shaved, untanned hides made from the skins of sheep, goats, or calves were stretched

and smoothed. They were easy to write on and more durable than papyrus. In China, people used silk to write on: typically the leftover material from silk production. However, the manufacture was expensive and the material quite weak, so it did not find widespread acceptance. Wax tablets were also used and were especially suitable in business and schools, as writing could easily be erased and the tablets written over. Tablets made from wood or ivory were covered with colored wax, which was then engraved

with a stylus. Finds from Egypt and Pompeii testify to their being employed in antiquity.

From the outset, paper provided an easy medium for longer, more durable manuscripts. Paper made from hemp was available in China before Cai Lun made his discovery. And following in his footsteps, the processes involved in the manufacture of paper were quickly improved upon. Mulberry tree fiber was mixed with ash and ground until the mixture dissolved. The fibrous mash was then shaped in a frame. The paper produced after drying was smooth and good to write on. Starch and gums were added as supplements, which strengthened it and made it more difficult to tear. Natural coloring agents not only were used to enhance its appearance but also to afford excellent protection against insects.

At the beginning of the seventh century, this groundbreaking invention reached Japan and Korea. It was carried by prisoners of war into Arabia 150 years later. There the paper business thrived; and paper quickly made its way into the entire Islamic world. Introduced into Europe around the year 1000, its use soon spread throughout the countries bordering on the Mediterranean. Paper mills began to spring up in France Spain, Italy, and Germany. Paper then replaced the use of parchment in monastic scriptoria and with the advent of printing, it became the accepted material for public and private writing. ❑

Cai Lun at his desk in his pagoda (Chinese woodcut)

PTOLEMY'S *GEOGRAPHIA*: THE NEW WORLD MAP

Alexandria, 147

Claudius Ptolemaeus, or Ptolemy (A.D. c. 90-168) was an Alexandrian Greek, whose most famous work, Alamagest, informed the Western world's knowledge of astronomy for nearly five-hundred years, and whose eight volumed Geographia accomplished a similar feat in cartogeographical science.

In Geographia, Ptolemy presented a conspectus of the most up to date cartogeographical knowledge of not only the Roman Empire , but of the oikoumenè — the entire inhabited world. In Book I he presents the data he has compiled and how it is to be used to create a new world map. His most innovative technique was to assign coordinates to known locations using latitude and longitude. He also presented

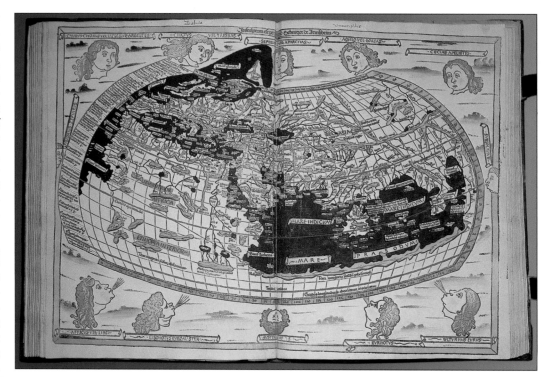

World map by Ptolemy from a medieval manuscript (Royal Navy Museum, Greenwich, 15th century)

various ways to draw the map, introducing the ground-breaking use of "equal-area" projection and subsequent books offered topographical specifics and the presentation of various regional maps as well as his new world map. Because the contemporary tools and methods of calculating distances were relatively imprecise, his world map, which longitudinally spanned from the Cape Verde Islands to China, and latitudinally from the Shetland Islands to the North African east coast, was oddly mishappen. It was, however, a remarkable achievement, which set a cartographic standard that would inspire and guide the Renaissance era voyages of discovery. ❑

discussing its complex relation to alternative stereographic and conic representations. Concerning this, he wrote: "Drawing a map on a sphere gives the likeness of the shape of the earth … but it is not easy to make it large enough to provide room for the many details that will need to be indicated, and it is impossible to fix one's sight on the whole shape at one time … Making the map on a plane surface is altogether free from these inconveniences, but requires a certain adjustment to correspond to the spherical form, in order to make the distances … on the unfolded surface commensurate with the real distances." The

NOK CULTURE SCULPTURES

Point of Interest

The Nok culture was the product of an Iron Age African people who inhabited the Jos Plateau area in central Nigeria, between 500 BC and AD 200. Considered Nigeria's earliest inhabitants and possibly lineal ancestors of the great Yoruban culture, their exact tribal identity remains a mystery. The designation "Nok" comes from the name of the village near which, beginning in 1943, exquisite terracotta sculptures were found.

The Nok Terracottas are hollow clay representations of humans and animals. The most renowned of these are large, elongated heads with ornately rendered hair and jewelry, and triangular eyes with perforated pupils. The disproportionately large heads are thought to signify

A Nok head made of clay

wisdom. Many of the sculptures representing complete torso and head are in postures of genuflection, suggesting that they served a religious function. ❑

ROMAN RELIGIOUS SYNCRETISM

Roman world, second century

Roman religious syncretism, the melding of Eastern and Mystery cults with gods of the traditional state religion, had been practiced as far back as 200 BC with the Senate's adoption of the Great Mother cult. By the second century AD, as the empire expanded its hegemony over ever more diverse cultures, this practice had grown exponentially. Nowhere was more indicative of this trend than the trading city of Lugdunum (present-day Lyon) in

Gaul. The city had a multicultural population, most significantly, immigrants from Asia Minor and the Syria-Palestine area. These diverse peoples brought with them the Phrygian cult of Cybele and the Persian cult of Mithraism, both of which featured the practice of *taurobolium* (the sacrifice of bulls and the use of its blood in baptismal rites), the worship of Egyptian Isis, and a new esoteric religious practice called Christianity. ❑

CLAUDIUS PTOLEMY

Brief lives

Born around 100 in Upper Egypt, Ptolemy lived in Alexandria where he gained fame as a geographer, mathematician, and astronomer. In *Geographia* he developed a model of the then known world based upon astronomical and geographical principles. His *Almagest* (*The Great Treatise*) was preserved in an Arabic translation from the original Greek. It was translated back into Latin in the twelfth century and became the standard work on astronomy until the Copernican revolution. In addition, he wrote on astrology, optics, and various philosophical questions. ❑

ROME'S CAPITAL IN THE NORTH

Germany, c.180

Augusta Treverorum (present-day Trier) became a vital urban center on the Roman-German border. The history of the city reflects the rise of commerce and culture in the areas conquered by the Roman legions.

Around 180, the northern gate of the city, the *Porta Nigra*, was completed. The impressive

The Porta Nigra in Trier.

stonework was designed to secure the main road connecting the German provinces. The history of Trier as a Roman city began in 54 BC with the conquest of Gaul by Julius Caesar who subjugated the Treveri, the Celtic-Germanic people who had settled between the Rhine and the Meuse Rivers. In 29 BC the inhabitants tried unsuccessfully to throw off the yoke of their conquerors. Eight years later, Augustus gave the region provincial status, named the city Augusta Treverorum, and made it the political and religious center of the province. Under the reign of Tiberius, it became capital of the province of Belgica. A further attempt to gain independence in the year AD 21 also met with failure. After that the city became prosperous and heavily populated. An amphitheater was built to hold 20,000 people in 100 and the city was also famed for its luxurious thermal baths. The Roman garrison stationed there was responsible for overseeing the *limes*, the northern boundary line of the empire. ❑

THE EMPEROR MARCUS AURELIUS

Vienna, 180

Statue of Marcus Aurelius

The shared emperorship in 161 of Marcus Aurelius and Lucius Verus was an unprecedented event in Roman history. The circumstances that gave rise to this can be traced to 136, when Emperor Hadrian adopted Lucius Aelius Verus and designated him as a successor. This was probably an error on Hadrian's part and perhaps due to his declining health. In any event, Lucius, who was self-indulgent and in poor health, died two years later. With his desire to control imperial succession temporarily thwarted, Hadrian finessed the accession of a surrogate choice, the 50-year-old Antoninus (who became known as Antoninus Pius), with the unusual tactic of adopting him, and then offering to name him successor with the proviso that Antoninus would in turn adopt not only his real choice, the young Marcus Aurelius, but also Marcus' stepbrother, Lucius Verus. Antoninus did so. At the death of Antoninus, the Senate called on the gifted young Marcus to ascend to the throne. He agreed to do so, but only if he could share the title with his stepbrother Lucius. The Senate, at first perplexed, conceded to this request, awarding to both all imperial titles, save *pontifex maximus*, which was to be held by Marcus alone.

Historians generally agree that the brilliant Marcus shared his title with Lucius more out of principled loyalty than out of genuine recognition of his stepbrother's worthiness. Marcus was the born leader and as a young man it was his extraordinary seriousness of purpose, his philosophical bent, and his commitment to service that inspired Hadrian to groom him as his eventual successor. Lucius, on the other hand, has been described as robust, cheerful, full of life, and perhaps somewhat irresponsible.

In spite of two wars and plague, Marcus brought a kind of *pax romana* to the empire. In the east there was the difficult Parthian campaign, the ultimate triumph of which was soon overshadowed by a chickenpox pandemic borne back to Rome by the Roman army. Then there were the Germanic Wars, which would occasion the death of Lucius continue after Marcus' death in 180.

Marcus's reign was seen as one of enlightened stewardship. Based on the Stoic principles of common sense and one's societal duties promulgated in his philosophical classic *Meditations*, he efficiently reorganized Italian political and bureaucratic infrastructure, and encouraged a form of democratic inclusiveness in the Senate by opening its doors to African and Oriental officers. Marcus was killed during a campaign in Germany in 180. Four years earlier he named his son Commodus as his successor. This would prove to be his most serious error. With the death of Marcus Aurelius what the historian Edward Gibbon described as the period in which humanity was happiest came to an abrupt end. ❑

OVERTHROW OF THE ARSACIDS

Persia, 200

The Arsacids, the royal dynasty of Parthia, ruled Persia for more than four centuries. Descended from nomadic tribes, possibly Scythian or Dahan, who came from east of the Caspian Sea, they established their capital at Ctesiphon on the Tigris River. In 250 BC, their first king, Arsaces I, invaded Parthia, then a province of the Seleucid Empire. He overthrew Seleucid hegemony and founded a kingdom whose power would eventually rival that of Rome. Even repeated defeats at the hands of the Romans, including the sack of Ctesiphon by Septimus Severus in 197, could not dislodge the Arsacids from a suzerainty that stretched from Mesopotamia to India.

Palace of Ardashir I dating from 3rd century

Indigenous Persians, however, were never reconciled to the presence of the Arsacid intruders. In 226, led by the Sassanian rebel Ardashir, they won a stunning victory over the Arsacid forces at Hormizdagan, killing their king, Artabanus. This victory heralded the beginning of the Persian Sassanid Dynasty, with Ardashir as it first king. ❑

ROMAN EGYPT

Egypt, 2nd century

The Roman occupation of Egypt, begun in 30 BC, ushered in an era of prosperity in the province that lasted a century. Supplying Rome with grain, Egypt was also a source of prodigious tax revenue, which was administered with efficiency and fairness. However, in the second century AD, the expanding empire's need for cheaper grains and greater tax revenue resulted in a more confiscatory approach toward the Egyptian province. This state of affairs became so oppressive that rebellions broke out, initially in the agricultural area in the Alexandrian delta, and soon spread. These revolts, known as the Bucolic Wars, were a serious threat to Rome under the reign of Marcus Aurelius. Under growing financial strain, the long-standing harmony between the Egyptian Jewish and Greek communities deteriorated, adding to the province's destabilization and the collapse of the Egyptian economy. ❑

THYSDRUS FLOURISHES

North Africa, c.200

The North African Roman town of Thysdrus flourished in the second and third centuries as a major center of the olive oil trade. Imperial estates were farmed under procurators, who parceled out the estates to bailiffs, who then divided those bequests among tenant farmers. These tenants were allowed to plant vineyards; the harvest was theirs to keep and sell for five years, after which a third of the yearly bounty would be due the bailiff. The productivity of this system made Thysdrus, like Carthage, a vital North African economic center and allowed for the construction of an amphitheater, whose 30,000-seat capacity rivaled that of the Roman Colosseum. ❑

END OF THE HAN DYNASTY

China, 220

The Han Dynasty began to totter in the late first century under the fractious reign of Emperor Ling (r.168–189). Peasant revolts, chaos within the Han regime, and the looming presence of warlords, were harbingers of the approaching collapse.

On the death of Emperor Ling, the battle to place his successor began with those loyal to the Empress Dowager He, who sought to elevate Ling's oldest son, Liu Bian, to the throne. General Dong Zhou was summoned to secure this accession by overseeing the extermination of the influential court eunuchs, whose choice for successor was Ling's younger son, Prince Liu Xie. Instead, Dong murdered the Dowager Empress and the new emperor, ignored the now ineffectual presence of the eunuchs, and placed Prince Liu Xie on the throne as the puppet Emperor Xian, effectively making himself China's new ruler.

Within a year opposition to Dong arose with a coalition of provincial officials and warlords. However, Dong's downfall came at the hands of one of his trusted officials, Prime Minister Wang Yun, who on May 22, 192, had him assassinated.

Chaos ensued until the arrival of the warlord Cao Cao in 196. The competent Cao quickly took the reigns of power, ingratiating himself with officials, generals, and the

Burial figure 120 BC

feeble emperor, but made it clear that the real power of the state resided in him. Emperor Xian was in no position to resist this benign warlord, and so accepted his role as puppet emperor.

The end of the Han Dynasty came in 220 with the death of Cao Cao, the leadership role was assumed by his son, Cao Pi. It was Cao Pi who effected the abdication of the last of the Han Emperors: Emperor Xian stepped down, relinquishing his title to Cao Pi, thereby ending 400 years of Han rule. ❑

ROMAN CITIZENSHIP EXTENDS THROUGHOUT THE EMPIRE

Rome, 212

Under the reign of terror of the Emperor Caracalla, the empire underwent a period of extreme crisis. Even his measure to extend citizenship to all inhabitants of the empire was only a way to increase the tax revenue his reckless spending demanded.

According to Caracalla's *Constitutio Antoniana*, all free members of the empire received the full rights of Roman citizenship. Thereby, the provinces were put on equal footing with Rome and

Caracalla

Italy. Before this, only a privileged few were able to enjoy the benefits this conferred and citizenship was limited to those whose parents were citizens and whose marriage was deemed valid. It could also be conferred on freedmen and to specially designated individuals or groups. When the right was extended it had been on a limited basis only.

The consequences of Caracalla's reform were twofold. First, the new Romans were entitled to vote for the people's assembly and enjoyed special protections under Roman law. The reverse side of these benefits was that they were now subject to all of the obligations born by citizens, especially direct taxation. This was the real reason for Caracalla's measure. In addition to his financially ruinous military campaigns, a new expense arose—Caracalla's building of the luxurious thermal baths known by his name, whose ruins still are seen in Rome.

Marcus Aurelius gave Caracalla his name because of the Celtic hooded cape he wore. Caracalla was named coemperor by his father Septimus Severus in 198. After his father's death, he and his brother Geta shared the imperium.

Within a year, Caracalla openly revealed the darker side of his character. He had Geta murdered in the arms of their mother, Julia Domna. When the citizens of Alexandria satirized his claim that the murder was self-defense, he had his troops rampage through the city causing an untold number of deaths.

Once he assumed sole power, Caracalla invested his mother with the regency in Rome, and went off on what were at first successful military campaigns. In 213–214, he defeated Germanic tribes on the Main and Danube Rivers.

Caracalla raised the pay of his soldiers. To keep them happy he was forced to devalue the silver coinage. Seeing himself as another Alexander, he set off to conquer the Parthian kingdom. En route he was murdered by the Praetorian Macrinus, who succeeded him to the imperial throne. ❏

Above: Floor mosaic from the baths of Caracalla. Below: View of the baths. Nearby were other areas for recreation.

THE DIOCLETIAN REFORMS

Nicomedia, 284

Diocletian, Roman Emperor from November 20, 284 to May 1, 305, ascended to imperial rule during a time when the Roman Empire was unstable. In efforts to gain control over the widespread territories of the Roman Empire, Diocletian developed the tetrarchy in 292—a system consisting of four emperors, two Augusti, and two Caesars. Diocletian appointed Maximian as the second Augustus and each of them chose a Caesar, Galerius and Constantius respectively, naming them as their heirs. Diocletian's system of government split the empire in half allowing each Emperor to control a specific territory. Remaining in Nicomedia, Asia Minor, Diocletian ruled in the east, while Maximian had control over the west. Additionally, each Caesar was given a quarter of the empire to rule. In order to legitimize his new system of government, Diocletian gave himself the title of Jovius and Maximian the title of Herculius, thereby aligning with Jupiter and Hercules and giving their positions divine justification. With the division of power, Diocletian and the other emperors were able to settle conflicts with the Persians, Germans, and English, as well as the unrest in Africa and the barbarian invasions.

The tetrarchy, while helpful, brought a huge burden of taxation onto the empire. Both Augusti required their own set of officers and the duplication of state servants caused the need for a tax increase during a time of high inflation. Diocletian reformed the taxation system, removing the old one and putting into place a simplified system based on land acreage. Romans were accustomed to irregular and ineffective tax collection; Diocletian's system was effective and regulated, causing an uncomfortable period of adjustment during its implementation and an increase in taxation. Senators were expected to collect a specific amount in taxes based on census data for their district. If their district was unable to produce the full amount, be it in cash or produce, the difference came out of the senator's personal

fund. Unwilling to face the increase in taxation, many citizens chose to flee the country for tax relief. Other citizens joined monasteries or entered into serfdom with the impression that barbarian invasion would bring harsh rule but the tax burden would be lighter. The discontent was universal in the Roman community; craftsmen, clergy, and intellectuals alike all sought avenues for tax relief. In 301, Diocletian began to address the issue of inflation with his *Edict on Maximum Prices*. This edict instituted wage and price controls. The maximum wage rates for all professions, from laborer to lawyer, were fixed. The price controls covered a range of more than a thousand goods including bread, meat, vegetables, fruit, footwear, leather, carpets, and clothes. Punishments for vi-

Head of Diocletian

olating any of the laws on wages and prices were exile or death. Despite these harsh punishments, the edict did very little to curb inflation. Many goods were sold on the black market creating shortages, and in some areas the edict was completely ignored. In time it was withdrawn as a failure.

Although Diocletian's reform of the economic system failed, his reform of the imperial system met with success. He separated civil and military departments and implemented an unbroken chain of command in each department, starting with the emperor and ending with the lowest official of the most distant province. Diocletian's reforms and his ability to efficiently end the domestic uprisings and foreign invasions at the empire's borders brought peace and stability. In 305, Diocletian retired to his palace in Dalmatia, the only Roman emperor to voluntarily relinquish the throne. He died there eleven years later. ❑

CIVILIZATION IN MESOAMERICA

Point of Interest

Throughout Central America, archaeologists have found evidence of highly developed cultures, some dating as far back as right before the Christian era. Sites have been excavated in Mexico, Guatemala, Honduras, Nicaragua, Costa Rica, and Panama.

At the time of the Spanish conquest, these areas were home to many different Indian tribes at different levels of cultural sophistication: hunters and gatherers, subsistence farmers, and highly developed urban civilizations could be found in relatively close proximity to one another. Common traits were powerful religious sentiments and lives governed by cult and ritual. Weapons and tools were made primarily of stone. Copper was rarely used and evidence for the use of bronze dates from the time just before the arrival of the Spanish. Iron, glass, and pottery, and both the plow and the wheel were unknown.

The classic culture of Teoti-

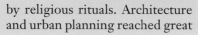

Mixtec codex (detail)

huacan emerged around 200 BC; it reached its peak around 500 AD. Its influence was felt throughout Central America, and its cultural hegemony lasted until the time of the conquistadors. The center of the kingdom was the city of Teotihuacan, effectively governed by a priestly class and ordered by religious rituals. Architecture and urban planning reached great heights, along with commercial endeavors. The works of artists and artisans also flourished.

Decline set in around the seventh century AD. Some archaeologists have argued that the city fell to invading forces, possibly the Otomi, a tribe from the North Mexican plateau, who descended on the kingdom and set fire to the city. Others have suggested that because only the major cult buildings were burned, the city might have fallen prey to an internal revolt.

There were other highly developed cultures in pre-Colum-

THE ACHIEVEMENTS OF MAYAN CIVILIZATION

Mexico, c.300

Left: Maya observatory. Right: Warrior's Temple. Both from Chichen Itza, Yucatan Peninsula.

Mayan civilization flourished in the area of present-day Mexico and Guatemala. Its architecture and technological expertise were more highly developed than any of the other Mesoamerican cultures.

Around 300, there existed many kingdoms in this region that despite their small size were rich in culture. Temple pyramids, monumental sculpture, mathematical knowledge, and writing testify to their high level of development. These semiautonomous states were all connected, but they often feuded with each other. At their head stood hereditary monarchs, the focus of an elaborate ceremonial repertoire. Political and religious ritual required the use of many ceremonial objects and fostered a class of artisans. They lived in the cities with the priests and state officials, forming an elite class in relation to the majority of people who lived as subsistence farmers in outlying areas.

The Mayan peoples were the first ones in Pre-Columbian America to master the art of writing. They used two calendars, one of 365 days based on the solar year, and a second ritual calendar in which a year consisted of 260 days. These two calendars were combined to form a synchronized period of 52 calendar cycles. Mathematical calculations were based on a vigesimal system (based on the number 20), which was adopted by most of the peoples in the surrounding areas. Mayan mathematicians discovered the concept of zero early on and were able to generate highly complex computations.

Where religion was concerned, Mayan belief was characterized by an encompassing fatalism. Without hope of salvation they felt themselves helpless before their gods. The gods themselves were closely bound to natural phenomena. They worshiped the maize god, who some identify as Yum Kaax. Itzamna, the sun god, and Chac, the rain god, were also important members of their pantheon. The gods were nourished with human blood, and human sacrifice was instituted by the state so that the people and the land might flourish. Cult festivals were an expression of their devotion to the gods. In this regard, a ballgame they developed was of particular importance. The forward and backward rolling movement of the ball symbolized the peregrinations of the sun, which would never end. At the end of the game, the losing team was sacrificed to the sun god. To be sacrificed at the altar was considered to be a high honor. Along with death in battle or in infancy, it was the only way one could reach paradise. Everyone else was condemned to a shadowy existence in the afterlife. Living conditions for the great majority of people were primitive. Houses were little more than stone-age shelters; the plow and work animals were unknown. ❑

bian Mesoamerica. The Zapotec culture was centered in Mitla and Monte Alban and reached its highest point around 500 AD. On Mexico's Gulf Coast, the Classic Veracruz culture flourished around the same time and was based in the city of El Tajin.
In the southern part of Central America, there were numerous tribes and groups rich in cultural and technological diversity. In the Nicoya region of Costa Rica and Nicaragua, a culture using finely carved stone tools and ceremonial objects flourished from about 300 to 500 AD. Fine polychrome pottery has been found in the Chiriqui province of present-day Panama that was probably made by tribes that originally lived in South America. They also brought with them their knowledge and skill as goldsmiths. The Coclé culture was located in central Panama. Excavations have uncovered ruins and burials sites rich in artifacts made from gold and other metals, fine jewelry and ceremonial objects made from ivory, as well as pottery and textiles. ❑

Chichen Itza: Chac Mool—Toltec sacrificial altar at the entrance to the temple.

ADVANCED CIVILIZATIONS IN INDIA

There are very few written records of the history of India. The reasons for this lie in the Indian philosophy of life. Because change is accepted so readily, the individual's personal destiny is unimportant in the discovery of everlasting truth. The uniqueness of a historical event is of very little importance. Only that which remains valid beyond time is worth preserving.

Our knowledge of the history of pre-Islamic India is drawn from sources that in the case of other advanced civilizations would be considered as secondary sources: archaeology, coins, inscriptions, literature, and legends, as well as records by foreign travelers.

For a long time it was accepted that the foundations of Indian history were laid only after the invasions of the Aryans in the second millennium BC. But when in the nineteenth century the ruins of the city of Harappa, and later also those of the city of Mohenjo-Daro, were found in the Punjab (West Pakistan), traces of an earlier civilization that had existed for more than 1,000 years, from 2500 to 1700 BC, were revealed. This Indus civilization of the Bronze Age was called the Harappa civilization, after the first site where it was discovered.

Even more important for the Indus civilization than Harappa itself was Mohenjo-Daro ("the place of the dead"), an urban development with the character of a big city. It was founded between 2300 and 1750 BC. The settlement had a perimeter of almost three miles (5 km). The rural population had to pay taxes in kind, which were processed in urban workshops and then sold by merchants overseas. Mohenjo-Daro revealed a system of irrigation and drainage unique in antiquity, and it also had numerous multi-story houses. The main streets and side streets, laid out at

Ornate masterpiece: the northern entrance gate to the Great Stupa of Sanchi (second century BC–first century AD)

right angles to one other, preserved their layout unchanged for almost 1,000 years. They formed carefully measured urban districts in which the population lived separately, grouped according to trade. It is believed that the caste system based on heredity and occupation or profession, which still exists today, had its roots in this strict division.

The religion of the Harappa civilization had many similarities with Hinduism. For instance, archaeological finds have included clay figures in the shape of animals and mother goddesses that are similar to those still seen today on domestic altars in India. At that time, cows were already sacred animals. The script of the Harappa civilization has not yet been deciphered, but it appears that its inhabitants must have been very peaceful since their cities do not include any signs of military installations. As a result, the people were powerless when they were attacked and invaded by the Aryans in 1500 BC.

THE AGE OF THE ARYANS

The origin of the fair-skinned pastoral people who bred cattle and called themselves "arya" (noble) has not yet been explained with certainty. The Aryans spoke a primitive form of Sanskrit, an Indo-European language; it

is therefore concluded that they came from the Indo-European part of the world. In about 1500 BC, they conquered large areas of northern India; they continued to extend their sphere of influence across the whole area between the Himalayas and the Vindhya mountains.

The Aryans worshipped several nature deities. The highest-ranking among their gods was the god of war, Indra. The oldest surviving literary Aryan work, the *Vedas* ("The Knowledge," 1500–1200 BC), a collection of popular songs, magic spells, and other references, dates back to these first centuries of Aryan rule in India.

Over the course of the centuries, the civilization and religion of the Aryans merged with those of the native population. This led to the development of Brahmanism, a religious idea of the universal soul (Brahma) in which the souls of individual people are absorbed. To achieve this integration with the universal soul, the individual must strive to discover the transcendent reality, since only in this way will he be able to overcome suffering.

It was also during this period that the teachings of reincarnation and *karma* were developed. According to these teachings, it was the actions of man in his present life that determined his lot and the caste to which he would belong in his next life. The power of the warrior and war god Indra decreased. In the *Upanishads* (*The Book of the Paths*, about 800 BC), all the nature gods of the Aryans were replaced by the idea of a universal soul.

A number of small royal courts formed the centers of Aryan power. The Aryans adopted the institution of caste from the Indus people, reorganizing it in a hierarchical four-caste system. The *Brahmins* (priests) were at the top, followed by the *Kshatriya* (warriors), the *Vaishya* (craftsmen), and at the bottom, the *Sudras* (farmers or servants). In addition to these four fixed categories that made up society, there were the "Untouchables," members of tribes that had not yet been assimilated and those with so-called unclean occupations. The Aryans occupied the top ranks in this system, and even today the higher castes include predominantly fair-skinned Indians.

THE TEACHINGS OF BUDDHA

In about 500 BC, a new civilization and power center developed in Maghada (present-day Bihar). This was where Siddhartha Gautama, the Buddha (the "Illuminated," "Who has achieved full understanding;" c.560–480 BC), displaced the Brahminic priesthood with his doctrine. He proclaimed that it was possible to be released from the cycle of rebirth not through sacrifice and asceticism but through meditation, self-perfection, and, lastly, the surrender of one's own self. Buddha had been born into an aristocratic family in Kapilavastu in the border region between India and Nepal. At the age of 29, he felt dissatisfied with his life as a rich nobleman and therefore left his castle, his wife, and his newborn son Rahula. As a traveling ascetic and the pupil of several yoga teachers, he wandered round the country for seven years until he finally found the redemptive knowledge (*bodhi*) that enabled him to become a Buddha. Wandering through northeastern India and surrounded by a group of followers, he taught the doctrine of salvation and redemption he had discovered.

The foundation of Buddhism is the idea that each life is suffering. Salvation can only be achieved through the knowledge that must encompass all the planes of man's life and must inevitably also affect man's way of life. According to Buddha's teachings, there is no lasting "self." The belief in the existence of an immortal soul and the concept of matter are delusions that cause the unredeemed to remain bound in the cycle of lives, dependent on the law of retribution for good and evil deeds (*karma*) that regulates the type and level of the reincarnation. The aim of salvation is to enter *nirvana*, the state of absolute release from which there is no return to the world of phenomena.

The kingdom of the Mauryas

The Buddha's doctrine laid the foundation for the development of the Maurya Dynasty that began shortly after the invasion of India by Alexander the Great (327–325 BC) and lasted until the second century BC in the north and northwest of India.

The capital of this dynasty was the ancient city of Pataliputra, present-day Patna in Bihar. By maintaining a well-organized and at the same time repressive state administration and a vast regular army, by controlling the most important trade routes, and by claiming to be a universal Indian monarchy, the Mauryas developed a new and very effective way of ruling their people. Many written records and documents date from that period; the Mauryan ruler Kautilya gives an ironic description of his era in his political textbook *Arthasastra*, while Asoka (about 268–232 BC) had his edicts carved into stone columns and rock faces. Because they contain the names of some rulers, these records also represent the first data in Indian history provided by their

own sources. Asoka pursued an expansionist policy and started his reign by conquering the federal state of Orissa. According to inscriptions, this campaign must have been very bloody. It left a lasting impression on this devout Buddhist ruler whose religion forbade the killing even of animals.

An independent, highly-developed civilization flourished during the Mauryan era, notable for its sumptuous architecture that can still be admired today. During excavations on the outskirts of Pataliputra, a royal palace from the Mauryan era (about 400 BC) was discovered with a wooden beamed ceiling resting on round, polished stone columns. Subsequently, three architectural styles have been identified: monolithic buildings built in rock, *stupas* (grave mounds), and temples. The caves in the Barabar Hills in Bihar and the Buddhist complexes near Bombay are extremely impressive. The constructions of Sanchi, Bharhut, and Amaravati are considered among the most important monuments of early Indian art because of their magnifi-

Representation of the Buddha (low-relief, sixth–seventh century AD)

cent reliefs carved on walls and gateways.

The influence of the Maurya Dynasty began to decline after Asoka's death and for some 500 years, rulers of various origins governed the land. At first it was the Greek Seleucid kings who expanded their realm southward. In about 95 BC, the Greeks were driven out of India by the Sakas, and they in turn were driven out by the Scythians. The state government and religion had become so well-established in India under the Mauryas that all conquerors sooner or later became Indian.

The Gupta Dynasty

After the decline of the Buddhist Empire, a Brahmin renaissance took place. Many small royal houses supported the Brahmins, who cost the ruling government less than the Buddhist monastic orders. In return, the Brahmin priests supported their princes' claims to power. In 320 AD, the Gupta Dynasty rose to prominence among these various smaller royal houses, forming special ties with them, comparable to those of the feudal system. The Guptas developed a new courtly civilization and returned to classical Sanskrit. The cultural influence of this period lasted for centuries. The reign of the Guptas is considered the Golden Age of medieval India. It is true that the caste system became even stricter than it had been before the Buddhist era, but the penal laws were less severe than under the reign of the Mauryas.

The Gupta Empire collapsed in the fifth century when it was attacked by the Huns, a Central Asian nomadic people. A period of conflict followed that was only briefly interrupted by the rule of the mighty monarch Harsha between 606 and 647. After the reign of this powerful king, India disintegrated again into separate little kingdoms, ruled by local dynasties. As a result, there was no common historical development in the north and northwest regions of India between the end of the Gupta Dynasty and the end of the twelfth century.

The south of India

The south of India developed its own civilization almost independently from the northern kingdoms. It is true that, like those in the north, many of the people in the south lived from agriculture and cattle breeding, but they were above all fishermen and sailors. Therefore, the Shatavahana Dynasty that ruled over large parts of the southern peninsula in the first centuries AD traded widely and had extensive business connections with the Mediterranean, as numerous discoveries of Roman coins demonstrate. ❑

TOLERANCE FOR CHRISTIANITY GUARANTEED BY THE EDICT OF MILAN

Milan, 313

After almost 200 years of persecution, the Emperor Constantine and his co-regent Licinius issued a decree that legalized the practice of Christianity. The once-persecuted Christians were now granted the protection of all the laws that pertained to Roman citizens. *The Edict of Milan* bore the title "On the Reinstatement of the Church." The emperors guaranteed Christians complete, unhindered freedom to practice their religion. They also provided for the restitution to the Church of all previously confiscated property, buildings, and lands. The emperor in the eastern half of the empire, Maximinus Daia, a particularly harsh enemy of Christians, was overthrown in the same year. Initial resistance to the new policy of tolerance soon evaporated.

The edict opened the way for the widespread acceptance of the Christian religion. When Constantine, who had himself converted to Christianity, assumed sole rule over the empire, the position of the new religion was secured.

He soon began passing laws that reflected the empire's new Christian sensibility. These included:

- Prohibition against branding the face: Prisoners, whether Christian or not, could no longer have their faces branded. Their hands and lower legs could be branded, but their

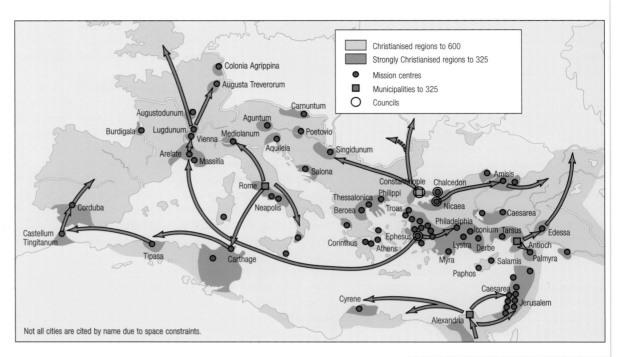

The spread of Christianity between the first and fourth centuries

Legend:
- Christianised regions to 600
- Strongly Christianised regions to 325
- ● Mission centres
- ■ Municipalities to 325
- ○ Councils

Not all cities are cited by name due to space constraints.

faces were protected since man was made in the image of God and the beauty created by heaven ought not be subject to desecration.
- The introduction of Sunday as a holiday. Other than farmers, all workers were required to observe the Sabbath.
- Privileges for clerics: Priests and other ecclesiastical officials were exempted from all public duties.
- Recognition of church law: The authority of canon law was fully recognized in all religious matters.
- The end of the use of cruci-

fixion and other cruel capital punishments for Christians.

The Edict of Milan provided Christians with unforeseen freedom and a huge influx of believers. In the days of persecution, prospective converts needed to possess great courage in the face of ever-present threats to life and limb. Now not only people motivated by the highest and noblest reasons could turn toward faith. Churches, financed by the regime, sprang up to meet the new demands, and the once-maligned faith began to take hold through the length and breadth of the empire.

Constantine made use of Christianity to strengthen his own power. The empire was faced with serious economic problems, and the diversity of religious practice could lead to conflict and divisions. A monotheistic religion such as Christianity had a certain stabilizing influence. Constantine endowed churches, enforced the writ of excommunication with civil penalties for those subject to it, and convened the Council of Nicea to resolve the Arian controversy. ❑

CHURCH FATHERS

Point of Interest

Development of the Christian movement into a religion was due mainly to the work of theologians and philosophers. The "Church Fathers" laid the groundwork of the faith by working through important doctrinal problems, such as the relationship between the three members of the Trinity. Most of their teachings were directed toward establishing dogma, a prerequisite for the growth and development of the Church. Where the scriptural text did not yield a clear, undisputed interpretation, believers turned to the writings of the Fathers for authoritative guidance. Among the most learned and influential of these early teachers were Tertullian (160–225), Origen (185–253/54), Athanasius (295–373), and Augustine (354–430). The work of John of Damascus Isidore of Seville (560–636), compiler of an encyclopedia of sacred and profane knowledge, brought an end to the age of the Church Fathers. ❑

Christians in the arena (mosaic, 2nd century)

CONSTANTINE'S ROAD TO POWER

Byzantium, 324

On September 18, 324, Constantine defeated his co-emperor Licinius at the Battle of Chrysopolis. That victory put the empire into the hands of a single individual after a period of divided rule.

In 306, while fighting in Gaul, Constantine was proclaimed by the army to be the successor to his father, Constantius Chlorus. At the same time, the army at Rome had given the imperium to Maxentius, son of the former emperor Maximian. The Western part of the empire remained divided until 312, when Constantine crossed the Alps from Gaul and attacked Rome. He won a decisive victory over the forces of Maxentius at the Battle of the Milvian Bridge and, along with his co-emperor Licinius, took control of the entire western half of the empire.

With his victory over Licinius in 324, Constantine finally realized his ambition of gaining sole control over all of the empire. To formalize his elevation to supreme authority, Constantine rebuilt the city of Byzantium and renamed it Nova Roma (New Rome). After his death, the name was changed again to Constantinople. As such it was destined to remain the imperial capital for over 1,000 years.

Constantine solidified his position by surrounding the person of the emperor with the loftiest ceremonial trappings, including *proskynesis* (prostration) in his presence as vice-regent of Christ on earth.

Constantine ascribed his unexpected victory at Rome in 312 to the intercession of the Christian God. He claimed to have received a vision of Christ before the battle and fought under the banner of the Cross. Constantine also played an important role in the establishment of Christian orthodoxy. To end the conflict over the teachings of Arian, he convened the first ecumenical council at Nicea in 325. Arius had taught that the person of Christ the Son was not equal with God the Father. The council branded this teaching as heresy and adopted the formulation of Bishop Athanasius, which became known as the Nicene Creed (parts of which are still in use today). It is reported that Constantine was baptized on his deathbed. ❑

THE GUPTA KINGDOM

India, 375

Samudragupta ascended the Gupta Kingdom throne in 335 and ruled for 40 years. He extended his rule from a tiny kingdom to an empire dominating all of northern and central India.

In his military campaigns, he subdued the Vakatakas in central India, the Nagas in northern India, the Maghas of Kausambi, the Kosalas of the Ganges, and the remnants of the Kushan Empire. Other territories came to Samudragupta through marriages and political alliances. Using his family to govern his provinces, and maintaining compliant rulers in his tributary nations, he ruled one of the largest empires of India.

Although a fervent worshipper of Vishnu, he followed a policy of religious toleration. A renowned a patron of the arts, this is reflected in his being memorialized on coins playing the lyre. ❑

THE KAMA SUTRA

India, c.300

The *Kama Sutra* (or *Aphorisms on Love*) is believed to have been written by an Indian philosopher named, Vatsyayana Mallanaga. He lived sometime in the Gupta period (fourth to sixth centuries) and was an adherent of a philosophical tradition known as *Carvaka* or *Lokyata*. A resident of the holy city of Benares, he was known not only for producing the *Kama Sutra*, but also for an authoritative commentary on Gautama's *Nyaya Sutras*. But it was the unique guidebook to the many and varied pleasures of sexual love, for which he is remembered. The *Kama Sutra* is one text of a series of writings known as *Kama Shastra*, whose mythical source was the utterances of Shiva's sacred bull, Nandi. *Kama* is a Sanskrit word that means desire or wish, in the sense of sexual pleasure.

The work contains 1,250 *slokas*, or verses, divided into 36 chapters.

Written in Sanskrit, it functioned as a guide to every aspect of erotic etiquette. Admittedly written to the male reader, it was also intended to serve as an instructional manual for brides to be.

The text is a veritable encyclopedia of sexuality that graphically describes not only hundreds of sexual techniques, but also offers a survey of all issues relating to the erotic, including the roles of courtesans and go-betweens, the sexual preferences of different nationalities, courtship and kissing, marriage and seduction, and a selection of magic spells.

Underlying the book is the Hindu philosophy that stresses that sexuality is a central part of human life, as fundamental as breathing. It is a basic part of nature, what Hindus call the Cosmic Dance of Shiva, and is as much a religious experience as it is a physical and sensual one. ❑

Erotic Indian sandstone relief

THE EMPIRE IS SPLIT

Milan, 395

Theodosius the Great was the last emperor of a single Roman empire. When he died in Milan, his testament called for the empire to be divided between his two sons. Honorius was given the rule of the western half, Arcadius the eastern half.

The boundary between the two parts ran north and south from Italy through Illyria. Constantinople was the cultural and political center of the Eastern Empire. Rome lost its preeminent position in the west and the new capitals were Milan (from 395) and then Ravenna (from 402).

Theodosius was born in 347 in Spain. In 378, Gratian made him emperor in the east. Upon Gratian's death, he ruled jointly with Gratian's half brother, Valentian II. But he was soon faced with a rebellion led by the disaffected general Magnus Maximus. Shortly after putting down the rebellion Valentian died under suspicious circumstances and a new imperial rival, Eugenius, had to be dealt with. Theodosius defeated him in battle in 394 and assumed sole control of the empire for the remaining year of his life. Theodosius had succeeded in protecting the empire from domestic and foreign dangers and preventing any loss of territory. His decision to divide the empire seems to have been based upon his fears of further invasions from Germanic tribes; he thought that the smaller realms could defend the borders of the empire more effectively.

Upon the death of Theodosius, his son Honorius appointed the Germanic general Stilicho as his co-ruler. Over the next years the empire suffered defeats from all sides. Frontiers that had remained defended for centuries collapsed. The wave of Germanic invasions could no longer be stopped. Between 401 and 403, Stilicho was able to halt the advance of the Visigothic king Alaric only by committing all available resources to the task. In so doing he was forced to withdraw his troops from the Rhine, leaving the way open for tribes to overrun the wealthy settlements of Gaul. Picts, Saxons, and Goths took over Britain, as the last Romans abandoned the island.

The Germanic invaders had become an irresistible force. This came at the end of a long period of decline of the empire in the west, which was hastened by the tetrarchy established by Diocletian and the relocation of much of the imperial administration to Constantinople. These developments conspired to make Rome, for so long the center point of the world, largely irrelevant in the course of future events. ❑

Ornamented bowl honoring Theodosius the Great (389)

ATHANASIUS AND ARIANISM

Point of Interest

The Arian Heresy of the third century plunged the Christian world into turmoil as bishops engaged in furious debate over the true nature of Jesus. The controversy was initiated by a priest in Alexandria named Arius who promulgated a notion that would eventually be judged heretical: God had created Jesus from nothing. Traditional Christian communities denounced this assertion on the grounds that this would have made Jesus not the *equal* of God the Father, but a rival demigod. This denunciation was made official in 325 when the Ecumenical Council of Nicea decreed that Jesus was "of the essence of the Father, not made, being of one substance..."

Arianism, however, managed to flourish because it received official sanction from a number of emperors. This sanction was supported by two church councils, one at Selencia for eastern Christian communities, and one at Rimini for those in the west; both asserted that the Son is only "similar" to the Father.

One of the most formidable and uncompromising opponents of Arianism was Bishop Athanasius, the patriarch of Alexandria, whose biography of St. Anthony inspired the spread of monasticism in the Western Empire. He taught that the true divinity of Christ was precisely because He was *of* the Father and not *made by* Him, and therefore, shared full equality *with* the Father. Holding tenaciously to this belief until his death in 373, he suffered imperial censorship and repeated exile from Alexandria. ❑

CONVERSION OF THE GERMANIC TRIBES

Constantinople, c.350

Ulfilas, the first Gothic bishop, was also the first to translate the Bible into Gothic. Ulfilas' father was a Goth, his mother a Cappadocian who was taken captive. He was raised in the Christian religion. In 341, he was part of a delegation sent to the Emperor Constantius, and Bishop Eusebius of Nicomedia named him bishop and gave him the mission of spreading the Gospel to the Goths. In the trinitarian conflicts taking place at the time, Eusebius was an adherent of the Arian party, and Ulfilas preached the Arian doctrine to the Goths.

Ulfilas' circle stood in open opposition to the Catholic bishops at the Council of Nicea. "I believe," wrote Ulfilas, "that the Son is subordinate and obedient to God the Father in all things as Scripture teaches us." According to Ulfilas, the Holy Spirit is "neither God nor master but rather the true servant of Christ, not equal to Him but in all things subordinate and obedient to the Son." This determination was far removed from the growing consensus of the Church.

With this as his foundation, Ulfilas translated the greater part of the Bible into Gothic. To do so, he not only had to coin new words to convey the sense of Christian theology, but also had to develop a new alphabet. He drew from Latin and Greek writing as well as in the prevalent letters of the Gothic tongue.

The simple beliefs of the German peoples came into conflict with the philosophical bent and symbolic repertoire of Arian teaching. Societies were structured around the belief in many gods of various powers. After intense struggle, and over the strenuous opposition of the upholders of earlier pagan traditions, Ulfilas finally succeeded in establishing Christian worship among the Goths. His translation of the Bible proved to be instrumental in the spread of Christianity among the Germanic tribes. ❑

Bernhard Rode, *Bishop Ulfilas*, etching

A page from the translation of the Bible into the Gothic language by Ulfilas

THE GOTHS

Point of Interest

The Goths played an important role in the late-antique world. Within a few centuries this people grew into a mighty European power. The Goths (meaning "men" or "heroes") originally came from the southern part of Sweden. By the second century AD, they expanded all the way to the Black Sea and established their sovereignty over much of the Ukraine. In 269, they invaded the Roman Empire but were defeated by Emperor Claudius II at the Battle of Naissus.

Sometime later the Goths split into two groups. The Ostrogoths (East Goths) under Ermanaric (r.350–375) built up a powerful state, but in 375 they came under the control of the Huns. After the death of Attila in 453, they once again gained their independence and settled in Pannonia (the region of present-day western Hungary). From there, their king Theodoric the Great (454–526) invaded Italy at the behest of the Byzantine emperor Zeno. He defeated the Italian king Odoacer, who had conquered Rome in 476. Theodoric wanted to unite all of the Germanic tribes under his leadership but was thwarted by the Frankish king Clovis I.

The Visigoths (West Goths) fled to the west before the invading Huns. They defeated and killed the Roman emperor Valens in 378 at Adrianople and forced his successor Theodosius to accept them into the empire. The Ostrogoth king, Alaric I, descended into Italy from Illyria and sacked Rome in 410.

After his death, the Ostrogoths migrated to southern France and Spain and under Theodoric I (r.418–451) established a kingdom with Toulouse as its capitol. He died in Catalonia in a victorious engagement against the Huns. The next great king of the Visigoths was Euric (r.466–484), who conquered almost all of Spain and much of Gaul. Their decline began under his successor, Alaric II (r.484–507), who lost most of his holdings in Gaul to the Frankish kings. The last Ostrogoth king was Roderic, who was killed by an invading Muslim army early in the eighth century, marking the beginning of the Muslim conquest of Spain. ❑

Visigoth soldier with chain mail tunic and spear (Mozarabic book illustration, 1109)

GERMANS, GOTHS AND HUNS

In August 410, an unbelievable event shook the world of the Mediterranean: Alaric I, the leader of the Visigoths, captured Rome and plundered it for three days. Those who were not Christians believed that it was a punishment for Rome's apostasy and its neglect of the old gods. In response, the church father Augustine wrote his famous work *The City of God* (413-426), in which he refuted this accusation. This treatise would have a crucial influence on theologians in the Middle Ages.

No matter which religion one subscribed to, it had become increasingly clear that the Western Roman Empire could no longer sustain itself. Among the reasons were the wars with Germanic tribes that had been going on for over 100 years. Its administrative and economic institutions could not meet the exhausting demands of imperial rule and confront the pressure of migratory warlike nations massed at its borders. The needs and upkeep of a military state had ruined the Empire's agriculture and its once flourishing urban system. For a long time the army had consisted mainly of Germanic soldiers with German generals commanding them. Even high-ranking officials were people of German origin who had become Roman citizens. By the time the Germanic tribes crossed the Rhine, the Roman Empire seemed already to have become "Germanized" from within. So it was that Alaric's main opponent in Rome was Flavius Stilicho, a general who was of Vandal origin; his murder in 408 made the Visigoths' attack on Rome much easier. The Western Roman Empire with its capital in Ravenna continued to exist formally until 476. But in reality the Goths had been its rulers for some time.

THE GERMANIC TRIBES AND ROME UP UNTIL 375

The military expeditions launched by the Germanic tribes against Rome were nothing new. As early as 100 BC, Rome had to contend with the attacks of Teutones and Cimbri tribes from Jutland. The attempt made during the reign of Augustus to incorporate large parts of Germania as far as the Elbe into the Roman Empire had been thwarted by the Roman defeat in the Battle of Teutoburger Forest in AD 9. In the third century Germanic tribes crossed the *Limes Germanicus* (the line of frontier forts) between the Rhine and the Danube and pushed forward as far as Gaul and northern Italy before they could be repulsed. These military campaigns were connected with the continuous movements of Germanic tribes, parts of tribes, or just small groups of people, who went on military expeditions and plundering raids for booty.

The reasons for these movements have not yet been completely explained. Worsening climate conditions, catastrophic floods along the north coast of Europe, and temporary overpopulation of many regions may have contributed to them, and the rich south had an irresistible attraction. Not to be discounted is that the ethos of these tribes glorified battle: it was custom that every spring young men would go on military campaigns as a rite of passage. Whatever the reasons, since the third century tribes and parts of tribes, ready for war, had gathered into larger and more dangerous groups, led by warlords. In the middle of the third century, tribes of Goths began to harass the Romans in regions near the lower Danube and even attacked the shores of the Black Sea.

In 269, the various Gothic tribes divided into two big groups, the Ostrogoths, who under their king Ermanarich controlled the vast regions of European Russia, and the Visigoths, who were more concentrated in the Balkan regions. Smaller tribes gradually became absorbed into them.

HUNS, VISIGOTHS, AND VANDALS

Soon the migration and foundation of kingdoms by these tribes had triggered the movement of other Germanic tribes. In 375, the Goths themselves were invaded by a nomadic people, the hordes of Hun horsemen who were pushing westward from the steppes of central Asia. At home their migratory movements had met with resistance from the neighboring Chinese empire. They were in search of fertile land in the West. The Black Huns defeated the Ostrogoths in the Volga region and drove those who did not submit farther to the west. The Visigoths consequently entreated the Romans for the right to settle along the lower Danube. But differences between the Visigoths and the East Roman central power led to the battle near Adrianople (378) that ended with the crushing defeat of the empire and the death of the Emperor Valens. While the Hun advance in 451 came to a halt after the defeat of Attila, the king of the Huns, by Roman and Germanic auxiliary troops on the Catalaunian Plain in France, the Germanic tribes that had started to migrate in large numbers could no longer be contained. The partition of the Western and Eastern halves of the Roman Empire, which from 395 were now each ruled by a separate emperor, had significant consequences. In 400 the Visigoths turned their attention to Italy, and the need to defend it resulted in the army being moved from the border along the Rhine, thus leaving it exposed and undefended. As a result, the Vandals, Alani, and Suebi crossed the Rhine into Gaul and from there to Spain. Here the Vandals, led by their chief Gaiseric, settled in the south (Andalusia), where they learned the art of shipbuilding and then built a fleet. In 429 they sailed to Africa where in 439 Gaiseric founded the first independent Germanic kingdom with Carthage as its capital. In 455 he set off from Carthage for Rome and plundered it again without opposition.

THE GERMANIC TRIBES AS "ALLIES"

At first the creation of new Germanic states within the empire by invading peoples was not

Galla Placidia, a Roman princess and queen of the Visigoths, with her two sons (wood relief, 5th century)

politically motivated. The newcomers were simply looking for places to settle, and since the numbers involved were probably only between 20,000 and 100,000, the Romans were easily able to incorporate them into the existing social framework. Those who chose to remain were integrated within the empire as *foederati* (allies), and they were given one-third of the land on which they settled. This approach was based on the tried and tested Roman policy that enabled the expanding empire to assimilate and "romanize" foreign peoples. Very often the new arrivals abandoned their own language after a few generations and merged with the rest of the population. Only a few words of their original vocabulary, such as the names of colors, the cardinal points, and the names of places and regions, might survive in the Roman language they used. Coexistence was made easier since most Germanic tribes soon converted to Christianity. With the weakening of centralized authority, however, the benefits of Roman citizenship diminished, and the prosperity and wealth seemed to be there for the taking. As a result, the forcible occupation of land became increasingly frequent.

The new Germanic kingdoms

After the Italian campaign of Alaric I, the Visigoths settled first in southern Gaul and then later in Spain, where they remained until 711 when their kingdom was overpowered by the Arabs. Only the name of the region of Catalonia ("Gotalandia") points to the one-time existence of their kingdom. In about 490, the Ostrogoths, who had grown strong again after the end of the Hun Empire, marched into Italy. Their most important ruler, Theodoric the Great (474-526), ultimately extended his rule over the entire Alpine region and the northeastern regions of the Balkans. Ravenna became one of the great cultural centers of the late ancient western world. After the death of Theoderic, his kingdom was conquered—as was that of the Vandals—by the armies of the Eastern Roman emperor Justinian I (527-565). It was Justinian's ambition to restore Roman rule over the entire Mediterranean. The Eastern Roman Empire had not been so seriously affected by crises and was now currently enjoying an economic recovery. While the Western Roman Empire collapsed under the attacks and invasions of Germanic tribes, the emperor in Constantinople ruled over the only stable empire in the Mediterranean.

Although the Vandal's power collapsed in the face of the first attack by the Eastern Roman armies, the conquest of the rest of Italy lasted almost twenty years and was not completed until 553. By 550 the Visigoths had already lost the southeastern corner of Spain between Cadiz and Cordoba. However, the effort involved in extending its control over the Empire's former lands debilitated Constantinople. Not long after it was barely able to resist the attacks of the newly emergent Persian Sassanid Empire, and subsequently that of the conquering sword of Islam. From 568 on, the Lombards occupied most of Italy. The northern region, Lombardy, is named after them. This meant that the new settlement areas were occupied by only a small number of Germanic tribes.

Originating from the central Elbe region, the tribe of the Alamanni occupied present-day Swabia in the third century, then in the middle of the sixth century pushed further south into the Alpine regions and towards the upper Rhine valley. But they too were unable to establish their rule permanently; in the eighth century they were subjugated by the Franks. The Angles and Saxons came from Jutland. The Saxons pushed further south and conquered present-day Lower Saxony, Westphalia and Thuringia; meanwhile some of them, together with Angles, occupied the British Isles and there founded several small kingdoms that were finally unified to make an Anglo-Saxon kingdom in the ninth century. The Saxons, who had succeeded in maintaining a coherent tribal identity without their own kingdom, were finally able to found a kingdom that developed into one of the more powerful Germanic realms. Charlemagne finally conquered this tribal state after a war lasting 30 years and converted it to Christianity. When the Lombards, and eventually also the Bavarians who had originally come from Bohemia, submitted to Charlemagne, his empire became the only one founded by migratory tribes to still survive on the European continent.

The Franks as heirs to the Romans

The Frankish migration was the shortest and at the same time the most successful, and it influence the history of the West for centuries to come. In the third century the Franks created a series of small tribal settlements on the right bank of the Rhine and these formed an alliance. In the fourth century they began to push deeper into Gaul. Where they merged with the local Roman population, they left only small vestiges of their presence in the Roman dialect and names of places. The situation was different in northern Gaul around the Somme. Here the Roman-Germanic language boundary shifted from the Rhine to a line running parallel to it, diagonally across Belgium and the ridge of the Vosges.

After eliminating all the rival powers, Clovis I, King of the Salic Franks since 482, finally established himself as overall ruler of all the Franks. By the time he died in 511 he had expanded his empire as far as the Pyrenees. Politically he benefited from the fact that in 498 he and several thousands of his followers officially converted to the Christian (Catholic) faith. For the first time in west European history, a Germanic tribe chose the orthodox religious faith of the Roman Catholic Church, rejecting both Arianism and paganism. The Church of Rome was also strengthened by this conversion. The reforms set in motion by Pope Gregory I increased its political influence and reestablished its moral authority through its commitment to the monastic principles of holiness and asceticism. At the threshold of the Middle Ages, these two polities, the Frankish Empire and the Catholic Church, were best able to embody the recollected authority of Rome's empire. Their mutual cooperation and periodic clashes determined the political dynamics of European society for the next three hundred years.

The civilization of the period of migration

The migrations, which can be reconstructed on a map with historical hindsight, are only partially supported by written sources. The archaeological remains left by the Germanic tribes provide more accurate information. From an archaeological point of view, the period of migration concluded when the custom of adding burial objects disappeared in the eighth century. The civilization that emerged in the fifth and sixth centuries during the migratory period can be classified into several groups, each of which can be traced back to the various dominant Germanic tribes. From the sixth to the middle of the eighth century Merovingian culture, known mainly from the objects found in the row-graves, seems to dominate. Customarily, bodies were fully dressed: the women were adorned with jewelry, while the men were given weapons. Celtic motifs were particularly widespread in the western regions and the British Isles; they would later play an important part in the art of illuminated manuscripts. Besides blacksmiths, who could also forge weapons, there were resident and traveling goldsmiths. In the fifth century production grew to such an extent that objects were exported far into northern Europe. In the glassworks of the Rhineland regions, the art of making glass—already practiced in Roman times—continued to flourish. Compared to metalwork, ceramics became less important from an artistic point of view, although here too an individual style developed. The most important example of architecture in the period of migration is Theoderic's tomb at Ravenna. ❏

THE TEACHINGS OF ST. AUGUSTINE

Hippo, North Africa, 426

St Augustine, or Bishop Augustine of Hippo, (354–430) was born of Berber descent in the North African provincial Roman city of Tagaste. Acknowledged as one of the founding Church Fathers, his journey to the Christian faith was chronicled in *Confessions*, a work generally recognized as not only a major influence on Christian theological thought, but also Western literature's first "autobiography." He is to this day recognized by both Catholics and Protestants as one of the most influential Fathers of the Church.

His great work, *The City of God*, completed in 426, was inspired by the Visigoths' sack of Rome sixteen years earlier. A central theme in this series of meditations is the question "Why did God allow Rome to fall to the Barbarians?" Many of the old-guard faithful saw the state's neglect of the traditional pagan gods as the cause of Rome's fall. Deprived of proper homage, the gods withdrew their centuries-old protection. Augustine rejected this belief, arguing that the old gods did not save Troy or prevent Roman defeats in the past. Addressing the issue from the perspective of his uniquely conceived Christian theology, which

put forth the ideas of predestination and original sin, Augustine asserted that Rome fell because, *a priori*, no secular city could be founded on goodness or justice. Only the City of God, to which all Christians should aspire, was eternal and would survive the ruin of the old order. He asked: "In this short life what does it matter under whose dominion a man lives, so long as he does not commit impious acts?" Whether it be the rise and fall of cities or the exertions of the individual, all worldly matters were meaningless without understanding these events or one's own life within the context of God's will. ❑

Michael Pacher, *St. Augustine and Devil* (right wing of the Altar of the Church Fathers, c.1480)

VISIGOTHS SACK ROME

Rome, 418

Given imperial sanctuary in 375, the Visigoths under King Alaric were enough of an internal danger to the empire to warrant Rome's hiring of barbarian mercenaries, including Vandals, to meet the burgeoning threat. Emboldened by relative autonomy, the Visigoths eventually turned on their hosts. They invaded Italy and confronted Emperor Honorius at Ravenna, demanding he bestow on them tributes of gold, and that he recognize Alaric as his equal. When Honorius rejected these demands, the Visigoths left Ravenna and proceeded to Rome where they sacked the city. Despite the devastation, there was a general sense of relief as the attack had little military significance. The core of the Roman army and government remained intact and unassailable at Ravenna.

In the aftermath, many blamed the growth of Christianity and the neglect of the old gods for Rome's weakness. It is more likely that the real reason was that Roman leaders had abdicated their responsibility for defending themselves, and so, were vulnerable to this barbarian enemy within.

It wasn't until 418 that the relationship with the troublesome Visigoths stabilized. Under an agreement between the barbarian King Wallia and the Emperor Honorius, the Visigoths were ceded the province of Aquitaine, which extended from Toulouse to the Atlantic. In return for the bequest of this "homeland," the Visigoths were to defend the Atlantic coast from raids

Alaric's entrance into Rome (woodcut, 19th century)

by Saxon pirates.

Their integration into the empire was further facilitated by a willingness to establish peaceful coexistence with Aquitaine's Gallo-Roman ruling class. In addition the Visigoths were Christian, albeit Arian, and as such had ready ties to the region's indigenous Christian community. ❑

THE ANGLO-SAXON TRIUMPH

Britain, c.450

After the departure of the Roman Army from Britain in 407, the indigenous Britons continued to battle the Picts and Scots. Eventually, Germanic tribes comprised of Saxons, Angles, and Jutes were drawn into the struggle, enlisted by Vortigern, leader of the Britons. The alliance was short-lived. In 442, the Saxons turned on their hosts and by 449 a full-scale Germanic invasion had begun. It was a power struggle that would push the Scots and Picts into what is today Scotland, the British Celts into Wales, Cornwall, Ireland, and Brittany, and end in triumph for the Anglo-Saxon tribes, whose rule would continue unrivaled until the Viking invasions of the late eighth century. ❑

Arrival of the Anglo-Saxons in Britain

ST. PATRICK IN IRELAND

Ireland, c.460

St. Patrick was born near present-day Carlisle in Britain (date unknown) and was the son of a landowner named Calpurnius. At the age of fourteen, Patrick was captured by Irish raiders and taken to Ireland as a slave. He escaped after six years and made a three-day voyage to Gaul. He trained as a priest in Gaul and Britain and, prompted by dreams and visions he believed were direct and specific guidance from God, he returned to convert Ireland in around 430. Of these dreams he wrote that the people of Ireland "...cried out, as with one voice: 'We appeal to you, holy servant boy, to come and walk among us.'" He succeeded in bringing most of the kings in Ulster, Leinster, and Munster, into the Christian faith. In this endeavor he became known as "Bishop of Ireland," and is one of Ireland's three patron saints, along with Brigid of Kildare and Columba. The date of his death has been surmised as either 461 or 493.

The most famous legend about him was of his driving the snakes out of Ireland. Zoologically suspect—Ireland was apparently devoid of snakes at the time of his mission—nonetheless there have been theories that the snakes were a metaphor for various "heresies," including the practices of the Druids and beliefs associated with the Pelagian Mysteries. ❑

GERMANIC TRIBES

Point of Interest

When speaking of the Germanic peoples historians refer to groups occupying northern Europe whose languages and cultures were closely related. Among the most important tribes were the Visigoths, Ostrogoths, Franks, Burgundians, and Vandals. The Huns from central Asia are also often included under this rubric. Before the birth of Christ, these tribal groups were already in movement: the Vandals, Goths, and Lombards had departed from their settlements in Scandinavia and moved south. Some of the tribes pushed farther west, displacing Celtic settlements and crossing over the Rhine during the time of Julius Caesar. By the end of the third century, these peoples had by and large resettled. Just east of the Rhine and north of the Main were the Franks; south of the Main were the Alamanni (from which the French name for Germany *Allemand* is derived) and the Burgundians. The Friesens and Saxons had settled on the North Sea coast, what is today Holland and Germany, with the Angles in Jutland. The tribes that had occupied the Oder-Neisse region had moved to the southeast: the Ostrogoths to the Ukraine and the Visigoths to the Roman province of Dacia, which was located north of the Danube, while the Vandals were to their west.

With their push into the heartland of Europe around 370, the Huns set off a chain reaction leading to further movements of peoples. The fall of the Western Roman Empire can be seen as the most striking result of these migrations. The Visigoths occupied the lower Danube region, pressing into what was formerly part of the empire. The Angles and Saxons settled in England, and the Franks occupied the northern part of France. The Burgundian Kingdom centered in Worms was destroyed by the Huns in 436. At that point the tribe moved to Savoy and the Rhone Valley. To their west, the Visigoths established their capital in Toulouse. The Suebi moved south to Spain in 409, followed by the Vandals, who established their own kingdom in North Africa in 429 under the rule of King Gaiseric. The Lombards, after wandering through the northern and eastern parts of present-day Germany, settled in Pannonia (roughly equivalent to present-day Hungary). Then driven out by the Huns, they finally gained permanent lands in the north part of Italy. Their kingdom centered on the town of Pavia. Their former territories in eastern Europe were gradually taken over by Slavic peoples. ❑

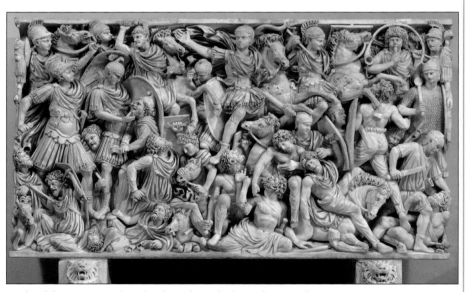

Battle of the Romans and Goths (from the Ludovic Battle Sarcophagus, c. 251)

ATTILA'S ARMY DEFEATED

Gaul, June 20, 451

In June of 451, an extraordinary alliance of Romans and barbarians, with imperial troops fighting alongside Visigoths, Franks, and Burgundians, won a pivotal battle over Attila the Hun on the Catalaunian Plains. The Visigoth king Theodoric died in battle, but Gaul was saved. The Roman general Aetius allowed Attila to retreat to Pannonia (Hungary).

It had been two years since Attila abruptly changed his policy of maintaining friendly relations with the Western Empire while he concentrated his efforts on extracting confiscatory tributes from its Eastern provinces. His demand to marry Honoria, the sister of the Emperor Valentinian III, and possessor of a dowry representing half the empire, was refused by the emperor. Attila responded by invading Gaul. The Hun troops were returning eastward after this incursion, their baggage trains laden with the spoils of war, when the alliance struck. This stinging defeat, and the retreat into Pannonia, marked the beginning of the end of Hun presence in the waning Roman Empire.

After his defeat in Gaul Attila and his Hun army found themselves confined to the small province of Pannonia, their ability to wage war vastly diminished. It was here that their fifty-year reign of terror in the Roman Empire came to a symbolic end with Attila's death in 453. Ironically, this warrior demigod, who had unified unruly bands of bow-wielding horseman from the Steppes into history's most fearsome army, died not on the battlefield, but at a feast celebrating his wedding. ❑

Raphael, *Meeting of Leo the Great and Attila*, fresco, 1511, Apostolic Palace, Vatican

ATTILA KING OF THE HUNS

Brief Lives

As the Western Roman Empire continued to decline Attila, (b.410) along with his brother and co-ruler Bleda, created a sizeable and fearsome empire. The reach of the Huns extended from the Caucasus over Hungary almost as far as the Rhine. Between 440 and 450, the Huns raided the territories of the Eastern Empire and commanded an annual payment in gold from Constantinople. During this time, Attila murdered his brother to set himself up as a sole ruler. In 451, Attila's army met with an allied force of Romans and Visigoths and was forced to retreat. He withdrew from Italy, laying waste to the cities on the way. Pope Leo I persuaded him, however, to leave Rome unharmed.

Attila returned to Pannonia. He died during the celebrations of his marriage to the Burgundian Queen Ildiko, possibly a victim of foul play. Attila's name lives on as emblematic of cruelty and barbarism. ❑

THE DEATH OF VALENTINIAN AND THE TRIUMPH OF THE VANDALS

Italy, September 21, 454

In September of 454, the Emperor Valentinian III stabbed to death his commander in chief, Aetius, during a meeting of the imperial council at Ravenna. A heated argument had erupted after the emperor accused Aetius of plotting to take power. It was believed by some of Aetius' retainers that this was a planned political assassination. In his thirty-year role as the empire's most powerful general, Aetius had shrewdly managed to form alliances with every group of barbarians he had defeated, and it was two of these barbarian retainers who then avenged his death by murdering Valentinian in March of 455.

The death of these leaders made the Western Roman Empire increasingly vulnerable to a new wave of barbarian attacks.

The latest threat came from the Vandals led by King Gaiseric, whose army had achieved a foothold in North Africa in 439 with the sacking of Carthage. Valentinian had maintained peace by signing treaties with the Vandal king but after his murder, Gaiseric declared those treaties void and proceeded to advance on Rome. In June of 455, Gaiseric's army sacked Rome for two weeks, plundering the city and taking thousands of captives, among them the Empress Eudoxia and her daughters. The only saving grace was their heeding pleas from Pope Leo and agreeing not to burn the city.

This second sacking of the city in 50 years highlighted the utter inability of the empire to defend itself. ❑

END OF THE WESTERN ROMAN EMPIRE

Ravenna, 476

With the abdication of the last emperor of the Western Roman Empire, a historical epoch came to a close. Germanic tribes ruled its possessions from their capital in Ravenna. Germanic troops overthrew the Emperor Romulus Augustulus and set up their leader, Odoacer, in his place.

The emperor of the Eastern Empire, Zenon, charged Odoacer to replace Romulus, who was still a child. Odoacer was the son of the chief of the Scirian tribe, which was closely allied with the Huns and had come into conflict with Rome in days of Attila. Since 470 he had served as an officer in the Roman army.

In 476, he brought together a Germanic army at Zenon's behest, took power, and exiled the young emperor to Campania.

For most citizens of the Western Empire, living conditions did not change significantly. Odoacer had no intention of refashioning the empire into a Germanic kingdom. In fact, he assumed a subordinate role to the Eastern emperor, renouncing the title of emperor and becoming in effect Zenon's representative in the West. Odoacer ruled from Ravenna, made no fundamental changes in the administration of government, and respected the will of the Senate. He commissioned renovations of the Colosseum in Rome and reinstated games there.

Zenon recognized Odoacer's claims, but suspected that he might develop into a military rival. Accordingly, in 488 he sent the Ostrogothic leader and consul, Theodoric the Great, to Italy to overthrow Odoacer by force. In two battles in the North of Italy, Theodoric emerged victorious, forcing Odoacer to withdraw to Ravenna. The city withstood a siege that lasted for two and a half years.

Through the mediation of the Bishop of Ravenna, the two warring generals reached a compromise, agreeing to rule jointly. Odoacer opened the gates of the city to his rival. Ten days later on March 15, 493, Theodoric stabbed Odoacer to death and assumed sole rule.

Theodoric maintained Roman manners and ways of governance. While the Goths observed their own laws and customs, Roman citizens were subject to Roman law and could claim its protections. His advisors were drawn from the ranks of the empire's educated class. Among those enlisted into his service were the philosopher Boethius and the author Cassiodorus, who wrote about the new emperor's policies. Like his predecessor, Theodoric left the local governments largely undisturbed, exercising power only in military matters and those relating to foreign relations. He practiced tolerance toward the church and provided Italy with a period of peace that had been sorely lacking.

The change in government meant a dramatic revival for the city of Ravenna, clearly evidenced by an upsurge in municipal building projects. Earlier in the century, Galla Placida, the half sister of the Emperor Honorius and from 425 to 437 empress herself, had many churches and mausoleums built in the city, but the city benefited from its newfound wealth and prestige.

Under the Gothic rule of Theodoric many more churches, mausoleums, and aqueducts were erected. These public works hinted at Theodoric's ambitious plan to establish a pan-Germanic union that would incorporate the Burgundians, Visigoths, Vandals, and Franks with the ultimate goal of restoring the West Roman Empire and putting it on an equal footing with the East. The plan remained unrealized due to the opposition of Theodoric's brother-in-law and rival, the Frankish king, Clovis I. ❑

Mausoleum of Theodoric in Ravenna

THE COUNCIL OF CHALCEDON

Asia Minor, October 451

In 451, the Fourth Ecumenical Council was summoned by the bishop of Rome, Pope Leo I, at Chalcedon (near present-day Istanbul). There the Council decreed a reversal of the decisions of the Council of Ephesus of 449, specifically condemning its acceptance of the Monophysite heresy. The congregants at Chalcedon reinstated the primacy of the Nicene Creed and the teaching that after the incarnation, Christ had a double but indivisible nature, both divine and human. Promulgated by the abbot Eutyches at Ephesus, Monophysitism asserted that the person of the incarnate Christ had but a single, divine, nature. Like Arianism and Nestorianism, Monophysitism was considered a misleading interpretation of Jesus' nature at variance with orthodox canon. ❑

Pope Leo I (Leo the Great)

THE MIDDLE AGES

AD 500–1500

- ■ Africa
- ■ Asia
- ■ Europe
- ■ North America
- ■ Oceania
-   South America

AD 500–599

Gaul, c.500. Clovis, the Frankish king, is converted to Catholicism, becoming the only orthodox Catholic Christian sovereign. The kings of the Visigoths, Vandals, Burgundians, and Ostrogoths are Arians.

American Southwest, c.500. The Anasazi culture is developing in Utah, Arizona, and New Mexico. For protective reasons, the Anasazi construct their villages on cliffs.

South America, c.500. The Huari civilization, based in the Ayachucho valley of the central Andean region, is expanding its power by conquest as far as the northern coastal region of Peru and the Nazca area to the south.

South America, c.500. The Tiahuanaco civilization, centered on the south coast of Lake Titicaca, shares religious and cultural beliefs with the Huari society and is amassing a large empire. There are signs that the power of Tiahuanaco—at 12,000 feet, the highest city in the world—derives from its control of trade in hallucinogens for ceremonial purposes. Its influence spreads south from Bolivia into Argentina and Chile.

Britain, 500. The Britons defeat the Saxons at Mount Badon and check the Saxon advance westwards, following the recent founding of the kingdom of the West Saxons (Wessex).

Gaul, 29 March 502. At Lyons, Gundobad, the King of the Burgundians, issues a new legal code that brings the Romans and Burgundians under the same law.

China, 502. Xiao Yan marches on Nanjing, forcing the Qi rulers, his own kinsmen, to cede their power. He founds the Liang Dynasty.

Gaul, 506. Alaric II, the King of the Visigoths, publishes a code of laws, the *Lex Salica*, inspired by the Theodosian code.

Gaul, 507. Allied with Gundobad, the Burgundian king, Clovis, crushes the Visigoths and kills their king, Alaric II, at the battle of Vouille. The Franks take Aquitaine; the Visigoths are pushed back into Spain.

Gaul, 508. At Tours, Clovis receives imperial recognition from Anastasius of his rule over Gaul.

Gaul, 508. Theodoric the Ostrogoth drives the Franks out of Provence and takes it over. His armies also rapidly recover Septimania (Languedoc) for the Visigoths, and Theodoric acts as regent for the infant Visigothic king, Amalaric, his grandson.

Paris, 27 November 511. Clovis, King of the Franks, dies, and his kingdom is divided up among his four sons: Theuderic in Reims, Chlodomer in Orleans, Childebert in Paris, and Clothar in Soissons.

Gothic Kingdom, 511. The Ostrogothic king Theodoric the Great assumes the crown of the Visigoths as well.

Korea, 512. The Japanese imperial chieftain Otomo no Kanamura agrees to the accession of the four provinces of Mimana in southern Korea to Paekche, a larger state in southwest Korea.

Burgundy, 516. Gundobad, King of the Burgundians, dies. His son Sigismund, who had shared power with his father, succeeds him and establishes Catholicism in place of Arianism among his people.

Constantinople, July 518. Anastasius, who came to the throne of the Eastern Empire in 491, dies. Anastasius reestablished the empire's finances, reforming the coinage and taxation systems. The new emperor, Justin, opposed to the Monophysitism of his predecessors, reestablishes orthodoxy and relations with Rome. The 35-year schism between the Western and Eastern Churches comes to an end.

North Africa, May 523. Hilderic succeeds Thrasamund as King of the Vandals.

Burgundy, June 524. After killing King Sigismund, the Frankish kings Chlodomer and Theuderic invade Burgundy. Chlodomer dies in battle at Vezerone, and the Burgundian king, Godomer, holds on to his kingdom.

Italy, 524. King Theodoric imprisons his minister Boethius, a Roman aristocrat and philosopher, on a charge of plotting with the Eastern emperor, and then has him executed.

Arabia, 525. The Ethiopians win back the Yemen from the Jewish prince, Dhu Nuvas, and reestablish Christianity there.

Italy, 30 August 526. King Theodoric dies of dysentery. His daughter Amalasuntha becomes regent for her young son Athalaric.

Rome, 526. Dionysius Exiguus, a monk of Scythian origin, produces Easter Tables and propounds the AD (*anno Domini*) system of dating from the birth of Christ.

Constantinople, 4 April 527. Seriously ill, Justin crowns his nephew Justinian as his co-emperor. He dies later the same year.

Constantinople, 528. The Emperor Justinian commissions the Justinian Code, the foundation of later Roman law.

Japan, 529. A serious revolt in Kyushu prevents a Japanese army from crossing to Korea to support the group of southern states known as Mimana, which are under threat of domination by Silla, a powerful kingdom in the southeast of the country.

Athens, 529. The Academy, which was founded by Plato, is closed by Justinian's order, making a decisive break with pagan culture.

Italy, 529. Benedict of Nursia founds the monastery of Monte Cassino and with it the tradition of European monasticism.

Persia, 530. Khosrow I succeeds to the throne, reorganizes the government, and inaugurates a flourishing period for the Sassanid Dynasty.

Rhineland, 531. Thuringia is conquered by the Franks Theuderic and Lothar.

Ethiopia, 531. The Byzantine Emperor Justinian tries to recruit Axum to help him in his fight against Persia.

Constantinople, January 532. A popular revolt against Justinian's rule causes panic in the capital, until thirty thousand rebels are massacred in the circus by imperial troops. The domed building of Hagia Sophia is erected.

Persia, 532. After a seven-year war, the new Persian king Khosrow signs a "treaty of eternal peace" with Justinian.

Burgundy, 534. The kingdom of the Burgundians, founded in 442, is annexed by the Franks.

North Africa, 534. The Byzantine forces, led by Belisarius, conquer the Vandal kingdom and capture the last Vandal king, Gelimer. Much of North Africa is now controlled by Byzantium.

Italy, 30 April 535. Theodahad, the new King of the Ostrogoths, has his wife, Queen Amalasuntha, the daughter of Theodoric, strangled. His action gives Justinian a pretext for his planned invasion of Italy.

Sicily, 535. Belisarius begins the conquest of the Ostrogothic kingdom by occupying the island of Sicily.

Rome, 9 December 536. Having captured Naples earlier in the year, Belisarius takes Rome. The Ostrogoths depose their inactive king, Theodahad, and elect a general, Vitigis, to replace him.

Rome, 537. Having secured his rear by conceding Provence, in Ostrogothic hands since 508, to the Franks, Vitigis moves on Rome and lays siege. The Franks now control all of Gaul except Visigothic Septimania (Languedoc) and Armorica (Brittany).

Japan, 538. Gilded bronze Buddhist images and sutras start to arrive in Japan from Korea.

Italy, March 539. Milan, one of the most important cities in Italy after Rome, is recaptured by the Ostrogoths and destroyed. The men are massacred and the women sold as slaves.

Italy, May 540. Vitigis, the King of the Ostrogoths, is tricked into surrendering to Belisarius, who takes possession of Ravenna. The reconquest of Italy south of the Po seems complete. Belisarius returns to Constantinople, taking Vitigis with him.

Ethiopia, c.540. Ethiopian scholars have begun to translate the Bible into their Geez language.

Kush, 540. Kush, to the south of Egypt, is divided into three Nubian kingdoms—Nobatia, Alodia, and Mukurra.

Syria, 540. Khosrow, the King of the Persians, resumes the war against Justinian by invading Syria. Antioch, the most important city in the area, is sacked.

Italy, 541. The senator Cassiodorus, once the chief minister of Theodoric, the King of the Ostrogoths, founds a monastery and famous library in his retreat at Vivarium in southern Italy.

Spain, 541. The Franks attack the Visigothic kingdom in northern Spain, but are driven back at Saragossa.

Constantinople, May 542. An epidemic of bubonic plague, which started in Egypt in 541, reaches Constantinople, killing hundreds of thousands of people. It spreads throughout the Byzantine Empire and is carried to Italy.

Italy, 543. With the departure of Belisarius, the imperial forces are in disarray. Totila, the new King of the Ostrogoths, advances to Italy, where he takes Naples after a siege. Belisarius is forced to return to Italy.

Kush, 543. The Nubian kingdom of Nobatia is converted to Christianity by Coptic missionaries from Egypt.

Rome, 17 December 546. The Ostrogothic king, Totila, captures Rome after a year's siege. The city has been deserted by all but 500 of its civilian inhabitants.

Rome, 547. Belisarius, the Byzantine general, reoccupies and repairs the defenses of the deserted city of Rome.

North Africa, 547. The Berber tribes of the interior, which have long been rebelling against the Byzantines, are crushed. After a series of civil wars and revolts, Africa is now at peace.

Constantinople, 548. Justinian summons Pope Vigilus from Rome and induces him to sign his edict condemning "The Three Chapters"—certain theological works accepted at the Council of Chalcedon in 451, but regarded as Nestorian heresy by the Monophysites. In this way Justinian hopes to reconcile the Monophysites to the Catholic faith as expressed at Chalcedon. This action causes protests in the West.

Constantinople, 28 June 548. Theodora, the wife of the Emperor Justinian, dies. She had been a highly influential figure at court, but was unable to get Justinian to favor her Monophysite faith.

China, 548. General Hou Jing, a Toba northerner who entered the service of the Chinese Liang in the south, heads a rebellion against his masters and leads his troops on Nanjing.

China, 549. Hou Jing lays waste to Nanjing.

Britain, c.550. The Anglo-Saxons again begin to push westwards, driving back or subjecting to their rule the Romano-British population.

Kush, 550. The Nubian kingdom of Alodia is converted to Christianity by Coptic missionaries.

Italy, 550. After Belisarius, frustrated by lack of imperial money and reinforcements, is recalled from Italy, Totila recaptures Rome.

Italy, 552. Justinian finally responds to the crisis in Italy by sending out a huge force led by Narses. He defeats and kills Totila in battle at Busta Gallorum.

Constantinople, 552. Two monks smuggle in two silkworm eggs from Ceylon, launching the silk industry in the West.

Egypt, 552. The patriarch, Apollinarius, reestablishes Catholicism in Alexandria by bloody repression, with the help of imperial troops. Coptic resistance, however, remains strong.

China, 552. While General Chen Baxian drives out the mutinous Toba general,

Hou Jing, from Nanjing in the south, Gao Yang deposes the last Emperor of the Northern Qi, thereby gaining control of most of northern China.

Italy, 553. The Byzantine general Narses defeats Teias, Tortila's successor as King of the Ostrogoths, at Mons Lactarius. The reconquest of Italy is almost complete.

Constantinople, 553. The historian Procopius completes his *Wars*, an account of Justinian's conquests.

Italy, 13 August 554. The Emperor Justinian launches a program to reorganize the administration of Italy after the chaos of the 20-year war with the Ostrogoths.

Spain, 554. Justinian's troops, invited to Spain two years previously by Athanagild, the pretender to the Visigothic throne, continue to occupy the southern part of the country after Athanagild becomes king and has no further use for them. They establish their capital at Córdoba.

Constantinople, December 557. An earthquake rocks the city, damaging the great church of Hagai Sophia.

Constantinople, 7 May 558. The dome of the church of Hagai Sophia collapses. Its immediate rebuilding is ordered by Justinian.

France, 558. Clothar I, the Merovingian King of France, unites the Frankish kingdoms after the death of his brother and nephew.

Central Asia, c.560. The Turkic peoples break their ties with the Juan-Juan or Avars, who created the first Mongol empire shortly after 400, to found two states. One is based in Mongolia (eastern Turks) and the other in Zungaria (western Turks). These events cause the migration of the Avar people toward the Caucasus.

Central Asia, 560. Khosrow, the King of the Persians, allied with the western

Turks, destroys the empire of the Hephtalites, which was set up on the borders of Persia and India about 100 years before.

Gaul, 561. Clothar, who has been the sole King of the Franks since 558, dies at Compiègne. The Frankish kingdom is divided among his four sons.

Constantinople, 561. Justinian establishes a new treaty with Khosrow by which the Persian frontier with the Byzantine empire is restored. The Byzantines, however, now undertake to pay an annual tribute.

Constantinople, 565. Justinian dies after a reign of 38 years. He leaves to his nephew and successor, Justin II, an empire at its territorial peak, but facing serious barbarian threats to its overstretched resources on most frontiers.

Gaul, 567. On the death of their brother Charibert, the sons of Chlothar redivide the Frankish kingdom. Sigibert takes Austrasia (eastern Gaul), Chilperic takes Neustria (western Gaul), and Guntram takes Burgundy (southeastern Gaul).

Pannonia, 567. The Lombards and Avars combine to crush the Gepids. The Avars take over their territory in the middle Danube.

Italy, 568. Under their king Alboin, the Lombards abandon Pannonia (Hungary) to the Avars and invade northern Italy.

Kush (Sudan) 569. Following the conversions of Nobatia in 543 and Ajodia in 550, the Nubian kingdom of Makuria is converted to Christianity.

Japan, 570. The Korean kingdom of Koguryo sends its first embassy to Japan.

Arabia, 570. Muhammad is born in Mecca.

Italy, 572. After a three-year siege, Pavia falls to the Lombards, who have overrun northern Italy; but their king, Alboin, is murdered by his Gepid wife.

Constantinople, 573. Justin II provokes war with the Persians, who ravage Syria and capture the strategic city of Dara.

France, 573. Gregory of Tours is named bishop. His history, *Gesta Francorum* (*Deeds of the Franks*), remains a crucial source of information concerning the Merovingian period.

China, 577. The dynamic emperor Wu of the Northern Zhou conquers the Northern Qi and reunifies China.

Constantinople, 578. Tiberius II succeeds Justin II as ruler of the Byzantine Empire. He has effectively ruled since 574, when Justin II went insane.

Italy, c.580. Cassiodorus, founder of a monastery and a renowned library on his estate at Vivarium, dies. He leaves a series of literary and historical works of his own, and many classical works survive in his library to be copied by future monks.

China, 581. The last Emperor of the Northern Zhou is overthrown by one of his own Chinese generals, Yang Jian, who founds the Sui Dynasty.

Balkans, 582. The Emperor Tiberius II surrenders Sirmium to the Avars and pays them a huge tribute to safeguard the rest of the Balkans. In August, he dies and is succeeded by Maurice, the general on the eastern frontier.

Spain, 585–586. Leovigild, the Arian king of the Visigoths, conquers the kingdom of the Sueves, in northwestern Spain. Leovigild dies, and the persecution of the Catholics ends with the accession of his Catholic son, Recared.

Spain, May 589. The Visigothic king Recared imposes the Catholic faith on his Gothic subjects at the Council of Toledo. Arianism, which has long hindered the fusion of the conquered peoples of the empire and the Germanic

tribes, is now virtually extinct except among the Lombards.

China, 589. After launching a successful combined naval and land attack against the Chen capital on the Yangzi river, Yang Jian takes the south and reunites China under the Sui Dynasty.

Persia, 589. Khosrow II is deposed from the throne of Persia in a military revolt and flees to Constantinople to seek support.

Rome, 590. Gregory, who founded six monasteries in Sicily as well as St. Andrew's in Rome, of which he is now abbot, is elected pope against his will.

Burgundy, c.590. The Irish monk and preacher Columba founds a monastery at Luxeuil.

Italy, 590. The Lombards survive a combined attack by the Franks and the Byzantines by retreating behind their city walls. They pay the Franks tribute to withdraw.

Persia, 591. The Byzantine Emperor Maurice restores Khosrow II to the throne of Persia. In return he receives significant territorial concessions; peace is once again established between the two empires.

Japan, 592. The Emperor of Japan has been put to death by Soga Umako. This is the latest stage in the continuing friction between the clans of the Soga, who support Buddhism, and the Mononobe, who maintain the supremacy of the indigenous *kami* deities.

Balkans, 592. Maurice begins warfare against the Avars and the Slavs, who have been periodically ravaging the Balkans and threatening Constantinople for the last decade.

Britain, 597. Augustine, sent by Pope Gregory, arrives in Kent on a mission to convert the pagan Anglo-Saxons to Christianity.

Italy, 598. After steady Lombard advances under King Agilulf since 591, the Byzantines finally conclude a treaty conceding northern Italy.

600–699

Britain, c.600. Augustine converts King Aethelbert of Kent to Catholic Christianity.

North America, c.600. Hohokam culture, which shows signs of Mexican influence, emerges in the southwest Arizona desert. Social organization is at a chieftainship level. At Snaketown and Pueblo Grande ball courts are erected, while at Mesa Grade low pyramid-type buildings are under construction.

North America, c.600. Hopewell has ceased to be the dominant culture of the Midwest and has almost disappeared as a cultural style.

South America, c.600. On Marajo island, in the mouth of the Amazon, social organization has developed to a chieftainship level. Very large and elaborate pottery styles are produced.

Peru, c.600. The Moche empire collapses possibly as a result of Huari expansion. Another cause of the collapse may be a major environmental change that caused the canals that irrigated the city of Moche to fill with silt.

Anatolia, 27 November 602. In the midst of a lengthy war against the Avars in which they have the upper hand, the Byzantine troops in the Balkans mutiny and choose the centurion Phocas as their leader. They march on Constantinople, where they get popular support. The Emperor Maurice flees but is captured and executed. Phocas becomes emperor.

Britain, 603. Aidan, the King of the Scots, attempts to stop the expansion of the Northumbrians under Aethel frith, but is defeated at Degsastan and forced to flee.

Persia, 605. The Persians under Khosrow II resume the war against the Byzantines.

India, 606. After the invasion of the Huns, King Harsha unites North India under his rule, which lasts until 647. Harsha is the last Buddhist King of India.

China, 606. The second Emperor of the Sui, Yangdi, expands and reorganizes the Confucian civil service examinations, introducing the prestigious Jingshi degree.

China, 607. A Japanese emissary, Ono no Imoko, is sent to China by Shotoku Taishi—crown prince under Suiko, the first officially recognised empress of Japan — in order to further good relations between the two countries.

Japan, 607. The Horyuji monastery is established at the instigation of Shotoku Taishi, who has done much to encourage the spread of Buddhism in Japan and the adoption of Chinese forms of culture and politics.

Asia Minor, 608. Having seized Armenia and Syria, the Persian army crosses the Taurus mountains into Asia Minor. Under the brutal, unpopular Phocas, the Byzantine empire is in total disarray.

Arabia, 610. Muhammad, a preacher of the Quraysh tribe of the Bedouin, begins to preach in Mecca, a prosperous oasis town and center of pilgrimage. He calls for an end to the demons and idols of Arab religion and conversion to the ways of the one god, Allah.

Constantinople, 5 October 610. Heraclius, son of the governor of Africa, attacks Constantinople with his fleet. The people rise in his favor; Phocas is seized and executed. Beset by barbarian attacks and religious and political divisions, the Empire is on the point of collapse.

Spain, 612. Sisebut, a poet and great patron of learning, becomes King of the Visigoths. He begins campaigns against the Byzantines and the Basques.

Paris, 15 October 614. Chlothar II, now sole king of the Franks after the execution of Queen Brunhilda, issues the Edict of Paris in an attempt to stamp out corruption in his kingdom. He establishes mayors of the palace to act as his chief ministers in the three parts of his united kingdom, Neustria, Austrasia, and Burgundy.

Palestine, 5 May 614. The Persians complete the conquest of Syria by capturing Jerusalem. They seize the True Cross, the most holy Christian relic.

Ethiopia, 615. Muslim refugees from Arabia are given refuge in the independent state of Axum.

China, 616. A rebellion breaks out throughout China against the Emperor Yangdi, who is building a great canal connecting the Blue river with the Yellow river.

Constantinople, June 617. The Avars and the Slavs arrive beneath the walls of the imperial capital and ravage the suburbs. The Balkans have been overrun by the barbarians; only a few towns remain in Byzantine hands.

China, 618. Li Yuan founds the Tang Dynasty.

Egypt, 619. The Persians complete their conquest of Egypt.

Constantinople, 619. The Emperor Heraclius buys off the *Kagan* (ruler) of the Avars, so that he can concentrate on defending the empire against the Persians.

Constantinople April, 622. Having raised money by melting down church treasures to mint coins, Heraclius launches a counterattack on the Persians. Three years before, he bought off the *kagan* (ruler) of the Avars in preparation for dealing with the Persian threat.

Arabia, 16 July 622. Muhammad is forced to leave Mecca and take refuge at Yathrib (Medina). His flight is known as the *hijra*.

Constantinople, August 626. The Persians ally with the Avars and launch a combined assault on Constantinople, but the Avar fleet is destroyed and the *kagan* raises the siege. Constantinople is saved.

China, 626. Li Yuan's second son, Li Shimin, engineers a coup d'état, known as the Xuanwu Gate incident, in which he kills his brothers. Shortly afterwards he forces his father to abdicate.

Britain, 627. King Edwin of Northumbria is converted to Christianity and baptised by Paulinus, who becomes bishop of York.

Persia, 9 December 627. Heraclius, allied with the Khazars, a people of Mongolian origin, penetrates deep into Persian territory and annihilates the fleeing Persian army at Nineveh. This victory opens up for Heraclius the route to the Persian capital, Ctesiphon.

Persia, 3 April 628. Following the murder of Khosrow II, his son and successor, Kavadh, sues for peace with the Byzantines. He hands back Armenia, Byzantine Mesopotamia, Syria, Palestine, and Egypt, as well as the True Cross.

Arabia, 628. After the Meccans lifted their seige of Yathrib, Muhammad and his supporters are granted permission to make a pilgrimage from Yathrib (Medina) to Mecca.

Gaul, 629. Dagobert, son of Chlothar II, succeeds to the Frankish throne.

Spain, 629. The Visigoths complete the recovery of southern Spain from the Byzantines.

Constantinople, 629. The Byzantine emperor, Heraclius, abandons the Latin imperial form of address—Imperator Caesar Augustus—and takes the Greek title of Basileus.

Arabia, 630. Having defeated the Meccans, Muhammad takes control of Mecca and declares the Kaaba to be the holy shrine and pilgrimage place for the new religion of Islam.

Arabia, 8 June 632. Death of Muhammad. Muhammad's closest followers select the ageing Abu Bakr to succeed the Prophet as leader of Islam. He takes the title of caliph.

Britain, 633. King Edwin of Northumbria is killed in battle by the Britons in alliance with the Mercians. Oswald becomes king after a brief pagan revival and restores Christianity with the help of Irish monks from Iona led by Aidan, who founds a monastery on Lindisfarne.

Red Sea, 634. Arab Muslims take Massawa on the Red Sea from the Ethiopian Axumites.

Balkans, 635. Aiming to keep the Avars out of the Balkans, Heraclius forms an alliance with Kuvrat, the Bulgar king.

Syria, 15 August 636. The Byzantine army is crushed by the Arab Muslims at the battle of Yarmuk. The Arabs, who took Damascus last year, now control all of Syria.

China, 638. The Emperor Taizong commissions the great scholar Yan Shigu to establish definitive versions of the classics, and orders Kong Yingda and other scholars to write detailed commentaries on them. Known collectively as the *Correct Meaning of the Five Classics*, these provide the foundation for classical Confucian education.

Jerusalem, 638. Jerusalem falls to the Arabs under Caliph Omar.

Central Europe, c.640. Led by Samo, a merchant of Frankish origin, the Slavs have established a kingdom in Bohemia independent of the Avars and the Franks.

Constantinople, 641. Heraclius dies after a thirty-year reign. Despite his spec-tacular successes against the Persians, he leaves an empire beset by religious controversies and now threatened by the Arabs. After a brief period of confusion—during which his two sons die within months of each other—he is succeeded by his youthful grandson, Constans II.

Egypt, 641. Egypt, invaded two years previously, surrenders to the Arabs. Alexandria surrenders, and its library is burned down.

Persia, 642. The Arabs defeat the Persians at Niharvand and put their king, Yazdgard III, to flight. This victory puts an end to the Sassanid dynasty.

Britain, 5 August 642. Oswald, the Christian king of Northumbria is killed by Penda, the pagan king of Mercia, at Maserfelth.

Italy, 643. Rothari, King of the Lombards, publishes an edict codifying the laws of the Lombards in Latin. Meanwhile, he is busy expanding his kingdom at the expense of the Byzantines.

North Africa, 643. The Arabs reach Cyrenaica and Tripolitania.

Arabia, 4 November 644. Omar is assassinated at Medina and is succeeded as caliph by Uthman.

Japan, 645. The Taika reform organizes Japan into a centralized monarchy following the Chinese example. This structure will remain in place until the beginning of the Shogunate in 1192.

North Africa, 646. With the support of the African Church and the Berbers, Gregory, the *exarch* (governor) of Carthage, rebels against the Emperor Constans II, who has espoused the Monothelete doctrine, a watered-down version of the Monophysite heresy.

North Africa, 647. The Arabs launch a raid into the Byzantine province of Africa, killing Gregory and effectively ending the African rebellion against Constans, the Byzantine emperor.

Syria, 647. Muawiya, the Arab governor of Syria, lays waste to Cappadocia in Asia Minor and takes the spoils home to Damascus.

India, 647. The Indian ruler Harsha, who became King of Kanauj in 606, dies after creating an empire in the north comparable to that of the Guptas.

Constantinople, 648. In an attempt to restore church unity, Constans II promulgates a doctrinal edict called the *Type*, but this simplistic attempt to prohibit discussion of the problem satisfies neither the orthodox nor the Monotheletes.

Rome, October 649. Pope Martin calls a council at the Lateran Palace which condemns the Monothelete doctrine and the recent compromise edict, the *Type*, imposed by Constans II.

Cyprus, 649. The Arabs, who have assembled a formidable fleet under the leadership of Muawiya, the governor of Syria, storm the island of Cyprus.

China, 649. After the death of the Emperor Taizong, Gaozong succeeds to the throne.

Tibet, c.650. The highland nomadic tribes join together to found a state. This marks the beginning of Tibetan history.

Italy, 652. Aripert, who has succeeded the Arian Rothari as King of the Lombards, is baptized a Catholic at Pavia. Catholicism has almost vanquished Arianism among the Lombards.

Spain, 653. At Toledo, Recessuinth, the King of the Visigoths, draws up a code, the *Liber ludiciorum*, based on Roman law and aimed at achieving equality between Hispano-Romans and Goths. It is the first territorial law code that applies to all regardless of racial and cultural differences.

Rome, 653. Pope Martin is arrested by the *exarch*, the governor of the imperial territory in Italy, and sent to

Constantinople, where he is convicted of high treason. His death sentence is commuted to banishment.

Rhodes, 654. The Arabs invade Rhodes and set about systematically pillaging the island.

Central Asia, 655. Yazdgard III, the last Sassanid king, who fled from Persia after its defeat by the Arabs in 642, is assassinated. The Arabs take Kabul and Kandahar.

Anatolia, 655. In a major sea battle of the coast of Lycia, the Arabs defeat the Byzantines, led by Constans II, and now command the eastern Mediterranean.

Britain, 655. At the battle of the river Winawed, Oswy, the King of Northumbria, defeats and kills Penda, the pagan king of Mercia.

Arabia, 17 June 656. Caliph Uthman is assassinated and succeeded by Ali ibn Abi Talib, Muhammad's cousin and son-in-law.

Arabia, 9 December 656. Rebels who dispute the succession of Ali are defeated by the caliph's forces at the battle of the Camel, near Basra. This conflict develops into a schism between the Sunni and Shia sects of Islam.

India, 657. Brahmagupta, a great mathematician, establishes the rules of calculation by introducing the concept of zero.

Central Europe, 658. Samo, who reigned over the Slav kingdom of Bohemia, which he had created, is dead.

Syria, 659. The Byzantines reach a truce with the Arab commander in Syria.

Mesopotamia, 24 January 661. Ali is assassinated in Kufa by an ex-supporter who has become a Kharajite.

Syria, 661. Muawiya succeeds Ali as caliph, founds the Umayyad Dynasty, and moves the seat of government to Damascus.

Italy, 663. Unpopular in his capital, and with Syria and Egypt under Arab control, Constans II sails west to Italy and makes a vain attempt to reconquer mainland Italy, which is now largely Lombard territory, for the empire.

Britain, 664. The plague which began in Egypt in the 540s and devastated Constantinople in 542, ravages the British Isles, having crossed Europe.

Britain, 664. King Oswy of Northumbria presides over the Council of Whitby, at which the nobles decide to join the Roman Catholic Church instead of the Celtic Church.

China, 664. The Chinese monk and pilgrim Xuanzang, who founded the Wei-shih school of Buddhism, dies at the age of 68. Xuanzang traveled to India in 629 to bring back sacred Sanskrit texts.

Korea, 668. The King of Silla recaptures Koguryo and Paekche, adjacent kingdoms in Korea, with the help of China, whose sovereignty he recognizes.

Sicily, 668. The Emperor Constans II is assassinated during a mutiny at Syracuse. He is succeeded by his son Constantine IV Pogonatos (the Bearded), who is in Sicily to put down the revolt that led to his father's death.

Central Asia, 670. Qutlugh reestablishes the khanate of Orkhon, an eastern Turkish empire which had been destroyed by the Chinese Emperor Taizong.

Central Asia, 670. The Tibetans take control of the Tarim basin and drive the Chinese from their four garrisons.

North Africa, 670. The Arabs complete their conquest of the region they call Ifriqiyah on the coast of North Africa (which stretches from eastern Algeria to Egypt).

Spain, 672. On the death of Reccesuinth at Toledo, Wamba is elected King of the Visigoths.

Britain, 673. Benedict Biscop founds a monastery at Monkwearmouth in Northumbria.

China, 673. Yan Liben, a painter of the Tang dynasty, is dead. He presided over the public works committee entrusted with the task of constructing the imperial palaces of the capital. He leaves behind his famous hand scroll of the Thirteen Emperors.

Constantinople, 678. The Arabs have attacked Constantinople by sea annually since 674. The Byzantines use "Greek fire," a new weapon invented by the Syrian Callinicus, to defend themselves. This is an incendiary mixture, fired from guns, that is fuelled by seawater rather than extinguished by it. It is a violent storm, however, rather than this lethal weapon, that destroys the Arab fleet and puts an end to their harassment. The Arabs and the Byzantines sign a peace treaty.

Syria, 678. Yazid succeeds as caliph on the death of his father, Muawiya, in Damascus.

Constantinople, 680. Constantine IV, until now forced to share power with his younger brothers Heraclius and Tiberius, becomes sole emperor.

Constantinople, 680. With the main Monophysite parts of his empire, Egypt and Syria, lost to the Arabs, the Emperor Constantine IV abandons his support for the now unnecessary Monothelete compromise. He holds the Sixth Ecumenical Council, condemning Monothelitism and restoring orthodox Catholicism.

Mesopotamia, 10 October 680. Al-Husayn, the son of Ali, is killed in combat at Karbala. His death gives birth to Shiism: the Shiites claim that the right of interpreting the Koran is confined to Muhammad's descendants. They maintain that Ali was immune from sin and error and had been divinely chosen as imam to transmit his office to his descendants. Al-Husayn is therefore regarded as a martyr.

Spain, 680. Count Ervig, taking advantage of an uprising by the Basques and of the discontent caused by reforms of the church and the army, overthrows Wamba, the King of the Visigoths, and as king makes concessions to the rebellious aristocracy.

Balkans, 681. After defeating the Byzantine army, the Bulgars found a new state on the delta of the Danube. Their ruler Asparuch pressures Byzantium into recognizing them and paying them an annual tribute.

Britain, 682. The controversial prelate Wilfrid, exiled from his Northumbrian bishopric, converts the South Saxons of Sussex to Christianity.

Near East, 682. Abdullah ibn Zubayr, who is supported by the people of Mecca and Medina, is acclaimed as caliph in Arabia, Mesopotamia and Egypt, and by the members of the Qais tribe in Syria.

Britain, 683. Benedict Biscop founds the monastery of Jarrow in Northumbria.

China, 683. On the death of the Emperor Kaozong at Loyang, his concubine Wu Zhao takes possession of the throne and founds the Zhou Dynasty.

Britain, 685. The Picts defeat the Northumbrians in battle near Forfar and kill their king, Ecgfrith. The Northumbrians are forced to retreat from conquered Pictish territory. The Firth of Forth becomes recognized as the boundary between England and Scotland.

Syria, 685. Abd al-Malik succeeds his father, Marwan, a distant cousin of Muawiya, as caliph of the Umayyads. The Sunnites, supporters of the Umayyads, believe—in contrast to the Shiites—that doctrinal authority changes hands with the caliphate. The new caliph makes Arabic the official language of the caliphate.

Japan, 685. Buddhism becomes the state religion.

Constantinople, 685. At the age of 16, Justinian II succeeds his father, Constantine IV, on the throne of the Byzantine empire.

Britain, 687. After its conquest by Caedwalla, King of Wessex, the Isle of Wight is the last area of Anglo-Saxon England to be converted to Christianity.

Britain, 20 March 687. The saintly Cuthbert, who lived as a hermit on the Fame islands and became bishop of Lindisfarne in Northumbria, dies.

Gaul, 687. After a series of conflicts between the Austrasian and Neustrian mayors of the palace—the real rulers of the Franks behind the facade of the increasingly ineffectual Merovingian kings—Pepin II, mayor of Austrasia, wins a decisive victory over his Neustrian rival at the battle of Tertry. The Franks are now united under one king and, more importantly, under one mayor.

Italy, 689. King Cunipert of the Lombards defeats a rebellious duke and succeeds in establishing religious unity. Arianism is finally stamped out.

Gaul, 690. Willibrord, a Northumbrian monk, travels to the continent and, with Frankish encouragement, begins to preach the Gospel to the heathen Frisians.

Sumatra, 690. The Malayan Kingdom of Srivijaya conquers the Indianized Kingdom of Malayu, setting up its capital at Palembang and adopting Buddhism.

Balkans, 690. The Byzantine emperor, Justinian II, defeats the Slavs, who are based in Macedonia and Thrace.

Mesopotamia, 690. Mus'ab, the governor of Mesopotamia and brother of the rebel ibn Zubayr, is defeated on the Tigris by the caliph Abd al-Malik.

Arabia, 690. Abd al-Malik's general al-Hajjaj captures Medina.

West Africa, c.690. The state of Gao is founded on the upper Niger.

Palestine, 691. The Dome of the Rock is completed in Jerusalem. The eight-sided domed structure is destined to become the second holiest place in Islam after the Kaaba.

Constantinople, 692. An episcopal council meeting confirms Eastern Orthodox practices over Western ways, ruling against the celibacy of the priesthood, and asserting that the patriarch of Constantinople is equal to the pope. The papacy rejects these canons.

Arabia, 693. Led by al-Hajjaj, the Umayyads put down ibn Zubayr's rebellion. Mecca is besieged and captured, and ibn Zubayr is killed. Abd al-Malik becomes master of the Umayyad empire.

Spain, 694. The Visigothic Council of Toledo decrees the enslavement of all Spanish Jews and orders their property confiscated. This is the culmination of a century of anti-Jewish legislation in the Visigothic kingdom.

China, 694. Manichaeism is introduced into China.

Constantinople, 695. The Byzantine emperor Justinian II is overthrown by the general Leontius. His nose is cut off and his tongue cut out. He takes refuge in the Crimea with the Bulgars.

Rome, 695. The pope consecrates the Northumbrian monk Willibrord as bishop of Utrecht, to serve his new converts to the Christian faith in Frisia.

Arabia, 696. The first Muslim dinar is minted. Abd al-Malik imposes Arabic as the official language in the Umayyad empire. The Koran is re-edited with vocalic symbols.

Venice, 697. The first doge is elected.

North Africa, 698. The Arabs occupy Carthage and bring an end to Byzantine rule in North Africa.

North Africa, 698. The Arabs put down a revolt by the Berbers in the Aures mountains, in the region which they call Ifriqiyah, on the North African coastline.

Constantinople, 698. Following another military revolt, the admiral Tiberius III becomes emperor. supplanting Leontius, who has his nose cut off.

700–799

Ireland, c.700. Adamnan, abbot of Iona, persuades much of the Irish church to come over to the Roman method of calculating the date of Easter, but fails to convince his own community and its daughter monasteries in Ireland.

North America, c.700. The use of bows and arrows, which are gradually replacing spears as the favorite weapons for hunting, has transformed activities in Indian society. The invention of the hoe has improved the efficiency of agriculture.

Mexico, c.700. The city of Teotihuacan is largely destroyed by fire and deserted by most of its inhabitants. The cause may have been social insurrection. Another theory is that the valley of Mexico could no longer sustain the huge population of Teotihuacan. Environmental deterioration caused by deforestation—to produce the vast amounts of lime plaster needed to cover the city walls—may also have been a factor.

Mexico, c.700. Possibly as a consequence of the collapse of Teotihuacan, Monte Alban is abandoned.

Mexico, c.700. The Temple of the Inscriptions and Temple of the Cross are under construction at Palenque, an important Maya religious centre.

Britain, c.700. The *Lindisfarne Gospels*, the finest of all Anglo-Saxon illuminated manuscripts, are produced. At around the same time, the *Book of Kells* is completed in Ireland.

West Africa, c.700. The kingdom of Ghana is growing in strength because of its control of trade routes, in particular the gold trade route.

Constantinople, 705. Tervel, the Bulgar khan, attacks Constantinople in support of the exiled Justinian II. The ousted emperor regains the Byzantine throne, and Tervel receives the title of Caesar.

China, 705. The Empress Wu is deposed in a coup d'état organized by her own ministers, who have grown sick of her frivolous excesses. The Tang Dynasty is restored in the person of the son she had previously deposed, Zhongzong.

Syria, 8 October 705. The Umayyad caliph Abd al-Malik dies in Damascus. He is succeeded by his son Walid.

Japan 710. Nara is established as Japan's first permanent capital. The Nara period is one of great artistic flowering.

Anatolia, 711. Bloody acts of suppression by Justinian II provoke a serious revolt in the Crimea, which is supported by the Turkish Khazars. After marching on Constantinople, the rebels defeat and kill the emperor in a battle in northern Asia Minor.

Spain, 711. A small Arab expeditionary force under Tarik crosses the Straits of Gibraltar and crushes Roderic's Visigoths in battle on the river Euadelete. Much of Spain rapidly capitulates to the Arabs.

Italy, 712. Liutprand becomes King of the Lombards. He aims to reunite Italy by conquering the Byzantine territories and the semi-independent dukedoms of Spoleto and Benevento.

China, 712. The Emperor Xuanzong succeeds to the throne, bringing to an end a period of instability during which the nominal emperors, Zhongzong and Ruizong, were forced to share power with the corrupt Empress Wei and the formidable Taiping Princess, both of whom aspired to follow the Empress Wu's example.

Gaul, 714. On the death of Pepin II, one of his illegitimate sons, Charles Martel (the Hammer), overcomes the other claimants and succeeds his father as mayor of the Austrasian palace, the effective power behind the Frankish throne. He goes on to defeat his Neustrian rivals at the battle of Ambleve.

Britain, 716. The wandering bishop Egbert, Northumbrian by birth, wins the monks of Iona and the monasteries under its jurisdiction over to the Roman dating for Easter.

Constantinople, 717. An Arab army of eighty thousand men and a fleet of eighteen hundred ships besiege the capital of the Byzantine empire. In the following year, Emperor Leo III the Isaurian triumphs over the Arabs, thanks to Byzantine superiority at sea. Further Arab expansion is blocked.

Rome, 719. The West Saxon monk Winfrid is sent by the pope to preach the Christian faith to the heathens in Germany. The pope gives him the name of Boniface.

France, 721. Having overrun Visigothic Septimania (Languedoc), the Arabs attack the Franks, but Duke Eudo defeats al-Sanh ibn Malik outside Toulouse and prevents an Arab invasion of Gaul.

Britain, 725. The Northumbrian monk Bede publishes a treatise entitled *De ratione temporum* (*On the reckoning of time*). He follows Dionysius Exiguus in reckoning dates from the birth of Christ. Through his works, this system is rapidly disseminated throughout Western Europe. In 731, he completes his *Ecclesiastical History*.

Constantinople, 726. Leo III the Isaurian bans the worship of religious images. His measures meet violent popular opposition throughout the empire. In the following year, Pope Gregory II condemns iconoclasm. Byzantine Italy breaks with the Empire. Leo's iconoclasm initiates a crisis in the Eastern Church that will last for a century.

France, 17–25 October 732. Charles Martel stops the Muslim expansion into Europe at the Battle of Tours.

Constantinople, 733. In response to a revolt in Italy against iconoclasm supported by Pope Gregory III, Leo III withdraws all the Balkans, Sicily, and Calabria from the jurisdiction of the pope and puts them under the control of the church at Constantinople. The break between the papacy and the Eastern Church is almost complete.

Gaul, 737. After the death of Theuderic IV, the throne of the Frankish kingdom is left vacant for a time by Charles Martel, the mayor of the palace and the effective ruler.

Egypt, 737. Christians invade Egypt from the south to protect the patriarch of Alexandria.

Spain, 739. Alfonso (the Catholic), the son-in-law of King Pelagius, becomes King of the Christian kingdom of the Asturias. He makes frequent raids on Arab territory.

Asia Minor, 739. The Arab invaders of Asia Minor are defeated by the Byzantine forces at the battle of Akroinon.

Rome, 739. The pope vainly appeals to Charles Martel for help against the expansionist policies of Liutprand, King of the Lombards.

Gaul, 739. The Anglo-Saxon monk Willibrord, who evangelized Frisia, dies at the age of 81 in the Echternach monastery which he founded in 698.

East Africa, 740. Muslims from Arabia and Persia are trading on the coast.

Japan, 741. The Japanese government decrees that Buddhist temples shall be established throughout the nation.

Gaul, 22 October 741. Charles Martel dies at Quiezy. His mayoral power is divided between his two sons, Pepin III and Carloman.

Constantinople, 741. Constantine V succeeds his father, Leo III the Isaurian, on the throne. A supporter of iconoclasm, he begins to persecute the image worshippers.

Constantinople, 742. Constantine V storms the capital, which had been seized by his rebel brother-in-law Artavasdus and the opponents of iconoclasm. Having regained control, he intensifies his attacks on image worship.

Constantinople, 745. An outbreak of bubonic plague sweeps Constantinople and spreads through Europe.

Egypt, 745. Nubians invade Egypt and temporarily occupy Cairo.

Cyprus, 746. The Greeks, having destroyed a large Arab fleet, regain control of Cyprus.

Gaul, 747. Carloman, who was sharing power with his brother Pepin, abdicates and retires to a monastery in Rome. Pepin III (the Short) becomes sole effective head of the Frankish kingdom.

Syria, 749. Marwan, the last Umayyad caliph, is defeated by the Abbasids at the battle of the Zab. In the following year, the Abbasids overthrow the Umayyad sect and gain spiritual and political control of most of the Muslim world.

South Africa, c.750. The culture associated with early users of iron in Africa reaches the Transkei area of the eastern Cape. This culture developed around Durban in Natal from about 380. Further south it becomes increasingly mingled with and indistinguishable from Khoisan herding culture. Bantu languages of the area borrow the click sounds of the Khoisan languages.

France, 751. After obtaining papal approval, Pepin III, the mayor of the palace, dispenses with the fiction of rule by the long-ineffective Merovingian kings and takes the title king for himself, founding a new royal dynasty, the Carolingians.

Italy, 751. Ravenna, the last Byzantine possession in northern Italy, falls to the Lombards under King Aistulf.

Central Asia, 751. After having occupied Tashkent, Samarkand, and Bokhara, the Chinese are crushed by the Arabs on the river Talas. Islamic influence spreads through central Asia.

Japan, 752. The Empress Koken attends a ceremony before the great bronze Buddha in the Toshodaiji temple in Nara. She attests that she, as empress, is the servant of the Three Jewels of Buddhism.

Arabia, 752. Two Chinese prisoners reveal the technique of making paper to the Arabs. The first paper mill in the Arab world is established.

Japan, 754. The Chinese monk Chienchen, who is almost blind, reaches Japan after making five unsuccessful attempts.

Gaul, January 754. Assailed by the Lombards and with little prospect of help from the Byzantines, Pope Stephen II appeals to the Franks for help. He and Pepin conclude the treaty of Quiercy. Pepin makes a donation of land to the pope, forming what becomes known as the Papal States. In return Pope Stephen recognizes the Carolingians as the legitimate rulers of the Franks. Defeated in battle by Pepin, the Lombard king Aistulf swiftly submits.

Mesopotamia, June 754. Al-Mansur, the brother of Abdul Abbas, the first Abbasid caliph, succeeds to the caliphate.

Spain, 756. The Umayyad prince Abd al-Rahman creates the emirate of Córdoba.

Britain, 757. After a very successful forty-year reign, King Aethelbald of Mercia is murdered at Seckington by his bodyguard. He is succeeded by his kinsman Offa.

Mesopotamia, 762. The second Abbasid caliph, Abu al-Mansur, makes Baghdad the capital of his empire. Meanwhile the Shiites revolt against the Abbasids in Mesopotamia, and a similar revolt is in progress at the town of Medina in Arabia.

Anatolia, 765. Constantine V steps up his persecution of the image worshippers. Icons and mosaics are smashed. The monastic order as a whole is violently attacked; many are martyred in the process.

Gaul, 24 September 768. Pepin III (the Short) dies. His dominions are divided, according to custom, between his sons, Charles (Charlemagne) and Carloman.

Gaul, 4 December 771. With the death of his brother Carloman, Charlemagne becomes sole ruler of the Frankish empire.

Rome, 772–774. Pope Adrian appeals to Charlemagne for help against the Lombard king, Desiderius, who has taken over part of the Papal States. Charlemagne conquers the Lombard kingdom and makes it part of the Frankish kingdom. Desiderius withdraws to a monastery. Charlemagne declares himself King of the Lombards. He then becomes the first Frankish king to visit Rome. He confirms the "donation" of the Ravenna region to the pope, which was made by Pepin the Short, his father.

Iraq, 772. Al-Mahdi succeeds his father, al-Mansur, as caliph of the Abbasids.

Constantinople, 775. On the death of Constantine V, his eldest son, Leo IV, succeeds as Byzantine emperor. Although an iconoclast like his father, he pursues a more conciliatory religious policy.

Malaysia, 775. The kingdom of the Srijaya (in Sumatra) conquers the whole of the Malaysian peninsula. A ninety-foot-high temple is built in honor of the Buddha.

Spain, 778. Charlemagne's forces invade Spain, where an Umayyad Dynasty was established in 756, but meet heavy resistance at Saragossa. As the Franks retreat from Spain, one of Charlemagne's most trusted generals, Roland, is killed in an ambush by the Basques at Roncesvalles. His death in battle becomes the subject of the *Song of Roland*, written in the French vernacular around 1100.

Saxony, 782. After three years of fighting, Charlemagne makes Saxony a Frankish province and imposes the Christian faith on the natives. But their leader Widukind soon leads a revolt and massacres a Frankish army. Charlemagne slaughters rebel prisoners and invades again. In 785, Widukind is baptized and reconciled to Charlemagne.

Baghdad, 786. Haroun al-Raschid becomes caliph in Baghdad, and the Islamic world enters a cultural and political golden age.

Byzantine Empire, 787. After heated debate, the second Council of Nicea, called by the Empress Irene, condemns iconoclasm and restores the veneration of images.

Gaul, 789. Charlemagne issues the *Admonitio Generalis*, a decree setting out his plans for the revival of culture and education in his dominions.

Britain, 8 June 793. Vikings raid the Northumbrian coast, sacking the monastery on Lindisfarne and slaughtering many of the defenseless monks.

Japan, 794. The Emperor Kammu moves the capital to Kyoto, away from the power of the Buddhist sects of Nara.

Ireland, 795. After attacking the Shetlands, the Vikings sail down the west coast of Scotland, sack the monastery on Iona, and plunder Ireland for the first time.

800–899

Rome, 25 December 800. The pope crowns Charlemagne emperor in St. Peter's.

Gaul, 806. Charlemagne makes provision for the division of his empire after his death. According to Frankish custom, he allots equal shares to each of his sons, Charles, Pepin, and Louis.

Baghdad, 807. Haroun al-Rashid grants the Franks a decree protecting the Holy Places in Jerusalem.

Persia, 24 March 809. The caliph Haroun al-Rashid dies at Tus in eastern Persia.

Gaul, 811. With the deaths of his brothers Pepin and Charles, Louis is Charlemagne's sole surviving heir.

Gaul, 812. The Byzantine Emperor Michael sends an embassy to Charlemagne and formally recognizes him as Emperor of the West. In return the Franks concede Venice and Dalmatia to the Byzantines.

Gaul, 28 January 814. On the death of Charlemagne, his son Louis (the Pious) becomes Emperor of the West.

France and Germany, 817. The Emperor Louis issues the *Ordinatio Imperii*, his plan to divide the empire among his sons while retaining its notional unity under a single emperor, the eldest, Lothar. His two younger sons, Louis the German and Pepin, are made kings of Bavaria and Aquitaine, respectively.

Constantinople, 25 December 820. The unpopular Leo V, emperor since 813, is assassinated in St. Sophia by supporters of the commander of the guards, who becomes the Emperor Michael II.

Britain, 825. King Egbert of Wessex wins a decisive victory over King Beornred of Mercia at Ellendun (near Swindon) and assumes for himself the title King of the English.

France, 826. Harald Klak, a pretender to the Danish throne who is backed by the Franks, is baptized at Louis's palace at Ingelheim. He takes back with him Anskar, a Frankish monk, who begins the slow and hazardous process of bringing Christian faith to the Danes.

France, 829. Louis angers his three older sons by amending the inheritance settlement of 817 to make provision for Charles, his infant son by a second marriage to Judith of Bavaria.

Rome, 831. The pope appoints the Frankish missionary Anskar bishop of Hamburg and gives him responsibility for all the northern peoples.

Constantinople, 832. Theophilus, Michael II's son and successor, expels all painters from the Byzantine empire as part of his bloody and violent drive against icons.

France, 833. Louis the Pious, the Emperor of the West, is deserted by his army and imprisoned by his eldest son, Lothar, who acts as sole ruler.

Mesopotamia, 833. Al-Mamun dies. During his twenty-year caliphate, Abbasid culture reached new heights; commerce and industry flourished, and international trade extended to India, China, Africa, and Europe.

France, February 834. After being rescued by loyalists, Louis the Pious is re-invested as emperor in Metz cathedral. His son Lothar capitulates and returns to his sub-kingdom in Italy.

France, 20 June 840. Louis the Pious dies at Ingelheim. Lothar succeeds him, but civil war between the surviving brothers looms.

France, 25 June 841. Charles the Bald and Louis the German, sons of Louis the Pious, defeat their elder brother Lothar, the Emperor of the West, at Fontenay.

Constantinople, 20 January 842. The Emperor Theophilus dies; iconoclasm dies with him. His wife Theodora, ruling as empress regent on behalf of their infant son Michael III, soon restores images as part of religious ceremonies and worship.

France, August 843. Lothar, Charles, and Louis conclude the treaty of Verdun. Lothar is recognized as emperor but has no power over the kingdoms of his brothers.

England, 844. Under their king, Kenneth MacAlpin, the Scots conquer the Picts and establish the Kingdom of Albion. This marks the beginning of Scotland as an autonomous nation. MacAlpin's heirs will rule Scotland until 1286.

China, 844. Emperor Tang Wuzong outlaws the widespread practice of Buddhism. He confiscates the wealth of the richly endowed Buddhist monasteries and has statuary melted down and made into coins.

France, 845. Hamburg is sacked by the Vikings. Anskar's church is destroyed, and he is forced to flee, but his missionary work to Denmark and Sweden continues from a new base at Bremen.

Rome, 847. On becoming pope, Leo IV sets about repairing and extending the city walls, which had been badly damaged by Arab pirates.

Iraq, 847. Caliph al-Mutawakkil tries to restore Abbasid authority in Mesopotamia by winning the support of the orthodox Sunnis. He persecutes the Mutazilites and the Shiites.

France, 28 September 855. The Emperor Lothar dies. His kingdom is divided among his three sons with the eldest, Louis II, taking Italy and the title of emperor.

Iceland, c.860. Intrepid Viking sailors land on Iceland (as they call it) for the first time. Within fifteen years, they establish permanent settlements. In 941, a national assembly is convened. Still in existence, the Athling is one of the world's oldest existing parliaments.

Russia, 862. The Varangian Prince Rurik conquers the important trading center of Novgorod, located in the region between the Neva and Oka Rivers. The dynasty he founds rules in Russia until 1598.

Eastern Gaul, 862. The Maygars (Hungarians), a nomadic people based in the Ukraine, launch their first raid on the west, attacking the kingdom of Louis the German.

Constantinople, September 867. Having risen spectacularly to power, the emperor's favorite, Basil, murders his benefactor and takes the throne.

Constantinople, 869. The Eighth Ecumenical Council, called by the Emperor Basil and Pope Adrian II, papers over the divisions between the Eastern and Western Churches, which have come to a head over Plotius, the irregularly appointed patriarch of Constantinople. Plotius is deposed, but the divisions remain.

France, 870. With Lothar II dead, Charles the Bald and Louis the German divide his kingdom between them. Lothar's only surviving son, the Emperor Louis II, controls Frankish Italy.

Britain, 874. The Danish army moves into Mercia, meeting little resistance. Mercian king Burgred abdicates and goes on a pilgrimage to Rome. The Danes appoint a puppet king, and effectively control Mercia.

Rome, 25 December 875. With the death of the Emperor Louis II, Charles the Bald hurries to Italy and is crowned emperor by Pope John VIII.

France, August 876. After the death of Louis the German, his three sons divide his kingdom.

France, 6 October 877. Charles the Bald dies, and Louis (the Stammerer), his only surviving son, succeeds him.

Britain, May 878. King Alfred of Wessex emerges from hiding and decisively defeats the Danes at the battle of

Edington. The Danes agree to evacuate Wessex.

Ethiopia, c.880. Falasha Jews have settled in Ethiopia.

Rome, 12 February 881. Charles III (the Fat), the son of Louis the German, becomes the first eastern Frankish ruler to be crowned emperor. But his "empire" is in reality a series of small, completely independent principalities.

Ukraine, 882. Under Oleg, Kiev replaces Novgorod as the main center of the Rus (Russians). Kiev remains the Varangian capital until 1169.

France and Germany, 887. With the deposition of Charles the Fat late in 887, the Carolingian empire has finally fallen apart. Arnulf becomes King of Germany, and a non-Carolingian, Odo, the count of Paris, becomes King of France. The rest of the empire—in southern France, Burgundy, and Italy—is subdivided into a series of warring kingdoms.

Balkans, 894–897. Having succeeded his brother in 893 as ruler of Bulgaria, Simeon invades Thrace. The Byzantines appeal to the Magyars for help, whose attack forces Simeon to make peace with Byzantium. Then in 897, Simeon allies with the nomadic Pechenegs, who force the Magyars across the Danube, where they establish their homeland (Hungary). With the Magyars out of the way, Simeon is able to defeat the Byzantines and exact tribute from them.

France, 1 January 898. With the death of Odo, the Carolingian Charles (the Simple) is recognized as king.

France and Germany, 899. Arnulf dies and is succeeded by his minor son, Louis, whose actions are dictated by his guardian, the Archbishop of Mainz.

900–999

China, 907. The Tang Dynasty, in power in China for almost 300 years, is at an end.

France, 910. The Benedictine monastery of Cluny is founded by William, the Duke of Aquitaine.

Britain, August 910. Edward, Alfred's successor as King of Wessex since 899, defeats the Danes at Tettenhall. With the aid of his sister Aethelfiaed, the regent of Mercia, he begins to drive back the Danes and reoccupies London and Oxford.

Germany, November 911. With the death of Louis, the last Carolingian, nobles meet at Forchheim and agree to elect Conrad, the Duke of Franconia, as their king, but part of the kingdom, Lotharingia (Lorraine), is seized by Charles the Simple, the King of France.

Constantinople, 913. Provoked by the Byzantines' failure to pay their annual tribute, Simeon, who now regards himself as Tsar of Bulgaria, invades but is stopped by the walls of Constantinople. He obtains major concessions from the regent, the patriarch, Nicholas Mysticus.

Spain, 914. Ordono II becomes King of Asturias and makes León the capital in place of Oviedo.

Bulgaria, 917. Having gone back on the agreement of 913 and seen Thrace overrun by Simeon as a result, the Byzantines launch a counteroffensive but are routed by Simeon at Anchialus. Simeon controls the Balkans.

Britain, 924. Having recovered East Anglia and the whole of Mercia from the Danes, Edward (the Elder) dies at Farndon. His son, Aethelstan, is chosen to succeed him as Anglo-Saxon king. Aethelstan, who rules until 939, extends his domain to encompass the greater part of England.

Bulgaria, 927. Simeon dies and is succeeded by his son Peter, who makes a peace treaty with the Byzantines.

Italy, 928. Pope John X dies in prison. His attempt to strengthen the independence of the papacy brought him into conflict with Princess Marozia, wife of the King of Lombardy and effective ruler of Rome.

Spain, 929. Abd ar-Rahman III, the most important Umayyad emir, takes for himself the title of caliph, directly challenging the Abbasid caliphate. In 931, he wins Morocco from the Fatimids.

Germany, 15 March 933. Henry the Fowler routs the raiding Magyars at Merseburg. On his death in 936, his son Otto is elected as his successor, paving the way for a hereditary monarchy to be established in Germany.

Vietnam, 939. Vietnam gains its independence after almost a thousand years of Chinese rule.

England, 940. Edmund, the Anglo-Saxon king, has to make peace with Irish-Norse Vikings led by Olaf, who have taken the Kingdom of York.

Mesopotamia, 943. The Byzantines penetrate deep into Arab land and recover the Mandylion, an icon of Christ.

England, 944. Aided by Danish settlers, Edmund recovers the land yielded to Olaf in 940.

Constantinople, 944. The Byzantine empire and the Rus make a new trade treaty.

Constantinople, January 945. Since 920 Romanus had ruled as co-emperor with his ineffectual son-in-law, Constantine VII, hereditary ruler since 913. In December 944 Romanus was ousted by his sons, but they in turn have been arrested and exiled by Constantine who now rules in his own right.

Mesopotamia, January 946. Caliph al-Mustakfi is blinded and deposed by Muiz ud-Daula, the Buwayid Sultan, who becomes the real power in Baghdad. He installs al-Muti as the new caliph.

Germany, 10 August 955. Otto unites his nobles against the Magyars and defeats them in battle at Lechfeld. They retreat to Hungary and abandon the raids that have caused havoc for 56 years.

Poland, 960. Prince Mieszko defeats the Slav tribes between the rivers Oder and Vistula, and founds the Piast Dynasty.

China, 960. Faced with an invasion from the north, the palace guards mutiny and place their commander, Zhao Kuangyin, on the throne. He rules as Emperor Taizu. He founds the Northern Song Dynasty, with its capital at Kaifeng.

Rome, 2 February 962. After an appeal by Pope John XII for aid against Berengar, the King of Italy, Otto invades Italy and is crowned Holy Roman Emperor in Rome.

Greece, 963. Monks taking vows as cenobites found the first monastery on Mt. Athos, Megisti Lavra.

Rome, 963. Pope John XII is deposed on charges of murder, incest, and perjury.

Rome, 964. Otto starves Rome into surrender and reinstates his nominee, Leo VIII, as pope. He is soon succeeded by Otto's choice, John XIII.

Vietnam, 968. Dinh Bo Linh adopts the title of Emperor of Dai Viet (northern Vietnam), which is now independent. He founds the Dinh Dynasty.

France, 966. A Benedictine abbey is founded on the island of Mont St. Michel off the coast of present-day Normandy.

Constantinople, 969. The Emperor Nicephorous II is murdered by John Tzimiskes, who succeeds him. John restores trading relations with the Rus (Russians), annexes much of Bulgaria, and forces the Abbasids to retreat in Syria and Anatolia.

Hungary, 974. The Hungarian Prince Géza is baptized, thereby opening his country to Christianity and Western Europe.

China, 975. The southern Tang kingdom submits to the Song, ending the era of Five Dynasties and Ten Kingdoms.

Constantinople, 10 January 976. John Tzimiskes dies and is succeeded by Basil II.

Italy, 7 December 983. Otto II dies suddenly and is succeeded by his infant son, Otto III. A power struggle within the aristocracy ensues. The Slavs take advantage to recover their independence east of the Elbe.

Greenland, 986. The Icelandic exile Erik the Red begins to colonize Greenland, which he discovered four years previously.

France, 987. After the dissolution of the Carolingian Dynasty, Hugh Capet becomes King of France. He founds the Capetian Dynasty, from which will come all the rulers of France until 1848 (except for the years 1792–1814).

England, 991. Olaf the Norseman overcomes a heroic defense at Maldon and advances deep into England, now ruled by Aethelred (the Unready).

Poland, 992. Boleslav succeeds Mieszko as ruler of Poland. He battles against the Holy Roman Emperor until 1018 and is crowned king in 1025.

Venice, 992. A treaty is signed with Byzantium that gives Venice free access to the harbor of Constantinople and reduces the duties assessed. This is the foundation of Venice's power as a commercial center.

Norway, 994. Olaf I becomes the first Christian King of Norway. He tries to convert Norway, Iceland, and Greenland.

Central Asia, 998. The Persian doctor and philosopher Avicenna is invited to take up residence at the court of Bukhara. There he writes his massive philosophical encyclopedia. He plays an important role in preserving and transmitting the work of Greek thinkers, most of which was unknown in the West.

1000–1099

Hungary, 25 December 1000. Duke Stephen, in power since 997, is crowned Hungary's first king with regalia sent by Pope Sylvester II.

Poland, 1000. Otto III, the German emperor and king, founds the archbishopric of Gnessen at the grave of Bishop Adalbert and thereby sets the Polish Church on an independent course. Gnessen remains Poland's capital through the tenth and eleventh centuries. Otto II strives for a renewal of the Holy Roman Empire and promotes the spread of Christianity.

North America, c.1000. The Norse explorer Leif Ericson sails from Greenland to the east coast of North America. He calls his discovery Vinland. Remains of a Viking settlement have been found in Labrador.

Peru, c.1000. With the fall of the Huari kingdom, the Chimu culture rises to a controlling position in northern and central Peru. It remains a force to be reckoned with until conquered by the Incas in 1470.

Italy, 23 January 1002. Emperor Otto III dies at Paterno. Henry II succeeds him.

Spain, 1002. Muhammad ibn Abu Amir, popularly known as al-Mansur, the chief minister of Caliph Hisham II and effective ruler of the Umayyad caliphate of Córdoba, dies and is succeeded by his son Abd al-Malik.

Spain, 1005. Sancho III becomes King of Navarre and makes his kingdom the strongest Christian power on the Iberian peninsula. In 1026, he conquers Castille and the Basque territory. Under his son the domain incorporates Aragon.

India, 1008. Under Mahmud, the armies of the Turkic Ghaznavid people sweep through India from their base in Afghanistan, defeating the armies of a Hindu confederacy on the plain of Peshawar.

Jerusalem, 1009. The Fatimid Caliph al-Hakim destroys the church of the Holy Sepulcher, apparently in a fit of madness, prompting calls for a Christian crusade to recover the Holy Land.

Ireland, 1014. The Vikings are defeated at the battle of Clontarf by the Irish army of King Brian Boru, who is killed in the battle. After his death, Ireland reverts to warfare between petty kingdoms.

Persia, 1014. The epic poet Firdawsi completes his masterwork, the *Shahnameh* (*The Book of Kings*), which tells the story of Persia from the beginning of time.

Russia, 1015. Vladimir, the Prince of Kiev, dies. He was converted to Christianity in 988 when he married Anne, the sister of the Eastern Emperor Basil II, thus opening Russia to Byzantine influence.

England, 30 November 1016. Edmund Ironside, who succeeded Aethelred as King of England earlier in the year, dies, leaving Canute as unchallenged ruler of England. Three years later, England and Scandinavia are unified under the rule of Canute.

Afghanistan, 1019. Mahmud founds the great mosque at Ghazni, capital of the Ghaznavid domains. His armies now occupy most of northern India.

Italy, 1024. Emperor Henry II dies on 13 July; a revolt then breaks out in Lombardy. Henry was the last of the Ottonians. After his death, Conrad II is elected king, beginning the Salic Dynasty.

Italy, 1025. The composer Guido de Arezzo, a Benedictine monk, founds the modern scheme of musical intervals and notation in his work entitled *Micrologus de musica*.

Rome, Easter 1027. Conrad II is crowned emperor in the presence of Canute, the King of England and Denmark, and Rudolf III of Burgundy.

Afghanistan, 1030. On the death of the great Ghaznavid ruler Mahmud, his son Masud blinds his brother Muhammad and takes the throne. His empire stretches from Persia to the valley of the Ganges.

Spain, 1031. The deposition of the last Umayyad caliph, Hisham III, brings an end to the caliphate of Córdoba.

France, 2 February 1032. On the death of the childless King of Burgundy, Rudolf III, the Emperor Conrad II claims the throne, as agreed in the treaty of succession of 1027.

India, 1035. Rajaraja the Great dies after a fifty-year reign has seen decisive Chola supremacy in the south of India.

Russia, 1037. In Kiev, Jaroslav I (the Wise) donates the church of St. Sophia as a metropolitan church. He leads the Kiev kingdom to its greatest flowering and codifies Russian law (*Russkaja prawda*).

Spain, 1037. Ferdinand I (the Great), King of Castille since 1035, unites in his person Castille with the Kingdom of León.

France, 4 June 1039. The Emperor Conrad II, who succeeded Henry II in 1024 and founded the Salian (or Franconian) Dynasty, dies.

England, 1042. After the withdrawal of the Danes, Edward the Confessor becomes last king of England from Wessex. He is a dedicated supporter of churches and monasteries, in particular of Westminster Abbey. He is buried there, and it becomes a national shrine.

Burma, 1044. The regime of King Anawrahta brings stability and power to Burma. From its capital, Pagan, the king extended his empire to the Indian Ocean.

Rome, 1046. Emperor Henry III forces the abdication of Pope Gregory VI on the grounds of simony and confirms the depositions of Sylvester III and Benedict IX. He installs Clement II as pope.

Persia, 1052. The Seljuks seize Isfahan.

Italy, 23 June 1053. Pope Leo IX raises an army to expel the Normans from Italy. The papal forces are defeated at Civitate, and Leo is captured.

Britain, 1054. Earl Siward of Northumberland leads an army into Scotland in support of Malcolm Canmore, whose father, King Duncan, was murdered by Macbeth, the Earl of Moray, who then took the throne. Macbeth is defeated at Dunsinane, near Perth.

Constantinople, July 1054. The patriarch of Constantinople, Michael Cerularius, is excommunicated by the papal legate, initiating a schism between the Eastern and Western Christian Churches.

Baghdad, 1055. The Seljuk Tugrul Beg enters Baghdad as the liberator and protector of the Abbasid caliphate against the Shiites. He restores the Sunni branch of Islam and installs himself as the temporal master of the caliphate.

Rome, 6 December 1058. Pope Nicholas II issues a decree restricting the right of electing the pope to the cardinals.

Italy, 1059. Robert Guiscard, the Norman Duke of Apulia and Calabria, receives from Nicholas II the feudal overlordship of Sicily. The Normans conquer Messina in 1061 and Palermo in 1072.

France, 1060. Henry, the King of France, is succeeded by his son Philip under the guardianship of Baldwin V, the Count of Flanders.

North Africa, 1062. After the Almoravid conquest of the Zanata in Morocco, Yusuf ben Tashfin succeeds to the throne.

Morocco and Spain, 1062. Abu Bakr, ibn Yasin's successor, founds Marrakesh and invades Spain.

Venice, 1063. St. Mark's Basilica receives its final form under the Doge Domenico Contarini.

Portugal, 9 June 1064. Coimbra is captured by Ferdinand, the King of Castile.

England, 14 October 1066. William of Normandy defeats King Harold at Hastings and becomes King of England. On Christmas Day, William is crowned king in Westminster Abbey.

Italy, 16 April 1071. The Norman Robert Guiscard takes Bari after a three-year siege. Byzantine rule in southern Italy is thus brought to an end after five centuries.

Anatolia, 1071. The Seljuks defeat the Byzantines under Romanus IV Diogenes at Manzikert. Taken prisoner, Romanus is replaced as emperor by his stepson Michael VII. He is freed and returns home, aiming to regain power from Michael, but dies in the ensuing struggle. The Byzantine Empire is forced to abandon its holdings in the greater part of Anatolia.

Spain, 1072. Alfonso VI becomes King of León and Castile after the assassination of his brother Sancho. On the death of their father, Ferdinand, in 1065, Alfonso received León but lost it to Sancho (who received Castile) shortly afterwards.

Italy, 1073. Robert Guiscard takes Amalfi from Gisulf II of Salerno, securing Norman control of the maritime trade routes but alienating the pope.

Rome, March 1075. Pope Gregory VII declares in his bull *Dictatus pape* that the bishop of Rome is absolute sovereign over the Church.

West Africa, 1077. The nomadic Almoravids overrun Kumbi Saleh, the capital of the African Kingdom of Ghana.

Italy, 1077. Emperor Henry IV, excommunicated by Gregory VII, submits to the pope at Canossa, yielding to him in the controversy over the investiture of bishops.

Byzantium, 1081. Through a military coup, Alexis Comnenus seizes power, initiating the Byzantine Empire's last period of prosperity and influence.

Rome, 1084. After conquering a part of Rome in the previous year, Henry IV deals with his rivals in Germany and then again turns his attention to Rome. The Romans submit, although Pope Gregory VII holds out in the Castel Sant'Angelo until rescued by the Norman Robert Guiscard. Meanwhile Henry enthrones an anti-pope, Clement III.

Spain, 25 May 1085. Alfonso VI of León takes Toledo, the old capital of Visigothic Spain and the greatest city that the Christians have captured in the *reconquista*. Alfonso takes the title Emperor of Toledo. Strategically, the loss of the city is a serious setback for the Muslims in that it penetrates their territorial power bloc.

England, 1086. William the Conqueror orders the creation of the Domesday Book, a record of population and economic production of the country's 34 shires.

France and England, 1087. On his death, William the Conqueror is succeeded in Normandy by Robert Curthose and in England by William Rufus.

Malta, 1091. Roger of Sicily, brother of Robert Guiscard, takes control of the island.

Middle East, 1092. The Islamic sect known as the Assassins murder the Seljuk vizier, Nizam al-Mulk.

Venice, 1094. The basilica of St. Mark is consecrated.

Spain, 1094. The Spanish knight El Cid carves out a territory for himself around Valencia. He will be celebrated as a national hero and is the subject of the oldest known saga written in Spanish, *Cantar de Mío Cid*, which dates from around 1140.

France, 27 November 1095. Pope Urban II calls a synod in Clermont at which he urges a crusade to free the Holy Places, saying that it is God's will.

Italy, 1096. The world's first university is founded at Salerno.

Portugal, 1097. Alfonso VI of León gives his son-in-law Henry of Chalon the land between the Minho and Tagus Rivers to hold as a hereditary county. This is the beginning of Portugal.

Middle East, 30 June 1097. The Crusaders defeat the Turks at Dorylaeum, opening the way to Asia Minor (Anatolia).

France, 1098. The Cistercian Order is founded at Citeaux by the Benedictine monk Robert de Molesme. It will be formally sanctioned by the pope in 1119.

Middle East, 1098. The Byzantines retake Smyrna, Ephesus, and Sardis. The Crusaders take Antioch. The Fatimids recover Jerusalem from the Turks, but in the following year, the city falls to the Crusaders, precipitating the wholesale slaughter of Muslims and Jews.

1100–1199

Jerusalem, 18 July 1100. On the death of his brother Godfrey of Bouillon, Baldwin becomes King of Jerusalem.

England, 2 August 1100. William Rufus is killed in a hunting accident in the New Forest. He is succeeded by his brother Henry.

France, 1108. Louis VI (Louis the Fat) becomes King of France. He increases royal prerogatives vis-à-vis the restive noble houses.

Hungary, 1114. Koloman, who conquered Croatia and so brought it within the orbit of Latin Christendom, dies.

France, 1115. Bernard founds a monastery at Clairvaux.

China, 1115. The Jurchen from Manchuria, allied with the Song, overthrow the Khitan Liao, their former masters, and found the Jin Dynasty.

Middle East, 1118. Hugues de Payens founds the Order of the Knights Templar to watch over pilgrims en route to the Holy Land. It resolves to fight for the defense of the Holy Land.

Spain, 1118. After four years of combat with the Moors, Alfonso, the King of Aragon and Navarre, retakes Saragossa and makes it his capital.

Holy Roman Empire, 1122. The Concordat of Worms ends the investiture controversy. Henry V relinquishes his claim to invest bishops with the ring and staff but receives a guarantee that either the emperor or his representative will be present when a bishop is chosen.

Germany, 1125. Emperor Henry V dies without an heir. The main candidates are Frederick of Hohenstaufen, the Duke of Swabia, and Lothar of Supplinburg, the Duke of Saxony. Lothar is chosen, but civil war ensues. The Salic Dynasty comes to an end.

Italy, 1127. Conrad III, the brother of Frederick of Hohenstaufen, becomes King of Italy.

England, 17 June 1128. Geoffrey V of Anjou, known as Plantagenet, marries Matilda, daughter of King Henry of England and widow of the Emperor Henry V.

France, 1128. Bernard of Clairvaux achieves recognition of the Order of the Knights Templar and drafts its rules.

Hungary, 1128. The Magyars are defeated by the Byzantine Emperor John II on the Danube, near Haram.

North Africa, 1132. The Almohad Abd al-Mu'min is recognized as caliph.

France, 1 December 1135. Henry I, the King of England, dies, and the crown passes to his nephew Stephen of Blois. Henry's preferred candidate was his daughter Matilda. A civil war over succession ensues.

Germany, 1138. Conrad III of Hohenstaufen succeeds Lothar III on the imperial throne. Civil war erupts when he seizes Saxony and Bavaria.

Poland, 1138. Boleslav III dies after a 36-year rule. He strengthened Poland and expanded his rule to the west and north. His will splits Poland into four principalities.

Rome, April 1139. A Lateran Council called by Innocent II settles the Anacletus schism, which arose when rival factions of cardinals elected two popes in 1130.

Portugal, 1139. Afonso defeats the Almoravids at Ourique and assumes the title of king. He makes Coimbra his capital. In 1143, he is recognized as king by Alfonso VII of Castile and in 1179, by the papacy.

France, 1142. Peter Abelard, the scholastic philosopher and author of the work *Sic et non*, dies in the monastery of St. Marcel. Abelard is best known for his ill-fated love affair with Heloise.

Middle East, 25 December 1144. The Crusader Kingdom of Edessa is taken by Zangi (Atabeg of Mosul), leading to the organization of the Second Crusade. After conquering northern Syria, Zangi goes to war with Damascus.

North Africa, 1146. Pursuing the "holy war" begun against the Almoravids by his predecessor, ibn Tumart, the Almohad caliph Abd al-Mumin conquers much of Morocco. In the following year, Marrakesh, capital of the Almoravid empire, falls to the Almohads under Abd al-Mumin.

Greece, 1147. Roger II of Sicily takes Corfu from the Byzantines and pillages Corinth, Athens and Thebes.

Middle East, June 1149. After the murder of Zangi, his son, the sultan Nur ad-Din, takes possession of Edessa. He kills Raymond of Poitiers, the prince of Antioch, near Apamea. In 1148, Raymond had urged the leaders of the Second Crusade to join him in an attack on Nur ad-Din, whom he saw as the major threat, but they had preferred instead to attack Damascus.

England, 1149. A university is founded at Oxford.

Syria, 1149. The Second Crusade, led by Conrad II and Louis VII, ends in a debacle before the gates of Damascus, with none of its expressed goals having been achieved.

Germany, 4 March 1152. Frederick Barbarossa (Red Beard), the nephew of Conrad III, who died in February, is chosen as emperor and unites the two factions that emerged after the death of Henry V.

France, 20 August 1153. Bernard dies at the monastery of Clairvaux, of which he had been abbot since 1115.

England, 1153. The death of King Stephen's son Eustace leads Stephen to recognize Matilda's son, Henry Plantagenet, as heir to the English throne. Henry becomes king in 1154, founding the Plantagent Dynasty, which will rule in England until 1485. With his marriage to Eleanor of Aquitaine, Henry also controls one-third of France.

Rome, 14 December 1154. Nicholas Brakespear, an Englishman, is elected pope and takes the name Adrian IV. In the following year, he crowns Frederick Barbarossa emperor, who has come to the pope's aid and put down a revolt led by the fiery reformer Arnold of Brescia.

Italy, 1158. The university of Bologna secures its first privileges from the emperor.

Rome, 1159. The election following the death of Pope Adrian IV produces a schism.

Milan, 1162. Emperor Frederick seizes and destroys Milan. Its inhabitants are dispersed among four villages.

Italy, 1167. The cities of northern Italy establish the Lombard league in opposition to Emperor Frederick.

Rome, 1167. Frederick seizes Rome. Pope Alexander III leaves the city.

Egypt, 1169. Saladin becomes vizier of the Fatimid caliphate of Cairo. By now, the viziers hold the real power, and the caliphs are little more than puppets.

Italy, 1170. The Lombard league allies itself with the pope and founds a new town in his honor, Alessandria, which gives it command of the routes of western Lombardy.

England, 1170. Henry II orders the death of Thomas Becket, Archbishop of Canterbury, since 1162. Becket had come into conflict with the king over ecclesiastical prerogatives.

Ireland, 1171. Henry II invades Ireland, which had been granted to him by Pope Adrian. He forces the Irish king, Rory O'Connor, to swear fealty to him, thus beginning the English colonization of Ireland.

Egypt, 1171. Saladin abolishes the Fatimid caliphate in Cairo and reestablishes Sunnism, thus becoming the effective sovereign of Egypt.

Arabia, 1173. Saladin seizes Aden.

West Africa, 1175. Under its chief Bilali, the Kingdom of Mali reaches the acme of its power and influence.

Italy, 1176. Defeated at Legnano by the Lombard league, Emperor Frederick Barbarossa concludes terms with the pope at Agnani.

Anatolia, 1176. The Seljuk Turks crush the Byzantine army at Myriocephalum. Byzantium loses its dominant status in the region.

Middle East, 1177. Saladin is defeated by Baldwin IV of Jerusalem at Ramleh.

Rome, March 1179. The Third Lateran Council decrees that a candidate will be elected pope only if he receives two thirds of the cardinals' votes.

Middle East, 1180. After a defeat by Saladin last year, Baldwin IV of Jerusalem agrees to a truce.

Constantinople, 24 September 1180. Manuel is succeeded as emperor by his 11-year-old son, Alexius II Comnenus. His widow, Maria, is regent.

Constantinople, 1182. A revolt led by Andronicus Comnenus against the Empress Maria prompts a massacre of Italians. The Emperor Alexius is forced to sign his mother's death warrant. Andronicus and Alexius rule jointly until Alexius is himself murdered.

Middle East, 1183. Saladin conquers Syria and becomes sultan.

Germany, 25 June 1183. The Peace of Constance ends the conflict between Emperor Frederick and the Lombard League.

Italy, 1184. A church council at Verona condemns all heretics. Pope Lucius III and the emperor agree that bishops shall excommunicate offenders and that their goods and property shall be confiscated.

Constantinople, 1185. The Emperor Andronicus is killed in a rebellion.

Japan, 1185. Minamoto No Yoritomo annihilates the Tairas, establishes himself at Kamakura, and sets up a military government.

Egypt, 1185. The Jewish philosopher and doctor Moses Maimonides publishes his masterwork, *Guide to the Perplexed*.

Middle East, 1187. After his victory at Hittin, Saladin picks off the Frank-ish garrisons. He takes back Jerusalem. Soon only Tyre, Tripoli, and Antioch remain unconquered.

France, 21 January 1189. Philip Augustus, Henry II of England, and Frederick Barbarossa assemble their forces for the Third Crusade.

France, 1189. Henry II is succeeded as King of England by his son Richard (Lionheart).

Japan, 1189. Having helped his brother Yoritomo in his fight against the Tairas, Minamoto no Yoshitsune becomes the target of Yoritomo's attacks. Defeated, he commits suicide with his family and partisans.

Anatolia, 1190. En route to take part in the Third Crusade, the Emperor Frederick Barbarossa falls off his horse and drowns in the Saleph River.

Japan, 1191. Shortly after returning from a period of study in China, Eisai founds the Rinzai Zen sect.

Middle East, 1191. Richard Lionheart seizes Cyprus. He and Philip Augustus then take Acre. Philip Augustus falls ill and abandons the crusade to return to France. His army remains, led by Hugh of Burgundy. After two years of fighting, Richard and Saladin agree to a treaty in 1192, whereby the Crusaders are allowed to keep their coastal kingdoms and have free access to the Christian shrines of Jerusalem.

Rome, 1191. Henry VI, the son of Frederick Barbarossa, is crowned emperor in Rome by Pope Celestine III.

India, 1192. After taking Delhi, Muhammad of Ghur installs Qutb-ud-Din Aybak as India's first Muslim ruler.

France, 1193. Philip Augustus seizes the Vexin, part of the English territory in France.

Central Europe, 1193. Richard Lionheart is taken prisoner in Vienna and given up to the Emperor Henry VI, of whose rivals—Tancred of Sicily and the Welf faction within Germany—he is an ally. He is freed in the following year for a ransom of 100,000 silver marks.

Middle East, 1193. The death of Saladin at Damascus sparks off a civil war among his heirs.

France, 1194. Philip Augustus is crushed at Freteval by Richard Lionheart, who reconquers his French fiefs. They sign the Truce of Verneuil.

Sicily, 29 September 1197. Emperor Henry VI, crowned king at Palermo three years before, dies at Messina. Henry granted wide concessions to win the pope's cooperation in the preservation of the union of the Empire and Sicily.

India, 1197. The celebrated monastery of Nalanda, a center of Buddhist studies, is destroyed by the Arabs.

Rome, 8 January 1198. On his election as pope, Innocent III calls for a new crusade.

Germany, July 1198. Otto of Brunswick is crowned king by the Welfs. Philip of Swabia, the leader of the Hohenstaufen faction, was elected king by his supporters in March. Civil war is inevitable.

1200–1299

Peru, c.1200. The city of Cuzco is founded by the Inca leader Manco Capac.

Near East, 1200. Al-Malik al-Adil, who became sultan on the death of his brother Saladin, restores the unity of the Ayyubids' possessions and annexes Mesopotamia.

Italy, 1201. Otto IV is recognized as Holy Roman Emperor by Pope Innocent III.

Central Asia, 1202. The Tartars are crushed by Genghis Khan.

France, 1202. The fiefs of King John of England within the jurisdiction of the kingdom of France (Aquitaine, Anjou, and Poitou) are confiscated by King Philip, who grants the lands to John's nephew, Arthur of Brittany. In the ensuing war, John's army wins a great victory at Mirabeau.

Mediterranean, 1203. The Almohads begin a conquest of the Balearic archipelago.

France, April 1203. Brittany rebels against King John of England. Arthur of Brittany, arguably the rightful King of England, vanished the previous year and was believed murdered by John.

Constantinople, 1204. The crusaders under the leadership of Venice seize the city and replace the Byzantine empire with an Eastern Latin empire that lasts until 1261. The Byzantines hold out in Trebizond under Alexius Comnenus.

France, 1204. The whole of the Duchy of Normandy, apart from the Channel Islands, is now in French hands. By 1206, Philip has driven the English from all of France north of the Loire.

France, 1205. Anjou is conquered by Philip Augustus.

Greece, 1205. The Duchy of Athens is founded by the crusader Othon de la Roche.

Asia Minor, 1206. Theodore Lascaris, son-in-law of the former Emperor Alexius III, is crowned emperor at Nicaea.

India, 1206. After the murder of the last Ghurid sultan, Qutb ud-Din Aybak founds the Muslim dynasty known as "the Slaves."

France, 15 January 1208. Peter of Castelnau is killed by a vassal of Raymond IV of Toulouse. Raymond is held responsible and excommunicated, and the pope calls for a crusade against the heretics. This begins the persecution of the Albigensians, (the Cathars) that will

last until 1228. The Albigensians dismiss church doctrines concerning the priesthood and sacraments and preach poverty and asceticism.

Rome, 1208. King John of England opposes Pope Innocent III on his nomination for archbishop of Canterbury. The pope places England under an interdict, forbidding the clergy to administer the sacraments. King John is excommunicated.

Central Asia, 1208. Genghis Khan conquers Turkestan.

France, 22 July 1209. In the crusade against the Cathars, Simon of Montfort sacks Beziers. Thousands, including many Catholics, are killed.

Rome, 1209. Recognized as emperor after the murder of his rival Philip of Swabia, Otto IV is crowned by the pope.

England, 1209. A group of scholars leaves Oxford as a result of unrest in the town and settles in Cambridge, forming England's second university.

Italy, 1210. Francis of Assisi founds the Order of Friars Minor (the Franciscans). It receives papal sanction in 1223.

Germany, December 1212. With papal backing, Frederick II of Hohenstaufen is crowned King of Germany.

England, 15 May 1213. King John submits to the pope, offering to make England and Ireland papal fiefs. Innocent III lifts the interdict of 1208.

France, 12 September 1213. Simon de Montfort defeats Raymond of Toulouse and Peter II of Aragon at Muret.

France, 1214. John of England is defeated by Philip Augustus of France at the Battle of Bouvines. In the following year, John is forced to sign the Magna Carta, in which the barons' feudal privileges are guaranteed and the king acknowledges himself bound by the law.

Rome, 1215. At the Fourth Lateran Council, Dominic petitions the pope to found a new order of preachers. The principal mission of the Dominicans will be the conversion of heretics. The Council also recognizes Frederick II's claims to the imperial throne over those of Otto IV.

China, 1215. Genghis Khan occupies Beijing.

France, April 1216. Philip Augustus and his son resolve to invade England. Rebellious English barons recently opened negotiations with France for support against their king.

Italy, 16 July 1216. Pope Innocent III dies at Perugia while busy with preparations for the Fifth Crusade. He is succeeded by a Roman nobleman, Honorius III.

England, 19 October 1216. King John dies at Newark. He is succeeded by his nine-year-old son Henry. William Marshall is made regent.

Europe, 1217. A severe famine affects central and eastern Europe.

England, September 1217. The barons make peace with the new regime.

Asia, 1218. Ghengis Khan occupies Kashgar and the Tarim basin. Korea acknowledges its vassal status.

Spain, 1218. Alfonso IX founds the University of Salamanca.

Rome, 22 November 1220. Frederick II is crowned emperor by Pope Honorius III after promising to go to the aid of the Fifth Crusade within nine months.

West Africa, c.1220. The Yoruba settle in the southwestern part of Nigeria. A priest-king rules from their holy city of Ife.

Iceland, c. 1220. The bard and statesman Snorri Sturluson writes the *Prose Edda*, a collection of Norse mythological stories.

Ethiopia, 1225. Lalibela, the Emperor of Ethiopia, dies. He moved the capital from Axum to Lasta (Lalibela), where he presided over the building of rock-hewn churches.

France, 8 November 1226. Louis IX succeeds Louis VIII as King of France. His mother, Queen Blanche of Castile, acts as regent.

Japan, 1227. On his return from a journey to China, the Japanese monk Dogen introduces Soto Zen Buddhism to Japan.

Rome, March 1227. On the death of Honorius III, Ugolini dei Conti, Innocent III's nephew, is elected pope. He takes the name Gregory IX.

Palestine, 1229. Frederick II, leader of the Fifth Crusade, negotiates with the Sultan of Egypt, al-Kamil, and gains possession of Jerusalem, with the exception of certain Islamic holy places such as the al-Aqsa Mosque. He also obtains Nazareth, Bethlehem, and a strip of land from the coast over which pilgrims can travel.

Majorca, 1230. Following his capture of Palma, James of Aragon overcomes Muslim resistance on the island. In 1238, he takes Valencia.

Spain, 24 September 1230. On the death of Alfonso IX of León, Ferdinand III of Castile is accepted as King of León, unifying the two kingdoms. In 1236, he conquers Córdoba.

Germany, 1230. The Teutonic Knights are invited into Prussia to help with the forcible conversion of the Prussians and Yatvags.

Rome, 1233. Pope Gregory IX establishes the Inquisition.

China, 1234. The Mongols take K'aifeng, completing the destruction of the Jin empire.

Spain, 1238. The Moorish ruler of Granada, ibn Ahmar, declares his independence from the caliph of Córdoba.

The kingdom of Granada remains under Moorish control until 1492.

Poland, 1241. After conquering a large part of Russia, including Kiev, the Mongol warlord Batu, a grandson of Genghis Khan, defeats a combined force of German and Polish knights at Liegnitz. In the following year, the Mongols withdraw from Hungary and Dalmatia, cross the Carpathians, and return to the lower Volga. Batu then founds the city of Sarai as the capital of the Golden Horde, a Mongol kingdom that stretches into Western Siberia and lasts until 1480.

Middle East, 17 October 1244. After sacking Jerusalem, the nomadic Khorezmian Turks join with Egypt to push the Crusaders out of Gaza.

Spain, 23 November 1248. Seville surrenders to Ferdinand III of Castile after a two-year siege. Most of its Muslim inhabitants flee to Granada. Most of Moorish Spain has now been recaptured by Christians, a process known as the *reconquista*.

Egypt, February 1250. Louis IX is taken prisoner at the battle of al-Mansurah. Two years before, he had launched the Sixth Crusade.

Egypt, 1250. The assassination of the last Ayyubid caliph of Egypt marks the takeover of power by the Mamluks.

Italy, 1250. Following the death of Emperor Frederick II, rebellions break out in northern Italy against the feudal lords.

Anatolia, 1254. John III Vatatzes, ruler of Nicea since 1222, dies at Nymphaeum near Smyrna. His alliance with Bulgaria in 1235 won much of Thrace. In 1246, he took Bulgarian territory and deposed Demetrius, the despot of Salonika. The Nicean empire could claim to be a rival to the Byzantine empire.

Persia, 1256. Hulegu founds the Mongol Dynasty of Persia. Two years later on 10 February 1258, he destroys Baghdad, bringing an end to the Abbasid caliphate.

England, 1258. Led by Simon de Montfort, the rebellious English barons wrest various concessions, known as the Provisions of Oxford, from Henry III. They include the institution of a parliament, which will meet three times a year, and the presence of a permanent council to advise the king.

Paris, 1259. By the Treaty of Paris, Louis IX recognizes Henry III's claim to Gascony, but it remains a fief of the French crown. Henry gives up all claims to the Plantagenet fiefs of Normandy, Anjou, Touraine, Maine, and Poitou.

France, 1260. The Cathedral of Chartres is dedicated in the presence of Louis IX.

Constantinople, 15 August 1261. Michael VIII Palaeologus seizes Constantinople, putting an end to the Latin empire and restoring the Byzantine empire.

Rome, 1263. Charles of Anjou, who is being groomed by Urban IV for the role of papal champion against German influence in Italy, is elected senator for life by the Romans. In 1266, he defeats and kills Manfred of Sicily, the natural son of Frederick II, at Benevento. He is invested by Pope Clement IV with the crown of Sicily and enters Naples.

Middle East, 1268. After seizing Caesarea in 1265, the Mamluk sultan, Baybars, takes Jaffa and Antioch.

Italy, 1268. Conradin, the last Hohenstaufen, invades Italy but is defeated by Charles of Anjou at Tagliacozzi. Caught trying to flee, he is tried and executed.

Tunisia, 1270. Louis IX of France dies at Tunis on the way to the Seventh Crusade, his second.

Italy, 1270. Charles of Anjou becomes master of Tuscany.

Middle East, May 1272. The Crusaders, led by Edward of England, reach a truce with Sultan Baybars at Caesarea. In October of the same year, Edward inherits the crown upon the death of Henry III.

Germany, 1 October 1273. Rudolf of Habsburg, an elderly Swabian count, is elected emperor, putting an end to the great interregnum that began with the death of Conrad IV in 1254.

France, 1274. A general council at Lyons, summoned by Gregory X, regulates the election of the pope by instituting the conclave.

China, 1275. The Venetian merchant and explorer Marco Polo reaches China after traveling overland from Italy with his father and uncle. He is befriended by the Chinese Emperor Kublai Khan.

Central Europe, 1278. Backed by Ladislas of Hungary, the Emperor Rudolph defeats his rival Otokar of Bohemia at the Battle of Marchfeld.

China, 1279. Kublai Khan overcomes the last Song resistance and reunifies China under the Yuan Dynasty.

Japan, 1281. The Mongols make a second attempt to invade Japan. A storm (*kamikaze*) drives them off its coast.

Constantinople, 1282. Michael VIII Palaeologus dies. He restored the Byzantine empire, which is now threatened by the Turkish tribes of Asia Minor.

Sicily, 30 March 1282. An uprising known as the Sicilian Vespers drives the hated French from the island. In September of the same year, Peter of Aragon, who had married the Hohenstauffen Princess Constanza, is crowned King of Sicily.

Spain, 4 April 1284. Alfonso X, King of Castile and León since 1252, dies at Seville. He protected Moorish and Jewish culture and contributed to the Spanish cultural renaissance.

England, 1284. Edward II is born at Caernavon Castle. In 1301, he is given the title Prince of Wales, which becomes the hereditary title for the oldest son of the reigning monarch.

France, 7 January 1285. Charles of Anjou, the ruler of Naples and Sicily, dies after losing Sicily and failing to realize his hopes of conquest in the east.

Middle East, 29 April 1289. The Sultan of Egypt captures Tripoli, leaving Acre as the only major remaining Christian stronghold. That falls to the Mamluks two years later.

Switzerland, 1291. On the death of Rudolf of Habsburg, emperor since 1273, the three Forest Cantons—Uri, Schwyz, and Unterwalden—sign a pact.

Rome, 23 December 1294. Boniface VIII is made pope in succession to Celestine V, who abdicated after five months.

Scotland, 1296. The castle of Dunbar surrenders to Edward of England, who invaded Scotland earlier in the year. He brings the Stone of Scone back to Westminster.

India, 1296. Ala-ud-din, Sultan of Delhi, founds a dynasty and extends his power over much of India.

Scotland, 1297. Led by William Wallace, the Scots rebel against the English and defeat them at Stirling. Wallace is captured by the English in 1305 and executed for treason.

Germany, 2 July 1298. Adolf of Nassau, elected King of Germany in 1292, is defeated and killed near Worms by his rival the Habsburg Albert of Austria. Albert is chosen as king later in the year.

1300–1399

Italy, 1300. Pope Boniface VIII decrees a Holy Year, which entails special indulgences. Since 1475, it has been celebrated every 25 years.

Florence, 1302. Charles of Valois and his French troops, called in by the pope, connive at the return of the extreme Guelf faction known as the "Blacks," involved in a power struggle with the moderate Ghibellines, the "Whites." Leading Whites flee, including the poet Dante Alighieri.

Flanders, 18 May 1302. The weaver Peter de Coningk leads a massacre of the Flemish oligarchs. Later in the year, an army of French knights, led by the count of Artois, is routed by Flemish pikemen.

Italy, 1303. Boniface VIII issues the papal bull, *In Unum Sanctam*, which declares the supremacy of the spiritual over the temporal powers. In response, the King of France, Philip IV (the Fair), has him imprisoned in Anagni. He is set free by a Roman army but dies in Rome the following year.

Paris, 20 May 1303. The war between France and England over Gascony is settled by a treaty restoring the prewar position.

Greece, 1303. Mercenaries employed by the Byzantine emperor, Andronicus II, defeat the Ottomans, but then turn against the empire.

Rome, 5 August 1305. Under pressure from Philip IV, Bertrand de Got, the archbishop of Bordeaux, is elected pope and takes the name Clement V.

Scotland, 25 March 1306. Robert the Bruce, an opponent of English rule, is crowned king. In June of 1314, English forces of Edward II suffer a major defeat by the Scots at Bannockburn, and Scotland achieves its independence.

Poland, 8 August 1306. Wenceslas III is murdered a year after succeeding his father, Wenceslas II.

France, 1307. Philip IV has the members of the order of the Knights Templar arrested and charged with heresy. Their substantial wealth becomes property of the crown, providing much needed relief to the royal treasury.

France, 1309. Clement, who was crowned pope in Lyons, moves the papal residence to Carpentras, near Avignon. Clement is destined never to set foot in Rome. This marks the beginning of what becomes a papal sojourn in France of almost seventy years, which has become known as the Babylonian Captivity.

France, 6 May 1312. A general council at Vienne abolishes the Order of the Knights Templar, intervenes in the Franciscan dispute about poverty, and condemns the heresy of the Beguines (self-appointed holy beggars).

India, 1312. Ala-ud-din's forces conquer the Deccan.

North Atlantic, 1312. A French ship discovers the uninhabited Canary Islands.

Italy, 24 August 1313. Henry VII, emperor since 1309, dies near Siena. His unfulfilled ambition had been to revive imperial power in Italy.

Switzerland, 1314. By their victory at the Battle of Morgarten over the army of the Austrian Duke Leopold I, the allied cantons of Uri, Schwyz, and Unterwalden secure Swiss independence.

Italy, c.1317. The frescoes in the Arena Chapel in Padua and the Church of Santa Croce in Florence are the masterpieces of the pioneering Renaissance artist, Giotto.

Norway, 1319. With the death of King Hakon V, the first Norwegian royal dynasty comes to end. From this time forth, it will be part of Sweden (1319–1343, 1362–1363, 1814–1905) or of Denmark (1380–1814) until its inception as an independent state in 1905.

Poland, 1320. Vladislav, the ruler of Kujavia on the lower Vistula, is crowned king in Cracow. He succeeds in unifying the country.

Italy, 1321. The poet Dante Alighieri dies shortly after completing *The Divine Comedy*. It is the first European literary masterpiece to be written in a vernacular language rather than Latin.

Anatolia, 6 April 1326. Orkhan, the son of Osman, who founded the Ottoman empire, captures Brusa from the Byzantines and makes it his capital. In the years that follow, he captures Nizaa and Nicomedia, expanding Ottoman territories at the expense of Byzantium.

England, 1327. With the Treaty of Northampton, England renounces its claim to Scotland.

Russia, 1328. The Prince of Moscow, Ivan Kalita (Ivan Moneybags) comes to an agreement with Great Khan of the Golden Horde that solidifies Ivan's position and lays the groundwork for Muscovite hegemony of Russia.

England, 1330. Edward III takes power. He sends his mother, Isabella, into a nunnery and executes her lover, Roger Mortimer.

Serbia, September 1331. Stephen Urosh IV overthrows his father, Urosh III, who is murdered. Under Urosh III, Serbia had become the leading Balkan power. Stephen's reign, the highpoint of the medieval Serbian state, is one of effective expansion. He maintains his father's control over Bulgaria and conquers Macedonia, Epirus, and Thessaly. In 1346, he assumes the title "Emperor of the Serbs" when crowned in Skopje. He dies in 1355 while marching to attack Constantinople.

Poland, 1333. Casimir III accedes to the throne and abandons the war with the Teutonic Knights, which was started by his predecessor, Vladyslav.

Japan, 1333. The Ashikaga Shogunate is established. This is the beginning of the Muromaki era, a period of constant warfare between feudal lords. The imperial court is based in Kyoto.

England, 1336. Edward III renews his claim to the French throne.

England, 1337. Edward III begins a war against France by securing allies among the German princes, including

Louis of Bavaria. He also withholds wool exports to Flanders to stir up unrest there. His landing in Antwerp with an army marks the beginning of the Hundred Years' War.

Moscow, 1339. Construction begins of a grand ducal palace called the Kremlin.

Flanders and France, 1340. The English fleet defeats the French fleet at Sluys, off the Flemish coast. The French fleet is all but destroyed, and Edward III gains control of the sea. But both sides are no longer able to pay their troops, and Edward III of England and Philip VI of France agree to the Peace of Esplechin.

Rome, 1341. Petrarch is crowned poet laureate. His poetry is immensely influential in both content and form.

Flanders, 1345. Jacob van Artevelde, who led a Flemish uprising against the French, is murdered in Ghent by a mob in revolt against his dictatorship. Flanders withdraws from active involvement in the war between France and England.

Germany, 11 July 1346. Charles IV of Luxembourg is elected Holy Roman Emperor at the instigation of Pope Clement VI, who has declared Ludwig of Bavaria deposed. Most of Germany, however, continues to support Ludwig.

France, 26 August 1346. The English army led by Edward III hands France and Philip IV a crushing defeat at the Battle of Crécy. Two weeks later, Edward lays siege to Calais.

India, 1346. Vijayangar is founded, the last great Hindu kingdom of South India. Its history is marked by continuing conflict with Sultanate of Delhi, which under the Tughluq Dynasty, widens its territory to include the greater part of India.

Rome, 20 May 1347. The demagogue Cola di Rienzo, whose ambition is to revive Rome's classical role as capital of Italy and assert its supremacy over pope and emperor, is given power by the people and takes the title of tribune. He is soon excommunicated and forced to flee.

Europe, 1348–1352. The Black Death spreads through Eastern Europe, England, France, and Germany. Much of the fabric of daily life is destroyed, and in some places as much as 75 percent of the population dies.

Prague, 1348. Emperor Charles IV, who became King of Bohemia on the death of his father at Crécy, founds the university of Prague.

Germany, 1349. William of Occam, the Franciscan philosopher, dies at Munich. He is best remembered for his law of economy (Occam's razor) in which he exhorted scholars to keep their theories short. He believed in the absolute power of God.

Germany, July–August 1349. Large-scale massacres of Jews occur in Frankfurt, Mainz, and Cologne, associated with the activities of the Flagellants. Many survivors flee to Poland. Soon after Pope Clement VI condemns the Flagellants and forbids their processions.

Southeast Asia, 1350. Ramathibodi, the King of Ayutthaya (Siam), leads an expedition against Cambodia. The previous year, he conquered neighboring Sukhotai and made its king, Lu Thai, a vassal.

Anatolia, 1354. Gallipoli, the key to the Dardanelles, is occupied by the Ottomans, furthering a conflict between John V Palaeologus, the son of the late Emperor Andronicus III, and John Cantacuzene, a former army commander. Both sides have turned to the Turks for help. Cantacuzene was responsible for their entering Europe the previous year.

Rome, 1355. Arriving in and leaving Rome in one day, Charles IV is crowned emperor by a papal legate. His haste, mocked by the Italians, demonstrates that he has abandoned any pretensions to real imperial authority in Italy.

France, November 1355. Edward III of England resumes the war with France. His son, the Black Prince, begins with a devastating raid in Languedoc.

France, August 1356. Taking advantage of the unrest throughout the French realm, the English organize a great expedition under the Black Prince, who launches a series of raids across Limousin and Berry in southwestern France. In September, English forces win an important victory at the Battle of Maupertius.

France, 1360. France and England reach accord in the Treaty of Bretigny. the French King, John the Good, who had been taken captive by the English, is freed and returns to France.

Anatolia, 1363. Defeated at the Battle of Adrianople, the Byzantine emperor is forced to acknowledge his dependency upon the Ottoman Empire. The victorious sultan, Murad I, makes Adrianople his capital and takes the title of caliph.

Spain, 1363. Backed by Peter IV of Aragon, Henry of Trastamara, the illegitimate half-brother of King Pedro, lays claim to the throne of Castile.

London, 8 April 1364. John the Good dies in captivity at the Tower of London. He is succeeded as King of France by Charles V (the Wise).

Brittany, 12 April 1365. By the treaty of Guerande, the house of Blois cedes its rights in Brittany to John IV de Montfort.

Spain, 1367. The Castilian king, Pedro the Cruel, aided by the Black Prince, defeats his rival to the throne, Henry of Trastamara, at Najera.

China, 1368. After the ruling Mongols retreat north in response to mass uprisings, Zhu Yuanzhang, one of the rebel leaders, captures Dadu (Beijing) from the Mongols and establishes the Ming Dynasty, with a capital at Nanjing.

Spain, 28 March 1369. Henry of Trastamara defeats Pedro the Cruel and besieges him in his castle of Montiel. Pedro is captured trying to escape and knifed to death by Henry.

Denmark, 1370. The peace of Stralsund gives trading privileges to the Hanseatic league of German towns.

Scotland, 1371. The death of David Bruce brings a new dynasty to the throne: the Stuarts. David's heir is his nephew, Robert II Stuart, the hereditary steward of Scotland.

Central Asia, 1370. The Mongol warlord Tamerlane conquers Transoxania and proclaims himself the Great Khan, heir to Genghis Khan.

Flanders, 1375. The English and the French reach a truce at Bruges whereby the English retain only Calais and a coastal strip of Gascony.

Rome, January 1377. In fear of losing control of the papal states, Gregory XI, pope since 1370, leaves Avignon and re-establishes the papacy in Rome.

England, 21 June 1377. Edward III is succeeded by his grandson Richard II, son of Edward the Black Prince. Richard is still a child; effective power rests with the royal council.

Morocco, 1377. The Arabic world traveler Ibn Batuta dies in Fez. His travels had taken him to North and East Africa, Russia, India, and China.

England, 1378. The poet William Langland is at work on Piers Plowman, an allegory of the soul's journey to find salvation.

Germany, 1378. On his death in Prague, Emperor Charles IV, who had been German King since 1346 and Emperor since 1355, is succeeded in the empire and Bohemia by his son Wenceslas.

Italy, 1378. The archbishop of Bari becomes Pope Urban VI. Gregory XI died on 27 March, when he was already considering a return to Avignon. Under pressure from the Roman mob, the cardinals hastily elected an Italian pope. The election of Robert of Geneva as anti-pope by discontented cardinals precipitates the Great Schism that will last until the Council of Constance (1414–1418). Gregory resides in Rome, and Robert, who takes the name Clement VII, takes up residence in Avignon.

France, 3 November 1380. Charles VI, who succeeded his father, Charles V, in September, is crowned king.

England, 1381. With death of its leader Wat Tyler, the Peasants' Revolt comes to an end. Tyler had marched with his followers on London, where they forced King Richard II to lower taxes and institute land reform.

Flanders, May 1382. The rebel leader Philip van Artevelde captures Bruges. Louis de Male, the Count of Flanders, appeals for help to Charles VI and Philip of Burgundy.

England, 1382. The Blackfriars council condemns the principal tenets of Lollardy—the teachings of John Wyclif—and takes steps to stamp out heresy within Oxford, thereby threatening the university's independence. Several of Wyclif's leading followers submit. Wyclif leaves Oxford.

Flanders, 1384. Philip II (the Bold), the Duke of Burgundy, inherits Flanders, Malines, Antwerp, and Artois, becoming count of Flanders.

Central Europe, 1386. The Swiss confederation defeats Leopold III, the Habsburg Duke of Austria, at Sempach; Leopold is killed in the battle. War broke out the previous year, prompted partly by Leopold's growing power in Swabia.

Middle East, 1387. The Tartar conqueror Tamerlane captures Isfahan and Shiraz and attacks Armenia.

Balkans, 28 June 1389. Ottoman Sultan Murad I defeats the Serbs at the Battle of Amselfeld.

Anatolia, 16 September 1389. Bayezid Yilderim succeeds his father, Murad, as sultan of the Ottoman Turks. He makes Bulgaria a province of the Ottoman Empire. Bulgaria will not regain full independence until 1908.

Italy, 1395. Gian Galeazzo Visconti buys the title of Duke of Milan from King Wenceslas, which gives him the status of a legitimate prince. Visconti had been pursuing a successful policy of expansion, making Milan the leading power in Northern Italy.

Scandinavia, 20 June 1397. The Union of Kalmar unites Denmark, Sweden, and Norway under one monarch. The Union lasts with some interruptions until 1523.

England, 29 September 1399. Richard II is deposed. His cousin Henry of Lancaster declares himself king under the name Henry IV. Richard dies under suspicious circumstances while imprisoned in Pontefract Castle.

Constantinople, 1399. John II of Boucicaut, the Marshal of France, with western troops holds Constantinople against the Ottomans. Emperor Manuel II leaves for the West in an attempt to raise further help, leaving his nephew John VII as co-emperor.

1400–1499

Germany, 1400. Wenceslas IV, an indolent drunkard, is deposed as King of the Romans (the title held by emperors who were not crowned as Holy Roman Emperor), though he remains King of Bohemia. The choice of Rupert of the Palatinate to replace him causes a schism when Wenceslas and his supporters refuse to accept the election.

England, 1401. Geoffrey Chaucer, author of *The Canterbury Tales*, dies before its completion.

Anatolia, 1402. The Ottoman sultan Bayezid is defeated by Tamerlane in battle near Angora. Tamerlane captures Smyrna and reaches the Bosphorus. Bayezid is taken prisoner and dies in captivity.

Prague, 1402. The reformer Jan Hus begins to preach in the Bethlehem chapel, founded in 1391 by two laymen as a center of religious revival.

France, 27 April 1404. Upon the death of his father, Philip II, John (the Fearless) becomes Duke of Burgundy.

Paris, 23 November 1407. Louis, the Duke of Orléans, is murdered on the instigation of John the Fearless, the Duke of Burgundy. With Charles VI prevented from governing by madness, a deadly struggle developed between Louis and John, and their supporters form factions known as the Armagnac and Burgundian parties, respectively.

Italy, May 1410. Following the death of Alexander V at Bologna, John XXIII—said to have poisoned Alexander—is elected pope. His election marks an important stage in the rise of the Medici family, his backers.

Peru, c.1410. Under the leadership of Viracocha, who became ruler of the Incas in 1400, the Inca Empire is expanding and the rigidly hierarchical structure of Inca society is growing more formalized.

West Africa, 1410. Kanajeji Sarki, the King of Kano, dies. He introduced iron helmets and quilted horse armor to the Hausa cavalry.

Hungary, July 1411. Sigismund of Hungary, the brother of Wenceslas, is elected Holy Roman Emperor. Of the two candidates who were rivals for the title in 1400, Rupert died in 1410 year and Wenceslas is retired with a pension.

England, 20 March 1413. On his death, Henry IV is succeeded by his son Henry V, who sets out to regain lost territories in France. He adopts the French claims of Edward III as his own and asserts his right to the inheritance of the Plantagenets.

Paris, 1413. Demands for reform of finance and justice made by the Paris craftsmen under the patronage of the Burgundian faction result in an ordinance that all officials, both central and local, should be elected. This utopian measure is overturned when the Armagnac faction seizes control of Paris.

Germany, 6 July 1415. Having appeared before the Council of Constance, Jan Hus is convicted of heresy and burned at the stake.

France, 25 October 1415. Henry V, who landed in France in August, secures a major victory over French troops at the Battle of Agincourt. The occasion is marred by the murder of French captives, whose presence was feared could threaten the English lines.

Morocco, 1415. King John of Portugal conquers Ceuta in Morocco. Keen to acquire gold and slaves from Africa, he is also motivated by a dream of allying with Africans against the Muslims of the Maghreb.

Germany, 1417. The Council of Constance arrives at a consensus candidate, and Martin V (born Odo Colonna) becomes pope, reestablishing the unity of the Church. Three years later he returns the papacy to Rome.

China, 1420. The Yongle emperor moves his main capital to the former Yuan capital Dadu, renaming it Beijing (meaning northern capital), the better to defend the country against resurgent Mongol power. Nanjing becomes the secondary capital.

North Atlantic, 1420. Prince Henry of Portugal encourages the settlement of Porto Santo and Madeira.

France, 31 August 1422. By the Treaty of Troyes, signed in 1420, Henry V of England became heir designate to the Kingdom of France. But he dies at Vincennes with his heir, Henry VI, only nine months old.

Constantinople, 21 July 1425. The Emperor Manuel II dies and is succeeded by his son John VIII Palaeologus. Manuel had ruled only Constantinople itself, while his brothers ruled other fragments of the former Byzantine empire.

Ethiopia, 1427. The Emperor Yeshaq sends envoys to Aragon in Spain to forge an alliance against Islam.

France, 8 May 1429. A farmer's daughter, Joan of Arc, appears before the Dauphin, Charles, at his castle in Chinon and tells him of the visions she had been granted that call upon her to liberate France. In September, she makes a triumphant entry into Paris.

Rheims, 18 July 1429. Charles VII is crowned King of France.

Greece, 29 March 1430. Sultan Murad II captures the Thessalonica, held by Venice since 1423.

France, 14 July 1430. Joan of Arc, taken prisoner by the Burgundians in May, is handed over to Pierre Cauchon, the bishop of Beauvais. She is found guilty of heresy and burned at the stake.

Central Europe, 1431. The Hussites (followers of Jan Hus) win a series of victories in Bohemia against German armies sent to oppose them. The church council at Basel, which opened in July, resolves to negotiate with them.

Belgium, 1432. The Van Eyck brothers, Jan and Hubert, complete work on the *Adoration of the Lamb*, an altarpiece for St. Bavo's church in Ghent. It ranks as the highest achievement of early Flemish art.

North Atlantic, 1432. The Portuguese discover an archipelago, which they name the Azores.

Rome, 31 May 1433. Sigismund is crowned emperor by Pope Eugenius IV, who hopes for his support against the council at Basel.

Switzerland, 30 November 1433. The readiness of the Council of Basel to open negotiations with the Hussites splits the movement between the moderate Utraquists and the radical Taborites. In the following year, the Taborites are defeated at Lipany by the army of the Emperor Sigismund, with the support of both Catholics and Utraquists.

Southeast Asia, 1434. The capital of the Khmer kingdom is moved from Angkor to Phnom Penh.

Florence, 1434. Cosimo de Medici, who was exiled by his enemy Rinaldo d'Albizzi in 1433, returns and seizes power in the city. Although Cosimo remains a private citizen within an independent republic, he is the city's de facto ruler.

France, 21 September 1435. By the Treaty of Arras, Philip the Good of Burgundy breaks with the English and recognizes Charles VII as the only King of France. Charles cedes some territory, but by so doing he can concentrate on defeating the English invaders without having to worry about Burgundy.

Bohemia, 5 July 1436. The agreement made with the Hussites in 1433 is confirmed, and Sigismund is recognized as King of Bohemia. In exchange a Hussite theologian is confirmed as Archbishop of Prague.

Italy, April 1438. Taking advantage of a split in the Council of Basel over the best place to meet a Greek delegation seeking the reunion of the churches, Pope Eugenius invites the Greeks to Ferrara. A minority of the council joins them there, while the majority remains at Basel and declares the pope suspended.

France, 7 July 1438. Charles VII promulgates the Pragmatic Sanction, which limits papal authority over French bishops and gives the king a say in the appointment of prelates.

Scandinavia, 1438. Peasant rebellions and nationalist tensions prompt King Eric to flee from Denmark. He takes refuge on the Swedish island of Gotland, where he becomes a pirate and preys on Baltic shipping.

Basel, 5 November 1439. The delegates who refused to follow the council to Italy declare Eugenius deposed and elect their own pope. He is a layman, Duke Amadeus VIII of Savoy. Famous for his wisdom and wealth, he adopts the name Felix V.

Mexico, 1440. Montezuma becomes ruler of the Aztecs and begins the conquest of tribes outside the valley of Mexico. A triple alliance formed in 1428 among the cities of Tenochtitlan, Texcoco, and Tlacopan led to the final overthrow of Tepanec power in the valley of Mexico. The Aztecs have gradually taken over the area of Tepanec domination.

Florence, 1441. The Ethiopian Church sends a representative to the Latin Church council. An act of union is signed between the Church of Ethiopia and that of Rome.

Naples, 12 June 1442. Alfonso V, King of Aragon since 1416, is crowned King of Sicily and Naples after conquering the town.

Bulgaria, 1444. The Ottomans defeat the Hungarians at Varna on the shores of the Black Sea. This opens their way to Constantinople.

Milan, 1447. On the death of Filippo Maria Visconti, the last of the male line, a republic is proclaimed by the citizens, who hire Francesco Sforza as their general. In 1450, he takes the title Duke of Milan.

Germany, 1448. Leaving Strasbourg, where he has lived for the past few years, Johannes Gutenberg—who has invented moveable printing characters—returns to his native town of Mainz.

Constantinople, 6 January 1449. Constantine XI succeeds his brother John VIII Palaeologus as emperor.

Normandy, 15 April 1450. With a victory over the English at Formigny, the French complete their reconquest of Normandy.

Anatolia, 2 February 1451. Muhammad II succeeds Murad II as sultan of the Ottomans.

Constantinople, 29 May 1453. After a two-month siege, the Ottoman Turks seize the city. The Byzantine Empire is at an end.

France, 17 July 1453. France defeats England at Castillon, ending the Hundred Years' War. England has surrendered all territory on the continent with the exception of Calais.

Venice, 18 April 1454. The Doge Francesco Foscari signs a treaty with the Ottoman Sultan Muhammad I, that grants the city trading privileges with his Empire.

Rome, 18 February 1455. The Dominican monk and painter Fra Angelico dies in Rome. He painted only religious subjects, combining the spirituality of the Middle Ages with Renaissance naturalism.

England, 22 May 1455. The Duke of York, dismissed as protector when Henry VI recovered his senses at the end of last year, defeats the king's forces at St. Albans and seizes power in his name. This marks the beginning of the War of the Roses.

Germany, 1455. The inventor and printer Johannes Gutenberg completes a 42-line Bible. The book printed with moveable type comes to be seen as the beginning of a new era in the transmission of information and ideas.

Greece, 1458. The Turks occupy Athens.

England, December 1460. The Yorkists are defeated at Wakefield. Richard, the Duke of York, is killed in the battle.

Anatolia, 1461. Muhammad II annexes Trebizond, the last fragment of the Byzantine empire.

England, 1461. Edward, the son of Richard, the Duke of York, is crowned Edward IV after defeating the Lancastrian forces at the battle of Towton. Henry VI flees with his wife Margaret to Scotland.

Russia, 1462. Ivan III (the Great) succeeds Vasily II as Prince of Muscovy.

Paris, January 5. The poet and vagabond François Villon is sentenced to death, but that is later commuted to exile. After this he vanishes without a trace.

Burgundy, 15 June 1467. Philip the Good is succeeded as Duke of Burgundy by Charles (the Bold).

Florence, 3 December 1468. Lorenzo (the Magnificent) and his brother Giuliano succeed their father, Piero de Medici, as rulers of Florence.

Spain, 1469. Isabella of Castile marries Ferdinand, heir to the throne of Aragon, creating the conditions for the unification of Spain.

Italy, 1471. Cardinal Francesco della Rovere is elected Pope Sixtus IV. He promotes art and science but engages in nepotism and the selling of Church offices.

Anatolia, 1471. Muhammad II conquers the last surviving Turkish emirate, Karamania. All the lands from the Taurus mountains to the Adriatic are now under Ottoman rule.

France, 11 June 1474. Louis XI ratifies the Perpetual Peace, signed by the Habsburgs and the Swiss.

England, 1474. The Treaty of Utrecht gives the Hanseatic league generous trading privileges in England.

France, January 1477. On the death of Charles the Bold, Louis XI invades Burgundy, Franche-Comte, and Artois.

Flanders, 18 August 1477. Maximilian of Austria, the son of the Emperor Frederick III, marries Mary of Burgundy, the daughter and heir of Charles the Bold. The house of Habsburg is now heir to the duchy of Burgundy, one of the richest states in Europe.

Florence, 1478. Giuliano de Medici is killed as a result of the Pazzi conspiracy against him and his brother Lorenzo. Lorenzo, however, gains the upper hand and becomes the de facto ruler of the city. Called Lorenzo the Magnificent, he presides over an unparalleled flowering of arts and science.

Spain, 1479. Ferdinand, the husband of Isabella of Castile, succeeds his father, John II, as King of Aragon. In prior years, Ferdinand and Isabella introduced the Inquisition into Spain.

France, 7 August 1479. Maximilian of Austria halts Louis XI's incursions into Burgundian territories.

Milan, 1479. Ludovico Sforza seizes power from his nephew Gian Galeazzo, the youthful grandson of Francesco Sforza.

Russia, 1480. Ivan the Great stops paying tribute to the Mongols. The Tartars pull back from Moscow. In the following years, he creates a unified Russia.

France, 23 December 1482. Burgundy and Picardy are absorbed into France by the Treaty of Arras. Artois becomes the dowry of the two-year-old Margaret of Burgundy, daughter of Mary and Maximilian, who has been promised in marriage to the dauphin. The rest goes to her brother Philip.

England, 9 April 1483. Edward IV dies at Windsor. During his second reign, he reestablished stability after the Wars of the Roses, but his achievements are threatened by the fact that his heir,

Edward V, is only twelve years old. In August, his brother Richard is declared regent for the young king. Two years later, Richard usurps the throne and installs himself as Richard III. His responsibility for the subsequent death of Edward V and his brother continues to be a subject of debate.

Rome, 5 December 1484. Pope Innocent VIII issues a bull deploring the spread of witchcraft and heresy in Germany and authorizing the Dominican inquisitors to deal with it.

Flanders, June–July 1485. Maximilian takes Bruges and Ghent by siege. Although accepted by Holland, Zeeland, and Hainault, Maximilian's claim to authority in the Low Countries as guardian of his son Philip had been rejected by Flanders and Brabant.

England, 22 August 1485. The victory of Henry Tudor (Henry VII) over Richard III at the Battle of Bosworth establishes the Tudor Dynasty.

Spain, 1487. Ferdinand and Isabella take possession of Malaga, which had been an independent Muslim principality.

South Africa, 1488. The Portuguese explorer, Bartholomew Dias, rounds the Cape of Good Hope.

Cyprus, 14 March 1489. The purchase of the island by the Venetians from Catherine Cornaro, the last of the Lusignan Dynasty of Cyprus, ends several centuries of Frankish sovereignty.

Brittany, 1491. When the French occupy the duchy of Brittany, neither England nor Spain sends help to the Bretons. The proxy marriage between Anne of Brittany and Maximilian of Austria, arranged the previous year, is annulled, and Anne has no choice but to marry Charles VIII, the King of France. The independence of Brittany is effectively ended.

Spain, 2 January 1492. Ferdinand and Isabella take Granada, the last Muslim kingdom in Spain, which had resisted Christian conquest for two centuries.

Spain, 30 March 1492. A royal edict is issued decreeing the expulsion of the Jews.

Rome, 10 August 1492. On the death of Innocent VIII, the Valencian Rodrigo de Borja (Borgia) is elected pope. He takes the name Alexander VI. His time in the curia is one of moral deterioration, his main concern being the advancement of his children Cesare and Lucrezia.

Caribbean, 12 October 1492. Christopher Columbus lands on an island he calls San Salvador (in the present-day Bahamas).

Rome, 4 May 1493. The Spanish-born pope, Alexander VI, decrees that all new lands discovered west of the Azores are Spanish.

Spain, 29 September 1493. Columbus, who returned to Spain in April, leaves Cadiz on a second voyage of exploration.

Netherlands, 1494. Philip (the Fair), son of the Emperor Maximilian, becomes ruler of the Low Countries.

Rome, 1494. Charles VIII enters Rome with the consent of the pope. Ludovico Sforza, allied with the French king, takes the title Duke of Milan.

Florence, 1494. Piero de Medici is driven out of Florence by the Dominican friar Savonarola, who sets up a form of religious dictatorship.

Spain, 7 June 1494. With the treaty of Tordessilas, Spain and Portugal divide the New World between them.

Italy, 31 March 1495. Venice, Milan, Spain, the pope, and the Holy Roman Emperor set up a holy league against Charles VIII of France, who seized Naples last month.

Europe, 1496. The alliance between the Habsburgs and Castile is strengthened by the marriage of Philip the Fair to Joanna of Castile, daughter of Ferdinand and Isabella.

Canada, 24 June 1497. The Italian navigator John Cabot, in the service of the English crown, reaches North America after a journey lasting 35 days, and starts to explore the coastline from Cape Breton to Labrador.

South Africa, 1497. On order of Manuel, the King of Portugal, Vasco da Gama sets sail for India via the Cape of Good Hope. He rounds the cape on 22 November.

Florence, 23 May 1498. The fundamentalist preacher Savonarola is excommunicated by the pope, tried, and burned at the stake.

Milan, 1499. Backed by the pope, Venice, Florence, and the Swiss cantons, Louis XII of France claims his right of succession to the duchy of Milan. The French, led by the mercenary Trivulzio, seize Milan. The usurper Ludovico Sforza flees.

Brazil, 1 January 1500. The Portuguese explorer Pedro Alvarez Cabral discovers the coast of Brazil. Later in the same year, he creates the first Portuguese trading posts on the west coast of India. ❑

KING CLOVIS FOUNDS FRANKISH KINGDOM

Gaul, 511

Upon the death of his father, Childeric I, Clovis I assumed control over a small Frankish kingdom in the vicinity of Tournai. With a combination of political maneuvering, armed force, and guile, he was able in a short time to unite all of the Frankish tribes in Gaul under his authority.

He defeated Syagrius's Roman army at Soissons in 486 and advanced the Frankish frontier to the Loire. In 502 he pushed further east by defeating the Alamanni, a Germanic tribe.

Clovis married Clotilda, a Catholic Burgundian. He is said to have vowed during the battle that he would be baptized if God helped him defeat the Alamanni. He kept his promise, and the Franks marched southward under their Christian king to defeat the Burgundians at Tolbiac. Clovis then turned on the Visigoths. Like most of the Germanic tribes, the Visigoths were Arian Christians, denying the Trinity, which gave the orthodox Catholic Clovis theological justification for his conquests. "It grieves me to see that the Arians still possess the fairest portion of Gaul. Let us march against them, vanquish the heretics, and share out their fertile lands," he announced from his capital, Paris, before marching to Poitiers.

Clovis, the king of the Franks, defeated Alaric II, the king of the Visigoths, who died in the fierce battle at Vouille ten miles from Poitiers. His victory left Clovis master of all but southeastern Gaul.

The four sons of the Frankish king Clovis: Childeric, Clothar , Chlodomer, and Theuderic (Miniature 1493)

Clovis's conversion hardly made him into a model of Christian meekness. Of Christ's crucifixion, he once exclaimed: "Had I been there at the head of my army of valiant Franks, I would have avenged his death!"

In the following year at Tours, Clovis was formally recognized by Anastasius, the Emperor in Constantinople, as the king of Gaul. He died at the age of 45 in 511, leaving his kingdom to be divided among his four sons. ❑

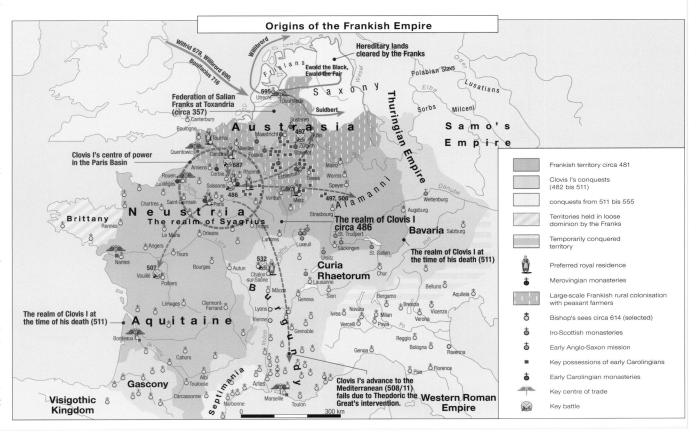

RESTORATION OF THE ROMAN EMPIRE UNDER JUSTINIAN

August 1, 527

Follower and co-emperor to his grandfather Justin I (c.450–527), Justinian ascended to the imperial throne. For his co-emperor he named his wife Theodora, who had once been an actress. Justinian set himself the goal of restoring the Roman empire to its former glory through military expansion and wide-reaching political and legal reforms.

His first priority upon taking office was to quell domestic dissent. The Nika riots, which were initially sparked by rivalries among teams of charioteers, spread throughout the city of Constantinople, almost causing the emperor to flee the city. After five days of fighting, the revolt was finally suppressed and its leaders exiled or killed.

Justinian pursued an aggressive foreign policy. His chief general Belisarius waged a victorious campaign against the Vandals in North Africa, then led his army into Italy against the Ostrogoths where he met with limited success. Military action was also taken against the Visigoths, Slavs, and Sassanid Persians. These actions expanded the bounds of Justinian's empire, but at great monetary cost. To rectify the drain on the public purse, Justinian raised taxes, provoking social unrest. His program of government reforms was intended to reduce corruption and guarantee that tax revenue found its way into the treasury. But the plan did little to allay the vast disparity in the living conditions between rich and poor.

One area in which the emperor's efforts met with unqualified success was legal reform. He compiled the vast body of Roman civil and criminal law into one all-embracing code, *Corpus Juris Civilis.* This still forms the basis of many European countries' legal systems.

Justinian I, Byzantine emperor from 527-565 (mosaic from Ravenna, 6th century)

Justinian and Theodora considered themselves servants of God called upon to protect the interests of the Church. They considered the Roman empire, Roman Law, and Christianity to be inextricably bound together. They actively suppressed paganism and heresy. One notable example is the forced dissolution of the Academy in Athens, which had been founded by Plato, on the grounds that it fostered pagan ideas.

The work of unifying the Church, occupied much of his later years. The Church was faced with the Monophysite controversy, which centered upon the singular or dual nature of Christ. Though Justinian tried to reconcile opposing viewpoints at a number of ecumenical councils, he succeeded in pushing the two sides farther apart.

Justinian ordered expansive reconstruction projects in Constantinople and elsewhere and saw to the rebuilding of the Church of Haggia Sophia. Justinian died at Constaninople in 565. ❑

The domed church Hagia Sophia in Constantinople, built between 532 and 537. The minaret was built after the Ottoman conquest of the city in 1453.

THE LEGACY OF POPE GREGORY I

Rome, 590

Gregory I was the first writer and the first monk to occupy the papal chair. The years preceding his election were difficult ones. There was a decided rupture between the Byzantine and Roman churches. In 568 the Lombards had invaded Italy, bringing with them their belief in Arianism. Gregory reorganized the lands and properties that made up the papal holding. He paid rent to the landholders, initiated construction projects, and set up a department to oversee church finances. His first great success was in liberating Rome from the Lombards by paying a large ransom. Within six years he had negotiated a peace agreement between the Lombards and Byzantium. His close relationship with the Lombard queen, Theodelinda, made it possible to bring a great portion of the tribe from Arianism into the Catholic fold.

In the year before Gregory took office, the Visigoths were converted to Catholicism. He was the first pope to recognize the importance of the Germanic peoples to the future of the Church. He was cognizant of the lessons of the Evangelists, who taught that the Gospels should be preached to the gentiles. Upon encountering some English boys

Carlo Saraceni, *Pope Gregory the Great*, c.610

brought into the Roman slave market, he was reported to have remarked, "Non angli, sed angeli." (They are angels, not Anglo-Saxons.) When a deputation appeared from England, Gregory took advantage of the moment and assembled missionaries to accompany them back to England. Following the lead of Augustine, a monk from Greg-

ory's own monastery in Rome, the delegation received permission from the Anglo-Saxon king to found a monastery near the royal residence in Kent upon the ruins of an old Roman city. The town, Durovernum, was called Cantwarbyrig in Old English (now Canterbury). It became the center of the Church in England. According to Church accounts, Augustine presided over the conversion of ten thousand Anglo-Saxons.

Relations between the Byzantine and Roman Churches were a high priority for Gregory. He opposed the head of the Eastern Church, John IV, when he assumed the title Ecumenical Patriarch (that is, chief prelate). Gregory forcefully responded that the title was godless and arrogant and did great harm to the faith and peace within the Church. ❑

THE MONASTIC ODYSSEY OF ST. COLUMBANUS

Italy, 590

Born in 543 in Leinster, Ireland, Columbanus was a great Irish missionary. He founded a number of monasteries in the Frankish and Lombard kingdoms. The codification of his legacy survives as the *Monastic Rule of St. Columbanus*, which sets out rules of conduct for abbots and monks, with penitential practices that are renowned for their severity.

His dedication to monastic life began under the tutelage of Abbott St. Comgall at the Bangor monastery in County Down, where he stayed until his early forties. Around 590, believing that God was instructing him to preach the Gospel beyond Ireland, Columbanus and twelve followers set sail for Brittany and the Frankish Kingdom in Gaul. He was welcomed by the Burgundian King Gotram, who gave

him an old Roman fortress at Annegray in the Vosges Mountains. As his monastic following grew, Gotram offered a second location at Luxeuil and finally a third at Fontaines. St. Columbanus oversaw these monasteries for twenty years, until he ran afoul of the royal household under Theodoric and his imperious grandmother Queen Brunehault by attempting to rid their court of vice.

Now *persona non grata*, Columbanus began a missionary odyssey that took him through modern-day Germany and Switzerland and ended with a warm welcome from the Lombard King Agilulf. The Lombard king's largesse allow him to open an abbey at Bobbio in the Apennines on the river Trebbia, where he continued his monastic mission until his death in 615. ❑

REUNIFICATION OF CHINA

China, 581

Emperor Wendi, founder of the Sui Dynasty (581–618), and his son Emperor Yandi unified China after years of discord between the Southern and Northern Dynasties. Using first arranged marriage and then military force, Wendi claimed the Northern Zhou throne. His army then overwhelmed the Southern Zhou Dynasty, thereby unifying China under the Sui imperial aegis.

The father and son emperors instituted sweeping reforms that centralized China's civil service along the lines of Confucian principles, created a more inclusive equitable land distribution sys-

Chinese clay figure (7th century)

tem, and increased agricultural productivity. They also completed massive construction projects including the Grand Canal and the Great Wall.

Although their accomplishments were impressive, their methods were harsh and ultimately self-destructive. Excessive spending, compulsory labor, and heavy taxation resulted in popular revolts, imperial in-fighting, and a bankrupt economy. Emperor Yandi's ill-conceived invasion of the Korean kingdom of Goguryeo resulted in total defeat of the Sui army and facilitated the rise of the Tang Dynasty. ❑

THE BENEDICTINE ORDER OF MONKS

Italy, 530

While studying in Rome at around 500, St. Benedict (c.480–543) became so scandalized by the city's rampant immorality that he left for the wilderness of the Subiaco region, where he lived in a cave as a hermit monk. His experience eventually led him away from holy solitude toward a belief that the joy of faith should be expressed in a communal setting. To that end, in 529, he founded the Monte Cassino Monastery. It was here, in 530, that he began to write his *Rule of St. Benedict*.

The precepts of the *Rule of St. Benedict* continued a legacy of monastic observance begun in the third century by the Desert Fathers of Egypt, the *Rule of Augustine* of Hippo, and the anonymous *Rule of the Master*, but were less rigidly austere and, most importantly, aimed at laymen and women. The monastery was to be as a family governed by an abbot elected for life by the monks. Central to the Rule was the daily Divine Office, or *horarium*, which was organized in eight canonical hours, with regular periods of communal and individual prayer, study, manual labor, and sleep.

The Rule of St. Benedict represented a moderate path to monastic observance that sought to express a loving relationship with God more through an inclusive human community and less through the exclusivity of individual effort and discipline alone. To this day, this inclusive approach has influenced the community ethos and daily routines of Orthodox and Catholic monasteries alike. ❑

Illumination from manuscript of the *Rule of St. Benedict* (c.1430)

PROHIBITION AGAINST PRIVATE PROPERTY

From the Rule of St. Benedict

This vice especially is to be cut out of the monastery by the roots. Let no one presume to give or receive anything without the Abbot's leave, or to have anything as his own—anything whatever, whether book or tablets or pen or whatever it may be—since they are not permitted to have even their bodies or wills at their own disposal; but for all their necessities let them look to the Father of the monastery. And let it be unlawful to have anything which the Abbot has not given or allowed. Let all things be common to all, as it is written (Acts 4:32), and let no one say or assume that anything is his own.

But if anyone is caught indulging in this most wicked vice, let him be admonished once and a second time. If he fails to amend, let him undergo punishment.

Let us follow the Scripture, "Distribution was made to each according as anyone had need" (Acts 4:35). By this we do not mean that there should be respecting of persons (which God forbids), but consideration for infirmities. She who needs less should thank God and not be discontented; but she who needs more should be humbled by the thought of her infirmity rather than feeling important on account of the kindness shown her. Thus all the members will be at peace.

Above all, let not the evil of murmuring appear for any reason whatsoever in the least word or sign. If anyone is caught at it, let her be placed under very severe discipline. ❑

BUDDHISM TAKES HOLD IN JAPAN

Japan, 592

Buddhism was brought to Japan during the Yamato Period (c.250–710) in the sixth century by Korean monks. Seen as a threat to traditional Shinto beliefs, it was opposed by a number of prominent ruling families, but was embraced by the powerful Soga clan, whose patriarch Soga No Iname believed it could unify Japan under the Emperor.

His son, Soga No Umako, was Buddhist but a ruthless politician whose ambition was to establish the Soga family's supremacy in the Yamato court. He was able to install his nephew, Sujun, as a puppet Emperor, and in so doing consolidate the Soga clan's imperial influence and elevate Buddhism to official status. When Emperor Sujun attempted to assert himself, Umako had him assassinated and replaced with his niece, the Empress Suiko. It was at this point that Umako's cruel court intrigues were palliated by the presence of Empress Suiko's nephew, Prince Regent Umayado. It was he who united Japan under the Emperor and Buddhism.

A true devotee to Buddhist teachings, the enlightened Prince was a Sutra scholar possessed of great administrative skill. An admirer of the Chinese model of centralized government, he sought to bring true unity to Japan under the aegis of Buddhist wisdom and to that purpose created a seventeen-article constitution that directed members of the ruling class to believe in Buddhism and to unite under the authority of the Emperor. It also stressed the virtues of harmony and obedience, elements that derive from Confucianism. ❑

Shaka Sanko, Shinto divinity

Persian Glory under the Sassanids

Persia, 613

After a 48-year reign, Khosrow I, the king of the Persians, died during a third war with the Romans. In 613, his son, Khosrow II, would extend their rule to the gates of Damascus, witnessing a return to the grandest days of the Persian empire.

In 531, when Khosrow I came to the throne, the Sassanid empire was embroiled in seemingly endless conflict with Byzantium, was paying tribute to the Hephtalite Huns, and was suffering internal disturbance from the Mazdakite revolutionary movement. His first step was to make peace with Byzantium, the "Eternal Peace" concluded with Justinian in 532.

Turning to domestic matters, he restored to their owners all goods confiscated by the Mazdakites, who believed in sharing everything. Women, whom they had

Ruins of the palace of Taq I Kisra of King Khosrow I in Ctesiphon

abducted, were allowed to choose whether or not to return to their husbands. Khosrow reduced taxes,

especially for the old. He kept the aristocracy under control by installing four military governors, answerable only to him. He was tolerant toward the Christians and had a good relationship with the patriarchs of the Nestorian Church, one of whom was his old doctor. He ordered the construction of many fine new buildings, including the Takhti Khesra at Ctesiphon. In alliance with the Turks, Khosrow withdrew tribute from the Hephtalites, and then went on to destroy them in campaigns between 565 and 568, when he annexed Bactria.

Having consolidated his position Khosrow renewed the war with the Eastern Roman empire, under Emperor Justinian. In 540 he attacked Syria, sacked Antioch, and deported its citizens to Ctesiphon. He made peace again in 562. ❏

The Sutton Hoo Burial Ground

England, c.615

Sutton Hoo (*hoo* meaning "spur of a hill") is the site of two sixth- to seventh-century Anglo-Saxon burial grounds located on bluffs overlooking the Deben River estuary in Suffolk, England. Consisting of over twenty burial mounds, it includes what is apparently a king's tomb, loaded with riches, in a massive burial ship measuring 90ft × 14 ft, (28 m × 4.3 m).

Unearthed in 1939 by an elderly woman who owned the estate on which it was located and an amateur archaeologist, the sites have yielded a treasure trove of information about Anglo-Saxon culture. The artifacts found at these sites have provided historians with invaluable evidence

about the daily life of this society in the Dark Ages, for which there are few written records.

Whose coffin it was at Sutton Hoo has been disputed by historians, but many believe it was that of the Anglo-Saxon King Raewald (r. c.599–c.624). Historians know that Raewald lived at the time of St. Augustine's mission in Kent, on which Pope Gregory sent him. It may well have been that Raewald and his sons and *aethlings* (lords) were among the first Englishmen to have accepted Roman Christianity.

This horde-rich method of burial was recorded in the contemporaneous Anglo-Saxon epic poem, *Beowulf*, which refers to the hero's interment being located on

a headland (*hoo*) "high and broad and visible to those journeying the ocean." The poem goes on to say that rings and jewels were put into the barrow with "all such adornments that warriors had claimed from the hoard."

The objects buried throughout Sutton Hoo suggest a proto-Christian presence in the culture. They also show evidence of an extensive foreign trade and highly sophisticated indigenous crafts. Beautifully engraved Anglo-Saxon and Swedish gold ornaments, exquisite bowls from Constantinople and Alexandria, and coins from Gaul bear witness to a society far more cosmopolitan and advanced than the previous, limited historical record may have indicated. ❏

Spanish Visigoths Impose Catholic Creed

Point of Interest

After being riven by controversy over the true form of Christian doctrine, Spain finally repaired the split between the Arianism of its Visigothic occupiers and the orthodox Catholicism of its subject population. The council at Toledo decreed that Spain would have a single creed, that of the orthodox Catholic Church.

The conflict between Arians and Catholics—the former refusing to accept the full equality of the Son with the Father—had persisted since the Council of Nicea in 325. The Visigoths, who seized control in Spain in 458, had always been Arians, but until the reign of Leovigild (568–586), their faith had not been a contentious issue.

In 578, having successfully fought off the Franks and the Byzantines, Leovigild decided that religious unity would promote national solidarity. He began persecuting Catholics, but few changed their beliefs. His elder son Hermenegild actually converted after marrying a Frankish Catholic princess, and attempted to overthrow his father in 583. The revolt ended in 585 and Hermenegild died in prison, still a stalwart Catholic.

Leovigild himself died in 586 and was succeeded by Recared, his younger son. Recared, too, saw the need for religious, and thereby national, unity, but in 587 he chose the Catholicism of the majority. He summoned Spain's leaders to Toledo to insist they declare their adherence. Some Visigoth priests remained diehard Arians, but most bowed to the changing realities and agreed accepting the declaration. ❏

THE GOLDEN AGE OF THE TANG DYNASTY

China, seventh century

The collapse of the Sui was exploited by the Tang dynasty's Li family when their patriarch Li Yuan was temporarily installed as Emperor Gaozu through the military prowess of his son Li Shimin. The son then ruthlessly claimed the throne when he killed his elder brothers and their families. He deposed his father in 627. As Emperor Taizong, he quickly consolidated his grasp on China, making the borders safe, penetrating into central Asia, and establishing trade routes to the West.

Taizong was to become one of China's great emperors, ushering in a golden age of peace and prosperity. His creation of the Confucian scholar-official bureaucracy, his agrarian land reforms that empowered the general populace, and his patronage of the arts would serve as the standard for future emperors. To this day the Tang period is seen as China's unparalleled renaissance era in which was produced its finest art and poetry.

Perhaps most significantly, Emperor Taizong introduced to this historically class-driven society a species of comparatively democratic social organization. He achieved this by decreeing an end to primogeniture, thereby divesting the powerful nobility of birth-right entitlements, and then extending more liberal inheritance rights, and therefore power, to his vast army of scholar-officials. In essence, he had shrewdly dismantled an ancient class system that gave noble families too much power and be-

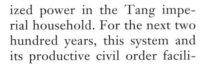

Tang Dynasty statuettes

stowed the privilege of social mobility on his newly created managerial class, whose loyalty would ensure the consolidation of centralized power in the Tang imperial household. For the next two hundred years, this system and its productive civil order facilitated the extending of China's territorial boundaries beyond those achieved by the Han Dynasty. ❑

THE DEATH OF QUEEN BRUNHILDA

France, 613

The sharing of power between the sons of King Clovis, upon his death in 511, became a clear source of friction. Two major blocs came into conflict with each other. In the west stood Neustria with Paris as its capital; in the east, Austrasia with Reims and later Mainz as the royal residence. The discord within the dynasty diminished its authority and ability to govern. Nobles exploited this weakness to increase their own power, though under the harsh rule of the Neustria's King Chilperic (r.561–584) they suffered for their presumption. Marriage bound Chilperic and his chief rival Sigebert I, king of Austrasia, when they were wed to sisters, Galswintha and Brunhilda, daughters of the Visigoth king Athanagild. In 575 Chilperic conspired with his mistress, Fredegund, and murdered Galswintha. Later Fredegund also had Sigebert murdered, and his wife Brunhilda was imprisoned in Neustria. Brunhilda was, how-

ever, able to escape and promptly assumed control over Austrasia in the name of her minor son, Childebert II. With a desire for power and few scruples, Brunhilda pursued two goals: to shrink the power of the nobility and to unify all of France under her guiding hand.

Thus she came into conflict with the King Clothar II, who had been ruling in Neustria since 584. At the same time her policies toward the aristocracy provoked rebellion in her own land. Bishop Arnulf of Metz set himself at the head of the resistance. He joined forces with Clothar and succeeded in capturing and imprisoning the queen. For three days she had to endure the severest tortures, and then she was dragged to death by a horse. Thus Clothar gained sovereignty over France, but at the price of acceding to the demands of the higher nobility.

Death of the Frankish Queen Brunhilde (miniature from a French chronicle)

Islam and the Arab world

Islam, the youngest of the world religions, originated in the early seventh century in a region that is among the most inhospitable on earth: in a hot, parched landscape that covers four million square miles between Asia and Africa. In the sixth and seventh centuries, the area was inhabited predominantly by nomadic Bedouins. Blood feuds between tribes were common, and children were often killed immediately after birth so as not to diminish the already scant food supplies. Generosity, loyalty, and courage were considered the preeminent human virtues.

In the middle of the sixth century, northern Arabia held three important cities, all situated in the mountainous region of Hijaz, bounded to the east by the great desert and to the west by the Red Sea. In the center of the Hijaz was the city of Yathrib, present-day Medina, situated in a region of small, fertile oases. Some 250 miles (400 km) south, in the cooler mountains, is the city of Ta'if, and to its northwest the city of Mecca, situated in a hollow surrounded by barren mountains.

Because of its location at a crossroads, Mecca flourished most; it profited from the tolls paid by richly laden camel caravans that frequently passed through. The leading citizens in the city belonged to the Quraysh clan, which ruled Mecca on the basis of its military and financial power. Pilgrims traveling to the Kaaba in Mecca, the holiest place in the Arab world, contributed further to its prosperity. Today Muslims still consider the Black Stone (a meteorite) at the Kaaba a sacred object. Allah, who later became the only god in the Muslim religion, was at the time one of the main gods worshipped in Mecca, among some three hundred other gods and goddesses.

Muhammad and the teachings of Islam

Muhammad was born in 570, the son of an impoverished member of the Quraysh tribe. As a young man he earned his living as an employee of the rich widow Khadija, who was fifteen years his senior. When Muhammad was 25 years old, she married him, and they had several children.

In 610 the archangel Gabriel appeared to Muhammad on the mountain of Hira and told him that he was the apostle of God and God's prophet. Muhammad doubted the genuineness of this revelation. But soon afterward Gabriel appeared to him again and entrusted him with the task of rousing people and warning them of the impending judgment of God. So it was

that in 613 Muhammad began preaching what the angel had told him to the public in Mecca. He declared that Allah is the only god, that in Allah's eyes all the faithful are equal, and that, although Allah determines the fate of men without their participation, they must answer to him on the Day of Judgment. The rich must share their wealth with the poor. Muhammad's followers called these new teachings *Islam*, meaning "Surrender to the will of God."

With his sermons, Muhammad elevated the aspirations of the Bedouin tribespeople. Until then, death for the Arabs was the end of all life. The only standard of personal success was the wealth that a person was able to amass during his lifetime. The prophet's early adherents were by and large poor. The wealthy Qurayshi fought a bitter battle against him because he questioned their way of life. After many of his followers had fled Mecca due to the growing pressure of the city's wealthy citizens, Muhammad also secretly left the city in 622, seeking refuge in Yathrib, which was given the name Medinet al-Nabi (City of the Prophet), or Medina for short. This emigration of Muhammad, called the *hijra*, marks the start of the Islamic calendar.

The spread of the new religion

With the preaching of the true faith and the purging of the old religion, Muhammad also acquired political responsibilities. He set forth social and legislative guidelines. He improved the condition of Arab women. In pre-Islamic times, a man could marry as many wives as he wanted. Although women remained in a subordinate position, Muhammad reduced the number of wives permitted to four, and a husband was responsible for his wife's welfare. For a long time, Muhammad also tried to convert the Jews and Christians to Islam because he did not see Islam as a new religion but rather as the final revelation of the Judeo-Christian prophets, whom he recognized as his precursors. According to the revelations granted to him, the Quran, the Holy Book of the Muslims, was a repetition of an original book that is in heaven, from which the Torah of the Jews and the Gospels of the Christian were also derived—which explains the similarities between the three religions.

Realizing that he could not convert the Jews of Medina, he rejected the use of Jewish ritual. He created new rituals that were unique to Islam. For example, instead of bells, a *muezzin* would call the faithful to pray at set times during the day. Prayers were to be said facing Mecca. He also instituted a fast that would last through the month of Ramadan, when Muslims

The new-born Muhammad in the arms of his mother.

were required to abstain from food and drink from sunrise to sunset.

Soon the Prophet acquired followers among the warlike Bedouin tribes. A common faith enabled them to overcome ancient tribal rivalries. This in turn resulted in political unification. Under Muhammad's leadership, Islam became the foundation for a theocratic political community that developed a militant sense of mission, initially directed toward the Quraysh. As the Muslims won victory after victory, they acquired large numbers of followers. The fight for Allah offered a double incentive: after a battle the booty was shared among the soldiers, and those who died in battle would go straight to paradise. In 630 the Muslims captured Mecca. Muhammad had all the idols in the Kaaba destroyed and declared the site an Islamic shrine, giving the religion a geographical and spiritual center. Muhammad died in 632.

THE FIVE PILLARS OF ISLAM

The life of the Muslim is determined by five ritual duties: faith, prayer, alms, fasting, and the pilgrimage. These are known as the five pillars of Islam.

Islam is based on the sentence, "There is no God but Allah, and Muhammad is his Prophet." Once a believer has uttered this sentence, he or she becomes a Muslim without the need for any special ritual. The most important virtue is obedience to Allah. Muslims believe that Muhammad was the last prophet, and that his word will guide the faithful until the Day of Judgment.

The second pillar is prayer, which must be said at five fixed times during the day. In addition, the faithful must perform ritual ablutions before prayer, without which the prayers are invalid. The times for prayer are called out by the muezzin from the minarets of the mosques. The holy day is Friday.

The third duty or pillar is giving alms (*zakat*). The alms are collected by the state and used to help the needy.

Fasting during Ramadan is the fourth duty of the faithful. Eating and drinking are only allowed after sunset and before sunrise.

The fifth and last duty is the pilgrimage to Mecca (*hajj*), to be carried out at least once in the life of each Muslim.

One of the main differences between Islam and Christianity is their attitude to war. Whereas Jesus sent his apostles to preach the true faith peaceably, Muhammad encouraged his followers to spread Islam with the sword. The *jihad* (struggle) is the holy war of the Muslims against all nonbelievers. A Muslim who dies fighting "on the way to Allah" is a martyr and goes directly to paradise. In practice this difference between Islam and Christianity is imperceptible: the persecution of heretics under Christianity has often been much more cruel than the proselytism of Islam.

ISLAM AS A WORLD POWER

After the death of the Prophet, the religious community of Islam developed through conquest into a powerful political entity. Because Muhammad had failed to name a successor, bloody conflicts ensued to secure the office of Caliph, the religious and political head of Islam. The first of the four orthodox caliphs, founders of the Golden Age of Islam, was the Qurayshi, Abu Bakr, the father of Muhammad's favorite wife Aisha. He led successful campaigns against apostate Arab tribes and expanded the sphere of influence of Islam into much of Persia and the Byzantine Empire. When Abu Bakr died in 634, he was succeeded by Omar I. During this caliph's rule of ten years, Islam made its most important conquests. The Arabs annexed Palestine, Syria, Egypt and almost the whole of Persia. The native population in these regions welcomed the conqueror as liberators from their Byzantine and Persian rulers. Followers of the "religions of the book" (Jews, Christians, and Zoroastrians) were allowed religious freedom in return for paying a poll tax. Those who joined Islam acquired the status of *mawali* (allies), but they could not become Arabs.

The Kaaba in Mecca, is the destination of the Islamic pilgrimage, the *hajj*.

DIVISIONS AMONG THE MUSLIMS

After the murder of Omar by a Christian slave, the caliphate passed to his son-in-law Uthman, who was a member of the Umayyad clan. Uthman incurred the hatred of many Arabs because he filled important posts with members of his own family, overlooking more able men. After ruling for twelve years, he too was murdered. The Islamic elders chose Ali, a cousin and son-in-law of Muhammad, to become the fourth caliph. But an anti-caliph came forward and opposed his election; this was Muawiya, the governor of Damascus and a nephew of the caliph Uthman. He reproached Ali for not atoning sufficiently for Uthman's murder. While preparations were made for the battle against Muawiya, Ali was murdered. As a result, his followers contested the legitimacy of the transmission of the Prophet's teachings. Islam split into two branches: Shia Islam, which considered Ali and his descndants as the sole legitimate heirs of Muhammad, and Sunni Islam, the belief of the majority of believers, which accepted the authority of the caliphate. Muawiya founded the hereditary Umayyad caliphate (661–750), a type of hereditary leadership that does not seem to be in keeping with the strict teachings of Islam. He moved the capital of the country from Medina to Damascus. It was under the Umayyad rulers that Islam spread to North Africa. Then in 711 the Arabs crossed the Strait of Gibraltar to invade Europe. They conquered almost the whole of the Iberian peninsula and brought down the Visigoth Empire. In the same year they also spread east as far as India.

In the following decades, the power of the Umayyad dynasty was weakened by inner conflicts. Led by Abul Abbas, the Abbasids rebelled against the Umayyads. In 749 Abbas became the first of the Abbasid caliphs. Marwan II attempted to restore Umayyad rule, but he suffered a devastating defeat in 750 near the upper Zab river in Iraq. It was only in Córdoba in 750 that the Umayyad Abd al-Rahman was able to perpetuate the dynasty. Science, art, trade and administration flourished under the first Abbasid caliphs, in particular Harun al-Rashid (786–809). Arabic became the unifying educated language throughout the realm, and the country lived in relative peace both at home and abroad. Islam had succeeded in establishing itself as a religious and political power.

THE UNIQUENESS OF THE NEW RELIGION

A new development emerged for the first time in the early Middle Ages: cultural and political conquest by a world religion. Until then it had always been the case that the person who won by the sword was defeated spiritually by the victim. For instance, having subjugated the Greeks, the Romans became subject to their spiritual influence, and later the Romans were converted by the religion of people of the Near East whom they had conquered. Similarly, the Germanic tribes who defeated the empire of ancient Rome became Romanized. But Islam seemed to follow different rules. Wherever the flag of the Prophet Muhammad was raised, it also supplanted the traditions and civilization of the country it conquered. This is what happened in Egypt, in the Near East as far as the gates of Constantinople, in the north African countries where Tertullian and Augustine had established a seemingly an unshakeable Christian tradition and even as far as southern Spain. ❑

THE TRIUMPH OF ISLAM

Medina, 622

Muhammad is the prophet of Islam. His teaching of perfect surrender to God's will had, by the time of his death, gained the allegiance of almost all of the tribes in Arabia.

When he was 40 years old, Muhammad had the first of many visions on Mount Hira near Mecca. He was convinced that he had heard the voice of God and been graced with a vision of the archangel Gabriel. In vivid colors, he painted a picture of the last judgment that would come at the end of history and separate the evil from the good, who would inherit the joys of paradise. He called upon his compatriots to leave behind their godless ways and submit to God's will. Muhammad did not see his mission as a new one; it had been undertaken by the prophets of Judaism and Christianity—Abraham, Moses, and Jesus—before him. Unfortunately, their followers had misunderstood or willfully distorted their message. Muhammad considered himself to be the Seal of the Prophets, that is, his revelation was the last that would be vouchsafed to humanity. Muhammad's teachings were transmitted orally. During the time of the third caliph, Uthman, they were written down to form the Quran.

Muhammad's message, *Islam*, "submission to God," found few adherents in Mecca. But a hundred miles away in Medina, his teaching rapidly took hold and gained wide support. In AD 622 Muhammad undertook what had come to be

Ali ibn Abi Talib, the fourth Caliph according to Sunni Islam, the legitimate successor to Muhammad according to Shia Islam.

known as the *hijra* (migration) to Medina. This became the first year of the Muslim calendar. It was in Medina that the basic institutions of Islam were established, fundamental teachings that still govern the lives of Muslims. Islam requires five basic duties of its adherents: first of all, a confession and recognition of God's unity, "There is no God but God"; followed by engaging in prayer five times each day, giving alms, observing a fast during the month of Ramadan, and the performance of a pilgrimage to Mecca at least once during one's lifetime.

Eight years after his emigration, Muhammad returned in triumph to his home city of Mecca. He rid the city of the numerous images of deities that had accumulated around the Kaaba, the city's central shrine. According to Islamic teaching, Abraham had received a revelation from God, and together with his son Ishmael built the Kaaba upon the site of its occurrence. Muhammad's message spread with incredible speed. Religious life had found a new definitive form. The mosque (from *masjid*, "place of prostration") acted as the spiritual and social center of the new community of believers.

At the head of this newly organized society stood the caliph. The era of the first four caliphs—Abu Bakr, Omar, Uthman, and Ali ibn Abi Talib—is looked upon by Muslims as a golden age. The Arabian armies swept away all resistance. Arab troops conquered Syria in 635, Egypt in 641, and Persia in 644. All of the long-established powers of the Middle East, with the exception of Byzantium, fell to the power of the Arabian sword and the message of Islam. A key element in the propagation of Islam was *shariah*, Islamic law, which makes no distinction between civil and religious matters, both having been set out in the Quran. ❏

THE SCHISM BETWEEN SUNNIS AND SHIITES

Point of Interest

At the end of the eighth century, a civil war split Islam, caused by differing understandings of the succession from the Prophet Muhammad. Three main groups came into being.

Sunni Islam, which now comprises 83 percent of believers, cleaves to the *sunna* (tradition). Its transmission and expression is found in the *Hadith*, collections of sayings and acts of the Prophet. In conjunction with the Quran, the *Hadith* are the authoritative guide to Muslim practice and belief. The Sunnis consider all of the caliphs—whether Umayyad, Abassid, or Osmani—as legitimate successors to Muhammad.

In contrast, Shiites (from the Arabic word meaning "sect") recognize only Ali (602–661), cousin and son-in-law of Muhammad, who became caliph in 656. The descendants from Ali's marriage to Fatima, Muhammad's daughter, are considered to be the imams by Shia Islam and the only true successors to the Prophet. The Shiites themselves are divided on the question of how many imams are to be considered legitimate successors, some saying five, others seven, others counting twelve visible imams.

The third sect, the Kharidjites (renegades), do not respect dynastic succession, but rather hold that the worthiest person should be leader of the faithful ❏

Muhammad, Prophet of Allah, on his throne (Islamic miniature)

MUHAMMAD, FOUNDER OF ISLAM

Brief Lives

Muhammad was born in 570 in Mecca. His full name was Abul Kasim Muhammad ibn Abd Allah. He was a member of the Hashim clan, a small part of the tribe of the Quraysh. He was an orphan and raised by relatives. He married a widow, Khadijah, and was a merchant by profession. He was deeply impressed by the Jewish and Christian teachings to which he was exposed and devoted himself to intensive consideration of religious matters. He had visions, heard voices, and felt himself to be a prophet called upon to announce God's revelation to him. His following grew upon his return from Medina to Mecca, where he finally won the support of the populace, including those members of his own tribe who had resisted him. He had already abandoned his mercantile career and devoted himself exclusively to the needs of the fledgling community. After a short illness, he died in 632 and was buried in Medina. ❑

THE GLORIOUS QURAN

Arabia, 653

The third caliph of Islam, Uthman, formed a commission to codify oral transmissions and written transcriptions of the revelations given to Muhammad. The result of this work is the Quran, which has been faithfully passed down in Arabic since that day.

Muhammad himself had transmitted the content of his visions orally. Between the time that he initially communicated them until the teachings received their final canonical form in the Quran, his words had circulated widely. The faithful would recite them in their assemblies. According to Islamic tradition, Muhammad received his first revelation on February 1, 610. Further revelations took place over the course of the next 22 years, until the time of his death.

Uthman, who was personally familiar with the process of transmission of the Prophet's words, collaborated with other companions of Muhammad to establish an authoritative text. It was said that they gathered together the teachings from "pieces of paper, stones, palm leaves, and the hearts of men." The canonization of the Quran confirmed its authority as the indisputable vehicle of revelation. To prevent confusion, translations of the holy text out of Arabic were strongly discouraged. According to Islamic teaching, the Quran preexisted the revelations to Muhammad. Whether it was created by God or existed in and of itself since eternity is a subject of some dispute within orthodox Islam and certain sects. The Quran is not only divine and eternal, it is a mirror held up to humanity, revealing humankind's weaknesses and the necessity to rely upon God. In it are found teachings regarding what God expects from people, details of the Day of Judgment, and cultic proscriptions and requirements. The Quran is made up of 6,236 verses divided into 114 suras (chapters). Because it is considered to contain God's own words, it is regarded as a sacred object per se worthy of considerable veneration.

Second only to the Quran in its authority are the Hadith, traditions drawn from the life and words of the Prophet. The third source of authority in Islam are the schools founded by the great Islamic legal scholars. Together these sources guide the daily lives and vibrant faith of Muslims throughout the world. ❑

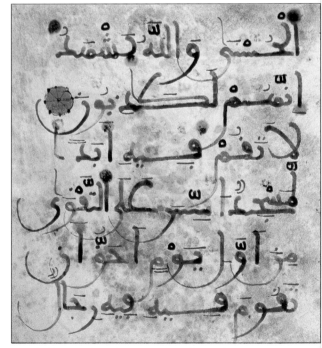

Detail of a Sura from the Quran in Arabic script

NARA: JAPAN'S FIRST PERMANENT CAPITAL

Japan, 710

Japan's first permanent capital, Nara, was founded in 710 beginning what is known as the Tenpyo Culture. Previous to this, the imperial households would move to a new capital after the death of the sitting emperor; this practice was based on the traditional Shinto belief that a dwelling place was polluted by death. The new city was modeled after the Chinese Tang capital, Chang'an (Xian).

For years Japanese culture had looked to the Chinese Tang as a role model in governmental and cultural matters. The building of Nara represented a turning point in Japanese history, heralding the awareness of a Japanese cultural identity. During the Nara period, the first histories of Japan, the *Kojiki* and the *Nihon shoki*, were produced. Indigenous Japanese poetry, *waka*, and art were created. Perhaps most importantly, a Japanese variant of Buddhism was established that influenced every aspect of the culture, including affairs of the state. In essence, the brief Nara Period (710–794) was a golden era, traces of which survive in today's culture. ❑

The Buddhist Horyu-ji temple in Nara.

MAYANS BUILD A GREAT CIVILIZATION

Central America, c.700

Emerging around 100, the Mayan people succeeded within six hundred years in creating a civilization that was the rival of any on earth. By 700, Mayan states stretched over vast areas of Central America. The main cities—Copan, Tikal, Quirigua, Palenque, and Uxmal—were populous and sophisticated administrative, cultural, and religious entities. Copan, site of the ancient kingdom of Xukpi, was especially renowned for its huge complexes of step-pyramids, plazas, and palaces. Mayan civilization was divided up into various theocratic kingdoms ruled by kings, who bore the title of "Great Sun."

The Maya religious complexes were sacred places whose stone pyramid and towers rivaled those of ancient Egypt. The Maya developed a system of writing in use from the third century until the arrival of the conquistadores. Another of their most impressive and enduring achievements was the development of calendars. Two of the most significant of these were the 260-day *Tzolk'in* and the 365-day *Haab*, the former still being used in regions of central Mexico and Guatemala. ❑

NORTHUMBRIA AND THE PICTS

Forfar, May 21, 685

Thirty years of Northumbrian domination of the Picts ended in May of 685 when King Ecgfrith (645–685), was killed in a battle with the Pictish King Bridei, son of Bili. By so doing, the Picts laid the foundation for the independent kingdom of Scotland.

The origin of this conflict dated to pre-Roman occupation, when battles raged between the combined armies of Pictish and Scottish tribes from north of the Firth of Forth with, initially, indigenous Britons, and later, the tribes of Germanic origin, the Angles, Saxons, and Jutes. These latter were enlisted by the Romans to quell the strife in the area of northern Britain that would become known as Northumbria. From the earliest Roman occupation of Britain until their departure in 407, the Picts staged continual raids to the south, occasioning the building of Hadrian's Wall. After the Roman troops left Britain, the Picts, along with the Scots, continued attacking the now Anglo-Saxon-dominated kingdom of Northumbria.

These attacks resulted in a stalemate until 603, when the Northumbrian kingdom under King Aethelfrith won a major victory over a combined army of Picts and Scots. Skirmishes continued after this, interrupted by short-lived treaties. When King Oswy became ruler of a unified Northumbria in 654, that kingdom's power relegated the Picts to a tributary relationship to their new masters, who now controlled domains up to the Forth. With their northern border secured, Northumbria grew to become Britain's most powerful kingdom, and remained so until their defeat by the Picts in 685. ❑

BOOK OF KELLS

Meath, c. 700

Illuminated capital from the *Book of Kells*

The Book of Kells is the most celebrated illuminated manuscript produced in the Middle Ages. Consisting of over 340 vellum folios (680 pages), this exquisite example of medieval Celtic art presents transcriptions of the four Vulgate Gospels, rendered in an ornately elaborate, colored, majuscule insular script.

Among its pages of lavish illumination is one of the earliest representations in Western art of the Madonna and Child.

The work was created by monks at the monastery of St. Columba on the island of Iona or by monks closely associated with the monastery. At some point, it was brought to the Abbey of Kells in County Meath, whence its name. Hidden in Dublin during Cromwell's invasion, it is now on display at Trinity College's Old Library. ❑

THE DOME OF THE ROCK

Jerusalem, 691

Begun in 687 by Abd al-Malik, the fifth Caliph of the Islamic Umayyad dynasty, the Dome of the Rock, or Qubbat as Sakrah, was completed in 691, making it the world's oldest standing Islamic building.

It commemorates two epochal events in Islam and Judaism. According to Islamic tradition, the Prophet Muhammad and the angel Gabriel ascended to heaven for a night journey from this spot. There they were received by Abraham and Moses, and given holy Islamic prayers. In the Jewish tradition, it is identified with Mount Moriah, where the binding of Isaac by the patriarch Abraham occurred. Jews also see it as having been the rock inside the Holy of Holies on which the Ark of the Covenant was placed.

Caliph Abd al-Malik commissioned the Dome of the Rock to serve not as a mosque, but rather as a pilgrimage shrine. To this day, it is the third holiest Islamic shrine after Mecca and Medina, and contains Islam's oldest *mihrab*, a niche indicating the direction to Mecca. ❑

Dome of the Rock in Jerusalem; top left inset: view of the interior

THE END OF THE MOCHE CULTURE

Peru, c.700

The pre-Columbian Moche people developed a highly sophisticated culture in the valleys of Peru's northern coast. At the beginning of the eighth century the area was conquered by the invading Huari tribe and incorporated into its kingdom.

The Moche had occupied these valleys for over 500 years. A great pyramid to the sun stood in their capital city. Nearby was the Moon Pyramid, which was might also have been used as a residence for an aristocratic family. Their government was a theocracy. Social ties were strong and strictly hierarchical. Agriculture benefited from an impressive system of irrigation and canals. Hunting and fishing contributed to the people's everyday diet, and a flourishing trade existed with the Andean highlands.

Clay figurine from the Moche Culture of Peru (c.700)

A SHIA MARTYR

Karbala, October 10, 680

Husyan ibn Ali, grandson of the Prophet Muhammad, was killed at the Battle of Karbala on 10 October 680. He was the son of Ali ibn Abi Talib, the Prophet's cousin and son-in-law. Ali is also considered to be the first Shia imam.

This battle and the death of Husyan were pivotal in Islamic history, defining the rift between the Shia and Sunni faiths. The Shia believe that Husayn, being Muhammad's grandson, was the rightful heir to the Prophet and that the recognition of this was the authentic expression of true Islamic faith. The Sunni tradition was represented by the powerful Umayyad Dynasty, whose founder, Muawiya ibn Abi Fufyan, believed that his companionship with Muhammad validated his and his son Yazid's claim to succession. It was Yazid's forces that engaged and defeated those of Husyan at Karbala. Against all odds, leading only seventy men, Husayn's sacrifice in defense of the true faith has come to represent to the Shia the quintessential example of Islamic martyrdom. To this day, the Shiites commemorate the date of his death as the holy day, Ashura. ❑

The Moche could also boast of their artistic production. Gold and metalwork showed a high degree of technical mastery. Buildings were decorated with turquoise mosaics, frescoes, and clay ornaments. They made tools, utensils, and weapons out of copper, and their ceramic work provides a vibrant portrayal of their daily life.

The advancing Huari proved too strong for the Moche and gained control over almost all of present-day Peru. Where the Moche had once dwelled, they erected garrisons and new cities. ❑

ARAB ADVANCE HALTED AT TOURS

France, 732

A crucial victory was won at the French city of Poitiers by the Frankish general, Charles Martel (The Hammer) over a seemingly unstoppable Arab forces, whose battle cry (from the Quran) was "Paradise lies in the shadow of the sword."

In the century following the death of the Prophet Muhammad, the Arabs carried their faith to the limits of the known world, with the exceptions of the Byzantine Empire and northern Europe. Early in the eighth century, they crossed the Pyrenees from Spain and seized Narbonne. In 732, led by Abd al-Rahman, a member of a zealous Muslim sect, they sacked Bordeaux and Poitiers and advanced on Tours, with its monastery of St. Martin, one of Christendom's richest.

Eudo, the duke of Aquitaine, reeling under the Arab onslaught, sent a desperate appeal to Charles, who came riding south with his Frankish warriors. Tours was saved, and for six days the two armies skirmished warily. On the seventh, Abd al-Rahman attacked Poitiers. The Arab leader was killed in the day-long battle, and the Arabs decamped the next morning.

The Frankish victory marked the highwater mark for Muslim armies in Europe. The Battle of Tours was followed in 737 by another significant battle between Charles Martel and the son of Abd al-Rahman near Narbonne. Once again the Moors were unable to withstand the Frankish cavalry charge. These two victories essentially established the Pyrenees as the border between Christendom and Islam. They also provided the impetus for the founding of the Carolingian dynasty. Charles became the mightiest ruler in western Europe, yet he never claimed the title of king, instead referring to himself as mayor of the palace or as duke. By the time of his death in 741, the old Merovingian dynasty continued to exist, but its kings had lost all real power.

Charles was the illegitimate son of the Frankish ruler Pepin II; he fought his rivals for three years before gaining possession of the Frankish territories between the Rhine and the Loire, thus uniting both Neustria and Austrasia under his rule. He went on to subjugate Burgundy and Provence and force German tribes to pay tribute. He was an outstanding general, pioneering the use of cavalry. He died on October 22, 741 and was buried in Saint Denis Basilica in Paris. ❑

In the Battle of Poitiers of 732 Charles Martel (Charles the Hammer) stopped the Moorish invasion (woodcut, c.1865).

A LASTING ALLIANCE BETWEEN CHURCH AND STATE

France, 754

Pope Stephen II and King Pepin III of Gaul, the son of Charles Martel, concluded a treaty at Quiercy, the center of the Merovingian court, that was to have to have far-reaching consequences on the balance of power in northern Europe. It marked a decisive step in the evolving relations between the papacy and the rulers of Northern Europe.

Under the treaty, Pepin the Short, as he was known, guaranteed the protection of the papacy by endowing it with 23 towns in central and northern Italy that were at that time under the suzerainty of the Lombard king Aistulf. This endowment became known as the Patrimonium Petri (St. Peter's Patrimony). Aistulf's expansionist policies had been jeopardizing the political existence of the pope, and soon after signing the treaty, Pepin invaded Lombardy and forced him to sue for peace.

In return for these services, a new dynasty of Frankish kings was given legitimacy. Although effective rulers for years, Pepin's line remained in name only mayors of the palace (chief ministers). In 751, the Pope authorized the ousting of the last Merovingian king in favor of Pepin. Part of the agreement required, under pain of excommunication, that the kingship reside only within the Carolingian bloodline. Pepin and his successors were given the title Patricus Romanorum (Protector of the Romans). ❑

Pepin III (Pepin the Short), Frankish king, 751-768

BUDDHA'S TEMPLE AT BORUBUDUR

Java, c.775

The Sailendra rulers of central Java built a magnificent temple complex in honor of the Buddha, although it may fairly be said that the awe-inspiring shrine was more the embodiment of earthly power than of the Buddhist ideal of nonattachment. They named the temple Borobudur, meaning "many Buddhas." It epitomized the confidence and proselytizing zeal of the Sailendra rulers, who had declared Buddhism the official religion on the predominantly Hindu island.

On a rounded hilltop, terraced and clad in stone, Borobudur rises out of the flat rice fields of the Kedu plain, girdled by distant volcanic cones. The lower six terraces are cut square, with stairways on the cardinal points that are adorned with an uninterrupted sequence of bas-reliefs portraying the life of the Buddha. If placed end to end, the reliefs would stretch for three miles. The upper terraces are round, with 72 *stupas* shaped like cupolas and carved in stone lattice work, each covering a seated Buddha. At the pinnacle is a larger stupa. The temple complex, its skyline resembling the City of God, is meant to symbolize the pilgrim's progress from worldly life to ultimate enlightenment. ❑

The central stupa from the Buddhist temple complex of Borobudur in Java. In the foreground is a statue of the Buddha.

BAGHDAD BECOMES A CULTURAL METROPOLIS

Baghdad, 749

With the fall of the Umayyad Dynasty, the Abbasids took over the caliphate. In the meantime, the first independent Arab state was established in Spain.

Abdul Abbas was chosen as caliph by his political dependents. He defeated the last Umayyad caliph and wiped out almost his entire family.

Since the time they first rose to power, the position of the Umayyads had been contended. The dynasty's founder, Muawiya I, belonged to the Meccan Banu family, which had been opposed to Muhammad in his early days in Mecca. The Umayyads had great military triumphs, extending the bounds of the Islamic rule through North Africa and as far east as India. They were, however, unable to capture Constantinople, and their advance into Europe was halted at Tours by Charles Martel.

Despite their military success, the Umayyads were not popular. Pious Muslims balked at their apparent worldliness and sought to reserve the caliphate for the relatives of the Prophet. Laws that distinguished between Arab fighters who were freed from paying taxes and converts to the faith upon whom a proportionately greater share of the burden fell exacerbated social tensions.

In 749, open rebellion led to the removal of the last Umayyad caliph, Marwan II, in favor of the leader of the Abbasid family, Abdul Abbas as Saffiah. He could claim decent from Abbas, the uncle of Muhammad. The annihilation of the Umayyad clan was almost total, but one member, Abd ar-Rahman ad-Dakhil, escaped to Spain, where he founded an independent Muslim emirate in Córdoba.

Baghdad flourished with the Abbasids in possession of the caliphate. In Harun al-Rashid (r.786–809) it experienced a golden age of culture and prosperity. It became the major trading center for goods traveling between Europe and India. Poets, artists, scientists, and scholars all gathered here and participated in a cultural flowering that drew elements not only from Islamic

1001 ARABIAN NIGHTS

Point of Interest

1001 Arabian Nights is a collection of over three hundred Persian, Arabic, and Egyptian stories ranging across many different genres: love stories, legends, adventures, and anecdotes of sea and land voyages. The story that frames the collection derives from Persian and Indian traditions. It tells of a young monarch from Samarkand; the unfaithful actions of his first wife transforms him into a wicked, misogynistic despot. Every evening he marries a maiden and then has her killed on the following morning. Scheherezade, the daughter of the Grand Vizier,

Sinbad the Sailor and the Old Man of the Sea.

finding herself in this predicament, puts her resourcefulness to work in order to survive. Each night she tells the king stories, breaking off at dawn. The king is so desirous of hearing how they turn out that he keeps postponing her sentence for 1,001 nights.

Over the course of her storytelling, she succeeds in winning the king's love.

Versions of many of the tales found their way into medieval Europe. Among the best-known stories are the adventures of Sinbad, the tale of Aladdin and his lamp, and the story of Ali Baba and the forty thieves. ❑

teachings but from the Hellenistic, Jewish, and Christian traditions as well. During a period of cultural impoverishment in Europe, Baghdad was the unrivalled center of civilization. ❑

THE RISE OF VENICE

Venice, 789

The invasion of the Huns into Italy in 452 drove many of its inhabitants to seek refuge in the easily defended lagoon islands that make up present-day Venice. There they built a new city. Because of its unique placement, Venice quickly developed into a port city and concentrated on building up its naval power. Accessible only by water, it was naturally protected from the growing might of the Lombard Kingdom, which dominated the north of Italy at that time.

In 715, Venice was given special trading privileges by Byzantium. Its main export was the salt that it produced, but soon a trade grew up in grain, skins, and slaves, mainly Slavs taken from the coast of Dalmatia. The Venetians traded with the Italian cities on the banks of the Po and became the point of transit for goods traveling from Byzantium and the Arab world into Europe. Despite Lombard pressure, Venice remained within the orbit of the Byzantine Empire.

Beginning in 726, Venetian noble families gathered to elect a doge (from the Latin *dux*, "leader"). By the end of the eighth century, the doge's power had grown to the extent that he was able to name his own successor, encouraging dynastic ambitions. In 811, the doges moved their residence to the Rialto, a well-protected island. They built impressive palaces and churches following Byzantine models. The first basilica in honor of St. Mark was erected in 828, though later it was moved and later still rebuilt. It followed the design of the Apostle's Church in Constantinople.

The Venetians came to an agreement with Charlemagne that opened the Frankish possessions to its merchants. Its favorable geographic location and its skilled diplomacy made Venice the meeting point between East and West. This, coupled with the extraordinary enterprise of its citizens, guaranteed its prosperity and autonomy over many turbulent centuries. ❑

Francesco Guardi, *Palace of the Doges,* 18th century

THE CAROLINGIAN RENAISSANCE

Aachen, c.789

In 789, Charlemagne, King of the Franks, issued his *Admonitio Generalis* (General Admonition), a declaration of his plans to revive

Carolingian gatehouse from the monastery in Lorsch, Germany

scholarship and the arts throughout his dominions. This initiative was pivotal in creating what became known as the Carolingian Renaissance.

Although semiliterate himself, Charlemagne was the first European king to encourage a form of universal education. Many of the most learned men in Europe came to his court in Aachen, where a school was established for the education of his own sons, young nobles, and even poor young men with the great scholar Alcuin of York as its head. He especially stressed the importance of the historical legacy of learning. In fact, many of the surviving works of the classical Latin canon were first preserved by Carolingian scholars.

A great patron of the visual arts, Charlemagne's decision to reject iconoclasm and, therefore, to allow for the use of some aspects of Classical art's human representation in painting, had profound consequences on Western art. It helped define the content of Romanesque and Gothic art, which to this day remain templates for creativity in the visual arts.

The avant-garde of this revival was to be a clergy who had a proper understanding of the Bible and the Christian faith. Priests were to be the emissaries

Carolingian art, a moneychanger.

of this Christian-based learning, which they would disseminate to the general populace. Theological as well as classically humanistic, Charlemagne's revival of scholarship and the arts was a melding of the aesthetic with the didactic. ❑

THE EMPEROR CHARLEMAGNE

Rome, 800

It was under Charlemagne (c.745–814) that the Frankish kingdoms became a Frankish Empire whose territory spanned most of today's Western and Central Europe. Inspired by his respect for scholarship, his court in Aachen served as the center for a revival of art, religion, and learning, which would become known as the Carolingian Renaissance. Because of the breadth of his sovereignty and the comprehensiveness of his unifying influence, some historians have referred to him as the father of Europe and the founder of Western Civilization.

Charlemagne's Frankish empire evolved from the kingdoms carved out by the first Carolingians, his grandfather Charles Martel and his father, the first King of the Franks, Pippin the Short. Upon Pippin's death, this legacy was bequeathed to Charlemagne and his brother Carloman, with Charlemagne taking Neustria, western Aquitaine and northern Austrasia, and Carloman receiving southern Austrasia, eastern Aquitaine, Septimania, Burgundy, Provence, and Swabia. From the first, the sibling's co-rule was strained and threatened by internecine rivalries. Their initial attempt at a joint effort, the suppression of a rebellion by Aquitaine and Gascony in 769, ended with Carloman retreating from campaign and Char-

lemagne taking the spoils of victory, thereby increasing his share of their joint legacy.

The enmity between the brothers nearly broke out into full-scale war after Charlemagne entered an alliance with Duke Tassilo III of Bavaria, effected by marriage to the daughter of the Lombard King Desiderius. When Charlemagne quickly dissolved this marriage, the outraged Desiderius appealed to Carloman for help in a military redress of this affront to his family's honor. Seeing a chance to gain the upper hand over his brother, Carloman considered the request. His death at an early age in December of 771 intervened.

Now unrivaled as King of the Franks, Charlemagne aligned himself with Pope Adrian I, becoming his defender and receiving from him the title "Protector of the Romans" and papal support for his invasion of Lombardy against the beleaguered King Desiderius. His victory there in 774 made him King of the Lombards and ruler of northern Italy. He was never able to subdue southern Italy, but his victory in the north was significant because it broke the vital connection of interests between the Pope and the Byzantine empire, thereby laying the groundwork for his elevation to imperial status.

His ascension to the impe-

Pope Leo II crowns Charlemagne emperor (book illustration)

rial throne took place on Christmas Day, 800. After Mass in St. Peter's, Pope Leo III produced a crown and, placing it on the head of Charlemagne, proclaimed him Emperor of the Romans. According to contemporary accounts, the Roman notables there assembled cried in unison: "To Charles, the most pious Augustus, crowned by God, the great and peace-loving emperor, life and victory." This marks the beginning of the Holy Roman Empire.

The dramatic scene was the climax to an extraordinary series of events that began when hostile aristocrats had Leo seized, beaten, and deposed. The humiliated Pope sought refuge with Charlemagne, who restored him to the Holy See.

Charlemagne claimed to be displeased with Leo's gesture in proclaiming him Roman Emperor. It was thought that he did not wish the title to be seen as a gift

of the Papacy. Their encounter was to have a significant influence on the course of medieval history and presage future battles between pope and emperor.

In 812, the Byzantine Emperor, Michael I, recognized Charlemagne's imperial claims in the West. Charlemagne named his son Louis the Pious as his co-emperor and successor. Charlemagne died in Aachen in 814. ❑

The marble throne of Charlemagne from the Cathedral of Aachen

Reliquary bust of Charlemagne

VIKING CONQUESTS

England, c. 800

The ninth century was the age of the great Viking invasions of Europe. Population growth in Scandinavia led to a hunger for land and booty and coincided with a breakthrough in nautical technology: the development of the longboat. The Viking craft could sail with the wind or into it, or be rowed; it held up to thirty warriors, had a hull flexible enough to bend in heavy seas without leaking, and drew only three feet of water below the waterline while carrying ten tons of booty.

The Vikings traveled far distances in their longboats in search of plunder and would attack by night without warning and with unbridled ferocity. Their attacks terrorized most of western Europe. No place seemed beyond their reach. Their attacks reached as far as Lisbon and Morocco, Hamburg and Tuscany. In 818, the Irish mystic Blathmac went to Iona in search of martyrdom at Viking hands. He waited seven years before they landed and tore him to pieces for refusing to reveal where the monastery's treasure was hidden.

Churches had always been respected by warring Christian factions, but they were singled out as soft targets for easy plunder by the Vikings.

The Vikings disdained the cultural heritage of the peoples whose settlements they overran. Artwork and priceless libraries, such as the one on the Isle of Iona, were all consigned to flames. The list of ruined places in Britain alone is staggering: Lindisfarne (in 793); Jarrow; the Shetlands, Hebrides, and Orkney (about 794); Skye (795); Rathlin (Antrim); Iona (at least four times from 795 onward); most of Scotland; much of Ireland, including Armagh; Sheppey; the English Channel coast. In continental Europe, towns such as Dorestad, the West's greatest trading center, near the mouth of the Rhine, and in Gaul, monastic and com-

mercial centers including Noirmoutier and Rouen—all fell to the invaders.

The victims of the attacks struggled to find reasons for the devastation. Alcuin of York suggested in a letter to the King of Northumbria, Ethelred, that it was God's judgment on the English for widespread fornication.

The Vikings continued to ravage Europe through most of the century.

They shifted their tactics. Formerly the Vikings arrived in the summer, plundered along the coasts and up the rivers, and sailed home with their booty before winter set in. Gradually they chose to winter in unoccupied territories. As a consequence, they could carry out their raids from these nearby bases. The raids continued with unceasing frequency and ferocity, with numerous towns—including Cologne, Paris, Nantes, and London—suffering bloody assaults. To the north, Iceland was occupied, the Scottish highlands and islands were colonized, and Vikings sailed around Ireland, creating new coastal towns such as Dublin. In England, they overran more than half the country before being checked by Alfred, the king of Wessex.

Viking landing (miniature, England 12th century)

But under the treaty of 886, the former Anglo-Saxon kingdoms of Northumbria and East Anglia and the east Midlands were

HAITHABU A CITY FOUNDED BY THE VIKINGS

Point of Interest

The Viking settlement of Haithabu was founded in the ninth century in present-day Schleswig-Holstein. It was well planned out with wide streets, houses, and halls enclosed with fences. Artisans settled there, and the city minted its own coins. It became a central point of trade between the lands on the east cost of the Baltic Sea, Scandinavia, and the Frankish Kingdom. A key factor in its growth was the importation of furs and slaves. From Haithabu's workplaces is-

sued fine handmade wares including articles crafted from metal, ceramics, and textiles. Products made from horn and bone, such as

Attempt at a reconstruction of the Viking village of Haithabu

yielded to Danish rule and called the Danelaw.

The Viking threat abated as the century drew to a close. As the invaders founded more permanent settlements, they turned their energy to commercial activity. Rollo, the veteran leader of a Viking warrior band, and the king of the western Franks concluded a treaty that ended nearly fifty years of violent Viking assaults upon

Norman bronze helmet

the Franks. In return for the concession of some territory, Rollo swore homage to Charles and accepted baptism. The treaty led to the establishment of Normandy, the duchy of the Northmen, the Normans. ❏

nails and knife handles, were to be found there as well.

In 890, a band of Vikings from Sweden occupied the city, which at the time covered about sixty acres of land, and fortified it with a semicircular wall made from wood and mud. The city was conquered by Henry I of Germany in 934, who forced its king, Knuba, to let himself be baptized. From the year 1000, on it stagnated under Danish rule, until it was finally burned down in 1050. In the area around the city, many burial sites have been discovered, some of which contained rich hoards of goods. ❏

THE TREATY OF VERDUN

Verdun, August 843

In 817, Louis the Pious, the son and successor of Charlemagne, passed a law regulating imperial succession. The *Ordinatio imperii* stipulated that the oldest son of the emperor would inherit the crown. In accordance with the law's provisions, Louis sought to reserve the throne for his eldest son Lothar. Lothar's brother, Charles the Bald, objected to the planned succession and raised a rebellion that for a time drove Louis from the throne. By the time he returned to power, three years later, he had lost much of his authority. Thus the death of Louis in 840 left open the question of succession to the empire founded by Charlemagne. Louis's two younger sons, Charles the Bald and Louis the German,

Louis the Pious (miniature, c.840)

swore oaths at Strasbourg, in local languages rather than Latin so combined against their brother Lothar, and they and their armies that the troops could understand. Louis addressed Charles's men in *lingua romana* (early French) and Charles spoke in *lingua teudisca* (early German). They forced Lothar to renounce sovereignty over their kingdoms.

But after violent struggles, the three sons met at Verdun and agreed to partition the empire. Bavaria and other eastern lands became the fief of Louis; the west, including much of old Gaul, was entrusted to Charles; the eldest son, Lothar, retained the title of Emperor and took the territory between the other two, from Italy to the Channel coast, keeping the Frankish capital, Aachen, and Rome. The treaty ended the divisions that had embroiled the Frankish empire in civil war. ❏

THE IDEAL CLOISTER

St. Gallen, c.825

Louis the Pious, the King of France, was a strong supporter of the monastic orders. Concerned that they were becoming too worldly, he sought to distance them from secular concerns by promoting the *Rule of St. Benedict.*

Gozbert, the abbot of the cloister of St. Gallen, drew up a master plan for the ideal monastery. The richly detailed drawing preserved on vellum shows a plan that would enable Benedict's instructions to be closely followed.

Ora et labora (prayer and work) were Benedict's watchwords and what he asked from the monks of his order. Teaching and handicrafts, medicine and agriculture, the preservation and copying of manuscripts, and caring for the poor—all were part the program laid out by the founder of the order. In 817, the Synod of Aachen made the Rule compulsory.

Gozbert's plan for a monastery to be built in nearby Reichenau demonstrates the place and role of monastic orders in society at large during the Middle Ages. The plan included a library and living quarters, stables and refectory, a hospital, a school, and lodgings for pilgrims. ❏

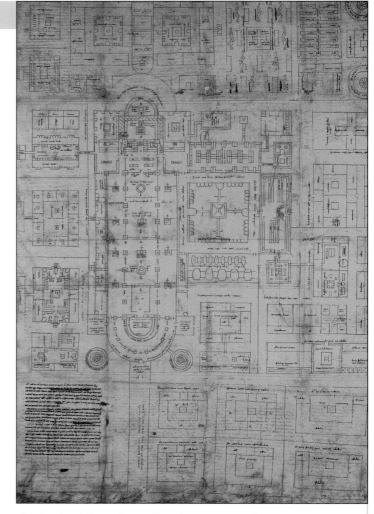

Plan for the Cloister of St. Gallen (drawing on parchment, c.825)

CONVERSION OF THE SLAVS

Moravia, c.850

The conversion of the Slavic peoples was a slow process that took most of the latter half of the ninth century and coincided with shifts in the cultural and political landscape in the Balkans. By the time of his death in 846, Mojmir, the prince of Moravia (present-day Czechoslovakia), had united for the first time the Slav tribes of Bohemia, Moravia, Slovakia, and Pannonia. This important military and political federation was known as Great Moravia.

From the beginning of the century, attempts had been made to convert the pagan Slavs to Christianity, first by missionaries sent by Rome, and then by the Frankish monarchs.

Mojmir became a Christian and within thirty years, the Slav peoples of Moravia had been converted to Christianity and given the foundations of their own literature, thanks to the work of two Byzantine monks. They devised a new alphabet that made it possible for the scriptures to be read in the vernacular. The alphabet was called Cyrillic in honor of the younger of the two brothers, who died in Rome at the age of 42.

Cyril's name was Constantine until he became a monk. He was born in Thessalonica, of Bulgarian extraction. He and his brother Methodius, who had been a provincial governor, both spoke Slavic.

They were chosen as missionaries by the Emperor Michael III at the request of Prince Rastislav, who wanted to counteract Frankish influence in Moravia. The brothers worked together to compose the Slavonic alphabet. It used Greek lettering, combined with the phonetic sounds of the Slavonic dialect of southern Macedonia.

Cyril and Methodus were both canonized by the Eastern Orthodox and Roman Catholic Churches. ❑

Cyril and Methodius (icon, 19th century)

THE VARANGIANS IN RUSSIA

Kiev, c.899

In 862 the Varangian general Rurik captured the town of Novgorod and from it ruled North Russia. Twenty years later, Rurik's successor Oleg took Kiev from the Khazars and made it his new capital. This created the first Russian state and a regular route from the Gulf of Finland via the River Dnieper to the Black Sea. Some Rus adopted Christianity. As traders, the Varangians traveled as far as Baghdad. The ultimate target was Constantinople and its repository of fabulous riches. One Rus attack on Constantinople in 849, by a fleet of two hundred ships across the Bosporus, almost succeeded. Sporadic attacks continued, but the prize remained out of reach. ❑

ALFRED THE GREAT HALTS THE DANISH INVASION

England, 896

The Anglo-Saxon kingdom of Britain was endangered by continuing Danish invasions. The Danes had dramatically changed their policy. Instead of plundering coastlines, they ravaged the country far inland and settled down, rapidly overwhelming Northumbria and East Anglia and collecting tribute. But through the efforts of King Alfred of Wessex, the Danes were forced to abandon their assault on southern England.

In 871, the West Saxons, under King Aethelred and his brother Alfred, were victorious at Ashdown, but they remained on the defensive. When Aethelred died, Alfred won a temporary respite by buying off the Danes. But they launched a surprise winter attack early in 878, forcing Alfred to flee into the Somerset fens. At this critical moment, Alfred rallied his people and won a crushing victory at Edington. The ensuing treaty entitled Alfred to call himself sole king of the Anglo-Saxons.

The Danes, however, retained much territory in England, and the war was by no means over. They continued to strike, mostly by sea. Alfred met this threat with limited success by ordering the construction of sixty-oar longboats similar to those used by the Danes. Much of Alfred's success was owed to a policy of creating fortified towns like Winchester and Buckingham. ❑

Alfred the Great (manuscript illustration, 14th century)

LAST DAYS OF THE CAROLINGIANS

France, 899

Struggles over succession and power brought to an end the Carolingian dynasty. Founded by Clovis shortly after the fall of the Roman Empire, it became under Charlemagne the most important political entity in medieval Europe.

With the death of Arnulf of Carinthia on December 12, 899, the last individual who could lay claim to the whole of the Frankish empire passed away. And Arnulf's authority was uncertain; in fact, he could exercise real power only over the eastern half of the empire. By the time of his death, centrifugal tendencies were irresistible.

The parceling out of the empire by the Treaties of Verdun (843) and Mersen (870), combined with the internecine scramble for power, tarnished the idea of a universal Christian kingdom that Charlemagne had bequeathed to his sons. The Treaty of Ribémont established the boundary between the western and eastern halves of the empire (the basis for the later French-German border), but it was shaped more by dynastic interests than concern for tribal or cultural differences. After the death of the West Frankish king and Holy Roman Emperor Charles the Bald, a rapidly changing cast of successors presided over a period of sharp decline. Following Charles were Louis the Stammerer, Louis III, and Carloman, upon whose death the throne reverted to the king of East Francia, Charles the Fat. For a brief time, Charles was able to unify the two Frankish kingdoms under his scepter. But unable to protect the land from Norman invasions, lacking the authority

Arnulf of Carinthia

to rein in the high nobility, and suffering from epilepsy, Charles was forcibly deposed in 887, and Arnulf of Carinthia came to power. With the death of Charles in the following year, the unraveling of the Carolingian Dynasty was nearly accomplished.

Arnulf was the Margrave of Carinthia and Pannonia, the illegitimate son of the Carolingian Carloman of Bavaria. He gained lordship over northern Italy, Burgundy, and West Francia but was little more than a figurehead in the territories outside of the domains of East Francia. He was defeated by the Normans in battle in 891. In 896, he received a call for help from Pope Formosus against the aggressive policies of the Lombard king Guido II. He traversed the Alps, conquered Rome, and became the last Carolingian to be crowned emperor. Nonetheless, his was a pale reflection of the glory of his predecessors. The annals of the Monastery of Fulda provide a revealing description of his reign. "During the time of Arnulf of Carinthia, numerous petty kings sprang up. Berengar, the son of Eberhard of Friaul, declared himself King of Italy; Rudolph, the son of Conrad, began to reign as King of Burgundy. Louis, son of Boso, ruled in Provence, and Guido son of the Duke of Spoleto contended for the crown of Belgium. Odo, the son of Robert the Strong, claimed the region lying along the Loire, and Ramnulf pressed his claim for part of Aquitaine." At the death of Arnulf, his six-year-old son Louis the Child succeeded to the throne. The Archbishop Hatto of Mainz acted as regent.

Louis the Child died on June 24, 911, and with that, the Carolingian Dynasty came to a de facto end. In East Francia, Conrad I was chosen by the lords of the kingdom as their king. He is considered the founder of the German kingdom. In West Francia, Odo of Paris assumed real governing authority. The Carolingians continued to rule in name only until 987. ❏

GOOD KING WENCESLAS

Bohemia, 929

An uprising of Bohemian nobles culminated with murder of Bohemia's king, Wenceslas. His pagan brother Boleslav was among those responsible for his death. Wenceslas was a devout Christian and pursued an alliance with the Christian King Henry of Bavaria, which may have been a source of resentment for Boleslav and the jealous nobles.

Wenceslas was the grandson of Borivoy, the first known prince of Prague, and was given a religious upbringing by his grandmother Ludmilla. Wratislaw, Wenceslas's father, was killed fighting the Magyars. Wenceslas restored order and built a number of churches. His piety was legendary and he was later canonized a saint. ❑

Assassination of St. Wenceslas (illumination from the Guelf codex)

CENTER OF GRAVITY IN ISLAM MOVES OUT FROM BAGHDAD

Islamic World, early tenth century

In 911, the last of the Aghlabid rulers of Ifriqiyah (Tunisia) were driven out of Kairouan (in Tunisia) by a popular revolt. Ubayd Allah Said installed himself in their princely residence. Styling himself al-Mahdi, "Prince of the Faithful," he would go on to found the Fatimid Dynasty.

The Aghlabids, though long since effectively independent of the caliphate, still acknowledging the Abbasid caliphate. The Mahdi, however, styled himself "caliph" challenging the authority of Baghdad. He was a Fatimid, claiming descent from the Prophet Muhammad's daughter Fatima, a claim he took as the source of his legitimacy.

The Mahdi's origins were obscure; He owed his prominence entirely to his chief propagandist, Abu Abd Allah, who forged links with the Ketama Berbers from 894. The Ketama, old adversaries of the Aghlabids, looked forward to being an elite army under a new regime.

Ubayd Allah settled in Ikjan, won over the people, and proceeded to advance into Aghlabid territory. He entered Rakkaba in 909, crushing the army of the dynasty's last sovereign.

These developments were not lost upon Abd al-Rahman III, the Umayyad emir of Córdoba since 911. He had himself proclaimed as caliph, establishing Spain as a major Muslim power and an in-

Palace of the Caliph Abd al-Rahman near Cordoba

dependent rival to the expansionist Fatimids of Ifriqiyah.

Spain had had a succession of emirs since the Arab invasion of 711, but the preceding century had seen a prolonged political crisis. The new caliph succeeded in crushing his rivals and reestablishing the authority of Córdoba, his capital. Under his rule Spain, with its flourishing commerce, fertile agriculture, and thriving intellectual life, became the cultural center of the Islamic world.

By 930, the Abbasid caliph-

ate was in serious decline. This was shown quite clearly when a breakaway group of revolutionary Muslims, known as the Carmathians after its founder Hamdan Karmat, sacked the holy city of Mecca and stole the Black Stone from Kaaba, the focus of the *hajj* (pilgrimage) and the center point of the Islamic world. Many pilgrims were killed. Their attack brought into high relief the growing impotence of the Abbasid caliphs, who proved unable to protect Islam's holiest shrine. ❑

THE BOGOMILS

Bulgaria, c.925

A strange religious sect, known as the Bogomils after its eponymous founder, gathered followers from all over Bulgaria. Denounced as heretics by the Orthodox Church, they faced severe persecution without giving up their fervently held beliefs.

The Bogomils were dualists,

believing in a good God and in an almost equally powerful Satan, who created the world, the body, and all material things. Their more fervent members, the "Perfect,", abstained from almost all the things of this world including sex, meat, and wine. They believed that they were the only true Christians, and that they would become incorporeal spirits after death. Accepting only the New Testament, the Psalms, and

the Prophets, they asserted that most of the Old Testament was Satan's work. Their uncompromising Gnostic ideas were clear threats to religious belief and the established order.

But the Bogomils were more than just a bizarre group of heretics. They were fiercely nationalistic, and their movement reflected Bulgarian resentment at Byzantine culture, imperial power, and Slav serfdom.

According to a contemporary account, the Bogomils "teach their people not to obey their lords, they revile the wealthy, hate the czar, ridicule the elders, condemn the boyars, regard as vile in the sight of God those who serve the tsar, and forbid every servant to work for his master." The Bogomils were, in fact, peasants united in a political movement by their religious beliefs. ❑

MONASTIC REFORM AT CLUNY

Burgundy, 910

In this year, a monastery at Cluny was founded by Berno, a Benedictine monk.

He had started a monastery in the Jura that had become too small for the many monks whom he attracted to it. In 910, he persuaded William the Pious, the Duke of Aquitaine and Count of Macon, to give him a hunting lodge at Cluny.

On September 11, 910, he won a unique charter for his new abbey there. It was put under the direct authority of the pope, but even he could only intervene in cases of "great disorder" among the Cluny monks. Otherwise Cluny was to be free of interference from both princes and pontiffs.

Berno established a monastic life devoted to prayer and religious services. The vow of silence encouraged meditation. External work and manual labor were more or less forbidden. Book production was restricted to religious works.

Because of Berno's spiritual leadership, he was named abbot of several other monasteries. In 927, Odo replaced him as abbot and went further than his predecessor. In 928, he convinced Pope John X to confirm the unusual charter, and in 931, he persuaded Pope Leo VII to allow him to bring other monasteries under the direct control of Cluny. In the last decade of his life, he expanded the network of satellite monasteries, making the Cluniacs the world's biggest monastic order. ❏

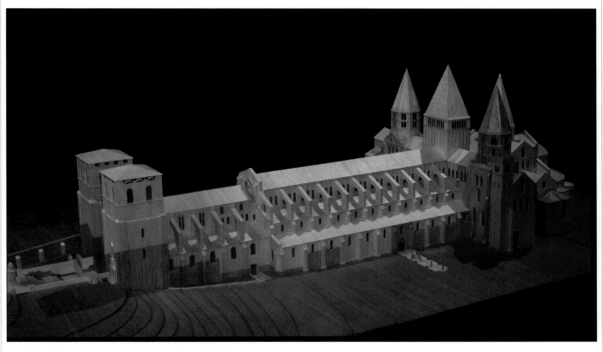

Model of the Monastery Church at Cluny built in 1088-1132

SIMEON I, TSAR OF BULGARIA

Bulgaria, 918

Simeon I, the Khan of Bulgaria since 893, laid claim to the title of Tsar of Bulgaria and Master of Greece. These titles expressed the reality of a resurgent and expanding nation.

Under his rule, Bulgaria succeeded in bringing the greater part of the Balkans under Bulgarian domination. However, his continual efforts to take Constantinople proved unavailing, and he never realized his ambition of becoming emperor in Byzantium. But he did install the first patriarch independent of the Byzantine church as a counterweight to the capital's cultural and religious influence. ❏

A DARK CENTURY FOR THE PAPACY

Rome, December 932

Popular discontent with the rampant corruption within the papacy and the noble family behind it culminated in a mob storming the castle in which Hugh of Provence, the king of Italy, and his bride were installed. Hugh escaped with his life, but his bride, the scheming Marozia, was jailed with her son Pope John XI.

As Hugh was also his bride's brother-in-law, the marriage contravened Church teaching, confirming the low opinion in which Rome's rulers and the papacy were held. Persistent and continuing scandals had already tarnished the reputation of the Church. Most dramatic was the notorious "cadaver council" of Pope Formosus 35 years earlier. Nine months after the aged pope's death, his body was exhumed, propped up on a throne in full papal vestments, and solemnly arraigned on charges of perjury. Formosus's corpse was found guilty. The three fingers he used for blessing were chopped off, and his body was thrown into the Tiber.

Formosus's successor and prosecutor, Stephen VII, was deposed and strangled; Benedict IV was probably murdered; Leo V was thrown into jail after only thirty days as pontiff, and later executed with Christopher, the anti-pope, by Sergius III. Sergius was so intimate with the wealthy, corrupt Theophylact family that he fathered a son by their 15-year-old daughter, Marozia. Marozia and her then husband, Guy of Tuscany, had John X imprisoned and eventually installed her son as Pope John XI. This proved too much to bear even in the lax moral climate of Rome. ❏

IOANNES X.
Sedit an.is.mens.
Romanus, ann.912.
Obijt an.928.

Pope John X (engraving)

THE MIDDLE AGES IN THE FAR EAST

After the expulsion of the Mongol rulers from China, Emperor Hongwu (1368–1399) marked the return of a pure Chinese dynasty, the Ming Dynasty. At this time, China experienced a long period of peace. The country developed a centralized system of government and a civil service reminiscent of the old traditions of Confucianism.

In this period of revival, China carried on a brisk trade with neighboring countries. This came to an end after almost 300 years amidst the chaos of peasant uprisings against the ever-growing burden of taxation, and raids from northern Manchuria, led by their chieftain Nurhaci. After warring with the Ming Dynasty for several decades, China fell under the foreign domination of the Manchurian Qing Dynasty that united China again. Its new ruler, Tiancong (1626–1634), was the son of Nurhaci.

THE MING PERIOD

The first Ming emperor, Hongwu, had all the generals who threatened his power executed immediately, and he made sure that all government power was concentrated in his hands. The death of this absolute monarch resulted in a civil war won by his fourth son, who seized power and ruled under the name Yongle (1402–1425). Yongle moved the capital from Nanjing to Beijing where he built an imperial palace. From there, the Ming emperors ruled the country that was divided into thirteen administrative districts. They were assisted by a network of civil servants, drawn increasingly from the emerging wealthy merchant class. The position of the officials within the administration depended on how well they did on a graded examination.

The most important cultural and technical achievements of this period included the building of the Great Wall, the compilation of a universal encyclopedia of 11,000 volumes, and substantial work on production and finishing processes that reveal a high level of technological development. Early on in the Ming Dynasty, China built a deep-sea fleet that carried out remarkable expeditions as far as the east African coast. In spite of initially intense trade with foreign countries, by the end of the Ming Dynasty, China had become increasingly isolated from the rest of the world. In 1514, the Portuguese landed on the coasts of southern China and began trading in pepper, ivory, sandalwood, and scents. In 1557, they were given permission to set up a trading post on the uninhabited Macao Peninsula. The Spanish arrived in China in 1575 and the Dutch in 1604

The sitting Buddha of Kamakura, Honschu, Japan, is 46 ft. high and was cast in 1252.

establishing a trading post in Formosa. The English did not establish a presence until 1637, but by the eighteenth century, they controlled the bulk of the Chinese trade in which, besides silk and porcelain, tea was becoming increasingly important.

Christian missionaries soon followed in the footsteps of the merchants. The Jesuits in particular showed themselves extremely skilled at adapting to Chinese customs. First, they dressed as Buddhist monks, then, when they realized that these were no longer highly regarded, they dressed as Confucian monks.

By the beginning of the seventeenth century, the internal political situation had begun to deteriorate. Political leaders were mired in conflicts involving the military, landowners, and civil servants. The peasant population suffered under the heavy burden of taxation and in 1628, they formed a revolutionary army. The Manchurian tribes in the north took advantage of this confusion. In 1644, they captured the capital Beijing that had been overrun by the peasant army. There the last Ming emperor, Chongzhen (1628–1644), hanged himself.

THE QING DYNASTY

Nurhaci and his son had already conquered and united all of the northern Manchu tribes. After the fall of Beijing, the third Manchu ruler, Shunzhi (1644–1662), proclaimed himself emperor of all of China and declared the founding of the Qing Dynasty.

The new ruler forced Chinese males to shave the top of their heads and wear a plait according to Manchu custom. The highest government posts were always occupied by both a Chinese and a Manchu, but military administration remained in the hands of the conquerors. A reduction in taxation and the building of irrigation systems benefited agriculture, and crafts and commerce also did well. The most important Qing ruler was the emperor Kangxi (1662–1723), whose reign witnessed a scientific and cultural renaissance.

Kangxi decreed that Christians were free to practice their religion. But as a result of the missionary wars in China between the Dominicans, Franciscans, and Jesuits, the emperor's successor revoked the edict of religious tolerance and Christians became targets of persecution.

Under Qianlong (1736–1795) China saw the greatest expansion in its history, but by the time his successor, Yongzheng (1795–1820), came to power, the decline of the Qing Dynasty had already started. Secret societies, some with hundreds of thousands of followers, formed shadow governments, and predatory tribes challenged the nations borders.

The Europeans took advantage of China's internal problems to increase their political and economic influence in the country. In the end, the problems plaguing this last emperor were the result of trade relations with western colonial powers. In about 1830, the British began importing opium, a drug that had devastating effects on the population that gave rise to the First Opium War of 1840. As a result of its defeat China became more dependent on the colonial powers. Up until the time that China became a republic in 1911, it was practically a colony of the West.

JAPAN UNDER THE SHOGUNATE

The shogunate—the rule by regional military leaders, or shoguns, chosen from among the warrior caste of the Samurai—completely changed Japanese society. The Tenno, or emperor, lost his political importance. As a result, Japan's existing feudal system was transformed into a centralized military state that lived almost completely isolated from the rest of the world.

By 1180, Yoritomo Minamoto (1147–1199), head of the victorious Minamoto family in the Samurai civil war, had established the family seat of his court in Kamakura, a small fishing village near present-day Tokyo. In 1192, Yorimoto had himself proclaimed shogun. He reinforced the power of his clan by incorporating the land of the enemies he had conquered into his own estates. The property was managed by administrators who in turn were supervised by a new police authority. After his death, the leadership of the clan passed to his wife who was of the Hojo clan, increasing mismanagement soon diminished her standing. As a result, the then emperor was able to restore his position for three years, until he was removed again by the shogun Takauji Ashikaga (1303–1358) who founded the Muromachi Shogunate. But the weakness of this shogunate invited the other territorial princes to try to expand their own territories. Japan was plunged into the worst civil war of its history.

The conflicts that started with the Onin War (1467–1477) lasted more than 100 years. In this chaos the Daimyos—powerful feudal lords with absolute powers—arose from different powerful clans. At the same time, there were important developments in the field of architecture, garden design, ceramics, painting, and literature. The monasteries of the Zen Buddhist monks played an important part in these extraordinary cultural achievements, and Zen became the quasi-official religion of Japan.

The unification of Japan after the war was the work of three men: Oda Nobunaga (1534–1582), Toyotomi Hideyoshi (1536–1598), and finally Ieyasu Tokugawa (1542–1616). Nobunaga had bought two muskets from the Por-

The Golden Pavilion (Kinkakuji) was built in 1394 as a country seat for a shogun in Kyoto.

tuguese and quickly had them copied. With these new weapons, his army was able to put an end to the supremacy of the Ashikaga Shogunate. After the death of Nobunaga, General Hideyoshi took over the task of unifying Japan. Although he overestimated his military power and invaded Korea without success, Nonetheless, Hideyoshi laid the foundation for the military supremacy of his successor and created a rigorous system of taxation.

Hideyoshi's death was followed by a series of feudal conflicts in the course of which Ieyasu succeeded in seizing power and establishing the foundations that would ensure the supremacy of his family for 250 years. Both the local Daimyo and the Tenno were deprived of power. In Edo, present-day Tokyo, he created a repressive police state. People could not change their residences or their professions. Relations with the outside world were restricted to a minimum. All foreigners, except for a few Dutch and Chinese merchants, were forced to leave, and Christianity was violently suppressed.

Japanese society was divided into three layers. At the top were the Daimyo, followed by the Samurai who were in the employ of the Daimyo, then the common people: the farmers, craftsmen, and merchants, as well as the so-called "unclean," butchers and tanners, beggars, and the physically deformed.

FALL OF THE TOKUGAWA

Japan began to experience growing economic problems around the mid-seventeenth century. One of the main reasons for these difficulties was the transition from the barter economy to the money economy. But the actual cause that led to the collapse came from outside. In addition to growing internal political opposition, there were also with Western countries. In 1853, Commodore Matthew C. Perry appeared in the Bay of Uraga and delivered a request from the American president to enter into a treaty of friendship that would lead to trade relations between the two countries. Fearing attack, the shogunate acceded to the request and signed the Treaty of Kanagawa on March 31, 1854, opening two Japanese ports to ships from the United States.

By entering into these negotiation the shogunate had usurped a prerogative of the emperor. Opposition groups criticized it for being too weak in the face of foreign influence. This led to an uprising of the young Samurai that collapsed after being attacked by American, French, British, and Dutch warships.

Finally on January 3, 1855 insurgent troops entered the palace of Edo and proclaimed a return of power to the emperor. The post of shogun was abolished and the rule of the Tokugawa family that had lasted for more than 250 years came to an end. ❑

PROGRESS IN CHINA UNDER SONG DYNASTY

China, 960

During a period of turmoil, General Zhao Kuangyin founded a new dynasty at Kaifeng. His brother Taizong was installed as the first emperor of the Song dynasty, which would last until 1279. China was faced with external challenges: the Xia on the west, who cut off all commerce with Central Asia, and the Liao Dynasty to the north, which was in power from 907 to 1125. The Liao was succeeded by the Jin Dynasty, which would last until 1234.

The commercial center of the regions controlled by the Song lay in the provinces south of the Yangtze River. By building dikes the amount of arable land was greatly increased. In the social order, the highly educated class of administrators assumed an increasingly important role. In addition to the large landowners, who jealously guarded their prerogatives, there emerged a new entrepreneurial class whose status almost equalled that of the government bureaucrats.

Large cities began to spring up, often with populations over 100,000 that included a middle class composed of artisans and traders. All professions were organized into guilds that closely regulated business practices and trade. The arts flourished as well, until the Mongol invasion brought an end to the dynasty. ❑

Chinese civil servants in their official garb

KOREA REUNITED

Korea, 936

The Wang dynasty unified the four rival dynasties that had divided Korea. General Wang Gon succeeded in bringing together a long-divided country into his kingdom of Koryo. It was from that kingdom that Europeans would later derive the name Korea.

Korean history is essentially the story of its relationship with its powerful neighbor, China. As early as 1100 BC, China founded its first colony near present-day Pyongyang. In 108 BC, this entire region was conquered by China. Over the course of time, three major kingdoms grew up in Korea that feuded with one another ❑

GERMAN KING BECOMES

Rome, 962

Amidst widespread speculation about his motives in taking the imperial title, the powerful German king Otto was crowned Holy Roman Emperor by Pope John XII in Rome on February 2, 962.

In 936, Otto succeeded his father Henry the Fowler as King of Saxony and was crowned at Aachen, Charlemagne's old imperial capital. Three years later, he scored a resounding victory over Eberhard of Franconia and other rebellious dukes at the battle of Andernach. From the start Otto made clear his determination to rule all of Germany, not just Saxony.

This approach upset Bavarians, Franconians, and even some Saxons; Otto's own brother Henry joined the unsuccessful rebellion. Years of anarchy, foreign invasion, and not least the rivalries of royal pretenders featured in the gradual break-up of the vast Frankish empire. With Otto's ascension, Germany came under the control of a single ruler and a single dynasty.

Otto continued to expand his power. In 955, he united his nobles and won a decisive victory against the Magyars at the Battle of Lechfeld. This put an end to decades of cross-border raids. Then he turned toward Denmark. There Harald Bluetooth, who had succeeded his father, Gorm the Old, as king in 935, had survived 25 long years of warfare before forsaking the old gods of the north and become a Christian.

Legend had it that he was converted as the result of an argument with a missionary, Bishop Poppo, during which Harald challenged Poppo to prove his faith by ordeal. The missionary agreed, and the next day he thrust his hand into a white-hot iron glove. When he withdrew his hand, the story goes, it was unharmed. Harald, in a state of astonishment, conceded that Christ was the one true God and that He alone should be worshipped in Denmark.

In point of fact, Harald had met defeat in an expedition against Otto and was forced to become a Christian as part of the price of defeat. There was strong resistance from those who clung to the old gods, but Harald realized the necessity of being on good terms with Otto, who continued to expand his influence in the north and was now the undisputed master of Denmark. Otto also expanded his influence into Scandinavia by supporting the candidacy of his sister Gunnhild and her five sons for the throne of Norway.

In assuming the imperial crown, Otto may have been motivated by aggrandizement pure and simple, but more probably it was due to his shrewd assessment of the political situation in Europe. When he became king, he was bent on gathering Saxons, Franconians, Bavarians, and others into one German kingdom. He also had an eye on the conquest and subjugation of Slav lands in the east. He knew that the title of Emperor would bolster his standing. It would also legitimize his claim to the lands of Lotharingia, the middle kingdom of the Frankish empire, comprising Italy, Burgundy, and eastern Gaul. By being crowned in Rome by the pope, he would to some extent take up the mantle of the previous Frankish rulers of that kingdom.

Otto's star rose over Italy when Adelaide of Burgundy was kidnapped by the Margrave of Ivrea, Berengar, who had sought to become King of Italy. Adelaide appealed to Otto, who rescued her, married her, and annexed part of the country. On his second visit, the pope appealed for help against troublemakers

HOLY ROMAN EMPEROR

in Rome. After his coronation, Otto made it clear who was master; he announced that in future no papal election would be valid until an oath of allegiance to the emperor had been taken, thus setting the stage for battles between the Church and Empire that would dominate European politics for the next 250 years. Unlike all other European monarchs, German kings were crowned as emperor in Rome by the pope until 1133.

In the Middle Ages, the pope and the emperor were representative figures in a world seen as wholly ruled by God, who was the source of their respective authorities. This was symbolized in the prevalent motif of the two swords, one representing temporal and the other spiritual power. Otto was the clear victor in the struggle for dominance between the two powers. In 963, Pope John XII was deposed on charges of murder and perjury. In the next year, Otto starved Rome into submitting to his choice for pope, John XIII. Otto died in 973 with the succession of his dynasty secure in the hands of his son, Otto II. ❏

Figure in gold of Otto I (Aachen)

BATTLE OF LECHFELD

Augsburg, 955

On August 10, the Magyar army, ravagers of Europe for over half a century, were dealt a decisive blow. They were destroyed on the Bavarian battlefield of Lechfeld by King Otto the Great of Germany. Otto had succeeded in uniting his often fractious lords in the common defense and driving back a fighting force that no one had been able to stop.

When the migrant Magyars conquered and settled in the Frankish region of Pannonia, east of the Alps, at the beginning of the tenth century, they used their new homeland as a base for raids that reached as far west as Orléans in France.

Germany bore the brunt of Magyar ferocity, despite a brief truce between the raiders and King Otto's father, Henry the Fowler. Otto came to the throne in 936 and managed to repel renewed Magyar attacks. They switched their attention to France and northern Italy, where they continued to carry out devastating raids. Then they returned briefly to their homeland and prepared to assault Germany again; fifty thousand Magyar troops besieged Augsburg in Bavaria, but its bishop Ulrich held them off until Otto arrived—with only ten thousand troops. Shortly thereafter, at nearby Lechfeld, Otto's mail-clad cavalry inflicted heavy losses on the lightly protected Magyar army, which fled in disarray.

The battle was fought on the day dedicated to St. Laurentius, who was especially revered by Otto. In his three-volume *Res gestae saxonicae sive annalium libri tres* (*The Three Books of the Deeds of the Saxons*), Otto's contemporary, the chronicler Widukind of Corvey, recounts that Otto went into battle armed with a lance that contained a piece of the True Cross. After his victory, his army acclaimed him as victor and were the first to urge him to go to Rome and accept the imperial crown. ❏

Battle of Lechfeld (book illustration by Hector Mulich, 1457)

BYZANTIUM EXPANDS WESTWARD

Bulgaria, 976

On January 11, Basil II became the Byzantine emperor. During his reign, he would be saluted with the honorific *Bulgaroktonos* (Bulgarian slayer), a tribute to his overwhelming defeat of neighboring Bulgaria in a gruesome war. After that Bulgaria was incorporated into the Byzantine Empire.

Bulgaria had been the strongest power in Eastern Europe under Simeon I (r.893–927), who was named Emperor at Constantinople. But after his death, its influence diminished. Its downfall began during the reign of Basil's predecessor, John Tzimiskes I (r.969–976), who forced the Bulgarian Tsar, Boris II, to renounce his imperial regalia and claimed Bulgaria for the empire. It fell to Basil to enforce that claim.

With its defeat of Bulgaria, Byzantium secured its western border from the repeated invasions that had plagued it. ❑

Emperor Basil II, conqueror of Bulgaria (manuscript illumination c.1017)

THE FATIMIDS RULE IN EGYPT

Egypt, 969

Having conquered much of Egypt, the Fatimids, Shiite Moslems from Ifriqiyah (Tunisia), set about making their capital of Cairo one of the most important cities in the Arab world. The able, well-led Fatimids were from a line of caliphs claiming descent from Fatima, the daughter of Muhammad. They built a palace and a mosque-university, al-Azhar (the Splendid), which became the center of Muslim learning in the world.

One of the main reasons for building a solid stone-walled city was fear of trouble from the local Sunni, or orthodox, Muslim population, which owed its allegiance to the caliphs of Baghdad. These Fatimids cut those links but had to face riots and resistance from local residents.

The Fatimids reached the high point of their prestige under their fifth caliph, al-Aziz Billah, who not only consolidated the dynasty's power in Egypt but strengthened its grip over Syria, which had just been conquered. His moves toward Aleppo in the north of the province set the Fatimids on a collision couse with Byzantium. ❑

The magnificent inner court of the al-Azhar Mosque in Cairo.

CHRISTIANS IN MUSLIM SPAIN

Spain, c.965

With the Muslim conquest and occupation of Spain, Christian began to adopt Arab culture while keeping their own religion. In cities such as Toledo and Córdoba, they had their own churches, bishops, and monks. They were known as Mozarabic, a word that comes from the name given them by the Arabs, *mustarib*, meaning would-be Arabs.

Churches architecture combined Moorish arches and ribbed domes with Roman columns. In addition, Mozarabic chant was used for the Latin liturgy.

The Christians moving out of Andalusia to Northern Spain brought with them remarkable techniques of Islamic decoration that they applied to Christian subject matter. One of the monks, Beatus of Liebana, wrote a commentary on the Book of Revelation in 786. known as the *Beatus Apocalypse* it is filled with glowingly painted pictures of saints and the beasts of the Revelation. ❑

POLAND ACCEPTS THE CATHOLIC CHURCH

Poland, 966

After his marriage to the Bohemian princess Dubravka, Mieszko I of Poland allowed himself to be baptized according to the rite of the Roman Church. The chronicler Widukind of Corvey lists him as the first king of Poland in his account of the year 963. He also notes his alliance with Otto I, the Holy Roman Emperor.

With Otto's support, Mieszko was able to expand his kingdom, conquering Silesia in 990. His close ties resulted in the bishopric of Posen's dependence upon the German Archbishop at Magdeburg. In the year 1000, the Emperor Otto III agreed to the establishment of an independent Polish church organization within the Catholic fold.

Twenty-five years later, the Polish duke Boleslav I was crowned king with the pope's blessing. From that point on relations with the Holy Roman Empire began to deteriorate. ❑

MOUNT ATHOS

Greece, 963

The monastery founded on Mount Athos remains the spiritual center of the Byzantine Orthodox Church.

On the top of Mount Athos situated on the Greek peninsula of Chalcidice, the monk Athanasius founded the monastery Megisti Lavra with the support of the Byzantine emperor Nicephorus Phocas in the middle of the tenth century. This remains the largest of the twenty monasteries built on the peninsula. The monks were cenobites, a tradition that emphasizes communal living. Whereas monastic practice in Western Europe was based on the ideals of poverty, chastity, and obedience, for the Eastern Church vigils, fasting and prayer were the guiding principles of cloistered life. On Mount Athos, monks devote as much as eight hours a day to prayer.

Mount Athos has been designated as a World Heritage Site and is a self-governing state within the Republic of Greece. ❏

Monastery on Mt. Athos, founded in 963

THE CONVERSION OF VLADIMIR OF KIEV

Kiev, 989

Vladimir (950–1015), the prince of Kiev and the first Christian ruler of Russia, married the sister of the Byzantine emperor, Basil II, in Kherson, which he returned to the emperor. He thus obtained his reward for helping the emperor to defeat a military rebellion. But for the marriage to take place, he had to agree to accept Christianity and impose it on his people. Prior to this, he had

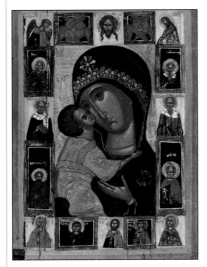

Madonna and Child (Byzantine icon)

been a devout pagan, worshiping Perun the God of Thunder. He was rumored to have had as many as eight hundred concubines.

When Vladimir arrived back in Kiev with his princess, he ordered that the idols should be overturned, cut to pieces, or burnt. The great idol of Perun was tied to a horse's tail and dragged to the river. Twelve men were appointed to beat the wooden idol with sticks to chastise the demon that had deceived its worshippers. It was then cast into the river Dnieper.

The next day, Vladimir proclaimed that all the citizens of Kiev should assemble on the river bank. When all his people had gathered he led them into the water. In an act of mass baptism, some went in up to their necks, with children in their arms.

Prince (and later Saint) Vladimir of Kiev (Russia book illustration c. 1500)

The Christianizing of Kiev had cultural as well as religious consequences. It signaled a closer relationship with Byzantium. In addition to embracing the rite of the Eastern Church, Kiev adopted the Slavic alphabet and Byzantine law. These changes were also reflected in the nation's architecture. Churches followed Byzantine models, prominently featuring mosaics and frescos. It was at this time that the ground-work for the Russian tradition of icon painting was laid.

The rest of his reign was for the most part a peaceful one. He convened a council of *boyars* (major landholders) and divided the kingdom into twelve administrative units, each administered by one of his sons. Vladimir was canonized. His feast day is celebrated on July 15 by both the Catholic and the Orthodox Churches. ❏

VIKING DISCOVERY OF NORTH AMERICA

Greenland, c.1000

As early as the beginning of the tenth century, the Viking explorer Gunnbjorn landed on the Greenland coast. By the end of century, Vikings were bringing reports of a "lush land" far west across the Atlantic. Until that time no one had explored so far, or if they had, did not return to tell the tale, but the land-hungry Vikings were seeking new places to colonize. The latest expedition told of a native people with whom they traded goods and milk—from cows they took with them—for furs and skins. The Viking leader Thorvald was killed by an arrow in a fight with the natives.

Almost twenty years before, Erik Thorvaldsson, nicknamed "the Red" for his hair color, used his period of banishment for murder to seek out new land to the northwest. He arrived at a good farming country that his predecessor had discovered and established a colony of three thousand Vikings and called the country Greenland. Settlers on Greenland ventured north, eventually establishing a second colony as well.

Soon afterwards, in 986, Bjarni Herjolfsson, sailing from Iceland in search of Greenland, was blown too far south and saw a country "well forested with low hills." Some years later, Erik's grandson Leif bought Bjarni's ship in Greenland, sailed west, and discovered what he called Vinland, "land of wine," where he stayed through the winter. His brother Thorvald repeated the journey in the following year, intending to set up a colony. Thorvald's crew also spent the winter in Vinland before returning with news of his death.

Recent excavations at L'Anse aux Meadows at the northernmost point of Labrador show evidence of a sizeable Viking settlement with at least eight

Reconstruction of Viking earth house from the time of their landing in North America

buildings.

Historians have suggested that, in addition to Labrador, Viking expeditions landed in the southern part of Baffin Island and somewhere between Newfoundland and Cape Cod. The hardships of these journeys are hard to imagine. The distance between Greenland and the coast of Canada is eighteen hundred miles across open water. The Vikings used some form of astrolabe as well as a sundial and were able to take readings from the sun, moon, and North Star. Although seaworthy, their flat boats were vulnerable to the choppy Atlantic seas, and any major swell would inundate them. ❑

THE BEGINNING OF THE CAPETIAN DYNASTY

France, 987

After the death of the last Carolingian king, Louis V, Hugh Capet founded a new dynasty in western France. Hugh Capet was the son and heir of Hugh the Great, who ruled over a territory that lay between the Seine and the Loire. Upon his father's death, he was crowned King of France. The dynasty that he founded lasted until 1328, but collateral lines (the Houses of Valois, Bourbon, and Orléans) would rule in France continuously until 1848—with the exception of the years 1789–1814 following the Revolution, when France was first a republic and then acknowledged Napoleon as emperor. All French kings were descended from Hugh in the paternal line.

Historians see the installation of Hugh as the birth of the French nation. As early as 843, the kernel of what would become the French realm had effectively freed itself from Carolingian rule. Powerful lords exercised their authority. To protect themselves against invading Normans, they built strong fortifications in Normandy, Aquitaine, Burgundy, Blois, Flanders, Anjou, and Toulouse. Because of the aristocracy's well-consolidated position, Hugh was unable to impose his will. His position can be seen as first of feudal lords, rather than that of a reigning monarch. Nonetheless he was able to secure the succession for his son Robert II. ❑

Hugh Capet receives the keys of the city of Laon, to bury the last Carolingian king (manuscript illustration, 15th century).

THE FOUNDING OF HUNGARY

Hungary, Christmas Day, 1000

The elevation of Stephen to kingship marked the birth of the state of Hungary. With the consent of the Holy Roman Emperor, Otto III, the Hungarian Lord Stephen was crowned king by Pope Sylvester II in the town of Gran.

Even before they had settled in the region, the Hungarians had been unreceptive to overtures from the Byzantinium. But in the time of Stephen's father Gezá, they were more welcoming to Catholic missionaries. Gezá allied with Otto, and his son Waik was baptized in 973, assuming the Christian name of Stephen. Stephen's marriage to the daughter of Henry Duke of Bavaria (later King Henry III) consolidated his relationship with the Empire.

After Gezá's death, Stephen was able to overcome rivals from in his family and other claimants to the throne. With Bavarian support, he further extended the reach of the Church in his homeland. In the year 1000, Otto founded the archbishopric of Gran. His goal was to tie Hungary, and Poland more closely, to his empire. Stephen, however, did not want Hungary to become an appendage to a greater state. He created another archbishopric as well as a number of monasteries. to enable Hungary's church to stand on its own and the nation to develop independently. In 1087, Stephen was canonized. ❏

Stephen I is crowned King of Hungary (painting, 18th century).

THE CHOLA KINGDOM OF SOUTH INDIA

Southern India, 1010

Under King Rajaraja of Chola, who extended his realm to encompass all of southern India, the Chola Empire became the most powerful and prosperous in India. Rajaraja initiated the construction of the Brihadisvara temple in his capital of Thanjavur. It reached a height of two hundred feet and stood as a symbol of Chola grandeur.

On Rajaraja's accession in 985, Chola power was in retreat after its initial expansion under Aditya I a century earlier. Rajaraja first turned south, defeating a revived Pandya power and invading Sri Lanka; then east, against the Gangas; and finally north, reducing the powerful Vengi state to a mere protectorate. His land conquests complete, he built a fleet that dominated the Indian Ocean, making Chola rich from Chinese and Near Eastern trade. ❏

DANISH RISE TO POWER

England, 1016

Following London's surrender to his Danish forces, King Sweyn claimed control of the whole of England. The deposed king of England, Aethelred, later named "the Unready," was forced to flee to France to join Queen Emma and their children, who had taken refuge with her brother, the Duke of Normandy.

The enmity between Sweyn and Aethelred went back to 1002 when Aethelred, his rule weakened by frequent Viking attacks, ordered the secret St. Brice's Day massacre of Danes living in England. Among those murdered was Sweyn's sister, Gunnhild. Sweyn retaliated by burning homesteads throughout the south for four years before accepting a substantial bribe to withdraw.

The uneasy truce was broken in 1012 when Aethelred persuaded one of Sweyn's top commanders, Thorkell the Tall, to defect. This led to the invasion, with Sweyn landing men on Humberside before marching south. His capture of London met with little popular resistance, despite an ingrained suspicion of Danish plans.

Sweyn's son Canute succeeded his father in 1014, and met with rebellion from the Anglo-Saxons. The resistance coalesced under Edmund Ironside, who controlled most of the north of England. Amid fluctuating alliances between Saxons and Danes, the treacherous Eadric supported first one, then the other.

In 1016, Canute defeated Edmund at Ashingdon in Essex, and the two agreed to divide the country. Edmund was murdered soon afterwards, and Canute eliminated potential rivals, including Eadric. In 1017, he married Aethelred's widow, Emma of Normandy. After that he espoused Christianity, established equal rights for Danes and Englishmen, and confident of his position, sent most of his army back to Denmark.

At the same time as he was recognized as king of all England, he was crowned in Denmark as King Canute II. From then on he sought to unify the two kingdoms. In 1030, he defeated Olaf, the king of Norway, at the battle of Stiklestad, adding most Scandinavia to his kingdom. ❏

Stone engraved with runes from Denmark set up by Harald Bluetooth.

TOLTECS AND MAYAS

Mexico, c.1025

A group of Toltec peoples settled in the old Mayan sacred city of Chichen Itza. According to some scholars, internal tribal disputes had precipitated a migration of some Toltecs from their homeland in central Mexico. From Chichen Itza, they were able to establish control over the better part of the Yucatan Peninsula. The Mayan people were still living in the area, cultivating subsistence crops, particularly maize. But the great days of the Maya had passed. Left behind was the evidence of their highly developed civilization. In the center of the city stood the temple of Kukulcan (Queztlcoatl) with stairways on all four sides reaching to the top. Other temples and palaces were also built on stone platforms. Also present were fine objects made from stone, jade,

Quetzlcoatl, the feathered snake, was venerated by the Toltecs as a god.

and bone.

One of the central tenets of the Mayan religion was the investing of the king and his family with divine attributes. This idea was adopted by other tribes and spread throughout Mexico.

The Maya were the first pre-Columbian people to develop writing beyond the rudimentary stage of pictographs. Texts in the Mayan language were inscribed on stone pillars and temples as well as on vases and walls. The Maya also developed a sophisticated vigesimal (i.e., based on 20) system of mathematics.

Mayan civilization is considered to have reached its highpoint around AD 300. By the time of the Toltec settlement of Mayan lands, it had all but collapsed. ❑

CHIMU CULTURE

Peru, c.1050

In the high plateaus of the Andes, the power of the Huari and Tiahuanuco peoples, bound together by close religious ties, came to an end. In the aftermath, a number of new states arose, the most notable of which was that of the Chimu.

Chimu gold figurine

The Chimu built a large kingdom in northwest Peru. The Chimu culture may have developed from the earlier Moche culture. The main city of the kingdom was Chan-Chan. At the time of its conquest by the Incas in 1470, Chimu lands stretched from Tumbez in the north, southward along the Peruvian coast almost as far as Lima.

The Chimu planned their cities in square-shaped districts surrounded by walls. Houses built of adobe were laid out on terraces, and their walls were decorated with sculptures. The mass production of implements, distinctive monochrome black pottery, and highly developed gold work were hallmarks of Chimu culture.

After the conquest, the Incas adopted many features of Chimu culture including their street and city plans. ❑

FIRDAWSI'S *BOOK OF KINGS*

Point of Interest

With the *Shahnameh (The Book of Kings)*, the Persian poet Firdawsi created one of the great classics of world literature.

After working for 36 years, Firdawsi finally finished his great epic. Comprising fifty thousand couplets, in some manuscripts sixty thousand, it tells the story of Persia from the creation of the world until the end of the Sassanid dynasty (c. AD 651). Mythical and legendary materials are interwoven with the historic narrative. A powerful dualistic strain runs through the entire work: it considers the relationship of good and evil, Persians and non-Persians, and town dwellers and nomads.

The poet constructed the work out of elements drawn from the oral tradition and earlier written texts. In the latter category are writings of the Zoroastrian priesthood, which were composed in the middle of the seventh century. The original source along with its prose translation into Arabic were

subsequently lost.

Not only because of its contents but also because of the purity of its Persian language, free of Arabic loan words, it became the Iranian national epic. Some episodes were elaborated over the centuries by singers and poets Although it belongs to the highest

rank of literary achievement, it contains much of the folklore and traditions of the common people, and it is the first work to describe a chess match. ❑

AVICENNA

Persia, June 18, 1037

Ibn Sina or, as Europeans call him, Avicenna, "the great master," died at Hamadan on this date, mourned throughout the Islamic world.

His mastery of every field of learning was unparalleled. He is particularly revered as the founder of modem medicine through his treatises on the pulse, fevers, symptoms and diagnosis, wounds, fractures, bites, poisons, and diarrhea, among the many conditions listed in his canon of medicine.

Ibn Sina was also famed as a philosopher, influenced by the Greeks. He believed that human knowledge could be unlimited. He also believed that the saint and the sage could both attain perfect clarity equal to that of the Prophet.

He was born in Balkh in present-day Afghanistan and spoke Persian. He taught himself medicine. He was said to have mastered all known science by the age of sixteen. He wrote his works at night very rapidly, while by day he served several princes as minister. He was often envied and forced to flee and hide, giving medical consultations to earn his living. He spent most of his last years at Isfahan. ❑

THE SALIC DYNASTY

Germany, eleventh century

The Salic Dynasty, established itself in 1028 with the accession of Conrad II to the German throne, lasted for almost a hundred years. Conrad's son Henry III succeeded him in 1039, ruled until 1056, and was followed by Henry IV and Henry V. All of the kings of the Salic dynasty were crowned emperor by the pope. Their dynastic name stems from the Salfrankish people of the age of great migrations.

The Salic rulers advanced the close relationship between church and state established by the preceding Ottonian Dynasty. Henry III attempted to carry out church reform by discouraging priestly marriage and the sale of indulgences. Henry IV, however, trod over the more controversial ground of the investiture of bishops, which precipitated a crisis between the temporal and spiritual powers. The struggle between emperor and pope became one of the defining dynamics of medieval society and governance. ❑

INCREASING POWER OF THE EMPERORS

Germany, 1024

With the death of King Henry II on July 13, 1024, the rule of the Ottonian Dynasty came to an end. The spiritual and temporal lords settled upon an outsider who was related to the former rulers through marriage. On September 4, 1024, the Graf Conrad of the Salic noble house, whose center of power lay in area around Worms and Speyer, was elected as the new German king. Under Salic rule the German emperors reached the zenith of their might.

Unlike the Ottonians before him, Conrad could neither read nor write and had only a minimal knowledge of theological issues. The election was conducted in the absence of any of the Saxon lords and against the wishes of Lothringia. Nevertheless a majority of those present agreed to recognize him. The transition from one dynasty to the next proceeded with no significant resistance, guaranteeing the perpetuation of the Holy Roman Empire.

Henry's foreign policy followed in the footsteps of the Ottonians. He strengthened the German rule over Italy. On his first trip to Italy, he was crowned king of Lombardy, and in the following year, Pope John XIX invested him with the emperor's crown in Rome. In 1033, he acquired lordship over Burgundy, supporting his claim through his wife Gisela's dynastic connections. Burgundy was of particular strategic importance because it controlled Alpine passes. He was also successful in his dealings with Poland and Hungary, using a period of relative peace among the German noble houses to extend the boundaries of his realm. ❑

Four Salic rulers: Conrad II, Henry III, Henry IV, Henry V (relief from the Cathedral of Speyer)

RUPTURE BETWEEN ROME AND CONSTANTINOPLE

Constantinople, July 16, 1054

Upon his election to the papal throne in 1048, Leo IX sought to assert his authority over the Eastern Church centered in Constantinople as the legitimate heir to St. Peter. This ambition took little account of the prestige and independent behavior of the Byzantine Church. It also showed little awareness of the deep distrust in the East of the papal alliance with the German emperor. At the same time, he was hoping that the combined forces of the two churches could mitigate the threat from Norman invaders who had made their way into Italy.

To accomplish his quest for supremacy, the pope sent Cardinal Humbert von Silva Candida as papal legate to make his case to Michael Cerularius, the patriarch of Constantinople. In the end his diplomacy came to naught. Not only was the patriarch unwilling to cede his authority, there were also serious doctrinal differences that remained unreconciled after some four hundred years. Catholic doctrine asserted the twofold nature of Christ, which the East rejected, and Rome insisted on celibate priests, whereas the East continued to allow its clergy to marry. The union of the Churches had depended on both sides turning a blind eye to these differences.

Frustrated in his diplomacy, the cardinal marched into the Cathedral of Saint Sophia and placed on the altar a bull of excommunication. Historians see this move as the final gesture of a desperate man who realized that his mission had failed. Patriarch Michael, enjoying the support of his people, was able to dismiss the pope's ban, which only succeeded in bringing about the final split between the Eastern and Western arms of the Church. In response, he closed down Catholic churches and monasteries in Constantinople and launched a campaign against what he alleged were the abuses of the Catholic rite. The papal ban of excommunication of the Eastern Patriarchs was not lifted until 1965. ❑

Pope Leo IX

SELJUK DYNASTY RULES BAGHDAD

Baghdad, 1055

In 1055, the weakened Abbasid caliphate invited the Seljuk dynasty into Baghdad. Though Baghdad had lost some its former glory, it had a population of approximately four hundred thousand and could still lay claim to being the economic and cultural capitol of Islam. Under their leader Tugrul Beg, the Seljuks occupied the city and became guarantors and effective rulers over the caliphs.

The Seljuks were a Turkic dynasty and practicing Sunnis, who converted to Islam in 970. In the eleventh century, they began a series of conquests, In Baghdad, they drove out the Shiite Buwayhids under whose protection the caliphate had stood. The Abbasids continued to rule in name after invasion, but the Seljuks were the real rulers. ❑

Seljuk mosque in east Anatolia (13th century) with hospital (at right)

THE FIRST SHEET MUSIC

Italy, c.1040

The development of Gregorian chant had created a need for the accurate transcription of musical compositions. An existing system, which consisted of marks placed above the text, was proving inadequate to the task. In his work *Micrologus de disciplina de artis musicae*, Guido da Arezzo, an

Drawing of the Guidonian Hand illustrating musical whole and half tones

Italian Benedictine monk who moved to Arezzo from a monastery on the Adriatic coast, developed the staff and thus presented a functional system of musical notation to represent whole tones. He used a red line for F, a yellow line for C, and in between was a black line for A.

He also laid the groundwork for *solfeggio* (the do-re-mi scale) and is credited with devising the Guidonian hand, which provided an easy way to memorize notes and intervals. ❑

UNION OF LEÓN AND CASTILE

Iberia, 1055

After a six-month siege, King Ferdinand of Castile captured the Muslim stronghold of Coimbra in the center of present-day Portugal. This proved to be a significant step in his campaign to regain Muslim territories in Spain for Christianity. Among other benefits, this victory brought enough territory under his control in Portugal and the south that he could exchange his title of King for that of Emperor.

Ferdinand's campaign, called the reconquista (reconquest), got under way when he imposed his authority over the old kingdom of León, overthrowing his brother-in-law Bermudo III, who had been its king, León's claim to the throne bolstered by his marriage to Bermudo's sister Sancha. Thus he united the kingdoms of Castile and León and gained control over Galicia, part of Navarro, and the Rioja. He did not set out to conquer the territories merely by force of arms, preferring instead to prevail by extracting tribute from them in return for protection. Coimbra, however, resisted his overtures, and it took battering rams to bring it to its knees. The conduct of the siege served as a warning to other Muslim cities. It suggested that if the citizens of a Muslim city surrendered immediately, they would be allowed to stay and carry on as normal. If they surrendered during the siege, they could depart with their lives and what they could take away with them. But if they went on fighting, their city would be stormed, and they themselves killed or enslaved.

Ferdinand adopted a policy of not forcing Muslims to change their religion. His goal was to increase the political power of the Christian community rather than the belief in the religion.

At his death in 1065, Ferdinand's kingdom stretched from the Ebro to the Tajus. ❑

NORMAN PACT WITH POPE

Italy, August 1059

At the Council of Melfi, the Normans led by Robert Guiscard achieved a vital agreement with their enemy, Pope Nicholas II. The alliance benefited both. Pope Nicholas had been under pressure, thanks to continuing quarrels with Byzantium in the east and the military threat from the Arabs in much of the Mediterranean. For Robert it meant that he could push on to drive the Saracens from Sicily without the fear that the papal armies would attack his rear.

According to the terms of the agreement, Robert promised loyalty to the Catholic Church. In return the pope invested him with the duchy of Calabria and Apulia—lands on the Italian peninsula that he had already conquered—as well as that of Sicily, which at that time was under Arab occupatiwon.

His campaign against the Saracens proved successful. In 1061, he captured the city of Messina, and within thirty years, the Norman conquest of the island was complete. In 1130, Robert Guiscard's grandson was crowned King of Sicily as Roger II.

Norman Cathedral of Cefalù in Sicily (12th century)

This was the era of great Norman achievement. While Robert occupied Sicily, his fellow Norman William was advancing into England. ❑

PAGAN IS HEART OF THE NEW BURMESE EMPIRE

Burma, 1044

The strictly disciplinarian regime of King Anawrahta brought stability and power to Burma. From its capital Pagan, the king extended his empire from the Mons kingdom of Thaton to the Indian Ocean.

Anawrahta exploited Pagan's location at the intersection of trade routes. He advanced farming techniques and strengthened his army. His revolutionary use of elephants added to his military might.

Conversion to Theravada Buddhism inspired Anawrahta to begin building the Shwezigon pagoda, but worship of many gods was tolerated inside the pagoda. The king said, "Men will not come for the sake of the new faith. Let them come for their old gods, and they gradually will be won over." ❑

The Shwezigon Pagoda built by King Anawrahta

THE GLORY OF VENICE

Italy, 1063

The Cathedral of Saint Mark was the visible sign of the dramatic ascent of Venetian naval and commercial clout. Ground was broken for the new cathedral in 1063. Thirty years later, it was formally dedicated. With its five cupolas, the cathedral followed Byzantium architectural models, but it also included elements drawn from the western European Romanesque tradition, as seen in its crypt. As the official church of Venice, it displayed the city's magnificence not only through its imposing façade, but also through the beautiful mosaic work found within.

Although Venice acknowledged the overlordship of Byzantium, from the eighth century onward, it had organized its own municipal government under the authority of the doges. With its battle-hardened fleet, it was of inestimable value to Byzantium. After Venice's navy drove back the Norman invaders from Constantinople in 1082, the Emperor granted the city exclusive trading privileges, which made its merchants the dominant players in the commerce with the Orient. ❑

Facade of the St. Mark's Basilica

THE BATTLE OF HASTINGS

Hastings, October 1066

Duke William II of Normandy, commanding a mixed force of around seven thousand French, Breton, and mercenary soldiers, crushed the army of his rival for the English throne and erstwhile lieutenant, King Harold, on a windswept Sussex down. The Normans claimed that William was the rightful heir to the English throne and that Harold had conceded this.

The battle was a struggle between two opposed styles, mobile French Norman archers against stoical, close-packed ranks of English infantry armed with lances and axes. Yet for much of the day, it seemed that the English had the upper hand. They approached through a wood near the top of Senlac Hill, eight miles

THE INDIAN TEMPLE OF KHAJURAHO

Central India, c.1060

Khajuraho is located in the north central region of India in the present-day state of Mahdya Pradesh. It was at one time capital of the Chandela Rajput Kingdom, which was the dominant power in the region for over two hundred years. As many as eighty temples were built at Khajuraho, most dedicated to Hindu gods, but a few were Jain in orientation.

The stupendous Kandariya Mahadeva Hindu temple at the Chandela capital of Khajuraho was completed in 1020. The Mahadeva temple surpassed the smaller temples built by the Chandela dynasty; it was the Chandelas' great masterpiece. Built in fine cream-colored sandstone, its main spire rises for 116 feet, though it appears even higher because of the deep basement and the vertical lines on the spire. It is surrounded by lesser spires.

Inside the temple is a *pradaksina*, or walkway, provided with shaded balconies. Outside are the friezes and sculptures. At the lower levels scenes from hunting, warfare, and courtly life are depicted. The higher friezes are reserved for representations of gods and goddesses, along with scenes of lovemaking, depicting couples and trios indulging in erotic play that bring to mind tantric practices. But most of the carvings are not sexual in nature; they depict Indian men and women engaged in the ordinary pursuits of life. Among the many representations are portraits of potters and musicians, of women putting on make-up, farmers, and other ordinary people. These sculptures are all at some distance from those representing deities.

The temple complex was lost to the jungle for many centuries and rediscovered in the mid-nineteenth century. It has now been named a World Heritage Site. ❑

ROMANESQUE ARCHITECTURE

Point of Interest

The Romanesque style of church architecture became established in Europe around 1000. Its mass and solidity created fortified castles in which God could dwell. For some constructions a tower would rise over the crossing where transept and nave intersected. In France most Romanesque churches had two towers. Other characteristic elements include load-bearing col-

Cathedral of St. Mary and St. Stephen (Speyer, Germany)

inland, dismounted and made a tight formation on the high ground. William's troops attacked with archers in front followed by armor-clad infantry. They rolled uphill in human wave after wave. William, on horseback, stayed close and so kept control over his men. He was a conspicuous target and had three horses killed under him. As the French front ranks at last panicked and fled, their own knights cut them down. William dismounted, removed his helmet to be recognized and, spear in hand, ordered them back into battle.

Many of the English, observing—so they thought—the beginning of a rout, and freed at last from their role as bowmen's targets, ran forward in hot pursuit, only to be hit on both flanks by French cavalry. It was probably the decisive moment of the battle. The French, turning near-disaster to advantage, now used the ploy to encourage the English to break ranks. In the confusion, the English leaders were exposed as ready targets. Harold's two brothers were killed in a hail of arrows and spears. Harold him-

The Battle of Hastings as depicted in the Bayeux Tapestry (c. 1077)

self, despite having lost one eye, fought on. His body, when recovered, was nearly unidentifiable.

Toward evening, the French continued to squeeze the core of Harold's army until only a few dozen remained standing. These survivors, who knew that all was lost, retreated in good order to make a last stand on ground that gave them the best chance to sell their lives dearly. This was a steep valley cut by ditches and unsuitable for cavalry. William, his lance broken, led a party of men from Boulogne into the enemy redoubt.

The battle provoked many questions about the events leading up the invasion. Why did Edward the Confessor, on his deathbed, disinherit his cousin, the duke, and nominate Harold? Why did Harold, after marching to York to defeat the Norwegian King Hardrada at Stamford Bridge only three weeks before, rush tired troops to Hastings and not wait for reinforcements? ❏

umns, groin and barrel vaults, and arches. The Romanesque period coincided with the rise of the great monasteries, many of which were built in this style.

Perhaps the earliest example of Romanesque architecture is St. Michael's Church in Hildesheim (Germany). Many fine examples of this style of architecture are still standing, including Mont St. Michel in France, Santiago de Compostela in Spain, Canterbury in England, as well as a number of churches in Germany, Eastern Europe, and in the Crusader Kingdoms in the Holy Land. ❏

DOMESDAY BOOK

Point of Interest

Despite his successful conquest of England at the Battle of Hastings, King William believed that he had not yet consolidated his hold on the country or harmonized its feudal system with that of his native Normandy. To remedy that, he instituted the Great Survey, a massive audit of the nation's wealth. Taking two years to complete, the Survey was compiled into two volumes called the Domesday Book. The information was arranged geographically, by shire, hundred, and village, providing the king

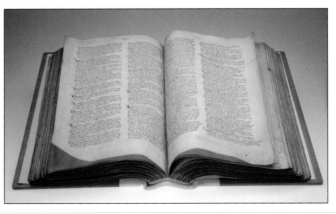

with a quick and reliable reference system for levying military taxation.

The Great Survey allowed William to achieve both his aims. The terms of the survey overhauled land tenure; from this point onward, all land in England was deemed to be held directly by the king or by his subjects on his behalf. ❏

Henry IV, Gregory VII, and the Investiture Conflict

Canossa, 1077

In the battle between Pope Gregory VII and King Henry IV over who had the authority to create bishops, the king appeared barefoot in the snow before the pope and succeeded in having the ban of excommunication that had been placed upon him revoked.

The conflict between these two dynamic individuals was a reflection of the complex relationship between the spiritual and temporal powers that would drive European politics over the next two centuries. Gregory VII asserted a radical new expansion of papal power. It was his conviction that the Pope's authority was paramount in all matters, having been granted by Christ through Peter the power to bind and loose souls. For his part, Henry was in the process of consolidating his position relative to a restless aristocratic class that had no intention of relinquishing any of its prerogatives.

The inevitable conflict came to a head over the very real problem of the investiture of bishops. At this time, bishops were not simply ecclesiastic officials; they were major landholders with considerable political power. Up until this point, the king's was the deciding voice in the choice of bishops within the confines of the Holy Roman Empire, but with the increasing momentum of the reforms originally set in motion by Gregory I, the bestowal of church offices by the laity was beginning to fall out of favor. Nonetheless, there was little disagreement that the ruler of the empire had a vital role to play in the choice of bishops, especially as they had considerable temporal responsibilities and prerogatives.

In 1075, the Episcopal See of Milan became vacant, and Henry exercised his customary right in choosing a replacement. Gregory, however, asserted that someone else was more suitable and that only he had the power to confer legitimacy. With this Gregory placed the question of investiture at the center of his program of reform demanding Henry's submission to his ruling. A synod convened by Henry unsurprisingly supported the king's position and set aside Gregory's choice. In response Gregory excommunicated Henry.

The submission that Henry offered at Canossa was a political necessity. Following his excommunication, the German bishops withdrew their support, and the nobility decided that it would no longer recognize his authority, if he were not able to convince the pope to lift the ban.

The successful solution to his problem did not immediately quell the nobles' discontent: they elected a replacement for him, whom Henry was able to defeat in 1080. A second ban levied by Gregory did

Michael Pacher, *Pope Gregory VII and King Henry IV* (painting for an altarpiece, before 1483)

not have the same effect as the first, as this time the German bishops, who were not in full agreement with the pope's strict reforms and growing assertions of power, chose to support Henry. The controversy over investiture was finally put to rest in 1122 with the Concordat of Worms. It was decided that a clear demarcation had to be created between the temporal and spiritual powers of the bishops, and the parties agreed upon procedures for joint investiture. ❑

Church Authority over the Choice of Pope

Point of Interest

To counter the prevailing influence of the rulers of the Holy Roman Empire in the matter of papal elections, Pope Nicholas II issued a papal decree in 1059 during the Easter synod that the authority to choose a new pope lay exclusively with the College of Cardinals. For a long time, the German emperors had played a decisive part in papal elections. In some cases their ambassadors actually directed the choice, in other cases the Roman participants in the election first had to swear that the election would only be official if agreed to by the emperor.

Just as problematic as the intervention of the emperors was the pivotal role of the Roman populace. So the choice of pope was dependent upon municipal politics and the friendly or hostile disposition of Rome's leading families. Nicholas sought to insulate the electoral process from outside influences. First the cardinals had to arrive at a choice, and then that choice had to be ratified by the clergy and the people of Rome. The decree had the effect of diminishing the emperor's power and freeing the pope from dependence upon him. The regulations were, however, not clearly formulated and could not forestall controversies such as those arising during the investiture crisis.

The Church's absolute freedom in papal elections was formulated by Gregory VII in 1075, two years before Henry IV appeared barefoot before him in snows of Canossa. His *Dictatus Papae* set forth his position unambiguously, stating that the authority of the Church is derived from God alone, and that only the bishops have the right to name their chief bishop. ❑

THE EBBING FORTUNES OF BYZANTIUM

Eastern Turkey, 1071

After the defeat of the army of the Byzantine Emperor Romanus IV at Manzikert, north of Lake Van, Asia Minor found itself at the mercy of the Turks. The emperor himself was captured.

This conclusive battle was the result of years of tension between the Armenian and Greek-speaking people of Asia Minor and the Turkish nomads infiltrating from the east with their flocks.

The enormous distances involved made it almost impossible for the Byzantine government to take effective punitive action against these nomadic bands, and gradually the indigenous population was being forced westward.

Earlier in the year, the new emperor resolved to drive the Turks out and raised a large army for the purpose. The Turks appealed for help to the Seljuk Sultan Alp Arslan, who came in person with his army. ❏

VALENCIA FALLS TO EL CID

Valencia, 1094

After a twenty-month siege the Moorish city of Valencia fell into Christian hands, defeated by starvation. The new ruler of the city was a man whom, ironically enough, the Arabs themselves

Title page from the Spanish national epic *El Cid* (1498)

ALMORAVID CONQUEST OF GHANA

Ghana, 1077

Thousands of Saharan nomads under the leadership of the Almoravid chief Abu Bakr swept through Ghana, destroying the richest empire in West Africa. The Almoravids were a Berber group from Mauritania. Their conquests began twenty years before when Abdullah ibn Yasim, preaching holy war and spiritual renewal, united the tribes of the western Sahara and advanced into Morocco with thirty thousand zealots.

Ghana had been an attractive target for them. Its prosperous capital, Kumbi Saleh, was the jumping off place for caravans traveling to Morocco and had become the wealthiest kingdom in West Africa through its trade in gold and salt.

While one Almoravid army crossed the Straits of Gibraltar into Spain, a second crossed the Sahara into Ghana, occupying its gold mines and making the Almoravids richer than the degenerate sultans they vowed to overthrow. Ghana became a tribute state of an empire that now stretched from the Niger to the Ebro in Spain.

The Almoravids withdrew to their stronghold in Morocco around 1100, but their success marked an important step in the spread of Islam throughout the region. ❏

dubbed El Cid Campeador (Lord Champion).

El Cid was born Don Rodrigo Diaz de Vivar in middle of the eleventh century, the scion of a noble Castilian family. He entered the service of King Alfonso VI of Castile and León. In 1081, Alfonso banished him for unauthorized raiding, and although nominally still in Alfonso's service, Don Rodrigo in effect became an independent traveling knight, serving both Muslim and Christian masters. He earned the title El Cid (from the Arabic *sayyid*, or *sid*, "lord") in the service of the Muslim rulers of Saragossa.

El Cid saw the chance to conquer the Muslim city of Valencia in 1092 as its ruler, al-Kadir, was under threat from the Berber Murabits (Almoravids) from North Africa, who had already conquered much of Muslim Spain. In October 1092, al-Kadir was killed by rebel Valencians with Almoravid backing, but before the Almoravids could seize the city, it was besieged by El Cid. Magnanimous in victory, El Cid promised freedom of worship for his Muslim subjects.

The figure of El Cid is celebrated in Spanish literature. An epic poem entitled *Poema de Mio Cid* dating from 1140, which exists in a manuscript composed a hundred and fifty years later, marks the beginning of Spanish literature. El Cid was also the subject of Pierre Corneille's great play by the same name (1636). ❏

THE *RECONQUISTA*

Point of Interest

The *reconquista* refers to the historical process whereby European Christians drove the Islamic Moors from the Iberian Peninsula into North Africa. The Moors had occupied Spain since 711. After Ramiro I of Aragon was murdered by a Muslim in 1064, the Christian effort to gain back land intensified.

Though there had been ongoing struggle between Christians and Muslims before, it was at this time that Christian Europeans began to cast the struggle in religious terms. The pope gave the fighting his seal of approval and pronounced that those who died in battle would be forgiven their sins, giving the conflict the character of a crusade. Early Christian victories included the captures of Toledo (1085), Lisbon (1147), and Córdoba (1236). The Reconquista ended with the capture of Granada, the last Moorish stronghold, in 1492. ❏

Ornamented capital from the Alhambra (Granada)

THE TEMPLE OF ANGKOR WAT

Cambodia, early twelfth century

The magnificent Hindu temple at Angkor Wat was commissioned by King Suryavarman II as a funeral monument. Its size alone made it a suitable memorial for this powerful king. The moat encircling the temple and its edifices measured 12 miles in circumference. The grand entrance guarded by the Nagas, part-dragon, part-human divinities, led to a splendid gatehouse, itself one of the grandest Khmer buildings ever erected. Inside was a raised courtyard surrounded by a gallery. On ground level and gallery level, exquisite reliefs represented the great epics of Hindu mythology. Within the court was a second court, also raised and galleried, and inside this court the third, innermost, and highest of the courtyards. Here upon a pyramid stood the great temple itself, dedicated to Vishnu and marked by five bell-shaped towers, one at each corner and one in the center, over 200 feet high. ❑

Aerial view of the main temple of Angkor Wat

SONG OF ROLAND

France, c.1100

Roland battling a Moor and giving St. Michael his glove (miniature from the *Chronicle of the World* of Rudolph von Ems, beginning of 14th century)

The *Song of Roland* influenced medieval literature throughout Europe. It is the finest example of Old French epic poetry. In all likelihood it was transmitted orally before being written down at the beginning of the twelfth century. It tells the story of Charlemagne's clash in Spain with the Moors, who are called Saracens in the poem. The poem is named after the bold and courageous nephew of Charlemagne.

Returning from their victories in Spain, Roland is betrayed by his step-father to the still undefeated Saracen king, Marsilius. Roland refuses to sound his great horn, Oliphant, for help, and he and his faithful companions, including his dear friend Oliver, are overwhelmed and massacred by the Saracens. Charlemagne arrives too late to save his nephew but succeeds in finally defeating the enemy.

Fashioned by an unknown author, the saga lived on in France and Germany and has been told and retold many times, in whole or in part. During the Renaissance, the great Italian poet Ludovico Ariosto wrote a satiric version, entitled *Orlando Furioso*, one of the most widely read works of its time. ❑

THE FIRST CRUSADE

Clermont, November 1095

The mounting of the First Crusade began at the Council of Piacenza in March of 1095, when the Byzantine Emperor, Alexios I Komnenos, requested the Pope's aid in ridding his empire of the Seljuk Turks. Subsequently, in November, at the Council of Clermont, Pope Urban II issued his epochal call to defend the Holy Land and Christendom.

Aimed at recruiting members of the nobility, the Pope skillfully appealed to their sense of noblesse oblige, vividly describing the atrocities visited by the barbaric infidels on helpless Christian pilgrims and the blameless Byzantine faithful and, further, offered to reward any who died in battle with a papal remission of sins.

Urban's successful call to arms was a significant moment in the history of the West. Rallying nobles and commoners together under the aegis of Christendom, the crusades developed into a culture-defining ethos that embraced the concept of holy war against not only Muslims but all non-Christians as well as Christian groups that were perceived as heretical. En route to Jerusalem, some of

THE KNIGHTS TEMPLAR

Point of Interest

The Order of the Knights Templar was formed in 1091 to protect Christian pilgrims from bandits as they traveled to Jerusalem. It was begun as a monastic order by two French Crusaders, Hugues de Payens and Godfrey de Saint-Omer, who, along with seven fellow veterans, took vows of poverty and celibacy, and swore to protect all Christian travelers and to continue the harrowing of

Knights of the Order of St. John

The capture of Jerusalem, 1099 (French miniature from the 15th century)

	Date	Goals	Crusaders, how many departed, reached Palestine	Leaders	Results
First Crusade	1096–1099	Guard the Christian Church in the Holy Land from Muslim attacks.	330,000 40,000	Robert of Normandy, Gottfried of Bouillon, Balduin and Robert II of Flanders, Raymond of Toulouse	Conquered Jerusalem. Founded the Kingdom of Jerusalem.
Second Crusade	1147–1149	Liberate the Crusader Kingdom of Edessa, which had been captured by the Emir of Mossul.	240,000 90,000	King Conrad II, Louis VII	Crusade failed.
Third Crusade	1189–1192	Take back Jerusalem, which had been conquered by Saladin in 1187.	350,000 280,000	Frederick Barbarossa, Richard Lionheart, Philip II of France	Treaty with Saladin guaranteeing free access to Jerusalem.
Fourth Crusade	1202–1204	Regain Jerusalem. Occupy Egypt.	30,000	Boniface of Montferrat, Louis of Blois, Balduin of Flanders	Conquered and plundered Constantinople.
Fifth Crusade	1228–1229	Fulfill a vow made by Frederick II, despite a papal ban.	70,000 60,000	Emperor Frederick II	Reconquered Jerusalem, Bethlehem, and Nazareth. Signed treaty with the Sultan of Egypt.
Sixth Crusade	1248–1254	Destroy Egypt, the center of Muslim power.	25,000 10,000	Louis IX (Saint Louis)	Louis captured and then ransomed. Kingdom of Acre fortified.
Seventh Crusade	1270	Attempt to convert the Sultan of Tunis.	25,000 10,000 (reached Tunis)	Louis IX, Charles of Anjou	Death of Louis. Charles calls an end to the Crusade.

the Crusaders, especially those from Germany, rallied against the Jews, and whole Jewish communities were massacred. It also occasioned the largest expansion of Western culture into Asia Minor since the fall of the Roman Empire.

Urban wanted the Crusaders to set out on August 15 1096. In fact, an army of one hundred thousand peasants and their families had set out months before, under the command of the monk, Peter the Hermit of Amiens. Known as the People's Crusade, they were an unwieldy mob that swept down the Danube toward the Muslim infidels.

In 1129, under the patronage of Bernard of Clairvaux, the Order was officially sanctioned by the Church at the Council of Troyes. This formal recognition led to an influx of nonmilitary laymen into its ranks, many of whom were from European nobility. Their influence helped maintain the Order's prominent role in European charities and banking for over two hundred years.

The Templar Order declined precipitously at the end of the thirteenth-century. Crusaders in the Holy Land suffered repeated defeats at the hands of the resurgent Muslims under Saladin, and the financial wing in Europe suffered the wrath of its greatest debtor, King Philip IV of France. In 1307, to abrogate his debts, he had the leaders of the Knight Templars arrested and executed, thereby extinguishing the Order. ❏

Knights Templar

Jerusalem, pillaging as they went. Disorganized and militarily inept, they were massacred by the Seljuk Turks as soon as they entered Asia Minor. Peter the Hermit survived and joined the second wave of Crusaders.

The second wave was made up of nobles and knights. Departing in August of 1096, as the pope had requested, they arrived in Constantinople between November 1096 and May of 1097 and pushed toward Jerusalem, defeating Muslims at the cities of Dorylaeum and Antioch. It took them two years to reach Jerusalem. Their siege began on June 7, of 1099 and ended in victory on July 15. Of the seven thousand knights who had originally responded to Urban's call, only fifteen hundred survived. Nonetheless they succeeded in founding a Christian kingdom in the Holy Land. ❏

PORTUGAL BECOMES AN INDEPENDENT KINGDOM

Lisbon, October 1147

After his defeat of the Moors at the battle of Ourique in 1139, the Portuguese Duke Afonso Henriques proclaimed himself King of Portugal. Portugal was at one time the Roman province of Lusitania. It had been overrun by the Visigoths after the fall of Rome and then taken by the armies of Islam during their push into Europe. The Christian reconquest of the Iberian Peninsula began with Ferdinand the Great, who united in his person the Kingdoms of Castile and León. Afonso was the son of the Burgundian lord whom Ferdinand had installed to govern the territory.

In 1147 Afonso launched a siege on Lisbon that lasted for seventeen weeks. It finally ended with the peaceful mass evacuation of its Muslim inhabitants after their surrender to an allied Christian force. The Muslims abandoned both shores of the Tagus and were forced to give up bases at Sintra and Palmela, leaving Afonso in control of most of the country's northern and western seaboard from his capital at Coimbra. The Muslims' northern border was forced back to Evora. Christian forces forecast a Muslim surrender soon after allied troops overran the main Muslim food cache stored in caves, but the defenders held out until English troops finally managed to get a mobile tower close enough to the fortress walls to drop a drawbridge over the parapet.

With the help of crusaders en route to the Holy Land, Afonso I wrested control of Lisbon from the Moors (etching).

Afonso then had to settle his debts with the large combined force of English, Flemish, and German Crusaders—some thirteen thousand men in 164 ships—whom he persuaded to help him. Under the alliance terms, which gave the Crusaders the spoils of the city, the new settlers were given incentives to stay, including the right to go on enjoying the customs and liberties of their native lands. Many Crusaders accepted the offer, with a group of Englishmen settling at Vila Verde. ❑

NEW KING CROWNED IN SICILY BY ANTI-POPE

Palermo, December, 1130

The Norman Roger II was crowned King of Sicily and special papal envoy by the anti-pope Anacletus on December 25, 1130. The ceremony was of special significance to both the new king, whose elevation to the throne was the end result of his inexorable rise in the Norman ranks, and to Anacletus, whose action enlisted an influential ally in his struggle with Innocent II for papal legitimacy.

The new king was the son of Roger I, Count of Sicily, who was one of the last of the Norman adventurers to come to southern Italy in the eleventh century to aid the Italian city-states in their battles with the Saracens. The victorious Normans eventually accumulated great power, becoming de facto rulers of southern Italy. Roger II continued this tradition by securing Sicily with victories over the Muslims in North Africa. His investiture in 1128 as the powerful Duke of Apulia made him Anacletus's logical choice for the throne.

Roger II's kingdom stretched from the Abruzzi to Malta and from Tripoli to Kabylia. His court was based on the French feudal system, but his Byzantine administration was cosmopolitan, including Greeks and Arabs. ❑

ANARCHY IN ENGLAND

England, mid-twelfth century

What is known in English history as "the Anarchy" began when Stephen, the last of the Norman kings, snatched the crown from his cousin Matilda in 1135. Matilda, putative heir to the throne after the death of her father Henry I, was challenged by Stephen, who claimed Henry's deathbed decree had named him heir. Asserting his claim, he won the backing of many of the powerful Barons who had previously backed Matilda.

In 1141, Matilda and her forces, led by the Earl of Chester, actually defeated Stephen, taking him prisoner and slaughtering many of the citizens of Lincoln. Shortly thereafter, Matilda's half-brother, the earl of Gloucester, was captured and used as ransom for Stephen's release and his subsequent restoration to the throne.

Stephen was continually at odds with the powerful bishops and exerted little control over the predatory barons who, in essence, created the anarchy with their penchant for robbery and pillage throughout the countryside.

It was not until 1153, at the Treaty of Wallingford, that a modicum of peace was restored, when Stephen agreed to recognize Matilda's son, Henry, as his successor. As Henry II, he was the first of the Plantagenet Kings. ❑

RISE OF THE CISTERCIAN ORDER

France, 1116

The first Cistercian monastery was founded at Citeaux in a desolate swamp some 14 miles from the town of Dijon on Palm Sunday in 1098. That date was also the feast day of St. Benedict, which was appropriate because the 21 monks, led by Robert from the Benedictine abbey of Molesme, saw themselves as renewing the Rule of St. Benedict.

In 1116, a young Burgundian nobleman, Bernard, established a new abbey at Clairvaux, the third daughter monastery of Citeaux. The Cistercians seemed to be dwindling in numbers, but the inspired teaching of Bernard and the organizing talent of the English abbot Stephen Harding transformed them into the fastest growing of all of the monastic orders.

The monks subjected themselves to severe discipline: they ate no meat or fat and did not wear comfortable clothing such as breeches or coats. They observed strict silence while they worked; all the monks were required to do physical labor in addition to their devotions. They chose remote deserted sites and lonely valleys for their abbeys and did much of their own farming. They also instituted a system of lay monks. The abbot of the mother house would visit once a year, and a general chapter was held yearly at Citeaux. The thrust of the movement was its focus on the inner life, to be fostered by severe discipline and inspired by awe of nature.

Bernard of Clairvaux grew to be one of the most influential voices in Christendom. He wrote, "Believe one who has proved it, you will find among the woods something you never found in books. Stones and trees will teach you a lesson you never heard from masters in the school." ❑

The Cistercian Abbey of Maulbronn was founded in 1147

AN END TO THE INVESTITURE CONFLICT

Worms, September, 1122

A compromise solution to the struggle between the papacy and the German emperor was forged with the Concordat of Worms. The controversy had dominated the relations between church and state for over fifty years and had given rise to extensive debates between adherents on both sides.

The battle began in earnest when Pope Gregory VII, seeking to impose papal power over kings, excommunicated the German emperor, Henry IV, in 1076. His successor, Henry V, followed in his father's footsteps. He tried to set up an anti-pope to support his position, forcing his rival to take refuge in a monastery. At their meeting, Pope Callixtus II persuaded Henry to renounce his right to invest bishops with the ring and crozier and allow their free election. In return the pope agreed to the emperor's presence at the election of bishops and authorized him to intervene in the disputes that frequently occurred.

In practice this solution left the emperor with some influence, but it went some way toward establishing the papacy as the supreme Christian authority. Expressed in the symbolism of the two keys given to Peter by Christ, the church was able to make its case as the ultimate authority based upon its power to bind and loose souls. The relative strength of *temporalia* (temporal power) and *spiritualia* (spiritual power), however, was by no means settled. The Church would reach the pinnacle of its prestige one hundred years later under the guidance of Pope Innocent III and then gradually relinquish its hold over secular matters. ❑

Pope Calixtus emerged strengthened from the conflict over the investiture of bishops.

Holy Roman Emperor Henry V

FAILURE OF THE SECOND CRUSADE

Damascus, September 1148

The Second Crusade, led by King Conrad III of Germany and King Louis VII of France, was inspired by the preaching of Bernard of Clairvaux. It ended in humiliating failure. Conrad lost much of his army to the Turks on his way East, and the entire episode was fraught with disagreement and disaster. When the French and German armies met in Jerusalem, the royal Crusaders foolishly decided that rather than retake Edessa, whose fall into Turkish hands had been the impetus of the crusade, the two armies would attack the commercial center of Damascus, which lay outside of the Crusader States. The Frankish barons of northern Syria refused to take part;

Crusaders besiege Damascus (book illustration, 15th century)

after all, the emir of Damascus, Dnur, was an ally against the dangerous ruler of Aleppo, Nur ad-Din.

When they arrived outside Damascus, the Crusaders learned that Dnur had appealed to Nur ad-Din, who had dispatched a relief force. After only four days, the Crusaders abandoned the siege and retreated. The road to Galilee was littered with corpses, and the legend of valiant knights from the west was shattered.

The sole bright spot for Christendom in the second crusade came from English and Flemish forces that, heading for the Middle East by ship, stopped in Portugal and were instrumental in the retaking of Lisbon from the Moors. This victory laid the foundation for the creation of the first kingdom of Portugal. ❏

BERNARD OF CLAIRVAUX'S EXHORTATION TO CRUSADERS

The Cistercian abbot Bernard of Clairvaux called upon the crusaders to renounce sin and look to the salvation of their souls:

"You noble knights … now you face a battle without danger, where victory brings fame and death salvation. Be wise men of business, great profit awaits you, do not turn your backs on it. Take up the sign of the cross, and you will achieve what you long for with a pure heart. The cost is cheap for what you are purchasing is the Kingdom of God." ❏

Bernard of Clairvaux (drawn from a fresco)

THE EMPEROR FREDERICK BARBAROSSA

Rome, 1155

Frederick Barbarossa (Red Beard) was a charismatic and powerful leader who was able to reassert imperial authority in Germany after a period of debilitation. With the pope's victory over the king in the investiture controversy, the German king had suffered a precipitous drop in prestige and an equally problematic loss of revenue. The great feudal lords had expanded their powers at the expense of the king. Under his predecessors, the king had control only of his own family's holdings. German politics was dominated by two great feuding noble houses: the Hohenstauffens, who were the descendants of the Salian dynasty, and

the Welfs, whose base of power was in Bavaria.

In 1152, Frederick Barbarossa was elected as king by the nobility, who asserted the old Germanic right of choosing their monarch. It was hoped that he would be able to alleviate the bitterness of the aristocratic rivalry, since he was a Hohenstauffen but also a Welf on his mother's side. The Welf connection did not, however, win over the Welf duke, Henry the Lion.

Historians have suggested that it was this continuing internal struggle that prompted Barbarossa to train his sights on Italy. The rich city-states that had grown up there over the

previous century were an obvious source of badly needed tax revenue. But perhaps just as important was the king's aspiration to revive the imperial monarchy. The writings of such thinkers as Otto of Freising and John of Salisbury were influential in the ongoing argument for a strong ruler with the authority and prerogatives of the old Roman emperors.

Frederick's first foray into Italy took place in 1154–1155. An uprising in Rome led by the firebrand Arnold of Brescia put Adrian IV, the only English-

TROUBADOUR POETS

Provence, c.1150

The first troubadour poets came from the Provençal region of France. Their verse displayed a new self consciousness. Most of their poems addressed themselves to the subject of love. They were generally sung to a musical accompaniment.

Troubadour poetry stemmed originally from courtly circles but also found exponents in the newly emerging cities of southern France. While many poets remained closely tied to their aristocratic patrons, others, called *jongleurs* (minstrels), wandered widely and included *chansons de geste* (songs of adventure) such as the *Song of Roland* in their repertoire.

The troubadours came from all rungs of society. There were even women troubadour poets, the best-known being Beatriz de Dia. The first troubadour seems to have been Duke William of Aquitaine (1071-1127), whose poetry reflected his aristocratic ideals and concerns.

One of the most enduring conventions of troubadour lyric was the love for a lady of a higher social position, whom the poet looked upon in an idealized fashion. Islamic culture also had an impact. It has even been suggested that the derivation of the word troubadour comes from the Arabic word for drum, though the more common derivation is from the French word *trouver*, meaning "to find." The Crusade against the Albigensians in southern France disrupted the Provençal tradition. ❑

Troubadour with a psaltery, an early form of a harp

KING HENRY II AND THOMAS BECKET

England, mid-twelfth century

Before Thomas Becket became the doomed archbishop of Canterbury, he was the Lord Chancellor of England under Henry II. Together the king and Becket taxed the Church and rode to hounds. When Henry appointed Becket as archbishop, he expected his dear friend to continue to do his bidding.

But Becket underwent a conversion. Donning a hair shirt, he defied the king and put the interests of his office and the Church above those of the state. Thus began a protracted debate between king and archbishop. On one occasion Becket waved his crozier at the king and told him he had no right to judge him.

For two years, Becket was forced to take refuge in France. When Henry had his son crowned in Westminster Abbey by the archbishop of York, assisted by six bishops, Becket denounced the action and excommunicated the bishop.

Soon thereafter, with all of Britain threatened by excommunication, Henry appeared to compromise and invited Beckett back on his own terms. In actuality the king's fury remained unappeased. He is reported to have finally demanded, "Who will free me from this troublesome priest?"

Four knights of the royal household gave Henry the answer. They struck down Becket in the transept of his own cathedral. The archbishop struggled for several minutes as his assailants hastened his martyrdom. The place of his death became a shrine visited by pilgrims from near and far, including Henry himself. Becket was canonized in 1173. ❑

Funerary monument of King Henry II (end of 12th century)

man ever to become pope, in a conciliatory frame of mind. Frederick put down the rebellion, executed Arnold, and in 1155, the pope crowned Frederick emperor.

But this was no sweeping victory. The Church continued to be divided between those who saw the emperor as a defender and those who considered him a threat; it opted for lending its support to the increasingly powerful city-states. The ascension of anti-imperial Alexander III to the papacy in 1159 decided the matter. Frederick embarked on three full-scale military campaigns into Italy over a twenty-year period. In 1174, the Italian city-states joined together in the Lombard League, won a decisive victory over the German forces, and the emperor was forced to relinquish all but nominal claims to Italy.

Meanwhile the German nobles, who had been expanding their territories east of the Elbe, continued to make trouble for him. Frederick brought his old enemy Henry the Lion to trial and succeeded in dispossessing him of the greater part of his holdings, but the benefit devolved upon the other noble houses rather than the emperor himself.

In 1189, Frederick left for Jerusalem as part of the Third Crusade. He died while crossing the Saleph River in Anatolia. ❑

THE EUROPEAN MIDDLE AGES

The period described as the Middle Ages in Europe begins with the fall of the Western Roman Empire in the fifth century. This period was marked by the supremacy and unity of the Catholic Church. It ended with the overseas explorations that started in 1492 and the Reformation, which destroyed that unity.

Geographically, the phenomenon of the Middle Ages was at first limited to the Roman-Germanic peoples of western and central Europe; seen from Italy, these were all situated to the west and were therefore collectively known as the Occident. Subsequently the Christians expanded and gradually incorporated north and east central Europe. Meanwhile the southern parts of the Apennine and Iberian peninsulas were wrested from Islamic occupation after fierce military conflicts. On the other hand, the Crusades failed in their attempt to incorporate the Byzantine Empire and Middle East within the sphere of influence of the West.

Medieval life was influenced both by Christianity and by the Germanic outlook and way of life. The encounter between the Celtic and Germanic tribes and the late Roman Empire resulted in the Germanic tribes' adopting Christianity and accepting the organization of the Church, as well as acquiring some aspects of the Roman cultural heritage and even parts of the Roman systems of law and administration. They also adopted certain forms of the Roman economy, particularly in the field of agriculture, taking on some of the methods of running large estates. They combined these with elements from their cultural tradition, such as the principle of personal allegiance and a social organization that divided society into noble-men, freemen, and slave-like half-freed men. Of especial importance to the development of arts and literature was their strong sense of the symbolic in an unpredictable world.

THE FRANKS AND THE BIRTH OF EUROPE

The early development of the western medieval world was influenced above all by the Frankish Empire. Under Charlemagne it included all of the territories that were still Christian in western and central Europe. Charlemagne also extended his authority in Spain, where he came up against Islam, and in the east, where he came into conflict with the non-Christian Germanic and Slavonic tribes. His greatest success here was the integration of Saxony, the dominant families of which later played a leading role in the European political arena (the Ottonian dynasty). The alliance of the Carolingian Empire with the papacy served to validate his claim to the title King of the Franks. In return Charlemagne's increased stature enhanced the status of the bishops of Rome, whose spiritual supremacy was now recognized by the whole of western Christendom. When Pope Leo III crowned Charlemagne emperor in 800, the Frankish Empire was linked to the Western Roman Empire that had fallen in 476. The West achieved its first cultural rebirth with the intellectual and artistic revival that has come to be known as the Carolingian Renaissance.

This empire was, however, too vast and too thinly populated to be able to resist external attacks for long. The main antagonists were the Normans, invaders from the north, who attacked and plundered the coastal regions. To make matters worse, there were also internal conflicts. Soon the Frankish Empire broke up into smaller empires in the Alpine region and in Italy, as well as into two larger parts: the West Frankish Empire, which became France and the East Frankish Empire from which the German Empire (*Regnum Teutonicum*) developed. Here the old regional office holders, the dukes and earls, retained their power.

FEUDALISM, SOCIETY AND THE STATE

The king gave these noble lords large estates, the yield of which provided their income. Many smaller noblemen and free farmers sought the protection of these lords who "gave" them land to work in return for part of its yield. Thus the ownership of a large feudal estate (in Latin, *feudum*) was a prerequisite for raising the funds necessary to maintain an army. Vassals had a feudal obligation to offer military service to their lord when called upon to do so. Over time feudal estates became hereditary, and as supreme feudal lord, the king often came into conflict with his powerful vassals. Feudal society developed as a result of this social organization. It was determined and shaped by a system that consisted of graduated social layers, starting with the emperor or king at the top, through the great vassals and down to the smaller "subinfeudatory" vassals. They all lived off their dependent subject farmers, to whom they owed protection in return.

POLITICAL ORGANIZATION

Another path was followed by the East Frankish, or German, kings, who with Otto I renewed their alliance with the pope, and in 962 became emperors. To reinforce their combined personal and imperial estates, they relied heavily on ecclesiastical authorities. They appointed bishops and abbots, who were given secular rights and carried out administrative and military duties. By the eleventh century, the popes had begun to assert their authority both in the spiritual matters of the Church and in the administration of ecclesiastical lands, and they contested the emperor's right to appoint bishops. The contest between secular and religious powers dominated European politics for almost two hundred years. In the end the power of both institutions was diminished in favor of the growing power of hereditary princes and dukes and newly emerging urban centers.

In contrast, the West Frankish kings (since 987, the Capetians) established themselves as hereditary monarchs and developed an efficient central administration. The same was

The Cistercians became the pioneers of a new ascetic philosophy: the Cistercian abbey of Fontenay was founded by Bernard of Clairvaux in 1118.

true of England, which was conquered in 1066 by the Norman duke, William the Conqueror. In due course the kings found it necessary to share power with the representatives of the aristocracy, especially when events required additional revenue. Out of these sporadic assemblies grew the notion of permanent representation in the form of the Estates General in France and the Parliament in England.

Town and country

A determining factor for life in the Middle Ages was the growth of towns and cities. Many towns developed around an Episcopal see or at the crossroads of regional and long-distance trade routes. A settlement became a town when a lord granted it the rights to hold a market, to build fortifications and to govern itself. The foundation of a town could serve to strengthen the sovereignty of a prince, or the town could be completely autonomous. There were fewer towns in Central Europe, springing up on the sites of ancient Roman urban settlements, many of which had fallen into serious decline. In the Holy Roman Empire, many towns were subject to the emperor alone, which meant that they were effectively independent. Citizens formed guilds based upon shared professions. They would regulate and oversee the production and sale of particular kinds of articles and goods. Many towns formed alliances, such as the Hanseatic League, which developed in the twelfth century. Meanwhile others—Venice and Florence, for instance—developed into independent city-states with large territories.

In rural areas, free and unfree farming communities developed along similar lines. The enforced associations of serf-farmers who were subject to the manor farm of a clerical or secular landowner developed during the twelfth and thirteenth centuries into associations with greater independence in village settlements. The growing displacement of the barter economy by money transactions made it easier to redeem burdensome obligations. But individually the farmers remained just as dependent as before, still committed to render services and pay contributions to their landlord. Nevertheless the reduction of encumbrances made it possible to increase agricultural production enough that it kept pace with the growth of the population, from about 5.5 million in central and western Europe in the year 650 to about 35.5 million in 1340.

Architecture, music and literature

The Middle Ages reached their cultural high point in the twelfth and thirteenth centuries. The first medieval architectural style, dating from 950, was Romanesque, characterized by massive walls and small windows. It found its chief expression in churches and was improved upon by the addition of arches and vaults. Technical innovations led to the development of the Gothic style, with pointed arches and ribbed vaults, that permitted a far greater use of glass. Earlier churches were dark closed spaces. Gothic cathedrals were filled with light, conceived with the express purpose of leading the worshipper to the contemplation of God. Characteristic of these monumental church buildings were their vast interiors, such as those of Notre Dame in Paris and the Cologne cathedral; such a church was no longer perceived as an assemblage of separate rooms but as a unit. Gothic architecture made its first appearance in about 1140 at St. Denis, and from there spread throughout Europe.

Sculpture, stained glass and the burgeoning art of painting on wooden panels developed in close parallel with church architecture. Music too was closely connected with the Church, but several forms of secular music also developed in the eleventh century, such as the songs of the southern French troubadours. Courtly literature was closely connected with chivalry and the nobility, and it included several genres, the most important being epic or heroic poetry, such as *The Song of Roland* and *The Song of the Nibelungs*, Arthurian legend and songs of courtly love. In Italy Dante elevated the vernacular into a vehicle that could express and encompass the totality of the medieval world view. In the thirteenth and fourteenth centuries, a more bourgeois form of literature developed that found its finest expression in English with Chaucer's *Canterbury Tales*.

Changing worldview

Gradually horizons widened both at home and abroad. This was partly influenced by increased and closer contacts with the neighboring cultures of Islam and Byzantium. At the same time, people began to call into question previously accepted knowledge and beliefs, including the perception of the Church as the sole arbiter of Western tradition. Even within the Church, theologians felt the need to prove a correspondence between the teachings of the Church and rational, intellectual thinking. Scholastic theology tried to arrive at the scientific knowledge of truth based on the doctrine of faith and, conversely, to substantiate the dogmas of the Church in a rational way, based on abstract thought. Opposing this was the Cistercian abbot Bernard of Clairvaux (c.1090–1153), who was the voice of conservatism and an ardent proponent of monasticism. In addition to the educational

Cupping was a widespread therapy in medicine in the Middle Ages (15th century).

role of the Church and monasteries, universities now emerged as centers for new ideas.

One of the reasons for the gradual weakening of the Church's dominance was that the stature of the papacy was diminished by the emergence of competing ideologies and widespread corruption. The election of two popes created a schism in the Church, and unity was restored only with great difficulty in the beginning of the fourteenth century after a series of Church councils. Medieval Europe was now characterized by great diversity in state systems, economic development, and spiritual and cultural achievements. In addition, there was a drastic change in consciousness in the wake of the plague epidemics that descended upon Europe since 1348.

The great plague epidemic known as the Black Death hit an overpopulated continent that was already devastated by famine. By the middle of the fifteenth century, one-third of the population of Europe had been killed by the plague. Entire villages were depopulated; fertile fields reverted into barren land. As a result of stagnant production and falling prices, Europe's largely agricultural economy entered a state of crisis. Many farmers abandoned the fields and fled to the towns.

The end of the Middle Ages was a time of misery and poverty, marked by religious longings for self-chastisement on earth as a preparation for the afterlife. But at the same time it heralded a flourishing revival in the field of literature and the arts that would become known as the Renaissance. ❑

HILDEGARD VON BINGEN

Germany, 1179

Hildegard died at the age of 81 on Setpember 17, 1179. At the time of her death, she was the abbess of the Rupertsberg Convent and well known for her transcriptions of her mystical visions. She was unusually outspoken for a woman of her time, offering her opinions on religious and political topics. In addition to the deep spirituality that infused her writings, her curiosity led her to examine the natural world closely.

Hildegard was born in 1098, the tenth child of a noble family. She received a religious education. Between 1147 and 1150, she participated in building the convent at Rupertsberg near Bingen and became its abbess in 1151.

Hildegard was the author of more than three hundred letters, which she sent to popes, princes, and bishops, and even some to Emperor Frederick Barbarossa.

Beginning in 1141, Hildegard began to write down her visions. These were collected in *Liber scivia* (*Book of Knowing*) and in *Liber vitae meritorum* (*Book of Life Worth Living*). These books contain descriptions of her encounters with God and her visions of the cosmos.

Hildegard saw the cosmos as the unique creation of God in which everything is wonderfully ordered, existing in perfect harmony. As God's "precious pearl," the human being has a very exalted position, but also grave responsibilities for contributing to the balance of the cosmic order.

The abbess was not only interested in theology; she was a devoted student of natural science as well. In addition to a comprehensive work on the subject, she also wrote a treatise on the causes and treatments of disease (*Causae et curae*). In this work, she discusses conception, pregnancy, and birth with clarity and concern for the patient's health. Her recommendations for the treatment of disease show a deep knowledge of natural remedies. Hidlegard was also a fine composer; 77 of her sacred hymns have been preserved. ❑

Cosmic Man from Hildegard's *Book of God's Works*

ARNOLD OF BRESCIA

Rome, 1155

The idealistic priest Arnold of Brescia, who preached the joys of purity and poverty, was sentenced to death and burned for heresy. His ashes were thrown into the Tiber. The Arnoldist movement, which stressed apostolic poverty for the clergy and held sacraments invalid if administered by priests who owned worldly goods, threatened to split the church, since Arnold allied himself with an anti-papal party. This is why Pope Adrian IV welcomed Barbarossa; he needed the German's help to suppress Arnold's movement. ❑

RISE OF CITIES

Point of Interest

The eleventh century witnessed a revival of commerce in Europe. By the following century, cities began to assume even greater importance as market and trading centers.

Existing settlements grew into cities and new cities were founded. Many grew up in previously undeveloped areas, such as the eastern part of Germany. Most important for the founding of a prosperous city was its geographic location along major trading routes, either rivers or well-traveled roads. A city's founders—whether kings, bishops, or lords—would often grant it special privileges, including exemption from some taxes or feudal duties, and allow it a measure of self-government. The relative freedom of the urban environment and the need for labor drew in people from the countryside. By the end of the Middle Ages, the political power of the semiautonomous cites rivaled that of the aristocracy and clergy. ❑

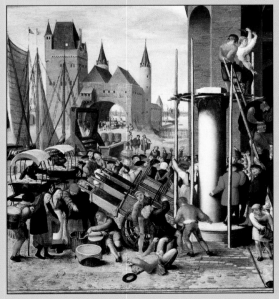

Founding of a city

Mayan Center Destroyed

Central America, 1179

During a period of considerable anarchy in Central America, the Mayan city of Chichen Itza was sacked and burnt by Hunac Ceel, the ruthless and ambitious king of neighboring Mayapan.

Hunac Ceel's rise typified the disorder of the time. He gained control of his own Mayapan people through cunning and military prowess, and then formed an alliance with the Izamal state to attack Chichen Itza. After his successful campaign, he turned upon his former allies of Izamal.

Chichen Itza, famed as the center of Maya civilization and reestablished by Toltec exiles from Tula two hundred years before, was abandoned. Its great monumental buildings—the Temple of the Jaguars, the Temple of the Warriors, the vast ball court, the pyramid-shaped Castillo, and the Caracol (the sacred well)—were deserted. Those who survived the sacking fled south into the wilderness around Lake Peten Itza, where the last survivors of Maya civilization maintained a precarious independence around their new capital, Tayasal. ❑

Europe's First University

Bologna, 1158

The laws surrounding the establishment of the University of Bologna facilitated the growth and spread of universities throughout Europe. The University of Bologna was founded as a school of law in 1119. In 1158, a charter by Emperor Frederick Barbarossa, *Authentica habit*, conferred economic and civil prerogatives on its faculty and students. They were absolved from their responsibilities to other powers and allowed to pursue their academic work under the direct protection of the emperor. The privileges were not, however, bestowed upon the university as an entity, but upon its members as individuals, giving them freedom of movement.

Within a few years, the university had enrolled as many as ten thousand students. Schools of medicine, theology, and philosophy were created in addition to its law school. Upon entrance to the university, students were required to take up a general course of study. This consisted of what was known as the *trivium* and *quadrivium*, the seven subjects that were considered to be the foundations of higher education: grammar, rhetoric, dialectic (the *trivium*), and arithmetic, geometry, music, and astronomy (the *quadrivium*). After completion of this course of study, the student could then concentrate on a more specialized field. Classes were conducted in Latin.

Following the model of Bologna, other existing schools transformed themselves into universities, offering a general education and then the opportunity to pursue a specialized curriculum. Early examples are the universities at Salerno and Montpelier.

In other places, schools attached to monasteries developed into full-fledged universities. Such was the case at Oxford and at the Sorbonne in Paris. New universities were created as offshoots of previously existing ones, as was the case with Cambridge and Padua. In the fourteenth century, a number of universities were established in Germany and Eastern Europe, the most well-known being those at Prague, Cologne, and Heidelberg. ❑

Lecturer at the University of Bologna

Muslim Kingdom in West Africa

Point of Interest

The Kingdom of Mali extended in the fourteenth century far to the north and east and prospered through a lively trade in salt and gold. Established around 1100 in the region of the Upper Nile, it first came to prominence at the end of the twelfth century. Over the next two hundred years, it became the leading power in West Africa.

All of the rulers of Mali were Muslims. At the beginning of the twelfth century during a period of fierce drought, their king had converted to Islam. According to the great Arabic geographer and traveler, Ibn Khaldun, the rain began immediately following the king's conversion, and the famine that had been afflicting the land came to an end.

A detailed account exists of a pilgrimage to Mecca undertaken by Mali's King Kanakan Musa (r.1312–1337). It was said that he distributed twenty thousand gold pieces as alms to the poor. With his death, decline set in. At the beginning of the fifteenth century, Mali fell into the hands of the Sonni from the neighboring Kingdom of Songhai. ❑

Great Mosque of Djenné (Mali)

Reliquary of the Three Kings

Point of Interest

A remarkable work of reliquary art was designed and built in the workshop of Nicholas of Verdun to hold relics of the Three Kings. Nicholas began work on the reliquary for Cologne Cathedral in 1181. Before this his most highly praised work was a magnificent altar built for the monastery church Stift Klosterneunburg (just north of present-day Vienna). Now known

Reliquary of the Three Kings

as the Verdun Altar, it is considered to be one of the finest examples of Romanesque metalwork. The altar features 67 engraved and enameled plaques showing scenes from the Old and New Testaments.

In 1164, the bones of the Three Kings were given to the archbishop of Cologne by Frederick Barbarossa, along with relics of Saints Felix, Nabor, and George. ❑

RISE OF THE SHOGUNS

Japan, 1192

The rise of the Japanese military class, the *samurai*, and their Shogun leaders, began in the Heian period (c.795–1185) during the waning fortunes of the powerful Fujiwara clan. The Fujiwara, who had exerted control over the Imperial throne for centuries, began to lose influence after 1016, and public order broke down. Wealthy landowners protected themselves by hiring members of the *samurai*. By the end of the Fujiwara reign, this class had created its own politically influential families.

The strongest of these were the Taira (or Heike) and the Minamoto (or Genji). The Taira assumed government positions previously held by the Fujiwara, and the Minamoto gained an increasing number of leadership roles in the military. Their competition with remnants of the Fujiwara clan and between each other broke out in earnest with the Hogen and Heiji Rebellions.

The Hogen Rebellion in 1156 was a civil war over imperial succession fought between Emperor Go-Shirakawa and his predecessor Emperor Sutoku upon the death of their father, Emperor Toba. The two sides called in the assistance of the Taira and Minamoto families. Some members of the Taira backed Go-Shirakawa, and others backed Sutoku; members of the Minamoto were similarly split. The result of this complex internecine struggle was a victory by Go-Shirakawa that elevated members from both samurai families to special imperial status.

The imperial recognition of both the Taira and the Minamoto not only vastly increased their respective power in Japanese society, but also set them on a collision course that would result in the Heiji Rebellion of 1159.

Again, it was fealty to different emperors, this time the cloistered Emperor Go-Shirakawa and his son Emperor Nijo, that inspired the struggle between the two powerful military clans. The outcome

Yorimoto Minamoto was the first to hold the title of Shogun (Japanese painting, Tokyo National Museum).

was even more significant than that of the Hogen Rebellion because, for the first time, a *samurai* family rose to a position of parity with the imperial household. Ending in the defeat of the Minamoto, the Taira had, if only temporarily, become rulers of Japan.

In 1168, Kiyomori, a member of the Taira family, was given the imperial appointment of *Daijo Daijin*, chief minister of the government, ruling through what was a figurehead emperor. Creating an administration dominated by *samurai* loyal to him, Kiyomori was the first of the military class to wield almost unrivaled power. By 1180, he had become an object of resentment, even among members

of his own clan. This resentment fueled the Genpei War and the founding of Japan's first true *samurai* shogunate, the Kamakura.

The war began in June 1180 with the Battle of Uji, at the Uji River near Kyoto. The Taira forces under Taira no Tomomori defeated the Minamoto, whose leader, Minamoto no Yorimasa, avoided surrendering by committing the first recorded act of *seppuku*, ritual suicide. The war raged throughout Japan for the next five years and ended on April 25, 1185 with the Minamoto winning the decisive Battle of Dan-no-ura. During this sea battle, the Taira installed child-emperor Antoku, and most of the Taira

nobles perished at sea and, with them, the reign of the Taira clan. When the fleets met at Dan-no-ura, in the straits between Honshu and Kyushu, it seemed at first as if the numerically superior Tairas would win. But when the tide changed and began to rip through the narrow straits, the Minamoto ships gained the advantage and, aided by nature, destroyed the Taira fleet.

The official ascendancy of the Minamoto to unrivaled leadership and the founding of Japan's first shogunate, the Kamakura Bakufu, took place on August 21, 1192, when Yoritomo Minamoto was named shogun by the emperor. ❑

The Death of Emperor Frederick Barbarossa

Asia Minor, 10 June 1190

In 1189, at the behest of Pope Gregory VIII, Emperor Frederick I Barbarossa, Philip II of France, and Richard I (Lionheart) of England embarked on the Third Crusade to drive the Islamic forces of Saladin out of Anatolia and to recapture Jerusalem. The 64-year-old emperor never reached the Holy Land. After crossing the Taurus mountains, the exhausted Frederick and his army were nearing the port of Seleucia, when traversing the shallow Saleph River (today's Göksu), the emperor fell off his horse and drowned. What caused the plunge has been disputed among historians; it has been suggested that he suffered a heart attack. ❑

Frederick Barbarossa as crusader (manuscript illustration, 1188)

Maimonides

Cairo, December 13, 1204

Maimonides, the controversial Jewish doctor and philosopher, died at the age of 69. His rationalism was seen by fundamentalists as being too unorthodox.

Born in Córdoba but forced out by the Almohads, Maimonides lived at Fez for ten years, where his family was obliged to convert to Islam. In a letter to the Jews of Yemen, he argued that forced conversion was no sin if loyalty to Israel was secretly maintained.

In Cairo, he became a doctor in the sultan's court and a spokesman for the Jewish community. He wrote the Mishneh Torah, summarizing Jewish law and ritual, in Mishnaic Hebrew. His most famous work is *The Guide for the Perplexed*. Written in 1190, it is the most complete expression of his religous philosophy. It

Maimonides wrote the central work of medieval Jewish philosophy

remains widely read as the

Maimonides exemplified the concept of the prophet-lawmaker, modeled on Moses, but played down traditional Jewish eschatology and stressed the eternal survival of the human soul. ❑

The Life and Death of Richard Lionheart

France, 1199

Richard the Lionheart, crowned king of England in 1189, spent his early life in France as Duke of Aquitaine, ruling the land of his mother, Eleanor, and fighting his father, Henry II. Henry had acquired vast territories in France by his marriage, and his sons were never satisfied with their shares. Richard's first act as king was to release his mother, who had been confined for supporting him against her husband.

Richard led the Third Crusade to the Holy Lands with Philip II Augustus of France. The English king fought valiantly and won battles against Saladin, the sultan of Egypt, but the Christian armies failed to hold on to their gains. After sixteen months of fighting, Richard had taken Acre, but Jerusalem was still in Muslim hands. Richard made the best of a bad job and patched up a truce with Saladin in 1192, under which the Christians would

keep a few coastal towns and were promised free access to the church of the Holy Sepulchre in Jerusalem.

On his return, Richard was captured by the Duke of Austria, who turned him over to the German Henry VI. A ransom of 150,000 gold marks was demanded. It was never paid in full, but even the first installment severely strained the resources of England.

Richard was rumored to have been homosexual, despite which he was portrayed as an exemplary knight for his efforts in the crusades and his military prowess. His nickname "Lionheart" was given to him in France, as *coeur de lion*. For the ten years that he was king of England, Richard spent no more than six months in the country. Indeed, he never learned English. He died in France besieging the castle of a disobedient baron. ❑

The Emperor Henry VI taking King Richard Lionheart prisoner

KING ARTHUR AND THE KNIGHTS OF THE ROUND TABLE

France, early thirteenth century

Arthurian legend was born out of the marriage between Celtic mythology and the French courtly tradition, in the concise formulation of the great Arthurian scholar Jean Frappier. There was apparently a real person named Arthur. A Scottish poem dating from the eighth century refers to a knight who, though brave, "was no Arthur." Another early source identifies him as *dux bellorum* (warlord). Whatever the historical reality, his figure soon attracted stories and legends. In Geoffrey of Monmouth's *Historia Regum Brittanorum* (*History of the Kings of England*), Arthur plays a prominent role. He is said to have fought a giant on what is now the island of Mont St. Michel.

But it was through the work of the French poet Chrétien de Troyes that the legend was cast in a form that would capture the imagination of the courts of Europe. Chrétien left behind four poems—*Eric and Enid*, *Lancelot*, *Yvain*, and *Perceval*—that provide the basic elements of the legend along with a

narrative structure that most of the retellings would follow. Here we find the King surrounded by his knights, who sit at a round table so that none has a higher place than another. Chrétien presented the ideal knight as one who embodies the code of chivalry, particularly in

Wolfram von Eschenbach with page

his reverent approach to women.

The many variants of the Arthurian legend delineate the rise and fall of Arthur's kingdom: the adulterous affair between King Uther Pendragon and the wife of his vassal, the Duke of Cornwall, which through the agency of Merlin led to Arthur's birth; Arthur's election as king; the establishment of justice in the kingdom; the fatal love between Lancelot and Arthur's queen Guinevere; the treachery of Arthur's nephew Mordred; and the death of Arthur with the promise that he would return in England's hour of need.

Upon this frame were attached numerous adventures. Most begin with Arthur and his court sitting in Camelot awaiting the arrival of some marvelous occurrence, whether a maiden harried by hounds, or a challenge thrown down by a giant green knight. In response one or more of the knights ventures out into the mysterious world that lay beyond the ordered society of the court and is

tested in various ways. His success or failure is then ratified by the assembled knights upon his return.

Although containing cursory reference to the Christian devotion of the knights, these stories were essentially secular in orientation. In response the church appropriated the legend for its own ends, Christianizing it with the story of the quest for the grail. As with the rest of the legend, the Grail story seems to have its ultimate source in Celtic mythology where are found stories of magical vessels stolen from the underworld. In outline: the vessel appears to the court, the knights are sent out in search of it, but to succeed in this quest requires holiness, not chivalry. In the story as told by Wolfram von Eschenbach, the knight who succeeds in locating the grail is Parzival, who is first seen as a parody of a knight, a country bumpkin who has to learn the ways of chivalry. It is innocence and purity that help him win. In other variants the grail is found by Galahad, Lance-

CRUSADERS DESPOIL CONSTANTINOPLE

Constantinople, June 1204

For three days, soldiers wrenched ornate crosses from the high altar, hacked anything of value from the walls, and burned works of art. The surprise in all this was not the destrction but that the pillagers claimed to be Christians who had taken religious vows three years before to join a crusade and respect places of worship.

The vows were discarded on the road to Constantinople, the the commercial hub of the eastern Mediterranean. It was also the seat of the Orthodox Christian Church. The pillage was carried out by Catholic Christians, mostly Frenchmen, with the backing of Venetian entrepreneurs. They did it in the name of religious unity. In fact, it was a short cut to repayment of a loan to fund the Fourth Crusade.

The whole expeditionary force was excommunicated by Pope Innocent III, who had called for a crusade to Palestine. The Venetian doge, Enrico Dandolo, contracted to supply ships for thirty thousand men, but only ten thousand volunteered. Their leader Boniface, the Marquess of Montferrat, agreed to seize Constantinople and share the city's wealth "to the honor of God, the pope, and empire," and pay the Venetians.

After the sack of its capital, the Byzantine empire was divided into three parts as war booty. A Latin was given the title of Emperor, displacing nearly a thousand years of Greek rule. Venice collected the Adriatic east coast, both shores of the Gulf of Corinth, islands such as Andros, and swathes of Albania, as well as the mantle of the leading

Domenico Tintoretto, *The Capture of Constantinople* (detail)

trade power of the Mediterranean.

Many territories that were "awarded" to the French Boniface and his henchmen—Macedonia, for example—had yet to be con-

quered. The new power arrangement in Constantinople foretold of increased instability in the region and would result in further warfare. ❏

SIEGRFRIED, LEGENDARY GERMAN HERO

Germany, early thirteenth century

lot's illegitimate son.

The allure of Arthur and his court was felt in all corners of Europe. The most widely read English version was set down by Thomas Malory late in the fifteenth century. His *Morte d'Arthur* tells the entire saga and remained the definitive retelling for hundreds of years. But tales of Arthur and his knights can also be found in German, Italian, even Hebrew. Its appeal has been remarkably durable. During the Gothic revival of the nineteenth century, Alfred Tennyson reworked Malory's material to reflect the concerns and ideals of Victorian interest. Novels, poetry, and movies continue to be made about Arthurian legend. Modern-day treatments have been undertaken by John Steinbeck, Edward Arlington Robinson, and C. S. Lewis. J.R.R. Tolkein was profoundly influenced by the legend and was in fact the editor of wonderful Middle English retelling of the story, Sir Gawain and the Green Knight. ❑

In the *Niebelungenlied (Song of the Niebelung)*, different strands of German heroic poetry are brought together and reinterpreted. Exactly what *Niebelungen* refers to is somewhat obscure, but the first part of the poem treats it as the lands and treasure of Siegfried, the poem's hero. The *Niebelunglied* was written around the beginning of the thirteenth century by an anonymous poet who resided somewhere in the region around the Danube. It describes the heroic death of the dragon-slayer Siegfried and connects it with the downfall of the Burgundian kingdom.

The poem consists of 2400 verses. Although replete with mythic and legendary motifs, the poem reflects historical events. It appears to hearken back to the marriage between a Merovingian king into the royal house of Burgundy. The fate of the Burgundians as described in the poem combines elements from their defeat at the hands of Attila the Hun in 436 and the destruction of their kingdom by the Franks in 538.

The story of the *Niebelungen* is a complex one involving treasure, betrayal, murder, and revenge. It was composed in two parts. The first part deals with Siegfried, his marriage to Kriemhild, sister of Gunther the king of Burgundy, and Gunther's marriage to Brunhild. Conflicts between these characters lead to Siegfried's murder. The second part treats of the downfall of the Burgundian kingdom. Written in High Middle German, it was widely read throughout the Middle Ages. It is an invaluable reflection of courtly life in the twelfth century. The poem formed the basis of Wagner's monumental opera the *Ring Trilogy*. ❑

The *Niebelunglied* is preserved in ten manuscripts

GERMAN POETS OF COURTLY LOVE

Point of Interest

The *minnesangers* were poets who entertained at the courts of German nobility. Their style and themes were derived from the Provençal troubadour poets and reflected the ideals and self-image of German courtly society.

In the first phase, which lasted until about 1200, their songs celebrate the knight's service to his lady love. The object of the knight's affection is wholly idealized, and service to her will ennoble him morally. With the advent of the crusades, a second element came into play. The poet debates with himself whether he should devote himself to his lady at home or take up the cross and transfer his devotion to God.

After 1200, the *minnesang* assumed more diverse forms and developed a self-referential quality. In Hartmann von Aue's "Day Songs," the coming of dawn forces two lovers to say their farewells. The subjects of Walther von der Vogelweide's poetry were not necessarily noble ladies, rather they were drawn from all ranks of society. In place of the ideals of courtly love and service to the lady, he speaks of a love that comes from the heart. Neidhart von Reuenthal's poetry signals the decline of this genre. He uses the elevated romantic vocabulary of his predecessors as parody. ❑

Walther von der Vogelweide

Tannhäuser dressed as Teutonic Knight

THE CAPETIAN MONARCHY CONSOLIDATES ITS POWER

Flanders, 1214

Starting from a position of nominal overlordship but little power, the Capetians were gradually able to expand their demesne and resources through war and dynastic marriage. Philip II, who succeeded his father in 1180, exploited political trends and feudal obligations to dramatically increase the standing of the monarchy

Horace Vernet, *Battle of Bouvines*

and reshape the geopolitical map of Europe.

Philip's main rival was the Anglo-Angevin dynasty, which then held sway over England, Ireland, Wales, and a large part of France. In Philip's favor were ties of vassalage that bound the Angevins to him, and Richard Lionheart's early death, resulting in the succession of his brother John. John was unequal to the challenge of retaining control of his widespread holdings. In 1204, Philip took back Normandy by force of arms and was able to seize adjoining

Angevin lands soon after.

A decisive battle fought in Bouvines pitted Philip against John's alliance that combined Flemish lords and the imperial forces of the Holy Roman Emperor, Otto IV, his close ally. Philip's victory signaled the end of the Anglo-Angevin kingdom.

A peace treaty made at Chinon deprived John of almost all his continental holdings, even Anjou, which had been the birthplace of his great-grandfather Henry I. John was able to hold onto Aquitaine only through the pope's intervention.

The victory was also an important one for the Hohenstauffen ruler of Germany, Frederick II. His rival was Otto IV, who had been crowned emperor in 1209, but had little support. Otto was an ally of John, bound to him by blood and marriage. Forced to flee the battlefield, he lost all his political backing. With Philip's support, the way was prepared for Frederick II to realize his claim to the imperial throne. ❑

MAGNA CARTA

England, June 15, 1215

Generally recognized as one of Western history's most influential legal documents, the Magna Carta (Great Charter) was, in reality, more of a peace treaty than an official codification of common law. In it, England's King John, under the threat of armed insurrection, acceded to a number of demands made by his powerful barons. Although many of its 63 clauses would serve as the fundamental tenets underpinning English common law, its true significance lay in the fact that, for the first time, a king agreed in writing to share power with his subjects.

In 1202, when John sought to secure ancestral holdings in Normandy and Anjou from France's King Philip II, military conflicts erupted that would last for over a decade and that John would attempt to prosecute by unilaterally raising taxes and demanding his barons' military participation. Chafing at John's abrogation of unwritten English feudal custom requiring

INNOCENT III ASSERTS PAPAL AUTHORITY

Rome, 1215

Pope Innocent III was one of the most powerful popes of the Middle Ages. He systematically extended the power of the papacy after his investiture in January 1198. He exploited the rapid decline of Germany's power in Italy, following the death of the Emperor Henry VI in 1197, by persuading Henry's widow, the Empress Constance, to recognize his authority over Sicily. When Constance died, Innocent became sovereign of Sicily and regent of Germany while her son and heir, Frederick II, was a minor. He defeated protesting German nobles and used his moral authority to get his suzerainty recognized by kings as far away as England, Portugal, Poland, Hungary,

and Denmark.

Innocent reclaimed papal supremacy in the Papal States and, over the protests of German princes, asserted that, since it was the pope's duty to crown the German emperor, then it was only right that the pope should decide on his fitness for office. He also forced King John of England to accept Stephen Langton as archbishop of Canterbury. The high point of his papacy was the Third Lateran Council of 1215, which instituted important church reforms regarding regulation of the clergy and the duty of confession. ❑

Emperor Frederick II fostered the growth of art and science

ST. FRANCIS OF

Rome, 1210

St. Francis was born in 1181, the son of a wealthy cloth merchant. As a young man, he was painfully aware of the contrast between his riches and the suffering he saw around him. Much to the chagrin of his father, at the age of 24 he began to eschew his material privileges by attending to lepers in the lazar houses near Assisi. He then experienced the first of many mystical experiences. While in the Church of San Damiano, an image of Christ addressed him: "Francis, Francis, go and repair My house which, as you can see, is falling into ruins." He responded by selling personal items to help rebuild that very church. The true turning point in his life was occasioned in

that the King first consult his Barons before instituting such measures, many of them resisted. The result was the complete loss of his French possessions in 1204 and another ten years of fruitless military engagements that sapped English morale and bankrupted the economy.

Having lost the crucial support of his Barons, King John increased his general unpopularity by running afoul of Pope Innocent III. In 1207, when John rejected the Pope's choice of Stephen Langton as Archbishop of Canterbury, Innocent placed England under Interdict, thereby banning any public worship and the administration of the sacraments. After being excommunicated in 1209, John recanted and made a bad situation worse by surrendering England and Ireland to the pope, who then leased these new papal fiefdoms back to John.

By May of 1215, the barons had had enough. Capturing London, they forced John to meet with their representatives at Runnymede, where on June 15, he affixed his Great Seal to a document called Articles of the Barons. Shortly thereafter, the Royal Chancery produced the official version of this document now known as the Magna Carta. Among its provisions are those that laid the groundwork for the right of *habeas corpus.* ❑

453.—Specimen of Magna Charta, engraved from one of the Original Copies in the British Museum. The passages are a portion of the

In 63 articles the Magna Carta sets out the right of the nobility and church with respect to royal prerogatives

ASSISI AND THE FRANCISCAN ORDER

1209 by a sermon he heard on Matthew 10:19 in which Christ tells his followers to proclaim the Kingdom of Heaven unburdened by money or even shoes. This was the moment of conversion in which he embraced a life of apostolic poverty.

He began to wander barefoot through Umbria, proclaiming the Gospel and preaching repentance. He soon attracted a small following of fellow mendicants who called themselves *fratres minores* (lesser brothers). The religious order that grew out of this was the Order of Friars Minor, known eponymously as Franciscans.

The order was officially recognized by Pope Innocent III in 1210 when, according to legend, he experienced a vision in dream admonishing him to bestow his papal blessing upon it. ❑

St. Francis preaching to the birds (from a medieval altarpiece)

THE MONGOLS CONQUER AN EMPIRE

In 1206, the Khwiltai tribe, who lived near the mouth of the Onon river, proclaimed Temujin the Great Khan of all the Mongols. He called himself Genghis Khan (1155–1227). It was under his rule that the fast, strategic expansion of a Mongol people from central Asia began. It would culminte in the great empire of Kublai Khan (1215–1294). The Mongol expansion, known as the Mongol storm, spread fear and terror from China to Europe.

As fast as the rise of the Mongol empire had been—at its peak it stretched from the Gulf of Arabia to the northern regions of the Siberian Forest, and from the Black Sea to the Pacific—its decline was equally rapid. In the fourteenth century the empire broke into several autonomous regions that had existed before the decline. The Khanate of the Golden Horde lasted longest, surviving until the end of the eighteenth century, albeit under Ottoman rule.

THE RISE OF GENGHIS KHAN

At the time of Genghis Khan's birth, the Mongchol tribe lived near Lake Baikal and, together with the Naiman, Oirat, Kereït and Merkit tribes, formed the core of the tribal group that was united by Genghis Khan's grandfather. The families and tribes of the Central Asian steppes were nomadic livestock farmers who used the steppe as common grazing land. Many historians believe that their society was based on an egalitarian tribal structure, but that social hierarchies developed based on the ownership of livestock. Their election of a leader to take charge of hunting and plundering expeditions soon led to the development of a military elite whose privileges increased considerably under Genghis Khan.

The influence of the family to which Temujin belonged had faded with the death of his father Yesügei in about 1165. In the *Secret History of the Mongols* (1241), the childhood of the future Great Khan is described as extremely poor and difficult. With the help of Tugrul, the khan of the Kereït tribe, he succeeded in acquiring the status of a minor prince. Like his grandfather and father before him, he formed alliances with other clans and so regained possession of his former property. In the course of a war lasting ten years, he subjugated or destroyed rival tribes then went on to defeat his former protector Tugrul, and in 1206 he was proclaimed Great Khan of all the tribes east of the Altai mountains. Although already 50 years old at the time, he

Representation of the siege of Baghdad by the Mongols (Persian, 14th century).

began building a military organization and set down a code of laws, the *Yassa*, to help him govern his fast-growing empire.

The aggressive nature of Mongolian warfare can be explained by their nomadic lifestyle. A large portion of the population could be under arms without affecting the tribal economy. Livestock breeding could not be expanded significantly, so the acquisition of more wealth was possible only through conquest and, more importantly, by taxes on trade caravans. Aiming to expand his influence, Genghis Khan first turned his attention to the east and southeast. The objective of his military campaign was the northern part of China, which had been conquered by the Jurchens in 1126 and had remained under the control of the dynasty they established, the Jin.

After conquering the Oirat and Kyrgyz people (1206–1209), as well as the Tanguts, he assembled an army of two hundred thousand men to attack China. By the end of the year, the army had crossed the Great Wall and was advancing in several groups on Beijing, where they regrouped again in 1214. The terms of a peace agreement that had been reached were violated by the Chinese. The emperor fled, and the Mongols destroyed Beijing in 1215, inflicting terrible carnage upon the civilian population. A year later the army had returned to its permanent camp in Karakorum,

to the south of Lake Baikal.

THE ADVANCE WESTWARD

Rebellion and unrest in the western territories of Turkestan and the Altai mountains caused Genghis Khan to send two Mongol armies to the troubled regions, bringing them back under control in 1218. This military campaign brought Genghis Khan into direct contact with the Shah Muhammad II, who ruled over the Persian Khwarezmid empire around Bukhara and Tashkent. Although the two rulers exchanged messages in which they both recognized each other's claims, war still broke out. A governor of the Shah had ordered the destruction of a Mongolian caravan of 450 people. Genghis Khan's ambassadors who went to demand satisfaction were themselves executed. The war lasted from 1219 until 1221 and ended with the Mongol conquest of the Persians. The Shah had died on an island in the Caspian Sea in the first year of the war.

During this military operation, two Mongol generals pushed as far as the lower reaches of the Volga, where they encountered an army eighty thousand strong assembled by Russian princes. On 31 May 1223 (some sources mention 16 June 1224), the Mongols smashed the Russian army in the Battle of the Kalka River. After this decisive victory, Genghis Khan resumed his conquest of China. He died in

1227 during a campaign against a coalition of the Jin and Western Xia.

THE PINNACLE OF MONGOL EXPANSION

Genghis Khan had entrusted his giant empire, which was already divided into administrative districts, to his four sons, designating his third son Ogodei as his primary heir. Upon Genghis Khan's death, Jochi took the land of the Kyrgyz, but he died in the same year and was succeeded by his son Batu, who extended his territories further westward. Chagatai had Central Asia, and Ogodei had the regions of the Altai mountains and the regions near the Irtysch River. Tolui, the youngest son, ruled in the tribal territories of the Mongols. In accordance with Genghis Khan's wish, Ogodei became Great Khan of the whole empire in 1229.

In 1235, after he had completed his conquest of China, the new Khan called a meeting of dignitaries to discuss a major military campaign to conquer the West. In the summer of 1236, about 150,000 horsemen gathered near the upper reaches of the Volga, and in 1237–1238, they occupied the first towns to the west of the river. The following winter, the Mongols continued their conquest of Russia, which culminated two years later in the fall of Kiev. Only the town of Novgorod, which was situated in the middle of marshes, was able to withstand the Mongol attacks, but because of the twin threat posed by the Mongols to the east and the crusaders to the west, it finally became politically dependent upon the Mongols.

Dividing their forces into several separate formations, the Mongols then pushed forward as far as Hungary and Poland, spreading fear and terror on their way. On April 9, 1241, a German-Polish army of horsemen led by Henry II, duke of Silesia, attempted to halt the Mongol invasion near Liegnitz, but they were soundly defeated by the highly mobile Mongol horsemen. At almost the same time, on April 11, a Hungarian army led by King Bela IV suffered a crushing defeat at the hands of the Mongol southern army. Now almost all of Hungary was under the control of the Khan, and the vanguard of the army was already in Austria. But the situation changed suddenly and dramatically. On December 11, 1241, the Great Khan Ogodei died unexpectedly in the capital Karakorum. According to Genghis Khan's legal code, all the successors of the first ruler had to take part in the election of a new ruler.

THE REIGN OF KUBLAI KHAN

When Ogodei died, the first signs of tension in the empire began to emerge. The Mongol Empire managed to hold together under Ogodei's son Göjük (1246–1248) and under Tolui's eldest son Möngke (1252–1259). Möngke's brother Hulegu conquered Baghdad in 1256–1258, but he was defeated by the Egyptian Mamluks in 1260; in Iran he founded the kingdom of the Ilkhane (which lasted until 1335). After Möngke's death, a grandson of Genghis Khan's, Kublai, was elected Great Khan and completed the conquest of China. In 1264, Kublai moved his capital from Karakorum to Chan-balisk (Beijing) and founded the Yuan Dynasty (so named in 1271).

With the final destruction of the southern Song dynasty in 1279, Kublai became the first foreign ruler to rule all of China. The roads in central Asia were safer than they had ever been. In China, major arteries were built and punctuated with watch posts. At the time the trading links among Europe, China and Mongolia were closer than ever. In particular, merchants traveling on the Silk Road brought reports about the Mongol rulers of China to Europe.

In 1271, the young Marco Polo, accompanied by his father Niccolò and his uncle Matteo, set off from their native city of Venice for the court of the Great Khan. They arrived after a voyage of three and a half years and were received with great pomp at the Khan's court. Marco was made an envoy of the Khan. When he returned to Europe in 1295, he described the splendor of the Mongol state and its magnificent cities of several million inhabitants to a Christian audience that found his account barely credible,

THE DECLINE

By the mid-thirteenth century, the giant empire of the Mongols was exhibiting the early signs of decline. An empire of such size—arguably the largest contiguous ever known—could not be governed from a central seat of power. In spite of a good communication system, it took months for information or news to reach Beijing. Technically the regional governors were still approved by the Great Khans, but independent territories soon developed, such as the Chagatai Khanate to the northeast of Tibet, the land of the Golden Horde to the north of the Black Sea and Caspian Sea, and the Ilkhanate in Persia.

A succession of popular revolutions against the Mongol rulers began in the fourteenth century. The driving force behind these uprisings was the Buddhist sect White Lotus. In 1368, the monk Zhu Yuanzhang (1328–1398) succeeded in driving out the last Mongol emperor and establishing the purely Chinese Ming dynasty. In 1410, the Chinese destroyed the Mongol capital of Karakorum.

The Great Khanate disappeared once and for all when the Khan's seal was handed over to the powerful Chinese Manchu rulers. The power vacuum created by the fall of the princes descended from Genghis Khan was filled by Tamerlane (1336–1405), a Turkish ruler who had family ties with the Mongols and considered Genghis Khan a role model. He built an empire to the east of the Caspian Sea and was the architectural inspiration behind many fine buildings, particularly in Samarkand. Tamerlane's armies advanced as far as Asia Minor and India. Between 1379 and 1385, he conquered eastern Iran, then between 1385 and 1387, Georgia, Armenia and Iran. In 1391, he advanced as far as the Volga; in 1395, he marched into Syria and Iraq; in 1398, he reached the Indus; and in 1402, he defeated the Ottoman-Turkish sultan Bajezid I. However, he was unable to consolidate the empire internally, and it collapsed under the rule of his grandson Ulugh Beg (d.1449).

The most important descendent of this last great Mongol emperor was Babur (1483–1530), who conquered the Delhi Sultanate in 1526 and so founded the Islamic empire of the Indian Moghuls that continued until 1858. In the west of the empire, the Mongols had largely converted to Islam, whereas the rest of Mongolia had converted to Lamaist Buddhism, a situation that put an end to their political activity. Mongolia has belonged to China since the seventeenth century; in 1911, Outer Mongolia broke away and declared its independence. ❑

Necropolis of Tamerlane in Samarkand,

GENGHIS KHAN AND THE MONGOL CONQUESTS

China, 1215

In 1215, Genghis Khan's Mongol horsemen swept through northern China and captured Beijing. The imperial palace of the Jin emperor went up in flames, the city was razed, and its inhabitants were butchered in a dreadful orgy of killing.

The emperor's treasury of gold and precious stones, silver and silk was carried away to Genghis, who camped near Lake Dolonor beyond the Great Wall. So confident of victory was he that he did not even appear before Beijing, leaving the conduct of the battle to one of his captains, Muqali the Jalair.

The fall of Beijing seemed inevitable. When Genghis first mustered his army before the city a year earlier, it was powerfully defended, and the Mongol leader cunningly sought easy ransom rather than a hard and expensive victory.

The Jin emperor gave him everything he asked for—treasure, horses, women, a royal princess for his own bed—and Genghis went away. But the Jin emperor knew that Genghis would be back, and in June 1214, he fled from the city. His departure demoralized the citizens, the army mutinied, and when Muqali appeared, Beijing was ripe for plucking.

Rather than pursue the Jin emperor, Genghis Khan left his forces in China under the command of Muqali and led his virtually invincible light cavalry back to the north, then west toward Turkestan, Transoxiana, and Afghanistan. It was a move that bode ill for the flourishing Muslim states of central Asia, for wherever the Mongols passed, they left nothing but death and destruction.

The Mongols emerged from the edge of the Gobi Desert as a feuding federation of tribes. It was Genghis Khan who welded them together into the fearsome fighting force that rampaged

Genghis Khan, founder of the Mongol Empire, holding an audience (Persian miniature)

across Europe and Asia.

Despite their conquest of many cities, and great stretches of China, and the mountainous country to the west, the Mongols did not settle down and establish their own civilizations as previous nomadic invaders had. For the Mongols, cities were not places to be lived in but places to plunder. After raping, slaying, and plundering a population, they would install a leader and move on. Theirs was a purely military organization, efficient and brutal. It was said the warriors lived on the very horses they rode, eating their flesh and drinking their blood when other food became scarce.

At its height, the Mongol empire stretched from the Pacific Ocean to Germany's Black Forest. ❏

GOTHIC CATHEDRALS

Europe, twelfth and thirteenth centuries

The great surge of the Christian faith in the thirteenth century found expression in stone cutting, statuary, and stained glass, woven together to make cathedrals of a new lightness and grace.

The wonders of Gothic architecture began in 1132 with the abbey church of St. Denis built by Abbot Suger outside Paris. Architectural advancements in columns, ribbed vaulting, pointed arches, and flying buttresses allowed the new cathedrals to soar as these features took weight from the walls. Windows could be enlarged to let in light. When Bishop Regnault began to raise the two great spires of Chartres, their height could be seen for twenty miles. He filled the cathedral with 160 stained glass windows, including the great rose window, bathing the interior with blue light. The portals were decorated with holy statues.

Rheims, where French kings were crowned, was rebuilt with 550 statues, "the smiling angels." Rose windows like those at Chartres and Rheims were added to the Cathedral of Notre Dame in Paris.

Meanwhile in England, King Henry III began rebuilding Westminster Abbey and employed the French architect Henry of Rheims to copy the rose window from St. Denis. Cathedrals at Canterbury, Lincoln, Wells, and Salisbury demonstrated the Gothic emphasis on vertical and horizontal harmony and the medieval marriage of science and art. ❏

Cathedral of Chartres is one of the finest example of Gothic architecture

ARCHITECTURE THAT REACHED TO THE SKY

Point of Interest

European ecclesiastical architecture of the Middle Ages is known as Gothic. Coined by artists in Renaissance Italy, this term was originally derogatory. For them the golden age of art and architecture was Greek and Roman antiquity, and the Middle Ages was a period of cultural decline. They named its art after the Goths, whom they looked upon as a barbaric people known chiefly for having sacked Rome.

In fact the Gothic style was a vital new expression of Christian thought. It made abundant use of symbols and allegory. The architecture incorporated sculpture to provide a largely illiterate population with lessons written in stone.

The characteristic feature of Gothic architecture was the spire, which stood in marked contrast to the rounded volumes of the preceding Romanesque period. ❏

CATHARS CONDEMNED AS HERETICS

Toulouse, 1215

The Third Lateran Council banned dualism as heresy, a direct assault on the Cathars. Their movement was very strong in regions of southern France. It was there that Cathar beliefs were first formulated by Niketas, a visiting bishop from Constantinople.

Cathars believed that there were two principles in the universe, good and evil, spirit and matter. They considered Jesus pure spirit. The Old Testament was seen as the work of the devil, and many Church rituals, including the sacraments, were considered useless pomp. They did not eat meat and disdained material possessions.

It was Cathar practices that raised most controversy. They made a distinction between the "perfect" and believers. The "perfect" devoted themselves to manual labor and lived a life of abstinence and fasting. Believers, because they were thought to be saved by the virtue of the "perfect," were given many liberties in their personal lives, leading enemies to accuse them of debauchery. Many Cathars were burned as heretics or fell victim to the zeal of crusaders. ❏

Court of the Inquisition (painting by Pedro Berruguete, c.1500)

JERUSALEM RECAPTURED BY FREDERICK II

Jerusalem, March 12, 1229

Frederick II of Germany, twice excommunicated by the pope for his delayed crusading, finally set off for the Holy Land in 1229.

It was in 1215 that the young king first vowed to join a crusade,

The Holy Roman Emperor Frederick II crowns himself King of Jerusalem (woodcut, c.1880)

but he did not succeed in getting away as expected in 1221. Two years later he said he would be ready to sail on June 24, 1225, but he was distracted by domestic problems, including a Mongol invasion, and a new date of August 15, 1227 was set. His troops sailed from Brindisi, without him, for he was unwell in Otranto. Without his presence, many other crusaders melted away.

When Frederick finally reached the Christian port of Acre in 1229, he didn't have much of an army. He did, however, have a secret card to play. For more than two years, he had been in clandestine diplomatic contact with the sultan of Egypt, al-Kamil. The sultan had been badly shaken by the crusaders' advance into Egypt during the previous crusade. He was happy to sign a treaty by which he surrendered Bethlehem, Nazareth, a corridor from Jerusalem to the coast, as well as most of the city.

A bloodless coup of this sort was a novelty in the history of the crusades, whose protagonists usually preferred to settle things by sword. Frederick remained in disgrace with the Vatican, however, since he had dared to negotiate with an infidel. ❑

EMPEROR FREDERICK II

Brief Lives

Under the direction of Frederick II (1194–1250), the Hohenstauffen dynasty reached the zenith of its power.

Born December 26, 1194, Frederick became King of Germany in 1196 and King of Sicily in 1198; he was crowned Holy Roman Emperor in 1226 and made King of Jerusalem in 1229. Clearly he was greatly honored during his lifetime.

Frederick showed himself to be a canny ruler in many respects. In 1220, he named his son Henry as his successor, retaining for the monarchy a privilege that had been traditionally allocated to the nobility. His governmental innovations and his intellectual stature, evidenced by his cultivation of poets, mathematicians, philosophers, and scientists, made him a model ruler in the eyes of Renaissance thinkers.

His reign was also marked by his struggles with the powerful German nobility, the independent cities of northern Italy, and the papacy. He died in 1250 in the midst of prepartions for another crusade, leaving behind an empire that had seen its finest days. ❑

ALEXANDER NEVSKY, VICTORIOUS RUSSIAN GENERAL

Russia, 1242

In a dramatic battle on the ice, Russian troops led by Prince Alexander Nevsky launched a successful counteroffensive against the Teutonic Knights, bringing to a halt their planned invasion of Russia. The decisive clash between the Novgorod Russians and the Teutonic Knights came on the ice at Lake Peipus in Livonia, where the German crusaders had gathered several elite armies.

The turning point in the day-long battle came when Nevsky, whose men had borne the brunt of the German assault, unleashed his elite droujina troops on the German flanks, crushing the enemy into submission. This was an unexpected victory: Russian foot soldiers had defeated knights on horseback.

Nevsky, who had been dismissed by Novgorod's Republican People's Council less than two years before, was proclaimed a national hero after agreeing to come out of retirement to lead the counterattack against the German invaders. In Novgorod, the victory was seen as the end of constant attacks by Catholic crusaders.

But Russia was also under attack from the East, and Nevsky did not attempt to battle the Mongols in the same fashion. In 1246, when appointed Prince of Kiev, he became a vassal of the Golden Horde and went so far as to help the Mongols in administrative tasks. Historians debate Nevsky's motives and the consequences of his actions. He may have been influenced by the Mongols' earlier assault on the city in 1240, and it is clear that his friendly dealings with the Mongols saved northern Russia from further devastation. ❑

Alexander Nevsky, Prince of Novgorod and Vladimir (fresco, 17th century)

BOOK OF MEDIEVAL LAW

Germany. c.1224

The *Sachsenspiegel* (Mirror of Saxony) is the oldest and most important medieval law book. It was written by an East Saxon knight, Eike von Repkow (c.1180–1233), first in Latin, then translated by the author into the German vernacular. Its stated aim was to hold a mirror up to the legal practices of the day, and it established legal standards for von Repkow's homeland.

The book encompassed issues dealing with civil and criminal law, as well as legal procedures and constitutional law. The author relied very little upon written sources but rather drew from the experience that he gained as vassal and legal advisor to Graf Hoyer von Falkenstein.

Although the *Sachsenspiegel* was the work of a private individual and did not have official standing per se, nonetheless it soon became looked upon as authoritative and served as the model for legal codes in other German duchies and cities (including Schwabia, Magdeburg, and Meissen). The work survives in more than two hundred manuscripts and was translated into Dutch and Czechoslovakian. The book was also used in Poland and in parts of Russia and Hungary. It was regarded as authoritative in parts of Germany until the enactment of the German code of civil law on New Year's Day, 1900. ❑

Illustrated edition of *Sachsenspiegel* (Heidelburg edition)

MONGOLS THREATEN EUROPE

Poland, 1241

A new wave of Mongol attackers entered Russia through the Caucasus, crossed the Volga in 1237, and rode north to sack Moscow. Forced by floods to turn south, away from the trading center of Novgorod, the Mongols attacked Kiev in 1240, before splitting apart to advance through Poland and south to Hungary. The seemingly irresistible invading force spread the fear throughout Europe that only the Atlantic Ocean could stop their progress.

The invasion by the Golden Horde started eighteen years earlier when Genghis Khan crushed the Russians at the Kalka River after an expedition through Persia. With Genghis's death in 1227, operations in the west were suspended. But after eight years, Tartar chieftains gathered at Karakorum, the capital of the Mongol Empire, and agreed to ride under the command of Batu Khan, the grandson of Genghis Khan.

Mongol warriors could travel four times faster than European heavy cavalry. The team that set out to conquer Poland covered the four hundred miles from the Vistula River to Germany in a month. In Legnitz, the Mongol horsemen broke an elite force of Teutonic Knights and contemptuously cut off an ear from each corpse to be bagged and counted later like rat tails. It was rumored that nine bags were collected. The Hungarians were also defeated.

Ruling entire countries through the local aristocracies that became their vassals, the Mongols created a vast empire that reached from the Pacific to the Danube. In the end, their relentless advance across Europe was not halted by arms. Closing in on Vienna, the Mongols were expected to continue west, pushing a shield of prisoners before them if necessary. But news reached Prince Batu, the commander of the conquering warriors, that the great khan, Ogodei, had died in Mongolia. Batu was a leading contender to succeed him and returned immediately to Mongolia taking his feared forces with him. They never returned. ❑

Death of Duke Henry II on the battlefield of Legnica

THE FIRST HABSBURG KING OF GERMANY

Germany, 1273

The election of the first German king from the House of Habsburg ended an interregnum of 20 years. On October 1, 1273 the electoral college decided upon Rudolph I von Habsburg as their new king. He was the most influential and wealthiest territorial lord in southwest Germany. The interregnum (during which there was no emperor) was the result of a disputed election. On May 17, 1257 Richard of Cornwall was chosen in Aachen as king. Just before this, however, some of the electors had decided in favor of Alfonse X (Alfonse the Wise) as their king.

Neither ruler could gain full acceptance. Alfonse avoided Germany completely. Richard visited Germany four times, but he had delegated most of his responsibilities to various proxies. On April 2, 1272 Richard of Cornwall died in England. Rudolph emerged as the most promising candidate.

In his 18 years Rudolph von Habsburg was able to revitalize the kingdom's fortunes. He was cleverly able to further the interests of his realm and those of his own house at the same time.

King Rudolph I from the House of Habsburg entering Basel in 1273 (19th century)

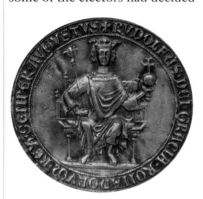

Royal seal of Rudolph I

Rudolph's main opponent, Ottokar II of Bohemia, received the lands of Austria and the Steiermark as a fief from Richard of Cornwall. He did not accept the new king's election. Rudolph placed Ottokar under the ban of the empire and defeated him in battle at Marchfeld in August of 1278. In this way he was able to secure Ottokar's holding for his sons Albrecht and Rudolph.

Rudolph was never invested with the emperor's crown, even though it was twice promised him (once in 1276 and then again 1278). The death of the then serving popes prevented him from realizing his plans. Rudolph died on July 15, 1291 in Speyer. ❑

SCHOLASTICISM

Point of Interest

Scholasticism was a movement associated with the great medieval universities that took a philosophical approach to theological questions. Leading lights of this movement included Albert Magnus, Peter Abelard, and John of Salisbury. Their works took the form of *Lectiones* and *Disputationes* (Readings and Arguments). Abelard's *Sic et Non* (1121–1122) was one of Scholasticism's central texts. Abelard raised various questions and then produced various authorities from Scripture and from Church teachings to arrive at a solution. His primary concern was the nature of being, as exemplified in arguments that sought to resolve whether universals independent of concrete things had actual existence or

The scholastic philosopher Albertus Magnus

were simply the product of human thought. ❑

ST. THOMAS AQUINAS

Paris, January 1274

St. Thomas Aquinas, philosopher and theologian, died on January 3, 1274, at the age of 48. His work marked a major watershed in Western thought with its synthesis of traditional Christian theology and the philosophical methodologies of the pagan Aristotle, as well as those of Muslim theologians such as al-Ghazali.

Aquinas was born of a noble family at Aquino, near Naples, around 1225. He entered the Dominican order, and in 1245 arrived in Paris to study under Albertus Magnus, a German Dominican who was one of the earliest Christian theologians to explore the application of Aristotle's rational analysis to theological questions.

By 1260, Aquinas had greatly expanded this mode of inquiry, systematizing it into a seamlessly rigorous discipline whose central principle was that Aristotelian reasoning and Christian faith were complementary and could be used to confirm each other. The arguments in his seminal works, *Summa Contra Gentiles* and *Summa Theologica*, would be the basis of Thomist philosophy and would serve as an authoritative standard against which future Catholic thought would be measured. ❑

St. Thomas Aquinas

THE MAMLUK DYNASTY'S DEFEAT OF THE MONGOLS

Palestine, September 1260

In September of 1260, the Mongols' inexorable westward movement was finally halted by the Mamluks, an Egyptian army of ex-slave mercenaries. Fighting for the Sultan Qutuz and under the command of the Turkish ex-slave Baybars, the Mamluks crushed the Asiatic forces led by General Hulegu at the Battle of Ain Jalut.

Grandson of Genghis Khan and brother of the reigning Mongke Khan, General Hulegu had crossed into southwest Asia four years earlier with the largest Mongol army ever assembled. Possessing a deep hatred of Islamic Arabs and simultaneously admiring Persian culture, his ultimate goal was to destroy the Abbasid caliphate centered in Baghdad and install himself as the first Khan of Persia. With his Christian general Kitbuqua, he first crushed the Muslim Assassin army at Alam-

ut and then, in 1258, marched on Baghdad, sacking the city and killing the caliph. From Baghdad the invasion moved to the Syrian capital, Damascus and finally to Aleppo. He then intended to invade Egypt, but on receiving word that Mongke Khan had died, he withdrew to Azerbaijan with most of his army, leaving what turned out to be too few men in Syria and Palestine.

The Mamluks began a series of attacks on Hulegu's diminished forces that ended in September 1260 on the coast of Palestine in the Battle of Ain Jalut (Goliath's Eye or Goliath's Spring). Historians have seen the Mongols' loss at Ain Jalut to the Mamluk forces commanded by Baybars as a historical turning point after which their influence in the Middle East began to wane.

After the Battle of Ain Jalut, the ambitious Baybars seized power

by assassinating Sultan Qutuz, making himself Sultan of the Bahir Dynasty. From humble beginnings as a Kipchak slave—the Kipchaks being a Turkic people of Central Asia—Baybars rose to power, fueled by a fierce military prowess that made him a hero in battles against the armies of the Seventh, Eighth, and Ninth Crusades. By the time of his death in Damascus in June of 1277, he had transformed an army of ex-slaves into the Mamluk dynasty, which would reign for more than a century. As the man who defeated the seemingly invincible Mongols and

Mamluk warrior in typical costume with round sword

saved the "civilized" world from "barbarian" Christians, he is to this day revered throughout the Islamic world. ❑

RUMI AND THE WHIRLING DERVISHES

Anatolia, 1273

The great Persian poet Jalal ad-Din Rumi was the founder of the Mevlevi order of Sufis, known as the whirling dervishes. Rumi is one of the greatest and best-loved poets in the Persian language. Like most of the best Persian poets, Rumi was a mystic, and a mystical Islamic fraternity, or *tariqah*, grew up around him at Konya (the ancient city of Iconium).

The hypnotic, whirling dance that is a key part of the rituals of the Mevlevi order is in fact a liturgical service, with every gesture carefully and meticulously prescribed; through it, members of the order seek to attain ecstasy and higher truth.

Music and dance are rare in Islamic ritual, but Sufi practices often ran counter to the standards of orthodox Muslims. The

first Sufi order to appear was the Qadirite sect of Baghdad, founded by Abd-al-Qadir al-Jilani, who died in 1166. This was followed by the Rifa'ites, founded by the Mesopotamian Ahmad al-Rifa'i, who died in 1183. Other major orders are the Chishti, the Halveti, and the Suhrawardi.

Rumi died in 1273 in Konya and is buried there in a shrine called the Green Tomb. ❑

KAMIKAZE: THE DIVINE WIND

Japan, 1281

The Japanese island of Tsushima was spared being overrun by Kublai Khan's Mongol hordes when his invading warships were wrecked by a typhoon off its coast. Seeing god's aid in their deliverance, the Japanese named the typhoon *Kamikaze*, the Divine Wind. Had the khan's 140,000 troops landed, Japan would have been conquered. ❑

ENGLISH BARONS IN REVOLT

England, 1265

Simon de Montfort, Earl of Leicester, was responsible for summoning England's first directly elected parliament. Due to a dislike of foreign influence, heavy papal taxation, and the extravagance of King Henry III's foreign dependents, the country's barons became restive. De Montfort became the leader of the baronial opposition, whose goal

was to curb Henry III's power. Along with the Earl of Gloucester, de Montfort presided over the Parliament at Oxford of 1258, where Henry consented to the Provisions of Oxford, which gave power to fifteen council members and forced the English monarchy to recognize the rights and power of parliament.

In 1261, however, Henry re-

neged on his promises, further antagonizing the barons and resulting in open warfare. On May 14, 1264, at the Battle of Lewes, de Montfort was victorious and captured Henry III and Prince Edward. De Montfort then set up a government and called a parliament consisting of knights from each shire and two elected officials from invited boroughs, as

well as barons and burgesses. Although his parliament gained national support, it alienated many of the barons including the Earl of Gloucester. With the escape of Prince Edward, they found a rallying point for their discontent. Simon de Montfort was defeated and killed by Edward's army at the battle of Evesham on August 4, 1265. ❑

Torrential Rain Causes Famine in England

England, 1316

In 1316, English farming collapsed after prolonged rainy spells that ruined harvests, resulting in a famine that left a tenth of the population dead. The weather of previous years had caused bad harvests in England and throughout northern Europe. Rains in the autumn of 1314 and the following two summers created food shortages for both humans and livestock. A shortage of salt, because the salt pans could not evaporate, exposed livestock to various diseases. In many areas, wheat yields were only a fifth of normal, and many sheep farmers saw their herds diminished by more than half.

The supply-demand shortfall also created severe economic burdens by drastically raising the price of a broad range of commodities. Taxes had already been increased, to finance royal campaigns against the Scots, and the rise in wheat prices hit the poor hardest. Emblematic of the famine's effect were the attack on wheat ships by hungry mobs in Sandwich and the mutiny of starving garrisons in Berwick. ❑

Marco Polo at the Court of

China, c.1282

Marco Polo, a young Venetian merchant, became a favorite of Kublai Khan's at the Mongol emperor's stately capital of Cambuluc (present-day Beijing). Marco Polo arrived with his father and uncle on the older men's second visit. On their first visit, Kublai had entrusted them with a message to the Pope, and in 1271, they set out for the east again with gifts from the Holy See. And they took the 17-year-old Marco with them.

The adventurous Venetians arrived at the khan's palace after being among the first westerners to travel the Silk Road. At Cambuluc they found an international group of advisers and military technicians, such as experts in siege warfare hired from Baghdad.

The khan was much taken by young Marco's wonder at the glories of the capital he had built on the ruins of the city razed by his grandfather, Genghis Khan, and he employed Marco on a number of diplomatic missions. The Venetian traveled throughout China on Kublai's business and reportedly became fluent in Persian and Mongolian.

The Battle of Morgarten

Switzerland, November 15, 1315

On November 15, 1315, a small army of Swiss foot soldiers, part of an alliance known as the Swiss Confederation, defeated the forces of Leopold I of Austria near Lake Zug. Leopold's army had come to the valleys of Schwyz and Unterwalden to subdue the peasant farmers and to bring central Switzerland within the domain of the Habsburg Empire. The Habsburgs had long enjoyed manorial rights in these valleys but had never pressed their claim to political power.

The cantons of Switzerland had become increasingly independent, the inhabitants of Schwyz having fortified the entrances to their valley. The valley was of particular interest to the Habsburgs because its Gotthard Pass afforded a relatively easy passage to Italy. Conflict was inevitable, especially when a dispute over grazing rights involved the men of Schwyz attacking the Einsiedeln monastery, taking some monks loyal to the Habsburgs hostage.

Leopold, the brother of Frederick of Austria, commanded an army of nearly five thousand knights on horseback and had devised a plan involving naval forces on Lake Lucerne to block off Unterwalden and attack Schwyz. However, the fifteen-hundred-strong Confederates ambushed the numerically superior Habsburg forces, trapping them in a narrow pass between Lake Aegeri and Morgarten, and rained down spears, logs, and rocks from above. With the utter rout of Leopold's men, the Battle of Morgarten ensured Swiss autonomy. It would be 70 years before the Habsburgs launched another attack on Switzerland. ❑

The soldiers from the Swiss Confederation defeat the heavily armored cavalry of the emperor (drawing from the Berne chronicle, 15th century)

KUBLAI KHAN

A sharp-eyed observer, Polo was impressed by the efficient Mongol administration, with its roads and postal system, its census, markets, and paper money, all of which Kublai adopted from the Chinese.

Of all the wonders of China, nothing impressed Marco Polo more than Kublai Khan's marble summer palace in the city of Shangdu (immortalized as Xanadu in the poem by Samuel Taylor Coleridge) where, it was said, the khan would drink "the milk of paradise."

Marco spent seventeen years in China and traveled back to Venice via Sumatra, Persia, and India. Upon his return in 1295, his fellow Venetians were dazzled by the jewels and stories he brought with him. His book, *The Travels of Marco Polo*, which he dictated while imprisoned in 1298–1299 after being captured in a battle against Genoa, was a huge success and lit the imagination of western Europeans intent on finding ways to the great wealth that lay to the East. ❑

Battle scene with riders and elephants from the Mongol invasion of Burma under Kublai Khan

KUBLAI KHAN, EMPEROR OF CHINA

Brief Lives

Kublai Khan succeeded his brother Mongke as ruler of the great empire founded by their grandfather, Genghis, the fearsome first great khan of the Mongols. Like all his family, Kublai was set on conquest and chose as his first victim the remnant of the Song empire in southern China.

Kublai set about the destruction of the Song with cunning rather than warfare. He sent an envoy, Hao Ling, to the Song court, ostensibly to discuss a peaceful settlement. He offered the Song a bargain: if they would acknowledge his reign as the "Son of Heaven" over all of China, he would allow them a measure of self-rule and the opportunity to benefit from the prosperity that would follow from a tolerant Mongol suzerainty.

Hao Ling embellished this offer by painting a picture of Kublai as a Chinese-style emperor, with Confucian advisers, governing in a civilized fashion. Hao Ling also pointed out that any military resistance would be useless, for

Kublai Khan

nothing could stand against the Mongol army, which was now as skilled in siege warfare as it was in the field.

The Song refused to acknowledge Kublai's claim to be the Son of Heaven and arrested Hao Ling. Eventually, in the face of the Mongols' war machine, they capitulated. The fall of the Song brought the whole of China under Mongol rule, the first and last time a foreign power would rule the Chinese. Kublai named his dynasty the Yuan dynasty.

Kublai Khan oversaw two unsuccessful invasions of Japan as he strove to expand his dominion. But his rule of China was inspired. He allowed a large degree of religious tolerance, supported vast public works, including the extension of a grand canal to his capital, and was a patron of the arts and learning. In his later years, however, he gave in to food and drink. The death of his son, his immediate successor, hastened the dissolution of the powerful Mongol empire. ❑

MARCO POLO DESCRIBES CHINESE ASTROLOGERS

From *The Travels of Marco Polo*, 1298–1299 (book pictured below)

There are in the city of Kanbalu, amongst Christians, Saracens, and Cathaians, about five thousand astrologers and prognosticators, for whose food and clothing the grand khan provides, and who are in the constant exercise of their art. They have their astrolabes, upon which are described the planetary signs, the hours, and their several aspects for the whole year. The astrologers of each distinct sect annually proceed to the examination of their respective tables, in order to ascertain from thence the course of the heavenly bodies, and their relative positions for every lunation. They discover therein what the state of the weather shall be, and thence foretell the peculiar phenomena of each month: that in such a month, for instance, there shall be thunder and storms; in such another, earthquakes; in another, diseases, mortality, wars, discords, conspiracies. As they find the matter in their astrolabes, so they declare it will come to pass; adding, however, that God, according to his good pleasure, may do more or less than they have set down. They write their predictions for the year upon certain small squares, which are called *takuini*, and these they sell, for a groat apiece, to all persons who are desirous of peeping into futurity. ❑

THE SHRINKING BYZANTINE EMPIRE

Byzantium, 1326

The rise of the Ottoman Empire began in 1301. Under Osman I, Ottoman Turks settled near the border of the Byzantine Empire and began to expand into its territory. The imperial army engaged with the invaders at Nicomedia in 1301, suffering a disastrous and wholly unexpected defeat. Osman, however, did not follow up his victory with an advance to Nicomedia; instead he began settling his forces closer to areas under imperial control, moving westward and pushing back the bounds of the Empire. After Osman's death, his son Orkhan continued the expansion through western Anatolia. In 1326, Orkhan had captured the Byzantine city

Bursa, and by 1337, he captured the Byzantine cities of Nicomedia and Pergamon. In 1361, the Ottoman Turks, under the rule of Orkhan's successor Murad, captured Adrianopole and forced the Byzantine Emperor to pay tribute. ❑

Osman I (1259-1326) was the founder of the Ottoman Empire

POPE CLEMENT V

Point of Interest

What is known as the Babylonian Captivity began in March 1309 when Pope Clement V moved his papal court to Avignon. The Dominican priory in which Clement's Curia settled became the Church's official papal residence until 1378.

The pope's desertion of his Episcopal see—he was, after all, the bishop of Rome—was precipitated by Clement's predecessor, Boniface VIII. Boniface came into conflict with Phillip of France over taxation of the clergy. Behind this lay Boniface's expansive vision of papal power, which reached its fullest expression in his bull, *In Unam Sanctam*. This was issued in 1302 at a council that took Phillip to task for his attacks on the church. When it became apparent in the following year that Boniface was preparing to

FLEMISH REBELS GET ENGLISH BACKING

Flanders, early fourteenth century

A shrewd economic power play by the king of England enabled a Flemish revolt to succeed against its French masters. An army of rich and poor led by Jacob van Artevelde, a wealthy burgher of Ghent, besieged Tournai and threw out Louis of Nevers, the Count of Flanders and a French ally. The revolt began when Edward III, seeking to drive up wool prices, restricted wool exports to Flanders.

The Flemish weavers were badly hit, many of them facing starvation. With memories still fresh of a previous revolt ten years before—when their peasant army was slaughtered by French cavalry and their leader horribly executed—the weavers prepared to fight back. They found a leader in van Artevelde. The revolt grew as other rich burghers took up arms with them.

Edward's lifting of the wool blockade gave both employers and workers a cause to fight for, and van Artevelde, an eloquent and en-

ergetic leader, used the opportunity to unite Flanders under one flag.

Edward was at war with France. His earlier friendship with John II of France had

soured. The alliance with Flanders was not only a thorn in his enemy's side, but also promised increased revenue from the wool trade. The Flemish relished their indepen-

dence but were not able to hold onto it for long. By the beginning of the fifteenth century, they had become a possession of the Burgundian House of Valois. ❑

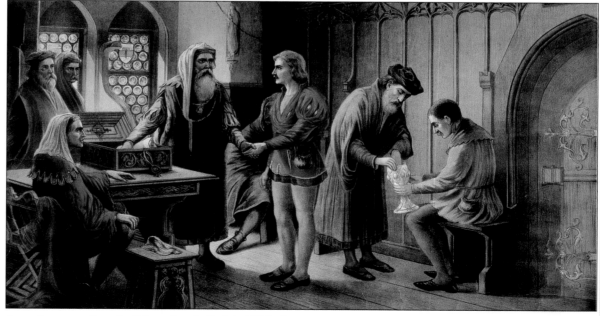

Scene from a meeting of guild members in the late Middle Ages

Fruity Pie

AND THE AVIGNON PAPACY

excommunicate him, Phillip had his minister attack the papal palace in the hilltop town of Anagni. Boniface was held captive and died three weeks later.

Bertrand de Got was elected pope in 1305 as Clement V. He was a native of Aquitaine, rose in French clerical ranks, and was named Archbishop of Bordeaux by Boniface in 1294. His immediate predecessor, Benedict IX, died after serving for only eight months. Clement's election to the papacy was in part to effect a compromise between the supporters of the French king and the guardians of ecclesiastical prerogatives. But the result was entirely one sided. Clement was a sick man and unable to stand up to the king. He was crowned in Lyons and never reached Rome. Soon after his coronation, the eleva-

tion of French clergy put the College of Cardinals firmly into the hands of the defenders of Philip and the secular power. Clement's inaction and the long papal presence at Avignon were indicative of the shift of power from the Church to the State. In 1306, Clement had *In Unam Sanctam* revoked. In retrospect, it can be seen as Boniface's basking in past glory rather than facing current reality. ❑

The Pope's Palace in Avignon was the resident of the popes from 1309-1376

THE DIVINE COMEDY

Ravenna, 1321

Exiled from his home city of Florence, Dante Alighieri (b.1265) died in Ravenna in 1321. His masterpiece, *The Divine Comedy*, is an all-encompassing vision of medieval European society and its spiritual aspirations.

Wandering a dark wood at the midpoint of his life, Dante is taken up by the poet Virgil, who guides him on a tour of the Inferno and Purgatory and then, as Virgil is not a Christian, and therefore cannot enter the heavenly realms, he entrusts Dante to the keeping of Beatrice, the young girl with whom Dante had fallen in love. Beatrice travels with him through Paradise. In the course of his journey, Dante encounters the souls of many of his contemporaries as well as historical and mythological figures. ❑

Dante as painted by Andrea del Castagno

GIOTTO

Padua, early fourteenth century

The Florentine Giotto di Bondone (c.1267/8-January 1337) is considered by art historians to have been the Italian Renaissance's first great painter. A student of Cimabue, Giotto moved beyond his teacher's iconographic Byzantine style, rendering figures that were more natural and life-like and introducing the illusion of depth. A sculptor as well as a painter, Giotto's experiments with perspective influenced other Italian painters, sculptors, and architects such as Pisano and Brunelleschi.

His extant masterwork is a cycle of frescoes in the Scrovegni (or Arena) Chapel in Padua that depict the life of the Virgin and Christ's Passion. ❑

The Ascension (Giotto di Bondone, fresco from the Arena Chapel in Padua)

IVAN I, MONEYBAGS, AND THE RISE OF MOSCOW

Moscow, mid-fourteenth century

In fourteenth-century Russia, princes acted as tax collectors for the Khans of the Golden Horde. The most successful of these was Ivan I (1288–31 March 1340), also known as Ivan Kalita (Moneybags). As Grand Prince of Vladimir, he became Khan Oz-Beg's most powerful Russian representative, a position he not only parlayed into great personal wealth, hence Moneybags, but also used to raise the Principality of Muscovy to unrivaled power.

Using his tax collection commissions, he contracted loans with other princes, many of whose lands he annexed upon default. Residing in the initially insignificant area of Moscow, he then used these default payments to expand his Muscovy holdings, leading to the eventual creation of the Moscow that would dominate Russian life.

He completed his consolidation of power by convincing the Khan to recognize his son, Simeon, as Grand Prince. In so doing, he began a dynastic lineage that would rule Moscow (and therefore Russia) for many years to come. ❑

Ivan Kalita (Moneybags) by Carl Peter Fabergé (c.1900)

THE FIRST FRANKFURT FAIRS

Germany, 1330

With the introduction of a spring trading fair, Frankfurt established itself as one of the major market centers in Europe along with Leipzig, Bruges, Ghent, and Lyons.

On April 25, 1330, the Bavarian king Ludwig granted the city of Frankfurt the privilege to hold a fair at Easter, in addition to the fall fair held in Frankfurt since 1150. The spring fair lasted fourteen days. Frankfurt had already been recognized as an important commercial center because of its location on the trade routes between Italy and Northern Europe. Following this grant, it became a major international hub. Among the many goods that passed through Frankfurt were wine, herring, furs, beeswax, horses and other farm animals, metal ware, luxury goods, and most importantly, wool. The explosion of trade led to the city's great prosperity. ❑

Textile market in the Netherlands (painting, c.1530)

THE ALLEGORY OF GOOD AND BAD GOVERNMENT

Siena, 1341

In 1341, the artist Ambrogio Lorenzetti painted a cycle of didactic frescoes called *The Allegory of Good and Bad Government* for Siena's government council chamber at the Palazzo Pubblico. A masterwork of early Italian Renaissance art, Lorenzetti's use of the relatively new naturalistic style contrasted greatly with the Byzantine style for which Siena was known. Its depiction of a civil rather than religious subject testifies to the rising wealth and pride of urban centers: they now had the wherewithal and the confidence to patronize the arts.

One series presents the effects of "Good Government." Set in an ordered landscape, it depicts ordinary citizens going about their daily tasks, such as weaving, agriculture, trade, and metalworking, all under the watchful eye of the one of the first female nudes in Western art, the allegorical figure of Security. Other allegorical figures depict Justice, Common Good, and Virtue, thus representing the civic and personal values required for society's orderly functioning. The fresco showing the effects of "Bad Government" is set in a ruined landscape and combines day-to-day realistic detail with the threatening allegorical figures of Tyranny, Discord, Treachery, Rape, Murder, and Plunder. ❑

SCOTLAND REGAINS ITS FREEDOM

Northhampton, 1328

Until the official founding of Great Britain in 1707 with the Acts of Union, the Scots succeeded in defending their hard-won autonomy from their English neighbors.

The English Queen Isabella and her lover Roger Mortimer, Earl of March, acting as regents for the young Edward III, signed a treaty on May 4, 1328 with Robert the Bruce at Northampton that guaranteed Scottish independence. The Kingdom of Scotland had been founded in 843 by Kenneth MacAlpin. With the death of Alexander III in 1286, the Canmore dynasty came to an end. Succession was granted to Alexander's granddaughter, Margaret. Daughter of the King of Norway and born in 1283, she died in 1290 at the age of seven on her way to Scotland on the isle of Orkney.

Already in 1174, the Scottish king William the Lion had to acknowledge the overlordship of Henry II of England, which explains why the successor to Margaret had to be approved by the then English king, Edward I. Surprisingly Edward chose John Balliol, who was crowned in 1292 in the traditional manner at the Stone of Scone. His election was greeted with mixed enthusiasm by the lords of the realm. Edward saw to it that his rights as overlord remained intact. This meant, among other things, that he had legal jurisdiction over the Scottish king. Later during his war with France, Edward requested the service of Scottish knights as required by feudal oaths. John's perceived friendship with England caused great resentment, and he was eventually forced to abdicate.

Edward regarded himself as the real king of Scotland. He brought the Stone of Scone with him to London and had it placed in the Chapel of Edward the Confessor at Westminster. The Scots under the leadership of William Wallace rebelled against their English masters. Wallace was executed in 1305, in the same year as Robert the Bruce gained the throne of Scotland, despite Edward's opposition. Edward, who was contending with wars both to the north and the south, died in 1307 while en route to once again subdue the Scots. In 1314, at the Battle of Bannockburn, the most disastrous defeat of the English since the Battle of Hastings, Bruce routed the English, who were led by Edward II, and secured de facto independence for his kingdom. The Treaty of Northampton provided legal recognition of that actuality.

At his death in 1329, Robert Bruce was succeeded by his son David II, who was the last of the Bruces to claim the title King of Scotland. In 1371, the Stuarts gained control of Edinburgh, which had functioned as the capital of the country since the eleventh century. A century later, James IV (r.1488–1513) married Margaret Tudor. This dynastic marriage provided the basis for the eventual unification of the two kingdoms under one monarch in 1603 by James VI (James I of England). ❑

Statue of Robert the Bruce at the entrance to Edinburgh Castle

THE ABDICATION AND DEATH OF EDWARD II

England, September 21, 1327

The failed Plantagenet king, Edward II (April 25, 1284–September 21, 1327), was murdered while imprisoned in Berkeley Castle, Gloucestershire, after having abdicated in January of 1327. Historians generally agree that Edward's failure as a ruler stemmed from his penchant for elevating questionable associates to royal positions. These appointments angered powerful barons and bishops and inspired his consort, Queen Isabella, and her lover, Roger Mortimer, to mount a successful coup in September 1326.

His conflict with the English body politic was exacerbated by his sybaritic life style and catastrophic ineptness as a military leader. His loss to the Scots at the Battle of Bannockburn made him universally unpopular. His abdication, which saw his fourteen-year-old son, Edward, become titular head under Isabella and Mortimer, was forced upon him by Parliament.

Theatrically immortalized in Christopher Marlowe's 1592 play, *Edward II*, Edward's single most enduring achievement was in being the first English king to charter colleges in Cambridge (1317) and Oxford (1326) Universities. ❑

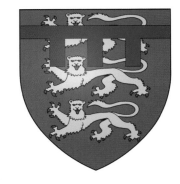

Coat of arms of the House of Plantagenet

THE BLACK PLAGUE

Europe, 1348

First reports of the plague came in 1345, when it emerged in the cities of the Golden Horde in southern Russia. From there it moved to Armenia and Azerbaijan, Scythia, Byzantium, and the Crimea. It then took hold in the Mediterranean, carried by merchant ships, and spread slowly westwards, engulfing city after city. By 1348, hundreds of thousands of men, women, and children were dying in every country in Europe, struck down by the Black Death. Not since the sixth century had such an epidemic attacked Europe.

Carried by infected fleas living on rats, the plague took three forms. *Bubonic* plague was seen in the swellings, or buboes, that inflated the lymph nodes at the neck, armpit, or groin; *pneumonic* plague affected the lungs, and victims choked on their own blood. A form of blood poisoning constituted the third deadly form of the epidemic.

The plague stunned Europe, affecting healthy and afflicted, rich and poor alike. Mortality rates ran as high as 75 percent. Those in the cities suffered more than those in rural areas, but the plague was democratic in choosing its victims. Even the most expert physicians could do little. Some recommended the burning of aromatic woods and herbs; others suggested special diets, courses of bleeding, new postures for sleeping, and many other remedies. The very rich tried medicines made of gold and pearls. Some chose to challenge the plague by bouts of riotous living; others sought protection by barring their doors and living as recluses. Still others sought safety in the remote countryside, but often they too fell ill. Attempts to bar sufferers from villages, towns, even whole cities also failed.

The outbreak shattered communities. Families were set against each other, and essential services collapsed; law and order, with so many administrators struck down, barely existed in some areas. A sense of panic pervaded Europe. Properties were deserted by desperate owners, and many of the sick died alone. Corpses were simply dumped in the street or buried in mass graves. Agriculture came to a standstill. Crops withered in the fields; cattle wandered untended.

Everywhere people were desperate for an explanation. Some blamed invisible particles carried in the wind, others talked of poisoned wells. Many, inevitably, blamed the Jews.

Estimates vary, but historians now think the plague claimed upward of some twenty million victims, killing one-quarter to two-thirds of Europe's population. The enormity of such destruction had a profound social, economic, and religious impact on the lives and culture of the medieval world. ❑

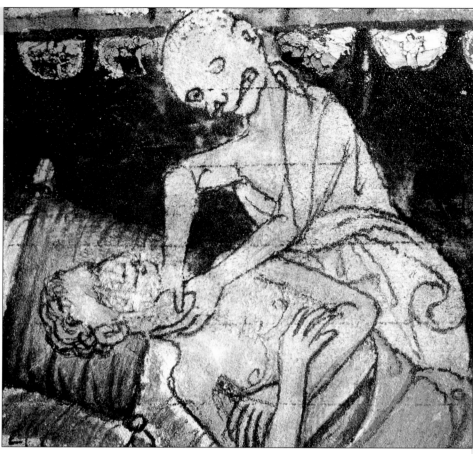

Death Strangling Plague Victim (Bohemian manuscript illustration, 14th century)

RELIGIOUS REVIVALS AND PERSECUTIONS

Point of Interest

The apocalyptic nature of the outbreak of bubonic plague, the Black Death, shattered the moral certainty of people across Europe. Among the most dramatic consequences were a frenzied religious revival and the mass persecutions of Jews.

Bands of hooded men, wearing white robes marked front and back with a red cross, traveled across Europe, attempting to atone for the ravages of the Black Death by whipping themselves in ritual public ceremonies. The Flagellant Brethren, as they were known, believed that the plague was a punishment for human sin, and that by scourging themselves they could show humankind's repentance.

They traveled in parties of fifty to five hundred men and were highly organized. Led by a layman, the master, they moved from town to town to perform their rituals. Singing hymns and sobbing, the men beat themselves with scourges studded with iron spikes. Blood gushed from their many wounds, and the spikes embedded themselves in the torn flesh. The ritual was performed in public twice each day.

They criticized church corruption and promoted a wave of savage anti-Semitism. Their exhibitions were highly influential, and the masses worshipped the flagellants as living martyrs whose deeds were to be admired and whose commands were to be carried out.

Jews were targeted by those needing a scapegoat. They were accused of poisoning wells and streams. Because of their traditions of ritual purity and better hygienic practices, Jewish enclaves were not as severely affected as the Christian nations surrounding them, which only heightened the suspicion and ill will directed toward them. Confessions obtained by torture spurred anti-Semites to mass murder. In German-speaking areas alone, some 350 Jewish communities were annihilated. ❑

The Battle of Crécy

France, May 1337

Long-standing English claims to the French crown, exacerbated by Salic law (which prohibited a woman in France from succeeding to the throne), competition for the wool market, unbridled personal ambition, feudal disputes, and a growing nationalism contributed to the fighting that plagued France and England for a century. The Hundred Years' War started when Philip VI of France announced that he would confiscate Gascony, an English feudal territory.

Some four years after declaring war, Edward III sailed from England to France with an army. He met the French at Crécy for the first pitched battle of the long war. Although heavily outnumbered, the army of Edward III won a great victory over French chivalry. Philip VI fled, leaving over fifteen hundred dead, and the way was open for Edward to advance on Calais.

Edward III landing with his army in France (French miniature from Froissart's Chronicles)

THE HUNDRED YEARS' WAR

1340	England defeats the French navy at the Battle of Sluys.
1346	England is victorious at the Battle of Crécy.
1347	Despite heroic resistance, England gains possession of the port of Calais.
1356	England wins at Poitiers, and French King John II is taken captive.
1360	Treaty of Brétigny
1415	England is victorious at Agincourt.
1420	Treaty of Troyes
1429	French resistance, led by Joan of Arc, stiffens, and England is forced to give up Orléans.
1453	With the French victory at Castillon, the war comes to an end.

The battle began with Philip's knights ignoring orders and vying with each other to be first to confront the invaders, but when the first ranks encountered the English, they turned and ran into their own allies. When the Genoese crossbowmen, on the side of the French, finally attacked in a heavy rainstorm, their bowstrings were soaked so their weapons were almost useless.

Then the English archers, equipped with the longbow, stepped forward and loosened a rain of arrows on the hapless Genoese, who fled into the swords of the French foot soldiers. In the melee that followed, the French presented a perfect target for the English bowmen, who could fire up to 24 arrows, each three feet long, within two minutes. The archers decimated the mounted French knights. ❑

A Contemporary Reflects on the Meaning of the Plague

From *Piers Plowman* by William Langland (c.1332–c.1386)

So Nature Killed many through corruptions,
Death came driving after her and dashed all to dust,
Kings and knights, emperors and popes;
He left no man standing whether learned or ignorant;
Whatever he hit stirred never afterwards.
Many a lovely lady and their lover-knights
Swooned and died in sorrow of Death's blows
For God is deaf nowadays and will not hear us,
And for our guilt he grinds good men to dust. ❑

TEUTONIC KNIGHTS

Germany, 1351

Under Winrich von Kniprode the Teutonic Knights attained their highest measure of influence and power. Winrich was the 22nd Grand Master of the Teutonic Knights. Elected for life, he was the order's political leader and founded a number of cities, expanded its trade and led the successful fight against Livonia.

The order was founded in 1198/99 in the Holy Land. Emperor Frederick II gave it the task of converting the Baltic Old Prussians; six years later the pope confirmed their mission. At the same time the Knights received from the emperor political control over the unconquered German lands that lay outside of the boundaries of the Empire. For the first half of the thirteenth century the Teutonic Knights were successful in overcoming the resistance of the Baltic Old Prussians. They constructed fortresses in the lands they conquered. The one at Marienburg served as the primary residence of the order. They created a highly organized and well-disciplined political state out of their conquests.

Starting in 1308 the order began to expand outside of the lands that were originally bestowed upon them. Through the acquisition of Pomerania and Danzig they became a naval power in the Baltic Sea. In 1410 a Polish-Livonian alliance crushed the order's army, and from then on their political power declined. ❑

Winrich von Kniprode, Grand Master of the Teutonic Knights

Hofmeister des deutschen Ordens.   Schwertbruder.

Grand Masters of the Teutonic Order

BOCCACCIO'S *DECAMERON*

Florence, 1353

The illegitimate son of a well-to-do banker, Giovanni Boccaccio was born in Tuscany in 1313. Having little interest in following his father's vocation, Boccaccio chose to indulge his passion for poetry after reading the works of Petrarch. The two would meet in 1350 and become mutually inspiring, lifelong friends.

Having been raised in Florence, Boccaccio moved to Naples, where he began writing poetry in earnest. Here, between 1336 and 1340, he produced two major works, *Filocolo* and *Filostrato*, the latter being the source for Chaucer's *Troilus and Criseyde*.

The work for which he is best known, *Decameron*, was written between 1349 and 1351, and was intended to be a poetic palliative to the Black Death that was ravaging Florence at that time. It consists of one hundred amusing stories told by seven young ladies and three young men taking refuge from the plague in the country, over a period of ten days (*decameron* suggesting ten in Italian.)

Although the story is written to console all unhappy lovers, the book's introduction relates Boccaccio's supposed eyewitness account of Black Death. Some scholars, however, question the veracity of his claim to having been in Florence at this time, believing he may have spent that period, like his characters, in the country outside of Ravenna. ❑

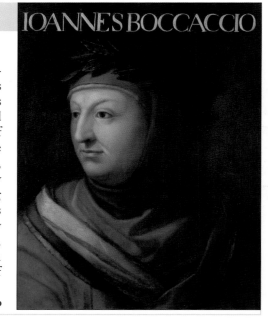

IOANNES BOCCACCIO

Giovanni Boccaccio

THE ORDER OF THE GARTER

Point of Interest

The origins of this elite group of knights, handpicked by the English monarch, are unclear. The order was founded by King Edward III reputedly after he rescued a lady's garter at a dance, wrapped it below his knee and rebuked onlookers with words that would become the Order's motto: *Honi soit qui mal y pense*, "Shame on him who considers this shameful." Some historians claim that in creating the Knights of the Garter, Edward was imitating Richard Lionheart's gesture of giving garters to knights on the Third Crusade. No doubt Edward was trying to kindle loyalty from his nobles, and some see connections to the Arthurian legends in his efforts. Or perhaps it was an indication that he was pursuing the French crown. Whichever interpretation is true, this order of knights was, and remains, the highest order of chivalry in Britain. Only 24 knights, the Prince of Wales, and the monarch are eligible for membership. On formal occasions they wear a blue garter below the left knee. ❏

Order of the Garter

THE RISE OF SIAM

Siam, 1350

The rise of the state of Siam as the dominant power in Southeast Asia can be said to have begun with the coronation of Ramathibodi I. Born as U Thong into a family of merchants, he took the name Ramathibodi upon his coronation and settled in the

Temple Wat Si Sanphet in Ayutthaya

capital city of Ayutthaya. There he declared Theravada Buddhism to be the country's official religion. He ruled until his death in 1369.

A new chapter in the history of the Thai people had begun when they freed themselves from Khmer rule in 1238. The earlier Kingdom of Sukhotai, which historians look upon as the first Thai state, was split up after the death of its king Ramkamhaeng among various petty Thai kingdoms in the area. This led to Ramathibodi's more powerful state establishing itself around the capital of Ayutthaya. ❏

THE GOLDEN BULL

Germany, January 10, 1356

The Golden Bull issued by Emperor Charles IV, from his residence in Prague was designed to end the successional disputes that had plagued the Holy Roman Empire. It also solidified constitutional aspects of the collection of German states and introduced the notion of majority rule. According to the Bull ("golden" because of the attached seal), the next king of Germany would be elected by an electoral college of seven lords. Under the new imperial edict, the electors could not discuss their choice before casting their vote, the new king could not be blocked by three votes, and at least in theory, the electors were to hold a Diet annually. Excluded from the Bull was the pope, who had frequently claimed that he should be allowed to confirm whomever was elected. ❏

The Gothic Vietsdom in Prague. Construction was begun in 1344.

CHARLES IV CROWNED EMPEROR

Rome, April 4, 1355

On this day Charles IV was given the emperor's crown. The papal legate of Innocent VI conducted the investiture ceremony. Charles had ascended the throne of Bohemia fourteen years before. He expanded the city of Prague, made it his capital. Under his influence it became a cultural center of Europe. In 1348, founded the first German university there. Through inheritance, conquest, purchase, and dynastic marriage, he extended his territories to include the Mark of Brandenburg. The chancellery in Prague contributed to the development of High German. ❏

Charles IV (15th century, after a 14th century original)

THE END OF THE MONGOL DYNASTY

China, 1368

After a period of social unrest, the Mongol Khan Dynasty was forced out of China. A peasant rebellion begun in 1351 succeeded in overthrowing the last Mongol emperor Shun-ti. The leader of the rebellion, Chu Yuan–chang, founded the Ming dynasty, which would last until 1664, and took the name Hongwu. The last years of the Khan's rule were marked by a series of natural catastrophes. The outbreak of an epidemic proved to be the last straw, triggering the uprising that eventually drove the Mongol emperor north out of the country.

The Ming Dynasty began with a thorough reorganization of government and society. The unrestrained powers of the emperor diminished, and the influence of the bureaucracy increased. ❏

Ming Dynasty porcelain dish

View of the Forbidden City in Beijing, the former imperial palace.

THE FORBIDDEN CITY

Point of Interest

The construction of the Forbidden City, the emperor's palace in Beijing, was begun in 1406 and completed in 1420. It was the residence of 24 rulers of both the Ming and Qin dynasties and was in use until 1911. Its name comes from the thirty-foot walls with four great gates that surround over 720,000 square yards, a territory which the normal retainers of the emperor were not permitted to enter. The city was the center of the imperial government. In the middle of it stand three imposing ceremonial halls. It has been named as a UNESCO World Heritage Site. ❏

THE GREAT SCHISM

Rome, September 20, 1378

With the election of Clement V as pope in 1305, the papal court established itself in France at Avignon. Although Clement and his immediate successors planned to go to Rome, a decaying and chaotic city, they never managed to depart their more opulent and safe surroundings, leaving the Church subject to French influence. In 1376, Gregory XI returned to the Eternal City. On his death in 1378, an archbishop from Naples, with a little help from the vocal Roman populace, was elected as Pope Urban VI.

French cardinals were in the majority at the conclave that elected Urban, but they were divided. Some supported Robert of Geneva, a cousin of the French king. The rest supported Urban, a man of lowly birth who they hoped would restore some spiritual authority to the papacy. But after his election, Urban delivered a violent attack on the luxurious life of the cardinals and the sale of church favors. Many French cardinals claimed that the election of Urban was invalid, since they were acting under fear of the Roman mob. They left Rome and elected Robert as pope. But Urban was determined to stay in office. His supporters considered that Robert (now Clement VII) was an antipope and charged that his election was an attempt by the French king to usurp the pope's power.

Thus was the Roman Catholic Church split into two hostile factions. The situation was further aggravated in 1408 when an attempt to resolve the situation led to the election of a third pope. The schism finally came to an end with the Council of Constance in 1414. ❏

Alexander V was one of three popes in 1409/1410 (copper engraving).

THE HANSEATIC LEAGUE AND THE RISE OF BRUGES

Northern Europe, 1356

In 1356, German Hanseatic towns formed an association to protect their trading network along the coasts of northern Europe, from London in the west to Novgorod in the east, helping to create the Hanse as an important commercial and military power.

German merchants had been extending their trading empire since the twelfth century, when they established a colony at Visby on the island of Gotland. Trading with Novgorod and Finland, Bremen serving the North Sea and North Atlantic, and eventually including London and Bergen. Flanders commanded the river-borne commerce of northern Europe.

The League allowed competition, but it imposed severe penalties on any member violating its rules of commerce.

Rising to prominence in this profitable admixture of laissez-faire and mutually respected constraints was the city of Bruges in Flanders. It was a nascent trading ness cooperative headquartered in Bruges, shrewdly gave foreign merchants significant privileges: import tolls were reduced, accounting methods simplified, and bills of exchange introduced. The Teutonic Knights opened a bank, and papal tithes from all over Europe were deposited in Bruges banks. Within a short period of time, Bruges grew to be the richest commercial staging post in Europe, prosperous not only in commerce but in the arts, in a gundian Valois dynasty was at its peak. Also bearing the title Count of Flanders, he was well positioned to help Bruges become an epicenter of European political influence. His championing of Bruges's economic and cultural development inspired him to become the official patron of a variety of professions, including woodcarvers, metalworkers, and artists like Jan van Eyck. He even went so far as to try to establish Flanders's independence from

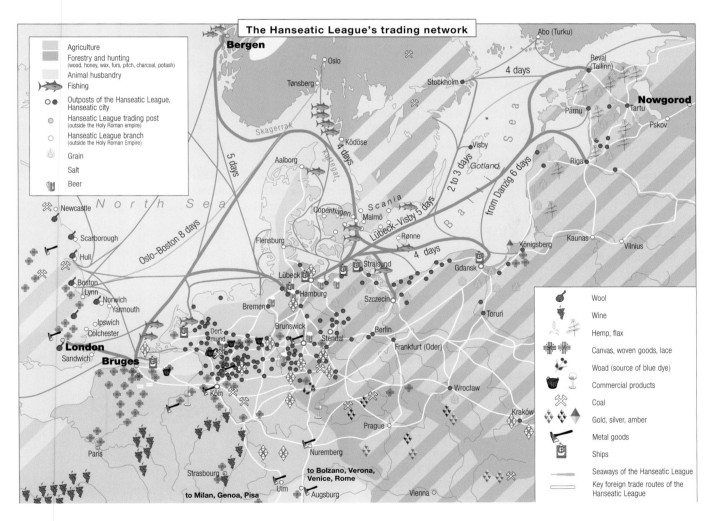

The Hanseatic League's trading network

Visby became a link with Western Europe, exporting Flanders cloths, salt, and beer to the Slavs, and importing their furs, hides, wax, and amber.

Beginning in the thirteenth century, the league established Lubeck as a focal point of Baltic commerce, with Hamburg and center in the thirteenth century, but because of its geographic position relative to England, France, Italy, and the Rhine states, the Hanseatic League built a factory there in 1336, which facilitated an enormous expansion of international commerce and banking. The Flanders Council, a business new international culture and lifestyle. Many of its merchants became very wealthy landowners and members of nobility whose cultural role model was the sumptuous court of Philip the Good, the Duke of Burgundy.

Philip was the Duke of Burgundy at a time when the Burgundian France but came into increasing conflict with the English, the result of which was intermittent warfare, which ended with the English being expelled in 1383. Here again, his royal patronage proved to be indispensable to the well-being of Flanders and Bruges. ❑

THE OTTOMAN INVASION OF THE BALKANS

Serbia, June 15, 1389

In the second half of the fourteenth century, the Ottoman Turks pushed farther into the former Byzantine Empire's European territories. Essential to their westward expansion was their subjugation of the Balkans, which at the time were being defended by a disorganized confederation of militarily skilled aristocrats and knights. Two crucial battles took place that established Ottoman sovereignty in the region.

The first battle was the Sultan Murad I's victory over the Serbs at Cernomen (on today's Greco-Turkish border) on September 26, 1371. After establishing this gateway to the Balkans, Murad was able to sweep westward, accumulating as he went numerous Balkan leaders willing to become Ottoman vassals.

The second was the Battle of Kosovo (also known as the Battle of Amselfeld), where Murad's forces defeated those of Prince Lazar of Serbia on June 15, 1389 at Kosovo Polje (Serbian for "field of blackbirds"). The battle achieved legendary status when both leaders were killed during the fight.

In the Ottoman tradition, the Sultan's heroic death during battle and the ultimate victory under his successor son, Bayezid I, have been recorded by chroniclers as epochal events in Islam's Holy War against the infidels.

The Serb version of Murad's death glorifies the heroic actions of Milos Obilic, who is reported to have snuck into the enemy camp and sacrificed his own life after assassinating the Ottoman ruler. His patriotic bravery, along with Lazar's death, have enshrined the Battle of Kosovo in Serbian myth as a defining moment in national identity. It is celebrated to this day on June 28, St. Vitus Day. ❏

Battle of Amselfeld (reproduction of a 20th century painting)

POLAND BECOMES A EUROPEAN POWER

Poland, late fourteenth century

King Casimir III ruled over Polish lands for almost forty years. The stability of a single leader helped establish strong economic growth. When he ascended the throne in 1333, Casimir's kingdom was threatened on all sides. He repulsed a Mongol invasion, annexed Galicia, and created well-defined national frontiers. He encouraged the immigration of Jews to serve as tax collectors and bankers, founded the University of Kracow, codified the laws of the land, established a firm, efficient administration, and gave peasants the right to migrate from one place to another. When he died in a hunting accident at age 60, the Polish throne passed to Louis, King of Hungary. Before Louis died, he arranged for one of his two daughters to inherit the kingdom.

Jadwiga, 10, was crowned Queen of Poland at the insistence of Polish nobles. Soon after, a marriage prepared the way for the union of the Polish and Lithuanian crowns, uniting the two countries against their common foe, the Knights of the Teutonic Order, the territory-hungry descendants of the crusaders. At a ceremony in Kracow, Jagiello, the 36-year-old Grand Duke of Lithuania, married Jadwiga, who was 12 at the time. The marriage ended the longstanding rivalry between the two countries, and the Lithuanians adopted Christianity.

Diplomatic maneuvering over the union was intense. Jagiello had long wanted to enter the sphere of western civilization, but Jadwiga resisted the idea of union with a pagan. She was finally persuaded by Polish lords and priests to sacrifice herself for Poland's sake. Although she was young, her royal dignity, legally equal to that of her husband, worked to her advantage. She was venerated by Poles after her death and was canonized by the Catholic Church in 1997. ❏

Jagiello II (lithograph after a painting by von Matejko)

THE DIVAN OF HAFIZ

Persia, 1390

The lyrics of the free-spirited Persian poet Hafiz mark the high point of Persian literature. They are still read in Iran by all classes of society.

Hafiz, "one who knows the Quran by heart," died in the town of Shiraz in 1390 at the age of 64. It was only after his death that his poetry was collected and published. His Divan (Collection) consists of almost six hundred poems. Written in the most elegant style, they reflect upon religious, political, and erotic themes. Hafiz attacked the bigotry of religious clerics, turned his back on orthodoxy, and wrote in praise of love and the virtues of wine, which is absolutely forbidden for Muslims. He saw wine as a gateway to ecstasy. Some readers have suggested that wine has a symbolic value in his poetry,

The Persian poet Hafiz

standing for the mystic's intoxication with the Divine.

Hafiz also considered the idea of love in an all-embracing sense. For him it meant love of God, existence, beauty, and other people. An unusual feature of his poetry is his use of the Persian pronoun "u," a form of "you" that can be either male or female. Whether Hafiz is addressing a woman or a man in his love poetry cannot be definitively established. ❑

AMSELFELD AS NATIONAL MYTH

Point of Interest

Amselfeld (Kosovo Polje) is an area that stretches westward from the city of Pristina. It was the center of medieval Serbia. After the Ottoman victory, June 28, 1389, St. Vitus's Day, became a national Serbian holiday.

After the Ottoman defeat of Hungarian troops in 1448, the area was for a time largely deserted. It was then settled by Albanians, who make up the majority in Kosovo to this day. In 1913 Kosovo, which had until then belonged to the Ottoman Empire, came under the control of Serbia and Montenegro.

In Tito's Yugoslavia, Kosovo was an autonomous province within the Republic of Serbia, but it lost that differentiation in 1989. Albanians were forced out of public life. A violent struggle for independence from Serbia was led by the Kosovo Liberation Army (KLA) and provoked Serbian massacres of civilians and attempted ethnic cleansing. In 1999, NATO forces inaugurated a bombing campaign against Serbia. From the summer of 1999, Kosovo was under the administration of the United Nations. In February of 2008 it declared its independence from Serbia. ❑

TAMERLANE, BRUTAL CONQUEROR

Samarkand, 1388

Tamerlane (also known as Timur Leng, Timur the Lame) saw himself as the heir to Genghis Khan. His trail of conquest, marked by extreme cruelty and bloodshed, reached from China through Central Asia to Turkey and Russia.

In 1388, Tamerlane accepted the title of Sultan. He felt that he was called upon to renew the Mongol Empire and act as a warrior for Islam. In 1360, he was able to take control of the area of Transoxiana (comprising present-day Uzbekistan, Tajikistan, and some of Kazakhstan) from the weakened dynasty of the Khans, who remained nominally in charge. He conquered Samarkand in 1363 and established that as a base for his campaigns of conquest. At the head of a mounted army, he brought Khorasan (1379) and Iran (1380–1386) under Mongol control. His victory over the Golden Horde in 1398

marked its last appearance on the historical stage. His army swept through India, capturing Dehli in 1398 and overrunning the Punjab in 1399. In the following year, he headed west, sacking Damascus, Aleppo, and Baghdad, wiping out the Mamluk army, and leaving hundreds of thousands of people dead.

Tamerlane did not succeed in his plan to conquer China. He died of a fever on the way, his dream of reestablishing the

Mongol Empire unrealized, but his descendant Babur went on to found the Mughal Empire in India. ❑

Invading Mongols (Persian miniature, 14th century)

THE PEASANTS' REVOLT AND THE ABDICATION OF RICHARD II

England, 1399

The end of the fourteenth century was witness to many uprisings in Europe, the most notable being the Peasants' Revolt in England. In June 1381, scores of rioters descended on London where they were joined by local workers in their protest against the continuing bonds of serfdom and an unpopular poll tax to finance military adventures. Led by Wat Tyler, the rebels burned and looted the city, while the 14-year-old king and his advisors fled to the Tower. On the second day of rioting, Richard II met with the rebels and allegedly agreed to some of their demands.

At the same time, rebels stormed the Tower and captured and beheaded the Lord of the Treasury and the Archbishop. Richard II agreed to meet Tyler the following day in what is now London's

Richard II greets rebellious peasants (lithograph)

Smithfield Market. Tyler's insolent behavior resulted in his being stabbed and his followers dispersed by the king's men. Order was regained four days after the uprising began, and Richard's promises went unfulfilled.

Richard II's reign continued to be beset by calamity until in 1399, under pressure from nobles, the king signed a deed of abdication. Among the delegation was Henry Bolingbroke, the son of John of Gaunt, who promptly claimed the crown for himself, becoming Henry IV. A document of more than thirty articles accusing the king of tyrannical rule was presented to parliament. Certainly, the wanton luxury of Richard's court, as well as his claim to be the source of England's law, caused great resentment, but the immediate cause of his overthrow was his inability to contend with hostile nobles. Richard died under suspicious circumstances in 1400 while imprisoned. ❑

GEOFFREY CHAUCER'S *CANTERBURY TALES*

England, 1400

Best known for the bawdy, humorous, and psychologically insightful characters that populate *The Canterbury Tales*, Geoffrey Chaucer (1343–1400) was the first great writer in the English language. At a time when most documents were written in French or Latin, and most literature focused on the deeds of the upper classes, Chaucer offered a refreshing and realistic look at the full range of English society.

Chaucer came from a well-to-do family of vintners and received a court education as a page. He fought for the English army in France, was taken prisoner in 1360, and later ransomed. He came back enthused by the French fashion for poems of courtly love. He read in four languages and on later travels to Italy was greatly influenced by his reading of Boccaccio. Chaucer enjoyed a successful career at court, where in addition to his duties as a diplomat and comptroller, he began writing and translating. His first literary masterpiece was *Troilus and Cresyde*, a love story set during the Trojan War. Eventually Chaucer turned his attention to detailing a band of pilgrims and the stories they told to one another as they traveled to Canterbury. In his narrative, Chaucer made immemorial the corrupt, the cuckolded, the pious, and the piteous. He drew his characters with a mixture of remarkable shrewdness and pithy humor, and his use of satire would inspire writers for centuries to come.

Chaucer's *Canterbury Tales*, which consists of both prose and verse, was incomplete at his death in 1400. In 1475 it was selected by William Caxton to be one of the first books printed in English. Chaucer was the first writer whose remains were put in what is now called the Poets' Corner in Westminster Abbey. ❑

Folio from the *Canterbury Tales* (manuscript)

THE KALMAR UNION

Sweden, June 20, 1397

With the creation of the Kalmar Union in 1397, three Scandinavian kingdoms were united under a single sovereign. Denmark, Sweden, and Norway became the second largest European territory under an arrangement conceived by Queen Margaret of Norway. The arrangement called for a common foreign policy and a royal succession to be determined by consensus. Legal structures within the kingdoms were not affected.

The agreement was a triumph for Margaret, an ambitious and skillful politician and a gifted diplomat. She became regent of Denmark on the death of her father, and of Norway on the death of her husband. She gained possession of Sweden after deposing Albrecht of Mecklenburg. Margaret's intention from the beginning had been to provide the union with a suitable male head, and her 15-year-old great-nephew, Duke Erik Vll of Pomerania, was crowned King of Scandinavia at Kalmar, although Margaret for all intents and purposes retained power. The union also grew to some extent out of a general trend toward the creation of larger political entities such as the formation of Poland-Lithuania and the expansion of Moscow.

The informal union among the three kingdoms lasted until 1523. ❑

Kalmar Castle, Sweden

PIRACY IN THE NORTH SEA

Northern Europe, late fourteenth century

The roots of the Kalmar Union lay in a war between Denmark and Mecklenburg in which piracy played a prominent role. Herzog Albrecht of Mecklenburg, who had served as King of Sweden since 1364, was defeated by the Danish-Norwegian Queen Margaret I at the Battle of Falkoping and put into prison.

Pirates who had been hired by Margaret to harrow her opponent's shipping now demanded their reward. In 1393, they took the city of Malmo and put it to the torch, then occupied Visby and Gotland. Despite the treaty signed by Albrecht and Margaret in 1395, which resulted in Stockholm's joining the Hanseatic League, the pirates continued to make the waters of the Baltic unsafe for shipping. To counter their influence, the Knights of the Teutonic Order took action. In 1398, they seized Gotland, the pirates' base of operations. Consequently many of the pirates made for harbors in the North Sea.

Once there they began to raid the coast of Germany and the Netherlands. The City of Hamburg decided to end the scourge. A joint Lubische-Hamburg fleet set sail in 1400. On its return, they reported that they had killed eighty of the pirates. In the next year, they captured two of the pirate chiefs, Klaus Stortebeker and Godeke Michels. They were executed along with their crews, about a hundred men in all. The Hanseatic League was, however, unable to organize a similar military action. Although the pirate crews attracted many criminals, honest seafarers and impoverished nobles were also drawn to a life of piracy. The pirates called themselves Likedeelers, meaning that the spoils were shared equally among the crews. ❑

Execution of the Pirate Klaus Stortebeker and Goedeke Michels in Hamburg (1402, etching)

DEFEAT OF THE TEUTONIC KNIGHTS

Prussia, July 15, 1410

The Teutonic Knights, a German religious order turned crusading military force, had invaded Prussia in 1243 to spread Christianity. They founded cities, built fortresses, and gained control over the region with the blessing of Rome. Eventually they turned their attention to present-day Poland and Lithuania. Recently united through the marriage of Jagiello, the Grand Duke of Lithuania, and the Queen of Poland, the Poles and Lithuanians managed, after years of skirmishing, to defeat the Teutonic Order at Tannenberg, and thus end the Order's two centuries of rule in the region. The fight was effectively about the control of Eastern Europe, and the defeat of the Knights ended a period of aggressive German expansion.

When it came time to fight, tactics proved the deciding factor, and the Polish gentry finally carried the day when the German charge failed. To this day remains a celebrated date in Polish history. ❑

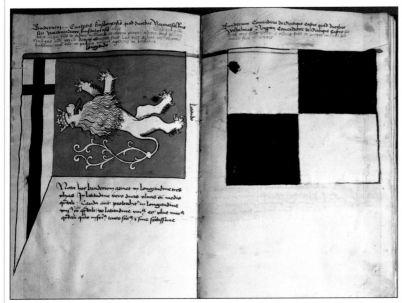

Battle standard of the German Order (drawing by Stanislaw Durink, 1448)

MILITARY ADVANCES UNDER THE RULER OF KANO

Kano, 1410

Kanajeji Sarki reigned in Kano (Nigeria) for twenty years. The West African monarch, who introduced war horses and gave his soldiers the protection of helmets and chain mail, raised the power of Kano to new heights. In the thirteenth century, Kano was an insignificant city-state whose writ ran little further than its city walls. Steadily Kano expanded its territories. By Kanajeji's accession, it dominated most of Hausaland (northwestern Nigeria); by his death, it had surpassed the power of the Mali empire and dominated West Africa. Not afraid of innovation, Kanajeji imported chain mail from the Egyptian Mamluks and, recognizing the tactical value of the horse, built a superb cavalry, its horses upholstered in quilted body armor. None could withstand them, and Kanajeji's army became one of most powerful on the whole of the African continent. ❑

THE BATTLE OF AGINCOURT

Agincourt, 1415

In 1338, England's invasion of northern France under Edward III set in motion a decades-long series of forays, skirmishes, battles, and extended truces marked by wanton destruction and violence and the ravaging of the French countryside. Of the few decisive engagements, the most notable was the English victory at Crécy in 1346 and its fabled triumph at Agincourt in 1415.

Immortalized by Shakespeare, the battle of Agincourt was fought and won by England's Henry V. Having invaded northern France, Henry was forced to do battle with an impatient French force between the ports of Harfleur and Calais. The English, numbering twelve thousand, knew that they were grossly outnumbered by the French, perhaps by as much as five to one. As they lay silent, legend has it that Henry V walked among them, talking quietly to archer, foot soldier, and knight alike. He had not wanted this battle and had been prepared to strike bargains to avoid it. Half a mile away, the French were jubilant, even parading a cart in which they intended to drag the English king through Paris.

Henry V took his position in front of his army as the French began their advance through a narrow muddy field and into a rain of English arrows. The English victory is often attributed in part to their use of the longbow, which was fired with quickness and accuracy and easily restrung compared with the cumbersome, anchored crossbow favored by the French. The French cavalry panicked, smashing their way through their own infantrymen, only to be turned back by palings constructed by the English in front of their archers. The French army literally choked on itself as horses and men piled atop one another. Breaches in the French ranks were quickly filled by English soldiers wielding swords and

ANDREI RUBLEV, RUSSIAN ICON PAINTER

Russia, c.1400

Byzantine influences were notable in the work of painter Andrei Rublev, the greatest Russian artist of his day. According to Byzantine tradition, icon painting had its original source in a "a painting not made by human hands." It was said that the face of Christ was impressed onto a towel that he had used. The task of the painter was then to copy this divinely inspired original, not invest the work with his own subjectivity.

Rublev's work demonstrates a remarkable marriage of spirituality and aesthetics. His work was more intimate and realistic in its contemplation of the divine than that of other icon painters, and he made use of the technique known as *sfumato*, the soft blending of light and shade. He was able to give simple expression to theologically complex ideas and convey a calm ecstasy in his singularly warm and intimate objects of devotion ❑

Icon (early 15th century)

axes. A massacre unfolded, and at day's end thousands of French soldiers were dead or wounded, with much lighter casualties recorded for the English.

The usual ransoming of lords and knights, which had made the long wars very profitable for some, was not observed at Agincourt. Fearing an attack from the rear, Henry had many of the French nobles who had been taken as prisoner slaughtered.

After months of negotiation, during which he laid siege to walled towns by cannon (and advanced the use of gun powder in modern warfare), Henry V married Catherine of Valois, daughter of the king of France, and was named heir to the French throne. He thereby nominally united the two warring nations. But in 1422, Henry died before he could succeed Charles VI of France. The fragile peace fell apart and the war continued another for thirty years. ❑

The Battle of Agincourt (manuscript illustration, 15th century)

PENINSULA OF MALACCA CONVERTED TO ISLAM BY INDONESIAN PRINCE

Malacca, 1414

Paramesvara was an exiled Indonesian prince who founded a kingdom on the Malayan peninsula. First, he declared Palembang in southern Sumatra independent from the Majapahit kingdom on Java.

Majapahit subsequently destroyed Palembang, forcing Paramesvara to flee to Tumasik (present-day Singapore) on the Malaccan peninsula. Again pursued, he reached Malacca on the narrow Malac-

can straits in 1401. There he established his new state. Malacca became prosperous thanks to its ideal setting for maritime trade. A center of international commerce, Malacca grew to rival Venice in

the wealth of its trade.

Paramesvara converted to Islam and took the title Raja Iskandar Shah. His conversion was critical to the introduction of Islam to the region. ❑

DEATH OF THE FIRST MING EMPEROR

China, c.1400

The founder of China's famed Ming dynasty was a peasant who became an emperor. Zhu Yuanzhang, began his rise to supreme power at age 17, when his family fell victim to the plague and famine. He became a monk to survive but found his real role when he joined the peasant revolutionaries, the Red Turbans.

He rose to power by his mili-

tary ability and bravery, and by refocusing his forces' attacks from the landowners to overcoming the Mongol Yuan dynasty, he achieved such success that, in 1368, he was able to take Beijing and drive the last Yuan emperor back across the Great Wall into the Gobi Desert.

He named his own dynasty Ming (brilliant) and ruled for thirty years. Scarred by the fate

of his family, Zhu Yuanzhang directed much of his energy toward establishing a stable social and economic order based on agriculture. He remained concerned with common people, and even when he grew despotic toward the end of his long life, his victims were more often nobles than peasants.

It has been suggested that he had been a member of the

White Lotus secret society, and although he denied this, he came to rely on his own web of secret agents and to look upon any opposition as proof of a conspiracy against him.

He was buried in the Purple Mountains outside Nanjing, his power base, and is lauded as the man who reunified China. The Ming dynasty would last nearly three hundred years. ❑

JAN HUS AND THE MOVEMENT FOR CHURCH REFORM

Constance, 1415

Jan Hus was a devoted scholar and teacher at the University of Prague. He was also a popular preacher who was sympathetic to many of the theological ideas of the Englishman John Wycliffe. Hus spoke out against corruption in the church. He opposed the selling of indulgences and the buying of ecclesiastical offices, and believed that communion should be extended to the laity.

Hus was from a humble background and preached his sermons in Czech. He was distressed by the Papal Schism, and declared that to rebel against an erring pope was to obey Christ. His preaching resulted in his excommunication by the pope and his being summoned to the Council of Constance. The initial task if the Council was to solve the problem of the split papacy, but it also tackled the issue of increasing heresy throughout western Europe.

Hus went willingly to Constance, seeing it as an opportunity to argue his points. He was guaranteed safe passage by the Holy Roman Emperor, but after appearing before church officials and refusing to recant his beliefs, he was imprisoned for seven months and ultimately condemned by the Council of Constance as a heretic. He was stripped of his vestments, crowned with a paper fool's cap painted with devils, and turned over to secular authorities. He was led out of the city and burnt to death. He died singing a hymn.

The condemnation and death of Hus divided Prague and Bohemia both politically and religiously. It helped awaken a growing Czech nationalism, as nobles and poor alike were shaken by the execution of a fellow countryman by foreigners. Many also felt that the efforts he made in challenging the Roman Church were entirely justified.

In the summer of 1419, the conflict between the Czech nation and the Church of Rome came to a head. During a mass demonstration in Prague, thousands of Hussites marched on the New Town Hall. After demands for the release of several of their preachers were ignored, the crowd forced its way into the building and threw several Catholic councillors out of the windows into the square. The event became known as The Defenestration of Prague.

King Wenceslas IV, who had at times supported both sides of the growing rebellion, died shortly after the Prague protest. His brother Sigismund, King of Hungary, inherited the kingdom of Bohemia. When he came to Prague with his German troops, he was denied entry into the city.

The next fifteen years were witness to the Hussite wars. The followers of Hus divided into two camps and fought each other as well as the armies sent against them by successive popes and German princes. In 1427, the Hussite armies went on the offensive and successfully attacked Austria, Poland, and Germany; they nearly made it to the Rhine before turning back.

A tenuous peace came in 1436 when the Emperor Sigismund, representatives of the Roman Catholic Church, and the moderate Hussites agreed that Bohemians would be allowed to take wine and bread during Mass, that the wealth of the Church would be limited, and that the word of God was to be freely preached. Such demands and policies would have a profound effect on the coming Reformation in Western Europe. ❑

Jan Hus burnt at the stake (Chronicle of Ulrich von Richental, 1482). The writing on his paper hat designates him as arch-heretic.

The Five Founders of Florentine Art: Giotto, Ucello, Donatello, Manetti, Brunelleschi (painting c. 1450)

BRUNELLESCHI'S DOME

Florence, 1421

When Filippo Brunelleschi (1337–1446) began work on the cathedral in Florence, all but its dome remained to be completed, but no one knew how such a massive structure could be built. He labored for fiteen years to meet the challenge. Taken with his work on the Church of San Lorenzo, the Pazzi Chapel in Santa Croce, and Santo Spirito, Brunelleschi could lay claim to originating a new architectural style. His reversion to classical models and search for harmonious proportions were a clear rejection of the medieval Gothic tradition. He is said to have been the inventor of linear perspective and the first to use it in a painting. ❑

Map of West Africa (1540, restored in the 18th century)

COUNCIL HEALS CHURCH SCHISM

Constance, November, 1417

The Great Schism did much to undermine the authority of the Church throughout Europe. By 1417, there were not two but three popes, and a council of national and clerical factions met to resolve the untenable situation. Instigated in part by the King of Hungary, Sigismund, more than two thousand attendees met in the German town of Constance.

The Pisan antipope, John XXIII, was the first to fall. He was found guilty by the council in May 1415 of adultery, incest, sodomy, the poisoning of Pope Alexander V, and the denial of the immortality of the soul. Gregory XII, the Roman pope, then decided that discretion was the better part of valor and resigned voluntarily in June. Benedict XIII, the Avignon pope, proved more obdurate, but he was finally deposed on 26 July 1417 as a heretic.

An Italian cardinal, Oddone Colonna, was elected Pope Martin V by the conclave. The new pope had no great reputation as a scholar or preacher. At Constance he was seen running with the hare and hunting with the hounds. Amiable and colorless, he was perhaps an ideal compromise figure, and his election signaled the increasing power of national interests over the papacy. ❑

Pope Martin V

PORTUGUESE EXPLORE AFRICAN COAST

Portugal, early fifteenth century

The European view of the physical world changed dramatically under the encouragement of a Portuguese prince known as Prince Henry the Navigator. Henry sent his squires and sailors on maritime adventures into the eastern Atlantic and eventually down the coast of Africa.

Henry's dreams of exploration were greatly aided by advancements in shipbuilding and by the rediscovery of Greek and Arab learning about cartography and navigation. Although he never left Portugal himself, the great sailor sent ship after ship out from his palace-observatory at Sagres. Henry's first commissioned voyage sent Goncalo Cabral to search for mythical islands in the Atlantic. Cabral eventually found the Azores.

Henry was determined that his vessels sail beyond the sandy bulge of the feared Cape Bojador on the coast of West Africa. Henry listened patiently to his captains' tales of the dangers of that awful place. They were terrified of the legends of the Sea of Darkness that lay beyond the cape. It was a place where white men turned black, and the currents would prevent any ship from returning.

Henry's expeditions established a foothold at Cueta, in present-day Morocco. When some of his ships were blown into Madeira and Santo Porto, those lands were claimed for Portugal, and by 1420, a settlement had been established. A Portuguese captain, Gil Eannes, continued to voyage south via Madeira and the Canary Islands. At last, in 1434, he rounded the feared Cape Bojador, thus fulfilling one of Henry's most fervent ambitions. Eannes found no indication of human habitation there and brought back only some plants called St. Mary's roses. The importance of his voyage, however, was that he proved that ships could sail the seas beyond Cape Bojador. The way south was now open.

Henry reacted promptly to Eannes's news. He sent Eannes to sea again along with another ship commanded by Alfonso Baldaya, a royal attendant, with orders to explore beyond the cape. By the time of Henry's death in 1460, Portuguese seamen had crept down the coast of Africa as far as the Gambia River. ❑

MAGNIFICENT EMPIRES IN BLACK AFRICA

Only a few decades ago, Sub-Saharan Africa was still seen as a continent without a history. It was only with the emergence of the young African states that the era before the European conquests came to the attention of historians, who discovered native African traditions and long-forgotten empires such as those of Mali and Ghana. When the former British colony of the Gold Coast became independent, it took the name Ghana in honor of the former power and importance of a region of Africa that had flourished between the fourth and sixteenth centuries.

The oldest Black African kingdom, south of the Sahara, was the "Land of Gold," Ghana. Its wealth was based on its plentiful deposits of gold. The old kingdom is in fact not at all the same as modern-day Ghana, which is situated near the Volta estuary. In 977, when the Kingdom of Ghana was at the height of its power, the Arab historian Ibn Haukal put it very simply: "The King of Ghana is the richest man on earth." His sphere of influence stretched from the Atlantic to Timbuktu on the Niger. He allegedly had an army of two hundred thousand men.

But danger lay in wait for Ghana in the form of Islamic missionaries, the Almoravids, leaders of a strict Islamic revival movement, the center of which was a monastery situated on an island in the Senegal River. In the middle of the eleventh century, they started a religious war, pushed northward and founded a capital, Marrakesh, for their new realm. In 1077, after fierce battles, the Almoravids conquered Ghana's trading capital, Kumbi Saleh, in the south of present-day Mauritania. Although the Almoravids were driven out after a few decades, Ghana never succeeded in regaining its former position of power, and in 1240 it was finally conquered.

THE KINGDOM OF THE MALINKE

The Kingdom of the Malinke (Mali) emerged as Ghana's successor. The tribal princes of Mali had already been converted to Islam. Under their legendary ruler Sundjata (1230–1255), who was also known as Mari Djata (the Lion of Mali), the Malinkes extended their sphere of influence. The kingdom lived off trans-Saharan trade; in addition they controlled rich gold deposits.

Mali reached its greatest expansion under Mansa (King) Kankan Musa in the first half of the fourteenth century. Musa's pilgrimage to Mecca in 1324 became famous for his vast and magnificent caravan of camels and slaves. Musa used the pilgrimage to establish economic and cultural relations with the Arab world.

Besides merchants, Musa also attracted white scholars and master builders. Timbuktu became the most important trading capital and cultural center in western Sudan. At the end of the fourteenth century, dynastic conflicts and the problems of invading Mossi tribes in the south and Tuaregs in the north weakened the Kingdom of Mali; then in 1435, the Tuaregs captured Timbuktu. Mali fell as Ghana had done before, and the kingdom of the Songhai took over its sphere of influence.

BOOKS, SLAVES AND HORSES — THE SONGHAI

Originally the Songhai lived in the region of the middle Niger, and their capital was Gao, about 220 miles (350 km) downstream from Timbuktu. Like the Malinkes, they too had converted to Islam in the eleventh century. They were then conquered by the Mali until their ruler Sonni Ali subjugated almost the whole of the former Kingdom of Mali. When Sonni Ali drowned in

An important example of west African art: Yoruba bronze head from Ife in present-day Nigeria.

a mountain river in 1492, one of his army commanders, a member of the Soninke tribe, seized power. Under the name of Askia Muhammad I, he founded the Muslim Askia dynasty, under which the kingdom of the Songhai reached the height of its expansion in the sixteenth century. In 1497 Muhammad I went on a pilgrimage to Mecca. He returned home with numerous Arab scholars, and the Songhai towns developed into centers of art and science; the Islamic school of Timbuktu, in particular, was highly respected in the Muslim world.

At the end of the sixteenth century, an army of Spanish conquistadors in the service of Morocco, armed with cannons, conquered Gao and Timbuktu, but they did not reach as far as the gold mines in the south. Morocco established a tyrannic rule over the country but was unable to subjugate it completely. Nevertheless the Askia were never able to regain their former position of power.

THE MURDER OF A KING AND HUMAN SACRIFICE

While the development of the Sudan region was marked to a large extent by the spread of Islam, the west African forest areas and coastal regions remained untouched by it. The tropical forest impeded penetration by the Islamic cavalry, and the history of that region until the fourteenth century is known only through archaeological research and stories, strongly influenced by legend, that have been handed down through the centuries.

It is known that the Yoruba kingdoms and the city-state of Benin played an important role in the history of that part of Africa. The oldest town and political center was Oyo, about 110 miles (180 km) to the north of present-day Lagos, and the religious center was Ife, some 60 miles (100 km) away. According to tradition, the greatest ruler, Oluascho, reigned for 320 years and fathered no fewer than 1,460 children. The bronzes of Ife are perfect examples of Yoruba art. They include heads of kings with faces entirely covered with parallel vertical decorative lines, reflecting their position of power, and emanating composure and calm, as well as groups of carved figures up to 6.5 feet (2 m) high, carved masks, and terracotta statuettes.

In the mid-twelfth century, the Ife-born Yoruba prince Eweka founded the city-state of Benin that became a center of the slave trade. It is reported that thousands of slaves were sacrificed in ritual killings.

The Kingdom of Benin is famous particularly for its bronze reliefs and its carvings in wood and ivory, as well as for its sculptures. Reliefs depicting the ruler and his exploits adorned the columns and walls of the royal palace. The technique of lost-wax bronze casting was copied from Ife, but it was further developed in Benin and became commonly practiced in the fifteenth and sixteenth centuries.

CONGO AND ZIMBABWE

In parallel to the Yoruba states and Benin, a series of smaller powers developed along the west African coast that stretched as far as the estuary of the Congo River. The center of these smaller groups, which gathered into a kind of federal alliance based on family relationships, was the Congo. The ruler of the Bantu people of Bakongo, Manikongo (Ruler of the Congo), derived his income from the tolls imposed on the trade with the interior, which was flourishing long before the arrival of the Europeans.

There were also numerous small states along the east African coast, mostly city-states under the influence of Islam such as Mogadishu, Malinde, Mombasa and Kilwa, but economically these were completely oriented toward the Asia, to which they exported gold, ivory and slaves.

Little is known about the states in the African interior. The only exception is the state of Monomotapa. This was the name given to the ruler of a state in the region of present-day Zambia and Zimbabwe, where the remains of some ancient monumental buildings have been discovered. The ruler lived behind an outer wall 33 feet (10 m) high, built around his fortress residence to protect him from the prying eyes of his subjects, who could approach him only on all fours or on their knees.

EXTERNAL INFLUENCES

The beginning of African history is marked by a natural catastrophe, the gradual transformation of the Sahara into a desert, which precipitated a mass migration of African tribes. The second major influence on African history was the spread of Islam, which led to a political and cultural flowering marked by the influence of the Arab world.

Christian kingdoms, such as those of Nubia and Axum, which became Ethiopia, developed independently, having been able to withstand the pressure of Islam for centuries. Ethiopia experienced a flourishing renaissance in the fourteenth and fifteenth centuries, inspired by close contacts with the Eastern Church.

In the fifteenth and sixteenth centuries, the attempts of Europeans to discover a water route to India eventually resulted in many kingdoms of Black Africa falling into the hands of colonists; others lost their influence or gradually disappeared. The slave trade that had been mainly in Arab hands was taken over by the Europeans and expanded considerably. ❑

Minaret of the Jinga-ber-mosque in Timbuktu (Mali). The protruding beams support the building and articulate the facade; they are also used as scaffolding by workers when repairing the building.

RISE OF THE AZTECS

Mexico, 1428

The Aztecs seemed to have stemmed from a tribe of nomads called the Mexica who migrated from the north into the well-settled area of central Mexico. There they established what

Aztec sacrifices

would become the Aztec capital, Tenochtitlán, in 1324.

At this point the Aztecs were subject to the powerful Tepaneca tribe. Over time they became assimilated into the more sophisticated cultures of the region. Through marriage with the royal family of another neighboring tribe, they founded their own dynasty, and within three generations under the leadership of Itzcoatl, they conquered the Tepanec capital. Along with his half-brother Tlacaelel, Itzcoatl can be said to have founded the Aztec empire, which began as a league with two other city-states, Tetzcoco and Tlacopan.

Tenochtitlán became an imposing political center. At its high point it was home to as many as two hundred thousand residents. Aztec life derived many features from earlier Toltec, Mixtec, and Zapotec cultures and was centered around its religion and pantheon of gods. The king ruled the empire in time of war, but in times of peace, the authority of the high priest went unchallenged. One well-known aspect of Aztec religious observance was human sacrifice, a ritual held to renew the strength of the gods and with them the forces of nature. ❏

THE MEDICI: FLORENTINE PATRONS

Florence, 1434

Without official positions, the Medici were able to establish themselves as the most powerful family in Florence. After a short period of exile forced by his rival Rinaldo degli Albizzi, the banker Cosimo de' Medici, called Cosimo the Elder, assumed de facto control of the city.

Cosimo was in many ways the embodiment of Renaissance virtues and vices. Despite his lack of an official title, he worked for the glory of his city through political and diplomatic actions and became the preeminent patron of

Pontormo, *Cosimo de'Medici*

the arts and sciences of his time.

JAN VAN EYCK: MASTER OF THE NORTHERN RENAISSANCE

Ghent, 1432

The Dutch master painter Jan van Eyck was largely responsible for an entirely new style of painting that represented and furthered a seismic shift in perception. For the first time since antiquity, painting had as its main objective the depiction of the world as it appears. Painting in the medieval period was a devotional art that sought to glorify God and inspire religious sentiments in the viewer. Van Eyck's painting are also devotional, his portraits aside, but his innovations with the embryonic technique of oil painting made possible a new way of depicting light and shadow and radically enhanced his colors. This, combined with his remarkable skill in rendering detail and a natural sense of perspective, produced tableaus that convey the sense and texture of seen reality. His masterpiece, the triptych The Adoration of the Lamb,

Jan van Eyck, *The Adoration of the Lamb,* **Central panel from tritych, Ghent, c.1430**

stands as one of the undisputed high points of Western painting. It can still be seen at St. Bavo's Cathedral in Ghent, where it has weathered the fires and storms of war and time. ❏

TWO KINDS OF CALENDARS

Point of interest

The Aztec calendars were based upon those devised by the Maya in the Classical period. A ceremonial calendar consisted of 260 days, and a solar calendar of 365 days. Each day was accounted for by both calendars. The two systems were synchronized on a cycle of 52 years; thus every 52 years, the first day of each calendar would coincide.

The Aztecs believed that the universe had been created and destroyed four times before the present age. They themselves lived in the fifth era, the age of the Sun God. Their mythology told of the gods' self-sacrifice bringing their age into existence. The God Qutelzcoatl had fashioned men from the bones of the dead in the underworld, which he sprinkled with his own blood. Human sacrifice was a sacred repetition of the gods' sacrifice and ensured that the sun would remain in its course. ❏

OF ART

He is said to have provided six hundred thousand gold guilders in patronage, a staggering sum equal to that of a Rockefeller or a Carnegie.

Cosimo's grandson Lorenzo followed his illustrious example. He became the city's leader upon the death of his father Piero in 1469. His early years in power were tainted by conspiracies at home and wrangling with the pope, but by 1480, he had fortified his position. During Lorenzo's lifetime, Florence became the preeminent center of High Renaissance culture. Florence became home to the humanist scholars Ficino and della Mirandola and gloried in the artistic productions of Verrocchio and Botticelli. Lorenzo himself was a scholar and poet of considerable merit. ❑

Joan of Arc at the stake (French miniature)

DELIVERANCE OF FRANCE BY JOAN OF ARC

Orléans, May 8, 1429

At the age of 13, Joan of Arc, a young peasant girl, began hearing voices in her father's garden. They told Joan that it was the will of heaven that the English should be thrown out of France and that she was to be instrumental in their eviction. She should tell the Dauphin that he must be crowned at Rheims, after which the English would not be able to stand against him. Remarkably, Joan succeeded in reaching the Dauphin's court and convinced him of her devoutness and sincerity. In return, he gave her a horse and a full suit of armor. She rode at the head of French troops to Orléans, which had been besieged by the English for seven months. Whether the French viewed the slight young girl as a mascot or an inspired leader cannot be said. But the troops were transformed into an elated crusading army that gave up swearing and harlots and attended Mass, where they vowed to follow Joan's voices.

The inspired French forced the English army into retreat, capturing the city of May 8, 1429. Shortly thereafter the Dauphin was crowned Charles VII, King of France. During the ensuing months, Joan played a major role in the attempted recapture of Paris, in which she was wounded, and in other smaller battles. Then she participated in an attack on Compiègne, where she was taken prisoner by the Burgundians. They sold her to their English allies for ten thousand gold crowns. An English escort took the Maid of Orléans to Rouen, where she faced a year of inquisition, torture, and imprisonment. She was charged on seventy counts. Joan conducted her own defense and stressed her purity and her devotion to France, but to no avail. She was declared a witch and, in May of 1431, was burnt at the stake. She asked for a cross to be held before her to see through the flames and her last word was "Jesus."

There is little doubt that this was a political trial or that Charles VII's complacency was one of the main causes of Joan's ordeal. And yet her short life had a profound affect on the fortunes of France. She sparked a patriotism hitherto unknown, and her appearance marked the beginning of the end of the English occupation of France.

Ten years after the death of Joan of Arc, a new trial declared her innocent. Nearly four hundred years after her ashes were thrown in a river, she was made a saint. ❑

NEW ARMOR CHANGES WARFARE

Europe, c.1430

Complete suits of armor made of metal plate began being worn on the battlefield with considerable success. They were developed to overcome the weakness of chain mail, which provided only limited protection: an arrow or a crossbow bolt could penetrate its openings. The new *harnais blanc*, or white armor, was a product of greater sophistication in metal manufacturing techniques.

Tougher iron and steel were heated in blast furnaces and then the white-hot plates were hardened by "quenching" in fluid. Improvements were also taking place in the workshops where the plate was fashioned, so that the armor offered greater resistance to missiles.

Of course, the use of full-plate body armor was not without some drawbacks. It was heavier and more tiring to wear. Accounts of Agincourt record that some armor-clad French lords drowned in the mud because their armor was so heavy. On the other hand, a lance rest at the side of the breastplate made heavy lances easier to handle. Knights could now lower their lances to the horizontal position and take accurate aim while charging at the enemy. ❑

FLOURISHING CIVILIZATIONS IN ANCIENT AMERICA

The rise of the Aztecs to the status of a great power in central America began under the reign of Itzcoatl, who died in 1440. By throwing off the domination of the Tepanecs and founding a triple alliance among the cities of Texcoco, Tlacopan and the Aztec Tenochtitlan, Itzcoatl laid the foundation for the Aztec empire. The first purification ritual recorded in Aztec history is also ascribed to him: Itzcoatl ordered all the historical codices dating from the time before his reign to be burned.

It was only in the fourteenth century that the Aztecs migrated from the north into the densely populated highlands of Mexico. Within a very short time, they adopted many aspects of the highly developed, tradition-rich civilization of the Central American people, ranging from the calendar system to pyramid architecture, from textile techniques to the art of sculpting gold.

In about 1370, the newcomers built the city of Tenochtitlan in an inhospitable area of marshes and lakes, where present-day Mexico City is situated. Just before the Spanish conquest, the Aztec capital had between one hundred and three hundred thousand inhabitants. (Archaeological records mention widely varying figures.) Not only was it one of the largest cities in ancient America, but it

was also one of the largest in the world.

Tenochtitlan bore a certain similarity to Venice with its lagoons and islands, because its numerous canals made the boat the main means of transport in a city where the horse and cart did not exist. As a result of the development of floating gardens (*chinampas*), the city was able to produce a large proportion of the food it needed. Many plants, unknown to Europeans at the time, were cultivated in pre-Columbian America, including maize, potatoes, pineapples and pumpkins.

THE SOCIETY AND RELIGION OF THE AZTECS

At the end of the fifteenth century, most of present-day Mexico paid tribute to the Aztecs, yet the Aztec state had only a low level of economic and political integration, so that large areas remained administratively independent; a few even retained their political independence.

The basic unit in Aztec society was the family clan, the *calpulli*. The land was the property of the calpulli, but its use was inherited by the members of the clan. Many of the functions performed by the clan were soon taken over by the fast-growing upper classes, who gathered around the ruler and his council of elders. In contrast to the general populace, the upper classes were allowed to be polygamous. Merchants and craftsmen

enjoyed a privileged position. Most of the general population was made up of ordinary people—that is, members of the calpulli—as well as the bondsmen and bondswomen, who were probably the original inhabitants of the regions ruled by the Aztecs.

Aztec prisoners of war served a particular purpose: they were sacrificed to the gods. So it was that one of the purposes of Aztec military expeditions was to find humans to use in ritual sacrifices. According to their religion, the Aztecs had to feed the gods with human sacrifices to ensure the continued existence of the world. The Aztec adoption of the gods worshipped by the people they conquered, a proven means to ensure political integration, led to an extraordinary complexity in the Aztec pantheon, whose leading gods were the Sun God and Rain God.

THE END OF THE AZTECS

The conquest of the warlike Aztec kingdom by a relatively small group of Spanish soldiers, led by Hernán Cortés, was made possible by several factors. From a technical point of view, the Spanish were armed with iron weapons and firearms, they rode horses and were accompanied by bloodhounds. Thus they were much superior to the Aztecs, who were armed only with stone and wooden weapons. In addition, the Aztecs, including

The Inca city of Machu Picchu is situated on a mountain peak and cannot be seen from the valley below. The building material (blocks of granite) had to be carried up the mountain.

their ruler Montezuma II (1502–1520), did not know what to make of the strangers. A prophecy announcing the return of the Toltec god Quetzalcoatl, who was mistakenly identified with the strangers, as well as a belief in predestination led to Montezuma's hesitant attitude. The aura of divinity and immortality surrounding the Spaniards disappeared only when the Aztecs succeeded in driving the invaders out of Tenochtitlan. The armies of other native peoples played a major part in the Spanish victory in 1521; these were traditional enemies of the Aztecs who had suffered from their stringent demands for tribute. The last Aztec ruler, Cuauhtemoc, was executed in 1525.

THE INCA EMPIRE

Contemporaneous with the Aztec empire was that of the Incas. It reached its greatest expansion at the end of the fifteenth century when it included the regions of present-day Peru, Bolivia and southern Ecuador as well as northwest Argentina.

Incan society was hierarchical. At the top of the pyramid was the god-king, the Sapa Inca, the son of the sun; his main wife was the incarnation of the moon goddess. The Inca ruler's family, the relations of the non-royal clan of Cuzco and the rulers of conquered tribes formed the upper class. At the bottom of the social pyramid were the peasant clans, the *ayllu*, among whom the land was redivided about every two years. Incan rule was based on the principle of services in return for land, so participation in new campaigns of conquest by those already conquered offered them compensation in return.

A policy of state-funded supplies of provisions prevented famine, and irrigation systems and terrace cultivation increased agricultural production. This system also included a network of controlling measures to which each individual was subjected from birth until death. The population was divided into groups following the decimal system. Officials used knotted cords, sometimes incorrectly described as a script, to record all data relating to these groups. The elevation of the sun cult as the empire's official religion and the enforcement of a common language promoted cohesion among the people.

The Spanish conquest of the Inca Empire, led by Francisco Pizzaro, was successful only because the country was in crisis. The end of military expansion at the beginning of the sixteenth century led to a rivalry among the upper classes that culminated in a fratricidal war between the Inca chieftains, Huascar and Atahualpa.

From their conquest of Mexico, the Spanish had learned that it was necessary to remove the indigenous ruler as soon as possible. They captured Atahualpa and killed him. Then Pizzaro succeeded in convincing some Indian tribes to join him as allies for the rest of his conquest. In 1533, he captured Cuzco and so destroyed the power structure of the Inca Empire. Only in the Andes mountains near Vilcabamba (Machu Picchu, to the north of Cuzco) did the Incas continue to fight the Spanish colonial power for three more decades. The execution of the last Inca ruler took place in Cuzco in 1572.

The Spanish conqueror Hernán Cortés lands in Mexico in 1519 (16th century).

THE EARLY CIVILIZATIONS

Another highly developed civilization in ancient America was that of the Mayas. Mayan civilization was at its peak between the third and tenth centuries, the period known as the classic period of pre-Columbian civilization. They settled in large areas of Mesoamerica, from northern Mexico along the Pacific coast as far south as northern Chile but never formed a unified country.

The height of Maya civilization was long past when the Spanish arrived. Having disintegrated into separate city-states, the Mayas on the Yucatan peninsula were soon conquered by the Spanish after they had completed their conquest of the Aztec empire. But the Mayas living in the southern forested regions continued to resist the Spanish invaders until the end of the seventeenth century.

Looking at their artistic output, the post-classic civilizations of the Aztecs and Incas do not bear comparison with the classic Mesoamerican civilizations. But our knowledge of the Inca and Aztec civilizations is much more extensive than that of the classic period, where facts depend mainly on archaeological sources, while in the case of the Incas and Aztecs many written records exist.

THE SPANISH COLONIZATION

After the arrival of the Spanish and Portuguese in South America, colonization of the New World soon followed. Here the sense of mission and national pride combined with brutality and greed soon led to unparalleled genocide. Initially, after Christopher Columbus landed in the Bahamas in 1492, the Spanish stayed mainly on the Caribbean islands and only made short expeditions to the mainland coasts. But reports of the fabulous wealth of the people living on the mainland eventually attracted bands of conquistadors to the interior of Central and South America in search of gold and silver. The native population was decimated as result. The reasons were partly the diseases introduced by the invaders, but also mass migrations provoked by *repartimientos*, a colonial labor system that was akin to unofficial slavery, whereby the Spaniards were allotted land, and the indigenous population on it was forced to work for them. ❑

THE INCAN EMPEROR PACHACUTI

Cuzco, 1438

Much of what we know about the emergence of the Incan Empire in the thirteenth century comes from *harawi* (songs), oral traditions, stone carvings, and pottery. Noted first by chroniclers of the Spanish conquistadores, they have served as the basis for modern-day analyses by archaeologists and historians. From these accounts have been gleaned references to Manco Capac, a semimythical figure who founded the Kingdom of Cuzco around 1200, considered the first of thirteen Incan emperors. By the time of the conquistadores' arrival in 1532, Manco's legendary domain near the present-day city of Cuzco had become the Incan Empire, the largest nation on earth at the time. Comparable to

the Roman Empire at its peak, it stretched 2,500 miles from present day Colombia to southern Chile, spanning four hundred thousand square miles and inhabited by up to twelve million people. Starting with the reign of the ninth emperor, Pachacuti Inca Yupanqui (r.1438–1471), credible documentation appears. From these sources we learn that it was under his leadership that the Incan Empire began its massive expansion.

Considered the greatest of the Inca rulers, the *Sapan Intiq Churin* (the Only Son of the Sun), Pachacuti rose to power with his victory over the rival Chanca nation in 1438. Taking over from his father, the Emperor Viracocha (named after the sun god), who had

abandoned Cuzco to the invading Chanca, the victorious Pachacuti named himself emperor. He soon expanded his domain to include much of modern-day Peru, then began organizing his growing empire into the *Tahuantinsuyu* (the United Four Provinces). He established a comprehensive, centralized form of governance featuring a rigid hierarchy, at the top of which were the emperor (the *Sapa Inca* or "Only Inca") and his wives, the *coyas*. Below them in descending order of importance: the high priests, the commander-in-chief of the army, the four *apos* (governors of the Four Provinces) and regional army commanders, temple priests, and government administrators. Because the emperor was considered a descen-

dant from the Inca god of creation, Viracocha, and his son, Inti, obedience to him was absolute. The protocol in the Inca social hierarchy was similarly rigid, and breaches were severely punished. Utopian in scope and totalitarian in implementation, Pachacuti's regime was essentially one of benign despotism that prohibited the accumulation of luxury goods to discourage both selfishness and crime, while providing employment, food, housing, and security for every level of society.

In addition to creating this highly evolved social organization, Pachacuti instituted an architectural renaissance in Cuzco that created Incan monuments rivaling those of Pharaonic Egypt. Still standing today are the remnants of his fortress, epicenter of the Inca civilization, the *Sacsahuaman* and the *Coricancha* (the Sacred Temple of the Sun God and the Temple of Gold). He also commissioned the building of the royal estate and religious retreat of Machu Picchu (old peak). This temple complex high in the Andes remains one of the great marvels of human enterprise.

Pachacuti was also a poet who composed the *Sacred Hymns of Pachacuti*. Still extant, these *haillikuna* were composed for performance at the *Situa* ceremony, a ritual festival whose celebration was to drive evil spirits out of Cuzco.

Upon Pachacuti's death in 1471, his son, Topa Yupanqui, became the tenth Sapa Inca It would be under Topa (r.1471–1493) and subsequently his son, the eleventh Sapa Inca Huayna Capac (r.1493–1527), that the Incan Empire would reach its territorial and cultural zenith. Within only a few years after Huayna's death, and less than a hundred years after Pachacuti's epochal first triumph, the Inca Empire would be destroyed by Francisco Pizarro and the conquistadores. ❑

The Inca capital of Cuzco (1576)

The Rise of the House of Habsburg

Austria, 1438

Duke Albert V, crowned as the German King Albert II, was not the first Habsburg to inherit the crown, but with his accession, the Habsburgs gained a throne that they would not relinquish (except briefly, 1842–1845) until the Holy Roman Empire was dissolved. They continued to rule in Austria until the end of the First World War.

The German electoral princes unanimously chose Albert to be their king. He succeeded his father-in-law, Emperor Sigismund, whose death in 1437 signaled the end of the male line of the Luxemboug dynasty. Albert also inherited Sigismund's title as King of Hungary and Bohemia.

Although Albert died soon after, on October 27, 1439, the crown remained in Habsburg hands, despite the fact that the family's ancestral seat lay in Canton Aargau in Switzerland. Frederick V Duke of Steiermark was given the crown in 1440, becoming King Frederick III, and in 1452, he was the last German king to receive the title of Holy Roman Emperor from the pope in Rome.

Through the marriage of Frederick's son Maximilian to Maria, heiress of Duke Charles the Bold of Burgundy, the Habsburgs secured for themselves, and thus for Austria, great power and status in Europe. Even though this marriage set him on a collision course with France, who also had claims in Burgundy, the Habsburgs were strengthened by the reunification of Austrian hereditary lands in the person of Maximilian after Frederick's death in 1493. Maximilian was now the sole ruler of the empire. To his title of German king, the pope added the title of Holy Roman Emperor in 1508.

The Habsburg Castle in the Swiss Canton of Aargau

In the ensuing generations, the Habsburgs ensured the growth of their power through a series of dynastic marriages. In 1496, Maximilian's son Phillip the Handsome married Johanna the Mad, daughter of the Spain's royal couple, King Ferdinand II of Aragon and Isabella Queen of Castile.

The early death of all the heirs to the Spanish throne and Johanna's melancholy, which rendered her unfit to rule, meant that after the death of Ferdinand, the kingdom fell to her son Charles, who was at the time ruling in Burgundy. He also inherited Naples, Sicily, and Spain's overseas possessions. Also heir to Austrian royal lands, he acquired the title Emperor in 1519, upon the death of his grandfather Maximilian. As Emperor Charles V, he became ruler of an empire over which the sun never set. In 1526, Charles's brother Ferdinand, who was also the brother-in-law of Ludwig II, the king of Hungary and Bohemia, inherited the Stephen's Crown, the mark of the Hungarian king, after Hungarian King Ludwig fell in battle. The Habsburgs were now at the zenith of their power. ❏

Habsburgs' Growing Power

Point of Interest

In the middle of the tenth century one finds the first documented mention of the House of Habsburg. At the time they were in possession of vast estates on the Upper Rhine.

Albrecht II was the fourth Habsburg to be crowned king of Germany. His predecessors were Rudolph I (1273-1291), Albrecht I (1298-1308), and Frederick III (1314-1330). Of these Rudolph I was the most prominent ruler. He succeeded in establishing the territorial foundations of Habsburg power in the southwestern part of Germany. After his defeat of his enemy Ottokar of Bohemia, he gained control of large parts of present-day Austria for his successors.

The Habsburg were able to connect their lineage to lands in the southeast in the fourteenth century through the acquisition of the Tyrol (1363), Freiburg in Breisgau (1368) and Trieste (1383). The term the House of Austria as a synonym for the Habsburgs was first used at this time. Simultaneously, however, they were forced to forfeit their hereditary possessions in Switzerland. Although by the fourteenth century the Habsburgs were the most powerful family in the German Empire, they never obtained the rank of *kurfurst* (Prince-Elector). Rudolph IV (r. 1358-1365) used forged documents to assert his claim to the title and privileges of archduke. The claim was finally recognized in 1453. ❏

FALL OF CONSTANTINOPLE

Constantinople, 1453

By 1453, the Ottoman Turks had surrounded Constantinople, the last vestige of the great Roman Empire. Having been driven out of central Asia by the Mongols, they had taken much of the Balkans. With victory at the battle of Varna in 1444, they cemented their hold on southeastern Europe.

In May, Constantinople, Queen of Cities and the impregnable capital of the once-great Byzantine Empire, fell to Ottoman invaders. Its thirteen-mile walls, forty feet high in places and further protected by moats, could not stand the battering of the Turkish cannons.

It was the end of an era. With its armaments outdated and its former allies deserting, Constantinople had been in decline for some time. Exploited by the Venetians and Genoese, betrayed by Slav and Byzantine princes, the city was friendless and hopelessly outnumbered by the armies of Sultan Muhammad II.

The siege of Constantinople was the realization of careful planning. The Ottoman army spent months maneuvering its heavy artillery into position, while several towns on the Sea of Marmara and the Black Sea were overrun. On April 6, the siege began in earnest with the sultan's great cannons directed at the Gate of St. Romanus, where the emperor and his Genoese soldiers had mustered.

Initial resistance was strong. A surprise attack was repulsed, and walls damaged by cannon fire were rebuilt. At sea the Turkish fleet suffered a reverse on April 20 when four relief ships battled through to the harbor. Then the sultan decided to transport 72 ships overland from the Bosporus to the Golden Horn, penetrating the harbor defenses. The sultan's cannon kept up the bombardment, and the besiegers dug in under the city walls.

The storming of the city began. There was fierce fighting, and the emperor was killed in the thick of battle, his head later to be displayed by the victors. Three days of looting began. Residents were dragged off to slavery, killed, or assaulted on church altars.

The 21-year-old sultan curbed some excesses. When the imprisoned Lucas Notaras, grand duke and admiral, was brought before him, Muhammad promised to put him at the head of the city's administration, with the state and court officials.

The fall of Constantinople, which was then renamed Istanbul, had many repercussions: a significant Christian foothold in Asia had been lost, and the center of orthodox Christianity moved to Moscow; the Europeans' loss of access to the Black Sea and overland trade routes to India provided impetus for voyages of discovery; and the Greco-Roman legacy and its scholarship migrated with refugees to Italy and helped fuel the nascent Renaissance.

The successes and excesses of the sultan's army at Constantinople also foretold of continued battles between Christian Europeans and the Muslim Turks as the latter set their sight on further European conquests. ❑

Turks besieging Constantinople (manuscript illustration, 1453)

ITALIAN CITY STATES

Italy, 1454

Milan and Venice signed a peace treaty at Lodi to which Florence, Naples, and the Papal States soon acceded, establishing in 1455 the Most Holy League. The treaty established a balance of power in Italy, which although fragile was able to last for fifty years until France's incursion onto the peninsula in 1494. By ceasing the infighting that had been so characteristic of Italian politics, the city-states of central Italy were better able to counter threats from the Ottoman Empire.

Through skilled diplomacy, these polities were able to assert their influence over cities in northern Italy and stand up to French expansionist policies while maintaining their close connection to the House of Aragon.

Economic flowering. In the second half of the fifteenth century, Italy was the leading econom-

A SHIFT IN

Point of Interest

Over the course of the fifteenth century, the hold of religion over hearts and minds began to loosen, its central place usurped by the individual's sense of self. This presaged a new sensibility among the educated elites in Europe that has come to be known as the Renaissance.

Material underpinnings. Italy's rich city-states were not dependent upon the clergy or upon an aristocratic order devoted to ideals of chivalry. They were governed by old families whose economic vitality provided the foundation of their influence. Cities attributed their success to the enterprise of these leading families and extolled the virtues of thrift, industry, and shrewdness in business. The new type of individual no longer sought the comforts of a religion that offered a paradise in the world to come as recompense for the misery of human existence, but instead looked

AGREE TO PEACE ACCORD

ic power in Europe. Built upon the rich agricultural production of central Italy and the control of trade in the eastern Mediterranean, Italy became the flag bearer for a new kind of economic organization, one based upon capital. Mercantile centers such as Venice, Genoa, Pisa, Florence, and Milan became home to powerful banking families.

Rivalry between cities. The development of Italy had been hampered by persistent conflicts among city-states. Petty but often bloody wars were the rule. Early on Milan, Florence, and Venice were the dominant powers. In 1406, Florence annexed Pisa; Venice had defeated Genoa in 1381, though the city came under French influence before submitting to the rule of Milan.

Internal organization. Most Italian states viewed themselves as

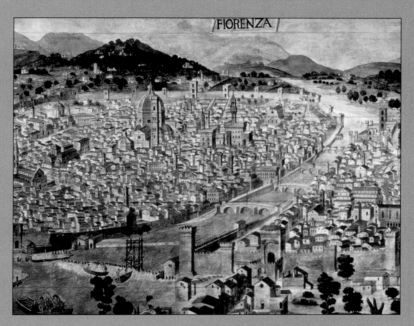

In the fifteenth century Florence was the center of the Italian Renaissance.

republics, though seen through a modern lens, they would be considered oligarchies, since actual

power was really in the heads of the leading aristocratic families and the wealthy merchants and

bankers. In Florence, the Medicis came to power with the rise of Cosimo de Medici in 1434. War broke out in the 1270s in Milan between the Ghibellines (supporters of the Emperor) and Guelfs (supporters of the pope). The Ghibellines defeated their rivals, and the Emperor elevated the Viscontis to the rank of duke. After the death of the last male heir in 1450, the Sforza family took the reins of power.

Venice was an exceptional case in that it had preserved and cultivated its own independent political and social institutions since the early Middle Ages. In addition to the doge, who was the city's political leader, there were the greater and lesser assemblies, the Council of Ten and the Council of Forty, amounting to a distinctively Venetian form of government. ❑

CONSCIOUSNESS

for the Divine in the harmony and beauty of the world. With the dissolution of the strict hierarchy of the feudal system, humanity revealed itself as "the measure of all things" (Protagoras).

Interpreting the past. Directing their attention to the world around them, people scrutinized their natural and political environment, trusting in their own power of reason and their experience. They began to understand natural processes and to assert their mastery over nature through technological development.

The Flight from Egypt (painting by Fra Angelico)

For them the world of classical Greece and Rome presented ideals of self-autonomy, the harmony of mind and body, and the deliberate cultivation of one's personality. The Ottoman conquest of Constantinople brought Greek scholars to the west, where they disseminated a body of knowledge that had been lost to Europe since the fall of Rome but had been preserved in Arabic translation. Thinkers such as Marsilio Ficino, who started an academy in Florence in homage to the one founded by Plato, turned to the study of classical texts as the source of wisdom and inspiration. Their researches in turn had a profound impact on the works of painters and sculptors.

Renaissance painting. The emerging interest in the earthly realities excited the imagination of artists. They saw their foremost task as the faithful recreation of the world around them

in all its depth and texture. The invention of linear perspective (the illusion of three dimensions on a two-dimensional surface) by the architects Filippo Brunelleschi and Leon Battista Alberti seems less of a coincidence than a necessary concomitant of this search to embody nature in art. Propelled by the discovery, such

Santa Maria Novella in Florence (façade by Leon Battista Alberti)

artists as Masaccio, Fra Angelico, Piero della Francesca, Andrea Mantegna, and Sandro Botticelli, established new standards for art, beauty, and the very meaning of representation. Italian painters reached heights never before achieved. Although religious motifs were central to their work—not surprisingly, as the Church was still the foremost patron of the arts—themes drawn from mythology and the celebration of civic life were readily adopted.

Secular architecture. Architecture also developed along classical models. As well as sacred architecture, buildings constructed to display worldly success and glory soon found their place. The wealthy city dwellers' pride in their own achievements was clearly echoed in the brilliant facades of their palaces. Architecture was now intended to exalt the individual, not reflect the glory of God. ❑

GUTENBERG INVENTS A NEW TECHNOLOGY

Mainz, 1455

Johannes Gutenberg (c.1400-1468) was born and died in Mainz, Germany. He was a goldsmith and printer, and is regarded as the inventor of Europe's first movable type printing press, and the first in the world to devise a process for typographic mass production. Although Chinese and Korean printers had invented clay movable type over five hundred years earlier, Gutenberg employed reusable metal typefaces and oil-based inks. He adapted these innovations to the already existent technology used in wooden wine screw presses.

Until his invention, European printers were dependent on the "technologies" of the handwritten manuscript and the woodblock. Although there is some evidence of a form of mechanized printing in the Netherlands a few years earlier, it wasn't until 1439 that Gutenberg himself began to hint at the existence of his new technology. In discussions with potential investors, he referred cryptically to his "secret," the nature of which he would disclose in 1440, in a paper entitled *Kunst und Aventur* (Art and Enterprise).

It is believed that the press was operational by 1450 in Mainz, and that its first work was a now lost German poem. It is known that in this year, Gutenberg borrowed 800 guilders from two investors, Johann Fust and his son-in-law Peter Schoeffer, and that he began to increase his output to include a relatively profitable series of Latin grammar texts. In 1452, he set up his workshop in the Hof Humbrecht, borrowed another 800 guilders from Fust, and was contracted by the Church to print thousands of Indulgences. He also began producing the work for which he would become best known, if not wealthy, the Gutenberg Bible.

The first Bible, a version of the Latin Vulgate, was printed between 1454 and 1455 and has been referred to alternately as the Gutenberg Bible, the 42-Line Bible (the number of lines per page,) and the Mazarin Bible. Within the year, 180 Bibles had been printed, 45 on vellum and 135 on paper, most bound in two volumes containing a total of 1,282 pages. As with the traditional Bibles from monastery scriptoria, each Bible was illuminated by hand, which regardless of the series's typographical uniformity, rendered each copy unique. Although today, only 48 Gutenberg bibles are extant, each is an iconic representation of a technological innovation that changed history. The technology that Gutenberg invented not only revolutionized the printing industry but also created a new template for the dissemination and, ultimately, the democratization of knowledge and learning.

Within a generation, Gutenberg's press would be a major factor in the rise of European Protestantism. When Luther posted his handwritten 95 Theses at Wittenberg, he had no idea how swiftly his declaration of religious independence would spread throughout Europe. Subsequent to this was the publication of his broadsheets protesting the use of Indulgences, which like his typeset replicated Theses, reached more people in a month than handwritten copies would have reached in a year. And with great irony, the same technology that sixty years before had printed thousands of Indulgences at the behest of the Church, now helped destroy their use. Additionally, Luther's broadsheets were the earliest form of what would become the single most important organ of information dissemination in the pre-electronic age: newspapers.

Not only instrumental in creating a sea change in European religious life, Gutenberg's press was also a technology that inspired an explosion of technological knowledge. Without the relative efficiency of information sharing that his invention facilitated, the rapid growth of Renaissance science could not have taken place. The ideas of Bacon and Galileo might have languished as arcane

Two pages from the Gutenberg Bible.

Gutenberg's press on exhibit at the Gutenberg Museum in Mainz. Above, a page is hanging on the line to dry.

academic subjects, known only to a handful of intellectuals.

Less than twenty years after the Gutenberg Bible, England had its own master printer, William Caxton. Inspired by Gutenberg, Caxton expanded the technology's mass market capabilities by producing the first printed advertisement, a poster extolling the virtues of Salisbury's thermal cures, and expanding on this approach, he used his Westminster press to publish a broad range of works including chivalric romances, history, philosophy, and an encyclopedia. He not only increased the dissemination of information, but also offered an early example of the democratization of that information.

Despite having developed one of history's most important technologies, Gutenberg never benefited financially. By 1455, he was so indebted to Fust and

Schoeffer that he had to declare bankruptcy and cede the control of his Mainz printing shop after the two investors won a lawsuit against him for defaulting on their startup loans. They themselves created their own imprint, and in 1457 produced the *Mainz Psalter*, Europe's first mechanically printed book containing the printer's name and date. Although they had used his presses, Gutenberg was not cited in the printer's credits.

The only recognition Gutenberg received in his lifetime occurred in 1465, when the Archbishop of Mainz, Adolph von Nassau, bestowed on him the title of Hofmann (Gentleman of the Court) and awarded him a small yearly stipend. As if this relative obscurity were not enough, after his death on February 3, 1468, the Franciscan cemetery in which he was buried was destroyed, his grave along with it. ❏

FRANÇOIS VILLON

France, c.1463

François Villon is considered to be the first French lyric poet. He lived a tumultuous life. Villon was found guilty of murder, but instead of the death penalty, he was banished from the city for a period of ten years. That is the last we hear of the poet whose ballads conjure the hard life of a wanderer and thief existing at the very bottom rung of the social ladder. Yet despite his unenviable circumstances and lack of high moral character, his passionate poetry offers keen self-awareness and a trenchant look at a society in the midst of upheaval. ❏

Woodcut from the first edition of Villon's poetry

CHARLES THE BOLD

Nancy, 1477

The tumultuous life of Charles the Bold, Duke of Burgundy, ended on January 5, 1477 at the Battle of Nancy. His army having been routed by a confederation of Swiss and Lorraine forces, Charles's body was found on a frozen pond, naked and half eaten by wolves, his skull cloven by a Swiss battle-axe. His face was unrecognizable; he could be identified only by the scars on his body.

The military failures and ignominious death of this once promising heir to the vast House of Burgundy helped precipitate the collapse of the Burgundian state and exacerbated the rift between the French and the Habsburgs.

In March of 1476 he suffered, in his own words, a "shameful defeat" at the hands of Swiss Confederation at the Battle of Grandson. He attacked Morat in revenge for this humiliation, but he was again defeated by the Swiss.

Charles's rival, Rene II of Lorraine, was encouraged by these defeats and reoccupied Nancy, calling for Swiss and French help against the determined Burgundy. It was here, outside the walls of Nancy that an anonymous Swiss pikeman took the life of the last Valois Duke. ❏

Battle of Morat between the Swiss Confederation and Charles the Bold

INTOLERANCE AND INQUISITIONS

Europe, c.1480

A special commission called by Pope Innocent VIII condemned as heretical part of the work of a brilliant 23-year-old philosopher, Pico della Mirandola. His *Conclusiones* comprised nine hundred propositions about God and humankind, and its introduction, "An Oration on the Dignity of Man," reflected his humanist view that "nothing in the world can be found that is more worthy of admiration than man."

Mirandola's work, which centered attention on human endeavor, potential, and the position of humanity in relation to God and Nature, has been called the manifesto of the Renaissance. It helped set the stage for the ascent and success of artists and writers in Renaissance Italy. Lorenzo de Medici was his great patron and frequently protected him from the wrath of the Church.

The son of a noble family, Mirandola began to study canon law at the age of 10 and philosophy two years later. He then moved to Perugia to study Hebrew and Arabic and was strongly influenced by Jewish scholars of the Kabbalah. He then went to Paris, where he met many humanist philosophers.

According to Mirandola, it is God's gift to humanity that one can be whatever one chooses to be! But Mirandola incurred the wrath of the Pope when he suggested Christ did not really descend into hell, and that cabalistic magic was the best way of proving the divinity of Christ. He was forced to write an apology, which he did, but failed to withdraw his beliefs. He fled Italy, was arrested in France, and spent the next few years of his life avoiding further trouble with the Church.

In the same year, 1486, the publication of an encyclopedia of witchcraft confirmed that the papacy was lending its support to the growing practice of persecuting and burning witches. For well over a century, Dominican friars had been burning witches, mainly in the villages of the Alps and the Pyrenees. In 1484, Pope Innocent VIII published a bull deploring the spread of witchcraft in Germany and authorized two Dominicans, Jakob Sprenger and Heinrich Kramer, to stamp it out.

Sprenger and Kramer published *Malleus Maleficarum* (*The Hammer of the Witches*). It asserted that witches could fly; that they could raise hailstorms, hurtful tempests, and lightning; that they could cause sterility and make horses go mad under their riders. Witches were said to eat children, have sex with devils, and engage in sexual and cannibalistic orgies. Voluminous evidence of these practices was provided, mostly obtained from torturing suspected witches. The two friars went to work trying and burning witches throughout the German states.

A lack of tolerance for religious thought and practice was most pronounced in Spain, where Jews, once an integral part of Spanish society and culture, were harshly persecuted after Catholic rulers replaced Arab ones. The Jews had benefited for centuries from forbearing Arab rulers and were highly assimilated; they operated their own autonomous administrative system, the *aljama*, and congregated in special districts, the *juderia*.

Urban anti-Semitism increased, and the state passed a series of punitive laws restricting the activities of Jews. The Inquisition, a systematic ecclesiastical court system founded in 1478 that tried the unfaithful, made matters worse by denouncing Jews as blasphemers and usurers, and encouraging every form of intolerance.

The inquisitors were led by Dominican friars, and their main target were *conversos*, Jewish people who had been forced to convert to Christianity, many on pain of death and so, not surprisingly, their Christian faith was not strong. Those convicted of being false Christians , were liable to be "relaxed," that is burned alive. All told, several thousand people were burned at the stake. The monarchy decided to end its Jewish problem in 1492 by expelling them. In a mass emigration reminiscent of the Biblical Exodus, the Jews were forced to leave Spain. The 150,000-strong community was given just four months to be gone. ❑

A "witch" being subjected to a trial by water (lithograph, 1848)

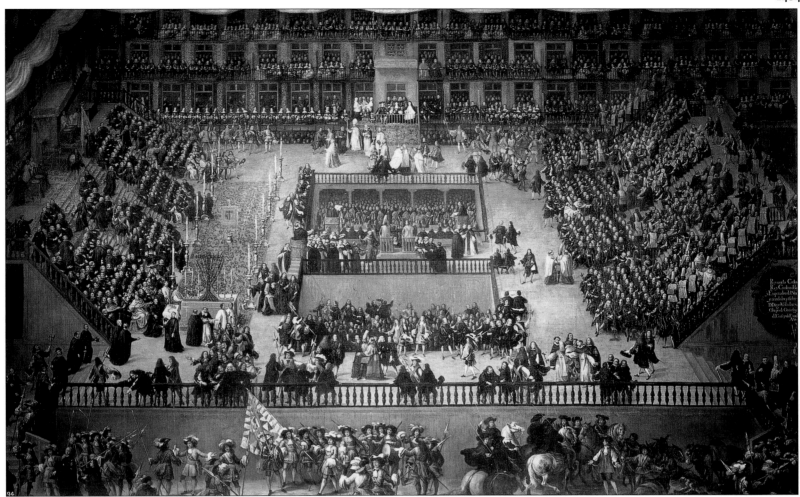

Auto da Fé in the Central Square of Madrid (painting by Francisco Rizi, 1683)

RUSSIA FREED FROM TARTARS

Moscow, 1480

For almost two hundred years, ever since the time of Tsar Ivan Kalita, the Tartar-Mongol army, also called the Golden Horde, had extracted confiscatory tribute from Russia. In 1476, Ivan the Great ceased paying this tribute, initiating a train of events that would reach a dramatic climax on the Ugra River in what became known as the Great Standoff. This would ultimately result in the Tartars' subsequent permanent departure from Russian soil.

Akhmat, Khan of the Great Horde, arrived on the banks of the Ugra River at the Lithuanian-Muscovite border in 1480, intending to punish the rebellious Russians. Wary of Ivan's forces, he waited for assistance from Lithuanian forces dispatched by his Polish ally, King Casimir IV.

The Lithuanians never arrived, and no significant battle took place. For a month both sides stared across the river at each other. In late autumn Ivan withdrew to Moscow. Akhmat fearing this to be some kind of ruse signalled a retreat, which degenerated into a panic-stricken flight. In the confusion the Khan was assassinated by a rival. His death marks the beginning of the disintegration of the Golden Horde. In the meanwhile Ivan had been gathering together the disorganized groups spread across Russian soil. In succession he established his sovereignty over Novgorod, Rostov, and Tver and established a strong central government. In 1494 Ivan was able to proclaim himself "Tsar of All Russia." ❑

PORTUGAL LEADS EXPLORATION

Lisbon, 1484

The first European manual of navigation and nautical almanac was prepared by a group of mathematicians appointed by King John II of Portugal. The king saw that his navigators were embarking on long voyages without charts or sailing directions.

The dead reckoning method of establishing a position by recording the distance and direction traveled was unreliable, and the North Star was not visible in southern waters. The king told the mathematicians to devise a method of finding latitude by solar observation. Studying a set of tables of the Jewish astronomer Abraham Zacuto of Salamanca, they developed a simplified version that allowed for a reading from which navigators would be able to calculate a ship's latitude.

Innovative techniques of maritime navigation such as these helped place Portugal in the vanguard of world exploration. Shortly after the Portuguese created their version of the Zacuto tables, the explorer Bartholomew Dias, at the behest of King John II, sailed down the west coast of Africa seeking a passage to India. During his two-year voyage, Dias sailed so far south that the North Star vanished below the horizon. For thirteen days, a strong wind carried him out to sea and still further south. When at last he was able to turn back, he found the lie of the land was to the east, not the south; Dias had rounded the Cape of Africa and in so doing had shown that the long sought after sea route to India did indeed exist. ❑

RECONQUISTA COMPLETE

Spain, 1492

With the conquest of the Moorish kingdom of Granada by King Ferdinand and Queen Isabella, the last Muslim bastion on the Iberian peninsula was lost.

Reconquista. Beginning in the eighth century, the Moors ruled Spain from the Ebro to Barcelona, governing the territory from their capital in Córdoba. The caliphs presided over a cultural Renaissance that united Arab, Christian, and Jewish scholars and scientists. The *reconquista* commenced from the center of Christian resistance, in Asturias, Navarre, and Aragon. The city of Toledo was retaken in 1085, followed by Lisbon in 1147, Córdoba in 1236, and Seville in 1248. It was during this long period of conflict that El Cid, the conqueror of Valencia, became a Spanish national hero.

Spain united. The process of forging a unified country out of the various kingdoms of Iberia received decisive momentum when the seventeen-year-old Ferdinand, the future king of Aragon, married the eighteen-year-old Isabella, heir to the throne of Castile and León. The marriage took place in October of 1469. Ten years later, the crowns of Castile and Aragon were united. Ferdinand succeeded to the throne of his father, John II. Isabella had inherited Castile five

years earlier when her brother, Henry IV, died. The couple successfully repelled the Portuguese

Isabella of Castille and Ferdinand of Aragon: Catholic rulers of the Iberian Peninsula (detail from the Altarpiece from the Royal Chapel in Granada)

army of Afonso V, who had been trying to claim the hand of Joanna, Henry's daughter, and with it

the Castilian crown. Their most pressing order of business was to integrate the two kingdoms. Whereas Castile possessed a strong central government, Aragon was a essentially a loose confederation of the small kingdoms of Aragon, Catalonia, Valencia, Sardinia, and Sicily, each with its own interests to pursue. Moreover, in both Aragon and Castile, the *cortes*, the parliamentary assembly of nobles, had developed considerable powers. The combined force of the Catholic monarchs was sufficient to reverse this trend, increasing both their political standing and the amount of money flowing into the coffers of the crown.

The rise of central authority was approved by the royal assembly of Castile, a kind of executive body that functioned as the highest court in the land. It was composed of lawyers and the members of the rising middle class, whose interests were opposed to those of the entrenched nobility. The assembly agreed that only the monarch had the right to impose taxation.

The Church as supporter of the crown. By exercising his privilege to suggest candidates for bishoprics and other ecclesiastical offices, Ferdinand gained considerable influence in church affairs. The first action taken in

THE WAR OF THE ROSES AND THE FIRST TUDOR MONARCH

England, 1455–1485

The War of the Roses was a series of internecine wars between the Plantagenet Houses of Lancaster and York, rival claimants to the throne of England based on their descent from Edward III. Its causes can be traced to 1399, when Henry Bolingbroke, the son of the first Duke of Lancaster, John of Gaunt, overthrew Richard II and was crowned Henry IV. Descendants of John's younger brother, Edmund of Langley, first

Duke of York, believed his issue were the rightful heirs.

The War of the Roses began with the reign of Henry VI, whose instability and poor leadership exacerbated the matter of succession, angering both royals and commoners and leading to armed rebellion by the Yorkists. In 1455, Richard Duke of York led his forces to victory resulting in his appointment as Protector and the cloistering of the men-

tally incapacitated Henry. After a period of compromise, hostilities resumed. A Yorkist victory at Northhampton in July of 1460 resulted in the Act of Accord in which Richard and his issue were recognized as successors to the throne upon the death of the Henry. Despite this compromise, the battles continued, with the line of succession going to Richard's son, Edward, upon Richard's death in 1460.

Edward was proclaimed king by Parliament, and his coronation as Edward IV took place in 1461. He reigned in relative peace until dissension within the House of York caused him to flee to Burgundy in 1470. After Henry VI was restored to the throne, Edward returned, reclaimed the crown and executed Henry. Upon Edward's death in 1483, his son was crowned Edward V. Edward IV's brother,

common by the king and his new wife Isabella was to establish the Inquisition, direct responsibility for which lay with the crown. Jews and Muslims were the victims of the royal policy to create a Catholic state. Immediately after capturing Granada in 1492, they issued a decree for the expulsion of all Jews from Spain.

The Court of the Lions of the Alhambra in Granada takes its name from the twelve marble lions that support the fountain in the middle of the court.

Jewish families were given four months to liquidate all of their holdings and leave or else convert. In 1499 and 1501, Muslims were given the same ultimatum. The Spanish Inquisition thrived in a climate of fear. Thousands were tortured and burned, and it produced an endless stream of refugees who sought havens in the Netherlands, England, Portugal, and North Africa.

Foreign policy. Although the attempt to secure the throne of Portugal for Spain through a dynastic marriage was unsuccessful, Ferdinand had much better luck in Italy. The French had waged campaigns 1494 and again in 1499 threatening Sicily, which belonged to Aragon. In 1504, Ferdinand launched a counteroffensive that succeeded in his winning a united kingdom of Naples and Sicily for Spain. Spain's future position as world power was clinched with Columbus's opening up the vast potential of the New World to Spanish trade. ❑

Richard, in his role as Protector, promptly arranged for Edward V and his brother to disappear into the Tower of London. Richard became King Richard III.

The end of the wars and the elevation of a new dynasty to the throne took place at Bosworth Field on August 22, 1485, when Henry Tudor, a descendant of both warring houses, defeated Richard and became the first Tudor king, Henry VII. ❑

The Death of Richard III at Bosworth Field **(etching after a painted original, 1774)**

THE FIRST GLOBE

Germany, 1492

The first globe to offer an accurate representation of the shape of the earth is attributed to a German businessman, Martin Behaim. Constructed in 1492, on the verge of the discoveries of the New World, it reflected earlier ideas of world geography.

Behaim, who lived in Nuremberg, financed the work, though his own scientific contribution was relatively small. He called it the *erdapfel* (earth apple), and it can still be seen in the German National Museum in Nuremberg.

Production. The work of constructing the globe was done by Ruprecht Kolberger, who made it out of a matrix of loam covered by successive layers of paper. The globe was cut into two hemispheres along the line of the equator and provided with an inner scaffolding of wooden hoops. The map of the world was painted by George Glockendon on vellum, who proceeded with the work in 24 sections. The map on which he based his painting was provided by Behaim, possibly from models that Behaim had copied during time spent in Portugal. The globe incorporates all of the Portuguese and Spanish discoveries up to that time

The globe's worldview. Obviously the globe does not picture the New World, but Europe and the greater part of Asia and Africa were included. Longitudinal measurements are distorted significantly, reducing, for example, the distance between Europe and the Pacific coast of China.

Inscriptions. The globe bears numerous inscriptions and drawings. They show, among other things, places where gold, gems, and exotic plants and animals were to be found. Knowledge that Behaim may have gained from a journey down the African coast has also been inserted. The globe incorporates much information drawn from the tales of medieval travellers such as Marco Polo, some of a fantatstic nature. In this regard the globe furnishes a remarkable expression of the world as it was then conceived.

Commercial aims. It appears that the globe was meant to be the prototype of a series that Behaim hoped to manufacture. The globes would be made using new printing processes. Behaim abandoned the idea and devoted his resources to funding new voyages of exploration.

The life of Behaim. Martin Behaim was born to a wealthy family in Nuremberg and raised in the Netherlands. In 1484, he went to Lisbon and from there journeyed to lesser known areas in Africa. It may have been that he performed some service for the crown of Portugal during his travels, because he was knighted on his return. After a brief stay in the Netherlands, he made Portugal his permanent home, dying in poverty in 1507, a victim of the plague. In the 1800s during a wave of German nationalism, Behaim was exalted as a groundbreaking scientist, navigator, and explorer. And although his reputation was overinflated, his globe shaped the discourse regarding the new vistas that were at that time being revealed to European eyes. ❑

THE AGE OF DISCOVERY

The period of the Renaissance, covering the fifteenth and sixteenth centuries, is also known as the Age of Discovery. Christopher Columbus discovered America in 1492, Vasco da Gama discovered the sea route to India in 1498, and Ferdinand Magellan sailed round the world between 1519 and 1521. The Renaissance voyages of discovery were mainly expeditions organized and financed by rulers and merchants who hoped to find new markets and increase their profits from trading with the rich countries in the Middle East and East Asia. Spain and Portugal also hoped that these voyages would bring them political and military advantages.

Besides these secular reasons, there was the crusading spirit and later the Christian missionary zeal to conquer new countries. The objectives were to halt Islamic influence in the Mediterranean and to spread Christianity throughout the world.

New scientific discoveries in the field of navigation as well as the development of seafaring techniques laid the foundations for the success of these voyages. Most explorers used the caravel, a new type of ship that was both easy to maneuver and suitable for long voyages. Equally important was the progress made in cartography. The discovery that the earth was round, a concept that gained acceptance in the fifteenth century led to a completely new image of the world. It replaced the belief that the earth was a flat disc.

THE RECONNAISSANCE OF THE AFRICAN COAST

Portuguese merchants were frustrated that the trade with East Asia was in the hands of the Mediterranean countries and depended on Arab middlemen, making goods more expensive as a result. In addition, trade could be adversely affected by political and religious conflicts.

The Portuguese saw shipping as the answer to the problem. In the first half of the fifteenth century Prince Henry, who would come to be known as Henry the Navigator, founded the first seafaring school in the world. It lay on the southernmost tip of Portugal at Sagres on Cape St Vincent. There, young seamen were trained. Prince Henry's aim was to bypass the Mediterranean and Muslim traders in North Africa through the systematic exploration of the African coast. This was not just a question of political advantage; it was also a matter of faith. As a Christian, Henry had fought the Muslims in North Africa in 1415 when he was 21 years

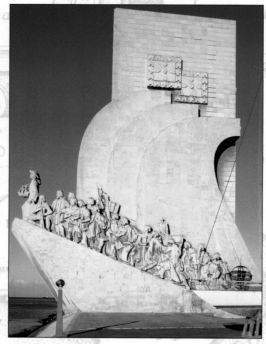

Commemorative monument in Lisbon: Henry the Navigator at the prow of a caravel.

old. He planned to move this battle, whose objective had been the liberation of the Holy Land, to the Atlantic.

In 1434 the Portuguese were the first Europeans to sail around Cape Bojador, south of the Canary Islands. From then on seafarers gradually felt their way further south down the African coast. In 1441 they reached Ras Nouadhibou and in 1441/42 Cape Verde; the route to the Tropics was now open. This marked the beginning of one of the most shameful chapters in the history of the West: human trafficking between Africa and Europe. In 1441, a ship brought the first slaves to Portugal.

As their ships sailed farther south, explorers discovered new territories. At the same time, the closer they came to the equator, the more frightened the sailors became. They had heard tales of terrible dangers lurking in these unknown regions. For instance, it was believed that the sea became increasingly viscous near the equator and sometimes even boiled. But in 1473, Lopo Conçalves sailed across the equator and neither he nor his crew came to any harm.

THE SEA ROUTE TO INDIA

The discovery of the sea route to India, which would make Portugal the richest nation in Europe for a time, was made by accident. In 1488 the explorer Bartholomew Diaz was caught in a violent storm off the west African

coast that pushed him far into the open sea. When he reached land again a few days later, he found himself in the area of the Great Fish River in the Mossel Bay. He had sailed round the southern cape of Africa.

Ten years later, in 1497, Vasco da Gama left Portugal with four ships. On the advice of his predecessor, he took a completely different course. When he reached the Cape Verde islands he left the coast and sailed across the open sea southward, arriving at the Cape of Good Hope after making a wide detour. After sailing round the Cape, da Gama made his way northward along the east African coast and reached the great seaport of Mozambique. This was where the sphere of influence of the Arab trade started. The Portuguese were not particularly welcome; the Arabs distrusted the foreigners from the West. They received a warmer welcome farther north in Malindi (on the coast of present-day Kenya). From there da Gama, accompanied by an experienced guide, set off on his adventurous voyage across the Indian Ocean.

On May 20, 1498, the Portuguese landed in Calicut on the west coast of southern India. Here the Europeans were greeted with great mistrust by the inhabitants; the resident Arab merchants in particular were hostile to the foreign arrivals, whom they rightly perceived as potential rivals. Because of this da Gama had difficulty exchanging the goods he had brought. In September 1499 he arrived back in Lisbon, after a voyage that had not been a great financial success. Even so, it would mark the beginning of a new chapter in the history of world trade.

THE DISCOVERY OF AMERICA

If the world really was round, then it seemed that it would be possible to sail westward from Europe to reach India, rather than going all the way around Africa. Christopher Columbus had this simple but revolutionary idea before Vasco da Gama set off on his expedition and spent almost ten years trying to convince the Spanish and Portuguese rulers of its soundness. It was only in 1491 that, after some tough negotiations, he was entrusted by Queen Isabella of Castile with the mission of sailing westward.

On August 3, 1492, Columbus left the Spanish port of Palos on the Rio Tinto with three ships. To plan his route, Columbus relied mainly on the map of the world drawn up by his fellow countryman Paolo Toscanelli. With no way of accurately calculating longitude, the distances between Europe and Asia (or, as it turned out, America) had been grossly underestimated. When Columbus eventually sighted land on October 12, 1492, he and his men had been at sea for 70 days. The newly discovered country was a small island in the Bahamas that he called San Salvador. He was convinced that he had landed on an island off the coast of Japan.

For three months the small fleet explored the Caribbean in the vain hope of discovering the rich countries of India and China. This first voyage was followed by three more expeditions in the course of which Columbus reached the North American mainland. Until his death he was convinced that he had discovered the continent of Asia.

When Columbus returned from his first voyage, a conflict broke out between Portugal and Spain as to which country had the right to the newly discovered territories. This dispute was settled by the Treaty of Tordesillas in 1494, which divided the world between them.

The first circumnavigation of the world (1519-1522) by Ferdinand Magellan confirmed the theory that Columbus and others had put forward. With Spain's backing, Magellan discovered the southwest passage and sailed between the South American mainland and the island of Tierra del Fuego through the strait subsequently named after him. The

sea route from the Atlantic to the Pacific Ocean had been discovered. Magellan himself did not live to see the end of the first circumnavigation of the world. He died in the Philippines in 1521 in a fight with its native people.

The Spanish moved aggressively to exploit the new world whose shape was gradually coming into focus. It took Hernán Cortés and his party two years to conquer the Aztec Empire. In November 1519 Cortés arrived in the Aztec capital Tenochtitlan. The Aztec ruler Montezuma II welcomed the foreign visitors to his country. But Cortés ruthlessly took advantage of the Aztec hospitality. Realizing that he could not conquer the Aztecs by peaceful means, he took Montezuma hostage and tried to blackmail the Aztecs into surrendering the city. Montezuma was killed in a subsequent battle, but Cortés was forced to retreat all the same. It was only later in 1521 that, at the head a large army, he succeeded in capturing the Aztec capital.

THE DISCOVERIES OF THE ENGLISH AND THE FRENCH

Compared with the successful Spanish and Portuguese voyages of discovery, the expeditions of the other European countries had less dramatic results. John Cabot, born Giovanni Caboto in Genoa, was awarded the right by

Henry VII of England to set off on a voyage of discovery. In 1497 he landed either in Newfoundland or Nova Scotia. Thinking he had arrived in China, he set off to explore large stretches of the North American east coast, possibly reaching as far south as Florida.

At the beginning of the sixteenth century the Florentine Giovanni da Verrazzano and the Frenchman Jacques Cartier explored North America. Both were looking for a northwest passage to the Pacific. In 1523 Verrazzano, in the service of the French crown, sailed from North Carolina as far as present-day New York. Between 1535 and 1541, Cartier explored the St. Lawrence Bay in Canada.

The attempts to find a northeast or northwest passage to India and China that had begun in the mid-sixteenth century continued to be unsuccessful. Thus, in 1556, Stephen Burroughs failed in his attempt to sail along the Russian north coast eastward, and in 1576 Martin Frobisher was equally unsuccessful in his attempt to sail in the opposite direction to the north of Labrador.

The age of discovery came to an end with these rather unsuccessful voyages. Spain and Portugal remained the leading exploring nations. Immense wealth flowed into Portugal, but it was not used efficiently to build up the country's home economy. After the death of the Portuguese king Henry, Philip II of Spain laid claim to the Portuguese throne, and in 1580 he proclaimed the personal union of Spain and Portugal (1580-1640). Portugal retained some autonomy, but the annexation of the country and its colonies made Spain the most powerful nation in the world for a time. ❑

The seafarer Magellan discovered the strait between South America and Tierra del Fuego: map of North and South America (engraving, 1596).

COLUMBUS DISCOVERS A NEW WORLD

Bahamas, October 12, 1492

Christopher Columbus was not the first European to land in the New World, but unlike previous forays of fact or legend, Columbus's voyage had a practical motive whose consequences would change history. His was a brilliantly innovative response to the need of Europe's developing nation states to generate new sources of income with which to grow their economies. Forty years before his voyage, the Ottoman Turks had conquered Constantinople, cutting off easy access to the lucrative land routes of Far East trade. Columbus's great insight was that Europeans could overcome the impediments to access to the East by sailing *west*.

His mission began in 1485, when he presented his visionary idea to John II, King of Portugal, who at first rejected the plan because of its questionable navigational calculations, and then because a native son, Bartholomew Dias, had just discovered a route around the horn of Africa. Henry VII of England showed interst, but on May 1, 1486, a historic meeting with Spain's King Ferdinand and Queen Isabella took place. Although they did not immediately approve the voyage, they saw its value and decided to keep Columbus from going elsewhere with his plan by putting him on a generous retainer that allowed him to live in Spain with practically all expenses paid. Continued lobbying of his hesitant benefactors seemed to pay-off in 1492, when Isabella at first agreed to fund his voyage and but then suddenly reversed herself. Defeated, Columbus was in the process of leaving Spain when King Ferdinand overrode Isabella's decision and officially granted his request. In contrast to popular historical wisdom, it was Ferdinand, not Isabella, who sent Columbus on his way to the New World.

The first of his four expeditions to the New World set sail

Columbus (painting by Ghirlando)

on the evening of August 3, 1492, from Palos, Spain, with three ships and a ragtag crew, many of whom were conscripted from the port's streets and jails. Of the ships, the largest was a carrack named the *Santa Maria* (nicknamed *Gallega*), and two smaller caravels, the *Pinta* ("the painted"), and the *Santa Clara* (famously nicknamed *Niña*, "Girl"). Stopping first at Hiero in the Canary Islands for provisions and repairs, the voyage over the "Ocean Sea" to what Columbus was sure would be an unimpeded and relatively short trip to the East Indies began on September 6.

Four days out of Hiero, Columbus noticed that needle of his compass was pointing markedly west-of-north. He knew that sailing the Atlantic coast of Europe, mariners had long since noticed that the compass pointed slightly East of North. It was as if the earth's magnetic fields, instead of being fixed, were subject to fluctuation and variation. With an unreliable compass, Columbus had to use a creative mix of dead reckoning (plotting his latitude on a chart) and his limited understanding of North Star celestial navigation, employing a quadrant and his astrolabe. He also used one of the most ancient navigational techniques: seeing large flocks of migrating birds, he set course to follow their southwesterly flight line.

Five weeks after leaving the Canary Islands, a crewman aboard the *Pinta* sighted what Columbus thought was his first landfall in the "Indies." On October 12, 1492, he stepped ashore on a small island in what is today part of the Bahamian chain. Grateful at having survived the perils of the Ocean Sea and mindful of his secondary role as a Christian missionary, Columbus claimed the island for Spain and named it San Salvador. Of the gentle natives who greeted him (prob-

Christopher Columbus and his brother Bartholomew (etching, 16th century)

FIRST ENCOUNTER WITH INDIGENOUS PEOPLE

New World, October 1492

ably Lucayan, Taino, or Arawak) he noted in his journal, "I could conquer the whole of of them with fifty men, and govern them as I please."

Believing that he had arrived on the eastern coast of Asia, Columbus continued, exploring the northeast coast of Cuba and finally Hispaniola, where on December 25, the Santa Maria ran aground and was abandoned. Here, in what is today Haiti, he founded the settlement of La Navidad, where he left 39 of his men to create Spain's first New World colony. After kidnapping twenty indigenous men whom he would present to the royal court, he set sail for Spain, arriving on March 15, 1493. ❏

Christopher Columbus made landfall on the Island of San Salvador on 12 October 1492. He describes his first meeting with the natives of the island:

"It appeared to me that they were a very poor people, in everything. They all go naked as their mothers gave them birth, and the women also, although I only saw one of the latter, who was quite young, and all those whom I saw were young men, none more than thirty years of age. They were well built with very handsome bodies and very good faces. Their hair was almost as coarse as horses' tails, and short, and they wear it over the eyebrows, except a small quantity behind, which they wear long and never cut.

Some paint themselves blackish, and some paint themselves white, some red, whatever color they find; and some paint their faces, some all the body, some only the eyes, and some only the nose.

"They do not carry arms or know what they are, because I showed them swords and they took them by the edge and ignorantly cut themselves. They have no iron; their spears are sticks without iron, and some of them have a fish's tooth at the end and others have other things.

"They are all generally of good height, of pleasing appearance, and well built: I saw some who had indications of wounds on their bodies and I asked them by signs if it was that and they

showed me that other people came there from other islands near by and wished to capture them and they defended themselves: and I believed and believe that they come from the continental land to take them captive.

"They must be good servants and intelligent, as I see that they very quickly say all that is said to them, and I believe that they would very easily become Christians, as it appeared to me that they had no sect. If it please our Lord at the time of my departure, I will take six of them from here to your highness that they may learn to speak. I saw no beast of any kind except parrots on this island." ❏

Christopher Columbus setting sail with three caravels to find the western route to the Indies (painting by Bejarano)

SAVONAROLA, THE "BLACK FRIAR"

Florence, 1498

Girolamo Savonarola was born at Ferrara in 1452 and became a Dominican friar. He began preaching in Florence in 1482 and in 1491 was named prior of the Church of San Marco. He lead a religious revival and became known as the "black friar." He railed against the corruption of the Church and the lax morals of its leader Pope Alexander VI, in particular. He condemned him for forsaking his vow of celibacy and bestowing church offices upon his illegitimate children. The Medicis, who were the leading family of Florence, also became targets of his wrath. He publicly denounced them as arrogant and lustful and accused them of robbing the poor and the widows and plundering the state's treasury. He said the art of Florence was immoral and charged Leonardo da Vinci and Botticelli with sodomy, though both were acquitted.

On Good Friday 1492 he revealed his vision of the destruction of Florence by flashes of lightning in a dense black sky. His congregation trembled when he drew vivid pictures of "barbers armed with gigantic razors" invading the city.

In 1494, on a wave of popular frenzy and with the help of the French king, he drove out the ruling Medici family. He set about to remake Florence into a puritanical republic, creating a "bonfire of vanities" sending books and pictures up in flames. The new atmosphere is clearly reflected in the works of Botticelli, who abandoned mythology as a subject. All of his paintings

Savonarola being burned at the stake (painting in San Minimato al Monte, Florence)

from this time forward were of religious subjects.

The Florentine experiment in popular theocracy came to an end in 1498. The city quickly recovered from its excess of piety. In 1497 Alexander excommunicated the friar. He was arrested in the following year and under torture confessed himself guilty of the charges against him. On May 23, he and two of his companions were burned as schismatics and heretics. ❑

TREATY OF TORDESILLAS

Tordesillas, Spain, June 7, 1494

Under the terms of a treaty signed here, Spain and Portugal divided between them all the new lands discovered in voyages of exploration. The agreed-to line of demarcation was 360 leagues west of the Cape Verde Islands (about 1100 nautical miles). Everything to its east was to be Portuguese and all the lands west of it Spanish.

The treaty was a response to the reports of Christopher Columbus whose stories about discovering a new world in the West, or maybe a new route to the Indies, alarmed Portugal's King John II. He had been planning his own expedition to India and became all the more worried when he learned that Ferdinand and Isabella had persuaded Pope Alexander VI to issue a series of bulls giving Spain all the lands that Columbus discovered, or would discover, west of the Portuguese Azores.

John II opened direct negotiations with Ferdinand and Isabella. Though as it turned out Spain received the lion's share of territory, Portugal was able to obtain Brazil as a colony. ❑

VASCO DA GAMA

Brief lives

Vasco da Gama was born in 1460, the year that Henry the Navigator died. It was Henry's enthusiasm for maritime exploration that gave Portugal the skills and experience vital for da Gama's expedition to discover the sea route to India. Henry had pre-

pared the way for him by initiating voyages of discovery down Africa's coast, and the rounding of the Cape of Good Hope by Bartholomew Dias provided da Gama with a jumping off place to India. After being promoted to the rank of admiral and then to the nobility, he died in India at the age of 64. ❑

THE SPANISH INQUISITION

Toledo, 1498

Despite the death of Tomas de Torquemada, a Dominican friar and guiding spirit of the Spanish Inquisition for twelve years, the inquisitions, in Toledo, Seville and Barcelona, continued to be vigorously prosecuted and began to spread to many cities in Aragon, despite local protests. All told, several thousand people had already been burnt at the stake.

In 1478 Ferdinand and Isabella obtained the consent of Pope Sixtus IV to appoint inquisitors. Their main target was *conversos*—Jews who had been forced to convert to Christianity on pain of death. Not surprisingly their adherence to their new faith was questionable.

An inquisition would begin with edicts offering people a chance to confess their own errors and also to denounce the sins of others. Only one informer was necessary for anyone to be charged. Those convicted were often burned alive. Confessions were obtained by torture and those "reconciled" by their confessions were sentenced to march for six Fridays to the cathedral, whipping themselves in the streets. Such penitents suffered heavy fines, were forbidden to wear anything but the coarsest clothes, and could not ride horses or bear arms. ❑

HROSWITHA, FIRST WOMAN PLAYWRIGHT

Germany, 1500

Works by the tenth~century Saxon canoness Hroswitha of Gandersheim (c.935 to 972). were discovered by the poet Conrad Celtes in the Benedictine monastery of St. Emmeram at Ratisbon, and were published in 1501 to an enthusiastic reception.

Her writings include six plays written in Latin. These establish her as the first known German woman writer and, more remarkably, the first European playwright since the classical age. Hroswitha's plays (*Abraham*, *Callimachus*, *Dulcitius*, *Gallicanus*, *Pafnutius* and *Sapientia*) deal chiefly with Christian virgin martyrs, and include some graphic torture scenes similar to those in early accounts of the lives of the saints, as well as moving scenes of the conversion of prostitutes. Her other works include narrative poems and legends of the saints. ❑

VASCO DA GAMA DISCOVERS THE SEA ROUTE TO INDIA

India, May 23, 1498

Almost a year after setting sail from Lisbon, Vasco da Gama arrived in Calicut on the Malabar coast, thus becoming the first European to discover a sea route round the Cape of Good Hope to India. During the long voyage he encountered many difficulties and dangers that tested both his seamanship and his qualities as a leader.

With a convoy of four ships with 20 guns and 170 well-armed men, he was able to fend off Arab traders, who feared the Christian Portuguese would challenge their monopoly of trade with India. After battling against hurricanes on its way round the Cape, da Gama's expedition met with hostility at almost every port of call in East Africa. At Mombasa, Muslims pretended to be Christians in order to get on board and prepare for an armed attack on the ships. Da Gama had to bombard Mozambique before he could obtain supplies of fresh water.

However, at Malindi, in what is present-day Kenya, a friendly welcome awaited the Portuguese,

Vasco da Gama's arrival in Calicut (Flemish tapestry, 16th century)

and they were able to recruit Ibu Majid, an experienced Gujarati seaman, who piloted them across the Indian Ocean.

When da Gama went ashore in Calicut he took presents for the king: hats, striped cloth, strings of coral and a case of wash basins. The king scorned them, saying da Gama had claimed he had come from a rich country, but all he had brought were cheap trinkets. After long tedious negotiations he finally arrived at an agreement and set sail to return to Portugal.

After his epoch-making voyage da Gama spent five years engaged in trade and armed raids in the Indies. He put down rebellions with unbridled ferocity, on one occasion sailing from Calicut to Cochin "doing all the harm he could on the way to all he found at sea." He discovered the Seychelles Islands and discovered and named the Admiralty Islands. During this time the Portuguese began establishing settlements along India's west coast. These served as trading posts as well as offering ports for their ships and were important factor in Portugal's mercantile dominance of the Indian Ocean.

Retiring to Evora, the residence of the Portuguese court, da Gama continued to advise the king on matters pertaining to India. He was created Count of Vidigueira, with special privileges of civil and criminal jurisdiction and church patronage.

Recalled from retirement by King John of Portugal in 1524 to replace an incompetent viceroy in the Indies, da Gama died in Calicut only three months after his arrival. ❑

THE BIRTH OF THE MODERN AGE

1500–1899

- ■ Africa
- ■ Asia
- ■ Europe
- ■ North America
- ■ Oceania
- South America

1500–1549

Brazil, 1500. En route to India via the coast of Africa, Portuguese navigator Pedro Álvares Cabral goes astray and discovers Brazil.

Spain, 12 February 1502. A royal edict orders the expulsion from Castile of all Moors who have not been baptized as Christians.

Persia, 1502. The Shiite Shah Ismail founds the Safavid Dynasty.

Spain, 20 March 1503. The Saragossa Instruction sets out a series of measures intended to encourage the Indians in the New World to adopt a settled way of life and to spread the Gospel among them.

Rome, 1 November 1503. Giuliano della Rovere, who takes the name Julius II, is the second pope to be elected in a year. He succeeds Pius III, who became pope on 18 August, upon the death of Alexander VI.

Spain, 26 November 1504. Isabella of Castile dies, leaving her daughter Joanna (the Mad) as heir to the throne of Castile, but effective power remains in the hands of Isabella's husband Ferdinand.

Afghanistan, 1504. Babur, a descendant of Tamerlane from Turkestan, seizes Kabul.

Florence, 1504. Michelangelo completes work on his statue of David.

Rome, 1506. Pope Julius II lays the foundation stone of the Basilica of St. Peter, the building of which has been entrusted to the architect Bramante. The work is to be financed by the selling of indulgences for the remission of sins.

North Atlantic, 1508. In search of a northwest passage, Sebastian Cabot reaches Hudson Bay.

Rome, 1508. Pope Julius II commissions Michelangelo to decorate the ceiling of the Sistine Chapel in the Vatican Palace.

Baghdad, 1508. The Safavid Shah Ismail seizes Baghdad.

England, 22 April 1509. On the death of Henry VII—the first Tudor king and victor of the Battle of Bosworth Field against Richard III—his only surviving son succeeds him as Henry VIII.

Florence, 17 May 1510. The Florentine painter Sandro Botticelli, a pupil of Fra Lippo Lippi, dies. Among his greatest works are *The Birth of Venus* and *Primavera*. He also painted superb portraits and illustrated Dante's *Divine Comedy* with pen drawings.

Caribbean, 1511. The first African slaves arrive in the New World.

Constantinople, 1512. Allied with the Janissaries, Selim, the son of Bayezid II, has his brothers and nephews killed and makes himself Ottoman sultan.

Rome, 1513. The Fugger bank is asked to sell indulgences to finance the work on the Basilica of St. Peter.

Poland, 1514. Astronomer Nicolas Copernicus returns to his native country after several years studying in Italy, convinced that the earth revolves around the sun—contrary to accepted belief.

France, 1 January 1515. The King of France, Louis XII, is succeeded by his nephew, Francis, who is determined to pursue France's claims in Italy.

England, 1515. Thomas Wolsey, the archbishop of York, becomes Cardinal and Lord Chancellor. His ambition is to make England the arbiter of European affairs.

Cuba, 1515. The Spanish found the city of Havana.

Spain, 23 February 1516. The Habsburg Charles I succeeds Ferdinand in Spain.

England, 1516. Future Lord Chancellor of England Sir Thomas More completes his work *Utopia*, a satirical critique of society and government.

Egypt, 5 July 1517. Sultan Selim makes his entry into Cairo. The Ottomans are masters of Egypt.

Germany, 31 October 1517. The Augustinian monk Martin Luther publishes 95 theses against the sale of indulgences granting the forgiveness of sins.

West Africa, 1517. The explorer Leo Africanus completes an expedition from Morocco to Timbuktu, Gao, Katsina, Kano, and Lake Chad.

Germany, 1518. At the Diet of Augsburg, Luther refuses to retract his widely circulated theses on indulgences.

Panama, January 1519. Accused of involvement in a conspiracy, Spanish explorer Vasco Nunez de Balboa is beheaded by order of his father-in-law, Pedro Arias Dávila.

France, 2 May 1519. Leonardo da Vinci, Italian painter, sculptor, architect, and engineer, dies.

Spain, 28 June 1519. Charles of Spain, King of the Netherlands and grandson of the late Emperor Maximilian, is elected Holy Roman Emperor and takes the name Charles V. Francis of France and Henry VIII of England were also candidates.

Spain, 20 September 1519. Portuguese-born sailor Ferdinand Magellan embarks on a voyage to cross the Pacific Ocean and circumnavigate the globe.

Mexico, 1519. Spanish explorer Hernando Cortés lands at Vera Cruz with a force of more than 500. He marches on Tenochtitlan, which Aztec leader, Montezuma II, surrenders without a fight.

Germany, 1520. Thomas Müntzer, a supporter of Luther with radical political aspirations, begins preaching in Zwickau.

Rome, 15 June 1520. Pope Leo X condemns Luther's *Ninety-Five Theses* as "heretical and scandalous" in his papal bull *Exsurge Domine*.

Constantinople, 21 September 1520. Suleiman (the Magnificent), son of Selim, becomes Ottoman sultan.

Germany, January 1521. After publicly burning the papal bull condemning his theses, Luther is excommunicated. Later in the year, Luther is "kidnapped" for his own safety by Duke Frederick of Saxony.

Balkans, August 1521. Ottoman forces take Belgrade.

Mexico, 31 August 1521. Cortés and the Tlaxcalans, who laid siege to Tenochtitlan on 28 April, capture and set fire to the city.

England, 21 October 1521. Henry VIII is named Defender of the Faith by the pope after defending the seven sacraments against Luther.

Mexico, 1522. On the ruins of Tenochtitlan, the capital of the Aztec Empire, the Spanish found Mexico City. They intend that the city become the capital of New Spain.

Netherlands, 1522. Charles V sets up a state-run inquisition to supplement the long-established papal Inquisition.

Switzerland, 19 January 1523. Ulrich Zwingli publishes his *67 Articles*, the first manifesto of the Zurich Reformation. After giving a summary of the Gospel, Zwingli attacks the authority of the pope, transubstantiation, and the cult of the saints.

Mexico, 1524. Cuauhtemoc, the last Aztec king, who has been held captive for three years, is hanged by the Spanish on a charge of treason.

Egypt, 1524. A rebellion by Ahmed Pasha against Ottoman rule—established in Egypt in 1517—is put down.

Germany, 1524. Led by theologian Thomas Müntzer, the peasants in southern Germany rise up and demand the abolition of feudal dues, serfdom, and tithes. The peasants' revolt is quelled the following year and Thomas Müntzer is imprisoned and beheaded.

Germany, 19 July 1525. The Catholic princes of the north form the Dessau League to fight the Reformation.

India, 1526. Mongol Lord Babur defeats the Sultan of Delhi at the Battle of Panipat and founds the Moghul Kingdom.

Spain, 14 January 1526. Francis of France, held captive by Charles V for a year, signs the Treaty of Madrid. He abandons Burgundy and gives up claims to Flanders, Artois, and Tournai. He also renounces all claims to Italy and pardons the rebel High Constable of Bourbon. Once released, he declares the Treaty of Madrid null and void.

Hungary, November 1526. John Zapolya of Transylvania has himself elected King of Hungary by a section of the nobility.

Germany, 1526. In response to the creation of the Catholic Dessau League,

Philip, Landgrave of Hesse, and Johann of Saxony establish the League of Torgau.

Austria, 1526. In accordance with the 1515 Treaty of Vienna, the Hungarian crown—in the absence of a direct heir—goes to Ferdinand, Grand Duke of Austria and brother of Charles V. The hereditary territories of Austria and the states of Hungary and Bohemia are thus reunited under the Habsburgs.

France, 1526. Francis of France forms an alliance with the Ottoman sultan, Suleiman the Magnificent, against the Emperor Charles V.

England, 1527. Henry VIII asks the pope to annul his marriage to Catherine of Aragon, who has born him one surviving daughter but given him no male heirs.

Germany, 16 April 1529. After the second Diet of Speyer, nineteen reformed states protest against the repeal of an imperial decree—passed in 1526, at the first Diet of Speyer—which allowed each prince to decide the religious allegiance of his state.

France, 5 August 1529. Louise of Savoy, acting for Francis of France, and Margaret of Austria, representing her nephew Charles V, sign the peace of Cambrai, known as the *Paix des Dames*. Under the treaty, France renounces all its rights in Italy, Flanders, and Artois, and agrees to pay a ransom of two million crowns. Charles V renounces any claims to Burgundy.

Hungary, 8 September 1529. The Ottoman Sultan Suleiman reenters Buda and establishes John Zapolya as the puppet king of Hungary.

England, 17 October 1529. Angered by Thomas Wolsey's failure to secure from the pope an annulment of his marriage, Henry VIII strips him of the office of Lord Chancellor. Thomas More replaces Wolsey as Lord Chancellor, becoming the first layman to hold the office in living memory.

Germany, 1–4 November 1529. On the invitation of Philip of Hesse, the reformers of Wittenberg, Strasbourg, and Zurich meet in Marburg to try to resolve the theological differences that divide the German Reformation. Luther, Melanchthon, Oecolampadius, and Zwingli fail to reach agreement on the Eucharist.

Italy, 24 February 1530. Charles V is crowned Holy Roman Emperor by Pope Clement VII at Bologna. He is the last emperor to be crowned by a pope.

Germany, 25 June 1530. At the Diet of Augsburg, the Lutherans deliver the *Confession*, a detailed statement of their faith prepared by Philip Melanchthon. It is designed to achieve reconciliation with the Catholic Church.

Hungary, 31 January 1531. John Zapolya and Ferdinand of Habsburg, both of whom were crowned King of Hungary in 1526, reach a truce.

Switzerland, 11 October 1531. During the second civil war between the Protestants and the Catholics, the Protestants are defeated at Kappel. Ulrich Zwingli dies in the battle.

Germany, 23 June 1532. Emperor Charles V signs the Peace of Nuremberg with the Protestant princes, who are granted freedom of worship in return for military aid against the Ottoman Turks.

Italy, 1532. *The Prince* by Niccolo Machiavelli is published posthumously.

England, 25 January 1533. King Henry VIII secretly marries Anne Boleyn.

Hungary, 22 June 1533. A year after invading Hungary, Suleiman the Magnificent, the sultan of the Ottomans, signs a peace treaty with Ferdinand of Habsburg, the brother of the Emperor Charles V. Hungarian rule remains divided between Ferdinand and the Ottoman puppet John Zapolya.

England, 11 July 1533. Henry VIII is excommunicated by Pope Clement VII.

Peru, 29 August 1533. On the orders of the governor, Francisco Pizarro, the Inca chief Atahualpa is executed, although the chief already paid millions of pounds for his ransom.

Russia, 11 December 1533. At the age of three, Ivan IV succeeds his father, Vasily III.

Germany, 1533. The radical religious sect known as the Anabaptists, which rejects infant baptism, takes power in Munster.

Persia, 13 July 1534. Ottoman armies capture Tabriz in northwestern Persia.

North America, 24 July 1534. A French expedition under Jacques Cartier, sponsored by King Francis, reaches the estuary of the St. Lawrence River of Canada after a three-month journey from St. Malo on the French coast.

Paris, 15 August 1534. The Spanish nobleman, ex-soldier, and monk, Ignatius Loyola, vows to found a society in honor of Jesus Christ (the Society of Jesus). In 1521, after an intense religious experience that began his conversion, Loyola went on retreat to Montserrat, in Spain.

England, November 1534. The Act of Supremacy separates the Church of England from Rome and declares the king to be its supreme head. The Act of Succession vests the succession in the children of Anne Boleyn; severe penalties are prescribed for anyone who opposes Henry VIII's marriage to her or its issue, and the king is given powers to demand an oath of allegiance to the act's provisions.

Peru, June 1535. The Spaniard Francisco Pizarro founds the city of Lima.

Germany, June 1535. The town of Munster, the stronghold of the Anabaptists, is taken by an alliance of Protestant and Catholic troops and its inhabitants are massacred.

England, 6 July 1535. After being imprisoned for fifteen months in the Tower of London, Thomas More is beheaded for refusing to take the oath demanded by the 1534 Act of Succession.

Canada, 2 October 1535. Having landed in Quebec a month prior, Jacques Cartier reaches a town he names Montreal.

London, 19 June 1536. Anne Boleyn, the second wife of King Henry VIII, is beheaded in the Tower of London.

England, 24 October 1537. Jane Seymour, the third wife of Henry VIII, dies after giving birth to a son who will become Edward VI.

Peru, 1537. After rebelling against Pizarro and capturing Cuzco, Manco Capac II establishes a new Inca state at Vilcabamba.

Germany, 10 June 1538. The German Catholic princes form the League of Nuremberg to counteract the Protestant Schmalkaldic League.

Europe, 1538. Pope Paul III, Charles V, and the Venetian Republic form a Holy League against the Turks.

Arabia, 1538. With the surrender of Basra to the Turks, the Ottoman Empire now reaches the Persian Gulf.

India, 17 May 1540. The Afghan chief Sher Khan defeats the Moghul Emperor Humayun at Kanauj. The emperor is forced to flee India and Sher Khan becomes *Sher Shah Suri*, ruler of northern India.

Hungary, July 1540. John Zapolya, who declared himself King of Hungary in November 1526, dies and is succeeded by his son John Sigmund.

Germany, c.1540. Maps published by the great cartographer Gerardus Mercator use the word America to describe the new lands discovered by Christopher Columbus.

North America, 8 May 1541. Hernando de Soto reaches a large river he names Rio de Espiritu Santo (the Mississippi).

North America, 23 August 1541. Jacques Cartier lands near Quebec on his third voyage to Canada. His expedition has been commissioned to found a permanent settlement.

Austria, 24 September 1541. The Swiss alchemist and doctor Theophrastus Paracelsus dies in exile in Salzburg.

Hungary, 1541. Ferdinand of Habsburg, King of Hungary and Bohemia, is defeated at Pest by the Turks, who seize Buda. Hungary becomes a Turkish province.

Rome, 22 May 1542. Pope Paul III summons a general council of the Church to meet at the imperial city of Trent. Its purpose is to achieve the reformation of the Church, the definition of dogma, and the reunion of Christendom.

Spain, 22 November 1542. New laws (*Leyes Nuevas*) are passed in Burgos giving protection against enslavement to the Indians in America.

Scotland, 14 December 1542. James V of Scotland dies and is succeeded by his one-year-old daughter, Mary Stuart, whose mother, Mary of Guise, becomes regent.

Switzerland, 1542. Recalled to Geneva, from whence he was expelled three years prior, the Protestant reformer John Calvin begins to implement his original scheme for the creation of a godly government.

Balkans, November 1545. The Emperor Charles V and Suleiman, the sultan of the Ottomans, reach a truce at Adrianople.

Germany, 18 February 1546. Martin Luther dies at his native town of Eisleben.

Rome, 7 June 1546. Bent on crushing the independence of the German states and restoring the unity of the Church, the Emperor Charles V makes a pact with Pope Paul III, who promises him money and troops in his fight against the Protestants.

Mexico, 1546. The first extractions are made from the silver mine at Zacatecas. The Spanish gain control of the Maya region after crushing a serious revolt by the Maya people.

England, 28 January 1547. Henry VIII dies and is succeeded by his nine-year-old son Edward VI.

France, 31 March 1547. Francis, King of France since 1515, dies and is succeed by his son Henry II.

Germany, 24 April 1547. Charles V's forces defeat the Protestant League of Schmalkalden at the Battle of Muhlberg.

Russia, 1547. Ivan IV (the Terrible) is crowned first Tsar of Russia in Moscow. To counter the power of the aristocratic *boyars*, he establishes a special council composed of personally selected advisers.

1550–1599

Germany, October 1550. Maurice of Saxony, entrusted with the execution of the decree passed at the Diet of Augsburg two years ago, lays siege to Magdeburg, the center of the Protestant opposition.

Italy, 1551. Henry II of France resumes the war against the Emperor Charles V and publicly disavows the Council of Trent.

Japan, 1551. The Spanish Jesuit Francis Xavier leaves for China after introducing Christianity into Japan. The Jesuit missionaries, two of whom stay behind to help to build up the nucleus of the new church, have come into conflict with Buddhist priests.

Germany, 2 August 1552. The Treaty of Passau, between Maurice of Saxony and Frederick of Habsburg, who is acting in the name of Charles V, revokes the Augsburg Interim of 1548 and promises religious freedom to the Protestant princes.

China, 3 December 1552. Francis Xavier, the "apostle of the Indies," dies of exhaustion near Canton, China.

Russia, 1552. Ivan the Terrible conquers the *khanate* of Kazan.

Spain, 1552. The Dominican friar Bartolomeo de las Casas publishes a book entitled *Brief Relations of the Destruction of the Indies*, attacking colonial practices in the New World.

England, 6 July 1553. Edward VI dies. Mary Tudor, the only surviving child of Henry VIII and Catherine of Aragon, enters London in triumph. She was recently proclaimed queen in Cambridge.

England, 1554. Mary Tudor, Queen of England, marries Philip of Spain, son and heir of Charles V. All the religious laws passed under Henry VIII and Edward VI are repealed by Parliament. Roman Catholicism is reestablished and the authority of the pope is recognized.

Germany, 3 October 1555. The Peace of Augsburg advocates that the religion of a prince should determine the faith of his subjects, thus sanctioning the existence of Lutheran states. It is decided that the imperial chamber should be composed of an equal number of Protestants and Catholics. Calvinists, however, are excluded from the agreement.

Europe, 25 October 1555. Charles V abdicates the sovereignty of the Netherlands to his son Philip.

Germany, 1555. Philip of Spain renounces his claim to the German throne in favor of Maximilian, son of Frederick of Habsburg.

India, 27 January 1556. The Moghul Emperor Humayun dies after falling from his library roof in Delhi. He is succeeded by his thirteen-year-old son Akbar.

Spain, October 1556. Charles V resigns the empire to his brother Ferdinand and retires to a remote monastery. He is succeeded as King of Spain by his son Philip II.

India, 5 November 1556. The Emperor Akbar defeats the Hindus at Panipat and secures control of the Moghul Empire.

Russia, 4 April 1558. Ivan IV grants the merchant Grigory Stroganov the right to use and cultivate the lands in the area of the Kama River and its tributaries.

France, 24 April 1558. Mary, the Queen of Scotland, the daughter of James V and Mary of Guise, marries the French dauphin, Francis.

Spain, 21 September 1558. Charles V, Holy Roman Emperor between 1519 and 1555, dies.

England, 17 November 1558. Queen Mary, the daughter of Henry VIII and Catherine of Aragon, dies at the age of 42. Mary's half-sister Elizabeth, the daughter of Anne Boleyn, becomes queen.

France, 3 April 1559. Philip II of Spain and Henry II of France sign the peace of Cateau-Cambrésis, ending the long series of wars between the Habsburg and Valois dynasties. The agreement is to be sealed by two dynastic marriages.

France, 10 July 1559. Henry II, King of France, dies. He is succeeded by his fifteen-year-old son, Francis II, the husband of Mary Stuart, the Queen of Scotland.

Scandinavia, 1559. Frederick II, the son of Christian III, becomes king of Denmark and Norway.

France, March 1560. In what is known as the "Conspiracy of Amboise," a group of Protestants launches an operation to capture the court and topple the Guise family. The Guises are warned, however, and the attempt fails. Several hundred Huguenots are executed and Louis de Bourbon, the Duke of Condé, is imprisoned.

Sweden, 25 June 1560. Gustav Vasa—whose capture of Stockholm in 1523 drove the Danes from Sweden, thus ending the great Scandinavian union that had existed for 126 years—abdicates. He leaves the foundations of a strong Swedish army and navy and a more settled system of administration.

Scotland, June 1560. The Scottish Parliament accepts a Protestant confession of faith drafted by John Knox, which forbids the saying of Mass and renounces the pope's authority in Scotland.

France, 6 December 1560. Francis II is succeeded as king of France by his ten-year-old brother Charles IX. The Queen Mother, Catherine de Medici, the widow of Henry II, becomes regent.

Scotland, 19 August 1561. Mary, Queen of Scots, returns to Scotland following the death of her husband, Francis II of France, the previous year. The Scottish nobility is bitterly opposed to her Roman Catholicism.

France, 1562. The Edict of St.. Germain supersedes the previous year's July edict, again giving limited toleration to Huguenots (Protestants) but obliging them to practice their religion outside town walls. Parliament refuses to recognize or register the edict. The massacre of an illegal Huguenot congregation at Vassy, by order of Francis, Duke of Guise, sets off a religious war.

France, 19 March 1563. The Peace of Amboise brings to an end the war of religion. Although the militant Catholic Francis, Duke of Guise, was just assassinated and the English allies of the Huguenots defeated, limited toleration is once more granted to the Huguenots.

China, 1563. Ming generals finally manage to gain the upper hand over resurgent Japanese piracy along the south China coast.

England, 1563. The *Thirty-nine Articles* of the Protestant Church of England are published.

Spain, 1563. Juan Battista de Toledo begins work in the Escorial Palace founded by Philip II of Spain outside Madrid.

Italy, January 1564. The decrees of the Council of Trent are published. They reaffirm traditional Catholic theology, but propose radical reforms in church orga-

nization, including the education of the clergy.

Rome, 18 February 1564. The sculptor and painter Michelangelo dies.

Switzerland, 27 May 1564. John Calvin, one of the dominant figures of the Protestant Reformation, dies in Geneva. He is wrapped in a coarse shroud and buried without a eulogy or a hymn.

Germany, 25 July 1564. Upon the death of Ferdinand, who inherited the Holy Roman Empire after his brother Charles V abdicated in 1555, his son Maximilian II becomes emperor.

Russia, January 1565. In an increasingly bloody reign of terror, Ivan the Terrible imposes his *oprichina*, a state within the state of Muscovy dominated by a private army called the *oprichniki*.

Brazil, 1 March 1565. A Portuguese colony is established at Rio de Janeiro.

England, 1565. A statute empowers the Royal College of Physicians in London to carry out dissections of the human body.

Netherlands, 2 April 1566. Backed up by Calvinist riots, two hundred noblemen petition the regent, Margaret of Parma, to demand the abolition of the Inquisition in the Netherlands. She promises to send a message to Philip II of Spain. The petitioners, led by William of Orange and Counts Egmont and Hoorn, acquire the nickname *les gueux*, "the beggars."

Scotland, 24 July 1567. Defeated by the Protestant nobility at Carberry Hill, Mary, Queen of Scots, is imprisoned and forced to abdicate in favor of her one-year-old son James VI.

Netherlands, 1567. Ferdinand, Duke of Alba, Philip's commander-in-chief, is sent to the Netherlands to help crush the Calvinist revolt. William of Orange, who opposes Philip II's policy of persecution of the Protestants and has tried to secure an agreement to ensure their religious freedom, is deprived of his office of *stadtholder*.

England, 19 May 1568. Mary, Queen of Scots, escapes captivity and flees to England, where Queen Elizabeth imprisons her.

Netherlands, 5 June 1568. Faced with continuing opposition from the province of Groningen, the Duke of Alba, the new viceroy, orders the execution in Brussels of twenty noble leaders.

India, 1569. Akbar captures the fortress of Ranthambore, bringing independent Rajput power effectively to an end.

Germany, 1569. The Flemish geographer Gerardus Mercator publishes a map in the form of a cylindrical projection showing all the lines of longitude as parallel.

Moscow, 25 July 1570. Tsar Ivan the Terrible attends the public executions of almost all his close advisers and ministers.

North America, c.1570. The Iroquois Indians in northeastern North America form a league of tribes whose aim is to meet and settle their differences peacefully.

Mediterranean, 20 May 1571. Venice and Spain form a Holy League with Pope Pius V to counter Ottoman expansion.

Mediterranean, September 1571. Don John of Austria, the illegitimate son of Charles V, and the navy of the Holy League defeat the Turks at the Battle of Lepanto, dealing a severe blow to Turkish naval power.

Philippines, 1571. The Spaniard Lopez de Legazpi founds the city of Manila.

Netherlands, April 1572. William of Orange returns to the province of Holland, where he is acknowledged as *stadtholder*.

Peru, May 1572. Tupac Amaru, the last of the Inca kings, is executed.

Paris, 24 August (St. Batholomew's Day), 1572. During celebrations for the wedding of Marguerite of Valois, the daughter of Catherine de Medici, and the Bourbon Huguenot, Henry of Navarre, thousands of Huguenots are slaughtered with Catherine's connivance. In the aftermath of the massacre, Henry of Navarre renounces the Protestant faith.

Japan, 1573. The *shogun* Ashikaga Yoshiaki submits to the nobleman Oda Nobunaga, spelling the end of the Muromachi *shogunate*, which was founded in 1335.

France, 1573. Catherine de Medici makes peace with the Protestants, ending the war that broke out after the St. Bartholomew's Day massacre.

Germany, 1574. With the Polish throne left vacant, the Emperor Maximilian II prepares to press his claims against Stephen Bathory, Prince of Transylvania.

Netherlands, February 1575. The Emperor Maximilian II mediates at a conference at Breda between the governor-general, Requesens, and Protestant representatives from Holland and Zeeland. Requesens agrees to withdraw Spanish troops and officials from the Netherlands.

Poland, 14 December 1575. Supported by the Turks, Stephen Bathory, Prince of Transylvania, is elected King of Poland.

France, 1575. The Duke of Alençon forms an alliance against his brother, King Henry III, with the Bourbon Henry of Navarre.

Prague, 12 October 1576. Rudolf II, King of Hungary and Bohemia, succeeds his father, Maximilian II, as Holy Roman Emperor. Maximilian died suddenly while preparing to invade Poland.

India, 1576. The forces of the Moghul Emperor Akbar conquer Bengal, the richest province of northern India. Akbar finishes the construction of Fatehpur Sikri, his "City of Victory."

Netherlands, 8 November 1576. By the Pacification of Ghent, the seventeen provinces of the Netherlands form a federation to maintain peace, suppress propaganda against heretics, and keep Spanish and other foreign troops out of the country. Negotiations between William (the Silent), leader of the rebels, and the states of Brabant were precipitated by the Spanish "fury" of Antwerp.

Netherlands, January 1579. The Union of Arras and the Union of Utrecht finalize the division of the former Netherlands. The United Provinces are formed.

North America, 1579. Aboard his ship, the *Golden Hind*, Sir Francis Drake docks outside of present-day San Francisco, in a bay that will bear his name.

Portugal, 1580. Philip II of Spain annexes Portugal, unifying the Iberian Peninsula.

France, 1580. Readers of Montaigne's *Essays* debate his "skepticism," which leads him to describe religion as an act of blind faith.

Argentina, 1581. Buenos Aires, founded in 1580 by the Spaniard Juan de Garay at the confluence of the Parna and Uruguay Rivers, is starting to assume an air of permanence.

Netherlands, 26 July 1581. The Estates-General of the Hague deposes Philip II as ruler of the seven provinces that formed the Union of Utrecht in 1579; by doing so, it declares both independence and war.

Rome, February 1582. To ensure that Easter falls on its proper date, Pope Gregory XIII decides to bring back the spring equinox to 21 March by removing ten days—those between 5 and 15 October—from the calendar. In so doing, he establishes the Gregorian calendar, which remains in effect to this day.

Russia, 10 August 1582. After 25 years of conflict, Russia makes peace with Poland and gives up its claims to the Baltic state of Livonia.

Spain, 4 October 1582. Teresa of Avila, who in 1562 reestablished the ancient Carmelite rule for nunneries, dies.

Russia, 1582. A large group of Cossacks, led by Yermak Timofeyevich, invade the Tartar *khanate* of Siberia and capture its capital, Kashlyk.

China, 1582. The statesman Zhang Juzheng dies. He had run the empire, on behalf of the Ming emperor, with a firm hand.

Japan, 1582. Oda Nobunaga, who reunified the country under his control, is attacked by Akechi Mitsuhide and dies. Akechi subsequently loses a battle with Toyotomi Hideyoshi and is killed.

China, 1582. The Italian Jesuit Matteo Ricci arrives in Macao and begins an intensive study of the Chinese language and civilization.

Moscow, 18 March 1584. Tsar Ivan IV ("Ivan the Terrible") dies in Moscow. Power passes to Boris Godunov.

Caribbean, 1 January 1586. Francis Drake, who left England on a new voyage to America in September, makes a surprise attack on the heavily fortified city of San Domingo then burns the Spanish city of San Agustin in present-day Florida. On his return to England, Drake takes on board Ralph Lane and other surviving English settlers from Roanoke Island.

Japan, 1586. Toyotomi Hideyoshi assumes the title of *kampaku* (civil dictator) and takes over the task initiated by Oda Nobunaga of uniting Japan under his sway.

England, 8 February 1587. Mary, Queen of Scots, is beheaded at Fotheringhay for complicity in the Babington plot. Its leader, Anthony Babington, and his five associates were executed the previous year. Babington had planned to assassinate Queen Elizabeth, free Mary from captivity, and rally support among English Roman Catholics for a Spanish invasion force.

Spain, April 1587. Francis Drake attacks and pillages Cadiz and ravages the Spanish coast, destroying naval stores. The incident becomes known as "the Singeing of the King of Spain's Beard."

Poland, 19 August 1587. Following the sudden death of Stephen Bathory at the end of the prior year, Sigismund III, the son of John of Sweden, is chosen to be King of Poland.

France, 20 October 1587. The latest Catholic-Huguenot conflict has developed into a struggle for the French succession between Henry of Guise, King Henry III, and Henry of Navarre, known as the War of the Three Henrys.

England, 15 September 1588. The Spanish Armada—an attempted invasion of England by Philip II—is defeated by the English led by Lord Howard of Effingham.

Japan, 1588. Toyotomi Hideyoshi institutes a "sword hunt" in order to disarm the peasantry.

France, 2 August 1589. Henry III, the last Valois king, dies after being stabbed by Jacques Clement, a fanatical Dominican friar. The Protestant King Henry of Navarre becomes King Henry IV.

Japan, 1590. Toyotomi Hideyoshi completes the political unification of Japan under his rule. His powerful vassal, Tokugawa Ieyasu, moves his administrative and military base to Edo (Tokyo), a strategic position for the domination of the great plain of eastern Japan.

England, 30 June 1593. The dramatist Christopher Marlowe dies in an argument in a tavern at Deptford near London at the age of 29. His rebellious and fevered spirit speaks through his tragedies: *Tamburlaine* (1587), a fierce indictment of ambition; *The Tragedy of Doctor Faustus* (1588), in which he affirms his belief in supernatural forces; *The Jew of Malta* (1589), a denunciation of the power of money; and *Edward II* (1592), a tragedy of human impotence.

France, 25 July 1593. King Henry IV abjures Protestantism and becomes a Roman Catholic. On 27 February 1594, he is crowned at Chartres.

Sweden, 1593. The Diet of Uppsala adopts the Augsburg Confession of 1530, imposing on King Sigismund the continuation of Lutheranism as the state religion.

Paris, 22 March 1594. Governor Brissac opens the gates of Paris to Henry IV. The opposition of the Catholic League, whose position was undermined by Henry's conversion to Catholicism the previous year, is on the brink of collapse.

Ireland, 1595. Hugh O'Neill, Earl of Tyrone, who became leader of the O'Neill clan two years prior, sets himself up as the champion of the Catholics and approaches Spain for help against the English.

Central Asia, 1595. The Emperor Akbar's troops annex Kandahar. All of India north of the Narbada River, as well as Kandahar, Kabul, and Ghazna, now acknowledge Moghul supremacy.

Arctic, 1597. Dutch explorer Willem Barents dies while on his third voyage to search for a northeast passage to China.

Russia, 17 February 1598. Boris Godunov, the *boyar* of Tartar origin, is elected tsar in succession to his brother-in-law Fyodor.

France, 13 April 1598. Henry IV, King of France, promulgates the Edict of Nantes to promote "union, concord, and tranquility" between his Catholic and Huguenot subjects. The edict grants the Huguenots a large measure of religious freedom.

Ireland, 15 August 1598. Two months after receiving a pardon for his rebellious activities from Elizabeth, Queen of England, Hugh O'Neill, Earl of Tyrone, leads an Irish force to victory over the English at the battle of Yellow Ford.

Persia, 1598. Shah Abbas embarks upon an ambitious scheme of urbanization. He plans to make Isfahan one of the most beautiful cities in the world.

Japan, 1598. Toyotomi Hideyoshi, who proclaimed himself civil dictator in 1586, dies after entrusting his son and his dynasty to Tokugawa Ieyasu and four other of his senior councilors. Following the death of Hideyoshi, Japanese troops withdraw from Korea.

England, September 1599. Appointed governor-general of Ireland earlier in the year, the Earl of Essex returns to England in defiance of Queen Elizabeth's orders. He was sent to Ireland to put down the revolt led by Hugh O'Neill, Earl of Tyrone, with whom he has concluded a truce.

London, 1599. Actor Richard Burbage pulls down the Shoreditch Playhouse on the south bank of the Thames and begins to build in its place a roofless summer playhouse, the Globe, to seat 1,200 spectators. The Blackfriars Theatre on the north bank, also built by Burbage, is to remain as a winter playhouse. Among Burbage's partners in the new enterprise is playwright William Shakespeare.

Scotland, 1599. In a treatise entitled *The True Laws of Free Monarchies*, James VI, King of Scotland, defends the principle of absolute monarchy by divine right.

1600–1649

Rome, 17 February 1600. The philosopher Giordano Bruno is burned to death as a heretic after a seven-year trial. Influenced by Neoplatonism, Stoicism, and Epicureanism, he believed in a pantheistic system based on Copernican astronomy.

London, 31 December 1600. The East India Company—"The Governor and Company of Merchants of London Trading into the East Indies"—is founded.

London, 1600. Shakespeare's new tragedy, *Hamlet*, about a reluctant young prince seeking revenge caught in the Danish court of Elsinore, opens.

Prague, 24 October 1601. The astronomer Tycho Brahe dies. He set up an observatory in Prague with the help of the Emperor Rudolf II, and worked there with Johann Kepler.

Netherlands, 20 March 1602. The Dutch East India Company is founded.

Beijing, 1602. The Italian Jesuit missionary Matteo Ricci visits Beijing for the second time and is given permission to stay.

England, 24 March 1603. Queen Elizabeth dies at Richmond having apparently named James VI of Scotland as her successor.

Morocco, 1603. Ahmed V, or Ahmed al-Mansur, dies. He came to power after his victory over Portuguese invaders in 1578, and was also known as the "Golden" or "Victorious." During his reign, Morocco was unified and prospered. He made an alliance with England against Spain, subdued Mauritania, and took possession of the wealthy Songhai Empire with its salt mines.

Japan, 1603. Out of the general conflict that followed the death of the civil dictator and prime minister, Hideyoshi (in 1598), Tokugawa Ieyasu has emerged victorious and is now appointed *shogun*. He goes on to found the Tokugawa Dynasty that will rule Japan until 1868.

Germany, 1605. Two hundred and five people convicted of witchcraft have been burnt in the last two years at the abbey of Fulda. Prince Abbot Balthasar von Dernbach supervises the witch hunts in the area, assisted by his minister Balthasar Ross.

London, November 5, 1605. A plot to blow up Parliament led by the Catholic Guy Fawkes is foiled. He and his coconspirators are arrested and executed.

Spain, 1605. Miguel de Cervantes publishes the first part of *Don Quixote*.

North America, 15 June 1607. Colonists finish building James Fort in Jamestown, to defend themselves against attacks by the Spanish and Indians.

England, June 1607. Beggars and homeless people around Northampton tear down enclosures recently erected near the town, in protest against the loss of common land. Several protesters are killed; after the actions have been stopped, three people are hanged as an example to the rest.

Germany, 19 May 1608. The Protestant states form the Evangelical Union of Lutherans and Calvinists under the direction of the elector of Brandenburg.

Canada, 7 July 1608. The first French settlement at Quebec is set up by Samuel de Champlain.

England, 1608. The English form an alliance with the United Provinces (the Netherlands) against Spain.

Bohemia, 9 July 1609. In a "Letter from the Crown," the Emperor Rudolf II grants Bohemia freedom of worship.

Germany, 10 July 1609. In response to the formation of the Protestant Evangelical Union, the Catholic states of the empire set up a league under the leadership of Maximilian of Bavaria.

Prague, 1609. The German astronomer Johann Kepler provides evidence for the elliptical rotation of the planets round the sun in his *Astronomia Nova*.

Paris, 14 May 1610. King Henry IV is assassinated by a monk who believes in tyrannicide as a means of putting an end to policies against the interests of Catholicism.

Italy, 18 July 1610. The artist Caravaggio dies of malaria in Porto Ercole at age 36, while waiting for permission from the pope to return to the Papal States. He fled in 1606 having killed an opponent in a duel.

West Africa, 1610. The Kingdom of Dahomey is established.

Italy, 1610. Using the newly invented telescope, Galileo observes the moons of Jupiter, and proves Kepler's theories about elliptical planetary rotation.

Sweden, 30 October 1611. On the death of Charles IX, the Swedish nobles and the council declare sixteen-year-old Gustavus II Adolphus of age, in exchange for a guarantee of their rights.

England, 1611. A new English translation of the Bible is published. It was authorized by King James in 1604, as a concession to the demands of Protestant clergy for reform.

London, 1611. Shakespeare's play *The Tempest* opens in London. It has a valedictory tone, with the hero, Prospero the magician, abandoning his magic, casting his wand and book of spells into the sea. He is attended to the last by his winged spirit Ariel, and plagued by his earthly servant, the half man, half beast, Caliban.

Russia, 1613. Michael Romanov is elected and crowned tsar. His descendants will rule in Russia until the Revolution of 1917.

Japan, 1614. The shogun Tokugawa Ieyasu issues an edict suppressing Christianity. Churches in Kyoto are to be destroyed and missionaries are taken into custody.

France, 1615. In accordance with the provisions of the Treaty of Fontainebleau, Louis XIII marries Anne of Austria.

Istanbul, 1616. The Sultan Ahmed Mosque (the Blue Mosque) is completed under the auspices of Sultan Ahmed I.

Italy, February 1616. Galileo is placed under arrest by the Inquisition for his astronomical theories, the most significant of which reaffirms the Copernican concept of the universe, placing the sun, not the earth, at the center.

Madrid, 23 April 1616. Cervantes, the creator of *Don Quixote*, dies.

England, 23 April 1616. William Shakespeare dies in his hometown of Stratford-on-Avon, four years after returning from London, where his plays were bringing him increasing fame and success.

Russia, 9 March 1617. The Treaty of Stolbovo ends the occupation of northern Russia by Swedish troops. Sweden also renounces plans for expansion toward the White Sea and in exchange the tsar, Michael Romanov, gives up Russian access to the Baltic Sea and the towns conquered by Boris Godunov.

England, 1617. King James makes poet and playwright Ben Jonson England's first "poet laureate."

New England, April 1618. A smallpox epidemic is raging throughout New England, and spreading down the coast as far as Virginia. Indian tribes from the Penobscot River (in Maine) to Narragansett Bay (in Rhode Island) are the hardest hit, and have lost up to 90 percent of their population. One of the latest victims is Chief Powhatan, whose daughter Pocahontas, the wife of a colonist, died of the disease the previous year in a ship off Gravesend after visiting England.

England, 29 October 1618. Sir Walter Raleigh is executed to appease Spain.

Bohemia, 1618. Count Thurn leads Bohemians in a revolt against the pro-Catholic policy of the regents in Prague, resulting in the second Prague Defenestration.

Germany, 28 August 1619. Following the death of the Emperor Matthias II, his cousin Ferdinand, King of Hungary since 1618 and until two days prior King of Bohemia, is unanimously elected emperor as Ferdinand II. Since Bohemia refuses to take an oath of loyalty to the new emperor, he makes an alliance with Duke Maximilian of Bavaria and the Catholic League against Bohemia and the Palatinate.

Virginia, August 1619. A Dutch frigate lands twenty Africans, who are to be indentured servants in the port of Jamestown. This is the first cargo of its kind to arrive in a British North American colony. As the status of slave does not exist in law, the way is open for total exploitation of the labor force.

France, 1619. Louis XIII recalls Richelieu from exile in Avignon to help defuse a rebellion by the Queen Mother, Marie de Medici.

Southeast Asia, 1619. The Dutch build a fortress and a colony on the remains of the first settlement, dating from 1596. They call the colony Batavia *Jakarta* after an ancient district in Holland.

London, 1619. William Harvey announces his discovery of the circulation of the blood.

England, 16 September 1620. A band of 35 religious dissenters sets sail in the *Mayflower* for Virginia, jubilant at the prospect of practicing their brand of worship in the New World without official harassment. On November 21, leaders of the expedition gather in the ship's main cabin to prepare a social contract designed to bolster unity. The document is meant to placate settlers angered by their arrival on land that has not been granted to them by charter. The Mayflower Compact establishes a civil body politic for the new colony that will set up "just and equal laws" based on Church covenants.

England, 1620. Francis Bacon publishes his *Novum Organum*, a scientific treatise promoting his belief that scientific research should be conducted in the interests of humanity.

Madrid, 31 March 1621. King Philip III of Spain dies and is succeeded by his son, who becomes King Philip IV.

Baltic, 16 September 1621. At the head of the most modern army in Europe, the Swedish king, Gustavus Adolphus, seizes Riga from the Poles.

Spain, 1623. Diego Velásquez becomes court painter to King Philip IV.

Persia, 1623. The Persian leader Shah Abbas takes Baghdad, Mosul, and the whole of Mesopotamia from the Ottomans.

London, 1623. Edward Blount and Isaac Jaggard obtain a license to publish sixteen hitherto unprinted plays by Shakespeare on 8 November. Later in the year, they publish a folio volume of nearly one thousand pages containing most of the original sixteen plays. Thirty-six pieces in all are brought together in the volume, and they are sold at £1 a copy. The plays are listed under three headings: "Comedies," "Histories," and "Tragedies."

France, 29 April 1624. Louis XIII appoints Cardinal Richelieu Chief Minister of the Royal Council.

Germany, 1624. Albrecht von Wallenstein is made Duke of Friedland. A Catholic convert of noble Bohemian stock, he has a sizeable army now at the service of the emperor.

England, 27 March 1625. Prince Charles succeeds to the throne on the death of his father King James. He is crowned King Charles I.

China, 1625. The first Manchu kings establish their capital at Mukden: Their kingdom is a threat to the weakening Ming Dynasty that rules China.

Germany, 27 August 1626. The Danes are crushed by troops of the Catholic League led by the imperial General Johann Tserclaes Graf von Tilly and the imperial army under Wallenstein. This marks the end of Danish intervention in the European wars, which have raged since 1618.

North America, September 1626. Following negotiations, a Dutch group led by Peter Minuit agrees to pay the Canarsee Indians the value of 60 *guilders*, or $24, in beads and trinkets, for the 22-square-mile island of Manhattan at the mouth of the river explored by Henry Hudson.

Canada, 25 April 1627. Control of New France passes to the Company of One Hundred Associates; it gains a fur monopoly and land from Florida to the Arctic.

India, 1627. Jahangir, the great Moghul emperor, dies.

France, 28 October 1628. After a fifteen-month siege, the Huguenot town of La Rochelle surrenders to royal forces.

Persia, 19 January 1629. Shah Abbas dies in Isfahan after a reign of 42 years. He is succeeded by his grandson, Shah Safi.

Germany, 1629. The Edict of Restitution, promulgated by the Emperor Ferdinand II, restores all ecclesiastical property to those who owned it in 1555. In this way the Emperor hopes to recover all German lands lost to Protestantism during the previous 75 years.

Australia, 1629. The Dutch sailor Francisco Pelsaert lands on northwestern Australia after his ship, the *Batavia*, is wrecked on Morning Reef.

London, 10 March 1629. Not able to have his way with a fractious Parliament, King Charles has it dissolved. It is not called back into session until 1640.

Massachusetts, 7 September 1630. Governor John Winthrop and his assistants pass a resolution declaring that Trimountaine, on the Shawmut Peninsula, "shall be called Boston." A resolution is passed that Boston will replace Salem as the colony's capital.

Sweden, 1630. King of Sweden, Gustavus Adolphus, invades Pomerania and Mecklenburg to counteract recent German military successes in Europe's long running wars.

Amsterdam, June 1631. Spurred on by his recent successes, Rembrandt leaves Leyden for Amsterdam, a fashionable center, to become a portrait painter.

Germany, 17 September 1631. After the Protestant town of Magdeburg is sacked by the troops of Tilly, the commander of the Catholic League, the Elector of Saxony concludes an alliance with Gustavus Adolphus of Sweden, who crushes the Catholic troops at Breitenfeld.

North America, 1632. With a grant from King Charles, Lord Baltimore founds a settlement in Maryland offering religious toleration to Catholics.

India, 1632. More than one million people have died in a famine in the Deccan, and some have only survived by cannibalism. The famine was caused by a drought in 1630–1631 and excessive rains the following year.

India, 1632. The Emperor Shah Jahan has begun the construction of the Taj Mahal in memory of his beloved wife, Mumtaz Mahal, who died a year before bearing her fifteenth child.

Rome, 1633. The Italian astronomer Galileo Galilei is forced to recant his stated views that support the Copernican theory of heliocentrism.

Germany, 5–6 September 1634. Imperial and Spanish troops under Archduke Ferdinand inflict a shattering defeat on the Swedes and other Protestant forces near the Bavarian town of Nordlingen. The victory ends Swedish influence in southern Germany.

Paris, 10 February 1635. King Louis XIII grants a letters patent to a new French Academy, a group of educated men under Valentin Conrart, whose function, following Italian models, will be to give precise rules to the French language and to compile a dictionary.

France, 19 May 1635. Cardinal Richelieu intervenes in the great conflict in Europe by declaring war on the Habsburgs in Spain.

Armenia, July 1635. The Ottomans capture Yerevan from the Safavid Persians.

Canada, 25 December 1635. Samuel de Champlain, explorer and founder of New France, dies in Quebec.

China, 1636. The Manchus, a new power in the northeast of China, adopt the Chinese dynastic name of Qing for their new state.

North America, 1636. The Puritan John Harvard founds the first American university, at Cambridge, Massachusetts.

Paris, December 1636. Pierre Corneille's tragedy *El Cid* is performed on stage for the first time, to great acclaim.

North America, 1636. Led by Englishman Roger Williams, the first colonists settle in Rhode Island. A Puritan and champion of religious toleration, Williams, who emigrated to New England in 1630, suffered persecution and banishment for his beliefs. He escaped to the shores of Narragansett Bay and purchased land from the Indians, which he renames Providence, to mark God's providence to him in his distress.

France, 1636. Following Richelieu's declaration of war on Spain the previous year, Spanish and Bavarian armies invade France, but are driven back.

Germany, 15 February 1637. Ferdinand II, Holy Roman Emperor since 1619 and staunch defender of Habsburg and Catholic interests during the great war in Europe, dies. He is succeeded by his son Ferdinand III, who became King of Hungary in 1626 and King of Bohemia in 1627.

North America, 5 June 1637. Supported by Indian allies, a Puritan force from the Connecticut River area attacks a Pequot village and slaughters 500 Pequot Indian men, women, and children. The battle brings to an end several years of war between the settlers and the Pequot.

France, 1637. The philosopher René Descartes publishes *Discours de la Methode* anonymously.

Netherlands, 1637. The tulip trade collapses after a boom the previous year led to massive speculation.

Scotland, March 1638. The Presbyterian opponents of King Charles's religious policy in Scotland sign a national covenant to preserve the purity of the Gospel. In November, a general assembly of the Scottish Church abolishes the episcopate and defies King Charles's orders to disband.

Paris, 5 September 1638. Anne of Austria, wife of King Louis XIII, gives birth to an heir to the throne after 23 years of marriage. He is given the name Louis.

Japan, 1638. Christians are persecuted throughout Japan. The Japanese are banned from leaving Japan and the country is closed to foreigners. Only the Dutch and the Chinese are permitted to maintain trading posts under guard in a walled compound on the island of Deshima, in Nagasaki Harbor.

France, 1639. The mathematician and physicist Blaise Pascal invents a calculating machine.

England, 13 April 1640. In order to raise supplies to resume the war against the Scots, King Charles convenes Parliament for the first time since 1629. Three weeks later the "Short Parliament" is dissolved after refusing the king money.

Portugal, 1640. Richelieu supports a revolution that frees the Portuguese from Spanish domination. John IV (the Fortunate) is declared king and founds the Braganza Dynasty.

London, 12 May 1641. Impeached for high treason by the Long Parliament (summoned by the king after his defeat in the second Bishops' War), the Earl of Strafford, King Charles's chief adviser, is executed.

Ireland, October 1641. In protest against despotic treatment and Protestant immigration to Ulster, Irish Catholics slaughter thousands of English settlers.

France, 4 December 1642. Upon the death of Richelieu, Cardinal Jules Mazarin becomes chief minister.

Australasia, 1642. Dutch navigator, Abel Tasman, discovers a large land mass (New Zealand) and a small island, Van Diemen's Land (Tasmania).

Nottingham, England, 22 August 1642. The king's declaration of war on Parliament sets off a civil war between royalists (Cavaliers) and Puritans (Roundheads). Under the command of Oliver Cromwell, six East Anglican counties raise a joint anti-royalist force—the nucleus from which a national parliamentary army could be formed.

France, 14 May 1643. Louis XIII dies at St. Germain. His will provides for a regency council consisting of his widow Anne, his brother Gaston of Orleans, the prince of Condé, and Cardinal Jules Mazarin, who will govern during the minority of the four-year-old King Louis XIV. Queen Anne, the widow of Louis XIII, is granted sole and absolute power as regent by the Paris parliament, overriding the late king's will.

England, 25 September 1643. The English Solemn League and Covenant, a national oath to increase the pace of religious reform, guarantees Scottish support of the parliamentary cause in England. The Scots see it as a way to impose Presbyterianism on England and Ireland and to preserve the constitutional liberties won by the Scottish and English Parliaments.

Chile, 1643. The city of Santiago is utterly destroyed by an earthquake.

England, 2 July 1644. Cromwell crushes the royalists at the battle of Marston Moor, near York, leaving some 4,000 dead, and taking 1,500 prisoners.

England, November 1644. The Puritan poet John Milton publishes a pamphlet on the freedom of the press entitled *Areopagitica*.

Australia, 1644. The Dutch navigator Tasman compiles a map of the north and west coasts of Australia.

Russia, July 13, 1645. Tsar Michael Romanov, founder of the Romanov Dynasty, dies in Moscow after ruling for almost 30 years. He is succeeded by his son Alexei.

Netherlands, January 1648. The Dutch and the Spanish sign a peace treaty ending 80 years of war. The seven Dutch provinces are recognized as an independent nation by Spain, which surrenders its rights to the "generality lands" and closes the port of Antwerp.

Paris, 26 August 1648. Parisians rise up in protest at the arrest of Councilor Broussel, who granted them their freedom. The royal family flees to St. Germain. This "day of the barricades" marks the start of the so-called *Fronde* uprising (named after a game played by children in the streets of Paris).

South Africa, 1648. Survivors from the Dutch ship *Haarlem*, which was wrecked in Table Bay the previous year, find the people and climate of the Cape of Good Hope hospitable.

England, 1648. The nonconformist George Fox, who started preaching last year, founds the Society of Friends (the Quakers).

Germany, 24 October 1648. The Treaty of Westphalia brings an end to the Thirty Years War.

London, 30 January 1649. King Charles is beheaded. Brought to trial by order of the Rump Parliament—the MPs who remained after Pride's purge the previous year—and Thomas Pride signed his death warrant.

England, 1649. Parliament abolishes the monarchy and the House of Lords. England is declared a Commonwealth or "Free State" by the Rump Parliament, with supreme authority vested in the House of Commons. The executive powers of the monarchy are now assumed by a Council of State composed of 40 members, 31 of whom are MPs.

Ireland, 11 September 1649. On the orders of Cromwell, 1,500 people are massacred at Drogheda.

1650–1699

England, 1650. England's first coffee house is opened in Oxford.

London, 9 October 1651. Parliament passes a Navigation Act favoring English shipping in an attempt to break the Dutch hold on the carrying trade. Under the terms of the new legislation, all goods imported to England must be carried in ships owned by Englishmen or colonials, with crews that are at least half composed of Englishmen.

Paris, 21 October 1652. Upon their entry into Paris, which has supported the monarchy against the Fronde rebels, the regent Queen Anne and fourteen-year-old Louis XIV receive a great welcome.

England, 1652. In an escalation of the conflict following the previous year's Navigation Act, England declares war on the Netherlands. The Navigation Act was specifically designed to hamper booming Dutch sea trade, and trouble has been brewing ever since it was made law.

New France, 5 November 1653. The Iroquois League has signed a peace treaty with the French. The Iroquois have been waging war against neighboring tribes for centuries, but most recently have nearly destroyed the Huron Indians, who have been forced to seek refuge with the French settlers.

London, 16 December 1653. Oliver Cromwell takes on dictatorial powers with the title of Lord Protector. The writer John Milton becomes his secretary.

London, 15 April 1654. The Peace of Westminster puts an end to the war between England and the Netherlands. The Navigation Act that caused the two-year war is retained and England asserts its supremacy over the seas.

New Amsterdam, 7 September 1654. A group of 23 Sephardic Jews arrives on board the *St. Charles*, a French armed vessel, following an order given to the 5,000 Jews in Recife, Brazil, that they have three months to leave.

France, 1654. An exchange of letters between the scientists Pascal and Fermat gives rise to a theory of probability.

Netherlands, 1654. The explosion of a gunpowder factory destroys a quarter of the town of Delft. Among the victims is Carel Fabritius, considered the most gifted of Rembrandt's pupils. He had just finished painting his *Self-Portrait*.

Madrid, 1656. Diego Velázquez paints *Las Meninas* (*The Maids of Honor*).

Amsterdam, 1656. Rembrandt is declared bankrupt and all his goods are put up for sale.

India, August 1657. Over the past year, the Moghul Aurangzeb has captured two fortresses in the Deccan sultanate of Bijapur and ravaged much of the land. It is only by the intervention of his father, Shah Jahan, that a complete conquest has been prevented.

England, 1657. The Dutch physicist Christiaan Huygens invents the pendulum clock—using Galileo's observations on the behavior of oscillating pendulums—and writes the first treatise on probability theory.

India, 25 June 1658. Aurangzeb proclaims himself Emperor of the Moghuls.

England, 3 September 1658. The Lord Protector, Oliver Cromwell, dies. He has ruled as a benevolent dictator since the dissolution of the Barebones Parliament in 1653, and in the year before, refused the offer of the kingship from Parliament.

Netherlands, 1659. The Dutch-Jewish philosopher and theologian Spinoza identifies God with nature in his *Short Treatise on God, Man, and His Well-Being*.

France, 1659. The Peace of the Pyrenees is agreed, which finally brings the Franco-Spanish War to an end. The treaty is sealed with the arrangement of a marriage between the Spanish King Philip IV's daughter, Maria Thérèse, and Louis XIV. The *infanta's* dowry will be paid in full only when she renounces all claims to the Spanish throne.

England, 29 May 1660. Charles II returns out of exile to London. He is crowned king at Westminster Abbey on 23 April 1661.

England, 1 October 1660. The crown strengthens the Navigation Act, requiring that certain colonial goods are to be shipped only to Britain. Such measures are directed against the Dutch, but they inevitably limit colonial trading outlets and are resented by settlers struggling to establish their communities.

Sweden, 1660. The Swedes mourn the death of Charles X in the course of a new campaign against Denmark. He is succeeded by his young son, Charles XI.

France, September 1661. Nicolas Fouquet, the superintendent of state finances, is arrested in Nantes at the instigation of Louis XIV. Jean-Baptiste Colbert, who worked for Mazarin until his death earlier in the year, and has been agitating for Fouquet's arrest, replaces him.

China, 1661. The Manchu Dynasty, which was still being opposed around 1655 by the last Ming partisans, is now recognized throughout China. Shunzhi becomes the first Manchu ruler.

Amsterdam, 1661. The brilliant Dutch painter Rembrandt receives his most important commission to date, a gigantic canvas, roughly five-and-a-half yards square: It is to be entitled the *Conspiracy of Claudius Civilis.*

France, 9 March 1661. Cardinal Mazarin, the king's prime minister, dies at Vincennes. Louis XIV confirms his wish to rule personally, without the assistance of a prime minister.

London, 1662. The Act of Uniformity is passed, stating that Church services are to be conducted in accordance with the revised prayer book.

London, 1662. Charles II gives a royal charter to the Royal Society, founded to promote scientific knowledge. The society emerged from meetings of scientists and philosophers first held in 1645, and was formally established in 1660.

Paris, 19 August 1662. The French mathematician, theologian, and physicist Blaise Pascal dies at age 39. When he realized he was dying, he asked to be moved to the hospital for incurables so that he could die there in the company of the poor.

London, 27 July 1663. Parliament passes a second Navigation Act, requiring all goods for the colonies to travel in British ships from British ports. An extension of the 1651 act, it aims to make England and its colonies less dependent on foreign trade.

New Amsterdam, 5 September 1664. After several days of tense negotiation, the Dutch settlement of New Amsterdam has surrendered, without firing a shot, to British forces. Britain now controls ports from Virginia to Massachusetts, and will be better able to enforce the Navigation Act, which provides for a British monopoly on colonial trade.

India, January 1666. The deposed Moghul Emperor Shah Jahan dies. Since 1658, he had been confined by his son Aurangzeb in the Agra Fort from where he could gaze over the Taj Mahal where his beloved empress lies buried.

Anatolia, May 1666. The religious leader Sabbatai Zevi, after a forced conversion to Islam, proclaims himself as the Messiah.

Paris, 1666. The English scientist and mathematician, Isaac Newton, develops his differential calculus.

Netherlands, 31 July 1667. The Peace of Breda ends the war between the English and Dutch.

Russia, 1667. The Cossack Stenka Razin leads a peasant uprising.

England, 1667. John Milton publishes his epic poem, *Paradise Lost*, in twelve books. He writes that his poem is meant to "justify the ways of God to man."

The Hague, 23 January 1668. During the War of Devolution, the Triple Alliance is formed between England, Holland, and Sweden to defend the Netherlands against the ambitions of the French king, Louis XIV, who is pursuing a claim based on his wife's rights as Spanish *infanta*. The war ends with the Treaty of Aix-la-Chapelle.

Lisbon, 1668. The Spanish sign a peace treaty recognizing Portuguese independence.

Crete, 1669. The Venetians lose the Mediterranean island of Crete, their last colonial possession, to the Turks.

England, 31 May 1669. The naval administrator and politician Samuel Pepys makes the last entry in the diary he began on 1 January 1660.

Amsterdam, 4 October 1669. The Dutch painter Rembrandt van Rijn dies in solitude and poverty, having defied the dictates of fashion to pursue his artistic genius. He survived both his son, Titus, and his common law wife, Saskia.

The Hague, 1670. The Dutch-Jewish philosopher Spinoza publishes his *Tractatus* anonymously. The work promotes democracy as the most natural form of government and is badly received by those in power.

New England, 1670. The English Hudson's Bay Company is formed.

Hungary, 1671. Following the abolition of the constitution, Hungary becomes a province of Austria.

Netherlands, 1672. Having declared war on the Dutch, the French cross the Rhine and capture city after city. To halt the invasion the Dutch open dikes, causing extensive flooding.

London, 1673. Parliament cuts off funds for England's war against Holland, forcing Charles II to drop the war, rescind religious liberties, and accept the Test Act, which is designed to prevent Roman Catholics from holding office.

Poland, 20 May 1674. John Sobieski is elected king with French support.

India, 1674. Francois Martin founds Pondicherry for the French East India Company.

India, 1675. Aurangzeb, the Moghul emperor, executes the ninth Sikh *guru*, Tegh Bahadur, for refusing to accept Islam.

London, 1675. The Greenwich Observatory is established.

Netherlands, 1675. The painter Jan Vermeer dies at Delft.

Massachusetts, 28 August 1676. Metacom, the chief of the Algonquin Wampanoags—known by the English as King Philip—is killed by English soldiers. His death ends a year of fighting between Indians and colonists.

England, 15 November 1677. Mary, daughter of the Duke of York and niece of Charles II, marries William of Orange. This marriage puts the seal on Anglo-Dutch rapprochement.

England, 1678. The Baptist preacher John Bunyan publishes his *Pilgrim's Progress*, an account of life as an allegorical journey with much vivid description and realistic narrative.

Netherlands, 5 February 1679. France signs the Treaty of Nijmegen with the Holy Roman Empire.

London, May 1679. In spite of King Charles II's opposition, the Act of Habeas Corpus is passed, making it impossible for anyone to be imprisoned without a court appearance.

London, May 1680. An Exclusion Bill, against the succession of James, Duke of York, is passed by the Commons but thrown out by the Lords.

Indian Ocean, 1680. The last dodos in Mauritius are killed by English sailors. These large, flightless birds were hunted for their meat and plumage.

Paris, 1682. The English astronomer Edmund Halley observes a comet and plots its orbit.

England, 1682. Isaac Newton discovers the law of universal gravitation, which identifies the nature of the earth's gravity and the pull of the heavenly bodies.

North America, 1682. The English Quaker William Penn founds Philadelphia and the colony of Pennsylvania.

France, 1682. The court of Louis XIV is installed at Versailles.

Vienna, 13 July 1683. Having invaded Austria earlier in the year, the Turks lay siege to Vienna.

Austria, 12 September 1683. A combined Austrian and Polish army, led by Charles of Lorraine and John III Sobieski of Poland, defeats the Turks at Kahlenberg.

Rome, 1684. Pope Innocent IX forms a Holy League with Venice, Austria, and Poland against the Turks.

England, 16 February 1685. At the death of Charles II, his brother James II, the Duke of York succeeds as the new King of England.

France, 18 October 1685. To force the French to practice the Roman Catholic religion, Louis XIV revokes the 1598 Edict of Nantes, which granted civil liberties and political powers to Protestants.

Russia, October 1686. Having joined Pope Innocent XI's Holy League and ensured the safety of Kiev by a treaty with Poland, Russia declares war on the Ottoman Empire.

Germany, 1686. The Emperor Leopold breaks the 1684 Truce of Ratisbon and joins the League of Augsburg, formed by Sweden and several German states to oppose Louis XIV of France.

Greece, 1687. The Venetians under Francesco Morosini, who have recently seized parts of Dalmatia and Morea, attack the Turks in Greece. They take Corinth and lay siege to Athens. The Parthenon, converted into a powder magazine by the Turks, is seriously damaged by a Venetian shell.

Istanbul, 1687. With the Ottoman Empire in a state of complete anarchy, Sultan Mehmet IV is deposed by the Janissaries. He is succeeded by his younger brother Suleiman II.

France, 26 November 1688. Louis XIV declares war on the Netherlands.

England, 28 December 1688. Invited by seven English lords, William of Orange and his English wife Mary enter London, having landed in England in November. James II flees to France.

London, 21 April 1689. William III and Mary II are crowned joint King and Queen of England, Scotland, and Ireland.

Europe, May 1689. England and the Netherlands join the League of Augsburg.

England, 17 May 1689. Following the decision by Louis XIV to send an expedition to aid James II in Ireland, England declares war on France.

London, 24 May 1689. Parliament passes the Act of Toleration, exempting

Protestants dissenting from the Church of England from the penalties of certain laws, as long as they swear oaths of allegiance and supremacy. Roman Catholics are specifically excluded from such relief.

Siberia, 6 September 1689. The Chinese and the Russians sign the Treaty of Nerchinsk establishing the boundary between their two countries along the Argun and Gorbitsa Rivers and the Stanovoi mountain range.

Russia, 1689. Tsar Peter (the Great), who ruled jointly with his half brother Ivan V since 1682, launches a successful coup and becomes sole ruler of Russia.

North America, 1689. The War of the Grand Alliance spreads to North America, where it is known as King William's War.

Ireland, 1690. William III lands in Ireland with an Anglo-Dutch army. On 11 July, William defeats James II at the Battle of the Boyne.

Canada, 11 May 1690. In the first major engagement of King William's War, British troops from Massachusetts, led by Sir William Phips, seize Port Royal in Acadia (Nova Scotia and New Brunswick) from the French. Their main objective is to take Quebec.

Netherlands, 1 July 1690. Led by Marshal Luxembourg, the French defeat the forces of the Grand Alliance at Fleurus. In addition to England, the Netherlands, and the Austrian Habsburgs, the alliance now includes Savoy, Sweden, Spain, the Holy Roman Empire, Bavaria, Saxony, and the Palatinate.

London, 1690. The philosopher John Locke publishes his *Essay Concerning Human Understanding* and *Treatise on Civil Government*.

Ireland, 1691. William III defeats the allied Irish and French at the Battle of Aughrim. Limerick, the Jacobite headquarters, surrenders to William III's forces after successfully resisting two sieges. By the peace of Limerick, Catholics are granted a measure of religious toleration, and Jacobite soldiers and civilians remaining in Ireland are granted security of life and property.

France, 1692. The French are heavily defeated by a Grand Alliance fleet at La Hogue.

Netherlands, 29 July 1693. The army of the Grand Alliance is crushed by French forces at the Battle of Neerwinden.

Persia, 1694. Hussein, a devout Shia, becomes Shah of Persia.

West Africa, 1695. Osei Tutu founds the Ashanti Confederation.

Poland, 27 June 1697. Frederick Augustus, Elector of Saxony, is elected King of Poland and takes the name Augustus II.

Hungary, 11 September 1697. Imperial troops under the brilliant commander Eugene of Savoy defeat the Turks at the Battle of Zenta.

Netherlands, 30 October 1697. The Treaty of Ryswick ends the war between France and the Grand Alliance.

Sweden, 1697. Charles XI, who confiscated large areas of land belonging to the aristocracy and transformed Sweden into an absolute monarchy, dies and is succeeded by his son Charles XII.

Siberia, 1697. Continuing their expansion eastwards through the vast territories of Siberia, the Russians reach and conquer the Kamchatka peninsula.

Europe, 11 October 1698. France, England, and the Netherlands sign a partition treaty to solve the problem of the Spanish succession after the impending death of the childless King Charles II. Under the treaty, Spanish possessions are to be divided between the dauphin, the electoral prince of Bavaria, and the Archduke Charles, son of the Emperor Leopold.

Austria, 26 January 1699. The Treaty of Karlowitz ends the war between Austria and the Turks that began in 1683. The Turks cede Transylvania and Hungary to the Austrians, Morea and Dalmatia to Venice, and part of the Ukraine to Poland.

1700–1724

Russia, 23 June 1700. Russia signs a truce with the Ottoman Empire, halting the war that began in 1695. Russia gives up its Black Sea fleet but retains Azov.

Boston, 24 June 1700. Judge Samuel Sewall writes *The Selling of Joseph*, the first outright appeal for the abolition of slavery to appear in America.

Denmark, 18 August 1700. Having invaded Denmark and captured Copenhagen, Charles XII of Sweden forces Frederick IV of Denmark to sign the Peace of Travendal.

Spain, 2 October 1700. Charles II, King of Spain, draws up a will in favor of the Bourbon Duke Philip of Anjou, the grandson of Louis XIV of France.

Spain, 1 November 1700. On the death of Charles II, Philip of Anjou comes to the throne as Philip V.

Baltic, November 1700. Charles XII of Sweden defeats the Russian forces besieging the city of Narva.

Germany, 18 January 1701. Frederick III, Elector of Brandenburg, becomes King of Prussia.

Netherlands, 7 September 1701. England, Austria, and the Netherlands form an alliance against France. The allies are fearful of a union between Spain and France following the choice made by Charles II, the late King of Spain, of a Bourbon as his successor.

Poland, 1701. Having occupied Lithuania, Charles XII of Sweden invades Poland and seizes Warsaw and Krakow.

London, 11 March 1702. The *Daily Courant*, the first daily newspaper in the world, begins publication.

England, 19 March 1702. On the death of William III of Orange, Anne Stuart, sister of Mary, succeeds to the throne of England, Scotland, and Ireland.

Europe, 4 May 1702. To stall the alliance of Spain and France, the Grand Alliance declares war on France.

Poland, 13 April 1703. The forces of Charles XII, King of Sweden, win a victory over the much larger army of Augustus II, King of Poland, at the Battle of Pultusk.

France, 1703. The military engineer Sebastien de Vauban imposes the use of the flintlock rifle by the French army and equips the soldiers with bayonets.

Russia, 1703. Peter the Great founds St. Petersburg.

Spain, July 1704. The English, led by John Churchill, Duke of Marlborough, seize Gibraltar.

Germany, 13 August 1704. The forces of the Grand Alliance, led by the Duke of Marlborough and Eugene of Savoy, defeat the French and the Bavarians at Blenheim.

England, 1704. Isaac Newton's treatise, *Opticks*, presenting his main discoveries concerning light and color, is published.

Japan, 1705. The Bakufu government accuses the House of Yodoya, the most prominent in Osaka, of ostentatious luxury and confiscates its entire wealth. In fact, the Yodoya has come to control the finances of many of the *daimyo* of Kyushu and western Honshu, whose huge debts to the Yodoya are cancelled by the confiscation.

Austria, 5 May 1705. Leopold, Holy Roman Emperor since 1658, dies and is succeeded by his son Joseph. Leopold tried to transform the Habsburg possessions into a modern state, strengthen-ing the political institutions and reorganizing the army and the finances. His struggle against the Turks led to the annexation of Hungary and Transylvania.

Britain, 1 May 1707. Scotland is united with England by an Act of Union.

Hungary, 1707. The Budapest parliament declares the fall of the Habsburgs and the independence of Hungary.

India, 1707. The great Moghul Aurangzeb dies at the age of 89, having secured control of most of the Indian peninsula. He is succeeded by Bahadur Shah.

Netherlands, 11 September 1709. After inflicting heavy losses on the enemy, the French forces are defeated by Marlborough and Eugene of Savoy at Malplaquet.

Afghanistan, 1709. The Ghilzai chieftain, Mirwais Khan, leads an uprising in Kandahar against the Safavid Persian rulers.

Poland, 1709. The Poles rise up against Stanislas Leszczynski, who flees, making way for the return of Augustus II.

Turkey, 1709. Charles XII of Sweden seeks refuge in Turkey after his defeat at Poltava.

Florence, 1709. Bartolomeo Cristofori, the famous maker of harpsichords, invents the pianoforte.

Spain, 28 September 1710. Charles III, Austrian King of Spain, takes Madrid.

Turkey, 30 November 1710. At the instigation of Charles XII of Sweden, Turkey declares war on Russia.

Spain, 10 December 1710. The French defeat the Austrians at Villa Viciosa, forcing Charles III to abandon Madrid and making Philip V Spain's first Bourbon king.

Paris, 1710. An income tax known as the "tenth" is introduced.

Vienna, 17 April 1711. On the death of the Emperor Joseph he is succeeded by Charles III, King of Spain, as Charles VI.

Boston, 25 June 1711. With the arrival of 64 British ships, carrying 5,000 troops and 6,000 seamen, preparations begin for an advance on Canada.

Afghanistan, 1711. Mirwais succeeds in defeating the Persian army sent to put down the Ghilzai rebellion and establishes the independence of the Afghan state.

Balkans, 1711. Supported by Venice and Russia, Danilo of Montenegro massacres the Muslims in his country and repels the Turks.

England, 1711. The South Sea Company is incorporated.

Pennsylvania, 7 June 1712. The assembly bans the importation of slaves into the colony.

Baltic, 1712. Russians and Danes defeat the Swedes in the Baltic and Scandinavia. Since 1700, in what would become known as the Second Northern War, the Swedish king, Charles XII, has been fighting to preserve Swedish supremacy in the Baltic. However, after these most recent defeats, as Charles is forced to sue for peace.

West Africa, 1712. The Bambara kingdom of Segu is founded upstream from Timbuktu. It is a non-Muslim state that challenges the declining Mali empire to the west.

Netherlands, 11 April 1713. The Treaty of Utrecht ends the war of the Spanish Succession. It confirms the permanent separation of the crowns of France and Spain and recognizes Philip V as King of Spain.

Germany, 1713. Emperor Charles VI issues the Pragmatic Sanction settling the succession to the Habsburg lands on his daughter Maria Theresa.

Prussia, 1713. Frederick William succeeds his father Frederick on the throne of Prussia.

South Africa, 1713. The first smallpox epidemic spreads from the sailors at the Cape of Good Hope, killing Khoisan hunters and herders in great numbers.

Russia, 1713. Peter the Great has a naval base built at Tallin in Estonia.

Britain, 1 August 1714. On the death of Queen Anne without a direct heir, she is succeeded as monarch of Great Britain and Ireland by George, Elector of Hanover since 1698 and great-grandson of James I of England.

Germany, 1714. The philosopher and mathematician Gottfried Leibniz publishes his *Monadologia*, according to which the universe is made up of "monads", divine mutually isolated creations. Each monad reflects the universe from its own point of view.

South Carolina, 15 April 1715. Yamassee Indians, goaded by Spanish agitation, kill hundreds of English settlers.

South Africa, 1715. Dutch burghers at the Cape of Good Hope elect their own commanders in an attempt to combat cattle rustling by Khoisan herders.

France, September 1715. Following the death of Louis XIV and the accession of his five-year-old grandson, Louis XV, the regency is put in the hands of Philip of Orléans.

Massachusetts, 1715. Three years after the first sperm whale was killed at Nantucket, the whale-oil industry is booming. Nantucket has a fleet of six 30-ton whaling sloops that can cruise for six weeks at a time.

Paris, 4 August 1717. A friendship treaty is signed between Russia and France.

New England, 1717. Colonial ships, now allowed to trade in the West Indies, begin bringing back French molasses, which they use to distill cheap rum in New England.

Vienna, 1717. The Schönbrunn Palace, built on the model of the Palace of Versailles, is completed. Intended as a place of leisure, its size and splendor serve to illustrate the magnificence of the imperial power.

Netherlands, 1717. A triple alliance, directed against Spain, is signed in The Hague by France, England and Holland. This is a response to Spanish expansionist ambitions: Philip V, as Louis XIV's grandson, wishes to gain the French crown, and his wife Elizabeth Farnese wants her children to inherit familial lands in Italy.

London, 1717. The Golden Lion coffee house is the first in London to admit women.

Austria, 21 July 1718. The Treaty of Passarowitz, negotiated by the Emperor Charles VI and the Venetians with the Ottoman Empire, ends the war begun by the Turks in 1714. Turkey cedes Temesvar to Charles, putting the whole of Hungary under Habsburg rule. The Turkish threat to Europe is effectively stamped out.

Europe, 2 August 1718. The Holy Roman Empire joins the triple alliance formed by Britain, Holland and France against Spain last year. The new quadruple alliance aims to uphold the terms of the 1713 Treaty of Utrecht, which Philip V of Spain has violated by invading Sicily and Sardinia.

Virginia, 22 November 1718. The infamous pirate Edward Teach, known as Blackbeard because of an immense beard that he tied with ribbons, is killed by an English naval officer.

Louisiana, November 1718. Governor Bienville founds a new city at the mouth of the Mississippi River, calling it New Orleans in honor of the French regent, the Duke of Orléans.

Norway, 11 December 1718. Sweden's king, Charles XII, dies in battle at Frederikshald (*Halderi*). He came to power in 1697 and has spent almost his entire reign engaged in the Second Northern War. Most recently he had been defeated by Russia and sued for peace, but then marched on Norway. He was killed by a musket shot fired from the fortress of Frederikshald.

Spain, 9 January 1719. In escalation of the conflict caused by the Spanish occupation of Sardinia and Sicily, and the drawing up of the quadruple alliance, Philip V of Spain declares war on France.

Netherlands, 17 February 1720. Spain signs the Treaty of The Hague with the Quadruple Alliance (Britain, Holland, France, and the Holy Roman Empire), ending the war begun in 1718. Philip V of Spain agrees to evacuate Sardinia and Sicily, the invasions of which started the conflict. He exiles his chief minister Alberoni, whom he holds responsible for the war.

Paris, 24 March 1720. Banking establishments close in the wake of financial crisis.

West Africa, c.1720. Biton Mamari Kouloubali makes himself leader of the Kingdom of Segu (*Mali*). Mamari was elected head of the *ton-den* brotherhood and began to conscript young Bambara into it destroying its previously egalitarian nature. He is establishing the *ton-den*, and himself, as the dominant powers in the community.

Austria, 1720. The Pragmatic Sanction—issued by Emperor Charles V in 1713, settling succession to the Habsburg lands on his eldest daughter Maria Theresa—is slowly recognized by the Habsburg states.

Russia, 25 January 1721. The Holy Synod replaces the Patriarchate of Moscow and steps are taken against the sect of the Old Believers. They object to the 1667 revision of Russian church ritual and liturgy in accordance with Greek practice, and are regarded as schismatics by the Orthodox Church.

Germany, 24 March 1721. The supremely talented musician Johann Sebastian Bach publishes the *Six Brandenburg Concertos.*

England, 3 April 1721. Following the collapse of the South Sea Scheme, the ambitious Whig politician Robert Walpole is made Chancellor of the Exchequer in the hope that he will restore financial order.

Greenland, 1721. Led by the Norwegian minister Hans Egede, the Protestant mission of Godthaab is established with the aim of converting the Eskimos.

Massachusetts, 1721. During an outbreak of smallpox Dr. Zabdiel Boylston of Boston experiments with inoculation at the prompting of Reverend Cotton Mather. Mather heard of the technique from his African slave Onesimus. Opponents to inoculation believe it has caused the disease to spread more rapidly, though all but six of the 240 Boylston inoculated have survived.

Russia, 12 September 1723. The Treaty of St. Petersburg puts an end to the Russo-Persian war that began last year when Peter the Great, made anxious by a Turkish push towards the Caspian Sea, launched an offensive.

West Africa, c.1723. King Agaja of the Kingdom of Dahomey at Abomey invades the Kingdom of Allada. Allada, founded about 150 years ago, was once the most powerful kingdom of the Aja peoples.

Louisiana, 1724. The Black Code makes it legal for slave owners to cut off runaways' ears, hamstring and brand them. It also bars Jews and Catholics from the colony.

1725–1749

Russia, 8 February 1725. Peter the Great dies in St. Petersburg. He is succeeded by his wife Catherine.

Austria, 30 April 1725. Philip V of Spain and the Emperor Charles VI sign the Treaty of Vienna ending Spanish and imperial adherence to the Quadruple Alliance. Philip guarantees the Pragmatic Sanction—allowing for the succession of the emperor's daughter on his death—and receives a promise of support in the recovery of Gibraltar and Minorca, though this does not extend to military aid.

France, 15 August 1725. Louis XV marries Maria Leszczynska, daughter of the deposed Polish king, Stanislav Leszczynski, by proxy in Strasbourg.

Netherlands, 1725. The composer Antonio Vivaldi publishes *The Four Seasons.*

Southern Africa, c.1725. Langa, the ancestor chief of Ngwane, Swazi and Hlubi nations, dies. Langa was tributary to the Tembe kingdom at Maputo Bay.

Russia, 16 August 1726. Russia becomes an ally of Austria and recognizes the Pragmatic Sanction guaranteeing the succession of Emperor Charles VI's eldest daughter, Maria Theresa.

Spain, March 1727. Spain breaks the terms of the Treaty of Utrecht, invades Gibraltar and attacks the English.

Philadelphia, 1727. The satirist and polemicist Benjamin Franklin sets up a philosophy club called the Junto, the aim of which is the "sincere enquiry after truth". The club's main rule bars the use of dogmatic remarks.

London, 29 January 1728. John Gay's *Beggar's Opera* opens to an enthusiastic crowd in Lincoln's Inn Fields.

Spain, 9 November 1729. In signing the Treaty of Seville, Spain renounces its right to Gibraltar, which remains in English hands. All English economic privileges in the Spanish American colonies are retained.

Africa, 1730. The Portuguese finally lose Mombasa to the native power of the Omani.

Southern Africa, 1730. Tau, king of Rolong and son of Thibela, ruler of the unified Rolong kingdom north of the Orange river, dies.

Southern Africa, 1730. The Dutch abandon their trading post in Maputo Bay, which they have held since 1721.

Austria, 16 March 1731. On the signing of the Second Treaty of Vienna, Charles VI obtains England's recognition of the Pragmatic Sanction.

West Africa, 1731. The slave trading Kingdom of Dahomey at Abomey, after defeats in battle, accepts the suzerainty of the Oyo Empire (the Yoruba people).

Persia, 1731. Tahmasp II, shah for less than a year, is deposed by his brother-in-law Nadir Kuli. Tahmasp's eight-month-old son, Abbas, is elevated to the throne as a puppet.

Caribbean, 1731. Robert Jenkins, master of the *Rebecca*, sailing from Jamaica with sugar and other commodities for London, has his ear cut off by Spanish coast guards. After prolonged torture of Jenkins and his men, during which the Spaniards repeatedly asked for money, they sliced off his ear with a cutlass and told him to carry it home to the king.

Germany, 11 January 1732. The German Diet meets in Ratisbon (*Regensburg*) and guarantees the implementation of the Pragmatic Sanction which allows for the succession of Maria Theresa, Emperor Charles VI's daughter.

France, 10 October 1733. France declares war on Austria over the question of Polish succession following the death of Augustus II. Augustus III, supported by Austria, Saxony and Russia, has been elected in preference to Stanislav Leszczynski, the candidate supported by France.

Japan, 1733. A large-scale food riot takes place in Edo (*Tokyo*) when some 1,700 people attack a rice store in protest against exorbitant prices. Such riots are becoming increasingly common, the earliest similar disturbance having occurred in Nagasaki in 1713.

North America, 6 February 1736. The young Anglican preacher John Wesley lands in Georgia.

Austria, 12 February 1736. Maria Theresa of Austria, heir to the imperial throne by the provisions of the Pragmatic Sanction, marries François-Stephane of Lorraine.

Austria, 13 April 1736. Franco-Austrian talks on Poland and Lorraine are resumed following the conflict that broke out over the question of Polish succession in 1733. Augustus III is to remain on the Polish throne.

Austria, 21 April 1736. Prince Eugene of Savoy—a great general and military tactician—dies. He was commissioned by the Emperor Leopold and went on to a glorious military career, famously cooperating with the Duke of Marlborough to win a decisive victory at Blenheim in 1704.

Italy, 18 December 1737. The master violin maker Antonio Stradivarius dies in Cremona.

Sweden, 1738. The "Hat" party is born during campaigning for the general election; they champion the French connection and advocate war with Russia. Their opponents, the "Caps" are led by Arvid Horn.

India, 20 March 1739. Nadir Shah of Persia occupies Delhi and takes possession of the Peacock throne.

England, 19 October 1739. England goes to war with Spain over borderlines in Florida and the mistreatment inflicted on British subjects. A British sailor, Robert Jenkins, attends a sitting of parliament exhibiting his ear that was cut off by Spanish coast guards. The conflict becomes known as "the War of Jenkin's Ear."

England, 1739. The 28-year-old philosopher David Hume publishes his *Treatise on Human Nature*. Hume opposes the commonly accepted ideas on the absolute power of reason and follows John Locke and George Berkeley in claiming that knowledge comes from experience. This empiricist position finds little favor with his educated audience.

South America, 1739. The Spaniards establish New Granada as an independent viceroyalty, encompassing all territories between the Amazon and the Orinoco.

Colorado, 1739. French explorers Pierre and Paul Mallet arrive in New Orleans after a nine-month trek across the Great Plains during which they discovered a mountain range known to the Indians as the Rockies.

Netherlands, 1739. Francois Voltaire publishes the *Anti-Machiavelli*, written by Frederick of Prussia, in Amsterdam.

Massachusetts, January 1740. Some 50 slaves are hanged after the exposure of alleged plans for an insurrection.

Florida, January 1740. Governor Oglethorpe, taking advantage of the protection of some friendly Indians, invades Florida, capturing Forts Picolata and San Francisco de Pupo.

Prussia, 31 May 1740. Frederick William dies and is succeeded by his son Frederick II.

Austria, 19 October 1740. The Emperor Charles VI dies. The succession rights of his daughter Maria Theresa, established by the 1718 Pragmatic Sanction, are challenged by Frederick II of Prussia.

Prussia, 16 December 1740. Frederick II invades Silesia starting yet another war in a Europe already beset by conflict.

South Carolina, 1740. The assembly makes it illegal to teach blacks to write or to hire them as scribes.

Sweden, August 1741. Sweden declares war on Russia, counting on support from France and intending to co-operate with the Russian Tsarina Elizabeth, who is planning a coup d'etat in St. Petersburg. The Swedes hope to take advantage of the fact that Russia is at war with Turkey.

Russia, 26 November 1741. In a palace rebellion, the Tsarina Elizabeth overthrows Ivan VI and his mother, the regent Anne Leopoldovna. This puts an end to the German influence in Russia, which had been encouraged by the regent.

Alaska, 9 August 1742. The remaining 31 members of Vitus Bering's expedition set off from their marooned ship on a timber raft, hoping to make it back to Russia. The Dutch navigator Bering, who was employed by the Russians to explore the lands east of Siberia, died of scurvy last year.

Ireland, 13 April 1742. The *Messiah* by the German-English composer George Frederick Handel is performed for the first time, in Dublin.

Germany, 11 June 1742. Maria Theresa of Austria and Frederick II of Prussia sign the Treaty of Breslau, which recognizes Frederick's claim to Silesia.

Sweden, 17 August 1743. By the Treaty of Abo, Sweden cedes southeast Finland to Russia and accepts the Empress Elizabeth's choice of a successor: Adolf Frederick of Holstein-Gottorp. This ends a disastrous war with Russia in which Sweden had intended to help the empress take the throne. In the event, the Swedish army was hopelessly disorganized, and Elizabeth herself seized power in a palace revolution.

France, 28 October 1743. Louis XV of France and Philip V of Spain forge a defensive and offensive alliance at Fontainebleau. This pact between the two Bourbon lines is known as the Second Family Compact.

London, 30 May 1744. The great satirical poet Alexander Pope dies. Among his masterpieces are *The Rape of the Lock* and the *Dunciad*.

Bohemia, September 1744. Having invaded Bohemia last month, Frederick II of Prussia takes Prague.

Paris, 8 December 1744. The beautiful and intelligent Madame de Pompadour comes into favor with King Louis XV.

East Africa, 1744. Mohammed ben Uthman al-Mazrui, who came to power as governor of Mombasa in 1739, declares himself independent from Oman.

Europe, 8 January 1745. England, Austria, Saxony, and the Netherlands form an alliance against Russia.

New England, August 1745. The French and their Indian allies carry out a series of raids on English settlements.

Germany, 25 December 1745. By the Treaty of Dresden, Frederick II of Prussia recognizes Francis, Duke of Lorraine and husband of Maria Theresa of Austria, as Holy Roman Emperor. Frederick's control of Silesia is also recognized under the treaty.

England, 1745. The painter William Hogarth completes *Marriage a la Mode*. Like his earlier *Rake's Progress*, the work is a moral narrative — a series of scenes exposing the follies and vices of his age.

Scotland, September 1745. Charles Edward Stuart, grandson of James II and pretender to the British throne, defeats a government army at the battle of Prestonpans. The "young pretender" — son of James Edward Stuart, the "old pretender" — landed in Scotland two months ago and rallied some of the Highland chiefs and other Jacobites against King George II.

Scotland, 27 April 1746. The young pretender Charles Edward Stuart is defeated by King George II's army at the Battle of Culloden and goes into hiding in the Highlands.

Austria, 2 June 1746. Austria forms an alliance with Russia against Prussia and the Ottomans.

Spain, 9 July 1746. On the death of Philip V, his son Ferdinand VI comes to the throne.

India, 20 October 1746. Following the spread the War of the Austrian Succession to India, Joseph Francois Dupleix, the French colonial governor, takes Madras.

Persia, 10 June 1747. The Persian ruler Nadir Shah is assassinated at Fathabad. After defeating the Afghan invaders in 1729, Nadir restored Tahmasp to the throne and went on to defeat the Ottomans in the west. Proclaimed shah himself in 1736, Nadir conquered Afghanistan and launched a campaign against India which culminated in 1739 in the sack of Delhi.

Afghanistan, June 1747. After the death of Nadir Shah, Afghanistan becomes independent of Persia.

Netherlands, 1747. The republic of the United Provinces is overthrown and the title of *stadtholder* (governor) is reinstated. William of Nassau, prince of Orange — grand-nephew of William III of England — is made hereditary *stadtholder*.

Beijing, 1747. The summer palace of the Emperor Qian Long is decorated and furnished in western style.

France, 18 October 1748. The Treaty of Aix-la-Chapelle ends the War of the Austrian Succession, giving general recognition to the Pragmatic Sanction and the Prussian conquest of Silesia.

England, 1748. The philosopher David Hume publishes his *Enquiry Concerning Human Understanding*.

England, 1748. Samuel Richardson, author of *Pamela*, publishes the last part of his seven-volume novel *Clarissa*, again written in epistolary form. The novel is described as showing the "distresses that may attend the misconduct both of parents and children, in relation to marriage".

Canada, 1749. Some 2,500 settlers sent by Lord Halifax to consolidate the British hold on Nova Scotia found the town of Halifax.

France, 1749. Georges Louis Buffon publishes the first three volumes of a great *Natural History*, the prospectus of which he issued last year.

England, 1749. Henry Fielding publishes *Tom Jones*, a comic novel of manners designed, like his *Joseph Andrews*, as a reaction to the moral conventionality of Samuel Richardson.

1750–1774

Portugal, 31 July 1750. John V dies and is succeeded as king by his son Joseph Emanuel, who appoints Sebastiao Jose de Carvalho e Mello, Marquis of Pombal, as his chief minister. Pombal immediately deprives the Inquisition of its rights.

India, 1750. By his victory at the Battle of Tanjore, Joseph Dupleix, the French governor of Pondicherry, wins control of the Carnatic region in southern India.

Tibet, 1750. The Tibetans rebel against China.

Paris, 1751. The Sorbonne condemns 14 propositions on evolution in Georges Buffon's *Natural History*. To avoid theological controversy, Buffon signs a declaration abandoning anything in his work that might be contrary to the account of earth's origins given in Genesis.

England, 1751. The poet Thomas Gray composes his *Elegy written in a Country Churchyard*.

Paris, February 1752. The parliament of Paris condemns the *Encyclopédie*, edited by Denis Diderot, the first volume of which appeared in 1751.

Philadelphia, June 1752. In his book *Experiments and Observations in Electricity*, Benjamin Franklin concludes that lightning is identical with electricity produced by friction.

India, July 1752. The English go on the attack. Robert Clive takes Trichinopoly and forces the French commander Bussy to evacuate Aurangabad.

Southeast Africa, 1752. The Portuguese southeast African coastal settlements of Mozambique, Zambezi and Sofala are placed under the governor at Mozambique; they are no longer subordinate to the Portuguese colony of Goa in India.

Austria, January 1753. Count Anton Kaunitz, the former Austrian ambassador in Paris, is appointed chancellor by the Empress Maria Theresa.

London, June 1753. A conference is held with the aim of ending the Anglo-French conflict over India.

England, 1753. The home of John Kay, who invented the flying shuttle in 1733, is destroyed by a riot.

London, 1753. The British Museum is founded.

New York, July 1754. At the Albany Congress, which brings together delegates from the 13 British colonies, Benjamin Franklin calls for the establishment of a common council of defense to fight the French and the Indians.

India, 1754. Joseph Dupleix, governor-general of the French possessions in India since 1741, is recalled to France after a brilliant colonial career. His departure leaves British primacy in India firmly established.

France, 1754. The French philosopher Jean-Jacques Rousseau publishes his *Discourse Upon the Origin and Foundation of the Inequality Among Mankind.*

Paris, 10 February 1755. The philosopher Baron de Montesquieu dies. His first great literary success was *Lettres Persanes*, published in 1721, which included a satire of French society. His most influential work was *De l'Esprit des Lois*, of which 22 editions were published in the two years following its first appearance in 1748.

England, 15 April 1755. Samuel Johnson's *Dictionary of the English Language* is published. The product of eight years' work, the *Dictionary*, which is both useful and entertaining, provides excellent definitions of the actual senses of words employed by the "best authors," without tracing their historical growth. It reflects Johnson's belief that the English language reached almost its fullest development in the days of Shakespeare, Bacon and Spenser.

Britain, 8 July 1755. As their land dispute in North America intensifies, Britain breaks off diplomatic relations with France.

North America, July 1755. George Washington takes command of the British forces after their defeat by the French at the Battle of the Wilderness, near Fort Duquesne (*Pittsburgh*). The British commander, Edward Braddock, was fatally wounded during the battle.

Lisbon, November 1755. As many as 30,000 people die in an earthquake.

Burma, 1755. King Alaungpaya founds a new capital at Rangoon.

North America, 1756. A stagecoach line opens between Philadelphia and New York. By traveling at 18 hours a day, the distance can be covered in three days.

Tunisia, 1756. Tunis is seized by troops led by the *bey* of Algiers.

France, 1756. The publication of Voltaire's *Essay on Universal History* confirms his reputation as a fine historian.

Versailles, 1 May 1756. The Austrian chancellor, Kaunitz, signs a treaty of alliance with France.

India, June 1756. Sirajuddaula, the new ruler of Bengal, captures Calcutta. Many of the British residents who surrender are condemned to die in a "black hole".

New England, 14 August 1756. Soon after arriving in America to command the French forces, Louis Montcalm de St. Veran takes Fort Oswego from the British.

Germany, 29 August 1756. Frederick II of Prussia invades Saxony, setting off a war in Europe. Prussia is allied with Britain against Austria and France.

New England, 31 August 1756. The British at Fort William Henry surrender to Louis Montcalm.

Britain, November 1756. On the resignation of the Duke of Newcastle as prime minister, William Pitt is appointed secretary of state and takes charge of the war against France.

Austria, 2 February 1757. Austria, already allied with France, forms an alliance with Russia against Prussia.

India, 22 June 1757. After retaking Calcutta and seizing the French station at Chandernagore, Robert Clive, leading the British East India Company's forces, defeats the ruler of Bengal's much larger army at Plassey, 100 miles up the Hooghly from Calcutta.

Germany, 5 November 1757. The Prussians, led by Frederick II, defeat a Franco-Austrian force at Rossbach.

Canada, 26 July 1758. British forces under James Wolfe capture Fort Louisbourg on Cape Breton Island from the French. The fort was taken by the British in 1745 but returned to the French three years later by the Treaty of Aix-la-Chapelle.

North America, 25 November 1758. After losing Louisbourg and Fort Frontenac to the British, the French are forced to evacuate Fort Duquesne (*Pittsburgh*), which the British rename Fort Pitt.

Prussia, 12 August 1759. The Austro-Russian coalition wins a resounding victory over Frederick II at Kunersdorf.

Canada, 18 September 1759. Quebec surrenders to the British after a battle that saw the deaths of both James Wolfe and Louis Montcalm, the British and French commanders.

France, 1759. Voltaire publishes a short story entitled *Candide*, a satire on the philosophy that "all is for the best in the best of all possible worlds."

India, 22 January 1760. British forces under Eyre Coote win a decisive victory over the French, led by the Count of Lally, at Wandiwash in southern India.

Quebec, 28 April 1760. French forces besieging Quebec defeat the British under James Murray in the second battle on the Plains of Abraham. The British retreat into the city.

South Carolina, 7 August 1760. The British garrison of Fort Loudon is overrun by Cherokee Indians after it was forced by starvation to surrender.

Germany, 15 August 1760. Frederick II defeats the Austrians at the Battle of Liegnitz.

Quebec, 8 September 1760. The French surrender the city of Montreal to the British.

Britain, 25 October 1760. On the death of his grandfather George II, George III comes to the throne.

Germany, 3 November 1760. Following the Russian capture of Berlin, his capital, Frederick II of Prussia defeats the Austrians at the Battle of Torgau.

North America, 1760. People of African descent are said to constitute 30 percent of the population of the 13 British colonies in North America.

France, 1760. Jean-Jacques Rousseau publishes *Julie ou la Nouvelle Heloise*.

China, 1760. Canton becomes the only port in China authorized to trade with other countries.

Scotland, 1760. The poet James Macpherson publishes *Ossian*, allegedly a collection of fragments of ancient poetry translated from the Gaelic. In fact, the author is Macpherson himself.

England, 1760. The Irish-born clergyman Laurence Sterne publishes the first two volumes of an eccentric novel entitled *Tristram Shandy*.

Spain, 1761. Spain is drawn into the war of European powers by the so-called third Family Compact, which makes its foreign policy subservient to that of France. This treaty of mutual assistance involving all the ruling Bourbon dynasties was drawn up by the duke of Choiseul, Louis XV's chief minister.

India, 1761. British forces under Eyre Coote seize Pondicherry from the French.

Britain, 2 January 1762. Britain declares war on Spain.

Russia, 5 January 1762. The Tsarina Elizabeth dies and is succeeded on the throne by her nephew Peter III, the maternal grandson of Peter the Great.

West Indies, 5 February 1762. Martinique, a major French base in the Lesser Antilles, surrenders to the British.

Russia, July 1762. Peter III is assassinated with the complicity of his wife, Catherine, who succeeds him on the throne as Catherine II. During his brief reign, Peter gave his support to Frederick II, restoring eastern Prussia to him.

Germany, 21 July 1762. Frederick II defeats the Austrians at Berkersdorf in Silesia.

Philippines, 5 October 1762. A British fleet bombards and captures the Spanish-held city of Manila.

Austria, 24 November 1762. Austria signs a truce with Frederick II of Prussia.

North America, 3 December 1762. France cedes to Spain all lands west of the Mississippi, the territory known as Upper Louisiana.

Portugal, December 1762. With British support, the Portuguese repel an invasion by French and Spanish forces.

France, 1762. Jean-Jacques Rousseau publishes *Du Contrat Social* (*The Social Contract*), which contains the opening sentence "Man is born free, yet everywhere he is in chains" and the slogan "liberty, equality, fraternity". He also publishes *Emile*, in novel form, which outrages church and state with its unorthodox views on monarchy and religion and causes him to flee into exile in Switzerland.

Paris, 10 February 1763. By the Treaty of Paris, ending the Seven Years War, France loses all its North American territories, including Canada, except New Orleans and the islands of St. Pierre, Miquelon, Guadeloupe and Martinique. Florida is ceded to Britain by Spain, which receives from Britain all conquests in Cuba.

Germany, 15 February 1763. Prussia and Austria sign the Treaty of Hubertusburg, by which Silesia is definitely ceded to Prussia. Frederick II fails to gain Saxony, however, which had been his objective in starting the war.

North America, November 1763. The Ottawa Chief Pontiac, who has inflicted several defeats on the British in the Great Lakes region, lifts a six-month siege of Fort Detroit after failing to gain French support for his rebellion.

North America, 1763. Two English surveyors, Charles Mason and Jeremiah Dixon, begin to survey a boundary line between the two colonies of Pennsylvania and Maryland.

New England, 1763. The Touro synagogue, the first major centre of Jewish culture in America, opens at Newport, Rhode Island.

Russia, 1763. Catherine II appoints a commission to determine the future of the Russian nobility.

France, 1763. The group of French economic and political thinkers known as the Physiocrats begins publication of a newspaper entitled *La Gazette du Commerce*.

London, 5 April 1764. Parliament passes a Sugar Act, its first law specifically aimed at raising revenue from the colonies.

London, 19 April 1764. Parliament passes a Currency Act banning the colonies from printing paper money.

Boston, 24 May 1764. The lawyer James Otis denounces "taxation without representation" and calls for the colonies to unite in demonstrating their opposition to Britain's new tax measures.

Poland, 6 September 1764. The pretender Stanislas Poniatowski, a favorite of Catherine II of Russia, becomes King of Poland.

Florida, 1764. The British farmer John Bartram discovers vast groves of wild oranges in Florida.

Dresden, 1764. The German archaeologist Johann Joachim Winckelmann publishes *The Art of Antiquity*, in which he defends the return to the classical tradition.

London, 22 March 1765. In order to raise money in the colonies to support British troops stationed there, Parliament passes the Stamp Act, taxing stamps affixed to certain printed matter.

London, 24 March 1765. Parliament passes the Quartering Act, requiring the colonies to provide shelter and food for British soldiers and their horses.

North America, 1765. The passage of the Stamp Act provokes widespread protests and riots in British colonies, and the campaign of non-importation of luxury goods from Britain is stepped up.

India, 12 August 1765. Robert Clive receives revenue authority over Bengal from the Moghul emperor.

Austria, 18 August 1765. The Emperor Francis dies and his wife, Maria Theresa, retires from public life. Their eldest son becomes emperor as Josef II.

Austria, 1765. When the Emperor Josef II cedes to the state the large private fortune bequeathed to him by his father, his mother, Maria Theresa, reassumes power and makes Josef co-regent.

England, 1765. James Watt refines and improves the steam engine invented by Thomas Newcomen by making the first engine with a separate condenser.

London, 4 March 1766. Parliament repeals the Stamp Act, the cause of bitter and violent opposition in the colonies.

New York, 19 December 1766. Thomas Gage, the commander in chief of the British forces, closes the New York Assembly, which has resolutely refused to comply with the controversial Quartering Act.

Spain, 27 February 1767. The new prime minister, Aranda, expels the Jesuits from the country.

London, June 1767. Parliament passes the Townshend Acts, spearheaded by Charles Townshend, the Chancellor of the Exchequer, imposing new taxes on the colonies and suspending the New York Assembly until it complies with the Quartering Act.

Russia, 1767. Catherine II gathers a great commission, composed of a representative of all social classes except the serfs, with the aim of drawing up a code of reforms.

Denmark, 1767. Christian VII, who was crowned king last year, extends his power over Schleswig and Holstein.

England, 1767. The chemist Joseph Priestley publishes the *History and Present State of Electricity*.

Boston, February 1768. Samuel Adams, the first American leader to deny the authority of the British Parliament over the colonies, calls for united action to oppose the Townshend Acts.

France, 16 September 1768. Rene-Nicolas de Maupeou is appointed chancellor in place of Guillaume de Lamoignon.

Boston, 1 October 1768. Lord Hillsborough, British secretary of state for the colonies, sends two regiments to Boston to quell unrest provoked by the Townshend Acts.

Istanbul, October 1768. Mustafa II, the Ottoman sultan, declares war on Russia, which has violated the 1711 Treaty of Pruth by occupying Poland.

New York, 5 November 1768. William Johnson, the northern Indian commissioner, signs a treaty with the Iroquois Indians to acquire much of the land between the Tennessee and Ohio rivers for future settlement.

Poland, 1768. An organization of Polish Catholic nobles, called the Confederation of Bar, is formed to oppose Russian influence and demands for religious and political equality for Protestants and Orthodox. When 20,000 Catholics and Jews are massacred in cold blood by advancing Russian armies, the rebels kill almost 200,000 people in three weeks.

Egypt, 1768. Having slaughtered the other beys two years ago, Ali Bey, leader of the Mamluks since 1763, is proclaimed sultan.

Russia, 1768. The great commission convened by Catherine II is dismissed without having achieved any positive results.

Switzerland, 1768. The botanist Albrecht von Haller publishes the final part of his eight-volume *Physiological Elements of the Human Body*, which lays the basis for the new discipline of physiology.

Switzerland, 1768. The mathematician Leonhard Euler publishes his *Institiones calculi integralis*.

England, 1768. The English naval officer James Cook leaves Southampton aboard the *Endeavour* on a voyage to the Pacific.

England, 1768. Richard Arkwright perfects a spinning frame and sets up a mill in Nottingham driven by horses.

California, 1769. The Spanish begin to settle in California, establishing a mission at San Diego.

North America, 20 April 1769. The Ottawa Chief Pontiac, who led a rebellion against the British from 1763 to 1766, is murdered by an Indian in Cahokia. It is rumored that the British had him assassinated.

Virginia, May 1769. The House of Burgesses condemns the policies of London. Dissolved by the Governor of Virginia, the House decides to boycott British merchandise.

North America, 1769. The explorer Daniel Boone penetrates the fabled territory west of the Blue Mountains which the Iroquois Indians call Kentake (Kentucky).

Virginia, 1769. Thomas Jefferson, recently elected to the House of Burgesses, calls for the emancipation of slaves.

Ottoman Empire, 1769. Continuing their war against the Turks, which began last year, the Russians rout the main enemy army along the Dniester river and overrun Moldavia and Wallachia.

Sweden, 1769. The "Hats" and the "Caps," the two major parties in the Stockholm government, come into conflict with King Adolphus Frederick.

New York, 19 January 1770. A group of New Yorkers called the Sons of Liberty engage British troops in a pitched battle in New York City over British demands for compliance with the Quartering Act.

Britain, January 1770. Lord North, who is in favor of King George III wielding personal power, succeeds Lord Grafton as prime minister.

Boston, 5 March 1770. In what immediately becomes known as the Boston Massacre, British soldiers open fire on demonstrators, killing five.

London, 12 April 1770. Parliament repeals all the duties on the colonies imposed by Charles Townshend except the tea tax.

Pacific, 19 April 1770. The British expedition led by James Cook sights the east coast of Australia.

France, 16 May 1770. The Dauphin Louis marries Marie Antoinette of Austria, the daughter of Maria Theresa.

Ottoman Empire, August 1770. The Russians defeat a Turkish-Tartar army attempting to retake Moldavia and force it to retreat.

India, 1770. During a great famine in Bengal which began last year the population has been reduced from 29 million to 19 million.

Paris, 1770. The first public restaurant opens in Paris.

Austria, 1770. While peasant revolts rage in Bohemia, the Empress Maria Theresa publishes a new penal code.

England, 1770. The American-born artist Benjamin West paints *The Death of General Wolfe*, in which he defies precedent by depicting an event from recent history in contemporary costume.

England, 17 August 1771. The Birmingham scientist Joseph Priestley discovers that oxygen is released from growing plants.

Crimea, 1771. Pursuing their war with the Turks, the Russians conquer the Crimea.

England, 1771. Richard Arkwright, the inventor of the spinning frame, opens England's first spinning factory, driven by water power, at Cromford in Derbyshire.

Scotland, 1771. A three-volume dictionary of arts and sciences edited by William Smellie and entitled the *Encyclopaedia Britannica* is published.

France, 1771. Nicolas Maupeou, who succeeded his father as chancellor of France in 1768, abolishes the parliaments and establishes new courts, incurring great unpopularity.

St. Petersburg, 5 August 1772. Russia, Prussia and Austria sign a treaty agreeing on the partition of Poland.

Russia, 1772. Catherine II abolishes the privileges of the Cossacks.

Portugal, 1772. The Marquis of Pombal, the prime minister, introduces the teaching of exact sciences at the University of Coimbra. He has made important reforms in the army, agriculture and commerce.

Sweden, 19 August 1772. Gustavus III, who became King of Sweden last year, destroys the rule of the parties in a bloodless military coup and re-establishes an absolute monarchy.

New England, 2 November 1772. In the face of a growing number of clashes between the English authorities and the settlers over the imposition of customs measures, radical Americans set up Committees of Correspondence.

London, 10 May 1773. To keep the troubled East India Company afloat, Parliament passes the Tea Act. The Act allows the company to export tea directly to the colonies and keeps the Townshend duty of three pence a pound on tea.

London, 1 September 1773. Phillis Wheatley, a 20-year-old slave from Boston, publishes a collection of poetry, *Poems on Various Subjects, Religious and Moral*, in London. The book had been rejected by American publishing houses.

Russia, September 1773. An army of Cossacks, led by Yemelyan Pugachev, besiege the towns of Orenburg and Kazan. Pugachev claims to be the deposed Tsar Peter III, who was killed in the coup of 1762.

Romania, 1773. Attempts to end the Russo-Turkish War at a peace conference in Bucharest end in failure.

India, 1773. Under the Regulating Act the British Parliament attempts to control the East India Company. Warren Hastings is made governor-general with superintending authority over the presidencies of Madras and Bombay as well as Calcutta. The crown asserts the right to set up a supreme court in Calcutta.

Near East, 1773. Revolts in Egypt and Syria against Turkish rule are put down.

Boston, 16 December 1773. Patriots board three British tea ships anchored in Boston harbor, hack open all the tea chests and throw their contents into the harbor.

France, 10 May 1774. Louis XV dies and is succeeded as king by his grandson Louis XVI.

London, 20 May 1774. Parliament passes the Quebec Act, enlarging the boundaries of Quebec to include French-speaking settlements (in Ohio and Illinois).

Ottoman Empire, June 1774. The Russians defeat the Turks in a battle near Shumla, almost wiping out the Turkish army.

London, 2 June 1774. Parliament reactivates the Quartering Act of 1765, requiring that all colonies provide housing for British troops.

Russia, July 1774. The Cossack leader Yemelyan Pugachev captures Kazan, to which he laid siege last year.

Ottoman Empire, 16 July 1774. The Russians and the Turks sign the Treaty of Kuchuk-Kainardji, ending their six-year war. Moldavia and Wallachia are returned to Turkish control and the Crimea becomes independent. Russia gains control of much of the northern Black Sea coast.

France, 13 September 1774. Turgot, the new controller of finances, urges the king to restore the free circulation of grain in the kingdom.

Russia, September 1774. The Cossack rebels led by Yemelyan Pugachev are decisively defeated by Catherine the Great's forces, ending their year-long revolt.

Philadelphia, 26 October 1774. A congress of colonial leaders criticizes British influence in the colonies and affirms their right to "life, liberty and property".

Paris, 12 November 1774. Louis XVI recalls the magistrates who were exiled by Maupeou in 1771 and re-establishes parliament. Maupeou himself was dismissed as chancellor in August.

Germany, 1774. Goethe's *The Sorrows of Young Werther* inspires a wave of hopeless passion among the book's admirers.

Austria, 1774. Maria Theresa grants religious tolerance to the non-Catholics of Hungary.

1775–1799

Brazil, 1775. The Church of Notre Dame is constructed in Rio de Janeiro.

London, 9 February 1775. Parliament declares Massachusetts to be in a state of rebellion.

Massachusetts, 21 February 1775. As the conflict with Britain worsens, the committee of public safety votes to buy military equipment for 15,000 men.

Paris, 23 February 1775. Beaumarchais' new comedy, *The Barber of Seville*, is a great success.

London, 22 March 1775. The statesman Edmund Burke makes a speech in the House of Commons urging the government to adopt a policy of reconciliation with America.

London, 13 April 1775. Lord North extends the New England Restraining Act to South Carolina, Virginia, Pennsylvania, Maryland and New Jersey. The act forbids trade with any country other than Britain and Ireland, and is bitterly resented in the colonies.

Massachusetts, 14 April 1775. General Gage gets orders to use force to halt colonial military build up.

Massachusetts, April 1775. Fighting breaks out between English and American troops—the Lexington Massacre in Massachusetts is followed by more bloody outbreaks at Concord.

France, 28 April 1775. Jacques Necker, a Genevan banker, publishes a book on the grain trade and laws, attacking the finance minister Turgot's reformist policies.

Massachusetts, 12 June 1775. General Gage, imposing martial law, proclaims all armed colonists traitors and offers pardons to those who swear allegiance to the crown.

Massachusetts, 17 June 1775. British troops led by General William Howe defeat colonists at the Battle of Bunker Hill. They take the stronghold overlooking the Charleston peninsula and Boston, but it is a costly victory.

Boston, 26 June 1775. George Washington of Virginia arrives to assume command of the continental army.

London, 23 August 1775. King George III rejects an offer of peace, declaring that the colonies are in open rebellion against the crown.

France, 27 October 1775. The Count of St. Germain, an ardent supporter of the enlightened Prussian King Frederick II's military strategy, is appointed secretary of state for war.

Ethiopia, 1775. James Bruce returns to Britain from a pioneer British exploration of Ethiopia and the Blue Nile to contribute to cartography and trade intelligence of the area.

Russia, 1775. Catherine II introduces major administrative reforms by which Russia is divided into 50 governments, which are then subdivided into districts. She gives assurances guaranteeing the freedom of trade and industry.

France, 12 May 1776. Louis XVI dismisses Turgot.

New England, 7 June 1776. A vote on a resolution for independence is taken. It is carried by twelve colonies. New York is the only colony which does not vote.

Philadelphia, 4 July 1776. The American colonies declare themselves independent.

Philadelphia, 9 September 1776. Congress resolves that the name of the colonies should be changed from United Colonies to United States.

Tanzania, 14 September 1776. The French make a treaty with the Kilwa sultanate to supply slaves for sugar plantations in Ile de France (*Mauritius*) and the Reunion islands.

Paris, 31 December 1776. The American Benjamin Franklin arrives in Paris to negotiate for French aid for American rebels.

Naples, 1776. The chief minister, Bernardo Tannucci, who has been legal adviser to the crown for 20 years, is forced to retire. Tannucci reformed the brutal Neapolitan legal code and restricted the feudal privileges of the nobility.

Britain, 1776. Edward Gibbon publishes the first of several volumes of his *Decline and Fall of the Roman Empire*. Readers are scandalized by his treatment of Christianity as the chief cause of Rome's decline.

Senegal, 1776. The Tukulor chiefs seize power. They are led by Suleiman Bal who replaces the worship of local spirits with Islam.

Spain, 1776. Charles III appoints the reformist Floridablanca as his prime minister.

Vienna, 1776. The composer Wolfgang Amadeus Mozart composes his *Serenade in D* for the marriage of Elizabeth Haffner.

Guatemala, 1776. Guatemala Nueva is founded.

New Jersey, 3 January 1777. American troops under Washington defeat the British at Princeton.

Paris, 13 February 1777. The Marquis de Sade is arrested. He was condemned to death in 1772 for various crimes, but escaped from prison before the sentence could be carried out.

Portugal, 24 February 1777. King Joseph dies and is succeeded by his daughter, Maria of Braganza. The prime minister, the Marquis of Pombal, is dismissed by the queen mother, Mariana Victoria. Pombal used the power which he gained following his masterful handling of the 1755 earthquake disaster in Lisbon to reduce the tyranny of the church, expelling the Jesuits in 1759 and breaking the Inquisition.

France, 29 June 1777. Following the dismissal of Taboureau des Reaux, Necker is made director general of finance.

New York, 7 July 1777. American troops give up Fort Ticonderoga, a huge complex of fortifications on Lake Champlain, to the British.

New England, 27 July 1777. The Marquis of Lafayette arrives to help the rebels. He is accompanied by other European officers, including Kalb, a German in the service of the king of France.

New England, 17 October 1777. The British troops from Canada are defeated at Saratoga.

New England, 15 November 1777. Congress adopts the Articles of the Confederation, codifying the division of power between the states and the centralized government, and submits it for the approval of the States.

France, 1777. The French chemist Antoine de Lavoisier perfects his theory of combustion.

Paris, 17 December 1777. Louis XVI recognizes the independence of the American colonies and agrees to negotiate with them.

France, 6 February 1778. France signs a trade agreement with the United States by which it agrees to enter the war against Britain. The treaty is the result of lengthy negotiations led by Benjamin Franklin, who is now seen as the permanent ambassador at Versailles.

France, 30 May 1778. The writer and philosopher Voltaire dies at the age of 84.

France, 2 July 1778. Jean-Jacques Rousseau, the Genevan political philosopher, dies insane after a sudden attack of thrombosis.

France, 10 July 1778. In support of the American rebels, Louis XVI declares war on England.

New England, August 1778. The French fleet gives up the idea of attacking New York and runs aground off Newport.

Paris, 1778. The composer Wolfgang Amadeus Mozart visits Paris and gives a performance of *Les Petits Riens*.

South Africa, 1778. Dutch settlers known as Boers have been trying to set up cattle ranches in the area west of Fish river known as Suurveld (sour-grass country), already occupied by Khoisan and Xhosa cattle herders.

Italy, 1778. A new opera house, called La Scala, is inaugurated in Milan.

England, 15 January 1779. The actor David Garrick dies aged 61. He retired as joint manager of the Drury Lane theatre three years ago.

France, February 1779. Lafayette returns from America and asks the king for more money for the revolutionaries.

South Africa, 1779. The Orange River is traced from the southern African interior down to its mouth on the Atlantic by H J Wikar, a Swedish explorer. The Dutch settlers call the river "Orange" in honor of the ruling house of their native land, but the native Sotho people of the upper river call it the *Ntshu*, meaning black.

France, January 1780. The finance minister, Necker, starts reforming the king's household in an attempt to improve the kingdom's disastrous financial situation.

Austria, 1780. The Empress Maria Theresa, who has ruled as co-regent with her son Josef II since 1765, dies. Her rule has been characterized by domestic reform, of the army, the church and the administration.

New Spain, 1780. Martial law (*estado de guerra*) is declared in New Spain (Mexico).

Uganda, 1780. King Kyambugu of Buganda dies, having ruled since 1763. Under Kyambugu, Buganda has developed a strong economy based on bananas, and has strengthened its army in order to open up trade routes with the east coast through Kenya.

France, 2 May 1780. Following Lafayette's latest departure for America, Louis XVI sends 6,000 men to New England under the command of Rochambeau to reinforce the revolutionary force.

India, September 1780. Under attack by the *nawab* (ruler) of Arcot - who is supported by the British - the Muslim ruler of Mysore, Haidar Ali, allies himself with the Marathas and retaliates. He launches an attack on the British coastal region of the Carnatic and the Marathas threaten

Madras, where the East India Company has its headquarters. British soldiers relieve Madras and the Marathas withdraw to make a separate peace.

New York, 1780. The Iroquois, who have occupied the valleys of the Mohawk River in central New York for generations, are devastated by American troops. In just over a month the Americans destroy their homes, barns, storehouses and cultivation. Most of the Indians flee. Washington ordered the offensive to discourage the Indians from attacking while the Americans are engaged in the war with Britain.

Mozambique, 1781. The Portuguese take the fort they call Lourenco Marques back from Austria, and resume control of Maputo Bay trade. This includes the slave trade from the southern Mozambique coast to Brazil, the French Indian Ocean islands and Arabia.

South Africa, 1781. The Suurveld War, which began in 1779, ends. The war was provoked by Boer ranchers to appropriate the Khoisan and Xhosa peoples' land in the Suurveld area around the Fish River.

Paris, 1781. The Marquis of Condorcet, a brilliant mathematician and radical thinker, publishes his *Reflections on Negro Slavery*, contributing to the growing debate on the slave trade.

India, 1781. The Governor General, Warren Hastings, founds the Calcutta Madrassah, a college designed to foster Arabic studies.

France, 19 May 1781. After having sought the position of minister of state in vain, Necker foresees his fall from grace and submits his resignation. His departure shakes financiers' confidence in the *Bourse* (the French stock exchange).

Russia, May 1781. An exchange of letters between Tsarina Catherine II and the Emperor Josef II establishes a defensive alliance between their two countries against the Ottoman Empire.

California, 4 September 1781. The Spanish name a tiny village near San Gabriel, Los Angeles.

North America, 19 October 1781. French and American allies defeat the British at Yorktown during the American War of Independence.

France, 1781. Jean-Jacques Rousseau's *Confessions*—a book of startling frankness is — is published posthumously.

Ireland, March 1782. Legislative independence is granted to the Irish parliament following the plea by Henry Grattan at last month's Convention of Dungannon.

Paris, 10 April 1782. Pierre Choderlos publishes *Les Liaisons Dangereuses*, which immediately causes a scandal.

France, 7 May 1782. Peace negotiations are begun between France and Britain.

Vienna, 16 July 1782. Mozart's opera *Abduction from the Seraglio*, telling the tale of an escape from a Turkish harem, is performed for the first time.

India, 1782. Haidar Ali, the Muslim ruler of Mysore, dies while engaged in the Anglo-Mysore War with the British. His son Tipu Sahib takes command, but military aid promised by the French arrives too late and Mysore is defeated.

Britain, 20 January 1783. Britain signs peace agreements with France and Spain, who allied against it in the American Revolutionary War.

Russia, 3 May 1783. Catherine II, thought of as an enlightened ruler by all of Europe, officially introduces serfdom in the Ukraine.

France, 4 June 1783. The Montgolfier brothers, Joseph Michel and Jacques Etienne, launch the first hot air balloon. Fascinated by the aeronautical ideas of a 14th-century Augustinian monk, Albert of Saxony, and the 17th-century Jesuit priest Francesco de Luna, they construct a balloon which takes off when a cauldron of paper is lit beneath it.

France, 3 September 1783. The Treaty of Paris formally ends the American Revolution.

Massachusetts, October 1783. A black woman is discharged from the army having served for three years under the name of Robert Shirtliffe.

Britain, 19 December 1783. William Pitt the Younger becomes the youngest-ever prime minister at the age of 24.

Spain, 1783. The jurist and economist Pedro Campomans, the procurator of the Council of Castile since 1762, becomes president of the council.

Paris, 1783. Jean le Rond d'Alembert, the mathematician and philosopher, dies. With Diderot he was joint founder of the influential, but controversial, *Encyclopédie*.

Angola, 1783. The Portuguese build a fort at Cabinda on the north side of the Congo river.

Maryland, 1783. The state prohibits the slave trade, which has now been banned in all northern states.

Austria, 1783. Josef II continues the reorganization of the church and takes action against the sects. He also makes a number of economic changes, abolishing private tolls and making the regulations for the sale of manufactured goods more flexible.

France, 1783. The chemist Antoine-Laurent de Lavoisier creates water from hydrogen and oxygen.

Prussia, 1783. The philosopher Immanuel Kant publishes *Prolegomena to any Future Metaphysic*.

Bohemia (Czechoslovakia), 1783. Peasant revolts break out following land reforms.

Istanbul, 8 January 1784. Vergennes, the French secretary of state for foreign affairs, intervenes to settle the long conflict over the Crimea between the Ottoman Empire and Russia.

France, 18 January 1784. Appointed finance minister on 3 November 1783, Charles Alexandre de Calonne joins the council and is appointed minister of state.

India, 11 March 1784. Tipu Sahib, the *sultan* of Mysore and Haidar Ali's son, signs the Treaty of Mangalore with the English, ending the Second Anglo-Mysore War. Both parties surrender their respective conquests.

Paris, 27 April 1784. Beaumarchais' *The Marriage of Figaro* opens at the Comedies Françoise theater. The play has been the talk of Paris for four years while the dramatist submitted it to censor after censor, repeatedly being refused permission for its performance. Louis XVI has condemned it as "unperformable" and ordered it to be banned, probably on account of its subversive morals, as it tells the tale of a handsome valet outwitting his master.

England, 13 August 1784. Pitt's India Act, which was passed soon after his re-election in May, becomes law. This effectively puts the East India Company under government control and amends the Regulating Act of 1773.

Philadelphia, 21 September 1784. *Packet and Daily*, the first daily publication in America, appears on the streets.

England, 13 December 1784. The lexicographer, poet and critic Samuel Johnson dies aged 75. He spent many years writing hack work for London's literary magazines to fend off encroaching poverty; but from 1762, a crown pension of £300 a year enabled him to take his place in high society and give free reign to his versatile genius.

Prussia, 1785. The philosopher Immanuel Kant publishes *Fundamental Principles of the Metaphysics of Ethics*.

Virginia, 16 January 1786. The Council of Virginia guarantees religious freedom.

Vienna, 1786. Mozart's opera, *The Marriage of Figaro*, based on the play by Beaumarchais, opens in Vienna. The story of the valet Figaro denying his master the feudal *droit de seigneur* of a night with his servant's new wife gives the piece a subversive flavor that delights the crowd.

Europe, 1786. The Count of Mirabeau, the well-known soldier, returns from fighting in the American War of Independence and tours Europe.

Sweden, 1786. King Gustavus III founds the Academy of Eighteen in Stockholm, based on the Prussian and French models. On his visits to Paris he attends meetings of the Académie Française, but he is more interested in art and literature than in the ideas of the philosophers.

Morocco, 11 July 1786. Morocco agrees to stop attacking American ships in the Mediterranean for a payment of $10,000.

Egypt, July 1786. The Ottoman sultan, Abdul Hamid, sends an expeditionary force of 1,500 men to Alexandria. They occupy the delta and drive out the *bey*, who takes refuge in upper Egypt and starts a civil war. The sultan blames him for having signed an agreement with France in 1785 guaranteeing safe passage for merchandise traveling from Suez to Alexandria.

Prussia, 17 August 1786. Frederick II (the Great), King of Prussia since 1740, dies and is succeeded by Frederick William II. Frederick the Great used his genius as a military commander to make Prussia into a great power.

Versailles, 20 August 1786. In order to bypass parliamentary opposition, the French finance minister Charles Calonne advises King Louis XVI to convoke an assembly of notables to agree on a plan of financial reform, including more equitable taxation.

India, 12 September 1786. Lord Cornwallis—the British general who distinguished himself in the American Revolution, despite being compelled to surrender at Yorktown—is appointed Governor General of India.

Massachusetts, 26 December 1786. Daniel Shays, a veteran of the revolutionary war, leads a rebellion of 1,200 farmers protesting seizures of farms, livestock and household goods for non-payment of debts.

Scotland, 1786. Robert Burns, an impoverished Scottish farmer, publishes *Poems Chiefly in the Scottish Dialect*, including the "Address to a Mouse".

Britain, 1786. The English naval officer Arthur Phillip is put in command of a fleet whose purpose is to establish a penal settlement in Australia. He is also offered the governorship of New South Wales.

Japan, 1787. Matsudaira Sadanobu is appointed chief senior councilor and launches a far-reaching program of bureaucratic reforms. He purges the government ranks of supporters of his predecessor Tanuma Ogitsugu.

Japan, 1787. Serious rice riots break out in Edo (*Tokyo*) following several years of famine and rising prices. Five thousand people go on the rampage, smashing rice shops and homes of rich merchants.

Southeast Asia, 1787. Following the signature of a friendship treaty between Vietnam and France, Count Thomas de Conway, the French Governor of Pondicherry, sends troops to Vietnam to restore King Nguyen Anh to the throne.

Versailles, 22 February 1787. At the opening session of the Assembly of Notables, the finance minister, Calonne, admits that there is a national deficit estimated at 112 million livres (£ 800 million).

Versailles, 8 April 1787. Calonne resigns under pressure from the Notables. He is replaced by Lomenie de Brienne.

USA, 25 May 1787. A convention to draw up the constitution for the United States of America, presided over by George Washington, opens in Philadelphia.

Versailles, June 1787. Lomenie de Brienne, the new French finance minister, replaces forced labor with a tax and allows the free circulation of grain.

Spain, 8 July 1787. At the instigation of his minister Floridablanca, King Charles III decrees the setting up of a ministerial council known as a *junta*. This is an attempt to modernize central government by creating a link between separate ministerial departments.

USA, 13 July 1787 Congress adopts the Northwest treaty regulating future colonization of the lands between the Ohio, the Great Lakes, the Appalachians and the Mississippi. It provides a framework for the incorporation of new states into the Union.

Paris, 30 July 1787. After having demanded a meeting of the Estates-General, parliament refuses to approve a new land tax.

Austria 1787. The Emperor Josef II promulgates the Josephine Code, guaranteeing the equality of all his subjects before the law.

England 1787. Following the pioneering anti-slavery work of Granville Sharp, the Committee for the Abolition of the Slave Trade is formed by the Reverend Thomas Clarkson, with William Wilberforce as its parliamentary representative.

West Africa 1787. Freed slave settlers from England land on the Sierra Leone estuary to found a "Province of Freedom". They elect James Weaver as their governor on the basis of a constitution drawn up by Granville Sharp.

Crimea 1787. The Russian politician Grigori Potemkin, a favorite of Catherine II, erects sham villages to impress his monarch during a royal tour. Potemkin was responsible for annexing the Crimea in 1783 and developing a Black Sea fleet.

Prague 1787. *Don Giovanni*, an opera by the Austrian composer Wolfgang Amadeus Mozart, is performed for the first time. Mozart's *The Marriage of Figaro* caused great excitement when it appeared last year.

Versailles, 4 September 1787. Louis XVI recalls parliament.

USA, 17 September 1787. The Philadelphia Convention publishes a constitution for the USA

Versailles, 29 November 1787. Louis XVI promulgates the Edict of Tolerance, granting civil status to Protestants.

Australia, January 1788. A British fleet led by Captain Arthur Phillip arrives in Botany Bay and hoists the British flag at Port Jackson in Sydney cove. Apart from officials, marines and 579 convicts, the ships carry agricultural implements, seeds, animals and provisions.

Paris, 29 January 1788. Parliament approves the king's decree granting civil status to Protestants, without guaranteeing either their freedom of religion or their access to office.

USA, 21 March 1788. Almost the entire city of New Orleans is destroyed by fire.

USA, 21 June 1788. The American constitution comes into force, ratified by nine states.

Finland, 21 June 1788. King Gustavus III of Sweden launches an invasion of Russian Finland without having declared war.

Black Sea, June 1788. The Russian Black Sea fleet, commanded by the American naval hero John Paul Jones, defeats the Ottomans in two naval battles near the mouth of the Dnieper River. Earlier in the year, the Russians repelled an Ottoman attempt to seize the Crimea and invaded Moldavia.

Paris, 6 July 1788. Ten thousand troops are called out as unrest mounts in the poorer districts.

Southeast Asia, 20 July 1788. Thomas de Conway, the governor of the French colony of Pondicherry, abandons plans to send troops to place King Nhuyen Anh back on the throne of Vietnam.

India, August 1788. Tipu Sahib, the sultan of Mysore—who supports France's campaign to prevent Britain from dominating India —sends three ambassadors to France.

Versailles, 8 August. In an attempt to ward off economic crisis, Louis XVI decrees that the Estates-General will meet on 1 May 1789.

Versailles, 25 August. In an attempt to save France from total economic collapse, Louis XVI recalls Jacques Necker, the Geneva born Protestant banker, who was disgraced in 1783, to replace Brienne as finance minister.

USA, 13 September 1788. New York is declared the federal capital of the USA and the seat of Congress.

Versailles, 23 September 1788. Louis XVI announces that the judicial reforms have been dropped and the traditional roles of the parliaments restored.

Paris, 24 September 1788. The parliament of Paris reassembles in triumph.

Poland, 6 October 1788. The Polish Diet, which has effected important administrative reforms since being forced to accept the partition of Poland in 1772, decides to hold a four-year session.

Prussia 1788. King Frederick William II issues a "religious edict" abrogating all freedom of worship. The freedom of the press is also abolished.

Ottoman Empire 1788. Continuing their war with the Ottomans, the Russians massacre the captured Turkish inhabitants of several towns in Moldavia and along the Black Sea.

Poland, 19 January 1789. The Diet suppresses the permanent council and takes over all its powers.

France, January 1789. Electoral rules for the meeting of the Estates-General are published. Third Estate patriots in Brittany and Provence condemn them as unfair and demand equal representation with the other two orders (the nobles and the church).

Sweden, 20 February 1789. King Gustavus III imposes the Act of Union and Security on the Riksdag, establishing despotism.

London, February 1789. King George III regains his sanity after three months of madness, during which the Pitt government framed a bill providing for a regency regulated by Parliament.

Pacific, 28 April 1789. After a mutiny provoked by his harsh treatment, the British sailor William Bligh, the commander of the *Bounty*, is cast adrift near the Friendly Islands in a small open boat with 18 men.

USA, 30 April 1789. George Washington is inaugurated as the first president of the USA.

France, April 1789. Members of the Third Estate condemn the heavy tax burden on the poor and demand a constitution to limit arbitrary royal power.

Versailles, 5 May 1789. The Estates-General is formally opened by Louis XVI.

Versailles, 11 May 1789. Debate at the Estates-General is deadlocked by the Third Estate's refusal to comply with the proposed voting system.

Versailles, 22 May 1789. The nobility follows the example of the clergy by giving up its fiscal privileges.

Southeast Asia, 14 June 1789. Captain William Bligh, cast adrift in April by his mutinous sailors on the *Bounty*, arrives at Timor, near Java, having sailed his small boat for more than 3,500 miles.

Versailles, 20 June 1789. Following the closure of the Estates chamber by

the king, the National Assembly deputies are sworn in at a meeting on the Jeu de Paume (the royal the tennis courts).

Versailles, 9 July 1789. The National Assembly declares itself the Constituent Assembly and sets about preparing a French constitution.

Paris, 12 July 1789. Louis XVI's dismissal of Necker, the highly popular finance minister, fuels the violence in Paris, which is on fire after two days of non-stop rioting.

Paris, 14 July 1789. The Bastille is seized by the people of Paris.

Paris, 15 July 1789. The electors of Paris set up a "Commune" led by Bailly, who is elected mayor of Paris, and Lafayette, who becomes head of the National Guard.

Versailles, 20 July 1789. Robespierre, a deputy from Arras, backs the revolutionaries.

New York City, 27 July 1789. The Department of Foreign Affairs, the first executive agency in the USA, is set up, with Thomas Jefferson at its head. Within in a few weeks its name is changed to the Department of State.

New York City, 2 August 1789. A United States war department is created, with Henry Knox at its head.

Versailles, 4 August 1789. The Constituent Assembly abolishes the privileges of the nobility, destroying the social structures of the Ancien Régime.

Versailles, 26 August 1789. The Constituent Assembly approves the final version of the Declaration of Human Rights.

New York City, 2 September 1789. A treasury department, headed by Alexander Hamilton, is created.

Paris, 16 September 1789. Jean-Paul Marat sets up a new newspaper, *L'Ami du Peuple*.

New York City, 24 September 1789. Congress passes the Federal Judiciary Act, creating circuit courts, district courts and a Supreme Court.

New York City, 25 September 1789. Congress proposes twelve amendments to the constitution known as the Bill of Rights. Ten of them are eventually approved.

New York City, 29 September 1789. Congress votes to create a United States army.

Paris, 7 October 1789. After a march by the women of Paris to Versailles to demand bread, the royal family is forced to return to Paris, where they take refuge in the Tuileries.

Serbia, 9 October 1789. Having invaded Serbia in the spring, Austrian troops defeat the Ottomans to take Belgrade.

Versailles, 10 October 1789. The Paris deputy Joseph Guillotin, a professor of anatomy, says that the most humane way of carrying out a death sentence is decapitation by a single blow of the blade.

Austrian Netherlands, 24 October 1789. The insurgents proclaim independence and strip the Emperor Josef II of his sovereignty over the country.

Black Sea, October 1789. The Russian general Suvorov takes Ochakov, the port at the mouth of the Bug, from the Ottomans.

France, 2 November 1789. All church property is nationalized.

France, 19 December 1789. Four hundred million francs' worth of government bonds, known as *assignats*, are issued to help to repay the national debt.

France, 24 December 1789. Protestants are given the vote on the same basis as Catholics.

North Pacific, 1789. A Spanish squadron lands at Nootka Sound, a small natural harbor (off Vancouver Island) in Canada, claiming it for Spain. A British trading settlement was established on the sound after its discovery by James Cook in 1778.

West Africa, 1789. The "Province of Freedom" formed two years ago in Sierra Leone collapses as settlers scatter after an attack by the local Temne ruler, "King Jimmy". The freed slaves had incautiously allied with local European slave traders against King Jimmy.

West Africa, 1789. King Abiodun, the great ruler of the Oyo state among the Yoruba people, dies. Oyo never recovered from its defeat in 1783 by the army of Borgu from the north, and Abiodun's son Awole, inherits a weakened kingdom.

India, 1789. Tipu Sahib, the Sultan of Mysore, attacks Travancore, an ally of the East India Company in southern India.

Ukraine, 1789. Polish nobles blame Russian infiltrators for new unrest among peasants in the Ukraine.

Vienna, 20 February 1790. The Emperor Josef II, an embodiment of enlightened despotism, dies at the age of 48. He is succeeded by his brother Leopold, the Grand Duke of Tuscany.

France, 26 February 1790. France is divided into 83 departments.

Paris, 31 March 1790. Robespierre is elected president of the Jacobin Club.

Algiers, 4 April 1790. A 100-year-old peace treaty between France and Algiers is renewed.

Paris, 7 April 1790. The publication of the *Red Book* listing gifts given by Louis XVI reveals that his secret expenses have totaled 228 million francs since the start of his reign. The destination of much of this money is unclear.

France, 17 April 1790. The government bonds known as *assignats* become legal tender.

Philadelphia, 21 April 1790. Twenty thousand people attend the funeral of the scientist and statesman Benjamin Franklin, who died on 17 April at the age of 84.

West Indies, 9 June 1790. Civil war breaks out in Martinique between white settlers and blacks campaigning for equality.

Paris, 19 June 1790. The Assembly passes a law abolishing the hereditary nobility.

Baltic, 9 July 1790. Pursuing their war with Russia, which broke out two years ago, the Swedes win the great naval battle of Svensksund, sinking or capturing a third of the Russian fleet.

Prussia, 27 July 1790. Prussia and Austria sign the Treaty of Reichenbach, giving Austria a free hand to take action against the Belgians.

USA, 1 August 1790. The first census taken in the USA reveals a population of nearly four million.

Sweden, 24 August 1790. The Treaty of Varala ends the war between Sweden and Russia and returns to the *status quo*.

West Indies, August 1790. An attempt by planters in Santo Domingo to win independence from France ends in failure.

England, October 1790. The politician and philosopher Edmund Burke publishes his *Reflections on the Revolution in France*.

France, 21 October 1790. The tricolor is chosen as the national flag of France.

Paris, 27 November 1790. The Assembly forces priests to swear allegiance to the church's Civil Constitution.

The Hague, 10 December 1790. Having completed the reconquest of the rebel Belgian states with his capture of Brussels a week ago, the Emperor Leopold II signs a treaty guaranteeing the restoration of Belgian national institutions.

Ottoman Empire, 22 December 1790. The Russians take Ismail in Bessarabia.

Paris, December 1790. Louis XVI seeks help from Frederick William II of Prussia, asking him to set up a "European congress backed by armed forces."

Southern Africa, 1790. Zwide succeeds his father, Yaka, as chief of the militaristic Ndwandwe chiefdom, centered on the Pongola River. Once subjects of the Tembe Kingdom at Maputo Bay, paying tribute in ivory and cattle, the Ndwandwe took advantage of the Tembe's involvement in civil war to build up power by attacking their neighbors.

Philadelphia, 25 February 1791. President Washington signs a bill creating the Bank of the United States.

West Indies, 26 February 1791. The leaders of a Mulatto uprising in Santo Domingo are executed.

Paris, 28 February 1791. After putting down a people's uprising in Vincennes, Lafayette rushes back to Paris to disarm revolutionary plotters.

London, 13 March 1791. Thomas Paine, a firm supporter of the French Revolution, publishes the second part of his *Rights of Man*, in which he rejects the arguments in Edmund Burke's *Reflections on the Revolution in France*.

Britain, 21 March 1791. Britain reaches an agreement with Prussia to oppose the expansionist ambitions of Russia.

Paris, 2 April 1791. Mirabeau, who has proved himself a highly influential force in the Assembly, dies. Poisoning is suspected.

Paris, 18 April 1791. National Guardsmen prevent Louis XVI and his family from leaving Paris.

Poland, 3 May 1791. Stanislas II, Augustus Poniatowski, the King of Poland, creates a constitution for his country providing for a hereditary monarchy and the separation of executive, legislative, and judicial powers.

Paris, 16 May 1791. Maximilien de Robespierre, an increasingly influential figure on the extreme left of the Assembly, persuades the deputies to vote against seeking their own re-election.

Paris, 26 May 1791. The Assembly forces Louis XVI to hand over all the assets of the crown to the nation.

Paris, 14 June 1791. The Le Chapelier Law bans strikes and abolishes all workers' associations.

France, 25 June 1791. The royal family returns to Paris after their attempt to flee ended with their arrest at Varennes.

Paris, 25 June 1791. The Assembly temporarily suspends Louis XVI's powers.

Brussels, 29 June 1791. The Count of Provence, the brother of Louis XVI, arrives in Brussels after successfully fleeing from Paris.

Paris, 15 July 1791. The Assembly decrees that Louis XVI was not responsible for his own actions in fleeing and that he can only be put on trial after his abdication.

Paris, 16 July 1791. Louis XVI is suspended from office until he agrees to ratify the constitution.

Paris, 16 July 1791. A major split opens up in the Jacobin Club over the future of the monarchy.

Paris, 24 July 1791. On the instigation of Robespierre, all Jacobins opposed to the principles of the Revolution—known as *Feuillants*—are expelled from the society.

Vienna, 25 July 1791. Chancellor Kaunitz opens talks with Prussia aimed at setting up a European congress opposed to the French Revolution.

Ottoman Empire, 4 August 1791. Austria and the Ottoman Empire sign the Treaty of Sistova, by which Belgrade is returned to the Ottomans.

West Indies, 12 August 1791. Black slaves on the island of Santo Domingo rise up against their white masters.

Prussia, 27 August 1791. The Emperor Leopold II and Frederick William II of Prussia issue a joint declaration at Pillnitz in support of the French monarchy.

Paris, 14 September 1791. Louis XVI solemnly swears his allegiance to the French constitution.

Paris, September 1791. The author Olympe de Gouges publishes *The Declaration of the Rights of Women and the Female Citizen*.

Paris, 1 October 1791. The National Legislative Assembly holds its first meeting. It comprises 745 deputies: on the right are 264 *Feuillants;* on the left 136 Jacobins, led by Condorcet and Brissot; and 345 independents.

Paris, 8 October 1791. Lafayette resigns his post as commander of the National Guard in Paris.

Belfast, 14 October 1791. The Protestant lawyer Theobald Wolfe Tone sets up the Belfast Society of United Irishmen, calling for the emancipation of Catholics—who are denied the right to vote—and parliamentary reform.

West Indies, 19 October 1791. An alliance is signed between the leaders of the Mulatto revolt in Santo Domingo and the royalist commanders who protect the white planters in west of the island.

USA, 4 November 1791. United States troops under Arthur St. Clair, the Governor of the Northwest Territory, suffer a humiliating defeat in a battle with Ohio Indians under Chief Little Turtle.

Paris, 11 November 1791. Using one of his few remaining powers, Louis XVI vetoes decrees ordering French émigrés, including his own brother, to return to France.

Paris, 28 November 1791. Maximilien Robespierre is elected president of the Jacobin Club.

USA, 15 December 1791. Virginia is the tenth state to approve the ten amendments to the constitution known collectively as the Bill of Rights. As three-quarters of the states have now ratified the amendments, they become law.

Japan, 1791. The famous author Santo Kyoden is sentenced to 50 days' house arrest in handcuffs for the publication of three risqué books that have fallen foul of new censorship regulations. The books have been banned and the publisher heavily fined.

West Africa, 1791. Uthman dan Fodio—a scholar and poet in the Arabic and Fula languages, who has became an itinerant missionary preaching strict Islamic doctrine—is appointed tutor to the Gobir royal family in Niger. After taking up his new job, he has visions under the influence of Sufism and becomes an influential figure at the Gobir court.

Australia, 1791. The third British fleet to arrive in Australia since 1788 increases the number of convicts and civilians in the new settlement at Sydney, putting extra pressure on supplies, already low as a result of crop failure from drought and inappropriate farming techniques.

England, 1791. The Scottish author James Boswell writes a biographical masterpiece entitled *Life of Samuel Johnson*.

Paris, January 1792. A split in the Jacobins between Robespierre and the Girondist party, led by Brissot, who favors war with the other European powers, is confirmed.

Ottoman Empire, 9 January 1792. The Ottomans sign a treaty with the Russians at Jassy ending their five-year war. Moldavia is returned to the Ottomans, but the Russians retain Ochakov and all the conquered lands between the Bug and Dniester Rivers. Under the treaty, Sultan Selim III also formally recognizes the Russian annexation of the Crimea, achieved in 1783.

Paris, 23 March 1792. A ministry dominated by Girondists is formed.

Paris, 24 March 1792. Political rights are granted to freed slaves in the colonies.

Sweden, 29 March 1792. Gustavus III, King of Sweden since 1771, dies from wounds sustained in an attack by a nobleman, Ankaestrom, on 16 March at a masked ball. He was one of the firmest backers of the restoration of absolute monarchy in France.

England, 1792. The chemist William Murdoch perfects a technique for the use of gas lighting.

Europe, 20 April 1792. Following Chancellor Kaunitz's refusal to dissolve the congress of European sovereigns, the French Legislative Assembly approves by a huge majority the king's proposal to declare war on Austria. Louis XVI's plan to attack his own nephew, the Emperor Francis II, violates the alliance that has linked France and Austria since 1756.

USA, 22 April 1792. President Washington proclaims American neutrality in the war in Europe.

New York City, 17 May 1792. A group of 24 merchants and brokers creates the New York stock exchange, on Wall Street.

Poland, 18 May 1792. Russian troops invade Poland.

Paris, 27 May 1792. The Assembly orders the deportation of all priests who refuse to swear allegiance to the church's civil constitution.

Paris, 20 June 1792. A huge mob overruns the Tuileries to demand that the royal veto of the latest decrees be withdrawn and their ministers recalled.

Paris, 29 June 1792. Lafayette makes an unsuccessful attempt to mobilize the National Guard to break up the Jacobin Club by force.

Germany, 14 July 1792. At Koblenz, the Duke of Brunswick, the commander-in-chief of the Prussian army, publishes a manifesto threatening Parisians with exemplary revenge if they do not submit to their monarch.

Poland, 24 July 1792. By approving the confederation formed at Targowica by Polish nobles who support Russia, Stanislas II Augustus Poniatowski, the King of Poland, yields to Catherine II of Russia. This marks the death of the Polish constitution.

Paris, 10 August 1792. The *sans-culottes* seize the Tuileries. The king is taken prisoner and suspended from office.

Paris, 11 August 1792. A revolutionary commune is formed. Antoine Santerre is made head of the National Guard. The Assembly appoints a provisional executive council of six members, including Georges Danton and Jean Marie Roland, and calls a national convention.

Netherlands, 19 August 1792. Lafayette is arrested by the Austrians. The fall of the Tuileries marked the final split between Lafayette and the revolution: the commander of the northern army was asked to hand over power to Dumouriez and chose to desert rather than face the guillotine, crossing the border into the Netherlands.

Paris, 5 September 1792. The Paris deputies, including Robespierre and Danton, are elected to the National Convention.

Paris, 19 September 1792. Thomas Paine arrives in Paris after fleeing from England, where he faces treason charges for views expressed in his *Rights of Man*, a defense of the French Revolution.

France, 20 September 1792. The French army under Kellerman defeats the Prussians under the Duke of Brunswick at Valmy.

Paris, 21 September 1792. At its first public meeting the National Convention decrees the abolition of the monarchy.

France, 22 September 1792. The French Republic is proclaimed. The Convention decides that all official rulings will from now on be dated from Year I of the French Republic.

USA, 29 September 1792. Despite widespread protests in Pennsylvania and the South, President Washington says that he plans strictly to enforce the whiskey excise tax introduced last year.

Netherlands, 6 November 1792. The French under Dumouriez inflict a crushing defeat on the Austrians at Jemappes.

Germany, 2 December 1792. The Prussians drive the French troops out of Frankfurt 40 days after they marched into the city.

USA, 5 December 1792. George Washington is re-elected president.

Paris, 11 December. Louis XVI appears for the first time before the Convention, to hear the charges against him.

Poland, December 1792. The Prussians occupy the towns of Torun and Danzig, and Little Poland.

Strasbourg, 1792. Rouget de Lisle writes the words and music for a *Chant de guerre pour l'armee du Rhin* (the *Marseillaise*).

West Africa, 1792. Freetown, Sierra Leone, is founded by 1,190 freed slaves who have landed from England.

England, 1792. *A Vindication of the Rights of Women* by Mary Wollstonecraft is published.

Paris, 21 January 1793. Louis XVI is guillotined.

Poland, 23 January 1793. Prussia and Russia agree on a second partition of Poland.

Ottoman Empire, January 1793. The sultan, Selim III, introduces a new administrative regime and reorganizes the Ottoman army on the European model.

Ireland, January 1793. Catholics are given the vote.

Europe, February 1793. Britain, Austria, Prussia, Spain, the Netherlands, Sardinia, Tuscany, and Naples form a coalition against France.

Corsica, February. A conflict develops between Pascal Paoli, who seeks Corsican independence from France, and the Francophile Napoleon Bonaparte.

Paris, 5 April 1793. Elected president of the Jacobin Club, Jean-Paul Marat orders the arrest of counterrevolutionaries and the ousting of the main Girondist deputies.

West Indies, 14 April 1793. A royalist rebellion in Santo Domingo is crushed by French republican troops.

Paris, 24 April 1793. The revolutionary tribunal acquits Marat of despotism.

India, 27 April 1793. The British orientalist Sir William Jones, who introduced eastern thought and literature, especially Sanskrit, to the west, dies in Calcutta.

Paris, 2 June 1793. After three days of street demonstrations, the moderate Girondists are ousted from the Convention by Jacobins.

France, June 1793. Outlawed by Pascale Paoli last month, Napoleon Bonaparte and his family are exiled from Corsica and forced to seek refuge on the French mainland.

Paris, 13 July 1793. Jean-Paul Marat is assassinated by Charlotte Corday.

Paris, 27 July 1793. Robespierre becomes a member of the Committee of Public Safety.

West Indies, 29 August 1793. Slavery is abolished in Santo Domingo.

Paris, 17 September 1793. The Convention passes an "anti-suspect" law by which all enemies of the revolution will be arrested and held until the war is over.

USA, 18 September 1793. In Washington DC, President Washington lays the foundation stone of the Capitol, the intended seat of the U.S. government.

India, 10 October 1793. Lord Cornwallis leaves India after greatly strengthening the British administration there. He has made a firm distinction between the commercial and administrative functions of the East India Company, Europeanized the administration and settled the revenue and land system of Bengal.

Paris, 16 October 1793. Marie Antoinette is guillotined.

North America 1793. Sir Alexander MacKenzie become the first white man to cross the North American continent, finishing his journey by canoeing down the Bella Coola river in Oregon territory to the Pacific.

Japan 1793. Matsudaira Sadanobu resigns from the office of chief senior councilor, which he has held since 1787, and goes into retirement. His departure follows a clash with the emperor and growing disaffection with his authoritarian style.

Paris, 25 December 1793. Robespierre gives his support to the Terror policy.

USA, 31 December 1793. Thomas Jefferson resigns as Secretary of State and retires from public life.

South Africa, 1793. The Second Suurveld War, which began in 1789, comes to an end. The war was provoked by the Xhosa chief Ndlambe's attempt to regain control of Suurveld. Under the peace agreement, the Boers have to concede to Ndlambe, but they blame their Dutch magistrates for the defeat.

Mediterranean, 27 February 1794. Austria and Russia reach agreement on the sharing out of Venetian possessions in the Mediterranean.

Poland, March 1794. Tadeusz Kosciuszko—who became leader of a group of exiled Polish patriots after the partition of Poland by Prussia and Russia last year—arrives in Krakow, wins the support of dissident Polish officers and proclaims a provisional constitution giving him dictatorial powers.

Scandinavia, 27 March 1794. The Scandinavian states create a league of armed neutrality.

France, 29 March 1794. Marie Jean Condorcet, the philosopher and mathematician who became president of the Legislative Assembly in 1792, is found dead in his cell in the town formerly known as Bourg la Reine. Condorcet, was condemned and went into hiding for several months before being recognized and arrested, is believed to have committed suicide.

Paris, 31 March 1794. Georges Jacques Danton and a group of his friends, including Camille Desmoulins, are arrested on charges of having connived with the foreign monarchs who are in league against the French Republic.

Poland, 4 April 1794. At Raclawice, the Polish insurgents under the leadership of Tadeusz Kosciuszko inflict a defeat on a superior Russian army.

Southern Africa, 1794. The Maputo Kingdom is victorious in the Tembe civil war, which has been raging around Maputo Bay for the past half-century. Maputo power, however, is limited to the bay and to trade with Portuguese ships, while the hinterland that stretches into South Africa (Natal) and Swaziland is left open to new militaristic powers, notably the Ndwandwe and Mthewa chiefdoms.

Paris, 5 April. Georges Jacques Danton and several of his supporters, including Camille Desmoulins, are guillotined.

Italy, 18 April. Napoleon Bonaparte, appointed a general in the French army in February, captures the port of Oneglia, a Piedmontese enclave on Genoan territory.

Poland, 19 April. Tadeusz Kosciuszko, the Polish rebel leader, enters Warsaw, which has been in revolt for two days against Russian occupation. The Russians withdraw from the city.

Netherlands, 19 April 1794. Britain, Prussia and the Netherlands sign a treaty against France in The Hague.

Paris, 4 June 1794. Robespierre is unanimously elected president of the Convention.

West Indies, 4 June 1794. British troops capture Port au Prince, the administrative capital of Santo Domingo, after a five-day siege.

Paris, 10 June 1794. A law is passed establishing the regime known as the Great Terror. In future there will be no preliminary questioning of defendants or witnesses in trials if the revolutionary tribunal states it has enough factual or "moral" proof. Defense lawyers are banned and juries will have to choose between two verdicts: acquittal or death.

Paris, 27 July 1794. The Convention orders the arrest of Robespierre and his followers. The Commune declares itself in revolt and hands them over.

Paris, 28 July 1794. Robespierre and 21 of his companions are guillotined.

France, 20 August 1794. Having been arrested on 9 August on suspicion of being a Robespierrist, General Bonaparte is released at the request of the commander-in-chief of the forces in the Alps and Italy in order to reinforce the Army of Italy's general staff.

USA, 20 August 1794. The revolutionary General "Mad Anthony" Wayne defeats the Ohio Indians at the battle of Fallen Timbers in the Northwest Territory, ending Indian resistance in the area.

Russia, 28 September 1794. The Anglo-Russian-Austrian alliance of St. Petersburg is signed, directed against the French.

Poland, 10 October 1794. The Russian General Alexander Vasilyevich Suvorov crushes the rebel Polish army at Maciejowice. The injured Polish leader, Kosciuszko, is taken prisoner.

Netherlands, 25 October 1794. Prussia denounces the Treaty of The Hague, signed between Britain, Prussia and Holland in April, and withdraws its troops from the Netherlands.

Poland, 9 November 1794. The Russians enter Warsaw, having successfully put down the Polish uprising led by Kosciuszko.

Britain, 11 November 1794. As part of a round of public order measures prompted by a fear of Jacobin activity, the British government suspends the ancient act of Habeas Corpus, which protects citizens against arbitrary arrest.

Philadelphia, November 1794. The uprising of the "whiskey rebels" comes to an end. The dispute began in June when farmers in western Pennsylvania and throughout the Appalachians refused to pay the federal excise tax on whisky. The rebellion disintegrated when President Washington personally took the field with a force of 12,500 militiamen.

France, 31 December 1794. France signs an armistice with the Austrians.

Persia, 1794. The brutal and ambitious chieftain Aga Mohammed overthrows the Zand dynasty, which has dominated Persia since 1750, and establishes the Qajar dynasty.

Britain, 1795. Having completed *The Marriage of Heaven and Hell*, the visionary poet William Blake goes on to write *The Book of Los*.

Russia, 3 January 1795. Russia and Austria hold a secret meeting to draw up plans for the partition of Poland.

France, 21 February 1795. The convention approves a decree restoring freedom of worship.

Basel, 5 April 1795. France and Prussia sign the Treaty of Basel ending hostilities between the two countries.

Paris, 10 April 1795. The Convention takes harsh measures following the protests of 1 April. It also takes the opportunity to root out *Thermidorians* (reformed Robespierrists) whom it suspects of trying to slow down the forces of reaction.

Budapest, 20 May 1795. Ignac Martinovics, the head of the Jacobin movement in Hungary, is executed, dashing the hopes of Hungarian revolutionaries.

France, 15 August 1795. The Convention creates a new monetary unit, the *franc*.

Prussia, August 1795. Prussia joins the talks between Russia and Austria on the partition of Poland.

South Africa, 16 September 1795. Following the royal Dutch government's overthrow by France and the local Jacobins, the *stadtholder*, William V, invites England to seize the Dutch colonial domain. England begins with Cape Town.

Netherlands, 29 September 1795. The government of the Batavian republic puts the *stadtholder* William V on trial on a charge of high treason.

Paris, 15 October 1795. An attempted armed takeover of the Convention by wealthy Parisians is put down, but only with heavy military intervention. From now on the Convention will have to take the army into account. One among the officers who attracted much attention was a young general, Napoleon Bonaparte.

Paris, 16 October 1795. Bonaparte is promoted to major-general.

Poland, 24 October 1795. The third partition of Poland is agreed between Russia, Prussia and Austria.

Paris, 31 October 1795. The Executive Directory, which replaces the Convention, is appointed. It consists of five Directors, nominated by the Council of Five Hundred and elected by the Council of Ancients.

Poland, 25 November 1795. King Stanislas abdicates following the partition of his country.

Paris, 9 March 1796. Bonaparte marries Josephine de Beauharnais.

Santo Domingo, 31 March 1796. A coup by a mulatto general fails.

Italy, 11 April 1796. Bonaparte starts the Italian campaign at the head of 40,000 men.

Italy, 22 April 1796. Bonaparte wins the battles of Montenotte, Millesimo, Dego and Mondovi between 13 and 22 April.

Piedmont, 28 April 1796. Bonaparte concludes a treaty in Cherasco with the King of Piedmont and Sardinia. He has exceeded his instructions from Paris in the signing of this treaty.

Italy, 10 May 1796. Bonaparte wins a brilliant victory against the Austrians at Lodi bridge.

Milan, 15 May 1796. Bonaparte enters the Lombardian capital of Milan in triumph.

Paris, 15 May 1796. The treaty between France and Piedmont-Sardinia is signed, ceding Savoy and Nice to the French republic.

Italy, 23 June 1796. Pope Pius VI signs an armistice with Bonaparte in Bologna.

Philadelphia, 17 September 1796. President Washington makes his farewell address.

Russia, 7 November 1796. Tsarina Catherine II (the Great) dies.

Italy, 2 February 1797. Bonaparte takes Mantua from the Austrians, opening up the road to Vienna.

Italy, 9 February 1797. Bonaparte moves into the Vatican states and occupies Ancona, with a view to forcing Pius VI to negotiate.

Paris, 2 March 1797. The Directory authorizes vessels of war to board and seize neutral vessels, particularly if the ships involved are American.

USA, 4 March 1797. Vice-president John Adams, elected president on 7 December to replace George Washington, is sworn in.

Austria, 31 March 1797. Bonaparte makes peace proposals to Archduke Charles of Austria.

Britain, 2 May 1797. A naval mutiny spreads from Spithead to the North Sea fleet.

Venice, 12 May 1797. The Grand Council replaces the doge with a democratic republic.

Philadelphia, 15 May 1797. President Adams calls Congress into a special session, hoping to resolve the crisis with France.

Persia, 17 June 1797. The *shah*, Aga Mohammed, is assassinated. He is succeeded by his nephew Fath Ali.

Paris, 26 October 1797. The Directory ratifies the Treaty of Campo Fòrmio, signed by Bonaparte and the Austrians on 18 October.

USA, 4 November 1797. Congress agrees to pay a yearly tribute to Tripoli in a deal similar to that concluded last year with the *bey* of Algiers. This is the USA's only way of protecting its shipping.

Prussia, 16 November 1797. King Frederick William II dies and is succeeded by his son Frederick William III.

Paris, 18 January 1798. Increasing pressure on British trade, the Directory passes a law authorizing the seizure of any neutral vessel carrying British goods.

Paris, 5 March 1798. Having shelved plans for the invasion of England, on Bonaparte's advice, the Directory accepts the idea of invading Egypt and puts Bonaparte in charge of the project.

Austria, 29 April 1798. Haydn's oratorio *The Creation* is first performed. Inspired by his hearing of Handel's oratorios in England, Haydn sets a text derived from Milton and James Thomson. It is scored for full orchestra, large choir and three soloists, and is a great success.

Caribbean, 2 May 1798. The black general Toussaint L'Ouverture forces the British forces to agree to evacuate the part of Santo Domingo still in their possession.

Ireland, 23 May 1798. Believing that a French invasion is imminent, the Irish nationalists rise up against British occupation.

Ireland, 21 June 1798. British forces suppress an uprising by Irish patriots at Vinegar Hill near Wexford.

Egypt, 29 June 1798. The first French frigate to arrive at Alexandria learns that Nelson's fleet put in the previous day in search of the French.

Egypt, 1 July 1798. Napoleon Bonaparte takes Alexandria.

Philadelphia, 11 July 1798. As the possibility of war with France grows, Congress passes the Sedition Act, aimed at curbing internal dissent. French negotiators are trying to intimidate the American envoys, and war at sea has already broken out, though it is undeclared. Under the Sedition Act American citizens may be imprisoned for obstructing the imposition of federal law or for seditious writings.

France, 1798. The American engineer Robert Fulton invents the first submarine. He arrived in France two years ago and submitted his plans to the Directory. Now the *Nautilus* has taken to the water in a successful demonstration. However, naval officers are not convinced.

England, 1798. William Wordsworth and Samuel Taylor Coleridge publish the *Lyrical Ballads*, a joint collection of poetry. The volume marks a significant departure from current poetic conventions and is a celebration of the imagination and creative originality. Coleridge, in particular, reacts against the poetic dictates of the eighteenth century, revitalizing his language by a skilful use of archaic diction, while Wordsworth is striving to transform everyday reality and to describe a mystical union of man with nature.

Austria, 1798. Ludwig van Beethoven presents his piano sonata, opus 13, known as the *Pathétique*.

Egypt, 1 August 1798. The French navy is destroyed by Nelson at Aboukir. The French army is virtually imprisoned in Egypt.

Ottoman Empire, 9 September 1798. The Ottoman Empire declares war on France because of its occupation of Egypt.

Caribbean, 22 October 1798. The black General Toussaint L'Ouverture's supporters drive the French government's last agent off the island of Santo Domingo.

Ireland, 19 November 1798. In prison awaiting execution, the Irish nationalist leader Wolfe Tone commits suicide.

London, 29 December 1798. A second military alliance against France is formed by Britain, Austria, Russia, Naples and Portugal. The first coalition collapsed when the Austrians signed the Treaty of Campo Fòrmio with France. Now plans are being made to challenge France in the Netherlands, Italy and Brittany.

Mozambique, 1798. The Portuguese reoccupy the fort of Lourenço Marques at Maputo Bay and reestablish trade with the local Maputo kingdom in ivory and slaves.

Britain, 1798. Thomas Robert Malthus publishes his *Essay on the Principle of Population as it Affects the Future Improvements of Society* in which he asserts that populations inevitably increase more rapidly than food supplies.

Japan, 1799. Following unrest fomented by the Ainu people, the whole of Ezo (Hokkaido) is placed under the direct control of the shogun at Edo.

Germany, 1799. The well-known writer Friedrich Schiller concludes his dramatic trilogy *Wallenstein*, about the famous general of the Thirty Years War.

India, 3 February 1799. British troops enter Mysore in order to subjugate Tipu Sahib, with whom Bonaparte is trying to establish contact.

Egypt, 10 February 1799. Bonaparte leaves Cairo for Syria, at the head of 13,000 men.

India, 4 May 1799. Tipu Sahib, the ruler of Mysore, dies fighting the British under the command of the governor, the Marquis of Wellesley.

Spain, 5 June 1799. The naturalist and explorer Alexander von Humboldt sets sail for America, planning to explore Venezuela, Colombia and Peru.

Britain, 12 July 1799. The Combination Act is passed, forbidding the forming of an association by two or more people with the purpose of obtaining wage increases or improved conditions of work. The measure is prompted largely by fear of revolutionary ideas spreading from France.

Egypt, 19 July 1799. A stone bearing ancient Egyptian hieroglyphics and *demotic* (ancient Egyptian script) and Greek is found near the town of Rosetta on the west bank of the Bolbitic arm of the Nile. The discovery will prove to be the key to the decipherment of hieroglyphics.

Egypt, 23 August 1799. Napoleon sails for France.

Paris, 13 December 1799. Having seized power in a military coup, Bonaparte has himself elected first consul.

Philadelphia, 14 December 1799. The retired president, George Washington, dies. His last words are " 'tis well."

Spain, 1799. The court painter Francisco Goya publishes *Los Caprichos*, a series of etchings that express his criticisms of a corrupt establishment. He withdraws them shortly after publication, fearing the Inquisition.

1800–1824

France, 1 February 1800. The new constitution, with Napoleon Bonaparte as first consul, is accepted by a referendum.

Philadelphia, 7 May 1800. Congress divides the Northwest Territory into two parts, with the border between them running north from the confluence of the Ohio and Kentucky Rivers. The western part will be known as the Indiana Territory, and the eastern sector keeps the name of Northwest Territory.

India, 1800. The British compel the *nizam* of Hyderabad to accept the status of protectorate.

South Africa, 1800. Dingiswayo seizes the chieftainship of the Mthethwa from his brother. The Mthethwa are a small clan on the Mfolozi river (in northern Natal), but Dingiswayo, who already has a considerable reputation as a hunter and warrior, determined that his kingdom should rival the powerful Ndwandwe kingdom of King Zwide. Dingiswayo allies with the Maputo of Laurenco Marques (Maputo) against the Ndwandwe with the aim of controlling ivory supplies from the interior to Portuguese ships.

France, 9 February 1801. The peace of Luneville puts an end to the war with Austria in Bonaparte's favor. This leaves Britain as the only survivor of the second coalition against France.

Washington DC, 4 March 1801. The House of Representatives chooses Thomas Jefferson as the new president and Aaron Burr as vice-president after the two men receive exactly the same number of votes in the electoral college.

Egypt, 6 March 1801. British troops land in Egypt, which is currently in the hands of the French.

Russia, 24 March 1801. Tsar Paul I is murdered, and Alexander I becomes the new tsar.

Tripoli (Libya), 14 May 1801. Pasha Yusuf Karamanli declares war on the United States after the United States refuses a demand for more tribute to protect U.S. ships from piracy. A U.S. fleet then arrives to blockade Tripoli.

France, 8 October 1801. France signs a treaty with Russia, reflecting their recently improved relations.

Vienna, 1801. Ludwig van Beethoven writes a sonata (Opus 27, number 2) which is nicknamed "Moonlight."

France, 27 March 1802. Bonaparte signs the Treaty of Amiens, ending war with Great Britain.

France, 2 August 1802. Bonaparte is proclaimed consul for life by a plebiscite.

Russia, 20 September 1802. The reformist Tsar Alexander I, who came to power the previous year, grants the senate legislative and judicial rights. Influenced by his education by the Swiss rationalist Jean Francois de Laharpe, he also grants an amnesty to all political prisoners and exiles.

France, 18 May 1803. Following Bonaparte's continued military activities in Italy, the Netherlands, Switzerland, and Germany, the British government makes a formal break with the Treaty of Amiens and declares war on France.

Ireland, 23 July 1803. Irish patriots rebel against union with Britain, which was established by law on 1 January 1801.

Caribbean, 29 August 1803. General Dessalines proclaims the independence of Haiti at the western end of the island of Santo Domingo. In January of the fol-

lowing year, Haiti becomes the first Black republic, having declared itself independent after eleven years bitter fighting.

Pittsburgh, Pennsylvania, 31 August 1803. Captain Meriwether Lewis leaves Pittsburgh on the first government-sponsored exploration of far western country.

USA, 20 December 1803. The United States buys the Louisiana territory from France.

Serbia, February 1804. Karageorges (Black George) leads a Serbian revolt against the Ottomans.

France, 21 March 1804. Napoleon Bonaparte promulgates a civil code unifying legal practices across France. A compromise between the old regime and the egalitarian principles of the revolution, it protects the rights of property ownership above all else.

New Jersey, 12 July 1804. Former treasury secretary Alexander Hamilton dies from wounds inflicted in a duel the day before with his political opponent, Aaron Burr.

France, 6 November 1804. A plebiscite ratifies the nomination of Bonaparte as hereditary emperor, and Napoleon crowns himself Emperor of France. He is known henceforth simply as Napoleon.

Europe, 6 November 1804. Austria and Russia sign a secret agreement against France.

Germany, 1804. Following Napoleon's coronation as emperor, Ludwig van Beethoven cancels the planned dedication of his Third Symphony and names it *Eroica*.

China, 1804. The major rebellion stirred up by the White Lotus secret society in 1796 against the Manchu government is finally put down. The Qing dynasty survives but is much weakened.

Tripoli (Libya), 4 June 1805. Yusuf Karamanli, *pasha* of Tripoli, signs a peace treaty with the United States, ending the war he declared in May 1801. He has been forced to surrender by the U.S. fleet patrolling outside his harbor and by that fact that his rebellious brother Hamed has been installed, with U.S. backing, in the eastern city of Derna.

Europe, 9 August 1805. Austria joins Britain, Russia, Sweden, and the Kingdom of Piedmont-Sardinia in the third coalition against France.

Bavaria, 8 October 1805. In a major battle, the outnumbered French army of Napoleon defeats the invading Austrian army at Ulm.

Prussia, 3 November 1805. Coerced by Russia, Prussia joins the third coalition against France by a secret treaty signed at Potsdam.

Pacific Coast, 7 November 1805. The expedition led by Meriwether Lewis and William Clark has reached the Pacific coastline after a journey of nearly four thousand miles over eighteen months. Their exploration opens a new era of westward expansion for the United States.

Austria, 2 December 1805. Napoleon defeats the combined Austrian and Russian armies at the Battle of Austerlitz.

France, 1805. Joseph Jacquard introduces the first weaving looms, thus enabling unskilled workers to produce beautiful and intricate patterns.

Britain, 16 May 1806. Advised by Charles Fox, the foreign secretary, the cabinet decrees a blockade of the European coast from Brest to Hamburg.

Netherlands, 5 June 1806. The Batavian Republic is established as the Kingdom of Holland under Louis Bonaparte, the Emperor Napoleon's younger brother.

France, 21 November 1806. Napoleon promulgates the Berlin Decree, which declares the British Isles to be in a state of blockade, and orders the confiscation

of British merchandise in French territory, the imprisonment of British subjects, and the closure of all French ports to ships coming from Britain or British territories.

London, 7 January 1807. Responding to the Emperor Napoleon's Berlin Decree blockading the British Isles, a British order in council closes the coastal waters of France and its allies to all commercial shipping.

Britain, 25 March 1807. Parliament passes an act abolishing the slave trade. A resolution for the abolition of slavery was first brought before parliament in 1789.

Ottoman Empire, 25 May 1807. A revolt by the Janissaries (foot soldiers recruited from slaves) leads to the deposition of Selim III and to his replacement by Mustapha IV.

Russia, 25 June 1807. At the Tilsit Convention, Napoleon and the Russian Tsar Alexander I agree an end to hostilities between their two countries.

Prussia, July 1807. The ministers Gneisenau and Scharnhorst reorganize the Prussian army.

Prussia, September 1807. Dismissed on 3 January by Frederick William III, Heinrich von Stein is recalled after the intervention of the queen, with the implicit agreement of Napoleon, who sees in his abilities as an organizer the guarantee that Prussia's war debts will be paid. Von Stein begins a series of reforms designed to turn Prussia into a modern state, including the abolition of serfdom and revising the privileges of the nobility.

Europe, 7 November 1807. After the Tilsit Convention in July, the Anglo-Russian alliance—at the heart of the third coalition against France—is broken.

Britain, 11 November 1807. Britain extends its blockade to the Russian seaboard following the collapse of the third coalition, and threatens neutral countries

with reprisals if they refuse to undergo verification of their merchandise.

USA, 22 December 1807. Congress passes the Embargo Act, which halts all trading completely and is immediately effective. Both import and export trade is banned, not only with Britain and France but with the whole world. President Jefferson hopes that this will force Britain and France to reconsider their harassment of U.S. ships. The act is viewed by merchants, sailors, and producers with dismay.

Spain, 6 June 1808. On hearing of Napoleon's decision to appoint his brother Joseph king of Spain, a *junta* that has withdrawn to Seville declares war on France.

Spanish America, July 1808. Following the capture of the revolutionary Francisco Miranda during an attempted coup in Venezuela, one of his followers, Simón Bolívar, seizes power in Caracas.

Europe, 14 October 1808. During their meeting at Erfurt that finished on this day, Napoleon and Russian Tsar Alexander I renew the Treaty of Tilsit, which both countries have broken since it was signed the previous year.

Prussia, 24 November 1808. Napoleon obtains the dismissal of the minister Stein whom he suspects of organizing an anti-French uprising.

Spain, 4 December 1808. Napoleon conquers Madrid, having put down the resistance in Somosierra the previous month.

Germany, 1808. Goethe publishes the first part of his *Faust*.

France, 28 January 1809. Having plotted against the emperor with Fouche, Talleyrand falls into disgrace. Stripped of every position he holds, he places himself at the service of Metternich, the Austrian ambassador to Paris.

North America, 2 July 1809. The government of the Western Territory announces that the famous Shawnee Indian Chief Tecumseh and his brother, the Prophet, have launched a campaign to unite the ten thousand Indians who live in the area west of the Mississippi river. The aim of this confederation is to halt American expansion in their lands.

Washington DC, 9 August 1809. President Madison reinstates the embargo on British trade following Britain's refusal to revoke the orders in council that justify harassment of American shipping.

Europe, 14 October 1809. Austria signs the Treaty of Schönbrunn, ceding its Illyrian provinces to France.

Mexico, 16 September 1810. A parish priest, Hidalgo, launches an appeal for Mexican independence.

Honolulu, 1810. The island of Hawaii is unified by King Kamhameha the Great.

USA, 2 February 1811. President Madison sends Britain an ultimatum, demanding that it revoke its orders in the council of 1807 that justify British harassment of U.S. shipping.

Britain, 5 February 1811. The Regency Act is passed, authorizing George, the Prince of Wales, to exercise the powers of regency in the place of his father, George III, who is insane.

Mexico, 30 July 1811. The parish priest Hidalgo, who called for Mexican independence the previous year, is executed, having been tried by the court of the Inquisition.

Europe, 17 October 1811. Prussia and Russia sign a military convention for joint action in the event of an invasion by France.

Egypt, 1811. The Ottoman sultan concedes supreme authority in Egypt to Muhammad Ali, an Albanian tobacco merchant who entered Ottoman service and led Albanian troops in the war against the French.

Venezuela, 1811. A congress proclaims Venezuela's independence and sets up a republican constitution. Simón Bolívar is a popular leader of the movement, as is the veteran revolutionary Francisco Miranda.

Finland, 9 April 1812. Russia and Sweden sign a treaty of alliance at Abo. Sweden cedes Finland to Russia and agrees to supply thirty thousand men to cooperate with Russian forces. Russia agrees to help Sweden annex Norway.

France, 9 May 1812. Rejecting proposals by the Russian Tsar Alexander I questioning the policy of the continental blockade, Napoleon breaks relations with Russia.

France, 1812. The naturalist Georges Cuvier publishes the first volume of *Researches on the Bones of Fossil Vertebrates*.

USA, 19 June 1812. Prompted by British interference with U.S. shipping and the press-ganging of U.S. sailors, the United States declares war on Britain.

Russia, 24 June 1812. Napoleon, at the head of the *Grand Armée*, crosses the Nieman and begins his invasion of Russia.

Spain, 22 July 1812. British forces under the Duke of Wellington defeat the French at Salamanca.

Spain, 12 August 1812. The British commander Wellington occupies Madrid, forcing Joseph Bonaparte, the King of Spain, to abandon the city.

Russia, 14 September 1812. Having forced the Russians to retreat after the Battle of Borodino earlier in the month, Napoleon enters Moscow, which has been set on fire by its fleeing inhabitants.

Russia, 19 October 1812. After failing to persuade Tsar Alexander I to come to terms, Napoleon begins a retreat from Moscow.

Russia, 5 December 1812. Napoleon decides to return to Paris to put down a

rumored plot against him and raise a new army.

Prussia, 20 December 1812. The remnants of Napoleon's *Grand Armée* reach eastern Prussia.

Lithuania, 30 December 1812. Having deserted the French after the catastrophic invasion of Russia, Prussia signs a treaty of neutrality with Russia at Tauroggen.

Germany, 1812. The folklore experts Jakob and Wilhelm Grimm publish a volume of *Fairy Tales*.

South Africa, 1812. During the fourth Cape Eastern Frontier War, the British under Colonel Graham support the land-hungry Boer ranchers and expel 22,000 Khoisan and Xhosa eastward across the Fish river. They then set up a line of forts along the river.

Ottoman Empire, 28 May 1812. The Ottomans sign a peace treaty with Russia at Bucharest whereby Russia acquires Bessarabia (Romania), and the Ottoman-Russian border is set along the Pruth river.

Austria, 30 January 1813. Austria signs an armistice treaty with Russia.

Prussia, 3 February 1813. Frederick William III of Prussia calls all his people to arms.

Poland, 18 February 1813. Tsar Alexander I enters Warsaw at the head of his army.

Prussia, 27 February 1813. Frederick William III signs an offensive and defensive alliance with Russia at Kalisz.

Germany, 4 March 1813. The Russians reach Berlin. The French garrison evacuates the city without a fight.

Prussia, 27 March 1813. King Frederick William III declares war on France.

Canada, 27 April 1813. U.S. troops capture York (now Toronto), the seat of government in Ontario, from the British.

Germany, 2 May 1813. Napoleon defeats a Russian and Prussian army at Grossgorschen near Lutzen.

Spain, 21 June 1813. French forces under Jourdan are defeated by the British under Wellington at the Battle of Vittoria. Joseph Bonaparte, the King of Spain, flees to France.

Germany, 27 June 1813. Russia, Prussia, and Austria sign the Treaty of Reichenbach, agreeing that the Duchy of Warsaw should be abolished, the Illyrian provinces restored to Austria, and French conquests in northern Germany relinquished. If France refuses to accept these terms, Austria will declare war.

Ottoman Empire, August 1813. Taking advantage of the war in Europe, the Ottoman forces occupy Serbia and destroy the forces of Karageorges, the Serbian independence leader.

South America, August 1813. While the Spanish are busy reconquering Chile, Simón Bolívar reoccupies Venezuela and its capital, Caracas.

Germany, 6 September 1813. While attempting to take Berlin, French forces under Marshal Ney are defeated by the Prussians under Butow at Dennewitz.

Germany, 9 September 1813. Russia, Prussia, and Austria sign the Treaty of Teplitz, an alliance guaranteeing mutual assistance against Napoleon.

France, 8 October 1813. Having liberated Spain from French occupation, British troops under Wellington invade southern France.

Mexico, 6 November 1813. José Maria Morelos proclaims Mexican independence from Spain at the Congress of Chilpancingo.

France, 31 December 1813. On New Year's Eve, the Prussian forces under Blucher cross the Rhine, beginning the allied invasion of France.

Italy, 11 January 1814. The King of Naples, Joachim Murat, enters into an alliance with the Austrians—whom he had crushed at Dresden the previous year—and occupies central Italy.

France, February 1814. At the conference of Chatillon-sur-Seine, the allies offer to return France to its 1792 borders, but Napoleon rejects the proposal.

France, 9 March 1814. The four allied powers—Austria, Russia, Prussia, and Britain—sign the Treaty of Chaumont, negotiated by British foreign secretary Lord Castlereagh. Under the terms of the treaty, each ally will supply 150,000 troops to defeat Napoleon, and Britain will provide a subsidy of five million pounds.

Paris, 30 March 1814. Encircled, poorly defended, and flooded with refugees, Paris surrenders to the allies.

Paris, 31 March 1814. Tsar Alexander I and Frederick William III of Prussia enter Paris in triumph.

France, 6 April 1814. Granted the sovereignty of the island of Elba and a pension from the French government, Napoleon abdicates at Fontainebleau. He is allowed to retain the title of emperor. Thus begins is first exile.

France, 2 May 1814. Having disembarked at Calais on 24 April, Louis XVIII issues the proclamation of St. Ouen, making known his intention to govern as a constitutional monarch. The following day he enters Paris.

Paris, 30 May 1814. The Treaty of Paris returns France to its 1792 frontiers. It is agreed that the final settlement of Europe will be made at a congress to be held in Vienna.

North America, 9 August 1814. By the Treaty of Fort Jackson, ending the Creek War, the Creek Indians are forced to cede 23 million acres, half of Alabama and part of southern Georgia, to the whites.

USA, 25 August 1814. The British capture and burn down much of Washington DC, including the White House, causing President Madison to flee.

USA, 13 September 1814. British troops make an unsuccessful attack on Baltimore. During the battle, the American Francis Scott Key composes a poem that later became the lyrics to "The Star-Spangled Banner."

Vienna, 1 November 1814. A congress opens that is composed of representatives of almost all the countries of Europe.

Netherlands, 24 December 1814. British and US representatives sign a treaty in Ghent ending their war. Territory seized by Britain will be returned to the United States. It will take at least a month for the news to reach America.

Connecticut, 5 January 1815. Federalists from all over New England draw up the Hartford Convention, demanding several important changes to the U.S. Constitution.

New Zealand, 24 February 1815. The Reverend Samuel Marsden is the first European to purchase land in New Zealand from the Nga-Puhi tribe.

France, 1 March 1815. Returning from Elba, Napoleon lands at Cannes with a force of fifteen hundred men and marches on Paris.

Paris, 20 March 1815. Napoleon enters Paris.

Vienna, 25 March 1815. Britain, Austria, Prussia, and Russia form a new alliance against Napoleon.

Austria, 10 April 1815. Austria declares war on Joachim Murat, the King of Naples, who has again given his support to Napoleon.

Italy, 3 May 1815. Murat, the King of Naples, is defeated by an Austrian army at Tolentino.

Vienna, 9 June 1815. Britain, Russia, Prussia, Austria, France, Sweden, and

Portugal sign the Act of the Congress of Vienna, establishing a comprehensive peace in Europe. An act is passed and creates a German confederation of 39 states to replace the old Holy Roman Empire. By the Treaty of Vienna, Belgium and Holland are united to form the Kingdom of the Netherlands.

Netherlands, 18 June 1815. Napoleon is decisively defeated by the British and the Prussians at the Battle of Waterloo. Four days later he abdicates for the second time, following the refusal of the parliamentary chambers to cooperate with him.

Paris, 7–8 July 1815. The victorious allies enter Paris. Louis XVIII returns to Paris.

France, 17 July 1815. After a futile attempt to escape to America, Napoleon surrenders to the British at Rochefort.

Europe, 26 September 1815. At the instigation of Tsar Alexander I, Russia, Austria, and Prussia sign a holy alliance by which they agree to act toward each other and toward their subjects in accordance with Christian principles.

South Atlantic, 17 October 1815. Napoleon arrives on the island of St. Helena, where he has been banished by the allies. Thus begins his second and final exile.

Poland, November 1815. The Duchy of Warsaw, which was annexed to the Russian empire by the Treaty of Vienna, is organized as the autonomous Kingdom of Poland and given its own constitution by Tsar Alexander I.

Scandinavia, 1815. Sweden and Norway ratify an act of union.

India, 2 March 1816. Gurkha tribesmen in Nepal sign a peace treaty with the British, ending their year-long war.

Argentina, 9 July 1816. The United Provinces of Rio de la Plata declare independence from Spain.

Germany, 5 November 1816. The Diet of the German Confederation, created by the 1815 Treaty of Vienna, meets for the first time, at Frankfurt.

USA, 4 December 1816. James Monroe, who served as Secretary of State under President Madison, is elected to succeed him.

France, 1816. A new science of comparative anatomy is born with the publication of Georges Cuvier's book on classifying the animal kingdom. Cuvier is also a brilliant paleontologist, able to reconstruct whole skeletons of long-dead animals from just a few bones.

England, 1816. Jane Austen, the author of *Pride and Prejudice* and *Mansfield Park*, publishes another novel, *Emma*. All of her works are published anonymously.

USA, December 1817. A war starts in earnest between U.S. troops and Seminole Indians, who the previously year had refused to leave the land in southern Georgia and northern Florida.

Australia, 1817. The Australian pioneer and wool merchant Elizabeth Macarthur retires from the management of Elizabeth Farm, the first great Australian estate. After taking over the business from her husband in 1809, she built up the merino flocks and traveled throughout Australia, expanding sales into the British market and establishing New South Wales as a major wool-producing region.

Argentina, 1817. Following his victories over the Spanish in Rio de la Plata, General José de San Martin embarks on a campaign to liberate Chile.

England, 1817. The Romantic poet John Keats publishes his first anthology of poems.

North America, 20 October 1818. Britain and the United States agree that the western border between Canada and the USA should be the 49th parallel.

Bohemia, 1 August 1819. Prince Metternich and Karl Hardenberg, the chief

ministers of Austria and Prussia, finalize the details of the secret Convention of Teplitz, which introduces reactionary policies throughout the German Confederation.

South America, 17 December 1819. At the Congress of Angostura, the Republic of Great Colombia—consisting of New Granada, Venezuela, and Quito—is established. Simón Bolívar is made president and military dictator.

South Africa, 1819. The Zulus under Shaka defeat the Ndwandwe at the Battle of Mhlatuze River and emerge as the dominant military power in the Natal region.

Britain, 29 January 1820. George III dies and is succeeded by his son George, Prince Regent since 1811, when George III was pronounced terminally insane.

Spain, 7 March 1820. To quell the mounting tide of revolt in Spain, King Ferdinand VII restores the constitution of 1812, which he abolished on coming to the throne in 1814.

USA, 15 March 1820. Congress reaches a compromise on the slavery issue by admitting Maine to the union as a free state and Missouri as a slave state. All future states north of a line between the 36th and 37th parallels, which came to be known as the Mason-Dixon line, are to be free.

England, 1820. The poet Shelley publishes *Prometheus Unbound*, and Keats publishes a volume of odes and ballads that puts him in the first rank of contemporary poets.

Mexico, 24 February 1821. General Agustin de Iturbide proclaims Mexican independence, declaring that the government should be a constitutional monarchy under Ferdinand VII of Spain or another European king.

Greece, February 1821. Archbishop Germanos of Patras calls for a Greek uprising against the Ottomans. In March, the Greek nationalist leader Alexander Ypsilanti invades Moldavia with a battalion, seizes its capital, Jassy, and occupies Bucharest.

South Atlantic, 5 May 1821. Napoleon dies on the island of St. Helena.

Ottoman Empire, 19 June 1821. Greek troops under Alexander Ypsilanti are heavily defeated by the Ottomans at the Battle of Dragasani, west of Bucharest.

Greece, 13 January 1822. At Epidaurus, nationalist rebels proclaim the independence of Greece and draw up a constitution. Although the independence movement is unsuccessful, the cause gains sympathy and support across Europe.

Ecuador, 24 May 1822. Antonio José de Sucre, a lieutenant of Simón Bolívar, defeats the Spanish royalist forces at the Battle of Pichincha, securing the independence of Quito.

Brazil, September 1822. Brazil declares its independence from Portugal. In October, Dom Pedro, the son of King John VI of Portugal, is proclaimed Emperor of Brazil.

USA, 12 December 1822. The United States grants formal recognition to Mexico's new revolutionary government headed by Agustin de Iturbide. The following June, President Monroe extends diplomatic recognition to Colombia.

West Africa, 1822. Encouraged and financed by the American Colonization Society, a group of U.S. white clergymen and businessmen, freed African Americans found a small settlement on the West African coast. The new colony becomes known as Liberia.

Vienna, 1822. Franz Liszt makes his debut as a pianist at age eleven.

Central America, 1 July 1823. Guatemala, San Salvador, Nicaragua, Honduras, and Costa Rica declare themselves sovereign states within the confederated United Provinces of Central America.

USA, 2 December 1823. In what is destined to become known as the Monroe Doctrine, President James Monroe declares that United States will not meddle in European affairs, but nor will it permit European powers to meddle in the affairs of the Western Hemisphere.

Southeast Asia, February 1824. Following the Burmese occupation of Assam and Manipur in northeastern India, war breaks out between Britain and Burma.

Britain, 6 June 1824. A law is passed recognizing the right to strike.

France, 16 September 1824. Louis XVIII dies, and the Count of Artois, his brother and the leader of the ultra-royalists, succeeds him as Charles X.

Peru, December 1824. Following the defeat of the Spanish by independence fighters under Antonio José de Sucre at the Battle of Ayacucho, the Spanish are forced to agree to the withdrawal of the royalist troops remaining in Peru. Peruvian independence is secured.

USA, 1824. An American invention makes it possible to harvest at three times the previous speed. Drawn by a two-horse team, Cyrus McCormick's reaper-harvester is an improvement on Patrick Bell's, which is pushed from behind.

Vienna, 1824. Ludwig van Beethoven composes his ninth symphony.

Britain, 1824. The Society for the Prevention of Cruelty to Animals is founded.

1825–1849

USA, 25 October 1825. The Erie Canal, linking the Great Lakes with New York City via the Hudson river, is completed.

Russia, 1 December 1825. Tsar Alexander I dies, and there is confusion about the succession. His brother Constantine has secretly renounced his claim in favor of the youngest brother, Nicholas, who refuses to believe in the arrangement until he has secured a further renunciation.

Russia, 26 December 1825. The Decembrist uprising calling for representative government, the abolition of serfdom, and social reforms is quickly crushed by Nicholas, who then accepts his succession as tsar.

Japan, 1825. After further encroachments on the Japanese coast by British and American ships, the shogun's government issues an edict calling for the expulsion of all foreign ships from Japanese waters.

USA, 1825. Guided by visions, Joseph Smith publishes his *Book of Mormon* and founds the first Mormon church at Fayette in New York state. He claims to be restoring an ancient, primitive Christian religion.

USA, 4 July 1826. On the fiftieth anniversary of the signing of the Declaration of Independence, two American founding fathers and former presidents, John Adams and Thomas Jefferson, die.

New Orleans, 1827. Students from Paris introduce a new Mardi Gras (Shrove Tuesday) celebration in New Orleans, supplementing the traditional masked balls.

Vienna, 26 March 1827. The composer Ludwig van Beethoven dies.

London, July–August 1827. France, Britain, and Russia sign the Treaty of London, threatening to use force if the Ottoman Empire does not agree to an armistice in their war with Greece. The Ottomans refuse.

Mediterranean, 20 October 1827. British, French, and Russian forces destroy the Ottoman-Egyptian fleet at the Battle of Navarino.

USA, 21 April 1828. *The American Dictionary of the English Language*, compiled by the editor and grammarian Noah Webster, is published.

Russia, 26 April 1828. In support of the Greek struggle for independence, Russia declares war on the Ottoman Empire.

Ottoman Empire, 8 June 1828. Pursuing their war with the Ottomans, the Russians cross the Danube.

South Africa, 22 September 1828. The Zulu leader Shaka the Great is assassinated by his brothers Dingane and Mhlangane, who become joint kings. After his mother's death in 1827, Shaka became mentally unbalanced and started arbitrary executions. Zulu conquests reached a peak in the Natal area, with a double victory over the last Ndwandwe remnants in the north in 1826 and 1828.

USA, 3 December 1828. Backed by the fledgling Democratic Party, Andrew Jackson is elected president, defeating his long-time rival John Quincy Adams, the sitting president.

North America, 20 December 1828. Cherokee Indians cede their traditional lands in Arkansas territory to the United States and agree to migrate to lands west of the Mississippi river.

Canada, 1828. Nominated as a member of the council, the French-speaking deputy Papineau draws up a powerful protest document, known as the Ninety-Two Resolutions, aimed at the British government.

London, 22 March 1829. At an ambassadorial conference, agreement is reached on the boundaries of an independent Greece.

Ottoman Empire, 14 September 1829. Following Russian victories at Silistria and Adrianople, Sultan Mahmud II signs a peace treaty with Tsar Nicholas at Adrianople. He recognizes Greek independence and accepts the terms of the London agreements of November 1828 and March 1829, which established the borders of Greece. Russia receives Moldavia and Wallachia from Turkey.

France, 1829. The Paris professor Louis Braille, himself blind since the age of three, invents a reading system for the blind.

Berlin, 1829. On Good Friday, Felix Mendelssohn and the choirs of the Berlin Academy perform Johann Sebastian Bach's *St. Matthew Passion*, which has lain forgotten for a hundred years.

Britain, 26 June 1830. George IV dies and is succeeded as king by his brother William IV.

Algiers, 5 July 1830. A French expeditionary force captures Algiers and deposes the *bey*.

France, July–August 1830. On 26 July, King Charles X issues five ordinances limiting political and civil rights. Led by the Marquis of Lafayette, liberals opposed to the king's ordinances seize Paris. Charles X abdicates on 2 August, and five days later Louis Philippe, the Bourbon Duke of Orléans, is proclaimed king by the liberals.

Netherlands, August 1830. Belgian resentment at forced union with the Dutch bursts into open rebellion in Brussels and throughout the provinces.

Netherlands, October 1830. A provisional government proclaims Belgian independence.

Britain, November 1830. Violent riots by farmworkers in the south of England are harshly repressed by the army. "Bloody assizes" condemn nine workers to the gallows. Nearly five hundred are deported and hundreds are imprisoned.

Italy, 1830. The French writer Stendhal (the pseudonym of Marie-Henri Beyle) publishes a novel entitled *Le Rouge et le Noir*.

Boston, 1 January 1831. William Lloyd Garrison publishes the first edition of a journal entitled *The Liberator*, calling for the complete and immediate emancipation of all the slaves in the United States.

London, 20 January 1831. The London conference of European powers signs a protocol delineating the boundaries of Belgium and Holland and establishing Belgium as a neutral state under the permanent guarantee of the powers.

Poland, January 1831. Following the Polish Diet's proclamation of the end of the Russian succession to its throne, war breaks out between Poland and Russia.

France, March 1831. The exiled Italian republican activist Giuseppe Mazzini founds a revolutionary society called Young Italy with the aim of uniting Italy through a general uprising and elevating Italian patriotism by moral fervor.

Brazil, 7 April 1831. Under pressure from both the army and the people, the unpopular Emperor Pedro abdicates in favor of his five-year-old son.

Belgium, 4 June 1831. The Belgians elect Leopold of Saxe-Coburg king, three months after the national congress had conferred the regency on its president, Baron Erasme Surlet de Chokier.

Virginia, 21 August 1831. The radical black preacher Nat Turner leads a band of slaves in revolt on a large plantation, killing 57 whites.

Poland, September 1831. Russian forces seize Warsaw, crushing the Polish rebels with whom they have been at war since January.

London, 4 June 1832. A bill of parliamentary reform is passed, giving the vote to men of substantial property.

Berlin, 22 March 1833. A customs treaty (*Zollverein*) is signed among Bavaria, Wurttemberg, Prussia, and Hesse-Darmstadt, notably excluding Austria.

London, July 1833. To enforce laws passed in 1802 and 1819 against child labor, an act is passed ensuring the appointment of factory inspectors.

Spain, 29 September 1833. Civil war breaks out between the Carlistas (supporters of Don Carlos, the pretender to the throne) and the supporters of Queen Isabella, who succeeded on her father's death.

Mexico, 1833. General Santa Anna is elected president of the republic. Santa

Anna supported General Iturbide, who was inspired by Napoleon's example to declare himself emperor in 1822, but was instrumental in his overthrow the following year.

London, 1 August, 1835. Slavery is abolished throughout the British Empire.

Texas, 20 December 1835. Leaders of the Texan secession movement issue a declaration of independence from the dictatorship of the Mexican President Santa Anna and officially proclaim the creation of the Republic of Texas. Full-scale civil war ensues.

Britain, 1835. The young writer Charles Dickens publishes a collection of his journalistic pieces under the title *Sketches by Boz*, receiving £150 for the copyright.

Texas, 24 February 1836. With five thousand soldiers, Mexican dictator General Santa Anna lays siege to the fortified mission station, the Alamo, defended by 187 Texans. On March 6 it falls to Mexican troops.

Texas, 21 April 1836. Texan troops led by General Sam Houston inflict a crushing defeat on the Mexicans at San Jacinto, taking General Santa Anna prisoner. In October, Houston is sworn in as president of the Texas republic.

South Africa, 1836. Following the end of the sixth Eastern Cape Frontier War the previous year, the Boers are disappointed when the British government hands back captured land to the Xhosa, with whom it makes friendship treaties. The Boers had joined the war in an attempt to gain land outside British domination following the abolition of slavery, but Christian missionaries had informed the government of the settlers' motives. The Boers are now *trekking* north to join hunters and raiders beyond the Orange and Vaal Rivers.

Britain, 20 June 1837. On the death of her uncle, William IV, Princess Victoria becomes queen of Great Britain and Ireland.

Florida, 25 December 1837. US troops rout Seminole Indians at Lake Okeechobee.

Canada, 1837. The speaker of the Lower Canada Assembly, Louis-Joseph Papineau, leads a rebellion by French-Canadians against the proposed union of the British provinces of Upper and Lower Canada. A similar rebellion in Upper Canada is led by the Scottish journalist and political activist, William Lyon Mackenzie.

Russia, 1837. The novelist and poet Alexander Pushkin dies of a wound received in a duel fought to defend his wife's honor. Unpopular and widely misunderstood in his liberal beliefs, Pushkin was forced into the duel by enemies at court.

South Africa, 6 February 1838. Having failed to obtain land by trickery from the Zulus, Boer leader Piet Retief is executed as a witch by Zulu chief Dingane.

Ohio, 30 October 1838. Oberlin College becomes the nation's first institution of higher education to admit women on an equal basis with men.

Paris, 19 August 1839. For the first time, a practical photographic process is presented to the public. Named daguerreotype after its inventor, Louis Daguerre.

China, 4 September 1839. Following the evacuation of Canton by British traders, the destruction of confiscated opium, the stoppage of foreign trade, as well as the denial of food and water to the British, naval forces fire the first shots in the as yet undeclared Opium War.

Paris, 1839. Frederic Chopin publishes his 24 preludes. Written the previous winter on the island of Majorca where he was staying with his lover, the novelist George Sand, they are dedicated to the piano maker, Camille Pleyel, a friend of the composer.

New Zealand, 6 February 1840. Through the Treaty of Waitangi with the native Maori, New Zealand becomes a crown colony of Great Britain.

London, 10 February 1840. Queen Victoria marries her first cousin, Prince Albert of Saxe-Coburg-Gotha.

Canada, 10 February 1840. Following the Durham Report of 1838, in which union was recommended, an act is passed uniting the British provinces of Upper and Lower Canada.

Prussia, June 1840. On the death of Frederick William III, his son Frederick William IV succeeds to the throne. Welcomed by liberals for his progressive leanings, he quickly disappoints them and comes under the influence of an effective, conservative court clique.

Connecticut, August 1840. A Spanish slave ship, the *Amistad*, arrives in Connecticut with 53 Africans in command. Slaves on board the ship rebelled while the ship was traveling from one Cuban port to another, killing the captain and all but two of the crew. Spain is expected to demand extradition of the rebels.

France, 1840. The essayist Alexis de Tocqueville publishes *Democracy in America*, a work of penetrating analysis that brings him almost instant fame.

China, 20 January 1841. Following lengthy negotiations between British and Qing representatives concerning the conflict known as the Opium War, and spurred by a British attack on the Bogue forts, the Convention of Chuanbi is concluded. Among other things, the Chinese negotiators agree to pay indemnities and cede the island of Hong Kong to Britain.

USA, April 1841. Edgar Allan Poe's new book, *The Murders in the Rue Morgue*, makes a new kind of story popular, the detective story.

USA, 4 April 1841. . President William Harrison, aged 68, becomes the first US president to die in office, only a month after being sworn in. He developed pneumonia soon after a bitterly cold inauguration day on which he refused to wear a hat or overcoat, made a two-hour speech, and went to three inauguration balls. Vice-President John Tyler becomes acting president. He is confirmed as president after appealing to Congress to grant him full powers. At this time, the US constitution is unclear on who succeeds presidents who die in office.

London, 13 July 1841. The Straits' Convention is signed by the leading European powers. In a deal largely the work of Britain's foreign secretary, Lord Palmerston, the powers agree that the Bosphorus and the Dardanelles should be closed to warships of all nations as long as the Ottoman Empire is at peace.

China, 29 August 1842. Britain's Opium War with China ends. Britain and China sign the Treaty of Nanjing, ceding Hong Kong island to Britain and opening five ports to foreign trade.

Britain, 1842. Lord Ashley's Mines Act comes into force, prohibiting the employment underground of women, girls, and children under ten years old.

Russia, 1842. The novelist Nikolai Gogol publishes *Dead Souls*, a somber portrayal of Russian life under serfdom.

Washington DC, 24 May 1844. The inventor Samuel Morse taps out the first telegraph message between two cities, to a friend in Baltimore forty miles away.

USA, 27 June 1844. Joseph Smith, the leader of the Mormon sect, and his brother Hyrum are killed by a mob in Carthage, Illinois, where they had been held on a charge of rioting. This follows months of tension between the Mormons who settled in 1839 at Nauvoo, Illinois, and locals who had come to resent and suspect Mormon political and economic power.

Morocco, 14 August 1844. France's Marshal Bugeaud attacks and defeats the army of Abd al-Kader, the Algerian resistance leader, and his Moroccan supporters at the Isly River. On 10 September, France and Morocco sign the treaty of Tangiers, ending their conflict. France agrees to withdraw from Morocco.

Denmark, 1844. *The Concept of Anguish*, by the philosopher Soren Kierkegaard, appears. It follows the publication of *Either/Or, Fear and Trembling*, and *Repetition*.

Britain, 1844. J.M.W. Turner paints his dramatically atmospheric *Rain, Steam and Speed*. The painting will be a major influence on the Impressionist movement.

North America, 28 March 1845. Mexico severs relations with the United States following the U.S. Senate's ratification of the annexation of Texas on 1 March.

USA, 29 December 1845. Texas joins the United States of America and becomes the 38th state in the union.

Germany, 1845. Friedrich Engels publishes his *Condition of the Working Classes in England*.

Ireland, 1845. Blight strikes the potato, the staple food of the Irish countryside, making much of the crop inedible. By 1852, one million people will have died of starvation and many more have emigrated.

USA, 13 May 1846. The United States declares war on Mexico.

USA, 15 June 1846. Britain signs a treaty with the United States agreeing to end its joint occupation of Oregon Territory. All the land west of the Rocky Mountains and south of the 49th parallel now belongs to the United States.

Denmark, 8 July 1846. King Christian VIII lays claim, under the Danish succession law, to the independent duchies of Schleswig and Holstein.

Panama, 12 December 1846. The United States and Colombia sign an agreement granting the United States transit rights on the narrow isthmus of Panama between the Atlantic and Pacific Oceans.

Britain, 1847. Among the new novels published this year are *Vanity Fair* by William Thackeray, *Wuthering Heights* by Emily Bronte, *Jane Eyre* by Charlotte Bronte, and *Dombey and Son* by Charles Dickens.

Britain, June 1847. In London, Karl Marx, Friedrich Engels, and Stefan Born found the Communist League.

Utah, 24 July 1847. A group of Mormons led by Brigham Young founds a settlement on the banks of the Great Salt Lake.

Mexico City, 14 September 1847. A US army storms and captures Mexico City, putting an end to the Mexican war.

Morocco, 23 October 1847. Having lost the support of the Sultan of Morocco, the Algerian resistance leader Abd al-Kader surrenders to the French.

Canada, December 1847. Following the victory of the reformists in a general election, Governor General Lord Elgin proclaims the birth of a parliamentary system.

Liberia, 1847. The state of Liberia, founded by the American abolitionists, proclaims its independence.

France, 23 February 1848. Following the outbreak of fighting between demonstrators and troops in Paris, Prime Minister François Guizot is forced out of office. The following day, King Louis Philippe abdicates and a republic is proclaimed.

France, 27 February 1848. The government, which recognizes the right to work, creates national workshops to relieve unemployment.

Austria, 13 March 1848. The Chancellor, Prince Metternich, resigns following demonstrations in Vienna.

Prussia, 17 March 1848. With the outbreak of a revolt in Berlin, Frederick William IV grants a constitution.

Hungary, 23 March 1848. Hungary proclaims its independence from Austria.

Denmark, 2 May 1848. Prussia invades Denmark over the Schleswig-Holstein question.

Paris, 4 May 1848. The Constituent Assembly elected in April holds its opening session. In the elections, the moderate republicans won a large majority over the socialists and the monarchists.

Poland, 7 May 1848. Prussian troops suppress a Warsaw uprising.

Paris, 15 May 1848. Demonstrators invade the assembly and proclaim it dissolved. The revolt is put down by the National Guard.

Prague, 17 June 1848. Austrian General Alfred Windischgratz crushes a Czech uprising in Prague.

France, 24 June 1848. The national workshops are disbanded by the assembly.

Paris, 26 June 1848. Another revolt in Paris is violently put down by Louis Cavaignac.

Vienna, 12 August 1848. Emperor Ferdinand, who fled to Innsbruck on 17 May, returns to Vienna.

Italy, 26 August 1848. Having continued to resist since the signing of the armistice, Giuseppe Garibaldi and his volunteers are defeated by the Austrians at Morazzone.

Hungary, 24 September 1848. Lajos Kossuth is proclaimed president of the committee for national defense.

Hungary, October 1848. Joseph Jellacic, commander of the imperial forces operating against the Hungarians, is driven out of Hungary.

Vienna, 31 October 1848. Prince Alfred Windischgratz forces Vienna to surrender after a third uprising.

France, 12 November 1848. A new constitution comes into force, providing for a single assembly of 750 representatives elected for three years by universal male suffrage, and for a president of the republic elected for a single term of four years.

Austria, 2 December 1848. The Emperor Ferdinand abdicates in favor of his nephew Franz Josef.

Prussia, 5 December 1848. King Frederick William IV dissolves the national assembly and grants a new constitution.

France, 10 December 1848. Louis Napoleon is elected President of the French Republic by a huge majority.

Hungary, 15 December 1848. The Austrian army, led by Prince Alfred Windischgratz, invades Hungary.

USA, 1848. The Declaration of Sentiments and Resolutions at the Seneca Falls Convention begins the women's rights movement in America.

Hungary, 5 January 1849. Budapest surrenders to the Austrians.

Italy, 23 March 1849. The Austrians under Marshal Radetsky crush the army of Charles Albert of Sardinia at Novara. The following day, Charles Albert abdicates in favor of the Duke of Savoy, Victor Emmanuel II.

Germany, 27 March 1849. Meeting at Frankfurt, the national assembly adopts a constitution that creates a federal state under an hereditary "Emperor of the Germans" (Kaiser).

Germany, 4 April 1849. Frederick William IV of Prussia, who was elected "Emperor of the Germans" on 28 March, rejects the imperial crown.

Italy, 25 April 1849. Asked by Pope Pius IX to intervene against the Roman republic, a French expeditionary force lands at Civitavecchia.

Rome, 30 April 1849. The republican patriot and guerrilla leader Giuseppe Garibaldi repulses a French attack on Rome.

Germany, 26 May 1849. Prussia, Saxony, and Hanover accept a draft constitution providing for a union of non-Habsburg Germany under the leadership of Prussia.

1850–1874

Germany, April 1850. At Erfurt, an assembly of German states—excluding, among others, Saxony, Hanover, Wurttemberg, and Bavaria—accepts the Prussian scheme for German union, which Austria strongly opposes.

Persia, 19 July 1850. Sayyid Ali Muhammad—known as the *Bab* (gateway) and the founder of *Babism*, a new Islamic mystical movement—is executed on the orders of Shah Nasir al-Din.

China, July 1850. Groups of pseudo-Christian God-Worshippers gather at Jintian, in Guangxi province, to stage a revolt.

Australia, August 1850. The British parliament passes the Australian Colonies Government Act, giving the colonies self-government.

USA, 9 September 1850. California becomes the 31st state in the Union.

China, January 1851. Hong Xiuquan, the leader of the God-Worshippers, plans to declare himself heavenly king and set up a "heavenly kingdom of great peace" in Guangxi province.

London, 1 May 1851. The Great Exhibition opens.

China, 11 September 1851. The Taipings break out of the Qing military blockade and begin their march northward into central China.

Ottoman Empire, October 1851. Tsar Nicholas insists that Greek Orthodox monks must be allowed to maintain authority over the Holy Places in Palestine, bringing Russia into conflict with France over protection of the region.

France, 2 December 1851. President Louis Napoleon Bonaparte overthrows the legislative assembly in a *coup d'état* and dissolves the constitution.

USA, 1851. Former whaler Hermann Melville publishes *Moby Dick*, a novel about a prolonged and obsessive hunt for a deadly great white whale.

Italy, 1851. Giuseppe Verdi's opera *Rigoletto* is performed for the first time.

South Africa, 17 January 1852. At the Sand River Convention, the British recognize the independence of the Transvaal Boers.

China, 10 June 1852. Feng Yunshan—the close friend, principal lieutenant, and first convert of Hong Xiuquan, the leader of the God-Worshippers—is killed in battle at the age of thirty.

Britain, 14 September 1852. Arthur Wellesley, Duke of Wellington, the great soldier and statesman, dies.

Italy, 4 November 1852. Count Camillo Cavour becomes Prime Minister of Piedmont.

France, 2 December 1852. Louis Napoleon is proclaimed Emperor as Napoleon III.

Balkans, 3 March 1853. Having been forced to withdraw from Montenegro, which they invaded the previous year, the Ottomans sign a peace treaty with Prince Danilo of Montenegro. Danilo, who came to power the previous year on the death of his uncle, Prince-Bishop Peter II, has embarked on a campaign to secularize the Montenegrin government.

China, 19 March 1853. Taiping forces capture the large city of Nanjing on the lower Yangzi River.

Japan, July 1853. A U.S. squadron under Commodore Matthew Perry arrives off Edo (Tokyo) and demands that Japan open to trade with the outside world.

Ottoman Empire, 4 October 1853. Following Russia's refusal to withdraw from the Danubian principalities, the Ottomans declare war on Russia.

Black Sea, 3 January 1854. The British and French fleets enter the Black Sea to protect Ottoman coasts and shipping.

South Africa, February 1854. Following the British annexation of the territories north of the Orange River, Boer leader Andreas Pretorius instigates a revolt and forces the British back.

Europe, 12 March 1854. Britain and France form an alliance with the Ottoman Empire and two weeks later declare war on Russia.

Japan, 31 March 1854. The United States and Japan sign the Treaty of Kanagawa, opening the ports of Shimoda and Hakodate to American trade.

USA, 30 May 1854. The Kansas-Nebraska Act is passed, allowing settlers of the newly created territories of Kansas and Nebraska to choose between free land and slavery. The Missouri Compromise of 1820 is repealed, which banned slavery north of the southern boundary line of Missouri.

Crimea, 17 October 1854. The allies lay siege to the Russian naval base of Sevastopol and win another victory a week later at Balaclava.

Egypt, 30 November 1854. The Frenchman Ferdinand de Lesseps obtains from Said Pasha a 99-year concession to build a canal linking the Red Sea to the Mediterranean.

USA, 1854. Groups opposed to the Kansas-Nebraska Act meet in Jackson, Michigan, to form the Republican Party.

Angola, 1854. The British explorer David Livingstone arrives in Luanda after a journey from Bechuanaland (Botswana) and Cape Colony.

Italy, 26 January 1855. Count Camillo Cavour, the Prime Minister of Piedmont, takes Piedmont into the Crimean War alongside the allies. He agrees to send fifteen thousand men to the Crimea.

Panama, 28 January 1855. The 47-mile Panama railway, linking the Atlantic and Pacific Oceans across the Isthmus of Panama, is completed.

Russia, 2 March 1855. On the death of Tsar Nicholas, he is succeeded by his son Alexander II.

Japan, December 1855. Much of Edo (Tokyo) is destroyed by the great Ansei earthquake. Many people lose their lives in the resulting fires.

USA, 1855. Walt Whitman publishes his first book of poems, *Leaves of Grass*.

Paris, 30 March 1856. Britain, France, Russia, the Ottoman Empire, Piedmont, Austria, and Prussia sign the Treaty of Paris, ending the Crimean War and securing the neutrality of the Black Sea.

Germany, 1856. At Neanderthal, near Dusseldorf, the remains of a *hominid*, probably dating from 70,000 BC, are discovered.

Egypt, 1856. The first railway line in Africa, between Alexandria and Cairo, is inaugurated.

India, 10 May 1857. *Sepoys* in the Bengal army at Meerut in northern India mutiny against their British officers and seize Delhi the next day.

Britain, 25 June 1857. Albert, the husband of Queen Victoria, is made Prince Consort.

Tunisia, 10 September 1857. In an effort to modernize Tunisia, the *bey*, Muhammad, grants a charter guaranteeing the equal treatment of Muslims and Jews.

India, 20 September 1857. The British recapture Delhi.

Cochin China (Vietnam), September 1857. The French occupy Da Nang and Saigon.

France, 1857. Charles Baudelaire begins the Symbolist movement in France with his collection of poems *Les Fleurs du Mal*.

India, 21 March 1858. British forces lift the siege of Lucknow, ending the Indian Mutiny.

Mexico, 4 May 1858. The liberal government led by Benito Juarez establishes a capital at Vera Cruz. The conservatives, meanwhile, who control the army and are supported by the upper classes and the church, are ruling from Mexico City under the leadership of Miguel Miramon.

China, June 1858. The Treaties of Tianjin—signed by Russia, the United States, Britain, and France—provide for aggressive expansion of foreign power in China.

Japan, 29 July 1858. After much pressure, Japan signs a commercial treaty with the United States. The treaty opens Edo (Tokyo) and Osaka to foreign residents and permits freedom of worship.

India, 1 November 1858. Queen Victoria is proclaimed ruler of India. The East India Company is abolished, and the administration of India is transferred to the crown.

New York City, 1858. The Irish immigrant John Stephens founds an Irish revolutionary society whose members are known as the Fenians, or the Brotherhood.

France, 19 January 1859. Following the secret meeting between Napoleon III and Count Cavour at Plombieres the previous July, France and Piedmont sign a treaty of alliance.

Egypt, 25 April 1859. Work begins on the building of the Suez Canal.

Italy, 26 April 1859. Count Cavour rejects an Austrian ultimatum to Piedmont to disarm. Three days later Austrian troops invade Piedmont.

France, May 1859. France declares war on Austria.

Italy, May 1859. Revolutions instigated by the National Society, which is campaigning for a unified Italy under the king of Piedmont, break out in Tuscany, Modena, and Parma.

Italy, 4 June 1859. Piedmont and France crush Austria at Magenta, and two weeks later defeat them at Solferino.

Italy, 11 July 1859. Napoleon III and Franz Josef of Austria reach peace terms at Villafranca, leading to the resignation in protest of Count Cavour.

Britain, November 1859. Charles Darwin publishes his *Origin of Species by Means of Natural Selection*.

Australia, 1859. Queensland is established as a separate colony, with its capital at Brisbane.

India, 1859. The first power-loom is set up in India.

Britain, 1859. John Stuart Mill publishes his essay *On Liberty*, stating the principle that individual freedom should be complete, provided it does not interfere with the liberty of others.

England, 1859. While exiled in London, Karl Marx publishes his *Critique of Political Economy*, putting forward a "materialist" interpretation of history.

Britain, 1859. Edward Fitzgerald publishes his verse translation of the *Rubaiyat of Omar Khayyam*, the mediaeval Persian poet and philosopher of resignation.

Germany, 1859. Richard Wagner completes his opera *Tristan and Isolde*.

Piedmont, 21 January 1860. Count Camillo Cavour becomes prime minister again, with the intention of uniting the duchies of Parma, Modena, Romagna, and Tuscany. In March the four duchies vote in favor of union with Piedmont.

Italy, 24 March 1860. France signs a treaty with Piedmont at Turin. Piedmont is to annex central Italy, while France is promised Nice and Savoy.

Italy, 11 May 1860. Garibaldi lands at Marsala in Sicily.

China, 21 September 1860. The American F. T. Ward enlists foreigners in a volunteer corps to defend Shanghai against Taiping rebels.

China, 21 September 1860. Fighting continues in the second Opium War. Anglo-French forces defeat Qing troops at Baliqiao on the road to Beijing. In October Anglo-French troops occupy Beijing after several days spent looting the Summer Palace, which is ultimately burned to the ground.

Beijing, 25 October 1860. Following the signing of the Sino-British Convention of Beijing on the 24th, the Sino-French Convention is signed on the 25th, ending the Second Opium War.

Washington DC, 6 November 1860. Abraham Lincoln is elected President of the United States.

USA, 20 December 1860. South Carolina secedes from the Union.

Russia, 1860. The port of Vladivostok is founded on the coast of the Sea of Japan.

Prussia, 2 January 1861. On the death of his father, Wilhelm becomes kaiser.

USA, 8 February 1861. Following the example of South Carolina, other slave states secede from the union and form the Confederate States of America.

Italy, 18 February 1861. Following the capture of Gaeta by Piedmontese troops four days previously, King Victor Emmanuel II of Sardinia is proclaimed King of Italy.

Russia, 3 March 1861. Serfs are emancipated by Alexander II as part of a program of westernization.

Washington DC, 4 March 1861. Lincoln is sworn in as president.

South Carolina, 14 April 1861. Fort Sumter in Charleston falls to Confederate troops.

Virginia, 21 July 1861. The first thrust by Union forces toward the Confederate capital of Richmond is repulsed at Bull Run.

Washington DC, 22 July 1861. The senate passes the Crittenden Resolution, stating the war's main purpose as the preservation of the union, not the abolition of slavery.

China, 2 December 1861. Following the death of the Xianfeng emperor on 22 August, and the accession of Zaichun on 11 November, the two dowager empresses, Ci'an and Cixi, become regents.

Britain, 14 December 1861. The prince consort, Albert, dies of typhoid, to the great sorrow of Queen Victoria.

Romania, 23 December 1861. The European powers recognize the principality of Romania (Moldavia and Wallachia), which is ruled by Prince Alexander Cuza.

France, 1862. The *velocipede*, a forerunner of the bicycle, is invented.

Cochin China (Vietnam), 13 April 1862. France and Annam sign the Treaty of Saigon by which France annexes Cochin China.

Virginia, 2 June 1862. General Robert E. Lee assumes command of the Confederate armies of North Virginia.

Prussia, 24 September 1862. King Wilhelm I names Otto von Bismarck as Prime Minister.

USA, 22 September 1862. In a deliberate attempt to cause social chaos in the rebellious southern states, President Abraham Lincoln proclaims the freedom of slaves in the Confederate states as of 1 January 1863.

Indiana, 4 November 1862. Richard Gatling patents a gun that fires hundreds of rounds a minute by using a cluster of rotating barrels.

Nevada 1862. Samuel Clemens becomes a reporter, using the pen name Mark Twain.

Poland, February 1863. Polish nationalists rise up in revolt against Russian rule. The rebellion was prompted by a new law conscripting almost the entire population of young Polish men.

Denmark, 30 March 1863. King Frederick VII separates Schleswig from Holstein and incorporates it into his states.

New Zealand, May 1863. Fighting between Maoris and British settlers breaks out in Taranaki. Conflict erupted in 1859 over a controversial land purchase, and the 1861 truce has failed to maintain peace.

Virginia, 3 June 1863. Setting out with 75,000 Confederate troops, General Lee begins a second attempt to invade the Union states. One month later, the Confederate advance is stopped at Gettysburg. It is the turning point of the U.S. Civil War.

Mississippi, 4 July 1863. Confederate forces surrender at Vicksburg. Now that the union troops have control of this strategic town, the Confederacy is effectively split in two.

Cambodia, 11 August 1863. The French establish a protectorate in Cambodia.

Germany, 1 October 1863. The German Diet decides to take action against Denmark following the Danish annexation of Schleswig earlier this year.

Virginia, 4 April 1864. Lieutenant General Ulysses S. Grant receives his commission to command the Union troops and plans a consolidated strike against Confederate troops in a bid to end the fighting.

Mexico, 10 April 1864. The Austrian Archduke Maximilian is appointed emperor of Mexico with the backing of the French army.

China, 1 June 1864. The Taiping ruler and self-styled "younger brother of Jesus," Hong Xiuquan, kills himself.

China, 19 July 1864. Nanjing falls to imperial forces. A hundred thousand Taipings either commit suicide or are killed by Qing troops. This marks the end of the Taiping rebellion.

Vienna, 30 October 1864. With the Treaty of Vienna, Denmark gives up Schleswig, Holstein, and Lauenburg.

Atlanta, Georgia, 16 November 1864. General Sherman wreaks havoc in confederate Atlanta, determined that it will no longer serve as a major supply center for the confederacy.

Geneva, 1864. A multilateral agreement on the Red Cross—a voluntary relief society dedicated to the care of those wounded in war—is signed at the Geneva Convention. This is largely the work of Henri Dunant, a Swiss humanitarian who organized emergency aid for French and Austrian wounded soldiers at the battle of Solferino in June 1859.

Virginia, 5 April 1865. Union troops leave the Confederate capital, Richmond, a smoldering ruin.

Virginia 9 April 1865. Confederate General Robert E. Lee surrenders at the Appomattox Courthouse. Six days later, President Lincoln is killed by an assassin's bullet while attending a performance at Ford's Theater in Washington DC.

Virginia, 27 April 1865. John Wilkes Booth, the accused assassin of President Lincoln, is shot dead.

Germany, 14 August 1865. A convention signed at Gastein between Prussia and Austria allots Schleswig to Prussia and Holstein to Austria.

Washington DC, 18 December 1865. The 13th Amendment to the U.S. Constitution abolishes slavery.

Paris, 1865. Edouard Manet's painting *Olympia*, echoing Titian's *Venus of Urbino*, but showing a very worldly model in the same pose, causes a scandal at the Salon des Refusés where works rejected by the Salon of the Academy are exhibited.

Tennessee, 1865. The Ku Klux Klan is founded in Tennessee.

New York City, 10 May 1866. At the first post-war meeting of the National Women's Rights Convention, a unanimous vote confirms the organization of the American Equal Rights Association.

Germany, 8 June 1866. Prussia annexes Holstein, which came under Austrian rule by the Convention of Gastein the previous year.

Austria, 12 June 1866. Austria signs a secret treaty with France as conflict with Prussia escalates.

Germany, 16 June 1866. Having declared the German Confederation dissolved two days previously, Prussia invades Saxony, Hanover, and Hesse. Four days later, Prussia's ally, Italy, declares war on Austria.

Bohemia, 3 July 1866. Prussian troops defeat Austrians in Sadowa.

Prague, 23 August 1866. A treaty is signed that brings the war between Prussia and Austria to a close. Austria relinquishes its claims to Schleswig and Holstein and agrees to pay Prussia war reparations. As Italy came into the war on the side of Prussia, Austria gives up Venice in its favor.

Russia, 1866. Fyodor Dostoyevsky publishes an epic novel, *Crime and Punishment*, which brings him instant popularity.

Germany, 24 February 1867. The parliament of the North German Confederation is opened. The crown of Prussia controls the league and represents the confederation internationally. It schedules the convocation of an imperial diet, elected by universal male suffrage, to meet in Berlin to enact federal laws. Count Bismarck becomes chancellor of the confederation.

USA, 30 March 1867. Russia sells Alaska to the United States for a price of 7.2 million dollars.

Mexico, 19 June 1867. The Emperor Maximilian, placed on the Mexican throne and then abandoned by Napoleon III, is seized by the republican President Benito Juarez supporters and executed.

Canada, 1 July 1867. Four provinces have united to form the Canadian Federation: Quebec, Ontario, Nova Scotia, and New Brunswick.

Britain, 15 August 1867. Parliament passes a Reform Act—spearheaded by Benjamin Disraeli, the Chancellor of the Exchequer—which adds nearly one million more voters to the electorate by enfranchising most male urban ratepayers.

Britain, September 1867. Karl Marx publishes the first volume of *Das Kapital*.

Japan, 9 November 1867. The last shogun, Tokugawa Keiki, resigns in favor of the Meiji emperor Mutsuhito. Before his resignation, he had become a virtual prisoner in his palace at Kyoto.

Austria, 1 December 1867. Johannes Brahms' *German Requiem* is performed for the first time.

New York City, 1 January 1868. Susan B. Anthony begins publication of a weekly Suffragist journal called *The Revolution*.

USA, 28 July 1868. The 14th Amendment to the constitution is passed. This landmark ruling declares that the federal government has the responsibility of guaranteeing basic rights, effectively diminishing the power of the individual states.

Japan, October 1868. Edo is renamed Tokyo, and the new era is named *Meiji*.

USA, 5 May 1869. The Union Pacific meets the Central Pacific in Promontory Point Utah to form the first American transcontinental railroad.

Europe, 10 May 1869. France signs a secret treaty against Prussia with Austria and Italy.

Egypt, 17 November 1869. The Suez Canal opens.

USA, 10 December 1869. Women in the territory of Wyoming are given the vote.

Russia, 1869. Count Leo Tolstoy publishes *War and Peace*.

USA, 10 January 1870. The Rockefeller brothers, John D. and William, found the Standard Oil Company of Ohio.

Prussia, 14 July 1870. Otto von Bismarck, the Prime Minister of Prussia, publishes a doctored version of the Ems Telegram—a communication between himself and King William of Prussia about the Spanish succession—which is extremely insulting to the French.

Italy, 18 July 1870. At the first Church Council to be held in three hundred years, Pope Pius IX announces the doctrine of papal infallibility.

France, 19 July 1870. France declares war on Prussia.

France, early September 1870. On 1 September, the French are decisively defeated by the Prussians at Sedan, and Napoleon III capitulates the next day. On 4 September, a republic is proclaimed and a government of national defense is formed to continue the war against Prussia.

Paris, 19 September 1870. The Prussians lay siege to Paris.

Rome, 20 September 1870. Taking advantage of the French defeat at Sedan, Italian forces enter Rome and expel the papal troops.

Turkey, 1870. The German archaeologist Heinrich Schliemann begins excavations at Hissarlik, believed to be the site of Troy.

France, 18 January 1871. Wilhelm of Prussia is proclaimed emperor (*kaiser*) of a united Germany at Versailles.

France, 28 January 1871. Beset by famine and surrounded by Prussian troops, Paris surrenders. During the siege, balloons were used to maintain contact with the rest of the country.

Paris, 28 March 1871. The Paris Commune is declared.

Germany, 14 April 1871. The imperial constitution is adopted, providing for the election of a parliament of 382 members, the Reichstag.

Germany, 10 May 1871. France and Prussia sign a peace treaty at Frankfurt.

Rome, 13 May 1871. Victor Emmanuel II, the King of Italy, issues the Law of Guarantees, assuring the pope that the Vatican remains outside Italian jurisdiction and granting him freedom in the exercise of his spiritual ministry.

Paris, 28 May 1871. The Paris Commune is suppressed by troops from Versailles after a week of fighting. Some twenty thousand of the *communards* are executed.

Germany, 8 July 1871. Bismarck launches a cultural struggle, the *Kulturkampf*, against the Catholic Church by abolishing the Catholic department for spiritual affairs.

Japan, August 1871. Feudal domains are abolished, and prefectures are created as the new units of local administration. In October, the tenets of equality in taxation laws and compulsory, fee-paying education are established. A modern postal system is introduced.

Chicago, 9 October 1871. A great fire kills three hundred people, makes ninety thousand homeless, and causes 200 million dollars' worth of damage.

Germany, 4 July 1872. A law is promulgated as part of the *Kulturkampf* (culture war) banning all religious assemblies, particularly Jesuit ones.

Germany, September 1872. The emperors of Germany, Austria-Hungary, and Russia form an alliance in Berlin.

New York City, 19 November 1872. William "Boss" Tweed, the former head of Tammany Hall, the city's Democratic organization, is jailed for fraud and corruption.

Vienna, 9 May 1873. A crash on the Vienna stock exchange leads to worldwide economic crisis.

1875–1899

USA, 30 October 1875. Mary Baker Eddy publishes *Science and Health with Key to the Scriptures*, arguing that illness is illusory and laying the basis for Christian Science.

Egypt, 27 November 1875. Facing bankruptcy, Khedive Ismail Pasha sells shares in the Suez Canal to the British.

Dakota Territory, November 1875. War breaks out between the Sioux Indians of the Black Hills and white prospectors.

Germany, 1876. The engineer Nikolaus Otto builds an internal combustion engine.

Germany, 1876. The Bayreuth theater opens with the first complete performance of Richard Wagner's *Ring* cycle.

India, 1 January 1877. Queen Victoria is formally proclaimed Queen-Empress of India.

USA, 1 May 1877. President Hayes withdraws all federal troops from the south, ending what has become known as Radical Reconstruction in the aftermath of the U.S. Civil War.

Ottoman Empire, 3 March 1878. Russia and the Ottomans sign the Treaty of San Stefano, granting independence to Serbia, Montenegro, and Romania. Bulgaria becomes an autonomous state under Russian authority, and Bosnia and Herzegovina are granted reforms.

Germany, 2 June 1878. The Kaiser is badly wounded in a second assassination attempt, by a radical student, Karl Nobling. As a result, Bismarck passes an antisocialist law, placing many restraints on socialist meetings and banning trade union activities.

Germany, 13 July 1878. At the congress of Berlin, Britain, Russia, Austria, Germany, France, Italy, and the Ottoman Empire reach agreement on the future of the Balkan states that supersedes the terms of the treaty of San Stefano.

London, 26 November 1878. The American artist James McNeill Whistler wins damages of one farthing in a libel action against the critic John Ruskin, who, on seeing *Nocturne in Black and Gold: The Falling Rocket*, accused Whistler of "flinging a pot of paint in the public's face."

South Africa, 4 July 1879. British troops defeat the Zulus in the battle of Ulundi, later capturing their king, Cetewayo.

Germany, 4 August 1879. A law is passed making Alsace Lorraine a part of Germany.

Ireland, 18 August 1879. Michael Davitt founds the Irish Land League, calling for the land to be returned to the Irish people. Charles Parnell, leader of the Irish Party in the House of Commons, is invited to be the League president.

Chile, 8 October 1879. The Peruvian iron-clad battleship *Huascar* is destroyed by the Chileans off Antofagasta in the conflict over nitrate-rich land in the Atacama desert that began earlier this year.

Denmark, 12 December 1879. Henrik Ibsen's *Nora or A Doll's House* has its premier at the Royal Theater of Copenhagen.

South Africa, December 1880. The Boers declare war on the British and drive them out of the Transvaal. The uprising is led by Petrus Joubert, Paul Kruger, and Marthinus Pretorius.

Afghanistan, 1880. The Second Afghan War with Britain ends with the accession of Abdur Rahman Khan, the grandson of the kingdom's founder, Dost Muhammad, who supports British interests.

St.. Petersburg, 13 March 1881. Tsar Alexander II is assassinated.

Washington DC, 2 July 1881. President Garfield is seriously injured by an assassin. At his death, the Vice President Chester A. Arthur becomes president.

Transvaal, 3 August 1881. At the Pretoria Convention, Britain recognizes Transvaal's self-government.

Sudan, 1881. Muhammad Ahmed ibn Abdallah proclaims himself *al-Mahdi* (the expected guide) and calls for a holy war against the Europeans and the Egyptians.

Vietnam, 1881. France declares its sovereignty over Vietnam and sends troops down the Red River to occupy Tonkin.

Germany, 1881. Doctor Karl Eberth discovers the typhoid bacillus.

Serbia, 6 January 1882. Milan of Serbia declares himself king.

Missouri, 3 April 1882. The bank robber and train hijacker Jesse James is shot dead by a cousin seeking the ten-thousand-dollar reward offered by the authorities.

Egypt, January 1883. Britain unilaterally abolishes its joint rule with France over Egypt, giving the general consul for Great Britain almost unlimited power.

New York, 25 May 1883. The Brooklyn Bridge, designed by John A. Roebling to link New York City and Brooklyn, is opened.

Indochina (Vietnam), 25 August 1883. While fighting continues with the French, a treaty is signed at Hue recognizing Tonkin, Annam, and Cochin China as French protectorates. This is rejected by the Chinese, however, who regard these territories as part of a vassal state.

South China Sea, 26–27 August 1883. A volcanic explosion on the island of Krakatoa devastates the island and causes the death of 36,000 people.

Chile, 20 October 1883. The Treaty of Ancon finally ends the war among Chile, Peru, and Bolivia for land in the Atacama Desert, which is rich in nitrates. By the treaty Peru cedes Tarapaca to Chile, and Chile keeps Tacna and Arica for a period of ten years.

Egypt, 1883. The fundamentalist leader, the *Mahdi*, defeats the Egyptian army under General William Hicks and occupies Darfur and Bahr al Ghazal.

Washington DC, 6 March 1884. Some hundred suffragists, led Susan B. Anthony, present President Arthur with a demand that he voice public support for female suffrage.

Paris, 13 March 1884. A new Arab review is published, the *Indissoluble Link*, aimed at thwarting British policy in the east by developing a pan-Arab, rather than pan-Islamic, consciousness.

Southwest Africa, 24 April 1884. Bismarck cables Cape Town that South-West Africa (present-day Namibia) is now a German colony.

China, 11 May 1884. Li Hongzhang signs a convention in Tianjin with the French negotiator Fournier over Indochina (Vietnam). China agrees to recognize all past and future Franco-Vietnamese treaties, to open Yunnan and Guangxi to French trade, and to withdraw its troops to the Chinese frontier.

China, 26 October 1884. With both sides disregarding the Tianjin Convention, the Chinese court declares war on France.

London, 1884. The Reform Act introduced by Gladstone's government allows householders in the counties to vote and increases the total electorate from three to five million. By a separate act, parliamentary seats are redistributed so that representation corresponds to population.

Missouri, 1884. Mark Twain publishes *The Adventures of Huckleberry Finn*, the tale of an orphan and a runaway slave's journey on the Mississippi River.

South Africa, 1884. The first black Southern African newspaper, *Imvo zaba Nshundu* (*Voice of the Black People*), is founded in Xhosa.

Washington DC, 4 March 1885. Grover Cleveland is inaugurated as the first Democratic President since before the Civil War.

Central Africa, 30 April 1885. Leopold II of Belgium proclaims himself sovereign of the Congo Free State (present-day Zaire).

New York City, 19 June 1885. The Statue of Liberty arrives from France.

Ireland, 14 August 1885. The new British government establishes close relations with Charles Parnell and passes the Land Act, providing large state loans for Irish peasants to buy lands from the English landowners.

Paris, 1885. European vineyards are being destroyed by a plant louse called *phylloxera vasatrix*, brought over in American vines. The louse eats at the roots of the vines and is devastating the European wine trade.

Bavaria, 13 June 1886. The mad King Ludwig II and his private doctor drown in the Starnberger Lake near Schloss Berg under suspicious circumstances.

Arizona, 4 September 1886. The Apache leader Geronimo surrenders to General Nelson A. Miles after a decade of guerrilla fighting designed to deter settlers in New Mexico and Arizona.

Germany, November 1886. Karl Benz patents the first motor car.

Atlanta, Georgia, 1886. A pharmacist, Dr. Pemberton, produces a nonalcoholic fizzy drink made from coca leaves, water, and sugar called Coca Cola.

London, June 20–21, 1887. England rejoices as Queen Victoria celebrates her Golden Jubilee.

Russia, 1887. Tchaikovsky composes his ballet, *Swan Lake*.

Germany, 9 March 1888. Kaiser Wilhelm dies, and his only son, the crown prince, succeeds him as Frederick III. On Frederick's death at Potsdam after a three-month reign, his son succeeds as Kaiser Wilhelm II.

Brazil, 13 May 1888. Slavery is abolished, despite fierce resistance by the planters, thanks to the efforts of two societies founded in Rio de Janeiro in 1880, the Sociedade Brasileira contra a Escradidao and the Associacao Central Emancipacionista.

USA, 1888. George Eastman perfects the first Kodak camera.

South Africa, 1888. Paul Kruger is re-elected president of the Transvaal.

Germany, 1888. The physicist Heinrich Hertz discovers electromagnetic waves.

France, 1888. The Dutch artist Vincent van Gogh moves to Aries, Provence, where he paints *Sunflowers*, *The Drawbridge*, *Yellow Chair and Pipe*, and *The Cafe Terrace*.

Austria, 30 January 1889. Archduke Rudolf, the liberal crown prince of the Austrian Empire, commits suicide with his mistress, Marie Vetsera, at Mayerling. Archduke Franz Ferdinand, the Emperor's nephew, becomes is his heir.

Britain, February 1889. Richard Pigott, an Irish journalist, admits forging a politically damaging letter purporting to be from Charles Parnell, the leader of the Irish home rule group of Ministers of Parliament.

Istanbul, 29 October 1889. Britain, Germany, France, Austria, Spain, Italy, the Netherlands, Russia, and the Ottoman Empire sign a convention declaring the Suez Canal neutral and open to all ships in wartime as well as in peacetime.

Germany, 20 March 1890. Kaiser Wilhelm II accepts the resignation of his Reich Chancellor Otto von Bismarck. Bismarck had been the determining force in Germany's policies since its inception in 1871.

Ethiopia, May 1890. The Italians proclaim a protectorate over the Red Sea coast (present-day Eritrea).

Berlin, 1 July 1890. Germany and Britain sign the Heligoland Treaty, by which Germany gives up claims in East Africa, including Zanzibar, in return for the British island of Heligoland, off the Elbe estuary.

Washington DC, 2 July 1890. The Sherman Anti-Trust Act, banning trade monopolies, is passed.

South Africa, 17 July 1890. Cecil Rhodes becomes prime minister of Cape Colony.

South Dakota, December 1890. The U.S. Seventh Cavalry kills 153 Minneconjou Sioux at Wounded Knee.

Britain, December 1890. Charles Parnell is forced to resign as leader of the Irish party at Westminster after being cited as corespondent in the O'Shea divorce case.

Rome, 15 May 1891. Pope Leo XIII publishes an encyclical on the condition of workers, applying Christian principles to the relations between capital and labor.

Germany, 6 May 1891. The triple alliance between Germany, Austria, and Italy is renewed.

Germany, October 1891. The Social Democratic Party adopts a Marxist program at its Erfurt conference.

Russia, 1891. Work starts on the building of a Trans-Siberian railway to link the Ural Mountains with the port of Vladivostok.

Russia, 1891. Thousands of Jews are evicted from Moscow and forced into ghettoes.

Britain, 1891. Arthur Conan Doyle publishes *The Adventures of Sherlock Holmes*, a collection of short stories featuring the "world's first consulting detective" and his chronicler James Watson.

New York City, 1 January 1892. An office is opened on Ellis Island to cope with the vast flood of immigrants to the United States, many of them fleeing from political and racial persecution in Russia and Central Europe.

Russia, 18 December 1892. Tchaikovsky's ballet *The Nutcracker* is performed for the first time.

Germany, 1892. Count Alfred von Schlieffen, the chief of the German general staff, devises a plan for offensive military action based on the premise that, in any future war, Germany would have to fight both France and Russia. The plan provides for swift, decisive action against France, while maintaining a defensive position against Russia.

Germany, 1892. The engineer Rudolf Diesel patents the first internal combustion engine.

Hawaii, 13 April 1893. U.S. troops are ordered to leave Hawaiian soil, ending a protectorate established four months previously, when Queen Liliuokalani was deposed.

Germany, 13 July 1893. A bill is passed that substantially increases the size of the German army and reduces the terms of military service in the infantry from three to two years.

Russia, 27 December 1893. Russia and France reach an *entente*, agreeing on mutual aid in the event of war with Germany.

USA, 1893. As a result of a stock-market crash, six hundred banks, 74 railways and fifteen thousand commercial businesses collapse.

Chicago, 1893. Swami Vivekenanda, who has founded a mission in India to preach the modern Hindu message of

Ramakrishna, makes a great impact at the World Conference of Religions.

Korea, 23 July 1894. Japanese troops take over the Korean imperial palace, carry off Queen Min and her children to the Japanese legation, and attack the Chinese offices.

Korea, 1 August 1894. War is formally declared between Japan and China.

South Africa, August 1894. Cecil Rhodes, newly appointed minister of native affairs in the Cape government, introduces a "native policy" to attract Afrikaaner support in the Boer republics. It includes depriving African landholders of the right to vote

France, 15 October 1894. Captain Alfred Dreyfus, a Jewish army officer, is arrested for betraying military secrets to Germany.

Russia, 1 November 1894. Alexander III dies and is succeeded as tsar by his son Nicholas II.

China, 21 November 1894. Japan defeats China at Port Arthur.

Hawaii, 24 November 1894. Sun Yatsen organizes the Revive China Society in Honolulu.

Chicago, 14 December 1894. Eugene Debs, the president of the American Railway Union, is jailed for six months for ignoring an injunction to end the Pullman railway strike, which began in July.

Japan, 17 April 1895. China and Japan sign the Treaty of Shimonoseki. China recognizes the independence of Korea and cedes Formosa (Taiwan), the Pescadores Islands, and the Liaodong peninsula to Japan. However, Russia, France, and Germany intervene in the settlement between China and Japan, forcing Japan to return the Liaodong peninsula to China.

New York State, 26 August 1895. A hydroelectric plant, designed by Nikola

Tesla and built by Westinghouse, opens at Niagara Falls.

China, 30 November 1895. China concludes a secret treaty with Russia, allowing Russia to build the Trans-Siberian railway through Manchuria to the Russian Pacific port of Vladivostok.

South Africa, 29 December 1895. Leander Starr Jameson, an agent of the British South Africa Company, invades the Boer republic of Transvaal with 470 men.

Vienna, 1895. In collaboration with Joseph Breuner, Sigmund Freud publishes *Studies in Hysteria*.

France, 1895. Armand Peugeot perfects a gasoline-driven engine and founds the Peugeot automobile company.

France, 1895. Emile Durkheim publishes *The Rules of Sociological Method*.

South Africa, 2–3 January 1896. Following his defeat on the 2nd by the Boers at Krugersdorp, Jameson surrenders at Doom Kop on the 3rd. Kaiser William II sends a telegram to Paul Kruger, the South African president, congratulating him on the suppression of Jameson. The telegram causes a storm of indignation in Britain, where it is seen as an attempt by Germany to expand its influence in Africa.

South Africa, 6 January 1896. Cecil Rhodes is forced to resign as Prime Minister of Cape Colony because of his implication in the Jameson raid.

Canada, 12 August 1896. Gold is discovered in a creek off the Klondike river in the Yukon Territory.

Sudan, 21 September 1896. Herbert Kitchener, who took control of the Anglo-Egyptian army in March with the object of reconquering the Sudan, seizes the town of Dongola.

Zimbabwe, 13 October 1896. Cecil Rhodes makes peace with the Matabele chiefs who revolted against his rule.

Ethiopia, 26 October 1896. The Italians and the Ethiopians sign the Treaty of Addis Ababa by which Italy recognizes the independence of Ethiopia and retains only the colony of Eritrea.

France, 1896. The Hungarian Jewish writer Theodor Herzl publishes *The Jewish State*, in which he advocates the formation of a Jewish state to solve the "Jewish Question."

Britain, 14 May 1897. The Italian physicist Guglielmo Marconi accomplishes the first communication by wireless telegraphy.

Britain, 22 June 1897. Queen Victoria celebrates her Diamond Jubilee.

China, 15 December 1897. Russian warships enter Port Arthur on the Liaodong peninsula.

France, 28 December 1897. The playwright, Edmond Rostand, establishes his reputation with the first production of *Cyrano de Bergerac*.

Egypt, 1897. Muhammad Abduk publishes his *Epistle*, a modern interpretation of Islam.

Switzerland, 1897. Theodor Herzl convenes the first Zionist Congress at Basel.

Britain, 1897. The physicist Joseph John Thomson discovers that atoms include very small, negatively charged particles called electrons.

Cuba, 15 February 1898. The U.S. warship *Maine* blows up in Havana harbor. Spanish sabotage is suspected.

USA, 25 April 1898. The United States declares war on Spain.

Philippines, 1 May 1898. U.S. forces under George Dewey destroy the Spanish fleet in Manila Bay.

China, 1898. Britain obtains the New Territories of Hong Kong under a 99-year lease. In addition, Britain obtains

Weihaiwei on the Shandong peninsula as a leased territory. France acquires Guangzhouwan in Guangdong province under a similar lease arrangement.

China, 1898. Devastating floods caused by breaks in the Yellow River banks in Shandong are followed by a prolonged and severe drought in northern China. This conjunction of natural disasters and foreign aggression contributes to the rise of the violent antiforeign Boxer movement.

France, 1898. The sculptor Auguste Rodin unveils his *Monument to Balzac*.

Moscow, 1898. Fyodor Chaliapin, the Russian bass, makes his first appearance as *Boris Godunov*.

Hawaii, 12 August, 1898. The sovereignty of the Republic of Hawaii is transferred to the United States.

Philippines, 13 August, 1898. Manila, the capital of the Philippines, falls to the United States.

Sudan, 2 September, 1898. Sir Herbert Kitchener leads the British to victory over the *Mahdists* at Omdurman and takes Khartoum.

Paris, 10 December, 1898. The United States and Spain sign a treaty ending their war in the Caribbean and the Pacific. The United States acquires Cuba, Puerto Rico, Guam, and for a twenty-million-dollar indemnity, the Philippines.

South Africa, 5 June 1899. Talks at Bloemfontein between Alfred Milner, the high commissioner in South Africa, and President Kruger break down over the issue of granting the vote to Uitlanders.

The Hague, 29 July 1899. A peace conference attended by representatives from 26 states establishes a permanent international court of arbitration.

France, 7 August 1899. The guilt of Captain Alfred Dreyfus, condemned and deported for treason in 1894, is confirmed by a court martial at Rennes. He is then pardoned by the French President Émile Loubet.

USA, 6 September 1899. The Secretary of State, John Hay, embarks on an open door policy toward China, urging the European powers and Japan to respect the territorial integrity of China and pursue a policy of free trade with the country.

South Africa, 12 October 1899. War breaks out between the British and Boers from the Transvaal and Orange Free State. The Boers surround Mafeking two days later, then lay siege to Kimberley.

Moscow, 27 October 1899. *Uncle Vanya* by Anton Chekhov is performed for the first time, at the Art Theatre. ❏

CABRAL AND THE FOUNDING OF BRAZIL

April 25, 1500

The navigator Pedro Álvares Cabral (1467–1520) was commissioned by the Portuguese king Manuel I to lead an expedition to India with the intention of establishing as many trading colonies and Christian missions as he could. He set sail from Lisbon on March 9, 1500, with fifteen hundred men and a fleet of thirteen ships, one of which was under the command of Bartholomew Dias, who twelve years prior had become the first European to sail around the Cape of Africa.

Based on charts supplied by Vasco da Gama, the expedition set a southwesterly course. On April 22, they sighted an unfamiliar coastline with a lofty, circular mountain (Monte Pascoal). On the next day Cabral's ship dropped anchor off the coast. Thinking he had come ashore on an island, he named it Vera Cruz (True Cross), and claimed it for Portugal by erecting a Cross. On April 25, the entire fleet sailed into a harbor, which they named Porto Seguro, and established the first European colony in what would eventually be Brazil, named after the region's abundant red-colored trees.

As many as 400 natives emerged to greet their new visitors. In his role as missionary, Cabral decided to show them an example of Christian piety. He knelt before the Cross and kissed it. But the natives, acquainted with only stone implements, seemed to be impressed more by the iron tools

The sea captain Pedro Alvares Cabral set sail from Lisbon March 9, 1500

used to create Cabral's object of veneration than they were with his attempts at conversion.

On May 3, leaving a handful of crew to oversee this inadvertently discovered land, Cabral and his fleet set out toward India. As they approached the Cape of Africa they encountered a fierce storm and half their vessels sank, drowning their crews, among them Bartholomew Dias. The

remaining fleet continued up the east coast of Africa making new discoveries, the most significant: present-day Madagascar. It finally arrived at Calicut, in India, on September 13.

After establishing a series of trade and Christian outposts, the four remaining ships of Cabral's fleet, loaded with spices, set sail for Portugal and arrived on June 23, 1501. ❑

JULIUS II

Rome, November 1, 1503

As elected successor to Pope Pius III, who died after only one month in the papal office, Cardinal Giuliano della Rovere took the name Julius II.

Politics. Julius was a typical representative of the Renaissance papacy in that his political ambitions and fostering of art superseded his concern for the pastoral needs of his flock. Through skilled diplomacy and beneficial alliances he succeeded over the course of his ten-year papacy in winning back much of the territory the Church had lost. He checked the ambitions of Cesare Borgia, illegitimate son of Pope Alexander VI (1492–1503), and ousted him from his office of administering the Papal States given to him by his father. Cesare had to return to Julius lands in Romagna, Umbria, and Siena. In 1506, Julius also regained Bologna and Perugia. He founded

Cesare Borgia

the League of Cambrai, an alliance with France that combined against Venice. When that collapsed, he reversed course and sided with Venice against France (the so-called Holy League), acquiring Parma, Piacenza, and

SHIISM ADOPTED IN PERSIA

Persia, 1502

In accordance with the firmly held religious beliefs of Shah Ismail, the new Safavid ruler of Persia, conversion to Shiism was mandated. The policy was carried out with ruthless dedication; Sunni dissenters faced execution.

Shah Ismail came to power in 1501 after routing an Ak Koyunlu force of 30,000 men at Sharur and

marching into Tabriz. The Safavids were natives of Persia and claimed to be descendants of the Prophet Muhammad. Under Khwaja Ali, head of the order from 1391 to 1427, they moved away from Sunnism to militant Shiism based on their belief in a line of twelve infallible *imams*, descending from the Prophet through Ali.

To assist the conversion of the Persian people, Shah Ismail imported *ulema* (Islamic legal scholars) from the Arab lands of Bahrain, Hilla in Mesopotamia, and particularly from Jabal Amil in Lebanon. Many leading Shiite theologians were of Amili origin, notably al-Karaki, the most important religious figure. ❑

Shah Ismail I, of Persia

POPE OF THE HIGH RENAISSANCE

Bramante: The Tempietto of San Pietro in Montorio, Rome

Michelangelo, *The Last Judgment*, fresco in the Sistine Chapel

Raphael, *The Sistine Madonna*

Reggio and driving the French out of Italy. With the expansion and consolidation of the Papal States Julius created the foundations of the political power of the modern papacy.

Architecture. In 1506, Julius commissioned the architect Bramante (Donato d'Angelo Lazzari) to build St. Peter's Basilica on the site of the old St. Peter's Church, which had been built in the fourth century. Traditionally considered to have been erected over the grave of St. Peter, the old church had fallen into disrepair and the decision was made to build a new church rather than repair the old

one. Bramante's design was profoundly influenced by classical models such as the Pantheon, attempting to achieve a balanced harmony of architectural elements that would at the same time meet traditional liturgical needs. The church was to take the form of a Greek cross with a domed chapel at each of the four corners. Although ground was broken in 1506, St. Peter's was not completed according to Bramante's design. After his death in 1513, the architects who took over the commission altered the plan and expanded the church so that the principal building now has a single dome and a Baroque façade.

Painting and Sculpture. Among the many artists who received commissions from the pope the most famous was Michelangelo. In 1513, he began his marble sculpture of Moses intended for the never-completed tomb of his patron. A masterpiece of the high Renaissance, Moses is invested with intense emotion and wonderfully rendered. Michelangelo captures Moses upon his descent from Sinai where he received God's commandments. His countenance suffused with anger, he is about to castigate the Israelites,

who in their faithlessness have built a golden calf and worship it. Also from the hand of Michelangelo came the perfect form of David, born from the artist's meditation upon classical models. The simple form of the marble block from which it emerges remains preserved in the finished work.

From 1508 to 1512, Michelangelo worked at the behest of Julius on the ceiling of the Sistine Chapel. Together with his painting *The Last Judgment*, it is considered to be a highpoint of Western art. The artist succeeded in solving the many compositional problems posed by such a large-scale work with numerous curved surfaces by submitting the overall work to an architectural scheme. The ceiling presents nine scenes from Genesis beginning with the separation of light and dark and

proceeding to Noah's ark. The central episode is God's creation of Adam, and the representation of God's hand reaching toward but not quite reaching Adam's compresses an entire worldview into one indelible image.

Other artists were hard at work decorating rooms in the Vatican Palace. In 1508, the pope commissioned the 25-year-old Raphael with adorning what was intended to be the pope's private library. His frescoes for what has come to be known as the Stanza della Segnatura rank among his greatest achievements. They include *Parnassus*, the *Disputa* and the *School of Athens*. Raphael, well-known for his beautiful Madonnas including the *Sistine Madonna*, also left behind a magnificent portrait of the aging Julius, which hangs in London's National Gallery. ❏

An Alliance of Capital and Politics

Augsburg Germany, 1515

The rise of the Fugger family of bankers perfectly illustrates the increasing importance of banking and capital interest in the political environment of Europe. The Fuggers became kingmakers; it was their money that bought Charles I of Spain the office of emperor. In return, Charles I granted them the right to exploit silver and mercury deposits in his Central American colonies.

It was 150 years prior that Ulrich Fugger, a poor weaver, settled in Augsburg and set up a small textile business that expanded into an industry exporting fustian, buying Levantine cotton from Venice, and dealing in spices. The industry was so successful that Ulrich was able to diversify into metals—obtaining, a monopoly of silver and copper mines in the Tyrol and much of the rest of eastern Europe. With the support of Count Sigismund of Tyrol, the Fuggers' syndicate was soon able to dictate the price of these precious metals.

Ulrich's sons built the House of Fugger into the most wealthy

House of the Fuggers in Augsburg, built in 1494 (picture postcard after a color drawing by Karl Nikolai, 1910)

and powerful bank in Europe. Jacob Fugger II was known as "Jacob the Rich." He had the right to mint coinage in Rome and controlled the biggest trade network on the Continent. Bankers had become strictly entrepreneurial, with the Fuggers vying with their rivals for more exploitation in the Americas. Their agents acted more like *conquistadores* than businessmen. At the same time, new powerful banks began to develop in Italy, notably in Genoa. ❑

The First Subsidized Housing

Point of Interest

Jacob Fugger with his bookkeeper

Jacob Fugger II (Jacob the Rich) benefiting from the handling of the Church's sale of indulgences, decided to lay up his treasure for the good of his soul by devoting some of the money he had made to charitable works.

In 1509, he built the Fugger Chapel in the old church of St. Anna. In 1516, he dedicated the first subsidized housing for the poor in his own name and that of his deceased brothers Ulrich and Georg. The project consisted of 67 small houses. The rent for a three-room home with kitchen and garden was one Rhenish gilder per annum. In the seventeenth century, the stonemason Franz Mozart, grandfather of the composer Wolfgang Amadeus Mozart, was one of the residents of the Fugger-built housing complex. ❑

Eastern Economy in Decline

Indian Ocean, 1510

The Mamluk Dynasty that had ruled Arabia for more than a century—weakened by a succession of incompetent, corrupt, and degenerate sultans—found itself faced with a devastating threat of economic decline. Since the eighth century, Arab traders dominated the lucrative routes to the east, cultivating extensive contacts with India. Their ships sailed across the Indian Ocean and their caravans brought goods overland to the great cities of the eastern Mediterranean.

However, the new adventurousness of European explorers put that monopoly in jeopardy. As soon as the Portuguese explorer Vasco da Gama discovered a new route to the Indies, sailing round the Cape of Good Hope, Portugal and other European nations began setting up their own trading posts. Attacks on Muslim shipping in the Red Sea and the Indian Ocean became increasingly frequent. The Portuguese set up a trading post in Calicut on the west coast of India. Despite a threat from the Mamluk sultan, Qansawh al Ghawri, to destroy Christian Holy Places, the Europeans continued to establish themselves as the new spice merchants. Further European exploration added to Arabia's difficulties, although the explorers headed west rather than east. The discovery of the New World in 1492 shifted the center of world affairs to the west. ❑

MACHIAVELLI'S *THE PRINCE*

Florence, 1513

In an attempt to regain favor with his former employers, a senior civil servant, Niccolo Machiavelli, wrote a remarkable study of political power, its uses and abuses, entitled *The Prince*.

In 1498, Niccolo Machiavelli, aged 29, was appointed secretary to the Council of Ten, the second most important executive tier in the republic of Florence. The council handled wars (at a time when war was an almost permanent feature among the Italian city-states) and internal security. In this capacity he met Cesare Borgia, upon whom many believe he based the prince in his book.

When the Medicis returned to Florence in 1512, Machiavelli suspected of participating in a conspiracy against them, lost his position, was imprisoned, and tortured. After his release he retired to his property in Tuscany and sought to rehabilitate his reputation through his writings. In 1513, Machiavelli wrote the work for which he is remembered, *The Prince*, though it was published only posthumously, in 1532.

The Prince offers a stark contrast with the medieval concept that the monarch should try to embody the highest ideals of Christian virtue, that he was God's representative on earth. Machiavelli eschewed considerations of ideals, and in keeping with developments in Renaissance art and culture sought to focus on the realities of political power. His prince needs to concern himself with getting and holding on to power. The ruler's primary concern is to preserve the essential nature of the state. Starting from a pessimistic view of humanity, Machiavelli insisted that the prince must distinguish between his personal convictions and the requirements of his office. Circumstances will arise that will require him to depart from ethical norms.

Machiavelli was able to regain some of the favor he had lost. In 1519, he was entrusted by the Medicis with carrying out various small commissions and in 1525, he oversaw the rebuilding of the city's walls. But with the installation of the Republic in 1527 he lost his position once again and died embittered shortly after. ❑

Title page of Machiavelli's *The Prince*

Niccolo Machiavelli (terracotta bust, Palazzo Vecchio, Florence)

MIXTECS: MASTER CRAFTSMEN

Mexico, 16th century

The Mixtecs inhabited what is now the Mexican State of Oaxaca. Their exceptional artistic abilities were, in turn, a major influence on Aztec culture. Recognizable features of their style include polychrome painted ceramics and bowls made from rock crystal, beautiful gold and silver jewelry often inlaid with pearls and precious stones, and turquoise mosaics and carvings.

Seven codices survive from the pre-Columbian period, among them the Borgia Codex. These are picture books that recount the history of the tribe. Some are made of deerskin, others of tree bark. ❑

Jeweled mask from the Mixtec site of Monte Alban

PORTUGAL CONTROLS SPICE TRADE

Malacca, 1511

Portugal positioned itself to dominate the lucrative spice trade with the east through the operations of its brilliant naval strategist, Alfonso d'Albuquerque. With his capture of Malacca, which commanded the passage from the Indian Ocean to the South China Sea, he established a string of naval bases and trading posts running from the Red Sea through Goa in India to the Far East. The siege of Malacca severely strained his resources in men and ships. Because of the stiff resistance of defenders and the problems caused by monsoons, he had to remain in the area for almost a year. During that time, Goa, a city built on an island and the center of a shipbuilding industry, almost fell to the Muslim sultan of Bijapur.

A Portuguese accountant assigned to the newly established royal factory at Malacca reported: "Should anyone ask what advantage to his exchequer the king, our lord, can derive from Malacca, there is no doubt that once the influence is finished that this ex-king of Malacca still exercises—the town is of such importance and profit that it seems to me it has no equal in the world."

Control of Malacca ensured the Portuguese a free hand in the trade of Oriental spices, such as pepper, cinnamon, nutmeg, and cloves. ❑

Portuguese cathedral in Goa

At the beginning of the sixteenth century, Europe was in a state of crisis. Economic changes—the first signs of a growing economic disparity between social classes, the introduction of new production techniques and organization, and the rise in prices combined with the stagnation of wages—had resulted in material problems. At the same time people also lived in fear of disorder, wars, coups, and the Ottoman threat to the West.

This atmosphere of crisis and people's awareness of it resulted in a strongly externalized devoutness, a heightened concern for salvation, and a growing criticism of the papal court and the clergy, which seemed to have abandoned spiritual values for the sake of worldly goods. Its continuous striving to increase its revenues was reflected in its growing bureaucracy and its materialistic approach to ecclesiastical means of grace and salvation. Many aspects of faith and pastoral services could only be obtained with money.

LUTHER AND THE GERMAN REVOLUTION

The Augustinian monk Martin Luther's *Ninety-five Theses* against the sale of indulgences, published on October 31, 1517, was the cause of the Reformation in Germany and resulted in the schism within existing religious structures, as well as the emergence of independent denominations besides the Catholic Church in Europe. The *Ninety-five Theses* aroused interest far beyond Church circles because they questioned not only the relationship between the individual and God, but also financial and economic matters relating to the Church.

In 1519 Luther broke all relations with Rome and in the following year he summarized his teachings in three pamphlets that soon enjoyed widespread circulation benefiting from the development of the printing press.

According to Luther's teachings, the way for man to ensure salvation was through faith alone, not through good deeds, and further, the mediation of the clergy between God and man was not necessary. When he appeared before the Diet of Worms in 1521, Luther was declared an outlaw of the Church. He was then exiled to Wartburg Castle where he translated the New Testament from the Greek original text into German.

In spite of the Edict of Worms, Luther's teachings spread throughout Germany. His followers formed a movement whereby the anti-clerical attitude of the people was often linked to economic and social demands. During the Peasants' War (1525), the peasants, referring to the Gospels and supported theologically by Thomas Müntzer, fought for the abolition of the corvée—compulsory, unpaid labor—and of serfdom, as well as the abolition of class differences. When Luther's exhortation to the peasants and princes failed to bring peace, he denounced the revolt and called upon the princes to put down the revolt in their capacity as authorities appointed by God. Subsequently the nobility promulgated principles of the Reformation in their

Martin Luther posting his *Ninety-five Theses* against the sale of indulgences on the door of the castle church in Wittenberg.

territories. By taking over former Church possessions, the evangelical princes were able to strengthen their position considerably in relation to the central administration of the Empire.

HOPE AND CHANGE

This development was encouraged by the imperial policy of Charles V. At first he saw the Reformation as little more than a tiresome rebellion that went against his interests. This was all the more so because the Reformation often took on a social revolutionary character and various interest groups all hoped to benefit from it. Such a change was only conceivable if it was at the expense of the emperor. Charles

V therefore tried to keep the movement under control by making small concessions. In 1530 he failed in his attempt to save the unity of the Church at the Diet of Augsburg; in the meantime large parts of the German Empire had adopted Luther's teachings, including Hesse and Saxony. Religious conflict was the order of the day, until the Treaty of Augsburg (1555) succeeded in reaching agreement between warring parties: from now on, people had to follow the religious denomination of their sovereign prince, albeit only the Lutheran and Catholic denominations were recognized. This led to a split within the Empire as well as the strengthening of the aristocracy and nationalist tendencies in relation to imperial rule. Charles V abdicated in 1556.

Meanwhile the Roman Church was also experiencing a period of renewal and change. The Council of Trent halted the secularization of the papal court and laid the foundation of modern Catholicism. The Roman Church made hardly any concessions in matters of doctrine but it did make some in its code of conduct for the clergy. The Counter-Reformation, initiated by the Jesuits, began to take hold in Germany.

ZWINGLI AND CALVIN

The Reformation did not remain restricted to Germany but found followers throughout Europe. There was a strong Reformation movement in Zurich introduced in 1519 by the pastor Ulrich Zwingli. His teachings differed from those of Luther in their stronger rejection of all Catholic rituals, particularly in the interpretation of communion. Zwingli saw the taking of communion merely as a symbolic act, a commemorative meal, while Luther believed, in accordance with the New Testament, that Christ was present in the bread and wine. Switzerland continued to play an important role in the Reformation after Zwingli's death (1531). In 1536 a new Protestant movement made its appearance in Geneva: Calvinism. The French-born John Calvin fled to Switzerland in 1534 because, as a Protestant, he feared for his life in France. In Switzerland he was able to develop his Protestant ideas. His aim was to completely "Christianize" human life and to submit the authorities to the control of the Church. The Spanish, on the other hand, should be free of state intervention. Calvin insisted on a strict code of behavior, forbidding dancing and gambling among other things.

According to Calvin's teachings, man's wealth on earth could well reflect his salvation after death and those chosen by God could be granted prosperity on earth. His Protestant movement spread to large parts western Europe (France, Scotland, and the Netherlands) and eastern Europe (Poland, Hungary, and Transylvania).

THE CHURCH IN ENGLAND

From the very beginning, the English Reformation was much more a political than a religious movement. The Reformation in England was not initiated by the Church or the clergy but by the English king, Henry VIII. Through a series of legislative acts, he gradually moved the English Church away from Rome. His initial reason was the pope's refusal to annul Henry VIII's marriage to Catherine of Aragon, who had failed to bear him a son. As a result he had his first marriage annulled by the Archbishop of Canterbury (1533) to enable him to marry Anne Boleyn (who later became queen). This decision was justified by the "Act in Restraint of Appeals," previously passed by Parliament, that denied all foreign powers—including Rome—jurisdiction in English matters. Henry's efforts to free the English Church from the pope's authority was also prompted by power politics. He proclaimed himself head of the English Church (1534), dissolved the monasteries, and confiscated their possessions.

After Henry VIII's death (1547), the reform movement was briefly interrupted under the reign of his daughter, Mary Tudor, married to Philip II of Spain, who tried to reintroduce Catholicism. After her death, Mary was succeeded on the throne by Elizabeth I, the daughter of Anne Boleyn, who was considered illegitimate by the Catholic Church. She completed the reform of the Church initiated by Henry VIII, not least because of her hostility to Spain. The Anglican Church became established during her reign and today its essential features are still as she determined them. Its dogma is based on Luther but its rituals are Catholic. Elizabeth did not tolerate any deviation in the Anglican faith. The radical Calvinists (Puritans) were oppressed and persecuted, later fleeing to the New World.

THE PERSECUTION OF THE HUGUENOTS

From the mid-sixteenth century, the Swiss interpretation of the Reformation had been spreading into France. The Huguenots, as the French followers of Calvinism were called, were mostly members of the aristocracy. Because of their efforts to have their faith recognized, including their civil and political rights, the Huguenots were oppressed by the French crown. The first of the eight Huguenot wars began at Vassy in 1562. In 1563, certain areas were set aside in which the Huguenots were allowed to practice their faith. But in 1572, the leaders of the Huguenot aristocracy, who had gathered in Paris to attend the wedding of the Huguenot Henry, King of Navarre, were all murdered together with thousands of their followers in the St. Bartholomew's Day Massacre.

When Henry of Navarre became the legitimate successor to the throne, King Henry III joined the Catholic League and Spain (1585) withdrew all of the rights that the Huguenots had been awarded and unleashed the eighth Huguenot war, at the end of which Henry of Navarre succeeded to the French throne as Henry IV (1589). To preserve France's national unity, he converted to Catholicism (1593), but he gave the Huguenots the freedom to practice their religion (1598). But later, in 1685, under Louis XIV, the Huguenots lost so many of their religious privileges that they were forced to live in hiding. Half-a-million of them fled France for North America, Great Britain, the Netherlands, Switzerland, and Brandenburg-Prussia.

THE THIRTY YEARS WAR

The religious conflict spread to other parts of Europe at the beginning of the seventeenth century, developing into the power struggle of the Thirty Years War. The opposition to the Catholicism was particularly strong in Bohemia. In 1618 this resistance culminated in an uprising in Prague and this in turn led to war against the imperial Habsburg rule. For the next 30 years, Germany became the battlefield of a war that involved most of Europe. The Treaty of Westphalia (1648) endorsed the Treaty of Augsburg (1555), and recognized both Catholics and Lutherans. The religion of the sovereign prince would determine the religion of his subjects, but greater toleration was afforded to dissenters for those regions not directly within Habsburg control. ❑

Henry VIII founded the Anglican Church. Illustration of the *Great Bible*, 1538/39.

THE SALE OF INDULGENCES

Rome, 1517

The advent of a money economy and the growing financial needs of the Catholic Church launched the practice of selling indulgences. Indulgences, which would come to be seen as a means of buying forgiveness for sins and a ticket to heaven, first became popular during the Crusades as a way to tempt knights to join forces to save the Holy Land. Indulgences forgave knights from doing penance for past sins. Indulgences were soon thereafter extended to those who sponsored a crusader. It wasn't long before indulgences were used to raise money from town folk and peasants.

In 1476, Pope Sixtus IV extended the opportunity to purchase an indulgence on behalf of loved ones assumed to be suffering from their sins in purgatory. In 1506, when Pope Julius II laid the cornerstone to rebuild St. Peter's Basilica he turned to the sale of indulgences to raise money for his cathedral. The

Johannes Tetzel selling indulgences (color lithograph, 19th century)

tactics of his envoys in selling them amounted to little less than emotional blackmail, according to his critics, as they depicted the voices of dead parents wailing in purgatory. Leo X, a Medici pope, continued Julius's policies and in 1513, a great effort to dispense indulgences was mounted

in Germany. The Pope granted Prince Albert, the archbishop of both Mainz and Magdeburg, the right to sell indulgences in Mainz for eight years if half the money collected was sent to Rome to be used to build the new Basilica of St. Peter.

By 1517, a popular local preacher, Johann Tetzel was carrying the papal bull allowing indulgences on a velvet cushion through towns in the region where Martin Luther lived and taught. Some of the Germans who paid for these indulgences brought their letters of receipt to Luther asking if they were valid. In response Luther posted the *The Disputation of Doctor Martin Luther on the Power and Efficacy of Indulgences*, which has come to be known as the *Ninety-five Theses*. They called for an academic debate on the subject. His actions launched a groundswell of latent criticism of the Catholic Church and its practices. ❑

CHURCH SPLIT BY

Wittenberg, October 31, 1517

Martin Luther was a 34-year-old professor and Augustinian monk when he nailed his *Ninety-five Theses* to the door of the Castle Church in Wittenberg. In it he issued a challenge to publicly debate the use of indulgences by the Church. The theses were written in Latin and mixed fine theological points with an emotional attack on the pope's men. They were sent to the archbishop of Mainz and the pope. Benefiting from the same printing technologies that facilitated the sale of indulgences, Luther was able to publish and distribute his call to arms throughout Germany within a few weeks.

In one thesis, Luther asserted that if the pope knew of his preachers' exactions he would rather have St. Peter's reduced to ashes than "built with the skin, flesh and bones of his sheep." In another, he asserts that any Christian who is truly repentant is entitled to forgiveness, with-

BY FAITH ALONE

Point of Interest

Martin Luther was above all concerned with the question of how man enmeshed in sin could attain God's grace. The answer to this question constitutes the heart of Protestant teaching. Luther became convinced that man could not free himself from sin through his own efforts. The only path to salvation was through faith in the resurrection of Christ. Luther found his proof passage in Paul's Letter to the Romans, 3:28 "Therefore we conclude that a man is justified by faith alone without the deeds of the law." The word "alone" is not found in the Greek text, but was added by Luther in his translation to emphasize the point.

Luther's teaching had broad logical consequences. By accepting it, the Church was then seen as the community of all believ-

ers, not an intermediary between God and the faithful. It did not possess the power to save. Priests were no longer to be considered the dispensers or mediators of grace, but rather as preachers and pastors. This leveled the distinctions between the priest and the congregation. For Luther, the Bible was the only authoritative source of teaching (*sola scriptura*). Church traditions and decrees were set aside. Of the seven sacraments (baptism, confirmation, communion, marriage, holy orders, confession, and last rites), Luther recognized only those two that he saw prescribed by the Bible: baptism and communion. Luther also repudiated the sacrificial character of the mass.

Almost 500 years after these ideas split the Western Church into two rival factions, Catholics

and Lutherans were formally reconciled in a common declaration: "Agreement on Fundamental Teachings." Human beings could only be saved by their faith and God's mercy. Good works were not preconditions for salvation but rather its "fruit." Nonetheless, the Catholic position remained that by agreeing to the working of God's grace people participated in their own salvation. The Luther-

ans denied that humans had it within their power to advance their own salvation; their only choice was total reliance upon God's grace. ❑

The Reformers: (from a painting by Lucas Cranach the Younger, in the Lutherhalle in Wittenberg). From right to left: Philipp Melancthon, Caspar Cruciger, Justus Jonas, Erasmus of Rotterdam, Johannes Bugenhagen, Martin Luther.

REFORM MOVEMENT

out any indulgences, but without repentance no forgiveness would be possible.

Luther's arguements were not especially radical, or different from what many other critics of the Church were saying. Luther was following in the footsteps of such reformists as John Wycliffe in England and Jan Hus, both of whom questioned the spiritual and temporal power of the papacy. In his lectures, Luther argued that priests should not stand between men and the Bible, and that faith was a gift from God.

As Luther's protests were talked about throughout Europe, he was summoned to Rome by Leo X who was determined to make "the drunk" German monk "sober." Luther resisted, and the pope allowed Luther to be questioned by Cardinal Cajetan at a diet held in Augsburg. Cajetan had made his reputation as defender of the Church in

disputations with the humanist Pico della Mirandola. The meeting did not go well, and Luther turned his attention to writing pamphlets in German that spoke out harshly against the Roman church. He denounced some of the sacraments and declared that faith trumped good works when it came to salvation. Forced to admit his opposition to the pope, Luther was excommunicated in January of 1521.

Charles V, the young Holy Roman Emperor, caught between his oath to defend the Church and popular support for Luther summoned the monk to appear before him at the Diet of Worms. The welcome of the German crowds showed that he had sturck a popular chord and the emperor feared that the revolutionary spirit might affect his power. Luther was again questioned, this time by the papal representative, Johannes Eck,

who offered him the chance to retract some of his works. He refused. It was on this occasion that he is purported to have said: "Here I stand. I cannot do otherwise. May God help me."

Luther was declared an outlaw in the Holy Roman Empire. He was fortunate to have a supporter in Prince Frederick III, the Elector of Saxony, who provided him shelter at Wartburg Castle from the storm he had started. There Luther continued to write, translated the Bible into German, refined his ideas challenging the papal claim to be the sole authority on the scriptures, and questioned many of the rights of priests. By now Luther also rejected transubstantiation—the belief the ritual bread and wine actually become the body and blood of Christ. He affirmed Christians' personal right to faith and encouraged priests and monks to marry. ❑

Lucas Cranach, *Portrait of Martin Luther*

Martin Luther was the son of an ambitious miner in Saxony. He was sent to university and was on his way to becoming a lawyer when he had a religious conversion and took holy orders, with the intention of becoming a monk. Ordained as a priest in 1507 and sent to teach at the new university at Wittenberg. In addition to launching the Reformation, Luther completed a translation of the Bible, a mass, a book of hymns, and one of catechisms. These works were not only written in German, they were written in plain language, making the scriptures accessible to ordinary Germans. After being excommunicated, rebellious German princes helped him to establish a new church.

A big, tough man with disturbing eyes, he was immensely proud of his peasant blood. He sang tenor and played the lute and had a happy home life. He married a former nun in 1525, and fathered six children. He was praised for his firm and eloquent style of speech, though he could also be vulgar and crude. It was said he had no sophistication or cunning and was open about his views and feelings.

Known for his violent temper, Martin Luther died in a mood of total serenity at age 63. His mind was sharp but his body was broken after years of overwork and illness. ❑

Debate between between Lutheran and Catholic preachers (woodcut, 1544, after an original by Lucas Cranach the Younger).

CHARLES V OF SPAIN ELECTED EMPEROR

Barcelona, July 6, 1519

The Spanish king, Charles V, a member of the Habsburg Dynasty, was chosen as the successor to his grandfather Maximilian I as Holy Roman Emperor. Charles sought to model himself after the medieval emperors who directed Christendom alongside the pope.

It took the courier fewer than nine days to ride at breakneck speed from Frankfurt across Europe to the gates of Barcelona to break the news to Charles that he had won the crucial election and would occupy the imperial throne of the Holy Roman emperor. Charles had successfully bribed the princes of Germany to cast their votes for him.

Charles had moved swiftly following the death of Maximilian of Austria in January. Within days of the news reaching him, couriers were urgently dispatched to Germany to negotiate with the princes—all seven of whose votes were vital for Charles to win. It was essential that he get his bid in before his rivals. He promised them not only a greater voice in governance but also an increased share of the tax revenue.

Once the diplomatic work was under way, Charles wrote a courteous note to King Francis of France advising him of his intentions. The king's reply came quickly: "Sire, we are both courting the same lady." There were four candidates in this election: Charles, Francis, Henry VIII of England, and Frederick (the Wise), the duke of Saxony. Charles was the favorite, particularly when it was known that he had borrowed freely from the Augsburg banking house of Fuggers, the biggest finance house in Europe, who backed him in preference to Francis of France. ❑

Emperor Charles V as a young man (c. 1516)

EXPLORER BEHEADED ON TREASON CHARGE

Panama, 1519

The famous explorer and conquistador Vasco Núñez de Balboa was executed by order of his own father-in-law, Pedro Arias Davila, the Spanish governor of Panama. Balboa's extraordinary career in Central America began seven years before, when he fled from his creditors in Spain by stowing away to Santo Domingo.

Hearing from the natives of a gold-rich land washed by an unknown sea, he led 190 men across the Isthmus of Panama. On September 29, 1513, he waded into the Pacific Ocean. He had discovered the overland route between America's western and eastern seaboards.

The Spanish governor of Panama, Pedro Arias Davila, promptly betrothed his daughter to this bold adventurer. Father and son-in-law worked together on a series of lucrative gold hunts, but at their first disagreement Davila had Balboa arrested and executed on a trumped-up conspiracy charge. ❑

Balboa at the Pacific Ocean

THE DEATH OF RAPHAEL

Rome, April 6, 1520

The sudden, early death of Raphael at age 37 plunged the papal court into grief and mourning. He was friend as well as painter to two popes and was in charge of architectural and decorative work at the Vatican palace. He died of a fever on Good Friday, his birthday, having divided his possessions among his students.

Raphael Sanzio, the son of a painter in Urbino, studied so successfully with Perugino that people could not tell his work from that of his master. After studying the work of Leonardo and Michelangelo in Florence, he went to Rome where Julius II appointed him to decorate the Vatican apartments with great semicircular frescoes, some of biblical scenes, some of classical antiquity, such as the philosophers of the *School of Athens*. He also drew the life-size cartoons for the tapestries to be woven for the Sistine Chapel. His secular portraits were as masterly as his serene Madonnas—that of Pope Julius was so lifelike that people trembled at it and that of Julius's successor, Leo X, also vividly alive. Leo sent Raphael's painting of St. Michael casting out Satan to the King of France. ❑

LUCREZIA BORGIA

Ferrara, June 24, 1519

Lucrezia Borgia, the duchess of Ferrara and daughter of Pope Alexander VI, died at age 39 after a life of family intrigue and broken marriages. Though beautiful and intelligent, she was essentially a pawn in her father's many power games. She was married at the age of 13 to Giovanni Sforza, the Lord of Pesaro. At the age of 18, she left him for a more politically favorable marriage to Alfonso d'Aragon the duke of Bisceglie, with whom she fell in love. Two years later, Alfonso became an embarrassment and was murdered, probably on the orders of Cesare, Lucrezia's brother. In 1501, Lucrezia was married for the last time to the duke of Ferrara. ❑

Lucrezia Borgia (portrait by an unknown artist, 16th century)

LEONARDO DA VINCI: UNIVERSAL RENAISSANCE GENIUS

Amboise, France, 1519

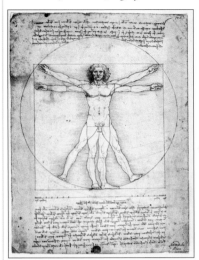

Leonardo da Vinci, *Vitruvian Man*

Leonardo da Vinci, *The Last Supper,* fresco in Santa Maria delle Grazie in Milan, 1495–1498

Leonardo da Vinci died at the age of 67 at the manor house of Clos Lucé near Amboise in the Loire region of France. His multifaceted creativity was grounded in his theoretical research. His work is a unique embodiment of the close connection between art and science; for Leonardo perception and understanding were inseparable. It was his conviction that the artist who has access to a precise awareness of nature and the ability to express that understanding is best situated to impart knowledge, in fact becomes a conduit for that knowledge. Leonardo himself conducted exhaustive studies into every area of art and science that bore upon a problem until he could see its solution clearly before his eyes. His countless drawings and sketches and extensive theoretical writings are incontrovertible witnesses to his complete immersion in the process of creation and discovery. His many volumes of notebooks in some ways are more powerful testimony of his genius than his finished works. As an artist, Leonardo was the supreme exponent of Renaissance aesthetics. His *Treatise on Painting*, his definitive theoretical work, emphasizes the supreme importance of the study of nature. In it he introduces a science of shadow and the concept of sfumato. The term derives from the Italian word for "smoke." It denotes the use of imperceptibly gradated layers of paint to produce the illusion of depth and texture.

In his research of natural processes he sought to discover their deeper structures through close observation and always looked for the underlying patterns behind phenomena. He studied of botany, optics, mechanics, and hydraulics. He was also an innovator in military technology. His notebooks are filled with sketches of siege weapons and cannons as well as designs for rudimentary helicopters and submarines.

Leonardo da Vinci, *Self Portrait*

Of special interest is his penetrating study of anatomy. He was one of the very first researchers to dissect a human corpse. His sketches showing a child in the womb of its mother, considered in the context of his time, have to be recognized as the product of staggering genius. ❏

Leonardo da Vinci, *Mona Lisa*

VASA LIBERATES SWEDEN

Sweden, 1523

Gustav Vasa is considered the architect of Swedish independence. He was brought up at the court of the old regent of Sweden. For two years he led a revolt against the King of Denmark, Christian II. Its success assured, the *Diet*—the Swedish parliament—elected him king of Sweden in 1523.

King Gustav's first step was to take Sweden out of the Danish-controlled Kalmar Union, which had united Norway, Sweden, and Denmark for 144 years. He then built a strong Swedish fleet of warships to protect its commercial interests in the Baltic. Gustav also embarked on a series of far-reaching reforms to modernize the administration of government. Wherever possible, he replaced nobles in local government with civil servants, responsible and loyal to the crown. One early challenge was to fill vacant bishoprics. Gustav leaned toward Luther's teachings and sought candidates favoring church reform. He encountered resistance especially in rural Sweden where Lutheranism was relatively unknown. ❑

Friedrich Pecht, *Portrait of Gustav Vasa*

PORTUGAL'S NEWFOUND WEALTH

Portugal, c.1521

For a time, the king of a small country at the southwestern corner of Europe became the Continent's wealthiest ruler. Sugar and spice, as well as gold from Guinea, enabled Manuel of Portugal to build the magnificent monastery of St. Jerome at Belem, encourage learning and artistic expression. To manage his newfound wealth and his many commercial operations, the king relied on Portugal's Jewish community. But he began to face pressure from Spain to expel all Jews. Manuel's plan was to tell the Jews that if they merely said that they had converted to Christianity they could stay with no questions asked. One notable Jewish scientist refused and left: Abraham Zacuto, the mathematician whose calculations enabled Portugal to produce Europe's first navigation manual. ❑

BIBLE TRANSLATED INTO THE VERNACULAR

England and Germany, Early 16th century

After being excommunicated and branded an outlaw by Pope Leo IX in 1521 at the Diet of Worms, Martin Luther sought refuge with the Elector of Saxony in Wartburg. Here he continued his work of reform by translating the Bible into German. His goal was to render the Holy Word into a vernacular that could be understood by the average German. Although a multilingual scholar himself, Luther had, from the outset of his mission, eschewed the use of Latin and purposely conveyed his message in language accessible to laymen. By September of 1522, he had created a translation of such colloquial vigor that historians have deemed his Bible the most important single work in the German language. It is still the most widely used Bible in Germany.

The creation and dissemination of Luther's work was in no small way aided by the era's technological advances in printing. Just decades before, the printing presses of Gutenberg in Germany and Caxton in England revolutionized society by dramatically increasing the accessibility of literature. The new wave of literacy helped to inspire William Tyndale's historic translation.

Encouraged by Martin Luther, William Tyndale produced the first translation of the New Testament from its original Greek text into English in 1526. Tyndale began his task in 1522 as a corrective to the ignorance of the local priests and his belief "that it was impossible to establish the lay people in any truth except when the Scripture were plainly laid before their eyes in their mother tongue, that they might see...the meaning of the text." A first-class linguist, he drew on the Greek Testament of Erasmus, published in 1516, for his translation. Like Martin Luther, Tyndale wanted his translation, especially of certain critical words and passages, to strip away what he saw were the embellishments of Catholicism and lay bare the original text. ❑

Page from the first complete Luther Bible.

CIRCUMNAVIGATION OF THE GLOBE

Spain, 1522

On August 10, 1519, Ferdinand Magellan set sail from Seville, Spain, on what would become the first circumnavigation of the world. Of the five vessels in his fleet, only one, the *Vittoria* returned; and of the 265 men aboard, only 15 survived.

Magellan, who sailed for Charles of Spain, was Portuguese, but because of the welcome Spain had given him, he became a Spanish citizen and persuaded Charles that the Portuguese domination of the spice trade with the east, around the Cape of Good Hope, could be broken by ships sailing west to find a passage around South America.

Sailing southwest, Magellan steered clear of the Portuguese coast of Brazil. He put in at the River Plate and farther south, at Port. St Julian, whose people he named *Patagonians* (Big Feet). As the ships sailed deeper into unknown waters, a mutiny broke out, which Magellan crushed, hanging the ringleaders. On October 21, Magellan rounded what he called the Cape of the Eleven Thousand Virgins and found himself at the eastern end of a passage he named All Saints Channel, later to be known as the Straits of Magellan. The channel ran through a maze of reefs, with snow-covered mountains on either side. He lost two ships, one wrecked by the violent winds, the other through desertion. After sailing past Tierra del Fuego, he emerged into a body of water so seemingly placid, he named it *Mar Pacifico* (Pacific Ocean). Continuing west, he arrived first at the present-day Marianas and the island of Guam. Finally, on March 16, Magellan and his fleet became the first Europeans to reach the Philippines. They had sailed a little over halfway around the world.

Soon after their arrival, his ships dropped anchor off Cebu, where the local chief agreed to convert to Christianity and then asked Magellan to help him conquer a tribe on the neighboring island of Mactan. It was there that Magellan died in battle with indigenous tribes on April 27, 1521.

Command then fell to Sebastian del Cano, who set sail with only two ships remaining. In the Moluccas, the men traded their merchandise for spices. Then, instead of heading home eastward back across the Pacific, they continued westward across waters where Portuguese merchantmen operated and seized one their ships, the *Trinidad*. With nearly all of the fleet gone, del Cano took the *Vittoria* across the Indian Ocean and arrived in Seville on September 6, 1522. ❑

Allegorical depiction of the discovery of the Straits of Magellan (copper etching, 16th century)

CORTÉS AND THE FALL OF THE AZTEC EMPIRE

Tenochtitlan, 1520

When the rogue soldier-explorer Hernán Cortés and his gold-seeking expeditionary force entered the Aztec capital of Tenochtitlan on November 8, 1519, they were warmly welcomed by its citizens and the Emperor Montezuma. This diplomatic graciousness had little effect. By November 16, Cortés—aware that he was vastly outnumbered by his hosts—put Montezuma under house arrest and assumed power in the Aztec capital.

Cortés tried to use Montezuma as his puppet emperor but lost control of the situation in June. In his temporary absence, his second in command, Pedro de Alvarado, ordered a massacre during a spring religious festival. Chaos ensued, with the citizenry in violent revolt against not only the Spanish but also the obsequiously compliant Montezuma, who, when appearing on the roof of his palace to exhort his people not to resist the Spaniards, was greeted with a hail of rocks and arrows.

Seeing that Montezuma was no longer of any use to him, it is believed that Cortés had him murdered. This event occasioned even more violence, leading to the deaths of over six hundred Spaniards in Tenochtitlan. The survivors escaped to the lands of their allies, the Tlaxcalans, an indigenous tribe who were foes of the Aztecs. By December, the Spaniards had sufficiently regrouped to mount an attack on the Aztec capital.

Tenochtitlan's fall was hastened by a devastating smallpox epidemic. Cortés's army began its siege at the end of December, and the three hundred thousand remaining defenders fought tenaciously for eighty days. They finally surrendered when Emperor Cuatemoc submitted to Cortés. In a final gesture, the conquistador accepted the emperor's surrender and then "...stared at him for a moment and patted him on the head." As of 1520, the Aztec Empire was no more. ❑

ALBRECHT DÜRER AND THE NORTHERN RENAISSANCE

Nuremberg, Germany, 1528

Albrecht Dürer is credited with bringing the Italian Renaissance to northern Europe. The outstanding German painter and engraver was born to a Hungarian goldsmith in 1471, and worked at an early age in his shop. He was later apprenticed to a painter and woodcut illustrator.

After a two-year visit to Venice, Dürer turned to oil painting in the Italian manner. He was inspired by the attention to perspective and science that he found in the south and attempted to render ideal human beauty in full-length paintings of Adam and Eve—the first full-size nudes to be painted in Germany.

Dürer continued to paint, engrave, and fashion woodcuts throughout his life. While in his twenties, he gained a reputation with his popular woodcut illustrations and copperplate engravings, such as *The Apocalypse*. His subjects were both secular and religious, and he is recognized for being one of the first painters to tackle a self-portrait.

His drawing talent combined with his studies of mathematics and his theory of art—he wrote texts on perspective, proportion, and optics—won him a kind of fame unknown for a German artist before his time. His reputation was greatly enhanced by the printing press, which allowed for the reproduction of his engravings and woodcuts and their distribution throughout Europe. Indeed, he set up his own printing press, and he and his wife sold his work at fairs.

Dürer was supported by patrons such as Maximilian I, the Holy Roman Emperor, and his successor, Charles V. He traveled extensively and was known for his friendships with such men as Erasmus and Martin Luther. He met Erasmus

Albrecht Dürer, *Knight, Death and the Devil*, copper etching, 1513

on his visit to the Netherlands in 1521 and drew his portrait in charcoal. Erasmus declared that that Dürer could express as much in black and white as other painters did with the use of color. His precision coupled with his lyrical line transforms his black-and-white work into a powerful representation of the natural world.

To this day, Dürer is seen as the greatest master of engraving on wood and metal. Some of his finest works are engravings like *Melancolia*—which contained the first magic square represented in art—and *The Knight, Death, and the Devil*, which he gave to Luther. He died at the age of 56 in 1528 in Nuremberg, the city of his birth. ❑

FRENCH KING CAPTURED AT PAVIA

Italy, February 24, 1525

When King Francis of France was not elected Holy Roman Emperor by the German prince-electors, he turned to war as another means of achieving supremacy in Europe. But his army was defeated at the battle of Pavia in Lombardy by the troops of his rival, Emperor Charles V, and he was forced to sign a humiliating peace treaty.

His last campaign in the Italian Wars began in the autumn of 1524. French guns broke down the defenses and the king's regiments stormed into the breaches. But new fortifications had been built inside the walls, and the French were routed by the defenders.

They retreated to mount a classic siege, hoping to starve Pavia into submission. But when the imperial forces marched on Pavia early in February, Francis found himself caught between the walls of Pavia and the attacking army. Francis led his knights in a disorganized charge without waiting for the infantry. His horse was shot from under him and in the shambles that ensued 6,000 French died and the king was taken captive. ❑

THE BATTLE OF PAVIA AND THE CHANGING FACE OF WAR

Europe, 1525

The firearms that killed King Francis' horse and destroyed the French army at the battle of Pavia were part of a revolution in military arms and strategy that was rapidly changing warfare in Europe as armies were modernized.

After Pavia, armored cavalry could no longer be regarded as the rulers of the battlefield. The day of the knight in armor was drawing to a close. New tactics were being developed for mounted troops using carbines and horse pistols.

Perhaps the greatest changes could be seen in siege warfare where the *trace italienne*, a circuit of low, thick walls punctuated by square bastions, was replacing the high, thin walls of the Middle Ages. These new defenses, developed in the long, protracted Italian Wars, were designed to absorb the punishment of the heavy siege guns that were now part of every successful army's battle armaments.

The adoption of the bastion defense was changing the entire pattern of warfare because protected cities could no longer be taken by the traditional methods of blowing a hole in the walls and pouring infantry through the breach. Towns now had to be encircled by siege works and batteries, and starved or frightened into submission. Warfare was becoming more and more a matter of engineering and logistics.

At sea, too, the advent of the big gun brought great changes. No longer did ships ram and board each other. Now formidable arrays of guns fired through ports in the ships' sides. The first such specialized gunship was built in England for Henry VIII's navy. It set a pattern that all maritime nations had to follow, or face inevitable defeat. ❑

THE PEASANTS' WAR

Germany, 1525

Inspired in part by Martin Luther's teachings and by radical Christian communities like the one based on common ownership set up at Allstedt in 1523, a series of peasant uprisings swept through Germany. The uprisings began in 1524 in Bavaria and spread rapidly. The revolt was not a concerted movement so much as a series of local uprisings against the oppression of princes, landlords, and the Church. Some peasant leaders, however, did get as far as drawing up a manifesto at Memmingen. It proposed the abolition of serfdom, the reduction of tithes, and the right of each community to choose and expel pastors. One of the revolt's leaders, the pastor Thomas Müntzer, preached the advent of God's Kingdom, where all men would be considered equal.

It was a program radical enough to drive the princes to take strong repressive measures. Moreover, the peasants lost Luther's support. He turned against them upon hearing of a murder at Weinsberg, when peasants speared the count of Helfenstein in front of his wife and child. Luther denounced the uprising in a four-page tract, *Against the Murdering Thieving Hordes of Peasants.* "You cannot meet a rebel with reason," he wrote. "Your best answer is punch him in the face until he has a bloody nose."

Title page from a tract written during the peasants' uprising.

Armed peasants (woodcut, 16th century)

In May of 1525, the revolt was crushed at the Battle of Frankenhausen. The peasant army of 8,000 was slaughtered and Thomas Müntzer was captured and beheaded. ❑

SACK OF ROME

Rome, May 6–16, 1527

In the midst of the war between Germany and France and bitter religious conflicts, Rome fell prey to the armies of Emperor Charles V subjected to the fury of 15,000 German mercenaries.

The majesty of the Renaissance papacy lay in tatters. The Vatican itself was occupied by Lutheran troops, its chapels used as stables, and the Raphael paintings in the papal apartments covered with graffiti. An appeal by Pope Clement VII to Charles to call off the men who were destroying the city came too late. The ensuing rape of the city was predictable once the German army—unpaid, starving, and now leaderless—came within sight of the city and its enormous wealth.

A year before, the Treaty of Cognac led to the formation of a Holy League under which Rome and Venice allied themselves with the pope to assist the French against Charles V. The emperor's swift response to this challenge caught the alliance unprepared. Two years later, the French and the Germans faced with a growing Turkish threat signed a peace treaty at Cambrai in France. France was represented by Louise of Savoy, acting for King Francis, and Margaret of Austria represented her nephew Charles. Consequently, the treaty became known as *La Paix des Dames* (The Ladies' Peace). ❑

MEMOIRS OF THE MOGHUL EMPEROR

Sakri, India, 1530

Babur, the descendant of Genghis Khan and Tamerlane the Great, worked wrote memoirs: an extraordinary document that provides insight into the life and times of the man who built an empire out of an impoverished central Asian princedom and conquered northern India.

The memoirs trace his childhood when at age 11, he became king of Ferghana. He lost and won that kingdom three times. He wrote sadly of tribesmen who had never seen guns before, laughing at the noise and confronting them with obscene gestures before being massacred, but had little sympathy for the supposedly sophisticated societies he conquered.

"Hindustan is a country that has few pleasures to recommend it. The people are not handsome. They have no idea of the charms of friendly society, of mixing frankly together, or of familiar intercourse. They have no genius, no comprehension of mind, no politeness of manner, no kindness of fellow feeling, no ingenuity or mechanical or artistic abilities, no knowledge of design or architecture, no horses, no flesh, no decent food, baths, no candles, not even a candlestick."

His work lists with loving detail the flora and fauna of his subject territories, describing parrots, rhinoceroses, the leaves of an apple tree and the changing colors of flocks of geese on the horizon. ❑

TUMULTUOUS REIGN OF HENRY VIII

England, 1532

Henry VIII ascended the throne in 1509. He and his new wife, Catherine of Aragon, were crowned at Westminster on June 24. Catherine was the widow of Henry's elder brother Arthur, and their marriage required a special papal bull to override objections to the marriage on the grounds of the closeness of the relationship. However, after seventeen years of marriage, Catherine had failed to give birth to a surviving male heir—her only surviving child was a daughter, Mary. Henry cast his eye upon the young Protestant Anne Boleyn. In 1525, Henry and his Lord Chancellor Thomas Wolsey, cardinal and papal envoy, began appealing to Pope Clement VII to annul Henry's marriage to Catherine.

The pope, however, balked at the annulment. His objections seemed to stem from Henry's earlier liaison with Anne's elder sister Mary, which raised the question of a forbidden blood link. Perhaps more telling was the fact that Catherine was the aunt of the Emperor Charles V, whose troops were occupying Rome at the time. Frustrated with Wolsey's ineffectual negotiations, a furious Henry charged Wolsey with abuse of power and stripped him of all offices. Summoned back to London to face charges of treason, Wolsey took ill and died en route.

To fill Wolsey's place, Henry appointed the lawyer and humanist scholar Thomas More, who earlier had been a defender of the king's prerogatives. However, More could not agree to open defiance of the pope and resigned his office in 1532. Thereafter the king had his way. He rid himself of Catherine and married Anne Boleyn. The price was the repudiation of papal authority in England. Assisted by his new first minister Thomas Cromwell, Henry persuaded Parliament to pass a series of measures that made him head of the Church in England and allowed the archbishop of Canter-

King Henry VIII with Bishop of Sherborne, 1519

bury to make all dispensations the pope had made in the past. Henry appointed Thomas Cranmer Archbishop of Canterbury. For appearances' sake, Cranmer took the oath of obedience to Rome, then promptly declared Henry's marriage to Catherine invalid and blessed the marriage to Anne. Anne, who was already pregnant, was crowned queen in June. In response, Pope Clement excommunicated Henry, leading to the final break with Rome. Parliament passed a Succession Act that commanded allegiance to Anne and her issue and made it high treason to challenge the king's title to the throne or criticize the marriage. It was his refusal to take this oath that led to Thomas More's execution on charges of treason. Another measure, the Act of Supremacy, made the king the supreme head of the Church of England, with full powers to deal with heresies, errors, and abuses. Consequently, taxes to Rome were stopped, the laws against heresy were amended to allow criticism of the Catholic Church, and a translation of the Bible into English was commissioned.

What had begun as a controversy over problems of marriage and succession turned into a po-

litical revolution. Not only did England break with the Catholic Church, but the king's need to carry public opinion also strengthened Parliament since it caused him to seek its support.

England's religious controversies had been taking place against a background of religious revolution in continental Europe. Martin Luther was preaching against papal indulgences and calling for German control of the German church. In Zurich, church reformation was in full swing; Sweden and Denmark also broke with the pope. But Henry had little patience with these radical reformers. His theology was strictly orthodox. In his younger days he had written a book denouncing Luther and his views, for which the pope had given him the title "Defender of the Faith." Despite its being cut off from the pope, the Church of England closely adhered to the Catholic Church in doctrinal matters.

In June of 1536, Henry dispensed with his second wife. Anne Boleyn was beheaded in the Tower of London, a victim of court intrigues and her own arrogance. She used to mock the king, though whether she was guilty of adultery is highly doubtful. She gave Hen-

ry a daughter, Elizabeth, but then miscarried, and the king decided the marriage was damned.

Henry began to pursue a policy of breaking up the great ecclesiastical estates. The program was implemented by Thomas Cromwell, who boasted that he would make Henry the richest prince in Europe. Cromwell had no difficulty in discovering excuses for suppressing the monasteries and confiscating their assets. Monastic property was put up for sale, the proceeds going to the king. Most of the Church lands were bought by the gentry via the Court of Augmentations and many of them turned into private homes. The king's additional income from the sale of nearly 800 Church properties soared to around £90,000 a year.

Though some abbots, monks, and nuns were given pensions, many monks sought to supplement their income by becoming village priests, causing clerical unemployment and doctrinal confusion. The dissolutions also caused hardship among the poor because the distribution of alms ceased. This was one reason for the demonstrations, known as the Pilgrimage of Grace, that broke out in the north.

In 1540, the last of England's big monastic houses, Waltham Abbey in Essex, was seized by the crown, bringing to a close a four-year campaign that saw more than 550 properties, with their treasure of plate and jewels, pass into the king's possession. The 370 smaller monasteries, which were the first to fall, brought Henry some £32,000 a year, and the 186 bigger ones that followed, £100,000. From this bounty Henry rewarded his supporters with gifts of property. Some other estates were put up for auction. Many of England's great family fortunes were founded on the suppression of the monasteries.

Though the suppression was due to Henry's desire for the wealth of the Church, it is also true that after his quarrel with Rome, the monasteries were an obstacle to the consolidation of his power over the Church.

After Anne Boleyn's beheading, Henry married Jane Seymour, who died while giving birth to the long-sought male heir, the future Edward VI. He would marry three times more. Of his fourth wife Anne of Cleves, the king said: "I liked her before I met her. Now I like her less." She was pensioned off, and Henry married Catherine Howard, the Duke of Norfolk's niece, who was beheaded for immorality. Henry's sixth wife was Catherine Parr, twice a widow before her marriage to Henry.

Henry was masterful and ruthless. He usually got his way in domestic affairs. In foreign affairs he was less successful, and in a war with France in 1545, he had the humiliation of seeing his finest ship, the *Mary Rose*, keel over and sink with 500 men on board as 200 French ships were riding up the Solent. That war cost more than £2 million and emptied the royal treasury.

On January 28, 1547, Henry VIII died at the age of 56 survived by his sixth wife Catherine. ❑

LATE GOTHIC WOOD CARVING

Germany, 1531

Tilman Riemenschneider, master sculptor and wood carver, died at the age of 70 in Wurzburg.

While Italy was undergoing a renaissance that looked to classical models and texts for its inspiration, German-speaking areas continued the elaboration of medieval ideas into much of sixteenth century. This manner has been termed the late Gothic. One main vehicle for this style was the winged altarpiece, examples of which were prevalent in what is now south Germany and Austria. The altarpieces were for the most part enclosed shrines with carved wood figures. They were displayed only on certain holy days. The outsides of the doors to the shrine were often painted; the doors' inner panels were decorated with carved reliefs.

Riemenschneider brought together divergent techniques in the service of a single vision, and his wooden altarpieces stand as

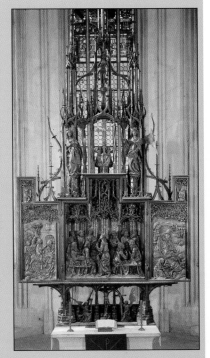

Altarpiece in Rothenburg, Germany, 1501–1504

complete integrated works unto themselves. ❑

SULEIMAN, THE MAGNIFICENT

Ottoman Empire, 1530

After the fall of Constantinople, the Ottoman Empire quickly became a force to be reckoned with, not only in Asia but in Europe as well. In 1520, Suleiman I ascended the throne. He would reign for 46 years, the longest ruling Ottoman sultan, and would come to be known as Suleiman the Magnificent.

Suleiman sought to extend his power westward into Europe, taking advantage of factional and religious conflicts that had the major European powers in their grip. In 1521, Belgrade fell to his forces. His victory confirmed the fact that the Danube was no longer a reliable line of defense. Charles V, preoccupied by German problems and Luther's revolt, had ignored pleas for help, and the defenders of Belgrade had no answer to the Ottoman cannon bombardment.

Four years later, Suleiman once again showed his strength, destroying the flower of Hungarian manhood on the battlefield of Mohacs. After one of the bloodiest battles of the time, the young Hungarian king, Ludwig II, lay dead with more than 20,000 of his troops.

Suleiman's next foray was his most ambitious: a march on Vienna—center of Habsburg power—in a dispute over territory with Charles's brother Ferdinand. Ferdinand was king of the part of Hungary that was still in Habsburg hands. Suleiman's chief problem was to reach Vienna before winter. He lost a month due to adverse weather and his army was exhausted and sick by the time it began its siege of the city on September 27.

The city's defenders were prepared. German diets had devoted 120,000 Rhenish guilders for defense against the Ottoman invader and promised an army of 16,000 men and 4,000 cavalry. In addition, France and Germany had reached an agreement at Cambrai, permitting Charles to concentrate his full attention on the invaders from the east. A well armed garrison repulsed the siege and finally the sultan gave the order to retreat.

In Asia, Suleiman was consolidating his control over Asia Minor. He established himself as the preeminent figure in the Muslim world. In 1535, he entered Baghdad with a conquering army. On the death of the last member of the Abbasid family, Suleiman assumed the title of *caliph*—successor to the Prophet Mohammed.

Under Suleiman's stewardship the Ottoman world attained its highest level of cultural development. His architectural achievements include the great Suleymaniye and Selimiye mosques, and he made support of the arts a government priority.

Finally on September 6, 1566, Suleiman died in Istanbul. The most powerful influence in the second half of Suleiman's reign was Hurrem Sultan (also known as Roxolana), a captive from Galicia. After bearing Suleiman a child, Roxelana became his wife according to Muslim law, a position no sultan's concubine had achieved for two centuries.

Suleiman was succeeded by his eldest surviving son, Selim, all potential rivals having been eliminated by intrigue or murder. ❑

ERASMUS: HUMANIST AND PREACHER OF TOLERANCE

Basel, 1536

Desiderius Erasmus (1470–1536), a Dutch humanist and religious scholar was admired by both Catholics and Protestants. Erasmus was a devout Catholic throughout his life despite his sympathies for Martin Luther and the Reformation's main complaints against the Catholic Church, but he believed that there could be reformation without radical change in church doctrine. Although he was an ordained priest, Erasmus preferred the life of an independent scholar. He authored many notable and important works during his life. In 1516, he prepared the first printed edition of the New Testament in Greek as part of the *Polyglot Bible*. His most famous work is *The Praise of Folly*, a satirical commentary on the shortcomings of his age, in which the Goddess Folly speaks in her own voice and extols her own virtues and unique sway over the minds of men. The preface to the work was written to his close friend Thomas More. Its opening paragraph reads as follows:

"At what rate soever the world talks of me (for I am not ignorant what an ill report Folly has got, even among the most foolish), yet that I am that she, that only she, whose deity recreates both gods and men, even this is a sufficient argument, that I no sooner stepped up to speak to this full assembly than all your faces put on a kind of new and unwonted pleasantness. So suddenly have you cleared your brows, and with so frolic and hearty a laughter given me your applause, that in truth as many of you as I behold on every side of me seem to me no less than Homer's gods drunk with nectar and nepenthe; whereas before, you sat as lumpish and pensive as if you had come from consulting an oracle. And as it usually happens when the sun begins to show his beams, or when after a sharp winter the spring breathes afresh on the earth, all things immediately get a new face, new color, and recover as it were a certain kind of youth again: in like manner, by but beholding me you have in an instant gotten another kind of countenance; and so what the otherwise great rhetoricians with their tedious and long-studied orations can hardly effect, to wit, to remove the trouble of the mind, I have done it at once with my single look."

Hans Holbein the Younger, *Portrait of Erasmus,* 1523

Other important works of his include: *Adages, Manual of the Christian Knight, The Education of the Christian Prince,* and *Colloquies.* ❑

ST. IGNATIUS OF LOYOLA AND THE JESUIT ORDER

Rome, 1541

Ignatius of Loyola was born in 1491 in the Basque town of Azpeitia. At sixteen he served as a page in the Castilian court where he enthusiastically adopted its sybaritic lifestyle. He lived as a free spirit until the age of thirty, when, as an officer engaged in battle with the French over a territorial dispute in Pamplona, he suffered a leg wound that would leave him disabled for life but also bring him to the worship of Christ. While recuperating in Loyola he studied literature on the lives of Christ and the Saints, and was so affected that upon his recovery he resolved to make a pilgrimage to the Holy Land. En route, he stopped at a Benedictine shrine disposing of his sword, giving away his fine military clothes, and donning a rough cloak and sandals. Continuing on, he sought refuge in a cave outside the Spanish town of Manresa. It was here that he experienced a moment of Grace (which he never specifically described) that awakened in him the awareness of God's presence in all things. That recognition would become central to Jesuit spirituality.

Eventually arriving in Rome, he requested permission from Pope Adrian VI to make a pilgrimage to the Holy Land. Denied his request due to the danger posed by the Turks' occupation of that region, Ignatius returned to Barcelona where he began studying for the priesthood and teaching others his method of worship, which included a controversial regime of prayer, fasting, and self-flagellation. This method would later be codified in his great work, *Spiritual Exercises*. His unorthodox proselytizing landed him in jail, first at the hands of the Inquisition in Barcelona and then by the Dominicans in Salamanca.

Ignatius enrolled in the University of Paris where his studies resulted in his ordination, and he gathered around him a coterie of students who began to practice his methods of worship. Barred from pilgrimage, he and his companions decided to go to Rome to take vows of poverty and chastity, and dedicate their lives in service to the Holy Father. In September of 1540, they were greeted by Pope Paul III, who formally recognized their society and its mission. On April 22, 1541, Ignatius and his companions took official vows, creating The Society of Jesus—the Jesuits.

The Jesuits' mission became the propagation of Christian faith through education. By 1548, the Society had opened schools in Italy, Portugal, the Netherlands, Spain, Germany, and India. Initially designed to teach Jesuit recruits, these "colleges" soon opened their doors to laymen. Of the education provided in these schools, Ignatius wrote "… good education in life and doctrine will be beneficial to many others, with the fruit expanding more widely every day." The Jesuits are, to this day, renowned as educators.

Ignatius died on July 31, 1556. He was canonized on March 12, 1622. ❑

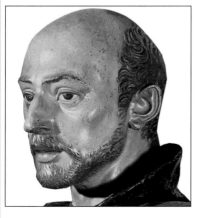

St. Ignatius of Loyola

THE CONQUEST OF THE INCAS

Peru, 1533

The European search for an empire on the west coast of South America was ignited by stories of an exotic and fabulously rich tribe called the *Viru* or *Peru*. In 1522 and again in 1524, Francisco Pizarro, a soldier of fortune who had been with Balboa when he discovered the Pacific, and his comrade, Diego de Almagro, led expeditions to find and conquer what was the Inca Empire.

Pizarro had received a royal warrant signed in 1529 allowing him to "discover and conquer" Peru, and he was made Spain's governor there.

He led an expedition of 180 men across the Andes—a monumental feat. They came into contact with the Inca leader Atahualpa who had recently won a bitter civil war against his brother. Pizarro invited Atahualpa to meet him in the upland valley town of Cajamarca. When the Inca leader came, he was handed a Bible, which he threw down. Pizarro sprang his ambush: Gunfire blasted at point-blank range into the packed ranks, followed by a cavalry charge. Panic did the rest. In two hours, 7,000 Indians died and their leader became a captive.

Atahualpa was ransomed for a fortune in gold and silver and agreed to become a Christian. But Pizarro feared that he could still rally against him and had the

Inca leader executed. Pizarro then marched on toward the Inca capital of Cuzco, which he conquered, thereby claiming the Inca Empire for Spain, a territory that stretched from the borders of Colombia to northern Chile and contained great wealth. He subsequently founded the port city of Lima.

The one enemy Pizarro could not conquer was his own greed. His companion, Almagro, to whom Pizarro had promised much, was disgruntled a few years later and after a fruitless search for gold in Chile, seized Cuzco. Internecine warfare followed. Almagro was executed in 1538 and three years later, in retaliation, the governor's palace at Lima was attacked. Pizarro, aged 63, was overpowered and killed, leaving a legacy of having vastly broadened Spanish influence in the new world, but having left its richest colony difficult to govern. ❑

Inca bringing gold treasure as a ransom for the chief, Atahualpa (etching, 1597)

EUROPE EXPLORES A NEW WORLD

Point of Interest

While Spain and Portugal were fighting for dominance over the southern half of the Western Hemisphere and establishing settlements and political institutions, the French and English were racing against each other to find a northern route to the Indies.

The search for a northern passage enticed the two maritime powers, hoping to find an alternative to sending their ships into the Portuguese controlled waters down the coast of Africa and around the Cape of Good Hope. Ultimately there was no northern route to be found, but the search for it revealed the outlines of a new and mysterious continent.

The French explorer Jacques Cartier arrived in Newfoundland with his expedition on May 10, 1534, and claimed it for the

French crown. This antagonized the English who argued that when John Cabot in set down on the North American coast in 1498, he had established England's rightful possession of Newfoundland and Nova Scotia.

The following year, Cartier traveled farther up the St. Lawrence River, convinced he had found the passage that would take him to the Orient. In 1535, he founded the town of Montreal on its banks and laid the groundwork for French colonial prerogatives in Canada.

In what is now the northern and central United States, attempts by the English throughout the sixteenth century to establish colonies met with failure. It was not until 1607 at Jamestown that the first permanent settlement was founded.

The Spanish had greater suc-

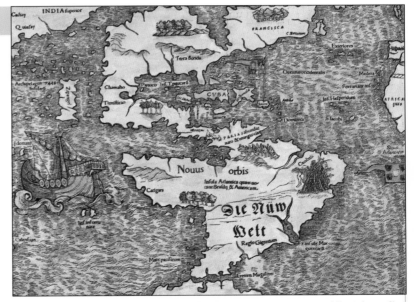

Map of the American continent (from Sebastian Münster's *Comographia Universalis*, colored woodcut, 1550)

cess in the southern region of the United States. Ponce de Leon arrived on the Florida coast in 1513. In 1539, Hernando de Soto discovered the Mississippi River, and between 1540 and 1542 Vásquez de Coronado

ventured as far north as present-day Arkansas. The Spanish were responsible for the first lasting European settlement in North America, St. Augustine on the coast of Florida. It was founded in 1565. ❑

TITIAN: VENETIAN MASTER

Venice, mid-sixteenth century

The Venetian painter, Titian, was considered the "prince among painters." During his long life (1485–1576) he painted portraits, landscapes, mythological, and religious subjects. In his early career, Titian studied with Giovanni Bellini and Giorgione, two seminal figures of the Venetian school of art. After their deaths, Titian inherited their mantle and was soon regarded as the finest painter in Venice.

Titian was the most notable portrait painter in Europe. He received commissions from Phillip II of Spain and the Emperor Charles V. His work influenced many artists, his sumptuous color and his brushstrokes, which became broader and more intense as his career advanced, gave his work depth, emotion, and a sense of dramatics. Titian's famous work *The Assumption* (1516–1518), with its brilliant red colors and three-tier structure, established him as the preeminent painter north of Rome. Other famous works include the striking, though unfinished portrait of Pope Paul III and his grandsons, the *Venus of Urbino, Madonna of Cherries*, and *Diana and Actaeon*. ❑

Titian, *Venus of Urbino*, c. 1538, Uffizi, Florence

NATIVE PEOPLE PROTECTED BY JESUITS

Brazil, mid-sixteenth century

Manuel de Nobrega, leader of Brazil's Portuguese Jesuits during the mid 1500s, used his role as missionary in Brazil to protect the indigenous people from colonists. Nobrega and the other missionaries stationed in Brazil had to battle against the cruel treatment of the natives and constant slave raids. Slavery was official policy and the Jesuits could not prevent native enslavement, but Nobrega found ways to curb the number of attacks on the natives. Part of Nobrega's strategy to improve their condition was to ask the king to establish episcopacy, a form of church governance. In 1551, with royal permission, Nobrega founded the country's first archbishopric. Brazil's capital was placed under the jurisdiction of its first archbishop, Dom Pedro Fernandes Sardinha. And in 1552, Nobrega founded the Jesuit College of Salvador, which worked closely with the native population. Although Nobrega and the other missionaries were intent on defending them, the natives did not embrace the Catholic religion. Having difficulties teaching the adults, Nobrega directed his efforts toward children. The Jesuits established elementary schools, using music to teach religion and language, and in the process became pioneers in music education. ❑

Jesuit Church of Sao Miguel (Paraguay)

CALVIN'S REFORM MOVEMENT

Basel, Switzerland, 1541

John Calvin published his personal testament of faith, *The Institutes of the Christian Religion*, in 1536. Its aim was to put an end to the divisions between the various strands of Protestantism. Its essential dogma is the omnipotence and omniscience of God.

While Martin Luther, Calvin's predecessor and in many ways his inspiration, concentrated on man and his sins, Calvin turned his attention to God and His awesome power. Calvin's worshippers must adore God; they must also show Him fear. As for sin, Calvin put forward the doctrine of predestination. God has already chosen the elect: those who will go to heaven. No one, however devout, can alter the divine decree. What determines whether one is chosen or damned cannot be explained. It is beyond human intelligence, only the immoral would dare question it.

According to Calvin, man is an insignificant creature dominated by the taint of original sin that followed the expulsion from Eden. Left alone, he is incapable of good; unless he devotes himself to the abject adoration of God, he is no more than prey for every tempta-

tion. Only by submitting himself to divine omnipotence can he live a proper life.

Calvin preached his message in France until he was forced to flee from persecution as a heretic. He arrived in Geneva and was persuaded to stay by William Farel, a fellow reformer. In 1537, Calvin joined Farel in demanding that every citizen swear to the Confession of Faith, on pain of banishment. The council rejected this reform, and the two men were expelled.

But Geneva city councilors, fearful of a return to Catholicism, relented and asked Calvin to return in 1541. He did so and set about publishing his *Ecclesiastical Ordinances*, which were accepted as the basis of government for both church and state.

The son of a lawyer, and a lawyer himself, Calvin relished the practical details of government. And, as a religious zealot, he could not conceive of a government that was not dictated by the religion of its citizens. The *Ordinances* laid down right and wrong. They demanded strict moral order and unswerving religious conformism. Within

the Genevan Republic, the laws of church and state became virtually inseparable. The *Ordinances* were administered by several groups of officials, all appointed rather than elected. Pastors dealt with religious orthodoxy and elders with public morals. The two groups met at the weekly consistory and examined the state of Genevan morals. They could summon and punish any alleged sinner. Doctors, appointed by the pastors, dealt with secular and spiritual education.

Calvin believed firmly in individual piety. Thus every vestige of one's life was to be controlled. Dancing was forbidden, as was the wearing of slashed breeches, the use of folk remedies, and many everyday pastimes. The clergy were required to visit all parishioners annually, to ensure that they were living proper Christian lives. By 1552,

and until his death in 1564, Calvin was the unrivalled ruler of Geneva, a city he re-created in the rigid image of his own Protestant orthodoxy. ❑

John Calvin (copper etching, 17th century)

PARACELSUS: MEDICAL PIONEER

Salzburg, September 9, 1541

Paracelsus was the most famous physician of his day. His medical ideas were deeply influenced by astrological and magical speculation, and he endorsed healing practices and principles drawn from alchemy. But at the same time he based his treatments on practical experience and his research into natural phenomena. This blend of empiricism and metaphysics identified him as a man on the cusp of the scientific age.

Paracelsus was the illegitimate offspring of a noble Schwabian family. Later in life he took the name Theophrastus Bombastus von Hohenheim. He received a

degree from the University of Ferrara, but as a doctor he was guided as much by the lessons he learned during his wanderings through Europe as by theoretical considerations. His travels took him through Germany, France, Scandinavia, and Hungary to Russia. From there he traveled to Constantinople and China. In 1527, he was nominated by Erasmus of Rotterdam to the Chair of Medicine at the University of Basel, but his candi-

Detail from title page from work of Paracelsus.

dacy was rejected by the medical faculty.

According to Paracelsus's teachings, the visible world is governed by invisible forces. Of special importance were the movements of stars and planets, which he thought had a decisive influence on the human organism. He seized upon a concept dating back to antiquity: The secret of medicine was to cooperate with or facilitate nature's own healing power.

From the stand-

point of modern medicine Paracelsus was a pioneer in pharmacology. He was the first to have patients ingest preparations made from chemicals. Since classical times their use had been restricted to external application for treatment of wounds or in surgery. He prescribed alchemical preparations made from copper, antinomy, arsenic, bismuth, gold, and lead.

He also subscribed to a theory of correspondences, seeing the human microcosm as a mirror image of the cosmic macrocosm. Paracelsus died in Salzburg, impoverished, on September 9, 1541. He was 48 years old. ❑

TSAR IVAN IV: REFORMER AND TYRANT

Russia, 1547

Ivan the Terrible

Ivan IV (Ivan the Terrible) was born in 1530, scion of the great Muscovy Dynasty founded by Ivan I. At the age of 17, he became the first Russian leader to be crowned *Tsar* (Russian for "Caesar"). He inherited a fragmented Russian state and a tumultuous political situation that was marked by the ouster of his mother as regent by the powerful *boyar*, the old nobility. Within a decade he would become one of Russian history's finest reformers; by the time of his death, one of its worst despots.

Envisioning a unified Russia, in 1549 he created a new form of parliament, called the *Zemsky Sobor* ("assembly of the land"), which consisted of a *duma* of nobles and high-ranking bureaucrats, the Orthodox clergy, and a "third estate"—a representative body made up of merchants and commoners. He revised the *Sudebnik*, the Russian code of laws, expanding the centralized codification of the legal system. He decreed the formation of a unit of Russian guardsmen called the *Streltsky*. He encouraged new routes of international trade on the White Sea and at the port of Archangel, engaging the Muscovy Company of English merchants.

In 1552, he expanded Russia's borders by dislodging remnants of Russia's age-old enemies, the Golden Horde, by first capturing the Kazan Khanate capital on the Volga, and then defeating armies of the Astrakhan Khanate. The annexation of territories held by these invaders brought the whole Volga basin as far as the Caspian Sea into the Russian Empire, thereby opening the way for Russian expansion beyond the Urals and as far as the Pacific Ocean. It was during these offensives that Ivan earned the sobriquet, *Grozny*, (the Dreaded or Terrible).

During this decade of great success Ivan began to undergo a disturbing personality change. Historians believe that two events, a near fatal illness in 1553, and the death of his first wife in 1560, triggered a form of paranoia, making him believe that the *boyars* had poisoned his wife and that many of his subjects were traitors.

Ivan's personal decline coincided with waves of drought, famine, plague, and the onset of the Livonian War. This conflict with a coalition of European states would last for 24 years, devastating Russia's economy and reversing many of Ivan's accomplishments. The deterioration occasioned by these events was exacerbated in 1565 when Ivan, increasingly suspicious of the *boyars*, created the *Oprichnina*, a region in northeast Russia that was to be his personal domain, functioning autonomously from the rest of Russia, defended by his private army, the *Oprichniki*.

By 1570, Ivan's mental instability made him increasingly unfit to lead. The *Oprichniki* took it upon themselves to attack the "enemies" created by his paranoia. Now acting as roving death squads, their indiscriminate murder of blameless peasants and members of the nobility culminated in the infamous Massacre of Novgorod of 1570 in which possibly up to sixty thousand people were killed. The sobriquet "Terrible" took on a new meaning.

On March 18, 1584, Ivan IV's tragic fall from enlightened reformer to mad despot came to a curiously ordinary end: The great leader, who once struck dread into the hearts of the Golden Horde and then into those of his own people, died suddenly while playing chess. ❑

THE COPERNICAN REVOLUTION

Poland, 1543

The astronomer Nicholas Copernicus was responsible for overthrowing one of the fundamental tenets of the Western belief system by asserting that the earth revolved around the sun, the center of our planetary system. Up until his time, it was an accepted truth of church dogma that the earth was at the center of the universe. His new, scientific view had profound effects not only on astronomy, but on questions regarding religion and science and human identity.

Copernicus died at the age of 70 in German-speaking Poland in the town of Frauenberg on the Baltic Sea. Just before his death, his groundbreaking ideas were first published in his work, *De revolutionibus orbium celestium* (*Concerning the Revolutions of the Celestial Spheres*), which supplanted the rudimentary astronomy that preceded him derived from the theories of Claudius Ptolemy. Copernicus showed that the planets, including the earth, were in circular orbit around the sun. Copernicus had studied Ptolemy's cosmology, which placed the earth at the center of a circle around which revolved the sun, moon, planets, and a region of the fixed stars, but he observed that this assumption led to inaccurate predictions in the long term. Copernicus referred to the Greek thinker, Aristarchus of Samos, who had raised the possibility of heliocentrism based upon his observations and calculations of the planetary orbital speed and their relationship with one another and with the sun. He may have been influenced by Muslim astronomers as well. Copernicus arrived at the conclusion that the earth rotated on its own axis. Beginning with this idea he found he could more easily and more accurately predict planetary movements.

The acceptance of the ideas of Copernicus entailed a turning away from centuries-old doctrines of the place of earth and man in the universe. The Copernican Revolution contradicted the idea of the Catholic Church that had promoted humanity to the central position in a sacred, universal history. ❑

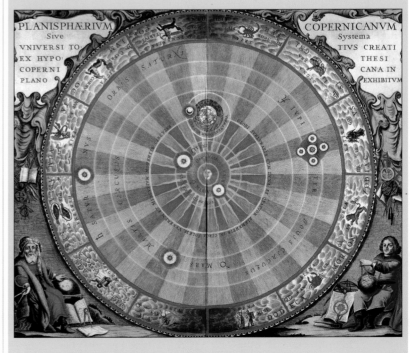

Copernican heliocentric solar system (etching, 1660)

TURBULENCE IN SPANISH COLONIES

South America, c.1545

Nicholas Copernicus offered a new way of looking at the universe

Following its initial phase of conquest, Spain began to set up the administrative apparatus to govern its colonies and ensure the continuing flow of silver from the mountains of the New World. The Spaniards also built up a fleet to transport the precious metal back to Europe.

However, the great inflows of wealth also brought problems as settlers battled to get a greater share of the riches, pirates found bountiful opportunities on the high seas, and the indigenous people of the Americas were conscripted to work in the mines and on plantations.

In 1541, Francisco Pizarro, the governor of Peru, was assassinated and the legacy of his murder continued to undermine attempts to govern Spain's richest colony. Pizarro had ignored intelligence about threats against him from a faction supporting his former companion in arms, Diego de Almagro. The two had become estranged and in 1538, Almagro was captured and executed by the Pizarro clan. On Sunday morning, June 26, 1541, twenty of his dispossessed followers smashed their way into the governor's palace. Pizarro was overpowered and killed.

In the meantime, debates about the treatment of the indigenous people of the colonies raged in Spanish intellectual and ecclesiastical circles. The issue was whether conquest, with its inevitable destruction of Indian culture, was morally justified.

The Dominican Bartolomé de las Casas stated the case against the conquest, condemning the brutality of Spain's troops. His opponent was Juan Ginés de Sepúlveda, a philosopher and theologian. Sepúlveda justified Spain's actions by the Biblical text: "Go out into the highways and hedges and compel them to come in."

He considered the Indians a barbaric race: "How can we doubt that these people—so uncivilized, contaminated with so many impieties and obscenities—have been justly conquered by such an excellent, pious and most just king?"

Bartolomé de las Casas ardently disputed that position. A former colonialist turned Dominican monk, he wrote *A Brief Account of the Destruction of the Indies*, an indictment of Spain's regime in the New World and demanded an end to the *encomienda* system, under which the native Indians were enslaved on the great estates.

He once ran his own estate, but was so appalled by the excesses of the Spanish forces that he abandoned his holdings and began campaigning for colonial reform. Apart from attacking Spanish cruelty, he also became an expert on the Indians, citing a mass of evidence to prove that their culture, while neither European nor Christian, was just as complex and sophisticated as their rulers'.

In 1542, he drafted the New Laws, demanding an end to slavery, and Charles V duly backed him up, suspending *encomienda* grants. But those who profited from the system rebelled and the New Laws were repealed in 1546. Despite this, the writings of de las Casas endured as a powerful witness to terrible events and were influential on later thinkers such as Montesquieu. ❑

Minting machine for silver coins from the New World.

ELIZABETH I ON THE THRONE OF ENGLAND

England, November 17, 1558

Henry VIII died in 1547 at the age of 56. Succeeding him to the throne was Edward VI, his son. Edward was nine years old when he was crowned king and reigned for a little less than six years. Upon his death his sister Mary Tudor came to the throne. Mary, the daughter of Henry and his first wife Catherine of Aragon, was England's first queen regnant. She ascended the throne with the intention of restoring papal authority over the English Church; when she died five years later, at age 42, she had caused 300 men and women to be burnt at the stake for their Protestant faith. Mary persuaded Parliament to abandon the independence of the English Church and to submit to papal authority; old Catholic services were revived and priests who, under the reforms of Henry VIII and Edward VI, were allowed to marry, were sacked.

Secret meetings of the English Protestants continued to take place in towns and villages in southern England as Catholic Mary's campaign of persecution spread. Some historians have argued that the queen was not directly responsible for the persecutions that earned her the epithet "Bloody Mary." Nonetheless, she had a political reason for seeking to restore Catholic authority. When Henry's marriage to Catherine of Aragon was annulled, in spite of papal condemnation of the action, Mary

became a bastard; by restoring papal authority over the English church she legitimized her birth. When Mary died in 1558, her half-sister Elizabeth I was

Marcus Geeraerts, *Portrait of Elizabeth I Queen of England, c. 1580*

crowned queen. She was born in 1533, the daughter of Henry's second wife, Anne Boleyn. Her reign was destined to last for 44 years.

At first, Elizabeth relied on the counsel of her Secretary of State, William Cecil, later to become Lord of the Treasury. She decided to reject marriage proposals made by the dynastic monarchies of Europe in an attempt to avoid becoming drawn into the various conflicts troubling the Continent, thus going down in history as the "virgin

queen."

Elizabeth set about consolidating the position of the monarchy in relation to Parliament. During her reign, the great noble houses lost ground to the landed gentry and the merchant class. One reason was her realization that the development of a navy was vital to England's national interests and that meant encouraging the development of seagoing mercantile interests.

After months of parliamentary maneuvering, and a shake-up of the Privy Council, Cecil achieved the religious settlement desired by his queen: Elizabeth reversed Mary's policy, reestablished the Church of England, and firmly repudiated papal au-

thority. In religious matters, Elizabeth tried to steer a course that promoted the Anglican rite, and despite some exceptions, discouraged harsh persecution of Catholics.

The gravest challenge to Elizabeth's rule in her early years as queen came from her cousin Mary Queen of Scots. Mary had been married to the dauphin of France and became the queen consort when he was crowned King of France as Francis II. But upon his death she returned to Scotland. As the great granddaughter of Henry VII she became the focal point for Catholic resistance to Elizabeth. But Mary found herself in the midst of a religious shift in her homeland. At a free Scottish Parliament meeting in Edinburgh, one hundred lairds heard a confession of faith drafted by the Calvinist reformer John Knox. This document aimed to embrace the "elect of all ages, realms, nations, Jews or Gentiles" and specifically rejected the rituals of Rome and abolished the pope's authority in Scotland.

Mary ruled in Scotland for seven years, but was forced to abdicate in favor of James, her one-year-old son. She fled to England and was imprisoned by Elizabeth. Elizabeth hesitated for almost twenty years before finally signing the order for Mary's execution, an act that provoked Catholic Spain into war with England. ❑

GUSTAV AND THE RISE OF SWEDEN

Stockholm, mid-sixteenth century

King Gustav, who almost singlehandedly made Sweden a European power, ensured an orderly handover of power by abdicating in favor of his son, Eric, after 43 years on the throne.

King Gustav, an elected monarch, had guaranteed a hereditary succession for his son

fifteen years before by passing laws establishing that the monarchy would pass through the male line.

Ever since King Gustav made Sweden independent of Denmark and took it out of the Kalmar Union, Sweden had been conscious that its sea and

land routes to the west—the narrow strip of water known as the Oresund— and Norway remained under Danish control, which could ultimately jeopardize its independence. To strengthen its hand, the new king, Eric XIV continued his father's policy of expanding

Sweden's diplomatic and trade links with powers in western and central Europe. Before his accession, the then prince had already tried—without success—to forge one such diplomatic alliance with England by negotiating a marriage with its Queen Elizabeth. ❑

IRRECONCILABLE DIFFERENCES DIVIDE PROTESTANTS FROM CATHOLIC CHURCH

Augsburg, 1555

At an initial meeting in Augsburg in 1530, Lutheran Protestants presented 28 articles of faith to the diet in an attempt to avoid a split with the Catholic Church. The Confession of Augsburg represented a sincere effort at compromise to secure unity. The first 21 articles were points on which both groups had already agreed. The last seven dealt with the controversial issues of confession and the celibacy of priests, leaving them open as being "under discussion."

The Confession was the work of Philip Melanchthon. Luther himself was unable to attend since he remained an exile from the empire. While Melanchthon was a loyal disciple and refused to compromise on matters of essential doctrine, he above all wanted to avoid making common cause with the more rebellious Swiss.

The emperor, Charles V, was also keen to achieve unity, as he needed the support of German Protestant princes in his continuing struggle with Suleiman's Ottoman armies that had laid siege to Vienna the year before. But despite the eagerness on both sides to reach an agreement, the *Confession* was able to do little more than paper over deep religious differences. And even though Luther continually made it clear that he would not go along with armed resistance to the emperor, his battle with the Catholic theologians remained as fierce as ever.

Presentation of the Confession of Augsburg to the Emperor Charles V

Fifteen years later, Catholics and Protestants met again at Augsburg: this time to sign a treaty ending the three-year war in Germany. The political and religious climate, however, had shifted in favor of the reformers, and the treaty also represented a clear recognition by the Catholics of coexistence for the new Protestant churches throughout Europe and a recognition by the emperor of the powers and rights of the German princes. The aging emperor had hoped to bring the Protestants back into the Catholic fold and to secure imperial power over both Catholic and Protestant princes in Germany. At the beginning of the year, riven by gout and under attack from the Turks on his eastern borders, he finally admitted that his dream was impossible. He nominated his brother, Ferdinand, to lead the Diet of Augsburg to find a compromise solution.

The principle established by the peace was *cuius regio, eius religio* (to each kingdom its own religion). In effect, it gave the princes power over the bodies and souls of their subjects. It did not grant ordinary people religious freedom, but they did have the freedom to move to adjoining states if their own prince did not permit their religion.

Charles V was able to take some comfort that the peace ensured the continuance of Catholicism in some German principalities. The Catholic princes, at odds with each other, could never have withstood the surging popularity of Lutheranism on their own. ❏

JESUIT MISSIONARY IN JAPAN

Japan, 1549

When Francis Xavier, a Jesuit missionary, landed in Japan on August 15, 1549, he was initially welcomed and was given permission to preach in the prince's lands. He made some 150 converts, including Barnabas who became his servant and guard.

What Xavier did not appreciate was that the warm welcome stemmed from the belief that rich Portuguese ships would follow the priest. When they did not materialize, an edict was issued making it a capital offense to convert to Christianity.

Xavier and two companions then set out as wandering missionaries. Poorly clad and with no money, they made their way to the capital, Kyoto, in the bitter winter. Francis was well-received among the poorer people but found that they had great difficulty comprehending his message, viewing Christianity as another Buddhist sect. Despite difficulties Xavier persevered and won many converts in other parts of Japan. Upon his departure for Goa after two years of missionary work, he left behind a number of fledgling Christian communities. ❏

Missionary Francis Xavier (unknown Japanese artist, 17th century)

Philip II and the Revolt of the Netherlands

Netherlands, 1567

When Philip II succeeded to the Spanish throne on January 16, 1556, he inherited from his father, Charles V, a vast empire. Taxes were required to govern the Habsburg possessions, and no one in the empire was more heavily taxed than the prosperous nobility and merchant classes of the Seventeen Provinces of the Netherlands. Having been born in Ghent, Charles V was relatively sympathetic toward his Dutch and Flemish subjects, allowing them limited self-government, and practicing toleration for their increasingly influential Protestant faith.

Philip II, an ardently devout Catholic, overturned these policies—reinstituting the Inquisition's harsh religious tribunals, increasing the centralization of Spanish control of the Provinces, and greatly raising taxes. Seen as draconian by not only the Provinces' trading classes but also by commoners, these measures led to the rebellion known as the Revolt of the Netherlands, or the Eighty Years War (1568–1648).

A major early outbreak was a popular revolt in August of 1566 in which a Catholic church in Flanders was ransacked. Fueled by the Calvinist iconoclasts' hatred of the Church's use of statues and other "idolatrous" imagery, the rebellion quickly spread throughout the Low Countries. As it gathered momentum, Philip's appointed Governor, Margaret of Parma, turned for help to William of Orange and members of the States General, a governing body of Dutch nobles. Of the latter, a group calling themselves *Les Gueux* (The Beggars) sought to arrange an accord through a petition to Philip, called "The Request," which guaranteed an end to the rebellion provided that the Spanish Government desist in its persecution of Protestants. The cessation of hostilities was very brief.

William of Orange, along with Lamoral, the Count of Egmont, and Philip de Montmorency, the Count of Hoorn, were Dutch nobles who had been appointed by Philip in 1556 as the Provinces' joint governors. By the time of the revolt, their allegiance had shifted, not so much due to Philip's religious measures, but more because of his policy of centralized Spanish control, and his imposition of confiscatory taxes. As Catholics themselves, they were unsympathetic to the popular revolt, but their growing commitment to Dutch autonomy inspired them to become leaders of the Dutch resistance.

With his Dutch proxy governors siding with the general opposition to Spain's rule and the

The cruelty of the Spanish overlords provoked Dutch resistance

continuation of Calvinist inspired Protestant rebellion, Philip decided in 1567 to restore order by sending the Duke of Alba and ten thousand troops into Brussels. Alba quickly imposed an iron-fisted regime. He wrested all power from Margaret of Parma and set up a new form of Inquisition known as the "Council of Troubles," whose "blood courts" arrested and executed more than one thousand alleged heretics. Two of the victims of these tribunals were the Counts of Egmont and Hoorn.

Alba's brutal tactics served only to inflame the rebellion, especially in the northern Provinces. On April 1, 1572, rebels cap-

Duke of Alba

tured the town of Brielle in Holland. This victory was seen as a turning point in the Dutch war of independence, bringing widespread support for its leader, William of Orange, and signaling the waning of Alba's power over the resurgent Netherlands. By 1573, Alba, was relieved of his command, and William, former Philip II proxy and faithful Catholic, was leading the Dutch resistance as a Calvinist convert. ❑

Tobacco Introduced into Europe

Spain, 1560

Tobacco made its first appearance in Europe at the court of Phillip II of Spain. It had been brought from America originally because its decorative broad green leaves and showy pink flowers had intrigued the European adventurers. The French ambassador Jean Villemain Nicot (from whom the term "nicotine" is derived) brought it to Paris where taking it as snuff soon became the height of fashion. Returning colonists from the failed Roanoke expedition brought the plant home with them to England. In the following century, the habit of smoking tobacco became widely popular. Songs were composed extoling its virtues.

Tobacco was not the only agricultural product that made its way to Europe from the New World. Potato plants were first imported as a kind of botanical oddity, but following its introduction into Ireland, became an important food staple. Sugar was considered a luxury item; the first sugar refinery in Europe was founded in 1573. Rubber's introduction into Europe preceded the discovery of its uses by some centuries. ❑

Smoker (Mayan art)

BRUEGEL'S EARTHY PEASANTS

Brussels, 1565

Toward the end of his life, Peter Bruegel, the genius of Flemish painting, moved to Brussels from Antwerp and began a series of detailed paintings of peasant life. Although he studied in Italy after becoming a master painter in the guild at Antwerp, his unflinching portrayals starkly contrast the idealized Italian style.

A brilliant draftsman, Bruegel found his subjects in the simple routines of haymaking, harvesting, children's games, or hunting in the snow. He liked to illustrate country proverbs, and

to show man in harmony with nature.

Among his most compelling works are *The Fall of Icarus* in which a plowman and a shepherd are quite unaware of the drowning man who has the presumption to fly, *The Tower of Babel*, and an *Adoration of the Magi*, which shows a rough stable crowded with peasant faces and a homely Joseph, listening to a peasant whispering in his ear. Bruegel's sons were both painters: Jan and Peter, who had the nickname "Hell", because he painted devils. ❑

Peter Bruegel the Elder, *Land of Cockaigne*, 1567

CATHOLIC CHURCH RESPONDS TO REFORMATION

Trent, Italy, 1563

A rapid series of votes over the last few days of the Coucil of Trent emphatically asserted the authority of the head of the Roman Catholic Church.

The hopes of the reformers, who wanted to entrust more power in the hands of the bishops, were dashed. Pope Pius called the

Council in the hopes of resolving the struggles between Catholics and Protestants, and particularly the bloody war between Catholics and Huguenots. The traditionalists, who feared that any weakening in the face of the growing power of the Calvinists in France and the Lutherans in Germany

would be fatal to the interests of the Catholic Church, won out.

The Council asserted the importance of the Mass and the authority of tradition and of the bishops. It contradicted the Calvinist assertion of predestination and the idea that ordinary people could interpret the scriptures

as well as the clergy. Reformers gained some ground. Bishops were urged to reside in their dioceses. The accumulation of wealth was prohibited. The ordinary clergy had to be properly trained. A new Bible, based on St Jerome's Latin version, the Vulgate, was endorsed as the ultimate authority. ❑

POLITICAL STRIFE IN FRANCE

Cateau-Cambrésis, 1559

Surrounded by the Habsburgs in Spain and Austria over the course of five wars, France managed to hold onto its territories. After the death of Henry II, his widow Catherine de Medici, who was the mother of the last three monarchs of the House of Valois (Francis II, Charles IX, and Henry III) was able to exercise considerable political influence.

The peace of Cateau-Cambrésis brought a temporary end to conflict. France agreed to recognize the abrogation of all claims on Burgundy. The treaty's terms had the result of strengthening Spain's hand in both Burgundy and Italy and consolidating Habsburg control over Italy. After the Ladies' Peace of Cam-

brai 25 years earlier, hostilities between France and Spain resumed. After suffering a number of painful defeats, France sought to find peace through marriage. The Spanish King Philip II had been a widower since the death of Mary Tudor in 1558. His hopes of wedding her half-sister were unrealized. One of the provisions of the Peace of

François Clouet, *Portrait of Charles IX, King of France*, 1561

Cateau-Cambrésis called for his marriage to Elizabeth, the daughter of Henry II.

The happy event had the unfortunate result of costing the French king his life. He met with an accident on the occasion of the wedding, while participating in a joust in celebration of the nuptials. Following his death, his

widow Catherine de Medici acquired great influence in French politics. Her fifteen-year-old son, Francis II, reigned for less than a year and was followed by his younger brother, Charles IX, who was only ten. She acted as regent until her son reached his majority and after that remained the power behind the throne. Catherine's primary aim was to preserve France's political unity in the face of the religious conflicts that were pulling it apart. The domestic strife was more than her diplomacy could handle. At first, she attempted to placate Huguenot interests, but when that failed, she lost control of the situation and precipitated the St. Bartholomew's Day Massacre. ❑

POWER STRUGGLES IN CHINA AND JAPAN

After the expulsion of the Mongol rulers from China, the emperor Hongwu (1368-1399) marked the return of a pure Chinese dynasty, the Míng Dynasty. At this time, China experienced a long period of peace. The country developed a centralized system of government and the civil service remembered the old traditions of Confucianism.

In this period of revival, China carried on a brisk trade with neighboring countries. This came to an end after almost 300 years amidst the chaos of peasant uprisings against the ever-growing burden of taxation, and raids from northern Manchuria, led by their chieftain Nurhaci. After warring with the Ming Dynasty for several decades, China fell under the foreign domination of the Manchurian Qing Dynasty that united China again. Its new ruler, Tiancong (1626-1634), was the son of Nurhaci.

THE MING PERIOD

The first Ming emperor, Hongwu, had all the generals who threatened his power executed immediately, and he made sure that all government power was concentrated in his hands. The death of this absolute monarch resulted in a civil war that was won by his fourth son. He seized power and ruled under the name Yongle (1402-1425). Yongle moved the capital from Nanjing to Beijing where he built an imperial palace. From there the Ming emperors ruled the country, having divided it into thirteen administrative districts. They were assisted by a network of civil servants, drawn increasingly from the lower but richer merchant class. The position of the officials within the administration depended on how well they passed a graded examination system.

The most important cultural and technical achievements of this period included the building of the Great Wall, the compilation of a universal encyclopedia of 11,000 volumes, and substantial work on production and finishing processes that reveal a high level of technological development. Early on in the Ming Dynasty, China built a deep sea fleet that carried out remarkable expeditions as far as the east African coast. In spite of trade with foreign countries that was initially intense, by the end of the Ming Dynasty China had become increasingly isolated from the rest of the world. In 1514, the Portuguese landed on the coasts of southern China and began trading in pepper, ivory, sandalwood, and scents. In 1557, they were given permission to set up a trading post on the Macao peninsula, which was uninhabited at the time. The Spanish arrived in China in 1575, the Dutch in 1604 (establishing a trading-post in Formosa), and the English in 1637; in the eighteenth century the English controlled the Chinese trade in which, besides silk and porcelain, tea was becoming increasingly important.

Christian missionaries soon followed in the footsteps of the merchants. The Jesuits did what they had done in Japan and adapted themselves to each particular situation so as to be able to work as missionaries. First they dressed as Buddhist monks, then, when they realized that these were no longer highly regarded, they dressed as Confucian monks.

The internal political situation had already begun to deteriorate by the beginning at the seventeenth century. The political leaders were

The Great Wall of China was constructed in the third century as a continuous defensive wall. It was later rebuilt and extended.

permanently involved in conflicts opposing the military, landowners, and civil servants. The peasant population suffered under the heavy burden of taxation and by 1628 had formed a revolutionary peasant army. The Manchurian tribes in the north took advantage of this confusion. In 1644 they captured the capital Beijing that had been defeated by the peasant army. There the last Ming emperor, Chongzhen (1628-1644), hanged himself.

THE QING DYNASTY

Nurhaci and his son had already conquered and united all the northern Manchu tribes. After the fall of Beijing the third Manchu ruler, Shunzi (1644-1662), could now proclaim himself emperor of the whole empire and declare his family the Qing Dynasty.

The new ruler forced Chinese males to shave the top of their heads and wear a plait according to Manchu custom. The highest government posts were always occupied by both a Chinese and a Manchu, but military administration remained in the hands of the conquerors. A reduction in taxation and the building of irrigation systems benefited agriculture, and crafts and commerce also did well. The most important Qing ruler was the emperor Kangxi(1662-1723), whose government was marked by a scientific and cultural renaissance.

Kangxi decreed an edict proclaiming that Christians were free to practice their religion. But as a result of the missionary wars in China between the Dominicans, Franciscans, and Jesuits, the emperor's successor revoked the edict of religious tolerance, and Christians were cruelly persecuted. It was under Qianlong (1736 to 1795) that China saw the greatest expansion in its history. When Yongzheng (1795-1820) came to power, the decline of the Qing Dynasty had already started, caused by the rebellion of various secret sects with hundreds of thousands of followers, together with attacks by a number of tribes at the edges of the empire.

The Europeans took advantage of China's internal problems to increase their political and economic influence in the country. In the end, the problems plaguing this emperor were the result of trade relations with western colonial powers. In about 1830, the British began flooding the country with opium, which had devastating effects on the productivity of the population. This led to violent conflicts that in turn developed into the First Opium War of 1840. After suffering a defeat, China became increasingly dependent on the colonial powers. Until the China became a republic in 1911, it was almost a colony of the West.

JAPAN UNDER THE SHOGUNATE

The shogunate, the rule by regional military leaders, or shoguns, who were chosen from among the warrior caste of the Samurai, completely changed Japanese society. The *tenno* (emperor) lost his political importance. As a result, the existing feudal system in Japan was transformed into centralized military state that lived almost completely isolated from the rest of the world.

By 1180 Yoritomo Minamoto (1147-1199), the victorious head of the Minamoto family in the Samurai civil war, had established the family seat of his court in Kamakura, a small fishing village near present-day Tokyo. In 1192, Yorimoto had himself proclaimed shogun. He reinforced the power of family clan by incorporating the land of the enemies he had conquered into his own estates. The property was then managed by administrators who in turn were supervised by a new police authority. After his death, the leadership of the clan passed to his wife who was of the Hojo clan, but her power soon diminished through increasing mismanagement. As a result, the then emperor was able to restore his power for three years until he was removed again by the shogun Takauji Aschikaga (1303-1358) who founded the Muromachi Shogunate. But this shogunate was so weak that the other territorial princes constantly tried to expand their own territories. Japan was plunged into the worst civil war of its history.

The conflicts that started with the Onin War (1467-1477) lasted over 100 years. In this chaos it was easy for the leaders of the mighty clans in the various regions, the *daimyos*, to develop into powerful feudal lords with absolute powers. During this period of conflict, there were important cultural developments in the fields of architecture, garden design, ceramics, painting, and literature. The monasteries of the Zen Buddhist monks played an important part in these extraordinary cultural achievements, and Zen became the quasi-official religion in Japan.

The unification of Japan after the war was the work of three men: Nobunaga Oda (1534-1582), Hideyoshi Toyotomi (1536-1598), and finally Ieyasu Tokugawa (1542-1616). Nobunaga had bought two muskets from the Portuguese. He quickly had copies of them made. The army, equipped with these new weapons, was able to put an end to the supremacy of the Ashikaga shogunate. After the death of Nobunaga, the general Hideyoshi took over the task of unifying Japan. But he overestimated his military power and invaded Korea without success. Nevertheless, Hideyoshi laid the foundation for the military supremacy of his successor and created a rigorous system of taxation.

Hideyoshi's death was followed by a series of feudal conflicts in the course of which Ieyasu succeeded in seizing power and establishing supremacy of his family that would last for 250 years. Both the local *daimyo* and the *tenno* were deprived of power. In Edo, present-day Tokyo, he founded a strict police state in which the streets were closely patrolled, and people could not change their residences or their professions. Relations with the outside world were restricted to a minimum. Foreigners were forced to leave, and all Christians were violently persecuted.

Japanese society was divided into three layers. At the top were the *daimyo*, followed by the samurai who were in the employ of the *daimyo*, then the people, who included the farmers, craftsmen, and merchants. At the bottom rung were those considered "unclean:" butchers and tanners, beggars, and the physically deformed.

FALL OF THE TOKUGAWA

Japan began to experience growing economic problems around the mid-seventeenth century. One of the main reasons for these difficulties was the transition from the barter economy to the money economy. But the actual cause that led to the collapse came from outside. In addition to growing internal political opposition, there were also problems with Western countries. In 1853, Commodore Matthew C. Perry appeared in the bay of Uraga and delivered a request from the American president to enter into a treaty of friendship that would lead to trade relations between the two countries. Fearing attack, the shogunate acceded to the request and signed the Treaty of Kanagawa on March 31, 1854, opening two Japanese ports to ships from the United States.

The internal opposition against the shogun was aware that the military ruler had seized power that only the *tenno* was entitled to enjoy. Opposition groups began to criticize the shogunate for being too weak in the face of foreign influence. This led to an uprising of the young samurai that collapsed after being attacked by American, French, British, and Dutch warships.

But on January 3, the troops of the insurgents finally entered the palace of Edo and proclaimed a return of power to the emperor. The post of shogun was abolished and the rule of the Tokugawa family that had lasted for more than 250 years came to an end. ❑

FRANCIS DRAKE: PRIVATEER

Plymouth, England, 1577

Sir Francis Drake was born around 1540 in Devon, England. He was a sailor by the age of thirteen. His fabled reputation as a privateer began with two expeditions he made to the West Indies between 1570 and 1572. After successfully pillaging ports throughout the Caribbean, his Spanish victims bestowed on him the sobriquet, *el Draque* (the Dragon.) Returning to England with a cargo of Spanish treasures, he was commissioned by Queen Elizabeth to lead an expedition to plunder Spain's Pacific coast colonies. This mission would result in his becoming the first Englishman to circumnavigate the globe.

He set out from Plymouth with five ships on December 13, 1577, adding a sixth commandeered Spanish galleon. En route to the Straits of Magellan, three ships had to be scuttled. On entering the Straits, they encountered violent storms that sank one of the remaining three and forced another to return to England. Only Drake's ship, the *Golden Hind*, reached the Pacific.

Drake continued up the South American Pacific coast, raiding ports and Spanish galleons, confiscating millions in jewelry, and ducats. He continued north, eventually reaching the latitude that defines the present-day United States/Canada border. Turning south again, in June of 1579, he headed to an inlet historians believe was just north of present day San Francisco. Upon landing, he claimed the port for England, naming it New Albion.

Setting sail across the Pacific on July 23, he began his journey back to England, stopping in the Moluccas and various Indonesian islands where he added spices to his Spanish loot. He arrived back in Plymouth on September 26, where shortly after, he was knighted by Elizabeth.

In 1585, he made another foray of plunder into the West Indies, after which he picked up survivors of the defunct Roanoke Island colony. No sooner had he returned to England when, in 1587, he staged a successful preemptive attack on the Spanish fleet at Cadiz and was subsequently named Vice Admiral of the English fleet that would de-

Sir Francis Drake

feat the Spanish Armada.

His death came on yet another raid through the Caribbean, where, in 1595, he contracted dysentery and died. Like a true sailor, he was buried at sea. ❑

THE BATTLE OF LEPANTO

Mediterranean Sea, 1571

The Turkish invasion of Cyprus by Selim II, the successor to Suleiman the Magnificent, brought the combined fleets of Spain, Venice, and Pope Pius V face-to-face with the larger Turkish fleet. Famagusta had fallen, and reports of unbelievable atrocities had incensed the Christians to a crusading fervor as they sailed from Messina in Sicily.

The two armadas met at Lepanto off the cost of Greece. The pasha's fleet was anchored in the gulf when the Christian fleet hove into sight. The Turks hesitated before moving out to attack in a crescent formation. It was then that the Spanish flagship *La Real* began her charge forward. The flagships struck so hard that they locked together. Fierce fighting continued for two hours with the fiery young Don John, the son of Charles V, leading his men onto the *Sultana*'s foredeck and confronting Ali Pasha in person. The Turkish Commander was killed by a bullet from an *arquebus*, his head struck off and

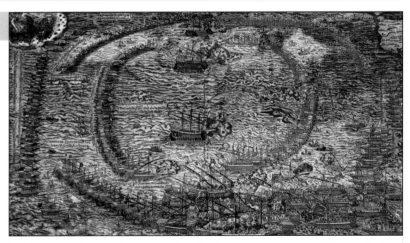

Jost Amman, *Naval victory of the Venetian-Spanish fleet over the Ottoman Turks*

presented to Don John.

The Turks lost 230 galleys in this battle; the Christians, 16.

All told, Lepanto was a grievous setback to Ottoman plans of European expansion. ❑

ENGLISH COMPOSERS ARE MAJOR FORCE IN EUROPEAN MUSIC

England, 1573

A hallmark of the Elizabethan era in England was the emergence of its composers, alongside Italy, in the front rank of modern European music. The 35-year-old Thomas Tallis was the most influential figure. He received a royal license to publish music with his gifted pupil, William Byrd, who like Tallis, was a Gentleman of London's Chapel Royal. Tallis was regarded as one of Europe's finest composers, although his early work was more old-fashioned than that of Christopher Tye (c.1505–1572) and lacked the festal qualities of John Taverner (c.1490–1545), who worked at the new Cardinal College (now Christ Church) in Oxford. The next generation included such figures as John Dowland and Orlando Gibbons.

But the mature Tallis was master of most forms and styles, from masses and other church music in Latin and English to small-scale instrumental works. A member of the royal household from 1543, he was one of the first to write music for the new Anglican liturgy and composed for the Catholic Queen Mary. One of his most remarkable pieces is an astonishing motet, *Spem in alium*, written for forty parts. ❑

MASSACRE ON ST. BARTHOLOMEW'S DAY

Paris, August 24, 1572

The followers of Calvin introduced Protestantism into France in the mid 1530s. But with the adoption of the new faith twenty-five years later by some of France's noble houses the religious differences became politicized and contentious. It was around this time that the term *Huguenot* came into general use to designate French Protestants.

Open warfare broke out between the Catholics and the Huguenots in 1562. Their quarrel split all levels of society from peasants to noblemen, with Gaspard de Coligny, the admiral of France, leading the Huguenots and the Duke of Guise championing the Catholics.

Ironically, the bloodshed stemmed from an attempt at reconciliation by the regent, Catherine de Medici. After her seizure of power, she stopped the persecution of the Calvinists and restored their leaders to influence at court, and in January 1562 her moderate chancellor, Michel de l'Hopital, granted them a degree of freedom of worship. This served only to enrage the fiercely Catholic citizens in Paris and other towns. Led by nobles opposed to religious reform, they began to attack the Huguenots. On March 1, soldiers of the Duke of Guise massacred a number of Huguenots as they prayed at Vassy.

The Protestant prince de Condé called the Huguenots to arms, and they retaliated by despoiling churches, murdering priests, and raping nuns.

This dangerous sparring continued on and off for the next few years, culminating in 1572 in what has become known as the St. Bartholomew's Day Massacre. It started just before dawn when a band of Catholics burst into the house of Gaspard de Coligny, disemboweled him, and threw him out of his bedroom window, still alive. It seems that he was marked for death because of his influence over the young

Charles IX. The king's mother, Catherine de Medici, fearing that Coligny was pushing the king into war with Spain, conspired with the Catholic leader, Henry of Guise, to have him removed.

An earlier attempt on Coligny's life had failed, and the king swore vengeance on the assassins. In order to save herself, Catherine convinced him that the Huguenots were about to rebel and begged him to authorize the killing of their leaders by the Guises.

Many of the Huguenots were in Paris celebrating the marriage of their leader, Henry of Navarre, to the king's sister, Margaret. A list of those to be killed was drawn up, headed by Coligny. But once the killing started, the people of Paris embarked upon a rampage. In all, nearly 10,000 people fell victim to the general, in and outside of the capital.

After the St. Bartholomew's Day Massacre, it became clear that the murder and intrigue that characterized the sectarian civil war in France was also a tactic embraced by the noble houses seeking advantage in the fluid political conditions caused by the weakness of the last kings of the House of Valois (Charles IX and Henry III).

Up until the violence that marked the marriage of Henry of Navarre, the Protestants had remained loyal to the crown. After the massacre, they became its enemy. Certain Protestant thinkers, called *monarchomachs*, propagated a theory of government based upon a social contract that permitted or even required tyrannicide in cases where the monarch violated his oath and attacked true religious faith. Though affirming the king as God's agent, their ideas had the effect of restricting the scope of his powers.

At the same time, challenges to the monarchy were rising on the Catholic side as well. In 1576,

François Dubois, *St. Bartholomew's Day Massacre*, 1572

Henry III granted wide-ranging religious freedoms to the Huguenots. In response, the militantly Catholic Duke of Guise entered into an agreement with the papacy and the Spanish crown designed to prevent the Protestant Henry of Navarre from succeeding Henry III to the throne of France. In 1588, despite the king's backtracking from his guarantees of religious freedom to the Protestants, the duke led a con spiracy that drove the king out of Paris and set the stage for the French crown to remain in Catholic hands.

Religious wars continued until 1598 when Henri IV promulgated the Edict of Nantes, giving Protestants freedom to worship, but discouraging them

Persecution of the Huguenots

from founding churches in regions that were controlled by Catholics. ❑

THE NETHERLANDS SPLIT ALONG RELIGIOUS LINES

Netherlands, January 1579

The seventeen provinces that made up the Netherlands united temporarily to fight against the common Spanish foe. But religious differences were so great that the overwhelmingly Catholic provinces in the south broke from the northern provinces and in 1579 signed a treaty with the Spanish. Then the northern provinces declared their total independence from Spain.

On January 1, 1579, the southern provinces of the Netherlands—Artois, Hainaut, and West Flanders—formalized their union with Spain in an agreement signed with the Spanish stadtholder, Duke Alessandro Farnese di Parma, forming the Union of Arras. On January 23, the northern provinces of Holland, Utrecht, Zeeland, Gelre, and Groningen joined together in the Union of Utrecht. Brabant and the rest of the south bound themselves to the principles of the Union of Arras.

In their struggle against their Spanish overlords, the Dutch were unable to form a united front. Political and, more importantly, religious divides remained unbridged. William Prince of Orange, who organized the resistance starting in 1568 and was named stadtholder by the breakaway provinces in 1572, was only able to unite the opposing factions for a brief time. On November 5, 1576, after bloody attacks by the Spanish on Antwerp and Brabant, the rebellious provinces of Holland and Zeeland entered into an agreement with those provinces not yet in open rebellion, which became known as the Pacification of Ghent. This bound them to mutual aid and cooperation in driving out the Spanish.

Both Catholics and Protestants exhausted their energies in increasingly brutal encounters. Many Catholics who supported the Counter-Reformation wanted to actively suppress what they considered to be heresies; while the Protestants wanted to permit only the practice of Calvinism.

The establishment of the Union of Arras and then the Union of Utrecht marked the bifurcation of the Netherlands. The Union of Arras established the southern provinces as their own state with its own constitution. They recognized the King of Spain as their sovereign and forbade any faith besides Catholicism. One attempt in the spring of 1579 to solve the religious disputes by peaceful means ended in failure. According to the Oath of Abjuration of July 26, 1581, the northern provinces—Holland, Zeeland, Utrecht, Gelre, Groningen, Overijssel, and Friesland—declared themselves independent and wholly free from the Spanish king's authority.

Until the Treaty of Munster of 1648, the northern provinces waged their war against mdSpain without any aid from the south. During the military conflict, a border was created between the north (the Dutch Republic) and the south (what is now Belgium and Luxemburg).During the course of the Counter-Reformation, the southern provinces lost much of their middle-class Calvinist urban population. These emigrants added to the vibrancy of the economy of the northern provinces. In the north, the conflicts came close to sparking a civil war, but a climate of religious tolerance emerged that may in part account for Dutch mercantile success and great prosperity throughout the following century. ❏

WILLIAM PRINCE OF ORANGE

Brief Lives

William I, Count of Nassau and Prince of Orange, was the leader of the Dutch war of independence from Spain and founder of the House of Orange.

He was born on April 25, 1533, and raised as a Catholic. In 1544, he inherited vast estates in the Netherlands and became stadtholder of Holland, Zeeland, Utrecht, and Franche-Comté. As the most powerful Dutch

Prince William of Orange

aristocrat, he naturally assumed a leading role in the movement to free Holland from Spanish rule.

In 1572, after some success against a weakened Spanish monarchy, he claimed the titles that the Spanish had revoked. In 1573, he converted to Calvinism. In 1576, he organized an assembly that enacted the pacification of Ghent, which guaranteed religious toleration in the Netherlands. It also marked an important first step toward establishing a sense of national identity among the various provinces that made up the Netherlands. William's popularity began to wane in the next decade. He was assassinated in 1584 by a French Catholic soldier. ❏

Dutch fighting for independence from Spain. Roderigo de Holanda, *The Battle of Nijmegen*, late 16th century

EL GRECO: VISIONARY ARTIST

Toledo, 1577

The paintings of El Greco marked a radical shift in the style of European painting. In a career that lasted for fifty years, he produced an exciting and dramatic body of work.

El Greco (the Greek) was born in Crete in 1541 and moved from his homeland to the Spanish city of Toledo, where he resided until his death in 1614. Schooled as an icon painter, he traveled to Venice where he came under the influence of Titian and Tintoretto. His attempts to find work in Rome were generally unsuccessful, probably because he did not hew closely enough to the style of Michelangelo.

El Greco developed his own style in Spain. His idealized human figures are attenuated, reaching upward, seemingly in the grip of some powerful religious emotion. He jettisoned the harmonious proportions that informed Renaissance art, as, for example, in Leonardo's *Vitruvian Man*, to achieve greater emotional tension and expression.

Religious elements are dominant in his work. The Catholic Church in the battles of Reformation and Counter-Reformation enlisted artists. Spain was particularly fertile soil for the mystical strain of Christianity—as evidenced by such figures as St. Theresa of Avila and St. John of the Cross. Accordingly, El Greco concentrated on the ecstatic and supernatural sides of religious experience. El Greco's paintings did not win the approval of the royal patron, Phillip II, who was very exacting in his tastes and may have rejected El Greco's overly free interpretation of Biblical themes. The artist did, however, gain commissions from religious organizations as well as from private individuals that enabled him to weather some economic difficulties and live comfortably in Toledo. ❏

El Greco, *Veil of Veronica*

ARCIMBOLDO: ARTIST AND JOKER

Prague, late sixteenth century

Giuseppe Arcimboldo was the master of the revels of Emperor Rudolf and his trusted friend. He was an exemplar of the later stages of Mannerism, a reaction to what was perceived as the overly static nature of Renaissance ideas of harmony and proportion. Mannerism applauded asymmetry and is noted for the torsion and attenuation of the human figure. Arcimboldo took this aesthetic to an extreme. He was especially known for his deceptive portraits. He could paint a collection of books to look like the face of a librarian, and would make up portraits out of animals or a tree trunk and its branches. He painted one portrait of the emperor himself entirely out of vegetables. ❏

Giuseppe Arcimboldo, *Fire,* 1566

SIBERIA BROUGHT UNDER RUSSIAN CONTROL

Russia, 1582

The Stroganovs, a Russian merchant family, received from Ivan IV the exclusive rights to establish trading posts in the vast area of the northeastern part of European Russia. They were given a twenty-year grant to exploit all of the land surrounding the Kama River and its tributaries. They hired the Cossack leader Yermak to defend their trading posts. The Cossacks were roving bands of warriors, as much brigands as regular soldiers. Yermak was a fitting leader, an imposing and energetic warrior.

In a bid to enlarge the territory under their control, the Stroganovs pushed east and came into conflict with the Siberian Tartars, the people native to the area. Using the Cossacks as a private army, the Russian merchants defeated the Tartars, whose troops were unable to withstand the Cossacks' superior firepower. Their ruler, Kuchum Khan, was driven into the steppes and his capital of Qashliq (near the present-day city of Tobolsk) was overrun. Some years later, counterattack caught the Cossacks by surprise, and Yermak was killed during the fighting. Yermak acquired the coloration of legend; he is featured prominently in the *Siberian Chronicles*. ❏

MOGHUL EMPEROR'S EXPERIMENT IN RELIGIOUS TOLERANCE

Fatehpur Sikri, India, 1582

Though illiterate, the great Moghul emperor Akbar (1542–1605) attempted to pursue a revolutionary program of religious tolerance. His reasons were as much political as they were spiritual in that he realized that only by rising above religious differences would he be able to unite India.

He built a "house of worship" (the *Ibadat Khana*) in his new city of Fatehpur Sikri, where he discussed religion with Sunnis, Shiites, Hindus, Zoroastrians, and Christians. All sought his conversion unaware of his aim of synthesizing the great religions and saving India from sectarianism.

At first Akbar invited only Muslims, but he was so disappointed by their bigotry that he renounced orthodoxy and adopted Jain ideas, becoming a vegetarian. Akbar put his ideals of religious toleration into practice, placing Hindus in high administrative positions and maintaining generally cordial relations with Jesuit missionaries. ❏

MISADVENTURES OF ROANOKE COLONY

North Carolina, 1590

In 1583, Sir Humphrey Gilbert tried without success to establish a permanent English settlement on the coast of Newfoundland. Two years later, Walter Raleigh organized and sponsored another colonial venture. A party of English sailors landed on the American mainland in what is today North Carolina to claim possession of almost 2,000 miles of American coastline. The leader of the endeavor was Sir Richard Greenville. He put 108 settlers ashore but did not leave them enough food. Their hunger led to hostility with the indigenous people. After a year, in June of 1586, they were rescued by Sir Francis Drake and brought back to England.

The following year, Raleigh sent out a second group of colonists under the command of John White, an artist who had accompanied Raleigh on earlier voyages of exploration. White's daughter gave birth in Roanoke to a daughter, christened Virginia Dare, the first English child born in the Americas.

Meanwhile Raleigh himself had been knighted for his initial discoveries and had won royal permission to name the new territory on the eastern seaboard "Virginia" in honor of the "Virgin Queen."

As conditions were deteriorating in the colony, it was decided that White would return to England to obtain further support for the settlement. His trip homeward was a perilous one and the attack of the Spanish Armada delayed his return to America, since every ship had been commandeered for England's defense. He finally made it back in 1590 to find that his granddaughter and 100 other souls of the little community had vanished, leaving no sign of violence and only one clue to what had happened: the word "Croatoan"—the name of an Indian tribe—carved on a post at the entrance to the empty palisade. Following this setback, plans to colonize Roanoke were abandoned. It would be almost twenty years before a permanent settlement would be established in Jamestown. ❑

Sir Walter Raleigh

DEFEAT OF THE SPANISH ARMADA

English Channel, July 20, 1588

Queen Elizabeth's execution of Mary Queen of Scots enraged the Spanish crown. It proved to be the final provocation that led to the launching of a fleet of Spanish ships for an attack on England. It would turn into a disaster for Spanish interests and signal the emergence of England as Europe's great naval power.

The Spanish Armada, commanded by the Duke of Medina Sidonia, set sail in May of 1588, and was sighted in the English Channel on July 20. During the night, with the Spanish anchored in close battle formation, the English slipped past to the Spanish rear. The Spanish outnumbered them two to one, with some ships of 1,000 tons and packed with soldiers with great grappling irons. But the English ships, though small, were highly maneuverable and superior in long-range gunfire.

By darting in, releasing their broadsides and escaping before the heavier Spanish cannon could be brought to bear, the English created havoc among the enemy, although they could make no impact on the stout Spanish hulls.

All afternoon and during the following night, the Armada pushed up the Channel, with the English snapping at its flanks. Medina Sidonia was expecting to rendezvous with reinforcements and landing craft from the Spanish Netherlands. They never made it. Patrols of rebel Dutch "sea beggars" saw to that. After a week of running fights, Medina Sidonia anchored off Calais. The English, standing off a mile distant, were ready with fireships stacked with wood, pitch, and explosives. They went in at midnight, the raging fires causing panic aboard the Spanish galleons. Ships collided and sank as anchors were abandoned and cables severed.

Daybreak found the fearsome Armada broken up and drifting. The English struck repeatedly. Some ships were sunk, others ran onto sandbanks, the rest fled. All told, the Spanish lost 65 ships and upwards of 10,000 men. The English lost fewer than 100 men and not one ship.

The ragged remnants of the Armada sailed north, seeking to escape into the Atlantic around the Orkneys and

The Spanish Armada attacked by English ships.

LONG RULE OF PHILIP II IN SPAIN

Madrid, 1598

Philip II of Spain, who had ruled the world's most powerful country for more than 40 years, died in his grim and gloomy Escorial palace outside Madrid on September 13, 1598, at the age of 71.

Under Philip, Spain became the richest and most formidable nation on earth, and he boasted of ruling the world from the Escorial with pen and paper. But Spain had been in trouble ever since he sent his "Invincible Armada" to face the English in 1588. The bid to punish England for its support of Dutch Protestants fighting against Spanish rule, and for plundering Spanish possessions in Mexico and South America, failed miser-

ably. Although Spain remained a major power after the defeat, its prestige was seriously damaged and its naval supremacy lost.

Philip's achievements, however, were many. Aided by the heroic defense of Malta by the Knights of St. John, he broke the power of the Turks in the Mediterranean. In 1580, he conquered the Philippines. In 1582, he annexed Portugal to give his country a new Atlantic seaboard, a fleet to help to protect it, and

Philip II of Spain

a second empire stretching from Africa to Brazil, from Calicut to the Moluccas. The accomplishment of the takeover required two years of political and diplomatic maneuvering and, finally, the dispatch of an army to his neighbor. Philip then convened the *cortes* (the parliament) at Tomar and took the oath to observe all the laws and customs of the realm. In turn, he was recognized as the lawful king of

Portugal.

But the Netherlands, one of the most valuable possessions in the empire, declared its independence in 1581 and a treaty with France shortly before Philip's death marked Spain's slow retreat from northern Europe.

Philip married Queen Mary of England earlier in his reign, at a time when the English looked upon Spain as their greatest enemy. He lived with her for only a little more than a year before returning to Spain. He regarded himself as a great champion of the Roman Catholic faith and supported the harsh measures of the Inquisition. ❑

Shetlands. The disaster would have been even greater had the pursuing English ships not been forced to turn back when they ran out of food and ammunition. But the Spanish fleet was further decimated by harsh weather conditions.

Relations between the two kingdoms had been strained for a considerable period of time. Philip of Spain's colonies and ships had suffered for years from the raids of Francis Drake, John Hawkins, and other English privateers. Whenever the Spanish ambassador protested, Elizabeth was noncommittal and the raids continued. After Spain signed a treaty with Henry III of France to make a common league against the French Huguenots, England threw its support to the Dutch independence movement. Elizabeth's dispatch of troops to aid the rebellion led to a

further deterioration in relations between the two countries. After strong threats from Spain and the discovery of a plot against the English crown, Elizabeth ordered the execution of her rival,

Execution of Mary Queen of Scots in Fotheringay (copper etching, 1588)

the Catholic Mary Stuart, who had been held prisoner since 1568. This was an open affront to France and Spain not only because of their shared faith, but because of the close relations

between Mary and their ruling houses.

Despite the fact that James VI, Mary's son and destined successor to the throne of Scotland, was a Protestant, Phillip saw the execution as tantamount to a declaration of war and the justification to force England back to the Catholic Church. In anticipation of coming hostilities, Sir Francis Drake attacked the Spanish navy in its harbor at Cadiz; just another incident in a long line of provocations.

Historians have suggested a number of reasons for the failure of the Armada. English ships were smaller and better suited to the constrictions of the Channel. They also were better able to employ their weapons and take advantage of unfavorable weather conditions. ❑

HENRY IV AND THE EDICT OF NANTES

France, 1598

Henry of Navarre ascended the French throne amid the turbulence of sectarian conflict. A few years into his reign, in what was considered a political masterstroke, he had a Mass said in Paris during which he formally rejected Protestantism and was received into the Catholic religion. The ceremony took place in the Basilica of St. Denis. Having made his confession and hearing Mass, he swore allegiance to the Church, reiterated

his renunciation of Protestantism, and received absolution. He left the basilica to the cheers of the Parisian crowd that saw in his conversion the promise of an end to the religious wars which had ravaged France for so long.

This was the second time that Henry had abjured his faith; the first time was during the St. Bartholomew's Day Massacre when he did so to save his life but afterward recanted. The second time he did it with the hard-won knowledge that he would never be recognized as the true king of France without becoming a Catholic. It is reported that as he looked down on the city from the hill of Montmartre, he said: "Paris is worth a Mass"

The culmination of his strategy to bring France together under his rule was reached in 1598. Despite his conversion, religious quarrels persisted. He gained popular goodwill with his victory over the Spanish and his successful suppression of a secessionist revolt in Brittany. With the country relatively peaceful,

A Protestant church built in Lyons after the Edict of Nantes

he was able to win back the Huguenot support he had lost upon his conversion. In April of 1598, he signed the "perpetual and irrevocable" Edict of Nantes, which granted Protestants freedom of conscience throughout the kingdom. The edict restored their old places of worship and granted them permission to build new ones. They now were granted equal civic rights with

the Catholics and allowed access to all public posts. The terms of the edict did not please many Catholics, but such was the war-weariness in France that they accepted the edict in return for peace. The following month the ailing King Philip of Spain signed the Peace of Vervins and his army marched home, leaving Henry the undisputed king of all of France. ❏

King Henry IV of France

WILLIAM SHAKESPEARE

Brief Lives

The Bard, as William Shakespeare came to be known, was born in 1564 in the English town of Stratford-upon-Avon where, it is believed, he attended grammar school learning a little Latin and less Greek. At eighteen, he married Anne Hathaway, daughter of a farmer, and they had three children. There are few records to consult as to how, after he left his provincial beginnings and moved to London to write and act, he became the greatest playwright of all time.

Scholars believe that Shakespeare began his writing career at the end of the 1580s, and probably worked on two or three plays at a time. In the course of his life, he wrote 37 plays, more than 150

sonnets, and numerous poems. He collaborated with others on dramas as well. He also acted, sometimes in his own plays (legend has it he played the Ghost in *Hamlet*), and he became a shareholder in the Globe Theatre, which produced much of his work in the 1590s. He grew up in the Elizabethan era, which celebrated plays and pageantry, although many topics were censored. Other playwrights of his time included Ben Jonson and Christopher Marlowe. While the plays of Jonson may have received more acclaim from his contemporaries, those of Shakespeare were more popular and his financial success as a dramatist was unrivaled. He earned enough money from theater and his real estate in-

vestments to retire to a fine home in Stratford. Shakespeare died in 1616 after contracting a fever. ❏

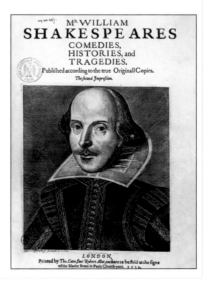

ENGLISH AND

London 1600

Trade with the east grew dramatically in the early seventeenth century as sea routes replaced ancient land routes. The defeat of the Spanish Armada opened up opportunities for England and the Netherlands to compete with Portugal and Spain to transport and trade valuable spices and silks. In England, Queen Elizabeth granted a Charter of Incorporation to the East India Company in 1600. It granted George Clifford, the Earl of Cumberland, and 215 knights, aldermen, and merchants the right to trade in the East Indies for 15 years.

The members of the Company put up £72,000 to finance a large-scale trading expedition and made plans to send a fleet

SHAKESPEARE AND THE GLOBE

London, 1599

The popularity of plays in Elizabethan England was remarkable. Prior to the 1570s, most dramas were morality plays or mystery cycles performed in the church or outside in an impromptu set up, but now, for the first time, freestanding theaters in London were being built and drawing large crowds.

Shakespeare came to London in the 1580s and associated with a group of players, or actors, called the Lord Chamberlain's Men (later the King's Men). In 1599, Shakespeare and members of the troop helped finance the building of the Globe Theater on the south bank of the Thames. It was here that Shakespeare acted and presented most of his best-known plays. The Globe was a partially covered, open-air wooden structure, three stories tall. It usually put on plays six days a week and occasionally two plays in a day were scheduled. Players rehearsed in the morning and performed in the afternoon. The core company of twelve performed year-round, closing only during Lent. It is estimated that the audiences numbered close to 1,500 to 2,000 a day. Playgoers came from all classes, commoners and aristocrats alike, and paid a penny to stand or two pennies to sit. Performers often played two and sometimes three roles in a play, which had virtually no props (save for the crucial trap door) and, of course, no lighting other than daylight. The company consisted of men and boys; women did not appear on stage until the 1660s. This accounts for the much larger roles, in terms of lines, given to men than women in the dramas of the time.

Shakespeare's plays, unlike his rhymed sonnets and poems, were written chiefly in blank verse. At the time they were first performed, they were not divided into five acts, nor were they usually printed, as the Globe did not want other theaters to gain hold of them.

Shakespeare wrote comedies, tragedies, and histories. His genius rests not only in his ability to capture the depth and range of human emotions, from jealousy to lust, from revenge to innocent love but, as a recent biographer said: "Shakespeare seems to have recycled every word he ever encountered, every person he ever met, every experience he ever had." His work is a rich parade of humanity. Many scholars believe that Queen Elizabeth so liked the fat, funny, and vital Falstaff that she insisted Shakespeare write a play about him being in love. Thus was born *The Merry Wives of Windsor*.

Equally remarkable was Shakespeare's use of language, which continues to inspire scholars and audiences. He had an enormous vocabulary (nearly three times that of the average English speaker) and introduced many new words into the English language. *The First Folio*, a collection of all but two of his plays, was published after his death in 1623. ❑

Scene from a performance of Shakespeare's *Julius Caesar*

DUTCH COMPANIES TRADE IN ASIA

of five ships to do business in the rich markets of Sumatra and Java. James Lancaster, who returned from a pioneering voyage to Sumatra, Malacca, and Ceylon in 1564, was appointed general of the fleet. In the early days of the East India Company, each voyage would have its own subscribers or shareholders.

Meanwhile, in the Netherlands various trading companies that had been engaged in cutthroat competition for spices and textiles in the East Indies were united in 1602 under one corporation. The Dutch East India Company was given a monopoly of Dutch trade and navigation east of the Cape of Good Hope and west of the Magellan Straits for an initial period of 21 years. The company, governed by a board of seventeen directors drawn from the Dutch states, was also granted sweeping powers to conclude treaties, keep a standing army, wage defensive war, and build "fortresses and strongholds" in the East Indies, thus becoming a state within a state. ❑

Founding of the East India Company

JAPAN CLOSES ITS DOORS TO THE WORLD

Japan, 1603

The closing of Japan to the West began at the end of the Sengoku Period with the beginning of Japanese unification under Toyotomi Hideyoshi. Having initially cultivated cordial relations with Portuguese Jesuit missionaries, Hideyoshi's growing disaffection with their Superior, Gaspar Coelho, resulted in his banning Christianity and ordering the Jesuits to leave the country. The issuing of this edict on July 25, 1587, came as a surprise to the missionaries. Only a day before, Hideyoshi had made a courtesy visit to Coelho. Within hours of the visit, Hideyoshi had sent a messenger back to him with an angry denunciation, accusing the Jesuits of selling Japanese as slaves and destroying Buddhist images. Some in the Jesuit community blamed the falling out on Coelho's mishandling of Hideyoshi.

With the rise of the Tokugawa Shogunate after its founder Ieyasu's victory at the Battle of Sekigahara in 1600, a new Japanese nationalism emerged, occasioning a growing intolerance of Western culture, especially the presence of Christian missionaries.

Ieyasu, who valued the profitable trade relations with the West and who had a close confidant in the English trader, William Adams, was initially well-disposed to Europeans. However, he became increasingly distrustful of the possible spillover effect that the dissension between European Catholics and Protestants might have on the Japanese Christian communities. His successors would inherit this legacy of distrust and transform it into full-blown xenophobia.

After Ieyasu's death in 1616, his successor, Hidetada, began instituting anti-Christian measures. He demanded the renunciation of the Christian faith throughout Japan, and went so far as to execute a number of Japanese and foreign faithful, and to force a leader of the Japanese Church to commit suicide. At heart, these actions were aimed at Christianity not as a religion, but because it was the faith of Japan's potential invaders.

With Shogun Iemitsu's Sakoku Edict of 1635, the closing of Japan to the West was complete. Its provisions were draconian: It prohibited travel outside of Japan; it banned Christianity entirely, calling for the hunting down and imprisonment of all Christian converts and Euro-

Siege of Osaka Castle

pean missionaries still working underground; it limited trade to a handful of Dutch East India Company and Chinese merchants, prohibiting all other commercial relations.

Not until the arrival of Commodore Perry in 1854, and the subsequent Treaty of Amity and Commerce with the United States in 1858, would Japan reopen its doors to the West. ❑

GIORDANO BRUNO CONDEMNED AS HERETIC

Rome, February 17, 1600

Giordano Bruno, one of the most important Renaissance philosophers, was born in Nola, in 1548, and became a Dominican in 1565. He advocated the ideas of Copernicus, who argued that the sun, not the earth, is the center of the universe, in opposition to the religious dogma of his time. Charged with heresy in 1576, he fled from the order and led the restless life of a wanderer traveling through England, France, and Germany. For a time he lived under the protection of the French king Henry III. He was first arrested by the Inquisition in Venice in 1592, but freed after he recanted the heresies of which he was accused. Later, after withdrawing his recantation, he was expelled from the Church as "an impenitent heretic" and sent to a secular court in Rome for punishment. On February 2, 1600, he was burnt at the stake.

Bruno hoped to heal the split between Protestants and Catholics and the Church and science.

Ettore Ferrari, *Giordano Bruno Burnt at the Stake by the Inquisition*, bronze relief, 1887, in the Piazza di Campo de' Fiori, Rome

He taught that nature's infinity corresponded to the infinitude of God, drawing metaphysical implications out of Copernicus's displacement of earth from the center of the universe, challenging the Church claim to be the only vehicle through which one could find salvation. ❑

ENGLISH AND SCOTTISH THRONES UNITED

England, March 24, 1603

Queen Elizabeth died at Richmond early in the morning of March 24, 1603, after a reign of 45 years. As she had no progeny, her successor was King James VI of Scotland, the son of Mary Queen of Scots, who became James I of England. James was the great grandson of the sister of Henry VIII and thus a direct descendant of the founder of the Tudor line, Henry VII. With his accession, the crowns of England and Scotland were united.

Elizabeth succeeded to an England riven by religious divisions, at war with France, and heavily in debt to the bankers of Antwerp. After a reign of 45 years, she bequeathed to her successor an exchequer which, for all her parsimony, had been drained by rebellion in Ireland and support for the Protestant revolt against Spain in the Netherlands.

But in her long reign, the arts flourished as never before, and they continued to ornament the years of James's kingship.

To her subjects, Elizabeth was England personified. Her bad habits—swearing, beer drinking, and spitting—did not lose her the affection of those who served her. As she said before the Armada: "Let tyrants fear. I know I have the body of a weak and feeble woman, but I have the heart and stomach of a king, and a king of England too; and think foul scorn that any prince of Europe should dare invade the borders of my realm."

The transition of power had been prepared before the death of Elizabeth and went without incident. However, five years later, a plot to overthrow the government was uncovered. Guy Fawkes, a Yorkshireman who served with the Spanish forces in the Netherlands after converting to Catholicism, was apprehended in the cellars under the Houses of Parliament with twenty barrels of gunpowder. Under severe torture, he confessed to plotting to blow up the House of Lords when the king and queen, Prince Henry, and members of both houses were assembled for the opening of Parliament.

Fawkes at first refused to reveal his accomplices, but King James ordered the torture to continue until finally Fawkes named Robert Catesby, a zealous Catholic, who had been involved in earlier plots against Elizabeth. Catesby and his fellow plotters planned to kidnap the king's daughter once Fawkes had succeeded.

The conspiracy was exposed after Lord Monteagle, a Catholic peer who had declared his loyalty to the king, received an anonymous note urging him to stay away from the opening of Parliament on November 5, because "God and man" would deliver "a terrible blow." Monteagle showed the note to Lord Salisbury, the king's chief minister, and the cellars were searched. Catesby and three others died resisting arrest. Guy Fawkes was tried, found guilty, and executed.

The unveiling of the conspiracy, known as the Gunpowder Plot, continues to be celebrated in England on the evening of November 5, as Bonfire Night. ❑

James I, King of England (1603-1625) and since 1567 James VI of Scotland (oil painting by Roland Lockey, 1621)

CARAVAGGIO'S DRAMATIC PAINTING

Rome c.1600

With his explorations of the technique of *chiaroscuro* (light-dark), Caravaggio developed into the most significant Italian painter of the early baroque period.

In 1600, Caravaggio (1573–1610, born Michelangelo Merisi) received a commission from his patron Cardinal del Monte for two paintings to adorn the Contarelli Chapel in the Church of San Luigi dei Francesi in Rome. The heightened realism of the two works, the *Martyrdom of Saint Matthew* and *Calling of Saint Matthew*, sealed his reputation. Matthew's depiction as an old man with a bald head and dirty feet shocked his contemporaries, as did Caravaggio's masterful use of light. He organized his paintings around areas of profound shadow juxtaposed with harsh illumination, which give the human actors in his dramas an intense emotional charge.

Caravaggio led a wild life. He was a notorious brawler and killed a man in 1606. His powerful patrons could do little to protect him, and he spent the most of his few remaining years as an outlaw. He supposedly died of fever, but the circumstances surrounding his death still remain mysterious. ❑

Caravaggio. *The Lute Player*, c. 1594. This early work shows the artist's mastery of light and shadow.

EARLY EUROPEAN SETTLEMENTS IN THE NEW WORLD

Point of Interest

When the Europeans first began their conquest of North America there were somewhere between one and eight million native inhabitants on the continent. They lived in hundreds of small tribes that exhibited a range of cultural practices and social organization, and they often fought among themselves.

England: The first encounters between the Indians and the English settlers were more or less friendly. Within a year of their arrival, the Pilgrim Fathers concluded a treaty of mutual assistance with the Indian chief Massasoit. The whites were allowed the freedom to build by the natives, who informed them about unfamiliar plants and the climate and soil of the new land. As the number of settlers increased so did tensions between the two populations. There was a fundamental difference in their ideas of property and land ownership. The colonists felt that they had a legitimate claim to the lands they were settling that derived from a royal grant. They also considered land as property

that could be bequeathed to their progeny. This concept of ownership was entirely alien to the native peoples. The newcomers referred to agreements that they used as proof of their right to dispose of the land as they saw fit and began to push the Indians out of their tribal lands.

In 1637, war between the combined forces of the Plymouth Colony and settlers from Connecticut with the Pequot Indians resulted in the dispersal of the tribe.

In 1675, the Wampanoag, Abenaki, Massachussetts, and Mohegan tribes formed a confederation under the leadership of the Wampanoag chief, Metacom, to oppose further incursions by the English settlers. But their resistance collapsed within a year and led to further massacres by the whites. Most of the survivors fled. By 1680, there were only about 15,000 natives still living in New England.

France: With the founding of Quebec Colony in 1608 the French began their colonization of the New World. In the previ-

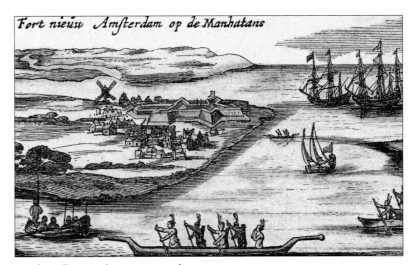

Fort nieuw Amsterdam op de Manhatans

Dutch trading post in New Amsterdam

ous century, French explorers had traveled through what is now Canada in search of a sea route to the Orient.

The French were much more interested in trade than in agricultural production or in building settlements in their North American colonies. They were also concerned about maintaining a balance with the other colonial powers. Accordingly, Louis XIV staked a claim to all of the central

area of North America. During his reign, French settlers traveled the length of the St. Lawrence River, through the Great Lakes, and down to the mouth of the Mississippi River. In 1682, the explorer Robert de la Salle named the territory along its banks Louisiana, in honor of his king.

Netherlands: In 1621, the Estates General of the Netherlands established the Dutch West India Company following the model

MIGUEL DE CERVANTES AND *THE MAN OF LA MANCHA*

Spain, 1605

Miguel de Cervantes Saavedra published *Don Quixote de Ia Mancha* in 1605 to immediate acclaim. Cervantes was born in 1547, in Alcala, to a noble but impoverished family. He left Spain at the age of 22 and enlisted in the army in Italy; wounded at the battle of Lepanto in 1571, he continued soldiering until in 1575 he was taken prisoner by the Turks. Despite many attempts at escape, he spent five years in Algiers before he was ransomed and returned to Madrid. He began writing, but poverty forced him into a variety of temporary jobs.

His first book, *La Galatea*, appeared in

Miguel de Cervantes

1585, but it was not until the publication of his masterpiece *Don Quixote* in 1605 that he experienced real success. The adventures of *Don Quixote de Ia Mancha* simultaneously poked fun at the traditional tales of chivalry and took a hard look at contemporary Spanish society.

Cervantes portrayed his hero as a keen consumer of just the sort of stories that Cervantes wished to mock; indeed, too much romance had driven Quixote mad. Accompanied by his squire Sancho Panza, whose earthy common sense contrasts with his master's fantasies, Quixote sets off on his aging horse, Rosinante, to

roam the world in search of adventure.

In his madness, the most ordinary things appear romantic or terrifying. In true chivalric style, he has his own fair lady, even if the girl he honors has no idea of his interest. Taking up his lance he tilts at what he thinks are giants, but in reality are only windmills. Quixote

Gustave Doré, *Don Quixote and Sancho Panza*, drawing

ENGLISH COLONIES AT JAMESTOWN AND PLYMOUTH

Jamestown, 1607

of the East India Company. It granted the company a monopoly on trade and the right to establish settlements in America, the Pacific Islands, and the west coast of Africa. In 1626, the Dutch acquired the island of Manhattan from the resident natives for a sum of about $24. The Dutch had already settled the area, but saw Manhattan as a secure defensive position as they pursued their trading activities. While the English built their houses close together around churches that stood at the center of their settlements, the Dutch residences were more widely scattered.

Competition for trade and sea routes between England and the Netherlands led to a war in which the English emerged as victor and the Dutch relinquished their claims to the colony of New Netherlands (most of present-day New York, New Jersey, and Connecticut). This possession was regained by the Dutch in 1673 but then reverted to England according to the Treaty of Westminster signed the year after.❏

searched for fine ideals, but the modern Spain in which he travels proves disappointing. Greed has replaced chivalry, and gold, looted from the New World, has taken the place of the knightly qualities he values.

Don Quixote was so popular that a "second part" appeared, written by an anonymous hack. Cervantes responded with a genuine sequel, as popular as the original. Cervantes also wrote plays, including *La Numancia* and *Los tratos de Argel*. In 1613, he published a set of short stories, which he called *Exemplary Novels*.

Just after completing his romance, *Persiles y Sigismunds*, in 1615, Cervantes succumbed to a sudden, fatal illness. ❏

Despite the failure of the Roanoke colony, Raleigh's venture had sparked considerable interest in England. The Virginia Company of London was founded and received a patent from James I to settle the east coast of North America. It financed an expedition consisting of over one hundred colonists hoping that they would find gold or spices in the New World. The company landed in Chesapeake Bay and founded the Jamestown colony. The hoped-for great riches, however, never materialized. Conditions were so harsh that many of the settlers did not survive the first few years.

The English took advantage of the troubled religious and sectarian climate on the Continent to expand its colonial reach. Unlike Spain, France, and Portugal, settlements were not the monopoly of the state. For England, as in Holland, the primary impetus for overseas enterprises rested in private hands.

A second venture to America was undertaken by a group seeking a place to freely practice their religion. After a hazardous voyage across the Atlantic, the *Mayflower*, a 180-ton ship normally used to carry wine, brought 120 anti-

Colonization of America. Arrival of the Pilgrim Fathers in Plymouth

Model of the *Mayflower*

Catholic Puritans to the shores of what they called "New England." It landed in what is now Plymouth, Massachusetts, on Cape Cod.

The colonists faced difficulties from the very start of their voyage. Even as the settlers rowed ashore, Dorothy Bradford, the wife of one of their leaders, fell overboard and was drowned.

Some colonists made it clear that they would obey no law once they landed. The sense of impending lawlessness grew when storms drove the *Mayflower* north of her destination to Indian territory known as Massachusetts. The response of 41 of the settlers was to draft their own "Mayflower Compact" a charter for civilization rather then anarchy.

During the first days ashore, the fitter members carried the ailing majority and built temporary shelters near the beach. Miles Standish, a leading settler, led armed settlers on a reconnaissance of the area. They came under attack from the native inhabitants after interfering with their gravesites but frightened the attackers away with gunshot.

With winter imminent, the settlers had to forage for food, including stores of Indian-grown corn. One useful source of food was a breed entirely new to the settlers—the turkey.

Within a year of landing, the Puritan settlement had reached a peaceful accommodation with the native Wampanoag people thanks to a remarkable pair of English-speaking Indians. One, named Tisquantum or "Squanto," was originally of the Patuxet tribe but had been living in a Wampanoag village. He was taken captive by George Weymouth in 1605 and brought to England where he lived for some years.

Squanto recrossed the Atlantic in 1614 to help Captain John Smith, only to be sold as a slave to Spain by the English explorer Thomas Hunt. The Indian escaped and reached England. From there he was able to return once again to America, before returning to Massachusetts. It was probably due to his efforts that the settlers were able to survive the first harsh winter and began to adapt to their new home. ❏

THE FIRST NEWSPAPER

Strasbourg, 1609

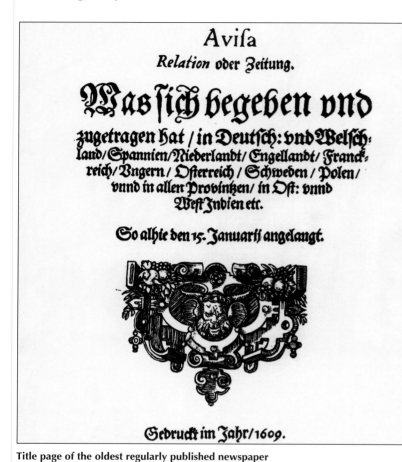

Title page of the oldest regularly published newspaper

The first weekly newspaper came out in German in 1609, and appeared regularly each week. The first daily newspaper, the *Einkommenden Zeitungen*, was published in Leipzig and had its first issue in 1650.

The printer and bookbinder Johann Carolus asked his readers in his first issue of *Relation Aller Furnemmen und Gedenckwurdigen Historien* (Collection of Important and Newsworthy Stories) for their indulgence with the new medium. If certain things were overlooked, he hoped they would put it down for the haste in reporting events that had occurred overnight. The four-page first edition combined news from Cologne, Vienna, Prague, Antwerp, Rome, and Venice.

Even before the first regularly appearing newspaper, kinds of newsletters were published to keep readers up to date with current developments in finance, law, and ecclesiastical matters. ❑

FLEMISH MASTER

Antwerp, early 17th century

In 1609, Peter Paul Rubens was appointed court painter to the Habsburg Archduke Albert. He and his compatriot, Anthony van Dyck, were the most celebrated painters of their day. Both painters had enjoyed the patronage of King Charles I of England, whom Rubens called "the greatest connoisseur in Europe." The king had them both knighted. Rubens decorated the ceiling of the Banqueting Hall at Whitehall Palace with three

Peter Paul Rubens

MONTEVERDI'S VESPERS

Italy, 1610

Born at Cremona in 1567, Claudio Monteverdi was appointed *maestro di cappella* (head of music) at the court of Duke Vincenzo Gonzaga at Mantua in 1601. He made a name for himself as an advocate of the new, expressive style of music known as the *seconda prattica* (second practice), and as a composer of two operas, *Orfeo* (1607) and *Arianna* (1608). Musical dramas with secular rather than sacred themes had been presented prior to this, as for example Jacopo Peri's *Daphne* (1598) and *Eurydice* (1600), but Monteverdi's were the first to show the true potential of this new genre. He also published five books of madrigals.

At the same time, Monteverdi showed himself a master of the older style of music, or *prima prattica* (first practice) of Palestrina and earlier composers. In 1610, he composed and published his *Vespers*, a magnificent set of church music dedicated to Pope Paul V, which established him as the most celebrated composer of his time. Both *prima* and *seconda prattica* are evident in the *Vespers*, a collection of pieces to be sung at the Church's early evening service. ❑

The composer Claudio Monteverdi

KEPLER'S LAWS OF

Prague, 1609

Looking to the heavens in 1572, Danish astronomer Tycho Brahe sighted a new star, more brilliant than Venus, where no star was supposed to be. He realized that the stellar object rested beyond the moon, in the constellation of Cassiopeia, in the realm of what were believed to be "fixed" stars. The scientific community was both intrigued and disquieted by his discovery. It meant that the stars were not, as depicted by Aristotle, immutable and eternal.

In his lifetime, Brahe logged no fewer than 777 stars and became the world's foremost astronomer. He vastly increased knowledge of the moon, regis-

PAINTERS

paintings glorifying the House of Stuart, as well as a famous one of Charles as St. George slaying the dragon.

Van Dyck was Charles's court painter for nine years, painting more than 30 portraits of Charles and his queen and especially beautiful studies of their children, full of spirituality along with elegance.

His house at Blackfriars, which the king used to visit by water for sittings, was kept in great style with his own musicians and fools. He was always richly dressed, and he fascinated women. His fiery English mistress, Margaret Lemon, in a jealous rage once tried to bite off his thumb to prevent him from painting. He married a lady-in-waiting a year before his death.

Rubens lived in even grander style as a diplomat, fluent in six languages, traveling Europe. He was sent to Spain by Isabella, the regent of the Spanish Netherlands, and to England by Philip IV of Spain to negotiate a peace treaty with Charles.

Charles bought much of his work, as did Philip and Marie de Medici, the queen mother of France, for the Luxembourg Palace. His vast output of canvases, crowded with nymphs, satyrs, and *putti* exhibiting the plumpest flesh, was the product of a factory of assistants who painted them from his sketches while he did the finishing touches. His energy was prodigious. "I have never feared to undertake any design however vast," he said. At 53, he gave up court life, retired to his chateau with a wife who was only sixteen, and painted landscapes. ❑

Peter Paul Rubens, *The History of Maria de Medici*, 1620–1625, detail

PLANETARY MOTION

Johannes Kepler

tered the refraction of light, and perfected a table of correction for the better identification of stars. Brahe's greatest contribu-tion to the science of astronomy was that he understood the need for constant observation of the skies and perfected instruments that enabled him to do this with accuracy.

In 1599, Brahe set up an observatory in Prague and hired Johannes Kepler as his assistant. In his work with Brahe, and later as astronomer to the emperor Rudolph II, Kepler started to apply the principles of geometry to the movements of the planets, in particular Mars. Unlike Brahe, Kepler believed in the Copernican sun-centered theory of the universe. He was a lover of music and looked for a harmony in the universe that would explain the motion of the planets.

Kepler based his work on data and mathematical calculations. His first law was published in 1609 and stated that the orbit of each planet is an ellipse, with the sun at a focus. (In 1610, using the newly invented telescope, Galileo, observing the moons of Jupiter, confirmed elliptical planetary rotation.) The circle, which had reigned supreme in explaining natural phenomenon, was suddenly displaced. Kepler's second law stated that the line joining the planet to the sun sweeps out equal areas in equal times. In other words, an object moves more quickly along the short radius of an ellipse than along the long radius. Kepler's third law, published in his book *Harmonices Mundi* in 1619, laid out that the square of the orbital period of the planet is proportional to the cube of its mean distance from the sun. Since the orbital period of the earth is one year, a planet that is twice as far from the sun as the earth would take nearly three years to travel its elliptical orbit. This last law was key to Isaac Newton's later work on gravity.

Kepler had a number of other firsts including explaining how the telescope works, how both eyes are used in depth perception, and how the tides are caused by the moon. ❑

THE ORIGINS AND RISE OF RUSSIA

The picture of Russia between the thirteenth and fifteenth centuries, the period in which it developed into a powerful empire, is uneven and fragmented in contrast with that of the previous Kiev Grand Duchy. The Kiev domain consisted of an alliance of princes that was able to protect Russia effectively against enemy attacks. The population had adopted the Greek Orthodox Faith after the baptism of Vladimir I in 988. Education and art flourished.

After Kiev was conquered by the princes of Vladimir-Suzdal at the end of the twelfth century, the previously strong unified empire broke up into several weak feuding principalities that were unable to repel enemy attacks effectively. When the Mongols invaded the Russian steppes for the first time in the thirteenth century, the Russian princes did not realize the serious danger they posed. Based on previous experience, they believed these nomadic tribes would soon become sedentary and assimilated into the native population, and then give up their warike behavior. This assumption proved to be wrong. In 1223, Russian and Mongol troops fought their first battle in the southern Russian steppe. The Russians suffered a crushing defeat. Soon the Mongols—also known as the Tatars—ruled over most of the Asian continent.

THE MONGOL EMPIRE

Batu, grandson of Genghis Khan, brought most of Russia—as far as Novgorod, the capital of the principality of Vladimir-Suzdal—under his control and destroyed Kiev. Under the fast-spreading influence of Islam—in the fourteenth century, all of the Tatar upper class had converted to Islam—order was restored throughout the country. During this period cultural, political, and economic relations were established with the east, south, and west.

The Mongols barely changed the political structure in the Russian principalities: The princes retained their territories, but their laws had to be approved by the Great Khan, and homage had to be paid to him. In addition, the princes had to make recruits available to the Mongols and pay tribute. The "Golden Horde" left the collection of compulsory taxes to the Russian princes.

Prince Alexander of Vladimir-Suzdal voluntarily submitted his principality to the Mongols and paid tribute to them in spite of the fact they had not conquered Novgorod. By declining help from the west, he succeeded in preserving his estates from the Mongol terror. After defeating the Swedes in 1240 on the Neva (hence his nickname "Nevsky"), and stopping the Livonian knights in 1242 in their push eastward, his principality and position were secure . Backed by the Great Khan who recognized his Grand Duchy, Alexander Nevsky developed an autocratic system of government.

THE RUSSIAN CHURCH

The Orthodox Church played an important role in uniting the Russian people during the centuries occupation by the Golden Horde. The Tatars pursued a policy of religious tolerance. They not only tolerated Christian churches, monasteries, priests, and monks but they encouraged them. In return, the clergy was expected to recognize the authority of the Tatars and to pray for them. So the priests proclaimed from the pulpit that the Mongols had come to Russia as a fair punishment for the sins committed by the Russian people in the past.

The Russian Church, accountable to the Greek-Byzantine patriarchs in Constantinople, was able to strengthen its position and expand during this period, while also acting as mediator between the Tatars and the Russians. The united Russian Church became the symbol of the united Russian people. The authority of the Church extended over

The Trinity monastery of St Sergius of Radonez was the seat of the Patriarch of the Russian Orthodox Church until 1988.

the whole country, beyond the borders of the principalities. It was this shared religion that held the Russian people together and separated them from the Muslim Mongols.

The gradual decline of the Golden Horde began in the mid-fourteenth century; it fragmented into several smaller Khanates that feuded among one other. However the resulting power vacuum was not filled by the Russians but by their traditional enemies. From 1350, the Poles ruled over the wealthy principality of Galicia in eastern Europe and in 1400, the Lithuanians ruled over a vast Grand Duchy that stretched from the Baltic Sea to the Black Sea.

THE RISE OF MOSCOW

The Grand Duchy of Moscow experienced a rapid upturn in the second half of the thirteenth century. In the early fourteenth century, Ivan I established himself as the "collector of Russian land." He bought up the small principalities that shared borders with the Grand Duchy of Moscow or brought them under his control through intrigues and treaties signed under duress. Having made a deal with the Mongol Khans, he obtained the right in 1328 to call himself Grand Duke of all of Russia. In addition, he was given the right to levy taxes in most of Russia. At this time, Ivan also moved the head of the Russian Church, the Metropolitans, and Patriarchs from Kiev to Moscow.

In 1378, the Moscow's Grand Duke Dmitri Donskoi, had become sufficiently confident in his own power to directly challenge the Mongols. His troops defeated a small Mongol army and following this the Grand Duchy refused to pay tribute. In 1380, the Muscovites, assisted by other Russian princes, defeated the Tatars at the Battle of Kulikovo on the Don. Two years later, the Mongols took their revenge and overran and devastated Moscow. But the Russian desire for freedom could not be stopped any longer. In 1480, Grand Duke Ivan III (1462–1505) formally put an end to Tatar rule. He continued Moscow's wars of conquest and toward the end of his reign he had conquered almost the whole of Russia. In doing so, Ivan III laid the foundation for the great Russian empire. The small principalities lost their independence and a new autocratic, centralized state was created supported by the dienstadel (a nobility with titles deriving from being in the sovereign's service), which was promoted at the expense of the old nobility and farmers.

After Ivan's marriage to the niece of the last Byzantine emperor (1472), he declared himself the protector of all Orthodox Christians, declaring Moscow the "third Rome," the seat of all Orthodox Christians, as the successor of Rome and Constantinople.

Under Tsar Peter I, the Great, Russia experienced one of the most important phases of modernization in its history.

IVAN THE TERRIBLE

Ivan III's grandson was the first ruler to be crowned "Tsar of all Russia." Under the name Ivan IV he continued the absolutist claims to power initiated by his predecessors. He consolidated his position internally by drawing up a new code of law (1550), introducing a central administration, and making reforms in the army. Despite his early reforms his irrational cruelty soon earned him the epithet "Ivan the Terrible." At the beginning of the 1560s, he began a campaign of extermination of the old aristocracy, while promoting the "service aristocracy" who were devoted to him. At the same time, he put into place the system of oprichnina, whereby lawful landowners in large areas around Moscow were dispossessed through mass resettlements and murder, and the ownership transferred to his Life Guards, drawn from the new aristocracy and foreigners.

Powerful at home, Ivan the Terrible was also very successful in his foreign policy. He extended his rule over the entire Volga region; this provided the important topographical prerequisite for future conquests. In the west, Ivan the Terrible tried to gain access to the Baltic Sea to free his empire from the isolation resulting from the Mongol occupation. But his attack against Livonia led to a war against Poland and Sweden (1558–1582/83) that ended with the defeat of the Russians and the loss of all conquered territories. This undoubtedly contributed to the economic and social decline of the empire.

On the other hand, trade relations with England proved very successful. The colonization of Siberia also contributed to an economic upturn. In 1582, on the instructions of the merchant family Stroganov, a Cossack division captured Isker and offered it to the Tsar. The foundation of Tobolsk (1587) and Tomsk (1604) opened the road to central and eastern Siberia. In 1647, Ochotsk was founded on the Pacific.

THE ROMANOVS PUT AN END TO A PERIOD OF CONFUSION

After the death of Ivan IV, Russia was plunged into a period of deep crisis and confusion. In theory, Ivan's son Feodor had succeeded his father, but in practice it was Boris Godunov, a member of the high aristocracy, who ruled. In 1598, after Feodor's death, Boris was finally elected Tsar. Severe famines and social unrest marked the beginning of the seventeenth century, and Poland and Sweden took advantage of the situation to conquer parts of the empire.

In 1613, a new tsar was elected, 16-year-old Mikhail Romanov. He was the founder of the imperial dynasty of Russia that ruled the country until the Russian revolution of 1917. The first Romanov on the Tsar's throne found ruling difficult. The empire was extremely unstable both at home and abroad.

In the mid-seventeenth century, Russia had opened up to the west and welcomed modernization at home. It was Feodor III who gave tsarism a firm base in 1682 by abolishing the system of mestnichestvo ("place of priority"), the feudal hierarchy that had formed the empire's military and civil administration. From then on, civil and military appointments were made on the basis of merit and performance.

The unexpected death of Feodor III, at the age of 27 in 1682, led to violent conflicts between claimants to the throne. Feodor's brother, Peter I (the Great) finally had the upper hand. Because of his comprehensive reforms at home and in particular his policy of westernization, he is considered the founder of modern Russia.

With his victory in the Great Nordic War (1700–1713), Peter I secured access to the Baltic Sea and a "window to the West." Thus, Russia acquired a predominant position in eastern Europe. In addition, the Tsar built a powerful Russian fleet, thereby establishing its reputation as a naval power. ❑

FIRST ROMANOV TSAR ON RUSSIAN THRONE

Moscow, 1613

Years of hardship and uncertainty followed the rule of Ivan the Terrible. Ivan's successor Boris Godunov was unable to gain the full support of the land-owning nobles. In addition, the country had been plagued by epidemics, unrest, and famine. In 1603, conditions had so detriorated that people were reduced to eating grass and birch bark, and there were even reports of cannibalism. The famine was the result of a series of disastrously poor harvests. Whole village populations, and at least 125,000 people starved to death in Moscow alone.

Two years later Boris Godunov died suddenly, ushering in what would become known as the "Time of Troubles." Boris was followed by Dmitri, a pretender claiming to be Ivan's son. His short and violent reign lasted little more than a year. The next few years were marked by a scramble for influence. Polish, Swedish, and Lithuanian interests competed with the *boyars* (major landholders) to fill the power vacuum.

Finally in 1613, Russia solved its dynastic problem by electing Mikhail Romanov as tsar. He was chosen by the *Zemsky Sobor* (the Assembly of the Land) after much deliberation. The new tsar had some claim to the throne since Ivan's first wife, Anastasia, had been a member of the Romanov family. Romanov was only sixteen and had received no training for the monarchy, having been brought up in a monastery. His father, who was the patriarch of Moscow, acted as regent and essentially ruled the country until his own death in 1633.

The Romanovs ascended the throne amid rejoicing, but they inherited a deserted land. Half the villages of Russia were empty of people and, because of the virtual collapse of authority, huge areas were vulnerable to wandering bandits. The treasury had been drained, and the new tsar needed loans in cash and kind—fish, salt, and grain—to meet the urgent demands of his military and civil officials.

Of pressing concern were relations with Poland and Sweden, who still occupied parts of Muscovy. In 1617, British mediation and helped secure the peace of Stolbovo between Russia and Sweden, which ended years of desultory fighting. For the price of 20,000 silver rubles, Sweden agreed to evacuate Novgorod and other areas of northern Russia and renounce its claim to the Russian throne. Sweden, however, retained the southern coast of Finland and its contact with its Estonian possessions; thus Muscovy was cut off from the Baltic and did not get back towns conquered by Boris Godunov.

Then in 1618, after the failure of an offensive that brought Polish troops close to Moscow, the two countries agreed to an armistice. Moscow had withstood the assault by the Polish forces. The Poles ran short of ammunition and provisions, and withdrew.

Under the terms of the treaty, Poland retained the provinces of Smolensk and Seversk. It recognized the election of Mikhail Romanov to the throne of Russia but did not renounce a claim to that throne. Poland had had Smolensk in its possession at the end of the "Troubles" and used it as the base for its offensive. This caused serious concern to Tsar Mikhail who was grappling with the domestic problems that he inherited when he came to the throne. Michael reigned until 1645. He was succeeded at his death by his son Alexis. ❑

OPENING GAMBITS IN THE

Prague, 1618

By the beginning of the seventeenth century, it had become apparent that a war in Germany between Catholics and Protestants was imminent and that it threatened to engulf the entire continent. Battle lines were being drawn up and fortunes spent on equipping private armies throughout Germany.

In the mainly Protestant north, whole cities were ringed with star-shaped walls, bastions, and moats; in the Rhineland and Bavaria, great new fortresses were built as Catholics braced themselves for war on a scale unprecedented in Europe.

Actual conflict was preceded by a flurry of intense diplomatic activity, particularly on the part of Prince Christian of Anhalt-Bernburg. As governor of the Protestant Palatinate, he sought alliances with every other Protestant power to combat the Catholic revival that had been growing since the beginning of the century. Overtures were made to England and France, with little success at first, but King James of England finally agreed to join an alliance with the Protestant Union of six princes and encouraged the union to make similar alliances with the Netherlands and Denmark.

With Louis XIII of France feeling more and more threatened as the war between Spain and the rebel Dutch had been resumed, the great powers now faced one another. On one side—though not necessarily Protestant—France, Holland, Denmark, Sweden, England, and Russia in the north and several Italian states in the south were lined up against the Catholic houses of Habsburg and Poland, with Philip IV of

Defenestration of Prague in 1618 (etching by Matthäus Merian the Elder)

HOLLAND FOUNDS A TRADING EMPIRE

Batavia, 1619

In competition with Portugal, Holland began to found colonies in the Far East. Jan Pieterszoon Coen established a base in Batavia (present-day Jakarta) for the Dutch East India Company. He served as governor for the colony from 1618 to 1623 and then again from 1627 to 1629.

The Dutch East India Company was founded in 1602 with the express purpose of breaking the Portuguese monopoly on trade with the East. Like similar companies in England, it received the exclusive right to exploit its

Spain prepared to strike at heretics everywhere.

The stage was set for the start of hostilities when Emperor Rudolph II's Letter of Majesty was revoked. Under pressure from Protestants, Rudolph had published this letter decreeing freedom of religious practice.

The first act in the conflict played out dramatically in Prague. Emotions had been running high in the city. The Holy Roman Emperor and King of Bohemia Ferdinand II refused permission for the building of two Lutheran churches. The Protestant leader, Count Thurn, called a meeting of nobles, gentry, and burghers from all over the province, to try two of Ferdinand's lieutenants for violating Rudolph's Letter of Majesty. He threw them out of a high window of Prague Castle along with the secretary who accompanied them.

Following the defenestration, the Bohemians set aside Ferdinand as king and chose in his place the Protestant Elector of Palatine, Frederick V. In so doing, they looked for support from England, since Frederick was married to the daughter of King James. Help was, however, not forthcoming. In November of 1620, the armies of the Emperor Ferdinand II invaded Bohemia from Austria. Frederick was confident that the enemy's forces were too weak with hunger or wracked with plague to fight and that his own army occupied an unassailable position on the White Mountain near Prague.

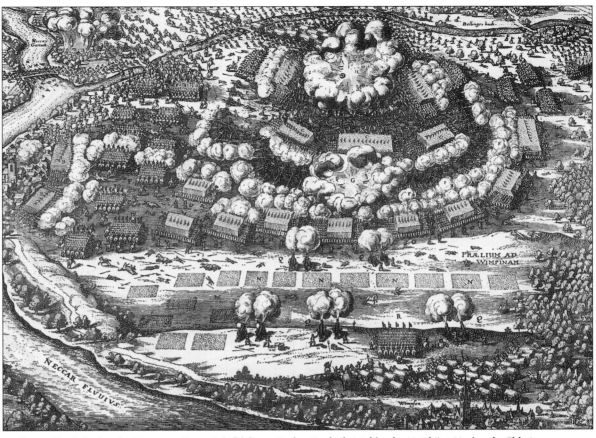

Graf von Tilly defeating the Margrave Georg Friedrich von Baden-Durlach (etching by Matthäus Merian the Elder)

His confidence was not justified. Ferdinand's general, Johann Tserclaes Graf von Tilly, led his army to victory: The emperor's banner flew over the White Mountain. Frederick's general returned to the city to break the news that the army had become mutinous during a lengthy artillery barrage, and many had refused to fight as they were overwhelmed by Bavarian and Spanish infantry.

Tilly oversaw a largely victorious campaign through Germany, culminating in the destruction of the Duke of Brunswick's forces at Stadtlohn. Over 15,000 of Brunswick's 21,000 men were killed; with Heidelberg and Mannheim firmly in Tilly's hands, the entire northern Palatinate was under the control of the House of Habsburg. When news of the defeat reached the elector, Frederick V, he abandoned further military ambitions and asked his father-in-law, King James of England, to mediate. James turned down the request. He was focused on his ambition of a "Spanish match" for his son Prince Charles.

Ferdinand handed over the Palatine possessions of Frederick to Maximilian I of Bohemia. Ernst II Graf of Mansfield was given complete command over Protestant forces. Bohemia remained in Catholic hands, and hostilities continued in Alsace and Hessen. ❏

country's colonial holdings. And it made tremendous profits.

Batavia was the center of its trading operations in Asia. Other large settlements included Malacca, Penang, and Makassar in the Celebes Islands. The colonies were ruled by native chiefs with whom the company entered into agreements for trade and protection. In the mid-seventeenth century, it was able to oust the Portuguese from Ceylon and take control of the cinnamon trade.

The company remained in existence until 1799, when it went bankrupt. The Dutch government assumed responsibility for its debts, but also inherited all of its holdings in the Orient. ❏

View of Batavia (copper etching 17th century)

CHRISTIAN IV OF DENMARK ENTERS THE WAR

Denmark, 1625

The entrance of Denmark against the Habsburgs raised the stakes in the Thirty Years War. Recognizing that the Habsburgs were intending to use their military success to consolidate their power in the north of Germany and impose the Counter-Reformation, Christian decided to lend his support to the Protestant side. His position as the Duke of Holstein gave him the credentials to assume the leadership of the anti-Habsburg forces.

The Treaty of The Hague of 1625 brought England and Denmark together with the Dutch Confederation in opposition to Spain. A coordinated plan of attack was agreed upon that marshaled the Protestant duchies and principalities against an army raised by Albrecht von Wallenstein and financed by the Habsburg Emperor, Ferdinand II. Wallenstein's early victories inspired Ferdinand to grant him the Duchy of Mecklenburg and appoint him head of all of his armies. Driven back, Den-

Wallenstein's army besieges a Protestant city defended by Denmark and Sweden (lithograph).

mark was forced to abandon Schleswig-Holstein. It sued for peace and the Treaty of Lubeck clearly reflected the empire's triumphs. At the zenith of his power, Ferdinand passed an edict of restitution that returned all lands and goods that had been taken away from the Church at the Treaty of Pas-sau (1552) and authorized the reimposition of Catholic doctrine on the lands taken from Danes. The war was clearly favoring the Habsburgs. ❑

REALISTIC AND SECULAR MOGHUL ART

Delhi, 1622

Jahangir, the third Moghul emperor, proved to be as great a patron of the arts as his father, Akbar the Great, who extended the empire of the descendants of Tamerlane throughout northern India and Kashmir.

Akbar gathered poets and painters around him, on the model of the Persian court. He recruited Hindu and Muslim painters and gave them the task of illustrating *The Romance of Amir Hamza.* The work is a unique combination of Hindu and Persian style and consists of 1,400 painted pages. Akbar also commissioned a translation into Persian of the vast Hindu epic poem the *Mahabharata.*

Jahangir encouraged portrait painting and pictures of his assembled courtiers as well as nature studies of animals and birds. He was a lover of nature and his favorite painter, Mansur, produced exquisite paintings of zebras, wild goats, pheasants, and turkey cocks. Jahangir gave Mansur the title of *Nadir al-Asr*—the Wonder of the Age.

Under Jahangir's patronage, Indian art even incorporated elements of Western painting. In one work, he had himself painted embracing Shah Abbas of Persia; the Great Moghul is shown surrounded by an enormous gold halo, a feature clearly copied from his European paintings. ❑

WALLENSTEIN

Brief Lives

Albrecht von Wallenstein was the most important and successful general in the service of Emperor Ferdinand II. After suppressing the uprising in Bohemia and Moravia in 1618–1619, the emperor rewarded him with extensive land holdings. The emperor provided Wallenstein with the Duchies of Friedland, Sagan, and Mecklenburg. But fearing that Wallenstein might harbor ambitions for the imperial throne, the emperor recalled him after his victory over the Swedes in 1630. Suspicions were raised that Wallenstein had offered his services to the emperor's enemies. In 1633, he was relieved of his command and while the emperor may not have ordered Wallenstein's assassination, he certainly did nothing to stop it. ❑

Velázquez: Painter to the Court of Spain

Spain, 1623

Diego de Velázquez (1599–1660), considered by many to be Spain's finest painter, was a master of realism. At the age of 23, he moved to Madrid and after painting King Philip IV's portrait a few years later, was given the post of court painter. He made two trips to Italy where he copied masterpieces and bought paintings, including Titians and Tintorettos, for the Spanish court.

Velázquez's mastery of technique—blending light, color, space, line, and rhythm in a unified manner—was complemented by his ability to pluck out the essence of humanity and nature. It is said that the figures in his paintings seem to breathe; his people and animals are full of life. When his painting *The Surrender of Breda* was installed in the king's new palace of Buen Retiro, viewers were astonished by its sense of actuality, as if it had been painted on the spot; in fact Velázquez had relied on eyewitnesses. His portrait of the pope, completed on one of his trips to Italy, was considered the finest portrait in Europe.

Velázquez never wearied of using the king as his model. Their friendship was illustrated by the directness and honesty of the portraits. In addition to his many portraits of the royal family and members of the Spanish court, Velázquez painted landscapes, and works with mythological and religious themes. His style and approach had a significant impact on many artists who have followed, including Pablo Picasso, Salvador Dali, and the impressionist Edouard Manet, who called him the "painter of painters." ❏

Velásquez, *Portrait of the Dwarf Sebastián de Morra*, 1642–1644

Richelieu: the Red Eminence

Paris, 1624

Cardinal Armand du Plessis (1585–1642), the great but unloved Duke of Richelieu, is regarded as the man who converted the absolutist theory of the French monarchy into practice. He displayed an iron will in carrying out his autocratic policies on behalf of King Louis XIII. Speaking on behalf of the clergy at the Estates General gathering in 1614, he declared to the young king that the clergy desired to have royal power like a firm rock that would crush all opposition. His speech and attitude launched his political career.

Born into a minor aristocratic family, he was destined for the army but gave up his military career to enter the Church. He prepared himself for politics by working to convert the Huguenots of La Rochelle before moving to Paris. There he began his devious but always logical acquisition of power.

Richelieu was initially appointed to serve Anne of Austria, the King's wife, but soon cultivated the favor of the queen regent, Marie de Medici and her Italian favorite, Concino Concini. However, those two proved to be unpopular in France, and when the young king had Concini murdered, Richelieu left court. He worked his way back into royal favor a few years later by acting as mediator between the king and rebellious factions of nobles. Made a member of the Council of State in 1624, he rapidly unseated the chief minister and assumed that position of power, which he maintained, through many trials and court intrigues and plots, until his death in 1642.

Within France, Richelieu relentlessly smothered any anti-monarchist movements whether religious or political. In 1626, he brought French nobles to heel by ordering the destruction of all fortified castles. In 1627, he laid siege to the Protestant stronghold of La Rochelle. He maintained a network of spies throughout France and Europe. During Richelieu's time, France was surrounded by an imperialistic Spain to the south and to the northeast in the Netherlands. In foreign affairs, he operated in a *realpolitik* fashion, making alliances with Protestants where it served French interests even while crushing them at home. Richelieu tried to keep France out of the Thirty Years War but did convince the king to declare war on the Habsburgs of Spain in 1635. His victories (at one time invading Spanish and Bavarian armies were a mere 50 miles from Paris) assured that France would emerge as one of the strongest European powers at the end of the war in 1648.

Needing money to cover the cost of maintaining his army, Richelieu raised taxes on the peasants. Resulting uprisings were summarily crushed. His relationship with Samuel Champlain assured a strong French presence in Quebec and was vital for the establishment of French power there and in Louisiana.

Richelieu was a leading patron of the arts and possessed one of the largest art collections in Europe. He was also a founder of L'Académie Française, which continues today to support French literature and the French language. He oversaw the rebuilding of the Sorbonne and is buried there.

Richelieu's legacy was his creation of a strong centralized government in France after centuries of feudal warfare and disputes. His policies made him many enemies, and he was immortalized in the works of the Alexandre Dumas in *The Three Musketeers* as the ruthless power behind the throne of France. ❏

Cardinal Richlieu was the dominant figure in French politics for eighteen years.

SWEDEN ENTERS INTO THE THIRTY YEARS WAR

1630, Northern Germany

Upon the death of the autocratic and capricious king of Sweden, Charles IX, in 1611, his sixteen-year-old son Gustavus II Adolphus, inherited a country facing external threats and internal disintegration. His first order of business was to deal with actual and potential conflicts with his neighbors, Denmark, Poland and Russia. Gustavus was fortunate in that the "Time of Troubles" in Russia had left it with little strength to threaten its neighbors. His more formidable enemy was his cousin Sigismund III of Poland, a devout Catholic who had designs on the Swedish throne. To counter his growing power, the king and his chief counselor, Axel Oxenstierna, instituted the draft and built up a disciplined fighting force that could rely upon regular pay (a novelty for the time). The conflict ended Sweden gaining the upper hand on the battlefield and in 1629, a peace treaty mediated by the French, was entered into at Altmark.

Meanwhile, his able first minister had been revitalizing the nation's economy and reorganizing the organs of government. A progressive tax was instituted and a permanent council served as the king's cabinet.

Gustavus now felt himself in a position to turn his attention to the war in Germany. The Thirty Years War was essentially a religious conflict, meant to decide the acceptance or rejection of Protestantism. But a number of other reasons for conflict fueled the aggression and determined the makeup of the opposing sides. On one hand were the Catholic Habsburgs, ruling in Austria and Spain, on the other German Protestants. But the Protestants found allies not only with their coreligionists in Holland and England, but also with the French who were primarily concerned with checking Habsburg imperial ambitions. In the confusion of opposing parties, independent players such as Albrecht von Wallenstein, ostensibly the imperial general but actually driven by his own appetite for conquest, could play determinative roles.

For Gustavus, the main objective was control over the Baltic, threatened by Wallenstein and the empire's push into northern Germany. That he also wanted to champion the Protestant cause cannot be ignored.

On July 4, 1630, the king

The Swedish king Gustavus Adolphus falls at the Battle of Lützen, 1632

landed with his troops on Usedom Island at the mouth of the Vistula River. Wallenstein, whose grandiosity had nettled the emperor, Ferdinand II, had been recalled with his army, and consequently, the Swedes faced little opposition as they turned west toward the Oder. With financial support from Cardinal Richelieu, the army continued its march through German territories capturing Berlin in the following year and handing the imperial forces under Tilly a major defeat at Breitenfeld, just north of Leipzig. This opened the way to the Catholic cities of central Germany. Both Mainz and Frankfurt fell to the Swedes. The following spring, Gustavus led his army across the Danube, where again he encountered and defeated Tilly, who was wounded in the battle and died shortly after. Unable to contain the Swedish army, the emperor turned once again to Wallenstein. On November 16, 1632, the two armies met at Lützen, a small village west of Leipzig. In the ensuing battle, the Swedes emerged the victors, but at the high cost of their king's life. ❑

GUSTAVUS II ADOLPHUS: DYNAMIC KING OF SWEDEN

Brief Lives

King Gustavus II Adolphus was a powerful leader who turned his country from a feudal backwater into a major European power. A huge man, blond and broad-shouldered, Gustavus displayed remarkable charisma, particularly with the common people. He came to the throne at the age of sixteen, and it was at this time that he was bullied into signing a charter of accession that allowed only nobles to take high office. Working with his astute chancellor, Axel Oxenstierna, Gustavus was able to surmount this and proceeded to remodel his country in every department. Government was streamlined, its council sitting permanently as a cabinet, making decisions in his absence.

Gustavus was an outstanding statesman and a brilliant military commander. In the siege of Riga, part of an ongoing conflict with Sigismund, King of Poland, he astonished his men by helping to dig trenches and came close to death leading the assault. He ensured that his conscript army was paid regularly—a rarity in the Europe of his day, since most soldiers were expected to live off the land. He built up a large navy to challenge Denmark for the mastery of Baltic.

Gustavus was killed as he led a cavalry charge into victory in a battle against the forces of Albrecht von Wallenstein at Lützen near Leipzig. He was only 37. ❑

Gustavus II Adolphus (oil on panel, 1631)

"Unutterable Distress:" the Destruction of Magdeburg

Account of Otto von Guericke, Burgomeister of Magdeburg

So then General Pappenheim collected a number of his people on the ramparts by the New Town, and brought them from there into the streets of the city... fires were kindled in different quarters; then it was all over with the city, further resistance was useless. Nevertheless, some of the soldiers and citizens did try to make a stand here and there, but the imperial troops kept bringing on more and more forces—cavalry, too—to help them, and finally they got the Krockenthor open and let in the whole imperial army and the forces of the Catholic League—Hungarians, Croats, Poles, Walloons, Italians, Spaniards, French, North and South Germans.

Thus it came about that the city and all its inhabitants fell into the hands of the enemy, whose violence and cruelty were due in part to their common hatred of the adherents of the Augsburg Confession, and in part to their being imbittered by the chain shot which had been fired at them and by the derision and insults that the Magdeburgers had heaped upon them from the ramparts.

Then was there naught but beating and burning, plundering, torture, and murder. Most especially was every one of the enemy bent on securing much booty. When a marauding party entered a house, if its master had anything to give he might thereby purchase respite and protection for himself and his family till the next man, who also wanted something, should come along. It was only when everything had been brought forth and there was nothing left to give that the real trouble commenced. Then, what with blows and threats of shooting, stabbing, and hanging, the poor people were so terrified that if they had had anything left they would have brought it forth if it had been buried in the earth or hidden away in a thousand castles. In this frenzied rage, the great and splendid city that had stood like a fair princess in the land was now, in its hour of direst need and unutterable distress and woe, given over to the flames, and thousands of innocent men, women, and children, in the midst of a horrible din of heartrending shrieks and cries, were tortured and put to death in so cruel and shameful a manner that no words would suffice to describe, nor no tears to bewail it. ❏

Hans Ulrich Franck, *Plundering Soldiers*, woodcut by 1643

Harvey's Discovery of the Circulatory System

London, 1628

For centuries, doctors subscribed to the theory of Galen, that the heart was a natural oven that kept the blood warm. Blood, it was thought, was subject to a kind of tidal ebb and flow. Dr William Harvey, an English physician, was the first to demonstrate that the heart beats through muscular contraction, squeezing blood out of its interior into arteries through one-way valves. Then it returns the blood back to the heart through the veins. What comes back to the heart is the same blood that left it earlier. It is recycled and not, as had been previously thought, freshly made in the liver with each heartbeat. Harvey's research was published in 1628 in his 72-page book, *Exercitatio Anatomica de Motu Cordis et Sanguinis in Animalibus*. It became an instant medical classic. Harvey recorded the results of experiments with animals. He made the bold assertion that the blood is constantly on the move, driven by the heart, a natural pump. His methods of observation and experimentation—he managed to measure the capacity of the heart—were an important stepping-stone in scientific research. A few years after his death, his work would be confirmed by the development of the microscope. Despite his scientific methods, however, he still adhered to the Elizabethan notion that the heart was the seat of life and vital forces.❏

Title page of *Exercitatio Anatomica* of William Harvey

Manhattan Purchased by Dutch

New York, 1626

The first known European to glimpse what was to become Manhattan was the Florentine, Giovanni da Verrazzano, who entered the island's harbor only as far as the Narrows. The first landing was made in September of 1609 by the Englishman and Dutch East India Company representative Henry Hudson. A crewmember on his ship the *Half Moon* recorded the name of the island as "Manna-hata." This name is believed to have been a phonetic rendering of the indigenous Lenape tribe's word meaning "island of many hills."

The island's first European settlers were the Dutch, who established a fur-trading base at "New Netherlands" (later New Amsterdam) on Governor's Island in 1624. In 1625, they built "Fort Amsterdam" on the tip of Manhattan. Historians recognize this event and year as the birthdate of New York City.

The fabled "purchase" of Manhattan took place on May 24, 1626, when the Director-General of New Netherlands, Peter Minuit, bartered for the island with a band of Lenape known as the "Canarsee." The Dutch goods traded have traditionally been valued at $24.00.❏

GALILEO FORCED TO RECANT

Rome, 1633

Galileo Galilei (1564–1642), the famed Italian mathematician and the first astronomer to extensively use the newly invented telescope, carries the mantle of "the first modern scientist." Galileo as a student, and later popular and successful professor, began developing hypotheses and experiments to test them. He challenged the Aristotelian view that objects of different weight fall to the earth at different times, and he used inclines to show the equal acceleration of objects. He described how the swing of a pendulum is affected not by its weight and its length of arc but by the length of its radius. He also invented the first practical thermometer and a number of other instruments used to measure natural phenomena.

In 1609, he began work on improving the telescope. While other things, that the Milky Way is a large collection of stars.

When he turned his telescope toward the planet Jupiter, Galileo observed that it was accompanied by four satellites he called the "Medicean Stars."

Galileo came under attack from the theological community for his advocacy of the claim by Copernicus that the earth revolves around the sun. He observed variations in the way planets move in the sky, which convinced him that Coperni-

The English poet John Milton visits Galileo.

Galileo before the Inquisition in Rome (color lithograph, 1631)

he did not invent this instrument, he was responsible for its rapid development. He may have been the first to build a telescope with a convex and concave lens so the image was upright (as opposed to the earlier upside down image), and could construct instruments with 32 times magnification. He showed that there are mountains on the moon, and he revealed many stars invisible to the naked eye, proving, among cus was right to put the sun at the center of the planets. The churchmen said that such a system conflicted with Holy Scriptures and were infuriated by Galileo's alleged impiety, and his success in communicating widely his novel ideas. The immense success of his book of astronomical observations, *Sidereus nuncius* (*The Starry Messenger*) was the deciding factor that led his opponents to denounce him to the Inquisition.

In 1615, he was summoned to Rome and managed to clear his name, but failed to overturn the ruling that the teaching of Copernicanism should be suppressed. Copernicus's major work, *De revolutionibus orbium coelesti libri VI* (*Concerning the Revolutions of Celestial Spheres*) was put on the Church's index of prohibited books and Galileo was ordered to abandon his views.

Galileo managed to steer clear of further run-ins for a time, but his criticism of a monk's treatise on meteors in 1623 rekindled anger toward him on the part of the Jesuits. Between 1626 and 1630, he wrote the fullest treatment of his ideas about astronomy: *Dialogue Concerning the Two Chief World Systems*, which reaffirmed his opposition to the idea that the earth is the center of the universe. The book was published in February of 1632, but distribution was halted in August and in 1633, he was called to Rome to stand trial for propounding his ideas in the book. In addition to criticizing Aristotle's and Ptolemy's cosmology, it also discussed at length the motion of stars, planets, and falling bodies and commented on the periodic nature of sunspots, all of which he held to be inconsistent with a stationary, pivotal Earth.

After a protracted hearing, Galileo was finally sentenced, having been found guilty by the Inquisition of teaching the banned Copernican doctrine. He was ordered to recant, which he did in a carefully worded formula renouncing his past errors. The pope commuted his sentence to house arrest.

What was on trial was not just the astronomical thoughts of one man, but a way of looking at the world that could not help but produce conflict. Galileo was a leading advocate of rational scientific thinking as opposed to belief, superstition, and supposition. For him, numbers were supreme. "The Book of Nature," Galileo contended, was written in mathematical characters, and his insistence on the value of observable phenomena was critical to the development of the methodology of science. ❑

REMBRANDT'S TIMELESS PAINTINGS

Amsterdam, 1639

With Rembrandt's work, painting freed itself from cultic and decorative impulses and sought to plumb the depth of the human character.

Rembrandt Harmensz. van Rijn settled in Amsterdam in 1631. With his marriage to Saskia van Uylenburgh, whose property made him an affluent man, he purchased a house and became a member of the city's social elite. Rembrandt was born in Leiden in 1606, the son of a miller. He studied in a Latin school and then attended the University of Leiden. Starting in 1620, he studied with a history painter, Jacob van Swanenburgh, who had himself studied painting in Italy. Later in Amsterdam, he worked for Pieter Lastman. In 1625, he went out on his own, working for a time with a fellow student Jan Lievens. Devoting his energies to establishing himself in Amsterdam, he executed a number of important works in the 1630s including *The Anatomy Lesson of Dr. Nicolaes Tulp*, *The Blinding of Samson*, and *Susannah and the Elders*.

In 1634, he married Saskia, who died in 1642. Only one of their four children, Titus, survived. By this time Rembrandt had come into the full possession of his artistic power. He acquired a considerable reputation for himself. He received an important commission to decorate a new hall for the Dutch militia, painting for it his most famous work, *The Night Watch*.

Rembrandt, *Self Portrait with Beret and Mantle with Fur Collar,*1634

His portraits from this period show his impatience with the overly mannered style of the high baroque, which he abandoned in order to explore the inner life of his subjects. Other major works from this period include *The Syndics of the Cloth Guild* and *The Jewish Bride*. Rembrandt learned from the Italian master, Caravaggio, the technique of *chiaroscuro* (light-dark). No one ever before or since has rivaled him in his matery of light and shadow.

In the following decade, the Dutch art market underwent an upheaval, and Rembrandt was forced to declare bankruptcy in 1656 and sell off his collection.

Rembrandt was the most impressive personality of seventeenth century Dutch art. He is known to have completed more than 600 paintings, 300 etchings, and as many as 1,500 drawings. His series of self-portraits stand as visual testimony to the odyssey of the painter; the later ones arresting the viewer with the artist's indelible gaze.

Rembrandt's common law wife, Henrickje, died 1663, his son Titus in 1668. Rembrandt died in 1669, impoverished and alone, and was buried in an unmarked grave at Amsterdam's West Church. ❑

RENÉ DESCARTES

Paris, 1637

An anonymously published work by the French mathematician and philosopher René Descartes entitled *Discours de la Methode* contained a phrase that encapsulated his radically new method of seeking after truth: "I think, therefore I am." Descartes wanted to break with tradition in more ways than one. His book was written in clear, straightforward French, not Latin, the preferred language of philosophers up until this point.

Descartes argued that only the existence of the mind cannot be doubted. One has to begin here as a first principle, and in a framework of skepticism and logic, build up to more complex truths. According to Descartes, reason reigns supreme. The route to scientific truth is through testing, selecting, and setting things in order; not simply accumulating knowledge, but systematizing it. From this cornerstone of certainty, Descartes derived a number of basic philosophical ideas such as the existence of God. No imperfect, finite human being, he argued, could have generated the idea of an infinite God. So God must have seeded the notion in us.

René Descartes extended his reputation by producing other important works that spread his ideas. In his *Meditations*, he developed the theme of doubt and skepticism. Indeed, he hypothesized that there may be a great malignant demon that deceives humanity into believing things, in which case there is only the secure base of being sure that one does oneself exist.

Meditations led Descartes into dispute and controversy with the Church, which leveled the accusation of atheism against him. Undeterred, he brought out his *Principles of Philosophy*. In this book, ranging over physics, chemistry, and physiology, he attempted to explain all physical phenomena through one system of mechanical principles. In so doing, he ushered in the Enlightenment and the scientific era. ❑

THE TAJ MAHAL

Agra, 1648

The Taj Mahal, the Moghul emperor Shah Jahan's enduring memorial in marble to his favorite wife, Mumtaz-i-Mahal (Elect of the Palace), took sixteen years to complete. Two years after work had begun, tectural masterpiece to emerge from the Moghul period leaves unmoved. It is both magnificent and serene.

The Taj reflected the variety of cultures in the

Mumtaz-i-Mahal and Shah Jahan

The Taj Mahal with reflecting pool

Mumtaz-i-Mahal died bearing her fourteenth child. Its designer, the Persian architect Ustad Isa Afandi, gathered together the finest craftsmen of the East. No visitor to the greatest archi- vast Moghul Empire. The architecture came from Persia, the concept of the ornate garden tomb came from Afghanistan, the decorative motifs from Shiraz, the dome from Turkey, and the use of water as a mirror from Kashmir.

The mausoleum, consisting of three buildings including a mosque, stands with a garden to its south, and sheets of water to reflect its domes and minarets. Everything is symmetrical. At its center is a two-storied cube topped by an onion-shaped dome and flanked by domed octagonal wings. ❑

MANCHU DYNASTY IN CHINA

Beijing, 1644

After a long decline in power, the Ming Dynasty came to an end with the suicide of its last emperor, in the face of a successful rebellion led by Li Zicheng. Peasant uprisings caused by heavy taxation, the Manchu incursions, and the breakdown of government combined to bring about the end of the dynasty. The conqueror Li's power was, however, short-lived. The Man- chu Qing Dynasty with the help of Wu Sangui, a Ming Dynasty general, defeated Li's troops, and the boy emperor Shunzhi was installed in Beijing. The Manchu took over the existing state bureaucracy, and though, at first, marriage between the conquerors and the defeated Chinese was forbidden, in time the Manchus succumbed to the influence of Chinese culture. ❑

CONSEQUENCES: WEAKER EMPEROR, STRONGER PRINCES

Point of Interest

In the long term, the Treaty of Westphalia resulted in the waning of the power and prestige of the emperor and the rise of principalities and nation-states. The Empire's vast holdings of land were essentially delimited by the boundaries of the Habsburg's hereditary fiefdom. France and Swe- den benefited greatly from the treaty, and a number of German princes also expanded their territorial holdings. This territorial realignment was significant, but in the long term more important still was the inescapable recognition that Protestant confessions had become permanent features of the European landscape.

The withdrawal of the emperor as a central force in European political stability led to shifting alliances among the remaining powers and a series of small conflicts that would plague the Continent until the advent of Napoleon. ❑

Detail of Treaty of Westphalia

Peace of Westphalia and the End of the Thirty Years War

Munster, October 24, 1648

Thirty years of bitter religious warfare ended with the signing of the Treaty of Westphalia. The conflict had drawn in almost every European power both on land and sea. Since 1645, negotiations had been underway in two cities—Catholic Munster and Protestant Osnabrück—to bring about the signing of the treaty.

France became the most significant player in the last phase of the war. Under the guidance of Cardinal Richelieu, who determined French foreign policy for its weak king Louis XIII, France allied itself with all the enemies of the Habsburgs, with the aim of weakening the power that threatened to encircle it. France lent financial support to Sweden and the Protestant princes in Germany. The tide turned against the Habsburgs with Swedish troops fighting in Prague—where the war started with a Protestant rebellion against the Catholic Habsburg Empire—and the French army winning a succession of victories in Bavaria. Finally Ferdinand III, the emperor, was forced to accede to the negotiations.

The treaty represented the failure by the Habsburgs to turn Germany into a Catholic monarchy. It guaranteed the full sovereignty of the German states and toleration for all three faiths—Catholicism, Lutheranism, and Calvinism—except in the hereditary lands of the Habsburgs. By the terms of the treaty, the Habsburgs recognized the independence of Switzerland and the separation of the United Provinces of the Netherlands from Spain. France acquired Alsace and other territories as reparation; Sweden secured Pomerania, giving her dominance in the Baltic.

But the war cast a long shadow. Whole towns had been razed by siege and fire, some losing as many as 50 percent of their population from plague borne by countless armies. Over 100,000 mercenary soldiers had to be paid and returned home lest they turn themselves into robber bands adding even more torment to a war-weary Europe. The high cost of war caused massive tax demands on both nobles and peasants who were already threatening revolt. So though the Treaty of Westphalia brought peace; it was an uneasy peace at best. ❑

Contemporary German map showing the campaigns, battles and troop movements in the Thirty Years War.

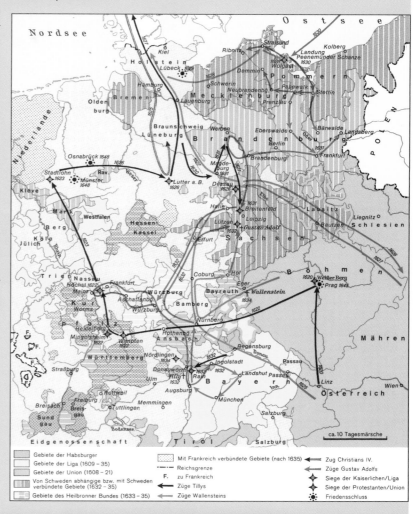

Gerard ter Borch, *The Ratification of The Treaty of Munster.* This treaty, signed in 1648, marked the end of the Eighty Years War between the Netherlands and Spain. According to its provisions Spain recognized the independence of the United Netherlands

THOMAS HOBBES'S *LEVIATHAN*

London, 1651

Born on April 5, 1588, in Wiltshire, England, Thomas Hobbes was one of the first great "natural law" philosophers whose materialist ideas reflected the burgeoning scientific rationalism inspired by his contemporaries Francis Bacon and Galileo.

Witness to the social chaos created by the English Civil War of 1642, Hobbes is best known for a political philosophy that pitted the individual's anarchic "condition of mere nature" against the civilized organization afforded by the "social contract." In his master work *Leviathan*, Hobbes asserts that the natural state of the individual is, on the one hand, "solitary, poor, nasty, brutish, and short," driven by predatory imperatives that disregard the need for society, but, on the other hand, is also possessed of the instinctual, "natural laws" of self-preservation and the fear of violent death. These "natural laws" lead the individual to accept a form of social contract under which he gives up his asocial liberties to the absolute power of the state. The underlying motivation to accept this "sovereignty by institution" is fear. It is ultimately in the individual's best self-interest to enter into a "covenant" with a government whose authority must be absolute and unlimited. Regardless of whether that government is a democracy, a monarchy, or a totalitarian regime,

Title page of *The Leviathan* by Thomas Hobbes (1651, London)

the integrity and success of the covenant can be effected only by complete submission to its authority. ❑

THE FIRST ANGLO- THE TREATY OF

London, 1651

The already deteriorating relations between England and the Netherlands were severely strained when Oliver Cromwell's Commonwealth Parliament passed the Navigation Act on October 9, 1651. Challenging Dutch mercantile supremacy, the Act proclaimed that goods from Asia, Africa, and America could only be imported into England by English ships. With the English economy severely depressed and Dutch maritime power on the rise, the move was seen as Britain's attempt to cut into Amsterdam's sea-trade monopoly at a time when the Netherlands were distracted by internal conflicts between the United Provinces' merchants and factions loyal to the House of Orange.

William II of Orange, who had died of smallpox in the previous year, had been determined to institute an absolute monarchy. With his death, a constituent assembly of the Netherlands' United Provinces met at The Hague in January of 1651 to block the creation of a monarchy and to create a republican government. William's close relationship with the House of Stuart, and his attempts to enlist the Netherlands in France's war with Spain offended the economically powerful assembly of burghers, who saw his actions as detrimental to their successful trading enterprises and as creating

POPULATION GROWTH STALLED IN EUROPE

Europe, c.1650

In the seventeenth century, during the period referred to by historians as the General Crisis, Europe experienced major changes that shaped the coming political configurations in Europe. Some trends had severely destabilizing effects, albeit temporary. One of these was a dramatic drop in population between 1648 and 1730.

A major factor for the population decline was the Thirty Years War, whose battlefield death tolls were increased by the spread of disease and the destruction of farmlands during the movement of armies across Europe.

Another was a high infant mortality rate caused partly by the era's unsanitary birthing procedures.

Also, couples were marrying later, and the subsequent births to older women resulted in an increase in unsuccessful pregnancies. In addition, these "late-in-life" couples produced smaller families. The cause of these later marriages was demographically complex but certainly had to do with the aforementioned diseases and wars.

Population decline was also caused by a combined occurrence of poor harvests, famine, and plague that was unusually common in many areas of Europe during this time period. After 1730, the triple threat of war, plague, and famine subsided, leading to a spike in population growth. ❑

DUTCH WAR AND WESTMINSTER

divisions within the United Provinces that could lead to civil war.

England soon used the provisions in the Navigation Act to justify declaring war on the Netherlands in July of 1652, after a confrontation off the coast of Dover, known as the Battle of Goodwin Sands, between the Dutch admiral Maarten Tromp and Britain's General Robert Blake. Sea battles raged on for two years, with the English eventually gaining the advantage, creating a blockade that crippled Dutch sea trade. However, by April of 1654, both countries were running out of manpower and funds to continue the conflict.

Cromwell initiated negotiations that led to the signing of the Treaty of Westminster on April 5, 1654. While the treaty ended the hostilities, it did not resolve the issues of maritime trade competition. Although they really had no intention of following through, the Dutch agreed to observe the provisions of the Navigation Act. But the real motivation behind Cromwell's initiative was embedded in a secret clause, the Act of Seclusion, wherein the Dutch agreed to exclude William III, Prince of Orange, from becoming a Stadtholder, thereby limiting the influence in the United Provinces of William's ally, and Cromwell's bête noire, the House of Stuart. ❑

Oliver Cromwell

CIVIL WAR IN ENGLAND

Whitehall Palace, January 30, 1649

After a show trial, King Charles I (b.1600) was found guilty and executed, and England became a commonwealth.

Religious conflicts and skirmishes with the House of Commons over taxes marked Charles's reign. He came to the throne on March 27, 1625, upon the death of his father James I. Charles's unshakable conviction that he had been elected by God to rule, soon led to confrontations with the members of Parliament. His third parliament pressured him into signing a Petition of Right wherein he relinquished his right to raise taxes without consultation, and he guaranteed certain personal freedoms.

From 1629 to 1640, Charles governed England without ever calling Parliament into session. His attempt in 1637 to force Scotland to observe the rite of the Anglican Church in its religious services led to open rebellion. Driven by a critical need for money and an impending religious war, he called back Parliament on April 13, 1640. He sent the MPs back to their homes on May 5, but they reconvened on November 3, and sat in continuous session until 1653, in what became known as the Long Parliament.

The conflict intensified in 1642 when Charles entered Parliament with an armed guard and tried to have five of his most bitter antagonists arrested on charges of high treason. Forewarned, his opponents were able to escape. Meanwhile, Charles was forced to flee with his family to York.

That signaled the beginning of a civil war. The king received support from the nobility and the Anglican Church; the Scots and the burgeoning middle class came down on the side of Parliament. On June 2, 1644, the Parliamentary party (the Roundheads) met the royalists (Cavaliers) on Marston Moor. A Roundhead cavalry charge led by Oliver

The execution of Charles I in 1649 before Whitehall Palace

Cromwell broke the ranks of the royalist army.

At the head of a superior force, Cromwell, now second-in-command under Sir Thomas Fairfax, met the king's army once again on the battlefield, this time at Naseby just south of Leicester, and once again was the victor. Charles fled to Scotland but the army under the command of Archibald Campbell, the Duke of Argyll, handed him back to the English. The Scots received the sum of 400,000 pounds, which they said was payment owed to them based on an earlier agreement. Charles accused them of betraying their king for money.

Charles escaped and was able to reach the Isle of Man; he turned once more to the Scots for help. But the Scottish troops were defeated at Preston in Lancashire and the last vestiges of support for the king were crushed.

With the king removed from power, various ad hoc arrangements were devised to fill the vacuum. Cromwell gradually emerged as the commanding figure. This deeply religious man, dedicated to Puritanism, conceived of himself as being guided by Providence. He wanted to rid himself of the king. In order to ensure that Parliament would rat-

ify the plan, the Rump Parliament convened with nearly 150 members excluded. Charles was led to the scaffold on January 30, 1649. His wife Henrietta returned to France and his son Charles found refuge in Holland.

On May 19, 1649, a council was established that hewed to Cromwell's line, formally designating the English state a commonwealth. That designation would last until the restoration of Charles II in 1662. The long civil war had, however, weakened the country. There were rebellions in Ireland and Scotland. Cromwell put both down, Ireland's with terrible brutality. In 1653, Parliament bestowed on Cromwell the title of Lord Protector. He declined the crown offered to him in 1657 but reserved the right to name his successor. He died in London on September 3, 1658. His son Richard succeeded him but ruled for less than a year before being forced to abdicate. Charles was entreated to return to England and entered London on the day of his thirtieth birthday, May 29, 1660. He was crowned Charles II King of England at Westminster Abbey on April 23, 1661. Upon the restoration of the monarchy, Cromwell's body was dug up and beheaded. ❑

LOUIS XIV: THE SUN KING

France, 1661

France's famed Sun King ascended to the throne in 1643 at age five. His 73-year reign remains the longest of any monarch in European history. His rule was marked by prolonged and frequent wars, the extension of French territory and influence in Europe, the consolidation of power within France, and a brilliant flowering of French culture.

It was not until the death of Louis XIV's chief minister, Jules Mazarin, when the king was 22, that he assumed full power over his kingdom. Louis was considered a bright and ambitious young man who had a devotion to regularity, an amorous disposition, and a strong distaste for civil unrest. In the early years of his reign, he surrounded himself with remarkably talented men. His chief minister, Jean-Baptiste Colbert, the son of a merchant, took control of fiscal matters and did much to make France the wealthiest state in Europe. Through taxes and incentives, he

modernized French industry and trade. He oversaw the enlargement of the French navy, the establishment of a more uniform tax system, and sought the means to take advantage of the natural resources of France. Roads and harbors were built and improved, industries—in particular the textile industry—were organized, and French colonies were exploited. The revenue stream tripled under his watchful eye.

While Colbert improved the finances of France, much of the money that came into the treasury went to support wars of expansion and Louis XIV's determination to make France's borders safe. François Michel le Tellier, Marquis de Louvois, like Colbert, a member of the bourgeoisie, was appointed the Minister of War. He limited the privileges of the nobles and brought much-needed discipline and to France's army. In 1667, the French army accompanied by Louis XIV, advanced into the Spanish Netherlands, claiming them for France

Hyacinthe Rigaud , *Louis XIV*

through inheritance rights of the queen. In 1681, the independent

city of Strasbourg was annexed to France. Many of the French

CONFLICT BETWEEN DENMARK AND SWEDEN

Baltic Sea, 1657

Between 1657 and 1660, Sweden and Denmark engaged in two conflicts that were part of a larger European war known as the Northern War (1655–1660.) At issue in all of the conflicts were the aggressive expansionist agenda of Sweden's Charles X

and control of maritime trade in the Baltic region.

The first Swedish-Danish War (1657–1658) was instigated by Denmark's Frederick III, who attacked Swedish provinces while Charles led an invasion of Poland-Lithuania. Charles respond-

ed by marching on Copenhagen, forcing the Danes to surrender. A temporary peace was achieved with the signing of the Treaty of Roskilde on March 8, 1658.
In August, Charles began the second Swedish-Danish War (1658–1660) by mounting an un-

successful siege on Copenhagen. Indecisive skirmishes continued until Charles's death in 1660. After this, Sweden ended their war with Denmark and the Northern War with the signing of the Treaty of Copenhagen on June 6, 1660. ❑

JULES MAZARIN

Brief Lives

Jules Mazarin (1602–1661) became chief minister of France upon the death of Cardinal Richelieu in 1642. Italian by birth and a naturalized French citizen, he continued the policies of his predecessor and mentor. He was very close to Anne of Austria, the wife of Louis XIII, and upon the latter's death in 1643,

Mazarin effectively ruled France on behalf of the young Louis XIV until his own demise in 1661. Under his leadership, the Thirty Years War was settled to France's advantage. A subsequent war with Spain ended with additional territorial gains and the fixing of France's southern border at the Pyrenees.

In addition, Mazarin, who was gifted in the art of diplomacy (and gambling), arranged a marriage between Louis XIV and Philip IV of Spain's daughter, Marie Thérèse.

Because of his support of higher taxes and his continued centralization of power in the hands of the French monarchy, Mazarin was

unpopular with French nobles and the general populace, and was the target of much enmity during the civil uprisings (*la Fronde*) of 1648–1653. ❑

Cardinal Jules Mazarin

military victories hinged on the weakened Spanish power and the focus of other European powers on keeping the Turks out of southeastern Europe. By 1689, a "Grand Alliance" was formed to counter Louis XIV's continued aggressions. England, Holland, Austria, Spain, and German princes fought to keep France out of Germany and the Netherlands. The War of the Grand Alliance ended in 1697, whereupon attention in Europe turned to the Spanish succession. With the Spanish king, Charles II, unable to produce an heir, the question of who would rule the worldwide Spanish empire was the center of European political attention. Louis XIV's grandson, Philip, the Duke of Anjou, was ultimately offered the Spanish crown, and war among the European rivals broke out again. France suffered heavy losses but ultimately retained most of the territory and power gained over the preceding decades.

At the beginning of Louis XIV's active rule, he tolerated various factions of Catholicism

Louis XIV at a court reception in 1714

and Protestantism in France. By the 1680s, however, French Protestants (Huguenots) were increasingly pressured to convert and began emigrating in large numbers. In 1685, Louis revoked the Edict of Nantes, signed by his grandfather in 1598, which had granted religious and political freedom to the Huguenots. The Huguenots included many wealthy merchants and skilled craftsmen and the exodus of some 200,000 had a severe impact on the French economy. This was followed by persecution of Catholic sects (in particular the Jansenists).

Louis XIV was a grand patron of the arts. Best known for his building of Versailles, he also oversaw the building of the Hotel des Invalides in Paris as well as a major renovation of the Louvre. He supported the playwrights Molière and Jean Racine, as well as painters and composers including Jean-Baptiste Lully and François Couperin. Ballet and opera were introduced to the French court and flourished. He fostered an elegance and opulent style that was copied throughout European courts. French fashion, food, and language set the standards even among his enemies. His extravagances combined with his military undertakings would leave the treasury bankrupt upon his death in 1715. The throne of France was inherited by his great grandson, the five-year-old Louis XV. ❏

MERCANTILISM

Point of Interest

Mercantilism involves the theory and practice of a national economic policy that strives for a treasury with a surplus of precious metals (gold and, to a lesser degree, silver). It developed in order to meet the growing financial needs of the absolute monarchies of Europe in the years of 1600 to 1800. It recognized that the most effective way to increase a country's economic clout was to boost domestic productivity and maintain a positive balance of trade. This was facilitated by the acquisition of colonies that provided raw materials and were then markets for finished goods. ❏

AURANGZEB: LAST OF THE GREAT MOGHUL EMPERORS

India, 1658

Aurangzeb (r.1658–1707), the last of India's great Moghul Emperors, rose to power in 1658 through a series of internecine intrigues that ended with the imprisonment of his own father, Emperor Shah Jahan. A power struggle with his three brothers, Dara Shikoh, Shah Shuja, and Murad Baskh, began with Shah Jahan's illness. When Aurangzeb moved to seize the throne, the brothers took action. Dara, the oldest and heir apparent, assumed the throne with the ailing Shah Jahan's blessing. The second, Shuja, named himself Emperor in Bengal and declared war on Dara. The third, Murad, was encouraged by Aurangzeb to claim the title of Emperor. In reality, Aurangzeb

only wanted to use him in his battle with Dara and Shuja.

Even when Shah Jahan recovered and Dara resigned the throne, Aurangzeb continued his ruthless drive for power, first defeating Dara's forces and subsequently executing him and then routing Shuja's, forcing him into permanent exile. He then had Murad assassinated. In August of 1658, after confining his father to lifelong house arrest, Aurangzeb claimed the Moghul throne. Aurangzeb's reign was noted for strict adherence to fundamentalist Islamic principles and intolerance toward Hindus. This would lead to his downfall and the subsequent end of Moghul power with

his defeat by the powerful Hindu Mahratta confederacy. Aurangzeb ruled India until his death on March 3, 1707. ❏

Aurangzeb, Grand Moghul of India (copper etching)

THE RISE OF PRUSSIA

Brandenburg, late seventeenth century

Frederick William, the elector of Brandenburg, joined the war between France and Holland which not only was dominating politics in Europe but also was beginning to spread to the New World in the West Indies.

Thirty-five years since he inherited a scattered group of lands ravaged by the battles of the Thirty Years' War. He consolidated them successfully, to become a real force to reckon with. Supporting the Dutch, he defeated their Swedish rivals at the Battle of Fehrbellin and proceeded to invade Bremen, Verden and Western Pomerania, Sweden's enclaves in north Germany. The elector's

intervention significantly altered the course of the war, discouraging France, Sweden's ally, from further commitments of money and manpower.

From the beginning Frederick William's goal had been the unifying of Prussia. Despite the antagonism of the landed aristocracy class he raised property

taxes. With the increased tax revenue he started building a small standing army. He also established a well-organized centralized government with a cadre of

The Battle of Fehrbellin of June 28, 1675 between the German Duchy of Brandenburg and Sweden (copper etching)

MOLIÈRE: FRENCH MASTER OF COMEDY

France, 1664

Molière was France's greatest comedian and playwright. His real name was Jean-Baptiste Poquelin. As a young man he joined the large theatrical family of Béjart to form L'Illustre Théâtre. They failed in Paris and toured France for thirteen years of varied fortunes, playing in tennis courts, with Molière in leading roles opposite Madeleine Béjart. In 1658, King Louis XIV became their patron. They took over the Palais Royal Theatre where Molière created a series of great comedies. Among his most famous works are Le Misanthrope (The Misan-

thrope), L'École des Femmes (The School for Wives), L'Avare (The Miser), Le Bourgeois gentilhomme (The Middle-class Gentleman), and Le Marriage Forcé (The Forced Marriage). Tartuffe, perhaps his best-known work, aroused bitter criticism for its savagely funny portrait of a religious hypocrite and was banned for years. In 1662, Molière married Armande Béjart, a girl of nineteen. She was the younger sister of Madeleine, Molière's leading lady.

In 1673, Molière died of a lung hemorrhage after collapsing on stage during his performance

as the hypochondriac in his own Le Malade Imaginaire. He was 51. The king's mourning for his favorite actor was not shared by many of the playwright's enemies at court and in the Church who had suffered from his ridicule. ❏

Scene from Le Monsieur du Pourceaugnac by Molière

civil servants loyal to the crown.

He concentrated on establishing a mercantile, political system for the economy by building a merchant fleet and canals for ships.

Frederick William tried to promote peace between the Lutheran Church and the reformed minorities, to which he belonged. He believed that religious tolerance and economic strength went hand in hand. He made it possible for fifty exiled Jewish families from Vienna to settle in Bran-

Businessmen showing their products

denburg on May 1, 1671, and permitted them freedom of trade. They were not allowed to work in financial businesses but could trade wool, textiles and clothing. They could, however, only practice their religion at home.

After the French King Louis XIV revoked the Edict of Nantes, many Huguenots were forced to emigrate. Almost 15,000 refugees found new homes in Brandenburg and Prussia. Here with the November 8, 1685 Edict of Potsdam,

Friedrich granted them full religious freedom, unlimited residential rights and extensive economic privileges. Many Huguenots were civil servants: noble officers, judges, doctors, teachers, financially sound business owners, and skilled trade workers. Prussia greatly benefited from their arrival.

Frederick William died on May 9, 1688 in Potsdam. He was succeeded by his son Prince Frederick III, later to become Frederick I, King of Prussia. ❑

Newton's Laws

Lincolnshire, England, 1666

Isaac Newton (1643–1727) was determined to lead a life of learning and invention, and eschewed the family farm in order to pursue his studies at Cambridge University, where he was influenced by his reading of Kepler, Galileo, and Descartes. He began to think about matter as being composed of particles in motion held together by various forces. In 1665, when the university was closed due to plague, Newton wrote up some of the notes he had compiled. One outcome of this was the essay *Of Colours*, which later became extended into Book One of *Opticks* (published in 1704). He experimented with a prism and found that white light could be separated into the colors of the rainbow and then return to white light, proving that white was made up of all colors. Newton further contended that light consists of minute particles of matter that emanate from luminous bodies such as stars and travel through space. (In 1678, Dutch scientist Christian Huygens would propose that light consists of waves that travel through the "ether" at great speed, in straight lines and with vibrations at right angles to their direction of travel.)

Newton went on to devise a mathematical method for ana-

lyzing the slopes of curves and the areas bound by them. Now known as calculus, it was the tool by which one could calculate variations that occur with the passage of time, such as the positions of an orbiting planet. (Gottfried Leibniz also arrived at the same conclusions at roughly the same time in Paris.)

In 1687, after two long, hard years of sustained effort, Newton published *Philosophiae Naturalis Principia Mathematica* (*The Mathematical Principles of Natural Philosophy*). Considered by many as the greatest scientific book ever written, it consisted of three parts. The first part was devoted to the motions of bodies in an unresisting medium—such as planets in orbit round the sun; the second looked at bodies in resisting mediums such as fluids; the third applied these mechanical theories to astronomical problems and demonstrated what the author called "the frame of the System of the World."

In the *Principia*, Newton formulated a law of gravity that he contended was universally applicable. Legend has it that it came to him at the age of 23 as he watched an apple fall from a tree. He supported this gravitational theory with detailed and

convincing mathematical proofs, including the use of calculus. Newton also explicitly defined such concepts as centripetal force, momentum, and mass, and stated three laws of motion.

The first law dealt with inertia; a body stays at rest unless acted upon by forces. The second law states that the change of motion in a body is in proportion to the force acting on it and is in a straight line. And the third law states that for every action in nature there is an equal and equivalent reaction.

It was the notion of a gravitational force that captured the imagination of his peers. In Newton's universe, every single piece of matter exerts a force on every other particle: "...all matter attracts all other matter with a force proportional to the product of their masses and inversely proportional to the square of the distance between them."

This universal gravitational law made sense of the whole structure of the cosmos from the paths of comets to the movement of the tides.

Underlying Newton's theories was the conviction that the operations of the universe were consistent and could be calculated and understood by man.

Newton completed much of his mathematical and scientific work before the age of 30. (He withheld publication of some of his work until later in his life because of disputes with his critics.) Late in life he became head of the Royal Mint in London and was the first scientist in England to be knighted. ❑

Isaac Newton studying light rays

WILLIAM PENN AND THE FOUNDING OF PENNSYLVANIA

Pennsylvania, 1683

William Penn was born on October 14, 1644, in London. The son of the highly regarded Admiral William Penn Sr., the young William rejected both Puritan and Catholic doctrine embracing instead the controversial ideas of freedom of religious expression and civil liberties. At 22, he became a follower of George Fox and the Society of Friends (Quakers). In 1664, he entered Lincoln's Inn, where he formulated a philosophy of common law and social justice that would result in the founding of Pennsylvania.

A formative event took place in August of 1670, when William and fellow Quakers were arrested and put on trial for defying the *Conventicle Act*, a law that banned religious dissent. When London's Lord Mayor overturned the jury's acquittal verdict and ordered not only the defendants but also the jurors themselves jailed, Penn mounted a "right to trial by jury" defense that was ratified by the Lord Chief Justice of England, freeing the Quakers.

This experience inspired Penn's vision of a community based on the Quaker principles of social and religious tolerance. To that purpose, he petitioned Charles II for a land grant in North America. Charles, who owed William Penn Sr. a considerable sum of money, agreed, creating the colony of Pennsylva-

nia ("the forests of Penn").

Arriving on the ship *Welcome* on November 8, 1682, Penn founded Philadelphia ("the city of brotherly love"). Designed as a haven for those persecuted for their religious beliefs, it soon attracted European Jews, Huguenots, and other victims of intolerance.

Penn codified the principles of this "holy experiment" in his *First Frame of Government*, a document establishing the community's commitment to private property, free enterprise, trial by jury, humane penal codes, and equal rights for women. Curiously, it ignored, and thereby accepted, the institution of slavery. Penn, himself, was a slaveholder.

Engendering cordial relations with the indigenous Susquehannock and Leni-Lenape tribes, Penn drew up the *Great Treaty*, which, among other provisions, contained the guarantee of fair value for lands purchased from them.

Eventually many of Penn's progressive programs were compro-

mised, but the spirit behind them served to inspire Thomas Jefferson, Benjamin Franklin, and the *Declaration of Independence*. ❏

The English Quaker William Penn founds the city of Philadelphia in 1683.

NEW PROTESTANT SECTS

England, seventeenth century

Coincident with England's civil war, a number of new independent religious sects sprang up. Generally known under the rubric of Dissenters, the believers endorsed a wide variety of practice and doctrine.

In 1689, religious freedom was granted to a number of these sects with the exception of Unitarians and Catholics.

The Baptists were dissenting Calvinists. The sect was founded in 1608 by John Smyth. It rejected infant baptism and considered the rite of baptism for adults of central importance.

The Quakers took the name the Society of Friends. The founder of the religion is considered to be George Fox (1624–1691), an itinerant

preacher, who taught that one's "inner Christ" is the only authority. The Quakers rejected all of religion's ritual trappings. Taking seriously Jesus' admonitions to be peacemakers, the Quakers were strict pacifists, abjuring any participation in war or violence and were thus easy targets for persecution. The name Quaker was initially

one of derision. George Fox responded that their critics call them Quakers because they tremble at the Word of God.

At the beginning, the Quakers faced harsh persecution. Many of their leaders were imprisoned and beaten. William Penn's new colony became their refuge, and the movement flourished there. ❏

EXPERIMENTS WITH STEAM

Paris, 1681

The second half of the seventeenth century witnessed many important scientific and technical discoveries. In 1681, the French physicist Denis Papin (1647–1714) first marketed a steam pressure cooker. Papin had observed that the temperature of water (as well as other liquids) depended upon the amount of pressure to which it was subjected. Putting this discovery to practical use, he made a hermetically sealed metal cooking pot with a special release valve at the top. This device, called a steam digester, was used to remove fat from bones and assist in the process of making bone meal. The steam release valve was a vital ingredient in the later development of the steam engine.

An inspiration for Papin and other early researchers of the power of steam were the vacuum experiments of Otto von Guericke. In 1654, Guericke made the first "Magdeburg hemispheres," two copper hemispheres joined together. With a pump he invented he forced the air out of the them, resulting in a vacuum and a seal that could not be broken. This led to a recognition of the existence of vacuums and the importance of atmospheric pressure.

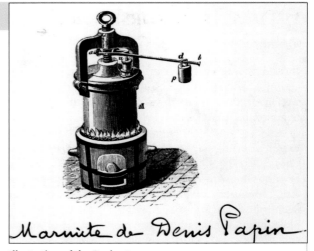

Illustration of the Papin steamer

To further understand the nature of the "power of nothing" more precise methods of measurement were needed. This led to many developments seminal to the Industrial Revolution such as a precision timepiece by the Dutchman Christian Huygens, who used a pendulum to regulate its motion, and a calculating machine by the mathematician and philosopher Gottfried Leibniz—the first that could add, subtract, multiply, and divide. ❑

THE WAR OF DEVOLUTION

Flanders, 1667

The War of Devolution (1667–1668) was fought between France and Habsburg Spain over territorial rights to the Spanish Netherlands. The seeds of the conflict were sown when Marie-Thérèse, the first daughter of the Spain's King Philip IV, married France's Louis XIV, renouncing her claims of Spanish inheritance in lieu of a future dowry. Upon the death of Philip in 1665, and the non-payment of the dowry by the Habsburgs, Louis claimed to be the rightful heir to the Netherlands holdings based on an old law of the Duchy of Brabant, which ruled that a disputed inheritance could "devolve" to the Spanish king's first daughter. Citing this law and the Habsburg's refusal to pay his wife's dowry, Louis instituted legal action. When this petition for redress was dismissed by the Habsburgs, he invaded the Spanish Netherlands.

On May 24, 1667, a French army of 70,000 swept into Flanders and took possession of dozens of inadequately defended towns, ending at Lille on September 25. Taking advantage of the Habsburg's vulnerable defenses, in February of 1668, a second French force invaded and swiftly occupied the Spanish ruled region of Franche-Comté.

Although nominally French allies, the Dutch United Provinces were so alarmed by these aggressive actions that they moved preemptively to protect themselves by entering a mutual defense pact with England and Sweden. Known as the "Triple Alliance," their combined presence as a potential military threat convinced Louis to end his expansionist activities. Agreeing to a peace settlement mediated by the "Alliance," France and Spain signed the Treaty of Aix-la-Chapelle on May 2, 1668. Allowed to keep Flanders, France withdrew its claim on the Spanish Netherlands and agreed to return the Franche-Comté to Habsburg control.

Peace was short-lived. Incensed by his former ally's perceived disloyalty and still intent on possessing the Spanish Netherlands, Louis invaded the United Provinces in 1672, beginning the Franco-Dutch War. It ended in 1679, with the Peace of Nijmegen, where Louis was again denied the Spanish Netherlands. ❑

EXPANSION OF CIVIL RIGHTS

London, 1679

In its battles with Charles II, Parliament forced the king to acknowledge some fundamental civil rights, particularly the protection against arbitrary arrest and imprisonment. Charles had resisted the principle of habeas corpus (you must produce a body), which prohibited trials in absentia and provided for due process to those who were arrested. It required that those holding others in prison be required to deliver them to a court for trial.

Charles, who was the son of the executed King Charles I, was returned from exile after the civil war had run its course. He chafed at Parliament's placing limits on his power and prerogatives. In 1640, Parliament had pressed for an expansion of habeas corpus, which Charles I had asserted was subordinate to the king's will. ❑

Session of Parliament (etching by Wenzel Hollar)

OTTOMAN INCURSION INTO EUROPE HALTED

Vienna, 1683

By the middle of the seventeenth century, the Ottoman Empire was in decline. Its fortunes were restored in 1656, with elevation of the 71-year-old Albanian, Mehmed Köprülü, to the position of Grand Vizier. Founder of what became known as the Köprülü Era, Mehmed was particularly keen on defeating the Austrian Habsburgs. During his five-year rule he wielded absolute power, renewing pride and discipline in the army, reviving Ottoman territorial expansion, and crushing internal revolts by having 35,000 rebels throughout the empire executed. Upon his death in 1661, he was succeeded as Grand Vizier by his son, Fazil Ahmed. Fazil recaptured Crete, but was not so fortunate with Habsburg Austria, where the Ottoman advance toward Vienna initiated by his father was temporarily halted at the Battle of St. Gotthard in 1664.

The Battle of St. Gotthard (at the present-day border between Austria and Hungary) was the end result of a series of conflicts that began with the Austrian Habsburg incursion into Transylvania in 1661. The Ottoman armies responded by invading Transylvania and Hungary. As the Ottomans under Fazil advanced from Belgrade toward Vienna, the Habsburgs under the Austrian General Montecuccoli with a coalition of French and German troops repelled the Ottomans, destroying most of their cannons and equipment. Although victorious, the Habsburgs knew the Ottomans would remain a threat and so were willing to negotiate a peace agreement by signing the Treaty of Vasvár, which gave far more to the Ottomans than it did the Habsburgs. It allowed the Ottomans to retain much of Hungary and Transylvania, while the Habsburgs agreed to pay a monetary tribute to the sultan to decamp from territories taken in their 1661 invasion of Transylvania, and recognize that region as being subject to Ottoman sovereignty. For their part, the Habsburgs received a commitment to what would be a temporary peace. The Battle of St. Gotthard's most significant result was that it halted the Ottoman invasion of Austria long enough for the Austrians to rebuild their defense force. Twenty years later, this would be crucial to a Habsburg victory in the epochal Battle of Vienna.

In 1682, after a Habsburg invasion of Hungary to root out forces under the Hungarian leader, Imre Thököly, the Ottomans' dormant plan to capture Vienna was set in motion by Grand Vizier Kara Mustafa Pasha, who mobilized an army and declared war on the Austrian Habsburgs. His 138,000 troops surrounded Vienna in July of 1683. On September 12, 1683, after a two-month siege, a 70,000-strong confederation of Habsburg forces co-commanded by King John III Sobieski of Poland and Charles V, Duke of Lorraine, arrived to Vienna's aid and met the Turks in battle before the walls of the city. Ottoman tactical errors and fatigue led to their decisive defeat within twenty-four hours. Although not the end of Ottoman incursions in Europe, the Battle of Vienna was a turning point in the 300-year conflict between European kingdoms and the Ottoman Empire. ❑

Battle before the walls of Vienna. The Ottoman army is decisively beaten.

"A CALAMITOUS DEFEAT"

Account of the Siege of Vienna by a Contemporary Ottoman Chronicler

... everything that was in the imperial [Ottoman] camp, money and equipment and precious things, was left behind and fell into the hands of the people of hell. The accursed infidels in their battalion (may it be crushed) came in two columns. One of them advancing along the bank of the Danube entered the fortress and stormed the trenches.

The other captured the imperial army camp. Of the disabled men whom they found in the trenches they killed some and took others prisoner. The men remaining in the trenches, some 10,000 of them, were incapable of fighting, having been wounded by guns, muskets, cannon, mines, stones, and other weapons, some of them lacking an arm or a leg. These they at once put to the sword and, finding some thousands of their own prisoners, freed them from their bonds and released them. They succeeded in capturing such quantities of money and supplies as cannot be described. They therefore did not even think of pursuing the soldiers of Islam and had they done so it would have gone hard. May God preserve us. This was a calamitous defeat of such magnitude that there has never been its like since the first appearance of the Ottoman state. ❑

JAMES II AND THE "GLORIOUS REVOLUTION"

England, 1688

The overthrow of King James II and the House of Stuart in 1688 by a confederation of Parliamentarians and the Dutch stadtholder, William III of Orange, resulted in an epochal shift in British political history. Known as the "Glorious Revolution" or the "Bloodless Revolution," it marked the end of the ancient British tradition of absolute monarchy and ushered in an era of a constitutional monarchy embodying the principles of parliamentary democracy. It also forever ended Catholic hegemony in British political life.

When James's father, Charles I, was executed during the English Civil War, James and his elder brother Charles fled to the Continent where they lived in exile until 1660, returning to England after Cromwell's death and the collapse of the Commonwealth. With the Restoration, James's brother was crowned Charles II, and James was named Lord High Admiral and the Duke of York and Albany. When James converted to Catholicism in 1670, his presence in such powerful positions, and the possibility of his succession to the throne, created fear in Parliament and the Anglican Church of the reprise of a royal Catholic dynasty.

In 1673, to block Catholic influence, Parliament passed the Test Act, which required that all government officials take an oath to the Church of England and denounce Catholic doctrine. James's refusal to do so strengthened the anti-Catholic mood in British society and led to Parliament's attempt to pass the Exclusion Bill, the sole purpose of which was to bar James from succeeding to the throne. Those supporting the bill became known as Whigs, those against it, Tories (beginning the British two-party system). Enraged, Charles II dissolved three parliaments between 1679 and 1681. The Exclusion Crisis came

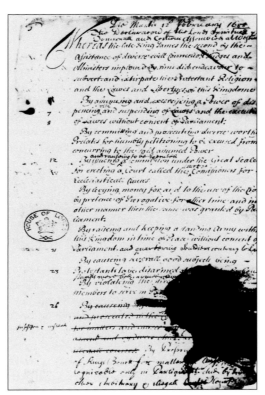

The Declaration of Rights of 1689 established England as a constitutional monarchy.

to an end with the uncovering of a plot to kill Charles and James, called the Rye House Plot. Creating sympathy for the Stuarts, it restored James to public favor.

When Charles died in 1685, James was crowned James II. Despite offering a bipartisan olive branch to Parliament, including pardons for many party to the Exclusion Crisis, serious armed rebellions were mounted by the Dukes of Monmouth and Argyll. The latter's rebellion, which ended in his defeat, led to a series of trials known as the Bloody Assizes in which 250 rebels were executed. The rejection of his palliative gestures and the outbreak of these rebellions hardened James's resolve. He instituted a number of defensive measures that contributed to the "Glorious Revolution."

Against English tradition, he ordered the creation of a large standing army. He then appointed a number of Catholics to high government positions, ignoring the directives of the Test Act, and going so far as to welcome to his court the first papal representative from Rome since the reign of Mary I. He weakened the Church of England's hold on education by elevating Catholics to leadership roles at Oxford. Perhaps his most radical act was to issue the Declaration of Indulgence. Requiring that its provisions be read from every Anglican pulpit, this act suspended all prohibitions against the doctrines and practices of Catholics and Protestant Dissenters. In April of 1688, the Archbishop of Canterbury headed a group of Anglican clergy, known historically as the Seven Bishops, in presenting a petition to James asking that he reconsider his issuance of the Declaration of Indulgence. James had them arrested and charged them with seditious libel, inflaming public outrage.

Predating this escalating conflict was an ongoing internecine intrigue. James's first two children were daughters, Mary and Anne. At his brother Charles's behest, they were raised as Protestants. In 1677, Mary was betrothed to James's nephew, the Dutch Protestant, William III, Prince of Orange. This Protestant marriage of convenience was arranged by Charles II largely to assuage the fears of anti-Catholic members of Parliament and the Anglican Church that the restored Stuart monarchy represented the return of a Catholic dynasty. At the time, James did not have a son, so upon his death, the Protestant Mary would succeed to the throne.

As the conflict between James II and the Protestant power structure became increasingly strident, some members of Parliament carried on clandestine talks with William, encouraging him, under the aegis of Mary's rightful claims to the throne, to invaded England and wrest the crown from James. William rejected such a move against his father-in-law without a formal request from Parliament.

On June 10, 1688, shortly after the arrest of the Seven Bishops, James's wife gave birth to a new heir apparent to the throne, a son, James Francis Edward. Sure to be baptized as a Catholic, he represented the anti-Catholics worst fear, the onset of a new Catholic dynasty.

This confluence of events begun by James's Declaration of Indulgence was brought to a head on June 30, 1688, on the day that the Seven Bishops were acquitted, when the Immortal Seven, the members of Parliament who had been conducting talks with William, sent him an official request to invade England.

On November 5, 1688, William landed with 15,000 troops at Brixham. Meeting with no resistance (therefore, "Bloodless Revolution"), he marched on London. On December 23, with William's consent, James fled to France. With James in exile, the "Glorious Revolution" had become reality with the crowning of William and Mary, as co-regents, at Westminster Abbey on April 11, 1689.

Before their coronation William and Mary agreed to the Declaration of Rights drawn up by Parliament, setting forth the underlying principles of a constitutional monarchy. Parliament proceeded to pass the bill on December 16, 1689. It ranks with the Magna Carta as one of the foundational documents of English government. ❑

THE CHATEAU VERSAILLES

France, 1689

The Chateau Versailles, built in 1623 by Louis XIII as a hunting lodge, underwent many changes during the reign of Louis XIV, becoming the official residence of the Court of France in 1682. King Louis XIV, whose regal splendor earned him the epithet the "Sun King," made renovations to the original chateau between 1661 and 1668. Upon their completion, Louis felt that the chateau was still too small and commissioned the architect Louis Le Vau to build a second building, called the envelope, which wrapped around the original chateau. In 1670, Le Vau died and François d'Orbay completed the envelope, which consisted of a white stone façade that served as a fine garden setting and a central terrace inspired by Italian Baroque villas.

The gardens of the chateau were landscaped by the Royal Gardener André Le Nôtre. Le Nôtre built the entire garden around a central and secondary axis with numerous statues and fountains; vistas opened up throughout the property and certain areas were dedicated to Apollo. The chateau housed the royal family and court members in its many apartments and buildings. Its apartments were lavishly decorated and consisted of many rooms that ranged from public to private in order to accommodate the requirements of public and private life as well as the king's private collections. In 1678, Louis XIV had the terrace of the New Chateau converted into the Hall of Mirrors. The Hall of Mirrors, decorated by Charles Le Brun, depicts the king's accomplishments on its ceiling. There are seventeen windows overlooking the garden and seventeen exceptionally large arcaded mirrors along the walls. On one end is the Salon of Peace, on the other, the Salon of War. The Hall of Mirrors has been seen as the heart of the French realm and it was here that Germany signed the Treaty of Versailles at the end of the First World War.

Life in the chateau was closely regulated. In order to escape its rigid protocol, Louis XIV bought the village of Trianon and demolished it; he then built a home for himself and his family where they could have light meals and be close with one another. The Trianon was originally decorated with Chinese-style ceramic tiles, but by 1687, Louis XIV had them replaced with marble. The Trianon had three groves; the Chestnut Grove, the Grove of Springs, and the Kings Grove, each adorned with fountains and sculptures, through which the king could promenade.

The last major feature added to the chateau by King Louis XIV was the Chapel Royal. The chapel was consecrated to Saint Louis (Louis IX); there the King attended daily mass. The architecture of the chapel is a combination of Gothic and Baroque and contains scenes from the Old and New Testament carved into every inch of stone. Further additions to Chateau Versailles were made by the Sun King's successors, Louis XV, Louis XVI and his queen Marie Antoinette. ❑

Palace at Versailles: the Hall of Mirrors. The Treaty of Versailles was signed here in 1919 marking the end of World War I.

IRELAND: RELIGIOUS

Drogheda, Ireland, 1690

Underpinning the seventeenth-century battle for Ireland between English Protestants and Irish Catholics was the confluence of the dynamic struggles taking place throughout Europe. A figurehead in these battles was James II, whose loss to William III of Orange at the Irish Battle of the Boyne in 1690 displayed the conflicts in high relief.

The seeds of this pivotal battle were sown earlier in the century. After the Elizabethan conquest of Ireland in 1603, Roman Catholic landowners were deprived of land and political power by the Protestant English, based mainly on their Roman Catholic faith. The English Parliament created a proxy Protestant government and installed new English and Scottish settlers on massive plantations, such as Ulster and Munster, carved out of confiscated lands. While some wealthy Irish gentry managed to hold on to their possessions, the general Irish Catholic populace suffered terrible hardships.

Plans for a bloodless coup in 1641, when it appeared that anti-Catholic Scots and members of the English Long Parliament were campaigning for an invasion of Ireland, were betrayed and subsequently foiled. Bands of ordinary Irish Catholics, seething with rage against years of Protestant occupation, began an anarchic rampage, murdering the hated English and Scottish landholders and plantation colonists. Known as the Irish Rebellion of 1641, it resulted in the massacre of thousands of Protestants.

Beginning in 1643, a series of alliances were formed by the English leader of Royalist forces in Ireland, the Marquis of Ormond, between the Irish Confederates and English and Scottish Royalists. This made Ireland a formidable supporter of both Charles I and Charles II in their battles with the parliamentarian Roundheads. Parliament chose Oliver Cromwell

AND **POLITICAL BATTLEGROUND**

Sea Battle between England and Holland off La Hogue, May 29, 1692 (etching)

to put an end to the Irish-Anglo rebellion. Temperamentally, the arch-Protestant Cromwell was an ideal choice for the mission. Possessing a hatred of Irish Catholics stemming from the massacre of Protestants, Cromwell prosecuted what amounted to a "holy war." His highly disciplined and well-armed forces quickly took Dublin. By 1652 most of the country had succumbed to his vengeful wrath. No conflict better represented this than, Drogheda, near the River Boyne, where Cromwell encouraged his forces to engage in the indiscriminant massacre of more than 3,500 Catholics.

The specter of Drogheda on the River Boyne would return to haunt the Irish and symbolize the complex historical forces that raged throughout Europe during the latter half of the century. The years leading up to James II's accession to the throne saw the concomitant rise of Louis XIV's absolutist ambitions. James's defeat at the Battle of the Boyne at the hands of William III of Orange (now William III of England) would be not only an epochal event in the Catholic-Protestant conflict in Ireland, which Irish Protestants celebrate to this day, but a blow to France's drive for supremacy.

William was the leader of the Grand Alliance, a confederation of European states formed to halt France; his defeat of James II in 1690 at the Battle of the Boyne, was as important to that struggle as it was to Ireland. James had the military backing of France as well as that of the Irish and the Jacobites, English supporters of the restoration of the House of Stuart. William, on the other hand, had an army made up of Protestants and Catholics from many European states, who were united against the concept of absolute monarchy, which was symbolized not only by Louis XIV, but also by his monarchist English proxy in the House of Stuart.

In a battle fought on July 1, 1690, near Drogheda on the River Boyne, William crushed James's forces. James made an ignoble retreat to France, enraging his Irish supporters. From there he would challenge William and the Grand Alliance one last time.

Between May 19 and May 24, 1692, a French fleet of ships carrying James and Franco-Irish troops toward England to restore him to the throne, was engaged and defeated by Anglo-Dutch naval contingent off the coast off the Cherbourg Peninsula, first at Barfleur and finally at La Hougue. The rout of the French fleet was the first great naval victory for the Grand Alliance and the end of James II's quest to regain the English crown. ❏

MAJOR **KINGDOMS OF** WEST AFRICA

Gold Coast, 1695

Osei Tutu (1695–1731) founded the Ashanti Kingdom in the 1670s, with its capital of Kumasi. Through war and the conquest of neighboring tribes as well as through negotiation and political cooperation, the kingdom became the center of a confederacy of West African tribes. Osei Tutu honored the chiefs of the various tribes in the confederation, respecting their sovereignty, and drew them into his inner circle of political advisors.

The Ashanti were famous for their artistic production, in particular their fine gold work. They also produced wooden statuary and terracotta funerary ornaments. Of commercial importance was their cultivation of yams and cacao as well as their trade in slaves.

Following the first Portuguese landing on the coast in 1471, the slave trade with European powers was conducted primarily by the Kingdom of Dahomey, which in contrast to the Ashanti, was an absolute monarchy. From its capital of Abomey, slaves were traded for weapons and munitions. Preceding both Dahomey and the Ashanti Confederation was the Yoruba Kingdom, founded in present-day Nigeria in the tenth century. The heart of the kingdom was the Oyo region with its capital of the same name. ❏

LOCKE'S **POLITICAL** THEORIES

England, 1690

Writing at the time of the English "Bloodless Revolution," the English philosopher John Locke asserted in his work, *Two Treatises on Government*, that each person has certain inalienable rights to life, liberty, and property, and that it is the task of government to guarantee those rights. In contrast to Thomas Hobbes, Locke considered sovereignty to derive from those governed and that neither a patriarchal or absolutist form of government corresponded to that reality.

For Locke, only the separation of powers between legislative, executive, and judicial branches of government could secure these natural rights. And the freedom of speech was the most effective bulwark against a government's sliding into despotism.

The legislature was to enact laws to serve the people. According to Locke, there were four principles that needed to underpin legislative

John Locke

power. Laws had to be openly decided upon and promulgated. Law could not be changed to suit particular cases. Taxes ought not be raised without the consent of the governed or their representatives. Finally, the legislature did not possess the authority to transfer its legislative authority to any other person or body.

The people had the right to resist any government that refused to acknowledge these basic principles and even oppose it by force of arms. Locke's ideas not only influenced Enlightenment philosophers, they were instrumental in guiding the thinking of America's Founding Fathers and the theorists of the French Revolution.

Locke's major philosophical work, *An Essay concerning Human Understanding* (1689/1690), founded the English empiricist school, influencing Hume, Berkeley, Mill, and later thinkers. ❏

RUSSIA'S EMERGENCE AS A GREAT POWER UNDER PETER THE GREAT

Moscow, 1696

Peter the Great (Peter I) was born in Moscow on May 30, 1672, to Tsar Alexis I and his second wife Natalia Naryshkin. He had two stepbrothers, sons of Alexis's first marriage to Maria Miloslavsky, Fyodor and Ivan. When Tsar Alexis died in 1676, Fyodor was named tsar, but upon his sudden death in 1682, a power struggle ensued between the Naryshkin and Miloslavsky families. The Naryshkins prevailed and placed the nine-year-old Peter on the throne. Within a month, the Miloslavskys, led by Peter's half-sister Sophia, had won the support of the *strelsky* (armed palace guards) and used them to mount a violent

takeover in which many Naryshkins were murdered. Becoming Regent, Sophia placed Ivan on the throne, but allowed Peter to assume the role as a "junior" tsar.

By 1689, the regime under Sophia had alienated the same *strelsky* contingent that had put them in power and, with Naryshkin complicity, staged a palace coup, restoring Natalia as Regent and Peter as "first" tsar. Sophia was divested of all power and Ivan relegated to a nominal position. Natalia was the de facto ruler of Russia until her death in 1694.

The newly elevated tsar soon displayed a seriousness of purpose and an aptitude for charismatic

leadership. He was nearly seven feet tall and indefatigably energetic; he set out to lift the Russian state out of its medieval stagnation, modernizing every aspect of its culture. Seeking to end Russia's cultural isolation, he welcomed the infusion of European ideas, especially advances in technology. Dismantling the old Muscovy hierarchies of social and political entitlement, he sought to create a culture of merit, in which citizens were rewarded, regardless of their social station. He began to build a standing army that could compete with any in the West. Inspired by his love for naval arts, he sought to put landlocked Russia to sea by building its first real navy.

Partly to enlist a coalition of European states to prosecute his war against the Turks, but also to learn about the West's latest technological advances and to recruit its experts to work in Russia, in March of 1697, Peter organized the "Grand Embassy." Leading 250 government officials and technicians, he visited Holland, England, Prussia, and the Habsburg Empire. Remarkably, at many stops he traveled incognito, using the name "Peter Mikhailov," and

as such, did stints as a common laborer in the shipyards of Holland and Britain. After eighteen months, he failed to receive any firm commitments to his anti-Turk coalition, but he accrued a vast amount of new technological information and hired nearly 800 European technical advisors.

In his absence, members of the *strelsky* still loyal to the Miloslavskys tried to restore Sophia to power. They were utterly crushed by Peter's forces, and the enraged tsar subjected the rebels to horrific punishment involving the cruelest forms of torture and execution. More than 1,000 *strelsky* died, some at the hands of

Peter the Great during his visit to England (painting by Daniel Maclise)

Caricature showing the "Beard Tax"

DRESDEN BAROQUE CAPITAL

Moscow, 1696

Like the other high lords of his time, August the Strong, Prince of Saxony and King of Poland, cultivated a taste for the fine arts. Under his rule Dresden became a leading cultural metropolis.

On September 15, 1697, the Electoral prince Frederick August I of Saxony was crowned August II, King of Poland. To receive the crown he had to pay enormous bribes and also convert to Catholicism. By changing his religion he was able to win Austrian support for his election.

August the Strong received his nickname because of his robust appearance and his numer-

ous mistresses, tried to emulate the model set by the French king, Louis XIV.

He was unable to overcome the resistance of the entrenched nobility in Poland and Saxony and rule as absolute monarch; however, in his lavish court and extravagant building programs he was the Sun King's equal. As a result he bankrupted his treasury.

The *Zwinger*, a palace surrounded by galleries and arcades is one of the finest examples of baroque architecture. Built in Dresden, its grand ballroom, which was not meant as a living space, is an impressive fusion of architecture

and sculpture. August assembled an extraordinary collection of gold, silver, and jeweled pieces in

the Zwinger's treasure chamber, the "Green Vault."

After his defeat in the North-

ern War, August had to give up the Polish throne, but with Russia's support he was able to regain it in 1710. After his death in 1733 his son, August III,

Pavilion at the Zwinger Palace in Dresden

Peter himself. Sophia was exiled to a convent.

His greatest military campaign, the Great Northern War, was against Sweden's Charles XII. It started in 1700 and ended on August 30, 1721, with the Treaty of Nystad, in which Russia won the Baltic coastline territories of Estonia, Latvia, and Finnish borderlands, which afforded crucial maritime access to Western Europe. Two years later, he made peace with the Turks with the signing of the Treaty of St Petersburg.

Despite the ongoing war effort, it was during this time that Peter moved Russia's capital to the newly created city of St. Petersburg (1703), and founded Moscow University (1705.) In the last years of his reign, he also instituted wide-ranging governmental and church reforms. A synod convened in 1721 effectively brought the Church under state control. He even instituted a tax on beards—a measure aimed at the strict practitioners of the Orthodox faith.

Having reigned for 42 years, his program of reforms only just begun, he died of an infection at the age of 52 on February 8, 1725. ❑

who became King of Poland and Electoral Prince of Saxony, had to fight in a war of succession to defend his claim to Poland, against Stanislav Leszcynski, who had served as king between 1706 and 1709.

In Saxony August the Strong and his son established a tradition of religious tolerance. Two baroque churches bear witness to this. The Catholic Hofkirche was King August's own church. Construction began in 1726 and finished in 1755. Work was begun on the Lutheran Frauenkirche in 1726. It had a central inner room built to accommodate Lutheran

THE SLAVE TRADE
London, 1698

With the passage in Parliament of a law encouraging private companies to engage in foreign trade, what had been up until that point a government monopoly was privatized. This began an era of booming trade between Europe, Africa, New England, and the Caribbean, exchanging rum, sugar, and slaves. Other goods traded included molasses, cotton, cacao, and coffee.

The slave trade had been in Arab hands for hundreds of years until Portuguese sailors explored the African coast in the fifteenth century. From then on, slaving assumed a central role in the commercial relations between African and European nations. The profits grew to be enormous. In the seventeenth century, a slave purchased for 45 *florins* in Africa could be sold for 210 *florins* in America.

By 1501, the Spanish in their colony of Hispaniola, had begun to cultivate sugar cane; four years later, the first slaves arrived from Africa. The islands of the Caribbean developed as the most important suppliers of subtropical agricultural goods for the European market. In Brazil, the first slaves were brought in within five years of the building of the first sugar mill. The other European powers had to press their claims against what had become a Spanish and Portuguese monopoly. England began to manufacture sugar in 1623, obtaining cane at first from the island of Jamaica. At first in conjunction with

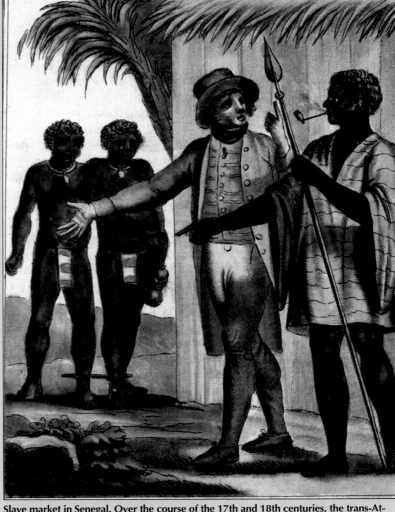

Slave market in Senegal. Over the course of the 17th and 18th centuries, the trans-Atlantic slave trade became a highly profitable business.

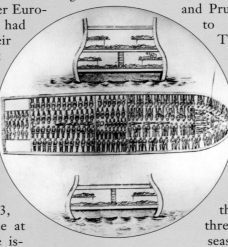

Sketch showing slave quarters between decks on a slave transport ship (copper etching, 18th century)

Portugal and then later on its own, England was able to secure for itself much of the trade with the West African coast. France, Holland, Sweden, Denmark, and Prussia all tried to follow suit.

The planters in the southern English colonies saw the greatest need for slaves. Because of climatic conditions, they enjoyed three planting seasons: first tobacco, then rice, and then indigo. The problem they faced was that there was not a large enough labor force to make use of the available land. Wage labor in the colonies was much more expensive than in England; slavery provided the perfect solution.

On the other hand, slavery was not profitable for the northern colonies. The agricultural conditions were different: There was only one planting season. Other livelihoods such as fishing or harvesting timber did not require a large work force. The cost of providing for slaves was actually higher than the benefits they produced.

By the time the traffic in humans was finally banned in the nineteenth century, more than fourteen million people had been transported from Africa. ❑

TURKEY'S EUROPEAN WARS

Point of Interest

The Turkish Wars refer to the ongoing conflicts between European Christian nations and the Islamic Kingdom of the Ottoman Turks that secured a foothold in Europe in the fourteenth century and had captured Constantinople in 1453.

At that point Turkey controlled a large part of the Balkans. Turkey's battles with the Habsburg Empire escalated in 1529 with the first siege of Vienna. In the middle of the sixteenth century the Habsburgs had to hand over to Turkey a large part of its holdings in Hungary as well as its vassal state of Transylvania. Poland lost the Ukraine to the Ottomans in 1676. The Great Turkish War began in 1683. A major Turkish defeat led to its conclusion in 1699 with the Treaty of Karlowitz, which signalled the departure of the Ottomans from the European political stage. ❑

Pierre-Denis Martin, *The Liberation of Grans from the Turks*

THE TREATY OF KARLOWITZ

Serbia, 1699

The Great Turkish War (1683-1699), in which the last enagement was the War of the Holy League, came to a conclusion with the signing of the Treaty of Karlowitz on January 26, 1699. The signatories were the vanquished Ottoman Empire and the members of the Holy League,

Austrian ambassador in Istanbul

which was headed by the Austrian Habsburg Empire and included the Polish-Lithuanian Commonwealth, the Republic of Venice and Muscovite Russia. Under its provisions, the Ottomans agreed to cede Hungary, Transylvania and Slavonia to Austria, Dalmatia and the Peloponnesian Peninsula to Venice and Podolia to Poland. After this treaty Ottoman presence in Eastern Europe practically disappeared.

Decline in Ottoman sovereignty in Europe began with their defeat at the Battle of Vienna in 1683. A resurgence of Ottoman territorial expansion took place again in 1690 with the occupation of Belgrade. Austria could not respond until 1697 and the end of the War of the Grand Alliance against France, at which point Prince Eugene of Savoy was enlisted to retake Belgrade. On September 11, 1697 he led Habsburg forces against those of Sultan Mustafa II at the Battle of Zenta, handing the Ottomans one of the worst defeats they had ever experienced. The Battle of Zenta resulted in the Sultan's surrender and the historic Treaty of Karlowitz. ❑

THE WAR OF THE SPANISH SUCCESSION

Spain, October 3, 1700

Since the Habsburg king, Charles II of Spain, had no direct heir, he chose as his successor his great nephew Philip Bourbon, in order to forestall the tumult that threatened to convulse Spain at his death. Philip was also the grandson of Louis XIV. The Austrian, Leopold, who was himself a Habsburg contested this choice.

When Charles died on November 1, 1700, fighting over the succession commenced. France received support from German duchies and principalities that were traditionally opposed to the Habsburgs. Bavaria had its sights set on Habsburg territory, perhaps even the imperial throne. Austria was joined by England, Holland and Prussia, all out of concern for a combination of Spain and France, which had become Europe's leading power. The war was mainly fought in the Netherlands and the Rhine region. In the war's decisive battle at Hochstadt on the Danube, France and Bavaria roundly defeated the Austrians. In the same year England took Gibraltar and Minorca while the French alliance had further successes in Italy and the Netherlands. The constellations of alliances and the balance of power in Europe continued to fluctuate, and a temporary halt to the fighting was achieved through the Treaty of Utrecht. ❑

Jacob van Loo, *King Philip V of Spain and Family*

THE DUCHY OF PRUSSIA BECOMES A KINGDOM

Königsberg, January 18, 1701

With considerable pomp and ceremony the Prince of Brandenburg and Count of Prussia, Frederick III, crowned himself Frederick I, King of Prussia. The Hohenzollern duke Frederick's elevation to king signaled the ascent of Brandenburg-Prussia from a petty principality into a formidable political power in the center of Europe.

The state placed on a firm footing: The king sought to unify Prussia and Brandenburg and saw his role as the embodiment of that union. His advantageous position was the result of territorial expansion and the consolidation of the Hohenzollern dynasty over the preceding decades. The scope of Frederick's ambitions was evident in his endeavors to enhance the honors due him and to play an even larger role on the international stage.

The emperor's endorsement: The proclamation of Frederick III as king proceeded with the endorsement of the Hapsburg Emperor Leopold I. Frederick was not yet powerful enough to fully realize his domestic and international projects. From 1690 on, he had entered into agreements with Vienna and sought to bribe members of the court in order to curry favor and to influence them on Prussia's behalf. A royal treaty of November 16, 1700 bestowed the hereditary title of king on the Elector of Prussia, after Frederick agreed to support the Habsburg claim in the matter of the Spanish succession. In the war that followed, Prussia supplied a contingent of 8,000 soldiers. In addition, in the next election for the Emperor, the Hohenzollerns supported the Hapsburg candidate.

The preliminaries: Frederick's coronation was a lavish affair. By December 17, 1700 the royal retinue from Berlin had already made twelve trips to Königsberg. On January 15, 1701, Prince-Elector Frederick III remained in Königsberg for the actual ceremony, and the elevation of the Duchy of Prussia to a kingdom was proclaimed. On January 17 he was awarded the Order of the

King Frederick I of Prussia

Black Eagle with the motto: "To Each His Own," thereby binding the Prussian Kingdom to the aristocracy.

A self-assured monarch: The coronation itself, performed on January 18 in the German Teutonic Castle at Königsberg, demonstrated the baroque splendor of a confident dynasty. Frederick himself put on his crown, and also that of his wife, Sophie Charlotte. Following that he was anointed in the castle church by a Reform bishop and a Lutheran minister. The costs of the celebrations were borne by the general populace through forced donations and tax revenue. A court wit summed up the beginning of the Prussian kingdom as follows: "The German subjects buckled under the weight of making donations; the court buckled under the burden of celebrations."

The rapidity of rise of Brandenburg-Prussia was remarkable. Between 1134 and 1157 the Margrave of Brandenburg was held by the Askanier dynasty. By 1417 the Hohenzollerns had been invested with the fiefdom of the Mark and the Electorate. Between 1657 and 1660 the Brandenburg Prince Electorate extended his sovereignty to include the whole Duchy of Prussia. ❑

Anton von Werner, *The Coronation of King Frederick I of Prussia*, c.1887

WAR AS AN INSTRUMENT OF ABSOLUTIST POLICY

Point of Interest

The era of absolutism was shaped by numerous wars, through which the European states sought to expand their power. While in the Middle Ages and early modern times military conflicts had had an ideological justification, for instance religion, now the reasons for going to war were frequently dynastic disputes; according to the doctrine of absolutism, wars were waged by kings to assert justifiable claims, such as the succession to the throne. These thinkers considered that the nation and its people were merged into a single entity.

The main opposition in Europe was between France, striving for dominance, and all of the other states, in particular Great Britain and the Holy Roman Empire, who were seeking to protect their interests by maintaining a balance of power. In northeast Europe the antagonism between Sweden and Russia predominated.

Jean Marc Nattier, *The Battle of Poltava*, 1717. Sweden suffered a great defeat against Russia.

Wars in Europe also had the effect of involving the overseas possessions of countries, especially in the case of Great Britain, which was becoming a dominant colonial power at this time. ❑

LEIBNIZ EVOKES

Hanover, 1710

As a typical representative of rationalism, the German scholar Gottfried William Leibniz stressed reason, but his entire his philosophical system was based on the idea of nature's perfection: God as beneficent creator was the indispensable key.

For his pupil, Queen Sophie Charlotte of Prussia, Leibniz published the *Essai de Théodicée* (*Essay of Theodicy*). In response to a essay written by Pierre Bayle, he refuted the position that God was the source of evil in the world. Leibniz asserted that because God was the only perfect entity and could therefore have no equal, all other entities, including the world, were to some extent imperfect. This position led Leibniz to declare his often famous, and most misunderstood, observation that our world is "the best of all possible worlds."

During his lifetime Leibniz was recognized as one of the greatest scholars in Europe. By

END OF THE WAR OF THE SPANISH SUCCESSION

Utrecht, April 11, 1713

The Treaty of Utrecht ended the war in Europe over the question of who would rule over Spain after the death of the last Spanish Habsburg king, Charles II.

England and the Netherlands entered the war to counter France's growing power on the Continent. The peace engineered by England sought to create a balance of power in Europe and to remove the threat of France and Spain under a united monarchy, given that the heir to the Spanish throne was the grandson of Louis XIV. Its most important provisions were agreed to in a series of meetings held in March and April of 1713.

- King Philip V would remain Spanish king.
- There would be no union between France and Spain.
- France recognized the succession of the House of Hanover to the throne of Great Britain.
- From France, Great Britain received the Hudson Bay Company's territories, Nova Scotia, Newfoundland, and an island in the Antilles, while from Spain it received Gibraltar, Minorca, and the right to the trade with the Spanish colonies.
- France ceded the Spanish Netherlands, which thus fell to the Holy Roman Emperor.
- The elevation of the Prince-Elector of Brandenburg to King in Prussia was recognized.
- Spain's Italian possessions went to Austria while Savoy received Sicily. ❑

GROWTH OF RUSSIAN MIGHT

Poltava, July 8, 1709

The Great Northern War (1700-1721) was a battle for control of the Baltic fought between Sweden and the combined armies of Russia, Denmark, and Saxony. The Swedish defeat resulted in Russia's sought-after dominance in the Baltic region. It also brought to a close the Swedish King Charles XII's years of expansionist aggression.

Led by Charles, Swedish troops initially penetrated into Russia but suffered a crushing defeat at the Battle of Poltava in the Ukraine on July 8, 1709. Badly wounded, Charles fled to Moldavia. He remained in exile under Ottoman protection for five years. The Battle of Poltava marked the turning point of the Great Northern War.

In order to break the Swedish hegemony, Tsar Peter I (Peter the Great), Augustus II of Poland, and Frederick I of Denmark had formed a pact of mutual assistance against the Swedish king in 1698/99. Fighting began when Poland invaded Livonia in 1700.

The first years of the war saw a number of Swedish successes. Denmark had to withdraw from the alliance after their army was routed in the summer of 1700, and in the same year Russia suffered a heavy defeat at the Battle of Narva in Estonia. Afterwards Charles XII turned against Augustus, who in 1706 had to relinquish the Polish crown in favor of Stanislas Lesczczynski after the Swedes had conquered Poland. But after the Russian victory at the Battle of Poltava, the tide turned in favor of the anti-Swedish coalition. With Russian assistance, Augustus was reinstated as

THE BEST OF ALL POSSIBLE WORLDS

the age of 21 he had become a Doctor of Law. His first position was in the service of the Elector of Mainz. From 1672 to 1676 he lived at the diplomatic mission in Paris and then became a librarian in Hanover where he wrote a history of the House of Brunswick. He initiated the establishment of the "Society of Sciences" in Berlin in 1700. He also was active as an adviser to various princely houses and was a close acquaintance of Europe's most renowned scholars.

With his mathematical and scientific achievements, Leibniz contributed substantially to the progress of the sciences, particularly his development of monad theory, which collated various logical propositions into a uniform philosophical system. Leibniz proceeded from the concept that the entire world was structured according to logical laws and was therefore also perceptible by human thought. In the course

of constructing a logical language of science operating with mathematical symbols, so as to avoid the misunderstandings that result from colloquial language, he produced some of the fundamental laws of higher mathematics.

The idea that space, time, and motion are only relative—in this respect Leibniz anticipated Albert Einstein's theory of relativity—arose, according to Leibniz, from the acceptance that the material world is mere illusion, because only the spiritual has any reality.

The introduction of force as a fundamental idea of physics was deduced by Leibniz from the idea that the entire world exists as small, indivisible mental force centers, called monads. In *Monadologia* Leibniz described his concept of the universal harmony of the cosmos, resulting from the interaction of monads. These were called "windowless" by Leibniz, that is, they do not in-

fluence each other. Correspondences in their modifications result rather from the fact that they all reflect the same universe, but in each case from another perspective and with a different degree of clarity. The monads are thus also in a hierarchical order in relation to each other. Individual humans consist of infinitely many monads, whereby the spirit as the highest monad is the only one that has true consciousness. The highest monad of all is God, who created this universal harmony and as such is the only being that can

Gottfried Wilhelm Leibniz

contemplate it in its totality. ❏

PORCELAIN FROM MEISSEN

Meissen, January 23, 1710.

Polish king, Swedish Pomerania was conquered, and by 1714 Russian troops had taken Swedish Finland and occupied the Åland islands.

In 1715, Hanover and Prussia also entered the war on the side of Russia. Eventually, Charles's army was no match for the Russian coalition forces. Charles himself was killed on December 11, 1718, during the siege of the Norwegian fortress of Frederikshald. The Swedish-Russian Treaty of Nystad in 1721 sealed the Swedish defeat: Finland was returned to Sweden, but Russia received Livonia, Estonia, Ingermanland and sections of Karelia, thereby gaining wide access to the Baltic Sea. After this expansion of the Russian sphere of influence, Tsar Peter I called himself "emperor of all the Russias." ❏

Böttger, the first European to successfully manufacture white porcelain, took over the management of a newly created porcelain factory.

When Augustus the Strong, Elector of Saxony and King of Poland, issued a patent for the establishment of a porcelain factory, it was publicly announced for the first time that a European, Johann Friedrich Böttger had invented hard porcelain. Two months later he opened the Meissen factory in Albrechtsburg.

Böttger was an alchemist, who claimed that he could transform base metals into gold. Augustus the Strong became his patron soon af-

Holy figurines, 1715

ter the turn of the century. By November 1707 Böttger was making red stoneware similar to Chinese ware, and in early 1708 he produced the first white (actually rather yellowish) porcelain; Meissen began producing truly white porcelain in 1717.

Böttger finally confessed to his sovereign that he did not know the secret of making gold, but the success of his new manufacturing process went far to alleviate any disappointment Augustus may have felt. Porcelain was not invented, as legend had it, "by mistake" in the course of alchemical experiments, but rather as the result of scientifically systematic trial and error. ❏

"WHITE GOLD" INVENTED IN CHINA

Point of Interest

White porcelain had been manufactured in China since the seventh century. In the middle of the ninth century, accounts of this reached Europe: "The Chinese possess fine clay, from which they make bowls; these have ... the refinement of glass, in which one sees the reflection of water." Europeans tried to copy the material, but for a long time had little success. In the sixteenth and seventeenth centuries, the first fine ceramics were produced, known as "earthenware" or "faience." Porcelain presented a challenge. Böttger's porcelain differed from the Chinese; in Asia feldspar was the predominant raw material, in Europe the main component was kaolin. ❏

FINANCIAL SPECULATIONS END IN RUIN

France and England, 1720

Two great financial scandals shook Western Europe in 1720. In France, the finances of the government note-issuing bank, Banque Royale, crashed as a result of the first paper money inflation in history, while in Great Britain the South Sea Company collapsed.

Paris, March 1720: Banque Royale closed its doors after its Scots-born chairman, John Law, fled the country. Middle-class investors and noble landowners were the hardest hit by the bank's collapse.

On September 1, 1715, the French king Louis XIV died leaving the country in a state of financial ruin; the national debt amounted to three and a half billion livres. In this situation, Law, a Scottish financial expert and speculator whose plans for the reform of banking in his own country had been thwarted by parliament, created the private issuing bank Banque Générale in 1716. This was renamed Banque Royale in 1718. Initially successful in re-

ducing the national debt, plots and speculations finally led to its collapse. Ironically, shortly before the collapse, Law had been appointed France's Controller General of Finances.

Law assumed that an excess of paper currency would promote public prosperity. He therefore systematically increased the number of notes in circulation, driving up the shares of his issuing bank. That institution also absorbed the West Indies company, likewise created by him, the shares of which also rose rapidly, fuelled by speculation occasioned by reports of extensive gold finds in Louisiana.

London, August 1720: The collapse of the "South Sea Bubble" shook the whole of British

Escape of the chairman of the Banque Royale, John Law (caricature, 1720)

society. It grew out of the rogue financial operations of the South Sea Company, which in 1711 had received the trade monopoly for South and Central America from the British crown against a loan of ten million pounds. Risky gambling in the company's shares took place as the price multiplied

ten times in a year. The public was systematically misled about the shaky financial position of the company. After the South Sea Company went bankrupt it was generally admitted that bribes had been paid to high government officials to not divulge its weaknesses. ❏

FEMALE SUCCESSION PERMITTED BY PRAGMATIC SANCTION

Vienna, 19 April, 1713

On April 19, 1713, Emperor Charles VI enacted the Pragmatic Sanction, which allowed female succession to the throne. In so doing, he ensured the indivisibility of the hereditary Habsburg lands and thus the continuation of the Habsburg Dynasty.

In this document, which was issued under both the law of the state and the dynastic law of the Habsburgs, it was determined that the succession to the throne according to the law of primogeniture would now apply to both male and female Habsburg heirs. Charles had been working to effect this change since the death of his one son left only his two daughters as heirs. According to the terms of the Pragmatic Sanction the succession was to be lim-

ited first to the direct descendants of the emperor. But if this line were to become extinct it could be passed to the daughters of his deceased brother Emperor Joseph I.

Emperor Leopold I (the father of both Joseph and Charles) had issued the succession pact in 1703. This decree declared that the succession of the Austrian line was placed ahead of the Spanish Habsburgs.

Charles's new regulation for the succession to the throne placed his daughters ahead of those of his elder brother Joseph I. By 1723 it had been officially ratified by all member states of the Habsburg Empire.

Acceptance of the Pragmatic Sanction throughout Europe became the main goal of imperial

foreign policy. In lengthy negotiations, which began in 1720 and in the course of which large concessions were made by Vienna, Charles VI managed to obtain the agreement of the European great powers. This formally protected the rights of his oldest daughter Maria Theresa, but after his death some powers no longer felt bound by the agreement. The electors of Bavaria and Saxony claimed greater rights: they were married to daughters of the House of Habsburg and aspired to the imperial throne. They received support from Spain and France. When Prussia took advantage of the weak position of Vienna to invade and seize Silesia, the European powers were once more on the verge of a military confrontation

over the distribution of power in Europe. ❏

Emperor Charles VI

HOUSE OF HANOVER RULES ENGLAND

London, January 8, 1714

Following the Act of Settlement, a Hanoverian acceded to the British throne after the death of Queen Anne. The law provided that Catholic descendants of the House of Stuart would be excluded from succession and that the crown would go to the House of Hanover.

So it was that Georg Ludwig, Elector of Hanover, became King George I of Great Britain. Designed to protect the Protestant succession to the throne, it became necessary because King William III (William of Orange) and Queen Mary II were childless, as was their successor Queen Anne.

The next Protestant successor in line for the throne was Sophia, widow of Ernest Augustus, Elector of Hanover, and granddaughter of England's King James

George I

Queen Anne

I. On her death, her son George became heir to the throne. This was how a man who did not speak English came to rule over a Great Britain, a country about which he knew very little.

Queen Anne had striven to the last to preserve the throne for the Stuarts, but in vain, since her nephew James Edward Stuart (the Old Pretender) was not ready to renounce his Roman Catholic faith and convert to Protestantism.

The most consequential matter to occur during the reign of Queen Anne was the passage of the Acts of Union in the Parliaments of first England and then Scotland. England and Scotland had been joined together under the same king since 1603, but after these acts they were truly united and were thenceforth referred to as Great Britain. ❑

ROBINSON CRUSOE

Great Britain, 1719

In his celebrated novel *Robinson Crusoe*, Daniel Defoe tells the story of an ingenious man shipwrecked on an island, where under adverse circumstances he brings Christianity and European civilization to the island's natives.

Defoe was 60 when he published *Robinson Crusoe*. The story was inspired by the fate of a Scottish sailor who had spent five years on an uninhabited island far off the coast of Chile, until he was rescued by a British ship in 1709. The novel was written as if it were an autobiographical account. It was an immediate success, going through four editions in the year following its publication. ❑

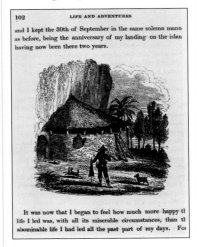

A page from *Robinson Crusoe*

TERRITORIAL GAINS FOR THE HABSBURGS

Passarowitz, July 21, 1718

Two years of renewed warfare between the Ottoman Empire and Austria came to an end on July 21, 1718, with the signing of the Treaty of Passarowitz.

The treaty brought substantial territorial gains to the Habsburgs. With the intercession of Great Britain, the Netherlands, and Sweden, the Habsburgs and the Ottomans came to a peace agreement by which Austria gained Banat, northern Serbia with Belgrade and Lesser Walachia. These regions were opened to development, and an organized, intensive settlement in the southeast took place immediately. In particular, country craftsmen and farmers came to the region from southwest Germany; they later became Banat Swabians.

For their part, the Ottomans agreed to treat their Christian subjects with tolerance. They consented to trade agreements with Austria; traders from the Danube monarchy would in the future enjoy freedom of trade and navigation throughout the

J. van Huchtenburgh, *Prince Eugene at the Battle of Belgrade*, 1717

Ottoman Empire. In fact, this was an advantage that the Austrians could hardly make use of, since they had no merchant fleet to speak of.

In 1711 after the Ottomans had won a victory against Russia, they trained their sights on Venetian possessions, first capturing Crete and then lands in the Peloponnese. Venice turned to Austria for assistance in April 1716. On August 5, 1716, the first major battle between the armies of the emperor and the sultan took place at Petrovaradin, near Novi Sad. Led by Prince Eugene of Savoy, the Austrians defeated the numerically superior Ottoman forces under the Grand Vizier Ali Pasha. On October 13, Prince Eugene took Temesvar, and on June 19, 1717, he besieged Belgrade. After an Ottoman attempt had failed to break through the siege, the fortress and city of Belgrade were taken by Austrian troops on August 22, 1717. ❑

Gulliver's Fantastic Travels

London, 1726

The Anglo-Irish writer Jonathan Swift's satiric masterpiece *Gulliver's Travels: Travels into Several Remote Nations of the World, in Four Parts. By Lemuel Gulliver, First a Surgeon*, lampooned the political and social customs of his time, and human nature in general. The four-part novel was begun in Dublin in 1721 and published in London in 1726. The book was received enthusiastically by the public and was soon translated into other languages.

Gulliver, who is both the protagonist and the narrator of the novel, is a clearly defined character. Although generous in some respects, he also displays credulousness and political naiveté, as well as a gift for language and a sense of humor. At the same time he can be seen as Everyman. As he proceeds through his adventures, his outlook on humanity darkens, until finally he seems to lose faith in human goodness.

In the course of four journeys into the Pacific, Gulliver visits four undiscovered islands, has meetings with miniature people and giants, and various animals, among them horses who are guided only by reason. The work consists partly of a fantastic journey, so that it has become a classic children's book; but at the same time it is a vitriolic allegory of the political situation of his time. Swift's venom was directed at the contrast between the English and the French, the senseless arguments between the Whigs and the Tories, and the conflicts between religious denominations, which appear in his work as a controversy over the question of whether a boiled egg should be cracked at the blunt end or the pointed one.

Swift plays again and again on contrasts, consistently presenting them to his disconcerted readers. Perhaps the most striking aspect of the novel, which has given rise to many varied interpretations, is its tendency to treat those who have faith in reason and in the progress of civilization with ever deepening skepticism. Swift also wrote contentious pieces in newspapers and pamphlets, most famously his *A Modest Proposal*, which suggested that the most efficient way to solve the problem of poverty in Ireland was to look upon Irish babies as culinary delicacies and feed them to the rich. ❑

Illustration from Gulliver's Travels, 1882

New Sea Route Discovered

Russia, 1728

At the request of the Russians, the explorer and cartographer of Asia, Vitus Bering, traveled to the easternmost point of Asia and subsequently discovered the Bering Strait, named after him, that separates Asia and North America.

As a Russian naval officer, the Danish explorer Vitus Bering undertook an expedition over the north coast of Russia on behalf of Tsar Peter I (the Great). In 1725 he had been commissioned to travel to Kamchatka to find a passage between Asia and America (Alaska) with an expedition of two ships. To the north of Lake Chukotka, Bering discovered St. Lawrence Island and the strait between the two continents that would be named after him. In 1741 he set off on a new expedition to the Arctic Ocean. Off the southern coast of Alaska he sighted Mount Elias and discovered the Aleutian Islands. The spread of scurvy, an illness caused by vitamin deficiency, combined with inclement weather, forced the expedition to return to Kamchatka. Bering died on the way home on December 19, 1741, on the largest of the Commander Islands, at the age of 61. ❑

Vitus Bering

The Safavid Dynasty Overthrown By Afghan Tribesmen

Isfahan, 1722

Aga Khan

Attacks by Afghan tribesmen gradually displaced the Safavids, who had governed Persia since 1501, and resulted in the establishing of Shia Islam as the state religion. When the Persian capital of Isfahan was conquered and plundered by the invading Afghan tribesmen, the Safavids were unable to muster more than token resistance.

The most illustrious ruler of the Safavids was Shah Abbas I, the Great, who died in 1629. Abbas moved the residence of the shahs to Isfahan and built a dazzling new capital there. Under his rule the building of the Ali Qapu Palace and the Sheikh Lotf Allah Mosque took place. Today these structures are recognized as masterpieces of Islamic architecture. The descendants of Abbas enjoyed the wealth that he had created, but their central power and authority declined.

The Afghan Dynasty of Kandahar, which controlled Persia after 1722, was driven out of the country in 1729 by the Turkmen Nader Shah, who achieved significant territorial gains in the east. He proclaimed himself shah in 1736, but his rule did not survive. After his death in 1747, Afghanistan became an autonomous state. In the meantime the Safavids returned to rule Persia until 1794 and the death of Aga Mohammed Khan. ❑

BACH'S SACRED MUSIC

Leipzig, May 5, 1723

Johann Sebastian Bach was appointed to the office of Cantor of the St Thomas School in Leipzig. The city council would have preferred Georg Philipp Telemann or Johann Christoph Graupner for the post and only decided on Bach after both of them had turned down the position.

Compared to his previous role as director of music for Prince Leopold of Anhalt-Cöthen (since 1717), his new position was in some ways a step down. Although he often tried to find another position, he remained in Leipzig until his death in 1750. As Director of Music he was also responsible for the overall musical life of the city.

Bach, who came from a family of professional musicians and organists, seemed destined to embark on a career in music. He was the fourth of five sons, and was twice married: to Maria Barbara (from 1707 until her death in 1720), and Anna Magdalena (from 1721). In total he fathered 20 children, ten of whom survived into adulthood.

Born in Eisenach on March 21, 1685, Bach received extensive training in piano, organ, violin, and singing. His knowledge of the techniques of composition was acquired through studying the works of other composers.

Bach's vocational career began in 1703 as a chamber musician at Weimar (1703). He then became organist in Arnstadt (1703–1707) and subsequently in Mühlhausen (1707–1708). Afterwards he returned to the court of Wilhelm Ernst, Duke of Weimar, but personal disagreements with his employer clouded this phase of his working life. With his appointment in 1717 to the court of Cöthen, his situation took a turn for the better, but his position there came to an abrupt end to 1723, after the Prince married a woman who had no interest in music.

In Leipzig, Bach composed numerous religious masterpieces: several volumes of cantatas (for Sunday services), of which

Bach's manuscript for the *St. Matthew Passion*

about 150 have survived: the *Magnificat* (1723), the *St. John Passion* (1724), the *St. Matthew Passion* (1727), the *Christmas Oratorio* (1734–1735), and the *B Minor Mass* (completed 1747). ❑

GENIUS AND TECHNICAL MASTERY

Point of Interest

Johann Sebastian Bach was appreciated by his contemporaries as an instrumentalist and master of improvisation on the organ, but the performances of his creative composition proved less appealing to the public. The Leipzig city council that employed him was more interested in him as a teacher than as a composer.

Many of Bach's compositions were recieved by the public as ponderously demanding and old fashioned; unlike Georg Philipp Telemann and Bach's son, Carl Philip Emanuel, his music was not composed in the currently popular courtly style.

Few of Bach works were printed during his lifetime. He frequently recycled his own compositions, using them to accompany another text, or transcribing them for different instruments.

By the end of the eighteenth century, however, Bach was rediscovered and his musical genius recognized. A greater understanding emerged of the ordering principles and profound musical intelligence underlying his compositions. Since then appreciation of his work has only grown.

Bach was a working musician. His compositions were never "absolute," intended only to meet aesthetic criteria (a concept that did not begin to emerge until the second half of the eighteenth century). They were functionally applied to meet the demands of his patrons or as part of religious services. Yet that in no way diminished their enduring power. Musicologists even go so far as to categorize Bach's late works, which were not composed in connection with his religious duties, such as the *Goldberg Variations* (1742/43), the *Musical Offering* (1747), and the *Art of the Fugue* (unfinished at this death), under this functional aspect. But these musical explorations, which were not intended to be performed, may perhaps more justly be considered as works in praise of God, whom Bach saw as the creator of the musical order, which he had been able to enter into.

Bach signed almost all his compositions with phrases such as *Soli Deo Gratia* (Glory to God alone.) In 1738 he told his pupils that music that did not serve "the honor of god and the recreation of the mind," was "a devilish bawling and droning." Bach left an extensive body of work, covering almost all musical forms with the exception of opera; apart from the cantatas and passions, he produced concerts and overtures, sonatas for violin, viola and flute, cello suites, English and French suites for the piano, the famous *Well-Tempered Clavier*, partitas, about 50 preludes and fugues for organ, as well as toccatas, fantasies, and organ chorales.

As was common in the baroque period, Bach's music expressed emotions. Partly using pre-ordained formulas, he perfected the compositional techniques of *cantus firmus* (fixed song) and counterpoint. His ability to improvise was extraordinary. He would give performances in which he would develop five-part fugues on themes suggested by his listeners. ❑

Johann Sebastian Bach

THE REIGN OF FREDERICK II

Potsdam, January 31, 1740

The distinctive characteristic of the reign of the Prussian King Frederick II, already known during his lifetime as "the Great," was enlightened absolutism: the ruler saw himself as the "first servant of the state."

Difficult youth: Frederick was born on January 24, 1712. His upbringing was extremely strict. When in 1730, Frederick tried to run away during a voyage with his father, King Frederick William I, and his plans were uncovered, he was incarcerated together with his friend, Lieutenant Hans Hermann von Katte. A military tribunal sentenced von Katte to life imprisonment for assisting Frederick, which his father rejected and instead imposed the death penalty; von Katte was beheaded on November 6, 1730, in front of Frederick.

Frederick remained in prison in Küstrin until 1732. The following year, on the orders of his father he married Elisabeth von Braunschweig-Wolfenbüttel, whom he did not love. In 1736 he was preparing himself for his future role in Schloss Rheinsberg. It was here that he wrote his *Anti-Machiavel*, a treatise in which he attacked the theories of the Italian Niccolo Machiavelli, arguing that a peaceful and enlightened rule was preferable to one of political expediency.

The "reason of state:" Having rejected Machiavelli's theories because of their contempt for the citizen and their rejection of moral principles in politics, Frederick, while still crown prince, formulated the principles that were to dominate his reign in Prussia. Admittedly, he still followed the path of absolutism, believing in the absolute power of the monarch and ruling with a rod of iron, but he saw himself as the defender of the state. The "reason of state" promulgated the welfare of the nation as a whole, and he required from his subjects that they subordinate themselves to the common good. He was dedicated to religious tolerance, declaring that "everyone should find salvation in their own way" and committed to reforms that redressed social grievances. Torture was to be abolished, and there was to be a constitutional state where law was to be applied without favor. He also supported a government-run education system for the general population. In addition, he introduced a plan for governmental administrative reform, demanding unconditional obedience from its officials.

General welfare: Frederick also proved himself to be an enlightened ruler in his market economy policies and in the systematic measures that he took to develop unsettled regions. Financed by the Prussian state, the Oderbruch, the Warthe-Netze, and other river plains were drained and turned into arable land. In this way thousands of acres of orchards and fields came into cultivation. The introduction of the potato and new farming methods improved the lot of farmers, as did laws that accorded them increased legal rights in relation to their landlords.

Patron of culture: Frederick had become familiar with the ideas of enlightenment through the French philosopher Voltaire, with whom he had corresponded from the age of 24, and whom he often entertained at his summer residence near Potsdam, Sanssouci, between 1750 and 1753. During these casual salons, literature, art, and philosophy were discussed, and Frederick played his own compositions and those of others on the flute. ❑

King Frederick II at Sanssouci

Frederick II, the Great, with his Anti-Machiavel

A TRIUMPHANT RECEPTION FOR HANDEL'S "MESSIAH"

Ireland, April 13, 1742

The premiere of George Friederich Handel's *The Messiah* took place on April 13, 1742 at the newly built Dublin Music Hall in Ireland. It was presented in London the following year. During Handel's lifetime this oratorio was performed over 50 times. To this day, it is a staple of Christmas music.

The Messiah has three sections. First, the birth of the Savior is announced primarily through the messianic predictions in the prophetic literature of the Old Testament. The second part consists of Christ's passion, crucifixion, and resurrection, while the third part deals with the salvation of mankind, drawn mainly from the Book of Revelation. The second part ends with the exuberant Hallelujah chorus. The music combines elements of arias from Italian opera and oratorios with traditional northern and central German church music as well as English anthems. In 1710 Handel went to live in London after a brief spell as *kapellmeister* (music director) to the court of the Elector of Hanover. In 1718 he was appointed music director to the Duke of Chandos, and in 1727 the composer received British citizenship.

In 1719 Handel was commissioned to found a royal opera house in London. He wrote further oratorios including *Samson* (1743) and *Judas Maccabaeus* (1746) in addition to numerous instrumental works including *The Water Music* And *The Royal Fireworks Music*. ❑

MARIA THERESA

Brief Lives

The Empress Maria Theresa at the Diet of Pressburg (chalk lithograph)

After the controversy that greeted her succession to the throne, Maria Theresa (b. Vienna, May 13, 1717, d. Vienna, November 29, 1780) instituted sweeping reforms in the army, the legal and the educational systems, as well in the state's administrative organization. She introduced general taxation against the protest of the estates and made the Austro-Bohemian territory an absolute state that was administrated centrally. Her mercantilist economic policy included the abolition of internal customs duties, the introduction of new industries, and rural development measures in the Banat and Natschka regions. The sovereign lived happily married to her husband, Franz Stephan, Duke of Lorraine, with whom she had sixteen children. ❑

M. van Meytens, *Portrait of Maria Theresa at Twenty-six Years of Age*

A WOMAN RULES AUSTRIA

Vienna, October 20, 1740

The ascent of Maria Theresa of Austria to the throne unleashed one of the longest-drawn-out wars in Europe. The Bavarian House of Wittelsbach refused to recognize the female line of succession and had the support of France and Spain, while the Prussian king, Frederick II (Frederick the Great), took advantage of the resulting frailty of the Austrian royal house to launch an illegal invasion of Silesia.

After the death of Emperor Charles VI, his eldest daughter, the 23-year old Maria Theresa, succeeded him to the throne. As she was not recognized by all European nations as the legitimate heir, her crowning as empress led to a war over securing supremacy in Europe.

Female line of succession: The trigger of the conflict was the question of the Austrian succession. Admittedly, after the death of his only son, Emperor Charles VI only had one heir. On April 19, 1713, the emperor had officially specified the female line of succession to the Austrian patrimonial lands with the declaration of the Pragmatic Sanction. This action had received the approval of most European powers, but some of them were not prepared to respect the agreement.

Older claims: The Bavar-ian elector Charles Albert of the House of Wittelsbach had never accepted the Pragmatic Sanction. Both he and the elector of Saxony were married to daughters of Charles VI's brother and emperor before him, Joseph I. He was now claiming part of the Habsburg monarchy and the title of emperor. He was supported in his claim by a large European coalition: besides the electors of Saxony, Cologne and the Palatinate, France and Spain were also on the side of the House of Wittelsbach.

Invasion of Silesia: Austria's isolation encouraged Frederick to invade the Austrian province of Silesia on December 16, 1740. He based his claim to this rich province on the rather unconvincing reference to testamentary treaties between the Hohenzollern and Piast dukes signed in 1537. This was the beginning of the first Silesian war.

By forming an alliance with Louis XV, Frederick also secured the support of France, which saw the possibility of some territorial gains because of the supposed weakness of Maria Theresa. But Great Britain unexpectedly intervened and joined the war on the side of Austria, in the interest of maintaining a balance of power in Europe. ❑

THE INFLUENCE OF MADAME DE POMPADOUR

Versailles, September 14, 1745

King Louis XV of France, great-grandson of and successor to the Sun King, followed a policy of favoritism and also had many mistresses. Because the problems of the realm remained unsolved, the dissatisfaction of the people with the monarchy increased as time went by.

Louis XV had acceded to the throne in 1715 when he was only five years old. The monarch distanced himself from the pomp and ceremony of court, turning instead to the pleasures of love and hunting. He was married to Maria Leszczynski, whose father, Stanislaus Leszczynski, had been King of Poland from 1706 to 1709.

In 1745 he elevated his official mistress, Jeanne Antoinette Poisson, to the rank of Marquise de Pompadour. She was only one of a long series of mistresses in the company of whom the king spent much of his time. Her immediate predecessors were three sisters. When the last of one of them, Marie-Anne de Mailly-Nesle, Duchess of Châteauroux, died on December 8, 1744, Jeanne Antoinette Poisson caught the eye of the king. She decided to separate from her husband Charles-Guillaume le Normant d'Etioles so as to enable her to become the king's official mistress.

Madame de Pompadour was rejected by the French people for being hard-hearted, ambitious, calculating, and extravagant, but she now became a patroness of the arts and sciences, with great influence on building activities at court: several summer residences were built on her instructions.

Many artists and writers enjoyed her patronage, including the painter François Boucher, as well as the writer and philosopher Voltaire. According to legend, it was the influence of Madame de Pompadour on Louis XV that made it possible for the enlightenment philosophers Denis Diderot and Jean le Rond d'Alembert to publish their celebrated *Encyclopédie*.

But most importantly, besides being the king's mistress, Madame de Pompadour, who had been given the title of duchess by the king in 1752, also became his political adviser. She calmly

Madame de Pompadour

SILESIA IN PRUSSIAN HANDS

December 25, 1745

After two wars, Prussia succeeded in incorporating the previously Austrian domain of Silesia. The Treaty of Dresden ended the Second Silesian War and endorsed the Prussian ownership of Silesia. The Prussian king, Frederick II, recognized Franz I Stephan, the husband of the Austrian ruler, as emperor.

In 1740, Frederick II invaded Silesia after perceiving the vulnerability of Austria occasioned by the refusal of many nations to recognize the succession of a female to the throne. After several military successes, he was ceded the county of Glatz as well as Lower and Upper Silesia by the Treaty of Breslau, signed on July 28, 1742. He committed himself to make no more territorial demands on Austria and to uphold the Catholic religion in Silesia.

What started as a Prussian-Austrian conflict gradually broadened into the War of Austrian Succession, in which Prussia was joined by France, Electoral Saxony, and the Wittelsbach electors of Bavaria, Cologne and the Palatinate, while the initially isolated Austria was joined in 1742 by Great Britain.

Besides Bavaria, Bohemia, and Moravia, the war also spread to Upper Italy, Alsace, and the Austrian Netherlands.

In 1744, after several Austrian successes in various battles and in diplomatic negotiations, Frederick II instigated the Second Silesian War. Resulting in a military stalemate, the war ended on October 18, 1748 with signing of the British mediated Treaty of Aix-la-Chapelle.

With this treaty, Maria Theresa gave up Silesia, France returned the Austrian Netherlands and occupied British colonies, the Hanoverian succession in Great Britain was recognized by all treaty signatories, as was the Pragmatic Sanction. ❑

Prussian troops at Hohenfriedeberg in the Second Silesian War

MISTRESSES AND INTRIGUE

Point of Interest

France's King Louis XV did not care for politics and left the business of governing to his ministers who, like himself, were often under the influence court favorites. Nevertheless, Marie-Jeanne Bécu, Comtesse du Barry, who became the king's official mistress after the death of Madame de Pompadour, was less politically inclined or ambitious. The king's sybaritic lifestyle and the absence of political continuity hastened France's financial ruin. As conditions steadily worsened, attempts were made to avoid national bankruptcy by the introduction of a new taxation system. This included a progressive income tax combined with the abolition of tax-free privileges of both the clergy and aristocracy. It failed because of the resistance of the royal family, the clergy, and the nobility. ❑

Madame du Barry

THE ROCOCO

Point of Interest

accepted the fact that the king satisfied his amorous needs in the company of younger, more exciting women while she exercised her influence on the appointment of officials; her aim was to fill the positions with her relatives.

Madame de Pompadour also conducted diplomatic negotiations with European courts. But after France's defeat in the Seven Years' War, the king's mistress became even more unpopular with the people.

She was also involved in domestic policies, arriving at decisions that went against tradition. Her opposition to the Jesuits resulted in their being banned from France in 1764. ❑

The last stage of Baroque was Rococo—a contraction of the French word "rocaille" (shell) and baroque—that began to spread throughout Europe around 1710.

Instead of the heavy, albeit dynamic, style that characterized the baroque, rococo displayed whimsicality and lightness. It delighted in ornamentation and harmonious elegance. A major influence in architecture and interior design, it also inspired trends in decorative arts, such as china figurines. Rococo found its expression in painting among artists such as Antoine Watteau, François Boucher and Jean Honoré Fragonard, whose paintings conveyed intimacy and depicted scenes of voluptuousness. In architecture, the German-speaking countries, especially Bavaria and Austria, were its most enthusiastic practitioners. The Asam brothers were brilliant church architects who created interiors of great theatricality by combining and merging sculpture, stuccowork, and architecture. A classic example of the rococo style is the Pilgrimage Church at Wies, designed by Dominikus Zimmerman. Inconspicuous from the outside, this small church's interior is a dazzling symphony of voluptuously sensuous decoration. In secular architecture, Sanssouci, and the Nymphen-burg palace near Munich are also fine examples of its ornately refined style. ❑

Pilgrimage Church in Wies

KING FREDERICK II'S SUMMER PALACE

Potsdam, 1747

Sanssouci, near Potsdam, the summer residence of Prussia's King Frederick II, is a masterpiece of the Rococo.

It took two years for the architect Georg Wenzeslaus von Knobelsdorff to complete Sans-souci (meaning "carefree"). An architectural triumph, the palace is intimate, single-storied and expressive of harmony, playfulness, and lightness.

Frederick II commissioned the residence from Knobelsdorff by showing him a sketch that he had drawn himself.

Reached through terraced vineyards and set in a large park, the summer residence was the expression of a relaxed style of life that favored relatively casual comfort and the proximity of nature to the rigid pomp and ceremony of the court.

It was here that the king performed his flute concerts, and also here that he met with luminaries such as Voltaire to discuss politics and philosophy. ❑

A view of the terraced garden at Sanssouci

THE CATHOLICS DEFEATED

Scotland, April 16, 1746

William Augustus, the brother of the British king, George II, was the commander of the British troops who defeated Scottish rebels, led by Charles Edward Stuart (the Young Pretender), in the Battle of Culloden, on April 16, 1746.

Culloden is a village just outside of the Scottish city of Inverness. The Jacobites (supporters of the Stuart dynastic claims, named after the Latin fom of James, *Jacobus*) had had some early successes marching as far as Derby, England before returning to Scotland to consolidate their forces. When the day of battle arrived the squabbling Scottish troops were overmatched and badly defeated. With this, the last revolt of the Scottish Catholics, Charles Edward had to abandon his rebellion against the House of Hanover. After Culloden, Charles, known as Bonnie Prince Charlie, was able to escape to the Isle of Skye and from there to the Continent, where he spent the rest of his days. ❑

THE ENLIGHTENMENT IN EUROPE

c. 1750, Europe

The eighteenth century is known as the Age of the Enlightenment. This philosophical and intellectual movement that spread throughout Europe sought to bring light into the darkness of a world steeped in superstition. This illumination was to be achieved through the use of reason.

In France philosophers of the eighteenth century laid the intellectual foundations for the fundamental change of French society that would result in the French Revolution (1789). The trend away from the medieval Christian view of the world that had already started during the Renaissance culminated in the Enlightenment: truth was no longer to be found in the dogma of Christian theology but rather in the unfettered use of human reason. Reason was espoused as the guiding principle for all laws, institutions, authority, and traditions.

As the Church's authority had been weakened by the development of new religious denominations, disputes in fundamental questions of faith in many European states were increasingly settled through civil and general wars, sowing doubt among the faithful regarding all Church dogmas. As a result, the Age of Enlightenment was also an age of secularization: worldly, secular explanations replaced established convictions pronounced *ex cathedra*. The Enlightenment's polemic against unquestioned tradition and prejudice led to a direct criticism of political absolutism. Its belief in the supremacy of individual immutable rights conflicted with the divinely absolute origin of governance.

The supporters of this political Enlightenment were the bourgeoisie, who, in the name of equality, turned against the institution of privilege that the upper echelons of the still extant feudal hierarchy assumed was their birthright. Convinced of the unlimited power of reason, the progression of the Enlightenment was accompanied by a new impetus in the field of education. Because all individuals were worthy of education, new philosophies promulgating the democratization of knowledge began to arise. Attention was directed not only to higher education but also to the system of primary school education. The latter was promoted in particular by the Swiss educational reformer Johann Heinrich Pestalozzi (1746-1826). ❑

Basic lesson in natural sciences.

THE AGE OF REASON

Europe, eighteenth century

In the name of Reason, rationalists subjected all traditional knowledge to criticism, because according to them truth could only be found through public discussion among rational individuals. Therefore tolerance and freedom of opinion were essential prerequisites. The embodiment of the Enlightenment was the 35-volume *Encyclopédie* that Denis Diderot and Jean Le Rond d'Alembert published with 200 collaborators between 1751 and 1780.

Natural sciences: The applied sciences, based on general investigation, were considered the field in which human rationality found its best field of activity. The success of modern empirical natural sciences, based on impartial observations, was indeed impressive. In physics, Isaac Newton and many others affirmed the orderly structure of the world, determined by natural laws. In astronomy, scientists started from the principle that the earth was not the center of the universe, while in medicine, man, as part of nature, was placed in the same category as other creatures. These scientific findings questioned the dogma of the Christian religion, displacing man from the center of creation. The medieval world view, in which a hierarchical society was deemed to reflect a divinely ordered cosmos, gave way to a mechanistic representation of a perceptible and explainable world. Unimagined possibilities opened up: man was able not only to perceive his environment, but he could also appropriate and dominate it.

Critique of knowledge: It is true that there were several different movements in the philosophy of Enlightenment, but they shared the aspiration to establish a solid foundation for knowledge. While Rationalism neglected experience in its unilateral emphasis of reason based on the laws of logic, empiricism, which was more widespread in Britain, recognized sensory experience as the means of acquiring knowledge of reality. It was Immanuel Kant who brought the two approaches together; perception produced data that was structured by reason. While Kant was aware of the possibilities of reason, he was also aware of its limitations, and so went beyond Enlightenment.

Moral philosophy: For Kant, reason was also the standard by which ethical actions must be measured. His categorical imperative states: "Always act according to that maxim whose universality as a law you can at the same time will." This transfers the claim of equality and universal validity of rationality to the field of moral philosophy. Here too, philosophy in Britain followed a different path because it postulated a "moral perception" that could lead man on the path of virtue and at the same time defined the "greatest good for the greatest number of people" as the aim of moral effort. The attempt to achieve happiness became the criterion for judging individual and state actions.

Social theory: Because the Enlightenment, in its belief in progress and reason, started from the point of view that man could achieve a state of earthly happiness, it concentrated on the basic conditions that either hindered or promoted the path to happiness. Typical of the Enlightenment is the concept that the authority to rule is not ordained by God. Using the model of a social contract, Enlightenment philosophers pointed out that sovereignty resides with the people. They choose to relinquish it but have the right to reclaim it. The postulate of a right to resist unjust authority, the idea of human worth and inalienable human rights rooted in nature, together with the idea that the relations of the state should be regulated by the law of nations, form the core of Enlightenment social theory. ❑

PHILOSOPHERS OF THE ENLIGHTENMENT

Point of Interest

François Marie Arouet, known as **Voltaire** (1694-1778) was one of the most important philosophers of the French Enlightenment. He was a fierce critic of injustice and unreasonableness in his criticism of religion, fanaticism, superstition, dogmatism, and mysticism. He was a tireless opponent of France's absolutist monarchy, which he compared unfavorably to the political conditions in Britain with its parliamentary system, tolerance, freedom of the press, and protection against torture and arbitrary imprisonment.

Voltaire

Jean-Jacques Rousseau (1712-1778), born in Switzerland, explained in his work of 1762 of political philosophy, *Du Contrat Social, Principes du droit politique* (*The Social Contract, or Principles of Political Rights*), the origin of the state, based on contract theory. This proposes that men contracted freely and that the individual subordinates him or her self to the general good. But according to Rousseau, the contract had been broken, so it was now a matter of restoring the position of the general will (*volonté générale*) and people's sovereignty. That is the reason why the interests of the individual must be subordinate to the general law. Rousseau started from the premise that man is naturally good; it is civilization that has led man into evil. As a result—in

Jean-Jacques Rousseau

contrast to the belief in progress expressed by the other representatives of the Enlightenment— Rousseau believed that the ideal state was based on a return to natural simplicity.

Denis Diderot (1713-1784) promoted deistic and materialistic ideas in the articles and entries he wrote for the *Encyclopédie*, the monumental work he published with the natural scientist and philosopher Jean le Rond d'Alembert. Deism only proceeds from rational arguments

Denis Diderot

for theological statements and rejects the authority of revelation. For Deists the knowledge of God was only possible when based on nature and the natural morality of man, independently from any Church or religious community. Diderot criticized the orders

and prouncements made by the Church and the state because they subjected people to an unnatural pressure. He demanded that the monarch be just and follow reason, and that the laws of justice apply to him too.

Charles de Secondat, Baron de la Brède et de Montesquieu (1689-1755), also a French philosopher, postulated the theory of the separation of powers into the legislative, executive, and judiciary, all completely independent from each other. He put forward these theories in his most famous

Baron de Montesquieu

work *De l'Esprit des Lois* (*The Spirit of the Laws*), published in 1748. He emphasized the role of conflict in a state with a republican constitution and asserted that the balance of interests between various social strata guaranteed the stability of a state and prevented the misuse of power. He believed that the aim of any form of government should be the legal guarantee of the freedom of the individual.

Immanuel Kant (1724-1804) led a withdrawn, inconspicuous life in Königsberg, Germany, but his critical philosophy, which rejected speculation and metaphysics, turned the intellectual world upside down in the same way as Copernicus had done with the natural sciences. The focal point of Kant's philosophy was the autonomously thinking and acting individual who was entirely re-

sponsible for himself. In his essay, *Answering the Question: What is Enlightenment?*, published in 1784, he starts with the programmatic, now famous, sentences: "Enlightenment is man's emergence from his own self-imposed immaturity. Immaturity is the inability to use one's own understanding without the guidance of another. This immaturity is self-imposed, if the reasons for it are not the lack of understanding but the lack of res-

Immanuel Kant

olution and courage to use one's own understanding without the guidance of another. *Sapere aude!* Have the courage to use your own understanding! This is the motto of the Enlightenment."

Gotthold Ephraim Lessing (1729-1781) like Kant, was a German Enlightenment era philosopher. In his best-known ideological drama *Nathan the Wise*, he celebrated the ideas of religious tolerance. ❑

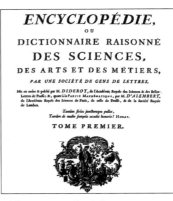

Diderot's *Encyclopédie*

THE LISBON EARTHQUAKE

Lisbon, November 1, 1755

On All Saints' Day, the Portuguese capital and surrounding regions were completely devastated by an earthquake that cost the lives of as many as 30,000 people. A large part of the town was destroyed. In the midst of the catastrophe, Count José de Carvalho e Melo, Marquis of Pombal and personal adviser to King Joseph I, distinguished himself in the aftermath of the catastrophe. "The dead must be buried and the wounded must be treated," he told the traumatized survivors. He organized rescue and medical services, then ordered and supervised the systematic reconstruction of the city destroyed in the earthquake.

With his work rebuilding the city as well as that in the political field, the marquis's zeal for reform and energy unsettled both the aristocracy and the clergy. After members of the aristocracy and Jesuits were accused of involvement in the attempt to assassinate the king in 1758, Pombal ordered all the assets of the Society of Jesus to be confiscated and their members expelled from the country.

In 1773 the marquis introduced a major program of reform in the spirit of enlightened absolutism. This included changes in the fields of financial administration and dispensation of justice, the army and navy, the economy, commerce, agriculture, and winegrowing.

The great German author Johann Wolfgang Goethe, described the effect the Lisbon earthquake had on him as a young man in his autobiography *Poetry and Truth* (*Dichtung und Wahrheit*): "The boy's equilibrium was deeply shaken for the first time by an extraordinary event of worldwide importance," he wrote. ❏

The Lisbon earthquake left an indelible impression on Enlightenment Europe..

CASANOVA'S MASTERPIECE

Venice, 1756

Accused of involvement in witchcraft, the Venetian gambler and womanizer, Giacomo Girolamo Casanova, was imprisoned in the "The Leads," a notorious prison attached to the Doge's palace.

His subsequent escape from what was considered the most secure prison in the world was only one of the exploits with which this illustrious adventurer confounded his contemporaries. Casanova's life took him to the four corners of Europe. Continually involved in quarrels and attempts to evade imprisonment, the much-traveled Casanova obtained a Doctorate of Law in his home town, became secretary to a cardinal in Rome, served as an officer in the Venetian army, worked as a lottery collector, and acted as a negotiator in the service of the French king, as well as being a secret agent for the Venetian Inquisition.

After this turbulent, unsettled career, he was appointed librarian to Count Waldstein's castle in northern Bohemia. There, at the age of 60, he began to write his memoirs, *Histoire de ma vie* (*The Story of My Life*). In nearly 4,000 pages, Casanova recorded a colorful account of the political and social life during the Rococo Age. In these memoirs, the man who had dedicated his entire life to sensual pleasures describes his numerous love affairs in detail. ❏

One of his many love affairs (an illustration from *The Memoirs of Casanova*)

PRUSSIA AND THE SEVEN YEARS' WAR

Saxony, August 29, 1756

The Seven Years' War, which involved several European nations, began with the Prussian invasion of Saxony. It developed into a conflict between Great Britain and France to secure political and economic supremacy.

Frederick II of Prussia, marched into Saxony to break up an anti-Prussian coalition, led by Austria. The issues that were fought over in the War of Austrian Succession still remained unsettled. Another cause was conflicting colonial interests, which inevitably led to deteriorating international relations in Europe.

Events in the New World also played a major part in this regard. The French and British settlers in the Ohio basin were fighting over land. That conflict was limited at first, but in the spring of 1756 there was an official declaration of war, and the conflict spread to the European continent. Both France's and Great Britain's search for allies gradually led to the formation of power blocs.

France tried to persuade Prussia to invade Hanover, which would have been a clear affront to England's Hanoverian monarch. When Frederick rejected France's request, good relations between Berlin and Paris soured. Instead Frederick and England's George II, signed an agreement in which Hanover was declared neutral. Frederick had signed this agreement in an attempt to isolate Austria; he also was concerned about a Franco-Russian alliance. However, since France had formed an alliance with Austria, and Russia had also become closer to Austria, Frederick's maneuver only contributed to accelerating the formation of a coalition against his own country.

At first the war did not go Prussia's way. In order to prevent his country from becoming a battlefield, Frederick launched several military campaigns. In 1756 he forced Saxony to surrender and won two battles against Austria in Bohemia. After Prussia's improving fortune in Silesia, Bohemia, Moravia, East Prussia, and Pomerania, Prussian troops suffered a crushing defeat at the hands of an Austrian-Russian army at the Battle of Kunersdorf on August 12, 1759. Now completely exhausted Prussia tried and failed to reach a negotiated peace. ❑

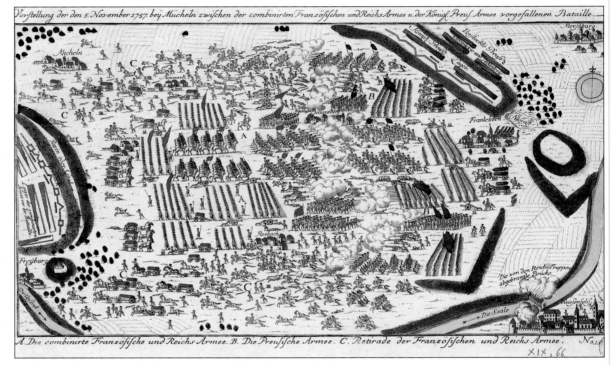

Battle formation near Rossbach (contemporary single-sheet woodcut)

VICTORY FOR GREAT BRITAIN AND PRUSSIA

Point of Interest

The Treaty of Paris, also known as the Peace of Paris, was signed on February 10, 1763, between Great Britain, Portugal, France, and Spain. This treaty, along with the Peace of Hubertusburg, signed five days later between Austria, Saxony, and Prussia, ended the Seven Years' War.

The peace treaties represented victories for Great Britain and Prussia, and the diminution of French colonial power. From France, Great Britain received Canada, Louisiana east of the Mississippi, and West Africa; from Spain it received Florida. In addition, the British established their supremacy in India. The acquisition of Silesia by Prussia was confirmed.

In 1760, after some catastrophic defeats, King Frederick II of Prussia succeeded in regaining the strategic initiative in spite of Russo-Austrian superiority. What contributed to this reversal of fortune was a change in foreign policy within the alliance during the winter of 1761/62. After the death of British King George II in 1760 and the retirement of William Pitt the Elder, Lord Bute, became the English Prime Minister in 1761. He pressed for an early peace in central Europe, because Britain had declared war on Spain in January 1762.

In Russia it was the ascent of a new monarch to the throne that brought about the change. Peter III, who was Tsar of Russia for only six months formed an alliance with Prussia and pressured Sweden into participating in the peace treaty. Peter's successor, Catherine II, withdrew from the Seven Years' War.

The Seven Years' War earned Prussia a position as a Great Power. In return the King of Prussia committed himself, as Elector of Brandenburg, to give his vote to the Austrian Archduke Joseph II in the Election of the Holy Roman Emperor.

The conflict in the overseas colonies also came to an end. After France had lost almost all its territories in Canada and the East Indies, it signed a preliminary peace treaty with Great Britain on November 3, 1762. ❑

BRITAIN: NEW IMPERIAL POWER

Paris, February 10, 1763

British officers in India; the victory of Britain in the Battle of Plassey in 1757 drove the French out of India.

The British were successful against the French both in North America and in India. After removing its most powerful colonial rival, Great Britain began to build its empire.

As a result of the Treaty of Paris, France was left with only a few possessions in North America, namely the islands of St Pierre and Miquelon just south of Newfoundland. From Spain Britain received Florida and all the land west of the Mississippi. The colonial war in America started in 1754. After a British squadron captured over 300 French merchant ships in November 1755 and the British government refused to pay compensation for damages, the Anglo-French war started officially on January 10, 1756. In 1757 the French were forced to go on the defensive in North America; among other things, the British conquered Louisburg in 1758. The outcome of the war in North America was decided with the conquest of Quebec on October 18, 1759. On September 8, 1760, the garrison in Montreal and all the French troops in North America surrendered their weapons. In India the war had already concluded. On June 23, 1757, the troops of the Nabob of Bengal, who had formed an alliance with the France, were defeated at Plassey. This put an end to the French dream of a colonial empire in India. ❑

The British General James Wolfe was killed during the capture of Quebec in 1759.

CATHERINE THE

Moscow, January 5, 1762

Despite far-reaching reforms carried out by Russia's most famous tsarina, the aristocracy still retained its privileged position.

After the death of Tsarina Elisabeth Petrovna, who ruled Russia from 1741 to 1761, her nephew Peter von Holstein-Gottorf, who ruled under the name Peter III (born February 21, 1728) became tsar. His ascent to the Russian throne marked a turning point in the Seven Years' War: as an admirer of King Frederick II (the Great) of Prussia, he withdrew Russian troops and signed a peace agreement with Prussia on May 5. But on June 29 he was forced to abdicate and on July 17, 1762, he was murdered at Ropsha, near Moscow.

Peter's wife, who was born Sophie Friederike Auguste von Anhalt-Zerbst in Prussia on May 2, 1729, succeeded him on the throne as Catherine II. Intelligent and educated, she corresponded with the leading intellectuals of her time as well as her numerous lovers (who included Grigory Grigoryevich, Count Orlov, and Grigori Alexandrovich, Prince Potemkin).

She initiated her reign with a series of reforms. Following a manifesto published by the tsarina in July 1763, the settlement of mainly German farmers in the fertile but until then almost uninhabited regions along the Volga began in 1764. In doing this, Catherine was guided by the same mercantilist ideas as the other territorial monarchs: according to the theory of population then current, an increase in the workforce would automatically lead to an economic upturn. The arrival of foreign settlers was particularly important for Russia, because the tsarist empire was populated by large landowners and their serfs. As a result it did not have enough free settlers to work the land. The colonists were promised all kinds of privileges: religious freedom, exemp-

GREAT AND THE RISE OF RUSSIA

tion from military and civilian service, tax exemption for up to 30 years, self-administration, and state support to resettle.

Catherine's enlightened despotism also included the introduction of reforms of the senate (1763) and government administration (1764), the secularization of church property (1764), and the foundation of numerous schools. In 1767 the Legislative Commission set up by Catherine began working on a new Code of Laws. The two-year long consultations fell short of expectations, but they did give an overall picture of conditions in Russia: illiteracy was widespread, and there were no banks, doctors, pharmacists, or schools in rural areas. European and Siberian Russia had about 17 million inhabitants, of which 7.5 million were peasants subjected to the so-called soul tax (a poll tax), and 1 million were aristocrats, merchants, clergy, and soldiers. The existing social tensions frequently developed into peasants' revolts, such as the great peasant and Cossack Rebellion led by Emilian Ivanovich Pugachev. He published a manifesto in September 1773, which he signed under the name of Tsar Peter III; in it he promised the Cossacks the restoration of their old privileges while calling upon them to rise against their lords. The Pugachev Rebellion brought together the dissatisfied population in the Volga region and the Steppe proletariat—Cossacks, peasants, and Orthodox Christians—to form a

large social-revolutionary movement. In the end Pugachev, who had a price of 20,000 rubles on his head, was handed over to the Russians by his own people and taken to Moscow in an iron cage. He was sentenced to death and executed on January 21, 1775, his death watched by the crowds as the nobility secured the best places for the execution of the man who had wanted to bring about their destruction. The free Cossack nation lost its autonomy, including its ancient oppositional character and became transformed into a border defense militia.

All attempts at introducing land reform were prevented by the hereditary aristocracy on which the tsarina relied. In a "charter bestowing them privileges" (April 21, 1785), she promised to maintain the prerogatives of their class. These included exemption from military service, taxes, and physical punishment, as well as full rights over the lives of their serfs. She also confirmed the right of the aristocracy to have collective federations with chosen representatives. ❏

Tsarina Catherine II, the Great, in Russian costume

ECONOMIC CYCLES

France, December 1758

The French national economist and physician to King Louis XV, François Quesnay (1694-1774) gave an account of economic cycles in his *Tableau économique*. He called his system physiocracy (Greek: natural government). It was the first attempt at a complete theory of economics on a national level.

The physiocrat system was based on the concept of natural rights and on the idea of a natural order desired by God. According to the physiocrats, the national economy was ruled by economic laws that were objectively determined by the productiveness of nature, and subjectively by the

principle of rationality.

The physiocrats saw only agriculture and forestry as productive, because only here a net product was achieved. The trading and manufacturing classes (sterile classes) could only transform materials produced by nature. Because this meant that the soil was the only source of wealth, a tax on land and soil had to be the only tax.

With its criticism of mercantilism and the call for laissez-faire (the non-interference of the state in the economy), physiocracy was the precursor to classic economic theory as articulated by Adam Smith. ❏

"PAPA" HAYDEN AND THE BIRTH OF THE SYMPHONY

Vienna, 1761

The Austrian composer Joseph Haydn (1732-1809) was a perfect representative of Viennese classicism. He was the founder of the classical symphonic form.

Haydn was a court musician in the service of Count Esterházy with whom he remained until his death, apart from a brief interruption between 1790 and 1795. Born into a north Austrian craftsman's family, he joined the Vienna Domkapelle (St Stephen's Cathedral) as a choirboy at the age of eight. It was in Vienna, the musical center of Europe, that he completed his musical training and began to compose. By the beginning of the 1790s, widely celebrated not only as a composer but also as an organist, he set out on two long concert tours in England.

Haydn's compositions captivated audiences with the power of their musical inventiveness;

in spite of their relatively tight structure, they were also very original. The composer has been recognized as the source of many of the compositional forms that have dominated classical music. Even such modern composers as Stravinsky and Prokofiev have acknowledged a debt to Hayden. The focal point of Haydn's creativity lay in his instrumental music: besides over 100 symphonies, he composed quartets and trios, as well as operas, and two oratorios, *The Creation* (1798) and *The Seasons* (1801). All have become staples of the classical repertory. ❏

An opera performance in Esterházy

THE INDUSTRIAL REVOLUTION

The Industrial Revolution occasioned profound, economic, political and social transformations. It began in Great Britain in the latter part of the eighteenth century and later extended to the European continent and the United States. Rapid economic growth and the increase in wealth also resulted in painful dislocations and exploitation of the poor.

The resulting economic growth increased national income, but at the same time it created a labor force faced with harsh working conditions. These conditions became the pivotal social issue during the industrial revolution.

In the mid-nineteenth century it became apparent that economic matters affected everyone. The economic crisis of 1857 was one such case where issues of supply and demand affected the entire world economy.

GREAT BRITAIN

Between 1700 and 1800 the population in Great Britain (excluding Ireland) increased from 6.7 million to 10.2 million, and by 1851 to about 21 million. Because of the relative cheapness of basic food compared to mainland Europe, the lower and middle income groups had a certain amount of excess purchasing power. This demand particularly benefited the British textile industry, which had a secure and plentiful source of raw material because of extensive sheep breeding.

In contrast to the continent economies where there was little scope for development because of government regulations and the constitution of guilds, Great Britain could boast of a relatively free market. In addition, its infrastructure was far superior; all large cities and industrial regions became linked by roads and waterways. The slowly expanding home market developed into a growing export market. Backed by a powerful navy, Great Britain was able to secure a significant share of world trade. The resulting wealth was used to finance new technologies. Great Britain was the first country to make the transition from an agricultural to an industrial nation.

The textile industry was in the vanguard of the new technologies. In 1764 the weaver, James Hargreaves, invented the first mechanical spinning machine, known as the "Spinning Jenny." As industry learned to harness the power of steam, factories became less dependent on local conditions. The speed, efficiency, output, and accuracy of work increased to a level never before achieved. The steam engine developed by James Watt in 1769 vastly

Machines transformed production processes: the steam hammer developed by the Scottish inventor James Nasmyth (1808-1890) made working with steel much easier.

accelerated this process and would undergo continuous technical improvements.

Following close on the heels of textiles, heavy industry began to benefit from significant technical advances. In 1784 Henry Cort invented the puddling process for refining iron ore, which considerably improved the techniques of steel production, while coke-fired blast furnaces and innovative rolling processes made possible the mass production of steel goods, introducing the concept of the modern foundry.

THE RAILWAYS — THE ENGINE OF PROGRESS

The modernization of industry encouraged more efficient modes of transportation, which in turn facilitated further growth. In Great Britain waterways were built early in the industrial revolution. Transport by water made the conveyance of heavy goods such as coal and iron much less expensive.

Besides the reduction in the cost, it was the growing speed of travel for both people and goods that became the main feature transportation at this time. Since the invention of the first steam engine, engineers had been trying to use it to power a vehicle. The first steam locomotive able to move under its own power was built by the British engineer Richard Trevithick. It made its maiden voyage in February 1804 in a foundry in Wales. In 1823 George Stephenson, who had studied the problems of locomotives in the pit wagon ways in the coal mines round Newcastle, set up the first locomotive factory in the world in that city. In 1825 he opened a stretch of railway from Stockton to Darlington, a distance of 19 miles (30 km). It was Stephenson who inaugurated the railway age with the "Rocket," built in 1829. This locomotive made its debut on September 15, 1830, at the opening of the Liverpool and Manchester Railway, where it provided regular passenger transport.

The railways not only attracted capital; they also changed the capital market. Joint-stock companies were created, a "railway fever" broke out, and a new group of "capital owners" was born who sought to invest their money in a profitable manner.

EUROPE AND THE USA

The process of industrialization started later outside Great Britain. Early in the nineteenth century Belgium, the Netherlands, France, and Switzerland were the first countries on the European continent to become industrialized. Germany followed suit by mid-century and the rest of Europe later still. The reason for this delay was mainly that the conditions that had made the industrial revolution pos-

The British railway engineer George Stephenson developed and built the "Rocket" locomotive.

sible in Great Britain were absent in the rest of Europe.

In France, agriculture rather than industry remained the main focus of the country's economic development throughout the nineteenth century. It was not only the French textile industry that lagged behind the British technologically; so did its iron and steel technologies. It was only in 1818 that the first coke-fired furnaces were introduced, and in 1820 that steel was first produced using the puddling process.

By the end of the nineteenth century, the United States had developed into one of the leading industrial nations, together with Germany and Great Britain. But it was only in 1850 that the foundations were laid for its industrial development, and for a long time cotton remained the only major export product. This was in spite of the fact that in 1830 the burgeoning railway industry had provided the necessary impetus for an expansion of the heavy industry that, together with oil production, would later become the mainstay of an expanding capitalism.

A CHANGING SOCIETY

The industrial revolution not only changed production processes; it also influenced the development of society. Besides the aristocracy, farmers, and small tradesmen, two new classes emerged: capitalists and wage laborers.

The mechanization of work processes resulted in the division of labor and the separa-

tion of work between individual production plants as well as inside the factories themselves. At the same time the skills needed to operate machines diminished as a result of mechanical production methods. Working processes were simplified and job qualifications were lowered, with the result that women and children could now also be employed.

Excessively long working hours, the remorseless intensity of the work, and the lack of sanitary conditions, combined with terrible housing conditions in the industrial regions, meant that factory workers in Great Britain had a much higher mortality rate than other occupational groups.

The unreasonable working and living conditions led to action by the workers, which was, at first, directed against the new machines in the textile industry. On March 11, 1811, in Nottinghamshire, textile workers destroyed all the machinery in protest against the threat of losing their jobs. This marked the beginning of the Luddite movement that continued until 1813. Then in 1838 the English working class formed their first political organization, the Chartists, and in the "People's Charter" demanded the introduction of universal male suffrage. In 1844 Friedrich Engels wrote *The Condition of the Working Class in England*, indicting the economic and social inequalities that would give rise to revolutionary movements. The novels of Charles Dickens also served to highlight the desperate living conditions of the urban poor. ❑

THE INDUSTRIAL REVOLUTION IN GREAT BRITAIN

Stanhill, England, 1764

In the second half of the eighteenth century, Great Britain was at the vanguard of far-reaching economic and social changes that led to the Industrial Revolution.

In 1764, the weaver and carpenter James Hargreaves from Stanhill near Blackburn invented the "Spinning Jenny," which he patented in 1770.

The spinning machine enabled one worker to run eight spindles at the same time instead of one because of its system of rovings and spindles. This invention marked the beginning of the Industrial Revolution, which would spread to the European continent and North America a few years later. The most important features of the Industrial Revolution were the replacement of human power by mechanical power (water power and steam power), the replacement of the spinning wheel by the spinning machine and of the hand loom by the weaving machine, as well as new techniques of iron extraction and processing.

In Great Britain there were several factors that contributed to this. Between 1700 and 1800 the population had increased from 6.7 million to 10.2 million; highly productive agriculture produced cheap basic food; as a result of migration to the cities available manpower increased; and economic liberalism together with increasing exports led to the development of a new entrepreneurial class.

The introduction of new techniques started in the textile industry in Great Britain in about 1750. The textile industry was the country's most important area of production, especially the manufacture of wool and cotton goods.

In 1733, John Kay invented the flying shuttle for the hand loom that enabled one worker to operate several machines at the same time. This resulted in protests by workers who felt that their jobs were threatened by this invention; disgruntled weavers stormed Kay's house, because with his invention one weaver was able to work faster and so produce more. This cost many workers their jobs.

But there was an imbalance of production between the process of spinning wool and weaving it: to keep a weaver busy for one day, ten workers had to spin wool all day. This led to the invention of machines for spinning wool. With the "spinning Jenny" spinners were able to spin much more wool than with the spinning wheel. The one disadvantage was that the machine was made of wood and was not strong enough for such heavy use.

It was Richard Arkwright who paved the way for the automatic spinning machine when he invented the "water frame" in 1769. Driven by water power, Arkwright's machine was able to produce excellently twined yarn. In 1775 Arkwright invented a mechanical machine to process raw fibres into combed rovings, moving across the grain, a process that until then had only been possible manually. It was Samuel Crompton who made the last step forward—for the time being—in the development of the mechanical spinning machine when he invented the "mule" in 1779; this combined elements of the two earlier machines and worked with up to 48 shuttles on one carriage.

Besides the textile industry, great progress was also made in heavy industry. In 1708 Abraham Darby invented the method casting iron using sand moulds, and in 1713 he was the first to use coke instead

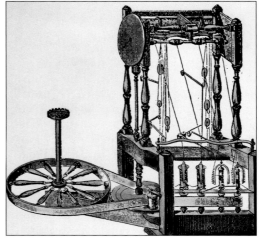

Arkwright's water frame was invented in 1769.

of charcoal as fuel for blast furnaces. In 1711, Thomas Newcomen, an ironmonger by trade, built the first steam engine for pumping water from a coal mine. In 1754 Henry Cort built the first iron-rolling mill to process steel into flat sheets, bars and sections.

At first water power was used to power these new machines. But as the use of spinning and weaving machines became ever more widespread, this was no longer sufficient. As a result of the invention of mechanical sources of power (in particular, the steam engine invented by James Watt) factories became independent of sources of natural energy. ❑

EMPEROR OF THE ENLIGHTENMENT

Vienna, August 18, 1765

The new Austrian emperor, Joseph II, was concerned with improving conditions in his empire and started a program of reforms in the Habsburg patrimonial lands, based on enlightened absolutism.

After the death of his mother Maria-Theresa in 1780, Joseph II succeeded as emperor and began his reform policies, described as Josephinism. On October 13, 1781, he published the Patent of Tolerance that ended the repression and persecution of all non-Catholics and allowed them to practice their religions. The Marriage Patent issued on January 16, 1783, introduced "civil marriage." By a legal decree issued on May 1, 1787, the judiciary was separated from the administration, special courts were abolished, and a criminal court was created.

In 1784, German was introduced as the official language in Hungary and the regional constitution was reformed, provoking several uprisings. The reforms in the Church in the Habsburg Netherlands and the abolition of the old constitution led to a revolution. This entrenched resistance forced Joseph to cancel all the decrees applying to Hungary with the exception of the Patent of Tolerance and the abolition of serfdom.

Joseph II died in Vienna on February 20, 1790. ❑

Radical reformer in Vienna: Emperor Joseph II

DAWN OF THE MACHINE AGE

Point of Interest

Changes in working processes were an inevitable consequence of the Industrial Revolution. Previously, goods had been produced manually. Now in mechanized factories, machines replaced hand tools. The mechanized working process led to clear divisions of labor.

At the same time, mechanized production affected the way in which workers were employed: work processes were simplified, lower skills needed, and the (low-paid) employment of women and children was made possible. Because the machines determined the rhythm of work, working days were long, ranging from twelve to sixteen hours, and hard. There were no provisions to prevent accidents. It was not until 1833 in England that it became illegal for children under nine years old to work in factories.

Notable advances were seen in the textile industry. Mechanization of the second stage of textile production—the processing of yarn into fabric—lagged behind other developments. Then in 1785, Edmund Cartwright invented the power loom. But it was only years later that the quality of hand-woven fabric was matched by mechanical weaving. The hand loom built by the Lyons silk weaver Joseph-Marie Jacquard in 1805 was an important step forward

Jacquard hand loom

because it also enabled complicated patterns to be woven.

While industrial methods of production strongly reduced the need for hand work, at the same time new jobs opened up as industrially-produced goods needed repair. The expansion of the commercial sector led to a growth in the buying and selling of goods, and in the nineteenth century this led to expanding infrastructure to provide channels of distribution. ❑

THE THAI NATION

Ayutthaya, 1767

The history of the first Thai kingdom ended with the destruction of Ayutthaya by the Burmese.

From this city the kings of Thailand had ruled a mighty empire. In 1350, King U Thong, who had proclaimed himself King Ramathibodi, founded the kingdom of Siam. He defeated several Thai principalities and conquered the Khmer state of Cambodia, including its capital Angkor.

There were numerous magnificent palaces, temples, and monasteries in Ayutthaya. Ramathibodi II (1491-1529) was the first Thai king to make contact with Europeans, and in 1686

the French were given the right to establish commercial settlements.

After the Burmese had been driven out, a Thai general ascended the throne (from 1782 until 1809), taking the name Rama I. He moved his residence to Bangkok and founded the Chakri dynasty that still rules today. His successors who ruled Siam—it reverted to its earlier name, Thailand, in 1939—went on to trade with most European countries. It was the only country in Southeast Asia to preserve its independence in the face of European colonial expansion. ❑

THE TRAVELS OF CAPTAIN JAMES COOK

Plymouth, England, August 26, 1768

Commissioned by the British Crown and the Royal Society, James Cook set sail in the *Endeavour*, a flat-bottomed ship, to the Pacific Ocean to observe and record the transit of Venus across the sun. In addition to making these astronomical calculations, he wanted to search for the mysterious southern continent, *Terra Australis Incognita*.

Cook was born in Yorkshire on October 27, 1728. He became a merchant navy apprentice in 1746 and was promoted to mate in 1752. In 1755, he decided to join the Royal Navy.

His voyage on the *Endeavour* took him round Cape Horn to the Pacific Ocean where on June 3, 1769, on Otaheite (Tahiti), he observed the transit of Venus across the sun, enabling him to calculate the distance between the earth and the sun. On October 7, 1769, instead of the southern continent, he sighted the north coast of New Zealand and discovered the passage between North Island and South Island (Cook Strait). Then he sailed westward and, on April 20, 1770, he reached the east coast of Australia at "Point Hicks." On April 29, Cook arrived in Botany Bay where he landed. Sailing through the Torres Strait (between New Guinea and Australia), he reached

Batavia (Jakarta) on Java. On July 13, 1771, Cook arrived back in Britain.

On July 13, 1772, Cook set sail again, this time with HMS *Resolution* and HMS *Adventure*. From the Cape of Good Hope Cook sailed southwards as far as the Antarctic Circle until he was prevented by ice floes from progressing any further. On March 27, 1773, he returned to New Zealand; then in June 1773 he left New Zealand and sailed on to Tahiti. The following year he reached 71°10' south until he was stopped by an ice barrier. Cook returned to Tahiti again and from there sailed westward where he discovered the New Hebrides and, further south, New Caledonia. He returned to Great Britain on July 29, 1775, after a voyage lasting three years and 18 days.

On July 12, 1776 he set sail on his final journey on the HMS *Resolution*; on January 18, 1778, he discovered the Sandwich Islands (Hawaii), then in March 1778 he reached the coast of America and sailed northwards in the direction of Alaska. On August 29 he had to interrupt his voyage through the Bering Strait. On November 26, 1778, Cook was in Hawaii again, where he was killed in a dispute with Hawaiians on February 14, 1779. ❑

James Cook was killed by the inhabitants of Hawaii on February 14, 1779

A Divided Poland

St Petersburg, August 5, 1772

Russia, Austria and Prussia agreed on the division of Poland, which, as a result, lost more than 72,000 square miles of its territory—about one-third—with more than 4 million people.

Poland's partition resulted from the civil war that followed the foundation of the Bar Confederation. On February 29, 1768, the Polish nobles, supported by France, had formed an association to defend the Polish-Lithuanian Commonwealth against the aggression of Russia. The resulting civil war weakened the country. Austria offered the Confederates bases in upper Hungary, and in the summer of 1770 France sent general Charles François Dumouriez with auxiliary troops. Thereupon, in October 1770, the rebels tried in vain to capture King Stanislav II, Augustus Poniatowski, but after the departure of the French and in the absence of Austrian help, the Confederates were defeated in the early summer of 1772.

The Partition Treaty gave Russia the territories of Polish Livonia and Belarus, embracing the counties of Vitebsk, Polotsk, and Mstislav, about 32,400 square miles in which about 1.25 million Belarussians, Russians and Latvians lived. Prussia took West Prussia (without Danzig, Graudenz and Thorn), as well as Ermland and the Netze District, an area of about 13,500 square miles with about 356,000 inhabitants of German origin and Poles. Austria took Zator and Auschwitz, part of Little Poland, including parts of the counties of Krakow, about 32,400 square miles, with about 2.6 million inhabitants, almost all Polish and Ruthenians. The region became the Kingdom of Galicia, and Lodomeria and was annexed by Austria. ❑

The rulers of Russia, Austria, and Prussia dividing up the map of Poland

Boston Tea Party

Boston, December 16, 1773

In the North American colonies, the outrage caused by the economic and political paternalism of Great Britain led to open rebellion.

On December 16, 1773, citizens of Boston, dressed as Native Americans, stormed three ships of the British East India Company and threw 342 crates of tea into the water.

The Boston Tea Party was a rebellion against the import taxes imposed on North America by the British government, and also against the existing monopoly of the East India Company.

Arguments about the validity of laws passed in London began in 1764, when the Sugar Act revised the tax laws on sugar imported into North America from the non-British West Indies. This was the prelude to extensive tax legislation that was intended to make the thirteen colonies in America more profitable to the British Crown, but at the same time marked the beginning of the colonies' disaffection with the motherland.

The cost of the war against France and Spain, which had ended in 1763, had been astronomical, and the British Prime Minister and Chancellor, George Grenville, wanted to recover at least a part of this cost through colonial taxation. The Stamp Act of 1765 was viewed by the colonies as confiscatory. It taxed

End of Sweden's "Age of Liberty"

Stockholm, February 12, 1771

Upon the death of the Sweden's King Adolf Friedrich, his son, Gustav III (b. January 24, 1746) succeeded to the throne.

He put an end to the "Age of Liberty" that had started in 1720, during which the *rikdag* (parliament) was the most important governmental institution. This period of a relatively weak monarchy was marked by the growing influence of various interest groups.

Supporters of France (the Hat Party) and of Russia (the Cap Party) were vying for power. On August 19, 1772, Gustav mounted a bloodless coup d'état and instituted a decidedly more absolutist rule. Foreign policy, the national budget, and the appointment of officials and bishops became his responsibility. Parliament retained the right of legislative initiative and the right to veto Sweden's participation in wars of aggression. It also shared in policy-making decisions involving the national bank and the levying of new taxes. For

his part, Gustav agreed to abolish torture, recognize liberalized press laws, and guarantee religious freedom to non-Lutherans. ❑

Gustav III

newspapers, magazines, pamphlets, official and commercial documents, playing cards, and even dice.

That taxes were raised without colonial representation seemed to the colonists to be an abrogation of English Common Law. Because the subjects in the colonies had no right to vote for members of the House of Commons, these laws could not, in their view, apply to them. On May 30, 1765, Patrick Henry arose in the House of Burgesses in Virginia and challenged the British House of Commons right to tax the property of the colonies without representation. A patriotic group, the "Sons of Liberty" used violence to stop the sale of revenue stamps. The resistance in the colonies bolstered the few members in the British Parliament who had originally voted against the laws.

Subsequently, in 1766, the

"Boston Tea Party:" British goods are thrown into the water by Boston citizens, encouraged by jubilant onlookers.

During the "Boston Massacre" British soldiers fired on civilians.

Stamp Act was repealed, although the king and parliament refused to relinquish its "full right and authority" to issue further laws and edicts for the colonies in America. The New York lawyer James Otis demanded that the Legislative Assembly of the colonists be given as many rights as the Parliament in Westminster. The slogan "No taxation without representation" became a popular catchphrase.

In 1767, the British chancellor, Charles Townshend, proposed an extensive body of laws. To finance the colonial administration and judiciary, these new laws included, among other things, a new import duty on six major imported goods. The Townshend Acts caused as much outrage as the earlier acts. There was further unrest in New York and Boston. On January 19, 1770, in the Battle of Golden Hill in New York, some 40 British soldiers, armed with bayonets, attacked

the "Sons of Liberty", followed shortly by the "Boston Massacre" on March 5, 1770, wherein members of the 29th regiment killed seven colonists.

Virginia declared an embargo on the import of British goods, which other colonies honored. The embargo was successful. In April 1770 the British parliament removed all goods from the taxation list, except for tea. The continued imposition of the tea tax eventually led to the Boston Tea Party. ❏

POTATO CULTIVATION IN EUROPE

Berlin, 1771

The cultivation of the potato was encouraged in the hope of solving the European food crisis caused by crop failures between 1770 and 1772.

Throughout Germany, especially in Brandenburg-Prussia, as well as in Switzerland, widespread famine resulted in a willingness to cultivate potatoes,

which in turn created a change in popular eating habits.

The first reports of the potato reached Europe via the Spanish conquistadors. Referring to it as a "truffle", Europeans initially ate only the leaves, believing that the potato itself was poisonous. Only much later did they discover its pleasant taste and nutritional value.

Cultivation in England began in the mid-seventeenth century and then spread through Burgundy and the Netherlands, eventually reaching Germany where King Frederick II enthusiastically promoted the humble but versatile new crop. ❏

Frederick II of Germany overseeing the potato harvest

FINANCIAL CRISIS IN FRANCE

Versailles, May 10, 1774

France's Louis XV died of smallpox on May 10, 1774 at the age of 64. He was succeeded by his grandson, Louis XVI (b. August 23, 1754), under whose reign the Ancien Régime's social and political tensions intensified.

During most of his reign, Louis XV's leadership was compromised by the questionable advice of court favorites and mistresses. It was not until 1770 that he attempted to introduce productive political reforms. These did not, however, effectively address the core problems of privileges enjoyed by the aristocracy and the clergy, and the destabilizing presence of a highly unfair system of taxation. In theory, parliament should have helped redress some of these inequities. Unfortunately, for years parliament had been the private domain of the aristocracy and functioned chiefly as a forum for its own, as opposed to societies', grievances. Louis sought to address this issue by dissolving parliament in 1771. He also introduced cautious tax reforms and abolished the freedom of the grain trade to guard against grain speculation.

This policy of reform was reversed during the reign of Louis XVI. He dismissed Nicolas de Maupeou, who had been appointed chancellor in 1768, and restored the aristocratic parliament. In opposition, his reform minded finance minister, Anne-Robert-Jacques Turgot, Baron de Laune, tried to implement the progressive ideas of the physiocrats and to introduce the principle of supply and demand in pricing and wages. He then abolished the hated "corvée," (unpaid, compulsory labor demanded by a lord or king), as well as mandatory guild mem-

Louis XVI

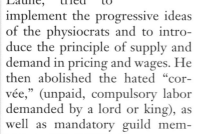

Marie Antoinette

bership and internal custom duties. In May of 1776, Louis XVI's parliament rejected Turgot's reforms and fired him. His successor, the Swiss banker, Jacques Necker, managed to publish the first national budget. In so doing, the extent of the benefits enjoyed by the aristocracy and the extravagant cost of running the royal household became common knowledge. Necker was subsequently removed from office. Exacerbating these problems occasioned by Louis's reactionary regime was the presence of his wife, Marie-Antoinette, whom Louis had married in 1770. This youngest daughter of the archduchess Maria Theresa quickly acquired the reputation of being frivolously extravagant and openly disdainful of the general populace. Her irresponsibly carefree life-style helped further tarnish the monarchy's reputation. Willfully ignorant of the living conditions of ordinary people, she came to represent all that the forces behind the French Revolution hated and ultimately overthrew. ❏

THIRTEEN COLONIES DECLARE THEIR

Philadelphia, July 4, 1776

The violent process of dissociation from the British Crown by the North American colonies started with the Declaration of Independence.

Two days after the decision of the Second Continental Congress to announce their independence from Britain, the Declaration of Independence was approved by the representatives of twelve colonies (New York gave its approval a few days later). The thirteen former British colonies—New Hampshire, Massachusetts, Rhode Island, Connecticut, New York, New Jersey, Pennsylvania, Delaware, Maryland, Virginia, North Carolina, South Carolina, and Georgia—formed the United States of America.

This proclamation was not only a morally audacious step but also a daring military and political enterprise. Left unsettled were the future internal structure of the

John Trumbull, *The Declaration of Independence*

COMMITTEE OF THE FOUNDING FATHERS

Point of Interest

The Continental Congress commissioned five men to draw up a document regarding the separation from the Great Britain.

In 1776 Benjamin Franklin (1706-1790), was sent to France as an ambassador at the court of Louis XVI (1776-1785). In 1778 he succeeded in persuading the French to sign the Treaty of Alliance with the Americans. In 1785 he became governor of Pennsylvania. He also became known for his scientific work, including the invention of the lightning rod.

The lawyer John Adams (1735-1826) was a delegate at the Continental Congress between 1774-1777. He later became the second President of the United States (1797-1801).

Robert Livingston from New Jersey and Roger Sherman from Connecticut were later also involved in drawing up the federal constitution. Livingston went on to become Governor of New Jersey.

Thomas Jefferson (1743-1826) was responsible for the initial draft. The son of wealthy landowner, he was a congressman between 1769 and 1775 and Governor of Virginia from 1779 to 1781. In 1785 he succeeded Franklin as the United States Ambassador in Paris and between 1789 and 1793 was foreign minister. He was elected president in 1801 and served two full terms. ❏

INDEPENDENCE

federal states and their relation to each other. There was also the question of slavery, a matter that affected the southern states, and that remained unanswered. Even the authors of the Declaration of Independence were skeptical about the successful outcome of their enterprise. Benjamin Franklin explained: "We must all hang together, or most assuredly, we shall all hang separately."

The War of Independence started on April 19, 1775, with the Battle of Lexington in Massachusetts. The British suffered losses as they did again at the Battle of Concord a little later. The second Continental Congress took place on May 10, 1775, in Philadelphia. On June 14, it unanimously elected George Washington as supreme commander and the following day the Continental Army was created out of the militia units. On January 10, 1776, Thomas Paine published his tract *Common Sense*, in which he explained the reasons why the colonies should become independent from Briatin and encouraged the colonies to form a republic.

A five-man committee, headed by Thomas Jefferson, was entrusted with drawing up a declaration that would explain the reasons for the separation from Britain. The emphasis on human rights, contained in it, can be traced to the Virginia Declaration of Rights, dating from June 12, 1776, originally drafted by George Mason, who was later instrumental in having the Bill of Rights added to the US Constitution. The Virginia Declaration of Rights was the first influential document to proclaim the natural rights of man, as formulated by John Locke and the philosophers of the Enlightenment. While the fight to secure basic rights was in reality a fight for freedom, the basic right and freedom to develop one's personality was of the utmost importance. This had to include additional rights such as religious freedom and the freedom of ideas, as well as the freedom of the press, which were all mentioned in the Virginia Declaration of Rights. This Declaration exerted great influence on European movements for independence and clearly inspired the French Declaration of the Rights of Man. ❏

Independence proclaimed in Philadelphia as a "freedom tree" is erected.

"LIFE, LIBERTY AND THE PURSUIT OF HAPPINESS"

Point of Interest

The Declaration of Independence

The American Declaration of Independence denied King George III of England the right to be king of the Americans because of numerous wrongdoings related to a fundamental belief in the concept of natural human rights. It begins::

"We hold these truths to be self-evident, that all men are created equal, that they are endowed by their Creator with certain unalienable Rights, that among these are Life, Liberty and the pursuit of Happiness.

That to secure these Rights, Governments are instituted among Men, deriving their just powers from the consent of the governed, That whenever any Form of Government becomes destructive of these ends, it is the Right of the People to alter or to abolish it, and to institute new Government, laying its foundation on such principles and organizing its powers in such form, as to them shall seem most likely to effect their Safety and Happiness.

Prudence, indeed, will dictate that Governments long established should not be changed for light and transient causes; and accordingly all experience hath shewn, that mankind are more disposed to suffer, while evils are sufferable, than to right themselves by abolishing the forms to which they are accustomed. But when a long train of abuses and usurpations, pursuing invariably the same Object evinces a design to reduce them under absolute Despotism, it is their right, it is their duty, to throw off such Government, and to provide new Guards for their security." ❏

Mozart's Precarious Career

Vienna, July 8, 1781

Wolfgang Amadeus Mozart (1756-1791), along with Joseph Haydn and Ludwig van Beethoven, was the major representative of Viennese classical music. He decided to give up a career as court musician because of its overly-demanding commitments. Disappointed by the rudeness and rough treatment of the Prince-Archbishop of Salzburg, Mozart quit his service and so became one of the first composers to be free of court obligations. This bold decision resulted in a loss of financial backing.

Mozart had caused a sensation as a child prodigy. His father, the musician Leopold Mozart, traveled extensively throughout Europe with Wolfgang and his elder sister Nannerl, impressing everyone who heard them with their musical talents. They spent time in many German cities, Paris, London, and Italy. As a result, Mozart became familiar with all of the important musical ideas of his time. He then integrated these into his own highly individual compositions. He began to compose at the age of five and at the age of nine he had already written his first opera, *Apollo and Hyacinth*.

In 1769 the then Prince-Bishop of Salzburg, Siegmund Christof von Schrattenbach, appointed the thirteen-year-old as his concertmaster. His activities in Salzburg were frequently interrupted by travels abroad. After Hieronymous von Colloredo was appointed Archbishop of Salzburg in 1772, Mozart's position became gradually untenable. In 1781 he drew his own conclusions and attempted to resign while in Vienna but was refused. In 1782 he married Constanze Weber, shortly after the performance of his opera *The Abduction from the Seraglio*. The following years were overshadowed by financial problems, but it was also the period during which he created most of his masterpieces. In addition to sonatas, symphonies, string quartets, and masses he also composed the operas *The Marriage of Figaro* (1786), *Don Giovanni* (1787), *Così fan tutte* (1790) and the *Magic Flute* (1791). Mozart's last work, the *Requiem*, remained unfinished.

Mozart's creativity was marked by melodic richness and a perfect balance between form and content, in particular in the instrumental genres. In his operas he distanced himself from the traditional fixed schematic representation by transforming his actors into characters. He also gave music greater weight through text-related expression, extending the key scenes, and emphasizing the ensemble. ❏

Stage design for Mozart's *Don Giovanni*.

America Gains its Independence

Yorktown, October 19, 1781

The War of Independence ended in favor of the American forces with the surrender of the British at Yorktown. In late summer of 1781 the British commander, General Charles Cornwallis, had made Yorktown on the Chesapeake Bay his base of operations.

1781 had been a low point for the Continental Army. New York was occupied by the British, whose fleet controlled most of the seaboard. It was at this dire point in the America's fortunes that the French committed themselves fully. Their fleet, half of which was in Newport with the other half in the West Indies, converged on Yorktown. By coordinating closely with George Washington and by taking advantage of the British Navy's tactical blunders, the French were able to hand England a major naval defeat and bring siege artillery into port where Washington's army was waiting. Washington conducted a textbook siege. Within three weeks, the British army of 8,000 men was forced to surrender to the combined American and French forces. Cornwallis raised the white flag on October 19 and formally surrendered to the American army. As the British troops laid down their weapons and marched out between ranks of American and French soldiers, the band played *The World Turned Upside Down*.

The surrender at Yorktown did not completely end the fighting. There were battles with loyalists in the Western Territories, but the British had lost their determination to continue the fight. Formal negotiations began in Paris in April of 1782, with Benjamin Franklin heading the American delegation. It was not until September 3, 1783 that the Treaty of Paris was signed in which Great Britain recognized the independence of the new republic. ❏

British surrender at Yorktown

THE VIENNESE CLASSICAL STYLE

Point of Interest

The period between 1770 and 1823 has been described as the era of Viennese classicism. Its greatest composers were Joseph Haydn, Wolfgang Amadeus Mozart, and Ludwig van Beethoven.

Haydn's words are characteristic of the era's musical ethos: "My language is understood throughout the world." He strove toward clear, natural expression; an artistically intricate, yet accessible, composition. Music was conceived to be universal and timeless. The emancipation of music from the task of entertaining a court helped create the era's innovative new musical forms. The richness of these new forms was in part linked to the vibrancy of its place of origin: at the time, Vienna was considered the political and cultural capital of the world, and its citizens were renowned as enthusiastic patrons of music. ❑

Mozart's autograph

ADAM SMITH AND "THE INVISIBLE HAND"

London, March 9, 1776

Scotland's Adam Smith (b.1723-d.1790) was a pioneering political economist. He published two influential treatises, *The Theory of Moral Sentiments* (1759), and *An Inquiry into the Nature and Causes of the Wealth of Nations* (1776).

His theories of free trade and of the mechanism of supply and demand as it affects commodity pricing served as formidable alternatives to the theories being propounded by the mercantilists and phyisiocrats.

Like the mercantilists, Smith supported the idea of "popular wealth." Unlike them, he believed that the accumulation of that wealth should not be sought through the strategies of state intervention, such as the use of protective tariffs and the creation of monopolies, but through the efforts of the individual pursuing his own self-interest in a free market economy. He argued that an economy based on this pursuit of individual self-interest created a healthy communal economy. He described this principal metaphorically as "the invisible hand." ❑

THE RUSSIAN ANNEXATION OF CRIMEA

Crimea, April 8, 1783

In 1783 the Russian Empress Catherine II oversaw the annexation of Crimea, the Tamam peninsula, and the region of Kuban. In doing so, Russia acquired vast, uninhabited, agricultural areas as well as strategically significant ports. The Ottoman Sultan Abdul Hamid I grudgingly accepted this annexation on January 8, 1784.

As a result of the first Russo-Turkish War (1768-1774), Crimea, which had been under Ottoman rule, became nominally independent. The last Khan of the Girai dynasty, which had ruled the Crimean peninsula since 1438, accepted the Russian proposal to take over the Khanate. He renounced the throne and was a given a pension by Russia. Renamed Tauris, Crimea became part of the Russian empire.

The new governor-general of Crimea, as well as another recently annexed region designated as New Russia, was a favorite of the Tsarina, Prince Grigori Aleksandrovich Potemkin (1739-1791). ❑

JAMES WATT AND THE STEAM ENGINE

Birmingham, 1781

The Scottish engineer and inventor James Watt (1736-1819) was the inventor of the steam engine whose widespread use, especially in the textile industry, was a major factor in the rise of the Industrial Revolution.

Inventors had experimented with steam power earlier: in 1690 in Marburg, Denis Papin had built a steam engine with pistons. The Englishman Thomas Newcomen further developed the technology in 1705 and in 1711. In 1769 Watt, who built the first practical, usable steam engine in 1769. One of his signature improvements to the technology was the addition of the planetary gear, which altered the up-and-down movement of the piston into a rotary motion, and then eliminated the resulting dead centers by adding a flywheel. This was the first time that rotary motion had been employed.

A Newcomen steam machine that had been brought to Watt's shop in Glasgow for repair was so improved by him that, compared to the conventional model, it consumed 75% less coal for the same output. Watt's separate condenser made the constant cooling of the cylinder unnecessary.

In January 1769 Watt, with the backing of the industrialist John Roebuck, registered a patent on a "new method to reduce the consumption of steam and fuel in steam engines." This was the birth of the low-pressure steam engine. In Watt's double-acting low-pressure steam engine, the steam acted on both sides of the piston.

When Roebuck went bankrupt, Watt entered into partnership with the manufacturer Matthew Boulton of the Soho foundry near Birmingham. In 1774 they set up the Boulton & Watt factory, which soon became extremely successful. In 1784 Watt improved his steam engine again. He introduced a centrifugal governor that kept the supply of steam constant. This last development brought the steam engine to its technical maturity. ❑

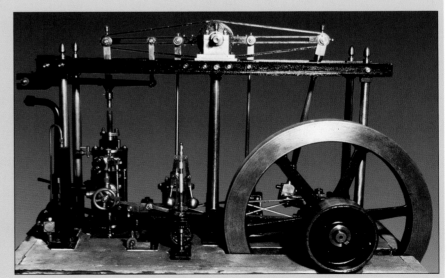

James Watt's steam engine

GEORGE WASHINGTON: THE FIRST PRESIDENT OF THE UNITED STATES

New York, April 30, 1789

On April 30, 1789, George Washington became the first President of the United States. The election took place in the eleven participant states (North Carolina and Rhode Island had not yet ratified the constitution). According to the Constitution as it was originally written each member of Electoral College cast two votes (only one of which could be for a candidate from his home state). All of the electors cast a vote for Washington, making him the only unanimously elected US president in history. John Adams, received the second largest number of votes and became vice-president.

Washington's election ushered in the age of presidential democracy, whose most distinctive aspect was the separation of powers, an idea derived from the French political theorist Montesquieu. This sharply contrasted with the parliamentary system of government in effect in England, wherein the legislative and executive function resided in one body.

George Washington was born on February 22, 1732, in Wakefield, Virginia, the son of a wealthy planter. Washington distinguished himself in the French Indian War, where as an aide to the British general Edward Braddock, he rallied the troops under his command after the general was killed in battle. At the outbreak of the Revolution in 1775 he was appointed

George Washington

general of the newly created Continental army by the Second Continental Congress. His army, consisting of regular troops and militia men, at no point exceeded 17,000 men. Despite several setbacks he succeeded in leading it to victory with the help of French troops. On October 19, General Cornwallis, commander in chief of the British army in North America, surrendered unconditionally to Washington at Yorktown. Two years later, Great Britain and the United States formally ended the war with the Treaty of Paris. In it Great Britain recognized its former colonies as "free, independent and sovereign." The area west of the Appalachians as far as the Mississippi went to the new nation, while Florida and the area west of the Mississippi were granted to Spain.

On December 23, 1783, he said farewell to his troops with the intent of retiring from public life.

Washington was called back into service to preside over the Philadelphia Convention that produced the Constitution. It was clear to the architects of the new nation that only Washington had the stature to unite a confederation of states whose interests did not fully coincide. The office of president as delineated in the Constitution was created largely with him in mind.

Washington's government succeeded in dealing with the national debt with the creation

THE BILL OF RIGHTS

Point of Interest

Of especial importance to the history of the United States and democratic movements throughout the world were the first ten amendments to the Constitution. Drafted by James Madison, they were intended to safeguard the rights of individuals from undue government intrusion. They came to be known as The Bill of Rights. They were ratified by the states in 1791.

Amendment I: Congress shall make no law respecting an establishment of religion, or prohibiting the free exercise thereof; or abridging the freedom of speech, or of the press; or the right of the people peaceably to assemble, and to petition the government for a redress of grievances.

Amendment II: A well regulated militia, being necessary to the security of a free state, the right of the people to keep and bear arms, shall not be infringed.

Amendment III: No soldier shall, in time of peace be quartered in any house, without the consent of the owner, nor in time of war, but in a manner to be prescribed by law.

Amendment IV: The right of the people to be secure in their persons, houses, papers, and effects, against unreasonable searches and seizures, shall not be violated, and no warrants shall issue, but upon probable cause, supported by oath or affirmation, and particularly describing the place to be searched, and the persons or things to be seized.

Amendment V: No person shall be held to answer for a capital, or otherwise infamous crime, unless on a presentment or indictment of a grand jury, except in cases arising in the land or naval forces, or in the militia, when in actual service in time of war or public danger; nor shall any person be subject for the same offense to be twice put in jeopardy of life or limb; nor shall be compelled in any criminal case to be a witness against himself, nor be deprived of life, liberty, or property, without due process of law; nor shall private property be taken for public use, without just compensation.

Amendment VI: In all criminal prosecutions, the accused shall enjoy the right to a speedy and public trial, by an impartial jury of the state and district wherein the crime shall have been committed, which district shall have been previously ascertained by law, and to be informed of the nature and cause of the accusation; to be confronted with the witnesses against him; to have compulsory process for obtaining witnesses in his favor, and to have the assistance of counsel for his defense.

Amendment VII: In suits at common law, where the value in controversy shall exceed twenty dollars, the right of trial by jury shall be preserved, and no fact tried by a jury, shall be otherwise reexamined in any court of the United States, than according to the rules of the common law.

Amendment VIII: Excessive bail shall not be required, nor excessive fines imposed, nor cruel and unusual punishments inflicted.

Amendment IX: The enumeration in the Constitution, of certain rights, shall not be construed to deny or disparage others retained by the people.

Amendment X: The powers not delegated to the United States by the Constitution, nor prohibited by it to the states, are reserved to the states respectively, or to the people. ❑

THE MONTGOLFIER BALLOON

France, 1783

of a national bank and putting national defense on a firm basis. He also was faced with organizing the executive branch to administer the government. A Cabinet was created with departments of war, state and finance, and later a postmaster-general and attorney general were added. The key cabinet members under Washington were Thomas Jefferson, Secretary of State, and Alexander Hamilton, Secretary of the Treasury. In 1789, in accordance with the Constitution, a Supreme Court was created with thirteen District Courts under it.

In 1790 it was decided to create a new capital, which would come to bear his name, on the banks of the Potomac river. The city's plan was designed by the French architect, Pierre Charles l'Enfant. On October 13, 1792, Washington laid the foundation stone for a new presidential residence, but he was not destined to occupy it. On March 4, 1797, he retired after two terms in office. He died on December 14, 1799, in Mount Vernon in Virginia. On October 1, 1800, Washington's successor, President John Adams, moved into the White House on Pennsylvania Avenue. ❑

The hot air balloon of the Montgolfier brothers made it possible for people to fly for the first time.

The age of manned hot-air balloon flight began on October 15, 1783. The 26-year-old physicist Jean-François Pilâtre de Rozier stayed aloft for four and a half minutes in a tethered balloon. The first free flight took place on November 21, when de Rozier and François Laurent d'Arlandes guided their Montgolfier balloon to a safe landing just east of Paris after a 25-minute flight.

Instead of using hot air like the Montgolfier brothers, the physicist Jacques Alexandre César Charles used hydrogen gas for his balloon, which had a diameter of 13 feet. He launched it above Paris on August 27, 1783. The silk fabric of the balloon was impregnated with rubber solution, and the lift was provided by the hydrogen in the balloon. The unmanned balloon landed near the village of Gonesse where the terrified farmers destroyed it with pitchforks. On December 1, 1783, César Charles and Nicolas-Louis Robert completed their first free flight. Two hours after taking off their balloon landed near Nesle. In honor of its inventor, the hydrogen-filled balloon was called a "charlière." ❑

A Montgolfier balloon in flight, 18th century

THE DISCOVERY AND SETTLEMENT OF AUSTRALIA

January 26, 1788

On January 26, 1788 six British warships, under the command of Captain Arthur Phillip, landed in Botany Bay by the shores of the future city of Sydney. On board were 732 convicts who were to be resettled there along with a troop of marines. The British Parliament had appointed Phillip as governor of its colony New South Wales, which would be renamed Australia in 1814 by the British explorer Matthew Flinders.

The ships had landed on what contemporary cartographers re-

ferred to as the "fifth continent." The unofficial name of this continent had been determined long before it was discovered. As far back as the sixteenth century cartographers surmised the existence of a large "southern land," which they named *Terra australis incognita*. On November 26, 1642, the Dutch explorer Abel Janszoon Tasman came close to this new territory during his discovery of the island of Tasmania, which he named Van Diemen's Land. On a second voyage he

traveled along the west coast of Australia, but the first European to explore the Australian coast in a systematic manner was James Cook in 1770.

At first the British crown was not interested in this newly discovered land. It was only when the French showed an interest in the islands in the Pacific and after the loss of their colonies in North America that the British became concerned and reoriented their colonial policy in that direction. ❑

British convicts in Australia working under guard

During the course of the French Revolution human rights are proclaimed. Von Béricourt, *The Peace Tree,* watercolor

Two political events in the Old and New Worlds stand out in the second half of the eighteenth century: the movement for North American independence with the creation of the United States of America in 1776, and the French Revolution in 1789. Both events had their origin in the philosophical ideas of the Age of Enlightenment, the great far-reaching and revolutionary cultural and intellectual movement of the eighteenth century.

The Enlightenment was the result and culmination of two centuries of secularization and of rationalism in philosophy and science. These changes entailed new perceptions of God and humanity's place in the world. Even though the Enlightenment did not have a unified philosophical system, it nevertheless became the unifying ideology for the intellectual elite of Europe. Initially also supported by the nobility, the Enlightenment was a primarily a bourgeois movement of emancipation to achieve the so-cio-political objectives of freedom and equality. But it went far beyond this, playing a decisive part in the emergence of the political awareness of the working class.

REASON DETERMINES MAN'S CONDITION

The central aspect of the enlightenment was its focus on reason, seen as the touchstone of knowledge and the means of providing an explanation for everything in the world. A tenet of the Enlightenment was the conviction that man had the ability to improve himself.

Enlightenment thinkers displaced God from the center of their philosophical systems with the deists going so far as to subordinate God to reason. For the first time philosophy was in prime opposition to Christianity. At the same time, the Enlightenment introduced radical political and social changes. Unlimited optimism and an enthusiastic, almost naive belief in progress replaced the previous faith in authority and tradition. Superstition and ignorance were the dark forces holding back humanity, and the solution was universal education. The dictum was education through self-discipline, and with it self-determination. In its attempt to spread this philosophical doctrine, the Enlightenment thinkers encouraged each individual to recognize and perceive his rights (women being for the most part left out of the equation) while claiming the right to share in decisions and involvement in public and political life.

In his teachings on natural law, the English philosopher, John Locke, presented as unconditional and inalienable every man's right to life, liberty, and the free enjoyment of his property. To safeguard these natural rights, people enter into social contracts in which they commit themselves to build an institution (the state) that will provide them the necessary protection. Locke's concept of a social contract was based on the premise that the resulting state authority would rest on the express approval or at least the tacit permission of the citizens.

Upon the principles that the state exists for the protection of its citizenry and lacked legitimate authority to abrogate basic freedoms, Locke founded the concept of human rights, which are expressed in the Declaration of Independence in the United States in 1776 and the Rights of Man in France in 1789. His ideas also gave rise to the political liberalism of the nineteenth and twentieth centuries.

SEPARATION OF POWERS AND SOVEREIGNTY OF THE PEOPLE

The concept of the separation of powers and of government's responsibility to parliament goes back to Charles de Secondat, Baron de la Brède et de Montesquieu. Based on the observation that freedom is less the result of particular moral qualities than the result of the restriction of the powers of the state, Montesquieu built the following model: the power of the state was to be divided into a legislature to write laws, an executive to implement them, and a judiciary to rule upon cases arising from these laws. The exercise of these separate powers had to be in the hands of different bodies or individuals. This was the most effective guarantee of mutual control. By limiting the accumulation of power of any one branch of government, checks were paced on its potential misuse.

The Geneva philosopher Jean-Jacques Rousseau pursued another course in his proposal for a political partnership between the people and the state. He developed a model of democracy that attempted to link the integration of the individual in society to the values of freedom and equality. Rousseau's ideas were based on a democracy practiced directly by the people. All citizens were equal, while at the same time the lawmakers and government were one and the same. The right of the majority came before that of the individual. Decisions were made according to the "general will" (*volonté générale*).

In the German-speaking language areas it was the philosopher Immanuel Kant of Königsberg who promoted the importance of a responsible government. His political theory was based on the creation of a "civil society" that would give the individual citizen the highest degree possible of freedom. The limitations of the freedom of each individual were determined by its compatibility with that of others. The legal system independent of the state under which a civil society lives is the guarantee of this freedom and the safeguard against its misuse.

THE EMANCIPATION OF THE NEW WORLD

The American Revolution was precipitated by the refusal of the thirteen colonies to pay taxes to their mother country, Great Britain, without enjoying the rights of political representation. The economic and financial conflict subsequently embraced fundamental political questions. In contrast to the French Revolution, the North American revolution was not triggered by economic oppression or social hardship, but by George III's encroachment on the vested rights of the colonists and his reluctance to grant them the protections instituted by English Common Law. The American Declaration of Independence formulated the people's right to resist any unjust form of government.

The United States Constitution drawn up in 1787 brought together the tradition of natural rights as formulated by John Locke and the American tradition of self-government. The Constitution and Declaration of Independence combined the liberal ideas of the British tradition of freedom (Magna Carta, 1215, Habeas Corpus Act, 1679) with the Locke's fundamental principles of democratic equality and political self-determination. These principles were fully articulated in the Bill of Rights (1791), the first ten amendments to the Constitution.

THE COLLAPSE OF THE ANCIEN RÉGIME

Important among the multiplicity of reasons that led to the French Revolution was the coincidence of a newly formed, rationalist view of society with a loss of confidence in the absolutist rule of the Ancien Régime. Monarchical authority was further shaken by economic crises and repeated crop failures, and the fact that the nobility and clergy were not prepared to give up any of their privileges.

The French Revolution was not a united movement. It comprised a dense tangle of several revolutionary movements that sometimes overlapped or sometime moved in opposite directions. Under the banner of "liberty, equality, fraternity," a political and constitutional revolution took place in France, supported by the middle classes (the constitutional monarchy in 1791 and the Republic in 1792). In addition there was a people's revolution (the storming of the Bastille in 1789, the *sans-culottes* uprising in 1793), originating in a politicized urban lower middle-classes as well as unrest in the provinces (the Reign of Terror in 1789, the counter-revolutionary uprising in Vendée in 1793).

In the end the French Revolution became the victim of its own radicalism (the Jacobin Terror 1793/94). Then Napoleon returned suddenly from Egypt, overthrew the Directory in the coup of 18 Brumaire of Year VIII (November 9, 1799 in the new calendar of the Revolution), and proclaimed himself First Consul.

The French Revolution destroyed the old class system of the Ancien Régime, but the conditions of the urban population and the peasants hardly changed. The main beneficiary was the politically and economically stronger middle-class or bourgeoisie. Nevertheless, the French Revolution's slogans of freedom created a permanent political awareness that would play an important in the national struggles for freedom in the nineteenth century.

THE ENLIGHTENED ABSOLUTISM OF FREDERICK II

In Prussia, the Enlightenment took the form of enlightened absolutism. The prototype of the enlightened absolutist ruler was the Prussian king Frederick II, the Great. Frederick called himself the first servant of the state. Although he believed that monarchy was a divine right, he also believed that an enlightened monarch had obligations towards his subjects.

Frederick II, who had always been interested in the arts and literature, was convinced of the benevolent effect of the monarchy on his subjects. It was, however, a distinctive feature of Frederick's enlightened absolutism that, on the one hand, it increased the individual citizen's confidence in the certainty of the law, on the other hand, it regulated the personal freedom of the individual through an expanded bureaucracy. In the end, the welfare of the individual was subordinate to the good of the state.

It was also Frederick's aim to maintain and expand the power of the Prussian state. It was for this reason that the enlightened monarch fought three wars in which heavy losses were suffered. These wars enabled Prussia to become a major European power but also sharply limited the rights of its citizens. ❏

Enlightened despot, Frederick II, King of Prussia.

THE LAST MEETING OF THE ESTATES-GENERAL

Versailles, May 5, 1789

The convening of the Estates-General at Versailles on May 5, 1789 was King Louis XVI's last attempt to remedy France's severe financial crisis.

The king had previously tried to avert the bankruptcy that threatened the country by calling a meeting of notables on February 22, 1787. But they refused to approve the plans for reform drawn up by his finance minister Charles Alexandre de Calonne.

There were only two possible ways of resolving the problem of the burden of debt, which was triple France's annual revenue: declaring the state bankrupt, or subjecting all citizens to an income tax. But the 144 representatives of the privileged estates refused to give up their tax exemption.

King Louis XVI

As a last resort the king convened the Estates-General. The last time the Estates-General had met had been in 1614. Upon opening the session, the king delivered an address urging the people's representatives to find solutions to the problems affecting the country's finances. Exhorting the Estates to find a way out of the crisis was the banker Jacques Necker. Necker had been dismissed as finance minister in 1781, but Louis recalled him in 1788. Necker explained the country's financial situation to the assembly and called upon the first two Estates to "make sacrifices."

There had been fierce discussions before the session opened concerning the election and composition of the Estates-General. Finally, on January 24, 1789, Louis XVI announced election rules that doubled the number of votes of the Third Estate.

Some 291 clerics, 270 nobles and 578 members of the Third Estate were selected. The greater number of delegates given to the Third Estate was soon revealed as a ruse. Under the rules the king laid down each Estate was given an equal vote, so the combination of clergy and aristocracy

King Louis XVI opens the meeting of the Estates-General in Versailles

was bound to prevail. The complicated voting system based on ancient administrative districts that dated back to the thirteenth century gave the middle classes within the Estates-General an advantage compared to the peasants. Only French males above the age of 25 who had a fixed abode and paid taxes had the right to vote. This meant that about 90 percent of adults did not have the right to vote.

After some six weeks of fruitless debates about technical questions, the representatives of the Third Estate decided to form a new national assembly that appropriated for itself the responsibilities of governance. The king's attempt to marshal the resources of the nation behind him had backfired. The middle class had found the vehicle it needed to wrest the power from the established orders. ❑

BACKGROUND TO THE MEETING OF THE ESTATES-GENERAL OF 1789

Point of Interest

Pre-revolutionary France was controlled by an assembly of privileged bodies, the structure of which was based on the Estates. The two politically privileged classes in France, the First and Second Estates, were the clergy with around 12,000 priests, monks, and nuns, and an aristocracy that comprised about 350,000 members. There were subtle differences within these classes, based on power and influence, but more than 90 percent of the population, which formed the Third Estate, had no political rights at all.

The clergy enjoyed special privileges. They formed a class of their own with their own administration and their own legal system. The duties of the clergy included the administration of baptism, marriage, and death registers. The high clergy, 18 archbishops and 121 bishops, were all nobles, as were most abbots and capitulars. The ordinary clergy were of humbler origin.

The nobility owned more than one-fifth of the land. High-ranking officers in the military were drawn from the ranks of the nobility, which filled all high Church offices and top administration posts as well. The nobility had its own hierarchy. The upper stratum of the aristocracy included some 4,000 people. A non-hereditary nobility was in charge of running the administrative and legal systems as well as the thirteen Parliaments of the realm, which functioned as High Courts. The landed gentry depended on the feudal tributes exacted from their peasants.

All those not of the nobility made up the Third Estate. The majority—over twenty million people—lived in the villages. Most peasants were tenants. It was the bourgeoisie, a non-noble propertied class that would drive the revolutionary impulses of the Third Estate. ❑

A peasant carrying a nobleman and priest on his back

THE STORMING OF THE BASTILLE

Paris, July 14, 1789

When a crowd of workers, merchants, and citizens stormed the medieval fortress that at that time served as a state prison, the hitherto "constitutional revolution" slipped from the hands of the bourgeoisie into the hands of the people.

The storming of the Bastille occurred on July 14, 1789. On that day, at 5 PM, the ill-defended Bastille, which was considered the symbol of despotism, surrendered. On the morning of July 14, a crowd of the people had occupied the arsenal (the Hôtel des Invalides) without meeting any resistance and had taken about 32,000 guns from the armory. The pamphleteer and journalist, Camille Desmoulins, who was an eyewitness, wrote: "As soon as they had armed themselves the people made their way to storm the Bastille." The idea of storming the Bastille came spontaneously, being a reaction to the concentration of troops around Paris and the dismissal of the popular finance minister Jacques Necker on July 11.

A total of 83 people were killed and 88 injured during the siege. The governor of the prison, Bernard René, Marquis de Launey, as well as four officers and three Swiss guards, were slain by the angry crowds. On the following day Louis XVI announced to the National Assembly in Versailles that he was withdrawing his troops. On July 16 he returned Necker to office, and on July 17 he reentered Paris, wearing a tri-color cockade as a sign of the "eternal alliance between the monarch and the people." The tricolor showed the colors of Paris (blue and red), with the white of the Bourbons in between them.

The Tennis Court Oath: In the prior month on June 20, the representatives of the Third Estate had gathered in the *Salle du Jeu de Paume* (the king's tennis court) and had sworn an oath to establish a new constitution for the nation. This was in reaction to the announcement by the government on June 17 of the closing of their former assembly hall after the majority of the clergy and the nobility had joined forces with the Third Estate.

On June 23, the representatives of the Estates were called to a "royal session." After the monarch submitted a reform program that would have laid the foundation for a constitutional monarchy (though it still included the nobility's privileges), the first two Estates followed the king out of the hall, but the Third Estate remained seated. Even under the threat of force, the people's representatives continued their meeting. Honoré Gabriel Riqueti, Comte de Mirabeau, made their position clear to the king's representative: "Tell those who sent you here that we are here because the people want us to be, and only the force of the bayonet will get us out of here."

The end of the feudal system: On August 4, the National Assembly put an end to all privileges—and thus to the feudal system—in a night session in the Palace of Versailles. The resulting decree was issued on August 11, stating: "The National Assembly … decrees that it abolishes the feudal system and that among the rights and dues, all those originating in or representing real or personal serfdom or personal servitude shall be abolished without indemnification." The provisions regarding the right to own land meant that in practice many peasants who were too poor to pay compensation to their landlords changed from unpaid to paid laborers.

Declaration of the Rights of Man and of the Citizen: On August 26, the National Assembly approved the *Declaration of the Rights of Man and of the Citizen*. It reaffirmed that the civil right to freedom already existed independently of the state. The National Assembly regarded the participation of the politically active citizen (*citoyen* as opposed to the inactive *bourgeois*) in public affairs as a guarantee of civil rights. Freedom and equality were constitutional rights.

Though the boundaries of freedom were not defined, it was agreed that the freedom of the individual should only be bounded where the freedom of another starts. The concept of equality was more clearly defined: it required equality of all citizens before the law, in access to public office, and in taxation.

Louis XVI in Paris: These decrees went too far in the eyes of the king, and even the right of veto that the people's representatives gave the king did not change his hostile attitude. A serious worsening of the food supply and the fear of a conspiracy by the aristocracy led to the march of 7,000 proletariat women on Versailles on October 5, an action that was perhaps not planned but was certainly supported by the influential leaders of the party, namely Louis Philippe Joseph, Duc d'Orléans and Marie Joseph Motier, Marquis de Lafayette, the leader of the national guard. The royal family was invited to move to Paris and the National Assembly accompanied them. The king moved into the Tuileries; he had put himself under the protection of the Revolution. ❑

Storming of the Bastille

Camille Desmoulins

Comte de Mirabeau

Declaration of the Rights of Man and of the Citizen.

THE ISOLATION OF REVOLUTIONARY FRANCE

Paris, June 20, 1791

The unsuccessful attempt by King Louis XVI to leave his country marked a turning point in the French Revolution.

After months of preparations, the royal family eventually succeeded in fleeing Paris. But on June 21, as they arrived in Varennes in northeastern France, an observant postmaster prevented them from reaching the border. This unsuccessful attempt by Louis XVI to leave the country was seen as evidence that he wanted to form an alliance with armies in other countries against his own people.

Louis XVI had, in fact, intended to join the army of the royalist general François Claude Amour, Marquis de Bouillé, go to Metz, and from there join up with the Austrian army in Belgium. That would have enabled him to return victoriously to Paris, abolish the National Assembly and the revolutionary clubs, and reestablish his absolutist rule.

The king's attempt to flee considerably weakened the position of the constitutional monarchists, who had supported him. They had recently lost their leader with the death of Honoré Gabriel Riqueti, Comte de Mirabeau on April 2, 1791. After his death a triumvirate made up of Antoine Barnave, Adrien Duport, and Alexandre Théodore Victor de Lameth had had some success in mediating between the aristocracy and the Third Estate. They were all members of the Jacobin Club, named for its meeting place in the Dominican monastery in the rue St Jacques. Its symbol was the Jacobin bonnet. Trying to expand its influence, the triumvirate enlisted the aid of Marie Joseph Motier, Marquis de Lafayette, the commander of the National Guard. This swing to the right resulted in a center-right majority in the National Assembly and the decree of a series of conservative laws.

Now the Jacobin barrister Maximilien de Robespierre demanded—albeit in vain—that the king be punished. In response the conservatives, led by Barnave, left the Club on 16 July. They then formed the Club des Feuillants, named after their meeting-point, the abbey of Notre-Dame-des-Feuillants. The name *feuillants* became synonymous with the terms 'aristocrats' and 'royalists.' The followers of Lafayette and those in favor of a constitutional monarchy also joined the club. Of the original 2,400 members, just under 500 remained in the Jacobin Club, of which only six were members of the National Assembly.

Meanwhile the radical Club of the Cordeliers—including Jean-Paul Marat and Georges Jacques Danton—seized the initiative. This Club and members of other secret societies called for a public meeting on the Champ de Mars. When at the instigation of the conservative majority of the National Assembly, a state of emergency was imposed, Lafayette ordered his National Guard to fire on the unarmed crowd. About 50 people were killed and several hundreds injured.

On September 3, 1791, the National Assembly approved a new constitution. The king and his cabinet were its rather weak executives. The National Assembly constituted the legislative body. It was permanent and composed of only one chamber. Its representatives were elected di-

Revolutionary poster

rectly according to their property qualifications (based on property and income), with the result that the lower economic stratum of society was excluded. The National Assembly had the final say over war and peace. The division of France into 83 departments established in 1789 remained in force. The king could not veto the actions of the National Assembly but could suspend it.

On October 1, the newly elected legislative National Assembly held its first session. Of

CONSTITUTION FOR THE KINGDOM OF POLAND

Warsaw, May 3, 1791

Poland was the first country in Europe to have a written constitution. On May 3, 1791 the Polish parliament (*Sejm Wielki*) adopted a constitution consisting of eleven articles. It established the separation of powers: the king and the state council formed the executive body, while the parliament, consist-ing of two chambers, was the legislative body. The throne became hereditary possession of the House of Wettin, thereby ending the country's tradition of electing its monarch, a situation that had been in effect since 1573.

In addition to the five ministers appointed by the king, the cabinet included two state secretaries, the catholic primate of Poland and the marshal of the *Sejm* (the president of the parliament). This body was subject to the control of the parliament, exercised through four committees for the main political areas.

The special constitutional position of the Grand Duchy of Lithuania was tacitly removed, and the two countries were formally united in 1791.

Although Poland had lost almost thirty percent of its territory to its more powerful neighbors in 1772, the country experienced a period of economic and cultural revival. ❑

THE CANNONADE OF VALMY

Valmy, France, September 20, 1792

As an eyewitness at the Battle of Valmy, the great German writer, Johann Wolfgang von Goethe wrote:

"Great consternation descended upon the army. They had thought of nothing else that morning but to ... skewer the French ... I usually warmed up the crowds with a few words, but this time I said: 'Today a new era in the history of the world will begin, and you will be able to say that you were there." ❑

The Cannonade of Valmy. On November 6, 1792 General Charles François Dumouriez defeated the Austrian army.

the 745 members, 264 belonged to the Club des Feuillants that henceforth represented the "right." The center consisted of 345 parliamentarians, "loyal to the constitution," while the "left" was represented by the 136 liberal members, known as the "*Girondistes*" because many of them came from the Gironde region.

A good month earlier, on August 27, 1791, the Prussian king Friedrich Wilhelm II and the Austrian Emperor Leopold II had met at Schloss Pillnitz and declared that the French king was not to be harmed or removed from power, and that this was a matter of fundamental importance to all the monarchist nations in Europe. With this Declaration of Pillnitz, they laid the foundation for the first anti-revolutionary coalition in Europe. In France this was seen as a declaration of war.

On April 20, 1792, the National Assembly declared war on Austria, with whom Prussia immediately sided, thus forming the First Coalition. An immediate cause was the refusal of Francis II, Leopold's successor, to disband the French emigrant army

gathering in Koblenz.

Underlying the triggering events were very real tensions between revolutionary France and the neighboring states, ruled by authoritarian monarchs. The declaration made by the Prussian general Karl Wilhelm Ferdinand, Duke of Brunswick, on July 25 clearly expresses the monarchist attitude. He announced that he "would take terrible revenge and give Paris a military execution and completely destroy it," if a single hair on Louis XVI's head was touched.

On April 28, the French advanced into Belgium but the army

was disorganized and lacked morale. Almost a third of the officers had left France. There was a shortage of weapons and ammunition, as well as an absence of discipline. The commanding generals, the Comte de Rochambeau and Marquis de Lafayette, resigned. But meanwhile in Paris 50,000 men were drafted into the regular army and 34,000 into volunteer battalions. Command of the army was handed over to Charles François Dumouriez. He engaged the Austrians at the Battle of Valmy, also known as the Cannonade of Valmy, on September 20. The French forced the Prussian and

Austrian troops to retreat after a fierce artillery duel. It was the turning point of the war.

With the *Marseillaise*, first sung by volunteers from Marseilles, the soldiers had a rousing war song. Although the composer of the tune remains unknown, the lyrics were written in the night of April 24–25, 1792, in Strasbourg by an officer in the corps of engineers, Claude Joseph Rouget de Lisle (1760-1836); he first called it *Le Chant de guerre de l'armée du Rhin* (*The Battle Hymn of the Army of the Rhine*). His song became France's national anthem in 1879. ❑

RENEWED CLASSICISM IN THE ARTS

Point of Interest

The classicism of the eighteenth and nineteenth centuries sought to revive Antiquity's ideals of order and harmony.

In 1791, the architect Carl Gotthard Langhals completed the building of the Brandenburg Gate in Berlin. Along with Karl Friedrich Schinkel, Langhals was one of Germany's leading neoclassical architects. Typical of this classical revival were the strict, simple purity of its buildings and their symmetrically structured facades.

In France architects such as Jacques-Ange Gabriel (builder of the Petit Trianon in Versailles, 1762-1764) and Jacques-German Soufflot (designer of the Church

of Sainte Geneviève and the Panthéon in Paris, 1764-1790) were the first architects to revive the classical style of antiquity laying the groundwork for the development of neo-classicism.

The newly rediscovered interest in Greek and Roman antiquity was inspired by the work of the German archaeologist and art historian, Joachim Winckelmann (1717-1768). In his writings he redefined Greek art, referring to its "noble simplicity and quiet grandeur," and the classical ideal of beauty that was also to exert its influence on the plastic arts and literature. ❑

Brandenburg Gate, Berlin (from a color print, 1825)

THE OVERTHROW OF THE FRENCH MONARCHY

Paris, August 10, 1792

The storming of the Tuileries heralded the end of the monarchy in France. The royalists and *Feuillants* were no longer represented in the National Convention.

On August 10, 1792, the radical *Sans-Culottes* (so-named because they did not wear the breeches of the upper class) organized the storming of the Tuileries, the residence of Louis XVI. The military failures at the beginning of the First Coalition War and the king's unremitting policy of obstructing the decisions of the National Assembly had roused popular indignation.

The National Guard posted in front of Tuileries went over to the rebels, but the Swiss guards stationed inside opened fire on the demonstrators once they enter the courtyard The fighting lasted for two hours until the crowd triumphed and massacred the remaining surviving Swiss guards and the Tuileries staff.

This act of violence brought about the end of the party of the *Feuillants*, which represented the aristocracy and the haute-bourgeoisie. A new political force emerged, the so-called passive citizens, the workers and small shopkeepers, who until then had been excluded from political decision-making. They demanded the abolition of the monarchy.

The day after the assault on the Tuileries, the legislative National Assembly took the royal family into custody and called for the convocation of a National Convention proclaiming: "The holder of executive power [King Louis XVI] is temporarily relieved of his authority until the National Convention has decided on the measures it deems necessary to safeguard the sovereignty of the people and the implementation of Freedom and Equality."

In preparation for the convention it abolished the property qualifications for voting in elections. The franchise was extended to all French males "21 years old, to have lived for one year in one's place of residence, to live off one's income or the earnings of work, and not to belong to the servants' class."

The Convention was called into session on September 21. It met, however, in an atmosphere of violence and chaos. Rumors of invading armies combined with food shortages and anti-clerical feeling had exploded into widespread rioting in early September. The violence was directed primarily at prisoners and priests, who were suspected of wanting to join with foreign invaders in restoring the monarchy. About 1,100 prisoners were murdered, more than half of whom were ordinary criminals, more than 300 were priests who had refused to take the oath on the constitution, 150 were members of the aristocracy, and about 50 were incarcerated Swiss guards.

A provisional government was established. Besides five ministers of the *Girondist* party, it included the radical Georges Jacques Danton as minister of justice. Danton and Jean-Paul Marat, the spokesman of the *sans-culottes*, had been the organizers of the September massacres.

In its first sitting the National Convention abolished the monarchy. September 22 became Day One in the first year of the new Republican calendar. ❑

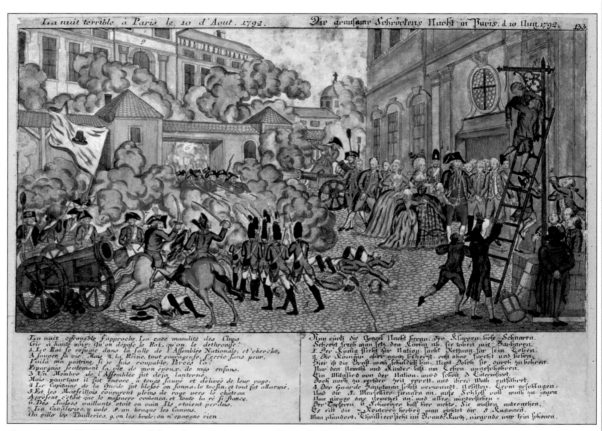

The Parisians with the support of the volunteers from Marseilles and Brittany storm the king's residence, the Tuileries Palace

THE GUILLOTINE

Paris, January 21, 1793

The guillotine owes its origin and name to the physician and politician Joseph Ignace Guillotin (1738-1814), a deputy in the first National Assembly.

On October 10, 1789, he proposed to the National Assembly the use of a mechanical contraption to carry out the death penalty in a more "humane" way, and one that in addition would apply to all social classes. Based on the advice presented to the National Assembly on March 7, 1792, by Antoine Louis, secretary to the Académie Royale de Chirurgie in Paris, the introduction of a mechanical decapitation machine in France was prescribed on March 25, 1792. On August 21 the guillotine was used for the first, but not the last, time. ❑

THE REIGN OF TERROR AND THE DEATH OF LOUIS XVI

Paris, January 21, 1793

The execution of Louis XVI signaled the radicalization of the French Revolution. As a result France cut itself off from all the monarchies of Europe.

On January 21, 1793, Louis XVI, the King of France, was beheaded in the Place de la Révolution (subsequently the Place de la Concorde). According to the indictment, the accused, named as Louis Capet and deprived of his title, was charged with preventing the sittings of the Third Estate and conspiring with foreign countries, among other things.

At first the *Girondists* who represented the haute-bourgeoisie tried to prevent the trial. It was only the discovery of incriminating documents during a search of the royal apartments on November 20 that overcame their objections. At that point it was impossible to ignore the arguments of the militantly anti-royalist Mountain party (*Montagnards*), led by Louis de Saint-Just. He declared on November 13: "I for my part cannot

see a middle way; this man must govern or die…"

After several hearings during which the king was interrogated, the Convention put three questions to the deputies: "Was Louis Capet guilty of conspiracy against public freedom and attacks on national security? Should the verdict

agreed by the nation be put to the vote? What punishment should be imposed on him?"

The king's guilt was unanimously agreed upon (with 14 abstentions) on January 15. On the evening of January 16 voting on the sentence started: 361 deputies voted in favor of the death penalty. A motion for a reprieve was rejected by the Convention by 380 votes to 310.

The execution was carried out with the enthusiastic participation of the populace. When the executioner showed the king's head to the crowd, the people danced round the guillotine in excitement. One of the direct consequences was, however, the widening of the First Coalition War. The British government expelled the French ambassador, causing the National Convention to declare war on both the Netherlands and Britain. On March 7, France also declared war on Spain.

On March 10, the National Convention set up a Revolution-

ary Tribunal against the decisions of which there was no appeal. Antoine Quentin Fouquier-Tinville, the public prosecutor, became the embodiment of legally sanctioned Terror. On April 6, the Committee of Public Safety (*Comité du Salut Public*), which had almost unlimited plenary powers, was founded as

the executive body of the National Convention.

On July 13 a *Girondist* sympathizer, Marie Anne Charlotte de Corday d'Armont, stabbed Jean-Paul Marat to death in his bath. In his newspaper *L'Ami du peuple*, Marat had demanded the death of all the leading enemies of the Revolution to achieve liberty, equality and fraternity.

On July 27 Robespierre took over the presidency of the Com-

Georges Jacques Danton

mittee of Public Safety and also, on August 22, of the National Convention. The Reign of Terror started on September 17 with the decree of a "Law against the Suspects." On October 31, twenty leading *Girondists* were executed. At the beginning of October 1793 there were about 2,400 people held in captivity. By December 21, 1793 the number had gone up to 4,525. On October 16, Queen Marie-Antoinette, was also beheaded.

On April 5, 1794, the former justice minister Georges Jacques Danton was executed together with his supporters, who had been imprisoned with him. They had called for the end of the Reign of Terror and through this "conciliatory act" they had become "suspects" in the eyes of the Committee of Public Safety.

This paved the way for the dictatorship of Robespierre, who preached terror as an expression of

the highest virtue: "Without virtue Terror is calamitous, without Terror virtue is powerless." On June 10, 1794, an even stricter Terror Law was passed. It abolished the preliminary investigation of the accused as well as their defense and the questioning of witnesses. All that was needed was a "proof of moral guilt." Now "heads began to fall like roof-tiles," to quote the words of Fouquier-Tinville. Between June 11 and July 27, 1,376

Maximilien de Robespierre

people were executed in Paris compared to "only" 1,251 in the previous twelve months. In all, 16,594 people were guillotined in France for political reasons between March 1793 and August 1794; in addition 20,000 people died as a result of mass executions by shooting or mass drowning, or as a result of famine and deprivation.

On July 27 Robespierre and his followers were overthrown. On the previous day, Robespierre had announced the "extermination of the conspirators against freedom." But because he did not mention any names, many felt threatened, including some of his earlier supporters such as François Fouché and Paul François Jean Nicolas, Vicomte de Barras. As a result they joined the moderates to save themselves.

On July 28 Robespierre, Saint-Just and twenty of their supporters were beheaded without trial. ❑

Execution of King Louis XVI at the Place de la Révolution

THE PARTITION AND DISSOLUTION OF POLAND

St. Petersburg, October 24, 1795

After a second and third partition by the Great Powers, Poland ceased to exist.

On October 24, 1795, Prussia became a signatory of the Partition Treaty of Poland that had already been negotiated between Russia and Austria on January 3 of that year. With this third partition, the independent state of Poland completely disappeared from the map of Europe. But the Polish question remained on the agenda.

The beginning of the end for the Polish State was its new constitution drawn up on May 3. Poland had been politically marginalized for a long time; it now became a commonwealth, capable of negotiating with other countries. This stirred up the opposition of its neighbors. Tsarina Catherine II of Russia called the large Polish landowners to a conference in St Petersburg where they agreed to form a confederation in opposition to the Polish Constitution. The plan was announced on May 14, 1792, in the border town of Targowica. On May 18, 1792, Russian troops entered Poland and after two months defeated the Polish army, under the command of Prince Joseph Poniatowski, the king's nephew, and General Tadeusz Kosciuszko. The constitution of 1791 was abolished.

Second partition of Poland: Because Austria was not interested in expanding its territory on this occasion, Poland's partition negotiated in St Petersburg on January 23, 1793, was between Russia and Prussia. Russia received an area of 91,000 square miles that included the Ukraine, the eastern part of Volhynia, and Podolien, as well as Polozk, Minsk, and the eastern half of Novgrodek. In addition, Russia also insisted on a Union Treaty that included a right of passage for its troops.

Prussia received about 21,000 square miles including Danzig and Thorn, as well as Poznán, Kalisch, and Gnesen (thereafter known as South Prussia). What remained of Poland after the Second Partition, including Kurland, still covered 88,800 square miles, with 4.4 million inhabitants.

The Kosciuszko uprising: On March 24, 1794, Kosciuszko called for the people in Kraków to rise up against this partition. After some initial defensive successes, Kosciuszko was defeated by the Russians at Maciejowice on October 10, and he remained a prisoner of the Russians until 1796.

Third Polish Partition: The Russian empire played a leading role in the ongoing negotiations regarding the Third Partition of Poland. The agreement was as follows: Russia received about 16,600 square miles, including Kurland and the rest of Lithuania, as well as all remaining Ukrainian and White Russian territory; Prussia received about 21,000 square miles, consisting of a small territory along the upper Warta (New Silesia) as well as Masowien as far as Memel (New East Prussia), and Warsaw. King Stanislaus Augustus Poniatowski formally abdicated on November 25 in Grodno. He was paid an annual allowance of 200,000 ducats by the three powers and died in St Petersburg on February 12, 1798. ❑

General Tadeusz Kosciuszko leading his men to victory

THE RISE TO

Paris, October 5, 1795

With the Directory (*Directoire exécutif*), the haute-bourgeoisie in France regained the political influence that it had lost during the rule of the Jacobins.

Thanks to the military leadership of the 26-year-old Napoleon Bonaparte a royalist coup in Paris on October 5, 1795 was suppressed. About 20,000 insurgents had occupied large areas of the city, but the uprising failed as a result of the opposition of the loyal troops summoned by the National Convention, under the overall command by Paul François Jean Nicolas, Vicomte de Paris, who gave Napoleon his command. Napoleon's successful suppression of the revolt first brought him to national attention.

The attempted coup was triggered by the arrival of 3,500 emigrants from Great Britain in Quiberon Bay in Brittany on June 23. They wanted to join forces with the rebels who were still fighting in Vendée (on the French Atlantic coast). There a fierce civil war fought against the Revolution since 1793 was still going on. But the majority of the population left the emigrants in the lurch, and the Republican General Lazare sealed off the invasion area. Now ruling in Paris were the Thermidorians, so named after the date of the fall of Robespierre on the ninth of Thermidor of Year II in the revolutionary calendar. On August 22, the National Convention drew up a new civil constitution. In an election that took place on September 23, over 900,000 citizens voted for the Directorial Constitution and 42,000 against.

It was the third Constitution since 1789, and it transferred the executive power to a Directory

François Babeuf

POWER OF THE FRENCH BOURGEOISIE

of five men. The Constitution, which guaranteed freedom of press, religion, opinion, and guilds, met the original demands that the bourgeoisie had insisted upon in 1789. The nation redefined itself as bourgeois society, while the aspirations of working people and peasants, as well as those of the aristocracy and clergy were ignored. A two-tiered voting system based on property qualifications prevented wage-earners from having any say in political matters. However, anyone who paid taxes could vote for representatives to the main assembly. The delegates were elect-

Napoleon Bonaparte firing upon royalist insurgents.

The rebels in the Vendée signing the peace treaty.

ed from those who could prove an income equivalent to 200 days of work (in the towns and cities) or 150 days (on the land). About 30,000 people in France met this qualification. The existence of a bicameral legislature was to prevent a recurrence of the Jacobin dictatorship.

To keep the royalists at a safe distance, the Convention decided that two-thirds of the delegates should come from its own ranks. The 750 elected legislators were divided into of the Council of the 500 and the Council of Ancients. The Council of the 500 proposed the laws, and the Council of Ancients passed them. One-third of both Councils had to be re-elected every year. A similar principle of rotation was applied to the five men of the Directory, who were selected by the Council of Ancients. They in turn decided on the appointments to the seven ministerial posts.

On October 31, the Directory of five men was elected. It was made up of two "leftists," Paul François Nicolas Barras (police and justice) and Jean-François Reubell (diplomacy, finance and justice), and two "moderates" Lazare Nicolas Carnot (army) and Louis François Honoré Letourneur (navy), as well as the former *Girondist* Louis Marie la Réveillière-Lépeaux (education). At first Carnot assumed the leading role, but later he was superceded by Napoleon's patron, Barras.

An attempted coup against the Directory, led by the revolutionary François Noël Babeuf, also known as Gracchus Babeuf, ended in failure; Babeuf had wanted to replace the Directory with a proletarian dictatorship. Babeuf and one of his supporters, Auguste Alexandre Joseph Darthé, were arrested and tried. They were executed on May 27, 1797. ❑

THE POLISH QUESTION

Point of Interest

Even after the third partition, the problem of Poland's annexation remained of paramount importance to European countries.

After the Peace of Tilsit in 1807, the Emperor Napoleon I created the Grand Duchy of Warsaw, formed by the Polish territories annexed by Prussia and Austria. He appointed King Frederick Augustus of Saxony regent in Warsaw (1807-1815). In 1815 the Congress of Vienna founded Congress Poland, which, although it had its own constitution, was associated with Russia in personal union. Austria kept Galicia while Prussia kept the Grand Duchy of Poznan; Krakow became a free city (the Republic of Krakow), until it was annexed by Austria in 1846. ❑

LAW CODE FOR PRUSSIA

Berlin, June 1, 1794

Ratified on June 1, 1794, the General Law of the Land for the Prussian States was the first modern code of law in Germany. A new legal system was introduced in Prussia, including state and administration regulations, class privileges and rights of investiture, ecclesiastical law, criminal law and civil law. Only procedural law and military law were excluded. General legal norms were described in its introduction.

Even after the reforms were introduced, the king retained the right to legislate. But the king and the administration were bound by the promulgated laws. The main features of the reforms were legal security, equality for all before the law, the autonomy of the judiciary, and the protection of the rights of the individual and of property. The country's new code regulated almost every detail of its citizens' lives.

Chief architects of the new law code and its provisions were the lawyers Carl Svarez and Johann von Carmer. ❑

Title page of Prussian law code with a representation of Justice

FRANCISCO DE GOYA

Madrid, 1797

Between 1797 and 1803, the Spanish painter and printmaker Francisco de Goya shocked the public with his paintings *The Naked Maja* and *The Clothed Maja*. The former resulted in Goya's receiving the unwanted attention of the Spanish Inquisition.

Goya was born on March 30, 1746, in Fuendetodos (Aragón) where his father was a gilder. He spent two years (1770-1771) in Italy, in Rome and Parma, where he won second prize in a painting competition. In 1775 he married the sister of the painter Francisco Bayeu and later worked at the royal court. Influenced by Giovanni Battista Tiepolo (1696-1770), his early work included wall paintings, altarpieces, and tapestry designs that were indebted to the rococo. His early portraits show the influence of the Spanish painter Anton Raphael Mengs (1728-1779), who painted members of the royal family. In 1786 Goya was appointed painter to King Charles III; then in 1789 he was made court painter by the King Charles IV. In 1792 he became president of the San Fernando Academy and in 1799 he was promoted to First Court Painter. In the same year he published his satirical aquatint etchings under the title *Caprichos*, then, in 1800, he painted the series *The Family of Charles IV*. By this time Goya had reached the peak of his popularity with the royal family. The Napoleonic Wars (1808-1813) extended the range of his activities: his etchings, *Disasters of War* (1809-1814) dramatically depicted its subect's horrors, while in *Tauromaquia* (1815) and *Disparates*

Francisco de Goya, *The Naked Maja*, 1797.

(1815) he displayed a poignant sense of empathy.

When Ferdinand VII came to the throne in 1814, he commissioned Goya to paint a portrait of him dressed in royal regalia. In the same year, Goya painted *The Third of May,1808: The Execution of the Defenders of Madrid*. Between 1819-1823, by then seriously ill, Goya retreated to his house in the country where he painted fourteen wall paintings of imaginary scenes. Because of their literal and spiritual darkness, they became known as the *Black Paintings*. In 1824 he left Spain and went to live in Bordeaux where he died on April 16, 1828.

The morally engaged art of Francisco de Goya created a link between traditional and modern painting. His last paintings revealed him as a precursor of Impressionism. ❏

EDWARD JENNER AND THE SMALLPOX VACCINE

Berkeley, England May 14, 1796

On May 14, 1796, a country doctor, Edward Jenner (1749-1823), was the first to inoculate a human with cowpox, and so discovered the smallpox vaccine. The word vaccination is derived from the latin word for cow, "vacca".

The process of vaccination was discovered by Jenner when he observed that cowpox, a particular variety of pox, produced a milder reaction in humans, and that having overcome it they became resistant to smallpox.

Jenner realized that vaccination with cowpox had considerable advantages over the current method used to immunize against smallpox, variolation. This treatment required the inoculation of healthy people with pus from those stricken with the illness. With cowpox vaccination, the vaccinated person did not develop pustules and there were no disfiguring scars. Neither was there any danger of a fatal outcome, (as there was with variolation's use of a smallpox derivative) since it posed much less danger to the person being vaccinated. The smallpox vaccination process developed by Jenner quickly spread throughout Great Britain and the rest of Europe, and ultimately all over the world. Smallpox has been virtually eradicated, but it is estimated that it claimed the lives of as many as 60 million victims. ❏

EDWARD JENNER QUOTE

"A Slight Affection to the System"

From Jenner's report on his new method of vaccination: "The more accurately to observe the progress of the infection I selected a healthy boy, about eight years old, for the purpose of inoculation for the cow-pox. The matter was taken from a sore on the hand of a dairymaid, who was infected by her master's cows, and it was inserted, on the 14th of May, 1796, into the arm of the boy by means of two superficial incisions, barely penetrating the cutis, each about half an inch long. On the seventh day he complained of uneasiness in the axilla, and on the ninth he became a little chilly, lost his appetite, and had a slight headache. During the whole of this day he was perceptibly indisposed, and spent the night with some degree of restlessness, but on the day following he was perfectly well. In order to ascertain whether the boy, after feeling so slight an affection of the system from the cowpox virus, was secure from the contagion of the smallpox, he was inoculated the 1st of July following with variolous matter, immediately taken from a pustule. Several slight punctures and incisions were made on both his arms, and the matter was carefully inserted, but no disease followed." ❏

THE QAJAR DYNASTY

Teheran, 1797

On June 6, 1797, the founder of the Persian Qajar dynasty and Shah of Persia since 1794, Aga Mohammed, was murdered by one of his servants. Originally the chief of the Turkmenic Qajar tribe, Aga Mohammed took advantage of the unrest following the death of Mohammed Karim Khan in 1779, and gradually succeeded in establishing his rule over the whole of Persia, having proclaimed himself Shah. The dynasty he founded remained in power until 1925.

Nadir Shah, who had seized power in 1736, was able to maintain the unity of the empire and to annex territories extending as far as Afghanistan, Hindustan, and Delhi. Soon after he was murdered on June 19, 1747, the empire splintered into smaller, regional kingdoms. Rising up in eastern Iran was the empire of the Afghans, while in western Iran several small kingdoms emerged, of which Mohammed Karim Khan's empire of the Zand, became the most powerful.

Khan's death in 1779, led to bloody feuds in the House of Zand until Lutf Ali Khan succeeded in restoring some stability to his country. But in the end he was unable to stand his ground against Aga Mohammed, who proclaimed himself shah, even though he was unable to claim lineal descent from the mighty rulers of the Safavid dynasty (1502-1736), the original holders of the title.

After the death of Aga Mohammed in 1797, his nephew, Fath Ali, assumed the title of shah and established his rule in the country through a series of military campaigns. These early successes proved to be only temporary. He suffered lasting setbacks in the border regions with Russia. Georgia, the object of fierce conflicts, was wrested from Fath Ali by Russia. Subsequently, Fath Ali lost his territories along the Caucasus to Russia in 1813 after the Treaty of Gulistan. Then, after another unsuccessful war (1826–1828), he lost his territories in Armenia. By the time Fath Ali died on October 20, 1834, Persia had lost much of its power and continued to be drawn into conflicts with Russia and Great Britain.

Further decline in the Qajar's Persian dynasty occurred during the reign of Nasir al-Din (r. 1848–1896). A reform-minded leader, his progressive attempts to modernize Qajar society failed because of the opposition of the orthodox clergy. His drive to reclaim some of the old Persian territories also failed. Although his Persian troops conquered

the city of Herat in Afghanistan in March 1852, they were forced to withdraw after the intervention of the British. In 1870 Persia established its neutrality and settled its borders through treaties with Turkey (1878) and Russia (1882). The murder of Nasir al-Din by a religious fanatic on May 1, 1896, did not completely halt his reformist policies. The country's infrastructure gradually improved with loans from the West, but these entailed a growing dependence on the Western powers. With the Anglo-Russian Convention of 1907, both Britain and Russia gained vast spheres of influence in regions that had once been ruled by the Qajar dynasty. The British were given the southeastern territories of Iran and the Russians received the north of Iran. ❑

Musicians and dancers at the court of Nasir al-Din

FRANCE SHOWS RENEWED STRENGTH

Campo Fòrmio, October 1797

The Treaty of Campo Fòrmio (present-day Campoformido) between Austria and France ended the First Coalition War. Austria lost Belgium, Milan, and Mantua but received Venetia, Istria, and Dalmatia. On April 10, 1792, France declared war on Austria, and Prussia came immediately in on the Austrian side. The execution of Louis XVI caused Great Britain, the Netherlands, Spain, and other countries to enter the war, forming the First Coalition, and the French victory at the Battle of Wattignies

(October 15, 1793) against Austria halted an invasion of France. The Austrians were forced to leave Belgium after the Battle of Fleurus (June 26, 1794). In January 1795 the French invaded the Netherlands and proclaimed the Batavian Republic. Prussia and Spain signed a peace treaty on July 1795. With Napoleon Bonaparte's series of brilliant military victories in his Italian campaign of March 1796, Austria bowed out as well. Only Great Britain chose to continue fighting. ❑

The Austrians occupied Venice in January 1798

NAPOLEON IN EGYPT

Cairo, July 21, 1798

In July of 1798 General Napoleon Bonaparte led a French army of 20,000 into Egypt in order to wrest control of the Ottoman province from the Mamluks. The French annexation of Egypt would not only protect its Mediterranean trade routes but also create an obstacle to Britain's India trade. A secondary goal of the expedition was the acquisition of Egyptian historical artifacts, and to that purpose, his military forces included a number of scientists. Their most significant find was the Rosetta Stone.

Managing to slip past the British fleet led by Rear-Admiral Horatio Nelson, Napoleon seized Alexandria from the Mamluks on July 1 and then proceeded toward Cairo. On July 21, at Embabeh, just north of the Pyramids his troops were met by the Mamluk leader, Murad Bey, and his army of 60,000 men, including his fabled cavalry. Although outnumbered, Napoleon employed one of his signature military tactics, the "divisional square," wherein he boxed in the enemy's larger force, pinning them to the banks of the Nile. Within twenty-four hours the Mamluks were routed, having lost as many as 3,000 men. Napoleon lost only 30. Known as the "Battle of the Pyramids," it secured Egypt for France but was a somewhat pyrrhic victory.

Although Napoleon's land forces subsequently invaded Syria, his fleet of twenty-one ships waiting at the mouth of Nile were overtaken by Nelson's British fleet on August 1. Known as the Battle of the Nile, it resulted in 1700 French casualties to 218 British. Most of the French fleet was destroyed.

Faced with volatile political conditions in France, Napoleon returned to Paris, leaving his army behind. In 1801 the French commander surrendered to the British and was allowed to return with his army to France along with the vast store of Egyptian antiquities that its scientific team had gathered. ❑

A Mamluk army of about 5,000 men was defeated on July 21, 1798 in the Battle of the Pyramids.

THE ROSETTA STONE

Rashid, Egypt, 1799

In 1798 when Napoleon Bonaparte began his conquest of Egypt, his troops were accompanied by a team of scientists whose mission was to collect Egyptian antiquities, formally known as the Commission of Science and Arts. The team opened a museum in Cairo to house these artifacts, the Institut de l'Egypte. Of their many historical finds, none was more significant than a 1700-pound stele. Discovered in July of 1799 near the port city of Rashid (Rosetta) and subsequently christened the Rosetta Stone, the dark blue, pink-tinged artifact was determined to be from the Ptolemaic Dynasty (305–300 BC). It represented a single text rendered in three scripts: hieroglyphic and demotic egyptian as well as classical greek. Because scholars were conversant in demotic (the commonly written egyptian script of its day) and greek, they were able translate the text, discovering that it was a decree issued by Ptolemaic priests honoring their pharaoh's wisdom, guidance and generosity during a period of travail.

Credit for the authoritative completion of this task goes to the French linguist Jean-François Champollion, who in 1824, after comparing the previous translations of the Rosetta Stone against its hieroglyphic symbols published *Summary of the Hieroglyphic System of the Ancient Egyptians*, and later (posthumously) *Dictionnaire égyptien en écriture hiéroglyphique*, a hieroglyphic dictionary.

Although both the French and the Egyptians would lose the Rosetta Stone to the British (it remains to this day in the British Museum), Champollion's accomplishment, as well as those of Napoleons' scientific team created and inspired a vibrant new interest in ancient Egyptian studies and archaeology in general. ❑

THE END OF THE REVOLUTION

Saint-Cloud, France, November 9, 1799

Upon his return to France from Egypt in October 1799, Bonaparte slipped into Paris and found the Directory besieged by the left and the right, its power slipping away. Plotting with Emmanuel Sieyès, a member of the Directory who wanted the constitution overhauled, Napoleon, supported by his generals, had himself voted commander of the troops in Paris. With the help of Talleyrand he secured the resignation of the members of the Directory. Then, in a *coup* that almost failed, Bonaparte marched at the head of his troops to where the Convention was sitting in Saint-Cloud. He received a hostile reception from the Council of Five Hundred, the neo-Jacobin legislative body at Saint-Cloud. He was shouted down and spat upon. He was accused of being an outlaw. The general appeared, by all accounts, to be paralyzed with indecision. A scuffle and his brother saved the coup. It was claimed that Bonaparte had

NAPOLEON

Brief Lives

Napoleon Bonaparte was born in Ajaccio on the island of Corsica. He attended a military school near Troyes and upon graduating received a commission as a second lieutenant in an artillery regiment. He distinguished himself at the capture of Toulon (December 20, 1793). He came to the attention of the Directory when he put down a royalist uprising in 1795 in Paris.

Soon after his marriage to Josephine Beauharnais (on March 9, 1796) he was named commander of the French "army of Italy." His invasion of northern Italy was an unqualified success and led to the establishment of several small sat-

The French defeating the Austrians at the Battle of Marengo on June 14, 1800

THE SECOND COALITION

Europe, January 1, 1799

While Napoleon was leading his army into Egypt, the Second Coalition formed with the goal of stopping the spread of revolutionary ideas in Europe and with the aim of regaining lost territories. The First Coalition of Austria, Prussia and Spain attempted to overturn the nascent French Republic after the execution of Louis XVI, but retreated in the face of determined French resistance. In 1798, Britain began preparing to fight France once again. Austria, Portugal, Naples, and the Ottoman Empire signed on.

In 1799, Tsar Paul of Russia agreed to join the Anglo-Austrian alliance. The Second Coalition attacked French forces in Italy, Switzerland, and Germany. The allies won a number of early battles, but when Bonaparte became head of the French government and its armies in 1799, the tide turned. In June of 1800, Bonaparte led a surprise attack into Italy, leading 40,000 troops over an 8,000-foot pass in the Alps, still covered with snow in May, and engaged the Austrian rearguard. The Austrians attacked at Marengo in Italy's Piedmont region led by General Michael von Melas but were repulsed with the help of reinforcements, and the French cavalry carried the day. The Austrians were soon driven out of Italy, and French dominance was reestablished. In December of the same year the French army soundly defeated the Coalition forces at Hohenlinden on the Rhine. This led to the end of the war. In 1801, the Treaty of Lunéville officially dissolved the Second Coalition. Great Britain signed a separate peace agreement in 1802 at Amiens, although the cessation of hostilities would be short lived.

Upon his triumphant return to Paris, Bonaparte was voted Consul for life. ❑

been attacked with a knife. His soldiers, incensed and incited by Lucien Bonaparte and Joachim Murat, marched into the council chamber. The legislators fled and Bonaparte declared himself first consul in a triumvirate that also included former Directory members Sieyès and Roger Ducos. He declared that he would abdicate when France was free from danger. Napoleon's seizure of power became known as the coup d'etat of 18 Brumaire, the day's date in the new calendar es-tablished by the revolution (November 9, 1799). The events of this fateful day are considered by many to be the end of the French Revolution (Other historians mark the end of the Revolution at the death of Robespierre.) A new constitution was issued in December 1799 that declared the revolution over. It also gave the lion's share of power to the consul, a post that Napoleon had reserved for himself.

Bonaparte quickly asserted himself. There was little popular resistance to the emergence of an autocratic leader. The country was at war and its economy in shambles. Napoleon began the process of writing a legal code for the republic. He began a dialogue with the pope with the view of reestablishing Catholicism in France and even reopened synagogues. He arranged for the regulation of tax collection and set about to create an army that would dominate Europe for the next fifteen years. ❑

BONAPARTE

ellite states. He then marched into Austria, which yielded its holdings in Italy to him with the Treaty of Campo Fòrmio. In 1798 he led an invading army into Egypt. He returned to Paris and overthrew the Directory and led a coup on 18 Brumaire (date equivalent to November 9, 1799 in the French Revolutionary calendar) and became first consul of the republic. He remained the ruler of France until 1814, crowning himself emperor in 1804.

Napoleon was a brilliant military tactician. His French army bulldozed its way through Europe overcoming all opposition. He was at the peak of power after his victory over Prussia (1806/07) and Austria (1809). He did, however, lose part of his army in the Peninsula War in Spain and Portugal (1809-1814). Fortune turned against him with his invasion of Russia. It ended in catastrophe and he was forced to retreat with his army in tatters. He was forced off of his throne and into exile on the Mediterranean island of Elba in 1814.

He returned and took power for 100 days in 1815 until his final defeat at the Battle of Waterloo. Following this he was imprisoned on the island of St. Helena, in the middle of the Atlantic Ocean, where he died on May 5, 1821 at the age of 51. ❑

Portrait of Napoleon Bonaparte

HUMBOLDT, THE EXPLORER

Ecuador, 1802

A scientific expedition that lasted a little more than five years brought new knowledge to Europe about South and Central America. On June 23, 1802, the German naturalist Alexander von Humboldt and the French botanist Aimé Jacques Alexandre Bonpland set a world record climbing almost to the top of the 20,560-foot peak (6,267 m) of Mt. Chimborazo.

On June 5, 1799, Humboldt and Bonpland left La Coruña in Spain on the corvette *Pizarro*. They arrived in Cumana, Venezuela, in mid-July. They first wandered through the coastal regions and the hilly hinterlands. They left Caracas on February 7, 1800, and headed south over the *llanos* (plateau) on to the Orinoco. They traveled downriver in hollowed tree trunks, making slow progress on a large tributary of the Amazon, the Rio Negro, until they reached Fort San Carlos.

From there the two travelers were able to return to the Orinoco via the Rio Casquiare, arriving after a 75-day river voyage at Angostura. They were back in Cumana on August 27, 1800. Their four-month journey provided important scientific data. It established the bifurcation of the Orinoco into two distinct river regions.

In November, the two intrepid explorers set sail for Havana. The following March found them traveling back to the mainland via Cartagena. They headed south on the Rio Magdalena to Bogotá, and in September they continued south on foot to Quito. After their ascent of Chimborazo, they traveled across the Andes to Cuenca, with its valley overlooking the Amazon, and the Cordillera Mountains (in present-day Peru), then on to Trujillo on the coast, finally arriving in Lima. They set off for Acapulco

Alexander von Humboldt and Aimé Jacques Alexandre Bonpland at the foot of Mt. Chimborazo,

in 1802, and in April 1803 arrived in Mexico City, where they explored the surrounding area. In January 1804, they left for Veracruz, from where they returned to Europe via Havana and the United States. They landed in Bordeaux on August 3, 1804. ❑

EXPANDING EUROPEAN KNOWLEDGE OF THE WORLD

Point of interest

Alexander von Humboldt (1769–1859) and Aimé Jacques Alexandre Bonpland (1773–1858) were celebrated upon their return to France as the second discoverers of the New World. They brought back 35 crates containing collections of botanical and ethnographic specimens.

Through his researches, Humboldt could lay claim to being the last cosmographer. His discoveries went beyond description and observation, leading to the recognition of laws governing nature and human culture, among them:

- The observation that the vegetation of a region is determined by climate and altitude became an axiom of botanical science.
- The first precisely stated descriptions concerning the climates of inland and coastal regions laid the foundation for

modern meteorology and climatology.
- The observation that the earth's magnetic field decreases as one approaches the equator opened up important vistas for geophysics.

Humboldt's description of Mexico's topography and mineral resources as well as its population, economy, and transportation systems is considered the first modern regional study. Humboldt analyzed the data he had brought back from South and Central America over the course of the next twenty years. His work *Voyage aux regions equinoxiales du nouveau continent* (*Voyage through the Equinoctial Regions of the New Continent*) was published in thirty volumes between 1805 and 1834. In 1829, he traveled through Asiatic Russia, and in the following year he began to assemble all of

the information about the earth known at the time, eventually publishing his five-volume work *Kosmos* (1845–1862).

Around the same time he turned his attention to Africa. The interior of the continent had remained largely unknown to Europeans. British naturalist Joseph Banks, who played a large part in the settlement of Australia, launched a society for the exploration of inland Africa in 1788. Until then few whites had ventured into the interior. Those who did were motivated by economic gain along with the thirst for conquest and adventure. As knowledge increased, opportunities for the exploitation of its natural resources and trade also increased. In 1790, the first credible map of the African continent was published. Despite many mistakes, it provided a guide to

areas that had been previously unknown. In June of 1795, the Scottish doctor and explorer Mungo Park (1771–1806) landed at the mouth of the Gambia River and traveled through the region of present-day Senegal, Sudan, and Niger. This was the beginning of the systematic exploration of Africa's interior. ❑

Alexander von Humboldt

SCHILLER AND GERMAN CLASSICISM

Weimar, 1799

The "Classic Decade" of German literature begins with Schiller's move from Jena to Weimar. Johann Wolfgang von Goethe invited the playwright Friederich

Goethe-Schiller Monument

Schiller to Weimar in 1799. During their friendly collaboration, Schiller wrote within a short period of time his great historical dramas.

Schiller was born on November 19, 1759, in Marbach. He was required by order of Duke Karl Eugen of Wurttemberg to attend military school, then he studied medicine and became a regimental doctor in Stuttgart. His play *The Robbers* premiered on January 13, 1782, in Mannheim. It was a defiant protest against absolutist forms of government, and it resulted in the duke's forbidding him to write anymore. Because of this Schiller left Stuttgart. There followed, among others, his plays *Intrigue and Love* (1784), and *Don Carlos* (1787). Schiller struggled financially. In 1789, his studies of history earned him professorship at the University of Jena.

Schiller's last creative period was marked by his friendship with Goethe, whom he met for the first time in 1788. In the summer of 1794, they began a friendly correspondence, and three years later, the two collaborated on a series of satirical essays they titled "Xenies" that were primarily directed at the literary critics of their time. Their wide-ranging discussions were instrumental in forging a new

Title page of *William Tell* with a portrait of Schiller

sense of aesthetics in Germany and encouraged Goethe to finish his masterwork, *Faust*, which he had set aside.

The classicism of the Weimar period followed the rationality of the Enlightenment and the *Sturm und Drang* epoch named after the play of the same name by Friedrich Klinger (1766). This was a deeply emotional period in German literature in which both Goethe and

Schiller played a part.

In his last creative burst in Weimar, Schiller wrote his great classical dramas: *The Wallenstein Trilogy* (Premier 1798–1799), *Mary Stuart* (1800), *The Maid of Orleans* (1801), *The Bride of Messina* (1801), and his celebration of freedom, *William Tell* (1804). Each has as its theme the conflict between duty and desire. Schiller died in Weimar on May 9, 1805. ❏

THE FIRST BATTERY

Paris, 1801

The "Voltaic pile" began the age of electricity. The Italian physicist Alessandro Volta (1745–1827) introduced this new source of electricity, which was in fact the first battery to generate a regular flow of electricity. Volta had developed his ideas after a close analysis of the research of Luigi Galvani (1737–1798), who used frog legs as electrical conduits.

Volta's battery consisted of dissimilar metals placed one on top of the other (copper or silver placed on top of tin or zinc), separated by layers made of cardboard or leather soaked in brine. The electricity flowed through the salt water solution. By placing a few voltaic cells in a series, he was able to generate a few hundred volts of electricity. (The measurement bears his name.) The battery had its limitations: the voltaic pile could be discharged only once. It was not until 1867 when Werner von Siemens (1816–1892) invented the electromagnetic generator that a reliable method of producing large quantities of electricity was available. ❏

THE BIRTH OF ENGLISH ROMANTIC POETRY

London, 1800

Two young poets, William Wordsworth and Samuel Taylor Coleridge, upended the conventions of English poetry, abandoning what they considered to be the artificiality of elevated poetic diction in favor of a more colloquial language that aimed at conveying the texture of felt experience. Their publication of a joint collection of poems entitled *The Lyrical Ballads* stands as a watershed event in English literature. In a famous preface to the second edition of the work, published in 1800, Wordsworth set out a hugely ambitious program for poetry and poets, demanding nothing less than the redirection of a society on the cusp of the industrial age. For Wordsworth the alienation from nature and the stress and overcrowding of city life was bringing about a craving for ever more intense forms of stimulation. It was the poet's duty to correct these tendencies.

Among the poems included in the *Lyrical Ballads* are Wordsworth's "Lines Written above Tintern Abbey" and "She Dwelt among Untrodden Ways." Coleridge contributed only four poems, the best known of which is "The Rime of the Ancient Mariner."

Between them Wordworth and Coleridge altered the course of English poetry, shifting its attention toward the powerful although at times problematic relationship with nature. They viewed the act of writing poetry as redemptive. Their fruitful collaboration and single efforts provided the impetus for a second generation of poets who stretched and reshaped the romantic paradigm: Byron, Keats and Shelley. ❏

NAPOLEON CROWNED EMPEROR

Paris, December 2, 1804

After the Treaty of Amiens (1802), which brought peace between England and France, Napoleon's power was further consolidated when, as "a token of national gratitude," he was elected Consul for life.

However, the English government became increasingly alarmed at French expansion throughout Europe, especially with a French-controlled coastline ranging from Genoa to Antwerp. With this in mind, it is probable that it financed an assassination attempt by the young Duc d'Enghien, a scion of the Royal House of Bourbon, on Napoleon's life.

Talleyrand and the police chief Joseph Fouché conspired to kidnap the young duke from neutral territory in Germany and had him tried and shot. This fostered anger among Royalist party members. To combat further assassination attempts and to further his own career, Fouché suggested that the Consulate

be transformed into an hereditary Empire; Napoleon needed little persuasion, and on May 28, 1804, the Empire was proclaimed.

Napoleon was determined that the observance marking his anointment as Emperor was to be far grander than any of the former kings of France. Fortunately for him, he had reconciled the Church of Rome with the French Republic in 1800, so he could invite Pope Pius VII to Paris to perform the ceremony.

The occasion took place in Notre Dame on December 2, 1804, and it was indeed a magnificent affair; more than one old revolutionary soldier looked on with resentment. The moment that most astonished and in some cases shocked was when Napoleon took the laurel wreaths from Pius' hands and crowned himself Emperor in the manner

Jacques Louis David, *Napoleon Crowns Josephine Empress*

of Charlemagne. Although perhaps an act of hubris, it was not, however, a calculated insult to the Pope; the act had been discussed with the Curia throughout the long planning for the ceremony. Thus it was that eleven years after the execution of Louis XVI, the monarchy returned to France. ❑

LOUISIANA PURCHASE

Paris, December 20, 1803

When, in 1801, news of a secret transfer of the Louisiana Territory from Spain to France reached Thomas Jefferson, he was gravely concerned. The third president of the United States knew well that a significant portion of trade in the new republic passed through New Orleans. Although having the decrepit Spanish Empire on the U.S. border did not worry him, having energized French soldiers under Napoleon Bonaparte did. Jefferson sent James Monroe to Paris with authorization to offer Napoleon nearly ten million dollars for the city and surrounding territory.

Before Monroe arrived for the discussions, however, Napoleon learned that French troops had fallen victim to yellow fever in Haiti, where they had been

sent to crush a slave rebellion. Haiti was the crown of France's New World empire, and without it, Napoleon Bonaparte's interest in keeping Louisiana waned considerably. The fleet he had prepared to send to Louisiana was trapped by ice in the Netherlands. Furthermore, France needed money to keep its continental enemies at bay. When Monroe began discussions with the French, he was surprised to be offered not only New Orleans but the entire Louisiana territory—800,000 square miles stretching from the Gulf of Mexico to the Canadian border and from the Mississippi River west to the Rockies.

The greatest land sale in history was concluded after months of negotiation. With the Louisiana Purchase, the United States

of America doubled in size overnight. The price was fifteen million dollars, and both the vendor, Napoleon Bonaparte, and the purchaser, the Congress of the United States, were delighted with the deal. Only Spain, complaining that France broke a pledge never to sell the land, objected.

There was no authority under the U.S. Constitution for Jefferson to acquire territory and grant citizenship to the settlers who lived there. He considered writing an amendment to accomplish the deed, but passing an amendment was a timely process. Fearful that Napoleon might change his mind, Jefferson presented a treaty to the Senate to approve the purchase. Congress then authorized him to take possession of the land. ❑

LEWIS AND CLARK EXPEDITION

Pacific Coast, 1805

After a hazardous eighteen-month journey across four thousand miles of the unmapped plains, forests, mountains, and deserts of North America, a United States government expedition reached the shores of the Pacific Ocean. The 28-man (and one woman) Corps of Discovery was led by Captain Meriwether Lewis, President Jefferson's secretary and a veteran of several Indian wars, and Captain William Clark. Its mission was to survey the newly purchased Louisiana Territory.

The woman—who carried her baby son all the way—was a sixteen-year-old Shoshone called Sacajawea, the wife of the expedition's interpreter, Toussaint Charbonneau. At one point, Sacajawea saved Lewis's life when he was threatened by an Indian chief. The last leg of the journey, down the dangerous rapids of the Clearwater and Snake rivers in canoes, brought them to the Columbia River and the sea. ❑

NAPOLEONIC CODE

Paris, March 21, 1804

After four years of debate, a new legal framework, the Napoleonic Code, was approved. Almost sixteen years after the Revolution, the civil code gave France its first coherent set of laws concerning property, the family, and individual freedom. Until that time, France was governed by a patchwork of legal rulings, grants, and privileges that often contradicted each other.

The code emerged from 84 grueling sessions of the State Council. Napoleon presided at 36 of these, all concerned with the family and property. The authority of husbands and fathers was strengthened, but the rights of illegitimate children were

BATTLE OF TRAFALGAR

Cape Trafalgar, Spain, October 21, 1805

By 1805, Napoleon had come to the realization that England was the prime obstacle to his plans for French domination of Europe. He assembled an invasion fleet around the Pas de Calais and surveyed the one impediment to his immediate plan. "Let us be masters of the straits for six hours and we shall be masters of the world!" Napoleon declared as he ordered Admiral Pierre de Villeneuve, to put to sea and engage the enemy.

Villeneuve and his captains were far from sanguine about the outcome of any battle that might ensue; their crews suffered from months of inactivity and new intakes of raw recruits. On October 19, 1805, with favorable winds, Villeneuve gave the order to weigh anchor to his combined fleet (eighteen French and fifteen Spanish ships) to leave Cadiz harbor. Almost immediately the wind began to die. The British frigate *Sirius* spotted the French sails and signalled: "Enemy's ships are coming out of port."

Upon receiving the signal, Admiral Horatio Nelson reacted quickly, directing his fleet toward the Straits of Gibraltar and then changing course northeast toward Cadiz. At about 6:30 am he sighted the French fleet off Cape Trafalgar. Nelson ordered his captains aboard his flagship *HMS Victory* to review and confirm his strategy. Nelson was determined to destroy the French fleet, and to this end, he eschewed the customary tactic of sailing in line parallel to that of the enemy and firing broadside into opposing ships as they sailed by. He intended instead to split his fleet into two squadrons, and attack the French at right angles. One squadron would strike at the rear of the French line, and Nelson's would engage the center, ignoring the lead ships.

In fair weather and calm winds, the two fleets approached each other. The English cleared their decks and ate what for many would be their last meal. Nelson asked lieutenant Pasco to send the signal "England confides that every man will do his duty," but for expediency the word "expects" was substituted for "confides"; the subtle change in meaning caused some resentment among officers and men as they ex-

The Battle of Trafalgar.

pected to do no less.

The first shots came at 11:40 AM. Fifteen minutes later, after sending the signal, "Engage the enemy more closely," Nelson and the *Victory* joined the battle, firing upon Villeneuve's flagship the *Bucenture*. The battle now became a desperate smoke-shrouded melee of ships, yardarm to yardarm, pounding each other into submission.

At 1:15 PM, as Nelson walked the quarterdeck with Captain Thomas Hardy, a marksman from the *Redoubtable* sent a musket ball through his shoulder, smashing into his spine. He was carried below as the battle still hung in the balance. But gradually the superior gunnery, by a three-to-two ratio, and seamanship of the British began to tell on the French, and one by one, they began to strike their colors. At 4:30 PM, Captain Hardy was able to tell the dying Admiral that twenty of the enemies' ships were captured and the rest had been dispersed or forced back into Cadiz. Nelson's last words were: "Thank God I have done my duty." ❑

reduced. Women had no legal equality, and colonial slavery was reintroduced. It did, however, liberalize divorce laws. For men, however, the code enshrined the principle of the equality of all individuals before the law and their freedom to work and to dissent from religious dogma.

Though not the first modern law code, it has been the most influential and was adopted by many other countries including the Netherlands, Portugal, Spain, and Italy. It also forms the basis for the civil code in many countries in South America. Elements of the Napoleonic Code can still be found in Louisiana's state laws. ❑

CODE CIVIL
DES
FRANÇAIS.

ÉDITION ORIGINALE ET SEULE OFFICIELLE.

GRAND JUGE ET MINISTRE DE LA JUSTICE.

À PARIS,
DE L'IMPRIMERIE DE LA RÉPUBLIQUE.

Title page of the Napoleonic Code

DEATH OF THE SLAVE EMPEROR OF HAITI

Haiti, 1806

Jean-Jacques Dessalines, the slave who became Emperor of Haiti, the Caribbean's first independent state, was killed at the age of 48. Born in Guinea, he came to the rich sugar-producing French colony of Haiti on a slave ship and took the name of his owner, Dessalines, as his own.

When Haiti's slaves revolted in 1791 under Toussaint L'Ouverture, Dessalines rose to become second in command. For seven years the two men led the slave army, first against the French, then against the Spanish and British, defeating all of them. When Napoleon reimposed slavery in 1800 and sent a military expedition to retake Haiti, L'Ouverture and Dessalines took to the field again. When L'Ouverture was captured—he died in a French prison in 1803—Dessalines took control of the army. He drove the French Army out of the country in October 1803.

On January 1, 1804, he declared Haiti independent; on 8 October, he crowned himself emperor. Unrestrained by the magnanimity and statesmanship of L'Ouverture, he gave his cruelty free reign. Hundreds were brutally killed and tortured. Indeed he proved so oppressive a tyrant that his leading general, Henri Christophe, had him assassinated in October of 1806. ❑

NAPOLEON'S CONQUEST OF EUROPE

Jena and Auerstadt, 1806

The English, using financial inducements, organized an anti-French coalition among Austria, Sweden, Russia, and Naples. To deal with this danger, Napoleon ordered his Grand Army away from Boulogne (ending the threat of invasion to England) and defeated the Austrians at Ulm in October, two weeks prior to the Battle of Trafalgar, and marched into Vienna in November 1805. It was possibly this victory and subsequent events that led Napoleon to ignore the significance of the British victory at Trafalgar.

On the first anniversary of his coronation as Emperor of France, December 2, 1805, Napoleon crushed a numerically superior alliance of Austrians and Russians in a decisive battle at Austerlitz.

Not for the first time he began the battle in a precarious position; outnumbered as he was, he forced the battle before the full weight of the Allies' armies could be brought to bear.

He pretended to retreat and gave an impression of weakness. Tsar Alexander was taken in by the deception and at daybreak advanced in an extended line against the French, who were massed behind the Goldbach Stream, west of Austerlitz. The Tsar's plan was to turn the French right wing and cut off their retreat to Vienna. Napoleon allowed the Allies to come on, with General Davout holding fast on the right wing. The movement down the heights of Pratzen weakened the Allies' center, where suddenly Napoleon ordered Marshall Soult to storm the heights. There was a desperate action between the Russian Imperial Guard and the French Guards, until at last the Russians gave way. The Allies were split in two and broke in an utter rout; they left behind 26,000 dead and Napoleon master of the battlefield.

In 1806, the Prussians entered the war against France. As always, Napoleon reacted swiftly and made a lightning offensive into Germany, where he won two spectacular victories against the Prussians on the same day: one at Jena, where he commanded the French, and the other a few miles north at Auerstadt, where the main Prussian force was routed by a force commanded by General Davout.

Napoleon faced his customary dilemma by defeating one ally before the other could arrive, in this case the Prussians before the Russians could arrive. Thinking that the main Prussian force was at Jena, he occupied the heights overlooking the Prussian camp and sent his men charging down on the enemy, driving them from the field.

Meanwhile at Auerstadt, Davout with only 26,000 men was engaged with the Duke of Brunswick's army of 70,000. As the battle raged, the Duke was mortally wounded, and his troops, retreating in disorder, became entangled with their defeated comrades fleeing from Jena. The result was utter confusion, and the victorious Davout was able to march on Berlin.

The Russians were now on their own, and Napoleon was able to bring them to battle at Eylau in February 1807 where, although putting up a stiffer resistance than the Prussians, the Russians were nonetheless defeated. In June of the same year, the French completely routed the Tsar's army at Friedland.

The defeat at Friedland demoralized Alexander, and he was by this time tired of his alliance with England. He was annoyed that, although they were prepared to finance his war, they would not commit any troops to the campaign. He met with Napoleon at Tilsit in Northern Prussia, and there on a raft on the river Niemen, they made a treaty that divided Europe between them. Russia was free to attack her ancestral enemies, the Swedes, the Finns, and the Turks. France would get the rest of Europe including the newly created puppet Duchy of Warsaw. But Napoleon's real aim was to isolate Britain. Through negotiation he persuaded the Tsar, already irritated by the British, to agree to his policy of barring British goods from Europe. Although beguiled by Napoleon, the Tsar still brooded over his defeat at the Emperor's hand, but believing the British were in some way at fault, he secretly agreed to declare war on them at some later date.

It seemed at this time that Napoleon's star would always be in the ascendant, with all of his continental enemies defeated or at least constrained to do his bidding. Napoleon was aware, however, that he had no heir to carry on his direct line. He divorced Josephine, with whom he had no issue, and set about finding a new Empress. He settled upon Marie Louise of Austria, marrying her on March 10, 1810, and almost exactly a year later an heir was born. ❑

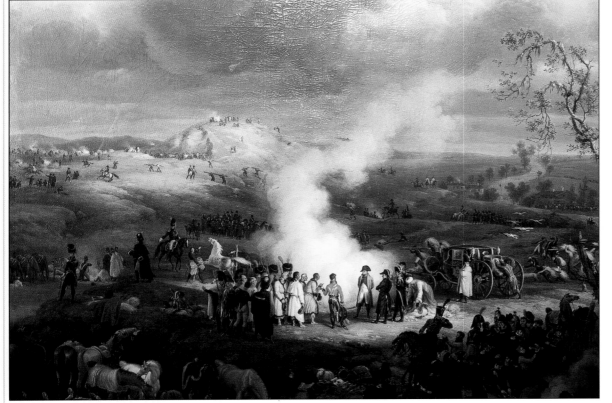

Louis François Lejeune, *Napoleon's camp on the Eve of the Battle of Austerlitz*

NEW EDUCATIONAL METHOD

Switzerland, 1806

Johann Heinrich Pestalozzi was a pioneer in teaching children as well as in teaching teachers. In 1806, he founded an educational institute in the town of Yverdon in Switzerland. It became a place to develop new approaches to teaching and learning and attracted students from all over Europe.

Pestalozzi, the son of a doctor, was born on January 12, 1746, in Zurich. In 1775, he started a reform school for around fifty orphans and neglected children in Neuhof in the canon of Aargau. His experiment of trying to help the poor turned out a failure, and he was forced to close the school in 1780, but it was the starting point for his new thinking about pedagogy.

Under the influence of the Enlightenment, he saw the opportunity to improve social conditions by developing a teaching method that combined practical work with theoretical knowledge, thereby increasing the child's capacity for independent thought and action. Once students began to think for themselves, they would be in a position to effect change on a broader scale.

In teaching young children, he emphasized building up their strength and encouraging them to become aware of their own abilities. He favored a natural style of education over the artificiality that dominated earlier teaching methods. Characteristics of a natural style of teaching were an interest in real-life situations rather than abstractions, and the fostering of self-expression. Pestalozzi combined these with his desire to offer everyone a basic education. He set down his experiences in his published works, *The Evening Hours of a Hermit* (1780) and *Leonard and Gertude* (1781).

After many disappointments, the school at Yverdon acquired international recognition.

In 1825, however, he was forced to close the establishment because of conflicts with his colleagues. Pestalozzi died on February 17, 1827, in Brugg in Aargau. ❏

Johann Heinrich Pestalozzi and students

BLOCKADING BRITAIN

Berlin, 1807

By 1807, Napoleon had defeated all of his continental enemies but became increasingly frustrated by England's willingness to finance alliances against him. Unable to defeat the Royal Navy and thus inflict a military defeat on home ground, Napoleon decided to launch a financial assault against this "nation of shopkeepers." To this end he introduced the Continental System, issued the Berlin Decree, which declared "the British Isles to be in a state of blockade," and ordered all continental ports to be closed to British shipping and all British goods to be seized.

At first the British received this news with derision, and cartoons appeared of Napoleon attempting to blockade the moon, but they became uneasy when Russia and Prussia were forced to comply by the Treaty of Tilsit.

For the blockade to be effective, it had to be enforced rigorously throughout Europe. Portugal, England's old ally, recognized that the sanctions were a two-edged sword and that they too would suffer economically, so they opened their ports to British commerce. At the same time, the more adventurous, both English and French among them, detected an opportunity and became increasingly more ingenious in their means of smuggling goods to the continent. ❏

Smuggled British goods being burned in public in Frankfurt (watercolor, 1810)

THE TIDE TURNS IN SPAIN AND RUSSIA

Beresina, November 26–28, 1812

In 1808, England seized the opportunity to form a coalition with Portugal and Spain, when Napoleon forced the abdication of the Spanish king Ferdinand VII and replaced him with his own brother Joseph. The British army in Portugal was threatened by an army of 75,000 in Madrid commanded by Napoleon and by Marshall Soult's army of Portugal. Soult was ordered to destroy the British and marched on Lisbon intending to capture the city, assuming that it would be the objective of their retreat. The British, under the command of Sir John Moore, surprised him by making forced marches over rough terrain to Corunna, where he successfully embarked his troops. He was, unfortunately, cut down by grape shot as he encouraged his men in their endeavors against the enemy.

However, under the command of Viscount Wellington, the British were able to make a bridgehead of the Iberian Peninsular. The Anglo-Spanish-Portuguese alliance achieved a series of decisive victories against the French, culminating in July 1812 when a force of British cavalry destroyed forty thousand French troops at Salamanca. This allowed Wellington to enter Madrid at the head of 28,000 soldiers to the wild enthusiasm of the populace; at the same time it dealt a great blow to Napoleon's prestige throughout Europe. It also silenced criticism in England for what was becoming a long and unpopular war.

Meanwhile in the east, after the Congress of Erfurt, Tsar Alexander had become less inclined to deal with Napoleon, as he no longer felt that Napoleon dealt equally with him. In an attempt to intimidate Alexander and bring him to the negotiating table, Napoleon massed an army of half a million in Poland in the spring of 1812. The threat failed, and on June 24, 1812, Napoleon crossed the Niemen River.

Under Mikhail Kutuzov, the Russians withdrew before the French, adopting a scorched earth policy while harassing the French supply lines. At the stream of Borodino, the Russians turned to do battle. The fighting was frenzied—a hundred thousand soldiers were killed—but inconclusive. Napoleon, however, was able to enter Moscow in September. Huge fires broke out in the city that night, the French were denied shelter, and to Napoleon's surprise, the Tsar refused to meet with him.

An early onset of winter forced Napoleon to retreat,

ENGLAND ENDS SLAVE TRADE

London, March 25, 1807

The royal assent for the act to abolish the slave trade marked the successful conclusion of a twenty-year struggle by one man. William Wilberforce, a 47-year-old independent Member of Parliament from Yorkshire, took up the anti-slavery cause in 1787. He had been converted to evangelical Christianity in 1785. His mentor told him told him to focus on the plight of the slaves: "If you carry this point in your whole life, that life will be far better spent than in being prime minister many years."

Wilberforce moved the first abolition bill in May 1789. But, despite the growing evidence of deaths and ill-treatment of African captives on the ships to the Americas, there were repeated delays in the Houses of Commons and Lords. The West Indian sugar lobby joined forces with the admirals, who saw the slave trade as a "nursery of seamen," and won support from landed gentry afraid of revolutionary movements. Wilberforce was finally able to prevail through the force of moral argument. ❑

PRUSSIAN REFORMS UNDER KING WILLIAM FREDERICK III

Berlin, 1807

At the outset of the Napoleonic Wars, King Frederick William III of Prussia managed to maintain Prussian neutrality. In 1805, he made the fateful decision to join Russia and its allies in the war against France. The Prussian army proved to be no match for Napoleon and on October 14, 1806, were utterly defeated at the Battles of Jena and Auerstedt. The subsequent surrender resulted in the Treaty of Tilsit, signed on July 9, wherein Prussia was forced to cede half of its territory to the victors, vastly reduce its army, and pay France an enormous indemnity.

After the treaty, it was clear to Frederick that Prussia was in dire need of reforms not only to modernize its army but also to reorganize his system of governance and liberalize the empire's near-feudal social structure. To effect these changes, he turned to an inner circle of advisors, not the least of whom was his wife, Queen Louise. She was a remarkable woman who was beloved by the Prussian people, and it was under her inspired leadership that the court's ablest administrators—

Prussian reformers: Boyen, King Frederick Wilhelm III, Gneisenau, Scharnhorst, von Grolman and von Stein

Baron H.F.K. von Stein, Count A. N. von Gneisenau, Prince K. A. von Hardenberg, and G.J.D. von Scharnhorst—were able to transform Prussia into a modern state.

To revamp Prussia's system of trade, a Zollverein, or customs union, was created to encourage free trade and economic cooperation among German states. Additionally, the Prussian Reform Edict was proclaimed. This called for a series of reforms that liberalized property relationships, streamlined the government, and most significantly, abolished serfdom, thereby removing the last vestige of Prussia's feudal past. However, it was the remaking of Prussia's army that would have the most profound effect. Under Scharnhorst's direction, a modernized Prussian army was created that would dominate Europe in the second half of the nineteenth century. Its victories over Denmark, Austria, and France would unify the German states into the German Empire of 1871. ❑

and because of the decimated state of his army, he had to retrace the route of his advance. The scorched earth denied the French any provisions, and they were soon reduced to a starving, freezing rabble, constantly under attack from Cossacks and regular Russian cavalry. Beginning with a rearguard force of 8,000, Marshall Ney made heroic attempts to protect the army, but his rearguard was quickly cut down to eight hundred.

At the Beresina, General Eble and his sappers constructed a bridge over the frigid water. The French army, now a terrified mob desperate to reach the safety of the far shore, streamed across under constant shelling from the Russians. Elbe delayed his deadline to destroy the bridge by two hours, but still thousands were left stranded to meet their fate with the merciless Cossacks.

Of the half million soldiers who crossed the Niemen River in June, only ten thousand returned to France in November fit for combat; the numbers bear witness to the scale of the disaster.

In the Peninsular War, Wellington continued to enjoy success, owing in part to good intelligence from the local population, which loathed the French: "The French never did or said a single thing I did not know, and they

Johann Adam Klein, *Napoleon's Retreat from Russia*. The march out of Russia inflicted huge losses on Napoleon's Grande Armée.

never suspected it." However, it was Wellington's determination to carry the war to the French on his own terms that would eventually bring an end to the five-year-long war. He was exceptional at coordinating operations extending from Catalonia, through central Spain, and to the Portuguese border with the 200,000 Spanish and English troops that made up his command.

Abandoning conventional military practice, Wellington would often retreat even after achieving victory. The weary French would be forced to pursue him, only to find him on a well-prepared battlefield of his choosing. He cornered the French at Vittoria in June 1813 and defeated them soundly. The French began their retreat out of Spain in July, with the British in pursuit, and by October the British were attacking their defenses north of the Pyrenees. ❑

The combined armies of Prussia, Russia, and Austria battled the French at Leipzig (copper etching).

DEFEAT AT LEIPZIG

Germany, 1813

The defeat in Russia encouraged the people of Europe to defy Napoleon, and with England as ever ready to finance them, a coalition was formed among the Russians, Prussians, Swedes, and Austrians.

Napoleon took to the field in the spring of 1813. The campaign began with two victories, first at Lutzen and then at Bautzen, but because of the weakness of his army, Napoleon was unable to capitalize on these victories.

Falling back toward Leipzig, Napoleon's cavalry became involved in an action on October 14, 1813, at Liebertwolkwitz that turned into the greatest cavalry battle in history, but it was inconclusive. On October 16, Napoleon engaged the Austrians and had the best of the day's fighting. He might have done better to have retreated at this stage, but he waited for reinforcements

that never arrived. The following evening, he began to withdraw toward Leipzig. At this point, his Saxon allies deserted him and went over to the allies.

Finally on October 18, the allied commanders were able to bring the full force of their 360,000 troops together to bear down on the French. For nine hours, the French withstood the allied onslaught before falling back into the city and continuing

the fight from street to street. By this time Napoleon had ordered a retreat. It began in an orderly manner, but then the only exit, the Lindenau bridge, was blown prematurely. This left twenty thousand French troops stranded, many of whom drowned while attempting to escape.

Although he was to stay in power for another year, the defeat at Leipzig sealed Napoleon's fate. ❑

THE AGE OF NATION STATES

The nineteenth century was the age of nation states in Europe and Latin America. On both continents, oppressed populations rose up against hereditary systems of rule. The process of emancipation, the long road to independence, often marked by the loss of the lives of many of its champions, overthrew long-cherished belief systems and changed the political and social structures of both the Old and the New World. The ideals of the French Revolution of 1789—Liberty, Equality, Fraternity—and the example of the American Declaration of Independence of 1776 were the origins of the modern nation state.

Eugène Delacroix, *Liberty leading the People,* 1830. Inspired by the people's rebellion against Charles X in July of 1830.

In contrast to the perception of a nation in former times, in a modern nation there is in theory no longer any difference between the privileged nobility and the people without rights. On the contrary, the people are sovereign and their representatives are the nation's voice. This notion of shared citizenship tended toward the creation of states that correspond fully with the aspirations of its citizenry.

The main characteristics that constitute a nation include, on the one hand, a common descent, language, and history (objective qualifications), and on the other hand, the political faith and deliberate self-determination of its inhabitants to be a single people, so that the country regards itself as a national community (subjective qualifications). In Europe, the Old World, the process of emancipation started at the beginning of the nineteenth century as a reaction against the oppression and hegemony of Napoleon I; in Latin America it was the reaction of the native population against the oppression of the old colonial powers, namely Spain and Portugal.

POLITICAL AND SPIRITUAL CURRENTS

The development of nation states would not have been possible without the great political and spiritual currents of conservatism and liberalism, including those of the democratic and socialist movements. These currents developed into a world view during the nineteenth century, that stemmed from the ideals of the French Revolution in reaction to the conservative ideas of the period of European restoration after 1815.

The democrats emphasized the principles of equality and of the people's sovereignty (that all authority of the state originates from the people). They rejected particularism and absolutism because neither of them reflected the true will of the citizen, and because they contradicted the principle of the sovereignty of the people. The conservative ideology stressed the importance of protecting and maintaining the established political, social, and religious order. Conservatism protected the authority of the throne and the altar, in the belief they were ordained by God. The thought of sovereignty vested in the people was tantamount to overthrowing the holy orders of the Ancien Régime.

BETWEEN RESTORATION AND REVOLUTION

The Congress of Vienna, convened in 1815, formalized the defeat of Napoleon I. The hegemony of the French emperor over Europe had come to an end, and he was banished to the island of St Helena. The Congress of Vienna gave Europe a new political order, but one based on old principles, that was to remain intact until the First World

War. It gave Europe, dominated by the five great powers (Great Britain, France, Prussia, Austria, and Russia), a long period of peace, but at the same time it oppressed the national and liberal hopes of the enlightened middle classes.

The order imposed by the Congress of Vienna was based on three political principles: restoration (the restoration of the old borders), legitimacy (the justification of the absolute monarchies' claim to power), and solidarity (the common policy of the conservative national leaders to deter revolutionary ideas and the Holy Alliance).

The principles of the Holy Alliance resulted in confrontation with liberal demand for national identity and democratic freedom. In Germany it was the students' societies in particular that expressed demands for national unity, a constitutional state, civil rights, and civil liberty. To protect the forces of reaction, the Austrian statesman Prince Metternich issued the Karlsbad Resolution in 1819. This was a kind of radical decree that enabled any form of action that did not conform with the will of the state to be prosecuted, thereby legitimizing press censorship, and the monitoring and persecution of rebel leaders.

It was a period of great change throughout Europe. In France, the July Revolution in 1830 gave the national movements in Europe a new impetus and resulted in the upper middle classes replacing the nobility as the most powerful class. In 1830, Belgium declared its independence from the United Netherlands; also in 1830, Poland, which was no longer an independent state after three partitions since 1795, rebelled against Russian rule. The rebellion was repressed, but Polish patriots who fled their country attracted sympathy elsewhere in Europe and were celebrated as freedom fighters. The restoration managed to survive, but the 1848 Revolution was already simmering during the forced internal political peace of the period.

LATIN AMERICA BECOMES INDEPENDENT

The process of political emancipation of the Latin American countries began with the gradual break-up of the Spanish and Portuguese colonial empires at the beginning of the nineteenth century. After Napoleon invaded Spain, political resistance began to grow in the colonies against the exploitation that had been going on for almost 200 years. Juntas were formed under the leadership of *caudillos* (strong men).

The instigators of these revolutions were the *criollos* (American born Spanish colonists), the prosperous but politically neglected colonial bourgeoisie. Their fight was mainly against political paternalism and economic exploitation rather than toward improving the lot of the native Indians and *mestizos* (mixed-race population). The attempt of the Spanish king, Ferdinand VII, to turn back the clock and restore the situation as it was before the Napoleonic era led to the radicalization of the independence movements.

The most important figures in the move towards Latin American independence were the two freedom fighters Simón Bolivar and José de San Martin. In 1823, President James Monroe issued a declaration that would become known as the "Monroe Doctrine." It warned against European intervention in American affairs ("America for the Americans"), and was formulated in response to Latin American independence movements, as the four former Spanish vice-kingdoms La Plata (Argentina/Paraguay), Peru (Peru/Bolivia), New Grenada (Columbia, Ecuador, Venezuela), and New Spain (Mexico) fought to secure their own national sovereignty. The Portuguese colony Brazil was the only one able to sever its ties with the mother country without bloodshed, declaring its independence in 1822.

But the old problems (economic underdevelopment, racial conflicts, unstable political conditions, nepotism, and illiteracy) did not disappear with the new independence. At the end of the nineteenth century, the old colonial powers were replaced by the United States with its policy of dollar imperialism.

UNIFICATION IN GERMANY AND ITALY

The revolutionary events of 1848 in France also caused ripples in Germany and Austria. In February the "bourgeois king" Louis Philippe was overthrown, while the future Napoleon III, nephew of the famous Corsican climbed the first rung of his career ladder with his appointment as president of the French Republic at the end of the year. In the small and medium-sized German states, liberal governments, *Märzministerien* (March ministries, named for the month of March 1848 when the popular uprisings occurred) were introduced and their demands granted: new constitutions, freedom of the press, and the convocation of a German national parliament. The national assembly gathered in Frankfurt to proclaim the German national state and drew up a constitution. The German revolution was finally crushed in a bloody defeat in the early summer of 1849. It failed because of the lack of unity of the liberal democratic movement, the lack of agreement over whether the small-Germany or large-Germany (Pan-German) solution should be followed—whether a national state should include Austria—and also because of the totalitarian policies of the conservative powers Prussia and Austria.

Nevertheless, in spite of the failure of the revolution, the desire for national unity remained alive. The liberal bourgeoisie was disappointed in its expectations, having pinned all its hopes on the economy and commerce, where there had been unity since the German *Zollverein* (customs union) of 1834. It was the Prussian statesman Otto von Bismarck who realized the dream of political liberalism when he finally created the German national state, after three wars of unification (against Denmark in 1864, against Austria in 1866, and against France in1870/1871). The liberals were divided about this unification that was "achieved from the top and through blood and iron."

In Italy too there were several attempts to achieve national unification. After the failure of the 1848/49 revolution, the Italian *Risorgimento* (rebirth) pinned all its hopes on the Kingdom of Piedmont-Sardinia, under the minister-president Camillo Count Benso di Cavour. While the victory in the Sardinian-French War against Austria had laid the foundation for a united Italy, the Italian people in the Kingdom of Naples and Sicily rose up. The "Expedition of the Thousand" led by the revolutionary general Giuseppe Garibaldi led to the downfall of the reigning House of Bourbon and the conquest of Sicily. In 1861 Victor-Emmanuel II became king of the first Italian nation state. The unification of Italy was completed in 1870 with the acquisition of Rome and the papal states, which had been occupied by French troops.

THE HIGH COSTS OF NATIONALISM

The development of nation states revealed two dangerous tendencies during the nineteenth century. On the one hand, the hardening of ideologies and the policies of strictly totalitarian states led to exaggerated national consciousness and pride, succeeded in turn by highly emotional nationalism and chauvinism . On the other hand, the people's desire for self-determination energized reactionary forces and led to the harsh oppression of national minorities, or strict policies of assimilation.

The aggressive, unbridled imperialism of the late nineteenth century that saw other countries invaded and their inhabitants mercilessly exploited through colonial acquisitions and military interventions was a negative result of the rise of nationalism. ❑

BEETHOVEN'S *FIDELIO*

Vienna, 1814

The premier of Beethoven's opera *Fidelio* took place on May 23, 1814, in its final version. The composer's struggles to perfect the work were arduous. He experienced many setbacks along the way. The first performance, which took place in Vienna in 1805, was greeted unfavorably by the public; reaction to the 1806 revised version was the same. In all, Beethoven composed four overtures for this, his only opera, including the famous *Leonora Overture*.

The themes of the opera are humanity and liberty. Florestan is unjustly imprisoned by Governor Don Pizarro, who plans to murder Florestan in advance of a visit from a government minister lest Pizarro's tyrannical actions be discovered. Florestan's wife, Leonore, disguised as a man named Fidelio, is able to sneak into the prison and reach Florestan in the dungeon. She succeeds in delaying her husband's murder until the arrival of the minister, Don Fernando.

Beethoven himself conducted the opera. In the audience was the seventeen-year-old Franz Schubert. Writing to his librettist, Georg Friedrich Treitschke, Beethoven said, "I assure you ... writing this opera will win me a martyr's crown." ❏

Sheet music from Fidelio

Carl Schlösser, *Beethoven Composing* (c.1890)

LUDWIG VAN BEETHOVEN

Brief Lives

Ludwig van Beethoven was baptized on December 17, 1770, in Bonn. The date of his birth is unknown. He was born into a musical family and received early musical instruction. His first public performance at the piano at age seven invited comparisons to Mozart, another child prodigy.

When Beethoven was seventeen, he was employed as a court musician—the only job he would ever hold. He soon was able to sustain himself as an independent artist. Although Beethoven received a stipend from three patrons in Vienna beginning in 1792, he was able to pursue his own artistic ideas without concern for outside influences. Beethoven supplemented his income with his work as a composer and conductor, but his performances became rarer as his deafness increased. He died on March 26, 1827, in Vienna.

In music history, Beethoven is considered as the bridge between two epochs. His early works with their cheerful universality come out of the Viennese classical tradition of Hayden and Mozart. To the Romantics of the nineteenth century, Beethoven stands as an Olympian presence who stamped musical composition with subjectivity and freedom. But despite such categories Beethoven developed his own unmistakable musical style. Especially in his later works, the composer extends the boundaries of musical systems, breaking down old ideas of form and content to reach a new aural synthesis. The most famous example is his *Ninth Symphony*. The last movement, the *Ode to Joy*, brings a full chorus together with the orchestra in a celebration of freedom. The *Ninth Symphony* had its first performance in 1820, seven years before the composer's death.

Beethoven was a titanic influence on later composers. Many of his musical compositions have left their mark on more modern music. Traces of his late string quartets can be found in the works of twentieth-century composers such as Bartok and Schoenberg. ❏

Ludwig van Beethoven

EXILE AND DEATH OF NAPOLEON

Point of Interest

Napoleon arrived on St. Helena in October 1815, with a small court that had voluntarily followed him into this, his second and final exile. He was given the freedom of the island on the condition that he be accompanied by a British officer. Tiring of this stipulation, he retired to his residence into a life of monotonous routine.

He soon became depressed, which could only be expected considering that he had dominated the politics of Europe for twenty years. His depression was exacerbated by his dislike of his jailer, Sir Hudson Lowe, and the silence from his wife and son.

He died May 5, 1821, at the age of fifty, of a stomach ulcer. ❏

Napoleon in exile on St. Helena

END OF THE NAPOLEONIC ERA

France, 1814

By January 1814, France was besieged on all frontiers and Napoleon was facing revolt from within his own government. In an inspired move to foment the rebellion and to provoke insurrection, the allies declared that it was Napoleon and not France who was their enemy. The initiative worked; the formerly docile legislature demanded peace, and Napoleon was betrayed by Talleyrand and deserted by his former comrade, Murat.

Encouraged by some small military successes, Napoleon refused to accept the allies' peace overtures, which would have allowed France to keep her natural boundaries. He left Paris, garrisoned with twenty thousand troops under Generals Marmont and Mortier, intending to attack the allied lines of communication in the east. Unfortunately for him, his plans fell into his enemies' hands. Persuaded by Tsar Alexander, the allies thrust toward Paris and at the same time increased their terms for peace, demanding that France fall back to her pre-revolutionary boundaries.

The French were beaten at La Fère-Champenoise and again five days later at Montmartre. Paris surrendered, and the authorities lost little time in negotiating a peace with the allies. In the meantime Talleyrand was already in talks with Louis XVIII, offering him the monarchy. Upon hearing this news at Fontainbleau Palace, Napoleon abdicated with the bitter comment, "You wish for repose. All right you shall have it."

As Napoleon made his way to exile in Elba, narrowly escaping assassination along the way, Talleyrand managed to obtain generally favorable peace terms for the French. They would suffer no humiliation and pay no indemnity.

During his confinement on Elba, Napoleon was heartened to learn that the French quickly lost their enthusiasm for the monarchy. The Bourbons had "learned nothing and forgotten nothing" during their years in exile. The allies became involved in petty disagreements, which combined with the intelligence that the English, who refused to pay his annuity or allow his wife to join him, planned to send Napoleon to an island in the Atlantic, prompted him to act: he landed in France on March 1, 1815. Regiments sent to arrest him instead embraced him with the old fervor. On March 20, he was in Paris.

To consolidate his position, Napoleon knew he needed decisive victory on the battlefield, so he mustered an army and marched into Belgium. He met and defeated the Prussians at Ligny on June 16. He then turned toward Brussels to engage the allied army commanded by the Duke of Wellington. Wellington was taken by surprise; at first report of the imminence of the French, he was attending the Duchess of Richmond's ball. Although it took Wellington some hours to bring his entire force to the field, he did offer determined resistance, and Napoleon was unable to push home his advantage. The fighting continued throughout the day, and as Napoleon's victory appeared to be at hand, Gebhard Blucher arrived to reinforce the British. Napoleon unleashed the Imperial Guard, but the British infantry annihilated them. It had been as Wellington commented, "The nearest run thing you ever saw!" ❑

The Prussian army arriving at the Battle of Waterloo (1815)

WAR OF 1812

Washington DC, 1814

The War of 1812 between the United States and Great Britain grew out of Britain's war with Napoleonic France. In order to halt trade with France, the Royal Navy set up a blockade along the U.S. Atlantic coast, effectively closing trans-Atlantic trade routes. In addition, during search and seizure of U.S. vessels, American sailors were impressed into duty on British ships. Another issue was Britain's aid to Native Americans in their conflicts with settlers in the Deep South and the West. The United States' response was to declare war on Britain on June 18, 1812.

With engagements on the Atlantic and the Great Lakes, along the Canadian border and in southern and western settlements, the conflict claimed 1,600 British and 2,260 American lives. The American siege of York (Toronto) in April of 1813 and the British "Burning of Washington" in August of 1814 were two of the most significant battles.

By late 1814, the war's stalemate resulted in peace with the signing of the Treaty of Ghent on December 24; its provisions returned the two countries' rela-

American troops under the command of Andrew Jackson defeat the British at the Battle of New Orleans (lithograph, 19th century).

tionship to its pre-war status. The last battle, the Battle of New Orleans, took place after the signing, on January 8, 1815. ❑

First Transatlantic Crossing under Steam

Liverpool, June 20, 1819

The first steamship to cross the Atlantic was the *Savannah*, which left its home port of Savannah, Georgia, on May 22, 1819, and arrived in Liverpool, England, on June 20. The extent of this technological feat was attenuated by the fact that the 109-foot vessel was under steam for a total of only eight hours and most of the voyage was made under sail. Nonetheless, its successful crossing represented a scientific triumph that validated the U.S. War Department's faith in the future of steam engine technology.

The War Department had previously commissioned five steam-powered paddle-boats to survey the Missouri River. The most successful of these had been the *Independence*, which traveled two hundred miles up the Missouri, and the *Western Engineer*, which reached as far as Council Bluffs, Iowa. The *Savannah*'s achievement proved the technology's global applications. ❑

The *Savannah* set sail across the Atlantic in 1819.

Congress of Vienna

Vienna, June 9, 1815

The Congress of Vienna succeeded in remaking Europe after the devastation wrought by the Napoleonic wars. The final act, signed after nine months of negotiations, confirmed the territorial arrangements of the Treaty of Paris and, among other measures, created a German confederation to replace the Holy Roman Empire.

According to the agreement, England retained its colonial possessions of Malta, Ceylon, Capetown, and the small North Sea island of Heligoland. The Swiss Confederation was reestablished with a guarantee of permanent neutrality. Legitimate dynasties were restored in Spain, Naples, Modena, Piedmont, and Tuscany. Prussia benefited hugely, getting Posen, Danzig, a slice of Saxony, Westphalia, and the former Swedish territories in Pomerania. Acceding to England's request, the Congress unified Belgium and Holland into a United Netherlands. Norway, which had freed itself from Danish influence, was required to enter into a union with Sweden. The map of France was redrawn to its 1790 borders, thus allowing it to preserve its status as a great European power.

The Congress also dealt with non-territorial matters, establishing the principle of free navigation on the Rhine and the Meuse, condemning, but not abolishing the slave trade, and extending the rights of the Jews. Another aspect of its work was the establishment of an internationally recognized system of diplomacy in which ambassadorial precedence and the rights of diplomats were acknowledged.

It was an exhausting time for the delegates, not only because of the amount of work they had before them but also because of the glittering social life surrounding the Congress. Tsar Alexander, convinced that he was responsible for the downfall of Napoleon, was the dominant figure in the dazzling crowd of monarchs and statesmen. Emperor Francis of Austria entertained 216 chiefs of mission and was so lavish with his hospitality that his treasury suffered severely. The Austrian court's festival committee arranged a rich program of events for Francis's guests. There were balls, concerts, sleigh and skating parties, hunts, horse shows, and galas. There was a choice of dinner parties every night, and the whole city was filled with diplomatic and sexual intrigue.

Most of the decisions were taken by the four leading allies—Austria, Britain, Russia, and Prussia—but Talleyrand, who had once been Napoleon's deputy, served his new master, King Louis XVIII, with great adroitness, weaving his way through the quarrels and the bargaining to France's advantage.

The Congress is generally considered to have succeeded in achieving its somewhat contradictory aims. On the one hand, it sought to regain the stability of Europe that existed before the French revolution; on the other, it redistributed territory to create a new balance of power.

As the Congress neared its end, news arrived of Napoleon's return from Elba. It issued a declaration in response: "Napoleon Bonaparte has placed himself outside the pale of civil and social relations and, as the enemy

Jean Baptiste Isabey, *Delegates to the Congress of Vienna.*

HEGEL'S PHILOSOPHY

Germany, 1818

After Immanuel Kant, Georg Wilhelm Friedrich Hegel was the most influential of German philosophers. He was a follower of Johann Gottlieb Fichte, dean of philosophy and first rector of the University of Berlin, which was founded in 1810.

Hegel (1770–1831) was born in Stuttgart and studied philosophy and theology in Tübingen. He taught in Berne, Frankfurt, and Jena. After Napoleon invaded Jena, the university lost most of its students, and Hegel worked for a time as a newspaper editor.

In 1808, he was appointed director of a *Gymnasium* in Nuremberg and finally was offered the chair in philosophy that had been vacated after Fichte's death. He was appointed Rector of the University of Berlin in 1830 and died during a cholera epidemic in the following year.

Along with Fichte and Friedrich Schnelling, Hegel was a leading exponent of Ger-

The philosopher Hegel

man idealism. The idealists took the position that reality and experience could be explained only in reference to some guiding intellectual principle. With his great works *The Phenomenology of Spirit* (1807) and *The Science of Logic* (1812–1816), Hegel developed an all-encompassing philosophical system. He conceived of reality as the self-development and unfolding of a universal spirit.

Hegel emphasized the concept of history, which he understood as the process of development as a dialectical engagement in which transformation derives from the clash of opposites and their resolution. His spacious view of the operation of history according to the dialectic had a decisive influence on the thinking of Marx and Engels. ❏

METTERNICH'S LASTING INFLUENCE

Point of interest

and disturber of the peace of the world, has exposed himself to public indictment." Nine days after the treaty was signed, Napoleon's hopes were dealt a final crushing blow at Waterloo.

Diplomacy continued after the Congress was formally concluded. In the fall of the year in Paris, the Russian Orthodox Tsar Alexander, deeply influenced by the mystical beliefs of Baroness von Krudener, formed a holy alliance with his more conservative allies, the Lutheran king of Prussia, Frederick William III, and the Catholic emperor of Austria, Franz I. The three powers agreed that "the precepts of Justice, Christian Charity and Peace must have an immediate influence on the Councils of Princes and guide all their steps."

With the exception of the pope, who refused to associate with heretics, and of Great Britain, the European monarchs gave lip service to the ideals expressed. But in private they were less kind to the idea. Von Metternich called it a "loud-sounding nothing," and according to Viscount Castlereagh, England's representative in Vienna, it was "a piece of sublime mysticism and nonsense." ❏

During the Congress of Vienna, secret meetings were being held behind the elegant facades of the imperial palace in Vienna, that would establish the shape of Europe until the mid–nineteenth century and would guarantee peace among its leading powers until the outbreak of the Crimean War in 1853.

In attendance were Emperor Franz I of Austria, Tsar Alexander I of Russia, King Fredrick William III of Prussia, and King Fredrick VI of Denmark. Also playing important roles were the English foreign minister, Stewart Viscount Castlereagh; the Prussian chancellor, Carl Augustus Count of Hardenberg; and the French statesman, Charles Maurice de Talleyrand. Talleyrand's exceptional diplomatic skills ensured that, despite

Charles Maurice de Talleyrand

its complete military loss, France could play an almost equal role at the Congress as the nations that had defeated it. The scion of an old aristocratic family, Talleyrand was appointed foreign minister under Napoleon in 1797, but from 1807 on he became opposed to the emperor's territorial ambitions and secretly tried to prepare the way for a return of the Bourbon monarchy. When the Bourbons did regain power, he was called out of retirement to serve as foreign minister again.

Most important of all was their host: Prince Klemens Lothar Wenzel von Metternich (1773–1859). Metternich was named Austrian foreign minister in 1809 and served as Chancellor from 1810 until 1848. He was both extolled and reviled. He was above all a political realist who sought to maintain the privileged position of the aristocracy and the balance of power among nations. At the Congress he succeeded in settling Russian and Prussian disputes over Poland, restoring France to its old recognized borders, and shaping a union of German states under the presidency of the Austrian emperor.

Metternich's later career was devoted to consolidating the polit-

Prince von Metternich

ical achievements of the Congress. He brought Austria into the Holy Alliance with Prussia and Russia and participated in a number of congresses convened to foster good international relations and quell the spread of revolutionary movements. Congresses were held at Aachen (1818), Troppau (1820), Laibach (1821), and Verona (1821). His domestic policies, which relied upon an increase in police powers, remained in effect until the March Revolution of 1848, which stripped him of his position. He fled to England, where he resided until his death in 1859. ❏

Father Hidalgo and the Birth of Mexican Independence

Point of Interest

The collapse of Spain's three hundred years of colonial domination in Mexico began when Napoleon placed his brother Joseph on the Spanish throne, forcing Ferdinand VII to abdicate. The confusion that ensued led to tension between the loyalist colonial ruling class, the Spanish-born *peninsulares*, and the middle class, Spanish-Mexican *criollos* (or Creoles). Among the latter were groups of intellectuals who saw the installation of a French usurper on the Spanish throne as cause for revolt. Most were essentially loyal to Ferdinand and did not want to break away from Spain, but rather wanted Mexico to become an autonomous nation within the Spanish empire. Others entertained the more radical belief that any such autonomy should include the elevation in status of the lower-class *mestizos* and other indigenous peasants. One of the most passionate champions of this inclusiveness was a *criollo* parish priest from the town of Dolores named Miguel Hidalgo y Costilla.

Along with other like-minded *criollos*, including the military officer Ignacio Allende, Father Hidalgo discussed these revolutionary ideas in the secret, and illegal, Queretaro Social and Literary Club. On Sunday morning, September 16, 1810, Hidalgo was warned that authorities were coming to arrest him. Instead of fleeing, Hidalgo delivered his historic "Gritos de Dolores" ("Cry of Dolores") sermon that served as a call to arms against the Spanish. This is seen as the beginning of Mexico's War of Independence.

Within hours, Hidalgo and Allende were leading an army of machete-wielding *indigenias* toward Mexico City. Picking up recruits along the way, the *criollo* leaders lost control of their lower-caste charges, who proceeded to massacre any Spanish in their path. Shocked at what they had wrought, Hildago and his adherents avoided further slaughter, bypassing the city, and headed toward the refuge of the Texas border to rethink their strategy.

On January 16, 1811, troops of the Royalist general Felix Calleja caught up with them at the Calderone River and routed the now disorganized rebels. Wresting command from Hidalgo, Allende led the survivors farther north where they hoped to receive assistance from President James Madison and United States forces. However, on March 21, they were intercepted in Chihuaha, and Hidalgo and Allende were taken prisoner. Tried and convicted as traitors, they were executed by firing squad, Allende on June 26 and Hidalgo on July 30.

With many twists and turns, the revolution, begun with Hidalgo's "Gritos de Dolores" sermon, would rage on for a decade, ending with Mexican independence in 1821. ❑

Independence for Spain's South American Colonies

Ayacucho, December 9, 1824

The Spanish South American colonies' wars of independence were waged from 1804 through 1824 and led by American-born Spanish colonists *criollos* (creoles) against the colonies' Spanish-born military and administrative officials (*peninsulares*). Inspired by philosophies of the Enlightenment and by the revolutions in the United States and France, the educated and well-to-do *criollos* began to entertain their own ideas of independence from Spanish rule.

Much of the impetus for these movements was occasioned by the turmoil that beset the Bourbon Spanish Empire in the late eighteenth century. The onset of the Napoleonic Wars brought tax increases that spread this dissatisfaction to all levels of the colonies' societies including the *mestizos* and the indigenous populace. Most importantly, Spain's distraction with the European wars presented the colonists with opportunities of self-governance that soon grew into the desire for full-blown independence.

Venezuela and Colombia. One of the earliest major revolts took place in 1806 when the *criollo* military leader, Francisco de Miranda, launched an unsuccessful attack on Royalist forces in Caracas. This began a Venezuelan revolt that saw the rise of *El Liberator*, Simón Bolivar, to leadership and the 1811 declaration of independence of Venezuela as the "First Republic." Although Royalist armies recaptured Caracas a year later, Bolivar returned from exile in New Grenada (present-day Colombia) and on August 6, 1813, routed Spanish forces and established Venezuela's Second Republic. In June of 1814, the royalists again took Caracas. Venezuela remained under Royalist control until the return of the indefatigable Bolivar in 1821, who, on June 24, defeated the royalist troops at the Battle of Carabobo, once and for all, establishing Venezuela as an independent nation.

Following his June 1814 loss, Bolivar repaired to New Grenada, where revolts against royalist forces were already under way. Here he participated in pitched battles with royalist forces in between his incursions into Venezuela. Finally on August 7, 1819, he led a surprise attack outside Bogatá. Leading a confederation of troops, including local *llaneros* (cowboys) as well as six thousand English and Irish fighters who were veterans of the Napoleonic Wars, Bolivar defeated royalist forces at the Battle of Boyacá. Three days later his triumphant entry into the city of Bogatá heralded the beginning of the new nation of Colombia. Bolivar was named its first President on December 17, 1819.

Bolivia and Peru. Even before the series of wars for independence that came to be known as Bolivar's Wars, Bolivia (then part of "Upper Peru") had declared its right to self-governance on July 16, 1809, when *mestizo* and *criollo* forces under Pedro Domingo Murillo defeated the royalist army at La Paz. However, not until the Battle

Simón Bolivar at the Battle of Zacatecas

of Ayacucho on December 9, 1824, when General Antonio Jose de Sucre defeated and captured most of the region's Spanish forces, would this region of "Upper Peru" be free of colonial rule. Officially declaring its independence from Spain on August 6, 1825, it took the name Bolivia in honor of Simón Bolivar.

The liberation of Peru began in earnest when the Argentinean revolutionary José de San Martin led troops in the siege of Lima on July 10, 1821. After ousting the Spanish viceroy, independence was declared on

EMANCIPATION OF BRAZIL

Brazil, September 7, 1822

This date marked Brazil's formal declaration of independence from its former colonial sovereign power, Portugal. The new state was organized as an independent country under the rule of the exiled Portuguese crown prince Dom Pedro.

Portugal's King in Exile. The independence movement in Brazil was triggered by the flight of the Portuguese court to Rio de Janeiro in 1807 after Napoleon's troops occupied Lisbon. Under the rule of Joao VI (1769–1826), Brazil had experienced dramatic economic growth. When the Portuguese court removed itself to Rio de Janeiro, Brazil became the center of Portuguese society. On December 16, 1815, Brazil was officially established as a kingdom, which included the mother country of Portugal as part of its domain.

Joao remained in Brazil. In Portugal a liberal constitutional movement gained momentum, demanding a new constitution and the return of the king. After the defeat of Napoleon, the country had been overseen by a British general, Field Marshall Beresford. A joint nation of Brazil and Portugal was envisioned but proved unwieldy. Beresford and his officers were expelled, and in 1821 Joao made his return. He was forced to accept the new constitution, which guaranteed civil rights and strengthened the role of parliament vis-à-vis the monarchy.

The Emperor of Brazil. After the departure of his father Joao VI, Dom Pedro took over the sovereignty in Brazil. The Cortes, the parliament in Lisbon, tried to reinstate Brazil's colonial status, which only served to provoke resistance in Rio de Janeiro. Dom Pedro acceded to his countrymen's desire for independence and founded his own dynasty. After the declaration of Ipiranga in 1821, he was crowned as Pedro I, first emperor of Brazil. This made Brazil the only South American country to achieve its sovereignty without recourse to warfare. In 1825, Portugal officially recognized Brazil as an independent country. ❑

Jean Julien Deltil, *Battle between Soldiers and Indians*

July 28. When royalists regained Lima in February of 1824, Bolivar arrived with his rebel forces and won a decisive victory at the Battle of Junin on August 6, 1824. Peru's previously declared independence was revalidated with the Battle of Ayacucho, the seminal engagement that effectively ended Spanish rule in South America.

Argentina, Chile, Uruguay. Argentina's war for independence was fought from 1810 to 1818, led first by Manuel Belgrano and later by José de San Martin. Its areas of conflict included Chile, Uruguay, Paraguay, and Bolivia. Having declared independence on July 9, 1816, its final engagement was fought near Santiago, Chile, at the Battle of Maipu.

Chile declared independence on February 12, 1818, after eight years of battles led by San Martin and the Irish expatriate Bernard O'Higgins, the latter becoming its first Supreme Director. In the later stages, Chile joined with Argentina's forces to win an important victory at the Battle of Chacabuco in February of 1817 and end the war at the Battle of Maipu on April 15, 1818.

Uruguay's independence was won not only from Spain but also from the Portuguese colony of Brazil. Originally united with Argentina as one of the Rio de la Plata provinces, Uruguay checked Spanish authority in 1811 when forces under José Artigas defeated Spain at the Battle of Las Piedras on May 18, 1811. Five years later, Portuguese troops invaded the region, leading to Uruguay's annexation by Brazil in 1821. A tentative liberation from Brazil was effected by an insurrection led by Juan Lavalleja with assistance from Argentinean troops in April of 1825. This resistance led to Uruguay's declaration of independence from Brazil on August 25, 1825, which would not be recognized by Uruguay's more powerful neighbors until the peace treaty ending the eight-year war between Argentina and Brazil. ❑

MONROE DOCTRINE

Washington DC, 1823

The principles defining what has become known as the Monroe Doctrine were first delineated by President James Monroe in his seventh annual address to Congress on December 2, 1823. He asserted that nations of the Western Hemisphere were sovereign and as such should not be subjected to any interference by European states. The doctrine promulgated four main ideas: (1) Countries of the Western Hemisphere were not to be regarded "as subjects for future colonization by any European power." (2) These countries' systems of government were different from those of Europe. (3) Any attempt by European countries "to extend their system" into the hemisphere would be viewed as a threat to "peace and safety." (4) The United States would not meddle in the affairs of European countries.

The doctrine was developed by Monroe and his cabinet members in response to word that France was enlisting the assistance of Russia, Austria, and Prussia in a plan to help Spain reclaim its former American colonies. France's motive was to restore the Bourbons to power in Spain, and then gain access to the reclaimed colonies' lucrative trade routes, which were currently controlled by Britain. Alarmed, British Foreign Minister George Canning sought to issue a joint declaration with the United States, whose principles would be similar to those being considered by the Monroe administration.

Former Presidents Thomas Jefferson and James Madison encouraged Monroe to pursue this bilateral approach, but Monroe's Secretary of State, John Quincy Adams, fearing both the Franco-Russian alliance and Britain's hidden motives, argued that sole authorship would not only state clearly the United States' position on the issue but also establish the young country's unique presence in world affairs. Monroe agreed and created the cornerstone of American foreign policy for the Western Hemisphere. ❑

James Monroe

GOETHE'S FAUST

Braunschweig, 1829

Goethe's drama, *Faust* Part I, had its first performance on January 19, 1829. As a five-year-old boy, Goethe had seen a puppet show that presented a version of Christopher Marlowe's *The Tragical History of Doctor Faustus*. Marlowe dramatized a German book entitled *Johann Fausten, the World-renowned Sorcerer and Black Magician*, which was published in 1587. In this work Faust is presented as an intellectual, hungry for knowledge and glory. He makes a pact with the Devil whereby the Devil agrees to serve him for 24 years, and after that time he agrees to resign his soul to Hell.

Goethe first produced an outline for a series of unconnected scenes. These were written down between 1772 and 1775 and have come to be known as the *Ur-Faust*. Although Goethe continued work on the piece, it appears that he had given up hope of ever completing it. In 1790, he published finished scenes as *Faust Fragments*.

Goethe found encouragement to persevere from his friend and fellow-playwright Friedrich Schiller. In 1797, he drafted a plan for the entire work and wrote its dedication.

He continued to work on Part I, and it was published in 1808. He finally completed work on Part II in 1831. It had its first staged performance in 1854.

Goethe's version deviated from the original. In Goethe's version, Faust need forfeit his soul only if his thirst for knowledge is eclipsed by the pleasure he derives from what life has to offer. Goethe also introduces the character of Gretchen. Seduced by Faust, she becomes pregnant and then drowns the child of their union. Later Faust visits her in prison and tries to help her escape. His attempt fails, but the play ends with heavenly voices announcing that she will find salvation.

Part II has a different tone. It is imbued with allusions to classical mythology. It ends paradoxically with Faust losing his wager but gaining admittance to heaven.

Goethe was employed for many years as a counselor to the Duchy of Weimar. It was there that he had his residence. He is considered to be the most important of all German writers.

Josef Schmeller, *Goethe Dictating to his Secretary John*, 1831

His complete works were published in an edition comprising 133 volumes. The breadth of his interests and work won him an international reputation. The many facets of his character and writings seem to share one common theme: the attempt to understand the nature of things and their organic development. ❏

THE LIFE OF GOETHE

Brief Lives

Johann Wolfgang Goethe was born on August 28, 1749, in Frankfurt to a well-to-do bourgeois family. He studied law but also showed interest in philosophy, philology, medicine, and drawing. He was passionately devoted to literature and began writing in 1771.

His first novel, *The Sorrows of Young Werther*, was published in 1774 and caused a sensation in Europe. It reflected his unrequited love for Charlotte Buff. This epistolary novel was a social critique. *Werther* and his dramas *Goetz von Berlichingen* (1773) and *Clavigo* (1774) were seminal works in the emotionally charged literary movement, *sturm und drang*.

Duke Carl August von Sachsen-Weimar invited Goethe to Weimar and offered him a job at court. He moved there in 1775. His first ten years in Weimar were occupied with administrative duties, unfinished literary experiments, and intensive scientific research in mineralogy and anatomy. During this period he was knighted by the duke and became Johann von Goethe. With his discovery of the human intermaxillary bone in 1784, Goethe made his most important contribution to the field of natural history.

Goethe came to feel suffocated by his personal relationships, a hopeless love affair, and the pressure of his duties at court. In 1786, he made his first trip to Italy. Upon his return he began a relationship with Christiane Vulpius. They lived together and finally in 1806 were married.

His friendship and collaboration with Friedrich Schiller encouraged him to complete many of his unfinished works. This stage of his career culminated in what is considered his greatest achievement, *Faust*. His novel *Elective Affinities* (1809) ignited passionate discussion. His memoir *Dichtung und Wahrheit* (*Poetry and Truth*) was published in four volumes between 1811 and 1831. In 1821, he completed *Wilhelm Meister's Journeyman Years*; *Wilhelm Meister's Apprenticeship* had been completed 26 years earlier. Goethe died in 1832 in Weimar. ❏

Johann Heinrich Tischbein, *Goethe in the Campagna*, 1787

DECEMBRIST UPRISING

St. Petersburg, December 18, 1825

A group of liberal military officers seized the occasion of the death of Tsar Alexander I in December of 1825 to attempt a military coup. Alexander had no male progeny, so his heir was his brother Constantine, who had waived his rights to the throne in favor of his younger brother Nicholas in 1822. But their agreement and its sanctioning by Alexander was not generally known.

At the beginning of his reign, Alexander I was identified with liberal causes that included governmental reforms. But after his victory over Napoleon, he became increasingly conservative and developed an affinity for Christian mysticism. The last ten years of his reign were marked by stagnation, religious intolerance, and the suppression of any opposition.

The attempted coup was motivated by the recognition of a greater political openness in the West. A whole generation of army officers had been instilled with the ideals of the French Revolution and hoped they could create a new political order. Aristocratic families also lent their support. In 1822, two groups sprang up, one in the Ukraine and one in St. Petersburg, which struggled for the overthrow of the tsar, the emancipation of the serfs, and a nationalism that would encompass all of Russia. After Alexander's death, the plotters refused to take the oath to Nicholas. In a day of mutinous turmoil, soldiers and sailors broke ranks, agitating for political reform for several hours before Nicholas gave the order to open fire. The uprising collapsed. In southern Russia, a mutiny was crushed after the fiasco in the capital was reported.

The new Tsar reacted harshly and swiftly toward the rebels. Five were given the death penalty, and 121 were sentenced to forced labor in Siberia. He tightened censorship and sought to stamp out all opposition. One of his more effective measures was the institution of a secret police force in 1826. ❏

FOUNDING OF THE MORMON CHURCH

Ohio, 1827

Joseph Smith was the founder of the Church of Jesus Christ of Latter-Day Saints (LDS). At the age of fifteen he received the first of a number of revelations. He was living at the time in Palmyra, New York, with his parents. He was awakened, he said, by a vision of God, who told him that all existing religions were fraudulent, and that Smith

Joseph Smith reads from the *Book of Mormon*

had been chosen to found the one true church. In 1827, Smith began dictating the Book of Mormon, which became the bible of his Church. He continued to work on it until his death.

From the outset Smith met with skepticism and actual persecution. In 1831, he moved with seventy of his followers, who call themselves Mormons, to the township of Kirtland in Ohio to build a new Zion. Dissensions within the community erupted over financial disagreements, and Smith moved west to Missouri to found a second center. It did not take long for the Mormons to run afoul of their new neighbors, and they were forced to relocate yet again, this time to Illinois, in the following year.

Smith and his brother Hyrum were arrested in 1842 and jailed for destroying the offices and press of a rival Mormon newspaper, the *Expositor*, which opposed their views. Despite an assurance of safety by the state governor, the jailhouse where they were imprisoned was broken into by an angry crowd. In the resultant tumult both Smith and his brother were shot and killed. ❏

ROSSINI'S *WILLIAM TELL*

Paris, August 3, 1829

On August 3, 1829, Gioachino Rossini's *William Tell* premiered at the Paris Opera. The opera is based upon Friedrich Schiller's drama of the same name. It

Gioachino Rossini

was not enthusiastically received at first, as it lacked the playful brilliance and virtuosity of his earlier works such as *The Italian Girl in Algiers*, *The Barber of Seville*, and *La Cenerentola*. With *William Tell*, Rossini engaged more serious and dramatic material.

Despite the initial cool reception, the opera found international success and recognition. Between 1808 and 1829, Rossini composed 39 operas; *William Tell* was his last. After this he devoted all of his energies to sacred music.

Characteristic features of his operatic style are the subordination of speech to music and *bel canto* singing, a highly legato and ornamental vocal style that emphasizes tone over volume. ❏

Scene from Rossini's William Tell (color etching)

GOLDEN AGE OF OPERA

Italy, mid-19th century

In the first decades of the nineteenth century, Gioachino Rossini was the undisputed master of Italian opera. After he retired from the operatic stage, two Italian composers competed for the laurels. Gaetano Donizetti (1797–1848) triumphed with his drama *Lucia di Lammermoor* (1835) and his comic opera *La Fille du Regiment* (1840). Vincenzo Bellini (1801–1835), whose best known works were *La Somnabule* and *Norma* (both 1831), was considered the master of the *bel canto* style.

Meanwhile, French grand opera was gaining more and more adherents: notable examples are Gaspare Spontini's *La Vestale* and Giacomo Meyerbeer's *The Huguenots*, which were crafted with an unexpected monumentality. ❏

THE JULY MONARCHY

France, 1830

As a result of the July Revolution in France, the reactionary Bourbon royal house was overthrown. The revolt propelled movements for broader freedoms in other parts of Europe as well.

Nonetheless France remained a monarchy. The cause of the uprising in Paris was the so-called July Ordinances enacted by King Charles X. The new laws stripped the press of the freedoms it had gained when liberals took control of the Chamber of Deputies and changed the franchise at the expense of the middle class. The attempt to set aside the constitution and return to the days of the absolute monarchy provoked the Parisians to take to the streets.

Barricades were set up in the city. Charles called out the army, but they were unable to engage the protesters successfully in the narrow alleyways of Paris. In bitter street fighting, the army was pushed back as throngs reinforced the rebel side. The July Ordi-

King Louis Philippe

nances were repealed, and the detested Chief Minister Prince Jules Armand de Polignac resigned. But it was too late to save the

July Revolution in Paris. Battle at the Louvre between protesters and the king's soldiers

king's crown. On August 2, he abdicated and fled to England.

The people had won, but they lacked a plan for how to proceed. Leading members of the upper middle class made use of this hesitation to present Louis Philippe, the Duke of Orléans, as the new king. He had shown himself to be a foe of absolutism, and his elevation would protect France from other European powers taking advantage of a vacuum of power to insert themselves into French domestic affairs. On August 3, the Chamber of Deputies extended the franchise to all males whose net worth exceeded 200 francs, which more than doubled the electorate. On August 9, Louis Philippe was chosen king.

With the new king's accession, the affluent upper middle class supplanted the aristocracy in the halls of power. However, despite some steps toward political openness, the great majority of people still remained essentially shut out of political life. Even with the extension of the franchise, only one percent of the population could vote. Crackdowns on dissent continued.

Nonetheless, the halting steps of the July Revolution were emulated throughout Europe. ❏

BELGIUM BECOMES AN INDEPENDENT STATE

August 25, 1830

In 1815, at the Congress of Vienna, Holland and Belgium were reunified as the United Kingdom of the Netherlands. The 1830 rebellion in Brussels against the authoritarian King of the Netherlands, Wilhelm I, successfully challenged his rule. In the weeks that followed, a provisional government was established, and on November 18, 1830, the National Congress in Brussels declared Belgium an independent country.

The Dutch tried to prevent the split, but the major European powers' support of Belgian independence was formalized in the London Protocol of January 20, 1831. On June 4 of the same year, Prince Leopold of Sachsen-Coburg-Gotha was crowned as the first King of Belgium. Holland finally accepted the reality of the situation and recognized Belgian independence in 1839.

The two countries, though bound together by history and geography, had experienced very different political and social development. The Dutch-speaking Protestant North relied on trade, shipping, and exploitation of its colonial possessions. The Flemish-speaking Catholic South supported itself with textiles and heavy industry as well as agriculture. ❏

Battle in Antwerp during struggle for Belgian independence (October 27, 1830)

RAILROADS USHER IN A NEW AGE OF MOBILITY

Great Britain, 1830

The first European railroads were developed and used at German mining sites in the latter half of the sixteenth century. Referred to as "wagonways," they featured horse-drawn wagons pulled along wooden tracks and were employed to carry ore up from the mines to the surface. A major technological advance occurred in the late 1760s when the Coalbrookdale Company in Shropshire covered the wooden rails with plates of iron. These "tramways" made conveyance faster and smoother. In 1789, William Jessup introduced both wagons with flanged iron wheels and iron-edged rails. In 1803, Jessup opened the first public railway for horse-drawn commodity transport south of London.

In 1804, Richard Trevithick built the first steam locomotive to be used on the Penydarren Railway serving ironworks in South Wales. It was also in Wales that the first fare-paying passenger service was introduced. Officially called the Swansea and Mumbles Railway, it came to be known as The Mumbles Train and was in service until the 1960s.

Perhaps the most important innovator in the development of rail technology was George Stephenson, who in 1814 built the "Blucher," a steam locomotive that represented a quantum leap beyond its predecessors. His next locomotive, the "Locomotion," became the centerpiece of the world's first public steam railway, the Stockton and Darlington.

Stephenson's innovations inspired the wealthy surveyor William James to draw up plans for a national rail network, much of which became the foundation of Britain's modern system. Stephenson and others eventually took over the implementation of James' ideas, but William James is referred to as the Father of the Railway.

The Stockton and Darlington inspired the first freight and passenger line to run on a published timetable, the Liverpool and Manchester Railway. A relatively short haul line, it in turn led to the building in 1837 of the Grand Junction Railway, the worlds first

The locomotive *Rocket* on its maiden voyage between Liverpool and Manchester

trunk line system, linking the Stockton and Darlington to Birmingham.

The Liverpool and Manchester was followed in 1836 by the London and Greenwich, the first passenger service to London. By the time of the Great Western Railway in 1841, linking London and Bristol, more than thirteen hundred miles of track had been laid in Britain.

In continental Europe progress was slower. However, by 1841, when the first international line was completed (from Strasbourg to Basel), France had 350 miles of railway. In Austria and Germany, the first steam railways began in 1835. Russia began work on a 404-mile Moscow to St. Petersburg line in 1850.

The United States' first railway was the Baltimore and Ohio Railroad, begun in 1830. With migration to the West, railroad growth was exponential, and by 1840, 2,800 miles of track had been laid. Within twenty years, track construction in the Western territories brought that figure to almost 40,000 miles. ❑

INDIAN REMOVAL ACT

Washington DC, 1830

At the beginning of the nineteenth century, an increasing number of white settlers emigrated to the southeastern regions of the United States seeking land on which to grow cotton. Much of this land had long been inhabited by Native American nations, the most prominent being the Cherokee, Creek, Choctaw, Chicasaw, and Seminole. The presence of these

Zachary Taylor

indigenous peoples on over 25 million acres of fertile territory thwarted the economic ambitions not only of the new émigrés but also of the United States government. Seeking to open these lands to the settlers, President Andrew Jackson signed into law the Indian Removal Act on May 28, 1830.

The Act called for treaties with Native Americans east of the Mississippi wherein they would cede their ancestral lands to the government in exchange for perpetual titles to lands in the west, financial assistance,

and a government guarantee of security. These were, ostensibly, voluntary contracts, but many tribes, facing increased violence from the settlers and no help from the government, signed the treaties out of fear for their lives.

Jackson had long been a foe of Native American presence in the South. The treaties signed under the Indian Removal Act were legalized excuses for forced relocation. The tragedy of this cruel diaspora was no better exemplified than in what happened to the Cherokee on the Trail of Tears.

George Catlin, *Sioux Ceremony with Peace Pipe*

Driven forcibly out of their Georgia homelands after signing the Treaty of New Echota, over four thousand died on their westward migration. ❑

POLITICAL TURMOIL IN SPAIN

Madrid, September 29, 1833

For much of the nineteenth century, Spain was troubled by domestic disturbances that led at times to violent clashes. The country was deeply polarized, and governments changed hands many times.

King Ferdinand VII died in 1833 leaving no male offspring. He had ruled since 1813, and after a brief period of increased political rights following the end of the Napoleonic Wars, the country reverted to monarchical absolutism. His successor according to Salic Law was his brother Don Carlos. Ferdinand had, however, married for the fourth time in 1829 and had a daughter by his wife Maria Christina. He invoked the Pragmatic Sanction, which permitted sovereignty to be passed to a female heir.

Thus upon Ferdinand's death his three-year-old daughter Isabella became Queen of Spain, with his widow serving as regent. Carlos rallied to his side the defenders of the rights of the male line, who took the name of Carlistas. The two camps stood on opposite sides of the political fence. Maria had the support of the liberals and the masses, as well as that of France and England. Carlos represented the conservatives. His support was based in the clergy and the large land owners, as well as cities in Navarre and the Basque regions that were afraid of

Theodor Hosemann, *A Band of Carlistas* (1849)

losing their special privileges.

The Carlistas were able to field an army of thirty thousand men. The regime assembled seventy thousand soldiers to march against them. Maria's army was led by the head of the progressive wing of the Liberal Party, General Joaquín Fernández Alvarez Espartero. With the Convention of Vergara, he was able to persuade a majority of the Carlistas to abandon the fight, and the brutal and costly civil war was finally decided in Isabella's favor. Carlos was forced into exile.

Maria Christine was not able to capitalize on her victory. Domestic politics remained highly divided and contentious. Liberal sentiment that had gained ground after Ferdinand's death pushed through a governmental reorganization resulting in the adoption of a bicameral legislature and a new constitution. The majority of liberals under the lead of Ramón de Narváez accepted the reforms. Espartero, leading more radical elements, aimed at a more thoroughgoing reconfiguration of civil society. By the end of the war, Es-

partero had become Prime Minister and then forced Maria Christina to leave the country, replacing her as regent to the young queen. His brutal style of governing soon alienated his supporters, and within three years, he was forced out by his old opponent Narváez, who declared Isabella of age and set her on the throne. Isabella's reign was marked with continued political turbulence. Between 1843 and 1868, the post of Prime Minister changed hands 27 times. Civil war broke out again with the Carlistas in 1847, who were again forced to concede defeat.

The Revolution of 1868 overthrew Isabella. In 1870, the *Cortes* (parliament) chose Amadeo, the son of the Italian King Victor Emmanuel, as their king, but he abdicated in 1873 after losing command of the army. Thereupon the *Cortes* declared the establishment of the Republic of Spain, but this form of government was also short-lived. Finally a semblance of order was regained when conservatives succeeded in setting Alfonso XII, the son of Isabella, on the throne. ❑

Isabella II, Queen of Spain (1833-1870)

POLISH STRUGGLE

Warsaw, 1831

The attempt by Polish nationalists to free their country from Russian domination ended in failure. After a ten-month-long uprising in Warsaw, the rebellious Poles were forced to submit to the forces of Tsar Nicholas I.

The Congress of Vienna (1814) confirmed the partition of Poland. The territory under Russian control was organized as a semi-autonomous polity called the Congress Kingdom of Poland. Poles began to chafe under increasingly autocratic moves from Russia. The July Revolution of 1830 in France brought the independence movement to a head. In November of that year, there was an assassination attempt on Grand Duke Constantine, Russia's hand-picked ruler of Poland, and within a week spontaneous demonstrations freed the Congress Kingdom from Russian influence. Leading the insurrection was an alliance of military officers, liberal aristocrats, and university students. A new government was formed in Warsaw.

Liberal circles of Western Europe rejoiced at the news of Polish steps toward independence, but their celebration was not followed by material or political support. The combined Prussian and Russian counterattack could

THE BOERS AND

South Africa, 1836

When in 1806 the English took over control of the Cape Colony, it appeared to make little difference to the Boers, who were the descendants of the original Dutch settlers in South Africa. Over time they became increasingly resentful of the policies coming from Government House and the influx of English settlers. They particularly disliked the change in the laws concerning slavery, which they believed encouraged relations between races, something anathema to their

FOR INDEPENDENCE

not be held back.

After the fall of Warsaw, the tsar clamped down. The Polish military was dissolved; properties of aristocrats who supported the uprising were confiscated; the university was shut down; and the Catholic Church was subject to rigid supervision. Poland became a province of Russia, deprived of its constitution and autonomy. Thousands of refugees fled. Their most favored destination was Paris, where the exiles split into two camps: the conservative-aristocratic "Whites" led by Prince Adam Jerzy Czartoryski and the democratic-revolutionary "Reds" with Ignacy Lelewel at their head.

After unsuccessful uprisings in Krakow (1846) and Posen (1848), the Poles made one final attempt to liberate themselves in 1863. Russia had just been defeated in the Crimean War, and the edict emancipating the Russian serfs may have raised hopes that their reaction would be tempered. As it turned out the hope was unfounded. The Russian army easily dispatched the thirty thousand or so poorly trained resistance fighters. Retaliation was harsh and complete. Rebels were executed or deported and their property confiscated. A policy of the total Russification of Poland had begun. ❑

MEXICAN-AMERICAN WAR

San Antonio, 1835

The first battle of the Mexican-American War was fought in Texas. In 1835, American settlers in Texas declared their independence from Mexico. The Mexican general, Antonio Lopez de Santa Anna, marched into Texas with five thousand troops. Surprised at the size of Santa Anna's army, Texan Colonels William Travis and James Bowie retreated to a former Spanish mission called the Alamo.

When an offer to surrender was rejected, Mexican artillery pounded the mission into a ruin. More than a thousand Mexican infantrymen were killed or wounded when they finally advanced, but it took them less than an hour to massacre the defenders.

Among the dead were Travis, Bowie, and Davy Crockett, the legendary frontiersman who had arrived in Texas only two weeks earlier. The only survivors were women who had sheltered in the sacristy below the mission. A year later, Santa Anna's army was defeated by the Texan army at the Battle of San Jacinto, and the general himself was captured. According to the Treaties of Velasco, Texas was granted its independence from Mexico. Ten years later it voted to become a state in the United States.

United States President James Knox Polk had further territorial

US soldiers attacking Mexico City (woodcut, 1847)

ambitions. The U.S. had wanted to buy New Mexico and California from Mexico, but Mexico had spurned the offers. The president finally found a *casus belli* when the news reached Washington that Mexican forces had crossed the Rio Grande and killed and captured US troops. "Mexico has ... shed American blood upon the American soil," Polk declared.

The US army was under the command of General Zachary Taylor, "Old Rough and Ready," and General Winfield Scott, "Old Fuss and Feathers." In the fall of 1847 after a daylong artillery bombardment, U.S. infantrymen stormed the Mexican capital, Mexico City,

winning a major victory. Santa Anna, the Mexican commander, was forced to flee with the remnants of his army, and Scott had the union flag hoisted over the National Palace. The battle cost more than a thousand American lives.

Finally after more than two years of fighting, in which nearly thirteen thousand US soldiers lost their lives, Mexican resistance finally collapsed. Under a treaty signed in Vera Cruz, Mexico surrendered Texas, New Mexico, and California to the United States in return for a payment of fifteen million dollars. The acquisition of these territories increased the size of the United States by a third. ❑

THE GREAT TREK

religious convictions.

When in 1833 slavery was abolished throughout the British Empire, the Boers, under the leadership of Louis Triehardt, began to move north toward the high veldt and Natal. Over the next ten years, about twelve thousand trekkers made the arduous journey to seek new pasturelands free from British intrusion.

To secure grazing rights, Piet Retief met in parley with Dingane, the Zulu Chief. They ap-

peared to have come to a mutual agreement, but perhaps fearing further encroachment from the whites, Dingane ambushed Retief and his party and killed them. He then attacked the Boer camp at Drakensburg, killed five hundred men, and made off with 35,000 cattle.

In 1838, Andre Pretorious gathered together another band of trekkers and headed back to Natal to seek revenge. At Blood River they defeated an army of ten thousand Zulus, forcing Din-

gane to resettle further north. The Boers perceived the victory as divine vindication of their practice of racial segregation and set up the first Boer Republic in the Natal. However in 1842, the British occupied Port Natal, now Durban, declaring it a Crown Colony, and forced the Boers to retreat to Drakensburg. ❑

Boer trekkers attacked by African warriors (after an original by Louis-Charles Bomblet)

DAWN OF THE VICTORIAN AGE

England, June 20, 1837

During the long reign of Queen Victoria, the reputation of the British royal house was greatly enhanced. The queen was one of England's best-loved monarchs, and the country became the world's dominant imperial power.

At the death of the childless William IV (b. August 21, 1765), the connection between England and the house of Hanover was severed. William's niece Victoria succeeded him.

Victoria was born on May 24, 1819, the daughter of the Duke of Kent (son of King George III) and the Princess Victoria of Saxe-Coburg-Saalfeld. Through her personal example of high moral rectitude, she restored the image of the British crown that had fallen into some disrepute during the tenure of the Hanoverian kings.

From a political standpoint, she was guided by the Prime Minister Viscount Melbourne, who would remain in office for the first four years of her reign. But there is no question that the most influential person in her life was her husband, Prince Albert of Saxe-Coburg and Gotha, whom she nicknamed Bertie.

Prince Albert was highly educated and was by nature liberal in his political leanings. His practical and well-thought-out approach to governance left a lasting mark on Victoria's reign. The crown was able to maintain its neutrality within a highly partisan political environment. The parliament's split along party lines served to augment the Queen's influence.

Albert was greatly influential in the political sphere, although he avoided becoming directly involved. He was active in promoting educational reform and held the post of Chancellor of Cambridge University. He was the force behind the London's great Exhibition in 1854 and was named Prince Consort in 1857.

Albert and Victoria had nine children. Indeed Victoria was called the "grandmother of Europe." Her eldest daughter Victoria was the wife of the 99-day-Kaiser Friederich Wilhelm II; her second child was her successor Edward, the Prince of Wales. He married a Danish princess and was

The young Queen Victoria with cabinet and the Prime Minister Viscount Melbourne (1838)

long kept away from political matters by his mother. He was almost 60 when he finally inherited the crown. Other direct descendants of Victoria and Albert included the rulers of Russia, Norway, and Spain.

After Albert's death in 1861, Victoria retired from the public stage and dressed in mourning for the rest of her life. The British Empire reached the zenith of its power during this period, and in 1877, Victoria was proclaimed Empress of India. Her Golden and then Diamond Jubilees prompted celebration and outpourings of devotion from her people. Victoria died on the Isle of Wight on January 22, 1901. ❑

TREATY OF WAITANGI AND THE FOUNDING OF NEW ZEALAND

New Zealand, February 6, 1840

New Zealand became part of the British colony of New South Wales, Australia, in 1788. With the arrival of European whalers in the late eighteenth century and an influx of lawless adventurers and land speculators, the stability and sovereignty of the indigenous Maori culture came under increasing threats. By the 1840s, the importation of firearms and the profusion of unscrupulous land deals made by Europeans with Maori chieftains prompted the British government to intervene. This intervention resulted in the Treaty of Waitangi and the founding of New Zealand as a modern nation state.

The treaty was to be a mutually beneficial agreement between the British and the Maori tribes in which the Maori would cede sovereignty to the Crown. In return they would maintain control of their own lands, receive protection from foreign aggression, and be accorded the rights of full British citizenship. The British wanted to neutralize the influence of other European nations, especially France, and to bring order to the lawless culture of European immigrants.

Co-authored by Lieutenant Governor Captain William Hobson and James Busby, a prominent merchant and fair-minded liaison between British commercial interests and the Maori, the

Treaty of Waitangi was signed on February 6, 1840, by Hobson and forty Maori chiefs. A Maori translation was created and circulated around the country, eventually being signed by over five hundred Maori representatives.

The two versions, English and Maori, created disputes that continue to this day. Significantly, in the treaty's reference to the "sovereignty" of the Crown, the British meant the Crown as "ultimate authority." Translated in Maori as *kawanatanga*, sovereignty meant only governorship

or stewardship. Despite this and other misunderstandings caused by translation, the Treaty of Waitangi is generally considered to be New Zealand's founding document. ❑

New Zealand: the Maori agree to become part of the British Empire.

QUEEN VICTORIA'S GOLDEN JUBILEE

Point of Interest

After the death in 1861 of her beloved husband, Prince Albert, Queen Victoria entered a long period of seclusion, during which she became increasingly unpopular with her once-adoring public. She began a gradual reemergence after being named Empress of India in 1877. By 1887, Victoria's fiftieth year of rule over the British Empire, the forgiving return of her subjects' affection was symbolized by their enthusiasm during her Golden Jubilee.

Celebrated on June 20 and 21, the Golden Jubilee began with a private breakfast in Windsor at Frogmore, Albert's burial site. That evening she was feted in Buckingham Palace at a lavish banquet attended by over fifty foreign kings, princes, and colonial governors. On the following day she rode through London to Westminster Abbey in an open landau past thousands of cheering subjects for whom ten miles of observation seating had been provided. As if in deference to those along the procession's route, Victoria wore not her crown, but a rather decidedly less regal bonnet. Returning to Buckingham Palace, Victoria ascended to the balcony where she received the tumultuous cheers from a crowd that attendee Mark Twain said "stretched to the limit of sight in both directions." ❏

Queen Victoria late in life

CHARTIST MOVEMENT

London, 1838

By the middle of the nineteenth century, Britain's radical political movements had inspired the growth of labor groups, such as the Birmingham Political Union, which agitated for electoral reforms that would enfranchise the country's growing middle and working classes. Parliament's passage of the Reform Act of 1832 only served to confirm the resolve of the advocates of reform insofar as it granted the right to vote only to upper and upper middle class males. Dissatisfaction with the Act's limited scope inspired the formation of aggressive new groups, of which one of the most active was the Chartists.

A confederation of working-class labor organizations, the Chartist Movement derived its name from a document drawn up in May of 1838 by six radical members of Parliament and six representatives from various labor groups, including William Lovett of the London Working Men's Association. The document, known as the *People's Charter of 1838*, was written to be presented as a petition to Parliament and contained six major stipulations:

- Universal suffrage for all males over 21 years of age
- Equality of electoral districts
- Voting by secret ballot
- Abolition of a property requirement for those seeking election to Parliament
- Pay for members of Parliament
- Annual Parliamentary elections.

Endorsed by the powerful Birmingham Political Union and by Fergus O'Conner, the publisher of the movement's most influential newspaper, the *Northern Star*, it became the centerpiece of a more comprehensive petition that was drawn up at a convention in London between February and May of 1839. Presented along with 1.25 million signatures to the House of Commons in July, the petition was overwhelmingly rejected by a vote of 235 to 46.

This rejection radicalized the movement and resulted in a series of violent clashes, the most significant of which was a three-thousand-strong march led by John Frost on the Westgate Hotel in Newport, Monmouthshire, on November 4, 1839. Intended to spark a national rebellion it instead ended in the deaths of twenty Chartists, the arrest and eventual deportation of Frost and other leaders to Australia, and temporary cessation of Chartist activities nationwide.

The Chartist Movement revived during the Depression of 1841–1842, taking the lead in strikes and adding economic demands to the still extant *Peoples' Charter*. During this period, riots and strikes broke out in northern England in protest against wage reductions. In May of 1842, the expanded petition was presented to Parliament, this time with three million signatures. Once again, the Chartists were rebuffed.

In 1843, seeing that the presentation of charters to Parliament and the use of force were ineffective, O'Conner developed a scheme whereby workers could become shareholders in a real estate corporation that would buy up large estates. These would then would be subdivided into parcels of two to four acres each. The workers could win a parcel in a lottery. This potentially successful venture was ended in 1848 after a financial subcommittee in Parliament decided that it was not feasible as a long-term economic project.

Stymied at every turn, the Chartist movement began to fall apart in 1848. One reason was the growing influence upon worker's groups of the writings of Karl Marx and Friedrich Engels. After

Chartist riots in Newport in 1839 (woodcut)

the publication of the *Communist Manifesto* in 1848, the Chartist Movement, with its comparatively moderate demands, found itself marginalized.

By the mid-century the Chartist Movement had completely dissolved. However, its fundamental goal, universal male suffrage, was taken up by the new Liberal Party and later by Conservatives, who under Disraeli, passed the electorate-expanding Reform Act of 1867. In fact, by the end of the century, every stipulation of the original *People's Charter* was enacted except for annual Parliamentary elections. ❏

Verdi

Milan, March 9, 1842

On this date, Giuseppe Verdi's opera *Nabucco* celebrated its premier at La Scala in Milan. This rousing work inspired his listeners and appealed to their patriotic sentiments.

Nabucco was Verdi's third opera. With it he found his own serious and personal dramatic voice. The plot deals with the hardships and freedom of the Jews during the time of Nebuchadnezzar. It was seen by his audience as a mirror that reflected the conditions and aspirations of the Italian liberation movement. The clearly defined rhythm of the prisoners' chorus "La pensiero sull'ali dorante" ("Thoughts fly on golden wings") became a kind of national anthem. At the end of the 1850s, as the political unification of Italy became a reality, Verdi's name echoed as a battle cry and an acronym for the new state, Vittorio Emanuele Re d'Italia—Victor Emmanuel, King of Italy.

Verdi had his first success with the opera *Oberto*, which was presented at La Scala in Milan. Following the triumph of *Nabucco*, he composed a dozen operas with pronounced political themes. By 1850, Verdi was at the height of his powers, composing his masterworks *Rigoletto* (premier in Venice, 1851), *Il Trovatore* (premier in Rome, 1853), and *La Traviata* (premier in Venice, 1853). The high point of these works are their great melodic arias. His later works include *Un ballo in maschera* (1859), *La forza del destino* (1862), and *Don Carlos* (1867). These operas display his greater interest in realistic drama and feature combinations of solo, ensemble, and choral passages.

On December 24, 1871, after a year's delay on account of the Franco-Prussian War, Verdi's opera *Aida* premiered in Cairo at the celebration of the opening of the Suez Canal.

Verdi's later operas, *Otello* and *Falstaff* are based on the theatrical works of Shakespeare. Verdi possessed the gift of writing melodies that conveyed to the audience the emotional lives of the characters in his operas. He was the most frequently performed composer of his time.

Verdi died on January 27, 1901, in Milan at the age of 87. ❑

The Italian composer Giuseppe Verdi

Treaty closes the Dardanelles

The Dardanelles, July 13, 1841

Under the terms of the Straits Convention signed by Britain, Russia, France, Austria, and Prussia, the straits between the Aegean and the Sea of Marmara were closed to all foreign warships as long as the Ottoman Empire remained at peace.

The agreement ended an unusual arrangement between Russia and the Ottoman Empire dating back to the Treaty of Unkiar Skelessi in 1833. That treaty supposedly provided for mutual support in the event of an attack, but a secret clause absolved the Ottomans of the need to come to Russia's aid, provided that the Dardanelles were closed to foreign warships, while the Russians were allowed free passage from the Black Sea. Austria and Russia agreed later the same year to take common action to protect the Ottoman Empire.

But Britain was suspicious of Tsar Nicholas' intentions toward the declining Ottoman Empire. "Russia . . . perhaps thinks it better to take the place by sap than by storm," said Britain's foreign minister, Viscount Palmerston in March 1834.

Anxiety over the Ottoman Empire's future increased after its defeat in June 1839 by Ibrahim Pasha of Egypt at the Battle of Nezib. France, Russia, and Britain competed with each other for influence. The treaty was of greatest benefit to Britain, which acquired the protectorate of Aden. ❑

The Oregon Trail

Point of Interest

The Oregon Trail was one of the main migration routes across the North American continent. It was over two thousand miles long and spanned Missouri, Kansas, Nebraska, Wyoming, Idaho, and Oregon. Travel on the trail was a six-month journey from end to end. By 1859, over fifty thousand people had emigrated to Oregon, and even more people continued from there south to California.

The first group of settlers to use the trail was guided by John Bidwell in 1841, and in 1842, Elijah White led the first wagon train to Oregon. During the Great Emigration of 1843, more than nine hundred people and a thousand head of livestock headed out across the Great Plains to Oregon. By 1845, more than three thousand emigrants had followed. The driving force that led thousands of people to emigrate was the government's offer of free land totaling 640 acres to married couples and 320 for single people. The trail was abandoned in 1870 after the completion of the transcontinental railroad, but it had helped the United States implement its cultural goal of Manifest Destiny. ❑

Campaign Against Child Labor

England, 1842

During the Industrial Revolution, coal was needed in large quantities, and mines began to employ women and children. The majority of the English public did not know about child labor in the mines until Lord Ashley, seventh Earl of Shaftesbury, published a report on mines and collieries in 1842. He became an advocate for more humane working conditions after learning that twenty-six boys and girls between the ages of eight and sixteen had died while working in a colliery. After the incident, he had a royal commission research the use of child labor in mines and collieries.

The report described children as young as five working as trappers in the mines, pregnant woman and young girls hauling heavy loads of coal, and young boys being used to squeeze into mine tunnels too narrow for grown men. These young children worked twelve-hour shifts and made only two pennies a day.

Within three months after the report was made public, the Coal Mines Act, prohibiting females and boys under the age of ten to be employed underground, was made into a law. ❑

FIRST OPIUM WAR

China, 1842

The First Opium War (1839–1842) was an Anglo-Chinese conflict instigated by Britain to open more Chinese ports to British traders and to reverse Britain's ruinous trade deficit. To effect these changes Britain used the narcotic opium.

For over a century, the ruling Qing Dynasty had protected its economic system from European control by imposing the restrictive Canton System on European traders. This trade policy allowed them the use of only one port, Canton (now Guangzhou), and prohibited direct trade with anyone other than a cartel of Chinese merchants known as the Hong, who limited imports and set high tariffs.

These stringent terms were exacerbated by a trade deficit created by British demand for Chinese silk, porcelain, and tea but little demand by the Chinese for British goods. The one commodity in demand, and the sole currency accepted by the Hong, was silver. Exporting more money than goods, Britain overcame this deficit by creating a Chinese demand for opium.

By the 1830s, massive quantities of the long-banned poppy distillate were being smuggled into the country by corrupt Chinese agents working on behalf of the English East India Company. In March of 1839, reacting to an epidemic of opium addiction, the Emperor demanded that the British turn over all their supplies of opium. Suspending all trade and holding some British merchants hostage, his agents proceeded to destroy Britain's most valuable export.

Viewed as destruction of Crown property, Britain dispatched warships to China. Arriving in June of 1840, the vastly superior British forces quickly subdued Canton, other coastal cities, and surrounding river basins. Utterly defeated, the Chinese were forced to sign the Treaty of Nanjing on August 29, 1842, followed by the supplementary Treaty of Bogue in October of 1843. Also known as the Unequal Treaties, China was forced to open four more ports to foreign trade, grant Great Britain most favored nation status, cede them Hong Kong, and pay reparations for the destroyed opium. In addition, the British were granted extraterritoriality status, exempting them from local Chinese laws. ❑

The British use opium to gain control of trade with China.

THE FIRST AFGHAN WAR

Kabul, 1842

The First Anglo-Afghan War (1839–1842) was one in a series of conflicts known as the Great Game between Britain and Russia over supremacy in Central Asia during the nineteenth century. After the British had secured control of India, it sought to fortify the colony's borders against Russian encroachment. The Governor-General of India, Lord Auckland, addressed the vulnerability of neighboring Afghanistan. In October of 1838, he issued the *Simla Manifesto* in which he recommended the use of military force to restore the long-exiled Shah Shuja to the Afghani throne. The ultimate failure of this strategy resulted in the First Afghan War being referred to as "Auckland's Folly."

In April of 1839, a coalition of five thousand British and Indian troops, along with ten thousand camp followers, entered Afghanistan unopposed and quickly took Kandahar. Two months later they overran Ghazni, defeating the army of the Emir of Afghanistan, Dost Mohammed. They then seized the poorly defended capital of Kabul. In August, after naming Shuja the new Emir, the troops and their camp followers settled in for what would become an increasingly problematic occupation.

The Afghani people were enraged by the British occupation. In October of 1841, a mob attacked and killed a senior British official in Kabul. When Britain's chief representative, William Macnaghten, tried to negotiate peace with Dost Mohammads's son, Mohammad Akbar Khan, he too was murdered.

By January of 1842, the British realized that their Great Game strategy was becoming too dangerous and expensive to continue. The British commander, General William Elphinstone, negotiated a safe-passage exit agreement with Akbar Khan's representatives. On January 6, all fifteen thousand of the British contingent (now including wives and children) departed Kabul for the garrison at Jalalabad. Only one person would arrive there.

Traversing passes along the Kabul River, they were attacked by Ghilzai warriors and Akbar Khan's army. After seven days, with many killed or taken hostage, the British reached Gandamak Pass. It was here, on January 13, that the final massacre occurred. The one known survivor, Dr. William Brydon, limped into Jalalabad bearing the news of one of the most catastrophic defeats in the history of the British Empire. ❑

British troops storming Ghazni in Afghanistan (lithograph, 1842)

REVOLUTION IN FRANCE

Paris, 1848

The revolutionary uprising in Paris lit a fuse that would set off similar actions throughout Europe. Two days of street battles in late February of 1848 led by a coalition of workers and middle-class citizens forced the Prime Minister François Guizot out of office. The "Bourgeois King" Louis Philippe abdicated and went into exile in Great Britain. A provisional government under Jacques Charles Dupont de l'Eure was formed, proclaiming France's Second Republic.

The immediate cause of the unrest was a law banning political assemblies. A marriage of convenience between workers and the middle class was formed to rally against the Guizot government, which was seen as defending the privileges and prerogatives of the upper middle class alone. Under pressure for change from the Parisian populace, the new coalition united a broad spectrum of political ideologies. Five of the eleven new ministers were moderate liberals. The journalist Louis Blanc represented the socialist movement for political reform. Two of the new government's important positions were given to moderate republicans: Alphonse de Lamartine became foreign minister, and the lawyer and journalist Alexandre Auguste Ledru-Rollin was chosen as Minister of the Interior.

In view of its highly diverse interests and ideologies, the new government tried to steer a middle course: a conservative foreign policy combined with a progressive domestic agenda. A high priority was to achieve relief for high unemployment through the establishment of "national workshops." Laws were passed that acknowledged a right to work, prohibited the death sentence for political offenses, protected freedoms of the press and assembly, and guaranteed universal male suffrage.

A coalition of conservative and moderate republicans gained the upper hand at a National Constitutional Assembly held in May. Disagreements over the establishment of the system of national workshops split the coalition between workers and the middle class and degenerated into armed conflict. The workshops were dissolved by a decree on June 21. Workers under 25 years of age were ordered to join the army where they would be employed in planned work in the France's rural areas. The outcome was the June Days Uprising. The uprising in Paris was poorly planned and brutally put down by the War Minister, General Eugène Cavaignac. About three thousand workers were killed and another fifteen thousand deported.

The victory for the forces of law and order was the signal for the resurgence of an authoritarian reaction to the liberation movements that were sweeping through Europe.

Lamartine rejects the red socialist flag in favor of the Tricolor.

A National Assembly held on November 4, 1848, approved a constitution that, among other things, consolidated power in the hands of the president. Surprisingly in an election held December 10, Louis Napoleon (the nephew of Napoleon Bonaparte) was elected president by a landslide. Apparently many workers joined the conservative cause in supporting him out of anger against the role played by the liberals in suppressing the June uprising. Louis Napoleon, who had been in exile in London, returned to Paris to assume the office of the presidency. ❑

MORSE INVENTS THE TELEGRAPH

Washington DC, May 24, 1844

Morse's invention of the telegraph was the first major step in the electronic transmission of information. Samuel Morse (1791–1842) sent the first telegram from Baltimore to Washington DC.

A highly successful portrait and landscape painter, Morse had developed a working model of a telegraphic system in 1837. Around the same time, the Englishmen Charles Wheatstone and William Cooke invented a five-needle telegraph, but it was inferior to that of Morse.

The Morse apparatus used a key to transmit a message. The sender pressed the key, resulting in short or long electrical impulses, which were received on the other end and converted into dots and dashes. Morse also invented a code that converted the sequences of dots and dashes into letters. Morse's telegraph and code quickly became the worldwide standard. ❑

The inventor Samuel Morse

CALIFORNIA GOLD RUSH

Sacramento Valley, California, 1848

The first strike in what became known as the California Gold Rush took place on January 24, 1848, in Coloma, California (near Sacramento), when James W. Marshall, the foreman of a work crew building a saw mill for entrepreneur John Sutter, found a few small nuggets of gold. This accidental find would change the course of U.S. history.

On February 2, a little more than a week after Marshall's discovery, California was ceded to the United States by Mexico. The provision of the Treaty of Guadelupe Hidalgo, which ended the Mexican-American War, required Mexico to give up not only all of its possessions from Texas to Oregon, but also the largest precious metal discovery in modern history. By the end of the Gold Rush in 1855, well over twelve million ounces of gold worth approximately seven billion (2006) dollars would be extracted from

Gold miner

California's mother lodes.

News of the find at Sutter's Mill was not widely known until publisher and merchant Samuel Brannan published a six-page supplement in the April 1st edition of his *California Star*. The official kick-off of the Gold Rush was occasioned by President James Polk's ringing endorsement of gold prospecting in his 1848 State of the Union address.

Over the next six years, 300,000 people from around the world flocked to California. 90,000 Forty-niners, a third of whom foreigners, arrived in 1849. This "gold fever" free-for-all had little oversight aside from codes of conduct developed by the prospectors themselves. Anyone could stake a claim. The lawlessness and violence that grew out of this chaotic system was not brought under control until California statehood in 1850, when government legislation imposed order. Finally in 1866, Congress set legal precedent for the distribution of claims with passage of the Chaffee Laws.

The Gold Rush changed the demographics of the United States. It inspired a mass mi-

Forty-niners panning for gold in the Sacramento Valley

gration that opened the American West and resulted in the first transcontinental railroad. The traffic in gold led to an exponential growth in the US economy. ❏

THE GREAT FAMINE

Ireland, 1845

From the early eighteenth century to the coming of the Great Famine (1845–1852), Ireland had experienced numerous food shortages due to the failure of its single most important crop, the potato. The worst of these was the Famine of 1741 during which a quarter of a million people died. Horrific as this famine was, its effects paled in comparison to those wrought by the epochal events a century later.

The Great Famine was unique, not only for its high death toll, but also for the profound effect it had on Irish culture. By the time it ended in 1852, one million peo-

ple had died. But the famine also caused a complex chain of events that altered the cultures of three nations. One was the emigration of nearly one and a half million Irish, most bound for America. Many died on the transatlantic "coffin boats," but those who survived eventually became a powerful force in the United States. The other was an increased radicalization of the Irish nationalist movement, which became dramatically more violent, creating a legacy of armed engagement that would politically destabilize Ireland and define the Anglo-Irish conflict for more than a century.

Remarkably, these major historical events were occasioned by an ordinary fungal infestation called *Phytophtora infestans* (potato blight). Transported to Europe in 1845 in potato exports aboard American ships, it destroyed the potato crop in a number of countries, but none as catastrophically as in Ireland, the majority of whose inhabitants survived in a subsistence

"monoculture" utterly dependent on the vulnerable tuber as their sole cash crop and source of nutrition. ❏

Irish immigrants in Queenstown (present-day Cobh)

GERMAN CONSTITUTIONAL ASSEMBLY

Frankfurt, May 18, 1848

Hopes for a unified German state as a parliamentary democracy foundered in the face of the concerted opposition of Prussia and Austria. The first elected German national assembly, the Frankfurt Parliament, met in St. Paul's Church in Frankfurt. In the spring of 1848, uprisings spread throughout Germany and resulted in the convocation of a representative body of almost all of the states in the German Confederation.

The enthusiasm generated by the February revolution in France first swept through the small states of southern Germany and crystallized in the issuance of "March Petitions." These demanded a new constitution, greater civil rights, freedom of the press, and the right to bear arms.

Various governments reacted differently. In some places the military was called out to put down demonstrations; this was the case in Vienna on March 13 and in Berlin five days later. In some places the authorities showed themselves more yielding, meet-

National Assembly at St. Paul's Church in Frankfurt (lithograph)

Battle of Kandern (lithograph, 1848)

ing some of the demands and appointing cabinets of "March ministers." But after the first burst of revolutionary fervor dissipated, these soon reverted to preserving the status quo.

German elections for 830 delegates were held in April. All adult males could vote. An uprising by radical ele-ments was put down at the Battle of Kandern. The assembly had a twofold task: to draw up a constitution and to prepare the way for a national government. The fundamental weakness of the assembly lay in its reliance upon the good will of its constituents. It had no way of enforcing compliance. Hence it could not overcome the decided resistance of the two major conservative powers, Austria and Prussia.

By the fall, counterrevolutionary forces had gained the upper hand. Although a constitution was drawn up and a plan was offered for a united Germany under Prussian direction and excluding Austria, it remained unrealized when Friedrich Wilhelm IV refused the imperial crown. ❏

POLITICAL IDEAS OF JOHN STUART MILL

London, 1848

John Stuart Mill's book, *The Principles of Political Economy*, cast fresh light on Britain in the age of the Industrial Revolution.

Mill (1806–1873) was a former civil servant and politician who would serve in Parliament in the 1860s. He was also the owner and editor of the influential *London Review*. Mill was a follower of Jeremy Bentham's utilitarian philosophy. He had also taken up and developed the economic theories of Adam Smith, David Ricardo, and Thomas Malthus. A firm believer in social welfare, he suggested that economic policy should be dictated by government legislation. To ensure that this happened, he advocated governmental involvement in an increasingly wide sphere of activities.

Mills best known work is *On Liberty*, which was published in 1859. In it he articulated a theory and defense of personal rights and liberty that has served as a basis for the workings of democratic governments since that time. ❏

DANCER COSTS THE BAVARIAN KING HIS CROWN

Munich, 1848

During the tumultuous days of the spring of 1848, the Bavarian King Ludwig I abdicated in favor of his son Maximillian II. Ludwig's affair with a dancer along with the revolutionary fervor of the time brought about the change in monarchs.

Despite her name, the woman known as Lola Montez was not a native of Spain. She was born in Limerick, Ireland in 1818, the illegitimate daughter of a Scottish officer and a Creole mother. In 1843, she gave her celebrated debut in London and made her first appearance in Munich on October 10, 1846. She soon won the affections of the king. He gave her the title of Countess of Landsfeld. This elevation to the rank of nobility caused intense controversy and was harshly criticized, primarily from the conservative politicians.

The dancer Lola Montez

King Ludwig I of Bavaria

The revolutionary events that were taking place in other German states spilled over into Bavaria in March of 1848. Ludwig agreed to many of the protesters' demands and called for a new cabinet with the appointment of a liberal interior minister. Rumors of the return of Lola Montez to the city of Munich, from which she had been banished, inflamed popular sentiment and caused renewed uprisings. As a result the king agreed to give up his crown to preserve the dignity of the monarchy.

Forced to leave Munich, Lola said farewell to the happiest time of her life. She traveled from London to Paris and emigrated to the United States in 1851. After numerous affairs and four marriages, she died in poverty in New York in 1861. ❏

HABSBURGS MAINTAIN THEIR POWER IN AUSTRIA

Vienna, 1848

Despite the revolutionary ferment of 1848, the Austrian monarchy succeeded in maintaining its position and halting nationalist movements in Hungary and Italy.

On March 13, Austrian Chancellor Prince Metternich resigned his office in the face of a popular revolution and escaped to England. Two days later the Emperor Ferdinand I promised concessions, including a new constitution. A kind of constitution was promulgated on April 25, but it had been arrived at without the participation of a representative body of the people. This only inflamed matters. An uprising on May 15 forced its revocation and a promise to establish a parliament. Two days later the emperor fled Vienna for Innsbruck.

On July 22, a constitutional parliament of representatives from German and Slavic states met in Vienna. News in September from Hungary, where the nationalist leader Lajos Kossuth had just become Prime Minister and was fighting against imperial troops, led to another revolutionary outbreak in Vienna on October 6. However Field Marshall Prince Windischgraetz moved his troops on Vienna from Prague, while from the east Croatian forces attacked the capital. After a bloody battle in the city on October 31, imperial troops gained the upper hand and control of the city. To stabilize the situation, Ferdinand I agreed to abdicate in favor of his eighteen-year-old nephew Franz Joseph I.

The Hungarian parliament, having refused to acknowledge Franz Joseph as their king, declared their independence from Austrian rule on April 14, 1849. But European states refused to recognize Kossuth's autonomous Republic of Hungary. With the help of Russia, the republican stronghold of Komorn was taken, and the short-lived republic collapsed.

Austria was also successful in maintaining its hold over Italy despite resistance in Milan. In August 1848, King Carl-Albert of Sardinia, who had hoped to lead the unification movement in Italy, was forced to sign a cease-fire after being defeated at Custoza. In the spring of 1849, the war flared up again, but after a second defeat, this time at Novara, Carl-Albert abdicated in favor of his son Victor Emmanuel, Italy's future king. The Italian uprising against Austria ended in Venice. The city capitulated to Austrian troops on August 24, 1849. ❏

Building the barricades at a citizen's uprising in Vienna, May 26, 1848.

SLAVERY DIVIDES A NATION

United States of America, March 12, 1852

The publication of the book *Uncle Tom's Cabin* gave the anti-slavery movement in the United States new impetus. Written by Harriet Beecher Stowe, it indicted the institution of slavery. She described in sentimental terms the hard lot of slaves in the southern United States. In no time at all, it became an international bestseller.

Since the sixteenth century, the tobacco-farming states of Maryland and Virginia had made extensive use of slave labor. Later, the Carolinas and Georgia, then the rest of the Deep South, including Texas, built economies based upon King Cotton and the slaves to harvest it.

When Congress passed a law banning the further importation of slaves in 1808, there were about 400,000 slaves in the South. That number increased by 250,000 by the beginning of the Civil War.

The westward movement by small farmers in the North and cotton planters in the South resulted in both free and slave territories. In 1820, Henry Clay shepherded the Missouri Compromise through the Senate. It tried to establish a balance between the two by granting Missouri statehood as a slave state and outlawing slavery above latitude 36'30°.

Meanwhile, the abolitionist movement was gaining momentum. In 1830, a slave revolt in Virginia led by Nat Turner was brutally suppressed. The same year, the Underground Railroad was organized to smuggle slaves from the South into the North and on to Canada. By 1860, some fifty thousand slaves had escaped to freedom.

After the Mexican-American War (1846–1848), Congressman David Wilmot sponsored legislation, the Wilmot Proviso, to prohibit slavery in the lands acquired from Mexico. This vast new territory consisted of present-day New Mexico, Arizona, Utah, Nevada, and California. Though it passed the House of Representatives, it failed in the Senate.

The entry of a slave-free California into statehood in 1849 threatened to split the Union. The California Compromise reached in 1850 allowed California's entrance as a free state but gave the Utah and New Mexico territories the right to decide for themselves whether or not they wished to permit slavery. In addition slavery was forbidden in Washington DC, the nation's capital. At the same time the passage of the Fugitive Slave Act recognized slaves as property

Harriet Beecher Stowe

and entitled slave owners to demand the return of those who had escaped to free states.

Four years later the two sides came to blows over the Kansas-Nebraska Act of 1854, which repealed the Missouri Compromise

LONDON'S GREAT EXHIBITION

London, 1851

Visitors from England and from all quarters of the globe flocked to the world's largest exhibition. It was opened by Queen Victoria in London's Hyde Park on May 1, 1851. By the time it ended on October 15, attendance had reached six million people.

Staged inside a giant iron and glass conservatory dubbed the Crystal Palace, the Great Exhibition of the Works of Industry of All Nations was designed to pay tribute to the industrial advances that had given Britain unprecedented prosperity and economic

mastery in the first half of the nineteenth century.

The thirteen thousand exhibits from around the world were grouped into six main categories and thirty classes. The displays were housed inside an 1,848-foot-long, 408-foot-wide, and 66-foot-high glass house with 108-foot-high transepts. Designed by Joseph Paxton, the building won the Great Exhibition design competition against over 254 international entries. It was based on the Lily House at the Duke of Devonshire's Chatsworth House.

The prefabricated structure took seventeen weeks to erect and used a million feet of glass. The main focus of attention was the Machinery Court, showing Jacquard looms, De La Rue's envelope machine, and an innovative reaping machine from America. The queen showed interest in the medal-making machine and the electric telegraph, using the latter to send messages

The Crystal Palace at the Great Exhibition in 1851 in London

to Edinburgh and Manchester.

The London Exhibition was only the first of many similar events. Especially noteworthy was the Chicago World's Fair of 1893 that announced to the world the growing commercial power of the United States. ❑

WELLINGTON, ENGLAND'S SOLDIER-STATESMAN

London, September 14, 1852

The Duke of Wellington, the victor of Waterloo and a former prime minister of Britain, died on this day at the age of 83. For almost half a century, "the Iron Duke" personified strength of will and public spirit. Although a rath-

er delicate boy, Arthur Wellesley, the third son of an Irish peer, became a disciplinarian who transformed the British army from, in his words, "the scum of the earth" into "worthy fellows." He served in India and distinguished himself

in Spain before vanquishing Napoleon at Waterloo. His career in politics after Waterloo suffered from his trenchant opposition to electoral reform, but it was impossible to form a Tory government without him. In 1848, he came out

of retirement to organize a military force against the Chartists. In later life, his advice was still sought. Faced with the problem of birds fouling the Crystal Palace, "Sparrow hawks, Ma'am," he said to the queen. He was right—as usual. ❑

LOUIS NAPOLEON BECOMES EMPEROR OF FRANCE

Paris, 1852

and gave settlers the right under the guise of "popular sovereignty" to choose or refuse slavery. As a result Kansas was plunged into a bloody civil war that continued until federal troops were called in.

One participant in the war of "Bleeding Kansas" was John Brown, who commanded a band of abolitionists. In October of 1859, Brown sought to incite a slave revolt in Harpers Ferry, Virginia. He was taken prisoner during an attack on an army arsenal and hanged in Charlestown on December 2. Most slave owners agreed with the justice of the sentence; for the abolitionists he became a martyr for the cause of freedom. Juliet Ward Howe wrote the lyrics to a popular tune sung about Brown, and the "Battle Hymn of the Republic" was born. ❑

The pivotal year of 1848 opened with the overthrow of the French monarchy and the proclamation of a republic. It closed with the election of Louis Napoleon as a prince-president. Louis was the son of Napoleon's brother. As a young man, he traveled throughout Europe. In 1836 and 1840, he failed in attempts to lead Bonapartist revolts against the July monarchy.

Louis was sentenced to life imprisonment for his abortive coups. Having escaped to England, he returned to France in February of 1848 and, despite the laws forbidding the Bonapartes' participation in politics, was elected to the National Assembly. In the presidential election, he was opposed by two left-wingers and a right-wing republican, General Louis Cavaignac. The leftist candidates

together received fewer than half a million votes. Cavaignac received a million and a half. But Louis Napoleon scooped up five and a half million, from workers and peasants as well as the bourgeoisie and upper-class conservatives.

Then on December 2, 1852, Louis Napoleon elevated himself from president to emperor, restoring the house of Bonaparte with a flourish of glory reminiscent of his famous uncle. He crowned himself Napoleon III on the grounds that Napoleon I had abdicated in favor of his son. Though his career in exile was largely undistinguished, on his return to France he exhibited great political adroitness, out-maneuvering his opponents and jailing thousands while gaining massive popular support with his program of tax and welfare reforms to ben-

The Emperor Louis Napoleon

efit the French working class. Foreign anxieties were somewhat eased by his declaration that "the empire means peace." ❑

ABOLITION

Point of interest

The Abolitionist Movement took hold in the United States from 1831 and continued until the end of the Civil War. It was a powerful and influential movement that sought the end of slavery on humanitarian, social, and political grounds. One of its earliest proponents was William Lloyd Garrison (1805–1879), whose newspaper *The Liberator* brought the movement to life.

On July 6, 1854, the Republican Party was founded in the state of Michigan and had in its platform unequivocal support for ending slavery. It united citizens from different parties in the common cause of abolition. In 1856, Abraham Lincoln entered the party, and four years later he became its candidate for presi-

Slaves working on a cotton plantation on the Mississippi River. Bottom left: The abolitionist, John Brown

dent.

Anti-slavery sentiment had already made itself known in Great Britain. The Committee for the Abolition of the Slave Trade was set up in 1787, and the Slave Trade Act of 1807 made the traffic in slaves illegal.

By the beginning of the nineteenth century, slavery had been made illegal in all of the northern United States. Southern whites defended the institution, which they believed was vital to their economic interests as well as supported by pseudoscientific

evidence proving the superiority of the white race. They accused abolitionists of trying to foment slave rebellions, such as the one led by John Brown at Harper's Ferry. The institution of slavery continued in the South until the end of the Civil War. ❑

FLORENCE NIGHTINGALE

Brief Lives

Florence Nightingale (1820–1910), at the request of Secretary of State for War, Sidney Herbert, arrived at the Barrack Hospital in Scutari (near Istanbul) on November 5, 1854. The conditions that she and her party of nurses found were appalling; the wards were infested with vermin and supplies were short. She also encountered hostility from the resident doctors, who resented her and the thirty-thousand pounds with which Herbert had furnished her; initially they forbade her access to the wards. However, the Battle of Alma and the subsequent worsening of conditions, with the wounded laying in their own filth on pallets in the corridors, forced the doctors to accept her assistance. Her first instruction was to order two hundred scrubbing brushes.

Florence Nightingale's innovative ideas on the sanitary conditions in hospitals and the introduction of a code of conduct and training for nurses had lasting effects. Despite the monumental task of caring for the wounded, she still found the time to make her rounds and in time came to be known as the Lady with the Lamp. ❏

The destroyed Russian fortress of Malakov near Sevastopol, September 8, 1855

THE CRIMEAN WAR

Turkey, 1853

In an attempt to test the resolve of the Turks and the British, Tsar Nicholas I occupied Moldavia and Wallachia, autonomous parts of the Ottoman Empire, in 1853. It was a fatal miscalculation in an ongoing dispute between Russia and France concerning the rights of the Orthodox and Catholic Churches in Jerusalem, and turned out to be the trigger for the Crimean War.

Both churches had claimed precedence to the Holy Places; the Catholic Church claimed its right through the Franco-Turkish Treaty of 1740, which had granted it the privilege of protecting all pilgrims to Jerusalem. In an attempt to divert public attention away from domestic issues, Louis Napoleon decided on championing their cause. Over time, however, the actual power had shifted naturally to the Orthodox Church due to the much greater numbers of Orthodox Christians living in the area, and Tsar Nicholas I had assumed the role of protector of the Orthodox cause.

The Turks, unhappy with the unfolding events on their territory, came up with an idea that they hoped would satisfy both parties. In February 1850, they sent the French two keys to the Great Doors of the Church of the Nativity; at the same time they assured the Russians that the keys would not fit. Unsurprisingly, this solution was rejected by both factions. The French took matters into their own hands and, by 1853, had seized control.

Through earlier meetings with British Prime Minister Lord Aberdeen, the Tsar had formed the misapprehension that England would not go to war over Turkey, and based on this, he sent the Menshikov Mission to Constantinople with the brief of securing a protectorate over all Orthodox Christians in the Ottoman Empire. British Ambassador Stratford Canning, who had warned his government that a crisis was brewing, had unofficially assured the Sultan of British backing and urged him to reject Menshikov's demands.

The Russians occupied Moldavia and Wallachia, prompting the Austrians to mobilize. This in turn caused the Prussians to do likewise. At a hastily arranged conference in Vienna, an agreement was reached that allowed the Russians to withdraw, with a face-saving stipulation making the Tsar the protector of the Orthodox Christians. However, the French had become more aggressive in the area. Confident of British support, which seemed confirmed by the arrival of a Franco-British fleet in the Straits (though this was, in fact, a coincidence), the Sultan declared war on Russia in October 1853.

A Russian victory in November over the Turkish fleet at Sinope caused a public outcry in England and France, and the British fleet was ordered into the Black Sea to protect Turkish shipping.

In May of 1854, a British army of thirty thousand landed at Gallipoli under the command of Lord Raglan, with the intention of engaging the Russians in Moldavia and Wallachia. But the Russians had already withdrawn, so still determined on a fight, the allies decided to attack Sevastopol.

The Franco-British army disembarked in confusion at Eupatoria on the Crimean Peninsula in September 1854 and was forced to leave a large part of its supplies on the beach owing to a lack of transport. They engaged the Russians at the River Alma, forcing them to retreat in confusion back to Sevastopol. By not taking swift advantage of their victory, the allies allowed the Russians to fortify the base, and siege warfare ensued.

On October 25, the Russians threatened the allied supply base at Balaclava. The British failed to capitalize on two successful engagements early in the battle. In the afternoon from the heights overlooking Sevastopol,

The British General Sir George Brown and his staff in the Crimea

PHOTOGRAPHIC REPORTS OF WAR

Point of Interest

The Crimean War (1853–1856) was the first modern war in many senses, not least of which because it was the first to be photographed. In addition, technological innovations such as the telegraph made it possible to obtain reports on events while they were happening.

British photographer Roger Fenton brought 312 photographic plates shot at the Siege of Sevastopol back with him to England. They were exhibited in London, then published in book form as well as made into woodblock prints to be reproduced in newspapers. His pictures of the fighting had the intent of countering anti-war sentiment, so they did not show the dark side of the conflict. There were no photos of the dead or wounded or the

Early war photography from the Crimea (1854)

awful sanitary conditions that claimed more lives than the enemies' bullets.

The English press was especially enthralled by the ill-fated cavalry charge of the Light Brigade, which became a symbol of British heroism and was immortalized by Alfred Lord Tennyson in his poem "The Charge of the Light Brigade." ❑

COMMODORE PERRY AND THE OPENING OF JAPAN

Japan, 1853

Lord Raglan noticed a party of Russians attempting to make off with naval guns from an isolated redoubt abandoned earlier by Turkish gunners. Through an intermediary, Lord Airy, Raglan gave vague orders "to prevent the enemy carrying away the guns." In turn these orders were delivered by Captain Nolan to the commander of the Light Brigade, Lord Cardigan, a man he held in contempt. Unable to see over the ridge to the intended redoubt, Cardigan could only view the guns in front of Sevastopol and asked where the guns were. Nolan impatiently waved his arm and said, "There!" The Light Brigade charged to their fate.

After another battle, at Inkerman where both armies got lost, the allies had to endure a winter siege, exacerbated by a gale that sank three million pounds' worth of supplies. The deprivations suffered by the army were well reported by William Russell of the *Times*, and when at last the allies took Sevastapol and claimed victory, the public mood was for peace. Viscount Palmerston, who had replaced Lord Aberdeen as Prime Minister, was able to negotiate a peace at the Treaty of Paris in 1856. ❑

When American Commodore Matthew Perry sailed into Tokyo Bay on July 8, 1853, his goal was to effect the Fillmore Administration's mandate to open Japan's ports to foreign shipping, thereby ending two hundred years of the ruling Tokugawa shoganate's policy of *sakoku*. This policy set severe restrictions on communications with the West and prohibited, under penalty of death, not only the entry of foreigners into Japan but also travel by Japanese out of Japan. Created to halt the aggressive trade policies of Spain and Portugal, it also sought to expunge the growing influence of Catholic missionaries.

In practice, *sakoku*, which literally means "locked-up country," was not a policy of total isolation. Japan extended a "most favored nation" status toward the Netherlands, China, and Korea, with whom it continued to pursue mutually profitable relations. Maintaining its entry and exit prohibitions, it allowed Dutch, Chinese, and Koreans to carry out trade on the island of Dejima off the coast of Nagasaki.

After the 1842 Treaty of Nanjing, by which Britain forced the opening of Chinese ports and wrought from China a series of one-sided concessions, Western

countries sought to impose similar terms on Japan. None was more determined than the US. The US government's first official attempt failed when, in 1846, the Tokugawa shogunate was unimpressed by the presence of a solitary warship in Tokyo Bay under the command of Commander James Biddle.

The breakthrough came in 1848 when Captain James Glynn successfully negotiated temporary terms with the shogun's representatives at Nagasaki. Upon his return home, he recommended the United States use force to open the ports of Japan. This set in motion the aggressive policy that would result in the arrival into Tokyo Bay of Commodore Perry's heavily armed "Black Ships" on July 8, 1853.

Known as *kurofune*, the four black warships were a symbolic show of force that convinced the shogunate to consider the Americans petition. Along with the obligatory tributary gifts, Perry presented a letter from President Fillmore to the Emperor that contained a series of proposals, concerned not with trade privileges but rather with the United States' desire to use Japanese ports for fleet maintenance. In addition, they called for the guarantee of safe passage for shipwrecked American sailors and

Admiral Perry being received by the Japanese (lithograph)

the permission to buy maritime provisions, especially coal, from Japanese merchants. After delivering this formal petition, Perry announced that he would return in the spring to receive their reply.

By the time Perry returned in February of 1854, this time with seven warships, Shogun Tokugawa Ieyoshi had already drawn up a document that agreed to all the proposals in President Fillmore's letter. The official ratification took place on March 31, 1854. Perry's accomplishment was to open Japan to the presence of American and other foreign ships. It did not establish commercial trading rights. Those rights would be won in 1858 by U.S. envoy Thomas Harris and the signing of the Treaty of Amity and Commerce. ❑

RAPID GROWTH OF THE STEEL INDUSTRY

London, 1855

An economical procedure for converting pig iron to steel was invented in 1851 by an American from Pittsburg named William Kelly. Calling it an air-boiling process, he discovered that by injecting air into molten iron, he could efficiently reduce its carbon content and other impurities, thereby dramatically cutting the time and cost of creating steel from iron. At about the same time, an Englishman in Sheffield, Henry Bessemer, had developed a similar process that he called decarbonization. Although Kelly had obtained a patent before Bessemer, it was the Englishman who has been credited as being the founder of the modern steel industry due to his creation of the Bessemer Converter. Patented in 1855 as the Bessemer Process, it was the first procedure for the inexpensive, mass production of steel. Bessemer Steel facilitated large-scale projects such as bridges, buildings, and ships and was a catalyst for the Industrial Revolution in Europe and America.

One of the beneficiaries of this new technology was Germany's powerful House of Krupp. A prominent German family for four hundred years, their role as leaders in steel manufacturing began in 1811 when Friedrich Krupp opened a small foundry in Essen. Specializing in casting steel into large blocks, its use of pre-Bessemer methods allowed for only a modest output. It was under Friedrich's son, Alfred, that the small foundry grew to be an industrial giant, renowned for its use of steel in structural engineering and in the making of railway materials, locomotives, ships, and most famously, weapons and ammunition. Europe's single most successful employer of the Bessemer Process, Krupp became the chief supplier of ordnance to the armies of Europe throughout the nineteenth century. ❑

Molten pig iron converted into steel at a nineteenth century foundry.

Decarbonization process using the Bessemer Converter

THE OIL BOOM

Pennsylvania, August 28, 1859

For hundreds of years, oil had been skimmed from naturally occurring "seeps" in western Pennsylvania by Native Americans and European settlers and used for medicinal purposes and lighting. Its use as a mass-produced industrial product began in the 1850s when a New York lawyer, George Bissell, teamed up with Yale chemist, Benjamin Silliman, to test its feasibility as a marketable illuminant. When the test results suggested its commercial potential, Bissell, along with Connecticut banker James Townsend, formed the Pennsylvania Rock Oil Company. It was their belief that oil could be extracted by the same well-drilling techniques used to obtain salt. Learning that this technique had long been employed by the inhabitants of Titusville in western Pennsylvania, Bissell chose Titusville as the site for the U.S. oil industry's first well.

By September 1861, the Empire Well at nearby Funkville was producing three thousand barrels a day.

The Pennsylvania oil boom heralded the arrival of thousands of fortune-hunters. In the once bucolic region of Oil Creek Valley, drilling towns sprang up overnight, chock-a-block with oil derricks. Oil wells were sunk so close to each other that huge conflagrations often broke out. The original Drake's Well survived only a short time before it too was destroyed by fire.

Production and profits saw exponential growth with the region's take-over by John D. Rockefeller and Standard Oil. Already producing ten percent of all petroleum output in the United States, Rockefeller expanded his Ohio-based company's monopoly when he bought out local oil interests bankrupted by the "Black September" stock crash of 1873. Under his stewardship, Oil Creek Valley produced half of the world's oil supply until the East Texas boom of 1901. ❑

THE SEPOY MUTINY

India, 1858

Staged by members of Nineteenth Bengal Native Infantry (known as "Sepoys") at Barrackpore, a mutiny quickly spread throughout north and central India. It inspired a rebellion by elements within the general populace. This spontaneous outbreak across has led some historians to see it as more than a "mutiny." Karl Marx christened it "India's first war of independence."

Diverse sectors of Indian society began to openly resist the British East India Company's intrusions into their traditional ways of life. The British were patronizing or outright dismissive of Hindu and Muslim religious practices, raising concerns that they sought to impose Christianity on their Indian subjects. They also overturned ancient practices governing the dispensation of property. Many in the old aristocracy had been deprived of their ancestral lands. Artisans and merchants resented the imposition of confiscatory taxes and tariff restrictions that favored the East India Company. The justice system provided no redress for the cruel treatment of the populace at the hands of Company overseers. The Sepoy Mutiny was the incident that symbolized these multiple grievances.

The British found allies in no less than twenty princely states including the fabled Gurkhas of Nepal. Sikhs and members of the Native Infantries of Bombay and Madras also aided the British troops.

Atrocities were committed by both sides, most notably by the Indians with the Bibighar Massacre at Cawnpore, where 200 British men, women and children were butchered and tossed down a well. For their part, the British committed mass murder after their siege of Delhi in September of 1857.

The major battles of the war ended with a British victory in June of 1858. In the aftermath the British government rethought its "insensitive" treatment of its Indian subjects. Divesting the British East India Company of all colonial power, the Queen issued a proclamation promising a more humane colonial stewardship and assumed direct rule of India. ❑

DARWIN'S *ORIGIN OF SPECIES*

London, 1859

Charles Robert Darwin (1809–1882) was born in Shrewsbury, England to a socially prominent family. After a brief stint as a medical student at Edinburgh, his interest in zoology and religion led him to Cambridge, where he studied for a vocation in the Anglican Church. Befriended by the botanist J. S. Henslow, he was encouraged instead to pursue his interest in botany and biology. Finishing his studies, he accepted an offer to serve as an unpaid naturalist aboard the *H.M.S Beagle* bound for South America.

During this five-year voyage 1831–1836, Darwin collected a trove of zoological specimens. He also kept copious notes, which formed the basis for his first work, *The Voyage of the Beagle*. It was during this voyage that he began to formulate his theory of natural selection and its logical, and more controversial, corollary, the theory of evolution.

Realizing that these theories would be misinterpreted as atheistic and therefore an affront to the Anglican Church, as well as to many of his fellow scientists, he revealed his ideas to only a handful of confidants. It was not until he received a paper from a colleague, Alfred Russell Wallace, which pro-

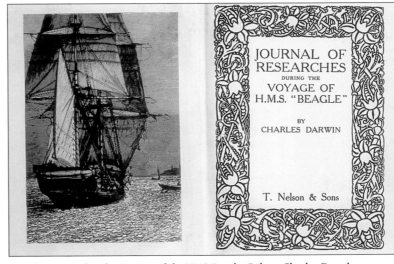

Darwin's Journals: *The Voyage of the* HMS Beagle. Below: Charles Darwin

pounded a theory of natural selection very similar to his own, that he decided to risk the controversy that might ensue. In May 1859, he and Wallace presented a joint paper to the Linnean Society. The response was dishearteningly anemic. Neither celebrated nor damned, it was practically ignored.

The situation was quite different on November 22 with the publication of his masterwork, *On the Origin of Species*. A comprehensive elucidation of his ideas, it only hinted that the processes of natural selection were applicable to the evolution of not only plants, sea life, and animals but to humans as well. For this mere hint, he was vilified by opponents, many of whom misunderstood his theories. Despite the outcry, the book was wildly popular and went through many editions. He would not fully address human evolution until 1871 with the publication of *The Descent of Man*. ❑

Massacre of women and children during the Great Indian Mutiny of 1858

THE AMERICAN CIVIL WAR

South Carolina, April 12, 1861

The question of slavery ignited a bloody conflict between the northern and southern sections of the United States.

Abraham Lincoln

The attack of General Pierre G. T. Beauregard on Fort Sumter in South Carolina on April 12, 1861, marked the beginning of the American Civil War. After the federal troops who were holding the fort surrendered, President Abraham Lincoln called up 75,000 militia men to prevent the secession of the southern states and dissolution of the Union.

The origins of the Civil War lay in the stark contrast between the economic and social orders of the industrial North and the agrarian South. The immediate cause of the South's decision to secede was the election of Lincoln as the sixteenth president in 1860. Lincoln was adamantly opposed to the extension of slavery into the new western territories and states. All of the 180 electors who voted for Lincoln came from the slave-free northern states.

In response to the election, South Carolina announced its secession from the Union on December 24, 1860. By the time of Beauregard's attack on Fort Sumter, six other southern states had followed suit: Alabama, Mississippi, Florida, Georgia, Louisiana, and Texas. North Carolina, Tennessee, Arkansas, and Virginia joined them shortly thereafter, and these eleven Southern states faced the remaining 23 Northern states.

Meeting in Montgomery, Alabama, on February 8, 1861, representatives of ten of the secessionist states ratified their joint decision to form the Confederate States of America (CSA). The following day, Jefferson Davis, a former U.S. Army officer who had served as Secretary of War under the fourteenth president, Franklin Pierce, was chosen as the Confederacy's first president.

Lincoln refused to recognize the breakaway republic. Attempts at mediation failed. After his inauguration on March 4, Lincoln made it clear that he would not attempt to eliminate slavery in those states in which it already existed, but at the same time he would not allow the Union to be divided. Some time later, he set forth his reasoning explicitly in a response to Horace Greeley, the publisher of the *New York Tribune*. Greeley, an unwavering Republican, had written an editorial entitled "The Prayer of Twenty Million" in which he urged the president to act to end slavery in the South. Lincoln set out his more moderate views, reasserting that his foremost concern was the preservation of the Union.

The first major battle took place on the Bull Run River in Virginia. The Confederate army under Beauregard's command succeeded in repelling the attack of Union forces led by Brigadier General Irvin McDowell. In

Pickett's Charge at the Battle of Gettysburg, 1863

the war's early engagements, the South gained ground, not in the least because many of its officers were drawn from the pre-war United States Army.

The Civil War provided the occasion for a broad development of military tactics and technology. On March 9, 1862, the first battle between armored ships took place in Chesapeake Bay. Neither the Union's *Monitor* nor the Confederacy's *Merrimack* was seriously damaged in the fighting, but they proved their superiority over the wooden warships and rendered them obsolete.

Military operations unfolded on two fronts: in the east between the Atlantic and the Allegheny Mountains, and in the west between Alleghenies and the Mississippi. The Midwest and Far West remained largely untouched by the conflict.

The South's master strategist was Robert E. Lee, first as military advisor to President Davis and then as commander of the Army of Virginia. His counterpart in the North was Ulysses S. Grant. Grant was commander in the West in 1863, and in the following year was brought in to command the Army of the Potomac, and then became commander of all Union forces.

Grant commanded the Union troops at the Battle of Shiloh, fought April 6–7, 1862, in Tennessee and barely prevented the South from routing his forces. Twenty-six thousand men lost their lives in the battle.

On April 25, 1862, Northern troops were able to take the Port of New Orleans and push their way up the Mississippi. In the following year, Grant captured the town of Vicksburg after a siege lasting seven weeks. With this victory he was able to gain control of the Mississippi River and split the Southern army. In the Battle of Chattanooga (November 11–13, 1863), Grant captured the crucial juncture of the Confederacy's railroad lines. Finally in December 1864, General William Tecumseh Sherman won a decisive victory for the Union at Nashville, effectively bringing the war in the West to an end. Sherman's march to the Atlantic was especially hard on civilian populations, marked by plundering and wholesale destruction of cities.

The decisive engagements, however, were in the East. At the Battle of Seven Pines (May 31–June 1, 1862), the Union army was stopped cold. Then at the Seven-Day Battle (June 26–July 2, 1862), Lee succeeded in thwarting Union General George McClellan's plan to take Richmond. Again at the second Battle of Bull Run (August 29–31, 1862), the South was victorious. Its intent

Union victory at Chattanooga

Fallen soldiers at the Battle of Gettysburg

to bring the battle to the North, however, was thwarted by McClellan at Antietam, Maryland (September 17, 1862), in what would turn out to be the bloodiest day of the entire war.

The Battle of Gettysburg raged for three days, July 1–3, 1863. In the end the Union troops under General George G. Meade defeated the Confederate Army of Northern Virginia. This was the high-water mark of the South's northward incursion and is considered to be the turning point of the war. After the fighting, 23,000 Union and 28,000 Confederate soldiers lay dead on the battlefield.

Gettysburg was the signal for the North to make more effective use of its human and economic resources. The population of the North was over twenty million, in contrast to the agrarian South's population of nine million, of which four million were slaves. A Northern naval blockade of Southern ports had devastating effects, preventing Southern states from reaping the benefits of their export of cotton.

Lee's army was able to halt Grant's advance at the Battle of Cold Harbor (June 1–6, 1864), but the losses were staggering, amounting to ninety thousand on both sides. After Sherman's occupation and devastation of Atlanta in September 1864, Southern resistance crumbled. Four months later the two rivals, Lee and Grant, met, and Lee formally surrendered, ending a war that had pitted brother against brother and changed the destiny of the United States. ❑

THE UNIFICATION OF ITALY

Italy, March 17, 1861

King Victor Emmanuel II of Piedmont and Sardinia was given the title King of Italy at the behest of the first Italian parliament. Victor Emmanuel (1820–1878) had been on the throne of his kingdom since 1849. He had turned over the responsibility for guiding the unification of Italy to his chief minister, Camillo Graf Benso di Cavour, the founder of the liberal newspaper *Il Risorgimento* (The Rebirth), from which this era in Italian history takes its name.

Sardinia had entered the Crimean War on the side of the French and British and had gained international recognition after the victory over Russia. Cavour called upon Napoleon III to help drive Austria out of Lombardy (through the Treaty of Plombières, 1858). In the war with Austria that followed, Italy received support from France and gained victories at Magenta and Solfierno in the spring of 1859. According to a treaty signed in Zurich in 1859, Austria ceded its Italian holdings to France except for the cities of Mantua and Peschiera. France then handed

Camillo Benso di Cavour (1810–1861)

Giuseppe Garibaldi (1807–1882)

over the territory to Sardinia. In return Sardinia gave France the cities of Nice and Savoy.

On May 11, 1860, the freedom fighter Giuseppe Garibaldi landed with over a thousand followers—the Expedition of the 1,000—on the western coast of Sicily with the intention of liberating the kingdom from the rule of the Bourbons. He arrived triumphant in Naples on September 7, the day after the last Bourbon king, Francis II, had fled his capital. On October 21, a

plebiscite resulted in the unification of the Kingdom of the Two Sicilies with that of Sardinia and Piedmont. Joining with them were the principalities in central Italy and Romagna.

Through its participation in the Prussian-Austrian War of 1866, the new Kingdom of Italy gained possession of Venice. After the withdrawal in 1870 of the French troops that had been stationed in Rome since 1848, the city of Rome became Italy's capital. ❑

HALF-HEARTED EMANCIPATION OF THE SERFS

Russia, 1861

Russia's defeat in the Crimean War convinced Tsar Alexander II that his empire needed to modernize its institutions. The ineptness of the army, which consisted largely of peasant serfs, was symbolic of his country's backwardness. Seeing serfdom as the primary obstacle to Russia's emergence from its feudal state to a westernized market economy, Alexander sought to convince wealthy landowners that freeing the serfs to work as independent agents would create a more profitable economic system.

Opposed to the loss of cheap labor and to the competitive threat that the freed serfs would

pose as independent farmers, the landowners negotiated a compromise wherein the serfs would remain beholden to them by becoming paying tenants on the existing estates. This adumbrated "freedom" was a major flaw in Alexander's Emancipation Reform of 1861.

Proclaimed on February 19 and codified in the Emancipation Manifesto, it granted the serfs the status of free citizens as well as the right to buy the lands on which they worked as tenants. This second provision inspired disdain in the serfs, who protested that the possibility of ever being able to buy their tenancies outright was very remote.

In fact, the new system of obligation was not very different from their old one. Economically, they were still serfs.

Tsar Alexander II

The Emancipation Reform also drew the ire of Russia's burgeoning socialist movement. Seen as benefiting only the ruling class, it became a symbol of the hated Tsar's duplicity. As such it helped feed the ideological fervor that resulted in Alexander's assassination by a radical socialist group on March 1, 1881. ❑

BATTLES OVER SCHLESWIG AND HOLSTEIN

Vienna, 1864

At the conclusion of the Second Danish-German War, Denmark lost control over the Duchies of Schleswig, Holstein, and Lauenburg. A peace accord reached in Vienna ended the hostilities between Denmark on one side and Austria and Prussia on the other. Denmark was forced to turn over possession of the three duchies to its opponents. In so doing, it lost two-fifths of its land and had to waive its rights to protect the interests of the Danish minorities in the relinquished territories.

The London Protocol of 1852 confirmed that Schleswig and Holstein would become semiautonomous areas within the Kingdom of Denmark. On March 20, 1863, Schleswig was fully incorporated into Denmark through the provisions of a new constitution. The status of Holstein and Lauenburg was not addressed at that time.

On November 15, 1863, when Danish King Friederich VII died without heirs, Prince Christian IX from the House of Schleswig-Holstein-Sonderburg-Glucksburg was given the throne of Denmark. His agreement with the decision to annex Schleswig ignited the war with Prussia and Austria. German-leaning residents of Holstein called for the Duke of Augustenburg to become its duke and that of Schleswig as well. He accepted and became Friederich VIII, the Duke of Schleswig and Holstein. He called on the diet of the German Confederation to come to his aid. As the Germans rallied to support him, the Danes withdrew their soldiers from disputed territory.

The Prussian Chancellor Otto von Bismarck used the conflict to his advantage. He accused Denmark of abandoning the London Protocol and by mentioning the Protocol challenged the legitimacy of the Duke of Augustenburg. On February 1, 1864, Prussia and Austria invaded Schleswig. The war lasted only seven weeks and ended with a Prussian victory.

On June 29, Denmark agreed to a settlement by which they gave up Schleswig, Holstein, and Lauenburg to Prussia and Austria. The shared rulership of the acquired territories soon led to a dispute between the two victors. The Gasteiner Convention prevented a confrontation:

Prussian troops fighting over Schleswig-Holstein

Austria received administrative control over Holstein; Prussia obtained Schleswig and purchased Lauenburg from Austria for 2.5 million Danish crowns.

After its defeat in the Austro-Prussian War of 1867, Austria ceded all claims to the duchies and Schleswig-Holstein became a province of Prussia. This disappointed the hopes of many of its residents that they could form a separate independent state. The incorporation into Prussia had important consequences for the new province: the introduction of the draft, the end of trade restrictions, the entry into the German *Zollverein* (customs union), administrative reform with the creation of twenty districts, and elevation of the city of Schleswig to provincial capital. The Prussian government's attempt to suppress the Danish language and sense of identity remained a source of friction in the new province. ❑

FIRST UNDERGROUND RAILWAY

London, 1863

The Metropolitan Railway was incorporated in 1853 but not until 1860 was enough money raised to begin construction. The railway tunnels were built using the cut-and-cover method; this had the unfortunate side effect of causing massive traffic disturbances, the demolition of houses that were located along the line, and frequent breaks in sewer lines. Despite these inconveniences, the railway was built to relieve traffic congestion in London, and on its opening in 1863, it carried thirty thousand passengers. The Metropolitan Railway ran east to west, from Paddington to Farringdon station, and by 1880, it carried over forty million passengers a year.

By 1884, other railways had been built and the inner circle, currently known as the Circle Line, was created. The Metropolitan Railway was electrified in the 1900s and became a part of the London Underground, which today covers an area of 253 square miles (655 sq km.) ❑

THE BURKE AND WILLS EXPEDITION

Australia, 1861

In August of 1860, Robert O'Hara Burke and William John Wills set out from Melbourne, Australia, leading nineteen men on an expedition to cross the continent from south the north. The expedition was to cover about 1,750 miles of unexplored territory, and none of the men had the experience to undertake the journey. Seven of the nineteen men died, including Wills and Burke; John King was the only man to complete the whole trip.

After reducing the group to Wills, King, and Charles Grey, Burke left the other men at Coopers Creek and continued to the Gulf. In February of 1861, the four men arrived at the Little Bynoe River but could not cross the swamps to reach the Gulf. During their return to Coopers Creek, Grey died. When they finally arrived in camp in April, the three survivors found that it had been abandoned seven hours earlier. Unable to follow the other men, they remained at Coopers Creek where Burke and Wills perished; King would have shared their fate, but he was instead rescued by aborigines and eventually returned to Melbourne. ❑

THE FIRST GENEVA CONVENTION AND THE RED CROSS

Geneva, August 22, 1864

Sixteen nations were invited to a conference sponsored by the Swiss parliament to address the laws of war and decide on conventions "for the Amelioration of the Condition of the Wounded and Sick in Armed Forces in the Field." Twelve of the attending countries signed the protocol that became known as the First Geneva Convention. By the end of the nineteenth century, 38 nations had signed.

Among other things, the Geneva Convention states that military hospitals and their personnel are neutral in war, civilians wanting to help the wounded ought to be considered as noncombatants, and all wounded soldiers, regardless of their nationality, should receive medical attention.

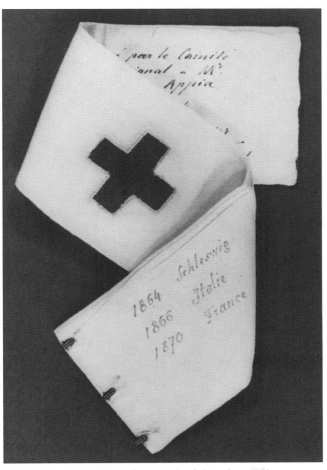

The Red Cross is a universally recognized sign of protection

This initiative was largely the work of Swiss businessman and philanthropist Henri Dunant (1828–1910). He was an eyewitness to the Battle of Solferino during the war between France, Sardinia, and Austria. His book, *A Remembrance of Solferino* published in 1862, was a passionate description of the suffering of the wounded in war and was instrumental in garnering support for the establishment of a relief organization. In 1863, the International Committee of the Red Cross was founded with the mission to improve the care and alleviate the suffering of victims of war. ❑

FIRST DISCOVERIES IN GENETICS

Austria, February 8, 1865

Mendel's Laws became the fundamental principles for the theory of reproduction and biological inheritance. After the systematic crossbreeding of peas and beans, the Austrian monk and naturalist Gregor Mendel presented his discoveries to the Society for Natural History in Brünn, the town in which he lived. Mendel showed that out of four crossbred plants, one had recessive traits, two were hybrid,

Gregor Mendel (1822–1884)

and one had dominant traits. This formed the basis for the science of genetics and proved a crucial component to the general theory of evolution. ❑

TAIPING REBELLION

China, July 1864

By the late 1840s, the Han population of southern China had become increasingly disaffected with the ruling Qing Dynasty. Seeking new leadership, thousands became followers of a heterodox Protestant convert named Hong Xiuquan. Believing himself to be Jesus's younger brother, Hong promised to lead the overthrow of the hated Manchu Qing and in so doing establish the Heavenly Kingdom of Peace.

The rebellion began in January of 1851 when an army of his followers, known as Taiping, defeated Imperial troops during the Jintian Uprising. This battle was the first in a series of victories over a fifteen-year period that nearly toppled the Qing Dynasty and saw more than thirty million Chinese convert to Hong's new religion.

Based in Nanjing, the Heavenly Kingdom of Peace was a theocratic, utopian empire in which private property was abolished, all intoxicants and polygamy were prohibited, and men and women were considered equals. The centerpiece of its strength was the three-million-strong Taiping Heavenly Army. Combined with allied Taiping rebel armies, Hong had over ten million soldiers with which to attack the Qing Imperial forces and their allies, who included British and French troops.

The Taiping Rebellion was finally suppressed. By its end in July 1864, it is estimated that twenty to thirty million Chinese had been killed, making the conflict one of the deadliest in history. ❑

GENEVA CONVENTIONS

Point of Interest

After the First Geneva Convention, further agreements followed that addressed the rights of the wounded and the victims of war. The laws of war were addressed at two conferences held in The Hague, in 1899 and 1907. What is now known as the Third Geneva Convention, the product of a conference held in 1929, addressed the treatment of prisoners of war.

All of these conventions were revised, updated, and ratified at a conference held in Geneva in 1949 and, taken as a whole, have come to be known under the general rubric of the Geneva Conventions. The articles in the Convention are directly concerned with *jus in bellum* (the laws for waging war). They outlaw torture, mutilation, and degrading forms of treatment of prisoners. They govern the treatment of civilian populations and provide definitions of protected persons. As of 2006, the Geneva Convention had been signed by 194 nations. ❑

AFTERMATH OF THE CIVIL WAR

Appomattox, Virginia, April 9, 1865

Confederate General Robert E. Lee formally surrendered to Union General Ulysses S. Grant at Appomattox, Virginia, on April 9, 1865, ending four years of bitter civil war. At the time of surrender, Lee had about thirty thousand men under his command, while Grant's army was 115,000 strong. Less than three weeks later on April 26, Confederate General Joseph E. Johnston laid down his arms in Durham, North Carolina. Finally on May 10, Jefferson Davis, President of the Confederate States of America, surrendered to Union troops in Irvinsville, Georgia.

The American Civil War is considered to be history's first modern war in that both sides mobilized their entire populations and harnessed all of their economic and technological forces to fight it. It cost over 600,000 military lives: 360,000 Union and 240,000 Confederate soldiers.

In addition to preventing the breakup of the Union, the war resulted in the end of slavery. President Abraham Lincoln had signed the Emancipation Proclamation on January 1, 1863, which outlawed slavery in all of the seceding states. Its provisions finally came into effect with the end of the war. With the passage of the 13th Amendment, the institution of slavery was brought to an end in all states and territories of the United States. This granted freedom to about four million slaves.

Lincoln, who was reelected to a second term as US president in 1864, had designed a plan for rebuilding the South at war's end. Unfortunately,

he did not live to realize it. On April 15, 1865, at a performance of *Our American Cousin* at Ford's Theater in Washington DC, Lincoln was shot and fatally wounded by a fanatical adherent to the Southern cause, the actor John Wilkes Booth. The original plan may have been simply to abduct the president. In any event, Booth was hunted down and shot while trying to escape.

Lincolns' successor was his Vice President, Andrew Johnson. Johnson had been the only senator from a Southern state (Tennessee) to side with the North. Lincoln had planned a policy of national reconciliation in hopes of quickly healing the wounds of war. At first Johnson was able to implement Lincoln's program, since the newly elected congress had not yet met. In the summer of 1865, he approved new elections for the South. Under the provisions of the 13th Amendment, the seceding states were readmitted into the Union.

Despite the North's victory and the formal end to slavery, one cannot speak of equal rights for freed slaves. Intentionally demeaning, racist legislation called Black Codes ensured that freed slaves would be second-class citizens and limited their mobility and access to legal redress. The radical wing of the Republican Party reacted harshly. It demanded that the Southern states be treated as conquered territories and at first refused Southern representatives' admittance to Congress. A fifteen-member committee, the Joint Committee on Reconstruction, was founded to supervise conditions in the South.

On April 9, 1866, Congress passed the Civil Rights Act that conferred citizenship on

Freed child slaves in Louisiana

all persons born in the United States, with the sole exception of the Native American population. The 14th Amendment added teeth to the act, and the 15th Amendment passed in 1870 went on to state, "The right of citizens of the United States to vote shall not be denied or abridged by the United States or by any State on account of race, color, or previous condition of servitude."

The radical wing of the Republican party gained seats in the election of 1866, winning a two-thirds majority and with it the ability to override presidential vetoes. They proceeded to make their Reconstructionist policies retroactive.

Revenge, corruption, demagoguery, and electoral fraud

Joyful former slaves celebrating freedom. Theoretically, blacks had equal rights with whites.

EMPEROR MAXIMILIAN OF MEXICO

Querétaro, Mexico, 1867

were the order of the day in the South, greatly damaging the country's recovery. Secret societies founded by white reactionaries, of which the most prominent was the Ku Klux Klan, terror-

Ulysses S. Grant

ized the black population. The election of the victorious Union General Ulysses S. Grant to the presidency in 1868 did little to lessen the South's antipathy for the new state of things. Under the presidency of Rutherford B. Hayes (1877–1881), Northern troops that had been an occupying force were finally withdrawn from Southern states. ❑

Robert E. Lee

On April 10, 1864, Maximilian, Archduke of Austria and brother of Emperor Franz Josef, was appointed Emperor of Mexico. The move came as part of France's attempt to establish a Catholic empire in the country and was inspired by the ambitions of Napoleon III.

Maximilian had been the governor of Lombardy-Venetia but was removed from office in 1859, having been blamed for Austria's failure to retain Lombardy against a Piedmontese-French attack. Until his appointment as Emperor of Mexico, he had lived in his castle at Trieste, pursuing his avocation as a botanist.

His reign as Emperor lasted for only three years. Seeing him as the agent of Napoleon III's failed imperialist ambitions to establish a Catholic empire in Mexico, Mexico's republican President Benito Juárez ordered Maximilian's arrest. He was executed in Querétaro on June 19, 1867 along with two of his generals, Miguel Miramón and Thomás Mejía.

Maximilian's brief rule, during which he managed to set up a stable government, followed the invasion of Mexico by France, Spain, and Britain and the subsequent 1861 Convention of London. At this convention, the three European powers demanded reparations from Mexico for various financial losses incurred during their occupation of Mexican territories while agreeing to eschew further colonial expansion. In 1862, Spain and Britain abandoned this provocative reparations scheme, but France continued and asserted its colonial intentions, thereby flouting the Convention. Faced with increased pressure from the United States, Napoleon eventually gave up his colonial plans and with them his emperor. Abandoned, the hapless Maximilian, an involuntary ruler at best, could only await his fate. ❑

Édouard Manet, *The Execution of Emperor Maximilian* (1867)

OPENING THE SUEZ CANAL

Egypt, November 17, 1869

With invited guests from around the world in attendance, the French Empress Eugenie officially opened the Suez Canal. The canal joined the Mediterranean and Red Seas, shortening the route from London to Iran or India by 42 percent and to Mombasa or Singapore by 30 percent.

Until this time, a traveler from Hamburg to Bombay had to go around the Cape of Good Hope at the southern tip of Africa, a journey of 11,200 nautical miles. By going through the Canal, that distance was cut almost in half. The Suez Canal is 100 miles (160 km) long, 65 feet (22 m) wide, and 25 feet (8 m) deep.

In 1854, the Egyptian viceroy, Said Pasha, sold a concession to the French diplomat and financier Ferdinand de Lesseps. Under his direction the canal was built ac-

cording to the design of an Austrian engineer, Alois Negrelli, at a cost of nineteen million pounds sterling.

The idea of constructing a passage from the Mediterranean to the Red Sea was not a new one. It had been considered as early as the second millennium BC. Around 1300 BC, Seti I and Ramesses II built the first canal from the Nile to Lake Timsah. On this waterway goods traveled back and forth between the Nile Delta and the settlement on the Red Sea coast. In the seventh century BC, the pharaoh Necho II began construction of a canal from Bubastis in the delta to the region around Pithom. The project was said to have cost upward of 120,000 laborers their lives, and then work was stopped because of an unfavorable oracle. The Persian king, Darius I (522–486 BC), completed Necho's canal. It was maintained

Celebration in honor of the opening of the Suez Canal, November 17, 1869

haphazardly thereafter and fell completely into disuse by the time of Arab conquest of Egypt.

After its opening the Suez Canal came under British control. Shares in the Suez Canal Company (Compagnie Universalle du Canal Maritime de Suez) were originally divided between the French and

the Egyptians. During a speculative crisis in 1875, British Prime Minister Benjamin Disraeli was able to acquire Egypt's shares for Great Britain with the help of a timely loan from the banker Lionel Rothschild. Britain occupied the Canal Zone in 1882 and remained there until the Suez Crisis of 1956. ❑

RUSSIA SELLS ALASKA TO THE UNITED STATES

Alaska, March 30, 1867

With the purchase of Alaska, the continental expansion of the United States came to an end. Russia sold Alaska and the Aleutian Islands, a territory of over 800,000 square miles (1.3 million sq km) to the United States for a sum of 7.2 million dollars. Called by many in the United States "Seward's Folly," after U.S. Secretary of the Treasury William Seward, the

sale was nevertheless ratified by Congress on April 9, 1867.

In 1733, the Danish explorer Vitus Jonassen Bering led a Russian expedition into Alaska across the straits that now bear his name. In 1799, a Russian-American company was given the rights to settle and exploit Alaska's resources for twenty years. In financial difficulties after the end of the Crimean

War, Russia offered it for sale. The first major wave of settlers arrived at the end of the nineteenth century as news came of gold strikes on the Alaskan coast and the Yukon River. In the year 1893 alone, gold finds amounted to over a billion dollars.

Alaska formally became a U.S. Territory in 1912, and in 1959, it

Gold rush in Dawson, the Yukon Territory

was admitted as the 49th State of the Union. ❑

MEIJI RESTORATION: THE WESTERNIZATION OF JAPAN

Japan, January 3, 1868

A western-influenced era in Japan began, ironically, with the "Restoration of Imperial Government" proclamation issued on January 3, 1868. Ending two hundred years of rule by the Tokugawa shogunate, it elevated the sixteen-year-old Meiji Emperor to the Japanese throne.

The shogunate's fall from power began when Tokugawa signed the Treaty of Amity and

Commerce (the Harris Treaty) with the United States in 1868. Forcing Japan to abandon its isolationist trade policies toward the West, it was an "unequal" treaty in that it gave the United States far-reaching concessions. Because it was seen as a defeat for the shogunate, the *shogun* asked the Emperor to sign the treaty to save face. Not wanting to appease the "barbarian" West,

the Emperor's Choshus and the Satsumas clan advisors refused, staging the coup that restored the Emperor to power and sparking a military confrontation with the Americans. The Choshus and the Satsumas clashed with the western navies but were quickly defeated. Their defeat convinced them of the impossibility of opposing western power, and that their only chance to maintain at

The Japanese Emperor Mutsuhito with his family

least the appearance of sovereignty was to assimilate western culture. ❑

KARL MARX AND *DAS KAPITAL*

Hamburg, September 11, 1867

The man credited with the philosophy and impetus behind the socialist and communist movements of the nineteenth and twentieth centuries was an exiled German bourgeois intellectual. Karl Marx (1818–1883), who co-wrote the *Communist Manifesto* with Friedrich Engels (1820–1895), was born to a German Jewish family that converted to Protestantism. Marx studied philosophy in Berlin before turning his attention to the struggles of class conflict and making his way in the world as a journalist.

In 1848, Marx and Engels published their famous 35-page pamphlet, the *Communist Manifesto*. It was a year in which revolution and unrest ignited Europe. None of the revolutions were inspired by their work, but the events played into the scientific view of history that Marx was developing in which the past was seen as a series of economic conflicts. The progressive line of this history was, in Marx's view, inevitably headed toward the overthrow of the reigning order and the ascendancy of the proletariat, or working classes, as the rulers of the political and social order. He encouraged the workers of the world to unite and take action in order to fulfill their destiny and to create a world without classes or private property. Marx and Engels wrote in Chapter 2 of the manifesto, "The immediate aim of the Communists is the same as that of all other proletarian parties: Formation of the proletariat into a class, overthrow of the bourgeois supremacy, conquest of political power by the proletariat."

Marx was expelled from Germany and later France for his revolutionary views and activities. He went to London in 1849 where he spent much of his time in the British Museum working on his magnum opus *Das Kapital*. In this three-volume economic history of the world, Marx turned conventional thinking upside down. He took issue with the Utopians that great thoughts changed social conditions. Rather, he argued, economic conditions determined men's thoughts. Human relations and government institutions were determined by economics. Capitalism, he claimed, was a temporary system that would be undone by its reliance on the exploitation of labor and its tendency to produce monopolies, in short, by its own internal contradictions.

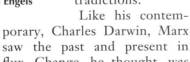

Friedrich Engels

Like his contemporary, Charles Darwin, Marx saw the past and present in flux. Change, he thought, was sometimes slow in coming, but eventually a sharp break would be made with the past, perhaps through revolution, and a new economic and social order would come into existence. Feudalism had thus been replaced by capitalism, and capitalism would eventually be replaced by the proletarian state. Marx's scientific approach to studying history through changing economic conditions has been labeled "dialectical materialism." The first volume of *Das Kapital* was published in 1867 in Hamburg in an edition of 1000 copies.

It was said of Marx that he was very bright and articulate and so convinced of his views that he was difficult to take on in discussion or debate. His views were not all original, but he had a great analytical mind and the ability to unite many threads into a powerful interpretation of the past, present and future. His writing partner Engels, who had lived and worked among the mills of Manchester, helped Marx put a human face on the misery of the working classes he wrote about. He also helped keep Marx and his family afloat.

Marx was quite isolated in London until 1864 when he helped found the International Working Men's Association. He was a leader of this diverse group, which focused on uniting workers in the name of socialism, until 1872 when the headquarters moved to New York. During his tenure he worked to rid the organization of anarchists who promoted terrorism to bring about change, in favor of setting up mass socialist parties.

Marx's ideas did not catch on quickly or uniformly. In industrialized England, the workers were involved in trade unionism and cooperative movements and essentially ignored his call to overthrow the current economic system. It was not until after his death that socialist and communist parties gained power and influence in Europe.

Marx himself lived in poverty. He and his wife Jenny had three daughters who reached adulthood, and he eked out a living writing articles for a number of publications. He was a prolific writer and many of his works (including the last two volumes of *Das Kapital*) were published after his death. He died at age 64 and is buried at Highgate Cemetery in North London. ❑

The German philosopher and political theorist, Karl Marx (1818–1883)

THE DEMISE OF THE PAPAL STATES

Rome, 1871

Pope Pius IX reads from his decree at the First Vatican Council (1869–1870)

The papacy had asserted its sovereignty over parts of Italy since the medieval era, although for much of the time its control was merely nominal. During the Renaissance, the Papal States encompassed most of central Italy. It lost a great portion of them to the newly formed Italian government in 1861. In 1870, Rome was taken by force, and the pope had to give up control of Rome, which had been under the protection of French troops. The city and the remaining papal holdings were incorporated into Italy by a referendum held in 1871. Pope Pius IX did not recognize the legality of Italian sovereignty, considering himself to be held prisoner in the Vatican. Finally in 1929, the papacy signed the Lateran Treaty, which ratified Italy's control over the former Papal States and established the State of the Vatican City.

A month before the Italian army marched into Rome to wrest it from the pope's control and make it the capital of the newly formed Italian state, the Vatican General Council passed a major new constitutional dogma by an overwhelming majority. The dogma, *Pastor Aeternus*, declared that the pope, when he speaks as "Shepherd and Teacher of all Christians," enjoys infallibility in defining doctrine on faith and morals. His definitions are "unalterable in themselves and not by virtue of the assent of the church." This represented a triumph for the conservative views of Pope Pius IX and a defeat for the liberal Catholic scholars. Pius had already displayed his militant views of ecclesiastical authority. In 1854, he announced the doctrine of the Immaculate Conception, which asserts that Mary the mother of Jesus was born free of sin. With the encyclical *Quanta Cura* (1864), the church defined its opposition to many of the intellectual currents of its time, including communism and rationalism. ❑

As the Catholic Church witnessed the diminution of its territorial possessions, it increased its claims of authority in spiritual matters.

FRANCO-PRUSSIAN WAR

Sedan, September 2, 1870

The Franco-Prussian War resulted in the collapse of the Second Empire in France and the founding of a united German state. After 44 days of warfare that devastated France and confirmed newly-unified Germany as the most powerful nation in Europe, a shattered Emperor Napoleon III, frequently in tears, surrendered his sword to the Prussian King Wilhelm I.

The beginning of the end came when Prussian troops encircled the emperor's relief force at Sedan as it tried to reach Metz, where the main French force had been penned in. The emperor, looking pale and dogged by illness, ended the squabbling among his generals and ordered the white flag to be raised. It was his reluctant acceptance that his 235,000-strong French army had been outmaneuvered, outnumbered, and outgunned by a 380,000-strong Prussian force.

The terms of surrender were negotiated at a poignant meeting in a tiny weaver's cottage between the emperor and the architect of his downfall, Prussian Prime Minister Otto von Bismarck, who used the war to unite the Rhineland states into a German confederation. The emperor was taken prisoner and housed in the comfort of the royal apartments at Wilhelmshohe.

Bismarck set about to deliberately fan the flames of war. The French had complained when a German was nominated to succeed to the Spanish throne. Bismarck had published a scornful Prussian response to France's concerns that inflamed French public opinion. Napoleon was forced to declare war, even though he knew that his army was weak.

Upon the defeat at Sedan, France declared itself to be a republic once more. Revolutionary crowds roamed the streets following the collapse of the twenty-year-old Second Empire. The new republic was fashioned by the emperor's opponents in the legislative body, anxious to head off a radical take over by the extreme left; the Empress Eugenie and the Imperial Prince fled to England. A provisional government of national defense was established under the military governor of Paris to combat the Prussian threat. But by the end of December, Prussian artillery was bombarding the city, and in January it capitulated.

While resistance continued in Paris, Wilhelm declared himself the Kaiser (emperor) of a new German *reich* amidst the glittering splendor of Louis XIV's Hall of Mirrors in the Palace of Versailles. For Bismarck it was the culmination of a carefully orchestrated military and political campaign. He became Germany's first chancellor.

The venue for the ceremony was a humiliation for the French, but the choice had as much to do with a desire to impress the numerous German princes, who had to be cajoled into joining the *reich* and giving up some of their privileges. The crushing defeat of France and the capture of Napoleon III by Germans who had accepted the Prussian military system stirred German public opinion; the German princes had to give way. ❑

PARIS COMMUNE

Paris, March–May, 1871

After Napoleon III's defeat at Sedan and subsequent imprisonment, the National Assembly, which had been toothless during the emperor's tenure, proclaimed the formation of the Government of National Defense on September 2, 1870. Republican members Léon Gambetta and Jules Favre announced the news of the emperor's abdication. The legislature was taken over by republicans, and the Empress Eugenie was forced into exile in Britain.

At an assembly in Paris, Louis Jules Trochu, the governor and military commandant of Paris, was put in charge of the new government, with Favre serving as Foreign Minister and Gambetta as Minister of the Interior. Trochu took over the direction of the war effort, but its outcome was hardly in doubt. By September 20, German troops had surrounded the city. Gambetta left Paris in a hot air balloon and transferred the government to Tours from where he tried to coordinate French military policy.

After the capitulation of Toul, Strasbourg, and Metz, the last remnants of the French imperial army melted away, and the German troops had little trouble with the forces assembled by the new

Uprising of the Paris Commune: barricades in rue d'Allemagne (photograph, March 18, 1871)

government. Efforts to break the German siege of Paris only raised hopes, then inflamed resentments against the government when those hopes were dashed. The supply of food dwindled. On January 28, 1871, Paris surrendered, and an armistice was signed with the German Chancellor Otto von Bismarck.

In the capital, a power struggle broke out between Trochu's government and socialist parties. A National Assembly was held on February 12 in Bordeaux, and the monarchist faction won a majority of seats. On February 17, the republican Adolphe Thiers was named president.

On March 18, an uprising of workers and the armed militia known as the National Guard took power in Paris, motivated by the harsh conditions dictated by Bismarck and the fear that the monarchist party might gain control. On March 26, a combination of socialist and radical democratic groups chose 85 members of a communal council and laid out a manifesto for the establishment of a sovereign commune of Paris. The new government combined the executive and legislative power in one body.

After a long siege and destructive bombardments, the resistance of the Commune was broken by government troops under Marshall Patrice Maurice Count of MacMahon in bloody street engagements. At the end of the battle, some twenty thousand of the *communards* faced firing squads. Another ten thousand were deported or imprisoned.

At the National Assembly held in Versailles on August 31, Adolphe Thiers retained his position with only the greatest difficulty in the face of strong monarchist sentiment. When in 1873 he tried to pass a law to strengthen the underpinnings of the republican form of government, he was forced out of office and replaced by MacMahon.

The return of the monarchy seemed inevitable, even imminent. But the Bourbon candidate for the throne, Henri Charles, Prince of Chambord and Duke of Bordeaux, turned the assembly against himself with his extravagant demands. He refused to endorse a parliamentary form of government and insisted that the tricolor flag be abandoned in favor of the Bourbon's *fleur-de-lis*. Even the monarchists felt that this went too far. In 1875, the assembly approved a series of laws that formally established the Third Republic. ❑

Peace treaty concluded in Frankfurt (lithograph, 1871)

GERMAN REICH UNITED IN VERSAILLES

Versailles, January 18, 1871

After the victory over France, the German national state was founded under Prussian leadership. In the Hall of Mirrors at Versailles, the Prussian king Wilhelm was proclaimed German *kaiser* (emperor). With German troops laying siege to Paris, the beginnings of the modern German state were established at the heart of the French monarchy exactly 170 years to the day after the crowning of the first Prussian king.

It took all of the persuasive skills of Prussian Prime Minister Otto von Bismarck to bring this about. King Wilhelm had not wanted it. He seemed almost disconsolate upon the issuance of the proclamation, telling his wife: "I can't describe to you how miserable I have felt over these last days.... It was especially painful to me to see the Prussian title disappear.... I only gained strength by fervently praying to God."

Before that Bismarck had to succeed in overcoming the Bavarian opposition to unification with Prussia's hereditary monarchy. He finally persuaded the states of southern Germany—Bavaria, Hessen, Baden, and Württemberg— to join the North German Confederation led by Prussia. In December the Confederation was renamed the German Reich (empire).

King Ludwig II of Bavaria, who was in constant financial trouble because of his obsession with castle building (e.g. Neueschwanstein and Linderhof), was promised financial aid in exchange for signing the letters to the emperor. These letters, which were written by Bismarck and the Bavarian statesman Maximilian Duke of Holnstein and sent on October 30, 1870, formally requested the Bavarian ruling house of Wittelsbacher to accept the Hohenzollern monarch, Wilhelm, as *kaiser* in the name of the German princes and free cities. Bavaria and Württemberg secured special privileges in regard to military and other civil posts.

This unified Germany was a constitutional monarchy, a confederation of states over which the *kaiser* was not absolute ruler but the "first among equals." The constitution of the Reich passed on April 16, 1871, had almost the same wording as that of the

Anton von Werner, *Imperial Proclamation in the Hall of Mirrors*, 1885. The artist places Otto von Bismarck at the center of the canvas.

North German Confederation of 1867. The Reich comprised 22 separate principalities and three free Hanse cities. It covered an area of nearly 350,000 square miles with 41 million inhabitants.

The central legislative organ in the newly formed German Reich was bicameral, consisting of the Reichstag, a directly elected lower house, and the Bundesrat, an upper house consisting mainly of important civil servants. The Bundesrat had the authority to initiate legislation, and no laws could be passed without its consent. It also had executive powers over governmental bodies as well as a series of extraordinary powers such as the power to enter into treaties and to dissolve the lower house.

With 17 out of 58 votes, Prussia held effective veto power. It put forward as Chancellor, Otto von Bismarck, who would serve in that position until 1890. The chancellor was the only minister of the Reich. All of the other state offices were placed under his jurisdiction. The chancellor served at the pleasure of the *kaiser*, who had the final say in matters concerning foreign policy and the military. ❑

OTTO VON BISMARCK

Brief lives

For almost thirty years, Otto von Bismarck-Schönhausen (1815–1898: photo at right) guided first Prussian and then German policy. He began his political career in 1846 serving in various positions in the Prussian government. He was an envoy to St. Petersburg from 1859 to 1862 and then for a short while Ambassador to France. On September 24, 1862, he was named Prime Minister of Prussia. His highest priority was rebuilding the military, which he did despite parliamentary opposition. He cleverly took advantage of the German wars of the 1860s (against Denmark and Austria) and France (in 1870–1871) to advance his goal of a German national state under Prussian leadership.

His foreign policy's chief goal was to prevent the formation of coalitions that would counter German interests. His domestic policies concerned themselves with limiting the influence of the liberal and progressive political agendas, paying particular attention to weakening the Catholic centrist party. After two attempts on the life of Kaiser Wilhelm I, Bismarck tried to make changes to the laws to respond to social grievances, essentially trying to co-opt the liberals' policies. He enacted laws that provided health, accident, and disability insurance. Kaiser Wilhelm II succeeded to the throne in 1888. Two years later, he forced Bismarck into retirement. The Iron Chancellor died on July 30, 1898. ❑

IMPRESSIONIST PAINTERS

Paris, April 15, 1874

In the mid-nineteenth century, Paris was the center and arbiter of western art. It was there that a group of artists who had been regularly rejected by the prestigious Salon put on their own exhibition in a former photography studio on the Boulevard des Capucines. The group included Claude Monet, Pierre-Auguste Renoir, Camille Pissarro, Edgar Degas, and Paul Cézanne—39 painters in all.

What defined their painting was their desire and ability to capture, not objects themselves, but light as it is directly perceived by the eye, being reflected from

Pierre-Auguste Renoir

Claude Monet

Claude Monet, *Impression, Sunrise*, exhibited at the *Salon des Refusés* in 1872

of the paintings, which appeared to them to be unfinished. Louis Leroy, the critic of *Le Charivari*, who was the first to call the group "Impressionists" wrote, "wallpaper in its embryonic state is more finished than that seascape." His reference was to a work by Monet.

The paintings of the Impressionists were characterized by a softness and fluidity, in contrast to the staid Classicism that preceded them. The shimmering glimpses they offered of landscapes suggest the passage of time; their devotion to capturing the quality of reflected light instilled quiet movement across the canvases. Among the painters was a wide range of subject matter and approach—the water lilies of Monet, the ballet dancers of Degas, the river landscapes of Pissarro, the café scenes of Renoir—and yet they all shared a determination to break with the past and capture a new sense of color and motion in the world around them.

The beauty and lyricism of Impressionism eventually won over both the critics and the general public, and the paintings of this period continue to be the most popular in Western art. ❏

objects in particular conditions. They used short brushstrokes of pure color and light tones, even in shadows, that blended to a shimmering effect when seen from a distance. Claude Monet declared that he sought to capture "the most fleeting effects." To do that they moved out of the studio and painted in the open air following the example of such painters as Gustave Courbet, Jean-Françoise Millet, and Eugène Boudin.

The style of art created by these painters came to be known as Impressionism, and the first public responses to it were incomprehension and ridicule. Outraged spectators objected to the formlessness and vagueness

VICTORIA PROCLAIMED EMPRESS OF INDIA

London, April 1876

Despite resistance from the Liberal opposition, Queen Victoria received a title she greatly desired, Empress of India. Some objected on the grounds that it had "bad associations" with Continental despots. But Prime Minister Benjamin Disraeli told members of parliament that "the amplification of titles" was often necessary to catch "the imagination of nations." He said the title was being anxiously awaited by the people of India; it would demonstrate to the world Britain's commitment to India at a time when Russia had advanced to within a few days' march of its frontiers.

After the King of Prussia became the German *kaiser* (emperor), Victoria said to Lord Ponsonby, her secretary, "I am an empress and in common conversation am sometimes called Empress of India. Why have I never officially assumed this title?" She argued that the title would once and for all settle questions of precedence with other European monarchs. ❏

THE AGE OF IMPERIALISM

The term "imperialism" refers to policies pursued from the mid-nineteenth century by the industrialized European powers, the United States, and Japan. Their aim was to make other countries economically and militarily dependent, to exploit them, and to dominate them through colonial acquisitions, capital export, and cultural influence. Even nominally independent states such as the Ottoman Empire, China, and the South American republics were subjected to this control because of their economic weakness and political powerlessness.

Between 1874 and 1914, politics were dominated by a form of imperialism, defined by extreme nationalism. Several factors played an important part in this: the competition for market outlets, the search for raw

race and its civilization ("the white man's burden"). According to this ideology, white European standards of progress and civilization would spread their light to all regions of the world while eliminating despotism and corruption. This latent racism was strengthened by the philosophy of Social Darwinism, a distortion of the idea of natural selection. The aggressive nature of imperialist politics was further facilitated by the inability of most of the countries involved to offer any effective resistance. The reasons for this were their economic and technical backwardness, combined with the absence of political systems able to challenge the invasion and occupation by the great powers. Any uprising (such as the Boer War or Boxer Rebellion) was brutally put down.

"Cape to Cairo" strategy, which was the conquest and domination of a continuous band of colonial territory in Africa.

French imperialism concentrated essentially on two areas: the subjugation of the Black African continent and the conquest of Indochina. The starting point for these conquests was the already existing French colonial possessions in North Africa (Algeria) and Cochin China (Vietnam). In the course of its long conflict with China, France acquired Tongking, Annam, and Laos. In 1887 the French founded the Indochinese Union, which included Cambodia.

French imperialistic politics were influenced by their defeat at the hands of Germany in 1870-71, which resulted in political isolation abroad. The avowed objective of French imperialism was to be recognized once more as a world power. The culmination of this policy was the Entente Cordiale with Great Britain (1904), an agreement that put an end to colonial political differences between the two world powers once and for all.

Imperial ruler: Germany's Kaiser Wilhelm II with his six sons in a parade (1913)

materials, and excessive nationalism that, combined with a sense of evangelizing mission and cultural xenophobia, developed into an imperialist ideology.

The "Great Depression" which had shaken the international economy beginning in 1873 put an end to economic prosperity. As European markets tightened as a result of growing industrialization and protectionism, interest turned to overseas territories as an area of expanding economic advantage. An imperialist policy became a means of guaranteeing both raw materials and captive markets. It was a one-sided exploitation by the great industrialized powers.

"THE WHITE MAN'S BURDEN"
The rise of modern imperialism was fed by a strong sense of mission and the belief in the fundamental superiority of the white

This imperialist ethos began in the 1870s in Great Britain and in the following decades it spread to all the world's great powers. Besides the traditional colonial powers of Great Britain, France, and Russia, new burgeoning imperial powers emerged—including the USA, the German Reich, Belgium, Italy, and Japan—and took part in the competition to acquire spheres of global influence.

BRITISH AND FRENCH CONQUESTS
British expansionist policies that began under the Prime Minister Benjamin Disraeli (1868/1874-1880) led to the creation of one of the largest colonial empires. The most pressing objective of British overseas policy was to secure the sea route to India, the most important and valuable of the British colonies. In the following years, the race to divide Africa led British imperialism to develop the

GERMANY'S "PLACE IN THE SUN"
The colonial policy of the German Reich began under the Chancellor of the German Reich, Otto von Bismarck, in 1884-85, when German West Africa, Cameroon, Togo, German East Africa and German New Guinea were put "under the protection of the Reich." Having become a unified nation only thirteen years earlier, Germany feared that it would be left behind if it did not join the race for colonial hegemony.

The building of a powerful naval fleet and the Kaiser's obsession with increasing the country's national prestige, led to a crisis in German-British relations and a rapprochement between Great Britain and France. Germany's decision to take part in global power politics was strongly and vociferously supported by the national press and imperialist agitation groups and led to chauvinism in many sections of the population.

THE "DOLLAR-IMPERIALISM" OF THE USA
Its victory in the Spanish-American War in 1898 transformed the USA from a thriving but relatively isolated economic power, into an imperial superpower with possessions in the Caribbean and the Pacific. The former Spanish territories of Cuba and Puerto Rico, as well as Guam and the Philippines, became US protectorates while Central America became the "USA's backyard" and the Far East, the showplace of American imperial politics.

Africa in colonial times: a scene in the Second Boer War, in which Great Britain fought against South Africa's Boer states, Transvaal and Orange Free State.

Being both an Atlantic and Pacific power, the USA could only protect its far-flung possessions in the long term by building two strong naval fleets. President Theodore Roosevelt's vigorous efforts to expand the US Navy transformed it into a naval power second only to Great Britain. The building of the strategically important Panama Canal linking two oceans created a naval geographic flexibility that made the effective control of the country's colonial possessions possible.

While "dollar diplomacy," that is, the indirect political control through financial means, proved successful in Central America, it failed in China. The Far Eastern policy of the US was based upon the unrealized hope of extensive trade with China. The imperial power politics of the US and the claim to equal economic opportunities in the Far East and the Pacific created a conflict of interest with the emerging superpower Japan. These conflicting imperialist agendas strained relations between the two countries until after the Second World War.

RIVALRY BETWEEN JAPAN AND RUSSIA

After Japan opened up to the West in the nineteenth century, its expansionist politics soon transformed it into a into a major superpower in East Asia. Its speedy industrialization and strong population growth (1867: 26 million, 1913: 52 million) laid the foundation for imperialist ideologies and power politics seemingly incommensurate with such a small nation.

Victorious in two wars (against China 1894-95 and against Russia 1904-05), Japan annexed Formosa and Korea, as well as Manchuria, an acquisition that was of prime importance because of its natural resources. In this way Japan gained political and economic influence in China. Japan's position as a great power was based on the military strength of its army and navy as well as its economic vitality.

In contrast to the other world powers, Russia's imperialism was more continental in nature. Driven by the tsarist desire for power and by the "pursuit of a border in the eternity of Siberia," Russian imperialism concentrated on two targets: access to the oceans in East Asia, and the control of the Dardanelles to permit access to the Mediterranean. The rigorous effort to build up the country's navy and

the construction of the vitally important and militarily indispensable Trans-Siberian railway (1891-1904) contributed substantially towards the realization of these objectives. The occupation of the much-coveted Manchuria in 1900 led to war with Japan. The motivating ideology behind Russian imperialism was Pan-Slavism, the idea of the political unification of all Slavs under Russian leadership.

THE COLLAPSE OF THE COLONIAL EMPIRES

The age of colonial imperialism came to an end with the decline of the European powers after the Second World War. But the concept of political imperialism continued to play an important part. On the one hand, the US and the countries of Western Europe followed policies to maintain and expand their sphere of influence in former colonies and dependent states in Africa, Asia, and South America through monetary incentives, trade agreements, and military aid. On the other hand, until the end of the 1980s, they supported national liberation movements to counteract Soviet supremacy in Eastern Europe and its attempts to create a sphere of influence in the Third World. ❑

THE BATTLE OF LITTLE BIGHORN

Montana, June 25–26, 1876

The Battle of Little Bighorn, also known as Custer's Last Stand and the Battle of Greasy Grass, on the Little Bighorn River in Montana Territory, was part of a resistance movement engaged in by a confederation of Lakota Sioux and Northern Cheyenne after key provisions of the 1868 Treaty of Laramie were breached. Fought on June 25–26, 1876, it resulted in the annihilation of a division of the U.S. Seventh Calvary led by Lieutenant Colonel George Armstrong Custer.

In the Treaty of Laramie, the federal government had acknowledged the Sioux's right to reservation lands in South Dakota and Wyoming, which included the Black Hills. In 1874, the discovery of gold there caused a gold rush that brought white prospectors streaming into the treaty-protected territory. When President Grant refused to stop this illegal intrusion, the Lakota Sioux and Cheyenne formed an alliance under the Lakota chiefs Sitting Bull and Crazy Horse and declared war. Defying govern-

ment orders, the tribes abandoned their reservations and set up encampments on land alongside of the Little Bighorn River.

Custer's Seventh Cavalry was one of three sent by President Grant to round up the rebellious tribes and return them to their reservations. The mission

Custer's Last Stand (woodcut, end of nineteenth century)

General Custer

failed utterly, not only because the plan of attack was poorly coordinated among the divisions, but also because the Seventh Calvary had no idea how many warriors were at the encampment.

When Custer arrived near the Bighorn encampment on June 25, he made the fatal tactical error of splitting his 655 troops into three groups, using his cadre of roughly 210 to lead the charge. By the time he realized that he was

Sitting Bull

facing as many as two thousand warriors, it was too late. Isolated on a bluff above the encampment, his valiant attempt to fend off the superior Sioux and Cheyenne forces ended in the deaths of all his men, himself included. ❑

FIRST PERFORMANCE OF THE RING CYCLE

Bayreuth, Austria, August 13–17, 1876

A huge banquet for five hundred people ended the musical event of the decade: the first performance of all four operas in Wagner's massive *Ring* epic, over three days in the new opera house he had had built for his own works. It was a triumph for Wagner's unabashed belief in his own genius. Construction of the opera house began years earlier with money raised by subscription and by donations from the eccentric King Ludwig II of Bavaria, always willing to spend vast sums on palaces and Wagner. The festival was attended by four thousand people, including the emperors

of Germany and Brazil as well as King Ludwig. Among the sixty correspondents were two from New York, reporting via the new transatlantic cable. ❑

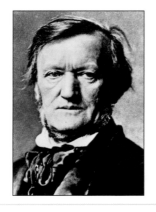

Richard Wagner

BAYREUTH MYTH

Point of Interest

From its inception, the operatic performances at Bayreuth were more than musical events; they were cultural and social experiences, as witnessed by the social prominence of the guests who patronized its opening season. In addition to two emperors, representatives from the most distinguished noble families of Europe found their places in the Green Circle. The composers Camille Saint Saëns, Anton Bruckner, and Peter Tchaikovsky were in attendance. Unlike most concert halls, the orchestra pit at Bayreuth is hooded and cannot be seen by the audience. Wagner had it con-

cealed so that the orchestra did not become a distraction, and it is considered an integral part of the orchestra's unique sound. In 1882, Wagner's *Parsifal* premiered at Bayreuth. It continues to be the site of an annual Wagner festival. ❑

Scene from *Parsifal*

EVERYDAY LIFE BECOMES EASIER

Point of Interest

Among the many groundbreaking inventions of the late nineteenth century are the telephone and the light bulb. Independently of each other, the Scottish teacher of the deaf, Alexander Graham Bell, and the American telegraph operator, Elisha Gray, applied for patents for devices that conveyed sound over distance. Although Gray's apparatus operated on the same principle as Bell's, it was Bell alone who obtained the patent and for that reason goes down in history as the inventor of the first practical telephone. On March 10, 1876, Bell spoke to his assistant over his telephone uttering the famous words: "Mr. Watson come here, I want to see you."

Precursors to Bell: The first attempts to devise a machine that would

Alexander Bell

convey sound over distance began in the middle of the nineteenth century. In 1849, the French technician Charles Bourseul, who had worked on the telegraph, built a transmitter that changed sound waves into electric current. In Germany, physics teacher Johann

Johann Philipp Reis

Philipp Reis built a model of the first functioning telephone, but the sound could not travel very far.

Electrical impulses from sound waves: Beginning with the ideas of

Thomas A. Edison

Bourseul, Bell arrived at the principle behind the modern telephone. The sound waves of an utterance traveled over a membrane, causing vibration in a metal reed that carried the overtones necessary for the reception of speech. The resulting impulse traveled to a receiver on the other end of the line, which then converted the impulse back into sound waves.

Rapid growth: The first overland message connected Boston and Cambridge, Massachusetts, a distance of almost two miles. In 1884, a connection was made between Boston and New York. A technical improvement in 1889 allowed the connection to be made automatically rather than by hand. The new invention quickly spread. By 1900, three million telephones were in service in the United States.

Edison, virtuoso inventor: In 1879, American inventor Thomas Alva Edison succeeded in

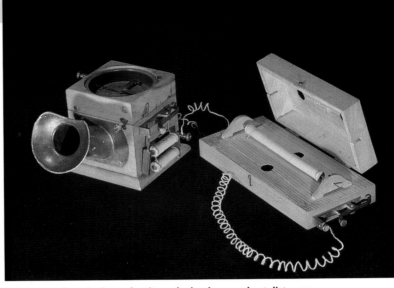

Reis invented a telephone, but it worked only over short distances.

creating a new light source, the first practical light bulb. As a precondition he had to first come up with a power source.

The arc lamp: In 1813, in the course of his research into electricity, English chemist Humphry Davy discovered that electricity would flow between two carbon rods and produce light when the poles were slowly moved away from each other. The use of the arc lamp as a light source was first made possible in 1866 upon the invention of a generator by the German electrical pioneer Werner Siemens. The first practical use of electricity as a source of illumination, the Yablochkov candle, named after its inventor Pavel N. Yablochkov, was produced in 1876, but it was designed for use on a grand scale.

Experiments with filaments: As early as 1854, a prototype of the light bulb had been constructed by German optician Heinrich Goebel using bamboo fiber for a filament. Other scientists and technicians experimented with diverse materials trying to find one that could survive the heat of the current passing through it. Edison came up with a thin cotton thread that would burn for as long as forty hours.

Practical use: Edison concerned himself with the practical applications of his inventions. He invented a suitable glass bulb and a socket so that when the bulb was screwed in, an electric current would travel through its filament. ❑

CONGRESS OF BERLIN

Berlin, July 13, 1878

The Congress of Berlin (June 13–July 13, 1878), resulting in the Treaty of Berlin, was another stage in the dismemberment of the Ottoman Empire. Largely concerned with the control of the Balkans, among its provisions was the ceding of the Caucasus to Russia and of Bosnia and Herzegovina to Austria-Hungary. It also recognized the independence of the principalities of Serbia, Romania, and Montenegro, while acknowledging the autonomy of the nominally Ottoman principality of Bulgaria. The participants—Britain, Austria-Hungary, France, Germany, Italy, Russia, and the Ottoman Empire—sought to revise the Treaty of San Stephano between Russia and the Ottomans, whose signing on March 3 had ended the Russo-Turkish War.

The specific issues at the Congress were the growing pan-Slavic independence movement and Russia's increasing sphere of influence in formerly Ottoman Mediterranean territories. The German Chancellor, Otto von Bismarck, adroitly mediated a settlement between Russian Chancellor Alexander Gorchakov and the opposition led by British Prime Minister Benjamin Disraeli. ❑

The Congress of Berlin

THE DISCOVERY OF BACTERIA

Berlin, March 24, 1882

The last third of the nineteenth century has been called the "golden age of bacteriology." Through the discovery of pathogenic etiology of many illnesses new methods of disease prevention and treatment were perfected.

At a meeting of the Berlin Society for Physiology the scientist Robert Koch made known his discovery of the bacteria that caused tuberculosis. He could thereby claim the first indisputable proof of a human disease being caused by a parasite.

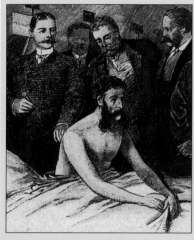

Koch demonstrates an inoculation against Tuberculosis

Tuberculosis, also known as consumption, was one of the most dangerous diseases of its time. In the nineteenth century, for example, it was responsible for one in every four deaths in England.

The Koch Postulates: To convince his critics of the results of his research Koch set out a set of principles for the proof of the bacterial nature of tuberculosis that later became known as the Koch Postulates, which served as the basis for further studies in bacteriology.

- A microorganism can only be considered as the pathogen of a specific disease, if it is always present in cases of the disease, but not found in cases of other illnesses.
- The bacteria have to be cultivated outside the organism and separated from other microorganisms.
- The transmission of pure strains in the course of experimental research has to produce the same illness.

For his work Koch used the latest discoveries in biology and its technology. One of these, de-

Robert Koch (1843–1910) received the Nobel Prize for Medicine in 1905

veloped by Carl Zeiss and Ernst Abbe, was the vastly improved microscope. Another was the use of aniline staining.

Louis Pasteur, pioneer: The decisive step forward for bacteriology came from the French chemist Louis Pasteur. In the 1850s he described the process of fermentation as the result of microorganic activity and disproved the theory of spontaneous generation. He showed rather that microbes were produced by biogenesis. During the observation of the fermentation of milk, Pasteur discovered that certain microorganisms could spoil food. This discovery led to the process of pasteurization. He first briefly heated wine in an unopened bottle and found that this killed the bacteria and therefore the process of decomposition did not occur.

Pasteur was also responsible for important medical findings.

EGYPT UNDER BRITISH CONTROL

Alexandria, 1882

Great Britain assumed de facto control over Egypt, thereby implementing an important stage in its expressed desire to spread its empire throughout Africa, "from the Cape to Cairo." In July of 1882, British warships

British and Egyptian troops battle a nationalist uprising at Omdurman.

opened fire on the fort protecting the Egyptian port city of Alexandria. The attack was called a punitive action against Egyptian nationalists, who had launched anti-European riots the month before. It served as a justification for a continuing British presence in Egypt and facilitated its expansion into the African continent. Of paramount importance to Great Britain was the security of the Suez Canal, which was vital to its connection with India. In 1914, Egypt formally became a British protectorate but regained its independence in 1922. ❏

DEATH OF ALEXANDER II

Russia, 1881

Alexander Romanov was assassinated in St. Petersburg on March 13, 1881. A terrorist society known as the People's Will ambushed him as he returned in his carriage to the Winter Palace after attending a military parade.

The first bomb thrown at the royal carriage left Alexander unharmed, but a second bomb left him gravely injured, and he died several hours later. This successful attack was preceded by several unsuccessful attempts, including one by an anti-tsarist who had gotten a job in the Palace and smuggled in dynamite.

The People's Will brought about Alexander's death for failing to summon a constitutional assembly. It was not until after his death that the public and the assassins learned that Alexander had agreed to reforms in his government just before attending the military parade. ❏

The fatally wounded Tsar Alexander II was brought back to the Winter Palace.

THE WAR OF THE PACIFIC

Santiago, Chile, 1879

In 1877 he observed that three kinds of bacteria that he accidentally put in the same dish filled with a nutrient solution prevented each other's growth. In 1881 he proved that in the case of cholera the introduction of other bacteria strengthened the subject's immunity. Pasteur thereby took the first step in developing vaccines to counter infectious diseases.

Early developments in bacteriology: A whole series of other pathogens were discovered before the end of the century: leprosy, cholera, diphtheria, tetanus, pneumonia, anthrax, meningitis and bubonic plague. Cures for these diseases were not yet known. It was not until the discovery of penicillin in 1928 by the British biologist Alexander Fleming that a class of drugs was created that could effectively combat many of these pathogenic disorders.
Nonetheless, Koch's discovery of the tuberculosis bacteria aroused hope that disease could be contained and cured. The new diagnostic possibilities made it possible to isolate the sick at an early stage and take preventive measure against epidemics. ❑

The War of the Pacific, also known as the Saltpeter War, was fought between Chile and the allied forces of Peru and Bolivia from 1879 to 1883. It began as a territorial dispute between Chile and Bolivia in which both sides laid claimed to the Atacama border region, which was rich in deposits of saltpeter and guano. Both resources were in high demand worldwide, the former for its use in making explosives, the latter for its use as fertilizer. In 1874, Bolivia asserted its right to the land but allowed for the cultivation of its resources by Chilean companies, whom it then taxed. When the tax was increased, and Chile refused to pay, Bolivia seized a Chilean company. Chile responded by occupying the disputed port of Antofagasta. In February of 1879, Bolivia countered with a declaration of war.

Peru, a diplomatic ally of Bolivia and wary of Chile's expansionist agenda, attempted to mediate a settlement. Chile not only rejected this effort but, on April 5, proclaimed its own declaration of war against both countries. Ironically, Peru, who had no part in the original dispute, carried the lion's share of the military burden throughout the war and was far more effective than Bolivia against Chilean forces.

But despite a valiant effort, the allies were no match for Chile. The naval war came to an end with Peru's defeat at the Battle of Agamos on October 8, 1879. Controlling the coastlines, Chilean forces then prosecuted a land war that culminated in the capture of Lima in January of 1881. Hostilities officially ended with the signing of the Treaty of Ancon on October 20, 1883. In its main provision, Chile won full possession of the border province of Tarapaca and a ten-year administrative rule over the additional border provinces of Tacna and Arica. Later, in the Truce of 1884, Bolivia ceded its entire coastline and the mineral-rich province of Antofagasta to Chile, and in return Chile agreed to build a Bolivian railway. ❑

After the Saltpeter War, Chile gained possession of the Atacama Desert

CONGO BECOMES PRIVATE PROPERTY

Berlin, 1884

The Berlin Conference of 1884 was convened to establish European rights to African colonization and trade, with special focus on the newly charted regions of the Congo. Of the fourteen nations represented at the conference, none was more determined to secure territory there than King Leopold II of Belgium.

Proactively, in 1876, Leopold had developed a Congo strategy wherein he enlisted the aid of the region's explorer, Henry Stanley, and formed a philanthropic organiza-

Leopold II

tion called the International African Society with which he merged the economic development agency known as the Congo Society. He used these organizations and his association with the respected Stanley as credentials of his worthiness to be accorded Congolese territory.

Leopold's petition was not on behalf of the Belgian people, but rather on his own. Remarkably, the Conference agreed to his request, ceding to his private ownership over nine hundred thousand square miles of Congo-

lese land.

Known as the Congo Free State, it became a personal business venture in which Leopold used slave labor to exploit the Congo's natural resources. Through the cruelty of his private army and through disease, between two and fifteen million Congolese died. By 1908, the international outcry against these abuses convinced Belgium to divest Leopold of his private possession and assume

Belgian industry exploited the Congo region.

the role of colonial steward over what then became known as the Belgian Congo. ❑

STATUE OF LIBERTY

New York, October 28, 1886

The Statue of Liberty was a gift from France in commemoration of the United States' centennial and represented the friendship between the two countries. Its iconic status as a symbol of democracy and freedom grew out of its association with the increasing number of immigrants arriving into New York harbor in the latter part of the nineteenth century.

Dedicated on October 28, 1886, the 300-foot-high, 225-ton, copper patina-clad statue represents "Lady Liberty" bearing a torch in her raised right hand and holding a tablet with the date "JULY IV MDCCLXX-VI" in her left. It was conceived by the French sculptor Frederic Bartholdi in collaboration with the designer of the Eiffel Tower, Alexandre Eiffel. Its 154-foot pedestal was constructed in the United States, and the 350 individual parts of the statue were cast in France and shipped to the United States aboard the French frigate *Isère*.

Its dedication date was delayed partly by difficulty in raising the funds, which came from public and private donations in France and the United States. ❑

INVENTION OF THE AUTOMOBILE

Europe, late 1800s

The first self-propelled mechanical vehicle, or automobile, may have been invented in 1672 in China by a Jesuit missionary named Ferdinand Verbiest. A more historically verifiable claimant for this honor is the French engineer, Nicholas Joseph Cugnot, who in 1769 created a steam-powered vehicle that was used by the French army to transport artillery. Steam-powered vehicles were also produced by the American Dr. J. W. Carhart in 1871 and by the Frenchman Amédée Bolée in 1873. Around 1832, Robert Anderson of Scotland introduced a carriage propelled by electricity.

Reconstruction of Otto's four-stroke gas engine of 1876

The dawn of the automobile as we know it began with the invention of the internal combustion engine. Many variants of the engine had been tried during the nineteenth century, but none more significant than the four-stroke Otto Cycle engine developed by Germany's Nikolaus August Otto in 1876. Although there is evidence that a similar engine had been developed earlier by a French engineer named Alphonse-Eugène Beau de Rochas, it is the Otto Cycle that is still cited today.

Credit for the invention of the first automobile of the modern era has been accorded to Germany's Karl Benz. Designing his own four-stroke, gasoline-powered engine, based on the principles of the Otto Cycle, Benz installed this engine in a three-wheeled chassis and called his creation the Benz Patent Motorwagen. Patented by his company, Benz and Cie, in January of 1886, it is considered the first true automobile. When he began to sell the Motorwagen to the general public in 1888, he became the first commercial automobile dealer. When French bicycle manufacturer Emile Rogers began selling the Motorwagen at his shop in Paris, sales increased exponentially. Thus it was the French who created the first high-volume, market-driven car dealership.

Simultaneous with Benz's work, a German team of Gottlieb Daimler and Wilhelm Maybach, who had help Nikolas Otto design his revolutionary engine, were pioneering new developments. In 1885, Daimler and Maybach introduced an improved version of the Otto Cycle, whose smaller size allowed for new automobile design. Installing this more structurally efficient engine into a four-wheeled vehicle, the German team built what became the prototype for today's cars. In 1889, they created a V-slanted, two-cylinder, four-stroke engine that became the template for modern engines. They were also the first to build their own automobile chassis instead of installing an engine into a preexisting carriage. Commercial production for this new vehicle began with the founding of the Daimler Motoren-Gesellschaft in 1890.

Benz, Daimler, and Maybach created the first automobile design templates, but it was the French team of René Panhard and Emile Lavassor who founded the first fully operational automobile manufacturing plant when they opened Panhard and Lavassor in 1887. Their Système Panhard used Daimler engines and introduced the first modern transmissions with front-mounted engines and radiators, pedal-operated clutches, and rear-wheel drive.

The Peugeot family founded the second automobile manufacturing firm. Originally a manufacturer of bicycles, the Peugeots under Armand Peugeot built the Serpollet-Peugeot in 1889, a three-wheeled, steam-powered car. In 1891, Armand Peugeot founded Les Fils de Peugeot Frères and introduced his own signature four-wheeled automobiles with Daimler engines. First to use solid rubber tires, they soon became leaders in the new sport of motor racing, the automobile's first form of mass-market advertising. In 1896, Armand founded Le Société des Auto-Mobiles Peugeot, which manufactured automobiles with Peugeot-designed engines. By 1899, of the twelve hundred cars produced in France that year, three hundred were Peugeots.

The first Americans to manufacture automobiles were Charles and Frank Duryea, two bicycle makers from Springfield, Massachusetts, who created their first gas-powered car in 1893. Founding the Duryea Motor Wagon Company in 1896, their signature model was an upscale limousine. Lagging slightly behind Europe, the Americans eventually made up for lost time and ultimately won the automobile manufacturing race when Henry Ford opened the Ford Motor Company in 1903. ❑

THE EIFFEL TOWER

Paris, 1889

The Eiffel Tower, an iconic representation of all things French, created a storm of controversy among Parisians at its dedication in 1889. Designed by the French architect Gustave Eiffel to commemorate the French Revolution's Centennial, the world's tallest structure to date was a remarkable technological achievement. But the 984-foot-high landmark alongside the Seine on the Champ de Mars was to some an aesthetic abomination. Artists and writers, including authors Alexandre Dumas and Guy de Maupassant, signed a petition of protest that compared the tower to a "gigantic black factory chimney" and labeled it "a dishonor to the city."

The controversy only served to assure its status as the city's most popular tourist attraction. One of its main draws was the glass-cage elevators that traveled to the top from each of the four semicircular arches at the base. The tourist trade benefited Gustave Eiffel, who received a percentage of visitor entrance fees for the first twenty years. As of 2006, the tower had received nearly 200 million visitors. ❏

View over the grounds of the Paris World's Fair of 1900 with the Eiffel Tower.

VAN GOGH: TORMENTED GENIUS

Auvers-sur-Oise, July 29, 1890

Vincent van Gogh was born in 1853 in the Netherlands into a Protestant pastor's family. He began working as an art dealer and moved on to preaching before becoming a painter, through his own determination and with his brother Theo's encouragement. He had little formal training before moving to Paris in 1886, where Theo managed an art gallery. Vincent, who was painting landscapes and working class scenes with a dark palette of colors, met Camille Pissarro, Claude Monet, and Paul Gauguin and began experimenting with color and with the short brush strokes characteristic of Impressionism.

In 1888, he moved to Arles in the south of France, where he worked day and night, producing close to two hundred paintings in eighteen months, but also damaging his physical health and emotional well-being. He was hoping to create an artist's community in Arles, but the only painter who joined him, Paul Gauguin, beat a hasty retreat after van Gogh, exhibiting increasingly unstable behavior, threatened him with a razor. Van Gogh later used the razor to cut off his own ear.

Van Gogh suffered from depression and epilepsy throughout his life. After the Gauguin incident, he spent time in a mental hospital. In 1890, after moving to a small town outside Paris, he stabbed himself and died a few days later. His brother Theo reported his last words as "the sadness will never end."

Vincent van Gogh,
Self-Portrait

Van Gogh produced more than eight hundred paintings and some seven hundred drawings. He was a master of color and movement on the canvas and, toward the end of his life, was placing oil paint on the canvas directly from the tube. Some of his most famous paintings include his sunflowers, painted to decorate his rooms in Arles, his rendering of night scenes, and his portraits of working people. Van Gogh found that, in his words, "color expresses something in itself." His dramatic use of bright and sometimes unexpected hues, coupled with the energy and intensity of his brushwork and perspective, produced masterpieces that have influenced many respected artists and continue to startle and delight even today. In the twentieth century, his paintings have commanded some of the highest prices in history on the art market, but Van Gogh sold only one work during his lifetime and died impoverished. ❏

MASSACRE AT WOUNDED KNEE

South Dakota, December 29, 1890

In February 1890, the United States Government broke a Lakota treaty by decreasing the size of the Great Sioux Reservation of South Dakota and breaking it into five small reservations. The Sioux were forced to learn farming, but because the arid climate was unsuitable for agriculture, they had to rely on the Bureau of Indian Affairs for food. The government reduced the Sioux food ration by half, and the tribes began to starve. At this time the Sioux tribe began using the Ghost Dance, which they believed would return the nearly extinct buffalo to the plains and cause white men to perish. The dance was supposed to be peaceful, but the armed forces saw it as threatening and outlawed it. Fearing an uprising from the Sioux, a Pine Ridge agent named Daniel Royer asked for military help and requested that tribal leaders be arrested.

That winter, Sitting Bull, a Lakota tribal leader, was killed in his cabin by an officer sent to arrest him. His tribe then fled the Standing Rock reservation to join the tribe of Big Foot, another chief, at the Cheyenne River. On December 28, 1890, Big Foot and about three hundred fifty members of his tribe left for the Pine Ridge reservation. They were captured by Samuel Whiteside and the Seventh Calvary Regiment and escorted to the Wounded Knee Creek.

At Wounded Knee, the tribe faced some five hundred soldiers and four Hotchkiss cannons, capable of firing about fifty shells a minute. On the morning of December 29, the tribe was ordered to disarm; while the soldiers were collecting weapons, a shot was fired, and the Calvary responded by opening fire. The resulting melee lasted for an hour and ended in the death of about three hundred Sioux men, women, and children and twenty-nine soldiers. In the twentieth century, the Wounded Knee Massacre came to represent the many injustices perpetrated by European Americans on the Native American population. ❑

Group picture around Chief Bigfoot on their reservation in South Dakota, 1890

WEALTH AND POVERTY

Point of Interest

By the end of the nineteenth century, the Industrial Revolution had raised the general standard of living with the creation of a middle class in the United States and Britain. However, set against this growing prosperity was the stark contrast between society's upper and lower echelons, where monumental wealth existed side by side with abject poverty.

The journalist and photographer Jacob Riis, a Danish immigrant, experienced this level of poverty upon his arrival in New York in 1870, and made it his life's work to raise public awareness of the brutal conditions in which his fellow immigrants were living. Attempting to appeal to the conscience of New York's middle class, he published the now classic book, *How the Other Half Lives*, in which he chronicled the pitiful squalor of New York's Lower East Side tenements. A pioneering polemic in the cause of social reform, it inspired legislation and public works programs that sought to ameliorate the suffering it exposed and had a profound effect on New York's then Commissioner of Police, Theodore Roosevelt. Its companion piece in Britain was William Booth's *In Darkest England, and the Way Out*, which helped to inspire reforms in London's educa-

Italian immigrants arriving at Ellis Island

tion, housing, and hospital systems.

These miserable conditions had no daunting effect on immigrants, who poured into New York at the rate of three thousand a week. Similarly in Britain, despite the fact that one in four Londoners was living in abject poverty, waves of immigrants continued to arrive weekly from Eastern Europe. ❑

MOVING PICTURES

Paris, 1895

The forerunner of movies was called the Stroboscope or Fantascope, created in 1832 almost simultaneously by the Austrian Simon von Stampfer and the Belgian Joseph Plateau. Their devices created the illusion of movement by using slotted spinning disks on which drawings were mounted. By the end of the nineteenth century inventors in France, Germany and the United States were all trying to develop a technology that would create this illusion of movement.

In 1895 the French brothers,

Cinématographe film projector

Auguste and Louis Lumière, created a hand-held moving picture camera that they named a "Cinématographe." This camera could not only record, but also develop and project. Discovering that the images created by the device could be projected onto a large screen, they presented a private screening of these "motion pictures" on March 22, 1895. The first public screening of such movies took place on December 28 of the same year at the Salon Indien at the Grand Café in Paris. At first attendance was sparse but within weeks they were presenting twenty shows a day.

The program ran for twenty minutes and consisted of ten short films, each lasting about 46 seconds and presenting ordinary moments in daily life. Among the topics shown were a baby being fed and workers leaving a factory in Lyons. One of the most popular was the thrilling experience of an oncoming train speeding directly into the camera. Another short used trick photography, showing a collapsed stone wall "uncollapsing" back to its original state. There was also a feature that was perhaps the first filmed comedy. Entitled, *L'Arroseur Ar-*

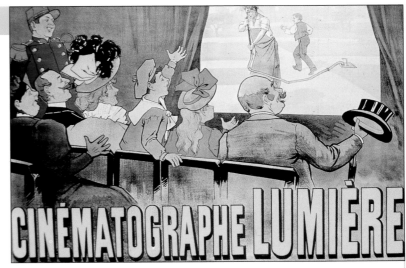

Poster advertising the "Cinématographe" of the Lumière Brothers, 1895

rosé ("The Sprinkler, Sprinkled"), it showed a young woman in a garden being sprayed by a misdirected water hose.

The images projected as moving pictures were animated by the use of perforated film strips, not unlike those used today, except, instead of celluloid, the strips were made from a special kind of coated paper. These image-bearing strips were secured by grippers and hand cranked in front of the projector's lighting mechanism.

At about the same time, Thomas Edison was experimenting with his own moving-image devices. Using the technology behind the Vitascope, a film projector

introduced in 1895 by Americans Charles Francis Jenkins and Thomas Armat, Edison and his employee William Dickson created a motion-picture camera called a Kinetograph along with a viewing machine called a Kinetoscope. One of the most famous Kinetoscope features is series of sneezes produced by Edison's assistant, Fred Ott. At its movie studio in West Orange New Jersey, called Black Maria, the Edison Company then developed their own unique projector named the Projectoscope. Like the films of the Lumière brothers, Edison's early films were "actuality" subjects, which portrayed every day occurrences. ❑

RÖNTGEN REVEALS NEW PATHS IN MEDICINE

Würzburg, November 8, 1895

The discovery of x-rays opened up many new possibilities in medicine and the natural sciences. In the course of an experiment with cathode rays the German physicist Wilhelm Conrad Röntgen discovered an enriched strand of energy with waves that were shorter than those of light, and that were able to penetrate and illuminate material. On account of the rays being straight-lined, he named them "X-rays." They would later be called "Röntgen Rays" in many languages after their discoverer. In 1901, his invention earned Röntgen the first

Nobel Prize for Physics.

In the field of medicine, applications of this new technology for diagnoses rapidly emerged. It became clear that bones were better able to absorb the rays than tissue. Doctors were able to look inside the human body without having to perform surgery. Many forms of cancer, tuberculosis, and heart disease could be diagnosed earlier and treated.

The spread of this new method was dramatic. The first X-ray department was established in 1906 at the Rudolf Virchow Hospital in Berlin. In 1921 the diagnostic pro-

cedure was enhanced through the injection of contrast dye into the bloodstream and body cavities.

In November 1896, the Viennese doctor, Leopold Freund, x-rayed a girl with a

Wilhelm C. Röntgen in his laboratory

disfiguring hairy birthmark. As a result of the procedure, the girl suffered sores on her skin. Such side effects did not raise red flags at the beginning, not even after severe radiation damage and burns occurred that sometimes led to amputations. Physicians

and technicians who were regularly exposed to the rays without protection suffered severe, often deadly, side effects. Many contracted leukemia. It was only as the twentieth century progressed that protective measures began to be established. ❑

An extraordinary congress took place in Basel, Switzerland at the end of August 1897. Delegates from Jewish communities from all countries met together to discuss the future of the Jews in a state that had yet to be created. The "Jewish State" would be founded on land from which they had been expelled in the First Century AD. The driving force behind this plan, which became known as Zionism, was the Budapest-born lawyer and journalist, Theodor Herzl, who remained the soul of the movement until his death in 1904. He picked up contemporary Zionist ideas and made them politically feasible. His plan was to garner an international approval for the foundation of a Jewish State on Palestinian soil through negotiations with the Ottoman Sultan of Constantinople and the European superpowers.

The new movement was in response to the failures of the experiment of Jewish Emancipation in the face of continuing anti-Semitism. There was ample evidence to suppose that anti-Semitism was on the rise. In Russia Jews were subjected to a disturbing increase of ever more bloody pogroms, while in France the conviction of Alfred Dreyfus convinced Jews that they were in fact not fully assimilated into European society. Herzl believed that the only solution for the long-term survival of the Jewish people lay in their possessing a state of their own. In Russia a movement began to emerge whose goal was the return of the Jewish people to their rightful homeland in Palestine where communal work and land ownership would regenerate them as a people. It was this movement that led to the first wave of migration (Hebrew: *aliya*, "to go up" [to Zion]) between 1881 and 1903, in the course of which some 25,000 Jews left eastern Europe to settle in Palestine. The second *aliya* (1904-1910) was also shaped by a pioneering spirit rooted in a social-revolutionary ethos. It laid the foundation of modern economic development. The settlers developed new forms of communal settlements (the first Kibbutz, Deganya, was founded in 1909). The land for the settlements was bought from wealthy Arab landowners.

FROM THE BALFOUR DECLARATION TO THE FOUNDATION OF THE STATE OF ISRAEL.

On November 2, 1917, the British Foreign Minister, Arthur Balfour, wrote an official letter to Lord Rothschild, representative of the Jewish people in England, in which he said that he believed that the Jews should have an nation of their own, but with the caveat that the civil and religious rights of the non-Jewish population be respected. Unfortunately, London had previously given the Sharif of Mecca, Hussein ibn Ali, assurances regarding a national Arab kingdom that would also include Palestine. When in 1922-23, Great Britain was ceded Palestine as a protectorate territory by the League of Nations, it was compelled to deal with these conflicting agendas. The result was Arab disillusionment. As they saw their own hopes for a nation state being dashed, they began to turn against the Jewish immigrants.

In 1939 the British announced their plan whereby a state, governed jointly by Arabs and Jews, would be created within ten years. Until then, immigration and the purchase of land was strictly limited. But with the help of the Jewish underground army Haganah and other clandestine organizations, some 100,000 illegal Jewish immigrants trying to escape Nazi-controlled Europe successfully made their way to Palestine. When, at the end of the war, faced with an overwhelming number of Jewish refugees the British continued to enforce strict immigration quotas, armed Jewish underground organizations turned against the British.

In 1947, the British government returned its mandate to oversee Palestine to the United Nations, and that body decided in a plenary meeting to divide Palestine into a Jewish and an Arab state; this was accepted by the Jews but not by the Arabs. As a result, on the eve of the expiration of the British mandate (May 5, 1948), the Jews declared the independent State of Israel. It included 56% of the formerly British territory (with the eastern part of Jerusalem), from which about 850,000 of

"Zion" is synonymous with Jerusalem, where the northeast hill built on by David and Solomon bears this name. A view of the Wailing Wall and the Dome of the Rock.

the 1,000,000 Arabs fled because they feared oppression by the Jews. The refugee camps to which they fled remain today as a primary source of conflict between the Israelis and the Palestinians.

WAR, PRESERVATION, AND CRISIS

The Israelis were attacked by neighboring states as soon as the State of Israel came into being, but they were able to repel these attacks In 1956 and 1967 there were further wars with neighboring states whereby the Sinai Peninsula, the West Bank and East Jerusalem, which were not part of the original UN grant to Israel, as well as the Syrian Golan Heights, were occupied. These victories did not bring lasting peace. In 1973, Israel eked out a difficult victory in the Yom-Kippur War. In 1979 a peace treaty was signed with Egypt after Israel returned the Sinai to Egypt, but tensions with the rest of the Arab world continued unabated.

The occupation policy pursued in the West Bank became one of annexation, of which southern Lebanon was included. Since Menachem Begin's tenure as Prime Minister (1977-1983), settlements by religious fundamentalists in the occupied territories were encouraged. With the first intifada, the uprising of Palestinians in the occupied territories, in 1987, the situation deteriorated further. An electoral win by a center-left coalition, led by the Prime Minister Yitzhak Rabin, in the summer 1992, changed the direction of Israeli politics. Following the maxim "Land for Peace," Israel entered into negotiations with neighboring Arab states and the Palestine Liberation Organization (PLO). In September 1993 the PLO leader, Yasser Arafat, and Rabin (who soon after was murdered by a Jewish fanatic for negotiating with the Palestinians) signed the Gaza-Jericho Agreement, which established the Palestinian Authority in the West Bank and the Gaza strip. The PLO recognized the existence of the State of Israel and abandoned its claim for Israel's annihilation. The second intifada declared in September 2000 was a serious setback in the peace process. This intifada was only officially ended in February 2005. The election of Hamas in 2006 as the governing partner in the Palestinian Authority and an ill-fated Israeli attack on Lebanon in the same year only served to exacerbate tensions, bedeviling hopes for peace in the region.

THE DREAM OF THE PAST

There are still some Jewish groups who dream of restoring the borders of the ancient Land of Israel (Eretz Yisrael) under its great Kings David and Solomon (1004-926 BC). At that time, Israel stretched from the Gulf of Aqaba to Damascus and far into east Jordan. Israel had been created by the migration of various nomadic tribes from Mesopotamia, who, in the fourteenth century BC, had settled in the Land of Canaan. In about 1200 BC they were joined by another tribe who were escaping from slavery in Egypt where they had originally migrated. Their leader, who had the Egyptian name Moses, preached the cult of Jahweh to his people. This cult was subsequently adopted by all the other tribes when they settled in Palestine. At the end of the eleventh century BC, this religious alliance was transformed into a political system, led by a king.

This had only been possible because the political weakness of Egypt and Assyria had created a power vacuum in this part of the Mediterranean region. But the internal differences within the Kingdom of Israel were so great that, after Solomon's death in 926 BC, it broke into the Northern Kingdom of Israel and the Southern Kingdom of Judah (Judea). In 722-21 BC the Northern Kingdom of Israel fell into Assyrian hands. In 587 BC Judea disappeared after the destruction of Jerusalem by the Babylonians. Its population was deported to Babylon but was allowed to return in 538 BC after Mesopotamia was conquered by the Persian King Cyrus II (the Great). On their return to Jerusalem they immediately began rebuilding the temple Solomon had dedicated to Jahweh. The period of the Babylonian Captivity played a major part in shaping the Jewish faith and its strict rituals, the aim of which was to strengthen Jewish identity in foreign lands. The Persian officials of Jewish ancestry, Nehemiah, who was Governor, and Ezra, a lawgiver, were the actual founders of Judaism. Its Holy Scriptures was the Tanaim, an anagram composed of the first Hebrew letters of the three constituent parts: the Torah, the Prophets (Navi'im), and the Writings (Ketuvim) became the mandatory guide for all Jews in the regulation of their everyday life. Although these texts underwent changes over time, their final form was fixed somewhere between 200 BC and AD 200.

In the Persian Empire, under Alexander the Great, and also during the period when it was part of the Ptolemaic Empire, Jews were not discriminated against by the country's rulers. But after Persia became part of the Seleucid Empire, the Jews suffered persecution. In addition, the growing Hellenization of the Jewish people was threatening Judaism from within. It was during this period that the belief arose in a Messiah (the Anointed One, Greek Christos), based on ancient promises, who would lead the Jewish people back to the glorious time of King David. Later, the administrative policies of the ruling Roman Empire made it temporarily possible for an independent Jewish state to co-exist with the Roman government, and in Alexandria where the Holy Scriptures were translated into Greek, thus being made accessible to educated people throughout the Mediterranean.

DECLINE, PERSECUTION AND DISCRIMINATION

The Roman expansion eastward finally led to the Jewish loss of independence when in AD 6 Judea became part of the province of Syria. The Jewish uprising in 66, triggered by excessive taxation, led four years later to the Roman conquest of Jerusalem and the destruction of the temple. The Jewish people became homeless but preserved their communal identity during the "Diaspora" (dispersal) through their adherence to their traditional laws and rituals. It was at this time, in the older Jewish community of Babylon that the Talmud (a compendium of Jewish teachings, instructions, and traditions) was created.

The fiercest enemies of the Jews were the Christians, who accused them of murdering Jesus and saw their enforced nomadic existence as reflecting God's will, presenting the Christian faithful with the example of an apostate people being punished by dispersal. Jews were used as a scapegoat upon which fear and anger could be projected, especially in times of social and economic stress. They were accused of the desecration of the Host, the ritual murder of Christian children, and the poisoning of wells. Whereas in Islamic countries Jewish communities were generally accepted, in the Christian West they had to be put under the special protection of the sovereign or sometimes the pope, and were segregated in sections of cities known as ghettos. It was eventually the Enlightenment that led to the emancipation of Jewish minorities in Western Europe. The French Revolution introduced equal rights for Jews, and these gradually became formalized throughout the nineteenth century. As a result, many Jews flourished in business as well as in art and science, but this in turn revived old prejudices, which took on a new, virulent cast during the Industrial Revolution. This prejudice eventually culminated in the horrors the Nazis "Final Solution," the attempted extermination of the entire Jewish people. ❑

THE DREYFUS AFFAIR: "J'ACCUSE!"

Paris, 1898

The Dreyfus Affair began when Captain Alfred Dreyfus, a Jewish military officer, was wrongfully arrested for treason. At the time of his arrest, France was openly anti-Semitic, although there were many Jewish officers in the military. In December of 1894, Dreyfus was convicted of treason and sentenced to life in prison on Devils Island. Dreyfus's conviction was based on the resemblance of his handwriting to the writing on a list, called the *bordereau*, that detailed secrets of the French military and was found in the German Embassy. In 1896, the matter surrounding Dreyfus's unfair conviction was highlighted when Col. Georges Picquart discovered evidence implicating Major Ferdinand Esterhazy as the author of the

Alfred Dreyfus

bordereau. Picquart was silenced by the French military, but during the following year, Dreyfus's brother made the same discovery and had the case reopened; Esterhazy was tried and acquitted.

The case split France into two camps: Dreyfusards were socialist, republican, and anti-clerical; anti-Dreyfusards were royalist, conservative, and supported the Catholic Church. On January 13, 1898, Émile Zola published a scathing letter in the newspaper *L'Aurore* titled "J'accuse," directed to French President Félix Faure that brought the facts of the Dreyfus case to public attention. The same year it was discovered that most of the evidence against Dreyfus had been fabricated. Esterhazy then fled to England, and in September 1899, Dreyfus's case was referred to an appeals court. The court martial found Dreyfus guilty with extenuating circumstances and sentenced him

to ten years in prison. This sentencing caused worldwide indignation, but President Émile Loubet immediately pardoned him. In 1906, the court of appeals exonerated Dreyfus, reinstated him into the army as a major, and decorated him with the Legion of Honor. The Dreyfus Affair helped to unite the French political left and prompted the 1905 law that separated church and state. ❑

Zola's accusation published on January 13, 1898

SPANISH-AMERICAN WAR

Cuba, 1898

In March of 1898, a photographer sent to Cuba to take pictures of Cuban insurgents fighting for their liberty sent a

A regiment from Spain leaves for the war against the U.S.

cable to his editor: "EVERYTHING QUIET STOP NO TROUBLE HERE." The reply came from the publisher of the *New York Journal*: "PLEASE REMAIN STOP YOU FURNISH THE PICTURES AND I WILL FURNISH THE WAR—HEARST." In three weeks the United States was at war with Spain.

From the moment that Cuban colonists rose up against their masters in Madrid, William Randolph Hearst's *Journal* and its bitter rival, the *New York World*, had been feeding and fomenting public opinion with stories of atrocities and brutality in Spanish concentration camps.

Despite the sincere reluctance of President William McKinley, the jingoism of the Congress and the public pushed him into declaring war. When the *USS*

Maine was blown up by a Spanish mine in Havana harbor and 252 men were lost, the United States was gripped by war hysteria. Washington's "hawks" had their way, and Congress dispatched an ill-equipped invasion force to Cuba. The bellicose under-secretary for the navy, Theodore Roosevelt, made a name for himself, perhaps for foolhardiness, by leading his "Rough Riders" in a near-suicidal charge up a hill at Santiago, resulting in a thousand casualties.

The war came to an end with the signing of the Treaty of Paris on December 10. According to its terms, Spain agreed to cede Cuba, Puerto Rico, Guam, and the Philippines to the United States for twenty million dollars. Secretary of State John Hay called the conflict "a splendid little war." ❑

THEODOR HERZL

Basel, Switzerland, 1898

The first World Zionist Congress was held August 29–31, 1897, in Basel, Switzerland. It was organized by Theodore Herzl. Herzl had been a reporter during the Dreyfus Affair, and after witnessing the display of anti-Semitism in France, he became convinced Jews would never be fully assimilated into European society and that a Jewish national State had to be established.

His efforts to bring that about made Herzl the founder of the modern Zionist movement. His vision for a Jewish state is described in his pamphlet *Der Judenstaat*, which was published in 1896 and introduced the idea of Zionism to the world. The final declaration of the Congress stated, "Zionism seeks to establish a home for the Jewish people in Palestine secured under public law." For the Jews this expressed

ATHENS HOSTS THE REVIVED OLYMPIC GAMES

Athens, April 1896

After a hiatus of over fifteen hundred years, the Olympic Games were revived In Athens. The first games were held on the nearby plains of Olympia in 776 BC in honor of the god Zeus. They included athletics, games, and contests of choral poetry and dance, and were held every four years until AD 393.

The new Games focused on athletics and sports. They were revived by Baron Pierre de Coubertin, a strong advocate of physical education in France. He began working on the idea in 1892 at a meeting of the French Athletic Sports Union. Two years later he won the unanimous support of an international athletics congress in Paris.

Coubertin was interested not only in physical prowess. He wanted to establish a venue where big nations would compete with each other in athletics instead of rushing into wars of national prestige. Although that mission has yet to be realized, the Games remain a symbol of the hope for a world at peace. ❑

The first revival of the Olympic games was sparsely attended. Inset: Baron Pierre de Coubertin

AND ZIONISM

a hope that had been carefully preserved since the destruction of the Second Temple in AD 70. A little more than fifty years later, in 1948, the State of Israel was born. ❑

Theodor Herzl

THE BOER WAR

South Africa, 1899

After the British annexed Natal in 1842, the Great Trek moved northeast into the Transvaal, and the Boers founded the first South African Republic. Subsequently, the British claimed all the land between the Vaal and the Orange Rivers, but the Boers who had settled the region resisted the incursion. The British withdrew, seeing no financial advantage to be gained, and in 1854, the Boers created a second republic, the Orange Free State.

Circumstances changed when large gold deposits were discovered in the Transvaal, and the British made it clear that they wished to annex the two Republics and unify them with the Cape and Natal Colonies. In 1896, Dr. Leander Starr Jameson, an associate of Cecil Rhodes, conducted a raid into the Transvaal with 470 mounted men, anticipating a general uprising of the Uitlanders (non-Boers). No uprising occurred, and he and his men were captured. The British, however, maintained the pressure for annexation.

The two Republics, tired of the British encroachment and armed with modern weapons supplied by Germany, united and made a lightning strike into the Cape and Natal in October 1899. They invested the towns of Ladysmith, Mafeking, and Kimberly. The British, with the offensive initiative denied them, were forced to send columns to their relief. The British commanders were woefully inept, and all the early successes of the war went to the Boers, who proved themselves excellent mounted infantry. However, by sheer weight of numbers—fielding an army of half a million—the British were able to relieve the besieged towns and enter Pretoria in June 1900, which they thought would end the war. The Boers formed commandos and engaged in guerrilla warfare, attacking and then disappearing into the vast veldt. The British retaliated by burning their farms and putting their women and children in concentration camps, where 27,000 died. The guerrillas were starved into submission, and the last commando surrendered in May 1902. Both Boer republics were incorporated into the Commonwealth. ❑

Boers defending against a British attack

The Twentieth Century and the World of Today

1900–2008

- ■ Africa
- ■ Asia
- ■ Europe
- ■ North America
- ■ Oceania
- □ South America

1900–1909

Nigeria, 1 January 1900. Nigeria becomes a British protectorate.

New York City, 2 January 1900. The first electric omnibus goes into operation.

South Africa, 10 January 1900. Lord (Frederick) Roberts replaces Sir Redvers Buller as commander-in-chief of the British forces in South Africa, with Herbert Kitchener as his chief-of-staff.

Britain, 20 January 1900. The art critic and social theorist John Ruskin dies after years of insanity.

South Africa, 24 January 1900. The British under General Warren take Spion Kop.

Rome, January 1900. Giacomo Puccini's opera *Tosca* is performed for the first time.

Britain, 27 February 1900. British trade unions create the Labor Party.

South Africa, 27 February 1900. The Boer General Piet Cronje surrenders to the British at Paardeberg after suffering a defeat.

South Africa, 28 February 1900. Following their relief of Kimberley earlier in the month, the British relieve Ladysmith.

South Africa, 13 March 1900. British forces under Lord Roberts take Bloemfontein.

USA, 14 March 1900. The US dollar goes onto the gold standard.

Crete, 19 March 1900. The British archaeologist Sir Arthur Evans begins excavations at the Palace of Knossos.

Brussels, 4 April 1900. Jean-Baptiste Sipido, a 16-year-old anarchist, attempts to assassinate the Prince of Wales.

South Africa, 9 April 1900. The Boers defeat the British at Kroonstadt.

Paris, 14 April 1900. The World Exhibition opens.

Pacific, 19 May 1900. Britain annexes the Friendly Islands (*Tonga*).

South Africa, 20 May 1900. The British relieve Mafeking.

China, 21 May 1900. Russia annexes Manchuria.

South Africa, 29 May 1900. Britain annexes the Orange Free State.

China, 17 June 1900. In response to the growing Boxer threat, the allied troops of Britain, Germany, France, Russia, the USA, Italy, Austria and Japan capture the Dagu forts.

China, 20 June 1900. Dong Fuxiang's Gansu troops and the Boxers begin attacks on the legations, churches and other foreign establishments.

Philippines, 21 June 1900. Arthur MacArthur, the US military governor, grants an amnesty to the Filipino rebels.

Britain, 29 June 1900. *The Dictionary of National Biography* is completed.

Paris, 19 July 1900. The *Metro* underground railway opens.

Italy, 30 July 1900. King Umberto is shot dead by an anarchist. Victor Emmanuel III succeeds.

USA, 10 August 1900. The USA wins the first International Lawn Tennis Trophy, established by Dwight F. Davis.

China, 14 August 1900. The allies enter Beijing and end the siege of the legations.

Germany, 25 August 1900. The philosopher Friedrich Nietzsche dies after 12 years of insanity.

South Africa, 1 September 1900. The British annex the Boer Republic of the Transvaal.

Britain, 17 October 1900. Lord Salisbury's Tory government is re-elected.

Europe, 20 October 1900. Britain and Germany sign a pact to continue the open-door policy towards China.

USA, 6 November 1900. The Republican President William McKinley is re-elected.

Canada, 8 November 1900. Liberals under Sir Wilfrid Laurier win the general election.

Britain, 22 November, 1900. Arthur Sullivan, the composer of the famous Savoy operas with librettos by W. S. Gilbert, dies.

Paris, 9 December 1900. *Nocturnes* by Claude Debussy is performed for the first time.

Paris, 30 November 1900. The Irish writer Oscar Wilde dies.

India, 1901. The famine and the epidemic of bubonic plague, which have ravaged India for the past four years, abate.

Australia, 1 January 1901. The Commonwealth of Australia comes into being.

Britain, 22 January 1901. Queen Victoria dies and is succeeded by her son Edward VII.

Italy, 27 January 1901. The composer Giuseppe Verdi dies.

Moscow, 31 January 1901. Anton Chekhov's play *Three Sisters* is performed for the first time.

India, 12 February 1901. The viceroy, Lord Curzon, creates the North-West Frontier province between Afghanistan and the Punjab.

Germany, 6 March 1901. An anarchist makes an attempt on the life of Kaiser Wilhelm II.

Germany, 31 March 1901. The first Mercedes motor car is built.

Venezuela, 9 August 1901. Colombian troops invade Venezuela.

Detroit, 21 August 1901. The Cadillac Motor Company is founded.

Britain, 4 September 1901. In the Taff Vale railway case, the House of Lords rules that trade unions are liable for the financial losses of companies affected by industrial action.

China, 7 September 1901. The Boxer Protocol is signed by China and the foreign powers, ending the Boxer rebellion.

France, 9 September 1901. The painter Henri de Toulouse-Lautrec dies at the age of 36.

USA, 14 September 1901. President William McKinley dies after being shot by an anarchist. Vice-President Theodore Roosevelt become president.

China, 16 October 1901. Russia signs a new agreement with China over Manchuria.

South Africa, October 1901. Boer commandos invade Cape Colony, coming within 50 miles of Cape Town.

USA, 18 November 1901. Britain and the USA sign the Hay-Pauncefote treaty, agreeing to terms for a canal through Central America.

London, 30 January 1902. Britain and Japan sign a treaty agreeing to respect each other's interests in China and Korea.

USA, 22 February 1902. The Yellow Fever Commission announces that the disease is carried by mosquitoes.

South Africa, 26 March 1902. The British colonial statesman Cecil Rhodes dies.

China, 8 April 1902. Russia signs a treaty with China over Manchuria, promising to withdraw its troops.

Russia, 15 April 1902. Sipyagin, the head of the secret police, is killed by socialist revolutionaries.

Martinique, 8 May 1902. An eruption of Mount Pele wipes out the whole town of St. Pierre.

London, 29 May 1902. The London School of Economics and Political Science opens.

Spain, 30 May 1902. King Alfonso XIII suspends the Madrid Cortes amid growing unrest.

South Africa, 31 May 1902. The Boers surrender to the British and sign the Treaty of Vereeniging, ending the Boer War and recognizing British sovereignty.

Europe, 23 June 1902. The Triple Alliance of Germany, Austria, and Italy is renewed for 12 years.

USA, 28 June 1902. The USA pays France $40,000 for the rights to the Panama Canal.

USA, 1 July 1902. The Philippine Government Act, under which Filipinos will be ruled by a US presidential commission, is passed.

Russia, 3 July 1902. To avoid the spread of riots, in which thousands have already died, Tsar Nicholas II offers talks with the people.

Britain, 12 July 1902. Arthur Balfour succeeds Lord Salisbury as Tory prime minister.

France, 29 September 1902. The writer Emile Zola, the author of *Germinal* and *Thérèse Raquin* and valiant champion of Captain Dreyfus, dies.

Germany, 22 November 1902. The steel magnate Friedrich Krupp, head of Germany's largest manufacturing firm and the richest man in the country, dies.

Vienna, 1 December 1902. Austria and Russia agree on joint supervision in Macedonia.

Venezuela, 9 December 1902. British and German warships seize the Venezuelan navy, demanding settlement of compensation claims arising from President Cipriano Castro's 1899 coup.

Egypt, 10 December 1902. The massive Nile dam at Aswan is completed.

Britain, 1902. Beatrix Potter publishes *The Tale of Peter Rabbit*.

India, 1 January 1903. A mighty *durbar* is held in the old Moghul capital of Delhi to proclaim Edward VII Emperor of India.

Central America, 22 January 1903. The US and Colombia sign a treaty to allow the construction of the Panama Canal.

Washington, DC, 13 February 1903. Britain, Germany and Italy sign a treaty agreeing to lift the blockade of Venezuela.

Balkans, 23 February 1903. The Ottoman Sultan Abdul Hamid II accepts Russian and Austrian proposals for reforms in Macedonia, in order to quell a rebellion there.

USA, 3 March 1903. A bill is passed curbing immigration and banning "undesirables."

Russia, 12 March 1903. Tsar Nicholas II issues a manifesto conceding important reforms, including the freedom of religion.

Nigeria, 15 March 1903. Following the fall of Kano last month, troops of the West African Frontier Force, led by British officers, take Sokoto. The sultan flees.

Finland, 26 March 1903. The Tsar appoints the Russian general Bobrikov virtual dictator of Finland.

Balkans, 14 April 1903. Bulgarians kill 165 people in a Muslim village near Monastir in Macedonia.

Balkans, 16 April 1903. In the latest act of Jewish persecution, peasants in Kishinev, in Bessarabia, massacre scores of Jews.

Serbia, 11 June 1903. King Alexander and Queen Draga are murdered by disaffected army officers and Prince Peter Karageorgevich is proclaimed king.

Germany, 16 June 1903. The socialists make large gains in elections to the *reichstag*.

France, 19 July 1903. Maurice Garin wins the first Tour de France bicycle race.

Switzerland, 19 August 1903. Delegates to the sixth Zionist Congress in Basel clash over proposals to set up a Jewish state in Uganda.

Britain, 17 September 1903. Joseph Chamberlain resigns as colonial secretary to have greater freedom to promote preferential trade with the empire.

Balkans, September 1903. The Ottomans have massacred 50,000 Bulgarians in the region of Monastir.

Britain, 10 October 1903. Emmeline Pankhurst founds the Women's Social and Political Union.

Germany, 1 November 1903. The historian Theodor Mommsen dies.

Russia, 17 November 1903. Vladimir Lenin splits the Social Democratic Labor Party, leading a majority breakaway group, the *Bolsheviks*.

Central America, November 1903. Panama declares itself independent of Colombia.

USA, 17 December 1903. Wilbur and Orville Wright fly a heavier-than-air flying machine at Kitty Hawk, North Carolina.

South-West Africa, 11 January 1904. Rebellious Herero massacre 123 German soldiers and male settlers near Okahandja, the seat of the Herero chief, Samuel Maharero.

Cuba, 5 February 1904. America ends its occupation of Cuba.

China, 8 February 1904. Provoked by Russian penetration of northern Korea and failure to withdraw from Manchuria, war breaks out between Japan and Russia with a Japanese attack on Port Arthur (*Lushuri*).

Europe, 8 April 1904. France and Britain sign an *entente cordiale* settling their colonial disputes in North Africa.

Britain, 26 April 1904. George Bernard Shaw's play *Candida* is performed for the first time.

New York City, 15 June 1904. About 1,000 die when the paddle-steamer General Slocum catches fire in New York harbor.

Finland, 23 June 1904. The Russian governor general, Bobrikov, is assassinated.

China, 24 June 1904. Japanese forces inflict a major defeat on the Russians at Telissu.

Austria, 3 July 1904. The Hungarian-born Zionist Theodor Herzl dies.

Switzerland, 14 July 1904. Paul Kruger, four times president of the Transvaal Republic, dies in exile in Geneva.

Russia, 15 July 1904. The playwright Anton Chekhov dies.

Belgium, September 1904. Leopold II, the king of the Belgians, appoints an international commission to investigate conditions in the Congo Free State.

Morocco, 3 October 1904. France and Spain sign an agreement on Morocco by which the northern part of the country is recognized as a Spanish zone of influence.

New York City, 27 October 1904. The subway opens.

USA, 8 November 1904. The Republican Theodore Roosevelt is returned to power in the presidential election.

China, 5 December 1904. The Japanese destroy the Russian fleet at Port Arthur (*Lushuri*).

Stockholm, 10 December 1904. The Russian physiologist Ivan Pavlov wins a Nobel prize for his work on the digestive system.

Russia, 26 December 1904. Tsar Nicholas II issues a decree offering liberal reforms, but warns that strikes and riots must stop.

Britain, 27 December 1904. James Barrie's play *Peter Pan* opens.

Russia, 1 January 1905. The Trans-Siberian Railway officially opens.

China, 2 January 1905. The Russians surrender to the Japanese at Port Arthur.

St Petersburg, 22 January 1905. The Tsar's troops shoot dead more than 500 strikers on "Bloody Sunday."

Moscow, 17 February 1905. Grand Duke Sergei, the uncle of Tsar Nicholas II, is assassinated.

China, 10 March 1905. The Japanese defeat the Russians at Mukden after a ten-day battle.

France, 24 March 1905. Jules Verne, the inventor of the science fiction, dies.

India, 4 April 1905. An earthquake in Lahore kills more than 10,000.

France, April 1905. The psychologist Alfred Binet invents intelligence tests.

Warsaw, 1 May 1905. Troops fire on May Day demonstrators, killing 100.

Sea of Japan, 28 May 1905. The Japanese annihilate the Russian fleet in the strait of Tsushima.

Norway, 7 June 1905. Norway declares independence from Sweden.

Athens, 13 June 1905. The prime minister, Delyannis, is assassinated outside the Greek parliament.

Odessa, Russia, 3 July 1905. Tsarist troops kill 6,000 demonstrators to restore order in Odessa. Unrest, for long underground, is coming to the surface. A general strike is declared in St. Petersburg.

South Africa, 4 July 1905. Dutch-speaking Boers protest that the new electoral laws imposed by the British favor the English-speakers and are an example of how Boers are discriminated against.

Russia, 8 July 1905. The crew of the battleship *Potemkin* surrender to the

Romanians, who say they will not be extradited because the mutiny was a political act.

USA, 16 July 1905. Commander Peary sets sail on his second expedition to the North Pole.

Finland, 24 July 1905. The German Kaiser, Wilhelm II, and Russia's Tsar Nicholas II conclude the Treaty of Bjoerkoe.

Russia, 19 August 1905. In a step towards constitutional monarchy, the Duma (a representative assembly) is established.

USA, 29 August 1905. Russian and Japanese delegates agree peace terms. An armistice is arranged for August 31.

Russia, 2 September 1905. The worst famine since 1891 is reported.

Central Asia, 5 September 1905. Hundreds die in battles between Muslim Tartars and Christian Armenians.

USA, 5 September 1905. The war fought in Korea and Manchuria between Russia and Japan ends today with the signing of a peace treaty at Portsmouth, New Hampshire.

Britain, 14 October 1905. The suffragettes Christabel Pankhurst and Annie Kenney opt to go to prison rather than pay a fine for assaulting a policeman at a political meeting in Manchester.

Russia, 30 October 1905. Tsar Nicholas II issues an imperial manifesto that transforms the country from an absolute autocracy to a semi-constitutional monarchy in an attempt to quell mounting unrest.

Russia, 8 November 1905. 1,000 Jews are killed in a pogrom in Odessa when a mob of 50,000 goes on the rampage shooting and stabbing Jewish men, women and children.

France, 6 December 1905. A law is passed separating the state and the church.

Alaska, 6 December 1905. The Norwegian explorer Roald Amundsen completes a two and a half year journey across the American Arctic coast from the Atlantic to the Pacific.

Russia, 7 December 1905. Revolutionaries occupy the fortress at Kiev in the Ukraine.

Germany, 9 December 1905. Richard Strauss's opera *Salome*, based on Oscar Wilde's play, has its first performance.

Moscow, 30 December 1905. Government forces crush an uprising by students and workers after a week of street fighting.

Austria, December 1905. The publication of *Three Essays on the Theory of Sexuality* by the psychoanalyst Sigmund Freud sparks off fierce controversy.

Britain, 10 February 1906. HMS *Dreadnought*, the most powerful warship in the world, is launched.

Nigeria, 20 February 1906. British troops arrive to quell protests by the Tiv people against Muslim Hausa rule.

Finland, 7 March 1906. Suffrage is extended to all tax-paying men and women over 24.

Britain, 8 March 1906. A government publication out today states that the empire occupies one-fifth of the land-surface of the globe and has a population of 400,000,000.

Russia, 20 March 1906. Army officers are massacred in a mutiny in Sevastopol in the Crimea.

Spain, 31 March 1906. A conference on Morocco closes in Algeciras having upheld French hegemony under the sultan.

Italy, 7 April 1906. Mount Vesuvius erupts, destroying the town of Ottaiano.

France, 19 April 1906. The Nobel prize-winning physicist Pierre Curie dies aged 47.

San Francisco, 18 April 1906. A major earthquake destroys most of the city.

Tibet, 27 April 1906. China reluctantly grants Britain control of Tibet, following the occupation of the capital Lhasa by British troops.

St. Petersburg, 24 May 1906. Tsar Nicholas II concedes universal suffrage but refuses to grant amnesty for political prisoners as suggested by the Duma.

Norway, 28 May 1906. The playwright Henrik Ibsen dies aged 78. Among his most controversial works are *A Doll's House*, *Ghosts* and *Hedda Gabler*.

Europe, 6 June 1906. Italy re-affirms its alliance with the Austro-Hungarian and German empires.

France, 12 July 1906. Captain Alfred Dreyfus is rehabilitated having been publicly disgraced 11 years ago on charges of espionage and treason.

Russia, 21 July 1906. The Duma is dissolved and martial law is declared.

Russia, 2 November 1906. The Jewish revolutionary Leon Trotsky is exiled for life to Siberia.

Belgium, 9 November 1906. Prince Albert is declared successor to Leopold as King of the Congo.

Japan, 15 November 1906. The world's biggest battleship, the *Satsuma*, is launched.

South Africa, 12 December 1906. The Transvaal is given autonomy with white male suffrage.

China, 1 January 1907. Four million people are starving owing to heavy rains and crop failure.

German East Africa, 16 January 1907. The great rebel leader Abdallah Mapanda, the head of *maji-maji* (*magic water*) uprisings since July 1905, is run to ground by the Germans.

Teheran, 19 January 1907. Mohammed Ali Mirza is crowned Shah of Persia. He is intent on a program of liberalization.

Washington, DC, 26 February 1907. President Roosevelt puts the US army in charge of building the Panama Canal.

Finland, 15 March 1907. The first women are elected to parliament.

South West Africa, 31 March 1907. The Germans end the state of emergency as all the Nama (*Hottentots*), except those led by Simon Koper, have been defeated.

Russia, 3 April 1907. Twenty million people are starving in the worst famine on record.

China, 15 April 1907. Japan hands Manchuria back to China under the terms of the Treaty of Portsmouth which ended the Russo-Japanese War.

France, 10 June 1907. The cinematographers Auguste and Louis Lumière invent a simple form of color photography which they believe will make moving pictures in color commonplace.

Russia, 16 June 1907. Russia's second *duma* is dissolved with the prime minister, Peter Stolypin, accusing 55 socialist members of plotting against the Tsar.

South Africa, 1 July 1907. The Orange River colony gains autonomy as the Orange Free State.

The Hague, 7 September 1907. The peace conference, determining the conventions of war, rules that all powers must give notice of war.

Brussels, 28 November 1907. King Leopold transfers the Kingdom of the Congo to the state.

Addis Ababa, Ethiopia 1907. The Emperor Menelik is paralyzed by a stroke and Ras Tasamma becomes regent.

South Africa, 1907. White miners strike to preserve a job color bar, reserving skilled jobs for whites only, after mines begin employing African and Chinese workers as operators of new mechanical drills.

France, 1907. The philosopher Henri Bergson publishes his most significant work to date: *Creative Evolution*.

Transvaal, 30 January 1908. Mohandas Gandhi, the leader of the Indian protest against new laws requiring Asians to register, is released from prison.

Lisbon, 1 February 1908. King Carlos and Crown Prince Luiz are assassinated following a failed revolution. Don Manuel is to succeed the king. The dictator Joao Franco and his cabinet resign following the king's assassination.

Ottoman Empire, 24 July 1908. The success of the Young Turks' revolution, which began on 3 July, forces Sultan Abdul Hamid II to restore the constitution.

USA, 12 August 1908. Ford's first Model T is produced in Detroit. Ford calls it, "a motor car for the multitude."

Balkans, 7 October 1908. Austria annexes Bosnia-Herzegovina. Though formally part of the Ottoman empire, the territory's predominantly Serbo-Croat population favors union with Serbia. Austria's unilateral move shocks other European powers.

London, 12 October 1908. Russia persuades Britain to participate in a congress on the Balkan situation.

London, 24 October 1908. The suffragette Emmeline Pankhurst and her daughter Christabel are jailed after a sensational trial in which two cabinet ministers are called as witnesses for the defense.

Balkans, 15 November 1908. Austria sends troops to the Serbian frontier.

Panama, 15 November 1908. The US President Roosevelt visits the city of Panama—the first president to travel abroad during his term of office.

China, 2 December 1908. The child Emperor Puyi succeeds to the throne as Xuantong.

Vienna, 9 December 1908. Austria and Turkey resume talks aimed at easing the Balkan crisis.

Stockholm, 10 December 1908. Professor Ernest Rutherford wins a Nobel prize for his work on radioactivity and the atom.

Britain, 1908. Kenneth Grahame publishes a delightful children's book: *The Wind in the Willows*.

London, 1 January 1909. Men and women over 70 draw their first old-age pensions.

India, 5 January 1909. Hindus and Muslims riot in Calcutta.

Balkans, 12 January 1909. The Ottoman empire accepts Austria's offer of 2.5 million Turkish pounds for Bosnia-Herzegovina.

Balkans, 24 February 1909. Serbia demands that Austria cede Bosnia-Herzegovina to it.

Balkans, 28 March 1909. The European powers agree to a formula for Serbia to renounce claims to Bosnia-Herzegovina.

North Pole, 6 April 1909. Commander Robert E Peary of the United States Navy is the first person to reach the North Pole.

Ottoman Empire, 23 April 1909. Muslim fanatics backed by the *sultan* have massacred at least 30,000 Armenians in the last week.

South Africa, 12 June 1909. Natal votes for union with South Africa.

Congo (Zaire), 12 June 1909. Belgian and British troops clash over the border of Congo and Northern Rhodesia (*Zambia*).

Persia, 26 June 1909. Mohammed Ali Shah annuls a new law which promised elections, and defers the promised constitution.

Persia, 13 July 1909. Nationalists opposed to the *shah* take Teheran.

Persia, 16 July 1909. The 12-year-old crown prince, Sultan Ahmed Mirza, is proclaimed shah.

Geneva, 13 September 1909. The Congress of Egyptian Youth demands British withdrawal from Egypt.

Spain, 13 October 1909. The anarchist Francisco Ferrer is executed by a firing-squad following the *Semana Tragica*, a week of rioting in Barcelona.

Brussels, 28 October 1909. The government announces major liberal reforms in the Congo.

Hawaii, 14 November 1909. The US president, William Taft, announces that a naval base will be built at Pearl Harbor to protect the US from a Japanese attack.

New York City, 28 November 1909. Sergei Rachmaninov gives the world premiere of his third piano concerto.

Russia, 29 November 1909. Maxim Gorky is expelled from the Revolutionary Party for his "*bourgeois*" high life on Capri.

London, 7 December 1909. The South Africa Act, bringing together the Cape of Good Hope, Natal, Transvaal and Orange Free State, is given the royal assent, as promised by the British at the end of the Boer War.

1910–1919

Africa, 15 January 1910. France reorganizes French Congo as French Equatorial Africa.

Persia, 31 January 1910. Russia and Britain decide to intervene as political unrest sweeps the country.

Africa, 7 February 1910. Belgium, Britain, and Germany fix the frontiers of Congo, Uganda and German East Africa respectively.

Tibet, 23 February 1910. The Dalai Lama flees to India as Chinese troops invade Lhasa. He returned from exile in Beijing only two months ago having fled in 1904 when British troops invaded.

China, 10 March 1910. Slavery is abolished.

Italy, 27 March 1910. Mount Etna erupts.

London, 14 April 1910. The House of Commons votes for bill to abolish the Lords' power to veto bills.

London, 7 May 1910. King George V succeeds the throne following Edward VII's death from pneumonia.

London, 20 May 1910. Halley's comet passes within 13 million miles of the earth.

London, 1 June 1910. Captain Robert Falcon Scott sets out on a journey to conquer the South Pole.

Russia, 3 June 1910. The *duma* is to abolish Finnish autonomy.

Germany, 22 June 1910. Nobel prize winner, Dr Paul Ehrlich, puts forward a new drug for syphilis, known as *salvarsan*.

South Africa, 1 July 1910. The Union of South Africa, formed on 31 May, becomes a dominion of the British empire.

Far East, 4 July 1910. Russia acknowledges Japan's occupation of Korea in return for a free hand in Manchuria.

New Jersey, 27 August 1910. Thomas Edison demonstrates talking motion pictures.

South Africa, 15 September 1910. Afrikaner nationalists win the first parliamentary elections.

Portugal, 17 October 1910. The provisional government banishes the royal family and abolishes the nobility.

Portugal, 9 November 1910. The republic is recognized by Britain, France, Germany, Russia, Spain, Norway, and Belgium.

Morocco, 3 December 1910. France takes the port of Agadir.

Britain, 1910. Bertrand Russell and A. N. Whitehead publish *Principia Mathematica*.

Germany, 26 January 1911. Richard Strauss's new opera *Der Rosenkavalier* opens to great acclaim in Dresden.

Britain, 6 February 1911. The Labor Party elect Ramsay MacDonald as its chairman.

Morocco, 30 March 1911. The sultan asks for French help to put down the uprising that began last October.

Paris, 23 April 1911. The cabinet agrees to send reinforcements to put down the Moroccan uprising.

Portugal, 30 April 1911. Women get the vote.

London, 4 May 1911. Lloyd George reveals the Liberal government's insurance bill designed to deal with sickness and unemployment.

Austria, 18 May 1911. The great composer Gustav Mahler dies at the age of 50. He will be best remembered for the song symphony *Das Lied von der Erde*.

Britain, 30 May 1911. The British writer and Sir Arthur Sullivan's librettist, Sir William Schwenk Gilbert, dies aged 75.

Mexico, 7 June 1911. A huge earthquake rocks Mexico City.

Morocco, 16 June 1911. The French army occupies Fez.

Morocco, 1 July 1911. Kaiser Wilhelm II dispatches a German gunboat to the Moroccan port of Agadir, to the alarm of the French.

North Africa, 3 August 1911. Airplanes are put to military use when Italians reconnoiter Turkish lines near Tripoli.

London, 10 August 1911. The House of Lords gives up its right of veto, accepting the Liberal government's parliament bill. The bill follows a general election and a threat by King George V to create sufficient peers to pass it.

London, 18 August 1911. The Official Secrets Bill gets royal assent.

Paris, 22 August 1911. Leonardo da Vinci's masterpiece the *Mona Lisa* is stolen from the Louvre.

Portugal, 24 August 1911. Manoel José de Arriaga is elected first president of the republic.

China, 4 September 1911. Flooding along the Yangzi River kills 100,000 people.

Berlin, 23 September 1911. France and Germany settle the Moroccan dispute.

Britain, 23 October 1911. Winston Churchill is appointed First Lord of the Admiralty.

Mexico City, 24 October 1911. Rebel supporters of Emiliano Zapata carry out raids around the capital.

North Africa, 5 November 1911. Italy announces the annexation of Tripolitania, Libya and Cyrenaica.

China, 10 November 1911. Imperial troops massacre republicans at Nanjing.

China, 29 December 1911. Dr Sun Yatsen, leader of the Chinese revolution, becomes provisional president of the Chinese republic.

Paris, 1911. Vaslav Nijinsky dances the lead role of Petrushka in Stravinsky's new ballet.

China, 1 January 1912. The Republic of China is officially proclaimed.

South Pole, 17 January 1912. The British explorer Robert Falcon Scott reaches the South Pole to discover that his Norwegian rival, Roald Amundsen, has beaten him to it.

Morocco, 30 March 1912. By the treaty of Fez, Morocco becomes a French protectorate.

Britain, 13 April 1912. The Royal Flying Corps is set up.

Russia, 5 May 1912. The first issue of the Bolshevik newspaper *Pravda* appears.

Britain, 22 July 1912. The admiralty recalls British warships from the Mediterranean to the North Sea to counter the growing German naval threat.

Far East, 7 August 1912. Russia and Japan reach agreement on their spheres of influence in Mongolia and Manchuria.

Balkans, 8 October 1912. Montenegro declares war on the Ottoman empire.

Balkans, 14 October 1912. The Ottomans invade Serbia.

Switzerland, 18 October 1912. The Ottoman Empire and Italy sign a treaty at Ouchy whereby the Ottomans cede Tripoli and Cyrenaica to Italy.

Turkey, 19 October 1912. The allied Balkan armies invade Turkey.

Balkans, 23 October 1912. The Greeks rout the Ottomans at Sarandaporos.

Germany, 25 October 1912. Richard Strauss's opera *Ariadne auf Naxos* receives its premiere.

Morocco, 27 November 1912. France and Spain sign a treaty outlining their respective spheres of influence in Morocco.

Albania, 28 November 1912. Albania declares independence.

Balkans, 4 December 1912. The Ottomans conclude an armistice with Bulgaria and Serbia. Greece refrains from signing.

Europe, 5 December 1912. Germany, Austria, and Italy renew the Triple Alliance for six years.

Switzerland, 1912. Carl Gustav Jung publishes his *Theory of Psychoanalysis*.

Turkey, 23 January 1913. The extreme nationalist Young Turks, led by Enver Bey, stage a coup d'état, overthrowing the Ottoman grand vizier, Kiamil Pasha.

New York City, 2 February 1913. Grand Central Station, the world's largest railway station, opens.

Antarctic, 10 February 1913. The British explorer Robert F. Scott and two of his companions, who were attempting to return from the South Pole, are found dead.

USA, 25 February 1913. Federal income tax is introduced.

Balkans, 6 March 1913. In a resumption of hostilities, the Greeks take Janina, capturing 32,000 Turks.

Australia, 12 March 1913. Canberra becomes the federal capital.

Greece, 20 March 1913. Following the assassination of King George, his eldest son Constantine, the Duke of Sparta, becomes king.

Balkans, 26 March 1913. The allies take Adrianople after a 155-day siege.

China, 8 April 1913. China's first parliament opens in Beijing.

Balkans, 22 April 1913. Scutari falls to the Montenegrins after a six-month siege.

The Hague, 26 April 1913. The International Women's Peace Conference opens.

Paris, 29 May 1913. *The Rite of Spring*, a ballet by Igor Stravinsky, receives its premiere.

London, 30 May 1913. The Ottomans sign a peace treaty with the Balkan League, ending their war.

Germany, 6 June 1913. A bill is passed providing for a large increase in the German army.

Turkey, 11 June 1913. Mahmud Shevket Pasha, the new *grand vizier*, is assassinated.

Balkans, 24 June 1913. Greece and Serbia break their alliance with Bulgaria over a border dispute.

Balkans, 30 June 1913. Bulgaria attacks Serbia and Greece.

Balkans, 1 July 1913. Greece and Serbia declare war on Bulgaria.

Balkans, 11 July 1913. Romania declares war on Bulgaria and invades.

Balkans, 10 August 1913. The Treaty of Bucharest ends the Second Balkan War.

China, 1 September 1913. A "second revolution," staged by the nationalist *Kuomintang* and other forces in reaction to Yuan Shikai's anti-democratic forces, ends.

Balkans, 21 September 1913. Turkey and Bulgaria settle their frontier dispute; Turkey keeps Adrianople.

Tunis, 23 September 1913. Frenchman Roland Garros completes the first flight over the Mediterranean.

Panama, 10 October 1913. The Panama Canal is opened.

Mexico, 11 October 1913. President Huerta declares himself dictator.

Mexico, 15 November 1913. The rebel Pancho Villa takes Ciudad Juárez.

France, 1913. Marcel Proust publishes the first volume of a novel entitled *À la Recherche du Temps Perdu*.

German East Africa, 2 February 1914. A 900-mile railway opens from Lake Tanganyika to Dar-es-Salaam.

London, 13 April 1914. *Pygmalion*, a play by George Bernard Shaw, receives its premiere.

Mexico, 21 April 1914. US troops opposed to President Huerta land and seize Vera Cruz.

Balkans, 28 June 1914. Archduke Franz Ferdinand is assassinated at Sarajevo.

Vienna, 23 July 1914. Austria issues a drastic ultimatum to Serbia.

Vienna, 28 July 1914. Austria declares war on Serbia.

Mexico, July 1914. President Huerta is expelled from office and civil war breaks out between Venustiano Carranza, the rebel leader, and his lieutenant Pancho Villa.

Berlin, 1 August 1914. Kaiser Wilhelm II declares war on his cousin Tsar Nicholas II.

Luxembourg, 2 August 1914. Germany invades Luxembourg.

Berlin, 3 August 1914. Germany declares war on France.

Belgium, 4 August 1914. The Germans invade Belgium.

Europe, 4 August 1914. Britain and Belgium declare war on Germany.

Turkey, 5 August 1914. The Ottomans close the Dardanelles.

Vienna, 6 August 1914. Austria declares war on Russia.

Serbia, 6 August 1914. Serbia declares war on Germany.

Europe, 12 August 1914. Britain and France declare war on Austria.

France, 17 August 1914. A British expeditionary force lands.

Belgium, 20 August 1914. German troops take Brussels.

Japan, 23 August 1914. Having issued an ultimatum to Germany, Japan declares war and attacks the German fortified port of Qingdao on Chinese territory.

Belgium, 23 August 1914. The British are forced to retreat after bitter fighting with the Germans around Mons.

France, 26 August 1914. The Prime Minister, René Viviani, forms a coalition government of national unity.

North Sea, 28 August 1914. The British sink three German cruisers and two destroyers off Heligoland Bight, opening the war at sea.

Japan September, 1914. Nine million people are reported to be starving.

London, 4 September 1914. Britain, Russia, and France agree not to make separate peaces.

Western Front, 14 September 1914. The Allies drive back the Germans on the Marne, relieving the threat to Paris.

Eastern Front, 14 September 1914. The Russians are forced to retreat from East Prussia after the Battle of the Masurian Lakes.

Hungary, 27 September 1914. The Russians invade Hungary.

Western Front, 9 October 1914. The Germans take Antwerp.

Western Front, 14 October 1914. French and British troops occupy Ypres. The Belgian government flees to France.

Western Front, 15 October 1914. Having captured Ghent and Bruges, the Germans take Ostend.

Egypt, 22 October 1914. Britain orders all foreign vessels out of the Suez Canal.

Black Sea, 28 October 1914. Turkey attacks Russian ports.

Eastern Front, 1 November 1914. Paul von Hindenburg becomes German commander-in-chief.

Europe, 5 November 1914. Britain and France declare war on the Ottomans, following Russia.

Indian Ocean, 10 November 1914. Australians sink the German cruiser *Emden* off Sumatra.

Istanbul, 14 November 1914. The sultan declares a *jihad* (holy war) on the Allies.

Poland, 6 December 1914. The Germans capture Lodz.

Egypt, 16 December 1914. Britain declares Egypt a protectorate.

China, January 1915. Seeking to extend its influence in China, Japan makes "21 demands" which severely undermine Chinese sovereignty.

New York City, March 1915. D. W. Griffith's epic film *The Birth of a Nation* opens.

Western Front, 5 April 1915. The French begin a broad offensive from the Meuse to the Moselle.

Western Front, 22 April 1915. The British launch a new offensive at Ypres.

London, 25 April 1915. Italy signs a secret treaty with Britain, France, and Russia agreeing to enter the war on their side in return for territorial gains.

Turkey, 26 April 1915. Allied forces establish themselves along the Gallipoli peninsula.

Italy, 23 May 1915. Italy declares war on Austria.

Britain, 25 May 1915. Herbert Asquith forms a wartime coalition.

Eastern Front, 5 August 1915. The Austro-Germans take Warsaw.

Eastern Front, 30 August 1915. The great Russian fortress of Brest-Litovsk falls to the Germans.

Poland, 1 September 1915. Following the partition of Poland by Germany and Austria, Joséf Pilsudski forms a movement for a free Poland.

Petrograd, 5 September 1915. Tsar Nicholas II takes personal command of the Russian army.

Bulgaria, 6 September 1915. Bulgaria signs a military convention with Germany and Austria.

Eastern Front, 19 September 1915. The Germans take Vilna.

Western Front, 26 September 1915. French and British troops launch two great offensives, in Champagne and Flanders.

Serbia, 9 October 1915. Belgrade falls to the Austro-Germans.

Brussels, 12 October 1915. The British nurse Edith Cavell is executed by a German firing squad for treason.

Paris, 29 October 1915. The socialist Aristide Briand becomes prime minister after the resignation of René Viviani.

Paris, 14 November 1915. Tomas Masaryk, a leader of the Czech nationalist movement, issues a manifesto calling for the establishment of a Czech national council.

Western Front, December 1915. Joseph Joffre is appointed commander of the French forces, Douglas Haig of the British forces.

Germany, 1915. Albert Einstein propounds a new theory of gravity.

Central Asia, 17 January 1916. The Russians launch an offensive against the Ottomans.

Britain, 27 January 1916. Military conscription is introduced.

Western Front, 21 February 1916. The Germans launch a major assault on the Verdun forts.

Britain, 28 February 1916. The novelist Henry James dies.

Europe, 9 March 1916. Britain and France sign the Sykes-Picot Agreement, specifying plans for the future division of Asiatic Turkey.

Mexico, 31 March 1916. Sent in retaliation for Pancho Villa's raid into the USA, in which 18 Americans died, US troops under Jack Pershing rout Villa's forces.

East Africa, 17 April 1916. The Boer leader Jan Smuts leads an anti-German drive from Kenya.

Dublin, 25 April 1916. A revolt breaks out against British rule.

Britain, 6 June 1916. Lord Kitchener dies when the cruiser HMS *Hampshire* is sunk by a mine off the Orkney Islands.

Arabia, 21 June 1916. Hussein, the grand sherif of Mecca, declares war on the Ottoman empire with the aim of achieving Arabia's independence from Britain.

Western Front, 24 June 1916. The Germans begin a new Verdun offensive.

Western Front, 1 July 1916. The British and French launch a major offensive on the Somme.

Petrograd, 6 July 1916. Russia and Japan sign a peace treaty.

Dublin, 3 August 1916. The former diplomat Roger Casement, famous for exposing slavery in the Congo, is sentenced to death for his part in the Easter Rising.

Italy, 27 August 1916. Italy declares war on Germany.

Western Front, September 1916. Tanks are used for the first time in battle, by the Allies on the Somme.

Prague, 16 September 1916. A provisional government of "Czechoslovakia" is recognized by France and Britain.

Western Front, 24 October 1916. French troops break German lines along a four-mile front as the second battle of Verdun opens.

Berlin, 5 November 1916. The Central Powers, Germany and Austria, proclaim the independence of Poland.

USA, 7 November 1916. Jeannette Rankin of Montana becomes the first woman member of the United States Congress.

USA, 11 November 1916. Woodrow Wilson is reelected president.

Austria, 21 November 1916. Franz Josef, ruler of the Austro-Hungarian empire since 1848, dies.

Britain, 7 December 1916. David Lloyd George succeeds Herbert Asquith as prime minister.

Petrograd, 30 December 1916. Gregory Rasputin, the infamous Siberian "seer" and "miracle worker", is murdered.

Berlin, 1 February 1917. Germany announces a resumption of unrestricted submarine warfare.

Ottoman Empire, 11 March 1917. The British enter Baghdad.

Russia, 16 March 1917. Tsar Nicholas II abdicates.

Ottoman Empire, 27 March 1917. The Ottomans are badly defeated by the British near Gaza.

Washington, DC, 6 April 1917. President Wilson signs a declaration taking the USA into the war.

Western Front, 16 April 1917. Allied troops launch an offensive against the Germans manning the Hindenburg Line.

Petrograd, 17 April 1917. On his return to Russia with the other Bolshevik leaders, Vladimir Lenin publishes demands for the transfer of power to workers' Soviets.

Western Front, 3 May 1917. The Battle of Arras ends following the Canadian capture of Vimy ridge.

Petrograd, 16 June 1917. The pan-Russian Congress of Soviets opens.

Western Front, 27 June 1917. The first US troops land in France.

Russia, 16 July 1917. The provisional government crushes a *Bolshevik* uprising; its leader, Vladimir Lenin, flees.

Portugal, 17 July 1917. Pilgrims flock to Fatima, where visions of the Virgin Mary have been seen.

Petrograd, 22 July 1917. Alexander Kerensky is appointed prime minister.

Western Front, 20 August 1917. The French break the German lines at Verdun on an 11-mile front.

China, 10 September 1917. Sun Yat-sen sets up the Republic of China military government in Guangzhou, in opposition to the Beijing government.

Petrograd, 15 September 1917. Kerensky proclaims Russia a republic.

Russia, 17 September 1917. The Germans drive the Russians out of the Baltic port of Riga.

France, 26 September 1917. The painter Edgar Degas dies.

Western Front, 6 November 1917. Canadian troops capture the village of Passchendaele, ending the third battle of Ypres.

Petrograd, 7 November 1917. Kerensky and the provisional government are ousted in a Bolshevik coup.

Britain, 9 November 1917. Arthur Balfour, the foreign secretary, unveils plans for a Jewish national homeland in Palestine.

Russia, 16 November 1917. Bolshevik troops take Moscow.

France, 17 November 1917. The sculptor Auguste Rodin dies.

Russia, 22 December 1917. The Bolsheviks open peace talks with Germany and Austria.

Russia, 28 January 1918. Lenin creates a Red Army and the *Cheka*, a security police force.

Britain, 6 February 1918. Married women over 30 win the vote.

Russia, 20 February 1918. On the breakdown of peace talks, the Germans resume attacks on the Russians.

Russia, 3 March 1918. Russia signs a peace treaty with Germany at Brest-Litovsk.

Russia, 5 March 1918. The capital is moved from Petrograd to Moscow.

Western Front, 21 March 1918. The Germans launch a great offensive on the Somme.

Western Front, 26 March 1918. Ferdinand Foch is appointed commander-in-chief of the allied forces in France.

Ireland, 19 May 1918. Five hundred Sinn Fein members, including Éamon de Valera, are jailed.

Russia, 26 May 1918. Armenia and Georgia declares independence.

Russia, 16 July 1918. The former Tsar Nicholas II and his family are shot in a cellar at Ekaterinburg.

Western Front, 18 July 1918. Allied forces launch a counter-offensive on the Marne.

Germany, 29 July 1918. Germany severs diplomatic relations with the Ottoman Exmpire.

Russia, 2 August 1918. A British-led force lands at Archangel to support the White Russian opposition to the Bolsheviks.

Western Front, 8 August 1918. The German line collapses as Allied forces go into action near Amiens.

USA, 15 August 1918. The USA severs relations with Russia.

Western Front, 3 September 1918. German forces begin a retreat to the Siegfried Line.

Czechoslovakia, 15 October 1918. The Republic of Czechoslovakia is proclaimed.

Hungary, 17 October 1918. Hungary declares independence from Austria.

Italy, 30 October 1918. The Austrian army completes its evacuation of Italian territory.

Ottoman Empire, 31 October 1918. The Ottomans surrender to the Allies. The Dardanelles are reopened to Allied shipping.

Vienna, 3 November 1918. Austria signs an armistice.

Germany, 9 November 1918. Kaiser William II abdicates and a republic is declared.

France, 11 November 1918. Germany agrees to an armistice at Compiègne.

Prague, 14 November 1918. Thomas Masaryk is elected the first president of Czechoslovakia.

Warsaw, 14 November. 1918 Joséf Pilsudski becomes president of Poland with dictatorial powers.

Britain, 21 November 1918. The German High Seas fleet surrenders to the British.

France, December 1918. The province of Alsace-Lorraine is reincorporated into France.

London, 13 January 1919. Sir Satyendra Prassano Sinha becomes the first Indian peer and thus a member of the House of Lords.

Berlin, 16 January 1919. Rosa Luxembourg and Karl Liebknecht, the leaders of the Spartacist uprising, are murdered by German soldiers.

Versailles, 18 January 1919. Peace conference opens.

Russia, 3 March 1919. Bolshevik leaders establish the Communist International (Comintern) as a vehicle for world revolution.

Europe, 11 March 1919. The Allies reach agreement to supply famine-hit Germany with food relief.

Italy, 23 March 1919. Benito Mussolini founds a party, the *Fasci di Combattimento*, to fight both liberalism and communism.

Versailles, 4 April 1919. The Allies sign an agreement with Germany making Danzig a "free city."

Ireland, 5 April 1919. Éamon de Valera becomes Sinn Fein's president.

Mexico, 10 April 1919. The rebel leader Emiliano Zapata is killed by government troops.

Afghanistan, 24 May 1919. Having defeated Afghan raiders in a clash on the Indian border, the British bomb Jalalabad and Kabul.

Versailles, 28 June 1919. Germany and the Allies sign the Treaty of Versailles.

Germany, July 1919. A republic is declared at Weimar and a new constitution adopted.

South Africa, 3 September 1919. Jan Smuts becomes prime minister following the death of Louis Botha.

Egypt, 19 November 1919. Britain grants Egypt a constitution.

Washington, DC, 19 November 1919. The US Senate votes against ratifying the Versailles Treaty.

London, 22 December 1919. David Lloyd George, the prime minister, announces plans for the partition of Ireland.

China, 1919. China refuses to sign the Treaty of Versailles, which has produced widespread anti-western sentiments in China and awakened interest in Marxism.

Britain, 1919. John Maynard Keynes publishes *The Economic Consequences of the Peace*.

1920–1929

Paris, 16 January 1920. The first meeting of the League of Nations is boycotted by the USA.

USA, 16 January 1920. The 18th amendment to the constitution, prohibiting the manufacture and sale of alcohol, comes into force.

Helsinki, 21 January 1920. The Baltic states decide to form a defensive alliance against Russia.

Paris, 24 January 1920. The death of the Italian painter Modigliani follows that of Renoir in 1919.

Russia, 20 February 1920. The Red Army captures Archangel.

Germany, 24 February 1920. The National Socialist Workers' Party, led by Adolf Hitler, publishes a program for a third reich.

Syria, 8 March 1920. Syria proclaims its independence from the Ottoman empire, with Emir Feisal, hero of the Arab Revolt, as king.

Turkey, 16 March 1920. Allied troops occupy Istanbul.

Ireland, 26 March 1920. Eight hundred special constables, the "Black and Tans," arrive from England to put down the republican revolt in the south of the country, where public order is rapidly deteriorating.

Budapest, 28 March 1920. The Hungarian parliament is dissolved and the regent, Miklos Horthy, becomes dictator.

Germany, 6 April 1920. French troops occupy Frankfurt.

Turkey, 23 April 1920. Turkish nationalists set up a provisional government at Ankara, with Mustapha Kemal as president.

Czechoslovakia, 27 May 1920. Thomas Masaryk is elected president; Eduard Benes is foreign minister.

Poland, 28 May 1920. War is declared between Poland and Russia.

Mexico, 8 July 1920. The guerrilla leader Pancho Villa surrenders to the Mexican government.

Syria, 24 July 1920. A French expeditionary force occupies Damascus and the port of Aleppo. Emir Feisal, installed in Damascus by the British three months ago, flees.

France, 10 August 1920. The Ottoman empire signs a peace treaty with the allies at Sèvres, confirming the loss to it of 80 percent of its land.

Near East, 1 September 1920. France proclaims the creation of the state of Lebanon, with the seat of government at Beirut.

India, 10 September 1920. The Indian National Congress votes to adopt Mohandas Gandhi's program of non-violent resistance toward the Indian government.

Latvia, 6 October 1920. Poland and Russia sign an armistice at Riga.

Russia, 14 October 1920. The *Soviet* government recognizes the independence of Finland.

Geneva, 13 November 1920. The first full session of the League of Nations opens, attended by 5,000 representatives from 41 countries worldwide.

Dublin, 21 November 1920. Fourteen British officers and officials are killed in their beds by IRA members, setting off a day of violence and killing in Ireland.

Norway, 10 December 1920. Woodrow Wilson, the former US President, is awarded the Nobel Peace Prize.

Geneva, 18 December 1920. Britain and France reach agreement on the frontiers of Syria and Palestine.

London, 23 December 1920. The Government of Ireland Act, providing for the partition of Ireland between south and north, becomes law.

Dublin, 22 January 1921. British tanks are sent into Dublin.

Russia, 5 February 1921. Anti-Soviet sailors mutiny at Kronstadt naval base outside Petrograd.

South Africa, 8 February 1921. Jan Smuts is elected prime minister.

Paris, 19 February 1921. France signs a military and economic pact with Poland.

Moscow, 26 February 1921. The Soviet government signs treaties respecting the territorial integrity of Persia and Afghanistan.

Germany, 8 March 1921. On account of Germany's failure to give a satisfactory response to demands for war reparations, Allied troops occupy Ruhr towns.

Moscow, 12 March 1921. Lenin announces that state planning of the economy will end and free enterprise will be permitted.

Russia, 17 March 1921. The anti-Bolshevik rebellion in Kronstadt is crushed by Red Army troops.

China, 10 April 1921. Sun Yat-sen is elected president.

Germany, 11 May 1921. Germany finally agrees to pay the war reparations demanded by the Allies.

Egypt, 23 May 1921. British troops are sent in to quell nationalist rioting in Alexandria.

Ireland, 22 July 1921. Éamon de Valera, the President of Sinn Fein, agrees to a truce with the British government.

China, 23 July 1921. The first congress of the Chinese Communist Party is held in Shanghai.

Ottoman Empire, 5 August 1921. Mustapha Kemal is appointed virtual ruler in the face of a Greek advance.

Baghdad, 23 August 1921. Emir Feisal is crowned King of Iraq.

Czechoslovakia, 26 September 1921. Eduard Benes becomes prime minister.

Berlin, 22 October 1921. The German government resigns as an economic crisis deepens.

Japan, 5 November 1921. Crown Prince Hirohito is made regent on the assassination of the Prime Minister, Takashi Hara Kei, the head of the first parliamentary government.

India, 17 November 1921. Riots break out in Bombay when Mohandas Gandhi, leader of the Indian Congress Party, burns foreign cloth during a visit by the Prince of Wales.

Kabul, 22 November 1921. Britain signs a treaty recognizing the independence of Afghanistan.

Ireland, 6 December 1921. An Anglo-Irish treaty is signed granting 26 counties of Ireland dominion status within the British Empire as the Irish Free State.

Britain, 1921. The novelist D. H. Lawrence publishes *Women in Love*, a sequel to *The Rainbow*, all copies of which were destroyed for obscenity in 1915.

Britain, 1921. Agatha Christie publishes her first detective novel, *The Mysterious Affair at Styles*.

South Atlantic, 5 January 1922. The British polar explorer Ernest Shackleton dies on the island of South Georgia.

Rome, 12 February 1922. Achille Ratti, the archbishop of Milan, is elected pope as Pius XI.

Egypt, 16 March 1922. Egypt formally declares independence under King Fuad.

Ireland, 16 June 1922. The pro-treaty party wins the first election in the Irish Free State.

Berlin, 24 June 1922. Walther Rathenau, the foreign minister, is shot—extreme right-wing nationalists are suspected.

Dublin, 13 July 1922. The Irish Army Council is formed under the leadership of Michael Collins.

Paris, 24 July 1922. The League of Nations Council approves the British mandate in Palestine and the French mandate in Syria.

Italy, 4 August 1922. Mussolini's Fascists, who have already taken Bologna and the areas around Modena and Ferrara, take Milan.

Ireland, 22 August 1922. The Irish nationalist leader Michael Collins is killed during an ambush in Cork. His death follows that of Arthur Griffith, the president of the *Dail Eireann*, the week before.

Balkans, August 1922. Romania, Yugoslavia, and Czechoslovakia sign a mutual defense agreement, establishing the "Little Entente."

Greece, 9 September 1922. The Greeks are ousted from Smyrna, ending their presence on the eastern Aegean seaboard.

London, 11 October 1922. Britain signs a treaty of alliance with Iraq.

Italy, 30 October 1922. Benito Mussolini becomes dictator.

London, 14 November 1922. The newly-formed British Broadcasting Company makes its first regular news broadcast by wireless.

Egypt, 26 November 1922. The archaeologists Howard Carter and the Earl of Carnarvon uncover the treasures of the Pharaoh Tutankhamen, buried 3,000 years ago, near Luxor.

Ireland, 5 December 1922. The Irish Free State is officially proclaimed.

Stockholm, 10 December 1922. The Danish physicist Niels Bohr wins the Nobel Prize for Physics for his work on atomic structure.

Russia, 30 December 1922. Soviet Russia is renamed the Union of Soviet Socialist Republics (USSR).

Paris, 1922. The bookseller Sylvia Beach brings out a limited edition of a novel by James Joyce entitled *Ulysses*, banned in the USA and Britain for obscenity.

Germany, 11 January 1923. In response to the German default in payment of reparations, French and Belgian troops occupy Essen.

China, 26 January 1923. A policy of co-operation (united front) between Chinese nationalists and communists is announced.

Germany, 27 January 1923. The National Socialist (*Nazi*) Party holds its first rally in Munich.

USSR, 9 March 1923. Vladimir Lenin retires from the Bolshevik leadership after a stroke.

India, 24 March 1923. The salt tax is restored.

Germany, 22 June 1923. The *mark* is trading at 622,000 to the pound sterling, having lost nearly half its remaining value since the start of the month.

Switzerland, 24 July 1923. Turkey, Greece, and the Allies sign the Treaty of Lausanne, whereby Armenia and territories in the Aegean lost after the Great War are restored to Turkey.

Berlin, 12 August 1923. Chancellor Cuno resigns as the German economy collapses. Gustav Stresemann takes over.

Geneva, 10 September 1923. The Irish Free State is admitted to the League of Nations.

Germany, 26 September 1923. President Friedrich Ebert declares a state of emergency throughout the country.

Palestine, 29 September 1923. The British mandate officially begins.

Rhodesia, 10 October 1923. Rhodesia, previously British South African Company administered, becomes a self-governing British colony.

Turkey, 12 October 1923. The Turkish capital is moved from Istanbul to Ankara.

Turkey, 29 October 1923. Mustapha Kemal proclaims Turkey a republic and himself its first president.

USA, October 1923. Albert Fall, the secretary of the interior, is implicated in the Teapot Dome oilfield-leasing scandal.

Berlin, 15 November 1923. A loaf of bread costs 200 billion marks.

Stockholm, 10 December 1923. The Irish poet W. B. Yeats wins the Nobel Prize for Literature.

China, 20 January 1924. The first congress of the *Kuomintang* (Nationalist Party) approves the "united front" of communists and nationalists.

Moscow, 22 January 1924. A council is appointed to succeed Lenin: Gregory Zinoviev, Leon Kamenev and Joseph Stalin.

USSR, 26 January 1924. Petrograd is renamed Leningrad.

Rome, 27 January 1924. Mussolini signs a pact with Yugoslavia, annexing the free city of Fiume.

Rome, 27 January 1924. Mussolini dissolves the chamber of deputies.

Britain, 1 February 1924. Britain recognizes the USSR.

India, 4 February 1924. Mohandas Gandhi is released from prison.

New York City, 12 February 1924. *Rhapsody in Blue* for jazz band and piano, by George Gershwin, is performed for the first time.

Ankara, 3 March 1924. Mustapha Kemal, Turkey's secular nationalist leader, who saved Turkey from Greek invasion, abolishes the *caliphate*.

Cairo, 15 March 1924. The first Egyptian parliament is opened.

Washington, DC, 28 March 1924. Harry Daugherty, the attorney-general, resigns in the Teapot Dome oilfield-leasing scandal.

Britain, March 1924. The airline Imperial Airways begins operation.

Germany, 1 April 1924. Adolf Hitler is jailed for five years for his abortive Munich beer-hall *putsch*.

Hollywood, USA, 16 April 1924. The new Metro-Goldwyn-Mayer film corporation is formed by merger.

Germany, 16 April 1924. Germany agrees to a new war reparations plan, drawn up by the American banker Charles Dawes.

Italy, 17 April 1924. Mussolini's fascist party wins a sweeping electoral victory.

Germany, 17 August 1924. Following the signature by Germany and the Allies of the protocol on German war reparations, French and Belgian troops withdraw from the Ruhr.

Arabia, 20 October 1924. Having forced the abdication of Hussein, King of the Arabs since 1916, Wahabi forces under ibn Saud enter Mecca.

London, 24 October 1924. The Foreign Office publishes the "Zinoviev letter," allegedly from Moscow, urging a revolution in Britain.

France, 28 October 1924. France recognizes the USSR.

Britain, 31 October 1924. The Tories win a huge victory in a general election following the scare over the Zinoviev letter.

Moscow, 26 November 1924. A special session of the Communist Party called by Stalin, Zinoviev and Kamenev denounces Trotsky.

Germany, 20 December 1924. Adolf Hitler is freed on parole after serving just eight months of his jail term for treason.

Britain, 1924. The novelist E. M. Forster publishes *A Passage to India*.

China, 12 March 1925. On the death of Sun Yat-sen, Chiang Kai-shek becomes leader of the *Kuomintang* (Nationalist Party).

Australia, 8 April 1925. The government announces a scheme to encourage large-scale immigration.

Germany, 25 April 1925. Paul von Hindenburg becomes Germany's first directly elected president.

Britain, 28 April 1925. Winston Churchill, Chancellor of the Exchequer, puts Britain on the gold standard.

Paris, April 1925. The *Exposition des Arts Decoratifs* reflects the growing popularity of "Art Deco."

South Africa, 8 May 1925. Afrikaans is made an official language of the Union.

South Africa, 29 June 1925. A law is passed further excluding Blacks, Coloreds (people of mixed race) and Indians from all skilled jobs.

China, 1 July 1925. The Nationalists begin a "northern expedition" to re-unify China.

Switzerland, 16 October 1925. Germany signs a mutual security pact with Britain, France, Belgium, and Italy at Locarno. The pact also affirms the postwar frontiers set out in the Versailles Treaty and accepts Rhineland demilitarization.

Persia, 31 October 1925. Reza Khan deposes Shah Ahmed Mirza, ending the Qajar dynasty.

Germany, 9 November 1925. The Nazi *Schutzstaffel* (Protection Squad), or SS, is founded.

Paris, 14 November 1925. The first Surrealist exhibition opens. Artists exhibiting include Max Ernst, Paul Klee, Joan Miro, and Pablo Picasso.

USSR, 21 December 1925. *Battleship Potemkin*, a film by Sergei Eisenstein, opens.

Germany, 6 January 1926. The airline *Lufthansa* is founded.

Berlin, 10 January 1926. Fritz Lang's film *Metropolis* opens.

Germany, 30 January 1926. British troops end a seven-year occupation of the Rhineland.

India, 24 April 1926. The first Hindu-Muslim riots for many years break out in Calcutta.

Berlin, 24 April 1926. Germany signs a friendship treaty with the USSR.

Persia, 25 April 1926. Ali Reza Khan Pahlavi is crowned shah.

India, 2 May 1926. Indian women are granted the right to stand for election to public office.

Poland, 13 May 1926. Josef Pilsudski takes control after leading a military *coup*.

Canada, 28 June 1926. The Liberal prime minister William Mackenzie King and his cabinet resign in the wake of a customs scandal.

Britain, 6 August 1926. Gertrude Ederle from the USA becomes the first woman ever to swim the Channel, cutting more than two hours off the record time.

Germany, 29 August 1926. A Nazi Party rally is held at Nuremberg.

Geneva, 8 September 1926. The League of Nations votes to admit Germany as a member.

Canada, 25 September 1926. Mackenzie King's Liberals are returned to power in an election.

London, 1 October 1926. Alan Cobham completes a record 28,000-mile round trip to Australia by air.

Italy, 7 October 1926. The Fascist Party is decreed the party of the state. Mussolini assumes total power and bans all opposition.

Britain, 14 October 1926. A. A. Milne publishes *Winnie the Pooh*, a book for children.

Moscow, 23 October 1926. Leon Trotsky and Gregory Zinoviev are expelled from the Communist Party central committee.

USA, 31 October 1926. The Hungarian-born escape artist Harry Houdini dies.

Italy, 15 December 1926. The Roman *fasces*, the symbol of authority and origin of the word "fascist", is adopted as the national emblem.

Japan, 25 December 1926. Hirohito ascends the throne on the death of his father, the Emperor Yoshihito.

Britain, 1 January 1927. The British Broadcasting Corporation comes into being.

India, 8 January 1927. The first scheduled London-Delhi flight arrives.

Paris, 6 February 1927. Yehudi Menuhin, a ten-year-old violinist of Russian-Jewish parentage, causes a sensation with his playing.

China, 21 March 1927. The victorious Nationalist army of Chiang Kai-shek enters Shanghai.

China, April 1927. Chiang Kai-shek carries out a coup against left-wing elements, killing trade union activists and communists, leading to the break-up of the united front. The communists are driven into the rural areas.

Saudi Arabia, 20 May 1927. Britain signs the Treaty of Jeddah, recognizing the independence of Saudi Arabia.

Paris, 21 May 1927. Charles Lindbergh lands at Le Bourget airport after the first solo trans-Atlantic flight.

Britain, 24 May 1927. Britain severs diplomatic relations with the USSR amid accusations of espionage and subversion throughout the British empire.

Czechoslovakia, 27 May 1927. Thomas Masaryk is reelected president.

Southeast Asia, 4 June 1927. Ahmed Sukarno founds the Indonesian Nationalist Party.

Geneva, 15 September 1927. Canada is elected to the League of Nations council.

China, 19 September 1927. The "autumn harvest uprising," which began earlier in the month under the leadership of Mao Zedong, suffers a serious defeat.

Iraq, 15 October 1927. Iraq's first oil strike is made at Kirkuk.

China, October 1927. Remnants of Mao's uprising move to the Jinggang mountains in Jiangxi province and set up the first revolutionary base there.

China, 15 December 1927. Russians are expelled from Shanghai following an attempted communist coup in Guangzhou.

Britain, 15 February 1928. The *Oxford English Dictionary* is completed after 70 years of work.

Near East, 20 February 1928. Britain recognizes the independence of Transjordan.

China, 7 April 1928. Nationalist troops launch an offensive with the ultimate aim of capturing Beijing.

Turkey, 9 April 1928. Islam is abolished as the state religion.

China, 3 May 1928. Seeking to impede Chiang Kai-shek's drive for national reunification, Japanese forces clash with Nationalists at Ji'nan in Shandong province.

London, 7 May 1928. Women over 21 win equal suffrage in British elections.

China, 11 May 1928. The Japanese win control of the stricken provincial capital of Shandong after three days of savage fighting.

New York City, 16 May 1928. Share prices plunge as panic selling hits Wall Street.

China, 8 June 1928. Beijing is taken by Nationalists, who have set up a government in Nanjing.

Mexico City, 17 July 1928. President Alvaro Obregon is assassinated at a lunch to celebrate his election earlier this month.

Egypt, 19 July 1928. Having dismissed the prime minister, Nahas Pasha, King Fuad ends parliamentary government in Egypt and makes himself dictator.

Japan, 22 July 1928. Japan breaks off relations with China.

Paris, 27 August 1928. Delegates of 15 nations sign the Kellogg-Briand pact, outlawing war.

Berlin, 31 August 1928. Bertolt Brecht's *Threepenny Opera* is performed for the first time.

Moscow, 6 September 1928. The USSR signs the Kellogg-Briand pact.

Rome, 20 September 1928. The Grand Fascist Council becomes the supreme legislative body in Italy.

USSR, 1 October 1928. Joseph Stalin issues a five-year economic plan to industrialize the USSR.

China, 6 October 1928. A new Chinese constitution is promulgated. Chiang Kai-shek becomes president of the republic.

USA, 6 November 1928. The Republican Herbert C. Hoover is elected president.

Japan, 10 November 1928. The 27-year-old Emperor Hirohito is crowned.

Moscow, 16 January 1929. Nikolai Bukharin resigns as head of the Comintern.

USSR, 23 January 1929. The OGPU, the secret police, arrest 400 Trotskyites for an alleged plot to start a civil war.

Vatican, 11 February 1929. The Vatican state comes into being.

Germany, 15 February 1929. Over three million are now out of work.

Paris, 21 February 1929. The exiled Leon Trotsky, Stalin's most feared opponent, is refused asylum.

Beijing, 2 March 1929. Martial law is declared after a mutiny is crushed among Nationalist troops.

Berlin, 3 May 1929. The city is declared to be in a state of siege as civil unrest escalates.

Bombay, 5 May 1929. A curfew is imposed in a bid to quell new Hindu-Muslim riots.

USA, 16 May 1929. The Academy of Motion Picture Arts and Sciences gives its first awards, the Oscars.

India, 27 May 1929. The nationalist Pandit Nehru calls for rebellion if India does not get dominion status by the year's end.

London, 7 June 1929. Ramsay MacDonald forms Britain's second Labor government.

China, 13 June 1929. Soviet troops cross into China in retaliation for raids on Russian consulates.

Tokyo, 26 June 1929. The government ratifies the Kellogg-Briand pact banning war, the last of the signatories to do so.

Russia, 17 July 1929. Russia breaks off relations with China and begins to mobilize on the border.

Italy, 19 August 1929. Sergei Diaghilev, the founder of the Ballets Russes, dies aged 57.

Jerusalem, 25 August 1929. The British declare martial law as Arabs and Jews continue fighting.

China, 9 September 1929. Heavy fighting between Chinese and Soviet troops is reported along the Manchurian border.

South America, 16 September 1929. Bolivia and Paraguay sign a peace treaty to end their ten-month-old border dispute.

Berlin, 22 September 1929. Communists and Nazis are involved in armed street confrontations.

Belgrade, 3 October 1929. Yugoslavia is declared the official name of the Kingdom of Serbs, Croats, and Slovenes.

Kabul, 17 October 1929. The Afghan national assembly elects the rebel leader Nadir Khan king.

New York City, 24 October 1929. The stock exchange crashes.

Germany, 8 December 1929. Hitler's Nazi, or National Socialist, Party, wins Bavarian municipal elections.

Lahore, 22 December 1929. The All-India National Congress demands independence.

Russia, 22 December 1929. The Sino-Soviet border dispute over the eastern railway ends with both sides agreeing to withdraw troops.

1930–1939

China, 13 January 1930. Two million have died of starvation and famine threatens millions more.

London, 31 January 1930. The Five Power Naval Conference, between Britain, the US, Italy, France, and Japan, aimed at curbing the arms race, opens.

USA, 18 February 1930. A new planet discovered beyond Neptune by the astronomer Clyde Tombaugh is named Pluto.

London, 21 April 1930. The London Naval Treaty, limiting the great powers' navies, is signed.

China, 23 April 1930. The nationalist General Chiang Kai-shek battles with the northern warlord General Yan Xishan.

India, 31 May 1930. New measures are introduced to curb civil disobedience, following the arrest of Gandhi on 5 May and the consequent civil unrest.

Baghdad, 30 June 1930. Britain recognizes Iraqi independence.

Germany, 30 June 1930. France pulls the last of its troops out of the Rhineland, five years before the date set by the Treaty of Versailles.

Central Asia, 12 August 1930. The Turkish and Persian armies launch an offensive on Kurdish rebels.

Australia, 18 August 1930. The two halves of the new Sydney Harbor Bridge are joined.

Beijing, 2 September 1930. General Yen Hsi-chan forms a rebel government.

Argentina, 6 September 1930. The radical president Hipolito Irigoyen is overthrown by army officers led by General Uriburu.

Germany, 15 September 1930. The Nazi leader Adolf Hitler is barred as an Austrian citizen from taking his seat in the *reichstag*.

Athens, 5 October 1930. A congress between the Balkan states opens, aimed at promoting cooperation.

Berlin, 13 October 1930. There is uproar in the reichstag when Nazi deputies turn up in uniform, which is illegal for civilians.

France, 16 October 1930. A line of defenses known as the Maginot Line is to be built along France's frontier with Germany.

Ankara, 30 October 1930. Turkey and Greece sign a treaty of friendship.

Brazil, 1 November 1930. President Vargas dissolves the congress.

Addis Ababa, 2 November 1930. Ras Tafari is crowned Emperor Haile Selassie of Ethiopia.

Iraq, 6 January 1931. A royal palace dating from 550 BC is found at the site of the city of Ur.

London, 23 January 1931. The Russian ballerina Anna Pavlova dies aged 49.

London, 26 January 1931. Winston Churchill resigns from Baldwin's shadow cabinet after disagreeing with the policy of conciliation with Indian nationalism.

Washington, DC, 3 March 1931. "The Star Spangled Banner" becomes the US national anthem.

India, 4 March 1931. The viceroy agrees to end the government's salt monopoly in return for an end to civil disobedience.

Spain, 12 April 1931. Election results show that republicans have swept the polls in most cities.

Spain, 14 April 1931. King Alfonso XIII abdicates.

Turkey, 20 April 1931. The Republican People's Party of Mustapha Kemal wins by a landslide in the national elections.

China, 30 April 1931. Rebels under General Chen Jitang split with Chiang Kai-shek and take control of Guangzhou (Canton).

New York City, 1 May 1931. President Hoover opens the 1,245 foot, 120-floor Empire State Building.

China, 17 June 1931. The British arrest Nguyen Ai Quoc, also known as Ho Chi Minh, founder of the Indochinese Communist Party.

Washington, DC, 22 June 1931. The President Herbert Hoover proposes that all war debts should be suspended for a year, in order to revitalize world trade.

London, 22 July 1931. Britain, the US and France renew recent credits for Germany for three months, to help Germany through financial difficulties.

China, 18 September 1931. Japanese troops occupy Shenyang in Manchuria.

London, 15 September 1931. Gandhi demands Indian independence at a conference.

Britain, 28 October 1931. The National Government stays in power after the largest election landslide in history.

China, 7 November 1931. The Chinese Soviet Republic is established, with Ruijin (*Jiangxi*) as its capital.

Germany, 15 November 1931. The Nazi Party wins elections in the state of Hesse.

China, 27 November 1931. Mao Zedong is appointed chairman of the central executive committee of the Chinese Soviet Republic.

London, 1 December 1931. The conference on India ends in failure.

Spain, 10 December 1931. Nicetor Alcala Zamora is elected as Spain's first constitutional president by the national assembly. Manuel Azana is prime minister.

India, 4 January 1932. Gandhi is arrested and the Indian National Congress outlawed.

China, 31 January 1932. Japanese forces take Shanghai in the war that began with the invasion of Manchuria.

China, 19 February 1932. The Japanese government has established a puppet regime in occupied Manchuria.

Berlin, 25 February 1932. Hitler is granted German citizenship.

China, 9 March 1932. Puyi, the last Emperor of China, is installed as head of the Japanese puppet state of Manchukuo (Manchuria).

Australia, 18 March 1932. Sydney Harbor Bridge is opened, the world's longest single-span bridge.

Ireland, 29 March 1932. Éamon de Valera, the hard-line republican leader of the *Fianna Fail* Party, will head the new government.

Germany, 10 April 1932. Paul von Hindenburg wins the presidency against Adolf Hitler after a second ballot to secure a majority.

Berlin, 24 April 1932. The *Nazis* lead in four state elections. In the Prussian state parliament their seats rise from six to 162.

China, 5 May 1932. Japanese troops withdraw from Shanghai after an armistice is signed.

Berlin, 31 May 1932. President Hindenburg invites Franz von Papen to form a government. He forms a cabinet that excludes the Nazis.

USA, 2 July 1932. Franklin D. Roosevelt wins the Democratic nomination for president.

Lisbon, 5 July 1932. Antonio de Oliveira Salazar is appointed Fascist prime minister.

Switzerland, 9 July 1932. The allies vote to ease Germany's economic crisis by suspending the repayments of war debts.

Germany, 31 July 1932. The National Socialists (Nazis) are now the biggest party in the *reichstag* following the general election, but without an overall majority.

Berlin, 30 August 1932. The Nazi Hermann Goering is elected president of the reichstag.

India, 24 September 1932. The Poona Pact is signed, extending the voting rights of Untouchables. Gandhi, who has risked unpopularity for supporting the Untouchables' cause, ends his prison fast.

USSR, 9 October 1932. Joseph Stalin expels two leading Bolsheviks, Gregori Zinoviev and Leon Kamenev, from the Communist Party and exiles them to Siberia.

USA, 8 November 1932. Franklin D. Roosevelt defeats the sitting Republican president, Herbert Hoover, in the presidential elections.

Berlin, 17 November 1932. The prime minister, von Papen, resigns after failing to form a government.

Berlin, 21 November 1932. Hitler refuses the chancellorship if it means combining with other parties as Hindenburg wants.

Germany, 24 November 1932. The Nationalists take seats from the Nazis in the election.

Berlin, 2 December 1932. General Kurt von Schleicher is appointed chancellor.

Berlin, 28 January 1933. Amidst growing violence General von Schleicher resigns as chancellor.

Germany, 30 January 1933. Adolf Hitler becomes chancellor.

Berlin, 28 February 1933. The *reichstag* burns down.

Germany, 15 March 1933. Hitler declares the Third Reich.

Germany, 20 March 1933. The Nazis open a concentration camp at Dachau, near Munich.

Berlin, 28 March 1933. Hitler orders a boycott of Jews and Jewish shops.

London, 29 March 1933. The Commons approves a plan for a federal constitution in India.

Berlin, 5 May 1933. Hitler proposes "eugenic laws" to ban mixed Jewish and Aryan marriages and to begin sterilization.

Madrid, 8 June 1933. Manuel Azana is dismissed as premier.

Vienna, 19 June 1933. The prime minister, Engelbert Dollfuss, bans all Nazi organizations.

Germany, 29 August 1933. It is officially confirmed that the Nazis are sending Jews to concentration camps.

USA, 5 December 1933. Fourteen years of prohibition come to an end.

Germany, 10 January 1934. The alleged *reichstag* arsonist Marinus van der Lubbe is guillotined.

Berlin, 26 January 1934. Germany signs a ten-year non-aggression pact with Poland.

Nicaragua, 22 February 1934. National Guardsmen gun down General Augusto Sandino.

Madrid, 25 April 1934. Martial law is declared as the government resigns.

Rome, 29 April 1934. The Italian parliament votes to remove its last remaining powers.

Vienna, 30 April 1934. The Chancellor Engelbert Dollfuss is made dictator of a rump parliament which then votes itself out of existence.

Germany, 30 June 1934. In the "Night of the Long Knives" Hitler purges the Fascist Party.

Berlin, 3 July 1934. The Vice-chancellor von Papen, resigns.

Germany, 13 July 1934. Heinrich Himmler is appointed head of the concentration camps.

Vienna, 26 July 1934. The government orders the round-up of Austrian Nazis following the murder of Chancellor Dollfuss.

Vienna, 29 July 1934. Dr Kurt von Schuschnigg is appointed chancellor.

Berlin, 2 August 1934. Hitler assumes the title "Fuhrer" on the death of Hindenburg.

Germany, 4 September 1934. 750,000 attend the opening of the Nazi party conference.

Spain, 8 October 1934. Martial law is declared following a bid to declare Catalonia independent.

Ankara, 25 November 1934. Mustapha Kemal tells Turks to adopt a surname by 1 January 1935. His will be "*Ataturk*", Father of The Turks.

Teheran, 27 December 1934. The government declares that Persia will now be known as Iran.

Africa, 15 January 1935. Mussolini unites Eritrea and Somaliland as Italian East Africa.

Rome, 24 January 1935. Mussolini dismisses the entire cabinet.

Italy, 23 February 1935. Troops set sail for Ethiopia as the border dispute over the Italian post at Wal-Wal inside Ethiopia escalates.

Switzerland, 7 March 1935. Nine-year-old Prince Ananda, now in Europe, is crowned King of Siam.

USSR, 9 March 1935. Nikita Khrushchev is elected chief of the Communist party.

Berlin, 11 March 1935. The German air force, or *Luftwaffe* is officially created in a proclamation by Hermann Goering.

Paris, 2 May 1935. France and the USSR sign a mutual defense pact in case of attack.

Britain, 19 May 1935. The soldier and writer Colonel T. E. Lawrence dies aged 46 in a motorcycle accident.

London, 22 May 1935. The government announces plans to treble the size of the air force in the next two years.

Rome, 24 May 1935. Pope Pius XI condemns the Nazi sterilization of 56,244 "inferior" German citizens.

Paris, 4 June 1935. Pierre Laval becomes prime minister.

Britain, 7 June 1935. Stanley Baldwin becomes prime minister again following the resignation of Ramsay MacDonald for health reasons.

Argentina, 12 June 1935. Bolivia and Paraguay sign an armistice to end their three-year-old war over the disputed Chaco area.

Britain, 29 July 1935. T. E. Lawrence's *Seven Pillars of Wisdom* is published posthumously.

Washington, DC, 14 August 1935. President Roosevelt signs the Social Security Bill, introducing welfare for the old, sick and unemployed.

Germany, 15 August 1935. On Hitler's orders the *swastika* becomes the national flag.

Ethiopia, 25 August 1935. The country is put on a war footing in anticipation of an Italian invasion.

Ethiopia, 3 October 1935. Mussolini's Fascist troops march into Ethiopia.

Ethiopia, 8 November 1935. The Italians complete their occupation of Tigre province, seizing the provincial capital, Makale.

China, 26 November 1935. Japanese troops march into Beijing to support a coup in Tokyo which has set up the autonomous state of Hebei province in the north.

Cairo, 12 December 1935. King Fuad restores Egypt's 1923 parliamentary constitution.

Czechoslovakia, 18 December 1935. Eduard Benes, the chosen successor to Masaryk, who resigned four days ago because of old age, is elected president.

Britain, 21 January 1936. Edward VIII is proclaimed king following the death of his father George V of yesterday.

India, 8 February 1936. Jawaharlal Nehru is elected president of the Indian National Congress.

Rhineland, 7 March 1936. German troops march into the Rhineland, in defiance of the treaties of Versailles and Locarno.

South Africa, 7 April 1936. The Native Representation Act bans blacks from office but lets them elect three whites to represent them.

Madrid, 17 April 1936. The parliament dismisses President Zamora for trying to dissolve it unconstitutionally.

Egypt, 28 April 1936. King Fuad dies and is succeeded by the 16-year-old Prince Farouk.

Addis Ababa, 5 May 1936. The Ethiopian capital falls to Italian troops.

Spain, 10 May 1936. The *Cortes* elects Manuel Azana president in succession to the ousted Zamora.

France, 8 June 1936. Within five days of sweeping to power as leader of a socialist popular front coalition, Leon Blum ends the strikes that have crippled France.

Spanish Morocco, 17 July 1936. General Franco heads an uprising against the government in Melilla.

Spain, 19 July 1936. General Franco lands in Cadiz heading rebel Spanish foreign legionnaires.

Spain, 24 July 1936. The government appeals for foreign help in the civil war.

Berlin, 1 August 1936. Adolf Hitler opens the Berlin Olympics.

Spain, 19 August 1936. The writer Federico Garcia Lorca dies shortly after his arrest, aged 37.

Egypt, 26 August 1936. An Anglo-Egyptian treaty ends the British protectorate over Egypt and gives Britain control of the Suez Canal for 20 years.

Spain, 29 August 1936. Following the rebels' capture of Badajoz, Spain is divided in half, with the nationalists holding the southwest and the north and the government controlling Madrid.

Spain, 17 September 1936. Franco's troops take Maqueda, between Toledo and Madrid.

Spain, 28 September 1936. Franco is made head of the rebel forces.

Baghdad, 29 October 1936. Pro-western Iraqi Kemalists come to power in an army coup.

Spain, 29 October 1936. Republican troops south of Madrid hold Franco's forces at bay.

Rome, 1 November 1936. Mussolini announces the anti-communist Axis with Germany, urging Britain and France to join.

USA, 3 November 1936. President Roosevelt is elected for a second term.

Spain, 7 November 1936. The government flees to Valencia.

Spain, 18 November 1936. Hitler and Mussolini recognize Franco's provisional government in Burgos.

Berlin, 25 November 1936. Germany and Japan sign an agreement to protect world civilization from the Bolshevik menace.

Spain, 1 December 1936. 5,000 Germans land at Cadiz to join Franco's rebels.

Britain, 11 December 1936. Edward VIII makes his abdication speech.

Britain, 12 December 1936. Prince Albert is proclaimed king as George VI.

Spain, 8 February 1937. Malaga falls to Franco, aided by 15,000 Italians.

Spain, 22 February 1937. Britain, France, Germany, Italy, Portugal and the USSR agree to a cordon around Spain to enforce the arms ban agreed on the 16 February.

China, 23 February 1937. Chiang Kai-shek, the head of the Chinese government, rejects Communist suggestions that they and the Nationalists should join forces to fight against the Japanese invaders.

India, 1 April 1937. The Indian constitution comes into being under the Government of India Act. Burma is separated.

Spain, 27 April 1937. Guernica is destroyed by the German air force.

Britain, 28 May 1937. Neville Chamberlain becomes prime minister following Stanley Baldwin's retirement.

Spain, 31 May 1937. Italy and Germany withdraw from the Spanish non-intervention cordon.

France, 3 June 1937. The ex-king Edward VIII, now the Duke of Windsor, marries Mrs. Simpson.

USSR, 12 June 1937. Eight top generals are executed as Stalin's purge extends to the Red Army.

Spain, 19 June 1937. Bilbao falls to Franco's rebels.

London, 7 July 1937. The British government announces plans to partition Palestine.

China, 7 July 1937. Japanese soldiers in night maneuvers outside their designated area attack Wanping at the southern end of the bridge near Beijing.

Eire, 21 July 1937. Éamon de Valera is re-elected president.

Germany, 1 August 1937. A new concentration camp has been opened at Buchenwald.

China, 14 August 1937. Hundreds are reported dead in a Japanese bombing raid on Shanghai.

Germany, 5 September 1937. The biggest-ever Nazi rally marks the opening of the Nazi congress in Nuremberg.

China, 25 September 1937. The Japanese bomb the Chinese Nationalist capital Nanjing.

China, 29 September 1937. Chiang Kai-shek, the Chinese leader, comes to an agreement with his Communist rival Mao Zedong in the face of the full-scale Japanese assault on their country.

Palestine, 20 October 1937. The British authorities limit Jewish immigration.

Moscow, 21 October 1937. Sixty-two party officials are executed in Stalin's latest purges.

Italy, 6 November 1937. Italy joins the anti-communist pact between Germany and Japan.

China, 9 November 1937. The Japanese take Shanghai.

China, 7 December 1937. The Japanese launch a general attack on Nanjing; bitter fighting follows.

Java, 10 December 1937. Parts of the skull of one of humankind's ancestors is discovered.

London, 6 January 1938. Sigmund Freud arrives in London, fleeing from Nazi persecution.

Romania, 10 February 1938. King Carol ousts the anti-Semitic prime minister, Octavian Goga, and becomes a dictator.

London, 21 February 1938. Anthony Eden resigns as foreign secretary in protest against Chamberlain's appeasement.

Vienna, 11 March 1938. Chancellor Schuschnigg resigns and the pro-Nazi Artur Seyss-Inquart succeeds. German troops invade on his invitation.

Vienna, 13 March 1938. The *Anschluss*, Germany's annexation of Austria, is declared.

Vienna, 14 March 1938. Vienna gives Hitler a tumultuous welcome.

Moscow, 15 March 1938. Another show trial ends in the execution of 18 top-ranking Soviet figures, including Nikolai Bukharin.

London, 24 March 1938. The prime minister, Neville Chamberlain, announces that Britain will fight for France and Belgium.

London, 1 April 1938. Britain and the US abandon the London naval treaty to allow for the building of battleships.

Vienna, 6 April 1938. Leading Jewish figures are sent to Dachau concentration camp.

Rome, 4 May 1938. The Vatican recognizes Franco as leader of Spain.

Prague, 20 May 1938. The government orders 400,000 troops to the Austro-German border.

China, 7 June 1938. *Guomindang* (Nationalist) troops burst the dykes of the Yellow River at Huayuankou to prevent the southward move of Japanese forces. The river floods disastrously.

Prague, 21 September 1938. The government agrees to Anglo-French plans to cede the Sudetenland to Germany; Czechs protest.

Germany, 30 September 1938. A solution to the Czechoslovakian crisis is announced following talks between Chamberlain, Daladier, Hitler and Mussolini. Sudetenland will be ceded to Germany.

Czechoslovakia, 1 October 1938. German troops march into the Sudetenland as Teschen, in Czech Silesia, is annexed by Poland.

Prague, 5 October 1938. President Benes resigns.

Budapest, 13 October 1938. Tension mounts amid calls for the annexation of southern parts of Czechoslovakia.

China, 21 October 1938. Guangzhou falls to the Japanese; fire spreads throughout the entire city.

US, 31 October 1938. Orson Welles' vivid radio production *The War of the Worlds* causes widespread panic because of its realism.

Czechoslovakia, 2 November 1938. Following "arbitration" by Hitler, Hungary annexes the southern parts of Slovakia and Ruthenia.

Germany, 9 November 1938. Jews across the country are subjected to violent attacks on what becomes known as *kristallnacht*.

Paris, 6 December 1938. France and Germany sign a pact on the inviolability of their present frontiers.

Cairo, 20 January 1939. King Farouk is declared the *caliph* (spiritual leader) of Islam.

Rome, 12 March 1939. Pope Pius XII is consecrated.

Czechoslovakia, 14 March 1939. The Germans march into Bohemia as the Hungarians occupy Ruthenia.

Czechoslovakia, 15 March 1939. Hitler enters Prague.

Madrid, 28 March 1939. Franco takes Madrid. The Spanish Civil War is over.

London, 31 March 1939. Chamberlain pledges to defend Poland.

London, 6 April 1939. Britain, France and Poland sign a mutual assistance pact.

London, 11 May 1939. Chamberlain warns Hitler that the use of force in Danzig will mean war.

Berlin, 22 May 1939. Hitler and Mussolini sign a "pact of steel" —a military alliance.

London, 26 May 1939. The Military Training (Conscription) Act receives Royal Assent.

Danzig, 20 July 1939. 2,000 Nazi guards arrive in the free city.

Moscow, 23 August 1939. Germany and the USSR sign a non-aggression pact, known as the Hitler-Stalin Pact.

Berlin, 26 August 1939. Hitler demands from Poland the port of Danzig (with its mainly German population), a corridor from Germany to Danzig, and the end of the Anglo-French pledge to Poland.

Poland, 1 September 1939. German troops invade at 5.45 am.

London and Paris, 3 September 1939. War is declared.

Germany, 4 September 1939. French troops cross the border into the Saarland.

Washington, DC, 5 September 1939. President Roosevelt declares US neutrality.

Poland, 17 September 1939. Soviet troops invade.

Warsaw, 29 September 1939. Polish troops evacuate as the city surrenders to the *Wehrmacht*.

USA, 4 November 1939. President Roosevelt announces that he will sign the Neutrality Bill, which will allow Britain and France to buy arms from the US.

Moscow, 28 November 1939. Stalin renounces the Finno-Soviet non-aggression pact.

Montevideo, 17 December 1939. The German battleship *Graf Spee* is scuttled after being chased by British warships into the river Plate.

Moscow, 23 December 1939. Stalin fires General Meretzkov, in charge of the war against Finland, as Finnish successes continue.

1940–1949

France, 6 January 1940. The Germans gain ground in a fierce onslaught along a 120-mile front north of Paris.

Britain, 11 February 1940. John Buchan, Lord Tweedsmuir, the governor-general of Canada, and author of great adventure stories such as *The Thirty-nine Steps*, dies aged 64.

Tibet, 22 February 1940. The new five-year-old Dalai Lama is enthroned.

Finland, 13 March 1940. Finland signs a peace treaty with the USSR, surrendering a large part of the territory.

Poland, 27 March 1940. Heinrich Himmler orders the construction of a concentration camp at Auschwitz, near Krakow.

Norway, 30 April 1940. The Germans claim they have advanced and taken the towns of Dombaas and Stoeren. Meanwhile, British and French troops hit back, particularly in the north.

London, 10 May 1940. Winston Churchill becomes prime minister.

The Hague, 15 May 1940. German forces occupy the city.

Belgium, 28 May 1940. Belgian troops surrender to the Germans.

France, 4 June 1940. Operation Dynamo evacuates British soldiers from Dunkirk.

France, 10 June 1940. The Germans are 35 miles from Paris; the government moves to Tours.

Italy, 10 June 1940. Italy declares war on Britain and France.

Paris, 14 June 1940. German troops enter Paris.

France, 16 June 1940. Paul Reynaud resigns as prime minister. Marshal Petain takes over and asks the Germans for an armistice.

Britain, 20 June 1940. The first New Zealand and Australian troops arrive.

France, 22 June 1940. The armistice with Germany puts half of France under occupation.

France, 11 July 1940. Marshal Henri Petain assumes supreme power in occupied France.

Baltic, 21 July 1940. Lithuania, Latvia and Estonia, occupied by Russian troops in June, vote to become part of the USSR.

Europe, 7 August 1940. Alsace-Lorraine and Luxembourg become part of Germany.

Britain, 18 August 1940. As *Luftwaffe* pilots home in on southern England, the Battle of Britain begins in earnest.

China, 20 August 1940. Japanese bombing of Chongqing, China's wartime capital, reaches its climax with raids which destroy most of the city.

London, 25 August 1940. The *Luftwaffe* carries out its first bombing raid on London.

Berlin, 26 August 1940. British planes bomb Berlin.

London, 30 September 1940. Hitler's long-awaited blitz on London has started.

Helsinki, 1 October 1940. Finland signs a military and economic treaty with Germany.

New York City, 21 October 1940. Ernest Hemingway's novel *For Whom the Bell Tolls* is published.

Spain, 24 October 1940. Hitler fails to persuade Franco or Petain to join the war against Britain.

Greece, 28 October 1940. Italy invades Greece.

USA, 5 November 1940. President Franklin D. Roosevelt is re-elected for a record third term.

London, 7 November 1940. Britain, Australia and the US agree on defense co-operation in the Pacific.

Britain, 14 November 1940. Coventry is devastated by the worst air raid of the war.

Warsaw, 15 November 1940. 350,000 Jews are now confined to a ghetto.

Budapest, 20 November 1940. Hungary joins the Axis.

Greece, 22 November 1940. The Greeks put the Italian invaders to flight in a great victory at Koritza.

North Africa, 9 December 1940. British troops launch an attack on Italians in the Western Desert.

London, 29 December 1940. In the biggest air raid of the war, the *Luftwaffe* razed one-third of the City, including the Barbican. St Paul's survives amid the flames.

North Africa, 14 February 1941. The advance guard of Rommel's Afrika Korps arrive in Tripoli.

Sofia, 14 February 1941. Bulgaria accepts German occupation.

Sudan, 16 February 1941. The last Italian troops are expelled.

Berlin, 19 February 1941. Hitler warns Greece to end the war with Italy or face Germany fighting with the Italians.

North Africa, 25 February 1941. Mogadishu, the Italian-held port of Somaliland, falls to the British.

Ankara, 4 March 1941. Turkey refuses to join the Axis.

Ethiopia, 6 March 1941. Haile Selassie's troops capture the Italian stronghold of Burye.

Britain, 28 March 1941. The novelist Virginia Woolf commits suicide aged 69.

Libya, 3 April 1941. British-led troops evacuate Benghazi in the face of Rommel's advances.

Iraq, 4 April 1941. The ex-prime minister, Rashid Ali, an Axis supporter, seizes power.

Yugoslavia, 6 April 1941. Axis troops invade.

Ethiopia, 6 April 1941. Allies occupy Addis Ababa, the capital of Ethiopia.

Yugoslavia, 17 April 1941. Yugoslavia falls to German forces.

Athens, 26 April 1941. The Germans march into Athens.

Crete, 29 May 1941. The Axis forces seize the capital, Canea.

Syria, 21 June 1941. British imperial forces take Damascus.

USSR, 22 June 1941. Germany invades along a 1,800-mile frontier with Finnish, Hungarian and Romanian allies.

London, 13 July 1941. Britain and the USSR conclude a mutual assistance pact.

USSR, 16 July 1941. German troops advance on Moscow.

Teheran, 19 September 1941. British and Soviet troops enter the city.

Teheran, 17 September 1941. The new shah, Mohammed Reza Pahlevi, promises to rule as a constitutional monarch.

USSR, 19 September 1941. Kiev falls to the Germans.

Leningrad, 2 October 1941. The Soviet army launches a counter-attack as the winter's first snows begin to fall.

Japan, 17 October 1941. The prime minister, Fumimaro Konoye, and his cabinet resign; General Tojo, a pro-Axis war minister, is appointed.

Hawaii, 7 December 1941. The Japanese bomb the American base at Pearl Harbor.

Berlin, 11 December 1941. Hitler and Mussolini declare war on the US.

Hong Kong, 25 December 1941. Hong Kong surrenders to Japan.

Philippines, 2 January 1942. Japanese troops take Manila.

India, 15 January 1942. Gandhi names Pandit Nehru as his successor.

Germany, 20 January 1942. Officials learn of Reinhard Heydrich's "final solution:" the extermination of the 11 million Jews in Europe.

Norway, 1 February 1942. Vidkun Quisling is appointed puppet prime minister by the Germans.

Singapore, 15 February 1942. Singapore surrenders to the Japanese.

Burma, 22 February 1942. Civilians are evacuated from Rangoon—battles rage 80 miles northeast of the city.

Germany, 26 March 1942. The Nazis begin the deportation of Jews to Auschwitz concentration camp.

Germany, 28 March 1942. The RAF begins a round-the-clock offensive on German munitions factories.

India, 29 March 1942. The British reveal a plan for Indian independence after the war.

Tokyo, 18 April 1942. US planes bomb Tokyo.

Yugoslavia, 3 May 1942. German reinforcements arrive to fight Tito's partisans.

Libya, 27 May 1942. Rommel's *panzer* divisions launch a long-expected offensive in the desert.

Czechoslovakia, 31 May 1942. Czech partisans assassinate Gestapo leader Heydrich.

Pacific, 7 June 1942. The Japanese withdraw after four days of serious fighting around Midway Island.

Libya, 21 June 1942. Tobruk falls to Rommel's troops; 25,000 Allied soldiers are taken prisoner.

USA, 25 June 1942. Major General Dwight D. Eisenhower is given command of all US forces in Europe.

Egypt, 25 June 1942. Axis forces threaten Cairo.

USSR, 29 June 1942. The Germans launch an offensive at Kursk, south of Moscow.

USSR, 6 August 1942. The Germans advance on Stalingrad.

North Africa, 6 August 1942. General Bernard Montgomery becomes commander of the Eighth Army.

Pacific, 7 August 1942. US marines land on the Solomon Islands.

Egypt, 30 August 1942. Rommel launches a new offensive in Egypt.

Warsaw, 2 September 1942. German SS troops "clear" the Jewish ghetto of 50,000 people.

USSR, 11 September 1942. The Germans drive a wedge through Soviet positions in Stalingrad.

Egypt, 30 October 1942. Montgomery is victorious at El Alamein.

Yugoslavia, 3 November 1942. The Bosnian capital of Bihacs falls to Tito's partisans.

North Africa, 7 November 1942. Allied troops land in Vichy-French North Africa.

North Africa, 8 November 1942. Rommel retreats into Libya.

USSR, 26 November 1942. Soviet troops smash through German lines in Stalingrad.

Morocco, 14 January 1943. Churchill and Roosevelt meet in Casablanca to concert a grand strategy.

USSR, 18 January 1943. The Russians break the 16-month siege of Leningrad.

Berlin, 28 January 1943. Hitler orders the mobilization of the whole population from 16 to 65.

Stalingrad, 31 January. The Germans surrender Stalingrad.

Pacific, 9 February 1943. The US navy secretary reports that Japanese resistance in Guadalcanal in the Solomon Islands has ceased.

Germany, 6 March 1943. The RAF pounds the Ruhr city of Essen, in Germany's industrial heartland.

Britain, 7 April 1943. The Keynes Plan for post-war economic recovery is published.

Tunis, 14 April 1943. Rommel evacuates his troops.

Poland, 26 April 1943. The unearthing of a mass grave of 4,000 Polish officers in the Katyn forest causes intense diplomatic friction. Germany accuses Russia of the murders.

Buenos Aires, 5 June 1943. A military *junta* is formed under President Arturo Rawson following yesterday's coup in which President Ramon Castillo was overthrown. The new Labor minister is Juan Peron.

Berlin, 19 June 1943. Goebbels declares the city "free of Jews".

USSR, 13 July 1943. Germany loses the greatest tank battle in history in the cornfields around Kursk.

Italy, 25 July 1943. Mussolini falls from power.

Poland, 16 August 1943. Jews in the ghetto in Bialystok rise up.

Poland, 2 September 1943. Inmates of concentration camps are being used for medical experiments.

Rome, 3 September 1943. The prime minister, Badoglio, signs a secret armistice with the Allies.

Yugoslavia, 14 September 1943. Partisans are advancing along the Dalmatian coast; Allied officers have reached Tito.

Italy, 13 October 1943. Italy declares war on Germany.

Yugoslavia, 19 October 1943. Italian troops aid Tito's partisans in their fight against the Germans.

USSR, 6 November 1943. The Russians retake Kiev.

Teheran, 28 November 1943. Churchill, Roosevelt, and Stalin arrive for their first big meeting together.

Europe, 24 December 1943. General Dwight D. Eisenhower is to be supreme commander of the Allied invasion of western Europe.

New York City, 1 January 1944. DNA is discovered by Oswald T. Avery.

Italy, 22 January 1944. Allied troops make a surprise landing at Anzio, 30 miles south of Rome.

Tokyo, 21 February 1944. Hideki Tojo becomes chief of staff of the Japanese army.

Burma, 19 March 1944. It is revealed that Allied troops have been landed by glider 200 miles behind Japanese lines.

Hungary, 5 April 1944. The Germans begin deporting Jews.

Berlin, 7 April 1944. Hitler suspends all laws and makes Goebbels dictator of the city.

France, 9 April 1944. General Charles de Gaulle becomes commander-in-chief of the Free French forces.

Britain, April 1944. Britain becomes an armed camp as Eisenhower oversees Allied preparations for the invasion of Europe.

London, 8 May 1944. The exiled Czech government signs a convention to allow the Soviet army to liberate the country.

USSR, 9 May 1944. The Soviet army takes Sevastopol, winning control of the whole Crimea.

France, 15 May 1944. Field-Marshal Erwin Rommel attempts to cut occupied France off from neutral countries to stop information being passed out to the Allies.

Italy, 18 May 1944. British and Polish troops capture Monte Cassino.

Italy, 23 May 1944. The Allies begin an offensive from Anzio.

Yugoslavia, 25 May 1944. Tito escapes to the hills as Germans capture his Bosnian headquarters.

Algiers, 3 June 1944. General de Gaulle announces a provisional French government to take over from Vichy when France is liberated.

Rome, 4 June 1944. The Allies take Rome.

France, 6 June 1944. Allied forces begin landing in Normandy —the invasion of Europe has begun.

Japan, 15 June 1944. US planes bomb the Japanese mainland.

USSR, 3 July 1944. Minsk, the last big German base on Soviet soil, falls to the Russians.

Lithuania, 13 July 1944. The capital, Vilna, is captured by the Russians as they advance through the Baltic states.

Berlin, 21 July 1944. Troops pour into the city following an attempt on Hitler's life yesterday.

France, 31 July 1944. The pilot and writer Antoine de Saint-Exupery is declared missing.

France, 31 July 1944. The Allies drive the Germans from Normandy.

Paris, 25 August 1944. General de Gaulle enters liberated Paris.

Poland, 27 August 1944. Polish and Soviet officials show the press the Maidenek concentration camp.

Germany, 11 September 1944. The US First Army under General Omar Bradley leads the Allies on to German soil.

Helsinki, 19 September 1944. Finland signs an armistice with the USSR.

Estonia, 22 September 1944. The Russians capture the capital, Tallinn.

Germany, 14 October 1944. Erwin Rommel takes poison rather than be executed for conspiracy against Hitler's life. Hitler had promised him a hero's funeral if he committed suicide.

Czechoslovakia, 18 October 1944. The Russians enter the country.

Philippines, 20 October 1944. General MacArthur lands on the central Philippine island of Leyte.

Belgrade, 20 October 1944. Tito's Partisans and the Red Army take Belgrade.

Washington, DC, 7 November 1944. President Franklin Delano Roosevelt wins an unprecedented fourth term in office.

Belgium, 28 November 1944. The first Allied convoy sails into the port of Antwerp.

Germany, 6 December 1944. Twenty million people are reported to be homeless after Allied bombing.

Moscow, 10 December 1944. De Gaulle and Stalin sign a treaty of alliance.

Indochina, 22 December 1944. Vo Nguyen Giap forms the Vietnamese People's Army.

Britain, 1944. The poet T. S. Eliot completes his Four *Quartets*.

Budapest, 13 January 1945. The city is now in Russian hands.

Warsaw, 17 January 1945. Soviet and Polish troops take the city.

Budapest, 21 January 1945. Hungary declares war on Germany.

Poland, 27 January 1945. The Red Army takes Auschwitz.

Germany, 31 January 1945. Soviet troops cross the river Oder north of Frankfurt, 40 miles from Berlin.

Philippines, 6 February 1945. MacArthur announces the capture of Manila and the liberation of 5,000 prisoners.

Burma, 5 March 1945. The British take the Japanese base of Meiktila, cutting Burma in two.

USA, 12 April 1945. The American statesman Franklin Delano Roosevelt, president four times, dies aged 63. Harry S. Truman is sworn in as president.

Poland, 15 April 1945. Allied troops liberate the concentration camp at Bergen-Belsen.

Italy, 28 April 1945. Mussolini is executed.

Germany, 30 April 1945. US troops liberate Dachau.

Berlin, 30 April 1945. Hitler shoots himself.

Europe, 2 May 1945. All one million German troops in Italy and Austria surrender.

Burma, 3 May 1945. The British 14th Army takes Rangoon.

Berlin, 8 May 1945. Field-Marshal Keitel signs Germany's final act of capitulation.

Berlin, 5 June 1945. Allied supreme commanders sign a pact for the occupation of Germany.

USA, 16 July 1945. The first atomic bomb tests take place in the New Mexico desert.

Hiroshima, 6 August 1945. An atomic bomb destroys the city.

Nagasaki, 9 August 1945. The city is destroyed by an atomic bomb.

Japan, 14 August 1945. Japan surrenders to the Allies.

China, 28 August 1945. Mao Zedong and Zhou Enlai discuss peace, democracy and unity with Chiang Kai-shek.

Hong Kong, 1 September 1945. British troops take control.

Tokyo, 3 September 1945. MacArthur formally accepts the Japanese surrender on the aircraft-carrier *Missouri*.

Korea, 8 September 1945. The USA and the USSR divide Korea.

London, 19 September 1945. The prime minister, Clement Attlee, promises India independence.

India, 21 September 1945. The Congress Party calls for the freedom of India, Burma, Malaya and Indochina from colonial rule.

USSR, 6 November 1945. The USSR says it will make its own atomic bomb.

Yugoslavia, 12 November 1945. Marshal Tito's National Front secures an overwhelming majority in a general election.

France, 13 November 1945. Charles de Gaulle is elected president.

Dutch East Indies, 17 November 1945. The Republic of Indonesia is declared.

USA, 18 April 1946. The USA recognizes the People's Republic of Yugoslavia, albeit with reservations.

USA, 19 April 1946. President Truman promises a million tons of wheat a month for Europe and Asia.

London, 1 May 1946. The USA and Britain publish a joint plan for the partition of Palestine between Jews and Arabs.

, 4 June 1946. Juan Peron is installed as the president of Argentina.

Calcutta, 19 August 1946. Over 3,000 people die in Calcutta in three days of intense fighting between Hindus and Muslims over Britain's plans for the future of India.

USA, 2 October 1946. A scientist claims that smoking could be a cause of lung cancer.

Washington, 12 March 1947. President Truman tells Congress that the USA must abandon its traditional isolationism in order to combat Communism.

USA, 29 August 1947. US announces discovery of plutonium fission, suitable for nuclear-power generation.

Budapest, 1 September 1947. Communists win Hungarian governmental elections.

USA, 14 October 1947. Chuck Yeager becomes the first man to travel faster than sound, as his Bell XI rocket plane exceeds 760mph (1,200 km/h).

India, 21 December 1947. 400,000 slaughtered during mass migration of Hindus and Muslims into the new states of India and Pakistan.

India, 30 January. Mahatma Gandhi is shot and killed by a Hindu extremist.

Prague, 10 March 1948. Jan Masaryk, Czech foreign minister and opponent of the Communist coup, is dead.

Israel, 14 May 1948. The British relinquish control and the new state of Israel comes into existence.

London, 7 June 1948. Allies agree to keep troops in Germany until "peace of Europe is secured".

Britain, 5 July 1948. The National Health Service, offering free treatment for the whole nation, is born.

North Korea, 9 September 1948. North Korea proclaims independence as the Democratic People's Republic of Korea, under President Kim II Sung.

Berlin, 18 September 1948. The Allied airlift reaches its peak since the Soviet blockade began three months ago, 895 flights landing in one day.

New York, 10 December 1948. The United Nations adopts a declaration of human rights.

India, 1 January 1949. A UN ceasefire comes into effect to halt fighting between India and Pakistan over the disputed state of Kashmir.

USA, 1 March 1949. Joe Louis retires, after successfully defending his world heavyweight title 25 times.

Moscow, 4 March 1949. Vyacheslav Molotov is ousted as Soviet foreign minister.

Berlin, 12 May 1949. The Soviet blockade is lifted.

Bonn, 14 August 1949. Konrad Adenauer wins the West German elections for chancellor.

New York, 25 August 1949. RCA announces invention of system for broadcasting color television.

East Germany, 12 October 1949. The Communists establish the separate state of East Germany.

China, 8 December 1949. Nationalist forces, defeated on the mainland, establish their capital on the island of Formosa.

1950–1959

London, 21 January 1950. George Orwell, author of *Animal Farm* and *1984*, dies of tuberculosis, aged 46.

London, 3 February 1950. Nuclear scientist Klaus Fuchs is arrested on suspicion of passing nuclear secrets to the USSR.

Jordan, 24 April 1950. Jordan annexes Arab Palestine, taking over West Bank territory and East Jerusalem.

South Africa, 11 September 1950. Jan Smuts, rebel Boer leader, and later, South African prime minister, dies aged 80.

Vietnam, 10 October 1950. French troops are overrun by the Viet Minh at Kaobang.

Tibet, 25 December 1950. The Dalai Lama is reported to have fled the country, following the Chinese invasion.

Korea, 17 February 1951. UN forces push north attempting to retake Seoul, captured by Communists six weeks ago.

Paris, 19 March 1951. France, West Germany, Italy and the Benelux countries agree to form a European Coal and Steel Community.

South Africa, 14 May 1951. The government removes the right to vote of "colored" (mixed race) people.

USA, 14 August 1951. William Randolph Hearst, flamboyant publishing tycoon, aged 88, dies.

Iran, 23 August 1951. British government fails to dissuade the Iranians from taking over the Anglo-Iranian Oil Company's oil fields.

West Germany, 31 August 1951. *Deutsche Grammophon* launches the first 33 rpm "long-playing" record.

Egypt, 19 October. British troops occupy the Suez Canal Zone.

Libya, 24 December. King Idris el Senussi proclaims independence from Italy.

Britain, 6 February 1952. King George VI dies peacefully in his sleep at Sandringham. He is succeeded by Princess Elizabeth, currently on a state visit to Kenya.

Gold Coast, 21 March 1952. Dr Kwame Nkrumah is elected the first African prime minister south of the Sahara.

Vietnam, 26 April 1952. French forces launch a major assault on the Viet Minh, north of Saigon,

London, 15 June 1952. *The Diary of Anne Frank*, describing two years in the life of a Jewish family hiding from the Nazis in an Amsterdam attic, is published in English.

USA, 1 January 1953. Country-and-western singer Hank Williams dies, aged 29.

Yugoslavia, 14 January 1953. Tito is elected president of Yugoslavia.

Moscow, 5 March 1953. Joseph Stalin dies after suffering a stroke.

Kenya, 8 April 1953. Jomo Kenyatta, leader of the Mau Mau rebels, is jailed for seven years.

Cuba, 26 July 1953. Government forces capture Communist insurgents, including their leader, Fidel Castro.

Moscow, 12 September 1953. Nikita Khrushchev is elected first secretary of the Communist Party.

Rhode Island, 12 September 1953. Aspiring young democrat senator John Kennedy marries Jacqueline Bouvier.

Moscow, 23 December 1953. Lavrenti Beria, Stalin's chief of secret police, is shot after he is found guilty of treason.

USA, 23 February 1954. Dr Jonas Salk's polio vaccine is given to children in Pittsburgh.

Cairo, 18 April 1954. Colonel Nasser emerges triumphant after a power struggle with Egypt's President Naguib.

Kenya, 24 April 1954. Security forces launch a campaign to round up members of the Mau Mau.

USA, 24 May 1954. IBM announces it is to market an electronic calculating machine for businesses.

Hanoi, 10 October 1954. Ho Chi Minh returns to Vietnam after France pulls out of the country.

Algeria, 1 November 1954. Nationalists riot in violent protest against French rule.

Kenya, 19 January 1955. The Mau Mau are offered an amnesty, to the fury of whites.

South Africa, 10 February 1955. Armed police start moving 60,000 blacks from a township that has been designated a future whites-only area.

Switzerland, 12 August 1955. Thomas Mann, Germany's greatest novelist, dies in Zurich, aged 80.

Alabama, 22 March 1956. Martin Luther King Jr. on his conviction of organizing a bus boycott, vows to use "passive resistance and the weapon of love" in the fight for black rights.

Egypt, 26 July 1956. President Gamal Abdel Nasser announces the nationalization of the Suez Canal Company, formerly under Anglo-French control.

East Berlin, 14 August 1956. Revolutionary playwright Bertolt Brecht dies, aged 58.

Hungary, 5 November 1956. Soviet tanks crush the Hungarian uprising. The poorly armed Hungarians are unable to mount effective resistance.

Hungary, 10 December 1956. The country is put under Soviet martial law.

USA, 14 January 1957. Actor Humphrey Bogart dies of cancer, aged 57.

Ghana, 6 March 1957. The British colony of the Gold Coast becomes the independent nation of Ghana.

Jordan, 14 April 1957. King Hussein successfully faces down an attempted army coup.

China, 24 April 1957. Critics of the government are urged to speak up, as Mao's "let 100 flowers bloom" movement gathers pace.

Moscow, 3 July 1957. Khrushchev defeats an attempt to remove him from power by three leading Stalinists.

London, 6 July 1957. US tennis star Althea Gibson becomes the first black player to win a Wimbledon singles title.

London, 4 September 1957. The Wolfenden report says homosexual acts between consenting adults should no longer be illegal.

Moscow, 4 October 1957. The USSR announces that it has successfully launched *Sputnik*, the first satellite, into orbit around the earth.

Stockholm, 10 December 1957. Frenchman Albert Camus, author of *The Stranger*, is awarded the Nobel Prize for literature.

Middle East, 1 February 1958. Egypt and Syria proclaim union as the United Arab Republic.

USA, 1 February 1958. America successfully launches its first space satellite.

Hungary, 16 June 1958. Imre Nagy, prime minister at the time of the Hungarian uprising, is hanged by the new regime.

Tokyo, 18 June 1958. The Japanese break tradition, letting Prince Akito choose his own bride.

Cuba, 17 September 1958. Fidel Castro leads an offensive against the government of General Batista. On 1 January 1959 Batista flees Cuba and Castro takes power.

Brussels, 19 October 1958. The World's Fair closes with a total of 41 million visitors.

Rome, 28 October 1958. After the death of Pius XII, a liberal cardinal is chosen as the new pope. He will be known as John XXIII.

France, 21 December 1958. Charles de Gaulle is elected French president, with an overwhelming majority in the electoral college.

Paris, 16 September 1959. President de Gaulle says Algeria can vote for its own future, after four years of peace.

USSR, 26 October 1959. The Soviet *Lunik III* spacecraft sends back the first-ever views of the dark side of the moon.

Stockholm, 7 November 1959. Seven non-Common Market countries, including Sweden, Britain and Portugal, form the European Free Trade Association.

1960–1969

Egypt, 10 January 1960. President Nasser lays the foundation stone of the Aswan High Dam.

Israel, 7 February 1960. Biblical scrolls, at least 1,700 years old, have been found in the desert.

Belgian Congo, 11 March 1960. Riot police stand by as fiery nationalist Patrice Lumumba is allowed to speak in public for the first time.

Hollywood, 5 April 1960. *Ben Hur* wins a record ten Oscars.

Brazil, 21 April 1960. The new city of Brasilia is inaugurated as capital.

Leopoldville, 30 June 1960. King Baudouin presides over a ceremony to grant independence to the Belgian Congo, which will now be known as the Congo.

USA, 26 September 1960. Millions watch the first-ever televised debate between presidential candidates, as Richard Nixon and John Kennedy go head to head.

London, 2 November 1960. A jury ends a vital censorship trial stating that D. H. Lawrence's *Lady Chatterley's Lover* is not obscene.

Washington DC, 9 November 1960. John F. Kennedy is elected President of the United States defeating Vice-President Richard M. Nixon in one of the closest elections in history.

Congo, 13 February 1961. Former premier Patrice Lumumba dies in mysterious circumstances.

Washington, 1 March 1961. President Kennedy announces the formation of the Peace Corps.

South Vietnam, 10 April 1961. Anti-Communist Ngo Dinh Diem is re-elected president in a landslide victory.

USSR, 12 April 1961. Russian cosmonaut Yuri Gagarin becomes the first man in space.

Cape Canaveral, 5 May 1961. Alan Shepard becomes the first American in space.

Washington, 25 May 1961. President Kennedy says that the USA aims to be first to put a man on the moon.

South Africa, 31 May 1961. Under attack for its apartheid policies, South Africa leaves the British Commonwealth.

London, 31 July 1961. Prime Minister Harold Macmillan announces that Britain is to seek Common Market membership.

Northern Rhodesia, 18 September 1961. UN secretary general Dag Hammarskjold dies in an air crash.

Israel, 31 May 1962. Adolf Eichmann, former SS officer responsible for implementing the "final solution", is hanged. Eichmann was captured by the Mossad outside of Buenos Aires, where he had been in hiding, and brought back to Israel to stand trial.

Mississippi, 30 September 1962. White protesters fail to stop enrolment of the state university's first black student.

Pretoria, 7 November 1962. Black nationalist leader Nelson Mandela is jailed for five years.

USA, 10 April 1963. The US submarine *Thresher* sinks: all hands are lost.

Addis Ababa, 25 May 1963. Leaders of 30 African nations found the Organization of African Unity.

Teheran, 6 June 1963. Rioting breaks out after the arrest of a leading Islamic opponent of the regime, Rouahallah Khomeini.

Saigon, 13 June 1963. A Buddhist monk burns himself to death in the street in protest against the government.

USSR, 16 June 1963. Valentina Tereshkova becomes the first woman in space.

Berlin, 26 June 1963. President Kennedy declares "*Ich bin ein Berliner!*"

Moscow, 8 August 1963. The USSR, USA and Britain sign a treaty banning atmospheric tests of nuclear weapons.

Washington, 30 August 1963. A telephone hot line between the Kremlin and the White House goes into operation.

Alabama, 10 September 1963. President Kennedy takes control of the state National Guard after it is used by Governor George Wallace to block school desegregation.

Dallas, 22 November 1963. President John F. Kennedy is assassinated. Lyndon B. Johnson is sworn in as his successor on *Air Force One*. Two days later the man determined to be his killer, Lee Harvey Oswald, is himself shot down by a Texas nightclub owner, Jack Ruby.

South Africa, 14 June 1964. African nationalist leader Nelson Mandela is sentenced to life on charges of treason.

Washington, 2 July 1964. President Lyndon B. Johnson signs the Civil Rights Act.

Washington, 27 September 1964. The Warren Commission reports that there was no conspiracy to kill President Kennedy.

Berlin, 5 October 1964. 57 East Germans escape under the Berlin Wall through a tunnel.

China, 16 October 1964. China explodes its first atomic bomb.

Africa, 24 October 1964. Northern Rhodesia becomes Republic of Zambia, ending 73 years of British rule.

Ottawa, 15 February 1965. Canada's distinctive maple leaf flag raised for the first time.

New York, 15 August 1965. Over 55,000 people attend the Beatles' concert in Shea Stadium.

USA, 11 October 1965. A Viking map from the fifteenth century of "Vinland" is published. It appears to show that they discovered North America well before Columbus.

Rhodesia, 11 November 1965. Prime Minister Ian Smith makes a unilateral declaration of independence from Britain.

Houston, 26 April 1966. American surgeon implants an artificial pump in a human heart.

Moon, 3 June 1966. An unmanned American spacecraft lands on and then takes off from the moon.

USA, 4 June 1966. 6,400 people sign appeal against Vietnam War, the largest political ad ever published.

California, 15 December 1966. Walt Disney dies aged 65.

Athens, 21 April 1967. A military junta seizes power in Greece and arrests leftists.

Britain, 1 June 1967. The Beatles release Sergeant *Pepper's Lonely Hearts Club Band*.

Prague, 28 June 1967. Czech writers sign a petition calling for liberalization of Communist government.

London, 14 July 1967. A bill to make abortion legal is passed by the House of Commons.

USA, 27 July 1967. Throughout this month race riots have ravaged several US cities, including Detroit, New York and Newark.

USA, 30 August 1967. Thurgood Marshall becomes the first African American named to the Supreme Court.

Vietnam, 21 November 1967. US bombers intensify their raids on North Vietnam.

Czechoslovakia, 5 January 1968. Liberal Alexander Dubcek, 46, becomes head of the Czechoslovak Communist Party and leader of the country.

Canada, 6 April 1968. Pierre Trudeau becomes prime minister.

USA, 9 April 1968. Within hours of the murder of Dr. Martin Luther King Jr, riots break out in a number of major US cities.

Paris, 13 May 1968. American and North Vietnamese diplomats meet to discuss the setting-up of talks to end the Vietnam War.

Los Angeles, 7 June 1968. Sirhan Sirhan, a young Palestinian Arab immigrant, is charged with murdering Senator Robert Kennedy, the brother of the late president, and assaulting five other people.

London, 8 June 1968. James Earl Ray, 40, wanted by the FBI for the murder of Dr. Martin Luther King Jr, is arrested en route to Brussels.

Rome, 29 July 1968. Pope Paul VI issues an encyclical, *Humanae Vitae*, condemning birth control.

Washington, 1 November 1968. President Johnson calls off the bombing of North Vietnam in an attempt to stimulate Paris peace talks.

Prague, 19 January 1969. Angry crowds gather after Czech student Jan Palach burns himself to death in protest against the Russian invasion.

Britain, 13 February 1969. Scientists announce they have successfully fertilized human eggs in a test tube.

Bethel, New York, 15 August 1969. 400,000 young people gather for three days of music and psychedlic experiences at the Woodstock Festival.

Libya, 1 September 1969. A group of army officers led by Colonel Muammar Gaddafi seizes power.

Nigeria, 2 November 1969. Biafrans face mass starvation because the Nigerian government will not let the Red Cross in.

1970–1979

Laos, 1 March 1970. American planes heavily bomb the Ho Chi Minh trail.

Washington, 10 March 1970. Army accuses five of murder and other crimes at Mylai in 1968.

Washington, 30 April 1970. President Nixon sends US troops into Cambodia to attack Communist military bases.

New York, 28 June 1970. Thousands of gay men and women protest against laws that make homosexual acts illegal between consenting adults.

Portugal, 27 July 1970. Dictator Antonio d'Oliviera Salazar dies, aged 81.

Northern Ireland, 10 April 1971. A more militant, "Provisional", wing splits from the official IRA.

Washington, 2 May 1971. Police eject 3,000 anti-war protesters from the banks of the Potomac.

London, 24 June 1971. Terms are agreed for Britain's entry into the Common Market.

USA, 6 July 1971. Jazz great Louis Armstrong dies aged 71.

New York, 1 August 1971. A galaxy of rock stars, led by ex-Beatle George Harrison, perform at Madison Square Garden to raise funds for Bangladesh.

Bangladesh, 30 January 1972. Sheikh Mujibur Rahman becomes prime minister of newly independent Bangladesh.

Northern Ireland, 30 January 1972. British troops fire on a crowd of civil rights protesters in Londonderry, killing 13 and injuring 17. Three days later the British embassy is destroyed by a crowd protesting the "Bloody Sunday" shootings.

Washington, 22 March 1972. The Senate passes the Equal Rights Amendment.

Hanover, 16 June 1972. West Germany's most wanted terrorist, Ulrike Meinhof, is arrested.

Vietnam, 11 August 1972. The last US ground forces withdraw from Vietnam.

Israel, 22 February 1973. Air force jets shoot down a Libyan Boeing airliner, killing 74.

Washington, 30 April 1973. The Watergate scandal forces four top White House aides—John Ehrlichman, Bob Haldeman, Richard Kleindienst and John Dean—to resign.

Washington, 17 July 1973. The Senate learns that Nixon regularly taped his own Oval Office conversations.

Middle East, 21 October 1973. Arabs put an embargo on oil to the US in protest against the US's support of Israel.

USA, 23 October 1973. President Nixon, faced with possible impeachment, agrees to hand over key Watergate tapes.

Washington, 15 March 1974. A federal grand jury has convicted President Nixon as a co-conspirator in the Watergate affair.

Britain, 6 March 1974. After an election created by the miners' strike, Harold Wilson forms a minority Labor government.

India, 18 May 1974. India tests its first nuclear bomb.

Toronto, 30 June 1974. Mikhail Baryshnikov, leading Soviet ballet star, defects to West.

Washington, 9 August 1974. Richard Nixon resigns, and Gerald Ford is sworn in as president.

India, 12 June 1975. The prime minister, Mrs. Indira Gandhi, is found guilty of electoral corruption.

Helsinki, 1 August 1975. 35 nations sign the Helsinki agreement on peace and human rights.

San Francisco, 18 September 1975. Heiress Patty Hearst, seized by the Symbionese Liberation Army 18 months ago, appears in court on a robbery charge.

Angola, 24 November 1975. Some 40,000 people are believed killed in fighting in the two weeks since independence.

Portugal, 25 April 1976. The first free elections for 50 years in Portugal produce a socialist government.

Lebanon, 16 May 1976. Fighting breaks out between Christians and Muslims in Beirut as the 30th cease-fire collapses.

USA, 17 January 1977. Gary Gilmore, the convicted killer, is shot by a firing squad in Utah. He is the first man in ten years to be executed.

Uganda, 18 February 1977. Idi Amin's latest wave of terror claims the life of the Archbishop of Uganda.

Spain, 15 June 1977. Spain goes to the polls for the first time in 41 years. Voters resoundingly voted for the center-right coalition of Prime Minister Adolfo Suarez.

Paris, 17 September 1977. Opera *diva* Maria Callas dies of a heart attack, aged 53.

South Africa, 2 December 1977. Police are cleared of causing the death of black activist Steve Biko while in their custody 12 weeks ago.

USA, 3 December 1977. The State Department proposes admitting 10,000 Vietnamese boat people fleeing from their troubled nation.

Switzerland, 25 December 1977. Cinema's greatest clown, Charlie Chaplin, dies, aged 88.

Afghanistan, 30 April 1978. Soviet-backed army officers take over, assassinating the president.

Russia, 14 July 1978. Three Soviet dissidents jailed to widespread protest from Western Europe and the USA.

Rome, 26 August 1978. Twenty days after the death of Paul VI, cardinals choose an Italian of peasant origins as Pope John Paul I.

London, 29 September 1978. A Bulgarian defector, Georgi Markov, is killed by a poisoned pellet from an umbrella point.

Rome, 30 September 1978. Pope John Paul I is found dead after only 33 days in office. On 16 October, a Polish cardinal, Karol Wojtyla, becomes Pope John Paul II, the first non-Italian pope for over 400 years.

Iraq, 6 October 1978. Iraq expels Iranian Ayatollah Khomeini.

Oslo, 10 December 1978. Israel's Prime Minister Begin and Egypt's President Sadat are jointly awarded the Nobel Peace Prize.

Cambodia, 8 January 1979. Vietnamese forces occupy Cambodia, ousting Pol Pot and the Khmer Rouge.

Jupiter, 7 March 1979. *Voyager 1* sends pictures showing Jupiter surrounded by a faint ring.

Uganda, 29 March 1979. Idi Amin flees the country while his capital is under siege by the Tanzanian-backed Uganda Liberation Front.

Pakistan, 5 April 1979. Former prime minister Bhutto is hanged on order of President Zia.

Poland, 10 June 1979. Pope John Paul II says mass to over a million in his native country in the first ever pontifical visit to a Communist country.

USA, 11 June 1979. Hero of many westerns, John Wayne, dies, aged 72.

Vienna, 18 June 1979. Carter and Brezhnev sign the SALT-2 arms limitation treaty.

Nicaragua, 21 August 1979. Sandinistas ban capital punishment and restore human rights laws.

Ireland, 27 August 1979. Lord Mountbatten is killed by an IRA bomb on his boat.

London, 21 November 1979. The Keeper of the Queen's Pictures, Sir Anthony Blunt, is revealed as a Soviet spy.

Seoul, 26 November 1979. President Park Chung Hee is assassinated.

Afghanistan, 26 December 1979. Soviet troops invade Afghanistan to support the new president, Babrak Karmal.

1980–1989

USSR, 22 January 1980. The USSR's most prominent dissident, Andrei Sakharov, is arrested and exiled to Gorky, a city closed to foreigners.

USA, 21 March 1980. President Carter urges the US Olympic Committee to boycott the Moscow Olympics in protest against the Soviet intervention in Afghanistan.

Paris, 15 April 1980. The funeral is held for France's leading philosopher and leftist thinker, Jean-Paul Sartre.

Hollywood, 29 April 1980. British-born thriller director Alfred Hitchcock dies, aged 80.

East Africa, 12 June 1980. A combination of drought and war threatens ten million people with famine.

New Delhi, 23 June 1980. Mrs. Gandhi's younger son and political heir, Sanjay, dies in a plane crash.

Egypt, 27 July 1980. The deposed Shah of Iran, Mohammed Reza Pahlavi, dies in a military hospital aged 60.

Poland, 24 January 1981. Millions of workers stay away from their jobs in support of Solidarity's call for a five-day work week.

France, 10 May 1981. The Socialist leader, Francois Mitterrand, is elected president.

Israel, 7 June 1981. Israeli planes destroy Iraq's nuclear reactor.

USA, 7 July 1981. Sandra Day O'Connor, becomes the first woman-named to Supreme Court.

Europe, 24 October 1981. Mass protests are held all across Western Europe against the presence of American nuclear weapons.

Nicaragua, 25 March, 1980. Fearing a US invasion, the Sandinista government declares a state of emergency.

Falkland Islands, 2 April 1981. Argentinian forces overrun the islands and capture the few British troops stationed there.

Falkland Islands, 14 June 1981. The Argentinian invaders surrender to the British task force.

London, 19 June 1981. Roberto Calvi, an Italian banker, is found hanged under Blackfriars Bridge.

Lebanon, 31 August 1981. The PLO is driven out of Beirut by invading Israeli forces.

Lebanon, 14 September 1981. President-elect Bashir Gemayel is killed by a bomb.

Monaco, 15 September 1981. Princess Grace dies in a car crash on a mountain road.

West Germany, 1 October 1981. Christian Democrat Helmut Kohl replaces Social Democrat Helmut Schmidt as chancellor.

Poland, 14 November 1981. Lech Walesa returns to Gdansk after 11 months internment.

Australia, 5 March 1982. Robert Hawke and his Labor Party oust the eight-year-old Conservative government.

Beirut, 19 April 1982. US embassy is bombed, killing 40 people.

Washington, 4 May 1982. President Reagan backs Contra guerrillas in Nicaragua in their struggle to overthrow the Marxist Sandinista government.

Oslo, 10 December 1983. Lech Walesa is awarded the Nobel Peace Prize; his wife accepts the award.

Argentina, 20 December 1983. Eight years of army rule have ended.

Washington, 23 April 1984. The virus that causes AIDS is identified.

India, 6 June 1984. Troops storm the Sikh Golden Temple at Amritsar to expel armed extremists.

Canada, 4 September 1984. Brian Mulroney and his Progressive Conservative Party win in a huge victory.

Beijing, 26 September 1984. China agrees to let Hong Kong keep its capitalist way of life after sovereignty reverts in 1997.

Oslo, 10 December 1984. Desmond Tutu, the Anglican bishop of Johannesburg, is awarded the Nobel Peace Prize.

South Africa, 19 February 1985. Hundreds are hurt in a police clash with blacks resisting relocation to a black township.

Auckland, 10 July 1985. *Rainbow Warrior*, a Greenpeace ship in New Zealand preparing for protests against French nuclear tests, is blown up.

France, 20 January 1986. Mrs. Thatcher and President Mitterrand confirm that Britain and France are to build a Channel Tunnel next year.

February 1986. Halley's Comet is visible in the night sky as it passes at its closest to Earth.

Iraq, 19 February 1986. Iranian forces capture the key Iraqi oil port of Al Faw during the Iran-Iraq War.

Stockholm, 28 February 1986. Swedish prime minister Olaf Palme is shot dead in the street.

Iceland, 13 October 1986. President Reagan and Soviet leader Gorbachev blame each other for the failed summit in Reykjavik.

Beirut, 21 January 1987. While on a church mission the Archbishop of Canterbury's special envoy, Terry Waite, is himself kidnapped trying to negotiate the release of other hostages.

Moscow, 29 January 1987. Mikhail Gorbachev calls for greater democracy, based on *perestroika* (reconstruction) and *glasnost* (openness).

Washington, 17 July 1987. Lieutenant Colonel Oliver North and Rear Admiral John Poindexter testify to Congress on the "Irangate" scandal.

Montreal, 16 September 1987. More than 70 nations pledge to save the Earth's ozone layer.

Sri Lanka, 12 October 1987. Indian troops, sent in as peacekeepers, battle Tamil separatists.

USA, 18 December 1987. Ivan Boesky, who gained over $80 million through insider trading, is given a three-year sentence.

Persian Gulf, 3 July 1988. A US warship shoots down an Iranian airliner, killing 286.

Chile, 6 October 1988. General Pinochet is defeated in the general election.

Washington, 14 December 1988. After Yasser Arafat renounces violence, the US says it will open a dialogue with the PLO.

Scotland, 22 December 1988. A Pan Am airliner is blown up in mid-air and crashes into Lockerbie, killing all person on board.

Libya, 4 January 1989. US Navy fight-pilots shoot down two Libyan jets.

Tokyo, 7 January 1989. Hirohito, Emperor of Japan for 62 years, dies, aged 87.

USSR, 26 March 1989. In the first free elections in the USSR, maverick politician Boris Yeltsin wins a vote of confidence.

South Africa, 15 August 1989. F. W. de Klerk becomes the President of South Africa.

Hungary, 10 September 1989. Hungary opens its border with Austria as thousands of East Germans flee to a better life in the West.

Cambodia, 26 September 1989. The last Vietnamese troops leave.

East Germany, 18 October 1989. GDR hard-liner Erich Honecker is forced to resign, and Egon Krenz is appointed to replace him as East German leader.

Prague, 24 November 1989. The Communist leadership quits in the face of massive public demonstrations.

Malta, 3 December 1989. Presidents Bush and Gorbachev announce an official end to the Cold War.

1990–1999

Moscow, 25 February 1990. Hundreds of thousands of demonstrators call for democratic reforms.

London, 31 March 1990. A huge march on the eve of the introduction of the poll tax ends in a riot.

Iran, 22 June 1990. Forty thousand people are feared dead in an earthquake in the north.

Geneva, 27 July 1990. Reports show that AIDS has become the main cause of death for women aged 20 to 40.

Islamabad, 8 August 1990. Prime Minister Benazir Bhutto and her government are forced to resign by President Gulam Ishaq Khan.

USA, 29 November 1990. President Bush wins UN backing for use of force against Iraq.

Poland, 9 December 1990. Lech Walesa is elected president.

Kuwait, 16 January 1991. Operation "Desert Storm" is launched to drive Iraq out of Kuwait.

Iraq, 18 January 1991. Iraq starts firing Scud missiles at Israeli cities.

South Africa, 1 February 1991. President de Klerk announces the abolition of the last remaining apartheid laws.

Budapest, 25 February 1991. Leaders of the Warsaw Pact vote to dissolve its military structures by 31 March.

Madras, 21 May 1991. A suicide bomber kills the former prime minister, Rajiv Gandhi.

Croatia, 26 October 1991. The historic port of Dubrovnik comes under siege by the Serb-dominated Yugoslav army.

Netherlands, 7 February 1992. Two agreements to bring closer European unity are signed in Maastricht.

Sarajevo, 1 March 1992. Bosnian Serbs begin a sniping campaign, after Croats and Muslims vote for Bosnian independence.

South Africa, 17 March 1992. White South Africans approve constitutional reforms giving legal equality to blacks.

Kabul, 28 April 1992. Rebels occupy the Afghan capital.

Sarajevo, 2 July 1992. UN troops take control of the airport in Sarajevo, besieged by Bosnian Serbs.

Canada, 26 October 1992. A national referendum votes against giving Quebec special status.

Britain, 11 November 1992. The Church of England votes its final approval for the ordination of women.

Europe, 1 January 1993. The Single European Market, encompassing 375 million people, comes into being.

Texas, 19 April 1993. The FBI ends a 51-day siege by storming the Branch Davidian religious cult headquarters in Waco.

Oslo, 15 October 1993. President de Klerk and Nelson Mandela are jointly awarded the Nobel Peace Prize.

Australia, 22 December 1993. Aborigines celebrate the Native Title Bill, an historic victory over land rights.

Israel, 25 February 1994. A Jewish zealot, Dr Baruch Goldstein, shoots 30 Palestinian worshippers in the Ibrahim Mosque, Hebron.

Italy, 28 March 1994. Conservative media tycoon Silvio Berlusconi wins the general election.

New York, 22 April 1994. The ex-president Richard Nixon dies of a stroke, aged 81.

USA, 17 June 1994. Millions watch on TV as former football star O. J. Simpson drives across Los Angeles, facing arraignment on murder charges.

Buenos Aires, 18 July 1994. A massive car bomb kills 96 people belonging to Argentinian Jewish organizations.

USA, 9 November 1994. The Republicans take control of both houses of Congress for the first time in 40 years.

Bosnia, 19 December 1994. Former president Jimmy Carter achieves a cease-fire accord.

Washington, 16 March 1995. Sinn Fein leader Gerry Adams is received in the White House.

Los Angeles, 3 October 1995. O. J. Simpson is found not guilty.

Washington, 16 October 1995. Louis Farrakhan leads a march of nearly half a million black men on the Mall.

Afghanistan, 1996. Kabul falls to the radical Islamic Taliban. In the following weeks and months the Taliban go one to take control of most of the country. The former communist president, Najibullah, under NATO protection since 1992, is kidnapped and murdered.

Great Britain, 23 February 1997. Geneticists at the Roslin Institute in Edinburgh announce the successful cloning of an adult sheep.

Great Britain, 1 May 1997. Labor wins a majority. Conservative Prime Minister, John Majors, is replaced by Tony Blair.

US & Switzerland, 7 May 1997. A US government report accuses Switzerland of being the "Nazis' banker," thereby indirectly prolonging World War II.

Zaire, 17 May 1997. After 32 years as President, Mobutu Sese Seko is overthrown. He dies on 7 September of the same year in Rabat, Morocco. Zaire's new leader, Laurent-Désiré Kabila, renames the country the Democratic Republic of Congo.

Hong Kong, 1 July 1997. The British colonial authorities returns the city after 156 years to Chinese control. The principal "one country two systems" is to be observed, preserving Hong Kong's capitalistic system for at least fifty years.

France, 31 August 1997. British Princess Diana dies in a car accident in Paris. She was divorced from Prince Charles, heir to the British throne, the year before. Her death sparks worldwide mourning.

Yugoslavia, 19 February 1998. Serbian troops launch an offensive against the Kosovar Freedom Army (UCK) in an area with an Albanian majority. A wave of refugees flee the fighting. On 13 October NATO pressures Serbian President Milosevic to call a temporary halt in the fighting.

Great Britain, 10 April 1998. Catholics and Protestants agree to the Good Friday Peace Accord. On 22 May, a wide majority of the population of both parts of Ireland approve of it and a representative body of Northern Ireland is seated on 25 June. The ratification of the agreement breaks down over the disarmament of paramilitary organizations.

India-Pakistan, 11 May 1998. For the first time since 1974 India conducts three underground nuclear tests. Strong international criticism ensues. On 28 May, its neighbor Pakistan conducts an atomic test.

Indonesia, 21 May 1998. After many weeks of antigovernment demonstrations, Premier Suharto, who had been in power since 1968, steps down. His Vice-President, Jusuf Habibie, takes over. On 29 October 1999, Abd ur-Rahman Wahid is elected president.

Europe, 1 January 1999. Eleven European countries institute a common currency.

Jordan, 7 February 1999. King Hussein II dies at the age of 63. His oldest son, Abdallah II, becomes king.

Washington DC, 12 February 1999. The US Senate dismisses charges of perjury and obstruction of justice against President Bill Clinton.

Yugoslavia, 24 March 1999. NATO begins an air campaign against Serbia to resolve the conflict in Kosovo.

Europe and Asia, 11 August 1999. Millions in Europe and Asia witness a total eclipse of the sun.

Russia, 31 December 1999. In a surprise move, Boris Yeltsin steps down as President of Russia and hands the reins of power over to Vladimir Putin.

2000-2008

The World, 1 January 2000. The whole world celebrates the arrival of the millennium. Concerns about widespread computer failures prove to be unfounded.

France, 25 July 2000. A Concorde departing from Charles de Gaulle airport crashes immediately after take off, killing all passengers and crew as well as four persons on the ground

Barents Sea, 12 August 2000. Explosions on board the Russian atomic submarine Kursk cause the death of the enitre crew. Nine days later British and Norwegian teams find the submarine on the sea floor.

Yemen, 12 October, 2000. The US destroyer Cole is the victim of a terrorist bombing that kills 17 seamen. Osama bin Laden is suspected to be behind the attack.

USA, 7 November 2000. With no clear victor in the presidential election between Vice-President Al Gore and Texas Governor George W. Bush, the matter is thrown into the courts. On 11 December, a decision by the US Supreme Court overturning a lower court ruling persuades Gore to abandon his run and concede victory to his opponent.

Israel, 6 February 2001. Hardliner Ariel Sharon wins the election for Prime Minister.

England, 21 February 2001. An outbreak of hoof and mouth disease leads to the slaughter of 3 million animals.

Italy, 22 July, 2001. Meeting of the G-8 Summit (with Russia as a guest participant) is overshadowed by mass demonstrations protesting increasing globalization.

United States, 11 September 2001. The world looks on in shock as terrorists fly two planes into the World Trade Center. Another one hits the Pentagon. A fourth hijacked plane crashes into a field in Pennsylvania, forced down by its passengers. The radical Islamicist, Osama bin Laden and his organization, Al Qaeda are responsible for the attacks that claim over 3,000 lives.

Afghanistan, 7 October 2001. The US begins a bombing campaign to bring down the Al Qaeda network and the Taliban government, which has been harboring it.

The Hague, 12 February 2002. The International Court begins war crimes proceedings against former Yugoslavian President Slobodan Milosevic.

England, 30 March 2002. The Queen Mother, Elizabeth, dies at the age of 101. She had won the deep affection of the British people.

Europe, August 2002. Historic flooding inundates much of Central Europe.

Bali, 12 October 2002. A terrorist bombing at a vacation resort kills over 200 people.

Moscow, 26 October, 2002. Chechen fighters seize a theater in Moscow holding 800 people hostage. In a rescue attempt gone wrong over 128 of the hostages die.

Yugoslavia, 12 March, 2003. The Serbian President Zoran Djindjic is gunned down by an assassin.

Switzerland, 12 March, 2003. The World Health Organization declares SARS as a global health threat.

Iraq, 20 March 2003. A US led coalition of forces begins its invasion of Iraq.

By the beginning of April, the coalition had seized Baghdad and toppled the regime of Saddam Hussein, who had gone into hiding.

California, 7 October 2003. One-time movie action hero, Arnold Schwarzenegger, is elected Governor of California.

Iraq, 14 December 2003. Former Iraqi dictator, Saddam Hussein, is captured by American forces.

Iran, 26 December 2003. A severe earthquake centered in the ancient city of Bam, causes the death of over 25,000 people.

Spain, 11 March 2004. Ten bombs explode practically simultaneously in four different Madrid train stations. The terrorist organization Al Qaeda claims responsibility for an attack that cost 191 lives.

USA, 28 April, 2004. The CBS television network broadcasts images of American soldiers torturing prisoners in Iraq's Abu Ghraib prison. The news causes worldwide outrage.

Afghanistan, 9 October 2004. Hamid Kharzai is elected president in Afghanistan's first election since the fall of the Taliban.

Ukraine, 26 December, 2004. Opposition candidate Victor Yushchenko wins the presidential election, despite his political opponents having poisoned him.

Southeast Asia, 26 December 2004. A powerful tsunami centered in Indonesia causes terrible devastation to a wide band of coastal regions. Hundreds of thousands are victims and millions lose their homes. The world responds with an outpouring of assistance.

Rome, 19 April 2005. Upon the death of Pope John Paul II, the German Cardinal Joseph Ratzinger is elected pope. He takes the name Benedict XVI.

England, 7 July 2005. A bomb attack in London's underground claims the lives of 50 people.

USA, August, 2005. Hurricane Katrina devastates the Gulf Coast, inundating New Orleans and surrounding communities. The government's slowness to respond is roundly criticized.

Montenegro, 21 May 2005. The Country votes to become independent of Serbia.

Lebanon, 12 July 2006. In an attempt to rescue three kidnapped soldiers the Israeli army invades Lebanon. They meet with an unanticipated level of resistance from Hezbollah fighters.

USA, 7 November, 2006. In congressional elections the Democratic Party regains control of both houses. Majority leader Nancy Pelosi becomes the first woman Speaker of the House when congress returns to session in January.

Iraq, 2 January 2007. Former Iraqi leader Saddam Hussein is executed. Pictures taken by a cell phone are broadcast worldwide.

Iraq, 10 January 2007. President Bush announces his plan to send over 20,000 more troops to Iraq to stabilize the security situation.

France, 6 May 2007. The head of the Conservative Union, Nicholas Sarkozy, is chosen as French President, defeating the socialist candidate Ségolène Royal.

England, 27 June, 2007. Gordon Brown succeeds Tony Blair as British Prime Minister. Blair had been Prime Minister since 1997.

Pakistan, 27 December 2007. Former Prime Minister of Pakistan, Benazir Bhutto, is assassinated after leaving a party rally. In October she had reached an agreement with Pakistani President Pervez Musharraf that allowed her to return to her native country and had hoped to bring reconciliation to a badly divided country.

USA, 4 March 2008. Arizona Senator John McCain secures enough delegates to assure himself of the Republican nomination for President. The Democratic nomination is still being contested by Senators Barack Obama and Hillary Clinton. ❑

THE BOXER REBELLION

China, August 14, 1900

By the end of the nineteenth century the Qing Dynasty's inability to defend China from the encroachment of Western powers had led to a nationalist movement that sought to expel all foreigners. The Manchu Qings' humiliating losses to the British during the Opium Wars and to the Japanese in the Sino-Japanese War exacerbated the populace's increasing frustration with a deteriorating economy. This frustration eventually broke out into what has become known as the Boxer Rebellion (November 1899-September 7,1901).

In November 1899 bands of a secret society known as the Boxers ("Society of Righteousness and Harmony"), began random attacks on foreign missionaries and their Chinese converts in the northern provinces. As the rebellion spread it received support from not only members of the Imperial army, but also from the

Dowager Empress Cixi.

On June 18, 1900, the Boxers mounted an attacked on the European legations in Beijing. When the Dowager Empress declared war on June 21, the Western powers deployed a multinational force of 20,000 troops. Known as the Eight-Nation Alliance, it included soldiers from Japan, Russia, the United States, Britain, France, Germany, Italy and Austria.

The rebellion was put down by August 14, although the Alliance continued for the next year to pursue rebels forces throughout the northern provinces. It is estimated that 50,000 Boxers were captured and executed. Of the as many as 115,00 people who died during the Boxer Rebellion, 32,000 were Christians.

The conflict officially ended with the signing of the *Boxer Protocol* on September 7, 1901. One of its harsher provisions required that the Chinese make indemnity payments to the member

A captured rebel is beheaded.

states of the Eight-Nation Alliance over a period of 39 years, totaling nearly $335,000,000 (present day). ❑

EDWARD VII'S ACCESSION TO THE ENGLISH THRONE

Isle of Wight, 1901

The death of Queen Victoria, the longest serving monarch (to date) in the nation's history ended the Victorian Age in which Great Britain enjoyed its great imperial power. At the time of his mother's death Edward was 59 years old. He was the second of nine children born to Victoria and Albert, her prince-consort.

As Prince of Wales, Edward had gained a well-deserved reputation as a playboy and man about town. It was therefore somewhat surprising when as a monarch he devoted his energies to politics and governance. He was particularly forceful in promoting British interests overseas, lending his support to the Triple Entente (between Great Britain, France

and Russia).

Edward's first son, Prince Albert Victor, died unexpectedly, and his second son, George, inherited the crown. During World War I he changed the name of his ruling house to expunge the association with Germany from Saxe-Coburg-Gotha to Windsor. ❑

Edward VII at the races on the Isle of Wight

SIGMUND FREUD AND THE FOUNDING OF PSYCHOANALYSIS

Vienna, 1900

With the publication of *The Interpretation of Dreams*, Sigmund Freud (1856-1939) fundamentally changed Western ideas about human psychology. Freud hypothesized the existence of unconscious drives that largely determine behavior. He described a process that he called the Oedipus Complex that accounted for the need to repress the most basic human wishes.

Freud saw dreams as the psyche's covert way of expressing these wishes. He believed that through the process of interpretation a patient could integrate unconscious drives into conscious life. The movement of psychoanalysis grew up around Freud's teaching and had an profound

influence on twentieth century thought. Freud emigrated from Vienna to London in 1938 to escape from the Nazis. He died in the following year. ❑

Sigmund Freud

THE FIRST ZEPPELIN

Lake Constance, Germany, July 2, 1900

The launching of the first zeppelin marked the beginning of a glamorous era of air travel. The maiden voyage of the first steerable zeppelin took place on Lake Constance in Germany. This giant glider was considered a wonder of aviation. Unlike motorized airplanes, it was able to fly because it was lighter than air. The zeppelins achieved lift off from rising gas (at first hydrogen and then later inert helium), powered by motors and steered by rear rudders.

Inventd by the Count von Zeppelin, the 440-foot, cigar-shaped "airship" was made of aluminum mesh, covered with fabric. Underneath the body of the balloon were two gondolas, connected by a passageway. One held two 16-horse-power gas motors, the other equipment needed to operate the ship.

Zeppelins were used by Germany in World War I to attack Great Britain. The zeppelins reached their peak of popularity in the 1930s when there were regularly scheduled transatlantic flights. The Hindenburg disaster of 1937, in which the largest zeppelin ever built went up in flames, marked an end to the zeppelin as a viable commercial mode of travel. ❑

The first zeppelin over Lake Constance, Insert: Ferdinand Graf von Zeppelin

SUFFRAGETTES AND THE RIGHT TO VOTE

England, 1903

Women's struggle to gain the vote had been a peaceful one for many decades. The suffragette movement employed a more aggressive strategy in pursuit of their goal.

Emmeline Pankhurst and her daughter Christabel founded the National Women's Society and Political Union with the expressed aim of enfranchising women. Their tactics included mass demonstrations, hunger strikes, and sit-ins. They practically laid siege to Parliament and courted arrest and imprisonment. The Pankhursts and their comrades-in-arms saw these public actions as the best way of directing attention to their cause.

After nearly fifteen years their perseverance bore fruit. On June 19, 1917 the House of Commons granted some women the right to vote. For a women to qualify she had to be a householder or be married to one. It was not until 1928 that the voting criteria for women became the same as for men.

New Zealand had given the franchise to women in 1893. Others that followed included Finland (1906), Norway (1913), the Netherlands, Sweden and Germany (1919) and the United States (1920). French women did

Emmeline Pankhurst (middle) being arrested.

not gain the right to vote until 1944, and full suffrage for women in Switzerland did not happen until 1971. ❑

NOBEL PRIZE AWARDED

Oslo and Stockholm, 1901

In what would become a tradition, the Nobel Prize was awarded for the first time on December 10, 1901, the anniversary of the death of Alfred Nobel. This award soon gained the reputation for being the world's highest honor in the fields of science, literature and culture.

The prize was designed "to recognize those individuals who in the past year had been of the greatest service to humanity." The initial honors went to Wilhelm Conrad Röntgen of Germany (physics), Emil von Behring also from Germany (medicine) and the Dutchman Jacobus van't Hoff (chemistry). The Nobel Prize for Literature was given to the French poet, René François Armand Sully Proudhomme. Recipients of the first Nobel Peace Prize were the Swiss philanthropist Henri Dunant, the founder of the Red Cross, and the Frenchman Frédéric Passy, who was responsible for the establishment of a society for the arbitration of international conflicts.

The Swedish chemist and industrialist Alfred Nobel (1833-1896), donor of the prize, was the inventor of dynamite. In his will he asked that the income from his fortune of 33.2 million Swedish kroner be divided yearly into five equal parts and given in the form of a prize.

Nobel's will stipulated that the Nobel Peace Prize winner be chosen by a committee elected by the Norwegian parliament. The Swedish Academy of Science was to designate the prizewinners in physics and chemistry. The prize for medicine was the choice of the Karolinska Institute for Medicine in Stockholm; the prize in literature was given by the Swedish Academy. ❑

PIONEERS OF AVIATION

North Carolina, December 17, 1903

On December 17, 1903, at Kitty Hawk on North Carolina's Outer Banks, Wilbur and Orville Wright completed history's first flight in an engine-powered, pilot controlled aircraft. Named *Flyer* I, the aircraft, designed and built in their Dayton, Ohio bicycle factory, had a wingspan of 40 feet, weighed 625 pounds and was powered by gasoline-fueled, 170 pound, 12 horsepower engine. Piloted by Orville, it flew at an altitude of 10 feet for 12 seconds and covered 120 feet. It was the first of four flights that day, the fourth and longest was Wilbur's 59-second, 852-foot effort.

Although the Wright Brothers introduction of the first successful engine-powered aircraft was a major event in aviation history, many historians believe that an equally significant achievement was their invention of the "three axis-control system" that made fixed wing aircraft flight possible. Coordinating their unique design for "wing-warp-

Wilbur Wright photographing his brother Orville in flight

ing" with a forward mounted elevator, and a rudder placed at the rear of the craft, the brothers introduced systems of steer-

ing and equilibrium control that remain to this day fundamental principles in aircraft design.

Variations on these basic prin-

ciples aided the French engineer Louis Blériot when he became the first to fly over a major body of water, the English Channel,

REVOLUTION IN PAINTING

Paris, 1907

An exhibition to honor Paul Cézanne was the occasion for the first public appearance of the Cubist paintings of the Spaniard Pablo Picasso and the Frenchman Georges Braque. Starting from Cézanne's work to objectify seen reality by portraying it at as a composition of geometric forms—spheres, cylinders, and cones—Picasso presented *Les Demoiselles d'Avignon*: the first attempt to fashion an abstract and anti-naturalistic art. At the same time the painting drew freely upon African art imbuing it with intense it vitality.

Cubism developed into different directions embracing collage and the deconstruction of figures on the one hand and adding a diachronic dimension to painting, most famously in Marcel

Duchamp's *Nude Descending a Staircase No. 2* (1912).

The impulse to abstraction was taking hold throughout the art world. In 1905 a group of young painters led by Henri Matisse, André Derain, and Maurice de Vlaminck was experimenting with electrifying color, unconstrained brushwork and intentional distortions. Their exhibition in the Salon d'Automne (an alternative to the official Paris Salon) garnered little critical approbation. One critic, Camille Mauclair, remarked that they had "flung a pot of paint in the public's face." Another, Louis Vauxelles, took offense at a Donatello sculpture occupying the same room as the group's paintings, famously remarking that it seemed as if "Donatello was sur-

Pablo Picasso, *Les demoiselles d'Avignon*, 1907

rounded by wild beasts" (French: "Donatello parmi les fauves"),

thus giving the movement its name, the Fauves. ❑

THE SAN FRANCISCO EARTHQUAKE

April 18, 1906

on July 25, 1909. Using "wing-warping" and aft rudder placement, Blériot piloted his *Blériot XI* monoplane, twenty-two miles from Calais to Dover. Powered by a 25 horsepower Anzani engine, the historic flight took 37 minutes and won Blériot not only a place in aviation history but also the £1000 prize that Britain's *Daily Mail* had offered for the first successful crossing. ❑

Orville and Wilbur Wright (from left to right)

A earthquake measuring 8.3 on the Richter Scale and the subsequent fires destroyed the greater part of the city of San Francisco, home to 300,000 residents.

Two intense tremors rocked San Francisco at about 5:00 AM, costing 498 people their lives and destroying about 30,000 buildings. The first tremor lasted for about 40 seconds, the second for 25 seconds. The city withstood the quake fairly well. Newer buildings with flexible steel frames weathered the event, but older wood and brick buildingscollapsed in on themselves. It was, however, fires

Survivors of the San Francisco earthquake look on as the city burns.

that were set by burst gas mains that caused the most damage. The city was in flames for three and a half days.

San Francisco is situated on the San Andreas Fault, which runs from north of the city south to the Baja Peninsula in Mexico. This makes the area one of the most earthquake prone on the globe. California has experienced two recent severe earthquakes: one in 1989 with its epicenter near Santa Cruz measured 7.1 on the Richter Scale; the second centered in San Bernardino measured only 6.0 but caused extensive damage in Los Angeles. ❑

RUSSIA: WAR WITH JAPAN AND UNREST AT HOME

Manchuria and Odessa, 1905

The Russo-Japanese War (1904-1905) was a conflict over the disputed territories of Manchuria and Korea. In the late nineteenth century the Russian expansion eastward with the Trans-Siberian Railway into Vladivostok threatened Japan's own plans to consolidate power in the regions south of this Russian port. Of particular interest to Russia was the creation of a second Far East naval base at Port Arthur.

After leasing Port Arthur from the Chinese in 1897, Russia proceeded to build a railroad to the port through southern Manchuria. This foreign intrusion into Chinese territory resulted in the Boxer Rebellion to which the Russians responded by occupying Manchuria. Japan interpreted this as a prelude to a Russian in-

cursion into Korea, which they were planning to annex. Seeking to avoid a clash, in 1904, Japan proposed a quid pro quo where they would forgo claims on Manchuria in exchange for a similar commitment from Russia vis-à-vis Korea. On February 8, 1904, after Russia's failure to even respond to this peace offering, Japan declared war.

In fact, the war had begun hours before the declaration when the Japanese launched a torpedo attack on the Russian fleet at Port Arthur, sinking two battleships and then mining the harbor. The Battle of Port Arthur, was, in fact, a protracted series of conflicts that ended on January 2, 1905, with a decisive Japanese victory. In retreat, the Russians were defeated again on

March 10 at the Manchurian city of Mukdan.

Their last hope was with the Baltic Fleet, whose arrival in May resulted in the Battle of Tsushima. It was fought on May 27 in the narrow straits separating Korea and Japan, and resulted in the destruction of the entire Russian fleet. With this devastating loss, Russia sued for peace.

Mediated by President Teddy Roosevelt, who won the Nobel Peace Prize for his efforts, Japan and Russia signed the Treaty of Portsmouth on September 5, 1905 in Portsmouth, New Hampshire. Gaining nothing other than an end to hostilities, Russia ceded Manchuria and the southern half of Sakhalin Island to Japan, signed over its 25-year leasehold on Port Arthur and recognized Japan's

hegemony in Korea.

Russia's defeat and the signing of a decidedly "unequal treaty" increased the instability in Nicholas II's administration, which for much of the war had been distracted by the communist led Russian Revolution of 1905. Emblematic of this movement, as well as the general public's dissatisfaction with the failing war effort, was the "Potemkin Mutiny." In June, while on duty in the Black Sea off Odessa, crew members of the battleship *Potemkin* staged a mutiny that they hoped would foment a general rebellion throughout the Russian Navy. Although they failed , the very fact that members of the Russian Navy would take such extreme action was a reflection of spreading discontent. ❑

THE *BLAUE REITER*

Germany, 1911

On December 18 an exhibition was held in the Munich Gallery of Heinrich Thannhauser under the rubric of *Blaue Reiter*. It was organized by two painters, the Russian-born Wassily Kandinsky and the German Franz Marc. It has been commonly supposed that the name of the movement derived from one of Kandinsky's paintings, but in an 1930 interview Kandinsky offered a different explanation: "Franz Marc and I chose this name as we were having coffee…Both of us like blue, Marc for horses, I for riders. So the name came by itself."

Artists associated with the movement offered a wide range of approaches. They included Kubin, Delauney, Braque, Derain and Malevitch among others. The *Blaue Reiter* Year Book of 1913 assembled their diverse works. The onset of World War I brought an end to the movement, but it provided inspiration for subsequent Expressionist painters. ❏

Wassily Kandisky

Wassily Kandisky, *The Blue Rider*, 1903

REVOLUTION IN MEXICO

Mexico, May 25, 1911

Porfirio Diaz, the Mexican president since 1876, was forced to resign, victim of a popular revolution that had been brewing since the previous October, when the liberal reformer Francisco Madero declared him an "illegal" president, and called on the people to overthrow his rule.

From then on Madero and his allies, the guerrilla bands led by Emiliano Zapata and Pancho Villa, advanced steadily towards power. Madero, temporarily exiled to Texas, first demanded an uprising in November of 1910, but few Mexicans responded. The situation changed when on February 14 Madero returned to Mexico to take the head of the guerrilla forces. Softened by years of power, Diaz's Federal troops could put up no real resistance to the uprising.

Aged generals, an ill-disciplined soldiery and an overall lack of strategy all combined to help the rebels. On May 10, the federal commander at Ciudad Juarez, where Madero had launched his first attacks, surrendered. From thereon the revolution gained momentum and the veteran president's support rapidly collapsed.

Diaz accepted a plan whereby he would resign and an interim president, who would immediately hold a general election, would be appointed. As guerrilla troops marched into Mexico City, Diaz was already en route for Paris. ❏

Zapatistas fight for land and liberty. Emiliano Zapata was murdered in 1919.

PEARY REACHES NORTH POLE

The Arctic, April 6, 1909

Robert Edwin Peary (May 6, 1856–February 20, 1920) was the American explorer who is credited with having been the first to reach the North Pole. Although to this day, the claim that he arrived at the Pole's geographically precise location is disputed in some circles, there is no doubt that his many expeditions to Greenland yielded a wealth of information regarding the Arctic, including a comprehensive understanding of the Inuit culture. What he learned from this culture aided his development of the "Peary System" of Arctic travel in which he devised a series of supply depots along various expedition routes.

Between 1886 and 1909, Peary led seven expeditions through Greenland, three of which, in 1893-94, 1905 and 1908-09, were attempts to reach the North Pole. It was on his third attempt that he is believed to have succeeded.

On his expeditions Peary was accompanied by his friend and most trusted fellow explorer, the African-American, Matthew A. Henson. It was with Henson and four Inuit guides that he planted the American flag on April 6, 1909.

On September 6, when Perry announced his achievement, he learned that a former expedition colleague, Dr. Frederick Albert Cook, had already claimed the honor a year earlier. After Cook's photographic "evidence" proved to be fraudulent, the honor was officially extended to Peary by an Act of Congress in 1911. ❏

Robert E. Peary plants the American flag at the North Pole.

REVOLUTION IN CHINA

Beijing, October 30, 1911

With Revolution sweeping across China, a desperate attempt to stem the tide was made by the reactionary but weak ruling Manchu clique headed by the Regent, Prince Chun. On October 11, Chun established a constitutional government and a cabinet of commoners. Acting in the name of his son, the five-year-old Emperor Puyi, the prince summoned his bitterest opponent, General Yuan Shi-kai, to be prime minister.

Yuan had betrayed Chun's reforming brother, the Guangxu emperor, and in revenge Chun had him removed from office in the most insulting manner. Yuan retired to his estates but retained the loyalty of the troops of his well-trained Northern army, who would not move against the rebels without him. But he returned Chun's insult, delaying until he could obtain power on his own terms.

The rebellion, which started prematurely when a store of explosives blew up in Hankou on October 9, forcing the rebels into action, caught everyone by surprise. Dr Sun Yat-sen, the revolutionary leader, was in Denver on a fundraising tour and learned of it from the American newspapers. The explosion enabled the government to arrest some of the rebel leaders, but the uprising took on a momentum of its own, with mutinous troops forcing unwilling officers to lead them.

Fanned by popular discontent, the movement spread rapidly through the western and southern provinces. Then on February 12, 1912 the Manchu dynasty fell after 267 years when the weeping Empress Dowager Longyu, the widow of the Guangxu emperor, read out an edict of abdication on behalf of the boy-emperor, Puyi. The edict designated the strongman General Yuan Shikai as the new ruler of China. The republican leader, Dr. Sun Yat-sen, agreed to step down as president of the republic in favor of Yuan in order to avoid civil war. The arrangement did not bring peace to China. Yuan ruled as a dictator and had himself crowned emperor in 1915. At his death in the following year China returned to a state of conflict between various military leaders. ❏

HENRY FORD'S MODEL T TAKES AMERICA BY STORM

Detroit, 1908

Henry Ford's automobile revolutionized the American way of life. The remarkable popularity of the automobile, led the one-time inventor to launch an entirely new production process that would alter the whole face of car manufacture and meet the ever-expanding demand for new cars.

Ford's Model T, "the motor car for the multitude", appeared in 1908, the product of an "assembly line" using mass-produced precision parts. Its successor, the car that some call the "Tin Lizzie" was put together on a 250-foot-long moving assembly line. Each worker was assigned a specific task and performed it over and over again as car after car rolled slowly by on the line.

With the new system a new chassis could be assembled in just two man-hours, a huge increase over the former schedule of 14 man-hours. It took only three man-hours to produce a complete new car; By his second year of production Ford's factory had turned out 250,000 vehicles. ❏

The Model-T Ford rolls off the assembly line.

WORLD WAR I: A PERIOD OF UPHEAVAL

The 1914-1918 war was the first time that a military conflict had spilled beyond the borders of Europe onto the five continents. The war was fought in the far-flung corners of the world: from Central Europe to the German colonies in Africa, from the Falkland Islands off the coast of Argentina, and from the Indian Ocean to the deserts of Mesopotamia.

There were two power blocs confronting each other. On the one side were the Triple Alliance, signed in 1882, consisting of the German Reich, Austria-Hungary, and Italy (which decided at first to be neutral and then in 1915 moved to the opposite side) as well as the Ottoman Empire and Bulgaria, allies of the Triple Alliance. On the other side were the Triple Entente with Great Britain, France, and Russia, together with their allies, Serbia, Belgium, and Japan, which by the end of the war had been joined by Italy, Portugal, Rumania, Greece, the USA, China, and most of the Latin American countries.

The war plunged the terrified world into a mechanized conflict of annihilation of unimagined size, with battles in which tens of thousands lost their lives, the deployment of new weapons such as tanks and planes, and the use of chemicals such as poison gas. The civilian population was also involved in that food was rationed, women were sent to work in arms factories, and air raids became both frequent and dangerous.

But most significantly, the socio-political structure of the old Europe broke down. The monarchies of the German Reich, of the multi-ethnic Austria-Hungary, and of Russia collapsed, as did the Ottoman empire. Socialist ideas were put into practice for a time in 1917 with the October Revolution in Russia. Germany and the succession states of the Habsburg monarchy made the transition from a monarchy to a democratic-republican form of government. When the USA entered the First World War, the center of gravity in world politics shifted. The United States now became the leading financial and economic power in the world.

In the Far East, Japan emerged from the war stronger than ever and directed its imperialist eye towards China, while the colonies of the European powers began their fight for independence. This was first seen in India, where Mahatma Gandhi led a non-violent opposition that refused to cooperate with the colonial power, thus forcing the seemingly all-powerful Great Britain to give in, albeit only after a second, even bloodier world war.

CAUSES AND COURSE OF WORLD WAR I

The causes of the general enthusiasm for war in August 1914 most probably lie, from a psychological point of view, in the unusually long period of peace. Germany had not fought a war for 40 years, so a brief period of conflict—everybody was convinced that the war would be ended by Christmas—seemed like a welcome distraction from daily grind.

There were a number of conflicting interests and tensions between the European powers, resulting from economic rivalry, the desire to acquire colonial territories, and the growth of nationalism. This included the naval rivalry between Great Britain and the German Reich since 1898; the Moroccan crises of 1905/06 and 1911 caused by tensions between Germany and France; the Bosnian annexation crisis of 1908/09 during the period of Austro-Hungarian expansion in the Balkans; and the two Balkan Wars of 1912 and 1913, which exposed the fast-growing national Slavonic awareness and associated independence movements, as well as the disastrous internal conflicts between the Balkan people themselves.

The tensions between the European powers led to a series of defensive alliances that finally, with the assassination of the Archduke Franz Ferdinand, the Austrian successor to the throne, in Sarajevo on June 18, 1914, and the Austro-Hungarian ultimatum sent to Serbia, started the war almost with the inevitability and certainty of a railway timetable.

REVOLUTIONARY CHANGES

After World War I, the military defeats, the catastrophic food situation, the bitterness caused by dictatorial government, and the example of the Russian Revolution, resulted in widespread revolutionary unrest in Germany

A new dimension in warfare: chemicals were used on a large scale for the first time. British soldiers blinded by a gas attack.

and Austria. In November 1918 this culminated in the fall of the monarchies and the proclamation of a republic. For fear of emulating "conditions in Russia," the social-democrat majority came to agreements with the military and later with middle-class parties. They rejected further revolutionary demands and took Germany on the road to parliamentary democracy.

In 1918/19, communist parties were emerging in almost all European countries. While social-democratic parties became the ruling party in many countries and were committed to policies of reform, communist parties everywhere became increasingly strong under the hegemony of the Communist International (Comintern) that controlled the development of the various national parties with their ever-changing directives.

ECONOMIC AND POLITICAL REALIGNMENT IN EUROPE

The Treaties of Paris (1919-1920), the peace treaties concluded by the Allies with the countries—or rather the succession states—of the Central European powers, left many conflicts unresolved, and these continued in the form of regional disputes. Tensions between the various nationalities dominated the political climate in the states of Czechoslovakia, Hungary, Poland, and Yugoslavia, created after the fall of the Habsburg monarchy. Disputed borders led to armed conflicts between Italians and Slovenes, Poles and Germans, and Armenians and Turks, among others.

The Treaty of Versailles, with its one-sided allocation of war debts, considerable territorial losses, and the high reparations demanded, caused outrage and a feeling of dishonor in Germany. Together with the so-called "stab in the back" by which the German army, "undefeated on the battlefield," was forced to lay down its arms only because of its fickle government, the Treaty of Versailles created reasons for future conflicts at home, while also giving the nationalist movement a new impetus.

The United States rejected the Treaty of Versailles and withdrew from European politics after the war. The country was not a member of the League of Nations, founded in 1920, although the League had been based on the fourteen-point program drawn up by President Woodrow Wilson to prevent war and promote cooperation between nations.

The external politics pursued by the European States were dominated by arguments

The assassination in Sarajevo had grave consequences. After the murder of the Austro-Hungarian successor to the throne and his wife, the Archduchess Sofia, the 19-year old Bosnian nationalist Gavrilo Princip (2nd from right) was immediately arrested. Gavrilo Princip (2nd from right) was immediately arrested.

associated with the reparations demanded from Germany. After Germany defaulted on its reparation payments, open confrontation followed with the occupation of the Ruhr by French troops. The situation was only defused by the Dawes Plan in 1924.

It was only gradually that Germany (having in 1922 surprisingly signed the Treaty of Rapallo with Soviet Russia (a country that had also been cast in the role of pariah), became involved in European politics, after the Treaty of Locarno in 1925 and its admission to the League of Nations in 1926.

Influenced by the high costs of the war, Europe's internal politics were dominated by recurrent economic crises, inflation, and unemployment. Great Britain, France, and Italy were in debt to the USA because of the loans they had taken during the war. At first the temporary solution of the reparations problem in 1924, when American credit was granted to the German Reich, led to a period of prosperity (the Roaring Twenties). The period between 1925 and 1928 was a period of recovery and modest prosperity, financed by credit from the USA and consequently dependent on the economic situation in North America.

THE EMERGENCE OF FASCISM

The crisis situation after the First World War led to a the emergence of Fascist movements in almost all European countries. These were organizations that paid homage to a fuhrer (leader) and pursued extremely nationalistic, anti-liberal, and anti-Marxist objectives, as well as expansionist ones. They advocated a single-party system and tried to secure power through terror. Their support came mainly from the middle classes, the members of which felt that their material existence was threatened by economic crises, inflation, unemployment, the growth of industrialization and monopolies with the resulting threat to small businesses, and the growing importance of the workers' movement.

In the early phases of the movement the Fascist parties adopted an anti-capitalist stance, but they soon formed alliances with industrialists and bankers, as well as with the military and civil rights parties.

The ways in which the Fascist movements in various countries evolved was influenced by the particular conditions in each country. In Germany, for instance, in the absence of a parliamentary democracy, the spread of Nazism was encouraged by the country's military and authoritarian tradition as well as its resentment about the repayment of the war debts. Fascist movements came to power in Italy in 1922, in Germany in 1933, and in Spain in 1936. ❑

RACE TO THE SOUTH POLE

Antarctica, December 14, 1911

The attempt to reach the South Pole became a dramatic race between an English party led by Robert Falcon Scott and the Norwegian expedition of Roald Amundsen. The parties were in communication with each other and wished the other well, but each was determined to claim the honor of the discovery. Amundsen and his four companions were the first to get there. Their British rivals arrived a month later; the trip back cost them their lives.

Amundsen set out from the Bay of Whales off the Ross Ice Shelf on October 20, 1911 with 52 sled dogs for the 600 mile journey across the ice. He had previously prepared ten depots with provisions along the route. The use of dogs from Greenland proved to be a great help. The dogs were able to complete the trip on light rations.

As Amundsen was running across the ice Scott and his party had set out from Cape Evans about 60 miles from Amundsen's base camp in the Bay of Whales. Scott began his trip on October 24 and reached the Pole a month after Amundsen. Upon his arrival he found the Norwegian flag Amundsen had planted along with a letter to him. Scott's disappointment was great. Scott's journals tell the dramatic story of their ill-fated return trip. His last entry was date March 29, 1912. His final words: "Every day we have been ready to start for our depot 11 miles away. I do not think we can hope for any better things now. We shall stick it out to the end, but we are getting weaker, of course, and the end cannot be far. It seems a pity, but I don't think I can write any more. Last entry. For God's sake look after our people." Six

Roald Amundsen is the first to reach the South Pole. The picture shows a member of his team, Oscar Wisting, with their sled dogs under the Norwegian flag.

months later a search party found the bodies of Scott and two of his companions along with the journals from expedition. ❑

THE *TITANIC* GOES DOWN

April 15, 1912

On its maiden voyage the British luxury liner *Titanic* struck an iceberg off the coast of Newfoundland and sunk. The disaster cost 1530 people their lives.

The ship was 882 feet long and weighed 46, 329 tons. It was built for the White Star line by Harland and Wolff of Belfast. It was the largest ship ever built and was billed as the most luxuriously appointed. A crew of 898 saw to the needs of 730 first-class, 560 second-class and 1200 third-class passengers. With a double hull and 16 doors that ran vertically through the ship dividing it into compartments, it was thought to be unsinkable.

The *Titanic* set out from Southampton on April 10, 1912 under the command of Edward John Smith. There was no thought of catastrophe as it steamed toward its destination of New York at a speed of 22 knots.

At 11:40 P.M. it collided with an iceberg. The lookout's telescope was missing and the iceberg was discovered too late. The stern of the ship was compromised and water poured in.

The ship builder, Thomas Andrews, who was on board at the time, immediately saw that the ship was going to sink. The doors couldn't hold the water out, which flowed from one compartment to the next and dragged the bows down.

For the 2206 people on board there were 20 lifeboats with room for only 1178, 200 places more than the security regulations required. Surviving were 315 men — despite the call for women and children first — 336 women and 52 children.

The CQD signal ("Come quick danger") as well as the newly adopted SOS were sent to the SS *California*, which was only 20 miles

Sinking of The *Titanic*

away. Unfortunately its radio tower was unmanned. When at 4:10 the first lifeboats were picked up by another vessel, the *Carpathia*, the *Titanic* had already broken up into two pieces and sunk. ❑

ASSASSINATION IN SARAJEVO

Bosnia-Herzegovina, June 28, 1914

In June of 1914 Archduke Franz Ferdinand, the heir to the Austro-Hungarian Empire, in his capacity as Inspector General of the Austrian Army was visiting the province of Bosnia-Herzegovina to observe the Austrian Army conduct maneuvers. Protocol demanded that he visit the Mayor of Sarajevo, although the Austrian authorities were concerned about the activities of the Serbian nationalists and their desire to include Bosnia-Herzegovina into Serbia proper. Counterintuitively Ferdinand became a target of the nationalists because of his liberal views toward Slav members of the Empire, whom he believed should enjoy equal rights. The nationalists feared that concessions would appease the Slavs, and they would not rise up in general insurrection in support of the union they desired.

On June 28 accompanied by his wife, Sophie Duchess of Hohenburg, Ferdinand drove through the sun-baked streets of Sarajevo toward City Hall; suddenly a bomb was thrown at them from the crowd by Nedjelko Cabrinovic. The Duke was able to deflect the missile away from his own car; however it exploded close to the one following, severely wounding personnel of the Duke's staff.

After his lunch at City Hall, unaware that Cabrinovic was just one of five would be assassins, Ferdinand insisted on visiting the injured members of his party. His car took a wrong turn, and it slowed to a stop five feet away from Gavril Princip who stepped forward pulling a revolver from his pocket. He fired once at Ferdinand and once at Sophie as

The Archduke Ferdinand, heir to the throne of the Austro-Hungarian Empire, shortly before his assassination

she threw herself across her husband's body: within ten minutes both were dead.

Bismarck's prediction that, "war in Europe will be over some damn foolish thing in the Balkans," had proved remarkably prescient. ❏

BALKAN WAR ENDED

Bucharest, August 10, 1913

After their defeating the Ottoman Empire, the four Balkan allies, Bulgaria, Serbia, Greece and Montenegro, quarreled among themselves over Macedonia. Their brief war, in which Bulgaria was pitted against the others, came to an end on August 10, 1913 with the signing of the Treaty of Bucharest.

Opposed to Macedonia becoming an independent state, (Albania) Serbia and Greece, began its occupation, which in turn prompted a Bulgarian invasion. The treaty ceded territory claimed by Bulgaria in Macedonia and Thrace to Serbia and Greece. Serbia and Montenegro were doubled in size and Romania, whose attack on Bulgaria ended the war, acquired Bulgarian territory.

In retrospect the unrest in the Balkans is seen as the prelude to the conflict that was about to engulf all of Europe.❏

King Ferdinand I of Bulgaria

OUTBREAK OF WAR

Great Britain, August 4, 1914

When the Archduke Ferdinand was assassinated in Sarajevo the Austrians accused the Serbian Government of being implicated. Confidant of support from their German allies, the Austrians issued ultimatums to the Serbs. The Serbs were allied with the Russians, but neither Germany nor Austria thought that Russia would go to war over Serbia.

Austria, with German backing, declared war on Serbia on July 28, 1914, and Russia immediately mobilized and called upon France, its ally, to do the same, which it did.

On August 1 Germany declared war on Russia. As the enormity of the situation became apparent, efforts were made to halt the progress of events. However key figures were unavailable to intervene; Kaiser Wilhelm was on a yachting holiday, the French President was on a state visit to Russia and the German Army commander, General von Moltke, was vacationing at a foreign spa.

On the August 3 Germany declared war on France and implemented the Schleiffen plan, which entailed outflanking the French Army by moving troops through Belgium, whose neutrality was guaranteed by Britain. The British Foreign Secretary, Sir Edward Grey, issued an ultimatum to the German Embassy, which was ignored.

On the August 4, Britain declared war on Germany. The British public met the news with enthusiasm and anti-German feelings ran high; the public had for a long time viewed the build up of the German navy as a threat to England's naval supremacy; German colonial ambitions in Africa were also observed with suspicion. However Britain had the smallest army in Europe and was the only country not to employ the practice of conscription. But the eagerness for war and the certainty that it would "all be over by Christmas," sent thousands of volunteers from all over the country and empire to the recruiting sergeants.

A more prescient view was expressed by Sir Edward Grey. "The lights are going out all over Europe; we shall not see them lit again in our lifetime." ❏

OPENING GAMBITS

Europe, 1914

The Russians took the offensive in the east, marching two armies into Prussia under the commands of Generals Alexander Samsonov and Pavel Rennenkampf, but because the railway gauge was different in Germany they encountered supply difficulties. The Germans, commanded by Erich Ludendorff and Paul von Hindenburg, taking advantage of the animosity between the Russian Generals, were able to surround Samsonov's second army at Tannenberg, taking him unawares. The Russians were destroyed by the superior munitions and infantry tactics of the Germans and lack of support from Rennenkampf. Russian losses were almost total in dead and prisoners taken. In September 1914 the Germans inflicted another defeat on the Russians at Masurian Lakes and although the army was able to retreat, 100,000 men were taken prisoner.

In the west the Schlieffen plan had not been as successful as the Germans had hoped, owing to the determined resistance of the Belgian Army, supported by two divisions of Marines sent by Winston Churchill, the First Sea Lord. The Belgians led by their king, Albert, fell back on Antwerp and while they had to sur-

render the port, they were able to retreat into France to continue the fight.

The British Expeditionary Force (BEF) under General French, was attempting to link up with the French army, when it came into contact with the Germans, under von Kluck, on August 24. The BEF, unaware that the French had already retreated from the Ardennes to the Marne and that the enemy heavily outnumbered them in men and guns, chose

German troops march into Brussels

to engage the Germans. The attacking Germans were surprised by the rapid fire from the British riflemen and believed them to be armed with machine guns: however although they suffered heavy losses they forced the British to retreat to Ypres. Desperate fighting ensued, but eventually the British were able to prevent a German breakthrough to the sea.

The Russians declared war on Turkey on November 2, in retaliation for aid given by the

Turks to the Germans in a naval bombardment of Russia: England and France, in support, declared war on November 5. England declared Egypt, which had been until that time part of the Ottoman Empire, a protectorate.

Colonel von Letto Vorbeck with a force of three thousand German troops and eleven thousand Asgaris began a guerrilla campaign against British and South African troops in East Africa that he would conduct successfully until the end of the war.

The German China Fleet commanded by Admiral Maximilian von Spee was attempting to sail back to Germany when it encountered Sir Christopher Cradock's fleet of aging battle cruisers off the Chilean coast at Corenel. Unwisely Craddock decided to engage the enemy, resulting in the first British naval defeat in a hundred years. Craddock, his ship the *Monmouth* and the battle cruiser *Good Hope* were lost. Spee continued on his voyage home, but then he too made an imprudent decision. He resolved to destroy the naval installations on the Falkland Islands and deviated from his course. He was surprised to find a British squadron at Port Stanley, commanded by Sir Frederick Sturdee. Sturdee was able to sink the *Schnarnhorst*, the *Gneissenau* and the *Nurnberg* and their supply ships; the *Dresden's* crew scuttled her to avoid capture.

By Christmas 1914 the trenches on the Western Front stretched for 440 miles from the North Sea to Switzerland and the soldiers of both sides wondered if they might be home for next Christmas. ❑

German troops in the trenches before Verdun

French soldiers preparing for a gas attack

FIGHTING TO A STANDSTILL

Europe, 1915–1916

The first Zeppelins appeared over London in December 1914, alarming the public, as the shelling of coastal towns by the German Navy in November had made them well aware that Germany was prepared to carry the war to England. At the beginning of the war airplanes were used only for reconnaissance purposes, but the more aggressive pilots began to take pot shots at each other with pistols and shotguns and also dropped handmade bombs on the infantry below. The public's fear was validated when Zeppelin raids on London were stepped up in April 1915. Technical improvements in aircraft design intensified the war in the air as the conflict progressed.

In February 1915 the Russians were being pressed by the Turks, and to relieve them the British mounted a naval attack on Turkish forts in the Dardanelles. The British devised a plan to attack the Gallipoli Peninsula with Constantinople as their objective, thus knocking the Turks out of the war and opening a third front for the Germans to defend; forcing them to withdraw troops from the Western Front. Unfortunately the plan failed through bad planning and general ineptitude; the British had made their intentions clear to the Turks and given them time to fortify and reinforce their defenses, and the British invasion in April met fierce opposition and was unable to make any significant advance. By November the British conceded defeat and withdrew, with a loss of about 220,000 men.

In 1915 at the Battle of Ypres, the Germans introduced a new horror to the misery of trench warfare, chlorine gas that choked and blinded the defenders allowing the Germans to make a four-mile gap in the defenses. In May of the same year the Germans had sunk the passenger liner "Lusitania" with the loss of 1,400 lives. These two acts combined to turn American public opinion against the Germans. In the meantime, German forces under the command of Generals Paul von Hindenburg and Erich Ludendorff were continuing to have successes against the Russians in Poland and against the Serbs in the Balkans.

In 1916 the German Fleet put to sea and from May 30 until June 1 engaged the British fleet off Jutland, 240 ships taking part in a battle that proved to be inconclusive. Both sides claimed victory: the Germans because they sank more British capital ships and the British because they forced the Germans back into port, where they remained for the rest of the war.

Hindenburg, Kaiser Wilhelm II, and Ludendorff .

In February 1916 General Erich von Falkenhayn launched his assault on the French at Verdun. Falkenhayn was convinced that the war could only be won on the Western Front and to that end he conceived a strategy that would entail the French committing more and more men to the defense of Verdun, thereby creating a battle of attrition. As the battle wore on the men came to call it the "meat grinder."

By the summer the French were desperate for relief and called on the British to start their offensive. On the morning of July 1, 1916, on a fifteen-mile front, nine divisions of British infantry, made up mostly of Kitchener's volunteers, went over the top. The British had done little to conceal their plans and after the week-long barrage was lifted, the Germans came out of their deep dugouts, set up their machine guns and slaughtered the oncoming infantry. On the first day the British suffered 60,000 casualties. The Battle of the Somme became a British byword for catastrophe. ❑

COMPLETION OF THE PANAMA CANAL

Panama, August 15, 1914

The Isthmus of Panama, in which a mere 48 miles separated the Atlantic and the Pacific, was an obvious candidate for a canal. In 1855 a railway had been built linking the two coasts. This, combined with success of the Suez Canal, hastened plans for its construction. In 1880 the man who engineered the Suez Canal, Ferdinand de Lesseps began work with French backing. But Panama was not a sea-level Suez and de Lesseps had not reckoned with having to build locks. A combination of extravagance on a grand scale and shady financiers linked to shadier politicians led to bankruptcy in 1889. The French plan was abandoned in 1893 af-

ter 22,000 workers had died from malaria and yellow fever.

In 1904 Teddy Roosevelt took up the cause. For his help in helping Panama gain its independence from Colombia, the U.S. was given control of the Canal Zone. But it wasn't until 1914 that the canal was completed and open to ship traffic. By that time disease had taken a further toll of over 5,000 men. In 1977 U.S. President Jimmy Carter agreed to turn the Canal back to Panama starting in 1999, which gained possession of it on December 31, 1999. ❑

The Panama Canal connects the Pacific and Atlantic with a series of locks.

THE RUSSIAN REVOLUTION

St. Petersburg, October 24–25, 1917

The Russian Revolutions of 1917 were two cataclysmic events which changed Russian and world history. The first was the February Revolution (February 23–27) which resulted in the overthrow of the three-hundred year old Romanov tsarist monarchy, and the installation of a moderate socialist Provisional government. The second was the October Revolution (October 24–25), which resulted in the rise to power of a Bolshevik (Communist) government, that became the Union of Soviet Socialist Republics (USSR).

Early twentieth century Russia was an extremely polarized society. Tsar Nicholas II's insistence on maintaining a near-feudal social structure had concentrated power in the hands of members of the royal family, nobles and business owners. The majority of Russians were landless peasants who lived in grinding poverty. In addition, as Russia made halting attempts to enter the Industrial Age, it created a new class of urban workers whose poor working and living conditions caused them to become increasingly angry at the tsarist regime and with its perceived representatives, the industry owners.

This widespread sense of alienation from Nicholas II's reign was pushed to the breaking point by Russia's entry into World War I. The devastation it wrought on the already weak Russian economy and the tsar's use of conscription proved to be the downfall of his regime.

In the late nineteenth century anti-tsarist groups had begun to form in Russia. A number of these groups came to embrace socialist philosophies, especially those promulgated by Karl Marx. As early as 1898, Russian Marxists had formed the Social Democratic Labor Party. It consisted of two factions, the radical Bolsheviks and the more moderate Mensheviks, both of whom

would be crucial to the events of 1917. As conditions worsened in Russia, these radical groups attracted members from all levels of Russian society.

A major precursor to the Revolutions of 1917 took place in St. Petersburg in 1905. Known as the Revolution of 1905, it started as a peaceful labor demonstration and ended with the "Bloody Sunday Massacre," when hundreds of demonstrators were gunned down by tsarist troops. This event occasioned nation-wide strikes and radicalized the Russian populace. It also inspired the creation of the workers "soviets," the democratic councils that would ultimately rise to power during the October Revolution.

By 1917 Russia's failing war effort led to decisive action by not only members of the moderate *Duma* (parliament) and those of the radical soviet factions, but also ordinary citizens. On February 23, 1917, "International

Vladimir I. Lenin speaking in Red Square on the first anniversary of the Russian Revolution

Women's Day," hundreds of women in St. Petersburg took to the streets. Soon joined by male workers, for four days over 385,000 citizens battled government troops, many of whom came over to the workers side. By February 28, the loyalist troops had surrendered and the tsar was forced to abdicate his throne. The monarchy overthrown, the February Revolution's Provisional Government took control of Russia.

This control proved to be ephemeral. The Provisional Government was made up of liberal and moderate socialist members of the *Duma*. Espousing

pro-capitalist democratic reform, it had little real connection to the workers' movement, which was represented in the new government by the more radical soviets. When the government moderates failed to address workers' grievances and insist on Russia's disengagement from the war, the soviet members rallied around the Marxist, worker-state, anti-war platform of the Bolsheviks. Two events occurred that resulted in the end of the Provisional Government and the rise of the Bolsheviks to power. One was the return from exile of the Bolshevik leader Vladimir Lenin; the other was the "Kornilov Affair."

Lenin's return in April came at a time when the Russian populace was becoming increasingly dissatisfied with the moderate policies of the Provisional Government.

The Storming of the Winter Palace

The Tsar and his family: Olga, Tsar Nicholas II, Anastasia, Alexei, Tatiana, Tsarina Alexandra, and Maria (left to right). Photo from 1907. They were all killed by the Bolsheviks on July 16, 1918.

THE UNITED STATES ENTERS THE WAR

Washington DC, April 6, 1917

Hailed as a conquering hero by members of the soviets, Lenin bided his time, waiting for the moderates to self-destruct. They did so in July when the Provisional Government's leader, Alexander Kerensky, attempted to purge the Bolsheviks from power by calling in support from troops led by General Lavr Kornilov. When Kornilov double-crossed Kerensky and attempted a military coup, it was the "Red Guard" of the Bolsheviks who defeated him. Kerensky's association with Kornilov severely damaged the Provisional Government's ability to rule. Lenin and the Bolsheviks became Russia's de facto leaders.

On October 10, Lenin and the Bolshevik party members called for the overthrow of the Provisional Government. The October Revolution, also known as the Bolshevik Revolution, took place in St. Petersburg on October 24 and 25. The Red Guard's near-bloodless coup ended with the storming of the Provisional Government's headquarters, the Winter Palace. On the night of October 25, Lenin, the soon-to-be head of the new Soviet Government, declared, "Long live the world socialist revolution!" ❑

Abandoning the Sussex Pledge, an agreement whereby U-boat commanders warned merchant vessels that they were about to be torpedoed and allowed the crews to take to the lifeboats, Germany resumed unrestricted submarine warfare in early 1917. What alarmed Woodrow Wilson, the American President, was that the policy was to be directed against neutral as well as allied shipping, if they were suspected of supplying the allies. In response he assigned US naval personnel to American merchant ships, declaring that the German course of action was piracy.

Throughout the month of March U-boats sank almost a million tons of shipping, including American merchantmen; but this was not enough to bring America into the war. The British had, however, broken the German code and were in possession of the "Zimmerman Telegram" which made clear that Germany was inciting Mexico to war against America. It was this information which turned American public opinion in favor of war and on April 6, 1917 America declared war on Germany. This news was greeted with enthusiasm on the part of the Allies, but the American Army at the time was small and unprepared for modern warfare; it would be at least a year before American troops could land in any force in Europe.

In the meantime the French and English mounted an attack at Passenschendale, or the third Battle of Ypres; however the French troops, exhausted from their exertions at Verdun, either mutinied or refused to go on the offensive. The heaviest rainfall in thirty years, combined with the intense shelling of the drainage systems turned the ground into a quagmire that swallowed men and horses and through which the British infantry was, after five months of fighting and at the cost of 350,00 casualties, able to make less than five miles of ground.

Taking what he considered a last chance of victory in the west, Ludendorff mounted a massive assault in late March 1918. On the first day gains of almost 40 miles of ground created a huge salient. But the British and French held with American assistance, and in July the German attack came to a halt.

In the summer of 1918 the allied command thought that the war would continue into 1919. However, in an attempt to straighten out their line, they counter attacked the Germans at Amiens. By abandoning the usual tactic of a preliminary bombardment in favor of a creeping barrage they managed to surprise the Germans. Using 400 tanks supported by British, Commonwealth and French infantry and air cover, they pushed the Germans back to their March positions. Ludendorff called it the "the blackest day of the German Army". It was a comment directed more at the collapsing morale of his army, which had in some cases surrendered in large numbers to smaller forces, than at the gains made by the allies.

The allies kept the initiative and by September the war had at last broken out from the trenches. In September, the American army was being used in force all along the front and by mid October the allies had retaken nearly all of German occupied France and Belgium. In the east T.E. Lawrence and Emir Faisal had taken Damascus with an Arab army and Turkey surrendered on October 30. In early November the allies had pushed the Germans back beyond the Hindenburg Line, and the Kaiser was forced to abdicate. ❑

France: May 20, 1918. US troops advance during a gas attack.

Above: US President Woodrow Wilson
Right: The passenger ship *Lusitania* was sunk by a German U-boat

THE OCTOBER REVOLUTION AND COMMUNISM

The October Revolution marked the conclusion of a revolutionary process that had started in the 1880s. Many representatives of the state lost their lives at the hands of revolutionary groups, including Tsar Alexander II (1881). Political reformers were targeted by the Tsarist police. It was not until 1898 that the Russian Social Democratic Labor Party (RDSLP) was formed (illegally) in Russia.

Although the number of factory workers increased 1.4 to 2.4 million between 1890 and 1900, the vast majority of the 126 million Russians were still agricultural workers, tied to the land. Revolution in Russia seemed an impossibility. The conditions stipulated by Marx and Engels as its prerequisites were missing. Capitalism did not play an important part, and industrial workers did not represent a large proportion of the population.

Yet, it was in Russia that the first revolution of the twentieth century in Europe took place: in 1905, a major strike provoked massive military intervention. Three years earlier, Lenin suggested in his book *What is to be done?* (1902) that for revolution to take hold, a party of determined professional revolutionaries was required. This approach divided the RDSLP (Russia's socialist party) at the party conference in London in 1903. The Bolsheviks (the majority) followed Lenin's line, while the others, the Menschenik (minority), wanted a party open to all.

THE BOLSHEVIKS IN POWER

Over the course of World War I, Russia's situation had gradually worsened after some initial successes. Military failures and dissatisfaction with the regime of Nicolas II resulted in the general strike of March 1917 in the capital Petrograd (St. Petersburg), in which the garrison later also took part. After the abdication of the Tsar, Russia was governed by two ruling bodies: that of the civilian government, and that of the workers' and peasants' representative councils (soviets). The Bolsheviks gained considerable influence in the soviets.

In his *April Theses*, Lenin urged the people to fight the government and to give power to the soviets. During the October Revolution, the Bolsheviks succeeded in toppling the government and setting up the Council of People's Commissars, led by Lenin.

The new government found itself in a difficult situation. Russia was at war with the Central European powers, and the generals loyal to the tsar were organizing themselves for a counter strike. By early 1918 Lenin withdrew Russia from the war and began to institute a policy of major land redistribution.

The struggles against Western troops (March 1918 to October 1919) and of the "Red" army against the "White" generals (1918-1920), together with the hasty socialist measures of "war communism," led to a central planned economy, whose initial effect was widespread famine, and near economic ruin. It wasn't until 1927 that industry managed to return to pre-war levels as a result of the "New Economic Policy" launched in March 1921. Meanwhile it had become obvious that the Bolshevik claim to leadership could not be guaranteed either through parliamentary democracy or by transferring power to the workers' and peasants' councils. The uprising of the Kronstadt sailors in March 1921 against the economic misery and domination by the party was violently put down, leading to a hardening of positions. Any opposition to the "general line" was now condemned as "fractionalism." As early as 1921 the party experienced its first purge, with the result that a quarter of its members were excluded.

After Lenin's death in 1924, the fight for his successor began. Finally Joseph Stalin emerged on top. Stalin was absolutely ruthless in pursuing his goal of transforming agrarian Russia into

May Day parade in Red Square in 1988, with a huge banner of Karl Marx, Friedrich Engels, and Vladimir Ilyich Lenin an industrialized power. His policies led to millions of deaths through starvation and other deprivations. This was combined with an absolute intolerance of dissent and the establishment of a terrifying internal security apparatus (the OGPU, forerunner of the KGB). He drove Leon D. Trotsky, the successful leader of the Red Army in the civil war, into exile in 1927, and during the 1930s paraded prominent Party figures in show trials that inevitably ended in confession and death. Hundreds of thousands of people were executed or sent to forced labor camps to die, in what has become known as the Great Terror.

SPECIAL COMMUNIST DEVELOPMENTS

Stalin died in March 1953. In 1956, the twentieth Party Congress turned into a trial of Stalinism: in his "secret speech," the general-secretary Nikita Khrushchev denounced Stalin as a cruel despot, condemning his personality cult and regime of terror. In 1961 the twenty-second Party Congress adopted a twenty-year plan for developing communism. Its goal was to overtake capitalist countries economically and have laid the foundation for the development of communism elsewhere: to create a social structure under which the principle of "to each according to his needs" could be implemented. These goals were never achieved.

Other socialist states challenged the leadership role of the Communist Party of the Soviet Union. The ideological divisions in the international communist movement clearly manifested themselves at the Berlin Conference of the communist and socialist parties in June 1971; the divisions between Soviet communism, the Yugoslav and Chinese systems, and Eurocommunism, were too great to be bridged.

Yugoslavia had freed itself from German occupation without outside help and claimed the right to develop its own independent form of socialism. Its leader, Josip Broz Tito, opposed what he saw as the degeneracy of Stalinism. In 1950, he introduced the "workers' self-administration," an economic model that was designed to rein in centralizing bureaucratic tendencies from developing.

Tito considered the task of the socialist state to be the attainment of social progress and the support of economic development. Eleven years after Tito's death (1980), the multi-ethnic country was the victim of its own internal conflicts. Through a number of bloody civil wars, the unified Slavic nation, dissolved into its constituent elements; Slovenia, Croatia, Bosnia-Herzegovina, and Macedonia all broke away from Serbian Belgrade.

THE CHINESE COURSE

The policies of the Chinese Communist Party, founded in 1921, were dictated by China's economic backwardness. In contrast to Russia, the revolution in China was not a coup organized by the intelligentsia, but the result of a mass peasant movement. As early as 1927, Mao Zedong had realized that only a strategy of peasant liberation could bring about a revolutionary change in society.

The "great leap forward" of 1958–1959, which was intended to lead to a spectacular increase in the country's industrial production, was a dismal failure and paved the way for a complete break with the Moscow. Mao's Cultural Revolution (1966–1969) had the ostensible aim of overcoming the divide between bureaucrats, the intelligentsia, and the people. In fact, it was a ploy to consolidate Mao's power and resulted in staggering social dislocation and misery.

The power struggle after Mao's death (1976) was finally won by Deng Xiaoping. The economic reforms initiated by him and continued by his successors were shaped by the rejection of a centrally planned economy, the decentralization of economic power, and the dissolution of agricultural collectives. Deng was also jointly responsible for the massacre in Tiananmen Square on June 4, 1989, when the army cracked down on protesters demonstrating in favor of democratic reform. He died in 1997.

EUROCOMMUNISM

The term "Eurocommunism" was coined in 1975 and refers to the theoretical self-image and political program of communist parties in Western Europe—in particular Italy, France and Spain—that promote a pluralistic model of socialism. These parties do not form a unified bloc, but nevertheless there are agreements over some fundamental points. The Eurocommunists are in favor of an independent foreign policy and unanimously condemned the invasion of Czechoslovakia in 1968 by the troops of the Warsaw Pact. They believe that socialist economic politics should be achieved first and foremost by controlling key industries and applying democratic planning. The Eurocommunists rejected the slogan "Dictatorship of the proletariat." In 1973 the communist party in Italy launched the slogan of "historical compromise," espousing cooperation with all democratic parties, especially the Christian Democrats, and the French communists formed a coalition government with the socialists in 1981. When the Soviet Union ended in 1991, world communism gradually disintegrated.

THE END OF THE COMMUNIST PARTY OF THE SOVIET UNION

Until 1989 the international political landscape was the direct result of the arrangements made by the Allied Powers at the end of World War II: two nuclear superpowers facing off in a Cold War. The economic pressures of a continuing arms race and military confrontations proved too much for the Soviet system in the long run. The election of Mikhail Gorbachev as general secretary of the Communist Party of the Soviet Union in March of 1985 triggered a political reform movement with the slogans *perestroika* (reorganization) and *glasnost* (a policy of openness and transparency). This led first to liberalization in the Soviet Union and then eroded the supremacy of the communist parties in all the countries of the Warsaw Pact. This was followed by the fall of the Berlin Wall in 1989, the end of the German Democratic Republic, and finally by the dissolution of the Soviet Union on December 25, 1991.

The political changes in Eastern Europe were also a consequence of failed economic policies. Socialist centrally planned economies had lost the competition with the capitalist industrial countries. This marked the end of state socialism. ❏

Soviet propaganda after the October Revolution: the Red Army calls for volunteers.

ARMISTICE SIGNED

Compiègne, November 11, 1918

The signing of the armistice between Germany and the Allied commanders as well as surrender of Austria-Hungary signaled the defeat of the Central Powers.

The armistice was signed in a railway car in the Compiègne Forest. The conditions as set down by Marshal Foch, the head of the armistice commission with Matthias Erzberger had the character of an ultimatum. Their intent was to see to it that it would be impossible for Germany to start another war.

With an offensive launched in March codenamed "Michael" Germany broke through between Cambrai and Saint-Quentin. They had hoped to gain a quick knockout punch before the arriving U.S. troops could be fully engaged. The offensive,

which included 59 divisions, saw early successes, but by early April it had come to a standstill. The German line was broken on August 8. The allied attack supported by tanks and air support routed the defenders. In the following weeks the German army was relentlessly pursued. The German army's supreme command demanded that then Chancellor Prince Max von Baden approach President Woodrow Wilson with a proposal to negotiate based upon the 14 Points he had announced in January 1918. But there was no mention of that in the negotiations between Foch and Erzberger.

Germany had to agree to surrender the greater part of its armaments and withdraw from territory it had conquered along with

the German-speaking areas on the western side of the Rhine. In addition there was to be a demilitarized zone that would extend some 20 miles east of the Rhine into Germany. In addition the German fleet was to be disbanded or put into Allied hands, and the naval blockade would remain in effect until a final treaty was signed.

Erzberger, a civilian who had called for negotiations to end the war as early as 1917, was chosen by Paul von Hindenburg as a more conciliating representative than a member of the German general staff. Despite his wish to continue negotiations von Hindenburg ordered him to sign the agreement. With Germany in revolt, the Kaiser had abdicated the throne two days before, the army supreme command realized that

British soldier and German captive

there was no point in delaying the inevitable.

The conditions of the armistice lasted until the signing of the Treaty of Versailles in 1919. ❑

REVOLUTION IN GERMANY

Berlin, November 9, 1918

Once the certainty of Germany's defeat became clear, the Kaiser and his government was driven out of power. At noon on November 9, the German Chancellor ,Prince Max von Baden, acting on his own authority, announced the abdication of Kaiser Wilhelm II. Initially the monarch had clung to the hope that he would be able to hold onto the Prussian crown, but his position was utterly untenable. By November 10, he was in exile in the Netherlands.

Rosa Luxembourg

Karl Liebknecht

The events of November had unfolded in a dramatic fashion. At approximately one PM, Prince Max von Baden announced that Friedrich Ebert, the leader of the Majority Social Democrats Party (MSDP) had become the new German Chancellor, and then he himself stepped down.

An hour later, Ebert's political ally Philipp Scheidemann proclaimed the establishment of a parliamentary republic from the balcony of the Reichstag. At around four PM, Karl Liebknecht proclaimed the birth of the German Socialist Republic. The Spartacist League (*Spartakusbund*) led by Liebknecht and Rosa Luxemburg, together with the so-called revolutionary coordinators working in factories, originally had planned to launch their rebellion on November 11.

That the Republic was proclaimed twice in the same day was clear evidence of the conflicts inherent in the November Revolution and the different goals of the major parties. The MSPD sought to save Germany

Revolutionary soldiers and sailors seize power in Hamburg on November 5th.

from civil war and famine, and to prevent any further radicalization. It therefore worked together with the Kaiser's administration and the old military apparatus.

The Spartacist League, called for a Democratic Coun-

cil based on the Russian model. The starting point for the revolution was the naval uprising in Kiel, which took place at the beginning of Novmber. Certain the war was lost, the sailors refused to follow a senseless order to head out to the English

US Emerges as World Power – Europe is Reshaped

Point of Interest

British tank near Cambrai

The destruction of old Europe and entrance of the US as a major

Channel and engage the British navy. In no time workers and soldier-councils throughout Germany had seized power for themselves.

The councils regarded themselves as distinct from the political parties and unions. As independent organizations, which had arisen spontaneously, they did not have a plan for political reorganization, but the majority allied themselves with the MSPD or USPD coalitions.

Over the next two months the Ebert-Scheidemann government gained the upper hand and led Germany in the election of the first national assembly on January 1, 1919, thereby paving the way for a parliamentary democracy.

The Spartacist Uprising of January 5 was unable to change this course. It was quickly suppressed and on January 15, 1919, soldiers assassinated the movement's leaders, Luxemburg and Liebkecht. ❑

international power was the result of four years of murderous war. The war's terrible toll upended the political configuration of Europe. Germany lost its status as a great power; its Kaiser went into exile and a republic was formed under a socialist president. The Austro-Hungarian Empire broke apart into new national states that jostled for advantage. Russia was undergoing a transformational change, and the nominal victors, France and England, emerged diminished, with the greater part of an entire generation either dead, wounded or demoralized. This decline weakened their hold on their colonial possessions as well. The political and economic

advantage shifted to the United States.

The map of Europe was dramatically reconfigured. Germany lost control over Alsace and Lorraine as well as North Schleswig, Posen and a part of West Prussia. The Habsburg Empire ceased to exist. Hungary and Czechoslovakia became independent. Serbia joined with Croatia and Slovenia to form an independent nation (from 1929 Yugoslavia).

The German-speaking Austrian heartland, which was forbidden from joining together with Germany, declared itself a republic one day after Germany signed the armistice agreement. Its first Chancellor was the social democrat Karl Renner. The Habsburg Emperor, Karl I, gave up his crown, ending a dynasty that had endured for six hundred years.

Karl also had to abdicate as King of Hungary. It became a republic on November 16, 1918. Three years later Karl tried unsuccessfully to regain the throne. Forced into exile, he died in the following year.

The Baltic lands of Finland, Estonia, Latvia and Lithuania had all previously been part of Russia. They now became independent states. German and Austrian troops that had been occupying Poland withdrew, and it once more was freed from foreign control.

The Ottoman Empire was in

its death throes and lost its little remaining influence on the European continent.

The real winners of World War I were The US and Japan. They had been at a disadvantage on account of the complex system of alliances and imperialist domination that had characterized pre-war Europe. The center of economic power moved from Great Britain to the United States. As Europe was squandering its treasure and blood the US benefited from the expansion of its markets and its emergence as the world's chief exporter.

The evolving technology of warfare with armored vehicles, air power and lethal artillery had turned France and Belgium into killing fields. The death toll of the war amounted to eight and a half million with over twenty million wounded. Millions were interned as prisoners of war, and in the war's aftermath millions more died from hunger, civil disorders and the terrible Spanish flu pandemic, which ravaged Europe's weakened population.

The war also created a spiritual vacuum on the continent giving rise to what became known as the "lost generation." It shattered cherished notions of the civilization and progress. In comparison the United States sustained relatively few losses. The ensuing decade was to be one of prosperity and a new self-confidence. ❑

The last Austro-Hungarian Emperor, Karl I, and family

Kaiser Wilhelm and family in exile.

GERMAN REACTION TO THE TREATY OF VERSAILLES

Versailles, January 10, 1920

The Treaty of Versailles dictated the final conditions for the end of World War I. It was signed on June 28, 1919 and came into effect on January 10 of the following year.

The terms of the treaty fueled rage in Germany and a deep sense of shame; it set the tone of political discourse for years to come

[map: Germany with regions labeled Dänemark, Danzig, Ostpreußen, Hamburg, Westpreußen, Niederlande, Berlin, Posen, Belgien, Preußen, Polen, Thüringen, Sachsen, Schlesien, Lux., Frankreich, Elsass, Württemberg, Bayern, München, Baden. Legend: Grenzen des Deutschen Reichs vor 1914 / nach 1918; abgetretene Gebiete; Abstimmungsgebiete, die beim Dt. Reich bleiben; Gebiete unter internationaler Kontrolle. 0 — 300 km]

and gave impetus to German nationalism. The protests against the treaty crystallized in radical movements that vehemently opposed the Weimar government, which sought gradually to ease the difficult conditions of the treaty in the process of fulfilling them. For their efforts they were accused of caving into foreign demands. An especially bitter pill

for the German public to swallow was the admission that Germany alone bore the guilt for the outbreak of the war. The allies used this as the legal basis for claims for reparations. The treaty did not, however, set down the exact amount that the Germans would have to pay. Specific terms called for Germany to give up the bulk of its merchant fleet, the surrender of most of its power lines and coal production.

In protest, the government of Philipp Scheidemann, which was composed primarily of social democrats, decided to go on strike on June 20, 1919. Three days later the National Assembly of Weimar elected a new leader, Gustav Bauer, and authorized him to sign the treaty. Germany's foreign minister, Hermann Müller, led the delegation to Versailles. The Treaty consisting of 440 articles that bore the stamp of the French President,

Georges Clemenceau and his British counterpart David Lloyd George, was intended to hamper the rise of Germany as an economic and political power for a long time to come.

Germany lost all it colonies and ceded about 45,000 square miles of territory. It sacrificed land in the east to Lithuania, Poland and Czechoslovakia. Alsace-Lorraine was given to France and Schleswig-Holstein to Denmark as well some territory to Belgium.

Danzig as a free city came under the jurisdiction of the League of Nations. The Saar region was also to be administered by the League for fifteen years. The German army was limited to a total force of 100,000 men, the navy to 15,000. Military aircraft, armored transport and heavy artillery were all strictly forbidden. A demilitarized zone was established stretching from the Rhine for 35 miles into Germany. Allied troops were stationed on the left bank of the Rhine to ensure compliance. The Treaty of Versailles provided for the founding of the League of Nations and backed by the agreement of England

and the United States to support France in any future conflict. Because the U.S Senate refused to ratify entry into the League the side agreement between England, France, and the U.S. did not come into effect. The United States decided in 1921 to enter into a separate peace treaty with Germany. ❑

VIOLENCE IN GERMANY

June 24, 1922

Humiliated by the Treaty of Versailles, right wing groups in Germany lashed out against members of the Weimar Republic's government.

Foreign Minister Walther Rathenau was assassinated by right wing extremist members, sharing the same fate as Matthias Erzberger, a centrist politician who had been murdered the year before. Erzberger's critics blamed him for signing the armistice with Marshal Foch, while Rathenau was seen as the enemy for agreeing to pay reparations. On June 26, the government enacted an "emergency decree for the protection of the Republic." A year later Adolph Hilter would lead an attempted coup in a Munich beer hall. ❑

Walther Rathenau (on the right) in Geneva 1922

RED ARMY DEFEATS THE WHITES

Moscow, November 16, 1920

Immediately following the October Revolution of 1917 the de facto leader of the new Russian government was the Communist (Bolshevik) Party. However, included in the government were members from other groups who had participated in the overthrow of the Kerensky Government. The ideological differences that existed between these groups led to the Russian Civil War of 1918.

Set against the Communists was a loose confederation which included members of moderate socialist parties, liberal Constitutional Democrats (Cadets), monarchists and pro-capitalist con-

servatives. Fearing a takeover of the Russian state by the Communists, these groups formed an alliance known as the Whites, whose White Army challenged and was defeated by the Communist Red Army. The Red Army victory in 1921 resulted in the creation of the Union of Soviet Socialist Republics (USSR) in 1922.

Despite initial support from Great Britain, France and the United States, the failure of the Whites was due to their inability to forge a cohesive military strategy. With the Red Army in control of Moscow and the surrounding industrial heartland,

the White forces were too scattered to mount decisive penetrations of the Communist defenses. In addition, the Red Army, having become a fearsome fighting force under the direction of Leon Trotsky, outnumbered their opponents ten to one.

The only goal that united the White's insurrection was their fear of a Communist state. Unable to create a unified political and social agenda of their own, they ultimately lost the support of the Russian populace. Their final defeat in 1921 in the Crimea left the Communist Party as the last surviving Russian revolutionaries. ❑

ALBERT EINSTEIN AND THE THEORY OF RELATIVITY

Stockholm, December 10, 1921

Albert Einstein (1879-1955) revolutionized our basic understanding of physics with his "theory of relativity." This phrase really refers to two theories, namely the theory of "special relativity," proposed in 1905, and the theory of "general relativity", proposed in 1919. Although he is most famous for these theories, his other work—on Brownian motion and the photoelectric effect—would have alone also made him famous.

Special relativity postulates that the speed of light is independent of the observer's state of motion. This simple sounding yet paradoxical idea requires radical changes in many of our common sense notions of space and time. After Einstein, it became impossible to conceive of space and time separately—they must ultimately be viewed as one indivisible reality. From this hypothesis, Einstein also derived the famous $E=mc^2$ equation, expressing the enormous amount of energy locked within matter. This led ultimately to the development of the atomic bomb.

General relativity is Einstein's theory of gravitation, which he conceived of as a distortion of the space-time continuum by the presence of matter, making it curved. One consequence of this theory is the prediction that light will be deflected by a gravitational field. This prediction was confirmed in 1919 when the British astronomer Arthur Eddington photographed a solar eclipse. This event made Einstein world famous overnight.

Albert Einstein and his second wife Elsa.

Nevertheless, there was much controversy surrounding his two relativity theories, and when he was awarded the Nobel Prize in 1921, it was "for his services to Theoretical Physics, and especially for his discovery of the photoelectric effect," with no mention of relativity.

The photoelectric effect refers to the observation that electrons are emitted from matter when light, or x-rays, are absorbed. Einstein hypothesized that light consists of particles, called photons. This assumption enabled him to explain the effect, and to make predictions about it which were later verified. Since this work seemed to contradict Maxwell's equations and the wave theory of light, it was strongly resisted. In 1915, Einstein's predictions were confirmed by Robert Andrews Millikan, and in 1921 he was awarded the Nobel Prize for this work. Ironically, it can be seen as one of the earlier successes of quantum mechanical reasoning, an approach to physics Einstein later expressed discontent with, due to its acceptance of randomness at the core of atomic phenomena. ❏

LEAGUE OF NATIONS FORMED TO STOP WAR

Paris, February 14, 1919

Following the bitter fighting of World War I delegates from 27 nations voted to set up The League of Nations to try to prevent future wars. The idea was first raised in January of 1918, when during a speech, President Woodrow Wilson offered his "14 Points." The last point read: " A general association of nations must be formed…for the purpose of affording mutual guarantees of political independence and territorial integrity to great and small states alike."

The league's charter was incorporated in the peace treaty with Germany. The founding members were 32 allied opponents of the Central powers along with 13 neutral states. The organization received a serious setback, when in the following month the US Senate refused to ratify the Treaty of Versailles. Most of the opposition related to Article Ten, under which the US would have to go to war if another member were attacked. There was also hostility to Britain and the dominions having six votes. There had been a long fight over the proposals. A compromise solution was worked out, but Wilson, incapacitated by a stroke, refused to support it. As a result the US never joined the organization that its president had inspired.

The League's first meeting was in Geneva on November 15, 1920. Germany joined the League in 1926 and in 1934 the Soviet Union followed suit. The League of Nations failed in its mission. It had no way of enforcing compliance with its determinations, and the unresolved antagonisms that remained at the end of World War I resurfaced to once again convulse Europe and Asia. The League lasted for 26 years. It was replaced in 1946 by the newly organized United Nations. ❏

LITERARY MODERNISTS

London and Paris, 1922

In what became a watershed year for English literature, 1922 saw the publication of two works that came to define Literary Modernism and continue to influence writers and readers to this day.

The first of these was the novel *Ulysses* by the Irish writer James Joyce. Based on *The Odyssey*, its eighteen chapters recount a single day in the life of Dublin advertising man, Leopold Bloom. The opening chapters had appeared in serialized form, but due to obscenity charges lodged in the United States, this was discontinued in 1920. The controversial book was finally published on February 2 by Shake-

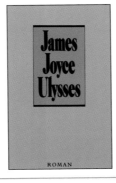
James Joyce Ulysses
ROMAN

speare and Company, a Paris bookstore run by Sylvia Beach. The work was banned in the United States until 1933.

The second was the poem *The Waste Land*, written in October by the London-based American expatriate, T. S. Eliot. A five part, 434-line conspectus of existential despair, the work was greeted by many critics as incomprehensible because of its complexly allusive and often obscurantist passages. After its initial appearance in Eliot's own literary magazine *The Criterion*, subsequent publications contained an appendix explaining the poem's many literary references. ❏

TURKEY BECOMES A REPUBLIC

October 29, 1923

Under the reforms inaugurated by Mustafa Kemal Pasha (known as Atatürk) Turkey became a modern state modeled after Western democracies.

The National Assembly meeting in Angora (now Ankara) proclaimed Turkey as a republic with Kemal Pasha as its first president. A constitution was enacted on April 20, 1924.

The Ottoman Empire was on the losing side in World War I and according to the Treaty of Sèvres it forfeited the region around Smyrna to Greece. This fueled a nationalist movement. When in 1922 Kemal Pasha drove the Greeks out of Anatolia and reclaimed Smyrna, he became a national hero. The Ottoman sultan, Mehmed VI and his successor lasted as caliph only until 1924, when Turkey abolished the caliphate.

The Treaty of Lausanne (July 24, 1923) gave the whole Anatolian Peninsula back to Turkey. The Allies removed their military and lifted the financial controls that had been put into place. Some 1.2 million Greeks had to leave Turkey.

The new Turkish state underwent fundamental reforms. It adopted a Western legal system, enforced strict separation of Church and State, replaced Arabic script with Latin characters, proposed equal rights for women, and laid the foundations for its own industries. Thoroughgoing land reform was proposed but not achieved. At the beginning Turkey was governed by one-party rule (The Republican People's Party).

Kemal Pasha ruled Turkey until his death in 1938, but his policies were followed by his successors. The army became the special guardians of the Kemalist ideology. ❏

KEMAL PASHA

Brief Lives

The politician Mustafa Kemal Pasha received the honorary title of Atatürk (Father of Turkey) in 1934. He had been active during World War I in the Young Turks movement and by war's end he was at the head of a growing nationalist movement. He is credited with the transformation of a backward-looking empire into a modern nation state. He was an especially dedicated advocate of education and the preservation and recognition of Anatolian culture.

Atatürk died in Istanbul on November 10, 1938. ❏

Kemal Pasha

THE BIRTH OF IRISH INDEPENDENCE

Dublin, 1922

By the end of the nineteenth century the Irish movement toward independence had become unstoppable. The nationalist Irish Parliamentary Party began a campaign for Home Rule, while a smaller group, Sinn Féin, sought outright independence. These nationalist movements resulted in the partitioning of Ireland, a war for independence, and civil war.

The partitioning of Ireland resulted from the passage of the Third Home Rule Act by the government of British Prime Minister H.H. Asquith in 1914. Faced with vehement opposition by the Protestant Ulster Unionists, Asquith made the fateful decision to exclude their six counties in northern Ireland, thereby dividing Ireland into the twenty-six counties that would come under Home Rule, and later dominion status, and the six Ulster counties that would remain part of Britain.

This act radicalized many in the Nationalist movement, some factions of which chose to reject this attenuated Home Rule and fight for a unified and wholly independent Ireland. This campaign began with the issuing of the *Proclamation of the Irish Republic* and the Easter Uprising of April 24, 1916. This attempted takeover of Dublin ended with the execution of the Proclamation signatories. The Uprising was the beginning of the Irish War of Independence.

In 1918 when Sein Féin won the Irish majority in Parliament, they declared independence from Westminster and formed an Irish Parliament, the Dáil. Naming Éamon de Valera president, this new Irish government organized a military wing out of the old Irish Volunteers, the Irish Republican Army. It was this army, under Michael Collins and Cathal Brugha that waged the Irish War for Independence against British troops between January 1919 and July 1921.

The conflict ended with the

Éamon de Valera, one the leading lights of Irish independence movement. He was later elected President of Ireland.

signing of the Anglo-Irish Treaty of 1922, in which Ireland agreed to become an autonomous dominion of the United Kingdom. Renamed the Irish Free State, it encompassed only twenty-six counties. The six Ulster counties chose to remain part of Britain, and so the partition of Ireland was made official.

The Irish Civil War (1922-23) was a direct result of the treaty. Pitting the "Free Staters", including Michael Collins, against the treaty's opponents, the Republicans, led by Éamon de Valera, the eleven-month war resulted in over 3000 deaths and the defeat of the Republicans. In 1937 Ireland passed a constitution declaring itself the wholly autonomous Republic of Ireland. ❏

MUSSOLINI AND THE RISE OF FASCISM IN ITALY

Rome, 1922

Mussolini's fascist regime valued nationalism, militarism, anti-communism, strict censorship and state propaganda.

Mussolini's climb to the position of dictator took years. He was appointed Prime Minister of Italy after the fascists March on Rome in 1922. The power base behind Mussolini's rise came from the working class and the industrial bosses, both of whom wanted peace, work, order and stability. To get support from the Roman Catholic Church, religious education was made compulsory in all elementary schools.

In February 1923, Mussolini and the Fascist Grand Council introduced the Acerbo Law. This law changed election results. Now if one party received just 25% (or more) of the votes, they received 66% of the seats in Parliament. The parliamentary del-egates themselves voted in a law that would end their careers under the intimidating and watchful eyes of armed fascist guards.

In the election of March 1924 the Fascist party took firm control of the Italian Parliament.

Also pivotal in Mussolini's rise to the role of dictator was the royal support he received from King Victor Emmanuel. The King was a reactionary who feared communism and disliked republicanism.

In November 1926 all rival political parties and opposition newspapers were banned in Italy. 1927 saw the creation of a secret police force called the OVRA.

Mussolini also changed Italy's constitution. He implemented a diarchy, a system in which he and the King were both political heads of state. This served Mussolini well since Victor Emmanuel was a weak man and unable to assert himself against Mussolini's will.

Mussolini continued to restrict free elections until in 1939 he simply abolished Parliament, establishing himself as dictator. ❑

Benito Mussolini marching in front of a battalion of black shirts.

GERMANY GROANS UNDER CRIPPLING INFLATION

Berlin, November 15, 1923

At the start of 1923 inflation in Germany began to spiral out of control. In January a loaf of bread had cost 250 marks—still high, compared with 63 *pfennigs* in 1918—and by July it had reached 3,465. By November the cost of the loaf had soared to 201,000,000,000 marks. A US dollar was worth four trillion marks - if anyone could be found who would sell a dollar. The pound sterling could buy 20 trillion marks.

In effect, German money had become worthless; barter was increasingly being adopted for trading goods and services, and middle-class families who kept their wealth in banks were wiped out.

In a desperate effort to rescue the country from runaway inflation, the *Reichsbank* (the German central bank) invented a new German mark. It was called the *rentenmark* and was tied to the country's real estate. Each *rentenmark* was pegged at a trillion existing marks.

Much of the blame for the financial meltdown lay on the government's shoulders. When French and Belgian troops occupied the Ruhr in order to enforce war reparations, the Germans encouraged resistance and printed marks in limitless numbers. That policy led to the destruction of the currency. ❑

ANDRÉ BRETON AND THE SURREALIST MOVEMENT

Paris, October 1924

French neurologist and art theorist, André Breton, published his *Surrealist Manifesto* to the profound bafflement of most in the art world. Like the Dada movement before it, surrealism, from its inception, was a deliberate provocation, but in place of the spontaneous creative eruptions of Dada, the surrealists sought to put their technical expertise in the service of the articulation of unconscious elements. Influenced by Freud, Breton saw the way forward as a receptivity to the hidden life of the unconscious and especially to dream motifs. He deplored what he saw as the domination of logical thinking, which he considered tantamount to the expulsion of the creative impulse under

Salvador Dalí

the guise of progress.

The first group show of the surrealists took place on November 13, 1925 in Paris. Among the artists exhibiting were former Dadaists Max Ernst and Hans Arp as well as Giorgio de Chirico. Joining them were Picasso, Klee and Miró, artists whose involvement in the movement was only a passing interest, although according to Breton, Miró was the most surrealistic of all. Later influential figures in the movement included the incomparable Belgian painter, René Magritte, as well as Yves Tanguy and Salvador Dalí, who espoused what he called the "paranoiac critical method" of accessing

Self-taught artist Max Ernst was one of the founders of the Surrealist movement.

the unconscious. By the early 1940s surrealism had become largely discredited. The spirit of art was moving towards abstraction and relocating from Paris to New York. ❑

THE BAUHAUS

Dessau, Germany, 1926

Bauhaus ("Building School") was an educational institution founded by the German architect Walter Gropius in 1919 in Weimar. The school operated from 1919 until 1933, during which time it moved from Weimar, first to Dessau and finally to Berlin,

The Bauhaus in Dessau, built according to the plans of Walter Gropius

where it was shut down by the Nazis for its "un-German" theories. Although the school was relatively short-lived, "Bauhaus Style," also known as "International Style," had a major impact on the twentieth-century architectural and design movements and remains influential today.

Its curriculum was a inter-disciplinary fusion of fine arts, crafts, architecture, and graphic, interior, and industrial design. Created by the merger of two existing schools, the Grand Ducal School of Arts and the Weimar Academy of Fine Art, it promulgated the idea that there was a synergistic interplay between technology and artistic expression, and that the form and function of any cre-

ated object, be it a building or a chair, was a unified whole.

Gropius was influenced by the nineteenth-century English designer William Morris's ideas that art could be useful and that the commonplace object inherently possessed artistic beauty. Applying these ideas to the processes of mass production, he sought to develop creatively designed products that were affordable and "adapted to our world of machines, radios and fast cars."

The Bauhaus School building in Dessau was opened on December 4, 1926. It is still standing and is a prime example of Gropius's melding of the functional with the aesthetic. ❑

DEATH OF LENIN

Moscow, January 21, 1924

Born Vladimir Ilyich Ulyanov on April 22, 1870, Vladimir Lenin was the son of a well-to-do educator and was baptized in the Russian Orthodox Church. At the age of seventeen he experienced two tragedies that many historians view as pivotal to his subsequent path in life. One was the death of his father from a cerebral hemorrhage. The other was the execution of his older brother, Alexander, who had been arrested for his role in a plot to assassinate Czar Alexander III.

Radicalized by his brother's death, he began to study the works of Karl Marx at Kazan State University. Espousing the Marxist cause, he was expelled but was later admitted to the University of Saint Petersburg where he took a law degree in 1891. After practicing law for two years, he became increasingly involved in communist propaganda efforts, which resulted in his arrest and exile to Siberia. There in 1898 he married a fellow Marxist Nadezhda Krupskaya.

Released from exile in 1900, he began a peripatetic existence in Europe. In 1901 he published one of his seminal works, the pamphlet *What is to be Done?* He became a leading spokesperson for the Bolshevik cause. After his election to the Presidium of the Russian Social Democratic Labor Party in 1906, he began a self-imposed exile in Europe that lasted until the Revolution of 1917.

On April 16, 1917, after the 1917 February Revolution and the abdication of Tsar Nicholas II, Lenin made his historic return to the Finland Station in Petrograd. Having continued to publish pamphlets promulgating Bolshevik ideas while in Europe, he was met as a conquering hero and quickly assumed the leadership of a movement that now sought to wrest control from Alexander Kerensky and the provisional government, whom he and his fellow Bolsheviks deemed too moderate. In July, under the threat of arrest by leaders of that government, Lenin

fled back to Finland to await the optimal time for the Bolshevik takeover.

That time came in October, when his return to Petrograd occasioned the October Revolution. By November 8 the Bolsheviks had overthrown the government and established the beginning of Soviet rule with the storming of the Winter Palace.

Named Chairman of the Council of People's Commissars on November 8, 1917, he quickly nationalized all business and industry, shops, banks and agriculture. When the Russian economy collapsed in the summer of 1921, he allowed a limited amount of private economic activity with his New Economic Policy. Questioned about this return to capitalism, he responded famously to purists' complaints with, "It's two

Vladimir Ilyich Lenin laid to rest in Moscow's Red Square

steps forward, one step back."

Despite numerous setbacks, Lenin successfully guided the formation of the Russian Communist state until his death from a heart ailment at the age of 54, on January 21, 1924.

His death set the stage for a power struggle that pitted the backers of the army's architect, Leon Trotsky, against those of Communist Party General Secretary, Joseph Stalin. The wily Stalin would win. Trotsky would be assassinated in exile in Mexico, his purported last words being, "I think Stalin has finished the job he started." ❑

LOUIE ARMSTRONG: KING OF JAZZ

Chicago, 1925

As leader of the jazz ensembles the Hot Five (1925-28) and the Hot Seven (1927-1928) trumpeter Louie Armstrong (known as "Satchmo") gained an international reputation.

Armstrong was born in New Orleans in 1900. He started playing with King Oliver and Fletcher Henderson who were major figures in the development the New Orleans style, which had been started by Buddy Bolden as a mixture of ragtime and blues.

The "Hot Five" gave its first performance in 1925 in Chicago. In the original group were Kid Ory on trombone, Johnny Dodds on clarinet, Johnny St. Cyr on guitar, and Armstrong's wife Lil Hardin Armstrong on piano. Armstrong's exuberant music was a key factor in the growing popu-

larity of jazz, and his vast musical talent was recognized outside of jazz circles. In 1944 he was the first jazz musician to be invited to

play at the Metropolitan Opera. From 1947 to 1963 Armstrong led the "All Stars." He died in 1971. ❑

Louis Armstrong, master jazz trumpeter

MICKEY MOUSE

Hollywood, 1926

Squeaky voiced and with ears like black ping-pong paddles, Walt Disney's iconic "Mickey Mouse," debuted as a talking character in *Steamboat Willie* at New York's Colony theater on November 18, 1928. History's first animated sound cartoon, *Steamboat Willie* was the third Mickey Mouse film, the two previous having been the silent films, *Plane Crazy* and *Gallopin' Gaucho*.

Conceived originally as a red velvet pantaloon clad mouse named "Mortimer," Disney worked with Ub Iwerks in 1927 to create what would become one of the world's most recognizable images. Thinking the name "Mortimer" "too pompous", it was Disney's wife Lillian, who christened their new creation "Mickey." ❑

LINDBERGH'S SOLO FLIGHT ACROSS THE ATLANTIC

Paris, May 21, 1927

At 7:52 A.M. on May 20, 1927, Charles Augustus Lindbergh took off from Long Island's Roosevelt Field in his monoplane, *The Spirit of St. Louis*, destined for Paris's Le Bourget Airport. He landed 33 hours and 32 minutes later to a gala welcome from 100,000 adoring French fans. Soon after, he was awarded the French Legion d'Honneur by President Gaston Doumergue. Not the first to fly across the Atlantic, (there had been 81 previous crossings) his was the first solo, non-stop flight.

The feat won him worldwide celebrity, earning him the sobriquets, "Lucky Lindy" and "The Lone Eagle." Awarded the Distinguished Flying Cross by President Coolidge, he was hailed as a conquering hero with a ticker-tape parade down New York's Fifth Avenue. He also won the $25,000 Orteig Prize, which had been offered by the Franco-American hotelier, Raymond Orteig, to the first person to fly the Atlantic nonstop.

His public acclaim as an aviator helped to popularize the idea of flying as a viable form of transportation. Having sparked the imagination of the general public, Lindbergh's virtuoso performance inspired the growth of commercial air travel.

Tragically, the ensuing fame and fortune made him and his wife, Anne Morrow Lindbergh, vulnerable to the predations of those who would exploit his celebrity status. In 1932 his first child, Charles Augustus Lindbergh Jr. was kidnapped and found murdered in New Jersey. Three years after the crime, a carpenter named Bruno Hauptmann was arrested, and after a

Pilot Charles Lindbergh with his *Spirit of St. Louis*

lengthy media circus of a trial, was found guilty and then executed.

Grief-stricken and tired of celebrity, the Lindberghs move to Europe, where they lived until 1939 and the onset of World War II. ❑

THE *THREEPENNY* OPERA

Berlin, August 31, 1928

The premier of Bertolt Brecht's *Threepenny Opera* took place at the Schiffbauerdamm Theater in Berlin, under the direction of Erich Engel who led the production to become one of the greatest theater successes of the Weimar Republic.

Bertolt Brecht and Kurt Weill offered, for the first time in a contemporary opera, a critique of social conditions. The work was inspired by John Gay's 1728 play, *The Beggar's Opera*. Brecht brought the seamy side of urban life to the stage with the story of the robber Macheath, called "Mack the Knife." Macheath comes into conflict with Peachum, the King of the Beggars, over Peachum's daughter Polly. Brecht used whores, thieves, and beggars as devices to reveal middle class capitalist ideals.

Weill's music, in the old tradition of strolling minstrels, incorporated elements from jazz and German folk music to create a parody of opera and operettas. The "Ballad of Mack the Knife" went on to become a popular standard.

The Rise and Fall of the City of Mahogany was a similar success. It triggered riots at the opening in Leipzig in 1930. ❑

The writer Bertolt Brecht

ST VALENTINE'S DAY MASSACRE

Chicago, February 14, 1929

In an outbreak of homicidal gangland warfare, seven members of George "Bugsy" Moran's gang, assembled in a garage at 2122 N. Clark Street, were machine-gunned to death by five assailants, all dressed as police officers.

The killings, which the press have christened "the St Valentine's Day Massacre" and which stemmed from rivalry over the lucrative market in bootleg liquor, were the work of the gang of Al "Scarface" Capone, who was fighting for supremacy among Chicago's mobsters. Capone arrived in United States from Sicily in 1914. His career and that of many others was launched by the passage of the Eighteenth Amendment and the Volstead Act in 1920 that banned the manufacture and sale of alcoholic beverages. It was soon quite clear that demand for alcohol would not dry up, and that millions were to be made by its illegal sale. Capone and other gangland bosses branched out into gambling, extortion and even murder for hire. Capone was finally arrested and sentenced to jail on charges of tax evasion in 1931. On March 23, 1933 soon after his first inauguration, Franklin D. Roosevelt signed a law repealing Prohibition. ❑

The gangster Al Capone

PREMIER OF TALKING PICTURES

New York, October 6, 1927

In the late nineteenth century a number of inventors who were pioneers in the creation of "moving pictures" began experimenting with ways of adding recorded sound. The earliest prototypes employed a synchronization of visuals and sound as separate technologies. These technologies were later integrated, allowing for "sound-on-film" synchronization and ultimately, the "talkies."

In 1888 the British photographer Edweard Muybridge and Thomas Edison considered ways to integrate Muybridge's image projecting Zoopraxiscope with Edison's cylinder phonograph. These discussions led to Edison's Kinetophone. Unveiled in 1895, it employed an individually viewed moving image apparatus with sound producing headphones.

In 1900 the technology experienced a quantum leap with a projected film and sound system created in France by Clément-Maurice Gratiolet and Henri Lioret. Named the Phono-Ciné-ma-Théâtre, its presentation at the Paris Exposition made it the first publicly exhibited projected sound-film.

The first commercially applicable sound-film technology was developed in 1919 by the American, Lee De Forest. By photographically recording sound on to a film strip, De Forest created the first "sound-on-film" technology, which made full length sound feature-films possible. His De Forest Phonofilms was the first to commercially screen movies using this technology when it showed a series of short films at New York's Rivoli Theater on April 23, 1923.

De Forest Phonofilms was soon driven out of business when two major Hollywood studios, Fox Film and Warner Brothers, developed their own "sound-on-film" systems. Fox Film's was called Movietone; Warner Brother's was called Vitaphone.

Warner Brothers presented the first feature-length sound film, albeit without dialog, with its release of *Don Juan* starring John Barrymore on August 6, 1926. Featuring only music and sound-effects it was not the first "talkie." A year later they presented the first feature-length "talkie" with the premier of Al Jolson in *The Jazz Singer* on October 6, 1927. ❑

Poster for *The Jazz Singer*

THE FIRST OSCARS

Hollywood, May 16, 1929

The film industry's growing maturity and self-confidence was on display as awards for outstanding achievement by actors, directors, producers and technicians were presented. The award is 12inch-tall model of a naked man plated in gold—-the Oscar. The honors were bestowed by the Academy of Motion Picture Arts and Sciences formed in 1927 by producers like Louis B Mayer of MGM as "an alliance of the creative elite of Hollywood".

The academy president, Douglas Fairbanks, gave statuettes to Janet Gaynor and Emil Jannings, the directors Frank Borzage and Lewis Milestone, the screenwriter Ben Hecht and the producer Jack Warner. A special award was given to Charlie Chaplin. ❑

THE DISCOVERY OF PENICILLIN

London, September 5, 1928

The discovery of penicillin in 1928 by the British bacteriologist, Alexander Fleming (knighted in 1944), began the era of antibiotics. Fleming came by accident to his discovery of penicillin. He observed that different kinds of mold produce an anti-bacterial substance through a metabolic process. Fleming identified the mold that destroyed bacteria as *penicillinium notatum*, which he extracted in 1929 and named penicillin.

Penicillin belongs to the class of antibacterial agents that are formed from living organisms. These had already been named antibiotics in the nineteenth century. Penicillin was introduced as the first antibiotic used for medical purposes. It proved itself effective against almost ninety different kinds of bacteria and was shown to weaken an additional sixteen strains. Many diseases that had been considered mortal were shown to be treatable with penicillin. It was first widely used in the United States. However, it was not until 1941-1942 that it was produced in sufficient quantities to make a substantial contribution to medicine.

The Nobel Prize in Medicine was given in 1945 to Fleming along with his compatriot Ernst

Alexander Fleming

Boris Chain and the Australian Howard Walter Florey, who further developed the penicillin extract as a therapeutic agent. ❑

EMPIRE STATE BUILDING

New York City, May 1 1931

United States President Herbert Hoover was the guest of honor to dedicate the opening of the world's tallest building. The Empire State Building rises to a height of 1250 feet (381m) with 102 stories over Fifth Ave. At the top is a lighted tower of glass, steel, and aluminum. Work on the building was completed in only 13 months from a design by the architect William F. Lamb.

The Empire State building remained the world's tallest building until 1973 when the World Trade Center surpassed it. The following year the honor went to the Sears Tower in Chicago with a height of 1453 feet (443m). Since the Observatory on the 86th floor opened to the

Construction worker on the Empire State Building

public, it has hosted over 110 million visitors. ❑

MAHATMA GANDHI

Brief Lives

Mohandas Karamchand Gandhi was born in Porbandar, India on October 2, 1869. He traveled to South Africa and worked there as a lawyer, representing the interests of the emigrant Indian population. It was here that he first put into practice the principles of non-violent resistance. In all, Gandhi spent 2089 days behind bars as a result of his many acts of civil disobedience. He attempted to improve relations between Hindus and Muslims and took the cause the Untouchables, India's outcasts, especially to heart. He was gunned down by a fanatical Hindu in 1948. ❑

Mohandas (Mahatma) Gandhi and Jawaharlal Nehru. Nehru rose to Congress President under Gandhi's tutelage and was recognized as his political heir. Both his daughter, Indira, and grandson Rajiv, would become prime ministers of India.

GANDHI'S CIVIL DISOBEDIENCE MOVEMENT

India, 1930

The march to the sea for salt led by Mohandas Karamchand (Mahatma) Gandhi initiated a new phase in his campaign of non-violent resistance devoted to gaining independence for India. On the morning of April 6, Gandhi reached Dandi on the Gulf of Cambay. Gandhi had started from Ahmedabad on March 12 with 78 companions on a march to the sea. By the time he reached Dandi, thousands of followers had joined him. Each of the marchers culled a handful of salt from the sea as a symbolic protest against England's salt monopoly. In the weeks that followed many peasants began using their own salt, The British responded with mass arrests. Among those imprisoned were Jawaharlal Nehru and Gandhi himself as well as other leading figures from the Indian National Congress, which had been established in 1885.

Gandhi had been struggling against British rule in India since 1919. His program of civil disobedience and non-violent resistance endowed him with a powerful moral authority. In 1919 he called for a general strike in response to the Rowlatt Act, which essentially continued martial law in India in the aftermath of World War I. Two years later he campaigned for homemade clothing to oppose British commercial interests.

Soon after the Dandi Salt March Gandhi was invited to London to participate in what became known as the Roundtable Conference. The results were disappointing and the British followed it up with a new round of suppression of dissent. ❑

Gandhi and the writer Sarojini Naidu on the march to the sea for salt

WALL STREET CRASH TRIGGERS GREAT DEPRESSION

New York City, October 24, 1929

The U.S. "Roaring Twenties" speculative bull market bubble burst on "Black Thursday," October 24, 1929. On that day panicked stockholders traded nearly 13 million shares, hoping to salvage anything they could from investments that for the previous five years had grown exponentially. On the next day, seeking to restore investors' confidence and so halt the market's precipitous slide, a consortium of Wall Street banks, including J.P. Morgan and Chase National, bought up massive amounts of "blue chip" company stocks at rates well above their market value. Any gain that this tactic achieved was wiped out on "Black Monday," October 28 and again on "Black Tuesday," October 29. By the end of the week, the market had lost $30 billion, a figure ten times greater than the federal government's annual budget.

These three days of staggering losses heralded the arrival of the "Great Depression." Though its immediate cause was the "black" days of October, the problem was really a result of a confluence of unsound financial practices employed after World War I. Two of the most prominent of these were the public's reliance on credit to buy consumer goods and the speculative process of buying stocks

"on margin." By the end of the 1920's these practices resulted in massive consumer debt and subsequent loan defaults. With consumers no longer able to buy goods, the industries that had created them collapsed, as did the value of those industries' stock.

By 1933, most manufacturing industries were defunct, 5000 banks had failed and 25 percent of the U.S. population was unemployed. The economic conditions in the U.S. had spilled over into Europe as well. The U.S. would not fully recover until World War II put its entire economy on a wartime footing. ❑

Above: Crash on Wall Street. Left: Unemployed German workers

THE BEGINNING OF THE SECOND SPANISH REPUBLIC

Madrid, April 14, 1931

The creation of the Second Spanish Republic began in 1930 when King Alfonso XIII ousted General Miguel Primo de Rivera as head of the military dictatorship that had ruled Spain since 1923. Originally a supporter of the military regime, Alfonso sought to accommodate a growing call in Spanish society for a revival of the *cortes* (parliament) and the formation of a constitutional

government. Despite knowing that his previous alliance with Rivera had made the monarchy an anathema to many of the groups campaigning for change, he directed Spain's provisional government to hold municipal elections on April 14, 1931.

Unfortunately for the King, the majority of the electorate were Republicans whose secular liberalism and anti-monarchist

platforms won a resounding victory at the polls, making them Spain's new ruling party. Their first act was to demand the King's abdication. Alfonso responded by signing a document renouncing the new government's mandate, after which he left Spain and took up residence in Rome, where he died in 1941 shortly after his official abdication.

By December 9, the Second

Republican government approved a new constitution introducing sweeping reforms, among which were freedom of speech and association, universal suffrage for women, the right to divorce, separation of church and state, and a recognition of the Spanish provinces' right to autonomy. There were also provisions that dramatically limited the power of the Catholic Church. ❑

ADOLF HITLER

Brief Lives

Adolf Hitler, dictator of Nazi Germany from 1933 till his death in 1945, was born in Braunau am Inn, Austria on April 20, 1889.

Hitler was born into the family of a low-level civil servant. His desire to become an artist was thwarted by his lack of talent. He served in the German army in WWI and was awarded an Iron Cross, a medal of distinction.

After Germanys' defeat and the humiliating peace terms forced upon her, Hitler became involved in anti-bolshevik, anti-Semitic, right wing politics. In 1921 Hitler became Leader (Führer) of the Nazi Party.

Hitler and his party spent the years from 1933, when Hitler was made Chancellor, to 1939 building a ruthless political organization along with a mighty military machine.

During the War Years, 1939 to 1945, Hitler's armies met with great success as they conquered nation after nation. These were also the years which witnessed what was perhaps the worst tyranny ever seen in Western, Central and Eastern Europe. Hitler's political machine carried out the execution of nearly six million Jews, gypsies, homosexuals, and political opponents, all of whom were deemed unworthy of life in a world ruled by National Socialism and Adolf Hitler.

After two years of military reversals, the winter of 1945 found Hitler ruling what was left of his empire from an underground bunker beneath the Reich Chancellery building. On April 30, 1945, with Soviet soldiers just 100 yards away, Hitler committed suicide ending his plans for a thousand-year Reich. ❏

NATIONAL SOCIALIST DICTATORSHIP IN GERMANY

Germany, 1933

On January 30, 1933, an ageing and somewhat befuddled President von Hindenburg was forced to appoint Hitler as Chancellor under pressure from leading army generals, bankers, industry leaders and right-wing politicians, all of whom were demanding a restoration of order.

Prior to this, Germany had been through three chancellors in as many years, none of whom were able to form a stable effective coalition. Unemployment had soared to six million, the currency was nearly worthless and the Nazis and Communists were fighting bloody street battles.

At the time, many people, including right wing politicians and those of more moderate thought, believed Hitler would be tamed and become more mainstream and less incendiary in his speech and actions. Others, perhaps those who had listened more carefully, had great trepidations about their new ruler and his private army of SA men.

It didn't take long for Hitler and his henchmen to begin disassembling the existing power structure. On February 28 the Reichstag, Germany's Parliament building, was set afire and gutted by flame. This monumental building had been the symbol of personal liberty, freedom of speech and the right to assemble. Many Germans saw the fire for the betrayal and treachery it represented. Others, whether unable or unwilling to see what appeared obvious, chose to believe the Nazi spin on events. They blamed a communist conspiracy even though the person actually accused turned out to be a simple minded Dutch communist caught on the grounds

Students in Berlin construct a bonfire of books of Jewish and dissenting authors

JAPANESE TAKEOVER OF MANCHURIA

Manchuria, September 18, 1931

In the war fought in 1905 Japan forced Russia to withdraw from southern Manchuria. Starting with their control of the Manchurian railroad (from Port Arthur to Harbin) the Japanese consolidated their position. This inevitably led to conflict with China.

Japanese troops, sent to Manchuria to guard the South Manchurian railway, which Japan had turned into a huge military-industrial complex, launched a surprise attack on the Chinese garrison in what became known as the Mukden Incident. The local Japanese commander used the pretext of a bomb explosion on the railway line to attack the Chinese garrison. It is widely recognized that the entire episode was manufactured by militant Japanese officers who had decided the time was right for military expansion.

The Governor of Manchuria, Zhang Xueliang, presumably under guidance from Chiang Kai-Shek, decided upon a policy of nonresistance. Chiang's hope that the League of Nations would intervene remained unfulfilled. International protests were lodged, but the Japanese refused to recognize them. Japan soon had control of most of Manchuria and in 1932 established a puppet government that was given the name of Manchukuo. The last Chinese Emperor, Puyi, was

Chinese, forced laborers for the Japanese

the titular head of state, but the country became a fiefdom of the Japanese army, which enslaved the population. Japan maintained possession of the territory until 1945. Its wealth of raw materials and agricultural production were essential to the Japanese war effort. ❏

of the Reichstag building.

Hitler took full advantage of the fire to further his claim that the communists were bent upon destroying the government and turning Germany into a communist state. This cowardly, heinous act he said was clearly "a God-given signal," for him to take firm control of Germany in order to save it from the communists.

Storm troopers unofficially became a "special" police force and began arresting socialists and communists and silencing opposition newspapers. The radio became a Nazi propaganda vehicle controlled by Dr. Josef Goebbels, Gauleiter of Berlin and Minister of Propaganda.

On March 23, against a backdrop of mounting Nazi violence, the Reichstag members, now meeting in another location, voted to give Hitler, rather than the president, full power to rule by decree. This effectively ended any chance of democracy or the possibility for opposition.

At the same time the Nazi campaign of terror against the Jews increased dramatically. Jewish shops were boycotted and shut down. Jewish professors were forced to resign their positions.

All of this occurred within three months and sadly it was the harbinger of things to come. ❑

Burning of the Reichstag, which Hitler used as a pretext to assume dictatorial powers

AUSTRIAN CHANCELLOR DOLLFUSS ASSASSINATED

July 25, 1934

On July 25, 1934 Engelbert Dollfuss was murdered in an unsuccessful coup d'etat in the Chancellery building in Vienna.

Dollfuss was a devout Catholic of humble origins who had risen to become Chancellor of Austria in the troubled economic and turbulent political times of the mid 1930's.

Dollfuss assumed the position of Chancellor in 1932 and presided over a parliamentary government with the smallest possible majority. In March 1933 he disbanded the Parliament and ruled by emergency decree effectively allowing him to rule as dictator until his death in July 1934.

Violently anti-socialist, Dollfuss admired Italian fascism and leveraged support from Mussolini's Fascist state against Hitler's Nazi Germany. Fearful of Germany's designs on Austria, Dollfuss banned the Austrian Nazi Party in June 1933 in an attempt to safeguard Austrian independence.

This act, along with agitation by German Nazis, led to the attack on the Chancellery and Dollfuss' murder. It has been widely believed that Adolf Hitler instigated this plot from Berlin. It had always been a clear intention of the German dictator to annex Austria to his German Reich, an event which did occur four years later. ❑

FDR AND THE NEW DEAL

Washington DC, March 4, 1933

On March 4, 1933 Franklin Delano Roosevelt was inaugurated as the thirty-second President of the United States. He took office as the country found itself mired in a deep depression. His predecessor, Herbert Hoover, seemed powerless to reverse an economic crisis that had left the banking industry in shambles and 14 million American unemployed. On the campaign trail Roosevelt promised a New Deal for Americans. He won in a landslide, carrying all but six states.

Roosevelt was, on the face of it, an unlikely populist. He was born in 1882 to a patrician family. While attending Harvard, his distant cousin Theodore assumed the presidency. He married another distant cousin, Eleanor, in 1905. He served as Assistant Secretary of the Navy under Woodrow Wilson. In 1921 he contracted a disease that left him permanently paralyzed from the waist down. From 1928-1932 he was the Governor of New York.

Supported by the voters' mandate, Roosevelt decided to use his first 100 days in office to institute radical measures to revive the economy. He persuaded the US Congress to pass the National Industrial Recovery Act, legislation that would have been considered unthinkable in a capitalist society before he became president. The act gave him power not merely to control industry but to bring unions and bosses together, shorten working hours, fix wages and regulate production.

Roosevelt made it clear that he was prepared to adopt near-dictatorial powers to save the country. He closed the banks, allowing federal aid only to the efficient; he bailed out farmers and homeowners who were behind with their mortgages. Three billion dollars were ploughed into public works programs throughout the states. The best known, the Tennessee Valley Authority, brought water and forests to the dustbowl, and a civilian "conservation corps" (the CCC) employed young people to plant trees. A Public Works Administration was set up.

Roosevelt's energy and optimism did much to reestablish confidence. It was during a banking crisis in 1933 that he uttered the famous line: "The only thing we have to fear is fear itself." He also won the thanks of a grateful nation by repealing Prohibition. "I think this would be a good time for a beer," he told Congress.

Congressional elections in 1934 gave Roosevelt's democrats a substantial majority and allowed him to effect lasting changes in the American political landscape. Among his most notable achievements were the establishment of Social Security, the Works Progress Administration (WPA) and the National Labor relations Act, which guaranteed the right of workers to strike. ❑

President Franklin D. Roosevelt and Vice-President John Nance Garner

ITALY INVADES ETHIOPIA

Ethiopia, October 3, 1935

Striving to achieve colonial territorial parity with Britain and France, and to further his dream of creating a new Roman Empire, the Italian dictator, Benito Mussolini, ordered the invasion of Ethiopia in October of 1935, beginning the Second Italo-Ethiopian War. One of Africa's few independent nations, Ethiopia's location between Italy's East African possessions, Somaliland and Eritrea, made its annexation highly desirable to Mussolini. In a breach of the Italo-Ethiopian Treaty of 1928, which set precise boundaries between Somaliland

and Ethiopa, Mussolini built a fort at the Walwal oasis in the Ogaden Desert. In 1934, an Ethiopian and British border commission surveyed this provocative territorial incursion and found Italy at fault. Britain, not wanting to offend its potential ally against Germany, called for no sanctions against Italy and recused itself from any further involvement. This lack of decisive action resulted in the Abyssinia Crisis, a military skirmish between Ethiopian and Italian forces in December of 1935, which left 50 Italians and 150 Ethiopians dead. When Ethiopia appealed

to the League of Nations, which included the unenthusiastic Britain and France, that deliberative body's ineffectual response served as a green-light to Mussolini's imperialist agenda.

Dispensing with the protocol of a declaration of war, 100,000 Italian troops, along with 25,000 Eritreans, invaded Ethiopia on October 3, 1935. On the following day, the League of Nations convened and drew up the Hoare-Laval Plan, which promised the Italians Ethiopian territories, if they would agree to end hostilities immediately, but the plan was

quickly scrapped. This lack of credible support by the major European powers doomed Ethiopia.

The Ethiopian military was no match for the well equipped and trained Italians. Its 250,000 irregulars often went into battle with only spears and bows and arrows. The only adequate forces were those of Emperor Haile Selassie, but these were too few to halt the invasion of 300,000 Italian troops. By May 6, 1936 the Ethiopian capital of Addis Ababa was captured, and on May 9, Selassie had fled and Italy's King Victor Emmanuel III was proclaimed em-

THE SPANISH CIVIL WAR

Spain, July 17, 1936

The causes of the Spanish Civil War were rooted in the struggle for power between the socialist Popular Front government of the Second Republic and the conservative Nationalists. Virulently anti-communist, the Nationalists had opposed the progressive liberalism of the Second Republic since its inception in 1931. By 1936, the Republican governments experiments in collectivization provided the Nationalists with a *casus belli*.

War commenced on July 17, 1936 when pro-Nationalist troops

in the Spanish Army in Morocco mutinied. Hoping to inspire the overthrow of the Popular Front government, they were soon joined by the right-wing nationalist, General Francisco Franco. Within days, Franco sent a portentously chilling telegram to the government in Madrid: "The Spanish Restoration Movement will triumph very shortly, and we will demand explanations of your conduct."

The three-year war was waged with the utmost ferocity, and atrocities were carried out by both sides. A "take no prisoners" mentality mirrored developments in the world at large, where extreme ideologies were creating polarization between nations that would soon result in global war. Spain proved to be a battleground for

the most totalitarian of these ideologies. Stalinist Russia backed the proto-socialist Popular Front while Italy's Fascist government and Germany's Nazis backed Franco and the Nationalists.

Casualties from the war and its aftermath were staggering. By the war's end, and the Nationalist victory on April 1, 1939, it is estimated that 500,000 people had died, including 75,000 executed by the Nationalists and 55,000 by the Republicans. At least 10,000 non-combatants were killed, most of them in bombing raids carried out by Hitler's German Condor Legion, the most horrifying of which was the incineration of thousands in the market town of Guernica.

The slaughter continued after the war with Franco's genocidal vendetta against Republicans. It is estimated that he had anywhere between 30,000 to 200,000 people executed.

Even the 500,00 refugees to France were not spared. After being declared prisoners of war by Marshall Pétain of the Vichy regime, over 5000 were deported to and murdered at the Nazi's concentration camp at Mauthausen. ❑

Solders loyal to Franco in the ruins of Guernica after the bombing and capture of the city. (October, 1937)

MAO ZEDONG

Brief Lives

Mao Zedong established the Communist Party in 1921. After the Japanese invasion of China in 1937 Mao joined forces with the Chiang Kai-Shek. Their alliance came to an end in 1946, and in 1949 Mao proclaimed the establishment of the People's Republic of China. He presided over the party and became party chairman in 1954, turning China into a communist country. His goal was to rapidly transform China into a modern economic power. His Great Leap Forward campaign was a tragic failure ending in a famine that took the lives of millions of Chinese. Faced with disillusion and challenges to his undisputed power he launched the Cultural Revolution (1966-1969), which entailed nothing less than a total upheaval of Chinese society. It provided him with the pretext to purge the party of all opposition,

but at the same time resulted in deaths of millions more. Mao died in Beijing September 9, 1976. ❑

Mao Zedong

OWENS UPSTAGES NAZIS AT BERLIN GAMES

Berlin, August 16, 1936

peror of a vastly enlarged Italian East Africa.

The Second Italo-Ethiopian war was marked by a host of atrocities committed by the Italian army. Particularly odious was Mussolini's authorization of the use of mustard gas against defenseless civilians. Over 760,00 Ethiopians died during the war. Even after the war, the Italian occupiers continued their cruelties. In February of 1937, when an attempted assassination of an Italian official in Addis Ababa failed, 30,000 civilians were slaughtered in the Massacre of Addis Ababa. ❑

The black American athletics star Jesse Owens (1913-1980) shattered two world class sprint records—and the Nazi regime's hopes of turning the eleventh Olympic Games into a showcase for its dogma of Aryan supremacy. The games drew 5,000 athletes from 53 nations. Owens, who won four gold medals in the 100 meters, 200 meters, 400 meters relay and the long jump, was the undisputed star of the games. Just as notable was Owens' upstaging of the Nazi leader Adolf Hitler who had intended to greet winners. The thought of publicly congratulating a Negro was too humiliating, and after Owens' second win Hitler stormed out of the stadium.

Sadly, in some ways Owens was treated better in Nazi Germany than in the United States. There he was able to stay in the same hotels as his white fellow athletes, Upon his return to New York, after being greeted by a tickertape parade, he had to use the freight elevator in the Waldorf Astoria to attend a reception in his honor. ❑

Jesse Owens at the 1936 Olympics

MAO'S LONG MARCH

Jiangxi, October, 16, 1934

Soon after the death of the republican leader Sun Yat Sen in 1925, China fell into two warring camps: the Soviet supported communists, whose leaders included Mao Zedong, and the Nationalists, or Kuomintang, led by Chiang Kai-shek. By 1928, the country tumbled into civil war. In October 1934 Chiang Kai-shek's nationalist army encircled China's communist forces in Jiangxi province. Chiang, who had failed to take Jiangxi by storm in four campaigns, adopted new siege tactics, surrounding the region with a network of barbed wire and blockhouses. Nearly half a million men and 400 modern aircraft were used to hem in the communists.

When the communists heard that Chiang Kai-shek was planning an attack on the city of Ruijim, their leaders decided that their forces must find the means to retreat. One 10,000-strong force under Fang Zhimin tried to break out in the summer of 1934 but faced overpowering opposition. Fang was captured and his head was put on display in Nanchang. His efforts though were a diversion for a larger operation: Zhu De and his political mentor

Mao Zedong broke out in the fall with 80,000 troops, accompanied by 20,000 non-combatants and began a flight to safety. Thus began the famous long march.

At the end of a year, Mao, who had emerged as the march's chief commander, and his armies had covered an estimated 8,000 miles (contested by contemporary westerners as closer to 3,700 miles) passed through 11 provinces, crossed 18 mountain ranges and 24 major rivers and broken through ten encircling armies. They fought against hostile warlords, ethnic groups, and nationalist troops all the way. Of the 100,000 that set out only 10,000 footsore, battered, emaciated survivors of the Communists' First Front Army reached the comparative safety of Yan'an in the wilds of northwest China. It is estimated that only 7,000 were part of the original group. They were joined within the year by the Fourth Red Army and the Second Red

Mao Zedong on horseback with Red Army soldiers on the "long march."

Army, which had endured similar circumstances.

The long march became a legend and a powerful piece of propaganda. There were many stories of bravery against impossible odds, none more remarkable than that of the 30 volunteers who captured the Luding Bridge over the Dadu river gorge in the teeth of murderous machine-gun fire. The march established Mao Zedong as the undisputed leader of China's communists. His claim

that the peasants (as opposed to urban workers) would prove the backbone of communism in China became accepted as did his adherence to guerilla warfare.

The nationalist forces of Chiang Kai-Shek and the armies of Mao Zedong forged an uneasy alliance to fight against the Japanese troops that invaded Manchuria in 1937. At the close of World War II, Mao would push the Kuomintang out of Mainland China to Taiwan. ❑

October 25, 1929 has gone down in history as Black Friday. It marked the end of the Roaring Twenties in the United States, where small investors poured money into a stock market that seemed incapable of retrenchment. As stock prices rose, the credit market became over-inflated. When in August 1929 professional speculators began to sell off their shares, the overall buying euphoria suddenly changed into a crazed selling hysteria. The consequence was a stock market collapse on an unheard-of scale. As the United States had by that time become the engine of the international economy, its crash brought down the rest of the world with it.

Between October 23 and 29, 1929, the Dow-Jones Index, quoted daily since 1896, slipped from 381 down to 261 points. In less than a week the equity market in Wall Street completely collapsed. The long period of prosperity in the USA gave way to a severe depression that triggered a worldwide economic crisis.

The effects of the American financial crisis were soon felt in Europe. Between 1924 and 1929, Germany and Austria in particular had relied on a massive inflow of capital from the USA. About half the German net investments were financed by foreign funds. When the USA lenders, driven by necessity, recalled their short-term loans from Central Europe, it became clear how insufficient the reserve funds of the German and Austrian banks were. On May 11, 1931, the collapse of the Austrian Credit-Anstalt bank alarmed the authorities; then on July 13, the Darmstädter and National Bank was the first major German bank to stop trading. The collapse of the entire banking system could only be prevented by emergency decrees and state intervention.

The banks' fight for survival further aggravated the economic crisis. In Germany, economic performance declined by 26% between 1928 and 1932, and by February 1932 the number of unemployed had risen to over 6 million. In 1932, the annual average unemployment rate was 29.9 % in Germany. In the USA some 15 million people were out of work at the beginning of 1933—one third of the workforce.

IN THE SHADOW OF FASCISM

The political impact was considerable. In October 1922 the leader of the *Partito Nazionale Fascista*, Benito Mussolini, was appointed prime minister by the Italian king Emmanuel III. The fear of the "red revolution" was such that the king, the Church, liberals, and democrats all yielded to the Fascist claim to power, thus enabling Mussolini to establish the Fascist autarchy of his party. By 1929, the establishment of the Fascist supremacy was complete in Italy, and "Il Duce's" legitimacy was accepted by a large part of the population.

The success of the Italian Fascists served as an example to the German National Socialist party. Nevertheless, the attempted coup in Munich on November 9, 1923, failed. Its leader, Adolf Hitler, used his subsequent—extremely light—sentence of one year's imprisonment to write his autobiography and political treatise *Mein Kampf* (*My Struggle*). He remained undeterred in his intention of seizing power in Germany remained; only the tactics changed: National Socialism would come to power through elections.

The economic crisis in 1930 gave the Nazis their political breakthrough. The NSDAP (National Socialist Workers Party, i.e. the Nazi party) was the strongest faction in the parliamentary elections both in July with 37% and again in November 1932 with 33.1% of the vote, but they failed to reach the absolute majority that they had hoped for. In fact, it was not the voters who ensured that Hitler became Chancellor but influential major landowners and industrialists. They persuaded the 85-year-old Paul von Hindenburg, president of the Weimar Republic, to appoint Hitler as chancellor of a presidential cabinet on January 30, 1933.

In the course of the next five months the NSDAP laid the foundations for what would be twelve years of National Socialist tyranny: basic rights were abrogated, political opposition was suppressed, the first concentration camps were built, and political repression in all areas of public life began.

JAPANESE EXPANSION IN EAST ASIA

When the 25-year-old Prince-Regent Hirohito ascended the imperial throne as emperor in 1926, Japan was facing a severe problem of over-population. Under the influence of a group of radical officers, a form of extreme nationalism spread among both the people and government officials. The only solution to Japan's economic difficulties and political problems caused by overpopulation seemed to lie in military expansion. On September 18, 1931 an incident near Mukden, staged by the Japanese military, was used as a pretext for the occupation of the three Manchurian provinces of China. These were merged into the new state of Manchuko in 1932. Because the great powers refused to recognize this Japanese vassal state, Japan gave notice of its withdrawal from the League of Nations.

This tension in Japan's foreign policy led to internal destabilization. In 1936, a military coup launched by a group of young officers failed, but the army assumed control of the most important positions of power in the country. With regard to foreign affairs, Japan began to forge closer links with the countries of the Axis Powers, namely Germany and Italy, with which it formed the Three-Power Pact in 1940. An exchange of fire between Japanese and Chinese troops

The USA entered the war in 1941: an attack by B-29 bombers that were used in the war in the Pacific.

near Beijing triggered open war between the two countries that lasted from 7 July 1937 until 1945.

"THEY HAD BEEN FIRING BACK SINCE 5:45 "

On September 1, 1939, German troops marched into Poland. To the end, Hitler had tried to isolate Poland from the West through mass propaganda, so as to limit the planned war on the eastern front. With this in mind, the SS had staged border violations by the Poles and a serious attack on the broadcasting station of Gleiwitz that provided the pretext for the Germans' "firing back." But the world could no longer turn a blind eye to Hitler's intentions. On September 3, France and Great Britain declared war on Germany.

Meanwhile National-Socialist Germany had been systematically been preparing for war. Between 1933 and 1939, annual defense expenditure had risen from 0.7 to 25.9 billion Reichsmarks (RM) and its share of the country's budget thus rose from 8.6 % to 61.4%. The result was a rapid increase in the national debt that went from 11.7 to 42.6 billion RM. At the same time the money in circulation rose from 5.7 to 14.5 billion RM (by 1945 it had risen to 56.7 billion RM). This huge military build-up was not matched by either France or England.

On March 16, 1935, Hitler announced the reintroduction of compulsory military service. In view of the military and political reluctance of the Western powers to intervene in the Sino-Japanese conflict or the Spanish Civil War, Hitler decided to implement his plans of expansion. In March 1938, he announced the *Anschluss* (annexation) of Austria, after sending an ultimatum to the Austrian president ordering him to appoint a cabinet designated by the German government. In October 1938, German troops marched into the Sudetenland, and in March 1939, Czechoslovakia was occupied to form the "Reichs protectorate of Bohemia and Moravia." In the autumn of 1939 Hitler wanted to make Poland a dependent state of the German Reich through the cession of territory.

When the Polish government rejected the German demands, Hitler decided to use force. In doing so, he was taking the risk of Great Britain declaring war, although the German Reich was yet not sufficiently prepared for a long struggle. The German attack on Poland was the final proof for London and Paris that the policy of appeasement had failed.

FROM EUROPEAN TO WORLD WAR

The European War (1939-1941) began with a successful blitzkrieg campaign by the German Wehrmacht. In the middle of 1940, the focus of the war shifted eastward, particularly to the Balkans but also to North Africa. The planned invasion of the British Isles had to be postponed "indefinitely" after German heavy losses incurred during the Battle of Britain in 1940.

The extension of the war from a European conflict to a global one occurred in 1941 and was marked by two events: the German attack on the Soviet Union (June 22, 1941) and the attack by the Japanese air force on

The Soviet occupation of Berlin: Red Army soldiers raising the flag of the Soviet Union on the roof of the Reichstag.

the American fleet in Pearl Harbor, Hawaii (December 7, 1941), which led to the USA entering the war. At the end of 1941, Hitler's objective "to defeat the Soviet Union in a brief campaign" failed as he approached Moscow, but because there was now no "second front" of the western allies, Hitler was able to launch a new offensive in the east.

During the third phase of the war, the military initiative that had been in the hands of the Axis powers was transferred to the allied coalition of Great Britain, the Soviet Union, and the USA. The British Royal Air Force began the carpet bombing of German cities (March 1942). In November 1942, the German-Italian troops were forced to withdraw from North Africa by the British, and in 1943 Germany was forced to end the U-boat war in the Atlantic. Germany was wearying of calls for "total war," the die-hard words distorted by propaganda and the (false) hope of Hitler's "wonder weapon." The disastrous engagement in Stalingrad that ended with the total loss of the German Sixth army did nothing to alter Hitler's conviction of invincibility.

At the same time, Germany was proceeding with the genocidal destruction of the Jews. Its methodical program of extermination showed humanity in it very worst light. Incredibly the imperative to annihilate the Jewish people took precedence over the war effort, with trains that could have been used to transport troops and military supplied rerouted to carry human cargo to concentration camps

The last phase of the Second World War started with the D-Day landings of allied troops in Normandy on June 6, 1944, and ended with the defeat of Germany and Japan. The German Reich was finished economically and militarily, and unconditional surrender in May of 1945 had become unavoidable. The War in the Pacific ended with the bombing of Hiroshima and Nagasaki. Faced with the loss of an incalculable number of soldiers that an invasion of Japan would entail, President Harry Truman's decision to unleash the nuclear genie would definitively shape the course of the second half of the twentieth century. ❑

GROWING PERSECUTION OF GERMAN JEWS

Nuremberg, 1938

The National Socialist genocidal war against the Jews began with incorporating anti-Semitism into the law. The first step was taken in 1933 soon after the Nazis came to power, when they passed a law stating that the Jews were not to be considered part of the German people but were to be treated legally as aliens.

From then on the areas of social life in which the approximately 500,000 German Jews (about .8% of the population) could participate kept shrinking. "The Jewish Boycott" of April 1, 1933 resulted in the dismissal of all Jewish civil servants (April 7), the revocation of the licenses of Jewish lawyers (April 10) and the removal of Jewish doctors (April 22).

The Nuremberg Law of September 15, 1935 officially declared that Jews were persons of diminished standing and rights. Hitler was personally respon-

sible for "The Law for the Protection of German Blood and German Honor" that prohibited the marriage or extra-marital contact between Jews and German citizens. The law also applied to "mischlings" those who had two or more Jewish grandparents. After the *anschluss* in 1938 the same restrictions were placed upon the Jews of Austria. The assassination of the German ambassador in Paris, Ernst vom Rath, on November 7, 1938 by the Polish Jew, Herschl Grynszpan, whose parents had just been deported from Germany, served as the pretext for vicious anti-Jewish demonstrations organized by the government. On the night of November 9 and into the following day more than 250 synagogues, 8000 business and countless homes of Jews were looted and destroyed. 91 German Jews were murdered and over 25,000 people deported to

concentration camps. This anti-semitic rampage became known as *Kristallnacht*. On November 12 the Jewish community was required to pay a fine of one billion marks as restitution for the damage they were accused of having caused.

Kristallnacht marked the beginning of a new phase in the Nazi persecution of the Jews. They were no longer to be hedged in by legal barriers, but rather interned in camps in preparation for their eventual extermination. ❑

Jews in Vienna forced to scrub the streets

SHOW TRIALS IN RUSSIA

Moscow, 1936-1938

Fully in power in 1934, Russian Communist Party leader, Joseph Stalin, still sought to eliminate any possible opposition. One potential threat was the popular Leningrad party leader, Sergey Kirov. When Kirov was assassinated in December, Stalin used the event as a pretext to have his secret police, the NKVD, round up those he accused of being "counter-revolutionaries." In truth, Kirov was probably murdered by the NVKD under Stalin's orders. The "counter-revolutionaries" were Bolsheviks and Trotskyites who Stalin had long wanted to eliminate. The arrest and trial of these party officials became known as the "Show Trials."

Lasting from 1936 to 1938, the "Show Trials" were a series of public trials in which many officials were arrested on trumped up charges and forced to falsely con-

fess to being enemies of the state. By the end of the trials, most of the Lenin-era party members had been tried and convicted. Most were summarily executed.

The first trials were held in August of 1936 and featured the conviction of two well known Bolsheviks, Lev Kamenev and Grigori Zinoviev. The next trials were held in January of 1937, the most prominent defendant being another Bolshevik, Karl Radek. The last trial was held in March of 1938 and included the conviction of long-time Stalin enemies Nikolay Bukharin and Aleksey Rykov, as well as the former head of the NKVD, Genrikh Yagoda, who confessed to the assassination of Sergey Kirov.

These trials were the beginning of Stalin's "Great Purge", in which millions of ordinary Soviet citizens died. ❑

ABDICATION OF KING EDWARD VIII

London, January 1, 1936

Born in 1894 to the Duke and Duchess of York, the future King George V and Queen Mary, Edward became King Edward VIII upon the death of his father in 1936.

Edward had a distinguished record of military service and was well-informed about policy matters and popular with the British people. However, a great rift

The Duke of Windsor and his wife, Wallis Simpson.

arose in 1936 when the new King made clear his intention to marry Wallis Simpson, a soon to be twice divorced American woman. The populace was opposed to having Wallis Simpson as the King's consort. Parliament refused to offer her any title and the government was threatening wholesale resignation if the King persisted with his plan to marry. In addition the Church of England, of which Edward was the titular head, censured divorced and opposed the marriage. Amidst all this controversy Edward remained determined to have his way and marry the woman he loved.

On December 10, 1936 after a reign of only eleven months, Edward signed the instrument of abdication in favor of his brother Albert, who became King George VI. ❑

HITLER'S OCCUPATION OF AUSTRIA AND THE SUDETENLAND

Munich, September 30, 1938

At 12:28 AM, Adolf Hitler, British Prime Minister Neville Chamberlain, Italy's leader Benito Mussolini, and the French President Édouard Daladier signed the Munich Agreement. The Czechoslovakian Government was not invited to take part in the talks. The agreement stated that the Czechoslovakia was to sign over the Sudetenland to the German Reich by October 10 1938. Chamberlain returning to England with treaty in hand, made the famously inaccurate prediction: "I believe it is peace for our time."

On October 1, 1938 the Wehrmacht (the German army) moved into the Sudetenland, appropriating twenty percent of Czechoslovakia. On October 5, Eduard Benes stepped down as president, an office he had held since 1935.

Six months earlier Hitler invaded Austria, declaring the union of the German peoples (*Anschluss*). The Austrian Chancellor, Kurt Schuschnigg, had been summoned to Berchtesgaden (Hitler's residence in

Left: German troops march into Prague. Right: Enthusiastic reception in Austria

Chamberlain and Hitler

the Bavarian Alps) on February 12, for what he thought was a friendly meeting. He was given an ultimatum to appoint the National Socialist, Arthur Seyss-Inquart, as Austria's new Minister of the Interior. Schuschnigg's pleas to France and Britain for help fell upon deaf ears. As he announced that a referendum would be held on March 9 for a " free und independent Austria," Hitler mobilized his troops. Schuschnigg was forced to resign, and Arthur Seyss-Inquart took power. His first act was to ask Berlin for help. German Soldiers marched into Austria on March 12, where they were enthusiastically received. On March 13, Hitler proclaimed the *Anschluss*, the formal unification of his homeland Austria with the German Reich.

Hitler's next target was the

Sudetenland, historically a German region. It had been included in the State of Czechoslovakia, which had been established at the end of World War I. Twenty-two percent of the population was German, the second largest group in the country.

Encouraged by Berlin, Konrad Henlein, leader of the Sudeten Germans, lobbied for an autonomy that Prague was reluctant to grant. On September 12, Hitler demanded the right of self-determination for the Sudeten Germans and urged them to take up arms.

Chamberlain met with Hitler in Berchtesgaden on September 15 and then again in Bad Godesberg on September 22, in hopes of mediating an agreement in the context of the mutual defense pact between France and Czechoslovakia. Hitler promised

that the Sudetenland was his last territorial demand in Europe but threatened war if it were not met. With the Munich Agreement France and Britain gave in to Hitler's demands, but this did not slake his thirst for further expansion. On March 14 of the following year, Jozef Tiso, in a move choreographed by Hitler, proclaimed an independent Slovakia. It would become a satellite of Germany. Two days later German troops seized the rest of the country and named a " Reichsprotector" for Bohemia and Moravia as an autonomous part of the "Greater German Reich."

Hitler breached the Treaty of Versailles numerous times, but neither France nor England was willing to stand up to him. The sacrifice of Czechoslovakia on the altar of appeasement was a low point for both nations. ❑

GERMAN PHYSICISTS SPLIT THE ATOM

Berlin, December 22, 1938

Two German physicists, Otto Hahn and Fritz Strassman, successfully performed the first demonstration of nuclear fission. In an article in a German scientific journal, scientists at the Kaiser Wilhelm Institute published the results of their findings. They had bombarded the element uranium (atomic weight 238) with a stream of neutrons and produced the element barium (atomic weight 116). The scientists were themselves startled by the results, which seemed to contradict all of the known principles of physics.

Their experiments had split apart the uranium atoms' nuclei producing new elements with less mass than the original uranium. In the process an enormous amount of energy was released. With their discovery the scientists ushered in the Nuclear Age. ❑

Otto Hahn's desk

GERMANY INVADES POLAND TO START WORLD WAR II

Polish-German Border, September 1, 1939

On August 28, 1939, Hitler and Stalin stunned the world when they united in signing the Soviet-German Non-Aggression Pact, in which they divided Poland between them. (Though this was not made public at the time.) Four days later, at 4:45 AM September 1, one and a half million German troops, using tanks supported by mechanized infantry and dive bombers, crossed the frontier on a broad front ranging from East Prussia in the north to Slovakia in the south, thrust into Poland presenting Blitzkrieg, lightning war, to the world.

The Polish army that faced this onslaught was ineptly led by generals who put their faith in cavalry rather than tanks and were dismissive of airpower. By September 3, when first England and then France (abandoning diplomatic efforts for peace) declared war on Germany, the Germans had already cut the Polish Corridor. The German general Guderian's tanks were on the outskirts of Warsaw by the September 8 and nine days later the Russians invaded from the east. By September 30, the Polish Army was defeated at the cost of 45,000 casualties for the Germans who killed or wounded 260,000 Poles and captured a further 700,000 But 85,000 thousand Polish troops escaped to Romania.

On September 17, a U-boat sank the British aircraft carrier *Courageous* and then four days later the battleship *Royal Oak*. Harmful as these losses were to the Royal Navy, Britain's main concern was Hitler's plan to take control of all neutral shipping, forcing uninvolved nations to divert exports to Germany. To achieve this aim he ordered unrestricted U-boat attacks on unarmed merchant ships from every nation, except for the United States.

German bombing of Dunkirk

Throughout October of 1939, the British sent troops to France to bolster the ninety French Divisions already in place along the French frontiers. The overall command of the army went to General Gamelan who, conscious of the allied numerical superiority, proposed an offensive against the 23 German Divisions ranged against him. He was overruled, the French Government preferring to put its faith in the Maginot Line, a strongly built series of forts and trenches, which stretched the length of the Franco-German border. Of the ninety divisions available to them the French committed 40 to this line of defense. 39 divisions, including the British Expeditionary Forces (BEF), protected the northern approaches into France, and the rest were held in reserve around Paris to be used where necessary.

In March of 1940, Winston Churchill called for the mining of Norwegian waters in an attempt to prevent iron being shipped to Germany. British and French forces were landed at Narvik, Trondheim and Bergen. However while the Allied governments were negotiating with the neutral Norwegians, the Germans, who

War begins: German troops crossing the Polish border

NAZI-SOVIET NON-AGGRESSION PACT

Moscow, 1939

As Hitler prepared for war his first target was Poland. Afraid of the prospect of a two-front war, he sent his foreign minister, Ribbentrop, to meet with his Soviet counterpart, Molotov.

On August 23, 1939 the two foreign ministers signed the Pact which stated the two countries would not attack one another. It was supposed to last for ten years; it was broken in less than two.

The Non-Aggression Pact also had a secret protocol, an addendum which was denied by the Soviets until 1989. The secret protocol divided Poland between the two powers, and in it Germany agreed to give the Soviet Union control of the Baltic States (Estonia, Lithuania and Latvia) in return for the Soviets' non-interference in Germany's war against Poland.

The terms of the pact and the protocol were honored until Germany's surprise attack and invasion of the Soviet Union on June 22, 1941. ❑

From left to right: Von Ribbentrop, Stalin, Molotov

had already drawn up a plan for the invasion of Norway, landed seven divisions and by April 9 had seized all major ports and occupied Denmark.

The British held onto Narvik but were forced to evacuate in May when their troops were needed for home defense.

Hitler had hoped to start his offensive into France in November 1939; however the Halder Plan, which had been conceived for this purpose, was rejected because of the high casualties it would have incurred. Generals von Rundstedt and von Man stein devised a plan that depended on the German armor breaking through the Ardennes, taking the Allies by surprise.

Hitler inspecting occupied Paris

The first phase of the plan was carried out on May 10, when Army Group B attacked through Holland and Belgium. Parachute and glider born troops managed to take key positions by May 11 and, as expected, the Allied response was to turn north to counterattack, unaware that to their south, Army Group A under von Runstedt had successfully penetrated the Ardennes. At the same time Army Group C was making feints against the Maginot Line and taking up positions to prevent an Allied flanking movement. Simultaneously with the ground operations the Luftwaffe launched an offensive against the allied air forces and flew sorties in support of the ground troops. The effect on the allies was catastrophic; reeling from the force of the combined attacks and the confusion brought about from the bombing to the rear they were unable to mount any counterattacks of any strategic significance.

On the May 17, Churchill, Prime Minister at that point for only ten days, visited the French Government in Paris and was shocked at the atmosphere of defeatism. Meanwhile, with short rests to eat and refuel, the German advance continued to the coast. On May 25, Boulogne surrendered and Dunkirk was surrounded; but astonishingly Hitler called off Guderain's tanks, which halted for three days allowing the British to fortify their positions and supervise the evacuation of 300,000 allied troops. A further 250,000 were evacuated from Le Havre and Cherbourg, in late June.

The Germans now turned south to attack Paris, and Army Group C outflanked the Maginot Line and raced toward the city to link up with their comrades. Paris fell on June 14. Prime Minister Reynard was forced to resign, and Marshall Petain sought an Armistice, which was signed at Compiègne (the site of the German surrender in World War I) on June 22, 1940.

German casualties for the campaign amounted to 156,000 killed, missing, or wounded. Allied losses including the capture of the French army were 2,292,000 killed, captured, or wounded. ❑

RETREAT FROM DUNKIRK

Dunkirk, June 4, 1940

Although the beaches of Dunkirk were littered with the wreckage of war and the bodies of those who did not make it to the ships, 338,226 men of the British Expeditionary Force, together with many French and Belgians, were rescued by the British Royal Navy and ferried across the Channel to England.

When the French line of defense was broken by the Germans at Sedan, and King Leopold ordered the Belgian army to lay down its weapons, the British pulled back to Dunkirk under relentless German air attacks and through thousands of fleeing refugees. It was thought at that point that no more than 45,000 troops could be saved.

The Luftwaffe continued the dive-bombing of the retreating British and allied forces trapped on the beaches. However, the advancing German army suddenly stopped outside of Dunkirk.

Off the coast was a fleet of British and French destroyers accompanied by by a host of ferries, fishing vessels and even river cruisers, all pressed into service to help transport the fleeing allies to safety.

Code-named *Operation Dynamo*, the rescue could not be described as a military victory, but its success made sure that the British army would live to fight another day. ❑

EXCERPTS FROM A SPEECH BY WINSTON CHURCHILL

Parliament, June 4, 1940

I have, myself, full confidence that if all do their duty, if nothing is neglected, and if the best arrangements are made, as they are being made, we shall prove ourselves once again able to defend our island home, to ride out the storm of war, and to outlive the menace of tyranny, if necessary for years, if necessary alone.

Even though large tracts of Europe and many old and famous States have fallen or may fall into the grip of the Gestapo and all the odious apparatus of Nazi rule, we shall not flag or fail. We shall go on to the end, we shall fight in France, we shall fight on the seas and oceans, we shall fight with growing confidence and growing strength in the air, we shall defend our Island, whatever the cost may be, we shall fight on the beaches, we shall fight on the landing grounds, we shall fight in the fields and in the streets, we shall

Winston Churchill

fight in the hills; we shall never surrender, and even if, which I do not for a moment believe, this Island or a large part of it were subjugated and starving, then our Empire beyond the seas, armed and guarded by the British Fleet, would carry on the struggle, until, in God's good time, the New World, with all its power and might, steps forth to the rescue and the liberation of the Old. ❑

GAINS FOR THE AXIS

European and Pacific Fronts, 1940–1941

When France fell in June of 1940, Winston Churchill declared that "...the Battle of France is over. I expect that the Battle of Britain is about to begin." He was right; the Germans were in the process of drawing up plans for Operation Sea Lion, the invasion of England. The German Navy stipulated that for the invasion to be a success it was necessary to have air supremacy.

The Battle of Britain began in July with the Germans attacking shipping in the English Channel. From August 12 through 23 the main focus of the Luftwaffe's campaign was against the RAF's airfields. Throughout this period both sides, but particularly the RAF, modified their tactics to adjust to their enemies methods. The critical stage of the battle lasted from August 24 through September 6. The RAF was hard pressed because of insufficient pilots and the damage caused by the raids on the airfields beginning to exhaust ground support personnel. It was at this point, perhaps because of an air raid on Berlin, that the Germans switched strategy and began to bomb cities, most notably London. The Blitz had begun and was to continue through May of 1941. The Battle of Britain ended in October when Hitler decided to postpone his invasion plans until the spring of 1941.

Then on September 27, 1940, Germany, Italy, and Japan signed the Tripartite Pact, which formally brought into being the Axis Powers; it divided their spheres of interest,

Surrender of a Russian soldier

and they pledged military support for each other in these spheres. It also warned the Americans that war on behalf of the Allies would entail war in the Pacific.

Mussolini, envious of Germany's military successes and seeking triumphs of his own, invaded Greece on 28 October 1940, expecting an easy victory. However the Greeks not only put up fierce resistance but pushed the Italians out of Greece and into Albania. The British sent troops from Egypt to aid the Greeks but in doing so alarmed Hitler, as he believed that the British would now be able to bomb his oil supply in Romania. When the Italian counterattack failed in March, Hitler recognized the need to go to his ally's help. On April 6, he invaded through Bulgaria, and although the Greeks and British fought with great resolve, they were driven out of Greece by April 30.

In Yugoslavia, the German army easily brought down the existing government. It did not, however, anticipate the resistance fighters' guerilla warfare. There were two camps: the royalist *chetniks* and the communist guerillas led by Josip Broz Tito. The communists held back until Hitler launched his invasion of Russia. From that point on they became a thorn in Germany's side, winning back large swaths of previously ceded territory.

On June 22, 1941, after years of planning, Hitler launched Operation Barbarossa, the largest military operation in history. It involved 5.5 million Axis troops along an 1,800- mile front. The Germans divided their army into three separate groups: Army Group North, to take the Baltic States and Northern Russia; Army Group Center to advance on Moscow, and Army Group South to take the Ukraine and on eastward to the Volga and the oil rich Caucasus. Astonishingly, this operation took the So-

Campaigning in winter: German truck stuck in the mud

viets by surprise, even though Stalin had been warned by his own intelligence services and Winston Churchill. The Luftwaffe destroyed over 2,000 planes in the first two days of fighting and hundreds of thousands of Soviet troops were either captured or killed. The Russians also faced uprisings in Lithuania and Estonia. The Soviet troops were urged to counterattack by Moscow, but this proved to be impossible owing to the complete destruction of their command structure. Although they met with determined resistance in some areas, the German Army Groups appeared to be invincible as they advanced toward their objectives.

Amid much secrecy and evasive action taken by HMS *Prince of Wales* to elude U-boat attack, Winston Churchill was able to meet President Roosevelt aboard the USS *Augusta* in Newfoundland in August 1941. It was here that they signed the Atlantic Charter, which stated that neither country was striving for territorial gain and that aggressor nations be disarmed. Roosevelt had already proclaimed America the "arsenal of democracy" and enacted the "lend lease" pact, which deferred British payment for American arms until the end of hostilities.

Following the attack on Pearl Harbor, Japan lost no time in attacking British and American positions in Southeast Asia. Manila was bombed on December 8, as Japanese troops were landed on Batan (not to be confused with Bataan) off the north coast of Luzon and elements of the Japanese 25th Army invaded Malaya. Singa-

pore was the linchpin that allied strategy depended on in Southeast Asia, and reinforcements in the form of two capital ships, HMS *Prince of Wales* and the *Repulse* had arrived in the South China Sea shortly before hostilities broke out. However, lacking air support, they were both sunk with their escort destroyers on December 10. On the same day Guam was lost, and on December 24, the Wake Island garrison surrendered. Hong Kong submitted on Christmas Day, with 6,000 troops falling into enemy hands.

However, the most shocking advance made by the Japanese was down the Malayan Peninsula, using light tanks and bicycle infantry, they had pushed back a numerically superior force all the way to Singapore by January 31. After a siege of seven days the garrison of 80,000 men surrendered to a force of 30,000 making it one of the worst British military disasters in history.

In the Philippines the Japanese began to land in force and make progress inland on the 22 December. General Douglas MacArthur, who was in command at the time, began a tactical withdrawal to Bataan. The seeming ease with which the Japanese had achieved victory was halted as the American defenders slowed their advance, making them pay dearly for the ground that they took. The continued defense of Bataan and then Corregidor bought time for the Allied war effort in the Pacific. But eventually they too fell to the Japanese. ❑

THE "FINAL SOLUTION"

Berlin, January 20, 1942

A meeting convened by the Security Chief of the German Reich, Reinhard Heydrich, in a villa in Am Großen Wannsee, a suburb of Berlin, had as its agenda the "final solution" of the Jewish problem in Europe. By this was meant the utter annihilation of the Jewish population. The thirteen second-level officials in attendance represented most departments of the central government and the governments for occupied territories. Adolf Eichmann had arranged the preparations for the conference and kept the minutes.

The first extermination camp had been built a year before at Chelmo, outside of Lodz in Poland, although the first shipment of Jews from the Lodz Ghetto did not take place until January of 1942. Auschwitz was visited around the same time by two civilians who instructed the camp officers in the use of Zyklon B poison gas. Mobile Killing Units had been following advancing German troops and conducting mass murders of Jews in the Baltic countries and in Russia, where with help from Ukranian troops they massacred 33,000 Jews at Babi Yar outside of Kiev in late September, 1941.

The goal of the Wannsee Conference was to organize and, in a way, industrialize these sporadic, inefficient killings. With a chilling command of euphemism Heydrich spoke about the change in policy from "emigration" (forced relocation) to "evacuation" (murder) given "the possibilities in the East" (extermination camps). Heydrich went on to outline the general procedures to organize this massive effort: the entire Jewish population of Europe was to be gathered up and placed in transit ghettos, "to be transferred from there farther to the East."

The Final Solution was given top priority, at times it conflicted with conventional war aims, as trains that could have been carrying military supplies or sol-

Polish Jews unloaded at Auschwitz.

diers were used for the transport of Jews. Mass deportations occurred from all countries of Occupied Europe except for Denmark, where King Christian X inspired his people to resist the Nazi demands. There was also sizeable resistance in Finland and Italy. But other countries were much more cooperative. In Poland about 3 million Jews were murdered (90 percent of the pre-war population); in the Soviet Union 900,000 (28 percent), 310,000 from Germany, Austria and Czechoslovakia (50 percent), 300,000 from Hungary (75 percent), 270,000 from Romania (34 percent), 130,000 from the Benelux countries (56 percent) and 70,000 from France and Italy (22 percent).

On April 19, 1943 resistance to deportation orders broke out in the Warsaw Ghetto. With makeshift arms the Jews were able to hold off the German army for a month. Almost the entire population of the ghetto was killed, over 56,000 people. ❑

ATTACK ON PEARL HARBOR

Hawaii, December 7, 1941

Tensions between the US and Japan had been growing steadily throughout the 1930s and were exacerbated by the Japanese invasion of Manchuria in 1931 which led to all out war between China and Japan in 1938. Both countries had drawn up plans for war in the Pacific, but the Japanese mistakenly believed that an attack on the British colonies in the Far East would precipitate a response from the Americans. To preempt this imagined response a plan was drawn up by Admiral Isoroku Yamamoto for an attack on Pearl Harbor.

At 3:42 AM (Hawaiian time) Sunday December 7, 1941, the USS *Condor* spotted a midget submarine in the approaches to Pearl Harbor, it radioed a warning to the destroyer USS *Ward*, which

spotted a submarine at 6:37 AM and sank it. The first shots of the Pacific war had been fired.

At 7:48 AM as crews of the US Pacific Fleet stirred from their bunks or made their way to the mess deck for breakfast, they heard the roar of 190 aircraft flying overhead and then the sounds of explosions as the payloads of the slow flying bombers found targets, and then from the ships speakers, "Air Raid Pearl Harbor. This is not drill." The first wave of the Japanese attack, lead by Mitsuo Fuchida, continued to find targets as the confused sailors and marines struggled to open ammunition lockers and man their battle stations. Half an hour later the second wave of 163 bombers commanded by Lieutenant Commander Shigekazu

Shimazaki hit the airfields at Ford Island, Barbers Point and Hickman Field. Only a few of the defending aircraft managed

Bombing of Pearl Harbor

to get off the ground, the rest were destroyed as they sat wing tip to wing tip on the tarmac.

In ninety minutes the Japanese sunk or damaged 18 ships including five battleships, destroyed 188 aircraft and killed 2,331 servicemen and 55 civilians, for the loss of 29 planes and five midget submarines. However, they had failed to sink any aircraft carriers, or damage the submarine pens or destroy the fuel storage facilities. They had also failed to declare war on America before the attack began, thus giving credence to Franklin D. Roosevelt's declaration that December 7, 1941 would be "...a date which will live in infamy." ❑

THE TIDE OF WAR TURNS

European and Pacific Fronts, 1942

On June 7, 1942, six months to the day after the Japanese attacked Pearl Harbor the Americans wreaked their revenge at Midway. It was the most significant naval engagement of the Pacific war and one in which the opposing fleets never glimpsed each other: the outcome depended entirely on airpower. The action took place over three days and ended with the sinking of four Japanese aircraft carriers and the loss of one cruiser. The Americans lost one carrier, but, significantly, had 29 already under construction and were developing training program for pilots. The Japanese had only one carrier left in action and three under repair, and they had lost 200 experienced naval aviators.

In July 1942 Winston Churchill and Arthur "Bomber Harris" conceived the plan "Operation Gomorrah" that would entail the sustained bombing of Hamburg by the RAF at night and USAF by day. On the night of July 24, 750 RAF bombers began the bombing of the city and on the following day, 68 American B17s continued the destruction. After two days the Americans ceased flying as the smoke cover was too dense. By August 3, when the operation came to an end, 10,000 tons of bombs had been dropped, destroying ten square miles of the city, including the submarine pens and factories employed in war manufacture; over 100,000 civilians had been killed and a million more made homeless due to the firestorms produced by the bombing.

Meanwhile in Africa, British General Montgomery had been given command of the Eighth Army in August 1942. Aware that neither side had been able to deliver the knockout blow after any initial success in the North Africa campaign, he dug in 50 miles from Alexandria and steadily built up his army, until it had gained at least a two to one advantage in men and equipment. The Battle of El Alamein began with a barrage on German positions on October 23, which successfully knocked out German communications. However the German defenses were five miles deep and heavily mined (the Devil's Garden) making Allied progress slow. But by October 30 Rommel considered the battle lost and sought permission to withdraw, which Hitler re-

El Alamein: German tank surrendering

Mussolini's corpse

fused. On November 5, the Allies achieved their breakthrough and Germany's Afrika Korps was in full retreat. In an address to the Americans Winston Churchill said "... this is not the end, nor is it the beginning of the end, but it is the end of the beginning."

The worst news for Germany was yet to come. The German Sixth Army under the command of General Friedrich Wilhelm Ernst Paulus, arrived at Stalingrad, a vital transport route, on July 24, 1942 and became immediately engaged in a ferocious and brutal battle. Stalin refused to allow any evacuation of the city, even of women and children, adopting a "not one step back" policy. Throughout the summer and early autumn the fighting continued from room to room, basement to stairwell, with no quarter being given. The city was reduced to rubble. In early October, the Germans were on the verge of success, but the Soviets held. In November, the momentum shifted, and Russian armies were able to encircle the city trapping the Germans inside. Hitler refused to allow Paulus to attempt a breakout, and Operation *Wintergewitter*, an effort to relieve the beleaguered army, failed. After 199 days and at the combined cost of 1.5 million casualties, Paulus surrendered the remnants of his army, 91,000 men. Only 5,000 would live to see Germany again.

Since the arrival of the Americans in North Africa in November 1942, the German Afrika Korps had been fighting on two fronts, with Montgomery on the east

and Eisenhower on the west. The Germans were dogged in retreat, and Rommel inflicted a defeat on the Americans at Kasserine Pass. However he was relived in March and replaced by General von Armin. The Allies pressed on and took Tunis on May 7 and captured von Armin in Bon Cap, where he was forced to sign the surrender of 150,000 Axis troops.

Following the success in North Africa, the Allies invaded Sicily in July, precipitating the fall of Mussolini. The Sicilian campaign lasted for six weeks and during this time the Allies entered into negotiations with the Italian Prime Minister Pietro Badoglio to arrange surrender terms. On September 3, Montgomery landed at Calabria in Southern Italy with the eighth Army, hoping to deceive the Germans into believing that this was the main invasion. The Germans were not taken in and withdrew. However, in the meantime Eisenhower accepted the Italian unconditional surrender on September 8, and the main Allied landings the following day at Salerno, although resisted by the Germans, were unopposed by Italian forces.

In the meantime the war in the Atlantic against the U-boat threat had turned in favor of the Allies. Improved submarine detection techniques, including sonar radar and the deployment of extra escort ships and aircraft carriers swung the balance to surface warships. Fewer U-boat commanders were prepared to venture out into the Atlantic and consequently more merchant vessels survived the crossing. ❑

Soldiers fighting in the rubble of Stalingrad

D-DAY: CROSS CHANNEL ATTACK

Normandy, June 6, 1944

Preceded by a massive aerial and naval bombardment British, American and Canadian forces landed on five beaches, (Sword, Juno, Gold, Utah and Omaha) along a hundred- mile stretch of Normandy coast on June 6, 1944. The night before British airborne troops had landed and successfully taken key bridges and crossing places, setting up defenses to protect the beachhead from German counter attack. The American airborne drops were less successful, as the troops, for the most part, missed their drop zones; however, they succeeded in confusing the Germans as they operated in pockets behind the lines for some days after the invasion.

The Canadian troops that landed on Juno beach, despite meeting stiff resistance, were the only troops to make their first day objectives. The British assaults on Sword and Gold took heavy casualties making an eight-mile incursion but failed to take Caen. The lightest casualties were on Utah beach and the Americans advanced to just short of their objectives. Omaha beach suffered the worst casualties of the invasion and at one point commanders considered withdrawing the men, but gradually small ad hoc units of infantry established two toeholds and they remained, gaining their objectives on D-Day +3.

The Germans, who had always thought that the main assault would come at the Pas de Calais and continued in this misapprehension, failed to mount significant counter attacks until it was too late, allowing the Allies to build up a superiority in men and equipment. The Allies made their breakout into France in mid July.

The German Army had been forced to withdraw along its entire Eastern Front during the winter and spring of 1943–44. The fighting was characteristically brutal, neither side giving or expecting quarter. In April the Red Army began its offensive into the Crimea with three armored attacks on the Pekekop Isthmus. The German and Romanian troops fell back toward Sevastopol, which they hoped to fortify and hold. The Russians pushed on and retook the Black Sea port of Odessa, followed by Kerch and the railway junction of Dzankhoi. The Germans realizing that the defense of Sevastopol was untenable attempted to evacuate as many troops as possible by sea, with limited success. By May 10, the Crimea was in Russian hands, and the Germans had lost 96,700 killed, missing or captured.

Eisenhower did not intend to divert his advance toward Germany by capturing Paris. He feared that the liberation of the city would be too costly in men and time, as it was then his intention to reach Berlin before the Russians. He was also concerned that the fighting might be like that in Stalingrad and the city reduced to rubble; Hitler ordered that the "...city not

The invasion of Normandy. Allied troops landed on a broad front on the Normandy coast.

fall into enemy hands unless in complete debris."

On August 19 the French Resistance, under Henri Rol-Tougay, took matters into its own hands and began to engage the German garrison in the streets of Paris. General de Gaulle pleaded with Eisenhower to be allowed to take his armored division to the aid of the fighters. However General Leclerc had already disobeyed General Omar Bradley and sent the French Second Armor to the city. On August 24 the tanks, commanded by Captain Dronne, arrived at City Hall. Leclerc arrived the following morning with the rest of the division and fighting continued throughout the city. At 10:30 AM, General Billotte sent an ultimatum to the garrison commander General von Cholitz that he surrender or face extermination if he continued to fight on. Although the Germans had laid explosive charges in key positions around the city, they decided against blowing them and on August 29, General Charles de Gaulle was able to lead a victory parade along the Champs d Elysées. ❑

WAR'S END IN EUROPE

Ukraine, February 4, 1945

When Churchill, Stalin and Roosevelt met at Yalta on February 4, 1945, the Russian Army was forty miles from Berlin and the Western Allies were preparing to cross the Rhine. The outcome of the war in Europe was no longer in any doubt; it was to decide policy in post-war Europe that the meeting was convened.

All three leaders had their own particular agendas; for Roosevelt it was the war in the Pacific. The atomic bomb program (Manhattan Project) had yet to be proved viable and estimates for American casualties in the taking of the Japanese main island ran as high as a million men. He also wanted to

persuade Stalin to join the United Nations after the war. Stalin was primarily concerned about the Soviet sphere of post-war influence, and it was in this matter that he met opposition from Churchill. Churchill wanted Poland to be unoccupied and free elections held when hostilities ceased. Stalin resisted this proposal on the grounds that Poland, which was already occupied by Russian troops, was vital to Russian defense although he conceded the right to have elections. Churchill's misgivings proved to be correct. It is generally accepted that the 1947 Polish elections were rigged in favor of pro-Soviet politicians.

They agreed on unconditional surrender terms for Germany and that the country would be divided into three occupied zones, of which the Russians would have the greater part, including the area around Berlin: although Stalin did agree to let the Allies have their own sectors in the city, establishing a joint control commission. Later the US and Britain would cede part of their

own zones to the French to create four occupied zones.

When the line of defenses that General Gotthard Heinrici had built along the Seelow Heights was broken after four days of fighting, the way to Berlin was open, apart

Dresden was almost entirely destroyed by Allied bombing.

from a few scattered and disorganized German units. The Russians assembled three army groups to attack the city: one from the north, the second from the east and the third from the south. On April 20, the Russians commenced an artillery bombardment on the center of the city that would not cease until it fell.

The strategically important actions for the capture of Berlin would take place outside of the city. General Weidling had gathered together a ragtag garrison made up of a few units of Waffen SS, Hitler Youth and the Volkssturm, a collection of men over the age of service, some of whom were WWI veterans. Aside from these, few had any combat experience.

Hitler had been advised to leave the city, but he chose to remain in his bunker where he continued to

direct the efforts to save Berlin. He called upon divisions to link up and form defensive perimeters in and around the key positions. But it was all a fantasy as most of the divisions he called upon were either too weakened to perform the maneuvers or had ceased to exist.

The Russians, conscious of the atrocities that had been committed against their own civilian populations in the German advance across their homeland, did not spare the Berliners. Rape and pillage were commonplace. These outrages reinforced the resolve of the garrison to fight with a bitter determination, leaving no room or basement uncontested.

On April 29, Hitler married his mistress Eva Braun and made out his will, in which he blamed the downfall of the Third Reich on the German people and a Jewish-

Clement Atlee, Harry Truman and Joseph Stalin at the Potsdam Conference.

THE JULY PLOT: THE ATTEMPTED ASSASSINATION OF HITLER

Rastenburg, Germany, July 20, 1944

Between 1939 and 1944 there were seventeen attempts on the life of Adolph Hitler. The most significant of these, the July Plot, was carried out on July 20, 1944 by a group of high-ranking officers of the German Reserve Army who had lost faith in Hitler's ability to lead the German people.

Ironically, one of the duties of these officers was to create a unit that would serve to protect the

Nazi regime from any internal threats. Assigned to create such an emergency contingency plan was Reserve Army General Friedrich Olbricht, who developed *Operation Valkyrie*. Hitler did not know that Olbricht had become a sworn enemy of the Nazi regime. He and co-conspirators Colonel Claus von Stauffenberg ,and a handful of other officers, planned to use their high security

clearance in *Operation Valkyrie* to stage a coup d'etat.

The opportunity to kill Hitler arose on July 20, 1944 when von Stauffenberg was summoned to a meeting at Hitler's headquarters, Wolf's Lair, in Rastenburg, East Prussia. He arrived with a bomb in a briefcase, which he proceeded to hide under the table where Hitler would be sitting. With bomb set to go off, von Stauffen-

Hitler and von Stauffenberg

THE BOMBING OF HIROSHIMA

Hiroshima, August 6, 1945

Bolshevik conspiracy. On April 30, Hitler committed suicide with his mistress; their bodies were cremated within the grounds of the bunker. On May 1 General Krebs met with General Chiukov, of the Russian First Army, who demanded unconditional surrender. Krebs stated that he was not authorized to make those terms, and returned to his HQ. Learning that Goebbels, the new Chancellor, was dead—also a victim of suicide—he gave orders for the survivors of the garrison to make a breakout for the allied line. He surrendered the city at 8:23 AM on May 2, having given his men a twelve-hour start; most were killed or captured by the Russians.

When the war in Europe was over and Allied troops were forced to pull back, in some cases as much as 150 miles, to the borders established at Yalta, there were some who argued that Roosevelt, in ill-health at the time and now dead, had given too much to Stalin at the conference table. The final dispositions for post-war Germany were agreed to by Stalin and Churchill (later Clement Atlee), and Harry Truman, Roosevelt's successor. The leaders met at Potsdam, outside of Berlin at the end of July 1944. They decided upon programs for de-Nazification of Germany along with war crimes trials and the return of all annexed territories to pre-war status. ❑

berg excused himself. The bomb exploded, killing several officers but, miraculously, Hitler escaped with minor injuries.

Von Stauffenberg, Olbrecht and their fellow conspirators were captured within days in Berlin. They were executed by firing squad in the courtyard of German Army Headquarters, now home to the Memorial to the German Resistance. ❑

The dawn of the nuclear weapons era broke over the Japanese city of Hiroshima at approximately 8:15 AM on Monday, August 6, 1945. It was at that moment, from the sunny sky over a city of 300,000, that a lone American B-29 bomber dropped a parachute cradling a 9,700 pound uranium bomb, code-named "Little Boy." The bomb detonated at 1,900 feet over the city center creating a fireball that reached 300,000 degrees Celsius. Within seconds some 70,000 people had been incinerated in a blinding white flash.

This original weapon of mass destruction, with an explosive power equal to 15.000 tons of TNT, was delivered by a B-29 Superfortress christened *Enola Gay*, so named after the pilot's mother, Enola Gay Tibbets. Stationed on the Mariana island of Tinian, the aircraft made the six-hour flight to Hiroshima under the command of Colonel Paul Tibbets with a crew of twelve. Forty-three seconds after dropping its payload and eleven miles away, the crew, looking back towards the target, watched as a mushroom cloud ascended 23,000 feet over Hiroshima.

At ground level, the blast was so bright that it burned shadows of bodies onto walls. Almost every building within a one mile radius of the impact center

disintegrated and windows as far as twelve miles away shattered. Minutes after initial impact firestorms engulfed the city. These firestorms and the attendant radioactive fallout would push the death toll to over 100,000. It is estimated that five years after the blast, over 200,000 Japanese had died due to the lingering effects of radiation.

With no telecommunications in the city the Japanese government had no way of assessing the extent of the destruction nor what had caused it. It was not until President Truman's address to the American people at 11:00 AM on August 6 that the Japanese learned that they had been history's first victims of atomic warfare.

After announcing America's use of "an atomic bomb", Truman demanded Japan's unconditional surrender, warning that "we are in possession of the most destructive explosive ever devised by man." And with chill-

ing emphasis, added, "This awful fact is one for you (the Japanese) to ponder, and we solemnly assure you it is grimly accurate." Truman did not give them much time to ponder. Three days later, on August 9, the B-29 Superfortress *Bocksar*, piloted by Major Charles Sweeney, dropped the worlds first plutonium bomb, "Fat Man," on the city of Nagasaki, killing 75,000 people. On August 14, Emperor Hirohito agreed to terms of surrender and on September 2, Japan signed the official document of surrender aboard the *USS. Missouri*.

Created at Los Alamos, New Mexico, in a project code-named the "Manhattan Project", the atomic bombs that ended the war with Japan were several years in the making, employing a workforce of 100,000 and costing two billion dollars. Although never used against them, the project was occasioned by the rumors of Germany's nuclear weapons program. ❑

The ruins of Hiroshima

The Second World War and the defeat of the Axis Powers completely changed the international political scene. Germany and Japan were forced to accept dependent roles and house occupying armies. The old Europe lost its leading role in world politics. This political power vacuum was quickly filled by two newly emerging world powers: the United States and the USSR. They would determine the course of international politics for the next fifty years.

The rules of international engagement underwent a dramatic shift after the US nuclear attacks on Hiroshima and Nagasaki at the end of World War II. The USSR lost little time in developing its own nuclear program. In the newly configured world the possession of a formidable nuclear arsenal became hallmark of military power. An arms race between the two powers led to ever greater destructive capacity with the development of the hydrogen bomb (1952 USA; 1953 USSR) and intercontinental ballistic missiles. Great Britain, France and China also developed nuclear programs, but on a much more limited basis. India carried out its first nuclear test in 1974 and Pakistan in 1998.

Nuclear diplomacy shifted world politics from multipolarity to bipolarity. This development to the "supremacy of two blocks" did not take place peacefully. It was characterized by continuous friction (the Cold War), and while both sides realized the dangers of

Meeting before the Cuba crisis: the US President John F. Kennedy with Communist Party leader Nikita Khrushchev (1961).

direct military confrontation, their competing agendas were played out in grim conflicts among surrogate nations, usually in the Third World. The battle for political dominance was further exacerbated by the conflicting political ideologies of the two powers.

FROM THE MODEL OF "ONE WORLD" TO THE COLD WAR

When Soviet and American soldiers shook hands on April 25, 1945, the war-weary world believed in a new beginning under the sign of peace and reconciliation. But appearances were misleading. The members of the anti-Hitler coalition could not agree amongst themselves. The USA favored the creation of a liberal global economy in which the USA would have the political lead, because it had the strongest economy. The USSR, on the other hand, supported the principle of international peacekeeping through hegemony. The USA as the "arsenal of democracy" promoted the right of self-determination, non-violence, international disarmament, free trade, and international cooperation in all areas. This model of "one world" was to apply to all people and introduce a new consensus in global politics.

The model for "one world" was rejected by the USSR so far as its sphere of influence was concerned. In accordance with what had been agreed at the Teheran Conference in 1943, the Polish borders were to move westward at the expense of Germany; the USSR was preparing to expand its sphere of influence and to create Soviet-friendly satellite states along the western borders of the Soviet Union after the war had ended.

This manifested itself first in Stalin's politics towards Poland. The appointment of the pro-Soviet Lublin committee and the non-recognition of the Polish government in exile, set up in London since 1939, marked a turning point in the Cold War. The unresolved German question became the test case of the confrontation and the Cold War sealed the division of Germany. The Soviet proposal made in the Stalin Note in 1952 to unite Germany as a neutral country was immediately rejected in the West.

THE UNITED NATIONS

On June 26, 1945 the Allies, including the USSR, founded the United Nations under the leadership of the USA, to guarantee and safeguard the peace. Unlike the largely toothless League of Nations of the 1920s and 1930s, the United Nations had better tools to fulfill its function of safeguarding world peace through mediation and decisions of arbitration, and through the observation and appraisal of conflicts. In addition to diplomatic and economic sanctions at its disposal, it was provided with the capacity to deploy UN troops. The United Nations is at the same time a world parliament and a permanent diplomatic conference with electoral blocks and changing coalitions. Politically, the most important organ is the Security Council with its permanent members: the USA, USSR (since 1991, Russia), France, Great Britain, and China. Since 1948, the United Nations has been sending peacekeeping forces with varying degrees of success to areas of conflict throughout in the world, including Palestine in 1948, Lebanon in 1958, Cyprus in 1964, and Somalia, Croatia, and Bosnia-Herzegovina in 1992.

CONFRONTATION INSTEAD OF COOPERATION

The USA pursued a policy of "containment" (the containment of the Soviet Union's striving for power), while the Soviet Union concentrated on the military protection and political isolation of its own national territories, particularly in Eastern Europe. Foreign policy in the USA became practically identical to anti-communism. The political and ideological conflict of the Eastern and Western blocs was the determining factor that dominated world politics throughout the 1950s. The Cold War was a reflection not only of the two blocs' readiness for confrontation even to the point of war, but also of their attempts at finding ways to coexist. In 1956, the Soviet Party leader Nikita Khrushchev formulated the concept of "peaceful co-existence of states with a different social structure." There were two occasions when this was put to the test, the Berlin crises from 1958 onwards, and the Cuban missile crisis in 1962, which brought the world to the brink of nuclear war.

At the end of the 1960s political relations between the two superpowers changed. The confrontational strategy of the Cold War gradually gave way to a more relaxed political approach. The deeper reasons for this change were the shock of the Cuban missile crisis in 1962, the military-strategic realization that the "balance of terror" of the superpowers made the arms race futile, and the recognition that the power politics of the Eastern and Western blocs must remain predictable. Important steps towards relaxation were the Nuclear Test Ban Treaty, signed in 1963, that banned nuclear weapons testing in the atmosphere, outer space, and underwater, and the Nuclear Non-Proliferation Treaty signed in 1968. In addition, new political factors were emerging that contributed to the relaxation of the political power blocs: Western Europe and Japan were asserting themselves as new economic centers in the world, and after the Cultural Revolution the People's Republic of China put an end to its self-imposed political isolationism.

DETENTE POLITICS

The main objectives of détente politics were to maintain the stability of East-West relations, the reduction of confrontation, and the development of trust through a willingness to negotiate. In addition to arms controls, detente politics involved economic and cultural aspects in the East-West balance. International cooperation eased the powerful political and ideological differences that still existed.

The treaty politics of the superpowers reached their peak in 1972 with the Strategic Arms Limitation Talks (SALT I). This Soviet-American agreement was a real step forward in the direction of a pragmatic arms control to end the arms race. In 1991, the START (Strategic Arms Reduction Treaty) was signed in Moscow; it included limiting the stockpiling of nuclear warheads to a maximum of 6,000 each.

The CSCE (Commission on Security and Cooperation in Europe) conference in Helsinki (1973-1975) emphasized both the process of international détente and the importance of a continuous exchange of opinions about power politics and ideologies. With its emphasis on the respect for human rights and other confidence-building measures, it gave

Political thaw: the presidents of the United States and the Soviet Union, George Bush and Mikhail Gorbachev, after signing the START Treaty (1991).

the opposition in socialist countries a considerable boost.

THE NON-ALIGNED MOVEMENT AND THE NORTH-SOUTH CONFLICT

The Non-Aligned Movement, founded in 1955, stimulated the bipolar East-West system and played an important part in world politics. With more than 100 members, the Non-Aligned Movement had no standard political line. It was a collaboration based on anti-colonialism, peaceful co-existence, and international disarmament as well as on respect for the integrity and sovereignty of states.

The emancipation of the Third World was closely linked to the Non-Aligned Movement. As a result of the gradual process of decolonization after the Second World War, the North-South opposition became a major factor in international political relations. The "rich North" with its industrial states stood in

stark contrast to the "poor South," with different socio-economic and cultural-political levels of development. These countries faced terrible issues of overpopulation, malnutrition, environmental degradation, shortage of raw materials, and distribution problems. The North-South Commission, under the chairmanship of Willy Brandt, concentrated on the relationship between the countries of the Third World and the industrial countries. The developing countries called for a new global economic structure that would eliminate all injustices. This objective would be achieved by a completely new redistribution of economic resources. However, this proposal was widely opposed by most industrial countries. Very few of the hoped-for new global economic structures have yet been put into place. The global problems of migration and environmental damage have given the North-South conflict additional explosive potential. ❏

AN IRON CURTAIN DIVIDES EUROPE

USA, March 5, 1946

After the defeat of Adolph Hitler, the victorious Allies soon parted ways. In a speech in Missouri, Former British Prime Minister, Winston Churchill, coined the phrase "iron curtain" to describe the division of Europe into two spheres of influence with the de-

Yugoslav leader, Josip Broz Tito

marcation line running through Germany and Berlin.

Soviet control of Eastern Europe: On January 11, 1946 Albania dissolved the monarchy and declared itself a People's Republic under the leadership of Enver Hoxha. Bulgaria followed suit in September voting to dissolve the monarchy and establish a Communist state in its place. In Romania the king was forced into exile by a Communist takeover in 1947. A coup d'état in Czechslovakia in 1948 forced Eduard Benes to resign and brought the Communist, Klement Gottwald to power. In Hungary the takeover was gradual. In 1946 the Communists under Mátyás Rákosi took power within the context of a parliamentary system, But in 1948 the Communists forced the opposition party to merge with them removing any pretense of a multi-party system.

Containment and the Marshall Plan: With George Marshall's appointment as US Secretary of State, a policy of containment of the Soviet Union in Europe was put into effect. In June of 1948 Marshall launched a program to assist in the reconstruction of post-war Europe, which became known as the Marshall Plan.

The Berlin blockade: children await anxiously for airlifted supplies from the Allies

The Berlin airlift: East-West tensions were exacerbated at this time. The Soviets brought the land and water routes into West Berlin under their control, restricting the flow of people and goods. At the risk of direct confrontation, the US and Great Britain began airlifting goods to alleviate Berlin's isolation. The blockade was lifted in May of 1949.

Yugoslavia goes its own way: Under World War II hero, Marshal Tito, Yugoslavia pursued its own model of socialism, which entailed decentralization and greater worker's rights. This brought it into conflict with the USSR and it was excluded from the Cominform (the association of Communist block states) in 1948. ❑

INDEPENDENCE FOR INDIA AND PAKISTAN

India, August 15, 1947

At the stroke of midnight, India won its long-awaited independence from Britain. And Muslims won a degree of freedom from Hindus. At the time the Indian subcontinent was home to 320 million inhabitants, more than 45 different cultural groups, speaking more than 200 different languages. The declaration divided it into two separate states: Hindu India and Muslim Pakistan, which was divided into West and East Pakistan (present-day Bangladesh).

The real hero of India's independence was absent from New Delhi when sovereign power passed to the Indian Assembly. Mohandas Gandhi, longtime leader of the Indian National Congress, was in Calcutta, trying to restore peace between Hindus and Muslims. He was praised by the president of the assembly, Rajendra Prasad.

Thousands of Indians crowd-

ed around the Council of State building as Prasad spoke. Pandit Jawaharlal Nehru, the prime minister of the dominion government, then informed Lord Mountbatten, who had ceased to be viceroy at midnight, that he was governor general of India. In Pakistan, Mohammed Ali Jinnah, the Muslim leader, took his oath as Governor General of that country. The ceremony took place in the capital, Karachi.

The partition of India resulted in mass migrations of the Muslim and Hindu populations. In Punjab and East Bengal where the borders were still in dispute fighting erupted between the two sides. The chief bone of contention was the Kashmir region. War broke out to determine the final status of this province, which was ruled by a Hindu Maharaja and had a

predominantly Muslim population According to a peace treaty signed in 1949 India received about 60 percent of its territory and Pakistan 40 percent. It still remains a flashpoint between the two often antagonistic nations.

Nehru spoke of the difficulties

facing his country when he praised Gandhi before the assembly, "The ambition of the greatest man of our generation has been to wipe every tear from every eye. That may be beyond us, but so long as there are tears and suffering our work will not be over." ❑

Pakistani refugees in New Dehli

THE STATE OF ISRAEL

Tel Aviv, May 14, 1948

Above: David Ben-Gurion bidding farewell to the last British troops leaving Israel. Right: Arabs in firefight with Israeli army.

The founding of the State of Israel fulfilled a dream that had sustained the Jewish people during a diaspora that lasted almost two millennia. At the same time it launched a bitter seemingly interminable conflict between the new state and its Arab neighbors.

After the withdrawal of British troops and the ending of the British Mandate in Palestine, the Jewish National Assembly under the leadership of David Ben-Gurion proclaimed the birth of the Jewish State of Israel.

Within a few days Arab troops attacked Jewish settlements, initiating the first Israeli-Arab War. The Israeli government turned to the Haganah, a paramilitary organization that had been formed to resist the British presence in Palestine, making it its regular army. Secret negotiations in Paris between Egyptian and Israeli delegations had broken down in the previous October over Israel's refusal to withdraw from Arab occupied territories.

The conflict produced a mass migration as Arabs fled from lands under Israeli rule. The Arab's hoped-for annihilation of the nascent state did not come about, and a cease-fire was declared in the following year. On February 17, 1949 Chaim Weizmann was named the first president of Israel. In May of the same year Israel became a member state of the United Nations.

The British had taken control of Palestine during World War I. At the end of the war it was put under British protection as a Mandate by the League of Nations. The Balfour Declaration of 1917—a letter written by the British Foreign Secretary—pledged Britain to support Jewish aspirations for a homeland in Israel with the caveat that it did not prejudice the rights of non-Jewish people living in Palestine.

In 1947 the United Nations General Assembly recommended that Palestine be partitioned into a Jewish and an Arab state. The resulting civil unrest took on the character of a civil war. At the time there were 1.2 million Arabs as against 600,000 Jews, although the Jewish population was continuing to swell with refugees from the concentration camps of Europe. The UN concluded that dividing the country was the only possible solution to the conflict. Both sides were consulted, but in the end neither chose to accept the recommendations. A cycle of attack and counterattack interrupted by periods of uneasy peace continues to this day. ❑

TWO STATES IN A DIVIDED GERMANY

Germany, 1949

The division of Germany began at the Yalta Conference in 1945, three months before the Nazi's unconditional surrender on May 7.

Here, the United States, Britain, and the Soviet Union agreed to partition Germany into zones of occupation. After May 7, France joined this coalition, and the four countries set up their respective regions of governmental jurisdiction. The official recognition of these zones of authority took place at the Potsdam Conference in July and August.

The eastern regions, consisting of the former German states of Brandenburg, Mecklenburg-Vorpommern, Saxony. Saxony-Anhalt, and Thuringia were claimed by the Soviet Union. Territories west of these were split between the United States, Britain and France, with all four powers sharing the administration of the city of Berlin.

Over the next four years a massive forced migration of German nationals took place, wherein millions were expelled from there homelands. This process was particularly brutal in the regions controlled by the Soviet Union. The resettlement process ended in 1949 with the creation of two separate German States commonly referred to as West and East Germany.

On May 23, 1949, the zones occupied by the Allies merged to become the Federal Republic of Germany. A liberal democratic republic adopting a capitalist market economy, it chose Bonn as its capital.

On October 7, the Soviet controlled regions became the German Democratic Republic. Following the Soviet's socialist model in government and economic structure, it located its capital in East Berlin. ❏

Konrad Adenauer signing documents recognizing the existence of two Germanys.

Demonstration in support of the establishment of East Germany

NATO IS FORMED

Washington DC, April 4, 1949

The confrontation between East and West led to the formation of NATO. Belgium, Canada, Denmark, France, Great Britain, Ireland, Italy, Luxemburg, the Netherlands, Norway, Portugal and the United States joined forces to create the North American Treaty Organization, a mutual defense pact, in which all members pledged to come to each other's aid in the event of an attack. The members established a defense force with a central command. In 1952 Greece and Turkey entered the alliance, in 1955 Germany was admitted, and Spain joined at the end of the Franco regime in 1982.

In reaction to West Germany's entry into the alliance the Eastern bloc formed the Warsaw Pact, a rival defense alliance.

The NATO defense force with a centralized command was established in September of 1950. On December 9, 1952 a strategy of massive retaliation in response to a nuclear attack was officially announced, becoming known as MAD, Mutually Assured Destruction. In 1967 this doctrine was replaced by a strategy of "flexible response." The NATO alliance did not officially participate in any armed conflict until its intervention in Kosovo in 1999. ❏

CHINA BECOMES A REPUBLIC

Beijing, October 1, 1949

A decades-long civil war in the most populous nation on earth came to an end with a Communist victory. The chairman of the Communist Party Mao Zedong proclaimed the birth of the Chinese People's Republic in Beijing before a mass rally held in front of the Imperial Palace. Zhou Enlai was named premier and foreign minister.

China had been torn by civil war between the communists and Chiang Kai-shek's Kuomintang since the 1930s. Chiang fled Mainland China in 1950 to Taiwan, where he established the Republic of China. ❏

Mao proclaims the People's Republic of China

EAST-WEST CONFRONTATION IN KOREA

Korea, June 25, 1950

When North Korea launched their initial attack on South Korea in June of 1950, the United States quickly came to South Korea's aid. American troops, under the command of General MacArthur, were joined by other United Nations contingents, including units from Britain and the Commonwealth and Turkey.

In September these forces launched a major amphibious assault at Inchon. The subsequent victory led to the collapse of the North Korean forces and the liberation of the South Korean capital, Seoul, on September 26.

UN forces were then able to drive northwards, capturing the North Korean capital of Pyongyang on October 20. As the UN forces advanced towards North Korea's border with China, the Chinese issued warnings that it would come to its Communist ally's aid. These warnings were apparently discounted by US intelligence.

However, in late November the Chinese army launched a massive intervention on the behalf of North Korea. The U.S and its allies had to retreat below the 38th parallel. By December 6, Chinese and North Korean forces had occupied Pyongyang, and on New Year's Eve they took Seoul.

By April of 1951, UN troops were able to win back Seoul and push on to the 38th parallel, along which was created a "demilitarized zone." Here the conflict reached a stalemate that lasted until July 27, 1953 and the

South Korean soldiers with a prisoner

signing of the Armistice Agreement by all combatants except the South Korea.

By the time of this signing, nearly twenty-five thousand US soldiers, and more than one million South Korean as well as one million North Korean-Chinese troops had lost their lives. The "demilitarized zone" created by the Armistice Agreement continues to function as a militarily fortified line of demarcation between North and South Korea. ❏

HILLARY AND TENZING CLIMB EVEREST

Nepal, May 29, 1952

Mountaineer Edmund Hillary, 34, of New Zealand and his Nepalese Sherpa guide Tenzing Norgay were the first men to conquer Mount Everest, the world's highest mountain. The two reached the pinnacle of Everest, more than 29,000 feet (8,835 meters) above sea level, at 11:30 AM on May 29, staying for only 15 minutes while Tenzing planted the flags of Britain, Nepal, India and the United Nations, and Hillary took photographs. Hillary dedicated his feat to the coronation of Queen Elizabeth II of England, which took place four days later.

Climbers had been trying to reach Everest's summit since 1921. It is not known whether the 1924 expedition of George Mallory and Andrew Irvine reached the top, since both perished in the attempt. ❏

Tenzing Norgay and Edmund Hillary

ELIZABETH BECOMES QUEEN

London, February 6, 1952

Queen Elizabeth II's accession to the British throne took place February 6, 1952 with the sudden death of her father, King George VI. The official coronation was held on Tuesday, June 2, 1953.

At the ceremony in Westminster Abbey, Elizabeth accepted the royal orb, scepter, rod of mercy and ring from the Archbishop of Canterbury and took the Oath of Coronation. At the end of the ceremony the cathedral rang out with the voices of the 8000 guests in attendance singing "God save the Queen!" ❏

Queen Elizabeth II and her husband, Prince Philip

KHRUSHCHEV DENOUNCES STALIN

Moscow, February 25, 1956

The USSR's de-Stalinization process peaked three years after the death of the Soviet Party President, Joseph Stalin. In a confidential address to the delegates attending the twentieth Party Day of the Communist Party of the Soviet Union, its first secretary, Nikita S. Khrushchev, disclosed the crimes committed by Stalin, who died on March 5, 1953.

Singled out for criticism were Stalin's personality cult, the "violations of socialist laws," and the persecution of so-called public enemies. About Stalin's personality, Khrushchev said: "The diseased megalomania bred in him a general mistrust of even outstanding party functionaries, whom he had known for years." Numerous victims of his purges were rehabilitated.

In view of protests, an investigation of the causes of Stalinism was not carried out. After Khrushchev was overthrown as Party President (1964), the preliminary attempts to overcome Stalinism slackened. ❏

Nikita Khrushchev at the UN

BERLIN THREATENED BY SOVIET TANKS

East Berlin, June 17, 1953

In the first uprising against a communist regime in the Eastern Bloc, the people of the GDR (East Germany) protested against political repression and the worsening of living conditions. The strikes of the construction workers in Berlin began on June 16 and then spread to the whole of the GDR. The strikers demanded that the increase in production quotas decreed on May 28, 1953, be reduced by at least 10 percent. Although the politburo backed down on this issue that evening, it could not arrest the spread of the mass movement any longer.

In 272 locations in the GDR, also in rural pockets, there was public unrest on June 17; some 300,000 to 400,000 persons in around 600 companies went on strike. Strike centers, apart from East Berlin, included Magdeburg, Halle and Leipzig, as well as the industrial stretch between Bitterfeld, Merseburg and Leuna.

In some cases town halls, party offices and prisons were attacked and political prisoners freed. Strike steering and action committees were set up; however, the spontaneous movement lacked leadership. In retrospect the strikers' demands seem wildly unrealistic. They included the resignation of the government, free elections, the release of political prisoners, the disbanding of the army, and the unification of Germany.

At around 1:00 pm on June 17, the occupying Soviet power announced a state of emergency in East Berlin and 167 of 217

THE SUEZ CRISIS

Sinai Peninsula, October 29, 1956

On July 26, 1956 the Egyptian President, Gamal Abdel Nasser declared the nationalization of the Suez Canal. He justified this on account of the refusal of Great Britain and the USA to share in the financing of the Aswan Dam. The conflict over the nationalization of the Suez Canal led to a military confrontation between Egypt and Israel, Great Britain, and France.

Nasser had been member of the secret society of "free officers" and on July 23, 1952, he was involved in a leading capacity in the coup against King Farouk, who had held office since 1936. On June 18, 1953, Egypt was declared a republic. In 1954, Nasser deposed General Ali Mohammed Naguib, who had replaced Farouk, and became President himself.

According to a 1954 pact between Great Britain and Egypt, Britain agreed to withdraw its troops from the Canal Zone. In exchange, Egypt committed to guarantee the free movement of ships in the Canal, under the authority of the International Suez Canal Corporation. The nationalization of the Canal violated this agreement and provoked an immediate response from Great Britain and France, who convinced Israel to seize the Sinai Peninsula and pave the way for their resumption of control over the Suez.

Israeli forces breached the border with Egypt on October 29. After the rejection of a British and French ultimatum to cease fire on both sides, the British and French launched an airborne offensive against Egypt and sent paratroopers on November 5 to Port Said and Port Fuad. But the military intervention had to be halted on November 6 under pressure from the USA and the USSR. Overseen by the UN, the Allies retreated by December 16 and by March 1957 Israel pulled back its forces as well. The Canal stayed blocked by sunken ships until April 1957.

Celebration around the successful State President, Gamal Abdel Nasser in Port Said

The successful resolution of the crisis from the Egyptian point of view proved a boon to Nasser. As a result, he became the recognized leader of the pan-Arabic movement. ❏

districts. Soviet tanks arrived to crush the uprising and rescue the regime. Around 20,000 persons were arrested and around 3,000 imprisoned. Some 2,000 demonstrators lost their lives, 21 were sentenced to death by martial law on June 17 and summarily executed. Ruling party President, Walter Ulbricht, consolidated his power through this uprising, with Moscow providing support. He was responsible for the slogan "building up of the basic principles of socialism" proclaimed at the second Party Congress on July 12, 1952. A period of increased repression and worsening living conditions followed. ❏

June 17: Demonstrators march through the Brandenburg Gate toward West Berlin.

THE WARSAW PACT

Warsaw, May 14, 1955

In response to the entrance of West Germany into NATO, the military alliance of the Warsaw Pact, led by the USSR, was established. Formed in the Polish capital it included Albania, Bulgaria, Poland, Romania, Czechoslovakia, the USSR, East Germany, and Hungary as member states. This collective defense alliance stipulated an obligation of support by the Pact troops under a unified High Command.

The course for this military alliance of the socialist states, with the exception of Yugoslavia, had been set in December 1954 at a security conference in Moscow. In recognition of the USSR as the leading power of the Eastern Bloc, the smaller states received only restricted voting rights. Issues of European and alliance politics were to be discussed within the framework of the political bodies of the pact, and a formal resolution was passed. Soviet commanders-in-chief and advisors as well as the orientation of the armed forces following the Soviet model ensured the military supremacy of the USSR in the organization.

In 1968, events in Czechoslovakia sparked a military response by the Pact. The suppression of the "Prague Spring" became the common concern of the Pact states with the exception of Romania and Albania, which formally declared its withdrawal on September 13, 1968.

The fall of the Soviet Union and the political turmoil in Eastern Europe rendered the alliance obsolete. On July 1, 1991, after the withdrawal of East Germany in 1990, the remaining member states met in Prague and rescinded the Warsaw Pact. With this, the division of the world into two blocks confronting each other in enmity, justified during the "Cold War," came to an end. Although the balance of forces may well have prevented a third World War, it was the cause of an exhausting arms race that continued into the 1980s. ❏

VICTORY FOR HO CHI MINH

Dien Bien Phu, Vietnam, May 7, 1954

The capitulation of French troops in Dien Bien Phu meant the end of French colonial power in Indochina. After a siege by the Vietminh lasting 56 days, the French defenders of the jungle fortification of Dien Bien Phu located 300 miles west of Hanoi, finally surrendered. With this, the French War in Indochina, which had raged since 1946, ended with the victory of the communist leaning Vietminh under the leadership of Ho Chi Minh. At the Indochina conference in Geneva on July 21, 1954, a cease-fire resolution was passed, which stipulated the division of Vietnam along the 17th parallel and free general elections in the year 1956. The kingdoms of Laos and Cambodia, which had been under French rule until that time, became sovereign states, on the condition of observing strict neutrality.

The USA did not sign the accord, and as the South Vietnamese government of Ngo Dinh Diem rejected talks with North Vietnam, fighting broke out anew. ❏

North Vietnam Premier, Ho Chi Minh

WAR IN ALGERIA

Paris, 1958

In the Algerian Aurès Mountains, a revolt of the National Liberation Front (FLN) had begun on November 1, 1954 with the aim of ending French colonial rule in Algeria. Years of bitter fighting ensued, which resulted in the fall of the French government and the founding of the Fifth Republic. The unrest in Algeria spilled over into France in the form of the army-backed putsch of May 13. The rebel officers demanded de Gaulle's appointment as head of government, as he was seen as an advocate of a "French Algeria."

A new constitution, which had been endorsed by a referendum on September 28, came into force on October 4, 1958 and the Fifth Republic was founded. Charles de Gaulle was elected as its first President on December 21. Perhaps because he saw it as inevitable, de Gaulle offered the Algerians self-determination, despite vehement opposition

The new French President, Charles de Gaulle

from the European population of Algeria. The settlers formed a radical "secret army" (OAS) and in addition to aborted uprisings, made several attempts on de Gaulle's life. In the spring of 1962, a ceasefire was declared in Evian. On July 1, 1962, 99.7 percent of the Algerians voted in a referendum for independence. The Republic was proclaimed with its first president, Ahmed Ben Bella. ❑

CASTRO'S REVOLUTION VICTORIOUS

Havana, January 1, 1959

In a revolutionary overthrow of the existing government Fidel Castro seized power in Cuba forcing the dictator, Fulgencio Batista y Zaldívar, to flee abroad. In 1953 the storming of the Moncade barracks in Havana, Castro's failed attempt at a coup d'etat against the Batista regime, brought him a sentence of 15 years of hard labor. After being

granted amnesty, he went into exile in the USA and Mexico. In December 1956, he returned to launch a successful guerilla campaign from the mountains of Sierra Maestra.

At first, the USA reacted sympathetically to the revolution. That changed when Castro introduced agrarian reforms in June 1960, which, among other things, entailed the dispossession of large landowners. Castro's efforts to weaken the strong US influence on the Cuban economy and his close relations with the USSR, led to the severing of diplomatic ties with the USA in 1961.

Fidel Castro stepped down from power in 2008, after ruling Cuba for almost 50 years, the longest of any leader in recent times. ❑

Fidel Castro with Ernesto (Che) Guevara

KING OF ROCK 'N' ROLL

New York, September 9, 1956

Superstar Elvis Presley in his film: *Jailhouse Rock*

Elvis Presley broke all records with his first appearance on the Ed Sullivan Show. Over 86 percent of all TV viewers, around 54 million people, tuned in to watch the idol of American teenagers.

Presley, born on January 8, 1935, in East Tupelo, Mississippi, was earning his living as a truck driver, when he recorded his first LP, "That's All Right, Mama" in 1954. In 1956, he enjoyed a series of hits with "Heartbreak Hotel," "Blue Suede Shoes," "Hound Dog" and "Love Me Tender,"

later with "All Shook Up" (1957) and "Jailhouse Rock."

Rock 'n' roll—a combination of elements of black blues and country music, dominated by white musicians—became the expression of the loosening inhibitions and youthful rebellion of the post-war generation in the US. After conquering America, Presley and rock and roll went on to become a worldwide phenomenon. Presley died in Memphis of a heart attack on August 16, 1977. ❑

EUROPE AGREES TO A COMMON MARKET

Rome, March 25, 1957

Europe came even closer together with the signing the Treaty of Rome and forming the Common market. At a meeting in Rome, representatives of Belgium, the Netherlands and Luxemburg, as well as France, Italy and the Federal Republic of Germany agreed upon the founding of the European Economic Community (EEC). This called for a common market for agricultural and industrial products to come into force on January 1, 1958.

This was in addition to its precursor, the European Coal and Steel Community (ECSC), which created a common market for coal and steel created in 1951. The European Atomic Community (EURATOM) for atomic research was founded along with the EEC. Common organs of the European Union (EU) were formed from July 1, 1967 onwards through a merger agreement.

The primary aim of the EEC was the establishment of a unified economic zone through the formation of a unified customs duty and the introduction of a common foreign customs duty (in force from July 1, 1968). This in turn led to the free movement of people, services, goods, as well as capital, across the borders of the member states, common policies in the agricultural sector, as well as joint foreign trade and currency policies.

As an economic-political counterweight to the EEC, the European Free Trade Association (EFTA) including Norway, Great Britain, Portugal, Austria, Switzerland, Denmark and Sweden came into existence on January 4, 1960. The EFTA proceeded with the step by step abolition of customs duties in the on industrial goods. In 1973 Denmark and Great Britain joined the EEC, with Ireland, Greece, Spain and Portugal following suit. The Maastricht Treaty of 1992 folded the existing EEC into a new organization, the European Union (EU), which brought the member states still closer, with the end goal of political integration. ❑

Statesmen of six countries sign the Treaty of Rome.

PEOPLE'S UPRISING IN HUNGARY BRUTALLY CRUSHED

Budapest, October 23, 1956

A mass demonstration by students in Budapest for democratic freedom rights set off an armed national uprising against the Soviet regime. Four months after the violent crushing of the Posen uprising in Poland (June 28), the political ferment created in the Eastern Bloc by de-Stalinization in the USSR, precipitated the most massive challenge to the Soviet claim to dominant status in Eastern Europe to that point.

After a peaceful rally, skirmishes erupted between demonstrators and Soviet tanks in front of the Parliament building. At the same time the communist leadership made efforts to calm things down.

On October 24, the reform-minded communist Imre Nagy was chosen as Prime Minister, and on the following day János Kádár, was to be named party head. In the following days, severe fighting in Budapest ensued between those opposing the regime and members of the state security service (AVH).

On November 4, Soviet forces intervened. The unequal struggle lasted until November 15. Then, the resistance in Budapest collapsed. ❑

Budapest, November 2: Stalin's head severed from its base at the Stalin memorial

YURI GAGARIN FIRST HUMAN IN SPACE

Baikonur, April 12, 1961

Yuri Gagarin, the Russian cosmonaut, was the first human to fly through space. As in the case of the first unmanned rocket launch in 1957, the Soviets were first in the space race.

At 9:07 AM Moscow time, at the rocket base Baikonur, Yuri Gagarin was launched into space in the spacecraft Vostok (East). The 27-year-old Soviet cosmonaut circled the earth in an elliptical orbit over 200 miles from earth at its farthest

point, reaching a speed of 18,000 miles per hour. Gagarin's flight lasted 108 minutes during which time the Air Force Major passed 70 minutes in a weightless condition. Gagarin could be viewed from earth through the television cameras installed in the capsule, the pictures from which were transmitted live. At 10:55 AM the space capsule landed in the region of Saratov on the Volga with its flight slowed in its last phase with the aid of para-

chutes.

Public rallies were held in the Soviet Union to celebrate this event. After 1945, the development of modern rocket technology had begun in the USA and the USSR, building on the experience of the purely militarily oriented German developments in rocketry (the so-called V weapons) of the Second World War.

The Soviets claimed first honors in space with the launch of the

Yuri Gagarin in the film *First Journey to the Stars*

WAR IN THE CONGO

Léopoldville, June 30, 1960

1960 was the year of Africa: 17 states gained their independence. However, political autonomy did not result in freedom from economic dependence and the solution to basic problems. In the course of the year, France granted independence to all of its west and central African colonies: Cameroon, Togo, Madagascar, Benin/Dahomey, Niger, Upper Volta, Ivory Coast, Chad, Central African Republic, Congo-Brazzaville, Gabon, Senegal,

Mali and Mauritius. Also Somalia (Great Britain/Italy) and Nigeria (Great Britain) became independent.

A bloody civil war erupted in the Democratic Republic of Congo (now, the Republic of Zaire), hastily granted independence by Belgium. Alongside Joseph Kasawubu, head of state and Patrice Lumumba, head of government, Moïse Chombé, who declared the mountainous province of Katanga on July 11 as independent, was

Patrice Lumumba (right) with Vice-President Okito

the third major political player. Lumumba and Kasawubu were deposed on September 14 by Army Chief Joseph Sese Mobutu with the assassination of Lumumba following in 1961. In 1963, UN troops ended the secession of Katanga. The final victor in the power struggle was Mobutu, who seized power on November 25, 1965. He remained in office until overthrown in the spring of 1997. He died shortly thereafter in exile, of prostate cancer. ❏

A WALL DIVIDES BERLIN

Berlin, August 13, 1961

The construction of a wall that divided the city of Berlin heralded an escalation of Cold War tensions.

In the early morning hours, armed soldiers of the DDR (East Germany) and members of the worker's militia first blocked the eastern sector of the divided city at the line of East Berlin's demarcation with the three Western sectors. On August 14, the Brandenburg Gate was closed to the West, and on August 15, the construction of a permanent concrete wall between East and West began. Up until then approximately 5,300 workers and 1,600 students passed daily from East Berlin on their way to work

or school in the Western sector of the city.

As the USSR expected, the three Western protectors were surprised by the sealing off of the city and lodged formal protests, but they left it at that because the blockade did not directly affect their interests.

The decision to construct the Wall had been finalized in Moscow on August 5 during a meeting of the General Secretariat of the Communist Party of the Warsaw Pact States. At first constructed simply with hollow blocks, during the following years the inner border was further strengthened. With the Wall, the western border of the DDR at 38 degrees lati-

tude between the north and south areas became the most securely guarded border in the world. The DDR officially declared the Wall to be an 'anti-fascist barrier' even though it was clear from day one that it was not built to defend against enemies from without, but rather to prevent its own population from escaping.

The barriers comprised 7.5 miles of wall and 85 miles of barbed wire. The DDR raised 116 watchtowers around West Berlin, 32 of

them along the sector border. Only one train station was open for travel to the West. Out of 81 above ground crossings, only 7 remained open. ❏

East German soldiers guarding the road out of the Eastern Sector of Berlin

first artificial satellite *Sputnik I* on October 1, 1957. On November 3, the dog Laika was transported on the *Sputnik II* as the first living creature into space. Gagarin's spectacular achievement meant yet another bitter defeat for the USA in the clearly prestigious space race. President John F. Kennedy declared to the press that he was sorry "to still be in second place after the Soviet Union in the space race."

The USA launched its first satellite into space in February 1, 1958. The Soviet Union was the first to leave the gravitational field of the earth with an artificial satellite on January 2, 1959. *Lunik I* flew past the moon at a distance of 4,600 miles. On October 4, 1959 *Lunik III* photographed the dark side of the moon.

In addition to national prestige, military considerations forced both sides to spend enormous amounts on space technology. Only gradual-ly did the broad applications of the new technologies for broadcasting and commercial purposes become apparent. On May 5, 1961 Alan B. Shepard became the first American in space. In the satellite capsule Liberty 7, he climbed to around 115 miles and landed in the ocean off the Bahamas after a 15-minute flight. On February 20, 1962, John Glenn, who flew in the spaceship *Friendship* 7 for four hours and 50 minutes was the first person to suc-cessfully orbit the earth.

NASA, the US space agency, declared that landing on the moon was the next target. The Mercury (1962–63) and Gemini (1965–66) programs served as preparation for the spectacular Apollo moon-landing program.

The manned Apollo flights began with *Apollo* 7 in October 1968. *Apollo 11* brought man to the moon for the first time, on July 20, 1969. ❑

THE CUBAN MISSILE CRISIS

Washington DC, October 23, 1962

The conflict between the USA and the USSR over the stationing of Soviet rockets on Cuban soil brought the world to the brink of nuclear war.

The United States President, John F. Kennedy, demanded the removal of Soviet mid-range rockets as well as the dismantling of the launching pads installed in Cuba, and announced the imposition of a naval blockade against Soviet cargo ships.

The US Air Force had photographed military installations on Cuba, which were identified on October 15 as rocket bases. This put Russian missiles, easily within striking distance of Florida. Since the severing of diplomatic ties with the USA (January 3, 1961), Cuba's head of government, Fidel Castro, had closely allied himself to the Soviet Union. The tensions between Cuba and the USA had become even more aggravated through the abortive landing of exiled Cubans supported by the CIA, in the Bay of Pigs on April 20, 1961. In September, each Super Power had blamed the other for the worsening of the crisis and had warned the other side not to take military action. After tense deliberations, Kennedy rejected the option of an air attack or an invasion of Cuba. A naval blockade of the island by American ships and aircraft was put into effect. Kennedy described this action as a "quarantine" in order to underline its defensive character.

However, as Soviet ships and submarines approached the exclusion zone, the danger of a military confrontation loomed. At almost the last moment the Soviet ships turned around or halted their progress. UN General Secretary, U Thant, conveyed a conciliatory proposal at the behest of 45 non-aligned states to Moscow, Havana and Washington. The situation eased as the Soviet Prime Minister, Nikita S. Khrushchev, accepted the proposal. In an exchange of notes, Kennedy and Khrushchev were successful in finally resolving the crisis with the US promising to undertake no invasion of Cuba in the future and Khrushchev issuing the order on October 28 to dismantle the Soviet rocket bases. ❑

BEATLES ON THE WORLD STAGE

Liverpool, March 21, 1961

Their music, their informal, unconstrained behavior and their long hair made idols of "The Beatles" from Liverpool for young people the world over in the 1960s.

The Beatles performed together for the first time in the legendary Cavern Club in Liverpool. This was followed by their first hit "Love Me Do" in October 1962.

The four Beatles, John Lennon, Paul McCartney, Ringo Starr and George Harrison, were stars of the concert halls of the world right up to their last public appearance on August 29, 1966, in San Francisco. With *A Hard Day's Night* (1964) and *Help!* (1965) they conquered the screen as well. At first restricted to rock 'n' roll, the Beatles, with their recordings from 1965 onwards, moved far beyond the conventional boundaries of pop music, and advanced to become the most influential band in the history of music. With as many as one billion records sold, they earned a place among the most successful artists of all times. Millions of fans the world over mourned when McCartney announced the end of the group on April 10, 1970. Lennon's assassination by a fanatical fan on December 8, 1980 in New York put a final end to any hope of a re-unification of the quartet. ❑

Left to right: Lennon, McCartney, Starr, and Harrison in New York

ISRAELI VICTORY

Middle East, June 5,1967

At 6:00 AM GMT, Israeli airborne forces attacked Egypt, Syria and Jordan for six days, and occupied the Egyptian Peninsula, the Gaza strip administered by Egypt, the Syrian Golan Heights and lands on the West Bank along with East Jerusalem. The strategy of a war with three fronts was the idea of Defense Minister, Moshe Dayan. This was the third Arab-Israeli war after those of 1948 and 1956. It was over in five days with Israel occupying lands equivalent to four times its size before the war began ❑

THE CIVIL RIGHTS MOVEMENT

Point Of Interest

The US civil rights movement reached a climax on August 27, 1963, with a march on Washington. Speaking before the 250,000 black and white Americans, Martin Luther King shared his "dream" of a free and equal society. The civil rights movement aimed at equal rights for black Americans through the consistent application of laws and Supreme Court decisions. The most important supporting organization was the National Association for the Advancement of Colored People (NAACP). In 1954, the Supreme Court decision of Brown v. Board of Education declared racial segregation in schools and universities as unlawful. After a boycott led by King in Montgomery, Alabama, segregated travel on public transportation was abolished in 1956. The decisive breakthrough came with the Civil Rights Act of 1964, which prohibited any kind of racial segregation in public places. ❑

Integration of public bus in the South

JOHN F. KENNEDY

Brief Lives

John Fitzgerald Kennedy (born May 29, 1917 outside of Boston) came from wealthy Bostonian family of Irish origin. Along with John, his younger brothers Robert F. (assassinated on June 6, 1968) and Edward M. Kennedy also entered politics. Kennedy was highly decorated during his service in the US Navy in World War II. He was elected to the House of Representatives in 1946 and served as Senator of Massachusetts from 1953 to 1961. He ran as the democratic candidate for president against Richard M. Nixon in 1960 and won in a very close election. He married Jacqueline Bouvier in 1953 and had two children Caroline and John. He received the Pulitzer Prize in 1957 for his book *Profiles in Courage*. ❑

John F. Kennedy

THE ERA OF MUHAMMAD ALI

Miami, February 25, 1964

In the Miami Convention Hall, the 22-year-old Cassius Clay, a 7-1 underdog, dethroned World Heavyweight Champion, Sonny Liston. Clearly delighting in his place in the spotlight, he announced to the world: "I am the greatest," and lived up to his promise to "float like a butterfly and sting like a bee." He would dominate professional boxing until 1967.

In 1964, he declared his allegiance to the Nation of Islam, put his "slave name" Cassius Clay aside, calling himself Muhammad Ali from then onwards. After ten successful world championship boxing matches, the title was taken from him because of his steadfast refusal to serve in the military.

In the year 1974, Ali regained the title of World Champion at the age of 32 against the George Foreman in Kinshasa (Zaire). After a total of two dozen world championship boxing matches, of which he had won 22 and lost two on points, Ali said farewell to the ring in 1979. He was awarded the Presidential Medal of Freedom in 2005. ❑

World champion Muhammad Ali

CIVIL RIGHTS ACTIVIST KING ASSASSINATED

Memphis, Tennessee, April 4, 1968

The black civil rights activist, Martin Luther King, was assassinated by a white racist in the state of Tennessee. King was born on January 15, 1929, in Atlanta, Georgia. Since 1954 he had been pastor in the Baptist Church in Montgomery, Alabama and founder of the civil rights organization Southern Christian Leadership Conference (SCLC). He followed in the footsteps of Mahatma Gandhi working for political change through non-violent resistance and civil disobedience. He organized numerous protest demonstrations, among these the legendary march to Washington, and calls for passive resistance against racial segregation. He was arrested by the police several times.

In 1964, he was awarded the Nobel Peace Prize. However, in the following years his influence waned as more militant voices such as Malcolm X and the black power movement emerged. King's assassin, James Earl Ray, was arrested by the police on June 8 in London and sentenced to 99 years in prison on March 10, 1969 in Memphis. He died in prison in 1998. ❑

Martin Luther King at the March on Washington

PRESIDENT KENNEDY ASSASSINATED

Dallas, November 22, 1963

At 12:30 PM, shots were fired at an open limousine carrying President John F. Kennedy Texas governor, John Connally, and their wives. A half an hour later Kennedy succumbed to his wounds in Parkland Memorial Hospital in Dallas.

At 1:50 pm, the presumed assassin Lee Harvey Oswald was apprehended, having shot and killed a policeman while being pursued. Two days later Oswald was shot dead by a nightclub owner, Jack Ruby on his way to prison.

There are still speculations about possible persons behind the assassination today, even after the Warren Commission,

appointed to investigate the circumstances of death, concluded that Oswald had acted alone.

Kennedy was the fourth US President to be assassinated, after Abraham Lincoln (1865), James A. Garfield (1881) and William McKinley (1901).

On board the Presidential airplane *Air Force One*, Vice-President Lyndon B. Johnson took his oath of office as the thirty-sixth President of the United States at 2:38 PM. Johnson vowed to continue Kennedy's policies, which aimed at easing East-West relations in foreign policy and abolishing racial segregation in domestic policy. On November 25, Ken-

nedy was laid to rest in Arlington Cemetery.

Kennedy, who was just 43 years old when he took office January 1961, made it his aim to solve current problems through the revival of the basic values of American democracy. With his "New Frontier" policy, he attempted to set new goals for society through domestic policy reforms. He was able to instill young people with a sense of idealism and interest in public service. One of his lasting achievements in this regard was the founding of the Peace Corps.

In foreign policy, his "Alliance for Progress", had the goal

of improved relations with the states of Latin America. The support of economic and social reforms was aimed at reinvigorating US policy toward Latin American and averting the danger of communism. At the same time his journey to West Berlin in June 1963 demonstrated the determination of the USA to stand by its allies.

Although Kennedy made efforts to ease Cold War tensions. at the same time he oversaw the Bay of Pigs fiasco in Cuba and a gradually deepening involvement in Vietnam. Whether or not he would have been able to chart a different course there remains unanswerable. ❑

Seconds after the fatal shots at John F. Kennedy in Dallas: A security man jumps onto the vehicle of the President and hurries Jackie Kennedy to safety.

Vietnam War Escalates with the Tet Offensive

Saigon, January 30, 1968

In the Vietnam War, the communist Vietcong fighting in North and South Vietnam were able to stand up to the military superiority of the USA. The Tet offensive of the Vietcong began with the commencement of the Buddhist New Year festival in 1968. The fighting was fiercest in Hué, Da Nang and in the capital, Saigon.

The first US military advisors arrived in South Vietnam in 1961; armed forces followed in 1964. The number of soldiers rose from 23,000 in January 1965 to 550,000 by 1969. Beginning in August 1964, the US attacked targets in North Vietnam, in hopes that a sustained bombing campaign would bring the North Vietnamese to the bargaining table. When it finally became apparent that would not happen, President Lyndon B. Johnson, ordered a cessation of the bombing and relieved General William C. Westmoreland, commander of US troops in Vietnam, of his duties.

Trang Bang (South Vietnam) 1972: Children flee after a bomb attack.

Meanwhile at home, the Vietnam War was opening fault lines. Antiwar demonstrations rocked university campuses throughout the country from such centers as the University of California in Berkeley, the University of Wisconsin in Madison, and Columbia University in New York. Students ran sit-ins, took over administration buildings, and had frequent clashes with police.

In May of 1968 American-North Vietnamese negotiations began in Paris. They would turn out to be protracted and often interrupted. Meanwhile, the war escalated further. In Laos, the US Air Force lent its support to the royalist government troops against the communist Pathet Lao, bombing the Ho Chi Minh Trail running through Laotian and Cambodian territory along the border with South Vietnam, the most important line of communication and supplies of the Vietcong.

On April 30, 1970, on the order of the new US President, Richard M. Nixon, US and South Vietnamese troops invaded Cambodia. Although the troops were recalled once again by the end of June, Cambodia had now been drawn into the Vietnam conflict.

The expansion of the Vietnam War met with international protest and in the USA anger over President Nixon's bombing campaign in Cambodia led to violent demonstrations. Four students were shot dead by police at Kent State University in Ohio. In one of the largest peace demonstration, around 300,000 people gathered in Washington on April 24, 1971 to demand the immediate withdrawal of US troops from Vietnam.

By war's end in 1975 more tonnage of explosives had been dropped on Southeast Asia than in all of World War II. Over one million Vietnamese and 58,000 Americans died in the war. ❑

Vietnam vet protesting the war

Prague Spring

Prague August 20, 1968

The military intervention of five states of the Warsaw Pact ended the attempt of "socialism with a human face" in Czechoslovakia. Troops of the Warsaw Pact nations USSR, Poland, Hungary, Bulgaria and East Germany occupied Czechoslovakia. With this, the "Prague Spring" experiment in democratization, followed with great interest internationally, came to a violent end.

After the election of Alexander Dubcek as the First Secretary of the Central Committee of the Communist Party of Czechoslovakia (CPC) on January 5, 1968, a phase of political liberalization supported occured. This was observed in the remaining socialist states, above all in the USSR as well as in neighboring Poland and East Germany, with increasing concern.

In place of politicians loyal to Moscow, reformers came onto the scene. They charted a new course that abolitished censorship and called for the separation of Party and state, and the authorization of a legal opposition. They envisioned the creation of a "socialist market economy."

On June 27, the highly regarded "Manifesto of 2,000 words," authored by Ludvík Vaculík, appeared in several newspapers, demanding an acceleration of the democratization process. Following this, the Communist Party leadership was put under increased pressure by Moscow. A conference was convened in Bratislava. Czech government and party leaders were joined by officials from the other Warsaw Pact nations. Although lip service was paid to Czech autonomy, at the same time it was indirectly threatened with "brotherly help." This help came in the form of Warsaw Pact troops and Soviet tanks.

Under Moscow Protocol of August 26, leading politicians

FIRST MAN ON THE MOON

July 20, 1969

US astronaut Neil Armstrong left the moon-landing shuttle and became the first earth dweller to set foot (at 2:56 AM GMT on July 21) on the moon's surface. He accompanied this with the words: "That's one small step for man, one giant leap for mankind."

Eighteen minutes after Armstrong, fellow astronaut Edwin ("Buzz") Aldrin joined him on the surface. They erected a metal plate, bearing the inscription: "Humans from the planet earth set foot for the first time on the moon here, July 1969 AD. We came in peace for the whole of mankind." An American flag was unfurled. The time spent on the moon lasted 21 hours and 37 minutes in all. On July 24, the three astronauts, Armstrong, Aldrin, and Michael Collins, landed safely in the Pacific.

The spacecraft, *Apollo 11*, blasted off from earth in April. After a journey of almost 220,000 miles, Aldrin and Armstrong landed on the moon in the shuttle, the *Eagle*, while Collins circled the earth's satellite in the mother ship.

The success of *Apollo 11* was the conclusion of a preparatory phase that had lasted eight years. On May 25, 1961, the then-US President, John F. Kennedy had called upon the nation to renew its efforts to reach the moon before the end of the decade.

With the Apollo program, the race between the Super Powers was decided in favor of the USA. The trip cost American taxpayers about 350 million dollars. Worldwide, around

"Buzz" Aldrin leaving the shuttle and stepping onto the moon.

600 million people watched the moon landing on television. The US would launch six further moon expeditions. ❏

NIXON GOES TO CHINA

Shanghai, February 28, 1972

Richard Nixon was the first US president to visit the People's Republic of China. Nixon was primarily interested in beginning the normalization of relations, which would eventually result in mutually beneficial trade agreements and the establishment of formal diplomatic ties.

Preparations for Nixon's visit began in July of 1971 when National Security Advisor, Henry Kissinger, twice conducted secret talks with Chinese officials in Beijing. Upon his arrival in Beijing on February 21, 1972, Nixon received a surprise invitation to the home the ailing Chairman Mao Zedong for a brief private meeting. Little is known of what was discussed at the meeting except that the two leaders engaged in a "serious and frank discussion." Only Nixon and a National Security staff member, Winston Lord, met with the Chinese leader.

After the meeting with Mao, the US delegation engaged in a week of meetings with Premier Zhou Enlai. Between meetings, Nixon and his entourage were treated to a series of tours, including a visit to the Great Wall and the Forbidden City. Pat Nixon's role as cultural ambassador to ordinary Chinese citizens was featured prominently in the attending international press corps news dispatches.

The fifteen hours of talks held at the end of the week resulted in the jointly issued the Shanghai Communiqué. One of the main points in the document was the status of the Republic of China (Taiwan). At issue was the interpretation of what was known as the One-China policy, which, according to Beijing, asserted that the Republic of China, as well as the "colonies" of Hong Kong and Macau, were in fact not separate national entities but rather came under the sovereignty of Mainland China. The United States declared that it agreed in principle to "understand" Beijing's position. However, it refrained from denying the independence of the Republic of China. This ambiguity would continue to be an obstacle until 1979 with the Carter Administration's official break with Taiwan and its endorsement of full diplomatic relations with Beijing. ❏

were forced to revoke the reforms. On April 17, 1969, Gustav Husák was chosen as the new Communist Party chief. Until his dismissal in 1987, he opposed every new initiative. The leading figure of the movement, Alexander Dubcek, became the Ambassador to Turkey for a short while. In 1970, he was relieved of all duties and expelled from the Party.

In the Western European communist parties in Italy and

Czech leader, Alexander Dubcek (left)

France, the crack down met with harsh criticism. Also Romania, Yugoslavia, the People's Republic of China as well as Cuba more or less clearly distanced themselves. ❏

THE FIRST HEART TRANSPLANT

Capetown, South Africa, December 3, 1967

A 55-year-old South African, Louis Washkansky, was the first person to receive a transplanted human heart. The donated organ came from a 25-year-old woman who had died in a car accident. Twenty doctors were involved in the operation in the Groote-Schuur Hospital under the direction of Christiaan N. Barnard. The operation was a success; however, Washkansky died 18 days later of a lung infection. Barnard carried out another 42 heart transplants until 1980 and, thanks to his pioneering efforts, the technique became widely used. Among the most important prerequisites for a heart transplantation was the invention of the heart-lung machine (1953).

Barnard himself became something of a media star. As a white South African he was an outspoken opponent of apartheid. He died in 2001 while vacationing on the Island of Cyprus. ❏

CIVIL WAR IN NORTHERN IRELAND

Londonderry, Northern Ireland, January 30, 1972

On what became known as "Bloody Sunday," British soldiers fired on an unauthorized demonstration of civil rights activists, killing thirteen civilians.

The British troops had become more and more a part of the problem that they were intended to solve. Between 1969 and 1999 more than 200,000 soldiers did their military service in Northern Ireland; around 500 of them lost their lives, and around 300 civilians were killed by the army.

The conflict between the English and Irish had deep historical roots. Ireland came entirely under English dominance in 1601 and became a part of the United Kingdom on January 1, 1801. The northeastern part, Ulster, was "purged" by Scottish-Presbyterian immigrants in the seventeenth century of its Catholic landowners. There were uprisings again and again, mainly by the Catholics, against economic and political oppression. On December 6,

1922, Ireland became an independent republic (with the exception of the six Ulster counties).

In the autumn of 1968, the Catholic population of Northern Ireland, which felt itself discriminated against by the Protestants, began a civil rights campaign. After Protestant extremists had stormed the Catholic Falls Road quarter in Belfast in August, 1969, without the police intervening, Prime Minister, Harold Wilson, sent troops to Northern Ireland.

In 1969 the Provisional IRA (Irish Republican Army) split from the Irish republican movement. In the following summer, it began a bombing campaign. The violence in Londonderry gave its activities further impetus.

Political efforts to find a solution to the conflict remained unsuccessful. The establishment of self-government in Ulster agreed upon at the British-Irish Sunningdale Conference (December, 1973) broke down in 1974 in the

Everyday life in Belfast: Catholic youth attack an army vehicle

face of resistance from the Protestant "unionists." They rejected any interference of the Republic of Ireland in Northern Ireland. On May 5, 1981, the prominent IRA member Bobby Sands died while on a hunger strike, encouraging IRA prisoners to seek recognition as political prisoners. More violence followed with attempts of reaching political agreement seemingly unattainable. Finally April 10, 1998 both sides benefiting from the active engagement of US President Bill Clinton, signed the Good Friday Agreement, which provided for the establishment of an independent government of Northern Ireland as a constituent country within Great Britain. As recognition of the peacemaking efforts in Northern Ireland, two politicians, the Catholic John Hume and the Protestant David Trimble, were awarded the Nobel Peace Prize in the year 1998. ❑

SOCIALIST ALLENDE DEPOSED—PINOCHET IN POWER

Santiago, Chile, September 11, 1973

A coup d'etat in Chile planned at the highest level of the military began in the early morning hours at the naval base of Valparaiso. At the same time, the other branches of the armed forces closed ranks under the leadership of General Augusto Pinochet Ugarte, who had been appointed Commander-in-Chief of the army just a few days before.

The military junta declared the government as deposed and demanded that the socialist President, Salvador Allende, capitulate after troops encircled the seat of the government in Santiago. When Allende refused, two planes opened fire on the building while troops stormed the building. In the melee Allende was killed. The junta then proclaimed a state of emergency and suspended the constitution. All

political liberties were revoked.

In the following months, the country experienced a wave of political persecutions, deportations, tortures and shootings. A system of political repression based on brutal violence under Pinochet was established. According to an official government report released later, around 3,000 persons were killed under the dictatorship, some 1,200 "disappeared" and thousands were tortured.

In 1970, Allende won the presidential elections with a popular front coalition (*Unidad Popular*). He aimed at a socialist transformation following a parliamentary process. Key industries were nationalized, large landowners dispossessed of their holdings, and the income of the lower social classes increased.

However, economic reversals

occurred after initial success. In 1972, the middle classes began striking against the socialist government for fear of further nationalizations. The flight of capital, the economic boycott by the USA, as well as lessening support from western democracies led Chile to the brink of collapse. Pinochet used the unrest to prepare for the coup. Documents that subsequently came to light trace the clear support and involvement of the CIA in Allende's overthrow. Pinochet established his supremacy over the moderate sections of the military and ruled Chile as president for sixteen years with sweeping dictatorial powers. In 1988, a referendum forced him out of office. He was charged with numerous crimes and human rights abuses but died before being convicted. ❑

Prisoners in the football stadium of Santiago

ATTACK ON THE OLYMPIC SUMMER GAMES

Munich, September 5, 1972

The attack on the living quarters of Israeli athletes by Arab guerillas at the XX Olympic Summer Games (August 26–September 11, 1972) shocked the world. The taking of hostages cost 17 people their lives.

In the early morning hours a group of Arab terrorists forced their way into the dormitory where the Israeli athletes were staying in the Olympic Village. Two Israelis were shot and nine were taken hostage. The terrorists demanded the release of two hundred prisoners from Israeli jails. The ultimatum was initially issued for 12 o'clock noon, but was later extended to 5 PM. At around 10 PM the Palestinians brought the hostages by helicopter to the Fürstenfeldbruck Airport.

After the landing police marksmen opened fire. In the

A masked terrorist on the balcony of the Munich Olympic Village

Swimming star Mark Spitz

ensuing exchange of fire all nine Israeli hostages, five Arabs, and one police officer were killed. The terrorists used hand grenades to destroy the helicopters. Three terrorists were captured.

On September 6, the Olympic Stadium stood in recognition of the funeral services for the murdered Israeli athletes. On this occasion the President of the International Olympic Committee (IOC), Avery Brundage, declared that it was intolerable that "a handful of terrorists destroy the core of international cooperation and good will for which the Olympic Games stand. The games must be continued!" The games continued on September 7.

There had been political controversy even before the opening. Four days before the opening, under pressure from 27 African states, which threatened a boycott, the IOC prohibited the participation of a racially segregated team from Rhodesia (present-day Zimbabwe).

The undisputed superstar of the games was the US swimmer Mark Spitz, who won seven gold medals (four in solitary swimming, and three in relay). Sawao Kato (Japan) followed with three gold and two silver medals. ❑

BANGLADESH INDEPENDENT FROM PAKISTAN

Dacca, Bangladesh, March 26, 1972

The leader of the East Pakistani Awami League, Mujibur Rahman, issued a proclamation that announced the formation of the Sovereign Republic of Bangladesh. With this, the conflict between East and West Pakistan, separated from each other by India, reached its climactic phase. The densely populated poor eastern section of the country had always felt itself neglected by the central government in Islamabad, over 1,000 miles away. Not unexpectedly, in the elections for the constituent East Pakistani National Assembly on December 7, 1970, the independence party won by a landslide.

The Pakistani President, Muhammad Yahya Khan, responded by imposing martial law and outlawing the Awami League. He then arrested its leader, Mujibur Rahman. In the fighting that ensued, the regular Pakistani army suppressed the Bengali uprising with brutal violence. By the end of the year, around 10 million Bengalis had fled to India, which intervened in the war on December 3 on the side of the Bengalis.

The third Indo-Pakistani War ended in just two weeks with the capitulation of the Pakistani troops in East Pakistan. On account of the military defeat, the Pakistani President, Yahya Khan, resigned on December 20, 1971, and Zulfikar Ali-Khan Bhutto became his successor.

This opened the way for the independence of Bangladesh. The Bengali government was constituted on January 12, 1972 under Mujibur Rahman. ❑

THE YOM KIPPUR WAR

Middle East, October 6, 1973

On the Jewish Day of Atonement, Yom Kippur, Egyptian and Syrian troops launched a surprise attack against Israel. It took only a few hours for the Egyptians to overrun the Suez Canal and seize the Israeli Bar-Lev Line of fortifications. However, the Egyptians did not advance up to the strategic passes in Sinai. At the same time, the Syrians captured the Golan Heights through a tank attack.

However, only a day later the Israelis began a successful counterattack. The Israeli Air Force bombarded military targets in Egypt and destroyed a large part of the Syrian land-to-air rocket batteries. When no clear victory was apparent for either the Arabs or the Israelis,

An Israeli tank battalion pushes back the attackers

PORTUGAL'S CARNATION REVOLUTION

Lisbon, April 25, 1974

An opposing "movement of armed forces" deposed the government of the Prime Minister, Marcelo Caetano, who had been in office since 1968. The coup brought to an end the dictatorship of the ruling party that Caetano's predecessor, Antonio de Oliveira Salazar, had founded in 1933.

The previous acting Commander-in-Chief, Antonio de Spínola, assumed leadership in the revolutionary junta on May 15 for four-and-a-half months. Based on a new constitution, Portugal became a republic in 1976. Between 1974 and 1987, fourteen governments made efforts toward social and economic reforms. For a long time Portugal was seen as the poor man of Europe. But a new era of prosperity was ushered in with its accession into the European Union in 1986.

Portugal had held onto its colonies longer than any other European colonial power. The Carnation Revolution meant freedom for the overseas provinces in Africa: Portuguese-Guinea (Guinea-Bissau, 1974), Mozambique (1975), the Cape Verde Islands (1975), São Tomé and Principe (1975) as well as Angola (1975) all become independent. ❑

Socialist leader, Mario Soares

DEATH OF FRANCO

Madrid, November 20, 1975

After the end of a dictatorship, which had lasted almost four decades, Spain made a peaceful transition to a constitutional monarchy. The death of Spain's dictator, Francisco Franco Bahamonde, at the age of 82, heralded a new era of political openness. In accordance with the agreements made earlier, Juan Carlos I, of the Spanish line of the Bourbons and the grandson of King Alfonso XIII who was deposed on April 14, 1931, was proclaimed King of Spain two days afterwards. Juan Carlos I and his Pre-

Francisco Franco

mier, Adolfo Suárez (from 1976 onwards), began dismantling Franco's institutions and pushing through democratic reforms. A new constitution called for parliament to be converted to a bicameral system. Elections on June 15, 1977 finalized the break with the dictatorship.

Franco had ruled Spain since his victory in the Spanish Civil War in April 1939. The military and the Church were the most important props of his regime. Franco held power in his hands as *Caudillo* (strongman); he was the last dictator of Western Europe from 1936 until his death. In 1940, he withstood pressure from Adolf Hitler and remained neutral in the Second World War. In the year 1947, he declared Spain to be a "Catholic Monarchy." Through an alliance with the USA in 1953, he was able to put an end to some of Spain's isolation. After his death an unsuccessful coup attempt by the members of the Guardia civil (civil guard) on February 2, 1981, collapsed not least on account of the resolute-

King Juan Carlos I addressing parliament in Madrid

ness of the king. It turned out to be the last attempt to turn the clock back. ❑

both sides agreed to a ceasefire. On November 11, Israel and Egypt signed a formal ceasefire treaty.

On October 17, the Arab Oil Ministers resolved to gradually curb oil production, for the duration of the Israeli occupation of Egyptian territories. The USA and the Netherlands were no longer supplied oil; other western countries such as West Germany were supplied only a portion of their previous allotment.

As a consequence, oil prices spiked. As an immediate measure, a prohibition on driving on Sundays was announced on November 25 in some EU states. In the US there were long lines at the gas pump and drivers were allowed to purchase gasoline only every other day. The oil embargo was revoked in stages and ended in March 1974. ❑

US Leaves Vietnam

Saigon, April 30, 1975

The 30-year Vietnam conflict ended with the victory of the communist Vietcong and North Vietnam. As units of the Vietcong entered the South Vietnamese capital, Saigon, helicopters were conveying the last American personnel off the roof of the American embassy. So ended an involvement that had begun with great idealistic fervor fifteen years before. The South Vietnamese government handed over all power to the communists. South Vietnam's President, Nguyen Van Thieu, had already announced his resignation nine days before.

On January 27, 1973, US National Security Advisor Henry Kissinger and the North Vietnamese politburo member, Le Duc Tho, had negotiated a ceasefire agreement in Paris, ending US military involvement. Fighting continued between North and South Vietnam until South Vietnamese forces retreated from the highlands in early 1975. The Vietcong rapidly occupied the territory given up and moved onto Saigon.

In Cambodia, the Khmer Rouge under the leadership of Pol Pot unleashed a four-year regime of terror. Its killing fields shocked the conscience of the world. It is believed that the Khmer Rouge murdered as many as two million Cambodians. The Vietnam War claimed around three million dead and wounded, 58,000 US soldiers lost their lives. Intense bombing and the use of herbicides (defoliants) devastated large sections of both North and South Vietnam. ❑

Mountain of skulls in Cambodia

The Watergate Scandal

Washington D.C., August 9, 1974

After the resignation of Richard M. Nixon, the Vice-President, Gerald R. Ford, was sworn in as the new President. On August 8, Nixon, the thirty-seventh President of the USA, announced that he was stepping down and so escaped threatened impeachment proceedings against him.

The reason for his resignation was the Watergate scandal. On June 17, 1972, the election campaign quarters of the Democratic Party at the Watergate Complex was broken into. The police apprehended five staff members of the Committee for the Re-election of the President with mini-cameras and bugging devices.

Nixon on the day of his resignation

In a sequence of events seemingly out of the pages of a political thriller, accusations were lodged against Nixon's closest aides. Among them, Nixon's Assistant for Domestic Affairs, John N. Ehrlichmann, the chief of staff in the White House, H. R. ("Bob") Haldeman, as well as Nixon's election campaign advisor, Jeb Magruder came under suspicion of covering up the burglary. All three, as well as Nixon's legal counsel, John Dean, were fired on April 30, 1973, by the President. All four men were convicted of crimes relating to the scandal and served time in jail.

At the same time, investigators began zeroing in on the President himself. Nixon denied any responsibility on his own part or on that of the Republican Party and his advisors. It was thanks to the reporting of the *Washington Post* journalists, Carl Bernstein and Bob Woodward, that the cover-up came to light. For their exemplary investigative journalism, they were awarded the Pulitzer Prize in 1973.

The investigation reached a turning point in July 1973. At that time it was revealed that Nixon had taped White House conversations and telephone calls. Nixon at first refused to part with the tapes. Although he dismissed Archibald Cox, who had been appointed by Congress as an Independent Counsel to investigate allegations of wrongdoing, this intervention could not stop the momentum of the investigation. Ten days after word of the taping became public the Judiciary Committee of the House of Representatives began impeachment proceedings on a petition of the Democratic Party.

On the basis of the investigations carried out there, on July 29, 1974, the motion for impeachment was passed. Nixon was accused of having known in advance of the break-in and then attempting to cover up the matter. Faced with the certain prospect of his removal from office Nixon finally agreed to step down. He was then given a pardon by his successor, Gerald Ford.

More than thirty years later, the Watergate scandal hit the headlines once again. On June 1, 2005, the *Washington Post* confirmed that a high official of the FBI, Mark Felt, was the informer with the cover name "deep throat," who had provided the reporters with information. ❑

RAID ON ENTEBBE

Uganda, July 3–4, 1976

On June 27 1976 two German and two Palestinian men hijacked Air France flight 139, which was carrying two hundred and forty-eight passengers and twelve crew members to Paris. The hijackers diverted the plane to Libya for refueling then proceeded to Entebbe Airport in Uganda where they demanded that the Israeli government release forty Palestinians and thirteen others being detained by July 1 1976. The hijackers threatened to begin killing hostages after the deadline. By the July 1 deadline the Israeli government negotiated for an additional three days, and the hijackers released most of the non-Israeli passengers leaving them with 83 Israeli hostages and twenty others who refused to leave. On July 3, the Israeli government approved a rescue mission led by Yekutiel Adam, Deputy Chief of Staff of the Israeli Defense Forces. That night four Israeli air force transport crafts secretly landed at Entebbe Airport. They were followed by two Boeing 707 jets, one of which landed at Jomo Kenyatta Airport with medical supplies. The second circled Entebbe Airport.

The assault team of the rescue mission used Ugandan President Idi Amin's transportation style, a Mercedes escorted by range rovers, to reach the hijackers. Because the Israeli troops had obtained the blueprints of the building in which the hostages were kept, they were able to complete the mission in thirty minutes. The rescue team shot and killed the hijackers, as well as two sentries, and they destroyed eleven Ugandan fighter planes. In all, forty-five Ugandan military personnel were killed along with seven hijackers, while only three Israeli hostages and one officer died during the fight. ❑

PEACE BETWEEN ISRAEL AND EGYPT

Camp David, September 17, 1978

On September 17, 1978 in a stunning breakthrough, Israel's Prime Minister Begin and Egypt's President Anwar Sadat announced that they had reached agreement at Camp David. President Carter, who shuttled tirelessly between the two often hostile delegations for 13 days, appeared exhausted but smiling after fashioning two remarkable agreements.

Carter acknowledged that the accords were only a beginning. "There are still great difficulties that remain," he said. Sadat praised Carter, and Begin congratulated him for achieving "a great victory." He said the summit would be called the "Jimmy Carter Conference," and added, "He worked harder than our forefathers did in Egypt building the pyramids."

Sadat and Begin signed two separate documents. The first, *Framework for Peace in the Middle East*, called for more negotiations to determine the future of the West Bank and the Gaza Strip. Israel agreed to withdraw almost all of its forces from the two areas and to not build any more settlements on the West Bank during the negotiations. The document did not guarantee the creation of a Palestinian state in the area, but one report says Begin did agree to "recognize the legitimate rights of Palestinians."

Six months after the Camp David Accord, Anwar Sadat made history by signing a peace treaty with Israel. In the process he isolated himself in the Arab world. The foreign ministers of eighteen Arab countries moved in Baghdad to cut diplomatic and economic relations with Cairo. Their decision, which was also approved by the

Begin and Sadat embrace, while Jimmy Carter looks on.

Palestine Liberation Organization, called for the immediate recall of ambassadors from Egypt, a complete termination of diplomatic relations within a month, an end to all financial aid and the imposition of economic sanctions. Egypt had been receiving a billion dollars a year from other Arab countries, mainly Saudi Arabia.

Sadat indicated he was aware of the risks when he signed the peace agreement with Israel's Prime Minister Begin at the White House. Sadat also recognized its historic importance, and he praised President Carter for his role in masterminding the accord. Sadly, Sadat was to pay a high price for his courageous efforts for peace: on October 6 of the following year he was assassinated by an Islamic militant ardently opposed to peace with Israel. ❑

SOVIET TROOPS MIRED IN AFGHANISTAN

Kabul, December 27, 1979

In Afghanistan the Soviet Union—like the United States in the Vietnam War—became entangled in an unwinnable military action. With the arrival of the Soviet armed forces in its capital, the former President, Hafizullah Amin, was assassinated and Babrak Karmal appointed as his successor.

The Soviet Union justified its intervention by citing the danger of a "counter-revolution" organized by the United States. The situation in the country had long been unstable. The monarchy was abolished in 1973, and the new ruler, Mohammed Daud Khan, was deposed in April 1978 by the pro-Soviet Democratic People's Party of Afghanistan. After a power struggle with Karmal and Nur Mohammed Taraki, Hafizullah Amin emerged the victor, only to fall victim upon Soviet military intervention in his country.

The West protested vehemently against the Soviet inva-

Soviet convoy in Afghanistan

The Year of Three Popes

Vatican City, October 16, 1978

Pope Paul VI died on August 6. He is credited with the appointment of bishops in the Eastern Bloc and the formation of new bishoprics thanks to his diplomatic relations with the governments of socialist states. He did antagonize some in the upper ranks of the clergy with his authoritarian style of leadership.

Albino Luciani, the Cardinal of Venice, was elected his successor on August 26 and took the name of John Paul I. However, his pontificate lasted only a single month; he died on September 28.

Then, for the first time since 1522, the Conclave of Cardinals elected a non-Italian as the pope. The new Supreme Head of the Church was the Pole, Karol Wojtyla, who took the name of John Paul II. Karol Wojtyla had been appointed the auxiliary bishop of Krakow in 1958 and then cardinal in 1967.

The pope made numerous journeys abroad, preaching a revivial of fundamental Christian values to huge crowds. Of great significance were his three journeys to his native country (1979, 1983 and 1987); they were seen as an endorsement of popular resistance movements against the Communist regime.

Pope John Paul II

However, his consistent and energetic opposition to birth control and the strict adherence to clerical celibacy and subordination of women in clerical life caused controversy and dissension among more liberal members of the Church.

On May 13, 1981, John Paul II was severely wounded, but survived an assassination attempt. He died on April 2, 2005 and was succeeded by the German Cardinal, Joseph Ratzinger, who took the papal name, Benedict XVI. ❏

Islamic Revolution

Iran, January 16, 1979

Visibly weakened by cancer, Shah Mohammed Reza Pahlavi left Iran after 37 years of autocratic rule, accompanied by Empress Farah Diba. On February 1, the 78-year-old Shiite leader, Ayatollah Ruhollah Khomeini, returned after fifteen years in exile and soon after proclaimed a "revolutionary government" under the leadership of Mehdi Bazargan. The Islamic Republic announced by Khomeini was endorsed on March 30 by a referendum. Many former associates of the Shah were sentenced to death by newly formed people's courts.

In order to force the USA to extradite the deposed Shah, who had flown to New York for cancer treatment, followers of Khomeini occupied the US embassy in Teheran on November 4, taking 52 Americans hostage and holding them for 444 days. With the occupation of the embassy, which ended on the day of Ronald Reagan's inauguration, January 20, 1981, all diplomatic relations between Iran and the United States ceased. ❏

A crowd of one million greets Khomeini in Teheran.

sion. The direct consequence was the boycott of the 1980 Moscow Olympics. With a some contrition the US President Jimmy Carter admitted that he had misjudged Soviet intentions. In Afghanistan a coalition of warring tribal groups, called *mujaheddin*, organized a guerilla campaign against the Soviets and the government troops. They were able to control the rural provinces to a large extent and received weapons from the West via Pakistan.

Over 100,000 Soviet troops were sent to Afghanistan. At least 14,000 Soviet soldiers died in Afghanistan; the cost in Afghani lives was immeasurably greater, with estimates ranging as high as two million killed.

But despite massive fire power the Soviets were never able to achieve their strategic aims. In accordance with a peace plan negotiated with the help of the UN in 1988, the Soviets retreated on February 15, 1989. The pro-communist President, Mohammed Najibullah, served as president, until rebel forces took over Kabul. In 1996, the radical Islamist Taliban took control of the country and remained in power until driven out by coalition forces after the attacks of September 11, 2001. The current government, headed by Hamid Karzai, who was elected president in 2004, is engaged in a continuing conflict with Taliban resistance fighters. ❏

The Shah of Iran

Brief Lives

Mohammed Reza Pahlavi was born on October 26, 1919, in Teheran, the eldest son of the Cossack officer, Reza Khan, who took over power in 1921 and in 1925 deposed the Qajar dynasty, which had ruled in Iran since 1794. On September 16, 1941, Mohammed Reza Pahlavi was proclaimed as Shah in place of his father, who was forced by the British and the Soviets to abdicate on account of his friendly relations with Germany.

Buoyed by oil revenues, he set the ambitious goal of modernizing Iran and making it a major player on the international stage. The reforms he instituted brought him into conflict with the clergy, and the negative consequences of industrialization, like inflation, migration into cities, and massive

The Shah crowns himself.

rent hikes, led to civil unrest 1977. His suppression of political dissent and the brutality of the *Savak*, his security police, resulted in more determined popular resistance. Shah Reza Pahlavi died on July 27, 1980, in exile in Cairo. ❏

MIKHAIL GORBACHEV AND THE END OF THE SOVIET UNION

Moscow, March 11, 1985

The Central Committee (CC) of the Communist Party of the Soviet Union (CPSU) elected 54-year-old Mikhail S. Gorbachev as the new General Secretary one day after the death of the previously serving General Secretary, Konstantin Chernenko. The decision to choose a younger man for the office came in part through his endorsement by the foreign minister, Andrei Gromyko.

Mikhail Gorbachev in Washington

Gorbachev, who was born on March 2, 1931, in Stavropol, had studied law and agriculture and became a full-fledged member of the Communist Party in 1950. He rose through the ranks, first serving in municipal governments and ascended in 1980 to the Politburo.

In his first months as General Secretary, Gorbachev dismissed one third of all ministers and 60 of the 158 district party secretaries. In this, he found backing from the KGB, which was represented by three persons in the thirteen-member Politburo. In a major shake-up he brought in Eduard Shevardnadze in place of his mentor, Andre Gromyko, who was shunted aside after 18 years in the Foreign Office to the ceremonial post of Supreme Head of State.

Gorbachev, along with his self-confident wife, Raisa, cultivated a new style of leadership in Russia. He wanted to renew the economy, tolerate freedom of opinion, end the arms race with the USA, allow the republicans in the USSR and in the socialist aligned states more autonomy, while still maintaining the claim of the CPSU to leadership. His key ideas were *glasnost* (openeness) and *perestroika* (restructuring). However, the problems in the conversion of the centrally administered economy into a mixed economy, the growing shortages in supplies, the nationalist movements in the south of the USSR and the quest of the Baltic States for autonomy proved insoluble within the context of the Communist-run Soviet system. The Soviet Union was formally dissolved in December 26, 1991.

Gorbachev was the recipient of the Nobel Peace Prize in 1990. His decision not to intervene militarily in response to the democratic revolutions in the former Warsaw Pact countries helped change the landscape of Europe. ❑

Gorbachev and Reagan (right) at the two-day summit meet in Geneva: The first summit meet since 1979 opens a new dialog of both the Superpowers.

THE UNITED STATES TURNS TO THE RIGHT

Washington D.C., January 20, 1981

The Republican, Ronald Reagan defeated the Democrat incumbent, Jimmy Carter in the general election of 1980. His inauguration signaled a more muscular US presence abroad and a more conservative governing style at home.

In the area of foreign affairs he pursued a hard anti-communist line. He increased the defense budget sizably, sent aid to rebel forces in Nicaragua and Afghanistan, dispatched US troops to Grenada (1983) and bombed Libya (1986). Arms reduction talks with the USSR broke down in the year 1986 on account of Reagan's program of Strategic Defense Initiative (SDI) for a space-based missile shield. Yet he was able to engage Mikhail Gorbachev in a dialogue that resulted in dramatic openings between East and West.

His economic policy ("Reaganomics") with its sharp reduction of taxes and spending on social programs combined with massive defense spending, caused deficits and the national debt to balloon. ❑

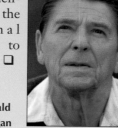

Ronald Reagan

RONALD REAGAN

Brief Lives

Ronald Reagan (born February 6, 1911 in Tampico, Illinois) was a sports reporter (1932-1937), film actor (1937-1942 and 1945-1957) and President of the Screen Actors' Guild (1947-1952). He was originally a liberal Democrat but joined the Republican Party in 1962. In 1966, he was elected Governor of California. After two unsuccessful attempts as presidential candidate (1968 and 1976), he gained the republican nomination and went on to win the general election against Jimmy Carter. He was elected to a second term by a landslide. He died on June 5, 2004 in Bel Air, California. ❑

THE *CHALLENGER* DISASTER

Cape Kennedy, Florida, January 28, 1986

The explosion of the US space shuttle, *Challenger*, was the most grievous disaster to date in the history of manned space travel. The fatal crash occured on the *Challenger's* tenth mission into space. It exploded 73 seconds after its launch. The crew, six professional astronauts and a co-passenger, the teacher, Christa McAuliffe, who had been chosen for the flight, all lost their lives in the tragedy. A solid rocket had come loose from its bearings and breached the outer tank, which exploded. ❑

GLASNOST AND PERESTROIKA

Point of Interest

The politics of reform ushered in by Mikhail Gorbachev were bound up with the catchwords *glasnost* and *perestroika*. *Glasnost* means "the public" or "openness" and was a slogan used by Gorbachev to express the principle of information being available for public discussion. In particular, he encouraged the media to bring transparency into political and economic processes. *Perestroika* means "rebuilding" or "restructuring" and stands for democratization, de-Stalinization, allowing market economic elements and limited forms of private ownership while maintaining the leading role of the Communist Party. Gorbachev's reform program gave rise to great hopes of a potentially enduring and more human kind of society within socialism. ❑

Raisa Gorbachev

The *Challenger* disaster

THE START OF THE COMPUTER AGE

New York, December 27, 1982

In place of its customary "man of the year" issue, the US magazine *Time* selected the computer as the "machine of the year" 1982. Since its beginnings in the 1940's, the devices for electronic data processing had become substantially more efficient, smaller and cheaper.

In 1941, the German structural engineer, Konrad Zuse, made use of "Zuse Z 3", the first working, electro-mechanical, digital processor in the world. In the summer of 1946, the "ENIAC" was working at the University of Pennsylvania. The 30-ton monster equipped with almost 18,000 electronic tubes could multiply ten ten-digit numbers with each other in about 3/100th of a second. The British mathematician, Alan Turing, was responsible for key work with algorithms that was the basis for many advances in computer science.

At the beginning of the 1970s, microprocessors were developed. This paved the way for IBM's introduction in 1981 of the first microcomputers to the market. A small commercial enterprise at that time, Microsoft, founded by Bill Gates in 1974, developed the operating system MS-DOS (disk operating system) at the same time. Intel built the processor, an 8088 with 4 Mhz clock frequency.

In competition with IBM, the firm, Apple Computer, created the Macintosh with a Motorola

Microsoft Head, Bill Gates

processor into the market. By the mid 1980s, Apple occupied the leading position in technology, as the graphic interface of the Mac was more user friendly than that of the personal computer (PC) with the DOS operating system. The first versions of Windows introduced from 1990 onwards were graphically designed masks for the operating system, MS-DOS. With this, Microsoft launched an economically successful competitive product to the Apple user interface. ❑

THE IRAN-IRAQ WAR

Middle East, September 22, 1980

A border conflict, which had been simmering for years, escalated with Iraqi troops attacking Iranian territory in an act of open aggression. The direct target of the attack was a border crossing at Shat al Arab. At the same time, the Iraqi head of state, Saddam Hussein, had set his sights on the annexation of the oil-rich province of Khuzestan.

After the initial territorial gains by the Iraqis, the conflict expanded to a bitter stalemate accompanied by high losses on both sides. Against a better-armed Iraq, Iran used "human waves" for winning back lost territories from 1981 onwards. This cost the lives of innumerable soldiers and "volunteers" fired with religious zeal.

After Iraqi aircraft bombarded Iranian oilfields and drilling rigs in March 1983, Iran threatened to expand the war to the entire Gulf area. A further escalation resulted from 1984 onwards, when Iraq sank tankers loaded with Iranian oil and Iran on its part focused on international shipping routes in the Persian Gulf.

On August 20, 1988, a ceasefire negotiated by the UN General Secretary, Javier Pérez de Cuellar, came into force, stipulating that both sides retreat to internationally recognized borders. The war was marked by Iraq's widespread use of chemical weapons against Iran and its own Kurdish citizenry. ❑

MITTERAND: A SOCIALIST PRESIDENT FOR FRANCE

Paris, May 10, 1981

François Mitterand was elected President of France defeating the incumbent Valéry Giscard d'Estaing with 51.75 percent of the votes. With the election, the Gaullist-liberal governmental era, which had lasted since 1958, ended, and socialists took charge.

Mitterand had entered upon a career in politics in 1944. Until the founding of the Fifth Republic in 1958, he held eleven Ministerial portfolios. He lost presidential elections twice: to de Gaulle in 1965 and to Giscard d'Estaing in 1974.

Mitterand called for new elections in June 1981 and led his left-leaning coalition to power. At the beginning, his

government pushed through its demands for nationalization and increased social spending, but Mitterand then severed his alliance with the communists and moved toward greater fiscal austerity. ❑

Francois Mitterand

PROTEST IN TIANANMEN SQUARE

Beijing, June 4, 1989

In Heavenly Peace Square (Tiananmen Square), the Chinese army put a violent end to the demonstrations of the democratic movement. Tanks ended the three-week-long mass demonstrations in a blood bath. According to unofficial estimates, the military action claimed 3,600 lives and left 60,000 wounded.

Since mid-April, students in Beijing, Shanghai and other Chinese cities had been demonstrating for more freedom and democracy. The criticisms of corruption and complaints of economic hardships were growing more vocal, as were the calls for democratic reforms. In addition to this, on May 13, several thousand Chinese students began a hunger strike. More and more citizens joined the protests.

For weeks, there was disunity in the Party leadership over how to deal with the protests. On May 19, Party Head, Zhao Ziyang, visited the students and made known his sympathy. Finally the hardliners around Deng Xiaoping, who was Chairman of the powerful Central Military Commission, won. He had troops from the entire country close ranks and fire on the demonstrators. During the "cleansing wave" after the massacre, around 120,000 persons were arrested and by the beginning of August at least 34 death sentences had been carried out. Zhao Ziyang was replaced by the mayor of Shanghai, Jiang Zemin, as the Head of the Communist Party, who, as Deng's successor, also took over the office of the Chairman of the Central Military Commission.

The massacre at Tiananmen Square evoked revulsion and horror in the international community. Even so, the West soon returned to "normal" policy vis-à-vis China. In the years that have followed China's economy had undergone liberalization, but any kind of political opposition continues to be suppressed. ❑

An unarmed man confronts the tanks of the People's Liberation Army.

ACCIDENT AT RUSSIAN NUCLEAR POWER PLANT

Chernobyl, Russia, April 26, 1986

The most serious accident to date in the history of the civil use of atomic energy occurred in a Ukrainian nuclear power plant. At 1:24 AM, a testing program in the nuclear reactor in Chernobyl went out of control on account of an operational error. A nightmarish sequence followed. A hydrogen explosion destroyed the reactor housing, nuclear fuel rods began to melt, and radiation of 50 million curies was released, 30 to 40 times more radioactivity than produced by the bombing of Hiroshima.

The reactor, which broke down, was a high productivity pressure pipe reactor with a thermal production of 3,200 megawatts. The greatest safety deficiencies were its inadequate shutdown system and a missing steel safety container.

Within 36 hours the evacuation of around 135,000 persons from almost 200 villages had begun. In all 180,000 persons were relocated. Officially, only 32 deaths were attributed to the disaster, but around 580,000 Soviet citizens were certified to have suffered from the consequences of the catastrophe. An area of around 75,000 sq. mi. (200,000 km²) was contaminated, with the radioactive cloud extending to north and central Europe. ❑

After the catastrophe: Destroyed parts of the building of the nuclear power plant in Chernobyl

THE WALL FALLS:

Berlin, November 9, 1989

In 1989, more than 40 years of a cemented post-war order in Europe fell apart. The citizens of the socialist states brought it to an end by choosing democracy over the powerful communist monopoly.

Germany: At 6:57 PM in a press conference broadcast live from the DDR (East Germany), the politburo member, Günter Schabowski, announced that the DDR State Council had approved a measure to permit short term "private travel and travel to foreign countries." At first no one understood the meaning of this news, but by 9:00 PM crowds were at East Berlin border checkpoints. Initially processing was slow, but at 11:14 PM the barriers were opened.

When earlier in the year, on May 2, Hungarian soldiers started to break down the "Iron

Hungarian soldiers secure the border

Curtain" at the Austrian border, a new escape route was opened to citizens of the DDR. On September 11, Hungary allowed all 57,000 citizens of the DDR to leave the country. On the night of October 1, over 6,000 refugees in the West German embassies in Prague and Warsaw were allowed to leave.

Protests for freedom and democracy in the DDR had been increasing since September. There were weekly prayers for peace at the Nikolai Church in Leipzig as part of regular "Monday Demonstrations." On October 23, more than 200,000 people took part.

In East Berlin there were protests even during celebrations of the fortieth anniversary of the founding of the DDR. On October 18, the State and Party Leader,

EASTERN EUROPE ON ITS WAY TO DEMOCRACY

Erich Honecker, who had been in office for 18 years, stepped down. Egon Krenz was elected as the new chief of the ruling party, but he also resigned on December 3. With the transition in the DDR, German unification was put back on the agenda.

Hungary: At a conference of the Hungarian Socialist Worker's Party (USAP) held on May 23, 1988, reforms precipitated the resignation of Party Leader János Kádár, and in February 1989 a multi-party system was approved.

On October 8, 1989, the USAP was disbanded and reorganized as the non-communist USP. The abolition of the "People's Republic" as a type of state was officially declared on October 23 with the proclamation of the Republic of Hungary.

Poland: *Solidarnosc* (Solidarity), prohibited since 1981, was re-registered on April 1 when the government and the opposition met at the "Round Table." A reform of political institutions allowed the Polish people to elect a third of the members of the Polish parliament (*Sejm*) and all the representatives of the newly created senate. In the first elections since 1945 the "Citizens Committee of Solidarity" received the majority of votes. On August 24 parliament announced the *Solidarnosc*

The Wall and the Brandenburg Gate were the partition between the opposing states of East and West for 28 years.

politician Tadeusz Mazowiecki as head of the government.

Bulgaria: On November 10 Foreign Minister Petar Mladenov replaced Todor Schivkov, who had held office since 1954, as the leader of the Communist Party (BKP). Mladenov immediately initiated reform, but at the same time, he also reaffirmed his firm hold on the socialist system. In the first free elections on June 17, 1990 the former communist state party was able to assert itself.

Czechoslovakia: On December 10, State President Gustav Husák, who had been in office since 1975, swore in a new parliament, consisting mainly of non-communists, and then resigned. The "Velvet Revolution" began on November 24 with the resignation of the Communist Party. On December 29 the author Václav Havel was elected president.

Romania: On December 25 State and Party Leader Nicolae Ceausescu was executed after having

been sentenced by a military tribunal. A day later the old guard communist Ion Iliescu became head of state. Open resistance against the regime, which according to an official statement had killed 1,038 people, began on December 16 in the states of Temesvar and Arad. Despite the actions of the army and security forces, the protests spread to Bucharest, where the army sided with the regime's opponents, leading to the fall of the government. ❑

The Czech politicians Alexander Dubcek (M.) and Václav Havel (r.) were guarantors of the democratic government.

The "Round Table" in Poland.

GERMAN REUNIFICATION

Berlin, October 3, 1990

Hundreds of thousands of Germans moved freely between the old East and West Berlins to celebrate reunification. After the peaceful revolution in the GDR (East Germany) brought down the Wall, the reformation of the GDR was topmost on the agenda: The SED (Socialist Unity Party) renamed itself under the leadership of Gregor Gysi as SED-PDS to begin with, and from February 1990, as the Party of Democratic Socialism (PDS). Party representatives and civil rights groups came to a consensus about political pluralism, the rule of law, and a market economy.

The clamor for the reunification started with demonstrations in the GDR. At the first free elections to the East German Parliament on March 18, 1990 a coalition government under Lothar de Maizière announced its aim to have the GDR unite with West Germany in accordance with Article 23 of the constitution.

On June 21, parliaments of East and West Germany passed a treaty on the creation of an economic, monetary, and social union. On July 1, 1990, the West German mark became the official means of payment in the GDR. Wages, salaries, pensions, rents, leases and scholarships were converted to the ratio 1:1, although for commercial transactions the West German mark was valued at a higher level.

On August 31, the Unification Treaty was signed. The four victorious powers of the Second World War reacted very differently to the process of reunification: The USA was positive, France and Great Britain guarded, the USSR hostile. After lengthy negotiations, on September 12, the USSR, the USA, Great Britain, France, and both Germanys signed the final document of the "Two Plus Four" Treaty in Moscow. The Allied Powers relinquished all claims and rights in Germany, and the country was granted its full sovereignty. The USSR accepted the NATO membership of unified Germany and the GDR withdrew from the War-

Hans-Dietrich Genscher, Hannelore and Helmut Kohl as well as Richard von Weizsäcker in Berlin (from left)

saw Pact.

With the signing of the accord, the borders of Germany were laid down in accordance with international law. On October 4, the first pan-German session of Parliament was held in the Reichstag in Berlin. With the added 144 members of Parliament of the former GDR, the number of parliamentarians increased to 663. October 3, Unification Day, became a federal holiday. A coalition of center-right and center-left parties formed a government after the first pan-German parliamentary elections on December 2, 1990 with center-right politician Helmut Kohl as Chancellor. ❑

WAR AGAINST IRAQ

Kuwait, February 24, 1991

A multinational force under the leadership of the USA put a stop to the expansionist impulses of the Iraqi Head of State, Saddam Hussein.

Early in the morning of February 24, 1991, the international force stationed in the Persian Gulf began air attacks on Iraq. After the breakdown of all diplomatic efforts, the liberation of Kuwait, which was occupied on August 2, 1990, by Iraqi troops, was handed over to the military. The UN Security Council had given Iraq an ultimatum on November 29, 1990 to withdraw by January 15, 1991.

Iraq had around 545,000 armed men; they were opposed by approximately 690,000 soldiers from 26 countries, including over 425,000 Americans.

After air attacks lasting five weeks, the ground offensive was launched on February 24. Within one hundred hours, Iraq was defeated and the war decided. On February 28, all acts of war ceased in Kuwait and Iraq and Iraq agreed to UN sanctions.

Around 100,000-120,000 Iraqi soldiers had fallen, the allies lost only 343. Some 5,000 to 15,000 Iraqi and 2,000 to 5,000 Kuwait civilians lost their lives. The environmental damage caused by the Iraqis was devastating: in Kuwait, 727 oil wells were in flames, and over 100 million gallons of oil had flowed into the sea. ❑

Oil wells burning in Kuwait. The massive clouds of smoke from over 600 burning wells turned day to night in Kuwait.

NELSON MANDELA

Brief Lives

Nelson Mandela (July 18, 1918 in Umtata) is the son of a Xhosa chieftain in the Transkei. After studying law, he became one of the first black South African lawyers. A member of the African National Congress (ANC) from 1944, in 1961 he founded the Umkhonto we Sizwe movement ("Spear of the Nation") and went underground. He was arrested in 1962 and sentenced to life imprisonment in 1964. Released on February 11, 1990,

Mandela became the first black president of South Africa on May 9, 1994. He received the Nobel Peace Prize in 1993. ❏

THE END OF APARTHEID

Capetown, South Africa, February 11, 1990

After almost 28 years of imprisonment the black leader, Nelson Mandela, was released to freedom. F.W. de Klerk, elected President of South Africa in August 1989, joined the black leader in ending racial discrimination. De Klerk announced the legalization of the Black Opposition and the end of the state of emergency. By the end of June 1991, all apartheid laws were essentially revoked.

In December 1991, the Convention for a Democratic South Africa met for the first time, with whites and blacks discussing South

Nelson Mandela after his release with his wife, Winnie

Africa's political future. On April 27, 1994 a provisional constitution took effect that terminated all race-based discrimination and declared the ten "homelands," of which four were formally independent (Bophuthatswana, Ciskei, Transkei and Venda), to be part of South Africa once again. Elections held at the same time gave the African National Congress (ANC) an overwhelming victory. Nelson Mandela became the first head of state in the post-Apartheid era and devoted himself to accomplishing a peaceful transition. A government of national unity, including de Klerk's National Party and the Inkhatha Freedom Party, alongside of the ANC, remained in power until 1999. ❏

GRIM CIVIL WAR IN YUGOSLAVIA

Ljubljana and Zagreb, Yugoslavia, June 25, 1991

Eleven years after the death of Josip Broz Tito, Yugoslavia, a multiethnic state, was torn apart by nationalist and sectarian conflicts. First the Republics of Slovenia and Croatia unilaterally declared their independence. This step led to war with the Serbian dominated federal army and Serbian paramilitary organizations.

While the war in Serbia ended on July 3, skirmishes between Croatian people's militia and commandos of the Serbian minorities escalated in the three Croatian regions dominated by Serbs: East Slovenia, Bajina, and Krajina.

On January 15, 1992 the EU recognized Slovenia and Croatia as independent. Following this, the UN Security Council endorsed the dispatch of a peacekeeping force to Croatia.

After the proclamation of the Republic of Bosnia-Herzegovina on March 3, heavy fighting broke out there between Serbs, Croats and Muslim Bosnians. On March 27, the Bosnian Serbs proclaimed a Serbian Republic. On July 3, the Bosnian Croats proclaimed a Croatian Republic of Herceg Bosnia.

With the arrival of the first U.N. troops in Sarajevo, airlift operations and food deliveries for the beleaguered civilian population commenced, but these were obstructed by the Serbs. Plans for a political solution, which allowed for a division of Bosnia, broke down due to the objections and unyielding position of the Serbs. On March 18, 1994 the Bosnian government and the Bosnia Croats joined forces against the Serbs and to jointly found a Federation of Bosnia-Herzegovina. In 1995, the Croatian army regained control over the territories occupied by the Serbs, at first West Slovenia on May 1, then the so-called Republic of Serbian Krajina on August 4.

On July 11, the Serbs marched into the East Bosnian Muslim en-

clave declared in 1993 to be a UN protected zone, and on July 25, Zepa fell as well. The Serbs, engaging in a deliberate policy of rape, murder, and ethnic cleansing, drove out the Muslim population. One terrible example of Serbian violence was the massacre at Srebenica, ruled genocide by the International War Tribunal, in which 8,000 men and boys were murdered.

After a Serbian air attack on a marketplace in Sarajevo, the NATO leadership reacted by sending 60 airplanes to bomb radar and telecommunication installations, anti-aircraft positions and munitions depots of the Bosnian Serbs. Two weeks later the Serbs bowed to international demands and on November 21, 1995 the broad outlines of a peace accord are reached during a US sponsored negotiation in Dayton, Ohio. The Dayton Accords established an independent Bosnia-Herzogovina. ❏

BEGINNING OF A NEW MILLENNIUM

The European Union grows from fifteen to twenty-five members: flags of the EU states flying at the European Parliament in Strasbourg.

The European Union (EU) was created by the Maastricht Treaty that came into force on November 1, 1993. Its twelve members included Belgium, Denmark, Germany, France, Greece, Great Britain, Ireland, Italy, Luxembourg, the Netherlands, Portugal, and Spain. The Maastricht Treaty accelerated the process of European integration and widened the scope of the articles of agreement of the European community, including the extension of political integration.

Besides establishing a common foreign policy and security policy, this expansion included the introduction of European Union citizenship and the further development of social policies, particularly the gradual development of economic and monetary union together with the foundation of a European central bank.

In 1995, Finland, Austria, and Sweden joined the EU. In May 1998 eleven of the 15 EU countries joined the Euro, the common currency of the EU, which was introduced on January 1, 1999; the national currencies of these countries were withdrawn from circulation in 2002. In May 2004, ten countries from eastern and southeastern Europe and the Mediterranean joined the EU, attracted by an increasingly strong Europe. The ratification of the text of the EU Constitution agreed upon in 2004 led to a crisis in 2005, when the French and the Dutch voted against the Constitution in a referendum.

TROUBLE IN THE BALKANS

As it had at the beginning of the twentieth century, the political situation in the Balkans in the 1990s once again led to a series of crises that affected the whole of Europe. In 1991, the multi-ethnic state of Yugoslavia violently broke apart. The main centers of the war were Croatia and more especially Bosnia-Herzegovina, where for decades the Bosnians (Muslims), Croats, and Serbs had lived together with relative good will. The declaration of independence of Bosnia-Herzegovina in 1992 developed into a bloody civil war. International mediation and negotiations, the deployment of UN troops, and the creation of protected zones for the Muslim population in Serbian-controlled areas could not prevent the growing violence.

The Bosnian Serbs drove other ethnic groups out of the areas conquered by them in a process of ethnic cleansing. As a result, the civilian population became the victim of massacres and mass rape. Political pressure by the USA and military strikes by NATO troops against the Bosnian Serbs led to the Dayton Agreement in November 1995. Bosnia-Herzegovina remained a state, inhabited by three ethnic groups, but peaceful co-existence was still a long way off.

Barely three and a half years after the Bosnian war, the Balkans were ablaze again: on the evening of March 24, 1999, NATO carried out air strikes against targets in Yugoslavia, while German soldiers were deployed for the first time since 1945. To put an end to the oppression of the majority population of Albanian origin in Kosovo, NATO became involved in the war to defend human rights, but without a mandate from the United Nations.

THE TINDERBOX OF IRAQ

The Iraqi president, Saddam Hussein, who had received military support from the West in the Iran-Iraq War (1980-1988), was declared "Public Enemy Number 1" by the USA in the 1990s. After Iraqi troops had invaded Kuwait on August 2, 1990, a coalition force, led mainly by the United States, was sent to liberate Kuwait. The ground offensive ended with a decisive victory for the coalition forces, which drove the Iraqi troops out of Kuwait but stopped short of toppling the Iraqi regime. In April 1991, an armistice was agreed to but Iraq remained a trouble spot. After months of political debate, including among other things argument as to the presence of weapons of mass destruction in Iraq, the USA took the initiative in March 2003. The second war since 1991 began, and the USA with its partner Great Britain deposed Saddam Hussein. Despite an intensive search for weapons of mass destruction, the existence of which had been the ostensible reason for the war, none were found. Iraq remained in the grip of sectarian violence even after the execution of Saddam, whom the USA had captured in 2003. Continuing bloodshed, approaching civil war, bombings, and suicide attacks continued to prevent the creation of democratic institutions.

NO PEACE IN THE MIDDLE EAST

After decades of confrontation, a certain level of communication between Israel and its neighbors was gradually established in the 1990s, albeit constantly interrupted by disagreements. The main points of contention were the creation of an independent Palestinian state and the future status of Jerusalem.

In 1993, the Palestinian leader Yasser Arafat and Israel's Prime Minister Yitzhak Rabin signed a declaration in which the PLO recognized Israel's right to exist and Israel recognized the PLO as the representative of the Palestinian people. In 1994, Israel vacated the Gaza strip. But when the government in Israel changed, the rapprochement came to a standstill again. In 2000, after the visit by the Israeli politician Ariel Sharon to the Temple Mount, serious unrest broke out that developed into a second *intifada* (uprising). The Israelis responded to the Palestinian acts of terrorism with retaliatory measures. In 2002, Israel began to construct a security barrier to separate the West Bank from Israel. After the breakdown in the peace negotiations, Yasser Arafat, the leader of the PLO, was somewhat marginalized. He was repeatedly put under house arrest by the Israelis and died in 2004. The Palestinian side is now divided into two factions. The more militant *Hamas* controls Gaza; it rejects Israel's right to exist. The West Bank is governed by the heirs to Arafat's organization, the Palestinian Authority. Its president Mahmoud Abbas has shown himself more willing to negotiate with Israel.

ENVIRONMENT AND NATURE

Nearly 100 government leaders and 3,000 diplomats from 170 countries took part in the Earth Summit held in Rio de Janeiro in June 1992 to discuss the most serious environmental problems. But the agreements were not binding and were only to be used as guidelines. In December 1997, the Kyoto Protocol, a wide-reaching agreement to reduce greenhouse gases that cause climate change, was drawn up. Most industrial countries were expected to reduce their carbon emissions by 8% by 2012. The refusal of the United States, China and India to sign on, however, dimmed the protocol's prospects for success.

The fragility of nature and its sensitivity to changes in the environment is clearly seen in the El Niño phenomenon, which attracted the attention of the world for the first time in 1997 when associated changes in the global weather system were observed. In December 2004, countries in the Indian Ocean were hit by natural catastrophe of Biblical proportions; a giant sea wave (tsunami), caused by an earthquake below the sea, cost the lives of more than 150,000 people.

GLOBAL ECONOMY

Globalization, the worldwide interdependence of the economy that has led to a single world market, was one of the most important topics in politics at the end of the 20th century.

Multinational corporations have taken advantage of the great potential offered by globalization, producing their goods where production costs are lowest.

In forthcoming decades, it is predicted that an explosion of knowledge and the internet will further increase levels of globalization. In addition, it is becoming evident that the booming economies of Asia will have a major influence on the stock exchanges of the world and the global economy. Significant economic growth is expected in the field of information technology and communications, in genetic engineering, in the development of new materials, and in the field of energy and the environment.

The world that was divided in two until 1989 has grown together with the internet as a means of communication and English as a universal language. Since the 1990s this has led in turn to cultural globalization that could result in the loss of national traditions.

INTERNATIONAL TERRORISM

The new century has been particularly influenced by the terrible events of September 11, 2001. Terrorists flew two hijacked passenger aircraft into the Twin Towers of the World Trade Center in New York. They also crashed a plane into the Pentagon near Washington. As a result of the attack both towers of the World trade Center collapsed, causing the death of over 3,000 people. The symbol of American economic and financial power had been hit, and the whole nation was shaken to the core. Osama bin Laden, the leader of the Al Qaeda terrorist network, was identified as the instigator of the attack.

Following the attack, the US planned military actions against the Al Qaeda terrorist network. Their main target was in Afghanistan whose militant Islamic Taliban government was thought to be harboring bin Laden. But before putting their plans into action, the US established a worldwide anti-terrorist network. In October 2001, US aircraft, supported by British units, carried out an aerial bombing campaign against Afghanistan. With the support of the Afghani Northern Alliance they succeeded in toppling the Taliban. The path to the reorganization of the country was now clear, but Osama bin Laden was still at large. At present Taliban forces seem to be regrouping, and the country's future remains uncertain. ❑

Terrorist attacks on 11 September 2001: the second hijacked aircraft explodes as it flies into the Twin Towers.

THE DAYTON ACCORDS

Dayton, Ohio November 21, 1995

Six weeks after the ceasefire in Bosnia and three weeks after the beginning of their talks at Wright-Patterson Air Force Base near Dayton, Ohio, the Presidents Slobodan Milosevic (Serbia), Alija Izetbegovic (Bosnia-Herzegovina) and Franjo Tudjman (Croatia) initialed a peace treaty. It would be signed on December 14, in Paris.

After four years of war, over 250,000 dead and hundreds of thousands of refugees in Bosnia-Herzegovina, the weapons were finally laid to rest. Massive NATO air attacks over two weeks beginning on August 30, had forced the Serbs to give in. Bosnia-Herzegovina remained a unified state within its current boundaries, to consist of two parts: the Muslim-Croatian federation, to whom 51 percent of the country was allotted, and the Serbian Republic in Bosnia, which received 49 percent. The Serbian stronghold of Pale belonged to this as well as the UN protected zones of Srebrenica and Zepa.

Sarajevo remained the capital of Bosnia and the seat of the central government. The Bosnian parliament was structured to consist of a lower House and an upper house and a presidency with representatives of the three ethnic groups.

The treaty was monitored by an international peacekeeping force (IFOR), which replaced the erstwhile UN protection force (UNPROFOR). One of the most difficult tasks was the rehabilitation of approximately 2.8 million refugees of the former Yugoslavia. To begin with, the approximately 1.3 million displaced, who found refuge in Bosnia itself, were to return; then approximately 820,000 in Serbia and Croatia; finally, approximately 700,000 refugees in the countries of western Europe. ❑

Milosevic, Izetbegovic, Tudjman coming to an agreement in Dayton, Ohio

MILESTONE ON THE ROAD TO PEACE IN THE MIDDLE EAST

Washington DC, September 13, 1993

After 45 years of enmity between Arabs and Jews, new hopes for peace and reconciliation were sparked as Israel's Prime Minister, Yitzhak Rabin, and PLO Head, Yasser Arafat, signed the Gaza-Jericho Accord for partial autonomy of the Palestinians. Their demonstrative handshake shake in the presence of US President, Bill Clinton, captured headlines in the newspapers around the world.

On September 10, both sides accorded each other recognition after decades of enmity. For the first time, the PLO formally accepted Israel's right to exist, while in return, Israel recognized the PLO as the representative of the interests of the Palestinian people. Secret negotiations bro-kered in Oslo paved the way to the peace accord.

The agreement stipulated among other things that the Palestinians in the Gaza Strip and in Jericho were granted the right to self-administration for a transition period lasting up to April 1999, and that Israel was required to withdraw its troops from the Gaza Strip and Jericho by April 1994.

These provisions were formalized after the signing of an interim agreement on May 4, 1994 in Cairo. On May 13, 1994 the area around Jericho was handed over to the Palestinians, and on May 18, the Israelis evacuated Gaza city. Administration of Palestine was transferred to a Palestinian Authority as the executive organ of government. It received control over education, health, and welfare as well as the economy, employment, and social welfare, environmental protection, and tourism. After 27 years in exile, Arafat visited the Gaza Strip on July 1; on July 5, he formed a government in Jericho. ❑

Handshake after the signing of the accord. Left to right: Rabin, Clinton, Arafat

THE DISINTEGRATION OF THE SOVIET UNION

Alma Ata, Kazahkstan, December 21, 1991

Boris Yeltsin, standing in front of the White House in Moscow, exhorts the people to resist

After 69 years the Soviet Union, founded in 1922, ceased to exist. Eleven of fifteen former Soviet republics joined together to form the Commonwealth of Independent States (CIS). With the resignation of the Soviet President, Mikhail Gorbachev four days later, the end of the USSR was sealed.

With the signing of an "Accord on the Union of Sovereign States" planned for August 20, Gorbachev had attempted to put the disintegrating USSR on a new democratic footing. The states of the union were granted the right to independence and self-determination. They were intended to decide on their political and territorial configuration themselves. However, on August 19, orthodox-communist forces attempted a coup d'état: an eight-member emergency committee declared that Gorbachev was no longer president and did not allow him to leave his vacation resort in Crimea. The putsch failed after three days due to popular resistance and the vacillation of the armed forces. On August 22, Gorbachev returned to Moscow. The beneficiary of the aborted coup was the Russian President, Boris Yeltsin, who portrayed himself as the defender of democracy, called for a general strike, and brought loyal army units onto his side.

On August 23, Yeltsin signed a decree in the presence of Gorbachev prohibiting the activities of the Communist Party in Russia, and Gorbachev resigned as the General Secretary of the CPSU. On September 5 in Moscow, the Congress of People's Deputies endorsed Gorbachev's plan for devolution of power with a two-thirds majority. With this the role of the centralized government in Moscow headquarters was radically weakened in favor of the individual republics.

The disintegration of the Soviet Union laid open the way for the Baltic States annexed by the Soviet Union in 1940 to regain state independence. At first, Soviet troops attempted to prevent the bid for autonomy in Lithuania and Latvia, but on September 6, Moscow finally recognized the independence of the Baltic Republics of Lithuania, Latvia and Estonia.

In the following weeks, Gorbachev made unavailing efforts to keep central institutions alive. On December 1, the people of Ukraine voted with an overwhelming majority for independence, giving the signal for the dismemberment of the USSR. All the Soviet republics joined the CIS founded on December 21 with the exception of the three Baltic States and Georgia, which was in the throes of a civil war. The leading member of the CIS, the Russian Federation, became a permanent member of the UN Security Council as the successor of the USSR. ❑

The CIS heads of state in Alma Ata with Boris Yeltsin (center)

LABOR VICTORY IN ENGLAND

London, MAY 1, 1997

With its largest victory in history, the Labor Party changed England's political course. Party head, Tony Blair, became Prime Minister and moved with his family into residence at 10 Downing Street.

With a 43.4 percent share of the vote, Labor won 419 of the 659 seats in Parliament. Blair was the youngest Prime Minister since 1812. Under his leadership Labor achieved the greatest electoral success of any British party since 1935. The country was clearly tired of the Tory leadership; they seemed to have lost their way after the departure of Prime Minister Margaret Thatcher. Blair's calls for reforms were well received, and the sizeable Labor victory began Labor's

Blair and family at 10 Downing Street

dominance in England, which has lasted until the present day. ❑

DOLLY, THE FIRST CLONED MAMMAL

Edinburgh, Scotland, February 23, 1997

In a breakthrough in the field of genetic engineering that awakened concerns worldwide about the possibilities of misuse, geneticists at the Roslin Institute announced that they had cloned an adult mammal. The clone was the seven-month old sheep "Dolly."

The researchers removed a cell, the nucleus of which contained the organism's entire genetic information, from the udder of a full-grown sheep. An unfertilized egg was taken from a second sheep and the nucleus of the cell removed. They then inserted the cell nucleus of the first sheep into the empty egg and implanted the complete egg cell into the uterus of a third sheep. This gave birth to "Dolly." ❑

The cloned sheep, "Dolly", in its pen

THE IMPEACHMENT OF PRESIDENT BILL CLINTON

Washington, DC, December 19, 1998

President Bill Clinton was an extraordinarily polarizing figure in America politics. Although for most of his tenure in office he retained high approval ratings, a significant minority, especially among those on the right end of the political spectrum, was vehemently opposed to him and leveled numerous charges of illegality and impropriety against him.

One area that raised questions throughout his presidency was the involvement of Clinton, then Governor of Arkansas, and his wife Hillary, along with James and Susan McDougal, in a real estate company, the Whitewater Development Corporation. To help fund this company, in 1982, McDougal purchased a savings and loan bank, naming it the Madison Guaranty. By 1989 the bank collapsed and was under federal investigation for questionable practices. The investigation by the Federal Resolution Trust Corporation also included the Madison Guaranty's dealings with Whitewater. In 1992, the RTC declared that the Clintons had been "potential beneficia-ries" of the bank's allegedly illegal practices. Accusations were also made against the Clinton by an Arkansas judge, David Hale, but he himself was convicted of fraud, and his testimony against the Clintons was inconsistent.

The death of Deputy White House Counsel, Vince Foster, added further complications. Though his death was ruled a suicide, many theories sprang up among Clinton foes that accused the presidential couple of involvement in his death. After his death, when the Clintons refused federal investigators access to his office, political factions in Washington began calling for an investigation into their White-water-Madison dealings. The Administration turned over documents, including Foster's, to the Justice department. Then, under increasing political pressure, Clinton authorized Attorney General Janet Reno to appoint an independent counsel to lead an inquiry. She appointed U.S. Attorney Robert Fiske. In the summer of 1994, Fiske was replaced by a former Reagan Justice Department official, Kenneth Starr.

As the Whitewater investigation progressed a number of pivotal events occurred. In the congressional elections of 1994 the Republican Party engineered a sweeping political victory. Under the leadership of the fiery minority leader Newt Gingrich, the Republicans took control of both the House of Representatives and the Senate. With their ascendance to power the tempo of investigations against the president accelerated.

In the meantime Paula Jones, a former Arkansas government employee, filed a civil lawsuit claiming that Clinton had sexually harassed her while he was Governor. In 1995 Clinton began an affair with a White House intern named Monica Lewinsky. When rumors of the Lewinsky affair began to surface in Washington, Lewinsky was transferred to the Pentagon where she was befriended by a fellow employee, Linda Tripp. Lewinsky engaged in phone calls with Tripp in which she admitted her liaisons with the President. Tripp recorded 20 hours of the conversations which she then to turn over to Kenneth Starr.

Having no success in proving any wrongdoing against the Clintons regarding the Whitewater matter, which he was originally mandated to investigate, Starr received approval to broaden his investigation to include other possible areas of wrongdoing, launching what many considered to be a fishing expedition to bring down the president. Most observers agreed that his staff included dedicated Clinton opponents. Starr shifted his focus away from Whitewater toward President Clinton's personal conduct. The Presidents response to these issues in the investigation is what led to the House of Representative's articles of impeachment.

Paula Jones' lawyer, still pursuing his client's harassment case, heard of the Lewinsky affair and subpoenaed her. Lewinsky confirmed the rumors to Jones' lawyer. On January 17 1998, Clinton gave a pretrial deposition to Jones' legal team who asked him about Lewinsky. Under oath, the President denied having had sexual relations with her. This denial under oath would become the basis of one the articles of impeachment: "Obstruction of justice related to the Paula Jones case."

In January of 1998, Starr had the FBI question Monica Lewinsky. In the same month Clinton went on the national television and denied he had had sexual relations with Lewinsky. On August 6, Lewinsky repeated her deposition at Starr's federal grand jury hearing. On August 17, Clinton appeared before the same grand jury via closed-circuit television where he again denied having had sexual relations with Lewinsky. This denial under oath would be the basis of a second article of impeachment: "Perjury before Independent Council Kenneth Starr's grand jury."

On September 9, Starr presented his final report to the House of Representative's Judiciary Committee. Responding to the report the full House of Representatives voted to open an impeachment, and on December 12, four articles of impeachment were drawn up and forwarded to the full House. On December 18 and 19 the House conducted deliberations. On Saturday 19 in a vote along strict party lines the House passed two articles of impeachment (that is the beginning of proceedings in the Senate, not the president's actual removal from office). Bill Clinton had become the second president in U.S. history to be impeached by the House of Representatives. (Andrew Johnson was the first.)

Removal from office required that the Senate also authorize the articles of impeachment. This did not occur. Hearings begun on January 7 ended on February 1; a two-thirds majority vote in favor was required to remove the president from office. The final vote was 45 votes for 45 votes for conviction and 55 against. Bill Clinton remained President of the United States. ❑

President Bill Clinton with Secretary of Defense William Cohen

DEATH OF A PRINCESS

Paris, August 31, 1997

Diana, the Princess of Wales was born on July 1, 1961 at Park House near Sandringham, Norfolk. Daughter of Viscount and Viscountess Althorp, Lady Diana Frances Spencer spent her childhood at Park House until 1975 when she and her two older sisters, Sarah and Jane, and her younger brother, Charles, moved with their then divorced father to Althorp, the Spencer family seat in Northhamptonshire.

Educated in a fashion befitting her noble station, Lady Diana first attended the preparatory school Riddlesworth Hall in Norfolk and then matriculated as a boarder at West Heath in Kent. In 1977, after briefly attending a "finishing school" in Rougement, Switzerland, she moved to London, working first as an au pair for an American couple and then as a kindergarten teacher in the Borough of Pimlico.

A social peer of the Royal Family, Diana had known her future husband, Charles, Prince of Wales, from her childhood at Park House. They met again as young adults in November of 1977 when the Prince was invited to Althorp. For the next few years the repeated sightings of Charles and Diana together at various social engagements led to speculation that Charles, thirteen years Diana's senior, might have finally found his Princess.

The speculation proved to be true. On February 24, 1981, Buckingham Palace announced that Charles and Diana were to marry. On July 29, 1981 Lady Diana became the first Englishwoman in 300 years to marry an heir to the British throne. The ceremony was performed at St Paul's Church by the Archbish-

op of Canterbury, Dr. Robert Runcie. Watched on television worldwide by many hundreds of millions of people, the wedding was one of the great social events of the twentieth century.

After a two-week honeymoon cruise through the Mediterranean aboard the Royal yacht *HMS Britannia*, the Prince and, now, Princess of Wales assumed their royal duties to their largely adoring public, setting off on a number of official domestic and international tours. From the start, Diana's presence on these official visits was electrifying. Enthralled by her graceful beauty and the naturalness of the warmth she displayed in public, the press soon made her the most photographed and sought after Royal in modern history. Although not obvious to the public, this elevation to icon-

Diana gave birth to her first son, next in line to the throne after Charles, Prince William Arthur Philip Louis. Three years later, on September 15, 1984, a second son was born, Prince Henry Charles Albert David. For the next several years she displayed a remarkable élan as both doting mother and symbol of the monarchy. Eschewing the frivolity of being a social and fashion icon, Diana gave much of her time and considerable prestige to over 100 different charities. She was especially tireless in her work on behalf of the homeless and those infected with HIV and to the eradication of landmines.

For reasons only she and Charles were truly privy to, the marriage bonds began to unravel. The slightest hints of marital trouble sent the press on a feed-

cember of 1992 the royal couple announced that they had agreed to separate. Diana moved into Kensington Palace while Charles remained at their family estate at Highgrove.

After their divorce on August 28, 1996, Diana, who retained the title of Princess of Wales, began devoting more time to her sons and less to charitable causes. Still revered worldwide, she became embroiled in personal relationships that became fodder for the tabloids, which broadcast her every move.

Although continuing to campaign against the proliferation of landmines, especially those in Angola and Bosnia, Diana increasingly retreated from public life, finding solace only in her sons and the companionship of Dodi Fayd, the son of the owner of Harrods department store.

Sadly, Diana's decline from fairytale princess to paparazzi prey ended tragically in Paris on August 31, 1997. Diana, Fayd and their driver, Henri Paul, were killed when their Mercedes crashed in the Pont de l'Alma road tunnel. Fayd's personal bodyguard, Trevor Rees-Jones survived. The official police report concluded that the fatal crash occurred during the couples' attempt to avoid paparazzi who were chasing them.

Diana's death stunned the world. The normally reserved British public displayed their deeply felt grief for the "people's princess," as British Prime Minister Tony Blair called her. Almost immediately upon the

Media event: Princess Diana in London

woman in 300 years to marry an heir to the British throne. The ceremony was performed at St Paul's Church by the Archbish-

ic status never appealed to Diana, and eventually became a role she could not continue to play.

On June 21, 1982 Princess

ing frenzy. This assault on her private life may have exacerbated the problems between Charles and Diana. In any case, in De-

broadcast of word of the tragedy bouquets of flowers began to appear in front of the gates of Buckingham Palace. ❑

RARE HEAVENLY PHENOMENON

The Atlantic Ocean, August 11, 1999

A fascinating natural spectacle caused millions of people in Europe and Asia to gaze enthralled at the heavens: A total solar eclipse turned day into night in many places when the moon came between the sun and the earth. Birds stopped singing and temperatures dropped up to 20 degrees Fahrenheit. The rare occurrence began over the Atlantic, about 180 miles (300 km) south of the Canadian province of Nova Scotia at about 9:30 AM GMT, when the deepest shadow of the moon impinged on the

Seconds before the total eclipse: The moon positions itself in front of the sun.

earth's surface for the first time. In three hours and seven minutes, it spread over a 8,700 mile (14,000 km) long band, which was 70 miles (112 km) at its widest, and moved at three times the speed of sound in an easterly direction.

At around 10:30 AM, the moon's shadow reached Europe and moved east further to India. In the Bay of Bengal, the deep shadow left the earth's surface at around 12:35 PM. In many places, thick clouds lowered visibility, much to the disappointment of the observers. The heavenly phenomenon, lasting not much over two minutes, was thereby observable only on account of the twilight-like darkness. ❑

GÜNTER GRASS HONORED

Stockholm, October 12, 1999

One of the most significant contemporary German authors was honored with the Nobel Prize in Literature for his life's work. The 72-year-old writer had been seriously considered for the award for many years. Günter Grass has "broken the evil spell that lay over Germany's past," stated the permanent secretary of the Swedish Academy, Horace Engdahl, in his speech given at the award ceremony. With his *Danzig Trilogy*, the author has "captured the forgotten face of history in lively yet dark fables" was how the Nobel Committee accounted for its decision. In 2006, Grass once

The author, Günter Grass accepts the award from Sweden's King Carl Gustav XVI.

again made headlines. In his autobiography he admitted that, as a 17-year-old at the end of 1944, he was a member of the armed SS. As someone who had written extensively on Germany's uneasy relationship with its own history, criticism was leveled at him in particular for his having kept this silent for many decades.

In the same year that Grass won the prize for literature the Nobel Peace Prize was awarded to the organization, Doctors Without Borders, for its dedicated work in war zones. The group was founded by French doctors in 1971 to assist in the crisis in Biafra. Since that time it as been on the front lines of humanitarian crises worldwide. ❑

YELTSIN RESIGNS

Moscow, December 31, 1999

In a New Year's Eve surprise, the Russian President, Boris Yeltsin, announced on national television that he was stepping down. The 68-year-old President stated that he was handing over his official powers, including the "nuclear suitcase," to his Prime Minister, Vladimir Putin.

Yeltsin appeared pale and unwell in his television appearance, which the Russian people watched with astonishment. He asked the people to forgive him for the mistakes he may have made in his two terms as President and announced: "On this last day of the century, which is coming to an end, I am stepping down from office…I have realized that I must do this. Russia must step into the new millennium with new politicians, new faces, and new, intelligent, strong and energetic persons…"

Prior to his resignation, accusations of corruption and misuse of office against Yeltsin had grown louder. After Yeltsin's resignation, Putin delivered the traditional New Year speech. The 47-year-old presented himself as a democrat and champion of freedom of speech

Boris Yeltsin (right) hands over the reins of power to Vladimir Putin.

and conscience, and freedom of the press. He signed an order giving Yeltsin immunity.

Putin took over his office as interim President until the early presidential elections designated for March 26, 2000, which he would go on to win.

Unable to run for president again in 2008 because of the law on term limits, Putin assumed the role of prime minister, with his hand-picked successor, Dmitri Medvedev, serving as president. It is widely assumed that Putin will remain the real power in Russian politics. ❑

RUSSIAN ARMY CONTINUES WITH THE CAUCASUS CAMPAIGN

Grozny, October 21, 1999

According to President Aslan Mashadov, 282 persons lost their lives and 400 persons were wounded in a Russian rocket attack on the Chechnyan capital of Grozny. Russian President, Vladimir Putin, at first denied that such an attack took place. Later the Russian government blamed the attack on Chechen rebels, charging that they had been dealing arms in the marketplace and that several explosions took place on account of a fight between the rebels. Survivors of the attack, however, disputed this account.

Bloody skirmishes between Islamic rebels and Russian troops led to a massive intervention of the Russian army in Chechnya. By the end of September 1999, Russian forces had marched into the Republic in the north Caucasian region for the second time since 1994. By their own account, the soldiers wanted to fight against Muslim rebels, who had entered in neighboring Dagestan at the beginning of August, in order to merge Chechnya and Dagestan into one theocracy. The multi-ethnic republic in the east Caucasian region, where around 70 different ethnic groups and 1.7 million people live, had been regarded as unstable for years.

Russian fighter planes began to attack targets in Chechnya as early as September 23. Russia explained the offensive as a desire to create a "safety zone" in order to isolate the rebels in the Caucasus. In addition to this, it was suspected that the Russian government wanted to unseat the elected President, Aslan Mashadov, and establish a leadership loyal to Moscow in the Caucasian republic.

In order to swell the number of his troops, Mashadov had made an alliance with the military commander, Shamil Bassayev, who was held to be the mastermind behind numerous terrorist attacks.

The Russian army controlled one-third of the country in the north after the Chechens withdrew from their last position on the left bank of the Terek river on October 19. Russia made use of artillery with a wide range and fighter planes. Around 220,000 persons fled by mid-November from the war zone, in which repeated artillery and bomber attacks took place on individual cities and villages. Even refugee convoys were not spared.

Numerous Western countries appealed to the Russian government to end the war in the Caucasus. Moscow however refused all foreign attempts at brokering a ceasefire. Even the support of the Organization for Security and Cooperation in Europe (OSCE) was refused by the Russian government. ❑

Mourning women: Russian air attacks devestated the civilian population.

THE WORLD GREETS THE NEW MILLENNIUM

The World, January 1, 2000

Full of revelry and of expectations, people the whole world over celebrated the beginning of the new millennium. All around the globe gigantic celebrations were held with splendidly colorful fireworks and a rollicking atmosphere. The fact that the new millennium would technically begin with the year 2001 did not worry anyone.

The first to celebrate the beginning of the third millennium were the inhabitants of Tonga and Kiribati in the South Pacific. The archipelago of Kiribati had had the date line shifted for the occasion and christened their most remote atoll "Millennium Island." Thirteen hours after the island dwellers, who celebrated the crossover into the year 2000 with traditional dances, Europe greeted the new millennium. Later, revelers in New York's Times Square witnessed the dropping of a 1,070-pound New Year's ball, six feet in diameter. The last place to make the start into 2000 was Samoa.

Shortly before midnight around the globe, however, tension mingled with the excitement: Numerous experts feared that some computers might turn back to 1900 instead of forward to 2000 and thus crash. Banks, hospitals, airlines, power suppliers, and telephone firms took commensurate preventive measures months in advance. But the much-ballyhooed computer chaos failed to happen, and the change in date took place without any great problems. Complications at nuclear power plants, which were most feared, also did not occur; seven atomic plants in the USA reported only insignificant problems while Japan reported that four plants had disturbances for only a short time. ❑

New Millennium party in front of Berlin's Brandenburg Gate

SUBMARINE DRAMA: SINKING OF THE *KURSK*

Barents Sea, August 12, 2000

At 11:30 Moscow time (9:30 GMT) Norwegian seismologists in the Barents Sea registered two explosions. On the same evening the commanders of the Russian marine division made an internal announcement that an atomic submarine had been in a collision. On August 14 the public was informed that there had been "trouble" on board the *Kursk*. The submarine had left with a naval unit on August 10, headed towards the North Sea. After a Russian rescue mission failed to release the crew, trapped at a depth of 354 feet (108 meters), Russia accepted international aid, which at first had been rejected. Nine days after the disaster Norwegian and British diving specialists found the flooded wreck on the floor of the Barents Sea. None of the 118 crew members survived the incident. ❑

The Russian atomic submarine *Kursk*

SERBIAN REGIME

Belgrade, October 5, 2000

A popular uprising in Yugoslavia forced the erstwhile President, Slobodan Milosevic, to hand over power to Vojislav Kostunica when hundreds of thousands supporters of the opposition alliance, DOS (Democratic Opposition of Serbia) demonstrated on the streets of Belgrade for the recognition of Kostunica's victory in the presidential elections on September 24. Finally the demonstrators stormed the parliament building and forced President Milosevic to admit defeat in the elections and to hand over power to Kostunica.

Two days after the September elections the official election commission reported that Kostunica had won 48.22 percent of the votes and Milosevic 40.23 percent. It announced that a run-off had to take place on October 8. The opposition denounced this as an election fraud and called for

NIGHTMARE AT KAPRUN

Austria, November 11, 2000

One hundred fifty-five persons lost their lives in Europe's most fatal cable car accident in the winter sports resort of Kaprun. The cable car caught fire after entering a two-mile (3.2 km) long tunnel, on account of a defective heater that melted the plastic casing of hydraulic fuel lines. The liquid fed the fire while causing the car to stop and the doors to stick closed. One hundred fifty-two skiers in the car, which was filled to near-capacity, perished. Some finally managed to escape the car and flee up the track only to be asphyxiated by the poisonous fumes and burnt by the flames, which were intensified by the tunnel's acting like a chimney. Three more lost their lives at the upper end of the tunnel, and the two persons in the descending car were killed by smoke inhalation. In all, only twelve persons managed to escape the flaming inferno

and reach safety. They descended through the tunnel behind the fire and below the smoke.

The 2.3 mile (3.8 km) long cableway, which began operating in March 1974, had functioned until then without mishap. A fire in the funicular, the cars of which

were made of non-inflammable material, was considered next to impossible. Therefore, sprinkler units in the tunnel, which had a diameter of twelve feet (3.6 m), were dispensed with, as were escape ways and manually operable gates. ❑

Rescue workers examine the gutted cable car at Kaprun

CRASH OF THE

Paris, July 25, 2000

Shortly after taking off from the Charles de Gaulle airport in Paris, an Air France Concorde crashed in a near-by field. All 109 aboard lost their lives; four more persons on the ground died on account of the debris that rained down from the skies.

It is believed a chain of technical glitches caused the tragic crash of the supersonic aircraft. Minutes before the Concorde attempted take-off, a Continental Airlines DC-10 had lost a 16-inch long segment on the runway of the Paris airport. Safety officials later speculated that during take-off a tire of the Concorde hit the metal piece and burst. The shreds of the torn tire ripped open a tank on the supersonic plane and the streaming fuel caught fire. When the airport tower informed the crew of the flames, they believed the fire to be in the engine. Given the tremendous speed of the

LOSES POWER

Vojislav Kostunica is the new President of Yugoslavia.

a general strike on October 2. The Constitutional Court then declared sections of the elections as invalid and demanded a new election. The DOS rejected this and called upon Milosevic to accept defeat.

Milosevic conceded power on October 6 in the face of the demonstrations. After the collapse of the regime, Russia, Yugoslavia's most significant ally, recognized Kostunica as the new President. Kostunica was sworn in on October 7. The moderate nationalist was the only politician in the opposition who had never allied himself with Milosevic. The change in Yugoslav leadership caused the European Union to lift its most severe sanctions against the country and grant the new President aid amounting to 200 million euros. Milosevic was later put on trial at the International Court at The Hague on charges of genocide and crimes against humanity for his role in the wars in Balkans following the break up of Yugoslavia. ❑

CONCORDE

aircraft, abandoning the take-off was not possible.

The pilot turned off the jet engine; shortly after this yet another engine went dead. The crew could not draw in the landing gear and, as a consequence, could not gain height. On attempting an emergency landing at the nearby Le Bourget airport, the Concorde crashed in a field close to a hotel, only a minute after it had left the ground.

Flight 4590 was bound for New York. It was the first and only crash of a Concorde, which began commercial flights in 1976. The Concorde cruised at approximately 1,350 miles per hour, cutting transatlantic travel time by nearly half, and could reach altitudes of up to 60,000 feet, or eleven miles.

The remaining Concorde fleet was grounded for a year following the accident. In 2003, Air France and British Airways ceased all Concorde flights. ❑

The Concorde's design was instantly recognizable.

GEORGE W. BUSH WINS DISPUTED ELECTION

Washington, D.C., November 7, 2000

The presidential elections in the United States ended with the closest election results since 1960. After the polls closed on election night, Al Gore, the candidate of the Democratic Party conceded defeat to his rival, the Republican George W. Bush. But then Gore retracted his concession. It was only after more than five weeks of an increasingly bitter tug-of-war carried out in various courts of law that it became clear that Bush would be sworn in on January 20, 2001 as the forty-third President of the United States.

television appearance in which he conceded defeat rather than subject the nation to continuing uncertainty. Although Gore had a lead of more than 500,000 in the "popular vote," the sum of all the votes cast throughout the country, in the decisive electoral count, Bush was the winner after the decision concerning Florida. Bush won 271 electoral votes to Gore's 267.

In the formation of his cabinet, Bush looked for experienced hands in the realms of foreign and security policy. He nomi-

Bitter electoral struggle for the office of the US President: First TV election debate between Vice-President, Al Gore (left) and the Governor of Texas, George W. Bush

The entire election came down to the state of Florida. Since Bush's lead there was only 0.5 percent, a recount was required. Finally it was not the will of the totality of voters but the highest court of the United States that decided the outcome of the election: The nine judges of the Supreme Court established on December 12, over one month after the election, that hand counting disputed ballots ordered by the highest court of the state of Florida was unconstitutional and could not be carried out in time. With this decision, Al Gore made a

nated Colin Powell as Secretary of State. Powell, born in 1937 in New York, the son of an immigrant from Jamaica, had a brilliant military career behind him; he was, among other things, the first black officer to be the National Security Advisor in 1987, and in 1989, as a four-star general, was appointed Chairman of the Joint Chiefs of Staff. Condoleezza Rice, another African American, was appointed by the new president to be the first female National Security Advisor. Both had already served under Bush's father, who was President from 1989 to 1993. ❑

WORLD TRADE CENTER BOMBING

New York City, Washington DC, Shankesville, Pennsylvania, September 11, 2001

The most devastating attacks in the history of international terrorism took place in the United States on September 11, 2001. In New York, Washington DC, and Shanksville, Pennsylvania over 3,000 people lost their lives. The attacks involved the hijacking of four passenger jets that had made morning departures from Boston's Logan Airport, Washington's Dulles Airport and Newark Airport in New Jersey.

In New York, at 8:45 AM, American Airlines flight 11, carrying 88 passengers and crew members crashed into north tower of the World Trade Center. At 9:02 AM United Airlines flight 175, carrying 59 passengers and crew crashed into the Trade Center's south tower. At 9:59 AM, the 110 story south tower imploded, as subsequently did the north tower at 10:28 AM. The collapsing towers destroyed five further buildings of the World Trade Center as well as four subway stations. The horrific devastation resulted in over 2650 deaths including some 350 firefighters, who had come to the aid of the estimated approximately 25,000 persons in the twin towers.

At 9:43 AM, American Airlines flight 77 crashed in to the Pentagon killing all 59 people aboard as well as 125 on the ground. The fourth hijacked airplane, United Airlines flight 93, went down in a field near Shanksville, Pennsylvania, killing all 40 passengers and crew. In the Pennsylvania tragedy, passengers, who had been informed over mobile phones about the attacks in New York and Washington, mounted a valiant resistance to the hijackers. Their heroic actions prevented the plane from being steered toward the presidential estate in Camp David, the White House or any other terrorist target.

The perpetrators of these heinous acts were members of the terrorist organization known as Al Qaeda, an Islamic fundamentalist group led by the Saudi Arabian, Osama bin Laden. Nineteen Al Qaeda operatives managed to slip through airport security at all three airports armed with box cutters and knives. Many were Saudi nationals who had been in the United States on student visas studying at flight training schools. Their leader was an Egyptian named Mohammed Atta. All nineteen terrorists died. It is believed that Al Qaeda had

First responders before the shattered remains of one of the Twin Towers

THE INVASION OF AFGHANISTAN

Kabul and the Hindu Kush, October 7, 2001

After the attacks on September 11, President George Bush quickly rallied world support for the creation of a military coalition whose aim was to attack Osama bin Laden and Al Qaeda's command center in the Hindu Kush mountains along the Afghani-Pakistan border. This invasion would also be aimed at removing from power bin Laden's protectors and allies, the Taliban.

Presenting the raison d'être for what would become known as the War On Terror, Bush declared: "We are fighting a war against terrorism in general…Success or the lack of it is dependent on wiping out of terrorism everywhere in the world, wherever it may exist." On October 2, NATO members responded to Bush's request for aid. Great Britain was the first to offer active military support, followed shortly by Germany. France announced that they had troops ready in Africa. Spain agreed to provide logistical support. In addition to this, Russia and China assured their assistance in the fight against worldwide terrorism.

Code-named "Enduring Freedom", the invasion began on October 7, 2001, with air attacks on Al Qaeda bases in the Hindu Kush. Targeting Al Qaeda strongholds that had been earlier reconnoitered by US special forces,10,000 US soldiers, along with platoons of British troops, scoured the rugged mountains. Aiding them were members of Afghanistan's Northern Alliance—local military cadres that had long opposed the Taliban, whose troops knew

F-14 fighter jet taking off from deck of aircraft carrier en route to Afghanistan

their way around the difficult terrain of the Hindu Kush.

Although their attacks inflicted major damage to Al Qaeda's network, the coalition forces did not capture bin Laden. On November 13, the troops of the Northern Alliance and coalition forces drove the Taliban out of Kabul.

The slow process of rebuilding Afghanistan's infrastructure and the drive towards democracy then began with Hamid Karzai as the head of the interim government. Karzai was elected the President of Afghanistan in 2004 but continues to be faced with a resurgence of Taliban fighters. ❏

INTERNATIONAL ALLIANCE AGAINST TERROR

Point of Interest

Osama bin Laden

In the wake of the attack on the World Trade Center, the US government was able to organize an international anti-terrorist alliance. President Bush promised to capture its mastermind, Osama bin Laden, and take the fight to Al Qaeda and its ally, the Taliban government of Afghanistan. Joining with the United States were Great Britain, which pledged its full support, France, which mobilized its forces in Africa, and Spain which offered logistic support. Germany provided troops for the invasion. Russia also offered its support, promising its partnership in anti-terrorist actions, and China, as well, assured the United States of its backing. The initial mission to Afghanistan was successful with the Taliban being unseated from power. But the United States lost much of the international good will that it had garnered with its invasion of Iraq. Osama bin Laden remains at large as of the time of this writing. ❑

An amateur photographer captured plane about to hit the second of the Twin Towers.

been behind a previous attack on the World Trade Center on February 26, 1993. At that time, the Iraqi terrorist, Ramzi Ahmed Yusuf, had driven a vehicle loaded with explosives into the basement garage, where it exploded. Six people died in that incident. ❑

KOFI ANNAN WINS THE NOBEL PEACE PRIZE

Oslo, Norway, December 10, 2001

On December 10, 2001, Secretary-General of the United Nations, Kofi Annan and the United Nations were co-recipients of the Nobel Peace Prize. Annan and the United Nations were the Peace Prize Committee's one hundredth awardees. The 63-year-old Annan, who began his tenure as Secretary-General in 1997, was cited for having "infused new life" into the United Nations. Both recipients were credited with having created a "better organized and more peaceful world." The Nobel Committee emphasized that the United Nations was the only world body that could generate international cooperation and maintain global peace.

The committee praised the Ghanaian for his efforts in keeping the UN vital both politically and financially. At the time the award was given, the United Nations had come perilously close to insolvency.

Some of the financial problems were due to the United States' reluctance to continue funding an organization that was perceived as opposed to US global policies. During his term

Kofi Annan receiving the Nobel Peace Prize.

of office, Annan had the difficult task of placating the host country's often vigorously articulated concerns while managing to accord proper respect to those of other member nations. Annan remained Secretary General until January 2007. ❑

ARIEL SHARON ELECTED PRIME MINISTER OF ISRAEL

Israel, February 6, 2001

On February 6, 2001, Ariel Sharon, chairman of the conservative Likud Party, was elected Prime Minister of Israel, defeating Ehud Barak, the labor party's sitting Prime Minister. With 62.5 percent of the votes, Sharon's decisive victory was seen as the electorate's expression of dissatisfaction with the deteriorating relationship between Israel and the Palestinians.

Fresh elections had become necessary when Barak announced on December 9, 2000 that he was stepping down, in response to increasing criticism of his policies, which aimed at renewing the provisions of the 1993 Oslo Accords. Many Israelis had long been uncomfortable with this Israeli-Palestinian peace treaty between PLO Chairman Yasser Arafat and the Israeli government under Yitzhak Rabin.

Barak had been seen as too conciliatory towards increasingly aggressive Palestinian factions. In contrast to Barak, the hawkish, ex-general Sharon was seen to be a hardliner whose get-tough policies would once and for all end the threats to Israel posed by radical elements in Palestinian culture.

Indeed, as Likud opposition leader, Sharon's highly publicized visit to the Temple Mount in September of 2000 was seen by some as a provocative act aimed not only at Palestinans but also at Barak's seemingly ineffectual Labor government. After his visit to this compound, which is of holy significance to both Jews and Muslims, Palestinians rioted. These riots, which were the beginning of what would become known as the Second *Intifada*, so alarmed the Israeli populace, that many became convinced that not only should the Oslo Accord provisions be scrapped but that the dovish policies of Barak's Labor Party need to be replaced with those of a hardline, right-wing

Ariel Sharon and Likud party members after their election victory

government. War hero Ariel Sharon had become the man of the hour. ❑

G-8 Summit Elicits Protests

Genoa, Italy, July 18-22, 2001

The twenty-seventh G-8 Summit was held in Genoa, Italy from July 18, 2001 to July 22. While politicians of the most powerful industrial nations met, demonstrators protested outside against the misery that they believed was being caused by globalization of markets.

In preparation for the summit, police had cordoned off most of the area around the meeting's venue. Despite the presence of up to 15,000 security personnel, militant demonstrators were undaunted and engaged in three days of running street battles. More than 500 people were injured. One demonstrator was shot dead by the security forces.

The summit members reacted to the protests by stressing what they felt were the beneficial effects of market globalization. In their closing joint communiqué representatives of the G-8 touted their commitment to humanitarian aid for poor and developing nations, including a 1.3 billion dollar fund to be used to fight global diseases. They also declared their willingness to confront the social and environmental challenges occasioned by climate change. To this end, they pledged to work towards the reduction of greenhouse gases over the long term.

The G-8 emphasized the need to make commodity markets of industrialized nations open to those of poor and developing

World leaders at G-8 Summit. Left to right: Junichiro Koizumi, Tony Blair, George W. Bush, Jacques Chirac, Silvio Berlusconi, Vladimir Putin, Jean Chrétien, Gerhard Schröder, Guy Verhofstdt (EU), Romano Prodi (EU)

countries, focusing especially on helping poorer trading partners to increase their exportable, indigenously created commodities. This was to apply to agrarian as well manufactured products. Related to this effort was the need to help stabilize those nations' economies through the reduction or retirement of debts.

Their human rights platform vowed to wage an internationally coordinated war on corruption, internet crime, child pornography, and human trafficking.

The modern prototype for the G-8 summits took place at

Rambouillet Palace near Paris in November of 1975. Initiated by German Chancellor Helmut Schmidt and French President Valéry Giscard d'Estaing, the leaders of six industrial nations— Germany, France, Great Britain, Italy, Japan and the United States—came together for the very first world economic summit. The group has met every year since that that first summit.

In 1977, Canada began participating in the summits and in 1997, Russia became the eighth member. The European Union participates as a silent member,

sending its representative, the Council President, to each year's meeting. The standard agenda of the participants is to align their nations economic policies and discuss matters of global interest. Paramount among these of recent years have been the issues of international terrorism, drug trafficking, and energy resources. In addition to the summit meeting, there are regular meetings of these nation's finance and foreign ministers as well as heads of governmental departments. ❑

The *Mir* Space Station

South Pacific, March 23, 2001

On March 23, 2001, after circling the earth for 15 years, the Russian space station *Mir*, was methodically de-orbited over the South Pacific. Upon reentry into the Earth's atmosphere the bulk of its 130 ton, 62 foot frame burned up, the residual debris falling harmlessly into the ocean in the vicinity of Fiji.

Mir, which means both "world" and "peace" in Russian, was the first space station designed and successfully used for long-term human habitation. Launched on February 19, 1986, it eventually consisted of seven linked docking modules. Except for brief periods, it was manned continuously from 1987 to 1999.

Of its 5,519 days in orbit the space station was occupied 4,592 days. The changing cast of visiting crew members came from ten different nations in addition to Russia.

Mir orbited at approximately 250 miles above Earth, completing 16 orbits per day at 90 minutes per orbit. Over its 15-year

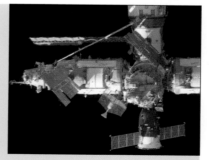

Mir space station

career, it covered 1,964,616,800 nautical miles. ❑

ONE CURRENCY FOR 360 MILLION EUROPEANS

Europe, January 1, 2002

The standardization of European currency, which began in 1999, came to fruition with the circulation of euro bills and coins.

The euro became valid in countries of the European Union that had elected to adopt a single currency. These were Belgium, Germany, Finland, France, Greece, Ireland, Italy, Luxemburg, the Netherlands, Austria, Portugal, and Spain. The euro was also circulated in Martinique, and Saint Pierre and Miquelon, San Marino, Andorra, the Vatican, and Monaco. Three EU countries, Denmark, Sweden, and Great Britain, were not signatories of the 1991 treaty on economic integration and a single European currency.

The new currency was first distributed among the population of 700,000 on Réunion Island to the southeast of Africa. Due to the time zone, the French Foreign Office distributed the euro there three hours before its release in other countries. Greeks and Finns followed at 10:00 PM (GMT). Almost everywhere the biggest currency conversion in history was carried out smoothly.

After only a few days transactions were predominantly in euros, despite long lines at banks, because proprietors were willing to exchange the old currency. On August 30, 2001 Wim Duisenberg, President of the European Central Bank, officially presented the first euro bills. "Starter kits" with the new coins could be gotten at banks so that people could

On New Years Day the inauguration of the euro is displayed in front of the European Central Bank

familiarize themselves with the new currency. The euro-packages proved so successful that some banks ran out after only a day. ❑

SLOBODAN MILOSEVIC TRIED FOR WAR CRIMES

The Hague, February 12, 2002

In October of 2001 the Yugoslavian ex-President, Slobodan Milosevic, became the first former head of state to be indicted by a world tribunal for war crimes. Charged with genocide for atrocities committed during the Bosnian-Croatian-Serbian War (1992-1995) his trial by the United Nation's War Crimes Tribunal began on February 12, 2002 in the Netherlands, at The Hague.

Milosevic refused to name an attorney until the last minute. In addition, he refused to recognize the court's authority to try him. The initial indictment pertained only to crimes committed in Kosovo: Milosevíc was accused of being responsible for the murder of at least 900 people in the war-torn region as well as forced displacement of 800,000 Kosovo Albanians between January 1, 1999, and the Serbian retreat from the province on June 20, 1999.

By February 1, the tribunal judges expanded the indictments to include crimes of genocide perpetrated during all the conflicts in Croatia, Bosnian-Herzegovina and Kosovo. The Swiss chief prosecutor, Carla Del Ponte emphasized that it was "neither a state nor an organization in court" but the accused who was to be held accountable "for his own deeds and for his share in the crimes, for which he stands accused."

Combative to the end, Milosevic escaped the tribunal's final judgment: before the hearings ended, he died of a heart attack in his prison cell on March 11, 2006. ❑

THE QUEEN MOTHER DIES

Windsor Castle, England, March 30, 2002

The Queen Mother died peacefully at the age of 101 at her home in Windsor Castle. Unmistakable with her pastel colored outfits and her warm smile, she was a symbol of British courage and civility. She was known affectionately as the "Queen Mum."

Born Elizabeth Angela Marguerite Bowes-Lyon, she became queen when her brother-in-law Edward VIII renounced the throne to marry, and her husband was crowned George VI. She supported her husband during the difficult times of World War II, and she remained at home in Buckingham Palace during the Blitz. This was seen as a great act of courage and secured her the enduring affection of the British people. Hundreds of thousands of mourners across England paid tribute to their one-time queen. A state funeral was

England's "Queen Mum"

given in remembrance of her. ❑

EUROPEAN CONSUMERS CRITICIZE PRICE INCREASES

Point Of Interest

After the initial excitement over the euro died down, the clamor over large price increases could be heard. In Germany, for example, the word for expensive, "*teuer*" was combined with "euro" to coin the term "*teuro*", which made the rounds. The accusation by consumers was that prices had already been raised in the summer of 2001 so that at the start of the euro prices, would appear to decrease. According to the results of a survey, Europeans surmised that early on there had been a distinct price increase for foodstuffs, and that the price of fruit and vegetables had increased by approximately 85 percent. Nearly three fourths of respondents believed that this was also the case for baking goods, meat, and cheese. ❑

"Operation Protective Barrier"

Bethlehem, April 1, 2002

16 people are killed by a suicide bomber in Haifa on March 31, 2002

In April of 2002, after Israel was subjected to a series of attacks by Palestinians, the Israeli army invaded a number of Palestinian cities.

On April 1, Israeli tanks entered Kalkilia, Tulkarem and Bethlehem. In the evening, they surrounded the Church of the Nativity of Christ in Bethlehem, in which over 100 armed Palestinians had barricaded themselves.

On April 2, Israeli troops also advanced into the refugee camp of Jenin. The occupied places were part of Palestine's autonomous zone. The advance occurred within the framework of the "Operation Protective Barrier," the largest military offensive in the West Bank since 1967. In a first step, Israeli military forces encircled the headquarters of the Palestinian President, Yasser Arafat, in Ramallah.

In the refugee camp of Jenin, the supposed breeding ground of many suicide bombers, heavy fighting broke out between the Israelis and the armed Palestinians. Parts of the camp were devastated and 4,000 Palestinians were arrested. The siege lasted until April 19.

The siege of the Church of the Nativity was abandoned on May 10. Thirteen Palestinians, who had barricaded themselves in the basilica, were eventually flown out in a British plane to Cyprus. A further 26 were brought to Gaza, and the remaining 84 Palestinians escaped.

The offensive into the West Bank took place after a series of suicide bombings in Israel, a tactic that had not been used in such high numbers since the founding of the state in the year 1948.

In March, over 100 Israelis died of the consequences of the attacks, for which Palestinian organizations claimed responsibility. As a justification for the acts of terror, Hamas and other groups cited Israeli actions in the Palestinian zones. ❑

Europe Hit with Devastating Floods

Central Europe, August 2002

In August of 2002 unusually heavy rainfall caused uncontrolled flooding throughout Central Europe. On August 17, the River Elbe at Dresden reached its highest peak ever recorded, spilling over its banks. Most of the old city was inundated, including world famous buildings such as the Semper Opera House and the Frauenkirche (Church of Our Lady.)

Throughout July heavy storms lashed Central Europe but the heavy rainfall in August and the ensuing massive floods along the Elbe, Danube, Moldau, and Mulde rivers created historically unprecedented destruction. The first wave of storms occurred in Bohemia and Austria on August 6 and 7. In the Czech Republic and Austria numerous villages were cut off from the outside world and thousands of people had to be evacuated. On August 12, the situation in Saxony reached a point of crisis when mountain streams and several dams overflowed. In Switzerland, the city of Bern suffered severe flooding as did a number of Alpine villages. In Germany, areas in the Erz Mountains were particularly hard hit. Along the Mulde River, the entire old city of Grimma was submerged on August 13.

While the situation along the Danube improved slowly, Dresden was inundated on August 15 by a second massive wave of floods. At the same time, sections of the chemical works "Spolana" near Aussig (Czech Republic) were under water. On August 18, around 19,000 soldiers of the Federal Army were called into service.

Dresden under water: the Zwinger Palace, the Semper Opera and Dresden Theater inundated.

The water damaged or destroyed at least 180 bridges, 500 miles of roads, 94 railway bridges and 250 miles of railroad tracks on the Elbe, Danube and their tributaries. At least 42 people died during the storms. The grim consequences of the floods occasioned an outpouring of humanitarian aid. In all, donations amounting to 500 million euros were received by the international contingent of Red Cross agencies as well as other local relief organizations. ❑

The Nebra Sky Disk

Saxony-Anhalt, Germany, September 25, 2002

Between 1997 and 1998, in Germany's Saxony-Anhalt region, archaeological "poachers" discovered and illegally absconded with the "Nebra Sky Disk," a 3,600-year-old bronze disk, depicting the Pleiades constellation.

Believed to be created by the Bronze Age Unetice culture, the artifact weighs around 4.5 pounds and has a diameter of 12 inches. With a blue-green patina and gold inlay, the disk is inscribed with various heavenly bodies in addition to the constellation.

Perhaps used as functional astronomical chart, it suggests that European Bronze Age cultures had a relatively sophisticated understanding of the heavens.

Retrieved by authorities from its unlawful owners at a hotel in Basel, Switzerland on February 23, 2002, it was presented at a press conference by the state archaeologist Dr. Harald Meller on September 25, 2002. It now resides in the Museum for Prehistory in Halle, Germany. ❑

CHECHEN REBELS SEIZE MOSCOW THEATER

Moscow, October 23, 2002

On the evening of October 23, 2002 Chechen rebels occupied a theater in Moscow, in which the hit musical *North-East* was playing, and seized over 800 hostages. The heavily armed rebels, among whom were several women, declared that they would release the hostages, who included spectators, cast and crew members, only upon the withdrawal of Russian troops from Chechnya. The rebels threatened to kill themselves and the hostages if their demands were not met. After a tense 58 hour standoff, the drama ended in tragedy with many of the hostages dying, not at the hands of the rebels, but from the siege tactics used by the military unit who had come to free them.

On October 26, at 6:20 AM, Russian soldiers of the Alpha unit began pumping an aerosol anesthetic into the theater's ventilation shafts in order to incapacitate the rebels. At 6:30 AM they stormed the theater. By 7:18 AM, the Alpha team had subdued the rebels and ended the siege.

The rescuers' victory was tragically pyrrhic: although all 41 rebels, including their leader Movsar Barayev, were killed 128 hostages also died, most of them from inhaling the anesthetic gas used by the security forces. It is believed that the concentration of the gas was too high and as such, was fatal to many of the hostages, weakened by two-and-a-half days without food.

Because authorities refused to disclose details about the chemical components of the gas, attending physicians were unable to prescribe timely and medically effective intervention for the sickened hostages. It was not until days after, and international outcry, that it was made known that the gas used was a fentanyl derivive. Had doctors known this, they might have been able to save many more lives.

Fentanyl is a synthetic opiate that is used medically as an anesthetic. Developed in France in 1963, high dosages can cause catastrophic respiratory depression. Its use in the theater siege sparked ongoing debates as to its status as a chemical or bioweapon. If it was considered as such, its use by Russian security forces would have been a breach of international provisions set out by the Chemical Weapons Convention prohibiting the use chemical weaponry under any circumstances.

In reaction to this debate, the Russian parliament passed stringent measures banning the press from publishing criticism of the actions of Russian security forces. ❏

Military and emergency personnel waiting outside theater in Moscow during hostage crisis.

THE CHECHEN CONFLICT

Point of Interest

After the hostage drama in a Moscow Theater in 2002, the Russian army launched new military operations against rebels in Chechnya.

Ever since the dissolution of the USSR in 1991, Chechnya had been a problem for the Russian government. In November of 1991, the republic split and a faction calling itself the Chechen Republic of Ichkeria declared independence from Russia. Russian President, Boris Yeltsin, waited until December 11, 1994, at which time he sent 40,000 troops to Chechnya, beginning the First Chechen War. The war ended in a stalemate on August 31, 1996.

The uneasy detente which followed ended in October of 1999 when Prime Minister Vladimir Putin launched a fresh offensive, beginning the Second Chechen War. This invasion was a reaction to the infiltration of Chechen fighters into Dagestan and a series of bomb attacks on residential blocks in Moscow and other Russian cities. The military action led to the storming of Grozny on February 6, 2000.

After the Second Chechen War, Russia was able to install a pro-Moscow leadership in Chechnya, but as the attack in Moscow showed, the rebel factions still remained a potent threat. ❏

THE *PRESTIGE* OIL SPILL

La Coruna, Spain, November 19, 2002

On November 19, 2002 the Greek-operated, Liberian registered oil supertanker *Prestige* broke up off the coast of La Coruna, Spain on the Galician coast, spilling approximately 65,000 tons of oil. One of the largest environmental disasters in Spanish history, the oil spill polluted several hundred miles of beaches on the northwest coast of Spain, reaching as far as the French Atlantic coast. The region's fishing industries were devastated.

The 800-foot tanker was on a course from Riga, Latvia to Gibraltar, when it ran into trouble on November 13, off Cape Finisterre during a storm. It sank after foundering for six days. In contrast to many tankers, the *Prestige* did not have a reinforced hull with a double-walled exterior.

The Spanish and Galician governments mounted a massive clean-up campaign, which, within a year, had achieved remarkable results. Many of the region's beaches were more pristine than they were before the spill. ❏

The tanker *Prestige* sinking

"Operation Iraqi Freedom"

Baghdad, Iraq, March 20, 2003

On March 20, 2003, a multinational force, led by the United States, invaded Iraq, beginning what was dubbed "Operation Iraqi Freedom." The invasion was launched to remove the regime of Saddam Hussein from power and to facilitate the building of an Iraqi democracy. Assisting in the invasion were troops from Great Britain, Australia, Denmark and Poland. The incursion's *casus belli* was the Bush administration's belief that Hussein possessed stockpiles of bio-weapons that he was clandestinely organizing into

Donald Rumsfeld, US Secretary of Defense, and architect of the military campaign against Iraq.

an arsenal of WMDs (weapons of mass destruction) to be used against Israel and other nations in the Middle East. It was also believed that Hussein was sponsoring international terrorism and was providing financial and logistical support to Al Qaeda.

The war began with heavy air attacks on the Iraqi capital. This first phase of the invasion was code-named "Shock and Awe." It sought to deliver a "decapitating stroke" against the regime of the dictator, wiping out the Iraqi leadership at the very beginning. To accomplish this, the US Air Force, which conducted the bombings, was supported by nearly 250,000 US soldiers, along with 45,000 from Great Britain.

In an address to the American people, President George W. Bush, justified the invasion, asserting that the Saddam Hussein's development of a bio-weaponry arsenal was a threat to the stability of all the oil-producing nations in the Middle East, as well as to America's only true ally in the region, Israel. He also linked Hussein's regime to Al Qa-

Statue of Saddam Hussein pulled down. The dictator was removed, but peace has yet to come.

eda, thereby making the case that the Iraqi dictator was a direct threat to the security of the United States. That neither of these charges was ever substantiated led to harsh critiques of US policy.

The international diplomatic community was split in its reaction to the war. On March 16, President Bush, British Prime Minister, Tony Blair, and Spain's Prime Minister, José Maria Aznar, addressed the UN Security Council, encouraging them to back a resolution condemning Hussein and supporting their belief that Saddam Hussein's Iraq was a terrorist-friendly rogue state that had become a threat to not only regional, but also world peace. This they said was justification for an invasion of Iraq to remove the Hussein regime from power. The Security Council however did not vote on the resolution, primarily because France and Russia opposed the measure and threatened to use their veto power if any such resolution were passed.

Despite the Security Council's inaction, a total of nine European countries supported the United States' position: Great Britain, Spain, Poland, Denmark, Italy, Portugal, Bulgaria, Hungary and the Czech Republic. France, Russia and Germany opposed a military attack and jointly proposed that Iraq indeed be disarmed but by peaceful means.

On April 4, the Battle for Baghdad began. The allied armed forces, which were vastly superior to Hussein's troops, reported remarkably swift progress. On April 9, US armed forces had secured much of the Iraqi capital. By May 1, President Bush was able to declare that the mission in Iraq had been accomplished. This would prove to be a premature assessment. As of January of 2008, the war in Iraq continues. ❏

The Assassination of Zoran Djindjic of Serbia

Belgrade, Serbia, March 12, 2003

On March 12, 2003, Serbian Prime Minister, Zoran Djindjic, was assassinated as he approached his government chambers in Belgrade. The death of the 50-year-old democratic reformer occasioned fears for the survival of the Serbian democratic movement.

In 1990, Djindjic was one of the co-founders of the Democratic Party in Serbia, serving as its chairman beginning in 1994. In 1996, with Vuk Draskovic and Vesna Pesic, he created the op-

Mourning the death of Zoran Djindjic

position alliance known as *Zajedno* (Together.) This alliance fell apart within a year. In 1997 Djindjic was elected as the first non-communist Mayor of Belgrade since 1945. In 2001 he became Serbia's Prime Minister.

Despite his political successes, his role as a moderate, democratic reformer made him anathema to a number of powerful political factions in Serbia. Serbia's former communists despised his capitalist orientation. Right wing nationalists saw his moderate and internationally accommodating policies as too liberal. They were particularly angered by his extradition of Slobodan Milosevic to face the War Crimes Tribunal in The Hague. He was also a target for Serbia's fearsome organized crime syndicates.

Djindjic's assassin, Zvezdan Jovanic, was a member of the JSO, an elite police unit also known as the "Red Berets." Dismantled after the Prime Minister's assassination, the JSO was known to have been admirers of Slobodan Milosevic's brand of ultra-nationalism. ❏

IRAQ DEFEATED IN THREE WEEKS

Point of Interest

March 17: US President gives the Iraqi Head of State, Saddam Hussein, and his sons a deadline of 48 hours to leave the country. Should this not happen, this would "bring with it a military confrontation, which will begin at a point of time decided by us."

March 18: The Iraqi leadership rejects the ultimatum of the USA.

March 19: Bush informs the US Congress that diplomatic efforts to diffuse the Iraq crisis are unsuccessful.

March 20: The war for Baghdad begins with heavy air attacks. The attempt to kill the Iraqi leadership fails.

March 21: Turkey, after months of negotiations, finally allows the US to use its air space for attacks.

March 22: The Third Infantry Division advances over 180 miles in just 36 hours through the Iraqi desert area, having faced almost no resistance.

March 23: The US troops face heavy resistance near Nassiriya.

March 26: 15 civilians die after cruise missiles hit a residential area of Baghdad.

March 27: 1,000 US paratroopers land in the North Iraqi Kurdish region; the Northern Front is set up.

April 4: US units control the Saddam Hussein Airport, 15 miles from central Baghdad.

April 6: British soldiers advance into the center of Basra.

On March 31 Iraq's capital, Baghdad, is rocked by heavy explosions.

April 9: US armed forces reach the center of Baghdad having faced almost no resistance.

April 14: US troops control Tikrit, the hometown of Saddam.

May 1: Bush declares the end of major combat operations in Iraq on board the aircraft carrier *Abraham Lincoln* anchored off San Diego. ❑

THE "TERMINATOR" WINS

Los Angeles July 10, 2003

In a surprising turn of events, Arnold Schwarzenegger, the Austrian actor and action hero, was elected the Governor of California. On November 17, he was sworn in as governor, succeeding the Democrat, Gray Davis, who did not serve out his second term. Schwarzenegger became the state's thirty-eighth governor.

Against the background of a weak economy, an energy crisis with frequent power outages, and an enormous budget deficit of 38.2 billion dollars, Davis's popularity plummeted. Capitalizing on this, the Republican, Daryl Issa, launched an initiative calling for the governor's recall. Over 1.3 million valid signatures in support of the measure were collected by July. Following this, the first recall of a governor in the US since 1921 was authorized. Though a Republican, Schwarzenegger was seen to be fairly liberal, which served him well in the predominantly Democratic state. However, in the electoral campaign he chose to present himself in the style of his films and spoke of whipping California back into shape once again.

Schwarzenegger began his career as a bodybuilder and won the "Mr. Universe" title in 1967. He emigrated to the US in 1968 and began an hugely successful acting career. His role as the "Termi-

Jubilation and celebrations over the electoral victory: Schwarzenegger with his wife, the former newscaster, Maria Shriver.

nator" (1984, 1991, 2003) made him a star the world over. ❑

EARTHQUAKE IN IRAN

Bam, December 26, 2003

A massive earthquake hit the ancient city of Bam in the Iranian province of Kerman approximately 600 miles southeast of Teheran. More than 25,000 persons lost their lives as a consequence of the disaster. Most of the inhabitants of Bam were rudely awakened from their sleep by the earthquake, which measured 6.3 on the Richter scale. Large numbers of buildings constructed out of clay bricks, suddenly collapsed, leaving many parts of Bam literally razed to the ground; for days afterwards heavy clouds of dust hang over the city.

The historic citadel of Bam, the oldest sections of which are about 2,000 years old, was also severely damaged. Electricity and the telephone network broke down and water and food supplies were dangerously low. The few roads still free of debris were crowded with ambulances and people desperately searching for relatives. Immediately after the catastrophe, international aid began to arrive; rescue teams from 44 countries provided support to local aid agencies. ❑

An Iranian woman stands near the ruins of her house in Bam.

THE GROWTH OF THE EUROPEAN UNION

Dublin, Ireland, May 1, 2004

On May 1, 2004, at ceremonies held in Dublin, Ireland, ten more countries joined the European Union. This was the largest single enlargement in the history of the EU. The new member countries were: Poland, Hungary, the Czech Republic, Estonia, Latvia, Lithuania, Slovakia, Slovenia, Malta and Cyprus. These additions brought the European Union's total membership to 25.

The Dublin ceremonies showcased what had become 1993, these prototype economic alliance organizations would become the European Union (EU).

The first enlargement took place in 1973 when Denmark, Ireland and the United Kingdom joined the original ECSC members that were already part of the European Community. In 1981 Greece became an EC member, followed by Portugal and Spain in 1986. In 1995, Austria, Finland and Sweden signed on to what had become

Celebrations in Riga after Latvia joins the EU

known as "European integration." This exponential growth of the European Union represented a major historical trend which began back in 1952 with the signing of the Treaty of Paris, creating the European Coal and Steel Community (ECSC). The founding members, Belgium, Luxembourg, France, Italy, West Germany and the Netherlands sought to expedite post-war economic recovery by pooling their resources.

This cooperative strategy was expanded in 1958 with the signing of the Treaty of Rome, establishing the organizational heir to the ECSC, the European Economic Community (EEC). This cooperative body would come to be known as the European Community (EC). In time, with the signing of the Maastricht Treaty in (after Maastricht) the European Union. With the May 2004 enlargement, the drive to create "One Europe" came dramatically closer to realization.

The Dublin ceremonies occasioned celebrations throughout Europe. The idea of a unified Europe was perhaps best expressed by the EU Expansion Commissioner, Günter Verheugen who marveled: "I have crossed so many borders today, that I do not know any longer, where I am. But that is not so important, because I am in Europe."

For others, the prospect of a monolithic European community was unsettling. The Czech President, Václav Klaus, stayed away from the festivities, fearing that his country would cease "to exist as an independent unified state" if the trend continued. ❏

THE ABU GHRAIB SCANDAL

Iraq, April 2004

In April of 2004, America's *CBS News* broadcast pictures and video taken in 2003 of US troops engaged in the torture of inmates at Iraq's Abu Ghraib prison. This irrefutable evidence of the military's abuse of war prisoners resulted in a major scandal that for many seriously damaged the United States' claim to moral authority in its War on Terror.

Appearing on not only American network stations but also on two stations based in the Middle East, *Al Arabiya* and *Al Hurra*, President George Bush condemned the "shameful occurrences" and declared that he was outraged by the allegations of torture. He went on to say that such behavior was not a normal reflection of the US military.

The US Army tabled an official report on July 22 concerning cases of mistreatment not only within Abu Ghraib but also in Iraq generally as well as in Afghanistan. The report had presented a total of 94 confirmed or suspected cases of mistreatment of prisoners,

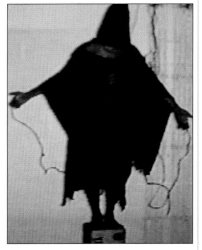

CBS News photo showing Iraqi prisoner of war being tortured

which took place between October 1, 2001 and June 9, 2004.

In the immediate aftermath, a number of members of the Abu Ghraib military staff were indicted on a range of charges stemming from the photographic and videotaped evidence. During these initial stages of the investigation, no Army higher-ups were implicated. ❏

VIKTOR YUSHCHENKO'S ORANGE REVOLUTION

Kiev, Ukraine, December 26, 2004

In the Ukraine's first free elections, a new era of democratic reform was begun when Viktor Yushchenko was elected as its new President on December 26, 2004. Despite vote tampering by the opposition and even the attempt to poison him with the chemical dioxin, Yushchenko managed to win 52 percent of the vote, defeating his opponent, Prime Minister Viktor Yanukovich. Yushchenko's victory was the beginning of what came to be known as the "Orange Revolution."

In an earlier runoff election in November, Yushchenko was almost denied a spot in the December contest when the Yanukovich faction engaged in voting fraud. In that runoff, exit polls indicated that Yushchenko had won by a considerable margin. The official count, which was monitored by Yanukovich's minions, gave the Prime Minister a 3 percent majority. After massive street protests, the Ukrainian high court invalidated those results, setting the stage for new elections in December and, ultimately, Yushchenko's rightful victory.

The December results were indicative of the trend in Ukrainian culture to move away from the Moscow-dependent, old style power structure, represented by Yanukovich and his mentor, former President Leonid Kuchma, towards a more democratic, westernized form of government. ❏

THE TSUNAMI OF 2004

Indonesia, December 26, 2004

On December 26, 2004, a massive tsunami caused by an earthquake at the bottom of the ocean hit the coasts of South and East Asia, claiming untold thousands of lives and rendering millions homeless.

The epicenter of the 9.0 magnitude earthquake was located in an area beneath the ocean bed northwest of Sumatra where two continental plates converge. The cataclysmic shifting of these tectonic plates created the seismic chain reaction that occasioned the creation of the tsunami.

The enormous wave hit without warning, utterly destroying

Tsunami victims in Aceh

coastal areas on which were located some of Southeast Asia's the most popular tourist haunts. Holidaymakers and locals had no time to escape the towering 30-foot-high wall of water. The only sign that there was anything amiss was an unusual ebbing of coastal waters. By the time the tsunami could be descried on the horizon, it was too late to escape.

In the immediate aftermath there was no way of knowing how many people had died. The estimated fatality figures grew dramatically on an hourly basis in the first days after the tragedy. Although it would be impossible to ever calculate the exact number of deaths, the United Nations estimated the number to be more than 165,000. That number would later be adjusted to 280,000. Many of the corpses that were recovered were never identified, and, in order to prevent the spread of disease, many were either quickly buried in mass graves or incinerated.

Tourist fleeing from oncoming wave

The single most stricken area was in the province of Aceh on the island of Sumatra, where more than 100,000 were feared to have died in the tidal waves. The capital of Banda Aceh resembled a war zone.

The world community reacted with an astonishing outpouring of humanitarian aid and financial support. World governments, corporations, private groups and individuals quickly raised funds and organized relief efforts in a show of genuine global unity.

After these initial relief efforts a summit of donor and affected states took place in the Indonesian capital of Jakarta in January 2005. One of the resolutions passed was a call for the establishment of a regional advance warning system for future catastrophic events in the Indian Ocean. ❑

THE MADRID TRAIN BOMBINGS

Madrid, March 11, 2004

On the morning of March 11, 2004 ten bombs exploded almost simultaneously on four different commuter trains in Madrid, killing 191 and wounding 1,755. All four trains were servicing the same line to Madrid's Atocha Station. The first affected train was at Atocha when three IED's (improvised explosive devices) went off at 7:37 AM. At 7:38 AM, two IED's exploded on a train just leaving the suburban El Pozo del Tio Raimundo Station. At the same time, one bomb exploded on a train at another suburban station at Santa Eugenia. At 7:39 AM, four bombs exploded on the Calle Tellez train just as it was arriving at Atocha Station.

One of the worst terrorist acts to have occurred in Europe since the 1988 bombing of the Pan

American 747 over Lockerbie, Scotland, the Partido Popular government of Jose Maria Aznar at first suspected members of the Basque separatist movement, the ETA. However, security experts doubted whether the ETA, weakened by numerous arrests, would have been in any kind of position to carry out these logistically extravagant actions. Also, in the past the ETA had always given warnings of impending attacks. With the Atocha bombings, there had been none.

The use of IEDs and other elements of the attacks led police to suspect Islamic terrorists. On March 13, a video surfaced in which a supposed military spokesman for Al Qaeda, claimed responsibility. He called the bombings an act of revenge for

Few survived the terror attack on Madrid's Atocha train station.

Spain's participation in the Iraq war.

The official Spanish government investigation linked the bombings to an Al Qaeda inspired cell, although no direct link has been established. Spanish security forces eventually

apprehended 29 suspects, most of whom were Moroccan, Syrian and Algerian Muslims. The mastermind behind the attacks, a 35-year-old Tunisian, avoided capture by blowing himself up during a police raid in suburban Leganés, on April 3. ❑

ELECTIONS IN PALESTINE

Palestine, January 9, 2005

The election of Mahmud Abbas as the President of Palestine, gave rise to the hope that the Middle East peace process might get a boost. Mahmud Abbas, also known as Abu Mazen, won the presidency with 62.3 percent of the ballots cast. He had served as Prime Minister in May 2003, but resigned after only a short term in office following differences of opinion with the then Palestinian President, Yasser Arafat. After Arafat's death in November 2004, Abbas took over the leadership of the Palestinian Liberation Organization (PLO).

The demise of Arafat and the election of his successor strengthened the hope that the peace talks, which had collapsed, could be renewed. The Israeli Prime Minister, Ariel Sharon, congratulated Abbas on his success two days after his election. Both agreed to the continuation of the Israeli-Palestinian dialogue in the "near future." To start the process Israel offered to withdraw troops from some Palestinian cities, and Ab-

Arafat died in November 2004

Palestinian President, Mahmud Abbas

bas took preliminary steps against militant Palestinians. The process was severely disrupted in early 2006, when Prime Minister Sharon suffered a serious stroke and was replaced by Ehud Olmert. ❏

UNREST IN FRANCE

Paris, November 8, 2005

The death of two young men in Clichy-sous-Bois, a suburb of Paris, home to many poor immigrants, triggered weeks of rioting. Two teenagers, aged 15 and 17, had fled from a police patrol on October 27 and climbed over the barrier of a power substation and were accidentally electrocuted. In the aftermath, heavy rioting and street battles ensued. Cars were set on fire, windowpanes smashed and bus stops destroyed. The unrest escalated with each passing night and on November 7 claimed its first life. France's conservative government imposed a state of emergency the following day, making use of a law that was passed in 1955, at the time of the Algerian War. It allowed the authorities to impose curfews. Originally it remained in force for only 12 days, but on November 16, the French parliament endorsed an extension of three months. The riots diminished in intensity after the emergency law came into force.

The rioting came as a surprise to many in France, who took pride in the country's progressive views on immigration and social welfare. But tensions among immigrant communities that felt isolated from France's mainstream had long been simmering. ❏

Youth riots starting outside of Paris challenged France's self image.

HURRICANE KATRINA CAUSES CHAOS

New Orleans, August 29, 2005

Along the USA's Gulf Coast, Hurricane Katrina left a trail of devastation, dealing the city of New Orleans was a near fatal blow. With wind speeds of over 120 mph and torrential rains, Hurricane Katrina swept across the Gulf Coast. It was one of the most destructive hurricanes ever to have hit the United States. Government sources reported that it claimed a total of 1,119 lives.

As the hurricane approached, the Mayor of New Orleans, Ray Nagin, ordered the evacuation of 470,000 inhabitants on August 28. On the overcrowded highways, all the lanes were cleared for travel in only one direction, north. For the 100,000 citizens of New Orleans, who did not own a car, the Superdome, the city's football stadium, was declared as an emergency shelter.

New Orleans is particularly vulnerable to floods since 70 percent of the city area is below sea level. It is surrounded by water on three sides – from the Gulf of Mexico, the Mississippi river, and Lake Pontchartrain. After hours of pouring rain, the city's sewage system broke down. However, the worst of the catastrophe occurred after the storm had passed. Two dams on Lake Pontchartrain burst, and the water poured into the city. At other spots, dykes were washed away.

As the images of waters rising over rooftops and terrible human suffering began to fill television reports, serious questions were raised about the Federal Government's actions or lack thereof. FEMA (Federal Emergency Management Agency) took days before it could get a handle on the situation. At one point its head, Michael Brown, seemed taken by surprise when informed by a reporter that the situation in the Superdome was becoming critical. Apparently he had no idea that the stadium was being occupied by evacuees, even though it had been reported by major news organizations for over 24 hours. ❏

Waiting for help: New Orleans residents caught in the flooding

INDEPENDENT MONTENEGRO

Montenegro, May 21, 2006

With its declaration of independence, Montenegro became the last of the six former Yugoslavian republics to attain self-governance. In a referendum initiated by the European Union, 55.5 percent voted for the dissolution of the confederation with Serbia. Montenegro was merged with the kingdom of the Serbs, Croats and Slovenians in 1918 and, from 1929 onwards, was part of the successor state of Yugoslavia. The Parliament of Montenegro proclaimed independence in the middle of June, and Serbia recognized the outcome of

The majority of the Montenegrins welcomed the independence of the country.

the referendum. ❏

NORTH KOREA TESTS NUCLEAR DEVICE

Pyongyang, North Korea, October 9, 2006

North Korea's official sources reported that it had conducted a successful test of an atom bomb to the consternation of the international community. According to the South Korean Defense Ministry in Seoul, the bomb was exploded in the southeast of the communist country. There were also fears that the country had been exporting nuclear technology to other nations.
In July, North Korean tests had moved the UN Security Council to condemn the country's actions. As of this writing six-party talks are underway to reach a final

Protest against the North Korea's nuclear tests in Seoul, South Korea

resolution of the issue . ❏

ISRAEL'S ATTACK ON THE HEZBOLLAH

Beirut, July 12, 2006

A comparatively insignificant incident caused the powder keg of the Middle East to explode once again. Reacting to the kidnapping of two soldiers by the radical Islamist Hezbollah militia, as well as their rocket attacks on the north of the country, Israel launched an invasion of Lebanon, attacking from the air and the sea, with the expressed intent of rescuing the two soldiers. On July 13, the air force bombed Beirut's international airport, which suspended operations as a consequence. Subsequently Is-

rael imposed a blockade on Lebanese ports. Meanwhile, Israeli cities and villages were being fired upon by Katyusha rockets of the Hezbollah, launched from South Lebanon.
On July 14, Israeli fighter planes bombarded the headquarters of the Hezbollah in Beirut. Its leader, Sheikh Hassan Nazrallah, responded by threatening Israel with "open war." Hezbollah's resistance was far tougher than assumed by the Israelis. An advance of troops into the south of Lebanon led to heavy fighting

with the Hezbollah and to a mass civilian exodus on July 19.
Katyusha attacks continued to plague northern Israel; on July 16, eight persons died in Haifa. In response, Israel launched further air attacks. The international community reacted only with declarations of intent, proposing to work toward a ceasefire and station a peacekeeping force under UN control in South Lebanon.
The Lebanese government's proposal to send 15,000 of its own soldiers to the south of the

country was a first step toward a cessation of hostilities. The UN Security Council agreed to Resolution 1701 during the night of August 12, which, among other things, called for a ceasefire. Both Israel and Lebanon agreed to the Resolution, and the blockade of Lebanon was lifted. The brief war dealt a severe blow to Israel's reputation for military invincibility and strengthened the hand of Hezbollah in Lebanon. The fate of the two captured Israeli soldiers remains unknown. ❏

SADDAM HUSSEIN EXECUTED

Baghdad, January 2, 2007

A video shot with a mobile telephone documented Saddam Hussein being insulted and ridiculed as he stood upon the gallows. Its appearance on the internet aroused great resentment and anger. The government in Baghdad announced an investigation into the circumstance surrounding the execution and vowed to capture and punish those responsible.
The 69 year old ex-dictator was executed by hanging on

This photo of Saddam Hussein before his execution taken on cell phone soon circulated in the media and on the internet.

December 30. According to official sources, he expressed no remorse. His corpse was buried in his native village close to Tikrit. His execution did not, however, have the calming effect on the politi-

cal situation in the Iraq that the US and Iraqi governments had hoped for. Violent confrontations between Shiites and Sunnis increased.
Following this, the US President, George W. Bush, announced a shift in his policy of an egy. His implement forces has increase of Ameri situation. improved the se solutions to As of this wri dividing the the political sues emain elusive. ❏ populatio

SHIFTING POITICAL LANDSCAPE IN THE U.S.

Washington D.C., spring 2008

After twelve years in power the Republican Party lost its control of both the House of Representatives and Senate in the 2006. While the loss of seats in mid-term elections is to be expected, the Democrats achieved a sweeping victory, recapturing much of the ground it lost in the watershed election of 1994 that propelled the Republican Party to power. The Democrats won 31 seats in the House and 6 seats in the Senate. Most analysts saw the vote as a referendum against President George W. Bush, whose popularity was at an all-time low in the period leading up to the election. The outlook for the war in Iraq, upon which he had staked his presidency, was particularly bleak, as mounting sectarian violence seemed poised to drive the country into a protracted civil war.

As a result of the shift in power, the former Democratic Minority Leader, Nancy Pelosi, became Speaker of the House, the highest national office ever held by a woman. This placed her third in line for the Presidency.

Throughout 2007 Republicans and Democrats jockeyed for the nomination of their party in the upcoming November 2008 presidential elections. The Republican Senator John McCain from Arizona became the presumptive nominee in March of 2008, having secured a sufficient

Speaker of the House, Nancy Pelosi, presiding over the opening of the 110th Congress

number of delegates in primary contests to secure the nomination. Senator McCain has served in Congress since 1982. After serving two terms in the House he was elected senator in 1986 and has occupied that office since that time. Senator McCain served with distinction as a Navy flier during the Vietnam War, winning both the Silver and Bronze Stars. He was shot down in 1967. Badly injured, he was captured and held as a prisoner of war by the North Vietnamese for five years. Although a conservative in his political orientation, he gained a reputation as somewhat of a maverick, showing himself willing to oppose the party's pos-

tions and work with Democrats on such issues as campaign financing, the environment, and, most recently, a ban on torture and abusive interrogation practices.

In the Democratic Party the race came down to two candidates, Senator Hillary Clinton, wife of former President Bill Clinton, and Senator Barack Obama. Senator Clinton has presented her-

self as experienced and prepared for the high office of the presidency. She has long been identified with core Democratic issues such as health and child care, education and women's rights. Senator Obama brings a unique perspective to his campaign. He is the son of Kenyan father and a white American mother from Kansas. This mixed race background offers the promise that he can serve to unite opposing parties and perhaps heal some of the divisions plaguing the country. His youth also has a broad appeal, garnering enthusiastic support from young Americans. As of this writing the contest had not been decided, although Senator Obama had a slight edge in the number of deleagtes pledged to support him.

The Democratic nominating convention will take place in Denver, Colorado beginning August 25, the Republican Conventin begins on September 1 in St. Paul, Minnesota. The general election will be held on November 4, 2008. ❑

Handshake between Senators Clinton and Obama

Senator McCain on the campaign trail

CLIMATE CHANGE REACHES A CRITICAL STAGE

Paris, February 2, 2007

The 2007 Nobel Peace prize was awarded jointly to Al Gore and the Intergovernmental Panel on Climate Change (IPCC). In February of 2007, the IPCC issued its fourth report since May of 1990. More than 500 scientists

Polar bears are losing their habitat as polar ice melts.

from 113 countries spent six years in preparing the report. According to its most recent findings the process of global warming can no longer be stopped.

The diagnosis is beyond dispute. Human beings are responsible. In the language of climate experts, a probability of that being the case is over 95%, which is tantamount to a certainty. Rajendra Pachauri, the leader of the reporting group said that he

hoped people would be shocked and that governments would take steps to cut their emissions of carbon dioxide and other heat producing gases in half.

According to the latest study, the earth has warmed .74 °C (1.3 °F) in the last 100 years, and eleven of the last twelve years have been the hottest since scientists began keeping records. The reason for this is the burning of fossil fuels such as oil and gas that trap carbon dioxide in the atmosphere. There is now more CO2 in the atmosphere than at any time in the last 650,000 years and the rate of increase is growing.

Researchers predict that the average global temperature will

increase between 1.8 and 4 °C (3.2 and 7.2 °F) between now and the year 2100. The resultant melting of polar ice caps will produce a dramatic rise in sea levels. This will be potentially disastrous for island nations and other low-lying countries

The report went on to confirm that the rise in greenhouse gases has also been responsible for extreme weather conditions. It predicted continuing volatility and more storms, floods, droughts, and heat waves.

The report was endorsed by 190 countries. However, the United States and China, whose response carried the greatest weight, were seen as trying to weaken its provisions.

The first part of the report on global warming was followed by a second part on April 6, which detailed the consequences of climate change for humans and the rest of the biosphere. The final part of the report issued on May 4, contained recommendations for action.

Even if serious efforts are made to rein in the pace of climate change, the consequences will still be grave. The pessimistic prognosis of the second part of the report leaves little doubt that the effects will be felt throughout the world. By 2080 coastal regions that are now home to 2,500,000 people in Europe will

be under water.

North American can expect dust storms and tornadoes, flood, heat waves and brush fires. Hardest hit will be the Arctic region from the melting of the ice sheets, the islands of the Pacific Ocean, which will suffer from inundations and tidal waves, and Africa, which can expect severe drought. The densely populated coast regions of Asia have to prepare for severe flooding. Twenty to thirty percent of all animal and plant life will have their survival threatened if the temperature rises 2.5 °C.

The report called for immediate action. If the international community can summon the will to take the necessary steps to contain the temperature rise to moderate levels a catastrophe can be avoided. The goal is to have the emission of greenhouse gases peak in 2015 and then be reduced in half by the middle of the century. The scientists predicted that this would curb worldwide economic activity by a mere .12 percent, and as such should not pose insurmountable threats to political and social stability.

To achieve this goal the panel made pressing recommendations. First the use of much more fuel-efficient technologies to burn less coal, oil and gas. If fossil fuels are used then ways must be found to prevent the gas from entering the atmosphere. ❑

AL GORE

Brief Lives

Former US Vice-President Al Gore, Jr. was born on March 31, 1948. His father Albert Gore, Sr. was a longtime senator from Tennessee, an office that his son would also occupy. The younger Gore graduated from Harvard, enlisted in the military and served as an army journalist in Vietnam.

He was elected to the House of Representatives in 1976 and then to the Senate, where he

served until 1993, when he became Vice-President under Bill Clinton. In 2000 Gore ran for President against George W. Bush and lost in an election so close that the Supreme Court had to intervene in the outcome.

Gore has been a longtime champion of environmental causes. His book, *Earth in the Balance*, laid out the scientific ev-

idence of climate change and the moral imperative to take steps to counter it. His 2007 film, *An Inconvenient Truth*, addressing the problem of global warming, won an Academy Award. He was also the recipient in 2007 of the Nobel Peace Prize, for his advocacy of environmental causes, an honor he shared with the Intergovernmental Panel on Climate Change of the U.N. ❑

Former U.S. Vice-President, Al Gore

INDEX OF PROPER NAMES

William III of Orange 393. See William III< King of England
William III, King of England 401, 402, 403, 411
William IV, King of England 325, 326, 327, 328, 472
William of Aquitaine 221
William of Orange 286, 287, 295, 362, 368, 411
William Tell 451, 467
William the Conqueror 212, 213
William the Lion, King of Scotland 245
William the Pious, Duke of Aquitaine 199
Wills, William John 488
Wilmot Proviso 480
Wilmot, David 480
Wilson, Harold 542, 608
Wilson, Woodrow 521, 523, 555, 561, 564, 567, 577
Winchester 196
Winckelmann, Joachim 304, 441
Windsor, House of 532, 548, 582, 633
Wittelsbach, House of 415
Wittelsbacher, House of 496
Wittenberg 270, 284, 342, 344, 345
Wolsey, Thomas 282, 283, 352
Woodward, Bob 611
Wordsworth, William 318, 451
Works and Days 16, 74, 75
Works Progress Administration (WPA) 577
World Trade Center, the 546, 574, 621, 630, 631
World War I 548, 549, 552, 554, 560, 562, 565, 566, 567, 568, 574, 575, 583, 585, 595
World War II 499, 545, 563, 572, 575, 579, 580, 581, 584, 592, 593, 594, 602, 604, 606, 610, 618, 633
Wounded Knee Massacre 506
Wratislaw of Bohemia 198
Wright, Orville 550
Wright, Wilbur 514, 550, 551
Wu Sangui 390
Wurzburg 353
Wycliffe, John 258, 345
Wyoming 332, 474, 500

X

Xenophanes 79
Xerxes I 86, 87, 89

Xia Dynasty 64
Xian 134, 188
Xiang Yu 110

Y

Yablochkov candle 501
Yablochkov, Pavel N. 501
Yagoda, Genrikh 582
Yahweh 62, 81, 112, 509
Yalta Conference 596
Yamamoto, Isoroku 587
Yamato Period 181
Yan 65
Yandi, Emperor 180
Yanukovich, Viktor 638
Yathrib. See Medina
Yazid 156, 189
Yeltsin, Boris 544, 546, 623, 626, 635
Yemen 87
Yermak 288, 369
Yesügei 232
Ying 64
Yom Kippur War 509, 610
Yongle 174, 200, 364
Yongzheng 200, 365
Yoritomo Minamoto 201, 226
York, House of 274
Yorktown 308, 310, 432, 434
Yoruba 169, 260, 261, 403
Yu, Emperor 64
Yuan Dynasty 154, 170, 174, 183, 233, 241, 250, 257
Yuan Shi-kai 553
Yucatan Peninsula 208
Yugoslavia 524, 525, 528, 534, 535, 536, 537, 538, 545, 546, 555, 563, 565, 586, 594, 599, 607, 619, 620, 622, 628, 629, 641
Yushchenko, Viktor 638
Yusuf, Ramzi Ahmed 631

Z

Zababa 49
Zacuto, Abraham 273, 348
Zaire 517, 545, 602, 604
Zand, House of 447
Zapata, Emiliano 518, 523, 552
Zapotecs 137, 262
Zedekiah 77
Zeeland 287, 368
Zen Buddhism 201, 365
Zeno, Byzantine emperor 143
Zenon 96, 149
Zeppelin, Ferdinand von 549
Zeus 22, 30, 56, 68, 74, 82, 98, 100, 101, 111, 112, 113, 114
Zhangping 65

Zhao 65
Zhao Gao 110
Zhao Kuangyin 202
Zhao Ziyang 616
Zheng, Prince of Qin. See Qin Shi Huangdi
Zhou Dynasty 134, 153, 157, 180
Zhou Enlai 537, 597, 607
Zhou-Xian, Shang ruler 64, 67
Zhu 65
Zhu De 579
Zhu Yuanzhang 233, 257
Zimbabwe 609
Zimmerman Telegram, the 561
Zimmerman, Dominikus 417
Zinoviev, Grigori 582
Zionism 508, 510
Zola, Émile 510
Zollverein, 456
Zoroaster (Zarathustra) 16, 80, 86, 87
Zulfikar Ali-Khan Bhutto 609
Zulus 323, 326, 333, 471
Zurich 283, 284, 342, 352, 455 487, 539
Zuse, Konrad 615
Zwinger Palace 404
Zwingli, Ulrich 283, 284, 342
Zyklon B 587

PHOTO CREDITS